D1163103

MODERN AMERICA

Authors: LEON H. CANFIELD
HOWARD B. WILDER

Editors: HOWARD R. ANDERSON
ELLIS MERTON COULTER
JOHN D. HICKS
NELSON P. MEAD

MAP AND CHART EDITOR: ROBERT M. CHAPIN, JR.

MIFFLIN COMPANY · The Riverside Press Cambridge

ABOUT THE AUTHORS AND EDITORS

Leon H. Canfield, author, is Professor of History and Head of the Social Science Department, Fairleigh Dickinson College, Rutherford, New Jersey. He was formerly Supervisor of History, Townsend Harris High School, College of the City of New York, and Head of the Upper School and Master of History at the Brunswick School in Greenwich, Connecticut.

Howard B. Wilder, author, made the teaching of American history his primary concern during the 15 years he was Head of the Department of Social Studies, Melrose High School, Melrose, Mass. Subsequently he became Principal of that school. He is also co-author of *This Is America's Story.*

Howard R. Anderson, general editor, is associated with the United States Office of Education, where he is concerned with social studies problems and materials. He was formerly Professor of Education at Cornell University and Director of Social Studies in the Ithaca, N.Y., Public Schools. Prior to that he was Assistant Professor of History at the University of Iowa and Head of Social Studies in the University High School.

Ellis Merton Coulter, consulting editor, is Professor of American History, University of Georgia. He is co-editor of *A History of the South* and author of numerous books on southern history.

John D. Hicks, consulting editor, is A. F. and May T. Morrison Professor of American History, University of California, Berkeley. He was formerly Professor of History at the University of Nebraska, and Professor of History at the University of Wisconsin. Among his publications are *The Populist Revolt, The Federal Union, The American Nation,* and *A Short History of American Democracy.*

Nelson P. Mead, consulting editor, is Professor of History, College of the City of New York, and is the author of *The Development of the United States Since 1865.* He has given special attention to the preparation of American history teachers for the secondary schools.

Robert M. Chapin, Jr., map and chart editor, is map-maker for *Time* and has prepared maps for other publications, such as the *Look At America* series and *The Pacific World.* He has also been a lecturer at Clark University, Worcester, Massachusetts.

ACKNOWLEDGMENTS

For specialized assistance at various points in the preparation of the manuscript or in the illustration of this book, the authors, editors, and publisher wish to thank the following persons: Richard Bartlett, Harry D. Berg, Samuel H. Bryant, Duane Decker, William Diez, Jere Donovan, Mary Pieters Keohane, Dyno Lowenstein, Alastair M. Taylor, and C. Lester Walker. Permission to reprint passages from other publications is gratefully acknowledged on page xvi. Picture credits are also listed on pages xv–xvi.

The Making of Modern America is a new book based upon an earlier text, *The United States in the Making,* by the same authors.

COPYRIGHT, 1952, BY HOUGHTON MIFFLIN COMPANY
COPYRIGHT, 1950, BY HOUGHTON MIFFLIN COMPANY
ALL RIGHTS RESERVED INCLUDING THE RIGHT TO REPRODUCE
THIS BOOK OR PARTS THEREOF IN ANY FORM

The Riverside Press
CAMBRIDGE · MASSACHUSETTS
PRINTED IN THE U.S.A.

Contents

Part Two · MODERN AMERICA EMERGES

ix

Part Three · MODERN AMERICA MATURES

x

List of Maps

List of Charts

List of Charts (Cont.)

Special Features

Unit Organization Charts. At the beginning of each unit (as on page 18) there is a chart showing the full organization of the book. The white portion within each chart emphasizes the unit you are about to read. Use these charts to get your bearings before reading each unit.

Chapter Time Charts. Before reading each chapter, look at the dates and time chart at the lower left of the first page in the chapter (as on page 37). The dates tell what period is covered in the chapter, and the white portion of the chart shows that period in relation to the entire time covered in the book.

About the Illustrations

The illustrations in this book have been prepared or selected primarily because of their contribution to a fuller understanding of American history, but also with careful attention to their interest and "eye appeal." The following points call for special mention:

Maps. All of the maps were prepared by an outstanding map maker. His work was carefully correlated with the manuscript, so that every important geographical idea is shown on a map. Every place name mentioned in the text can also be found on a map, by reference to the Index if necessary. Full use has been made of all appropriate techniques of map making, old as well as new. Among the newer ones are the suggestion of "roundness" where this is helpful (page 647), choice of the best possible projection for a given purpose (pages 29 and 43), and clear representation of topography (page 278).

Charts. Statistical and organizational information has been dramatized and made easier to remember in the charts. Several of the statistical charts are continuous; that is, the reader's eye is drawn to the period he is studying, but he is also able to glance back to see what happened earlier or ahead to what he will presently read about (pages 197, 383, and 544). By this means the eye can "take in" the all-important continuity of historical statistics.

Drawings. The large pictures at the beginnings of units, as well as on the title page, part titles, and cover, were drawn to give a "photographic" effect. Dramatic as well as realistic, they symbolize important characteristics or events in American history. A great many small, spot drawings have been included to show houses, tools, furniture, clothing, weapons, and many other articles used at various times and in different places throughout our history.

Other illustration. All of the illustrations referred to above were made specifically for this book. Most of the other illustrations are halftone reproductions of existing pictures. You can add to your understanding of history if you will learn to recognize the kind of picture, or "copy," which was used to make a halftone reproduction. Very old drawings, paintings, and documents have sometimes faded or become soiled or otherwise damaged. When these are reproduced they may not be as clear as a picture made from a modern drawing, painting, or photograph. But they may be so important historically that they belong in such a book as this (page 211). Consider, too, the good results that can be obtained from very old, historic photographs (pages 297 and 350).

Acknowledgment of picture sources. The pictures used for halftone reproduction in this book were searched out in hundreds of books, from libraries and museums all over the country, and from files containing thousands of photographs. The authors, editors, and publisher express sincere thanks to all who helped. Except where credit appears elsewhere, special acknowledgment is made to the following for permission to reproduce pictures on the pages indicated:

Acme, 2 (bottom), 6–7 (bottom), 503 (top right), 551 (top right), 680 (top), 694, 700, 703, 746, 751, 754, 756, 765, 766 (bottom), 771, 772, 774, xxii; Agricultural Education Service, USOE, FSA, 553; American Petroleum Institute, 374; American Woolen Co., 508; Courtesy of the artist, Stanley Arthurs, 232; Atlanta University, 329; The Baltimore & Ohio Railroad, 234, 389; Bell Telephone System, 369; Bettmann Archive, 95; Bituminous Coal Institute, 525 (top); Black Star, xxxi; Brown Bros., 107, 115, 147, 259, 409, 427 (top right), 536, 684, 718, 735 (top right); K. S. Brown, 564; Bureau of Public Roads, GAA, 496 (2 – right, center); Canadian Pacific Railway Co., 646 (2), 647; J. I. Case Co., 399 (2); Caterpillar Tractor Co., 6–7 (top); Central City Opera House Assn., Inc., 347 (2 – top left, center); The Chicago Historical Society, 75 (top right); Colonial Williamsburg, 79 (except top right); Commonwealth of Mass. Dept. of Public Safety, xix (top); The Corcoran Gallery of Art, 199; Courtley, Ltd.: Courtley Men's Toiletries Collection, by Robert Riggs, 597 (bottom); Culver, 229, 289, 325, 381, 453, 456, 477 (top), 637, 652, 733; C. P. Cushing, 670; Dallas Historical Society, 349; The DoALL Co., Des Plaines, Ill., 228; Thomas A. Edison, Inc., 360; European, 750; Federal Public Housing Authority, NHA, 585 (right); FSA, 15; Gendreau, xxvi; Electro-Motive Division, General Motors, 364; Geological Survey, USDI, 283; Gilbert Paper Co., 33; Gimbel Pennsylvania Art Collection, 502 (top left); John Hancock Mutual Life Insurance Co., 77, 260, 436; *Harper's Weekly* (Oct. 16, 1869) 452, (Apr. 9, 1870) 406, (Sept. 6, 1873) 361, (Oct. 11, 1873) 455, (Nov. 12, 1880) 203, (Nov. 17, 1888) 465, (July 16, 1892) 395, (May 12, 1894) 467, (Oct. 25, 1902) 523, (Nov. 9, 1907) 533; Harris & Ewing, 164, 527, 589 (top); Hedrick-Blessing, 607; Lewis W. Hine Memorial Collection, 425; Historical Pictures, 474; The Historical Society of Pennsylvania, 159; The

Home Insurance Co.: courtesy of The H. V. Smith Museum, 596; Hughes Tool Co., 87, 273, 373, 565; Illinois Division of Parks, 241 (except top right); International, 692, 701 (photo of Roosevelt), 739; International Business Machines Corp.: Fine Arts Dept. Collection, 560; *Judge* (Nov. 7, 1896) 470; Kaywoodie Co., 368; Kennedy & Co., N.Y., 209, 254; Keystone, 253 (top right), 391 (top right), 664, 683, 717, 721; Laboratory of Anthropology, Santa Fe, N.M.: Ben Wittick Collection, 352; *Ladies Home Journal,* © Curtis Publishing Co., 405; Lambert-Frederick Lewis, 347 (left center); *Frank Leslie's Illustrated Newspaper* (Mar. 17, 1860) 247, (1865) 323, (1877) 457; Libbey-Owens-Ford Glass Co., 433; Library of Congress, 205 (top right), 211, 296, 297, 315, 321 (2), 556, 621, 738; LIFE photo by Thomas D. McAvoy, 767 (top right); Lockheed Aircraft Corp., 497 (center); The Magnavox Co., Fort Wayne, Ind., 608; *Marine Corps Gazette,* 1945, by Sergt. John Clymer, 479; Massachusetts Historical Society, 89; Mathison Aerial Surveys, 606; The Metropolitan Museum of Art, 194; Mexican Tourist Assn., 643; Mission Photo, 277 (except top right); John Morrell & Co., 25, 101, 270; Museum of the City of New York: The J. Clarence Davies Collection, 366; National Archives, 291, 354, 605, 678; The National City Bank of New York, 554, 558; National Cotton Council of America, 552 (photo by Ford Boyd); National Gallery of Art, Washington, D.C. (lent by Mrs. Arthur Iselin and her son, William Jay Iselin) 155; National Life Insurance Co., Montpelier, Vt., 74, 125; Nebraska State Historical Society, 350 (top); New England Mutual Life Insurance Co., 97; The New-York Historical Society, 103, 177, 431 (top); New York Public Library, 441, (Stokes Collection): 245, 285; New York Stock Exchange, 517; Northern Pacific Railway Co., 505; Office of Indian Affairs, USDI, 353 (bottom); Orlando, FPG, 519; Pan American Airways, 633 (top); Pennsylvania Dept. of Commerce, 133; Providence, R.I., *Sunday Journal,* 589 (bottom — photo by Scheer); Public Buildings Administration, FWA, by Tom Lea, 348, 401; Public Health Service, FSA, xviii; *Puck,* 371, 387, (Nov. 2, 1904) 512, (Aug. 20, 1913) 515; Fred H. Ragsdale, 347 (bottom); Rapho-Guillumette, 635; William Rittase, 317 (photo of Lincoln); H. Armstrong Roberts, 14 (bottom); James Sawders, 633 (bottom); Shostal, 1 (color photo by Brian Brierley); Courtesy of the artist, F. A. Schwarz, and Oregon State Board of Control, 168; The Society of California Pioneers, 437; Soil Conservation Service, USDA, 557, 570; Southern Pacific Railroad, 364; Standard Oil Co. (N.J.), 3, 10 (2), 11, 33, 496 (right center), 602, xix (bottom); Philip Suval, Inc., 236; Union Pacific Railroad, 2 (top), 363, 567; U. S. Air Force, 497 (top); U. S. Navy, 702 (from Acme), 715; U. S. Steel Corp., 502 (2 — bottom), 572, 755; University of Iowa, 257 (top); Utica Public Library, 110; Virginia Historical Society, 306 (top); Wide World, 189, 674, 708 (top) 760, 763, 766 (top), 776, xx; Courtesy of Wyeth Inc., by Dean Cornwell, N. A., 258, 434, 623; Yale University Art Gallery: The Mabel Brady Garvan Collection, 213; Courtesy of Young & Rubicam, Inc., 438; Jerome Zerbe, 347 (right center); Acme, xxiv–xxv; Adapted from Graphic Syndicate chart, xxiii; Sukert from Guillumette, xvii.

PERMISSION TO REPRINT

Grateful acknowledgment is made to the following publishers, authors, and other copyright holders, for permission to reprint copyrighted material:

Doubleday & Company, Inc., selections from Walt Whitman.

E. P. Dutton & Co., Inc., selection from *Conquering Our Great American Plains,* by Stuart Henry, copyright 1930, by Stuart Henry.

Hakluyt Society, selections from *The Journal of Christopher Columbus.* Translated by Clements R. Markham. London, Hakluyt Society, 1893.

Harper & Brothers, selection from *TVA: Democracy on the March,* by David Lilienthal.

Henry Holt and Company, Inc., selection from *Chicago Poems* by Carl Sandburg. Copyright, 1916, by Henry Holt and Company, Inc. Copyright, 1943, by Carl Sandburg.

Houghton Mifflin Company, selections from *The Log of A Cowboy,* by Andy Adams; *The Gathering Storm,* by Winston Churchill; and "American Letter," in *Poems: 1924–1933,* by Archibald MacLeish.

Alfred A. Knopf, Inc., selection from *Life With Father,* by Clarence Day.

A. C. McClurg & Company, selection from *Vigilante Days and Ways,* by Nathaniel P. Langford. McClurg, 1912.

The Macmillan Company, selections from *America in Mid-Passage* and *Rise of American Civilization,* by Charles A. and Mary R. Beard; and *A Son of the Middle Border,* by Hamlin Garland.

Virgil Markham, selection from "Lincoln the Man of the People," by Edwin Markham.

Charles Scribner's Sons, selections from *How the Other Half Lives,* by Jacob Riis; and *Across the Plains,* by Robert Louis Stevenson.

YOUR AMERICA

INDUSTRIAL GIANT

The United States of America is one of the mightiest nations that man has ever created. More important, it is founded on the highest principles that men of good will and common sense have been able to put into practice. We still face many perplexing problems, but we can be justly proud of what our nation has accomplished.

The next few pages will give you a quick view of what your country is today and how it compares in some ways with other areas of the world, especially with Soviet Russia, a vigorous contender for world leadership in the modern world. Then you can go on to read the full story of the way your country developed and of the important and inspiring principles which are the foundation of the American way of life.

• • •

America is above all an industrial nation, the greatest on earth. Its area — about 3 million square miles — is smaller than that of Soviet Russia and even of Brazil. Its population — over 150 million — is less than that of India or China. Yet its industrial power equals that of all the rest of the world combined!

AMERICAN INDUSTRY LEADS THE WORLD

OUTPUT OF INDUSTRIAL ESSENTIALS

	United States	Soviet Russia	Great Britain
Coal (millions of metric tons)	720	220	210
Pig iron (millions of metric tons)	65	14	9
Oil (millions of metric tons)	256	27	None
Electric Power (billions of kilowatt-hours)	326	65	10

OUTPUT OF MANUFACTURED PRODUCTS

	United States	Soviet Russia	Great Britain
Steel (millions of metric tons)	84	19	12.7
Cotton textiles (millions of square yards)	8.1	1.9	1.4
Shoes (millions of pairs)	470	110	137

(Figures for a recent year)

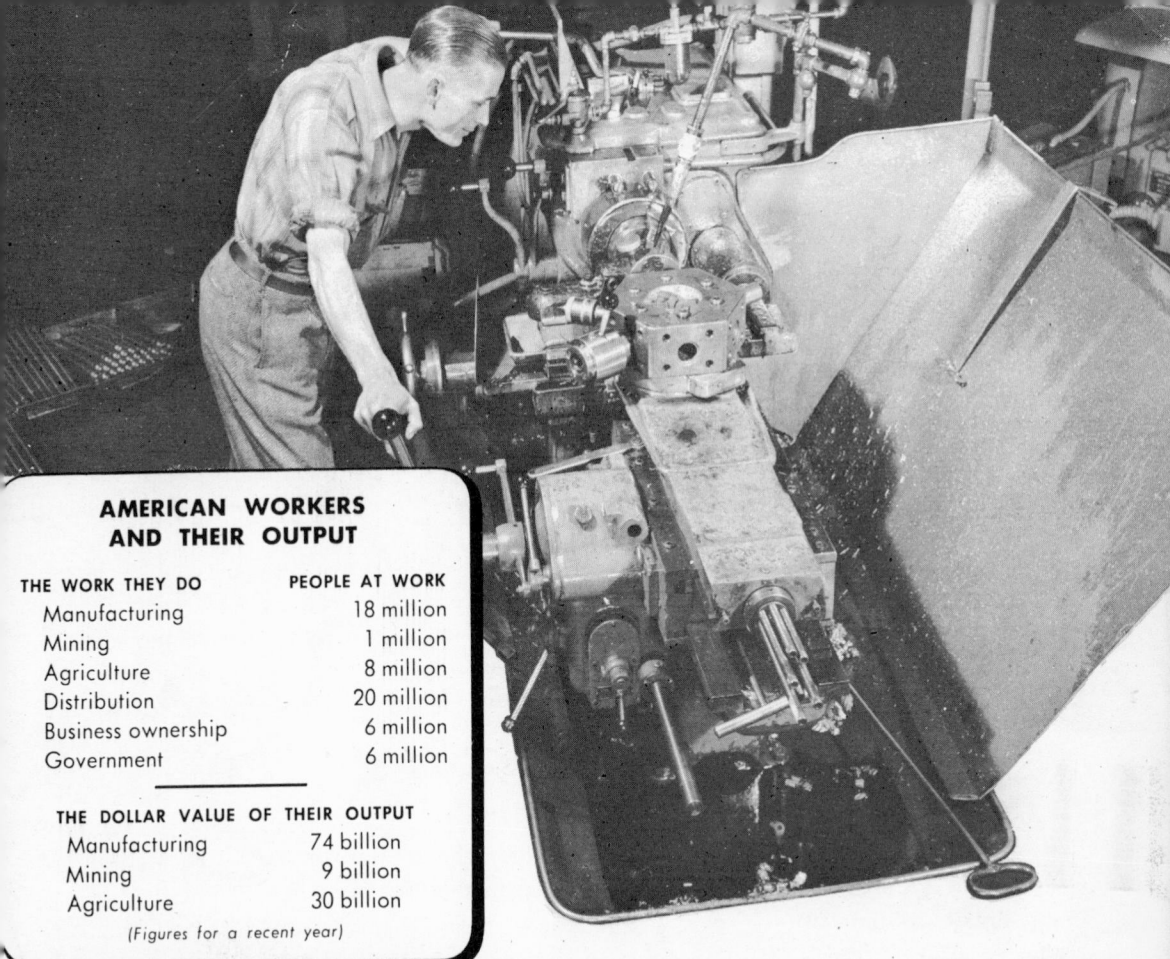

AMERICAN WORKERS AND THEIR OUTPUT

THE WORK THEY DO	PEOPLE AT WORK
Manufacturing	18 million
Mining	1 million
Agriculture	8 million
Distribution	20 million
Business ownership	6 million
Government	6 million

THE DOLLAR VALUE OF THEIR OUTPUT	
Manufacturing	74 billion
Mining	9 billion
Agriculture	30 billion

(Figures for a recent year)

How has this come about? In the first place, as the chart on page 2 shows, we have a high output of coal, pig iron, oil, and electric power. These basic materials and sources of power, among others, are essential in the manufacture of finished industrial products. Equally important, our nation has a large number of people to do its work, as shown in the chart above. The chart cannot show, however, that an unusually large proportion of these workers are highly skilled and have developed remarkable inventiveness and "know-how." Further, their natural ability has been multiplied many times by the ingenious machines they operate. Owners and managers of industries, at the same time, have developed techniques and qualities of leadership for which they are famous all over the world. Finally, there are millions of other workers without whom the men and women of industry could not exist — the all-important farm workers who provide them with food, and the workers who distribute the products of industry to people who need and want them.

Turn now to the industrial map of the United States on pages 4 and 5. As you look at it, imagine the mines and oil wells, the forests, the trains and trucks and ships, the countless factories, and especially the millions of busy people who run them. Then you may understand better why America is often called "an industrial giant."

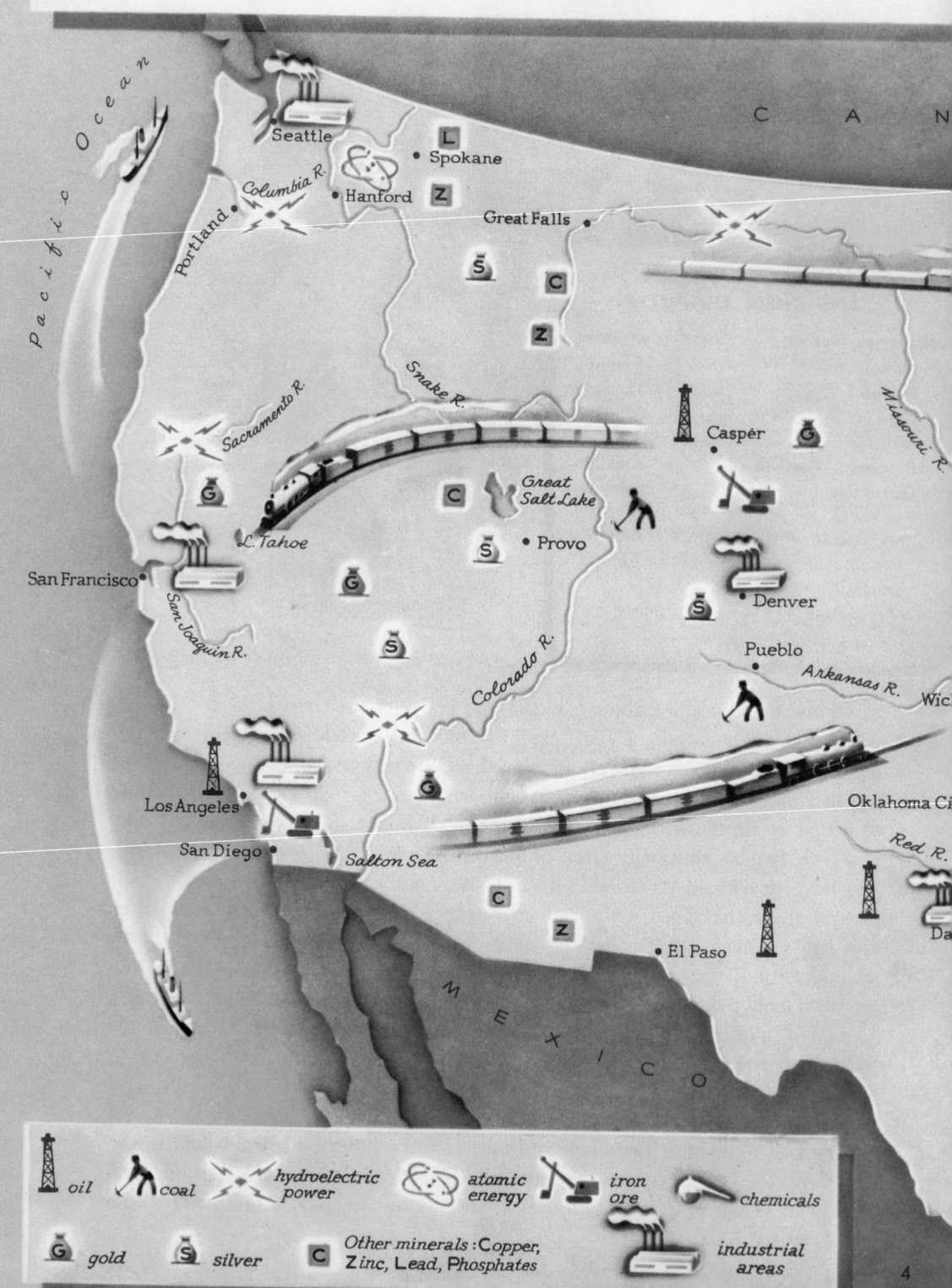

oil   coal   hydroelectric power   atomic energy   iron ore   chemicals

G gold   S silver   C Other minerals: Copper, Zinc, Lead, Phosphates   industrial areas

4

R. M. Chapin

LEADER IN AGRICULTURE

In an industrial society like the United States, large quantities of food must be on hand in stores and markets every day for industrial workers to buy. Great Britain, also an industrial nation, must import much of her food, since she does not have enough land on which to produce it. American farmers, on the other hand, have everything that it takes to provide the American people with a wide variety of nutritious foods. More than that, the farmers of America have raised such large crops and so much livestock in recent years that the United States has exported more than 2½ billion dollars worth of foodstuffs annually. Today the United States is the leading agricultural nation of the world, as well as the leader in industry.

The American farmer, like the industrial worker, has worked hard and has had to show remarkable ingenuity and skill to produce so much food. He has had the advantage of unusually fertile soil and favorable climate. The use of hybrid seeds and of other products of scientific research have aided him greatly. But the mechanization of American farms probably accounts more than anything else for his spectacular crops. Industry has manufactured the machines needed by the farmer, and the farmer has bought and used them in vast numbers.

The importance of machinery on the farm is shown in the chart on page 7. Russia was an agricultural country centuries before America was discovered, and Russian farmers are famous for their hard work and natural ability. But compare the figures. America has fewer people than Russia, and a much smaller percentage of them work on farms. Still, in terms of percentage, America has nearly twice as much of its land given over to crops, and American farmers produce more than two and a half times as much grain, for example, as Russian farmers can produce. An important reason for this is that American farmers have over five times as many tractors as the Russians. They also have correspondingly large numbers of planters, reapers, and other types of machinery to help them in their work.

6

AMERICAN AGRICULTURE LEADS THE WORLD

MEN, LAND, MACHINES, AND OUTPUT	United States	Soviet Russia
Total population	150 million	200 million
Agricultural workers	12 per cent	65 per cent
Cropland	21 per cent	11 per cent
Grain (in bushels)	6.8 billion	2.7 billion
Farm tractors in use	2.2 million	0.4 million

THE DOLLAR VALUE OF LEADING AMERICAN FARM PRODUCTS

Truck crops	3.8 billion
Milk products	3.7 billion
Corn	3.7 billion
Cattle sales	2.6 billion
Hog sales	2.3 billion
Wheat	1.7 billion

(Actual or estimated figures for recent years)

Turn now to the agricultural map of the United States on pages 8 and 9. It shows some of our important agricultural resources, and it dramatizes the land formation and the natural vegetation which are important in determining where certain agricultural products are raised. The map also shows a few of the cities which are important in the processing and shipping of farm products. As you look at the map, remember that rural America is made up of nearly 6 million farms, of which more than two thirds are operated by the people who own them. As you think of the 8 million workers who are growing and harvesting food, think also of the profitable work they create for mills and factories where food products are put into packages, bottles, and cans, and of the trains, trucks, and ships which carry such products to the markets of America and the world.

7

AN AGRICULTURAL MAP

salmon

Seattle

Columbia R.

C · A · N

Portland

Missouri R.

beef cattle

Pacific Ocean

Snake R.

Ogden

Platte R.

Sacramento R.

San Joaquin R.

San Francisco

Denver

sardines

Colorado R.

Los Angeles

Salt R.

Oklahoma C.

tuna

San Diego

Fort Wort

Rio Grande

Scale of Miles

0   50 100   200   300   400 mi.

M E X I C O

← Western Highlands →   ← Interior Plains →   ← Coastal Plains →
5 000 - 8 000 ft.   1 000 - 5 000 ft.   sea level - 1 000 ft.

desert shrub   grassland   prairie   forest

Sierra Nevada

Rocky Mts.

← 8 000 - over 14,000 ft.

plateaus

Great
Plains

100° W.

Appalachian Mts.
1 000 - over 6 000 ft.

8

lobster

fish

dairy cattle

L. Superior

L. Michigan

L. Huron

L. Ontario

L. Erie

Burlington

Boston

Providence

St. Paul

Minneapolis

Milwaukee

Rochester

Buffalo

Newark

New York

oux City

Grand
Rapids

Chicago

Cleveland

Omaha

Pittsburgh

Philadelphia

Baltimore

Cincinnati

Louisville

St. Louis

Kansas
City

Ohio R.

Richmond

oysters

Winston-Salem

Charlotte

Mississippi R.

Tennessee R.

Dallas

soybeans

peanuts

Savannah

rice

naval stores

Jacksonville

Mobile

Houston

Biloxi

shrimp

New Orleans

Atlantic Ocean

cane sugar

sponges

Tampa

truck farming

Gulf of Mexico

9

R. M. Chapin

NATION OF FREE PEOPLE

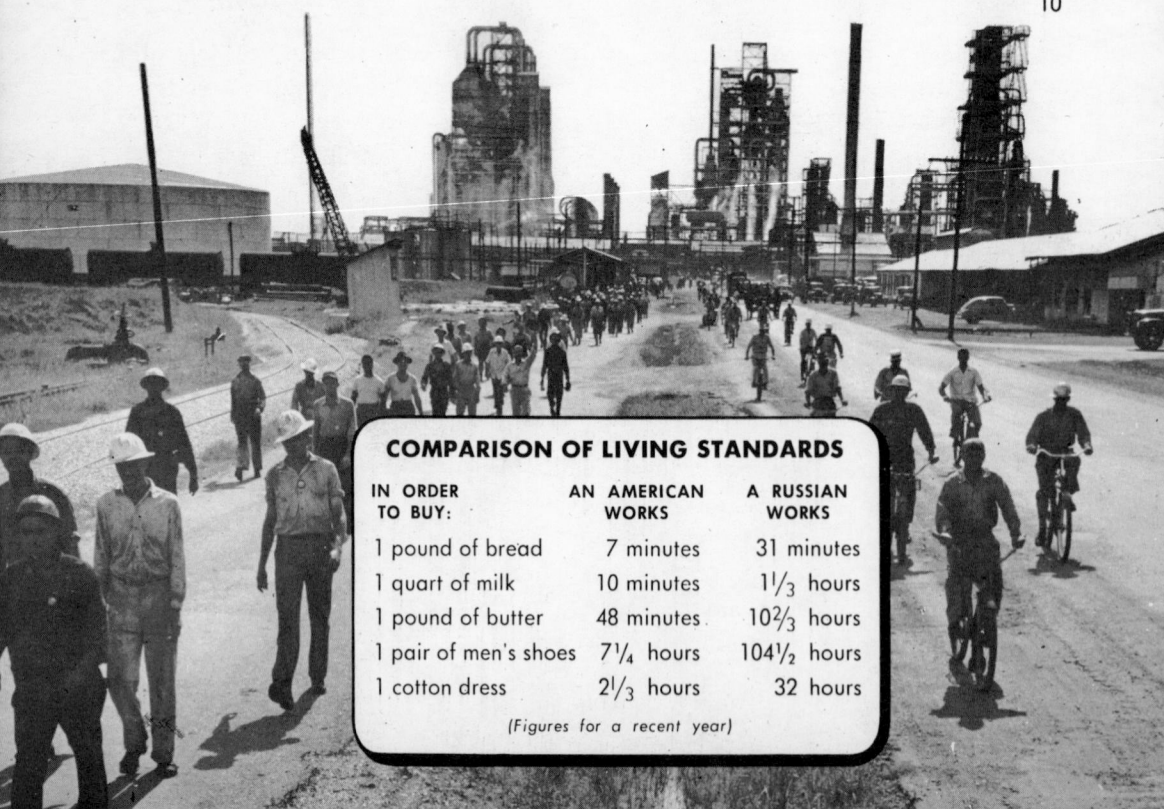

America leads the world in industry and agriculture, but how do the American people fare in this prosperous society? Few if any of us are as well off as we should like to be — and our discontent is an indication that we are an energetic and ambitious people. About one third of our families receive incomes of less than $2000 a year, which in our large cities is not enough to provide them with acceptable standards of living. Still, while there is room for improvement in the living standards of many Americans, the chart below shows that the American workman is a great deal better off than, for example, the Russian workman. He needs to work far fewer hours than a Russian citizen works to buy food and clothing for his family. Because of this advantage the American can afford to enjoy many things that are beyond the reach of workers in many other lands. For example, in one year recently American citizens drove 30 million passenger cars about 300 billion miles, of which nearly half was pleasure driving.

What kind of people are Americans, and what kind of lives do they lead? Some answers to those questions are contained in the chart on the next page,

10

COMPARISON OF LIVING STANDARDS

IN ORDER TO BUY:	AN AMERICAN WORKS	A RUSSIAN WORKS
1 pound of bread	7 minutes	31 minutes
1 quart of milk	10 minutes	$1\frac{1}{3}$ hours
1 pound of butter	48 minutes	$10\frac{2}{3}$ hours
1 pair of men's shoes	$7\frac{1}{4}$ hours	$104\frac{1}{2}$ hours
1 cotton dress	$2\frac{1}{3}$ hours	32 hours

(Figures for a recent year)

What the Average American Works For

HE WORKS 250 DAYS EACH YEAR

ITEM OF EXPENSE	DAYS WORKED
Food	72
Clothing	29
Shelter	43
Transportation	15
Personal expenses	10
Medical care	9
Savings	21
Recreation	11
Religion, private welfare, etc.	7
Taxes	26
Other	7
	250

which shows what the average American does with the money he earns. Out of the 250 days he works, 144 are spent in providing food, shelter, and clothing for himself and his family. The work of 34 days takes care of transportation, personal expenses, and medical attention. He puts into savings the earnings of 21 of his working days. Eleven days are spent in providing recreation for himself, his wife, and his family — for sports, trips, books, theaters and movies, music. What he earns for the greater part of seven days is given to his church or to the assistance of his less fortunate neighbors. For 26 days he works to pay taxes which provide the many services and protection of his government. Over 3½ billion dollars of these taxes are spent by his government on public welfare. He also sees to it that his government spends nearly 5 billion dollars each year for education of all kinds, for the American citizen believes that every child should have the opportunity to do better than he himself has done. His insistence on real opportunities for his children probably explains as well as anything else why America has reached its present position of leadership among the nations of the world.

A POLITICAL MAP OF

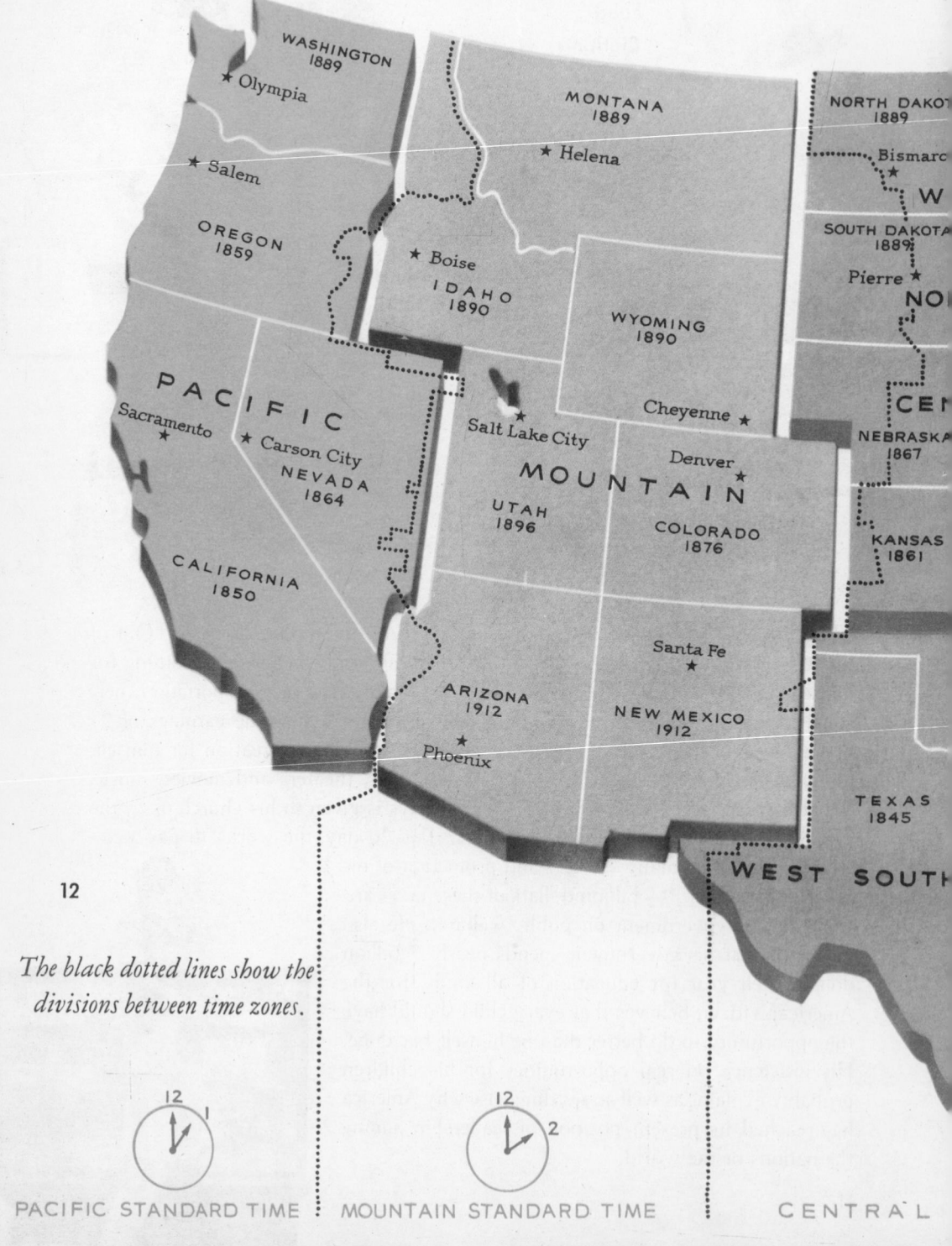

The black dotted lines show the divisions between time zones.

PACIFIC STANDARD TIME : MOUNTAIN STANDARD TIME : CENTRAL

THE UNITED STATES

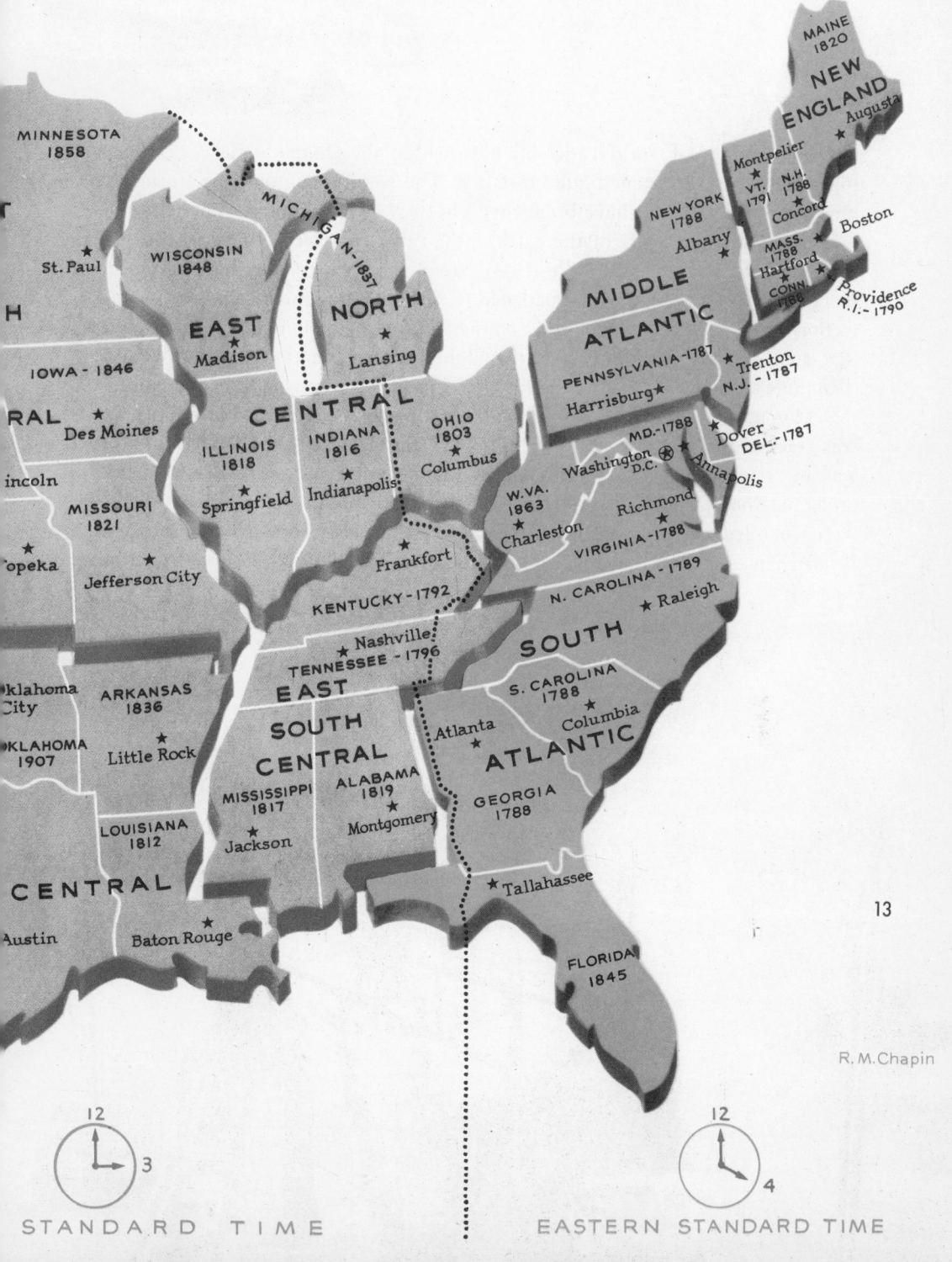

MAINE
1820

NEW
ENGLAND

Augusta

MINNESOTA
1858

Montpelier
VT.
1791
N.H.
1788

NEW YORK
1788

Concord

Boston

St. Paul

WISCONSIN
1848

MICHIGAN-1837

Albany

MASS.
1788
Hartford
CONN.
1788

Providence
R.I.-1790

MIDDLE

ATLANTIC

EAST

NORTH

IOWA - 1846

Madison

Lansing

PENNSYLVANIA-1787

Trenton
N.J. - 1787

Harrisburg

Dover
DEL.-1787

CENTRAL

Des Moines

ILLINOIS
1818

INDIANA
1816

OHIO
1803

MD.-1788

MISSOURI
1821

Springfield

Indianapolis

Columbus

Washington
D.C.

Annapolis

W.VA.
1863
Charleston

Richmond

incoln

opeka

Jefferson City

Frankfort

VIRGINIA-1788

N. CAROLINA - 1789

KENTUCKY - 1792

Raleigh

Nashville

SOUTH

klahoma
City

ARKANSAS
1836

TENNESSEE - 1796

EAST

S. CAROLINA
1788

KLAHOMA
1907

Little Rock

SOUTH

CENTRAL

Atlanta

Columbia

ATLANTIC

MISSISSIPPI
1817

ALABAMA
1819

GEORGIA
1788

LOUISIANA
1812

Jackson

Montgomery

CENTRAL

Tallahassee

13

Austin

Baton Rouge

FLORIDA
1845

R. M. Chapin

12
3

12
4

STANDARD TIME

EASTERN STANDARD TIME

A POWER IN THE WORLD

The position of world leadership now held by the United States is a responsibility that we have assumed quite recently. The picture-map on page 16 suggests how our world interests have broadened. In the 1700's, although American ships went trading to the ends of the earth, most Americans were concerned in their thinking only with the Old World civilization from which they had sprung. In the 1800's their thinking was broadened to include Latin America when, for protection of their own interests, they warned European nations not to interfere in that area. Finally, in the 1900's, the United States found itself looking in all directions and vitally concerned with affairs in the remotest parts of the globe.

Our new position as a world leader has brought many responsibilities and was reached through great sacrifice. In 1917 and again in 1941 we had to go to war to resist nations which threatened our security and were determined to undermine our way of life. Hundreds of thousands of American citizens died or were wounded in these great world wars. Americans also made material sacrifices. It has been estimated that the First and Second World Wars cost the American

14

people over 400 billion dollars. After World War II the largest items in our national budget were armaments, veterans' services, and aid to countries devastated by war. These were some of the costs which American citizens had to pay for national survival and for the preservation of the civilization they cherish.

Unlike other world leaders of past and present, the people of the United States have no aggressive designs upon any other nation, nor do they seek additional territory. Indeed, through agencies such as the Economic Cooperation Administration (ECA), the United States has contributed billions of dollars to strengthen nations weakened by war and to establish conditions throughout the world in which war will be less likely to break out. Through the United Nations, through regional defense plans for the Western Hemisphere and the North Atlantic, and in other ways, the United States has committed itself to resist aggression whenever it may threaten.

American citizens, always quick to defend their own rights, respect the right of other nations to lead their own lives and develop their own institutions, without outside interference, so long as they do not threaten the peace of the world. Since they are willing to concede this right to other nations, they quite naturally expect, or even insist, that other nations do likewise. Meantime, after two bitter experiences, the armed services of the United States stand guard to protect, if need be, the property, the institutions, and the lives of American citizens.

• • •

The foregoing pages have given you an over-all view of a few important characteristics of modern America — your America. You are now ready to begin the story of the exciting events, the profound ideals, and heroic acts which went into its making. It is a story of vital interest for every citizen — the Making of Modern America.

15

AMERICA
CHANGES
ITS VIEW
OF THE
WORLD

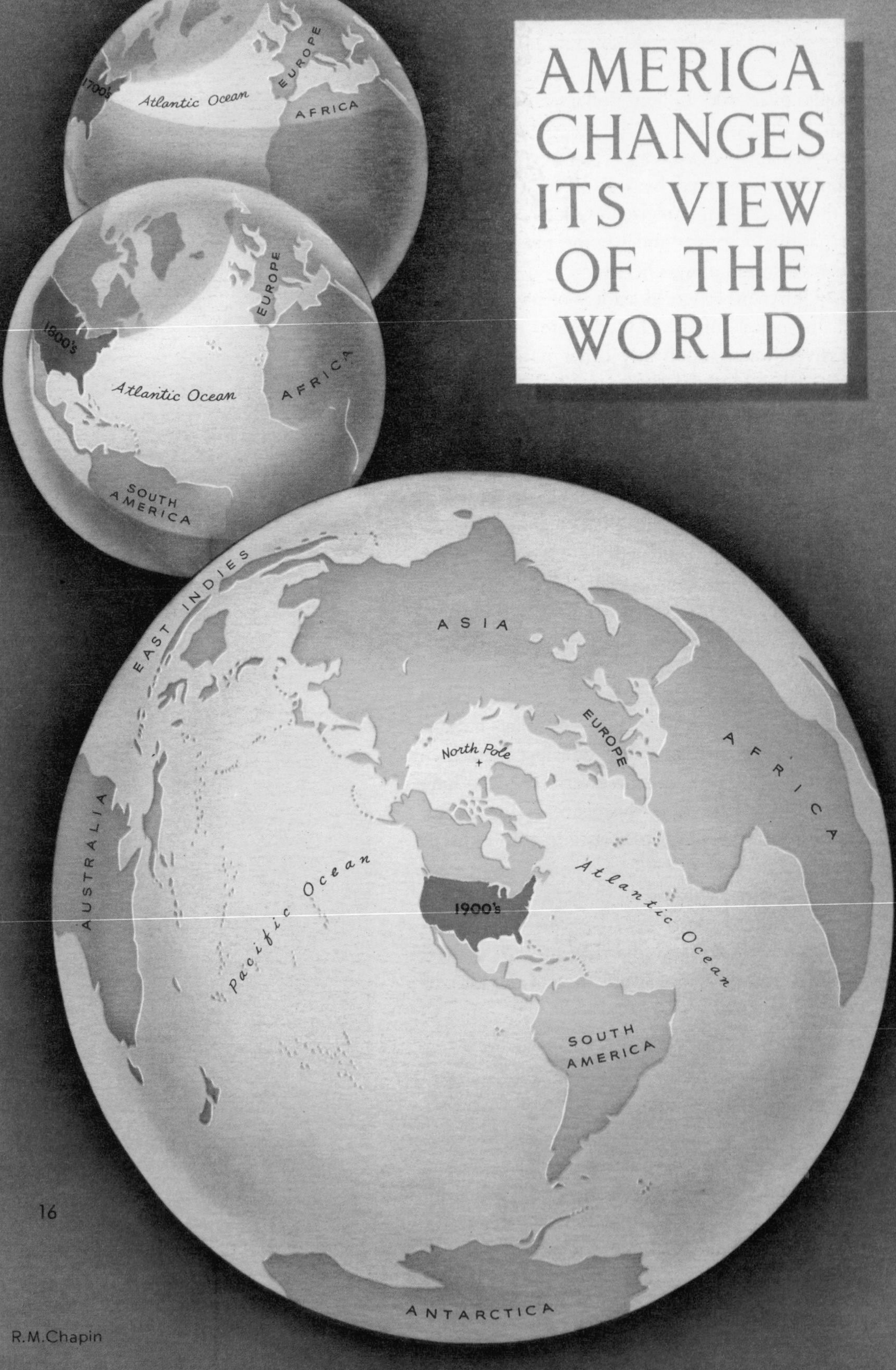

1700's
Atlantic Ocean
EUROPE
AFRICA

1800's
Atlantic Ocean
EUROPE
AFRICA
SOUTH AMERICA

EAST INDIES
AUSTRALIA
ASIA
EUROPE
North Pole
AFRICA
Pacific Ocean
1900's
Atlantic Ocean
SOUTH AMERICA
ANTARCTICA

16

R.M.Chapin

Part One

EARLY AMERICA DEVELOPS

"Independence has been declared!"

THE PLAN OF THE BOOK

Unit One

EUROPEANS ESTABLISH AN INDEPENDENT NATION IN THE NEW WORLD

America owes much to Europe. Europeans brought to the New World their religion, their institutions of government, and their ways of living. Yet there were two important reasons why colonial America — and especially the America of the thirteen colonies — was never merely a transplanted Europe.

First, the colonists were not completely representative of the peoples of the Old World countries. They were more venturesome and determined to get ahead. Usually they had been so dissatisfied with conditions at home that they had been willing to risk their lives crossing 3000 miles of ocean and settling in a wilderness. Many of them wanted greater freedom to govern themselves and to worship as they pleased.

Second, living conditions in the New World were far different from those they had left behind. A small population in a vast area made it easy for a colonist to own land. Because of distance, Great Britain, the mother country, found it difficult to enforce the regulations she laid down for the colonies. Necessity compelled the settlers to take care of themselves and develop ways of living which met their new needs.

After 1763 Great Britain tried to tighten her control over her thirteen colonies in the New World — but too late. For over 150 years Americans had lived under a tradition of self-government, and they were unwilling to accept further restrictions. Driven to take up arms against Great Britain, they later decided to declare their independence. Many of the colonists were doubtful about taking such an extreme step, but there were many others who greeted the Declaration of Independence with cheers. Among the latter, as shown in the picture at the left, were those who had volunteered to fight in the colonial army. Their way of life had prepared them for freedom. They were willing to risk their lives for what they thought right.

Chapter 1

Columbus

EUROPE FINDS AND EXPLORES

A NEW WORLD

. . . Here the people could endure no longer. They complained of the length of the voyage. But the Admiral cheered them up in the best way he could, giving them good hopes of the advantages they might gain from it. He added that, however much they might complain, he had to go to the Indies, and that he would go on until he found them. . . .

From the JOURNAL OF CHRISTOPHER COLUMBUS

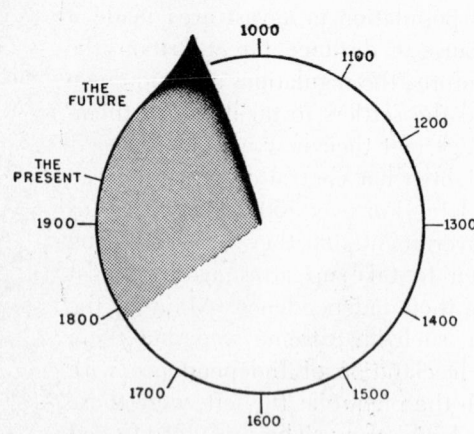

Middle Ages - 1782

One August day in 1492, a fleet of three little ships, under the flag of Spain, sailed westward across the Atlantic Ocean. For weeks the frightened crews looked out on unknown and uncharted seas. There was great rejoicing aboard the ships when land was sighted at last. Little did the sailors suspect, however, that their pilot — an Italian navigator named Christopher Columbus — had led them safely to a New World.

Nor did people in Europe have any way of knowing on October 12, 1492, what Columbus and his men had done. No radio networks stood ready to broadcast the first flash; no newsreel cameramen circled overhead in airplanes to snap pictures as Columbus set foot upon the shore; no newspapers rolled from mighty presses to feature the story in headlines.

Only gradually did Europeans learn of this historic voyage. At first, like Columbus, they thought a new route to Asia had been discovered. Finally the great truth dawned on them: Columbus had actually piloted his ships to an unknown land. That discovery brought many changes in European life. But they were only part of a larger pattern of changes that had taken place in Europe before 1500. New ideas and new interests were stirring everywhere. The Middle Ages were ending, modern times were beginning, and all Europe was swiftly awakening.

To understand this awakening is to understand better how the United States of America got its start. This first chapter explains some of Europe's new interests and ideas, and shows how they led to explorations all over the world — and especially in the Americas. Here are the important points in the chapter:

1. Changes in European life lead to voyages of discovery.
2. Adventurers explore the earth and discover a New World.
3. Spain builds a rich empire in the New World.
4. France explores and colonizes in North America.

---

1 **Changes in European Life Lead to Voyages of Discovery**

Europe lives under the feudal system. For a number of centuries before the days of Columbus, during a time now called the Middle Ages, western Europe was divided into many estates, or manors. Each manor was controlled by a lord or baron. Most of the common people lived as *serfs* upon these estates. The life of a serf was not much better than that of a slave. He was bound to the soil, and if the land changed ownership, he went with it. The serf made a bare living, but most of his labor went

to the support of the lord. In return, the lord of the manor acted as judge-and-jury in settling disputes that arose among his serfs. He also protected them from attack by enemies outside his estate. The lord of the manor usually received his estate from a more powerful noble, to whom he owed duties, chiefly military service.

Knight and Lady

Under this arrangement, called the *feudal system*, there was little peace and much brutality. Members of the ruling, or landholding, class usually had their own private bands of soldiers, and fighting was constantly breaking out between such bands. As long as Europe remained under the feudal system, with people dependent upon minor feudal lords for protection, kings and emperors were not very important. Closely-knit countries, as we think of them today, did not exist.

Feudalism gives way to nationalism. As time went on, however, members of the ruling class decreased in number. Powerful lords crushed weaker lords and took their estates. Strong families intermarried with other strong families. At last certain great rulers were able to create mighty kingdoms. National states under powerful governments, like Spain, England, France, and Portugal, were created in this way.

Under the new pattern of government serfdom began to decline. Although some of the duties that serfs had been required to perform still remained, people were at least free to move about and earn their living as they pleased. Feudal lords in turn left their estates to live around persons of greater influence —usually at the court of the king. Loyalty of the people to a common ruler rather than to a number of lesser nobles brought about a feel-

Serf

ing of national unity and encouraged patriotism.

Trade increases between Europe and the East. As the feudal system declined, trade with the outside world began to grow. Trade had not been much needed under the feudal system, when each estate took care of the needs of its own people. In fact, during the Middle Ages, trade in western Europe hit a very low point, and the city life that had been developed earlier by the Romans almost disappeared. Some cities in Italy, like Venice and Genoa, stayed large and busy, but by the year 1100 only a few such cities were carrying on any important trade.

During the next two centuries, however, trade was revived in an unusual way. From western Europe whole armies, led by noblemen in armor, journeyed by land and sea to the Holy Land in Asia Minor. There they fought battle after battle with

Crusader

the Mohammedans in heroic attempts to rescue the Holy Land and bring it again under Christian control. These religious expeditions were known as the Crusades.

People who took part in the Crusades became acquainted with eastern luxuries that they had never dreamed existed. They brought home from the Orient spices, rare drugs, brilliant dyes, perfumes, jewels, ivory, glassware, fine silks, and gorgeous tapestries. More and more Europeans longed to possess such luxuries, so that the demand for them grew rapidly. The merchants of the Italian cities, especially those of Venice, were quick to see the importance of meeting that demand.

Mohammedan expansion (shown in black) was checked by the Byzantine Empire in the East and by the Franks (of France) in the West. How are water areas shown on this map? What means is used to show land areas not controlled by the Mohammedans? To what does the explosion symbol in the Holy Land refer?

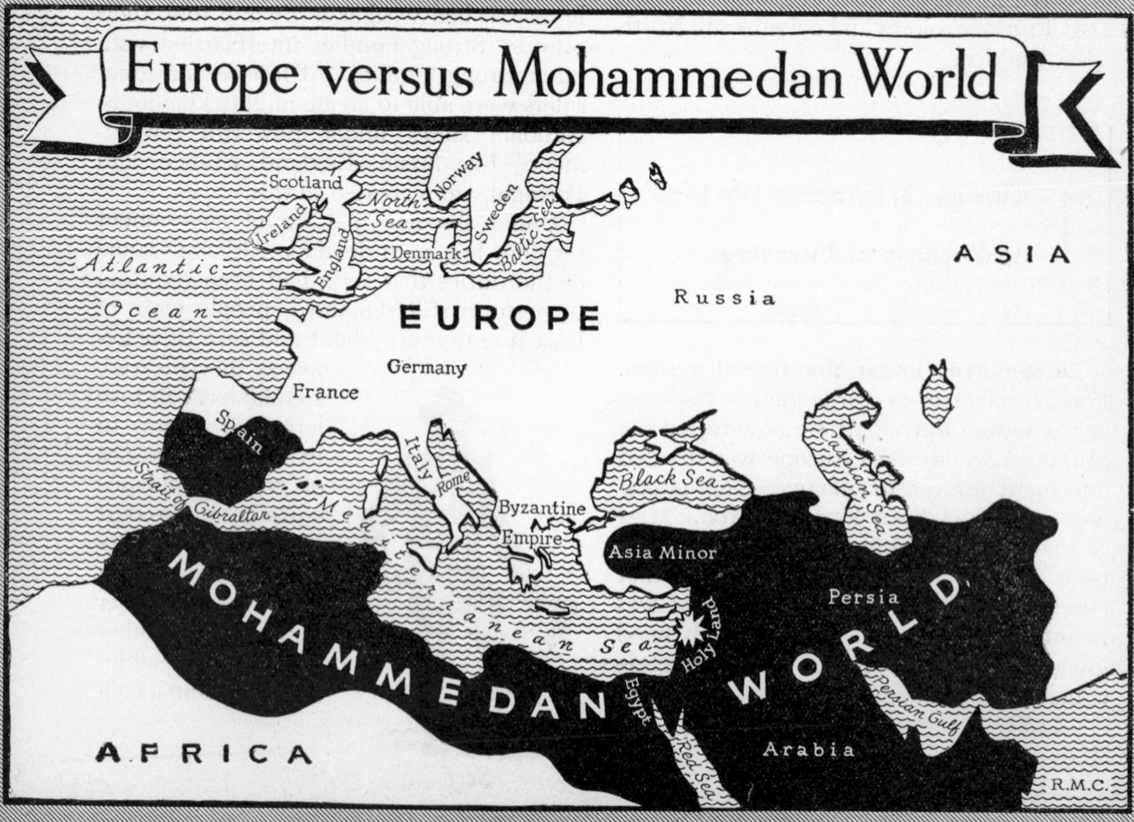

Europe versus Mohammedan World

Scotland · Norway · North Sea · Ireland · England · Denmark · Sweden · Baltic Sea

Atlantic Ocean

EUROPE · Russia · **ASIA**

Germany

France

Spain · Italy · Rome · Black Sea · Caspian Sea

Strait of Gibraltar · Mediterranean Sea · Byzantine Empire · Asia Minor · Persia

MOHAMMEDAN · Egypt · Holy Land · **WORLD**

AFRICA · Red Sea · Arabia · Persian Gulf

R.M.C.

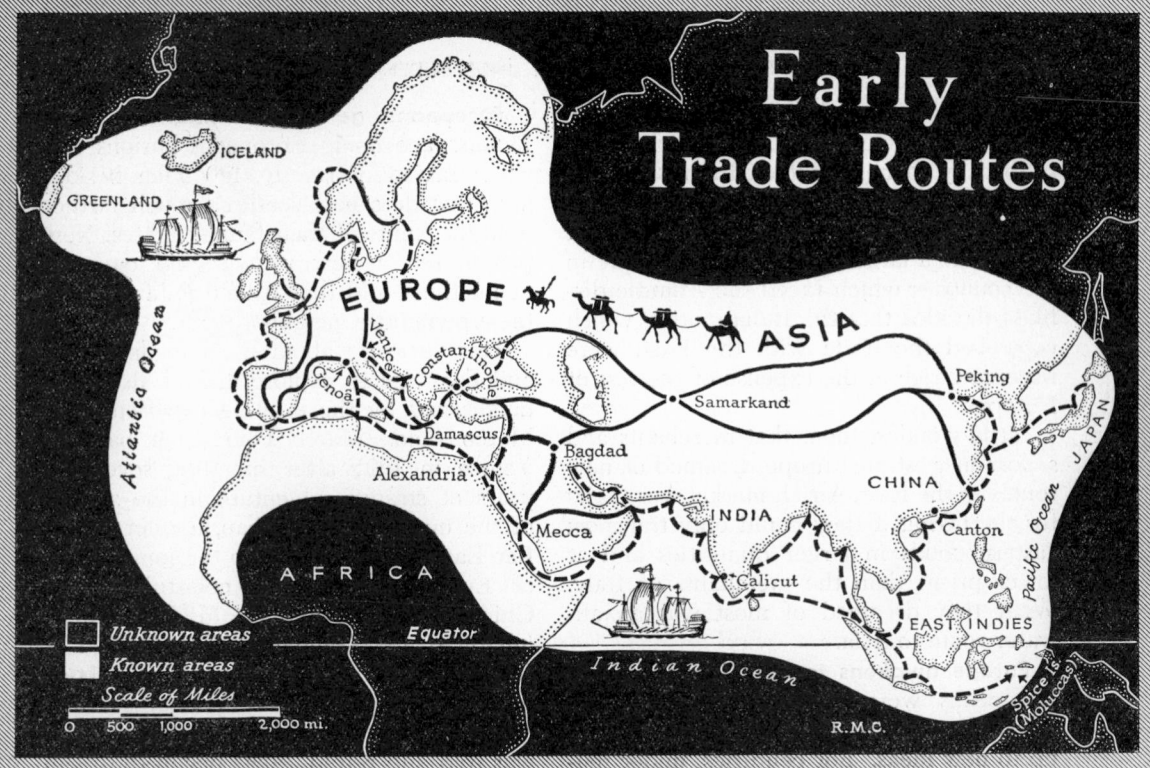

Early Trade Routes

Eastern goods reached Europe over land and water routes. How is each type of route shown? What European cities were most active in this trade? About how far was it from Damascus to Peking by the shortest route? What does the black area represent?

These merchants set out on buying trips to the ports of the eastern Mediterranean, returning to Europe with spices, perfumes, and other items. For centuries some goods had been trickling from many parts of Asia along land and water routes to the cities of the eastern Mediterranean. Now the trade routes became crowded as the riches of Asia began to flow to the Mediterranean Sea, to be shipped by Italian merchants to all parts of Europe. (Trace these routes on the map above.)

A commercial class arises. Somehow the eastern goods had to be paid for. As imports from the Orient flowed into Europe, European gold and silver, never very plentiful, drained out. Money became scarce, but the imports were as desirable as ever. So western Europe now began to produce a surplus of her own goods which could be traded for eastern luxuries. Woolen fabrics, wines, metals, furs, and grains were shipped to the East. Two-way trading became so brisk that it brought a rebirth of town life in western Europe. This

growth of industry and trade resulted · in the appearance of a new middle class — merchants, traders, professional men, and skilled workers.

The new middle class, to protect its own interests, favored national laws. Instead of the tangle of local feudal laws which touched only a few persons, they wanted laws that everyone in a country would have to obey. Because kings stood for national law and could put down feudal disorders, it is not surprising that the middle class became the chief supporters of kings. In this way the new national states were further strengthened.

Europeans desire new trade routes. People in Europe gradually became so used to enjoying the products of the Orient that, by the end of the 1400's, such products ceased to be luxuries; they became necessities. Spices, especially, were now needed to flavor and preserve food. Eastern goods were still brought to Europe by means of Oriental caravans and the galleys of Italian merchants. Many shipments of goods, however, never reached the European trade centers because caravans were waylaid and robbed by roving bands of thieves. Moreover, almost all the business with the East was in the hands of Italian merchants, who made a large profit from it. People in the countries which faced the Atlantic disliked the idea that the Italian cities, which controlled the trade with the East, were becoming rich at the expense of the rest of Europe.

Little wonder, then, that merchants and sailors in western Europe dreamed of new routes to the East. A rich market was theirs for the taking if they could only transport eastern goods in larger quantities and at lower prices than the merchants of Italy. What they dreamed of most was an all-water route to Asia.

Europe awakens to new ideas. While Europeans were learning to enjoy new physical comforts, they were also waking up to new ideas. For centuries, under feudalism, people's interests had been limited to the simple affairs of the small estates on which they lived. They had almost completely lost the desire to educate themselves. Few men had written books or produced works of art.

Now the relations with the East were bringing about a new interest in learning. Europeans not only came in contact with the rich culture of the Mohammedans but also rediscovered the advanced learning of the Greeks and Romans. The booming trade relations which grew out of the Crusades also stirred up an exciting exchange of ideas between Europe and the East. The result was a great revival of learning and of the arts.

This revival took many forms. Universities were founded and grew. Scholars began to study and enjoy certain literature and art of Greece and Rome which had been neglected or forgotten. Architecture and painting flourished. Stories and travelers' tales were written in the simple languages which common people understood, instead of in Latin. By the time of Columbus, this great intellectual movement was on the march. The movement is called the *Renaissance* (ren-eh-sahnss'), which means rebirth.

Europeans get the wanderlust. The Renaissance made Europeans curious and adventurous. Formerly, few men besides the Crusaders had ventured much farther than the limits of their feudal estates. Now people felt a new wonder and curiosity about the world that stretched far beyond their own little neighborhoods.

This curiosity about the outside world, and the urge to explore it, had also been heightened by the exciting experiences of Marco Polo. Marco Polo came back to Venice in 1295 after spending seventeen years of strange adventure in the service of the mighty Kubla Khan, a ruler of the Far East. He whipped up the imagination of Europeans with his colorful tale of China and Japan and the "12,700 islands, inhabited and uninhabited," in the sea of India — a tale which appeared in a book called *Concerning the Kingdoms and Marvels of the East.* As Marco Polo's story was told and retold, kings began to dream of new empires, merchants to search for new and richer markets, and missionaries to leave home in the hope of saving the souls of heathens. But most important of all, the story stirred up the restless spirit of seagoing men who pushed farther and farther in search of adventure and new discoveries.

Printed books inspire new learning. Just before the middle of the 1400's the art of printing from movable type was discovered in Europe. Until then, making a book had been a slow, tedious job. Every letter had to be written by hand, and it took months to copy just a single manuscript. Few people could afford these books. Since most people had no books, there was little reason for learning to read. With few readers, there were few writers. For hundreds of years learned men were chiefly to be found among the clergy. Monks in lonely monasteries struggled to keep alive an interest in learning during the Middle Ages.

After the invention of printing, conditions changed. Books now could be turned out in larger quantities at much less expense. The number of people able to own books increased. And the desire for education — especially in the new middle class — increased also. The change-over from medieval to modern life was advanced more by

Scandinavian Vikings actually reached the New World before Columbus. They colonized Greenland and Iceland, then landed on the shores of Labrador about the year 1000. They also explored the coast and part of the interior of North America but they founded no lasting settlements there, so that their exploits were generally unknown to Europeans of the late 1400's. A modern artist shows here what a Viking ship probably looked like.

the invention of printing than by any other single happening at that time.

The science of navigation improves. Another outcome of the Renaissance was the development of scientific knowledge, in particular the science of navigation. A belief that the earth was round — claimed by ancient geographers but forgotten by most people during the Middle Ages — was brought out, dusted off, and accepted again as truth. By this time, too, the compass for determining direction, and the astrolabe for measuring latitude, were being used. Although sailors still depended largely upon skill and experience, they could now get maps and charts that roughly traced Europe's coastline and showed fairly well

the position of Europe's seaports. Everything was pointing toward a period of exploration and discovery.

——— CHECK-UP ———

How did changes in European life lead to voyages of discovery?

1. By what means did Europeans make a living during the Middle Ages? How were Europeans governed?
2. What factors encouraged a revival of trade between Europe and the East? Who controlled this trade?
3. Why did Europeans become dissatisfied with the older trade routes?
4. What developments paved the way for the great voyages of discovery?

2 Adventurers Explore the Earth and Discover a New World

Portugal seeks a sea route to Asia. The Portuguese were the first to discover an all-water route to the Orient. Portugal was planted squarely on the path of the Italian ships which sailed out of the Mediterranean to trade along the Atlantic seaboard. (See map, page 23.) Watching the rich business of the Italian merchants go past their front door, the Portuguese naturally grew interested in commerce and exploration. It seemed to them that their own capital city, Lisbon, ought to share in the wealth coming from east-west trade that Venice and Genoa were cornering for themselves. Portuguese interest in exploration was furthered during the 1400's by Prince Henry

The Portuguese route to Asia differed from earlier routes in what way? How did Portuguese explorations extend the size of the known world?

the Navigator, a younger son of the royal family of Portugal. Prince Henry believed that scientists should know much more about geography than they did. He was also interested in the exploration of Africa. At the southern tip of Portugal, he set up a school for navigators.

Vasco da Gama reaches India by water. Prince Henry's enthusiasm for exploration spurred many Portuguese adventurers to head their ships southward along the western shores of Africa. Before many years, some of them had sailed past the Canary Islands, discovered Cape Verde, and reached Cape Sierra Leone. Starting out in 1486, Bartholomew Dias (dee'ahs) cruised down the entire length of the African coast and rounded the Cape of Good Hope before turning back.

Twelve years later, in 1498, Vasco da Gama finally made the dream of the Portuguese come true — he actually reached India by water. Da Gama sailed along the west coast of Africa, rounded the Cape of Good Hope, then crossed the Indian Ocean. (See map on this page.) At the end of the voyage, he dropped anchor off Calicut, in India. A little later, a navigator named Albuquerque reached the Spice Islands. Before long, Portuguese mariners were bringing back the spices, drugs, and fine fabrics of the Orient at a cost below what the Italian merchants had to pay for the same goods in the ports of Asia Minor.

Columbus seeks Asia and finds a New World. It was while the Portuguese were trying to reach Asia by sailing around Africa that Columbus insisted he could reach Asia by sailing straight west across the Atlantic. His bold plan was based upon the belief that the world was round, and upon maps which were wrong. These maps showed the distance west from Europe to China to be much less than it actually is. (See map, page 27.)

The obstacles Columbus met when he tried to get support for his trip, and the problems he faced in piloting his little fleet across the Atlantic, are a familiar story. His courage, in the face of such difficulties, marks the beginning of the vision and sacrifice out of which America has grown.

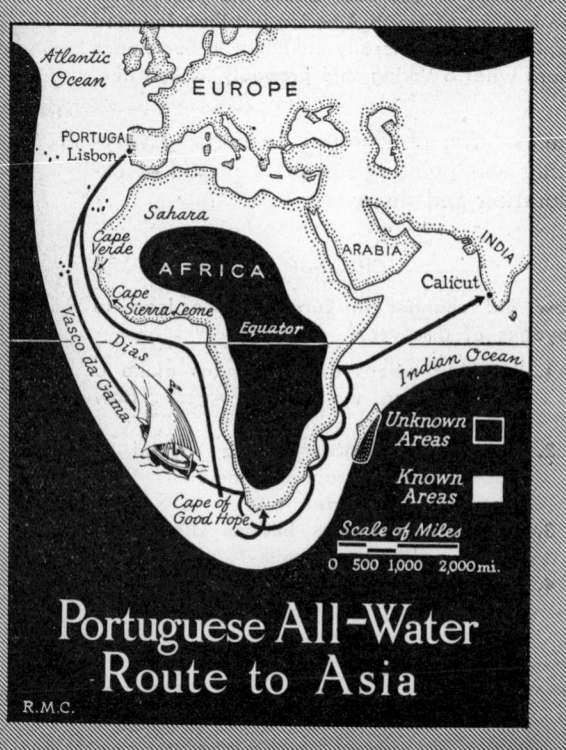

Portuguese All-Water Route to Asia

R.M.C.

Columbus Discovers the New World

Columbus thought that the world was smaller than it is and that Asia lay directly to the west of Spain (see map at right)

... With these mistaken ideas Columbus sailed westward and by accident discovered the New World (see map below)

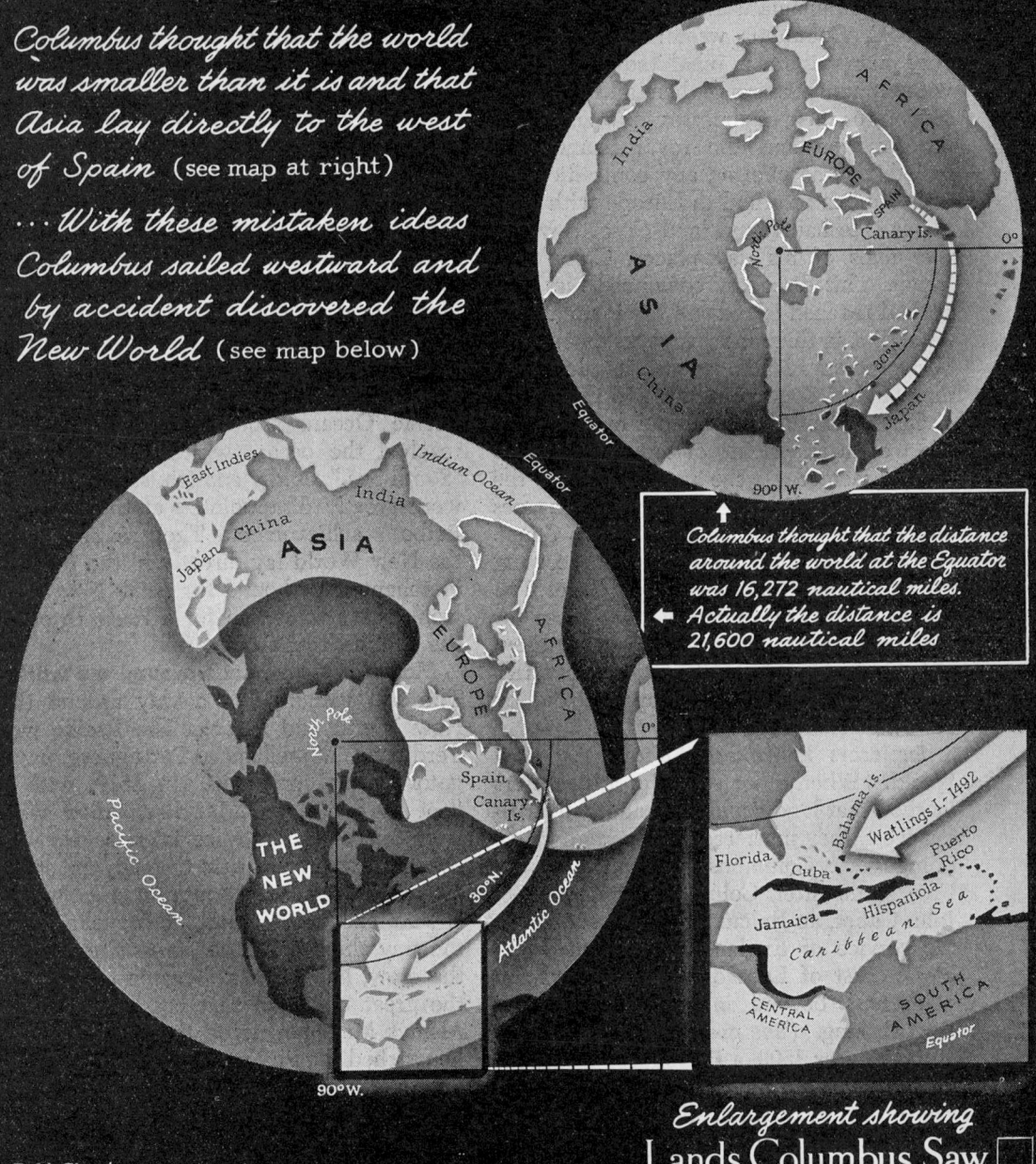

Columbus thought that the distance around the world at the Equator was 16,272 nautical miles. Actually the distance is 21,600 nautical miles

R. M. Chapin

Enlargement showing
Lands Columbus Saw

Expert navigators were few in the late 1400's, but Columbus was one of them. Still, owing to imperfect geographical knowledge at that time, Columbus made several errors. Compare the small globe at the upper right with the larger one at the lower left, and note two errors he made: (1) in locating the prime meridian (longitude 0°), and (2) in estimating the circumference of the earth. Compare the length of the voyage he planned with the one he actually made. Why did he discover the West Indies instead of Japan? Did Columbus know the true size of Asia? Note in the enlarged inset at the lower right the portions of the New World that Columbus actually discovered.

Some time after he had finally reached one of the Bahama Islands that October day of 1492, Columbus wrote: "I discovered very many islands, inhabited by people without number: and of them all I took possession for their Highnesses [of Spain] with proclamation and the royal banner unfurled, no one offering any contradiction."

Columbus returned to Europe with high hopes. He had found land close to where the maps of his day placed China and Japan. This discovery convinced him that he had reached islands off the mainland of Asia. But in three later voyages among the West Indian islands, as well as along the mainland of South America and the shores of Central America, Columbus failed to find the wealth and riches of the Orient. This failure seemed all the worse because the Portuguese kept bringing back rich cargoes along the sea route charted by da Gama. In 1506, Columbus died without receiving credit or honor for what he had done. The Spanish king and queen had little use for him because he had failed to bring them riches. Despite his great service to civilization, Columbus was never appreciated by his own generation.

Explorers learn more about the New World. When other seagoing adventurers learned that land could be reached by sailing west, they mustered the courage to try doing what Columbus had failed to do. Five years after Columbus' first voyage, John Cabot, an Italian navigator, set sail in the service of England. He reached the bleak coast of Labrador and claimed the wilderness beyond in the name of the English king. (See map, page 43.)

In the year 1500, a Portuguese navigator named Pedro Cabral (pay'-droh cah-brahl') was on his way south along the coast of Africa when strong winds and currents carried his fleet across the Atlantic. He landed on the eastern shore of South America in what is now called Brazil, and claimed it for Portugal. At about the same time, an Italian adventurer named Amerigo Vespucci (ah-may-ree'goh ves-poot'chee), sailing first for Spain and then for Portugal, skirted the shores of South America. Vespucci suspected that the land he sighted was more than an island off the Asiatic mainland. Finally he became convinced that he was looking at a new continent. In figuring out this fact, Vespucci made an important contribution to history — though it is clear that Columbus' contribution was far greater. Vespucci wrote so many letters about the New World upon which he had stumbled that the land came to be called America in his honor.

As the years went by, adventurers pushed even farther to the west. In 1513 a Spaniard named Balboa struggled through the fever-ridden jungles and deadly swamps of Panama until he reached a high point of land from which he could look upon the Pacific Ocean. Four days later Balboa reached the ocean, which he called the "South Sea." Oddly enough, seafaring men were greatly disappointed at the news of Balboa's achievement. They realized that the New World lay directly in the path of merchant ships bound for Asia. Now they would have to search for a route through the continent or around it.

Magellan's crew sails around the world. The first man to find a way around the New World and to cross the Pacific was Ferdinand Magellan, a Portuguese navigator sailing for Spain. In 1519, with a fleet of five ships, Magellan sailed west from Spain for the Spice Islands. He was the first explorer to pass through the strait at the southern end of South America, which is now called the Strait of Magellan. As the tiny ships sailed on across the Pacific, the crew, half-starved, became terrified at the great unknown that lay before them. Always Magellan urged them on. Finally he reached the Philippine Islands — a place he never left, for he was killed there by a poisoned arrow. The expedition pushed on without him. Finally, in 1522, one surviving ship, the *Victoria*, limped back into a Spanish harbor. Eighteen men were left of the original crew — the first men who had sailed all the way around the world. (See map, page 29.)

The world is divided between Spain and Portugal. When Columbus returned to Europe with the incorrect news that he had reached Asia, the Portuguese feared

Voyage of Magellan and His Crew

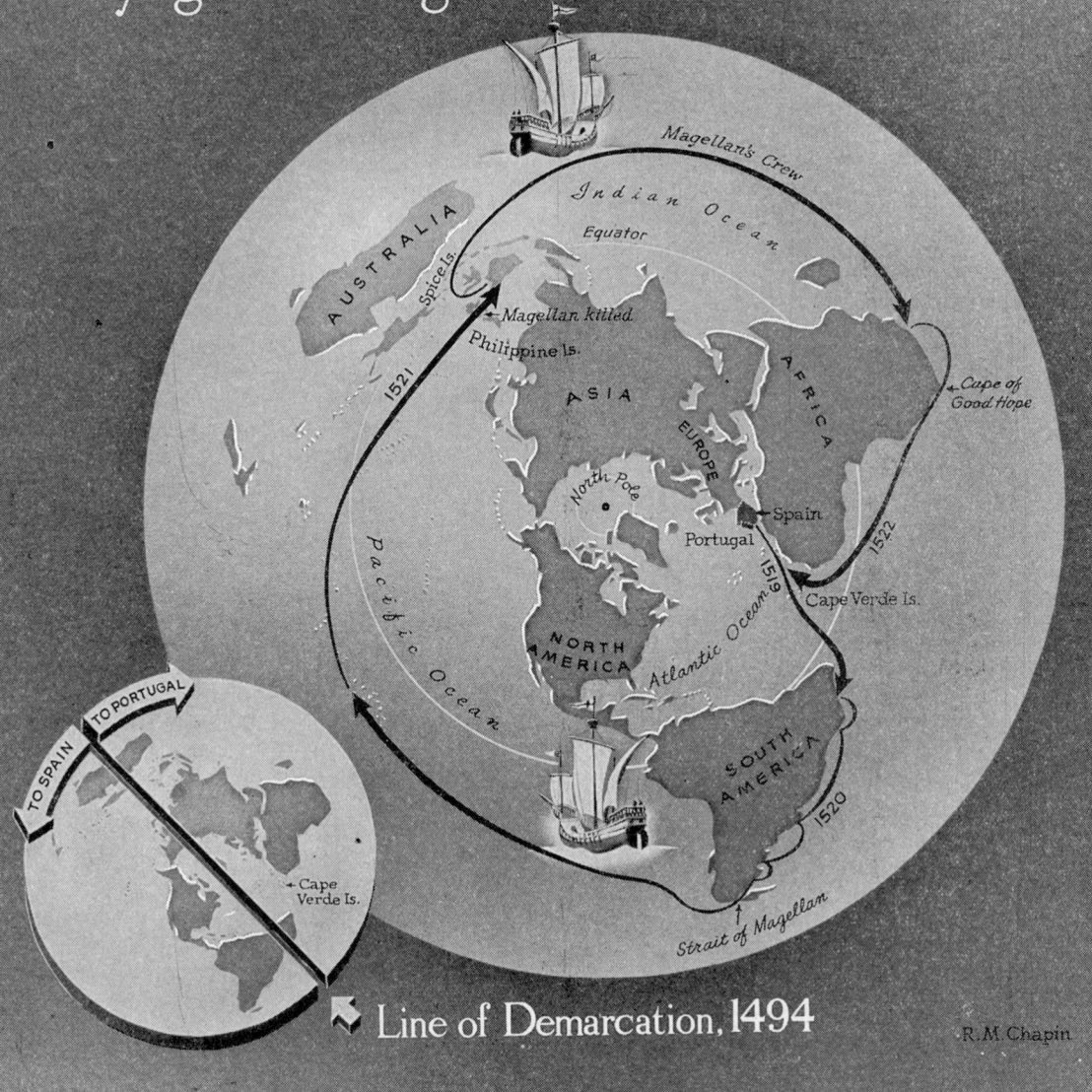

Magellan's Crew

Indian Ocean

Equator

AUSTRALIA

Spice Is.

← Magellan killed

Philippine Is.

1521

ASIA

EUROPE

AFRICA

North Pole

Cape of
Good Hope

→ Spain

Portugal

1522

1519

Cape Verde Is.

Pacific Ocean

NORTH
AMERICA

Atlantic Ocean

TO SPAIN   TO PORTUGAL

SOUTH
AMERICA

1520

← Cape
Verde Is.

Strait of Magellan

⬥ Line of Demarcation, 1494

R. M. Chapin

By the line of demarcation Portugal claimed to the right of the line all new lands **not** already ruled by a Christian king; Spain to the left. What direction did the line run? Note that it went around the earth. During what part of Magellan's voyage was he traveling through area assigned to Spain by the line of demarcation? How can you determine which direction is north from any point on this map?

that their plans for developing trade with the East might be upset. Portugal and Spain disagreed about ownership of other parts of the world. To end the rivalry, Pope Alexander VI, in 1493, drew an imaginary line 100 leagues west of the Cape Verde Islands. Portugal could claim all new lands east of this line; Spain could claim new lands to the west. The next year, Spain and Portugal drew up a treaty which moved this "line of demarcation" 370 leagues west of the Cape Verde Islands. Actually, Portugal was given rights to most of the East, plus Brazil in the New World, while Spain was allowed all the New World except Brazil. (See map, page 29.)

Portugal loses her advantage. After gaining so much land through the revised treaty, Portugal was able for a time to carry on a rich trade with the East Indies and had a monopoly of the slave traffic along the African seaboard. But Portugal was too weak to hold what she had gained. Within a century, she was under the rule of the Spanish king, and the Dutch had taken over her rich eastern trade.

––––––––– CHECK-UP –––––––––

What great discoveries were made by Spain and Portugal?

1. What discoveries were made by Portuguese navigators?
2. What miscalculations were made by Columbus? Why were these important?
3. Why was each of the following important? (a) Cabot, (b) Cabral, (c) Vespucci, (d) Balboa, (e) Magellan
4. What dispute arose between Spain and Portugal? How was it settled?

3 **Spain Builds a Rich Empire in the New World**

Spain becomes a great power. As the power of Portugal declined, Spain became the mightiest nation in Europe as well as in the New World. The line of demarcation gave Spain an excellent chance to build a great colonial empire – and she wasted no time in doing so. Led by soldiers of fortune called conquistadors (conquerors), large numbers of Spanish adventurers invaded the New World. (See map, page 31.) Most of them were looking for riches and a route to Asia. They also had hopes of converting the natives to Christianity.

Cortez conquers Mexico. The Spaniards had little trouble in subduing the natives of the Bahamas, Hispaniola, Cuba, and other islands off the mainland. The conquest of Mexico was more difficult. Here, the Aztec Indians lived – a highly civilized race of people who built splendid cities, fine temples, and excellent highways. They dug canals, raised plentiful crops, wove textiles, and worked rich mines of gold and silver. More than that, they had developed an accurate calendar and a form of picture-writing. They had a knowledge of astronomy and of mathematics. But advanced as their civilization was, the Aztecs were no match for the Spaniards when it came to warfare.

In 1519 a dashing Spanish adventurer, Hernando Cortez, landed on the mainland and pushed inland with a force of over 500 foot soldiers and with a few horses. Within two years this small but bold army conquered the Aztecs and destroyed their capital, now Mexico City. The Spaniards tore down Aztec temples, where human sacrifices had been made to the Aztec gods, and carried off untold wealth, which they shipped back to Spain.

Adventurers from Europe continued to flock into New Spain, as Mexico was called. They came for just one reason: to get rich. In general only the priests cared about the rights and feelings of the natives. The Spanish government, though aware that the natives were being treated shamefully, did not have enough control over the conquistadors to prevent their cruelty. Many Aztecs were forced to work in mines and quarries and in other ways were reduced almost to total slavery. Only around the many missions founded by the priests was the life of the natives easier.

Pizarro conquers Peru. Francisco Pizarro, a daring lieutenant under Balboa, heard stories about a rich empire in Peru, far to the south. Pizarro decided to strike out on his own. About 1531 he organized a small force and headed for Peru. The

Inca

Spanish Explorations in the New World

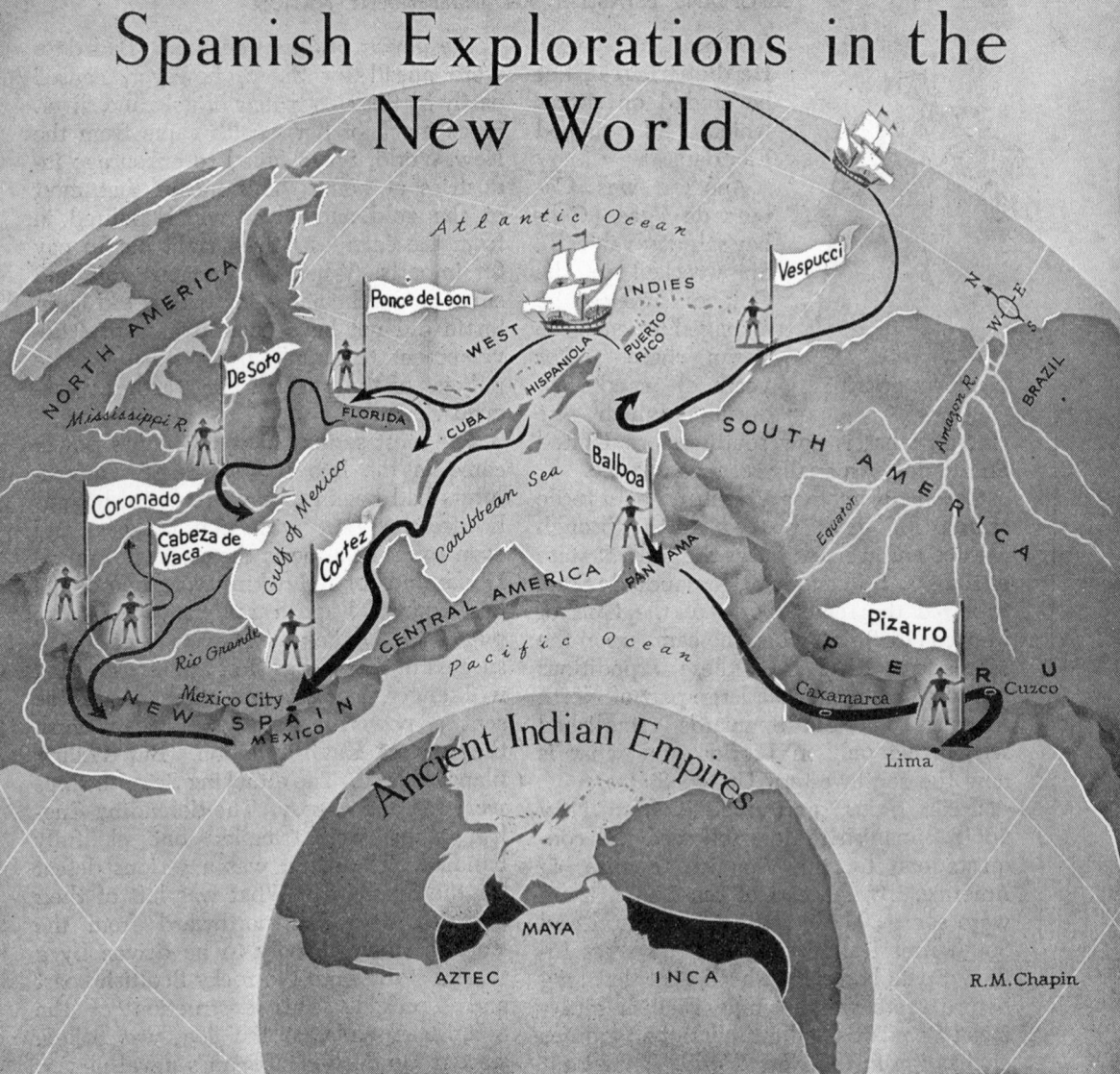

The unusual projection of this map emphasizes the portions of the New World explored by certain Spaniards. What present-day territory did each explore? What direction did Pizarro follow in going to Peru? Cortez in going from Cuba to Mexico? How can you tell from this map?

stories had been true. Pizarro found a native civilization superior in agricultural development, architecture, and government to any other in the New World. But Pizarro treated the Indians and their leaders, the Incas, in the same way that Cortez had treated the Aztecs. He had no interest in their fine civilization. He was interested only in the booty he could strip from their temples, tombs, and palaces. Faced by the military skill of the Spaniards, the Incas were powerless.

Spanish explorers push northward. There were other Spanish explorers who made names for themselves. None, however, uncovered such dazzling stores of wealth as Cortez and Pizarro had found in Mexico and Peru. One of them, Ponce de Leon (pohn'say day lay-ohn') set out in 1513 from Puerto Rico looking for a fabled

Spanish priest

fountain of youth. He didn't find it, but he landed on shores which he named Florida.

Another was Cabeza da Vaca (Cahbay'sah day vah'cah). Shipwrecked in the Gulf of Mexico, he managed to reach the Texan shore. After years of wandering, during which he crossed what is now southwestern United States, de Vaca finally reached Mexico.

Coronado, another adventurer on a futile search for gold, pushed north through Mexico and went as far as the present state of Kansas. Still another, Hernando de Soto, explored the region north of the Gulf of Mexico (1539–42), where he came upon the Mississippi River. All these expeditions gave Spain a claim to a large part of North America, but the Spaniards established settlements only in Florida and what is now the southwestern United States.

Spain gains great wealth from New Spain. Spanish settlers followed the conquistadors to the Spanish empire in America. By the end of the 1500's, there were some 200,000 settlers in Central and South America, Mexico, and the West Indies. Spain had such a head start that long before there was a single English settlement, Spaniards had established a vigorous civilization in the New World. They built beautiful churches and monasteries, prosperous estates, and thriving cities. They had printing presses, libraries, schools, and universities.

The Spaniards introduced horses and mules, fruits and cereals to the New World. They raised grain, sugar, and cattle in New Spain for shipment to Europe. The New World settlements, however, were important to Spain chiefly as a source of gold and silver. Huge amounts of the precious metals, plundered from the Aztecs and Incas and later obtained by working the mines of Peru and Mexico, were shipped to Spain.

The power of Spain declines. Bad days were ahead for Spain, however, caused partly by this steady flow of gold and silver. Since much of her wealth came from the New World, Spain failed to encourage industries at home. This meant that most of the gold and silver which poured in from the colonies flowed right out to pay for imports. When the precious gold and silver stopped coming in, as they did later, Spain did not have enough industrial development to supply her needs. Unwise policies of the Spanish king further weakened Spain.

The most serious blow to Spain's power came in the late 1500's. English adventurers had begun to capture Spanish ships headed for port with rich cargoes, and even to raid the ports themselves. Francis Drake and John Hawkins were two of the best known English raiders. (See map, page 43.) Drake and Hawkins became so successful that Philip II of Spain was stung with anger. For this and other reasons, he sent a powerful fleet in 1588 to crush the upstart English nation. But Philip's plans misfired. The attacking Spanish ships were big and clumsy. The defending English ships were smaller but skillfully handled. The result was a serious defeat for the Spaniards. What was left of their defeated fleet fled northward from the English Channel, only to be driven by a terrific storm onto the rocky Scottish coast and wrecked. This destruction of the Spanish Armada, as the fleet was called, started the decline of Spain's naval power.

——— CHECK-UP ———

How did Spain build a rich empire in the New World?

1. Why were the conquests of Cortez and Pizarro important? How were the Indians treated in the conquered lands?
2. What did each of the following accomplish? (a) Ponce de Leon, (b) Cabeza de Vaca, (c) Coronado, (d) De Soto
3. How far had Spanish settlements in the New World advanced by the end of the 1500's?
4. What factors contributed to the decline of the Spanish empire?

4 France Explores and Colonizes in North America

France stakes her claims. Back in 1524, the Italian seaman Verrazano (vehr-raht-sah'noh) had made explorations for France. He had cruised along the coast of North America from North Carolina to Nova Scotia, looking for a passage to Asia. Ten years later, Jacques Cartier (khar-tyay') sailed up the St. Lawrence River as far as the spot where Montreal now stands. These voyages gave France a strong claim to a large part of North America. (See map, page 35.) The defeat of the Spanish Armada in 1588, furthermore, brightened the outlook of both England and France for building empires in the New World.

France becomes established in the New World. The earliest permanent French settlement in America was made in 1608 at Quebec, by Samuel de Champlain, the "Father of New France." Other French pioneers followed Champlain, eager to find a passage to Asia, build up a profitable fur trade in North America, or convert the Indians to Christianity. First they blazed their way through to the Great Lakes region, then pushed down the Mississippi valley. Thus, in 1671, St. Lusson reached Sault Ste. Marie (soo sant mar-ee'), between Lakes Superior and Huron, taking possession of the whole area for France. Two years later, Marquette and Joliet (zho-lyay') made their way down the Mississippi to the mouth of the Arkansas River.

Robert Cavelier, Sieur de La Salle, added the last big area to the French empire in America. In 1682 La Salle floated down the Mississippi all the way to its mouth. He took formal possession of the vast Mississippi valley for France and named it "Louisiana" in honor of King Louis XIV of France.

Soon, along the waterways of the interior of North America, the French built a series of military posts. Besides serving for defense, these posts were used both as trading stations and as missionary centers. French traders persuaded the Indians to give them valuable furs in return for trinkets, hatchets, knives, brandy, and guns.

French explorers, like those of other lands, claimed new territory in the name of their king. Along the broad inland waterways they left on the land the names of France and Frenchmen: prairie, bayou, La Salle, Fond du Lac, St. Louis.

Jesuit priests labored courageously to convert the Indians to Christianity.

Farming is poor in New France. Three fourths of the colonists of New France took up farming as an occupation, but few of them were successful. The forest clearings were not large. Methods of farming were primitive. The French settlements were too far north to have a long growing season, and the soil was not always fertile. Settlers were barely able to raise enough crops for their own needs. Because these farmers, much like the peasants in France, had to pay rent for their lands, the younger men often quit farming to take up the freer, better-paying life of the forest ranger or the fur trapper.

Furs and fish bring profits. The fur trade of New France, which depended largely upon the Indians, was far more profitable than farming. To build up this trade, French fur traders learned to speak Indian languages and to live the way the Indians lived. Some of them took Indian wives. During the 1600's, Indians brought their furs each year to Montreal for trading. In later times the traders journeyed deep into the great forests to the west and did their bartering with the natives at Detroit, Green Bay, and Sault Ste. Marie.

Fishing also brought profits to New France. French fishermen had been sailing into the North Atlantic before the settlement of Quebec. But when Frenchmen settled Newfoundland, Cape Breton Island, and Acadia, the fishing industry in these northern areas became well established.

New France grows slowly. The French government tried various schemes to promote the development of New France. But there were several important reasons why few people were willing to move to New France.

(1) There was no chance for the ordinary settler to buy his own land. Huge estates in New France were parceled out among French noblemen, who in turn were expected to persuade tenants to leave France and work the estates under near-feudal conditions. Naturally, there was nothing in this system that was attractive to the average French farmer.

(2) There were no opportunities for religious freedom. The French king would allow no one to go to New France except Frenchmen who were members of the Roman Catholic Church. Thus the French Protestants, or Huguenots, who would have been glad to start a new life in New France, were not allowed to do so.

(3) There was little political freedom in New France. A royal governor was appointed by the king for the whole colony, and his powers were almost unlimited. Justice was handed down by royal magistrates under royal law, without jury trial. In their social and religious life as well as in their work and government, the people of New France took orders from representatives of the French king.

(4) Finally, the French home government treated New France as a stepchild without any rights — a country where the people were expected to live and work only for the benefit of the mother country. The colony was looked at merely as a convenient place to get raw materials and as a market for goods manufactured in France. Such an attitude killed any ambition the settlers might have to strike out in commercial and industrial ventures.

These were the reasons why New France failed to grow rapidly. When New France was finally surrendered to Great Britain in 1763, only 80,000 people lived there. At the same time, the English colonies had a population nearly 20 times as large.

——— CHECK-UP ———

How did France found colonies in North America?

1. How did France establish a claim to large parts of North America?
2. Identify each of the following: (a) Champlain, (b) La Salle, (c) Marquette and Joliet.
3. What ways of living and making a living were followed in New France?
4. Why did the population of New France grow slowly?

French fur trader

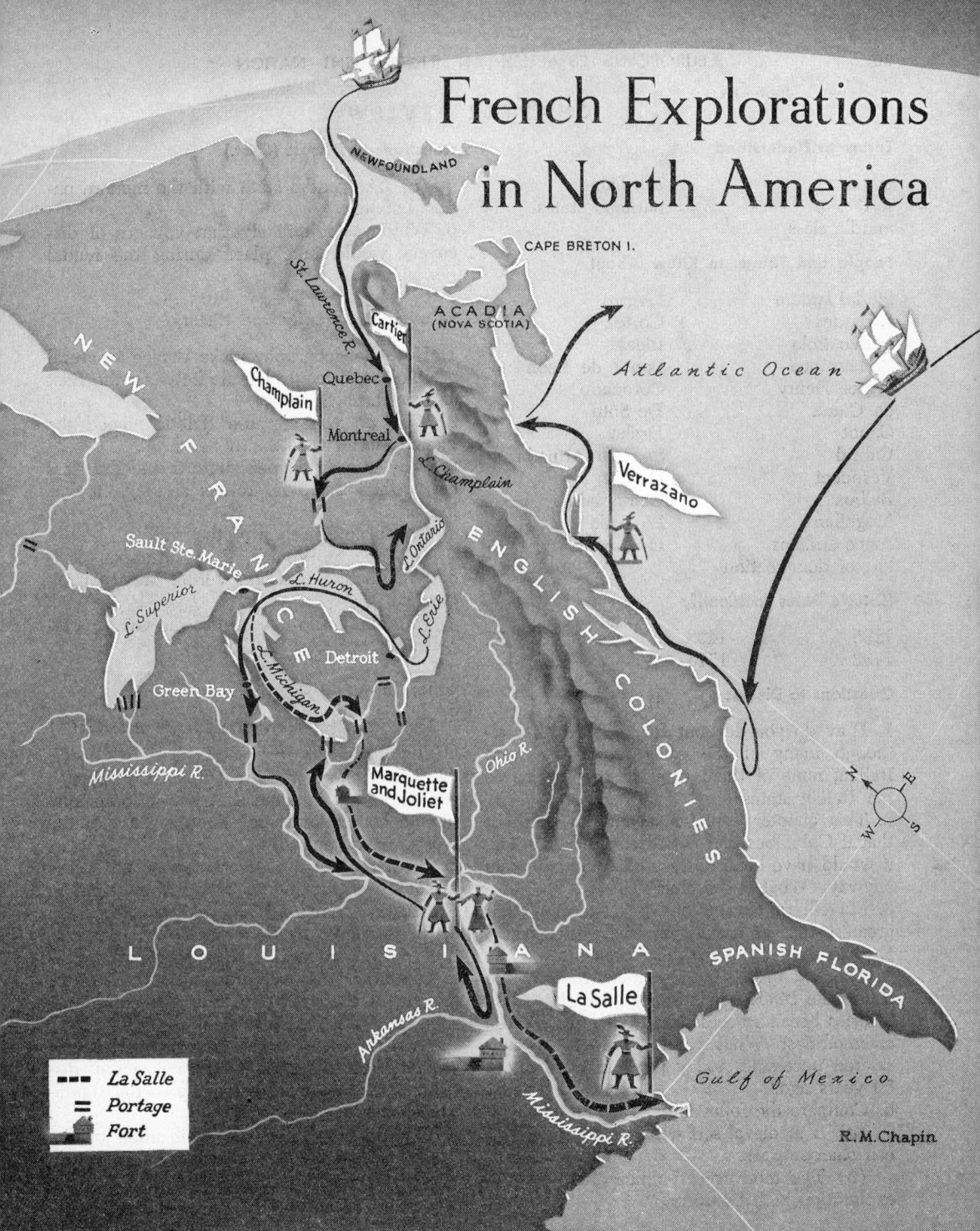

French Explorations in North America

NEWFOUNDLAND

CAPE BRETON I.

St. Lawrence R.

Cartier

ACADIA
(NOVA SCOTIA)

Champlain

Quebec

Atlantic Ocean

Montreal

L. Champlain

Verrazano

NEW FRANCE

Sault Ste. Marie

L. Ontario

ENGLISH COLONIES

L. Superior

L. Huron

L. Erie

L. Michigan

Detroit

Green Bay

Ohio R.

Mississippi R.

Marquette and Joliet

N
W — E
S

LOUISIANA

SPANISH FLORIDA

La Salle

Arkansas R.

Gulf of Mexico

Mississippi R.

R. M. Chapin

- - - La Salle
= Portage
 Fort

The projection of this map brings into the foreground that portion of interior North America which the French successfully explored. The routes of what explorers are shown? Why did they follow the routes they did? What direction did La Salle travel in reaching the Gulf of Mexico? How can you tell? What kind of line has the artist used in showing **La Salle's** route? What is the meaning of the word "portage"?

CHAPTER REVIEW

Terms to Understand

manor   astrolabe
serf   national states
middle class

People and Things to Know About

feudal system   Pizarro
Crusades   Cortez
Marco Polo   Incas
Renaissance   Ponce de Leon
Prince Henry   Coronado
da Gama   De Soto
Cabot   Drake
Cabral   Spanish Armada
Vespucci   Cartier
Balboa   Champlain
Magellan   La Salle
Aztec Indians   Huguenots
line of demarcation

Historic Dates to Identify

1295   1498   1519–22
1492   1513   1588

Questions to Discuss

1. How do you account for the fact that although many of the early navigators were Italian, none of them were in the service of the Italian states?

2. This chapter contains a clue to the fact that if Columbus had not discovered America, it would have been discovered in a few years anyway. What is the clue?

3. Magellan's voyage has been termed "the greatest feat of navigation ever performed." Explain the reasons for this statement.

4. The text makes the statement that by the end of the 1400's commodities which had been luxuries became necessities. What were these commodities? What products which are considered necessities today were luxuries about 50 years ago?

5. Compare the following:

   (a) A medieval serf with a modern American sharecropper.

   (b) The motives of France and Spain in exploration and discovery.

Questions to Discuss (Cont.)

   (c) The feudal state with the modern national state.

6. Why was it unlikely that voyages of discovery would take place during the feudal period?

Relating Geography and History

1. How did geography make Venice a natural middleman to control trade between the East and northern Europe?

2. Why do you suppose Balboa named the Pacific Ocean the "South Sea"?

3. Why was da Gama's route to the East less costly than the older routes although it was longer?

4. On an outline map of the world:

   (a) Locate: Venice, Constantinople, Calicut, the Bahamas, Cape Verde, Mexico City, Quebec.

   (b) Show the routes of: da Gama, Magellan, Cabot, Cortez, De Soto.

Other Things to Do

The activities marked with an asterisk(*) are for the whole class.

*1. Select one of the great Spanish or French explorers, and imagine that you accompanied him in his explorations. Keep a diary of the most eventful episodes.

2. Read the stirring description of La Salle's discovery of the mouth of the Mississippi in Francis Parkman's *La Salle and the Discovery of the Great West.*

3. Prepare a report on some important twentieth century discoverer or explorer. Be sure to discuss the area explored, the equipment used, and the significance of the work.

*4. Make a list of the chief developments which paved the way for the voyages of discovery. In a parallel column give the significance of each.

5. Prepare a talk on the civilization of the Incas or Aztecs at the time of the discoveries. Emphasize the cultural achievements of these peoples.

Read Carefully
50-51

Sec 5

scan quickly

Chapter 2

Roger Williams and Indian

ENGLISH COLONIES DOMINATE

NORTH AMERICA

Having undertaken, for the glory of God and advancement of the Christian faith and honour of our king and country, a voyage to plant the first colony in the northern parts of Virginia, [we] do by these presents solemnly and mutually, in the presence of God and one of another, covenant and combine ourselves together into a civil body politic; . . . and by virtue hereof to enact, constitute, and frame such just and equal laws, ordinances, acts, constitutions, and offices from time to time as shall be thought most meet and convenient for the general good of the colony. . . .

Adapted from THE MAYFLOWER COMPACT, 1620

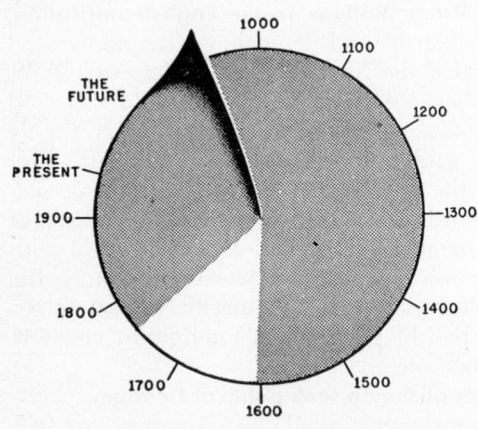

1606-1763

During the century after Columbus' discovery, far-reaching changes were taking place in the world. By the time that English colonization began in the New World early in the 1600's, the area of the earth that was known to man had doubled. Great colonial empires had been staked out. Trade and commerce had increased amazingly. The discovery of new lands promised to change the entire course of history.

Spain at the peak of her colonial power in the 1500's might well have laughed at the possibility of rivalry from England in the New World. The little kingdom of England, bearing small resemblance to the modern British Empire, consisted of only England and Wales. To be sure, a few promising signs of strength were appearing. During the reign of Queen Elizabeth

37

SUCCESSION TO THE ENGLISH CROWN (1485–1820)	
House of Tudor	**House of Stuart**
1485 Henry VII	1660 Charles II
1509 Henry VIII	1685 James II
1547 Edward VI	1688 "Glorious Revo-
1553 Mary	lution"
1558 Elizabeth	1689 William and
	Mary (1694)
House of Stuart	1702 Anne
1603 James I	
1625 Charles I	**House of Hanover**
	1714 George i
Commonwealth	1727 George II
1649 **and Protecto-**	1760 George III
rate	1820 George IV

(see chart above), the English people enjoyed stable government and generally peaceful conditions. The first of Elizabeth's daring sea captains were venturing on long voyages which proved highly profitable. Englishmen were beginning to be proud of their nationality.

After Queen Elizabeth's death, the crowning of James I brought England and Scotland under the same royal family, but for another century Englishmen thought of their Scotch neighbors as foreigners. Ireland was only partly conquered. In the New World, England could base her claims on the explorations of only one man, John Cabot. In the race for colonial power Spain was far in the lead and France was gaining. England seemed quite out of the running.

Yet the time was to come when England's colonial strength would be felt all over the world. In the early 1600's English settlers began founding colonies along the Atlantic seaboard in America. By 1733 there were thirteen of them — thirteen colonies which were to be the foundation stones of the United States of America. Wherever the English settled, they brought with them ideas which led to the creation of a freer way of life. In time personal liberty, self-government, and religious toleration became vital parts of our American democratic tradition.

By 1763 the English had established their control over the eastern half of North

America. To reach that enviable position, the British government, with the help of the colonists, had been obliged to fight a series of wars against the French and Indians. This chapter traces the growth of this English strength in the New World. It explains why Englishmen left the safety of their homeland to brave the dangers and uncertainties of the wilderness, how they planted their thirteen colonies and kept them going, and finally how they made their position firm in North America. These are the main points for the chapter:

1. Conditions in England favor colonization.
2. Virginia becomes the first permanent English colony.
3. The New England colonies are firmly settled.
4. Proprietors establish several vigorous colonies.
5. The British drive the French out of North America.

1 Conditions in England Favor Colonization

Many motives foster English migration. Spaniards and Frenchmen explored and settled the New World out of a craving for riches, a desire for a new route to Asia, and an urge to win Christian converts among the Indians. These motives played a part in the settlement of the English colonies, too — but a smaller part. Certain forces at work in England had far more to do with driving Englishmen westward across the Atlantic Ocean. Primarily, these forces were (1) political, (2) religious, and (3) economic.

Englishmen seek political freedom. Some Englishmen sailed for America because they were unable to live happily under the rule of James I or the other Stuart kings who followed him. (See chart above.) The Stuarts claimed for themselves the right to make and enforce laws without the consent of Parliament, the law-making body in England. They insisted that for whatever they did they were responsible only to God. Many Englishmen resented this theory of Divine Right which the Stuarts adopted, and the resulting conflict between king and Parliament lasted for many years. People left England in anger and resentment to look for homes in the New World. During the years when the king held absolute control, the English settlers in America came from among the king's opponents. Later, when Parliament held the upper hand, the settlers came from the group that supported the king.

A religious conflict arises. The political conflict was not the only one which drove Englishmen to America. There was also a religious conflict which was felt just as deeply. This conflict had its beginnings in a religious revolt which had broken out in Germany ten years after Columbus' death — a revolt which was called the Protestant Reformation. The Protestant Reformation did not end until half of western Europe had broken away from the authority of the Pope and from some of the beliefs taught by the Roman Catholic Church.

By the early 1600's there was only one accepted form of religion in England — the Church of England, or Anglican Church. This church acknowledged the king of England as its head and was Protestant in its beliefs and practices. Every citizen of the kingdom was expected by law to support this church. Anyone who failed to do so was subject to severe penalties.

Two groups object to the Church of England. The Anglican form of worship displeased two groups in England. The first group, the Roman Catholics, would not accept any change in their worship and would not recognize anyone except the Pope as head of the Church. On the other hand, certain Protestants did not feel that the Anglican Church differed enough from the Roman Catholic. Among this second group, some known as Puritans remained in the Church of England but sought to purify it according to their own beliefs. Others refused point-blank to agree or con-form to the established church. Referred to as Separatists, they set up their own little church organizations in open defiance of the law.

Dissenters seek religious freedom. Anyone who failed to conform to the established Church of England was called a *dissenter*. A dissenter's life was far from easy. During the years that Charles I ruled without Parliament (1629–40), thousands of Protestant dissenters sought refuge in America. Most of them were sturdy farmers, artisans, and mechanics, well fitted to face the hardships of settling in a new land. However, in 1640, Parliament gained control of the government, and the tables were turned. Since the leaders of Parliament were Puritans, the members of the Anglican Church, who had supported the Stuart kings, were driven into hiding or exile. Hundreds of them fled to the New World, particularly to Virginia. When the Stuart kings were restored to power in 1660, Protestant groups once more set sail for America as a refuge from persecution. Meanwhile there were severe laws against Roman Catholics in England, although they were not always rigidly enforced.

Englishmen seek a better living. More important than the political and religious unrest that sent Englishmen to the New World were the economic reasons for colonization. Though England did not have a large population, many people were finding it hard to make a living. There were three reasons why this was so:

(1) The market for wool was increasing, and greedy landlords were fencing in large stretches of land for sheep-raising. They would even take away the little farms on which their tenants had been raising crops and use them for pasturage. As a result, there were many hard-working farmers without lands to farm. America, with its abundance of unsettled land, tempted many Englishmen to leave their homes.

(2) Prices were high. Much of the gold and silver from the mines in New Spain found its way into England either through trade or through piracy. This meant more money with which to buy the limited supply of goods — inflation we would call it

today. The resulting high prices made life harder for the common people.

(3) There was widespread unemployment. Vast areas of land which had formerly supported a large number of tenant farmers now supported only the few herders needed to tend flocks. Unemployment led to lawlessness which filled the land with "valiant rogues and sturdy beggars." Severe laws were passed to check this crime wave. English prisons were filled with vagabonds who, according to a writer of the time, "for small robberies are daily hanged up in great numbers, even twenty at a clap." Justice, in many of these cases, was too harsh, for often the only guilt of the "criminal" was that he couldn't pay his debts. As punishment for some offences, a vagrant could be deported to the colonies.

The colonies offer a way out. Many of these Englishmen, then, the landless, the unemployed, and those who were just "broke," looked toward the New World as a place to make a fresh start in life. It took courage, though, to make the change. The voyage across the North Atlantic was long, disagreeable, and dangerous. Aboard ship, passengers had to live under crowded and unsanitary conditions. Some of them died before reaching America. Many, too poor to pay their way, sold themselves into service — to ship captains, or agents — in return for their passage to America. In America these *indentured servants* (or *redemptioners*), were turned over to landowners who paid the price of their passage. Then the indentured servants had to work for several years to free themselves from bondage.

Businessmen seek profits. Though hard times at home had much to do with the sudden surge of Englishmen to America, this was only one of the economic forces at work. Within England a prosperous trading and commercial group had sprung into busy existence. These men were on the lookout for new fields in which to invest money. The establishment of overseas trading posts and colonies seemed to offer just such opportunities. Merchants and men of means combined to form companies to promote colonial business and trade. By supplying money, leadership, and even many of the pioneers, these companies eventually made England the leading colonial power of the world.

Trading companies were expected to earn large profits for the persons who invested in them. The companies leased by charter great areas of land in the New World. Those who invested in the companies hoped that the lands would be rich in natural resources — lumber, furs, iron ore, gold, silver, or agricultural products. They figured that the cost of transporting settlers to America to help to develop these resources would be far less than the amount of money which the products would bring when sold at home or in other parts of the world. By obtaining charters from the king, the companies established legal claim to the lands. They could look to England and to English law for protection against any attempts to take the land away or to interfere with the companies' development. It was a trading company of this sort which planted the first permanent English colony in the New World.

Other motives inspire colonization. Other reasons, though not so important, played some part in encouraging English colonization of the New World. Love of adventure spurred courageous seamen to search unknown waters and rugged landsmen to explore the new continent. Then, too, England had an overpowering urge to break the power of Spain. Englishmen reasoned along the lines of the English travel-author, Hakluyt, who said:

If you touch him [the Spanish King] in the Indies, you touch the apple of his eye, for [if you] take away his treasure . . . which he hath almost [entirely] out of his West Indies, his old bands of soldiers will soon be dissolved, his purposes defeated, his power and strength diminished, his pride abated, and his tyranny utterly suppressed.

Farsighted Englishmen were sure that Spain's greatness rested upon her rich empire. The way to break Spain, they saw, was to set up a rival colonial empire.

What conditions in England encouraged colonization?

1. How did the conflict between king and Parliament lead Englishmen to settle in America?
2. How did the lack of religious freedom in England stimulate emigration?
3. What were the economic reasons that led Englishmen to look toward America?
4. Why was colonization closely linked to the interests of businessmen? What were still other reasons for emigration?

2 Virginia Becomes the First Permanent English Colony

Early efforts fail. England's first active interest in the New World was aroused during the closing years of Queen Elizabeth's reign. Daring English "sea dogs," such as Drake, Frobisher, and Hawkins, boldly challenged the might of Spain, pouncing upon her treasure-laden ships and raiding her rich ports in the New World. (See map, page 43.) At the same time, Sir Humphrey Gilbert and Sir Walter Raleigh sent expeditions to secure a foothold along the American coast. Gilbert and Raleigh [1] were not successful in their ventures, but their faith and vision set an example for other Englishmen who attempted to colonize a quarter of a century later.

The first charter is granted. During the reign of James I, England finally planted a

[1] Gilbert personally conducted an expedition to America in 1583; on the return voyage his little vessel foundered in a storm, and all on board were drowned. Gilbert's half-brother, Raleigh, spent a small fortune on his colony on Roanoke Island, off the coast of what is now North Carolina. It was here that Virginia Dare was born, the first child of English parents to be born in what is now the United States. During the exciting days of the Spanish Armada, the colony was left to its own resources, and when at last, in 1591, relief ships were sent out, the settlers had completely disappeared. To this day the fate of the "lost colony of Roanoke" has remained a mystery.

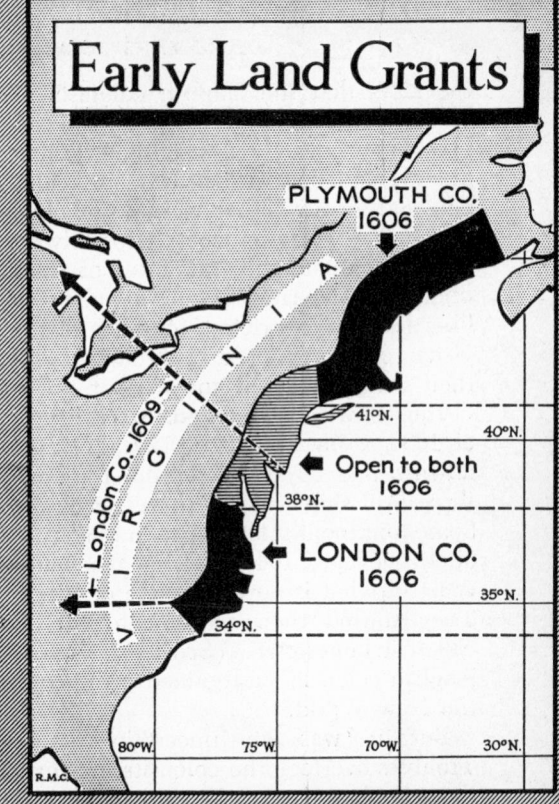

Early Land Grants

The London Company was granted rights to what lands? The Plymouth Company? What was the status of the land lying between the grants of the two companies?

permanent settlement in the lands claimed by Cabot. These lands, a long stretch of seacoast from present-day North Carolina to New England, had been called Virginia since the days of Queen Elizabeth. In 1606 King James issued to certain "Knights, Gentlemen, Merchants, and other Adventurers" a charter for the settlement of Virginia. The men to whom this first charter was issued were divided into two companies. One in London was called the London Company; the second group, centered in Plymouth, England, was called the Plymouth Company. (See map above for the extent of their grants.)

The English charter contained one provision that became of vital importance later on. It gave English colonists a right that neither the French nor the Spanish settlers in the New World enjoyed. This historic provision stated, in the words of the king, that the English colonists were to "have and enjoy all liberties, franchises, and immunities, . . . as if they had been abiding and born within this our realm of England, or any other of our said dominions." The early pioneers probably gave little thought to this guarantee of English liberties. But later colonists, when their liberties were restricted, found in this provision of the charter a strong basis for their struggle for self-government.

Jamestown is founded. Near the end of 1606, a small band of 120 adventurers, all men and boys, sailed from England in three frail ships for the shores of Virginia. Some four months later, after a long, roundabout voyage, 104 of them reached the coast of what is now the state of Virginia. They started their settlement there and called it Jamestown. (See map, page 53.) English colonists had gained a toe-hold in the New World.

But it was an uncertain toe-hold. Troubles overtook the colonists; misfortune dogged their steps. They had picked a poor spot to settle, a timbered area along the James River close to a marsh infested with malaria. They used the brackish river for most of their water supply. Many died from disease, others from hunger and from Indian attacks. The settlers did not really share the hardships equally, for some were "gentlemen" who felt it was beneath their dignity to do the hard physical work which was needed to start the settlement.

When things were at their worst, Captain John Smith took charge. Smith was a boastful man, but he was an able and courageous leader. He established the rule "No work, no food" and made it stick. Also, he dealt wisely with the Indians. Under Smith's firm grip, the little Jamestown band held together. But Smith returned to England, and a terrible "starving time" followed during the winter of 1609–10. At the end of the winter, the Jamestown settlement had only 60 gaunt survivors. Ill and discouraged, they made plans in the spring of 1610 to abandon the colony. Then, quite unexpectedly, several ships sailed into the James River with fresh supplies and more recruits.

Early Jamestown struggles along. The London Company financed the Jamestown venture, of course, in the hope of making a profit from it. This hope, however, failed to come true in those early years. Trade with the Indians was disappointing. Even cultivation of the soil was largely a failure. One trouble lay in the *common-store system* of the settlement. Under this system, whatever a man produced went into public storehouses. In return, he drew his supplies from the company. Since individual effort was not rewarded, the common-store system discouraged industry and ambition. Ten years after its founding, there were only about 600 people living in Jamestown — despite the London Company's investment of £80,000 in the colony. (See chart, page 69.)

Jamestown makes progress. After these difficult early years, however, conditions improved in Jamestown. New charters, granted in 1609 and 1612, gave the company rights to considerably more land and put greater powers of government into the hands of stockholders. Large numbers of new colonists arrived — sober, industrious men and skilled workers. Jamestown became more prosperous when John Rolfe[1] found a way to cure tobacco. Before long, Jamestown was exporting large quantities of tobacco to Europe. Meanwhile, the common-store system was abandoned. Under a new system, tracts of land were granted on easy terms to individuals and small companies. An historic event occurred in 1619, when a Dutch war vessel sailed into port with 20 Negroes aboard, who were sold as slaves. It was some time, however, before Negro slaves were used in great numbers.

Representative government begins. An even more important event took place in 1619 when an assembly met in the little church at Jamestown. It included representatives chosen by the settlers as well as the governor and a group of councilors appointed by the company. The fact that representatives chosen by the people were

[1] John Rolfe is also famous because he married Pocahontas, the daughter of the powerful Indian chieftain, Powhatan. Pocahontas, according to legend, had once saved John Smith's life.

included in this meeting was of great importance, for it marked the beginning of representative government in America.

Virginia becomes a royal colony. After its discouraging start at Jamestown, the colony of Virginia kept improving as a place to live, but it never did succeed as a business venture. In 1624 the charter of the London Company was withdrawn and Virginia became a royal province. Now the governor and councilors were appointed by the king. Fortunately, the House of Burgesses (the body of elected representatives) was allowed to continue, and in due time the framework of government in this colony

became a model for others. Within this framework, the council and the House of Burgesses were separate lawmaking bodies, while the governor retained the power to veto any laws not satisfactory to the royal government.

As a royal colony, Virginia continued to grow, though not very rapidly at first. Following the triumph of Parliament over Charles I in 1649, however, large numbers of the king's supporters flocked to the Virginia shores. By the middle of the century the population was more than 15,000. In the older sections along the coast, small farms had given way to plantations worked

Conflicts at sea between Spaniards and Englishmen are dramatized on this map. Why did Hawkins and Drake sail to the New World? How did Drake return to England from his longest voyage? The routes of what early English explorers are shown? Among other things, this map shows the extent of the Spanish empire in the New World. Why did it not extend farther into the interior of North and South America?

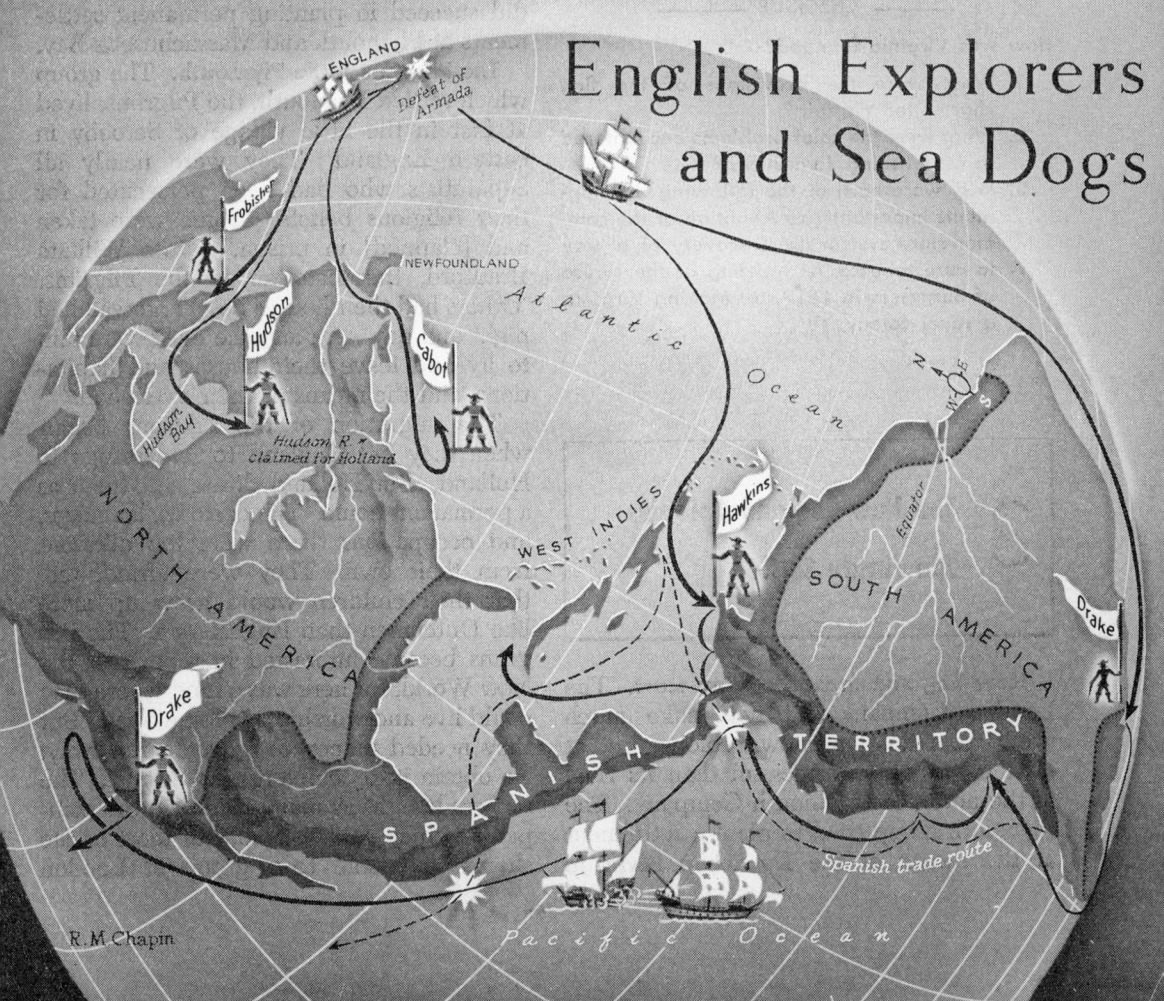

English Explorers and Sea Dogs

R. M. Chapin

by indentured servants and slaves. Slowly but steadily the settlers pushed inland, and the frontier yielded to the pioneer.

Bacon leads a frontier rebellion. In fact, by 1676 frontier settlements were so far removed from the coast that the coastal inhabitants were inclined to show little interest in the problems of the pioneer. In this year a serious rebellion was led by a frontier planter, Nathaniel Bacon, in protest against a government which failed to protect them from the Indians and to consider their needs. Bacon died at the height of his success, and his cause collapsed. In time, however, most of the abuses of which Bacon and his followers had complained were corrected. The rebellion is important in our history because it showed the unwillingness of frontier settlers to submit to a corrupt government which took no notice of their problems.

─────── CHECK-UP ───────

How was Virginia founded?

1. What were the provisions of the first charter for Virginia?
2. What were the chief problems encountered in establishing Jamestown?
3. Why were each of the following developments important? (a) Abolition of the common-store system, (b) Discovery of a way to cure tobacco, (c) Meeting of the House of Burgesses in 1619, (d) Making Virginia a royal colony

---

3 The New England Colonies Are Firmly Settled

New England makes a slow start. The London Company did not make much profit from the Jamestown colony, but at least it was more successful than its rival to the north, the Plymouth Company. The Plymouth group tried to plant a settlement at the mouth of the Kennebec River in

Early plantation house

what is now Maine, and then gave it up as a bad job. Reorganized as the Council for New England in 1620, the company was granted the right to colonize and govern the territory between the fortieth and forty-eighth parallels. Under the new charter, the energetic Sir Ferdinando Gorges (gor'jes) and Captain John Mason set up new colonies in what are now Maine and New Hampshire. They met with little success. Two groups of pioneers, however, did succeed in planting permanent settlements at Plymouth and Massachusetts Bay.

The Pilgrims settle Plymouth. The group which settled Plymouth, the Pilgrims, lived at first in the little village of Scrooby in eastern England. They were nearly all Separatists who had been persecuted for their religious beliefs. "Some were taken and [clapped] in prison," wrote William Bradford, the historian of the Pilgrims. "Others had their houses beset and watched night and day . . . ; and the most were fain to fly and leave their houses and habitations, and the means of their livelihood."

The migration of the Pilgrims began when they left England to find refuge in Holland. But Holland didn't suit them as a permanent home. The customs, language, and occupations there were too different from their own. They were afraid, too, that their children would grow up more like Dutchmen than Englishmen. The Pilgrims became interested in reports of the New World, for here was a land where they could live and worship as they wished. But they needed money to move so far away. To obtain it, a company was formed. The settlers bought as many shares in the company as they could afford, but most of the shares were sold to a group of London businessmen. All profits from the settlement for the first seven years were to be divided among the shareholders. That meant, of course, that most of the early profits would be sent to London.

About 100 people, including 35 Pilgrims from both Holland and England, set sail from Plymouth, England, across the Atlantic in the tiny *Mayflower*. They were bound for the shores of what is now Virginia, where they had a grant of land from the London Company, but storms blew them off their course. Finally they landed far to the north on the bleak shores of Cape Cod Bay in December of 1620. The Pilgrims made friends with some of the neighboring Indians and soon laid the foundations of a small community, which they called Plymouth. The first winter was a bitter time. Still, though half of the settlers died from sickness, the survivors were by no means ready to give up when spring came.

The Mayflower Compact is written. From the start, the Pilgrims were faced with serious problems. At first they didn't even have a legal right to make their home in Plymouth, which was outside the boundaries of the London Company. Nor had any definite plans been made for governing the settlement. Before landing, therefore, the Pilgrims drew up the *Mayflower Compact*, part of which is quoted at the opening of this chapter. In this famous paper, they pledged their allegiance to the king and agreed to pass and obey such laws as the good of the colony demanded. The Mayflower Compact did not actually provide a plan of government, but it contained the basic idea of American democracy — the idea that government depended for its authority upon the will of the people.

Bark house

Plymouth progresses slowly. Beyond contributing the Mayflower Compact and the example of their courage, the settlers at Plymouth did not greatly influence the growth of the country. The soil around Plymouth was not fertile, and the debts owed to the London merchants proved a handicap to the progress of the colony. Few new settlers were attracted because of the strict religious views of the Pilgrims. Also, the colony failed to get a charter from the king, and therefore could not set up a recognized government. In 1691 Plymouth was joined to the Puritan colony, founded nearby on Massachusetts Bay.

Puritans decide to emigrate. In 1628 a group of prominent Puritans were given permission to settle within the territory belonging to the Council for New England. Under the name of the Massachusetts Bay Company, these Puritans secured a royal

Frame house

charter which granted them a strip of land extending from three miles north of the source of the Merrimack River to three miles south of the Charles River. The charter also gave the company the right to dispose of its lands and to govern its colonists. Since the charter neglected to fix the office of the company in England, the leaders migrated to the New World, took the charter along, and set up an independent, self-governing colony.

Unlike the Pilgrims of Plymouth, the Puritans migrated in fairly large numbers. During the period from 1629 to 1640, when Charles I ruled without Parliament, the Puritans in England were severely persecuted. They felt they had little chance of winning acceptance of their beliefs by the

Church of England or of checking the king's power. Many of them decided to leave the country.

Massachusetts Bay Colony is founded. In 1630, under the leadership of John Winthrop, eleven ships filled with Puritans dropped anchor off the shores of Massachusetts. Less than ten years later, some 20,000 persons, mostly Puritans, had settled around Massachusetts Bay, particularly at Boston, Charlestown, and Salem. Some of the settlers were wealthy merchants, doctors, or lawyers. Others were Puritan clergymen, whose influence on the colony was very great. The best known of these was John Cotton. The group also included large numbers of farmers, mechanics, and tradesmen, all looking for a better life.

The Puritan Church dominates the colony. The rapid increase of population in Massachusetts made plenty of hands available for the work to be done and led to the growth of representative government. After 1634 an assembly called the General Court met four times a year at Boston to attend to the public business of the colony. This General Court included the governor, his assistants, and representatives of the freemen. But in spite of representative government, life in Massachusetts was severely limited along Puritan lines. Non-Puritans could settle in the colony, but they could not vote. The opinions of the ministers and elders of the Puritan Church carried great weight. The General Court was severe with Non-Puritans, not only in respect to their beliefs but even with regard to their behavior and dress.

Presently adventurous and dissatisfied groups broke away from the Massachusetts Bay Colony and formed other New England colonies. These restless persons were looking for freedom of thought and religion, or better land for farming, or both.

Roger Williams founds Rhode Island. One man who broke away from Puritan authority was a spirited young pastor, Roger Williams. His views were too advanced for the Puritan ministers who controlled Massachusetts. For instance, Williams asserted that "Persecution for cause of conscience is most evidently and lament-

ably contrary to the doctrine of Christ Jesus." He stood firmly against the election of colony officials by church members only. Further, he did not think these officials had any right to interfere with an individual's religious beliefs. This sort of teaching could not be overlooked by the strict Puritan authorities. In 1635, by order of the General Court, he was expelled from Massachusetts. Williams spent the winter with friendly Indians. Then, with a few followers, he founded a settlement at Providence at the head of Narragansett Bay in what is now Rhode Island.

Williams was not the only one exiled by the Puritan fathers. Mrs. Anne Hutchinson, "a woman of ready wit and bold spirit," held religious beliefs which were frowned upon in Massachusetts. She won over many to her beliefs, and when the General Court exiled her, a group of friends left with her. They planted a settlement at Portsmouth near Providence.

Rhode Island gets political and religious freedom. Other religious outcasts from Massachusetts found a welcome in Rhode Island, which grew steadily despite the contempt and scorn of other colonies. In 1644 the settlements around Narragansett Bay were united under a charter which Roger Williams secured from England. Williams and his neighbors insisted that there should be complete religious freedom in their colony. Some 20 years after the first charter, a new one formally gave Rhode Island citizens religious freedom, as well as the privilege of electing their own officers and making their own laws. Although the people of Rhode Island often quarreled over the affairs of the colony, they stood firmly for the principles of freedom of conscience and religious toleration — principles which were to become fundamental in the American way of life.

Pioneers settle the Connecticut valley. The pioneers who settled in the rich Connecticut valley were not exiled from Massachusetts because of their religious views. They were, instead, adventurers searching chiefly for better soil and a more liberal form of government. In the summer of 1636 a small band of them, led by Thomas

Slat-back chair   EARLY FURNITURE   Settle

Trestle table

Hooker, pastor of the church in New-town (now Cambridge), pushed southwest through the dense forests of Massachusetts. Hooker and his followers, who had the grudging consent of Massachusetts authorities to build homes along the Connecticut River, settled at Hartford. Soon there were some 800 people in the three towns of Hartford, Wethersfield, and Windsor. The settlement of Connecticut was the beginning of a westward movement that was to dominate American life for two and a half centuries. In the same way, generation after generation of pioneers left their homes in settled areas in search of new homes farther west.

Connecticut frames the first constitution. Besides starting the American march westward, Connecticut made a real contribution to our political institutions. In 1639 representatives from the three towns met at Hartford and drew up the first written constitution for the government of a commonwealth in America. The document was called the *Fundamental Orders*. Under the government set up by this constitution, the colony grew quite strong. It succeeded in almost wiping out the Pequot Indians who fought to block the advance of the white settlers.

In 1662 Charles II granted Connecticut a charter which not only assured colonists of their right to govern themselves but also extended their lands. Thus Connecticut gained the valuable harbor of New Haven. New Haven had been settled by John Davenport and his congregation, also pioneers from Massachusetts. Through the

new charter, political power was placed almost entirely in the hands of the qualified voters. In fact, the charter was so satisfactory that it was kept as a state constitution long after Connecticut — along with the other colonies — won its independence from Great Britain.

New Hampshire becomes a colony. The settlements started in Maine by Sir Ferdinando Gorges and in New Hampshire by Captain John Mason (page 44) were little more than trading posts for several years. Then pioneers from Massachusetts pushed northward into these areas, just as Hooker and his followers had moved into the Connecticut valley. The newcomers refused to recognize the authority of Gorges and Mason; they insisted that their allegiance lay with Massachusetts. Presently the Massachusetts colony extended its control over the area. New Hampshire remained a part of Massachusetts until 1679, when it was granted a charter making it a royal colony. Maine continued as a part of Massachusetts until 1820.

A New England Confederation is tried. In their early years, the New England colonies had acted quite independently of one another. They were almost like separate countries. All were conscious, however, of hostile people in neighboring areas — the Indians, the Dutch, and the French. In 1643 this common fear drove them to meet and act as a group for the first time. Delegates from the colonies of Massachusetts Bay, Plymouth, Connecticut, and New Haven met at Boston and formed a "firm and perpetual league of friendship and amity for offense and defense."[2] This league became known as the New England Confederation. Little came of the Confederation until 1675, when it put down a fierce Indian uprising called King Philip's War. Later, when the smaller colonies came to resent the overbearing attitude of Massachusetts, the Confederation fell apart. Nevertheless it was the first, faltering step toward a real union among the colonies.

The Dominion of New England is imposed. Of all the English colonies, Massachusetts was the most independent. While England was busy with the struggle between the king and Parliament, Massachusetts disregarded certain royal orders and adopted an oath of allegiance to the colony instead of to England. Angered by this attitude, Charles II and his successor, James II, decided to bring the colonies more directly under the control of the Crown. In 1684 the charter of Massachusetts was set aside. During the next four years the New England colonies, New York, and the Jerseys were united by royal order into the Dominion of New England. Almost all power was placed in the hands of a governor and council appointed by the king. The governor of the new dominion was Sir Edmond Andros, the former governor of New York.

The Dominion collapses. For good reasons, the colonists heartily disliked Andros as a leader. He saw to it that colonial liberties were cut down and heavy taxes levied against the colonies. Not only was Andros harsh but he made no effort to understand the colonial point of view. Resentment among the colonists smoldered. Luckily, Andros didn't last long as governor. In 1688, back in England, the "Glorious Revolution" took place. James II — last of the Stuart kings — had to flee from England. In his place, William and Mary of Holland were proclaimed King and Queen of England.[3] When New England heard about

this upheaval, Andros was forced out of office. In 1691 a new charter was issued to Massachusetts under which it regained its General Court, although it remained a royal colony. The governor was to be appointed by the king. The right to vote, formerly limited to Puritans alone, was given to all male adults who owned a certain amount of property. Religious toleration was assured to all Protestant sects. Plymouth and Maine were now absorbed by Massachusetts, while Connecticut and Rhode Island were permitted to govern themselves under their former charters.

——————— CHECK-UP ———————

How were English colonies firmly established in New England?

1. Why did the Pilgrims come to America? What was the Mayflower Compact? Why did Plymouth colony make such slow progress?
2. Who were the Puritans? Why did they come to America? What was the relationship of church to government in Massachusetts?
3. Why was Rhode Island colonized? How did it differ from Massachusetts?
4. Under what circumstances were settlements made in Connecticut and New Hampshire?
5. Distinguish between the New England Confederation and the Dominion of New England. Why did the latter collapse? With what results?

---

4   **Proprietors Establish Several Vigorous Colonies**

Who were the proprietors? Companies like the London Company and the

---

[2] Rhode Island was not invited to send delegates because it was looked down upon by the other New England settlements.

[3] To guard England against further attempts at personal tyranny, a Bill of Rights was adopted by Parliament and accepted by the new monarchs. Laws were not to be suspended by the King;

taxes were not to be levied without the consent of Parliament; nor was the right of petition to be denied. The Bill of Rights with its new guaranties of liberty and freedom was important not merely to the people of England, but to the colonists as well, for they too considered themselves entitled to the rights of Englishmen.

Linen chest

Bed

Cradle

Plymouth Company assisted certain colonies in getting started in the New World. But several other English colonies were founded under a different type of sponsor, called a *proprietor*.

The proprietor of a colony was usually an Englishman who was a favorite of the king, or one to whom the king owed a great debt. In either case, the man received a gift in the form of a land grant in the new continent. Except for certain restrictions in their charters, proprietors were given powers almost as great as the powers of the king over a royal province.

Maryland is founded. The first successful colony to be founded by a proprietor was Maryland. It was founded through the efforts of George Calvert, the first Lord Baltimore. Baltimore died before his plans could fully take shape, but the venture was carried on successfully by his son. In a charter signed by the king in 1632, Baltimore was granted land running from the south bank of the Potomac to the fortieth parallel (the latitude of the present city of Philadelphia), and from the Atlantic Ocean as far west as the source of the Potomac River. (See map, page 53.)

Late in the fall of 1633 a band of pioneers left England to settle in the Baltimore colony. The following year they established the settlement of St. Mary's on the shores of Chesapeake Bay. Under the guidance of the Baltimore family, Maryland made steady progress. The proprietary form of government continued there until the American Revolution, except for a brief period (1690–1715) when the colony was taken under royal control.

Maryland enjoys political and religious freedom. Lord Baltimore's original charter had stated that all laws for the government of the colony would have to be made with the "advice, assent, and approbation of the freemen of the same province." As the colony grew larger, representatives of the freemen were chosen for that purpose. The proprietor claimed that he was the only one who could write laws, while the assembly could do no more than accept or reject his proposals. But the assembly claimed the right to make laws too. The argument ended when the proprietor, with good grace, agreed to the assembly's point of view. In time, Maryland developed a legislature of two houses similar to the Council and the House of Burgesses in Virginia.

Being a Catholic, Baltimore planned to make Maryland a refuge for people of his own religion who were being persecuted. The number of Catholics in England who wanted to emigrate to America, however, wasn't large enough to found a prosperous colony. Furthermore, the charter stated that the Anglican Church must be established in the colony. For these reasons, the doors were left open to Protestants as well as to Catholics. Soon, Protestants actually outnumbered Catholics. To protect the latter in their beliefs and form of worship, a Toleration Act was passed in 1649. This law granted freedom of worship to people who professed belief in Jesus Christ. Religious toleration in Maryland, therefore, was not quite as complete as in Rhode Island.

The Carolinas are settled. The next proprietary venture developed in Carolina, farther to the south. In 1663 King Charles II granted to eight nobles the land between Virginia and Spanish Florida. Like that of Maryland, the charter gave these proprietors great powers, but recognized the right of the people to share in the law-making. The Anglican Church was established as the official church. To attract settlers, however, the charter also said that the proprietors could adopt a policy of "liberty of conscience in all religious or spiritual things."

From the start, Carolina seemed to separate naturally into two sections: North and South Carolina. (See map, page 53.) North Carolina was settled largely by Virginia frontiersmen, joined by some Quakers. Along the shores of Albermarle Sound they raised tobacco for shipment to England, and corn and livestock for their own support. South Carolina grew even more quickly. There were rich lowlands in this region, fine land for rice and indigo plantations. (Indigo is a plant from which dye is made.) For many years South Carolina had the only good harbor in the South — Charles Town (later Charleston). This community rapidly grew to be the political, social, and economic center of the entire colony. People of many faiths and nationalities migrated into South Carolina. They included Anglicans and dissenters from England, settlers from New England and northern Ireland, emigrants from the West Indies, French Huguenots (Protestants), and Germans.

The Carolinas become royal colonies. The political picture in the Carolinas was far from happy. The root of the trouble was the elaborate kind of government the proprietors tried to set up. Worked out by the English philosopher, John Locke, the scheme was called the *Grand Model.* Under this form of government the settlers were divided into social classes. The plan was obviously unsuited to frontier conditions in the American wilderness, where men were more likely to be judged by their accomplishments than by their family backgrounds. A government of the usual colonial type was finally established, but argument after argument arose between the proprietors and the popular assemblies. In 1729 seven of the eight proprietors sold their rights to the Crown. Thus North and South Carolina became royal colonies.

The Dutch settle New Amsterdam. Although it did not begin as such, New York developed into a proprietary colony at a later time. Even before the early Pilgrims made their historic voyage in the *Mayflower,* Dutch pioneers had secured a foothold in the Hudson and Delaware valleys. The Dutch East India Company had authorized Henry Hudson, an Englishman by birth, to hunt for a northwest shortcut to Asia. Hudson hoped his ship, the *Half Moon,* was China-bound when it worked its way up the Hudson River in 1609. (See map, page 43.) Traders quickly followed the explorer. In 1621 the Dutch West India Company was chartered to colonize this region and develop trade. Settlements were staked out on Manhattan Island, at Fort Orange (where Albany now stands), and in New Jersey and Delaware. The Dutch later took over a small colony named New Sweden which had been established by Swedish settlers on the Delaware River. (See map, page 53.)

The patroon system is established. The Dutch West India Company tried to promote the settlement of New Netherland (as the Dutch colony was called) by offering land grants to individuals called *patroons.* The patroon had his choice of a feudal estate running sixteen miles along one side of a navigable river or eight miles along both sides. On his part, the patroon had to bring 50 people to America and settle them on his land. The patroon was given a free hand — he not only owned his estate but he ruled over the people who lived on it.

The Dutch face serious problems in the New World. The patroon system created certain powerful family groups, such as the Schuylers and the Van Rensselaers. It failed, however, to attract a steady flow of immigrants because Dutchmen enjoyed a fairly liberal government at home. Dutchmen were further discouraged from settling in New Netherland because the Dutch West India Company tried to keep settlers from taking part in the profitable New World fur trade.

Moreover, the Dutch found themselves in a ticklish spot in New Netherland. Wedged between the growing English settlements in New England and the southern colonies, they were anything but welcome. The English called them the "Dutch intruders" and wanted to get rid of them because they interfered with a possible union of New England with the southern colonies. The Dutch also controlled some excellent harbors that the English wanted, as well as the rich traffic in furs that flowed down the Hudson River from the wilderness. At this time the English and the Dutch all over the world were engaged in keen commercial rivalry.

New Netherland becomes New York. The English decided to take steps against the Dutch in the New World. In 1664 Charles II made his brother James — then Duke of York — proprietor of a new English colony extending from the Connecticut River to the Delaware River. That same year, an English squadron boldly sailed into the harbor of New Amsterdam (now New York City) and demanded surrender of the town. The governor, Peter Stuyvesant, stamped his wooden leg and swore. He was eager to fight it out with the English, but the townsmen refused to back him up, because their cause seemed hopeless. Thus New Amsterdam passed peacefully under English control. The colony, as well as the city, was now called New York.

Politically, New York did not show an immediate improvement. Except during one short break of two years (1683–85), the Duke of York would not let an assembly share in the government of the colony. When he succeeded his brother to the English throne in 1685 (see chart, page 38), New York automatically became a royal province. Soon after that, it was annexed to the Dominion of New England under the administration of Governor Andros (page 48). When Andros was removed

Dutch house

after the "Glorious Revolution" of 1688, William III reorganized the government of the colony and at last made special provision for a representative assembly. New York remained a royal colony until the American Revolution.

New Jersey is founded. New Jersey, like New York, was simply taken over by the English from earlier settlers. With lavish generosity, the Duke of York in 1664 gave away part of his province even before he took possession of it. He gave all the land between the Hudson and the Delaware Rivers to two of his favorites, Sir George Carteret and Lord Berkeley. As you have seen, this region had already been settled by a small number of Dutch and Swedish pioneers, but its real development began after the English arrived. In 1665 the proprietors took over control of Elizabethtown, a Dutch settlement. The next year settlers moved in from Connecticut and built a stable Puritan community at Milford (now Newark). The full development of the Jerseys (East and West Jersey) is a confused story because they changed ownership so often, but the region emerged as a separate royal province of New Jersey in 1738.

William Penn secures a refuge for Quakers. The most successful proprietary colony was Pennsylvania. Its founder was William Penn, a man who had been converted in England to a religious sect called the Society of Friends, or Quakers. The beliefs of the Quakers often brought them into trouble with the authorities in England. It happened that Penn had inherited from his father a claim of £16,000 against Charles II. He asked the king to cancel this debt by granting him the territory of

Sylvania in the New World. His plan was to provide a refuge for his persecuted fellow-believers, as well as to promote a profitable business venture. The king accepted his offer.

The name Sylvania was changed by the king to Pennsylvania in honor of Penn's father. In 1681 when the king granted to Penn this vast tract of land (see map, page 53), he was not careful to note what land in the New World had already been given away. Because of overlapping boundaries, a dispute arose between the Penn and Baltimore families. It was finally settled more than three quarters of a century later when the famous Mason and Dixon's line was surveyed.

Penn's charter showed that the day of great powers for the proprietor had passed. His charter said not only that laws must be made, as usual, with the consent of the freemen but also that they must be sent to the Privy Council in England for approval or rejection. Taxes could be levied only with the consent of the colonial assembly "or by act of Parliament in England." Appeals from the decisions of the colonial courts might be made to the king.

Delaware is founded. Since Penn's land had no coast line, he persuaded the Duke of York to turn over to him three lower counties on the Delaware River, which had been seized from the Dutch. These counties were organized into the separate colony of Delaware in 1704, but remained under control of the Penn family until Revolutionary War days.

Pennsylvania prospers. Penn made a great success of his Pennsylvania colony, and for very good reasons. He combined the qualities of a warm-hearted leader and a sound businessman. He saw to it that the courts handed down justice tempered with mercy. He let people of any religion settle on his land as long as they were believers in "one almighty and eternal God." He realized that the best way to attract settlers was to make it easy for them to get land. Land could be bought on easy terms or rented for as little as a penny an acre. Penn made life even more attractive for his settlers by securing peace with the Indians, whom he treated fairly, even paying them for their land. He visited the colony in 1682 and again in 1701 to obtain firsthand knowledge of conditions.

Settlers flocked into Pennsylvania. The population was made up chiefly of Quakers from England, Wales, and Ireland, Scotch-Irish Presbyterians, and Germans of many Protestant sects. Philadelphia became not only "the city of brotherly love" but a brisk trading center and the largest city in all the colonies. There was some wrangling between the proprietor and the people now and then, but, taken all in all, Penn's "holy experiment" was a great success. Except for a brief period of two years when Penn was at odds with William III, the Penn family held the province until the American Revolution.

Georgia is settled. Pennsylvania was 50 years old before the last of the thirteen original colonies, Georgia, was planted on the American continent. Georgia was born as a charitable experiment, the idea of a man named James Oglethorpe. Oglethorpe was a wealthy and influential Englishman with a "strong benevolence of soul." He was outraged by the fact that poor but honest people were being put behind prison bars simply because they could not pay their debts. He wanted to find a refuge for them and other unfortunate people, and the New World seemed to be the answer.

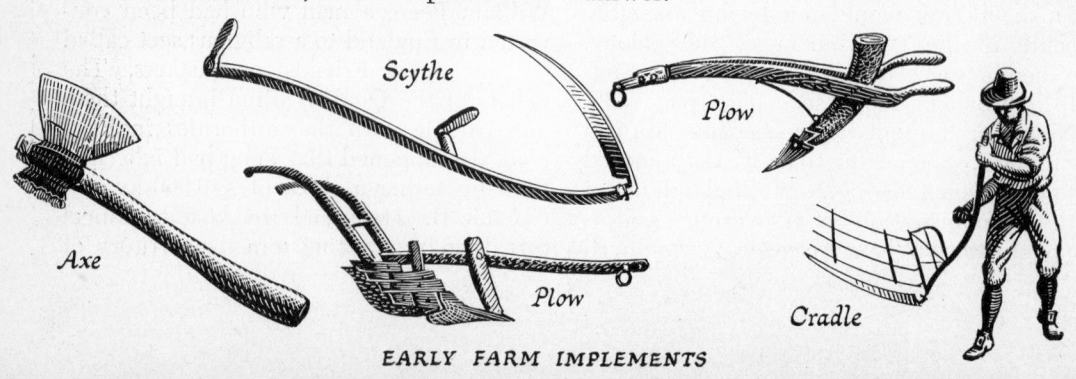

Scythe

Plow

Axe

Plow

Cradle

EARLY FARM IMPLEMENTS

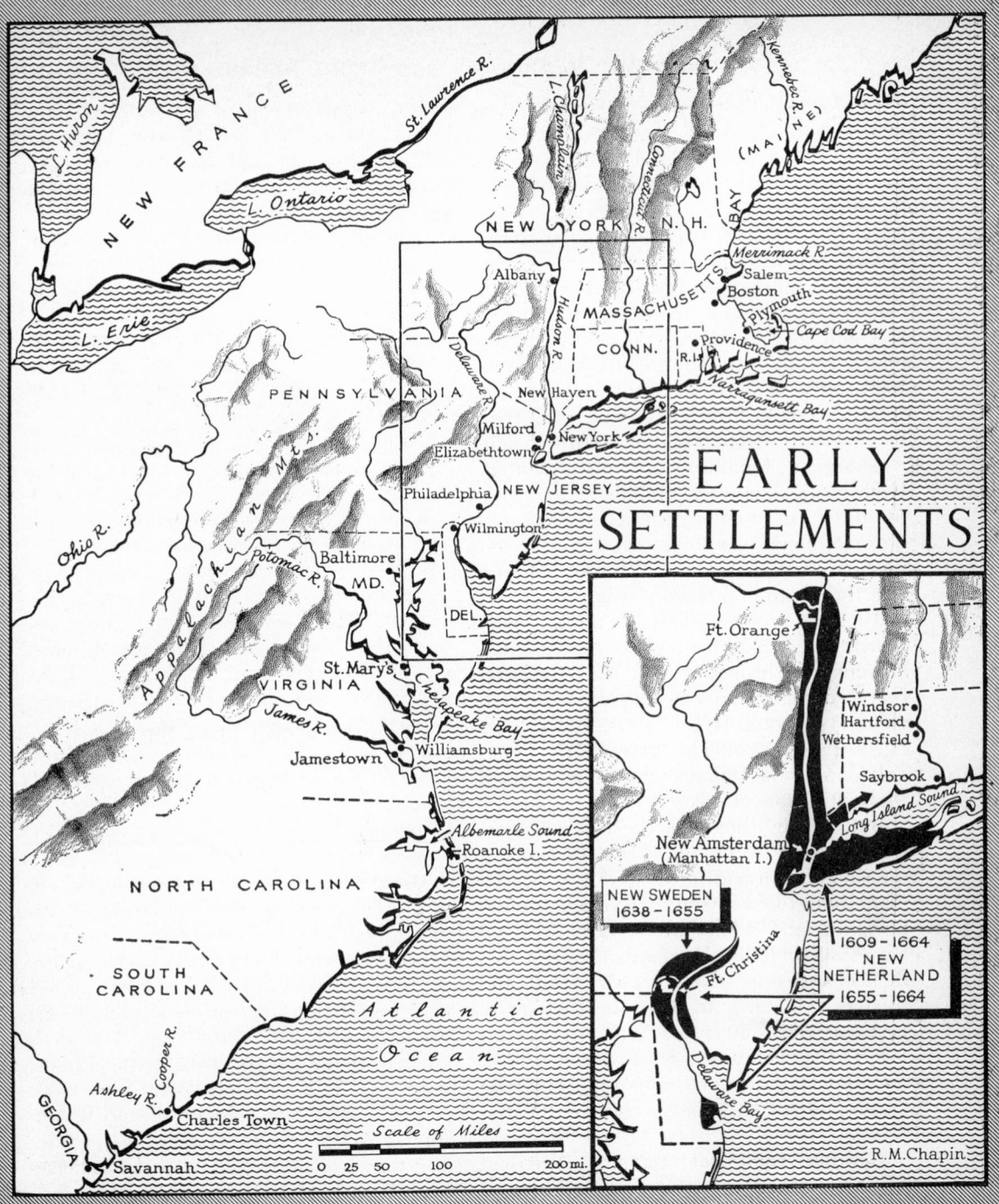

EARLY SETTLEMENTS

NEW FRANCE

L. Huron

L. Ontario

L. Erie

St. Lawrence R.

L. Champlain

Kennebec R.

(MAINE)

NEW YORK

N.H.

MASSACHUSETTS

Merrimack R.

Salem

Boston

Plymouth

Cape Cod Bay

Albany

Hudson R.

Connecticut R.

Delaware R.

CONN.

R.I.

Providence

Narragansett Bay

PENNSYLVANIA

New Haven

Milford

Elizabethtown

Ohio R.

Appalachian Mts.

Philadelphia

NEW JERSEY

New York

Wilmington

Potomac R.

Baltimore

MD.

DEL.

St. Marys

VIRGINIA

Chesapeake Bay

James R.

Williamsburg

Jamestown

Albemarle Sound

Roanoke I.

NORTH CAROLINA

Atlantic Ocean

SOUTH CAROLINA

Ashley R.

Cooper R.

GEORGIA

Charles Town

Savannah

Scale of Miles

0   25   50   100   200 mi.

Ft. Orange

Windsor

Hartford

Wethersfield

Saybrook

Long Island Sound

New Amsterdam
(Manhattan I.)

NEW SWEDEN
1638-1655

Ft. Christina

1609-1664
NEW
NETHERLAND
1655-1664

Delaware Bay

R.M.Chapin

English settlements in North America are shown in the large map; the inset at the lower right calls particular attention to Swedish and Dutch settlements. What happened to New Sweden? Why did the English believe it was necessary for them to take over New Netherland? Using the scale of miles, figure out how far it is from New York to Albany. Can the same scale of miles be used on the inset map? Referring to the map on page 41, figure out which settlements were made on land originally granted to the London Company. The Plymouth Company. The area lying between these two early grants.

In 1732 Oglethorpe persuaded George II to grant to him and a number of other trustees a large tract of land below Carolina for a period of 21 years. Besides offering a refuge for the poor, Georgia, as it came to be called, was intended to serve several practical purposes. It was to be used as a military outpost for the English colonies against the Spaniards in Florida. It could also be used, according to the plans, as a base for frontier fur trade, as a source of wine and silk, and as a haven for certain German Protestants who were then looking for protection under the British flag.

Georgia's founders are disappointed. High ideals filled men's minds as they pictured the sort of colony that Georgia would become. Land was to be given to new settlers in small holdings. The sale of rum was forbidden and slavery was prohibited. With such worthy plans in mind, Oglethorpe and a small band of settlers founded Savannah early in 1733. In the years that followed, many kinds of people moved into Georgia — Scotch Highlanders, Swiss, Salzburgers and Moravians (German Protestants), and some Italians who came to teach the cultivation of silk.

But the high hopes of the Georgia trustees were not borne out. Both slavery and the sale of rum had to be accepted. Large plantations tilled by slaves developed in the lowlands, and small farmers had to move back into the hills. Demands for even further changes in policy finally drove the trustees voluntarily to surrender the colony to the Crown 20 years after its founding. Georgia became a royal colony with a governor and council appointed by the king, and an assembly chosen by the people.

Georgia completes colonial America. With the founding of Georgia in 1733, all thirteen of the colonies which were to become the original states of our republic had been established. Only a century and a quarter had passed since those early "gentlemen" had landed at Jamestown. There had been even less time since Pilgrim and Puritan had first set eyes upon the shores of New England. Yet in that brief span of years, the Atlantic coast had been turned into a checkerboard of little hamlets, thriving ports, small farms, and huge estates. Meanwhile, hardy pioneers pressed farther and farther westward into the menacing wilderness.

——— CHECK-UP ———

What were the proprietary colonies?

1. What was the nature of a proprietary colony? Name the proprietary colonies.
2. How was political and religious freedom established in Maryland?
3. What developments paved the way for the British seizure of New Netherlands? How did New York fare under British rule?
4. Under what circumstances was Pennsylvania founded? Why was it successful?
5. What were the purposes in founding Georgia? How successfully were they carried out?

---

5   The British Drive the French out of North America

Great Britain and France battle for empire. The English colonists were to run into more serious competition in the New World than they had faced with the Dutch at New Amsterdam. While the English were building their thirteen colonies, the French were extending control of vast areas to the north and west of the English holdings. As both New World powers expanded, an increasingly bitter rivalry sprang up between them over (1) territory, (2) the fur trade, and (3) the fisheries. This rivalry led to open warfare.

The conflict which broke out between Frenchmen and Englishmen in North America was only part of a terrific struggle that France and Great Britain [4] were wag-

---

[4] In 1707 England and Scotland were united under the name of Great Britain. Throughout the colonial period, however, the terms "England" and "Great Britain" — as well as "English" and "British" — are commonly used with the same meaning.

WARS INVOLVING ENGLAND AND FRANCE

In Europe	In America
1689–1697 War of the League of Augsburg	1689–1697 King William's War
1702–1713 War of Spanish Succession	1702–1713 Queen Anne's War
1740–1748 War of Austrian Succession	1744–1748 King George's War
1756–1763 Seven Years' War	1754–1763 French and Indian War
1778–1783 War of the American Revolution	1775–1783 War of the American Revolution
1792–1802 Wars of the French Revolution	1790–1800 Undeclared French War
1803–1815 Napoleonic Wars	1812–1814 War of 1812

ing for power and empire all over the world. For the most part, the wars that flared up between them off and on from 1689 until 1763 (see chart above) were fought upon European battlefields. But hostility existed wherever there were French and English settlements.

Each side has certain advantages. In America the English had several important advantages: (1) They were superior in man power. By 1760 English settlers outnumbered French settlers 1,600,000 to 80,000 — twenty to one. (2) By that time, too, the English settlers had made such rapid strides in agriculture, commerce, and industry that they were far ahead of the French in the ability to equip troops in the field. (3) Furthermore, since the English controlled the seas, their fleets crippled French attempts to land soldiers and materials on American soil.

But the advantages were not all England's. The French, too, held some trump cards, especially in the early part of the conflict: (1) They had a highly centralized government in New France, and because of it, they could collect men and resources efficiently and unify their command. Since they did not have to deal with troublesome local governments or disputing assemblies, the French authorities in America were able to carry on the wars with a free and vigorous hand. This was in sharp contrast to the English colonies. (2) Another advantage for the French was that Quebec, the stronghold controlling the St. Lawrence River, appeared able to defy any attempts at capture. (3) Lastly, the French had many friends among the Indians. Except for the Iroquois and Cherokees, all the Indian tribes along the frontier were allies of the French.

The early wars bring no decision. The advantages and disadvantages of each side served to equalize the early French-English fighting in America. Altogether four wars were fought between the English and the French in North America. In the first three, which took place before 1750, neither side won or lost enough to make any real difference in their positions. To be sure, as a result of what was called Queen Anne's War, the English gained possession of Acadia (Nova Scotia) and Newfoundland, as well as a protectorate over the Iroquois Indians. Nevertheless, after a half century of conflict (1689–1748) neither the French nor the English had won supremacy in North America.

Rivalry develops in the Ohio valley. Fighting broke out again in America in 1754. This time the underlying issue between the two powers was clear. Which civilization — French or English — was to have the opportunity to spread westward and thus control the continent? Disputes arose between the rival English and French at several points along the frontier. But the most serious flare-up came when the representatives of the two nations met head-on in a struggle to take over the Ohio valley.

The French had been so busy extending their authority over the Great Lakes and the lower Mississippi River that they had failed to gain a foothold in the Ohio region. When the French finally did explore the Ohio country in 1749, they found that the English had also laid claim to the region. In fact, an ambitious group of prominent Virginians and British had formed the Ohio Company, planning to build settlements upon a 200,000-acre grant from the King of England. This news forced the governor-general of New France into swift action. He had several forts built along the upper reaches of the Allegheny River, one of the tributaries of the Ohio. The English viewed these military moves with alarm. The mother country wasted no time in instructing the colonial governors to repel the French invaders if they insisted upon staying "within the undoubted limits of his Majesty's dominions."

The French ignore Washington's warning. This order from England was quickly put into action. Governor Dinwiddie of Virginia decided in 1753 to send a mission to warn the French to stay out of the disputed area. For this job, he picked George Washington, a surveyor 21 years old and a major in the militia of the colony. Washington and his comrades faced many hardships and perils during the long wilderness journey, but with courage and skill they overcame them and delivered the warning to the French commander at Fort Le Boeuf. The French flatly refused to withdraw. In early 1754, Washington was sent again on a military mission to keep the French from gaining control of the fork where the Allegheny and Monongahela Rivers join to form the Ohio. In an armed clash, Washington and his men had to retire before stronger French forces. Meanwhile the French were able to strengthen their position at Fort Duquesne (doo-kain') at the forks of the Ohio. (See map, page 57.)

A plan for colonial union is rejected. With the menace of the French growing more real every day, farseeing Englishmen on both sides of the Atlantic were thinking seriously about the advantages of co-operation among the colonies. In 1754 seven colonies sent commissioners to Albany, New York, to a congress which had been called by the British government. A plan of union drawn up by Benjamin Franklin was adopted. In its final form the scheme provided for a president-general appointed by the king, and a council consisting of delegates to be selected by the colonial assemblies. The council was to be given power to manage Indian affairs. It could also make laws and levy taxes for the common defense, with the approval of the president-general and the Crown.

The Albany Plan, however, was not acceptable to the colonies. They did not wish to give up so much of their power to a central authority nor to shoulder any additional costs for defense. The British government didn't like the plan either, because it promised too much popular control to the colonies. "Everybody cries, a union is absolutely necessary," wrote Franklin in exasperation, "but when they come to the manner and form of the union, their weak noddles are perfectly distracted." The attempt at union failed. War had to be waged by Great Britain with more or less aid from thirteen individual colonies.

The French are victorious at first. The British side looked like the losing one at the start of the so-called French and Indian War which began in 1754. (See chart, page 55.) Inefficient government, poor military leadership, and lack of co-operation on the part of the colonies seriously hurt their cause.

The most serious blow was the defeat of General Braddock in an advance upon Fort Duquesne in the summer of 1755. Braddock's regulars and a small force of Virginians under George Washington had to build a road through the wilderness. (See map, page 57.) As they drew near Fort Duquesne, Braddock was overconfident. He knew little about Indian warfare, but he did not choose to listen to the hard-won experience of George Washington. The exhausted troops had almost reached Fort Duquesne when they were suddenly set upon by the French and Indians and were

French-Canadian
militiaman

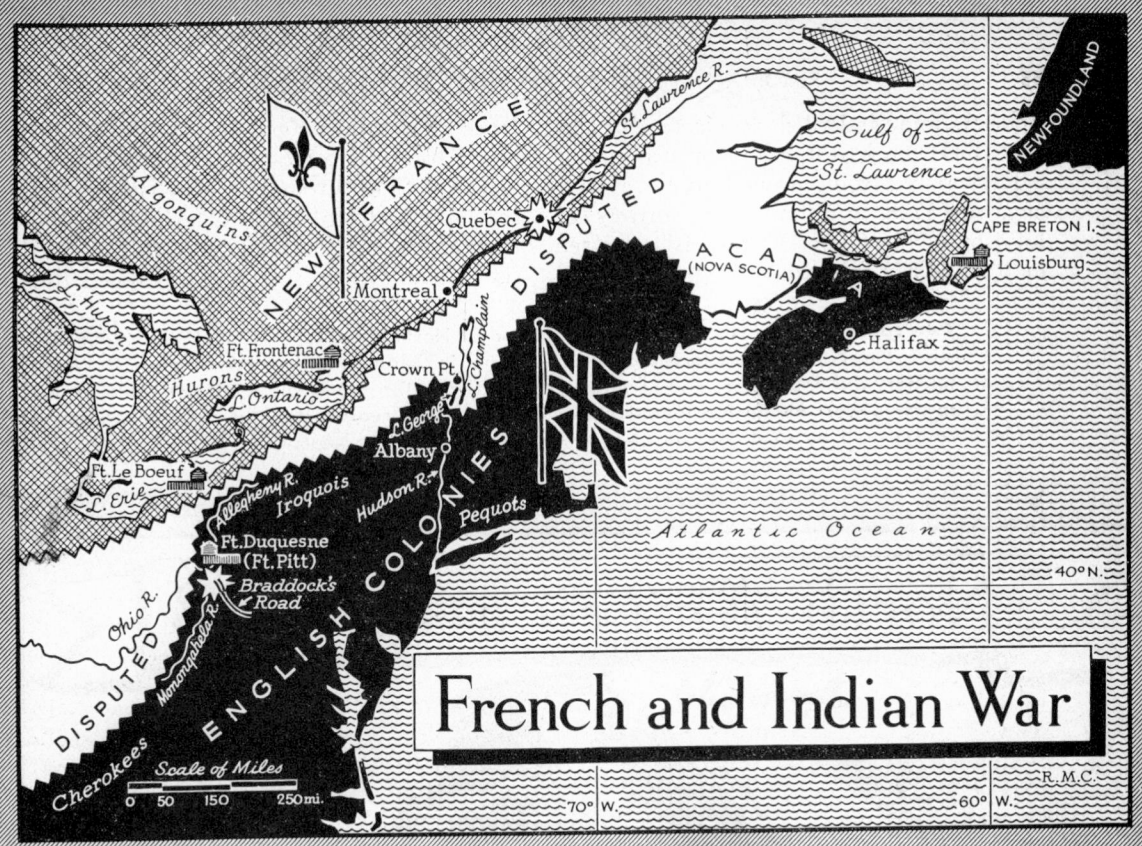

Control of eastern North America was at stake in the final war between the French and English. In what years did this war take place? What was its outcome? Which Indian tribes were allied with the French? The English? About how long was the road that Braddock had to cut through the wilderness? What modern city is built on the site of the French Fort Duquesne?

nearly wiped out. A withering fire seemed to come from behind every tree and rock. Braddock was mortally wounded, and young Washington and the Virginians had to struggle valiantly to save the rest of the force.

This defeat was a terrible blow to the British cause, which continued to grow worse during the next two years because of several defeats along the frontier. "These miserable English are in the extremity of distress," wrote a French captain in 1756, "and repent too late the unjust war they began against us."

The tide turns for the British. The turning point in British fortunes arrived when William Pitt the Elder became the leader of the British government in 1757. Pitt breathed a new spirit of determination into the government and brought about co-operation among the British armies and navy. He tackled the problem in America with a new plan in mind — not simply to hold back the French but to push them right out of the continent. He named new, more capable commanders to lead the British forces in America, of whom the most outstanding were Major General Jeffrey Amherst and Brigadier General James Wolfe. Next, Pitt made an urgent appeal to the colonies for at least 20,000 men to aid in "carrying war into the heart of the enemy's possessions." He promised that colonial officers would receive greater recognition than before, and that Parliament would be called upon to repay the colonial governments for military costs. Pitt's enthusiasm stirred most of the colonial assemblies, and they called for troops to join the British regulars in attacks upon the French strongholds in America.

Pitt's policy soon proved to be a wise one. In 1758, the important fortress of Louisburg on Cape Breton Island (see map, page 57) fell after a siege conducted "with great firmness and alacrity" by a combined force of troops and warships. The same year, Fort Frontenac, which controlled the approach to Lake Ontario and the French line of communication to the Mississippi valley, was seized. The French also

Two countries claimed most of the mainland of North America in 1763. Which countries were they? What territory did Spain acquire in 1763, and from what nation? What territory did Spain lose, and to what nation? The British government did not want settlers to move west of the Proclamation Line of 1763. The reasons for this and the trouble it caused will be explained in Chapter 4.

abandoned Fort Duquesne in the face of an approaching British expedition.

The British win Quebec. The crowning event of the war was the triumph of General Wolfe, in 1759, over the valiant General Montcalm at Quebec. Quebec, a fortress on a cliff, was secure against direct attack, as Montcalm knew. The British fleet was lying in the river below. Montcalm decided to sit tight, holding the fort until winter weather came along, when the British would have to withdraw. One night, however, Wolfe led his men up an unguarded part of the steep hill and gained control of the plains outside the fort. In the fierce battle that followed, both generals were mortally wounded, but the discipline and spirit of Wolfe's regulars carried the British to victory.

Great Britain triumphs everywhere. In the next year (1760) Montreal surrendered, and all of northern New France passed into the hands of Great Britain. Meanwhile, the British kept winning along other battle fronts of this far-flung conflict. Guadeloupe, Martinique, and other French islands in the West Indies were captured, while in India the forces of the British East India Company routed the French. To top it all, when Spain entered the war on the side of France, the British seized the Spanish territories in Cuba and the Philippines. "Our bells are worn threadbare with ringing for victories," wrote an English statesman.

Englishmen control eastern North America. The war was formally brought to a close by the Peace of Paris in 1763. France surrendered Canada and her possessions east of the Mississippi (except New Orleans) to Great Britain. New Orleans and the French territory west of the Mississippi passed into the hands of Spain. England returned Guadeloupe and Mar-

British regular
(Black Watch)

tinique to France, and restored Cuba and the Philippines to Spain. Spain, on the other hand, had to give up Florida to Great Britain. All that was left of the former great French empire in North America were two small fishing islands, Saint Pierre and Miquelon (mick-eh-lon′), off the coast of Newfoundland. (See map, page 58.) Thus, from this mighty conflict, Great Britain emerged the mistress of the seas and the owner of an empire destined to become the greatest and farthest-flung that the world has yet seen. After 1763 in North America, from the Atlantic Ocean to the Mississippi River and from Florida to Hudson's Bay, there was no one left except the Indians to challenge English authority.

——— CHECK-UP ———

How did the British drive the French out of North America?

1. Compare the advantages and disadvantages of the British and French at the beginning of the struggle.
2. What events led to the outbreak of the French and Indian War?
3. What was the Albany Plan of Union? Why was it not put into effect?
4. Why were the British unsuccessful in the early years of the war? What developments caused the tide to turn?
5. What were the results of the conflict with the French?

CHAPTER REVIEW

Terms to Understand

Anglican Church	royal colony	indentured servants	proprietary colony
dissenters	charter	representative gov-	patroons
Puritans	General Court	ernment	Quakers
Separatists	religious toleration	common-store system	Parliament

People and Things to Know About

Stuart kings	Sir Edmund Andros
London Company	George Calvert
John Smith	Maryland Toleration
John Rolfe	Act
Mayflower Compact	Henry Hudson
Massachusetts Bay	Peter Stuyvesant
Company	William Penn
John Winthrop	Mason and Dixon's line
Roger Williams	"holy experiment"
Anne Hutchinson	James Oglethorpe
Thomas Hooker	Albany Plan
Fundamental Orders	General Braddock
New England Con-	William Pitt
federation	Wolfe and Montcalm

Peace of Paris, 1763

Historic Dates to Identify

1607	1634	1681
1619	1636	1733
1620	1639	1754
1630	1649	1763
	1664	

Questions to Discuss

1. In which colony would you have preferred to live had you been (a) a Quaker, (b) a Catholic, (c) a Puritan, (d) a poor farmer, (e) a supporter of Charles I, (f) a Scotch-Irishman?
2. What institutions (ways of doing things) that are a part of the American system today do we find existing in the colonial period?
3. Compare the following:
(a) Puritans and Separatists.
(b) William Pitt and Winston Churchill in their respective wars.
(c) A royal colony and a proprietary colony.
4. What unique feature existed in the charter of the Massachusetts Bay Company? Why was it significant?
5. Was the treatment of criminals in England in the 1600's preferable to treatment in present-day America? Why?
6. What do you suppose that the English historian, Green, meant when he wrote: "With the triumph of Wolfe on the Heights of Abraham [outside Quebec] began the history of the United States"?

Relating Geography and History

1. The most important geographical factors influencing the development of the English colonies were a long and indented coastline, the Appalachian Mountains, and numerous

Relating Geography and History (Cont.)

comparatively short rivers. The French colonies were most influenced by the control of two great rivers, the St. Lawrence and the Ohio. How would the differing geographical factors help to account for differences between the French and English colonies?
2. Explain on a basis of geography why (a) the upper Hudson valley and (b) the upper Ohio valley would be of strategic importance to both the French and the British?
3. On an outline map of the United States:
(a) Locate: Jamestown, Plymouth, Boston, Providence, Hartford, New Amsterdam, Philadelphia, St. Mary's, Fort Orange, Elizabethtown, Savannah, Fort Duquesne, Charles Town, Quebec.
(b) Locate: Kennebec River, Connecticut River, Hudson River, Ohio River, Delaware River, Allegheny River, James River.

Other Things to Do

*1. In which of the English colonies in America would you have preferred to settle? Write a brief essay in which you bring out the reasons for your choice.
2. Do research to discover who were the first settlers in your own community. You will wish to find information on their nationality, religion, and reasons for coming. You will also wish to find out how they provided for the necessities of life. Your local library or your state historical society should be able to assist you. Newspaper files often contain historical sketches of particular communities.
3. You have discovered in this chapter that new colonies were often settled from nearby colonies. This was also true of the later states. Do research to determine the immediate origin of the first American settlers of your state.
*4. Make a three-column chart headed "English Colonies," "French Colonies," and "Spanish Colonies." Compare these colonies in a general manner as to population, economic activities, and government.
5. Make a comparative list of the chief features of your state's constitution and a colonial charter. You will find complete texts of charters in Commager, ed., *Documents of American History*.
*6. Make a two-column chart headed "Events in England" and "Effects of these events in the colonies."
7. Prepare a talk on the civilization of the French in Canada today. The object is to show how French institutions have survived.

Early windmill

Chapter 3

THE COLONISTS DEVELOP A LIFE OF THEIR OWN

When John Pory came over from England, in 1619, to write his account of Virginia, he wrote: "Our cowkeeper here . . . on Sundays goes accoutered [dressed] all in fresh flaming silk; and a wife . . . of a collier of Croyden wears her rough beaver hat with a fair pearl hatband . . ."

The New World did not care whether a man had been a knight or a cowkeeper before he came there. If he did well in the New World, his wife could dress in silk and nobody would think it odd. And that, too, has always been a part of the American dream — that a man should have a chance to do his best and rise in the world — that no man is better than another because his parents had money or titles or power.

Adapted from AMERICA by Stephen Vincent Benét [1]

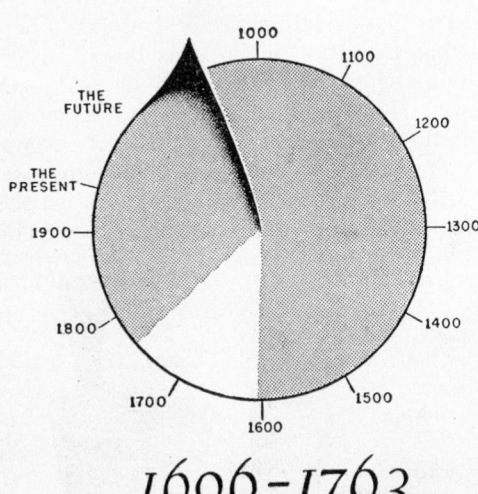

1606-1763

About the time of the Treaty of Paris in 1763, there were some 2 million people living in the thirteen colonies along the Atlantic seaboard. For the past 150 years settlers had been fighting the Indians, clearing the wilderness, pulling stumps, and hauling stones to clear their land. That kind of life was still seen on the frontier, but many more people now lived peacefully and prosperously on fertile farms and plantations or in villages, towns, and cities. The new country was primarily a land of farmers, but there were livelihoods to be made in the towns and cities too. Industries were getting a good start, and hundreds of merchant ships were loading and unloading in the harbors. Throughout the

[1] From AMERICA, published by Rinehart & Co., Inc. Copyright, 1944, by Rosemary Carr Benét.

colonies people were enthusiastic about what could be made out of this great new America.

But just what kind of people had carved out a new life in the English colonies? What kind of houses did they live in, and what kind of churches did they attend? How did they make their livings? How were they governed? What did they read, how did they get along together, and what did they do in the way of entertainment and fun? By answering questions like these, this chapter pictures the way of life that the colonists grew to cherish. The development of colonial civilization is discussed under the following major points:

1. Living conditions vary among the colonists.
2. Farming, industry, and trade flourish.
3. The seeds of liberty and self-government take root.
4. The colonists begin to enjoy the arts.

1 Living Conditions Vary Among the Colonists

Colonists come from many lands. The settlers along the Atlantic coast came from many places and had many different backgrounds. Although the English far outnumbered any other single group, other nationalities were well represented. Next to the English in numbers were the Scotch-Irish and Germans, who eagerly turned to the New World to escape religious persecution and economic hardship. The hardy Scotch-Irish — people originally from Scotland who had lived for a while in Ireland — settled chiefly along the frontier of New Jersey, Pennsylvania, Maryland, Virginia, and the Carolinas. The Germans not only pushed into the back country but made their homes in large numbers in the more settled parts of Pennsylvania. In addition there were in the colonies French, Scotch, Irish, Welsh, Swiss, Dutch, and Swedes.

"From this promiscuous breed," observed a French settler, "that race now called Americans have arisen." The colonies actually were a product not only of English effort but of Old World expansion.

Colonial population increases. After a slow start, population in the English colonies grew swiftly, partly because of immigration and partly because the colonists often had large families. Benjamin Franklin, for example, was one of a family of seventeen children. Families of fifteen, or even twenty children were not unusual, but the death rate was likewise very high. Large families were an advantage, because every member could contribute to the family's support.

In general, the population was scattered rather thinly along the Atlantic seaboard. Just before the American Revolution there were almost 3 million people in the colonies, but only one tenth of them lived in towns. Philadelphia had nearly 25,000 people. Boston and New York were close behind with about 20,000, and Charleston was fourth with only about 10,000. Cities and towns did not then have the conveniences which later made them very different from farm sections. As centers of wealth and progress, however, the cities exerted a great influence upon the development of learning and the fine arts.

Social classes develop. When the settlers came to America, they left behind them the sharp class distinctions of Europe, where a man's position in life was based largely upon the family into which he had been born. But as community life developed in the colonies, certain distinct groups emerged. There were three main groups:

(1) An aristocracy based on wealth was at the top of the social ladder. This

Mug
Piggin
Trencher
Scoop

WOODENWARE

group was made up of southern planters, great landholders of the middle colonies, rich merchants of the cities, and a few professional men like doctors and lawyers.

(2) Next came the small, independent farmers who were really the backbone of the colonial population. Also in this group were skilled workmen, small shopkeepers, and laborers.

(3) The third group included the indentured servants and the Negro slaves.

These early American social groupings were based upon wealth rather than birth. With the exception of Negro slaves, anyone who used his head and worked hard had a chance to improve his lot, so that it was reasonably easy to move into a higher social group.

Colonial homes, food, and dress vary. When building their homes, the early colonists did not follow any one style of architecture. The kind of house each man lived in depended upon (1) what he could afford, (2) the material available for building, and (3) his Old World background.

The homes of the very earliest pioneers, of course, were crude temporary structures. These were replaced as soon as possible by frame houses. The small farmers and townsmen built simple houses of wood, but on the great estates, large homes of stone or brick, as well as of wood, were erected. During the 1700's the houses of the wealthy people grew more elaborate. Splendid mansions appeared on the southern plantations. Wealthy people in the cities built spacious and elaborately furnished houses of wood or brick.

There was great variety also in the interiors of colonial homes. In a farmer's house, for instance, there was usually nothing but simple, homemade furniture and utensils. In the homes of the wealthy, on the other hand, there were tapestries, paintings, fine silver, glass and chinaware, and good furniture. Many of these articles had been imported or copied from English models. All houses had at least one fireplace. In the northern and middle colonies this was a necessity, not only for heating but for cooking meals and drying fruits and vegetables. Southern plantation houses

Early planter and wife

had fireplaces for chill evenings, but cooking and drying were often done in small buildings detached from the main house.

There were also noticeable differences in the way people ate and dressed. After the hardships of early settlement had passed, there was plenty of food for everyone, but there was not much variety and delicacies were few. The ordinary northern farmer and the poorer people of the South ate only what they raised or caught, except perhaps for a little salt or tea. But the southern planter and the northern men of wealth set a lavish table. As for dress, the small farmer wore plain homespun cloth or leather, produced in his own household. On the other hand, the "gentleman farmer" and the wealthy city dweller closely followed the fashions of London, dressing luxuriously in fine fabrics imported from Europe. George Washington once wrote to his London agent: "Whatever goods you send me, let them be fashionable."

Frontier life is rugged and democratic. Very different from this more or less settled life was that of the colonists on the frontiers. From the beginning of the colonies, restless settlers were constantly pushing westward against the virgin forest that walled in the coastline from Florida to Maine. The simplest way to break through it, pioneers found, was to follow the rivers — the Connecticut, Hudson, Delaware, Susquehanna, and their tributaries. (See map, page 67.) Along these rivers which stretched like fingers into the wilderness, the fur trader and the hunter blazed the

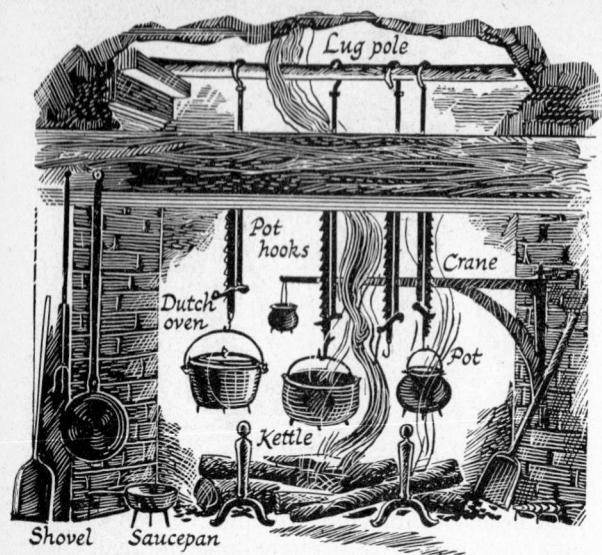

Lug pole

Pot hooks

Crane

Dutch oven

Pot

Kettle

Shovel Saucepan

that means a few hours to us took more than the same number of days in colonial times. Routes were blocked by almost impassable rivers. Along the way, it was hard to find overnight lodging.

Early transportation between important centers was by water or by horseback, but by the middle of the 1700's leading cities were connected by post roads. Soon stagecoaches traveled on regular schedules to and from Boston, New York, and Philadelphia. In the northern and middle colonies, away from the cities, however, travel remained primitive for a long time. In the South, where there were few large settlements, good roads were also slow to develop. Even along the settled routes, travel was work rather than fun. A traveler from Boston to New York near the end of the 1700's gives us this glimpse of his experiences:

We generally reached our resting-place for the night, if no accident intervened, at ten o'clock, and, after a frugal supper, went to bed with a notice that we should be called at three the next morning — which generally proved to be half past two. Then whether it snowed or rained, the traveler must rise and make ready by the help of a horn lantern and a farthing candle, and proceed on his way over bad roads . . . Thus we traveled, eighteen miles a stage, sometimes obliged to get out and help the coachman lift the coach out of a quagmire or rut, and arrived in New York after a week's hard traveling, wondering at the ease as well as expedition [promptness] with which our journey was effected.

Such were the joys of early travel! Remember also that there was no telephone, radio, nor any other modern convenience of communication. A postal system between Massachusetts, New York, and Pennsylvania was not set up until the late 1600's.

trails. In their footsteps followed the farmer, with his family, his household goods, and his animals, in search of fertile lands. Farther south, the growth of large plantations and the exhaustion of soil in the fertile lowlands forced the small farmers to clear fields in the back country.

Along the frontier it was hard to tell the differences between people from the northern, middle, and southern colonies. Here was America's first melting pot. All faced the same dangers. All had equal opportunities. Differences in nationality, religious belief, and social position were forgotten here. In this frontier life, therefore, there developed a spirit of democracy which vitally affected the course of later American history.

Although frontier life was difficult and dangerous, the westward urge was a strong one. So strong had it become on the eve of the American Revolution that a hunter-trapper-explorer named Daniel Boone was already trying to locate — for profit-hungry speculators — the best lands beyond the Appalachian Mountains. Before the war broke out, scattered settlements had arisen in the region of Kentucky and Tennessee.

Travel and communication are difficult. In spite of the continuous movement westward, many an early colonist died without ever setting foot outside his own colony or even his own town or county. To take any sort of trip was really difficult. A distance

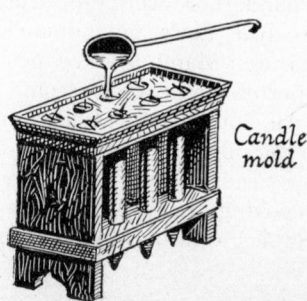

Candle mold

Candlestick

It was another 50 years before postal service reached the South. At best, the communication service in colonial times was poor and cost a great deal.

——— CHECK-UP ———

How did living conditions vary among the colonists?

1. What different foreign lands were represented in the English colonies? What different social groups developed?
2. How did the colonists provide for the necessities of life? Why was life on the frontier different from that on the coast?
3. Describe travel in colonial days.

2 Farming, Industry, and Trade Flourish

Colonists work at many different jobs. Self-reliance and resourcefulness were needed just to stay alive in those early colonial days. The distance between Europe and America was so great and ocean travel was so difficult that the early settlers had to depend on their own resources. Only by using all their energies and skill were they able to build homes and maintain families. Out of hard, unending toil, many different trades and occupations were developed.

Most colonists till the soil. All through the colonial period, at least nine tenths of the people made a living by farming. Soil in the South yielded fine harvests, thanks to mild skies and plenty of rain. The tidewater (coastal) region of the South was the home of the plantation system. Here tobacco, rice, and indigo were grown for export. Not much cotton was raised in colonial times. For home use, the southern colonies raised grain, vegetables, and fruits. The middle colonies produced wheat, corn,

fruits, vegetables, and livestock. They exported so much foodstuff to the other colonies and abroad — particularly to the West Indies — that they were known as the "bread colonies." Of the three sections, New England was least suited for agriculture. Its land was rugged and had a stony surface. Farms there were small, tilled with crude tools and by backward agricultural methods. A smaller percentage of people in New England made their living by farming than in the other regions.

Methods of land-holding differ. Farmers held their land under different systems in different colonies. In Virginia, for instance, there was the "head right" system. Under this plan, 50 acres of land were set aside for each immigrant, and given either to the settler himself or to the person who paid for his passage. Under this practice, plantations grew to hundreds and even thousands of acres. In some of the proprietary colonies it was possible to obtain large grants of land. For example, in early Maryland an "adventurer" who brought over five men received a tract of 1000 acres, subject to an annual quitrent (a small fixed rent payment) of twenty shillings. Landholders in all proprietary colonies had to pay such a quitrent. In New England, however, settlers received land from the town and did not have to pay rent.

The general trend was toward small land holdings. Since settlers could obtain land so easily, they did not long remain as tenants on great estates. New York was noted for many large manors tilled by tenant farmers, but even here — as well as in Pennsylvania and New Jersey — small farms were the general rule. In the South most of the land was at first handed out to small freeholders, and in the back country that situation did not change. In the tidewater region in the 1700's, however, large plantations spread over most of the land.

Large plantations use slaves. This growth of large plantations south of the Potomac River was caused in large part by the spread of Negro slavery. The planters found the slave a better investment

Lantern

than the indentured servant (page 40), who was free to go his own way when his debt had been worked out. The slave and his children after him were permanent possessions. It has been estimated that during the 1700's some 20,000 slaves were brought over to the New World every year, and a large number of them reached the English colonies. Soon after the middle of the century, Negroes made up about two fifths of the southern population. But in the North, slavery made little headway. Slaves there were used chiefly for household work and personal service. Except for the Quakers, hardly anyone — North or South — raised a voice against the use of slaves upon moral or religious grounds.

Industrial and commercial resources abound. Even though most colonists made their living by farming, the country had resources and facilities for many other kinds of work. New England, especially, had what was needed for a more varied economic life, with its waterfalls for power, its extensive fisheries, and its fine harbors along the irregular coastline for shipping. The middle colonies, too, had fine harbors and were richly provided with natural advantages, such as timber, fur-bearing animals, fisheries, and mineral deposits. The South was blessed with mineral wealth and dense woodlands, and had possibilities for manufacturing. Its exceptionally favorable soil and climate, however, kept southern people chiefly at farming until long after the end of the colonial era.

Fur-trading flourishes on the frontier. Next to farming in economic importance was the fur trade, which flourished along the entire frontier. Usually, the traders obtained their furs from Indians, driving hard bargains in which they bartered blankets, liquor, ammunition, and worthless trinkets for great quantities of fur. Frequently they got the Indians drunk with rum and then cheated them.

Lumbering is widespread. There seemed to be no end to the timber resources of the colonies, and lumber was very important before the modern age of steel, cement, and other manufactured materials. In New England grew cedar, spruce, various hardwoods, the valued sugar maple, and sturdy

white pines used for ship masts. In the middle colonies almost any type of tree could be found. Farther south, in the Carolinas and Georgia, the forests were full of the long leaf yellow pine. This was in demand not only for its easily-worked wood but also for the tar, pitch, resin, and turpentine taken from it and used for naval supplies.

Shipbuilding flourishes around the harbors. Ships were built along the seaboard of every colony, but especially in New England and in the middle colonies. Building materials were plentiful and cheap, and as commerce increased there was always a ready market for all sorts of vessels. The busy shipyards along the coast acquired a world-wide reputation for skillful and inexpensive construction.

Fishing and whaling bring profits. Fishing, in which New England led the way, was another important colonial occupation. "Let not the meanness of the word fish distaste you," warned Captain John Smith of Virginia, "for it will afford as good gold as the mines of Guinea." New England schooners sailed in fleets to the fishing banks. The hard work and boldness of their crews brought immense returns. At a fishing port after a good haul, acre upon acre could be seen covered with platforms on which fish were drying in the sun. But colonial fishermen wanted even greater profits. They pressed northward along the coast to Nova Scotia, the Gulf of St. Lawrence, and the Grand Banks of Newfoundland. (See map, page 57.) After 1763, when France had to surrender her lands in North America (page 59), the English colonists had less competition in these fishing grounds. Hundreds of ships were kept busy, carrying the better grades of dried and salted fish to Europe and the poorer grades to the West Indies to be fed to slaves.

People in the colonies had many things in common, but there were also important differences among them. What were the major occupations in New England? The middle colonies? The southern colonies? What were some of the reasons for these differences in ways of earning a living?

Life and Work in the Colonies

CANADA

St. Lawrence R.

L. Ontario

L. Champlain

Mohawk R.

Connecticut R.

furs

iron

Boston

L. Erie

Allegheny R.

Susquehanna R.

Delaware R.

Hudson R.

hemp and flax

shipbuilding

Ft. Duquesne

Monongahela R.

Ohio R.

Allegheny Mts.

Ft. Cumberland

New York

Staten I.

Philadelphia

Atlantic

furs

Shenandoah R.

Baltimore

Ocean

Kanawha R.

Blue

Ridge Mts.

Potomac R.

Chesapeake Bay

James R.

Norfolk

tobacco

Roanoke R.

naval stores
(tar, pitch, etc.)

rice and indigo

Peedee R.

Santee R.

Savannah R.

Charles Town

Savannah

BRITISH TERRITORY

FLORIDA

NEW ENGLAND COLONIES
Massachusetts
New Hampshire
Connecticut
Rhode Island

MIDDLE COLONIES
New York
Pennsylvania
New Jersey
Delaware

SOUTHERN COLONIES
Maryland
Virginia
North Carolina
South Carolina
Georgia

R. M. Chapin, Jr.

Betty lamp   *Bull's-eye lamp*

Whaling, too, became an important industry, especially among the venturesome New Englanders. Through this dangerous work, oil and candles were obtained both for local use and foreign trade. No other nation, declared Edmund Burke, the English statesman, "ever carried this most perilous mode of hardy industry to the extent to which it has been pushed by this recent people." Town histories of many old New England ports tell exciting stories about the daring of their townsmen in early whaling days.

Early manufacturing was in the home. While farming, hunting, and fishing gave the colonists food, there were other necessities of life which had to be manufactured. Some of the most important of these, particularly the making of textiles, centered in the home. The early colonist raised sheep for the production of wool. He also grew flax and hemp for clothing as well as for rope. His home was filled with the busy hum of the spinning wheel as his wife and daughters twisted these fibers into thread which was later woven at home into cloth. Most men and women were "clothed with their own spinning." The colonist's boots and shoes, and other clothing of fur or skins, were also made in his home. So were his furniture and his household utensils. Often he was his own carpenter, wagoner, and blacksmith.

Colonial industries compete with England's. In the later colonial period some of these home occupations spread beyond the household. Weavers in New England and the middle colonies began to make more than enough cloth for their own use. When they made more than they could sell nearby, they began exporting to the southern colonies and to the West Indies. The hat industry also boomed in New England and in the middle colonies, and colonial headwear found a wide market in the West Indies, Ireland, and southern Europe. Likewise, the northern and middle colonists went in for ironmaking. In time the production and manufacture of iron increased until New England's forges not only supplied local demands for farm tools, nails, and utensils, but also made iron articles for export to the other colonies and the West Indies. The cloth, hat, and iron industries grew so prosperous that English manufacturers became alarmed over their own loss of markets.

Rum is an important colonial product. Another profitable industry in the 1700's, particularly in New England, was the production of rum from cheap West Indian molasses. Slave and fur traders found rum important in their dealings with the natives. Numerous New England fortunes were founded upon the profits of the rum industry.

These industries — along with others of less importance — made the colonies largely independent of English products. In fact, by the middle of the 1700's the colonists took care of their own needs for the coarser and more essential manufactures. They continued, however, to import from the mother country goods of finer quality and various luxuries.

Colonial commerce is far-flung. As colonial industries grew, a considerable amount of trade developed. Commerce among the various colonies was carried on almost entirely in ships cruising along the coastline or up the rivers, for transportation by land was too slow, troublesome, and expensive. Of even greater importance was the commerce that sprung up with other countries. The southern colonies did business directly with England. Most of their exports, such as tobacco, rice, and indigo, were sent there, and in return England supplied most of their imports.

The northern colonies traded not only with England but with continental Europe and the West Indies as well. The West Indies produced most of the world's sugar; for their necessities they had to depend on foreign sources. New England and the middle colonies found them to be a ready market for wheat, flour, fish, and lumber. On the return trip, colonial merchants brought back cargoes of sugar and molasses for the distilleries of Massachusetts and Rhode Island, other tropical products, and a balance in cash. Sometimes colonial ships detoured to England and exchanged the products of the West Indies for English textiles and other manufactures.

The triangular trade develops. West Indian trade was closely tied up with the slave traffic. A slave trader took a cargo of rum from New England to Guinea on the western coast of Africa, where he bartered it for slaves. Then he took the slaves to the West Indies, the chief slave market of the New World. Here he exchanged the Negroes for molasses and sugar. On the third leg of this long triangular voyage, the molasses and sugar were brought to the New England distilleries to be made into more rum. New England traders made fat profits in this never-ending chain of transactions.

Colonial trade involves risk. Although great fortunes were to be made at sea, the colonial shipper faced very real dangers. Storms and uncharted reefs carried many a merchantman to the bottom. Pirates like Captain Kidd and Henry Morgan seem shadowy figures from the past to us, but to the colonial merchant, fearfully watching the horizon and hoping for the safe return of his ships, pirates often meant the difference between a handsome profit and a ruinous loss.

Money was a problem, too. There was no uniform and adequate kind of currency in the colonies. Gold and silver were scarce. Not much English money reached the colonies because the colonists bought more goods in England than they sold there. Spanish and Portuguese coins were in circulation, but not enough of them to meet

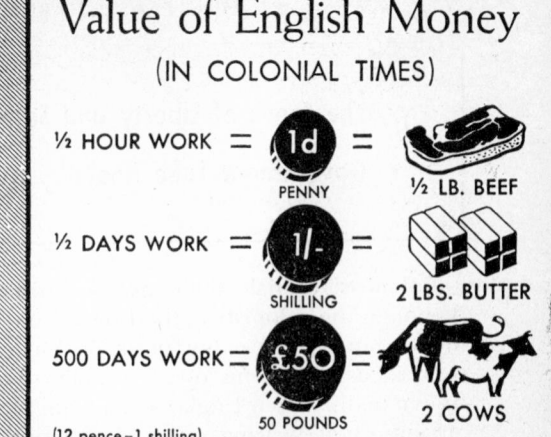

Value of English Money
(IN COLONIAL TIMES)

½ HOUR WORK = 1d = ½ LB. BEEF
PENNY

½ DAYS WORK = 1/- = 2 LBS. BUTTER
SHILLING

500 DAYS WORK = £50 = 2 COWS
50 POUNDS

(12 pence = 1 shilling)
(20 shillings = 1 pound)

The value of English money in the colonies is shown here in terms of the earning power of an average worker. Note that a man might have to save all of his earnings for nearly a year in order to buy one cow. A man worth £50 was considered quite well off in those days.

the needs of trade. Toward the end of the 1600's some of the colonies tried to meet the problem by issuing their own paper money. But colonial currency varied greatly in soundness and value and failed to solve the problem. Since money was so scarce, colonial traders usually bartered goods. In the southern colonies, tobacco and rice were accepted as legal currency. In the North such staple goods as wheat, corn, hides, and cattle were used to make payments, but they rarely had a fixed value in relation to each other.

———— CHECK-UP ————

How did the colonists make a living?

1. How did agriculture differ from one group of colonies to another?
2. What economic activities other than agriculture flourished? Account for their location.
3. What manufactured goods were made in the colonies? What was imported?
4. With what places did the colonies trade? What products were exchanged? What were the obstacles to commerce?

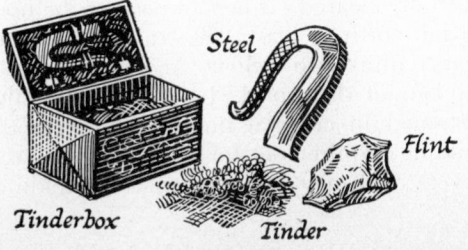

Steel

Flint

Tinderbox

Tinder

69

3 The Seeds of Liberty and Self-Government Take Root

Colonists cherish their political rights. Although the colonists in the English settlements came from many parts of Europe, their ideas and forms of government were drawn mainly from England. This fact had an important bearing upon the history of our country, since Englishmen of that day enjoyed greater freedom in government than the other peoples of Europe. That freedom was reflected in colonial representative assemblies and a judicial system based upon the common law of England. Trial by jury, free speech, and freedom from unreasonable imprisonment were some of the "fundamental rights of Englishmen" generally enjoyed by the settlers in the English colonies.

The colonial pattern of government emerges. By the end of the colonial period, the pattern of government in all thirteen colonies was more or less uniform. Each colony had (1) a governor, (2) a council which acted both as adviser to the governor and as the upper house of the legislature, and (3) a representative assembly. Divided according to the sources of authority, the colonies fell into three groups. (1) Rhode Island and Connecticut were self-governing. (2) Maryland, Pennsylvania, and Delaware were proprietary. (3) The rest were royal (under the control of the king). (See map, page 71.)

In the self-governing colonies, the governor, council, and assembly were all elected by qualified voters. In the proprietary colonies, final authority rested in the proprietor, or a governor chosen by him. In the royal colonies, the governor was appointed by the king. In both royal and proprietary colonies, the council was generally chosen by the governor. Since the governor represented royal authority, he had power to enforce laws, grant pardons, make appointments, and remove civil officers for good cause. He could recommend and veto (refuse to approve) legislation, and he could summon and dismiss the popular assemblies.

Popular assemblies are important. The colonial assemblies, as you will see, were elected by only part of the people. Nevertheless they stood for the principle of democracy. Like the House of Commons in the English Parliament, they had the right to vote for or against the spending of public funds. They used this power to check the authority of the governors and to advance the interests of the landholders, merchants, and planters whom they represented. "Every proprietary governor for this reason," shrewdly observed a writer of those days, "has two masters: one who gives him his commission, and one who gives him his pay." Again and again, colonial governors and elected assemblies disagreed violently on questions of taxation, defense, the authority of royal judges, the issuance of paper money, and particularly the enforcement of trade laws. These "perpetual broils" between governors and colonial assemblies were an important part of the struggle for self-government.

The right to vote is limited. If a man living in colonial days wanted to vote or hold office, he had to pass certain tests which seem undemocratic today. To him, however, they seemed very democratic when compared with the restricted suffrage (right to vote) in Europe. To vote, the colonist had to be an adult male who met certain property qualifications and — in some colonies — certain religious qualifications. In the South, where most of the population was engaged in farming, the ownership of land was the basis of the right to vote. Farther north, where many people made a living at trade or industry, the voter had to own real estate or a certain amount of personal property. If he lived in Pennsylvania, for instance, he had to own fifty acres of land that was at least partially cleared. If he had no land, he had to be worth at least £50. In addition, he was required to believe in Christ as the Saviour of the world. Land was so easily obtained in colonial times that the landholding requirement for voting was not as severe as it may seem. Chances of holding an office, on the other hand, were pretty slim, because most officeholders were appointed by the governor or chosen by the assemblies.

Local government takes root. Every colony was blessed with the English tradition of local self-government. Sometimes "local" meant town government, as it did in New England. The typical New England town was really a compact farming community. The colonist and his neighbors lived close together in homes clustered about the church, while their fields extended in all directions. The New England town corresponded loosely to the church congregation and served as a unit for the collection of taxes. The colonist rarely missed a town meeting, even though only those who had full town citizenship could vote. At the town meeting all the local problems were thrashed out, and representatives were elected to the colonial assembly. The town meeting was an example of pure or direct democracy in America.

Sometimes "local" self-government meant county government. In the South, where the colonists were scattered on large plantations, the unit of local government had to cover a much larger area than a New England town. County officers were usually appointed by the governor but the qualified voters of the county elected representatives to the colonial assembly. In the middle colonies there was a mixture of county and town government. For example, in New York the town was more important, while in Pennsylvania the voters of the county elected not only the members of the assembly but also such local officers as the sheriff and the coroner.

Religious liberty develops slowly. Though it was natural enough that principles of self-government should be rooted in America from the start, religious freedom was more slowly won. It was the belief in Europe that a *heretic* (a person who did not accept the prevailing faith) was a criminal and should be punished even more severely than other lawbreakers. Thus the idea of intolerance in religion was carried to the New World with the earliest settlers. Many who had come to find freedom of worship would not extend the same free-

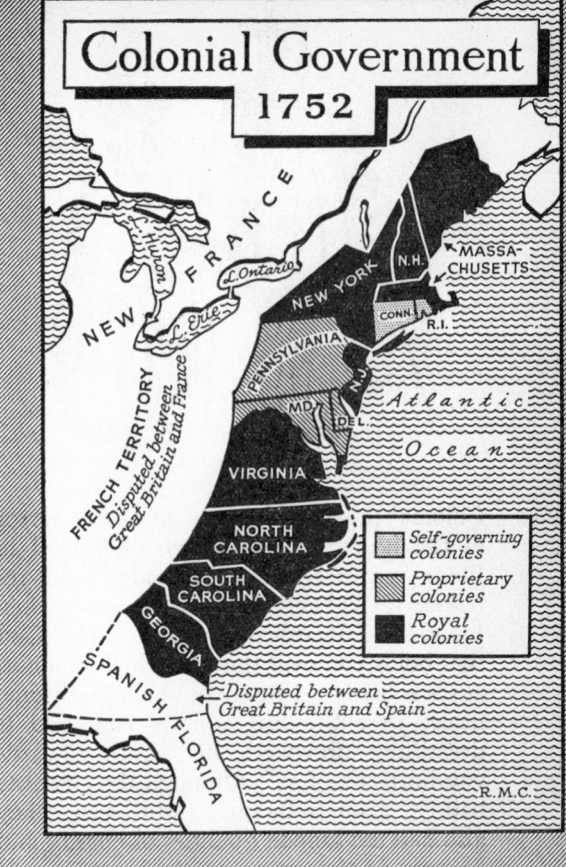

Colonial Government 1752

NEW FRANCE

L. Ontario
L. Erie

NEW YORK
N.H.
MASSACHUSETTS
CONN.
R.I.

PENNSYLVANIA
N.J.
MD.
DEL.

Atlantic Ocean

VIRGINIA

NORTH CAROLINA

SOUTH CAROLINA

GEORGIA

FRENCH TERRITORY
Disputed between
Great Britain and France

SPANISH FLORIDA

Self-governing colonies
Proprietary colonies
Royal colonies

Disputed between Great Britain and Spain

R.M.C.

Colonial governments were of three general types. What were they? In 1752, what colonies were included in each type? What territory was claimed by both France and Great Britain in 1752? What territory by both Spain and Great Britain?

dom to those who wished to worship differently.

Religion was vital in colonial times. In fact, religion affected the thoughts and actions of the people of the colonial period far more than it affects people today. In the 1600's particularly, colonists felt deeply about their spiritual life, and they had great faith in a divine system of rewards and punishments for what they did while on earth. Sunday was a day suitable only for going to church, praying, and reading the Bible. The colonists felt it was sinful — and in most colonies it was illegal — to do such things on Sunday as fish, travel, transport or sell goods, or take part in any amusement. Their beliefs made mixed dancing, cardplaying, and other kinds of amusement taboo on all days in many communities.

Quakers

Colonial preachers set out to arouse terror in the hearts of people who indulged in these "vices." During a widespread religious revival called the Great Awakening, Jonathan Edwards thundered: "The God that holds you over the pit of hell, much as anyone holds a spider, or some loathsome insect over the fire, abhors you, and is dreadfully provoked; his wrath towards you burns like fire." Although the colonists had a grim religious enthusiasm, they also had the human qualities of charity and humor. As time went on, the religious zeal softened somewhat, especially among the wealthy planters in the South.

There were many sects. No single religious group dominated all the colonies. The Anglican Church was the legally established church in the South. In Virginia, Maryland, and South Carolina, even dissenters had to give money toward its upkeep, because members of the clergy were supported out of public funds. In New England — excepting Rhode Island — the Puritans were far more powerful than any other religious group. Many New England towns were founded by Puritan groups which had come directly from England under the leadership of their pastors. New settlers were unwelcome in these towns, and in some cases could acquire land only with the consent of the town authorities. In most of these towns, only church members were allowed to vote. Non-believers were persecuted or banished, and the strictest observance of the Sabbath was maintained. The church was the center around which the life of the town revolved.

While Puritanism dominated in the North and the Anglican Church in the South, the middle colonies became the common ground for many religious groups. Here were Anglicans, Puritans, Dutch Reformists, Lutherans, and the Quakers, who were given that name because some were so fervent in their prayers that they actually shook and trembled. As you have read, the Quakers were members of the Society of Friends. They depended for guidance on the "inner light" of conscience. At their simple meetings, each man or woman spoke only when prompted by his own feelings. Quakers believed in a peaceful and orderly life and were opposed to war. Because of their religious views and independent attitude, the Quakers met with persecution almost everywhere and particularly in New England. They found a refuge first in Rhode Island, later in North Carolina and the liberal province of West Jersey, and finally in the colony of Pennsylvania. In addition to these various sects there were present in colonial America Roman Catholics (chiefly in Maryland) and a small number of Jews.

Religious toleration gains headway. Despite the intolerant attitude brought by the early colonists, the leveling influence of a new country helped in time to develop a greater spirit of toleration. It was aided by the firm stand taken by such men as Roger Williams and by the passage of such laws as the Toleration Act of Maryland. Furthermore, the fact that there were many different religious groups in the average colony prevented any one from keeping control of the assembly. In the later colonial period the colonies were far ahead of Europe in permitting freedom of worship.

Foot stove

Freedom becomes deep-rooted in the American colonies. Thus the idea of religious freedom, like the ideas of representation, popular control of finances, local self-government, and individual liberty, became established in the colonies. The experience of pioneering in a new continent, as well as the loose control exercised by England, had much to do with the upsurge of these principles. Later, when the British government sought to tighten control over the colonies, it was too late to change them. Such principles of freedom had become part of the fabric of colonial existence.

─────── CHECK-UP ───────

How did self-government get its start in the colonies?

1. What was the general pattern of colonial government? Compare the positions of the governor and the assembly. Who could vote?
2. Contrast local government in the New England, middle, and southern colonies. Why did different forms of local government develop?
3. How did religion affect the rights of the colonists? To what extent did religious toleration exist?

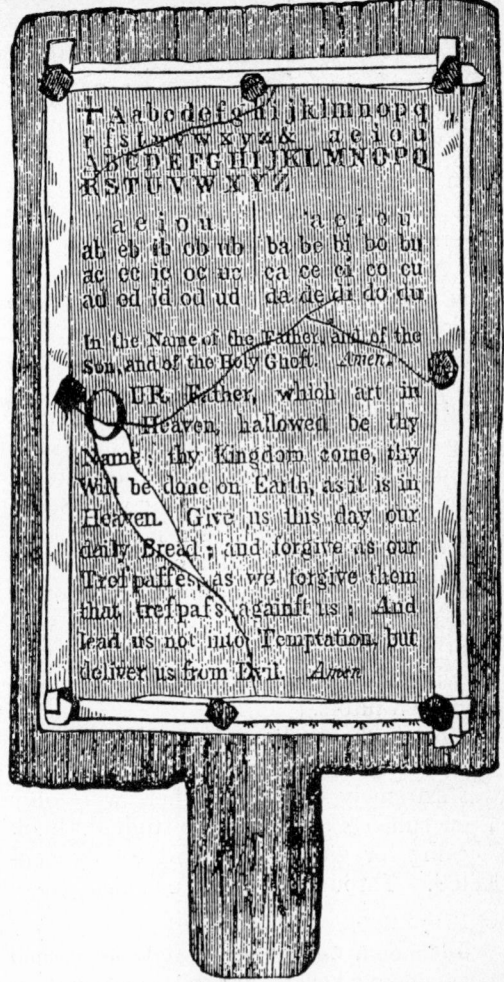

Complete books were expensive in colonial times, so children learned to read by holding a "hornbook" on which single printed sheets could be attached. Sometimes a thin, transparent sheet of "horn" protected the sheet, and from this came the word "hornbook."

---

4 **The Colonists Begin to Enjoy the Arts**

Interest in culture grows. The early pioneer found that just making a living was a full time job. He had little time for science or the fine arts. But in the 1700's the situation changed. Opportunities for education improved. A merchant and professional class, with a taste for the better things of life, was coming into existence. There was a growing interest in books, libraries increased, and America began to make contributions to the advancement of science. Benjamin Franklin's practical inventions and pioneer experiments in the field of electricity made him an international figure.

Colonial schooling was poor. Opportunities for education varied from colony to colony, but from a modern point of view they were not very good. New England was well in advance of other sections in providing for education. Early in its development (1647) Massachusetts attempted to establish a system of popular education. There, every town of 50 householders was ordered to appoint a teacher for "all such children as shall resort to him to write and read." Each town of 100 families was to maintain a grammar school which would prepare boys for college. But many towns were slow to carry out these requirements; even a half century later, it was evident that they were "shamefully neglected by divers [various] towns." Moreover, though the New England schools were "public," they were not "free," except to pupils who could not afford to pay.

Educational progress in other colonies was also disappointing. Even after the middle of the 1700's, a future president of King's College (later Columbia University) admitted that in New York "the state of learning is not very high among us." South of the Potomac River, farms and plantations were so far apart that a school system was impossible. The only boys who got an education in that area were those who went to one of the few private institutions or who lived on plantations which hired their own tutors.

Where schools did exist in the colonies, teachers were not well trained, discipline was extremely severe, and there were only a few subjects that could be studied. Book learning for girls was almost totally neglected. Throughout the colonies there

Dartmouth College in its early days could not afford a bell to summon students to class. Instead, a student blew a booming note on a conch shell to announce classes.

were thousands of men, and even more women, who could not read or write. Education, such as it was, was chiefly encouraged for religious reasons, as a means of helping young people to outwit that "old deluder, Satan."

Higher education is limited. The same emphasis on religious education was found in the colleges. In colonial America every college except one was founded to prepare young men for the ministry. The Puritans wanted young ministers educated to carry on their religious heritage, and so the Massachusetts General Court in 1636 established a college. Named after John Harvard, who gave his library to it, Harvard was the first college in the colonies. William and Mary, and Yale, were founded near the turn of the century, and six others came into existence before the Revolution began. Four of these, now known as Princeton, Columbia, Brown, and Rutgers, got their start under religious sponsorship. Dartmouth was organized to train Indians as missionaries to their own people. The Philadelphia Academy (later the University of Pennsylvania) was from its start the most liberal institution of higher learning in colonial America. Thanks to Ben Franklin, the curriculum included mathematics, accounting, science, natural history, agriculture, history, government, international law, and modern languages, in addition to the usual classics and Hebrew.

Books and libraries appear. The early settler did very little reading. Books were expensive and hard to get. The settler spent all his daylight hours in providing food and shelter, while the dim candlelight and flickering firelight did not encourage the habit of reading in the evening. With the growth of education, however, the colonist showed more interest in literature. Colonial booksellers started to do a lively business, mostly in foreign publications. Clergymen, lawyers, and rich merchants began to acquire more books for their libraries. In time, subscription and then public libraries appeared in the big cities.[1]

(Continued on page 76)

[1] Only the persons who contributed to the support of subscription libraries could borrow books from them.

Benjamin Franklin
(1706-1790)

Printer

BENJAMIN FRANKLIN has fittingly been called the "first civilized American." Better than any other individual he represented the highest accomplishments of colonial America. Born in Boston, Franklin ran away to Philadelphia at the age of seventeen and entered the printing business. Among his most noted publications were *The Pennsylvania Gazette* and *Poor Richard's Almanack*. The latter was widely appreciated throughout the colonies for its practical wisdom and enjoyed for its quaint humor.

Franklin was far more than a successful publisher; in fact his outstanding characteristic was his many-sidedness. In his outlook on education, science, and public questions he was truly "an apostle of modern times." The breadth of his interests and activities was amazing. He was responsible for starting subscription libraries and for founding the Philadelphia Academy, which later became the University of Pennsylvania. Here he insisted on the teaching of a wide variety of useful subjects. At a time when there was little interest in science in the colonies, Franklin became well known on both sides of the Atlantic for his researches in this field. This interest in science resulted on the practical side in the invention of the Franklin stove and the lightning rod, and many other useful devices.

Scientist

Franklin's services to America were numerous and valuable. He ably represented the colony of Pennsylvania as its agent in London. He was responsible for drawing up the Albany Plan of Union. When the colonies broke away from England, he realized the need of union and submitted his plan of confederation to the Continental Congress. Franklin was a skillful diplomat. He was influential in securing French aid during the Revolution and in bringing peace negotiations at the close of that conflict to a satisfactory conclusion. His presence at the Constitutional Convention, where he did much to bring opposing factions into agreement, was a fitting climax to a lifetime of public service and devotion to the welfare of his fellow citizens.

Diplomat

Pointing out the importance of this movement, Benjamin Franklin stated: "The libraries were augmented by donations; reading became fashionable; and our people, having no public amusements to divert their attention from study, became better acquainted with books, and in a few years were observed by strangers to be better instructed and more intelligent than people of the same rank generally are in other countries."

Colonists write books. With added leisure, colonists not only read more; they also grew interested in writing. Much of the early literature dealt with religious subjects. In the 1600's John Cotton, Roger Williams, and Thomas Hooker all wrote religious papers and sermons which exerted a great influence on colonial thinking. In the 1700's an outstanding New England churchman named Cotton Mather wrote wordy essays on many sacred themes. The last great defender of Puritan traditions — Jonathan Edwards — wrote brilliantly on religion and philosophy.

Religious writing, however, was not the only colonial literature to appear. Poetry, history, diaries, books of travel, and almanacs were published. Roger Williams wrote a book on Indian languages. Michael Wigglesworth, a poet of the late 1600's, wrote *The Day of Doom,* which terrified his Puritan readers long after its publication. A hundred years later, Philip Freneau wrote poems which were simple but showed true poetic feeling.

Historians describe early America. Among the early writings of a historical nature were John Smith's *True Relation*

Franklin fireplace

and *Generall Historie,* in which he told his own vividly colored, and not too modest, account of the early years of Virginia. Also written before the middle 1600's was William Bradford's *History of Plymouth Plantation,* in which he related the bitter struggle and perseverance of the Pilgrim fathers. Governor John Winthrop's *A History of New England* gave a clear glimpse of Puritan society in the earliest days of settlement. In the next century, Thomas Hutchinson, in his well-balanced *History of the Colony of Massachusetts-Bay,* proved himself the foremost colonial historian of his time. In the South, William Byrd II wrote colorfully about the life and manners of Virginia and North Carolina of the early 1700's. In the later colonial period, a leading diarist was Judge Samuel Sewall of Boston. Almanacs, such as Benjamin Franklin's *Poor Richard's Almanac,* set forth useful knowledge and rules of conduct in a way which won many readers among the colonists.

Newspapers and magazines appear. The first regular newspaper to come off the press in America was *The Boston News-Letter* in 1704. It was a four-page, two-column, weekly publication. After a halting start, the number of newspapers grew until, on the eve of the Revolution, every colony except Delaware and New Jersey had one or more papers. They didn't look or read much like the city dailies of today. News was far from up-to-date, since a long time elapsed before it reached the colonies from the Old World, or even traveled from colony to colony. Political writing that could be taken as criticism of the government might lead to punishment. Thus the early newspapers, when read today, look dull except to the historian. Nevertheless colonial newspapers did a great deal to mold public opinion. Benjamin Franklin, who published the influential *Pennsylvania Gazette,* was a leading figure in the newspaper world and in the development of the magazine as well. In 1741 he founded one of America's pioneer magazines, which struggled along under the weighty title of *The General Magazine, and Historical Chronicle for all the British Plantations in America.*

Printing was tedious work in colonial days, and also called for high skill. The type of metal or wood for a few pages was placed in the press and inked by hand. Paper was placed over this, and pressure applied. The printer then hung the paper up to dry before it was folded and bound with other sheets to make a book or pamphlet. These early printers were essential to the growth of an independent spirit in the colonies.

Freedom of the press is defended. The development of newspapers started a battle over freedom of the press. Living in a continent of open spaces and unlimited opportunity, the colonists naturally championed freedom of expression. In 1734 John Peter Zenger, a poor German printer and editor of *The New York Weekly Journal*, was brought to trial for publishing articles which criticized the governor of New York and his party. He was defended by Andrew Hamilton of Philadelphia, the most famous lawyer in the colonies. Hamilton's eloquent appeal in favor of the free discussion of public questions won the jury over. Zenger was acquitted (1735) on the ground

that his statements were not libelous. The decision of the jury in the case of John Peter Zenger was later called "the germ of American freedom, the morning star of that liberty which subsequently revolutionized America."

The arts get a slow start. In such fields as sculpture, painting, music, and drama, the people of the colonies contributed little. They accomplished more in architecture, though American architects largely followed European models. In the 1700's the mansions of the well-to-do townsmen and planters displayed a grace and beauty unexcelled in the development of American building design. Many of these are still standing. With their great halls, high ceilings, and stately staircases, these imposing houses were as comfortable and spacious as the best residences of English gentlemen of that day. Many of the furnishings for these homes were imported, but silverware and other household articles made by colonial craftmen had beauty which is greatly admired today.

A few painters, who worked principally at portraits, rose to distinction before the end of the 1700's. The best known were John Singleton Copley of Massachusetts, Benjamin West of Pennsylvania, Gilbert Stuart of Rhode Island, and Charles Willson Peale of Maryland. Sculpture did not appear until after the middle of the 1700's, and then it was confined to portrait busts and "figures in Paris plaster."

There were some evidences of a rising interest in music. Pipe organs were installed in a few city churches, musical instruments were common, and concerts in Boston, New York, and Charleston attracted good-sized audiences. As for the drama, Puritan New England was openly opposed to it, but in other colonies during the latter half of the 1700's, some of the best London plays were put on by professional English actors. It must be remembered, however, that a very small part of the population was influenced by these developments in the fine arts.

Medical science is backward. Medical science at this time, in Europe as well as America, was hardly worthy of the name. The ignorance and superstition of the 1600's are shown by the following typical prescription "to cure various disorders," including the plague, smallpox, and fever:

In the month of March take toads, as many as you will, alive; put them into an earthen pot, so that it be half full; cover it with a broad tile or iron plate, then overwhelm the pot, so that the bottom may be uppermost; put charcoals round about it and over it, and in the open air . . . set it on fire and let it burn out and extinguish of it self: When it is cold, take out the toads, and in an ironmortar pound them very well . . . Moderate the dose according to the strength of the party.

Doctors placed great faith in physicking and bleeding, and many a poor sufferer no doubt found the remedy worse than the disease. Even as late as 1799, George Washington was given just such barbarous treatment, and it may have hastened his death. Doctors with acceptable training were hard to find during most of the colonial period. A great forward step was taken when the College of Philadelphia established a medical school in 1765. Also, more and more Americans began to attend the medical centers in Europe. One well-known doctor was Benjamin Rush of Pennsylvania, who did pioneer work on yellow fever, and who was also one of the signers of the Declaration of Independence.

Colonial amusements were lively. Though the colonists lived strenuous lives, they still found some time and opportunity for amusement. The long winter months gave the farmer a rest from his ordinary work, and frequent holidays gave him a chance to relax and enjoy himself now and then. Horse racing and cockfighting were leading sports, especially in the South. Fishing and hunting were enjoyed in all colonies. Dancing, cardplaying, cricket, billiards, and ice-skating were other forms of recreation — except that some religious sects frowned on them. The colonist liked Sunday services, weddings, house-raisings and corn-huskings, elections, and even funerals, because these occasions brought him together with his friends in a group. Many colonists indulged in drinking, smoking and gambling.

The colonists' idea of a really gay event was a fair. Colonial fairs resembled those of Europe and were held once a year or oftener in most of the colonies. Usually they lasted for three or four days. Here, the colonist could take part in any sport from horse racing to climbing a greased pole or catching a greased pig. The fair offered him shows, fortunetellers, tightrope walkers, and traveling entertainers if he cared for such amusement. People from all around the countryside came to the fair. Friends and neighbors could gossip, people could argue on politics, and everybody could have a good time.

A common outlook united the colonists. Such was life in colonial days. It had its highlights and drawbacks, and contained

COLONIAL WILLIAMSBURG

A British flag rippled from the cupola of the Capitol, seat of the House of Burgesses, Council, and General Court.

Expert colonial craftsmen made pewter and silverware to augment furnishings imported from Europe and Asia.

The homes of wealthy citizens were large, but were simple in exterior design. Interior furnishings, however, were chosen with elegant and expensive taste.

The Great Building of the College of William and Mary was designed by Sir Christopher Wren, famous English architect.

This fireplace, used to warm food before serving, shows the graceful interiors prized by well-to-do colonists.

The city of Williamsburg, capital of Virginia from 1699 through 1799, has been restored in recent years to look as nearly as possible as it did in colonial times. Thousands of people visit there each year to wander through scenes familiar to a southern planter and his wife some 200 years ago. Few colonial communities, of course, were as splendid as Williamsburg, the political, economic, and social center for the oldest of the thirteen colonies.

many contrasts. The same colony which listened to stern Jonathan Edwards also produced the liberal and many-sided Benjamin Franklin. It was a far cry from endless sermons in a bleak New England church to the ease and warmth of a Virginia plantation. The lonely life of the frontier differed sharply from the bustling activity of Boston or Philadelphia or Charleston. Yet beneath these differences was a common outlook which bound the colonists together without their realizing it. The stern New Englander may have thought that half the world separated him from the carefree planter of South Carolina, but he was soon to realize that they were brothers in their ideas of political and economic rights.

——— CHECK-UP ———

How did the colonists begin to learn and enjoy the arts?

1. What provisions were made for education in the colonies? What were the purposes of colonial education?
2. Who were the important colonial writers? On what subjects did they write?
3. What were the chief features of colonial newspapers? What was the importance of the Zenger trial?
4. How did the colonists provide for amusement and recreation?

CHAPTER REVIEW

Terms to Understand

tidewater region
"bread colonies"
"head right" system
triangular trade
established church

heretic
religious toleration
town meeting
county
suffrage

People and Things to Know About

Daniel Boone
Cotton Mather
Jonathan Edwards
Thomas Hutchinson
Philip Freneau
Boston News-Letter
John Peter Zenger

Benjamin Franklin
Michael Wigglesworth
William Byrd II
Poor Richard's Almanac
John Singleton Copley
Gilbert Stuart

Historic Dates to Identify

1636   1647   1735

Questions to Discuss

1. Compare the following:
   (a) The self-sufficiency of the colonial farmer with that of the present-day farmer.
   (b) Colonial education with present-day education.
   (c) The colonial attitude toward religion with that of the present day.
2. Why would the mother country (England) encourage the raising of tobacco, indigo, and rice, be neutral on the raising of wheat, and discourage manufacturing in the colonies?
3. Why is not present-day manufacturing carried on as a household activity?
4. To what degree do you think that the statement that "Europe, not England, is the parent country of America" is correct?

Questions to Discuss (Cont.)

5. Do you think that colonial amusements were more desirable than present-day amusements? Why or why not?

Relating Geography and History

1. Why would life in the Appalachian region differ markedly from life on the seacoast? Why do you suppose that many settlers from Pennsylvania were found in the mountain region of North and South Carolina?
2. Show on an outline map of the world the chief trade routes of the American colonies as described on pages 68 and 69. Indicate the products exchanged and the directions which the traders followed.

Other Things to Do

1. Prepare a brief talk on the chief national groups which came to your state during its formative period. Why did they come? What customs did they bring with them?
2. Prepare a report on the layout and operation of some great southern plantation such as Mount Vernon. You may want to illustrate your talk with a blackboard diagram.
*3. Prepare a three-column chart headed "education," "form of local government," and "economic activities." Compare the New England, middle, and southern colonies on this chart.
*4. Write an imaginary letter describing a stagecoach trip from Boston to Philadelphia in the middle of the 1700's.
5. Prepare a more detailed report on colonial amusements.

Hauling tobacco

Chapter 4

ENGLAND'S AMERICAN POLICY

LEADS TO REVOLT

We cannot, I fear, falsify the pedigree of this fierce people, and persuade them that they are not sprung from a nation in whose veins the blood of freedom circulates. . . . An Englishman is the unfittest person on earth to argue another Englishman into slavery.

Edmund Burke in Parliament, March 22, 1775

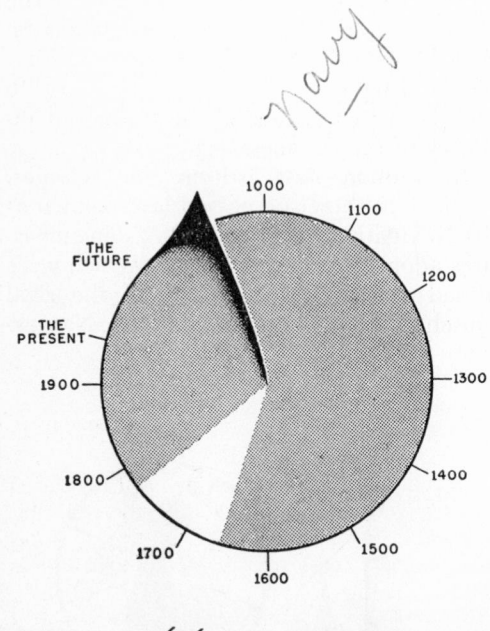

1660 -1775

The glitter of gold and the thirst for power had lured Spain and France to establish colonial empires in the New World. Both empires were tightly controlled by their mother countries. The colonial governments were put into the hands of royal officials, and the individual settlers were closely checked in all their actions.

England had treated her colonies in a very different way, as you have seen. In the first place, the desire for gold and power had not been the principal causes for the English migration to America. English settlers had come looking for homes, and they had come under the sponsorship of private agencies rather than through the help of the government. In the early days of settlement, England had shown little interest in the colonies and had kept only a loose control over them. As the commerce and industry of the colonies became more important, however, the mother country extended its control in order to share in the profits of colonial business. Even then, English colonists enjoyed more personal freedom than colonists ever had in the French and Spanish empires.

When the French and Indian Wars were ended with the Treaty of Paris in 1763, England had no real challenger left in North America. But greater power brought greater problems, and the British government soon found itself faced with certain "burdens of empire." To solve these problems, a firmer hold over affairs in America seemed necessary. England placed more controls on American settlers, controls which came into direct conflict with colonial ideas of rights and liberties. In the brief but dramatic period between 1763 and 1775, the colonists' loyalty to the mother country wavered and open resistance began. The struggle that developed between England and the colonists is described in this chapter under four headings:

1. England regulates colonial business.
2. Colonial controls are tightened.
3. A new British policy angers the colonists.
4. Open resistance flares up.

1 England Regulates Colonial Business

England follows the mercantile theory. England's early attempts to regulate her American colonies were directed at trade and industry. Like other European countries of that day, England followed the *mercantile theory of trade.* According to this theory, the wealth and power of a nation was measured by the amount of gold and silver it could accumulate. A country in England's position, lacking extensive deposits of these precious metals, had to acquire its wealth either by working mines in other parts of the world, or by building up a *favorable balance of trade.* An English economist of the 1600's expressed the

matter in this fashion: "The ordinary means therefore to increase our wealth and treasure is by foreign trade, wherein we must ever observe this rule: to sell more to strangers yearly than we consume of theirs in value . . ." In other words, if England exported to another country goods worth more than the goods shipped back to England, that country must send gold to England to pay the balance of its debt.

To build up a favorable balance of trade, England encouraged the production of English foodstuffs, raw materials, and manufactured products. Steps were taken to see that a maximum of manufactures were exported to other countries and that imports were kept at a minimum. England also stimulated her shipping, and built a strong navy to protect her commerce.

The colonies were extremely important to England under the mercantile theory. They were expected (1) to furnish raw materials not produced in England, (2) to serve as a market for goods manufactured in the mother country, (3) to ship their goods only in English vessels, giving English shipowners a chance for profit, and (4) to add directly or indirectly to the stock of gold and silver in England. So that the colonies might fulfill these requirements, England believed it necessary to pass laws that regulated the trade and industry of the colonies.

Navigation Acts irritate the colonies. Parliament therefore passed laws known as the Navigation Acts. Following some measures adopted during the 1650's, which were aimed at the carrying trade of the rival Dutch, Parliament approved the Naviga-

*Spinning-
high wheel*

tion Act of 1660. This act stated that goods imported into, or exported from, any British possession must be carried in ships built and owned in England or in the English colonies. Three fourths of every ship's crew had to be English. The act also enumerated, or listed, certain articles grown or manufactured in the American colonies which must not be sold directly to foreigners. They had to be sent first to England, in order to insure enough raw materials for the mother country, enlarge English shipping, and make possible the collection of import taxes. This list of enumerated articles included sugar, tobacco, cotton-wool (raw cotton), and indigo. Later the list was increased to cover the main products of the middle colonies and New England.

In a second Navigation Act, passed in 1663, Parliament went even further in her efforts to make the colonies dependent upon England. This law stated that all European cargoes headed for the colonies had to be sent to England first and reshipped from there in English vessels. A few exceptions were made, but the act was planned to give English merchants an almost complete monopoly over the colonial import trade and to let them collect commissions on all European goods that went to the colonies. Naturally, these acts of 1660 and 1663 aroused a wave of resentment in America. In public, colonial merchants argued loudly against them. In private, they evaded the regulations by smuggling.

Parliament enforces the Navigation Acts. British merchants kept complaining that the Navigation Acts were being violated. In 1696 Parliament passed an act to enforce them. Under this act, colonial governors had to take an oath that they would make colonists obey the Navigation Acts. Customs collectors and inspectors were given the power to search ships, wharves, and warehouses in order to seize unlawful goods. Colonial laws which interfered with these English laws were set aside. For a while, this sort of policing worked. The colonists had to import their merchandise from England, and the balance of trade turned in favor of the mother country.

Spinning - low wheel   *Big wheel*

The Molasses Act restricts trade. By far the most annoying of the acts affecting trade was the Molasses Act, passed by Parliament in 1733. This act was intended to break up the profitable trade between the American colonies and those islands of the West Indies which were not British, especially those controlled by France. The act was urged upon Parliament by Englishmen who wanted special protection for their heavy investments in British West Indian sugar plantations. The Molasses Act placed such high duties on sugar and molasses imported from the non-British West Indies that there was no longer any profit in the trade. If the act had been enforced, a major disaster would have struck the New England and middle colonies. The trade with the non-British West Indies gave the colonists a market for their products which brought in the money needed to meet their unfavorable trade balances in Great Britain.

The Molasses Act was ignored by almost everyone. The fact that the act existed, however, made the colonists bitterly resentful. They were angry that the interests of a small group of British West Indian planters were placed above their own. After all, weren't the colonists Englishmen too? Resentment of the Molasses Act turned many colonists into smugglers and lawbreakers, and fostered disrespect for law in general.

England restricts colonial industry. The colonists were further irritated by the attempts of Parliament to restrict their industry. Colonial manufactures had been increasing until they began to interfere with the American market for British goods. English manufacturers then joined with shippers and planters in demanding their share of protection. One by one, colonial industries were curbed by new English laws. The Woolens Act of 1699 stopped shipment of all woolen goods between one colony and another or between any colony and a foreign country. A colony could produce woolen fabrics only for use inside its own borders. The colonial hat industry received the same kind of blow when the Hat Act of 1732 was passed. Under this act, no hats or felts could be exported from one colony to another or from the colonies to Great Britain and Europe. Also, a colonial hatmaker could hire no more than two apprentices at a time.

In 1750 Parliament passed the Iron Act, which put a stop to all but the first stages of iron manufacture in British America. The colonies were encouraged to ship bar and pig iron to England, but this law made it clear that they were not to compete with British makers of tools, implements, and hardware. English controls covered even the timber industry, for lumbermen were not permitted to cut down certain giant trees which had been marked with a broad arrow to show that they were reserved as masts for the royal navy.

The colonies become part of a great empire. As a matter of fact, the laws regulating colonial trade and manufacture were only part of England's growing system of control over her various colonies. The ties which bound the British possessions together before 1700 had been very loose. These possessions had come into being

with little help from the home government. For the most part, the king and Parliament had followed a policy of *laissez faire* ("let them alone"). Left in such freedom, the American colonies had gone their own way, developing their own government, business practices, and ways of life.

In the 1700's, however, the picture changed. The British empire expanded, and the American colonies became part of a widespread system. At home, Scotland was joined with England, and Ireland was brought under British control. Abroad, British influence spread in India, control of the African slave traffic was secured, and the British West Indies proved a valuable source of trade. From this time on, British colonial policies were framed in the interest of the empire as a whole. The American colonies were just one part of that empire.

The Board of Trade handles colonial affairs. In England the affairs of the colonies were put in the hands of the Board of Trade. This group met often and kept a close watch on all colonial activity, including that in America, to make sure that British interests were protected. A British merchant or manufacturer who thought his rights were being disregarded in the colonies, or whose goods needed protection against colonial competition, could appeal to the Board. On the other side, any colony with a complaint could order its agent in London to present its case to the Board of Trade.

Colonial regulation tightens. In addition to the navigation and manufacturing acts, there was other proof that American colonies were being brought under closer control by England. By the middle 1700's the trend toward self-government had received a decided setback. All but five of the colonies had a royal governor, appointed by and responsible to the king. Colonial laws that conflicted with British policies were set aside by the home government. Judges in the royal colonies were appointed either directly by the king or by the governor with the consent of the council. To enforce the Navigation Acts, the British government sent to America

Tanning

like Eckhart brought its lunch
Eckhart eat it,

judges, royal collectors, and naval officers who did not receive their salaries from the colonial legislatures. Parliament even attempted to control colonial currency, claiming that the interests of British merchants depended upon currency regulation.

Some controls offer advantages. While the colonists were irritated by the navigation and manufacturing acts, these measures did not hurt commerce and industry as much as it might seem. Some of the steps taken by Parliament actually benefited the colonies. To encourage the colonies to produce naval supplies and indigo, for instance, the British government paid bounties for the shipment of these articles to England. To aid colonial tobacco growers, the planting of tobacco was prohibited in England and Ireland. When Parliament decreed that all goods had to be carried on English or colonial ships, a boom was started in colonial shipbuilding and shipping. Finally, as a part of the empire, the American colonies gained military and naval protection, as well as trade advantages with other British possessions.

Smuggling becomes a common practice. An even more important reason why the British trade regulations did not seriously affect commerce was the fact that they were widely evaded. Attempts to enforce the laws were not adequate, and the colonists were determined to ignore them. Smuggling was practiced on a wide scale. In 1721 a Boston merchant frankly admitted that it was easy to import many articles prohibited by the acts of trade "if you have a Captain you can confide in."

A fundamental conflict develops. While British regulations did not hinder colonial trade and industry very greatly, they did highlight the conflict between the policy of Great Britain and the self-interest of the colonial manufacturer and trader. The colonists felt that their own interests were being sacrificed to help make English merchants and manufacturers rich. The Board of Trade in England, on the other hand, followed a uniform policy for the entire empire. They acted on the theory that the colonies existed for the benefit of the mother country. The natural outcome of

Weaving

this situation was bound to be misunderstanding, bitterness, and evasion of the laws.

Hit 'em in the chin
Sock 'em in the jaw
put 'em in the grave-
yard
Rah!
Rah!
Rah!

––––––– CHECK-UP –––––––

How did England regulate colonial business?

1. What was the mercantile theory of trade? What part did colonies play in it?
2. What were the Navigation Acts? What was the Molasses Act? Why were they passed? How did the colonists feel about them?
3. What restrictions were placed on colonial industry by Parliament?
4. Why did not the colonists react more strongly against the restrictions on trade and industry before 1760?

2 Colonial Controls Are Tightened

Colonial self-reliance increases. The successful ending of the French and Indian War gave the American colonies a growing sense of their own strength and a pride in it. It is true that some colonies had not greatly helped the British cause, and that most of the victories had been won by British soldiers with the aid of the British Navy. Nevertheless colonial troops and

House   Bed   Coach

A WEALTHY MAN'S POSSESSIONS

commanders had played no small part in winning the war. The military experience the colonies had gained gave them confidence in their ability to take care of themselves. They felt secure from attack, since the French were no longer a threat to their safety. Moreover, colonial population was growing at a rapid rate. Benjamin Franklin, among others, looked forward to the time when the colonists would outnumber the people who lived in England. Franklin wrote: "The foundations of the future grandeur and stability of the British empire lie in America."

The colonies protest writs of assistance. Under these circumstances, the colonists were not inclined to submit meekly to strict regulation. If the king and his followers had kept themselves informed about the colonies, they would have heard rumblings of colonial hostility toward further increases in royal power. One such warning was the fiery protest of James Otis against British abuse of the right to search private property. To help enforce the acts of trade during the French and Indian War, Parliament had provided for the use of "writs of assistance." These papers were search warrants which did not mention the buildings or property to be searched but allowed the holder to enter any place he pleased and search for smuggled goods. Otis protested that writs of assistance violated the fundamental rights of English subjects. "A man . . . is as secure in his house," said Otis, "as a prince in his castle."

Patrick Henry attacks the Crown. An even more definite sign of colonial feeling developed in a dispute over the right of the king to set aside a colonial law. The par-

ticular dispute arose over a salary cut for the Anglican clergymen in Virginia. Their salaries had been fixed at 16,000 pounds of tobacco a year, collected from members of the parish. In 1755 and again in 1758 tobacco prices were high because of crop shortages. To hold salaries down to their intended level, the Virginia House of Burgesses passed a measure which temporarily allowed these salaries to be paid in money at a rate far below the market value of tobacco. The clergymen felt they were receiving unfair treatment and appealed to the British government. In 1759 the British government set aside the law.

Four years later this action led to a trial known as the Parson's Cause. The case was brought by a clergyman who wanted to collect damages for losses suffered while the law had been in force. The trial made a prominent figure of Patrick Henry, a young Virginian attorney. In a brilliant argument, Patrick Henry said that the people were being denied the right to make their own laws. He also charged that by the unnecessary use of his veto power, the king, "from being the father of his people, degenerated into a tyrant." The jury chosen to decide upon the amount of the damages awarded the clergyman one penny, a decision that almost openly defied the royal ruling.

The British face a defense problem. While the colonists emerged from the French and Indian War with greater self-confidence, the British government was finding pressing reasons for tightening, rather than loosening, control. The fact that the French were no longer in North America raised a problem of protection.

The problem was acute in the region between the Alleghenies and the Mississippi. The presence of the French along the frontier had blocked English expansion to the west. Now the frontier was wide open. Pioneers from the seaboard colonies, "with an insatiable thirst for land," began to pour through the mountain passes into the valleys of the Ohio country. The Indians there grew restless under the threat of losing their hunting grounds. They were further angered by the way they were being tricked and cheated by white fur traders. Finally they went on the warpath under the able leadership of an Ottawa chieftain, Pontiac. They terrorized frontier settlements and gained control of most of the British frontier posts. As long as the colonies remained under British control, it was a responsibility of the British government to protect them. Only after a bitter struggle was Pontiac's uprising put down.

The British face financial problems. The French and Indian War brought England face to face with another problem — the need for a greater national income. The cost of the war had about doubled the national debt and put a heavy financial strain upon the resources of the British government. When peace came, it was estimated that a standing army of 10,000 men was needed to protect British possessions in America. The cost of maintaining such a force would amount to more than £300,000. The British taxpayer, already carrying a heavy tax load, was in no mood to shoulder this additional expense alone. He felt that the colonies should pay their share of the military costs. As they were then organized, however, the colonies seemed either unable or unwilling to do so. The British government decided that a reform in colonial administration had to be made if the colonies were to assume their share of the costs of running an empire.

Violation of trade laws requires action. The French and Indian War also showed England the need to enforce the trade laws more vigorously. During the war, smuggling in the colonies had aided the enemy. French forces in Canada, for instance, had obtained meat and other provisions from Pennsylvania, New York, and New England. William Pitt strongly condemned this "illegal and most pernicious trade" by which the enemy got supplies that helped them "to sustain, and protract, this long and expensive war."

George III increases royal authority. These British problems of 1763 — defense, finance, and law enforcement — pointed toward less local self-government for the colonies and much closer supervision by the imperial government. The trend toward stricter control of the colonies was speeded up by a change in English politics. In 1760, George III mounted the throne. A young man of 22, he was unwilling to accept the idea that the king's power should be limited. His mother had always said to him, "George, be king!" When he be-

Dispossessed Indians were a constant menace on the frontier. These natives of Pennsylvania are collecting petroleum. They used it for medicinal purposes, as well as for tipping arrows and war paint.

came ruler this obstinate young man put his mother's advice into swift action. He set out to get his way not by ignoring Parliament but by building up a personal following. He made free use of bribes and appointments, and presently the "King's friends" were strong in Parliament.

The increase in royal power drove the wedge of misunderstanding deeper between England and the colonies. The king knew little about the colonies, but he did not like what he heard about their ideas of self-government. Whenever his followers in Parliament quarreled with the colonies over their rights, George III backed up his followers.

──────── CHECK-UP ────────

Why did England seek tighter colonial controls?

1. How did the French and Indian War make Americans more independent than ever?
2. What were the nature and significance of (a) James Otis' protest against the writs of assistance and (b) Patrick Henry's part in the Parson's Cause?
3. What were the great imperial problems produced by the French and Indian War?
4. How did the accession of George III affect British-American relations?

---

3 **A New British Policy Angers the Colonists**

Grenville launches his program. George Grenville became Prime Minister of England in 1763. Grenville was a conscientious though narrow-minded minister who

Brazier

Cream Pitcher

Tankard   SILVERWARE

could not grasp the colonial point of view. On taking office, he vigorously tackled Britain's problems of colonial defense, enforcement of the trade acts, and national income. He launched the following program:

(1) *The Proclamation of 1763.* Pontiac's rebellion had convinced the British government that all land and Indian questions should be settled in London. Upon the advice of his ministers, the king issued the famous Proclamation of 1763, which stated that the vast stretch of land west of the Alleghenies was formed "for the present" into a reservation for the Indians. From that time on, no one but the British government could buy land from the Indians. Any trader who wanted to do business with the Indians had to have a license. Settlers who had built homes in the reserved region had to get out at once, and would-be pioneers were forbidden to move beyond the mountains.

(2) *More rigid enforcement of the trade acts.* Grenville was convinced that reform was needed in the collection of colonial customs duties. Enforcement of the acts of trade was so lax, in fact, that the British government was paying £8,000 a year to collect less than £2,000. So many colonists took part in smuggling that the practice had even become respectable. Grenville sent more English ships to patrol American waters and called upon colonial governors to stamp out illegal trade.

(3) *The Sugar Act.* The most glaring example of smuggling in the colonies was in the molasses trade. The Molasses Act of 1733 was easy to disregard because customs officials closed their eyes to violations. Five sixths of the molasses imported into Rhode Island, for example, came from non-British islands in the West Indies. Grenville tried to break up the illegal molasses trade by securing the passage of the Sugar Act of 1764. This act cut the extremely high duty on foreign molasses from sixpence to threepence per gallon. It was thought that England might stand a chance to collect the lower rate. To make up for the cut in the molasses duty, the act raised the duties on refined sugar and

A royal seal, impressed on this receipt, shows that one shilling had to be paid to the government when a private debt was settled. Wide use of such "stamps" infuriated the colonists, who regarded them as an unjust form of taxation.

certain other foreign products that came into the colonies.

(4) *The Currency Act.* Grenville pushed his program of colonial control further with the Currency Act of 1764. This act made it unlawful for colonial governments to issue paper money, or for colonists who owed money to English merchants to pay these debts in colonial currency.

(5) *The Stamp Act.* British leaders soon saw that government income from colonial trade wasn't enough to pay the growing costs of colonial defense and enforcement of the trade laws. Grenville decided upon a stamp tax. This direct means of raising money had been used in England for many years and its extension to the colonies had often been suggested. Grenville seemed to sense, however, that such a tax might lead to a quarrel with the colonies, so he told them of the stamp tax plan a full year ahead of the time when the Stamp Act was actually passed. He invited the colonies, in case they opposed it, to suggest a better means of raising money. The colonial assemblies protested the stamp tax, but they were unable to propose any other satisfactory plan.

After a "languid debate" in Parliament, the Stamp Act was passed in 1765 by a wide majority. Revenue stamps costing from a halfpenny to £10 had to be attached to newspapers, pamphlets, licenses, com- mercial and legal documents, deeds, play- ing cards, advertisements, almanacs, and similar items. If a colonist tried to evade this Stamp Act, he could be brought before a court and tried without a jury. Grenville and his ministers expected that the tax would be so evenly and lightly distributed that few people would oppose it. To make the tax seem less disagreeable to the colo- nists, only Americans were to serve as stamp agents. Benjamin Franklin, who was in England at the time, was against the act, but assumed that the colonists would have to obey it. He even tried to obtain a stamp distributor's commission for one of his friends in Pennsylvania.

(6) *The Quartering Act.* The final step in Grenville's program was the Quartering Act of 1765, intended to reduce the cost of maintaining the new army of defense in America. The colonists were required to furnish the English troops with certain sup- plies and with living quarters wherever barracks failed to meet the need. Colonists were to be repaid for these services by the colony in which the troops were stationed.

Grenville's program arouses protests. Grenville was not long ignorant of the colo- nists' feelings. Almost every measure in his program brought loud complaints. Pioneers and land speculators, especially those who already had claims in the western areas, protested the Proclamation of 1763. Why

89

had the French been driven out of the western lands if English settlers were to be prevented from moving in? Six of the colonies challenged the proclamation on the ground that it included territory granted to them in their charters.

The colonists were also disturbed over the Sugar Act, which made it clear that England was taxing them to raise her own national income. The preamble to the act stated that it was "just and necessary" to raise money in the colonies to pay for their defense. The colonists had never seriously challenged Parliament's right to tax goods for the *regulation of trade,* but taxation for the purpose of *increasing England's income* was quite another matter. Samuel Adams of Boston summed up the deep resentment of the colonists over any move to tax colonial trade for revenue. He said: "If our trade may be taxed why not our lands? Why not the produce of our lands and everything we possess or make use of? . . . If taxes are laid upon us in any shape without our having a legal representation where they are laid, are we not reduced from the character of free subjects to the miserable state of tributary slaves?"

Colonial protests center on the Stamp Act. The Stamp Act caused greater anger and resentment than any other part of the Grenville program. The stamp tax fell most heavily upon publishers, lawyers, merchants, and bankers, who were loud in their protests. The Virginia House of Burgesses, led by the fiery Patrick Henry, adopted resolutions declaring that it alone had the "sole exclusive right and power to lay taxes and impositions upon the inhabitants of this colony."

Protests were registered on a wider basis when delegates from nine colonies met in New York in October of 1765. This body was called the Stamp Act Congress. It stated its continued loyalty to the king and obedience to Parliament, but it issued at the same time a declaration of colonial rights and grievances. This declaration asserted that the colonists were entitled to all the rights of natural-born British subjects, including the right to tax themselves. An Englishman living in England could be taxed only by act of Parliament. Since a colonist could not be represented in Parliament, he should not be taxed without the consent of his own assembly. The congress therefore asked for the repeal of the Stamp Act. The Stamp Act Congress was another milestone in the movement toward unity among the colonies (pages 48 and 56).

The colonists boycott English goods. Most colonists were upset not so much by the way the Grenville program affected their personal rights as by the way it touched their pocketbooks. Since the French and Indian War, business had been bad. Every step in the Grenville program made it worse. Hard times came, and colonial merchants bought smaller amounts of goods from England. When British merchants and manufacturers saw what was happening, they became alarmed.

Realizing that they could make their power felt in England through an organized *boycott,* or refusal to buy goods, the colonists made agreements which had a single purpose — to cripple British trade with the colonies. Thus merchants of New York and Philadelphia agreed among themselves not to buy European goods until the Sugar Act had been amended and the Stamp Act repealed. Prominent traders in Boston warned English business men that imports by the colonies would be cut to a mere trickle. Before long, British merchants and manufacturers felt the pinch and began to demand that Parliament repeal the Stamp Act.

Some colonists use violence. Meanwhile skilled workers and laborers who had been put out of work by the depression started to show their resentment through action. Societies known as "Sons of Liberty" held parades of protest, forced stamp distributors to resign, and destroyed stamps. In Boston, a mob hanged and burned a stuffed dummy of the stamp agent and tore down the frame of a building in which they believed the agent planned to sell the stamps. Rioters did great damage in the house of a customs official and almost completely destroyed the splendid mansion of Chief Justice Hutchinson because they mistakenly thought he favored the stamp tax. To this

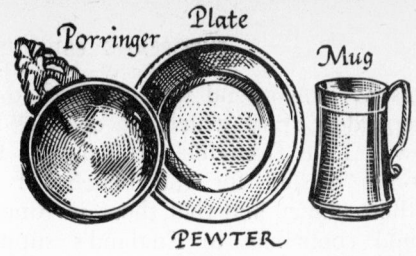

Porringer Plate Mug

PEWTER

day, the manuscript of Hutchinson's *History of Massachusetts-Bay* has stains around its edges from having been thrown into the mud of a Boston street. Similar disturbances occurred throughout the colonies. By November 1, 1765, when the stamp tax was slated to go into effect, every stamp distributor in the colonies had already quit his job.

The Stamp Act is repealed. Probably neither the arguments of the Virginia Burgesses nor the Stamp Act Congress carried much weight in England. There, Parliament was considered supreme, and its lawmaking powers had no limit. If such rule was satisfactory to Englishmen, why wasn't it good enough for colonists?

There was a wide difference between the English and the colonial ideas of representation. The colonists believed in direct representation of each community or colony by elected delegates. In England, on the other hand, each member of the House of Commons was looked upon as a man who represented no single community, but the nation as a whole. Towns or villages which had shrunk in population kept the right to elect members to the House of Commons, while new cities which had grown up more recently lacked direct representation in Parliament. A member might even be elected from a district in which he did not live. According to this theory of representation, the colonies were "virtually represented" in Parliament — at least as much as certain English communities were.

Business losses, however, could be passed over less lightly than a theory of government. British merchants sent numerous petitions to Parliament demanding immediate repeal of the stamp tax. These could not be ignored. In March of 1766, Parliament repealed the act. At the same time, the tariff on both British and foreign molasses was cut to a penny per gallon, and certain other duties were lowered.

Colonists ignore the Declaratory Act. These actions did not mean that Parliament had any thought of giving up its authority over the colonies. Along with the repeal of the Stamp Act, Parliament passed a Declaratory Act. This measure stated that the king and Parliament had the right "to make laws and statutes of sufficient force and validity to bind the colonies and people of America . . . in all cases whatsoever." But the colonists were too busy celebrating their victory to pay attention to the meaning of the Declaratory Act. A wave of loyalty swept through America, and statues were raised to William Pitt and the king. The breach between England and the colonies might have been healed except for a new series of blunders by the government of George III.

——— CHECK-UP ———

How did a new British colonial policy arouse the Americans?

1. What were the various parts of the Grenville program? What groups of people were affected by each? Why?
2. Why were the colonists more opposed to these acts than they had been to earlier ones? Why was the Stamp Act especially objectionable?
3. What various means were used to secure the repeal of the Stamp Act?
4. Which was the more important in securing repeal, the arguments of the colonists or the demands of British merchants?

4 Open Resistance Flares Up

The Townshend Acts reopen the quarrel. England was still faced with the problem of income. The chief responsibility for raising money rested on Charles Townshend, Chancellor of the Exchequer (official in charge of the treasury) in a new ministry. Townshend was opposed to the independent spirit which the colonies had shown. Like Grenville, he believed that colonies existed for the benefit of the mother country and that those in America should contribute to England's support. When William Pitt, still friendly to the colonies, retired from leadership of the cabinet to recover from an illness, Townshend proposed a new plan to raise money in the colonies.

Townshend realized that the colonists hated internal taxes, such as the stamp tax. His plan was to switch to external taxes — duties placed on articles that the colonists had to import. He led Parliament, in 1767, to put a tax on glass, red and white lead, painters' colors, tea, and paper. To discourage smuggling, writs of assistance were declared legal in the colonies, and cases that arose under this law were to be tried in courts without juries. The money raised by the new duties was to be used to maintain the army in America and to pay the salaries of royal judges and civil officers in those colonies where it was found necessary. By another act of the same session of Parliament, the New York assembly was suspended because it had refused to obey fully the terms of the Quartering Act.

The boycott is renewed. The colonists reacted against the Townshend Acts as they had against the Stamp Act. John Dickinson summed up their arguments in his *Letters from a Farmer in Pennsylvania.* He rejected Townshend's distinctions between external and internal taxes. He stated that the passage of any act or tariff in order to take revenue from the colonies was beyond the power of Parliament. The Massachusetts General Court, led on by Samuel Adams, circulated a letter to other colonial assemblies urging them to co-operate in standing up for their rights. These political outbursts received little attention in England until the colonists again started to boycott English goods. In Boston, New York, Philadelphia, and other commercial centers, pledges were made not to buy certain articles from England. Once more there was a sharp drop in imports from Great Britain.

Violence breaks out again. Men of independent income or merchants who were able to lay in a large advance stock of goods could afford to use the boycott as a form of protest. Boycotting, however, was a hardship to laborers and small shopkeepers, who needed a steady flow of English goods to keep business going. These men did just what they had done after the Stamp Act — they resorted to violence as a protest against the Townshend Acts. At Boston, customs officers were set upon by a mob "with clubs, stones and brickbats," and the windows of their homes were smashed. In Providence a customs employee was given a coat of tar and feathers. In Newport, Rhode Island, an armed revenue cutter was broken up and burned. There were outbreaks also in New York and Philadelphia. Angered at this "dangerous spirit of opposition to the authority of the laws," the British ministery ordered General Gage to transfer a military force from Halifax to Boston.

The Boston Massacre occurs. The presence of British soldiers in Boston was a constant reminder to the colonists that they were being forced to obey laws which they hated. They called the British soldiers "red coats," "lobsters," and "bloody backs." More than once they threw snowballs, stones, and oyster shells at them.

On March 5, 1770, these outbreaks reached a climax in the Boston Massacre. This massacre was described by a colonial writer as "a quarrell between the soldiers and inhabitants. The bells rang. A great number assembled in King Street. A party of the 29th [British regiment] under the command of Capt. Preston fired on the people — they killed five — wounded several others. . . ." The anger of the colonists boiled over. In a town meeting they demanded that the British regiments be removed from Boston. The incident closed with a trial of the soldiers in the squad. They were defended by John Adams and Josiah Quincy, Jr., who had no sympathy for the British but felt that the soldiers should receive a fair trial. All were acquitted but two, who were given light punishment for manslaughter. The trouble was patched up, but the Boston Massacre left deep scars.

The Townshend Acts are repealed. Relations between England and the colonies were improved when Lord North, who became England's prime minister in 1770, urged the repeal of the Townshend Acts. It wasn't that Lord North felt generous toward the colonists. He simply realized that the cost of enforcing the laws was greater than the revenue they brought into the treasury. All the duties were removed except the one on tea. The tea duty was kept as a symbol — to show the colonists that Parliament had the right to tax them. With the repeal of the Townshend Acts, colonial life resumed its former ways. Colonists smuggled tea into the country from Holland. Business improved and the boycott agreements were forgotten.

A new Tea Act angers the colonists. But the peaceful atmosphere was misleading. Samuel Adams and other colonial patriots were determined to fight regulation by the mother country at every turn. It was not long before the British government played directly into their hands.

The new trouble arose over the Tea Act. The British East India Company was almost bankrupt owing partly to the fact that the colonists were boycotting tea because it still carried the threepence duty. Parliament, wanting to save the company, passed a measure which permitted the East India Company to export tea from its warehouses in England without paying a heavy export tax. Thus the company could sell tea in America more cheaply than in England and even below the price of tea smuggled in from Holland. The East India Company would have almost a monopoly of the tea business in the colonies, and the English government would have an increased income from the tax of threepence per pound in America. "There must always be one tax to keep up the right," declared the king, "and as such I approve of the tea duty." The British government was sure that the colonists would disregard the tax in their eagerness to buy cheaper tea.

Boston patriots hold a tea party. The colonists responded to the Tea Act in quite a different way. Some of them regarded it

Glassmaking

as a scheme to make them forget their rights and liberties by appealing to their pocketbooks. Merchants and smugglers were against it because they were afraid of competition from the powerful East India Company. When British ships loaded with tea approached New York and Philadelphia, they were turned back before they entered the harbors. At Charleston, landing of the cargo was delayed until it had to be seized by customs officials and stored in the government warehouse. In Boston, Governor Hutchinson refused to grant clearance papers for the return of the loaded vessels to England. But a mass meeting of citizens led by Samuel Adams protested the landing of the tea and the payment of "one farthing of duty" on it. Matters were thus at a standstill on the night of December 16, 1773, when a band of men, disguised as Indians, climbed aboard the ships and emptied the chests of tea into the harbor.

The tea party brings on a crisis. Up to this point, feeling in the colonies had been fairly well united in opposition to the Tea Act. But it divided sharply over the "Boston Tea Party." Many patriots in the colonies applauded the daring deed. Colonists with a high regard for the rights of property, however, thought that the raiders had gone too far. Even the liberal-minded Franklin said that the East India Company should be fully repaid for "an act of violent injustice." In England there was disapproval on all sides. The British ministry looked upon the destruction of the tea as an act of lawlessness which called for punishment. The Boston Tea Party resulted in a crisis in the relations between the colonies and Great Britain.

Parliament passes the Intolerable Acts.
Feeling in England was expressed by the prompt passage of a number of new laws. Called in America "the Intolerable Acts" because of their harshness, these laws were intended to punish the defiant colonists.

The first act, the Boston Port Bill, closed the port of Boston until the owners of the tea had been repaid, and until "the trade of Great Britain may safely be carried on there, and His Majesty's customs duly collected." The second, the Massachusetts Government Act, greatly limited the privileges of self-government in Massachusetts. A third measure permitted English officials accused of serious offenses in connection with their duties in Massachusetts to be tried in another colony or in England. This act was intended to give such officials an opportunity for a fairer trial. In addition, a new Quartering Act gave local authorities the responsibility for finding suitable lodgings for troops. Finally there was the Quebec Act, which was not meant as a law to punish the colonists but was looked upon as such by some of them. The Quebec Act wiped out western land claims by adding to the old province of Quebec the stretch of wilderness southward to the Ohio River and westward to the Mississippi. Furthermore, the strict form of government in this area, though satisfactory to the French inhabitants in Canada, was looked upon by the English colonists as a threat to their free institutions.

To add insult to injury, General Gage was made governor of Massachusetts and four more regiments of British regulars were sent to the Boston area to help him keep the peace. "They will be lions, whilst we are lambs," the general assured the king, "but if we take the resolute part they will undoubtedly prove very meek."

Committees of correspondence are formed. The colonists had already faced enough troubles to know the value of united action. Even before the Intolerable Acts were passed, the more determined patriots had worked out a form of organization to exchange ideas and plans of action. In the fall of 1772, Samuel Adams had urged: "Let associations and combinations be everywhere set up to consult and recover our just rights." He led the way by urging the Boston town meeting to set up a *committee of correspondence*. Its purpose was to state the rights of the Boston colonists and make them known to the people of other towns. The example was followed all through Massachusetts, and the idea also took hold rapidly in other colonies. Soon public opinion was being expressed through each local committee. By the time of the Intolerable Acts, there were centralized committees of correspondence in every colony except Pennsylvania.

The colonists protest the Intolerable Acts.
The Boston Port Bill aroused colonial resentment anew. Three days after a copy of this bill reached Boston, a town meeting there urged all colonies to stop trading with England. The Virginia House of Burgesses set aside the day the Port Bill went into effect for "fasting, humiliation, and prayer." In return, Virginia's royal governor dismissed the Virginia assembly. However, the assembly met unofficially the next day at a local tavern and decided to sound out the colonies on the need for calling an annual congress to consider matters of common interest. Stirred by this suggestion — and led, as usual, by Samuel Adams — the Massachusetts House of Representatives invited all the colonies to send delegates to a congress in Philadelphia.

The First Continental Congress assembles.
This congress was more representative of all the colonies than any colonial group that had met before. It met in Carpenters' Hall, Philadelphia, September, 1774. There were 56 delegates, chosen by assemblies, by conventions, by committees of correspondence, or in other ways. Georgia was the only colony not represented.

Flax brake

Colonial resentment against unjust taxation and other repressive measures reached fever pitch soon after fighting broke out. Aroused patriots in New York are shown here toppling over a statue of George III, which they melted down to make bullets. Such an action would have been unthinkable a few months earlier.

The delegates included some of the ablest men in the colonies. Half of them were lawyers and eleven were merchants. They had one goal in mind — the defense of colonial rights — but they differed on the methods of defense. Although every shade of opinion was represented in the congress, it was soon clear that the patriots who did not fear to take strong steps were in control.

Proof of that fact came when the congress endorsed a set of resolutions drawn up earlier by a convention in one of the Massachusetts counties. These resolutions stated flatly that the colonists need not obey the Intolerable Acts. They charged that the new government of Massachusetts was "tyrannical and unconstitutional." In fact, the resolution advised the people to learn "the art of war" and to break off all trade relations with Great Britain, Ireland, and the West Indies. At the same time, though by only one vote, the Congress turned down a scheme of colonial union proposed by the conservative members — a scheme similar to the Albany plan of union (page 56).

The Continental Congress takes action. All groups in the Continental Congress united, however, in drawing up a declaration of rights and grievances. This declaration stated that Parliament had taxed the colonies unfairly and had burdened them with standing armies in time of peace. It went on to say that Parliament had broken up their assemblies, treated their petitions with contempt, and passed laws (the Intolerable Acts) which were unfair, illegal, and destructive of colonial rights. The declaration went even further, stating that the colonists were "entitled to life, liberty, and property," and "to a free and exclusive power of legislation in their several provincial legislatures . . . in all cases of taxation and internal polity."

Still the bolder members of the Congress were not satisfied. They wanted more than mere paper resolutions. They pushed through a plan known as the Continental Association. This was "a non-importation, non-consumption, and non-exportation agreement" which they thought would bring the British ministry to terms in a hurry. To make the Continental Association effective, committees were to be appointed in every county, city, and town to watch for violations of the agreement and to publish the names of offenders. This was a boycott on a much larger scale than had been tried before.

The boycott is enforced. The association did just what it was intended to do. English exports to the colonies fell off until they were only three per cent of what they had been. From all over England, merchants and manufacturers flooded Parliament and the ministry with petitions to repeal the Intolerable Acts. In the colonies, however, the association did not receive whole-hearted support. Colonial merchants protested that the boycott was ruining business. Many colonists felt that the new plan was a shift of control from Parliament to local vigilance committees. "If I must be enslaved," wrote the loyalist, Samuel Seabury, "let it be by a king at least, and not by a parcel of upstart lawless committee-men."

The British march to Concord and the retreat to Boston covered about how many miles? Why were British losses heavy? Why did the Americans first seek to fortify Bunker Hill and later occupy Dorchester Heights?

Where the War Began

MASSACHUSETTS

Scale of Miles
0 1   3   5 mi.

The British government refuses to give in. The appeals of the first Continental Congress made little headway with the British government. Lord North and the king's friends were in no mood to listen to petitions or to elegantly phrased statements of colonial rights. They realized the damage being done to British trade by the Association, but from their point of view, the colonies were in a state of rebellion, and rebellion had to be put down at any cost. "Blows must decide whether they are to be subject to this country or independent," remarked the king. The only move England made to satisfy the colonial protests was a half-hearted one — Lord North's resolution of February, 1775. In that statement, the British government offered to stop taxing any colony that paid its share of the costs of imperial defense and made provision for the support of royal officials stationed there.

Less than a month later, however, Parliament passed a Restraining Act. This act cut off the New England colonies from the Atlantic fisheries. It also limited their trade to Great Britain, Ireland, and some of the West Indies until "the trade and commerce of his Majesty's subjects may be carried on without interruption." Shortly afterward other colonies — New Jersey, Pennsylvania, Maryland, Virginia, and South Carolina — were subjected to the same laws. Again, Parliament had played right into the hands of the American leaders. The new controls enraged many colonists who had previously been neutral and forced them into the ranks of the patriots.

Blows are struck at Lexington and Concord. Feeling between England and the colonies was now running so high that it was only a step to the clash of arms. The first blows were struck at Lexington and Concord near Boston on April 19, 1775. General Gage heard that the colonists were collecting military supplies in Concord. He sent a force of about 700 soldiers to seize these supplies. At Lexington there was a group of newly organized militia called "minutemen." Warned of the British plan by William Dawes and Paul Revere, they waited for the British and tried to halt them. But the British soldiers routed the minutemen easily, and leaving eight colonists dead or dying at Lexington, they pushed on to Concord. Here they met more stubborn resistance from "embattled farmers," though they managed to destroy some military stores. The day was not over, however. As the British marched back to Boston, the colonists, like a swarm of angry hornets, stung the "red coats" from behind rocks, trees, and walls. The hard-pressed British grew panicky. They were reinforced at Lexington, but the British lost 273 men in killed, wounded, and missing before the weary detachment reached Boston.

The fight at Lexington and Concord inflamed the war spirit of colonists everywhere. From New Hampshire to Georgia expressions of sympathy and pledges of aid poured into Massachusetts. Thousands of armed New Englanders gathered just outside Boston, and General Gage with his army was shut up inside the city. In Great Britain, the news only made the government more determined to stamp out the spirit of rebellion in America.

The Second Continental Congress convenes. Before the First Continental Congress had broken up, it had made plans for a new assembly the next year in case colonial grievances still had not been settled. The Second Continental Congress met at Philadelphia on May 10, 1775. Many of the distinguished men who met this time were to play leading roles in America's fight for independence. The bolder patriots were in control again, but they moved carefully because the conservatives fought against extreme action. "Every important step," wrote John Adams, "was opposed, and carried by bare majorities."

In June, the forces around Boston were taken into the service of the Continental Congress. George Washington was made commander-in-chief of the troops "raised, or to be raised, for the defense of American liberty." The Congress sent another petition for relief to the king, to whom it again professed the loyalty of the colonies. Lord North sent an offer of conciliation, but it was turned down on the grounds that it did not propose to repeal the objectionable acts of Parliament nor did it state definitely that Parliament would give up its power to tax

Paul Revere warns a group of patriots that the British are on the move. Revere was Boston's most versatile citizen: a skilled silversmith, coppersmith, bell caster, cartoonist, engraver, and dentist.

the colonies. Thus the issue between the colonies and the mother country stood out clearly.

——— CHECK-UP ———

What developments resulted in open resistance?

1. What were the Townshend Acts? How did they differ from earlier measures?
2. What events in the colonies followed the passage of the Townshend Acts? Why were the acts repealed?
3. What was the Tea Act? How did it produce a crisis?
4. What was the purpose of each of the Intolerable Acts? What developments resulted from them?
5. Explain (a) the purpose, (b) the organization, and (c) the work of the First Continental Congress.

CHAPTER REVIEW

Terms to Understand

mercantile theory	internal taxation
customs duties	committees of corre-
laissez faire	spondence
writ of assistance	militia
resolution	enumerated articles
boycott	favorable balance of
direct representation	trade

People and Things to Know About

Navigation Acts	Quartering Act
Molasses Act	Stamp Act Congress
Woolens, Hat, and	Samuel Adams
Iron Acts	"Sons of Liberty"
Board of Trade	Declaratory Act
James Otis	Charles Townshend
Patrick Henry	Boston Massacre
Parson's Cause	Lord North
Pontiac	Tea Act
George III	"Boston Tea Party"
Proclamation of 1763	Intolerable Acts
Sugar Act	Quebec Act
Stamp Act	Continental Congress
Continental Association	

Historic Dates to Identify

1660	1765	1773
1733	1767	1774
1763	1770	1775

Questions to Discuss

1. Compare the following:

(a) Direct taxation with customs duties.

(b) The Grenville Acts with the Townshend Acts.

(c) The Molasses Act of 1733 with the Sugar Act of 1764.

(d) English ideas of representation with colonial ideas.

2. Explain how each of the following fitted into the mercantile theory: (a) the Navigation Acts, (b) the Molasses Act, (c) restrictions on industry. Do you think that the Townshend program was in harmony with the mercantile theory? Why?

3. Which British policies would have antagonized you most had you been (a) a manufacturer, (b) a southern planter, (c) a frontiersman, (d) a New England merchant, (e) a lawyer or newspaper editor?

4. The Acts of Parliament would come under such general headings as "regulation of trade," "regulation of currency," "regulation of public lands." Are these powers exercised at present by our state or national governments? Do you think that they could have been adequately exercised by the separate colonies? Why did

Questions to Discuss (Cont.)

Americans object to their exercise by the British government?

5. How would you react to each of the following statements?

(a) The British government was foolish to eliminate French power in America.

(b) Parliament may have had the authority to tax the Americans, but it was not wise to do so.

(c) Americans were too provincial-minded to appreciate the problems of governing an empire.

6. What do you suppose John Adams meant when he asserted that "Molasses was an essential ingredient in American independence"?

Other Things to Do

1. Debate: Resolved, That the advantages of being a part of the British Empire were greater than the disadvantages following 1763.

*2. Make a brief of the chief points in the colonial argument against the authority of Parliament over the colonies. Start with the argument, "Americans are possessed of all the rights of British-born citizens," and arrive at the conclusion that "Parliament has no authority to legislate for the colonies."

*3. Make a five-column chart headed "English Acts," "Provisions," "Reasons for Passage," "American Groups Affected," and "Means of Opposing." Fill in the various acts included in this chapter.

*4. Make a list of the provisions in our national Constitution, particularly those in the Bill of Rights, which were an outgrowth of the objectionable measures used by the British government to enforce the regulatory acts.

5. Prepare a biographical report on one of the leaders of the American cause. You will find biographies all together in one section of your library. Remember that they are arranged alphabetically according to the last names of the subjects and not according to the authors. For example, Tom Paine, American Godfather by W. E. Woodward would be found under the "P's" rather than the "W's." See if your library has a set of the Dictionary of American Biography. This highly useful 20-volume collection of biographies of important Americans is used in the same way as an encyclopedia.

*6. Imagine that you are an American merchant in 1774. Write a letter to an English merchant with whom you have been doing business and explain to him why you have decided to boycott his goods.

Frontier rifleman

Chapter 5

THE THIRTEEN COLONIES WIN THEIR

INDEPENDENCE

The battle, sir, is not to the strong alone; it is to the vigilant, the active, the brave. Besides, sir, we have no election. If we were base enough to desire it, it is now too late to retire from the contest. There is no retreat but in submission and slavery! Our chains are forged. Their clanking may be heard upon the plains of Boston! The war is inevitable — and let it come! I repeat, sir, let it come!

Patrick Henry in the Virginia Convention, 1775

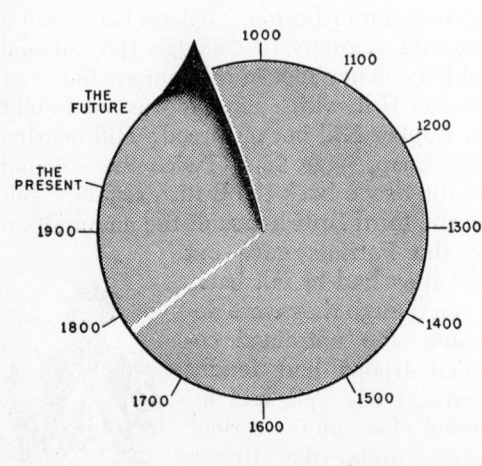

1775-1783

In the short space of twelve years between 1763 and 1775, the ties that had bound Great Britain and her American colonies were strained to the breaking point. The tension had started merely with protests by the colonists against certain English laws. Then, as disagreement followed disagreement, feeling became increasingly bitter. The colonies were torn between their sense of loyalty to the British empire and their desire for liberty. In the end, the desire for liberty proved stronger, and the American colonies declared their independence. A new nation was born in the New World.

To declare independence was simple; to establish it was another matter. The new nation, small but determined, was faced with the task of defending itself against the greatest power of that day. The unequal struggle dragged on for eight long years.

99

Hessian

Before the war ended, other nations became involved. Some of their citizens came to help the American cause and returned home with American ideas of human rights, ideas w h i c h presently had their effect in other countries. Thus the shot fired at Concord bridge was really "heard round the world."

This chapter is the story of the long, uphill fight for American liberty and independence. The major points are as follows:

1. The colonists declare their independence.
2. The Americans fight against heavy odds.
3. British military blows weaken the Patriots.
4. Patriot victories lead to American independence.

1 The Colonists Declare Their Independence

The colonists cling to old loyalties. Though blood had been shed at Lexington and Concord on April 19, 1775, the American colonists were not agreed on what course to follow. Most of the people who had protested Great Britain's policies wanted above all to keep their rights as British subjects. Only a few bold leaders talked about actual separation from the British empire, and they were looked upon as dangerous radicals. The reluctance to break with Great Britain was clearly shown in a declaration by the Second Continental Congress (July, 1775) on the reason for taking up arms. This declaration stated that armies had not been raised "with ambitious designs of separating from Great Britain." As late as the following autumn and winter,

North Carolina, Pennsylvania, New Jersey, New York, and Maryland went on record against separation.

British harshness makes matters worse. Colonists who still cherished a feeling of loyalty toward the mother country, however, were badly shaken by events of the year that followed the skirmishes at Lexington and Concord. Every new step the British government took added fuel to the fires of resistance. The king and his ministers seemed determined to force the colonists into accepting strict regulation. In August, 1775, George III proclaimed the colonies to be in a state of rebellion. Later in the same year, he approved an act of Parliament which prohibited all trade and other dealings with the colonies. Furthermore, George III began to hire German soldiers to help him put down the rebellion in North America. (The German soldiers were called Hessians, because most of them came from the German state of Hesse.) It seemed bad enough to the colonists to be policed by British regulars; it was even worse to watch hired foreign soldiers swaggering up and down the streets.

Colonists resort increasingly to force. Meanwhile the colonists had taken up arms on several occasions. In June, 1775, colonial volunteers began to fortify the heights of Charlestown, Massachusetts, in an effort to drive General Gage and his soldiers out of Boston. General Gage sent a force of regulars to dislodge the colonial soldiers. They met in the famous Battle of Bunker Hill, which actually was not fought on Bunker Hill but on Breed's Hill nearby. (See map, page 96.) Twice the colonial militia drove back the British regulars, but on the third British assault the ammunition of the Patriots gave out and they had to fall back. Even though they were defeated, the untrained colonial troops had fought courageously and had inflicted far more serious losses upon the British regulars than they themselves suffered. The following March, Washington

British regular

and the colonial troops fortified Dorchester Heights overlooking Boston and forced the British, now under the command of General Howe, to withdraw from the city.

Fighting had broken out elsewhere. In May, 1775, soon after hearing the news of Lexington and Concord, Ethan Allen and his "Green Mountain Boys" seized the British fort at Ticonderoga. (See map, page 111.) Then they captured Crown Point and opened the way to Canada. The Continental Congress sent two expeditions north late in 1775, one under General Richard Montgomery against Montreal, the other under General Benedict Arnold against Quebec. Montreal fell, but the combined forces failed to capture Quebec, and Montgomery was killed. Contrary to the expectations of Congress, the Canadians failed to rally to the colonial cause. After spending the winter outside Quebec, Benedict Arnold and his men were forced to withdraw to Crown Point.

In the South there was further fighting. (See map, page 113.) During February, 1776, Patriots won a sharp engagement against British sympathizers at Moore's Creek, North Carolina. A few months later, a force of 6000 militia successfully resisted a British naval attack on Charleston, South Carolina, and forced the British ships to leave.

Thomas Paine speaks out for independence. As the king's policy grew more hostile and armed warfare between British troops and Patriots spread, expressions of loyalty to the mother country seemed more and more foolish. Many colonists who had firmly opposed an open break with Great Britain began to waver. They now began to listen to the arguments of the so-called "radicals," who believed in outright separation. One of the most powerful arguments in favor of complete independence appeared in January, 1776, in a little pamphlet called *Common Sense*. It was written by Thomas Paine, an Englishman who had only recently come to the colonies. "I offer nothing more than simple facts, plain arguments, and common sense," wrote Paine. His logic was clear-cut and convincing, and he wrote so simply that the ordinary man

At the Battle of Bunker Hill, Americans hold their fire to make every shot count against advancing British. The Pine Tree flag was one of many used by New England Patriots early in the war.

could understand his ideas. Thousands of copies of his pamphlet were sold, and Paine's vision of a new independent democratic state became widely known in America.

"As Europe is our market for trade," argued the author, "we ought to form no political connection with any part of it. 'Tis the true interest of America to steer clear of European contentions, which she can never do while, by her dependence on Britain, she is made the make-weight in the scale of British politics." He asked what use it was to maintain allegiance to England if it brought only loss and injury to the colonists. " 'TIS TIME TO PART," was Paine's trumpet call. Some of Paine's statements were extreme, but his fearlessness and his vigorous words won many to his point of view.

The colonies declare their independence. The ties which held Great Britain and the colonies together finally snapped in the spring and summer of 1776. In April the Continental Congress opened American ports to the trade of all nations except Great Britain. On June 7, Richard Henry Lee, delegate to the Congress from Virginia, moved that "these united colonies are, and of right ought to be, free and independent states." A committee was appointed to draft a declaration of independence; it was made up of Thomas Jefferson, John Adams, Benjamin Franklin, Roger Sherman, and Robert R. Livingston. The motion for independence was carried on July 2. The Declaration of Independence, largely the work of Virginia's Thomas Jefferson, was formally adopted on July 4, 1776. (See pages 103–105.)

The Declaration proclaims human liberty. The Declaration of Independence stands out as one of the vital documents of history. What made it so extremely important was that it described a new kind of liberty and applied that liberty to conditions in America. Near the beginning of the preamble appeared a striking statement of the rights that every individual possesses. Then the Declaration stated that "the history of the present king of Great Britain is a history of repeated injuries and usurpations, all having in direct object the establishment of an absolute tyranny over these states." To prove the case against the king, a long list of grievances followed. The document closed with a formal declaration by which "these United Colonies" were proclaimed "FREE AND INDEPENDENT STATES."

The Declaration makes the issue clear. With the publishing of the Declaration, a great step had been taken. The climax of the first part of the Revolution had been reached. Only thirteen years had gone by since Grenville launched his colonial pol-

icy. In that time, a tremendous change had taken place in the minds of a very large group of American people. To them the future of America no longer depended on the progress of the British empire. They no longer looked backward at Europe, but forward to the West. Few, if any, had started with such an idea in mind, but the tide of events carried them along by main force. The Declaration of Independence cleared the air of many doubts and made the issue in America clear. But individual colonists still had to decide which was more important, their desire for independence or their loyalty to the mother country.

——— CHECK-UP ———

How did the colonists come to declare their independence?

1. What events of 1775 increased American bitterness toward England?
2. On what occasions did the colonists take up arms against the British?
3. What arguments for American independence were presented by Thomas Paine?
4. How did the Declaration of Independence present the American case for independence?

2 The Americans Fight Against Heavy Odds

American allegiance is divided. It would be a mistake to think that the Declaration of Independence suddenly changed the colonists into a united body of enthusiastic Patriots. At the time, only about one third of the colonists had "independence in view." This third was made up, for the most part, of the small tradesmen, mechanics, and farmers of New England, well-to-do planters of Virginia and other colonies, and pioneers all along the frontier. As the war went on, more and more colonists swung over to the Patriot side.

(Continued on page 106)

..We hold these truths to be self-evident...

Th Jefferson

THE

DECLARATION OF INDEPENDENCE

By the Representatives of the United States of America

in General Congress Assembled (July 4, 1776)

WHEN in the Course of human events, it becomes necessary for one people to dissolve the political bands which have connected them with another, and to assume among the powers of the earth, the separate and equal station to which the Laws of Nature and of Nature's God entitle them, a decent respect to the opinions of mankind requires that they should declare the causes which impel them to the separation.

We hold these truths to be self-evident, that all men are created equal, that they are endowed by their Creator with certain unalienable Rights, that among these are Life, Liberty and the pursuit of Happiness. That to secure these rights, Governments are instituted among Men, deriving their just powers from the consent of the governed, That whenever any Form of Government becomes destructive of these ends, it is the Right of the People to alter or to abolish it, and to institute new Government, laying its foundation on such principles and organiz-

ing its powers in such form, as to them shall seem most likely to effect their Safety and Happiness. Prudence, indeed, will dictate that Governments long established should not be changed for light and transient causes; and accordingly all experience hath shown, that mankind are more disposed to suffer, while evils are sufferable, than to right themselves by abolishing the forms to which they are accustomed. But when a long train of abuses and usurpations, pursuing invariably the same Object evinces a design to reduce them under absolute Despotism, it is their right, it is their duty, to throw off such Government, and to provide new Guards for their future security. Such has been the patient sufferance of these Colonies; and such is now the necessity which constrains them to alter their former Systems of Government. The history of the present King of Great Britain is a history of repeated injuries and usurpations, all having in direct object the establishment of an absolute Tyranny over these States. To prove this, let Facts be submitted to a candid world.

He has refused his Assent to Laws, the most wholesome and necessary for the public good.

He has forbidden his Governors to pass Laws of immediate and pressing importance, unless suspended in their operation till his Assent should be obtained; and when so suspended, he has utterly neglected to attend to them.

He has refused to pass other Laws for the accommodation of large districts of people, unless those people would relinquish the right of Representation in the Legislature, a right inestimable to them and formidable to tyrants only.

He has called together legislative bodies at places unusual, uncomfortable, and distant from the depository of their Public Records, for the sole purpose of fatiguing them into compliance with his measures.

He has dissolved Representative Houses repeatedly, for opposing with manly firmness his invasions on the rights of the people.

He has refused for a long time, after such dissolutions, to cause others to be elected; whereby the Legislative powers, incapable of Annihilation, have returned to the People at large for their exercise; the State remaining in the mean time exposed to all the dangers of invasion from without, and convulsions within.

He has endeavoured to prevent the population of these States; for that purpose obstructing the Laws for Naturalization of Foreigners; refusing to pass others to encourage their migrations hither, and raising the conditions of new Appropriations of Lands.

He has obstructed the Administration of Justice, by refusing his Assent to Laws for establishing Judiciary powers.

He has made Judges dependent on his Will alone, for the tenure of their offices, and the amount and payment of their salaries.

He has erected a multitude of New Offices, and sent hither swarms of Officers to harass our People, and eat out their substance.

He has kept among us, in times of peace, Standing Armies without the Consent of our legislatures.

He has affected to render the military independent of and superior to the Civil power.

He has combined with others to subject us to a jurisdiction foreign to our constitution, and unacknowledged by our laws; giving his Assent to their Acts of pretended Legislation:

For quartering large bodies of armed troops among us:

For protecting them, by a mock Trial, from Punishment for any Murders which they should commit on the Inhabitants of these States:

For cutting off our Trade with all parts of the world:

For imposing Taxes on us without our Consent:

For depriving us in many cases, of the benefits of Trial by Jury:

For transporting us beyond Seas to be tried for pretended offences:

For abolishing the free System of English Laws in a neighbouring Province, establishing therein an Arbitrary government, and enlarging its Boundaries so as to render it at once an example and fit instrument for introducing the same absolute rule into these Colonies:

For taking away our Charters, abolishing our most valuable Laws, and altering fundamentally the Forms of our Governments:

For suspending our own Legislatures, and declaring themselves invested with power to legislate for us in all cases whatsoever.

He has abdicated Government here, by declaring us out of his Protection and waging War against us.

He has plundered our seas, ravaged our

Coasts, burnt our towns, and destroyed the lives of our people.

He is at this time transporting large Armies of foreign Mercenaries to compleat the works of death, desolation and tyranny, already begun with circumstances of Cruelty & perfidy scarcely paralleled in the most barbarous ages, and totally unworthy the Head of a civilized nation.

He has constrained our fellow Citizens taken Captive on the high Seas to bear Arms against their Country, to become the executioners of their friends and Brethren, or to fall themselves by their Hands.

He has excited domestic insurrections amongst us, and has endeavoured to bring on the inhabitants of our frontiers, the merciless Indian Savages, whose known rule of warfare, is an undistinguished destruction of all ages, sexes and conditions.

In every stage of these Oppressions We have Petitioned for Redress in the most humble terms: Our repeated Petitions have been answered only by repeated injury. A Prince, whose character is thus marked by every act which may define a Tyrant, is unfit to be the ruler of a free people.

Nor have We been wanting in attentions to our British brethren. We have warned them from time to time of attempts by their legislature to extend an unwarrantable jurisdiction over us. We have reminded them of the circumstances of our emigration and settlement here. We have appealed to their native justice and magnanimity, and we have conjured them by the ties of our common kindred to disavow these usurpations, which, would inevitably interrupt our connections and correspondence. They too have been deaf to the voice of justice and of consanguinity. We must, therefore, acquiesce in the necessity, which denounces our Separation, and hold them, as we hold the rest of mankind, Enemies in War, in Peace Friends.

We, therefore, the Representatives of the united States of America, in General Congress, Assembled, appealing to the Supreme Judge of the world for the rectitude of our intentions, do, in the Name, and by Authority of the good People of these Colonies, solemnly publish and declare, That these United Colonies are, and of Right ought to be Free and Independent States; that they are Absolved from all Allegiance to the British Crown, and that all political connection between them and the State of Great Britain, is and ought to be totally dissolved; and that as Free and Independent States, they have full Power to levy War, conclude Peace, contract Alliances, establish Commerce, and to do all other Acts and Things which Independent States may of right do. And for the support of this Declaration, with a firm reliance on the protection of divine Providence, we mutually pledge to each other our Lives, our Fortunes and our sacred Honor.

JOHN HANCOCK, *President*

NEW HAMPSHIRE
Josiah Bartlett
William Whipple
Matthew Thornton

MASSACHUSETTS BAY
Samuel Adams
John Adams
Robert Treat Paine
Elbridge Gerry

NEW YORK
William Floyd
Philip Livingston
Francis Lewis
Lewis Morris

NEW JERSEY
Richard Stockton
John Witherspoon

NEW JERSEY (cont'd.)
Francis Hopkinson
John Hart
Abraham Clark

PENNSYLVANIA
Robert Morris
Benjamin Rush
Benjamin Franklin
John Morton
George Clymer
James Smith
George Taylor
James Wilson
George Ross

DELAWARE
Caesar Rodney
George Read
Thomas M'Kean

MARYLAND
Samuel Chase
William Paca
Thomas Stone
Charles Carroll
of Carrollton

RHODE ISLAND
Stephen Hopkins
William Ellery

CONNECTICUT
Roger Sherman
Samuel Huntington
William Williams
Oliver Wolcott

VIRGINIA
George Wythe
Richard Henry Lee
Thomas Jefferson

VIRGINIA (cont'd.)
Benjamin Harrison
Thomas Nelson, Jr.
Francis Lightfoot Lee
Carter Braxton

NORTH CAROLINA
William Hooper
Joseph Hewes
John Penn

SOUTH CAROLINA
Edward Rutledge
Thomas Heyward, Jr.
Thomas Lynch, Jr.
Arthur Middleton

GEORGIA
Button Gwinnett
Lyman Hall
George Walton

Colonial militiaman

However, there were Loyalists, or "Tories," in every colony. In 1776 they made up about another third of the colonial population. Everywhere men of wealth, education, and social standing, who feared that separation from England would mean ruin for them, remained loyal to the king. Thousands of them joined the royal armies. Other thousands left the colonies, many of them going to Canada. As the war grew more bitter and passions were inflamed, the Loyalists who remained in the colonies were harshly treated. They were disarmed, jailed, tarred and feathered, banished, deprived of their property, and even put to death. "A Loyalist," said the Patriot, "is a thing whose head is in England, whose body is in America, and its neck ought to be stretched."

The remaining third of the people stayed neutral for a while, waiting to see what would happen.

The Patriots have some advantages. At first glance, it might have seemed that the Patriots had bitten off more than they could chew. They were defying the mightiest power in the world. But they possessed certain advantages.

(1) Great Britain had to fight the war 3000 miles from her base of supplies, along an extensive coast line, and over a wide territory.

(2) The English people as a whole felt only lukewarm about pressing the war against the colonies. In fact, there were some leaders, like Edmund Burke and the Earl of Chatham, who openly showed their sympathy for the colonists. Many of the king's opponents at home felt that the Americans were fighting the cause of all Englishmen against tyranny. This attitude on the part of the English people led the king to hire German soldiers, especially Hessians, to do much of the fighting.

(3) The colonists knew the lay of the land while the British troops did not. All the colonists had to do was hold their territory, or even a considerable part of it, to be victorious.

(4) Many Americans entered wholeheartedly into the fight because they knew their homes and families were in danger.

(5) The Patriots were fortunate in their leaders, many of whom had seen action in the French and Indian War. In strength of purpose and nobility of character, George Washington was the foremost leader. It is doubtful if independence could have been won without him.

(6) The American cause benefited greatly from foreign aid. From the start, the Patriots had hoped for foreign assistance against Great Britain. It was natural for them to look first toward France. Not only were France and Great Britain deadly rivals of long standing, but certain groups of Frenchmen were sympathetic to the American cause. Early in the war, Congress sent Benjamin Franklin and two other commissioners to France. They had orders to obtain any kind of aid, secret or open, and to arrange a trade treaty. Later, John Jay was sent to Spain and John Adams to Holland, while still other agents were sent to other European capitals.

France withheld military aid at first because the odds against the colonists looked so great. She helped the Patriots, however, by shipping supplies. The French government also sheltered American merchant vessels and let them sell their cargoes in French ports. France finally entered the war in 1778 when the Patriot cause seemed more hopeful. Spain entered somewhat later, while Dutch aid to the Americans eventually caused Great Britain to declare war against Holland.

Many European officers crossed the Atlantic to help the Americans. The gallant young Marquis de Lafayette came from France. Baron von Steuben, from Prussia, drilled the raw recruits of the Continental (Patriot) forces during the long winter at Valley Forge. Other foreign offi-

French regular

cers who helped the Patriots were Baron de Kalb, from Germany, and Kosciusko (kahs-ee-us'koh), a noted Polish engineer, and Count Pulaski (poo-lah'ski), also from Poland. DeKalb and Pulaski gave their lives in the fight for American liberty.

Lack of unity injures the Patriot cause. In spite of these advantages, the Patriots suffered from tremendous handicaps. Their main weakness was a lack of co-operation. They were not a single, united nation fighting Great Britain, but thirteen independent republics. The Continental Congress took over the burdens of building an army and navy, of raising money, and of conducting foreign relations. But it had no real authority to do these things. When it wanted men, money, or supplies to carry on the war, it could only *ask* the state governments for help.

Fearful of a dictatorship, the Congress determined to keep important power out of the hands of any one man. It tried, for instance, to handle military matters in general meeting and through committees. Naturally there was neither efficiency nor speed in such a method. A sorry example of the result was Washington's bitter winter at Valley Forge, when he tried desperately to get the bare necessities of food and clothing for his shivering army. Instead of sending him what he needed, the Congress wasted its time on unimportant matters and listened to unjustified criticisms of the gallant commander in chief.

Raising money proves difficult. No problem gave the Americans more trouble than that of raising money to carry on the war. Congress tried various methods, none of which worked very well. During the first years of the war, it authorized the issue of nearly $250,000,000 in paper money called "Continental currency." The states on their own account printed another $200,000,000. Since Congress had no gold or silver for which its notes could be exchanged, it asked the states to find "ways and means" to redeem them. The value of the Continental currency depended upon the success of the Patriot cause and upon the willingness of the states to redeem it in gold and silver. During the dark days of the

Lafayette visits Washington during the bitter winter at Valley Forge. Undismayed, Lafayette kept pressing for aid from France. When French help came, it clinched the success of the American cause.

war, when the prospects of a Patriot victory seemed very doubtful, it took $80 of paper money to obtain one dollar in gold or silver. The currency was all but worthless, which explains the common phrase "not worth a continental."

The helplessness of Congress was clearly shown when it asked the states for money. It requested more than $100,000,-000 up to October, 1781, and got less than $4,500,000. Congress tried to get money, too, through loans, both abroad and at home. The results, again, were poor. Foreign loans brought in less than $8,000,-000, and loans at home resulted in an even smaller amount. Two Americans, however, contributed much, both in money and hard work, toward solving the perplexing financial problem. They were Robert Morris, who finally became superintendent of government finances, and Haym Salomon, a Philadelphia businessman.

Maintaining the army is a problem. While the problem of raising money was the worst that the Congress had to face, the task of recruiting and maintaining an army was almost as difficult. Washington was faced by problems that no general of today would envy. His forces and equip-

Continental

ment were always inadequate. Arms and munitions were scarce and many of the men were untrained and undisciplined, ready to desert at the slightest excuse. His forces were full of "summer soldiers" and "sunshine patriots," who were willing to serve in the militia, perhaps to repel invasion, but then wanted to go home to plow the fields or reap the harvest. Washington could not interest men in steady military service because his army was so poorly fed, clothed, and paid.

At its peak Washington's army numbered about 14,000 men "fit for duty." This was in the summer of 1776. During the winter of 1776–77 his effective force was cut to about 3000. The Continental army which marched from the Hudson River to help deal the final blow at Yorktown in 1781 was only about 2000 strong. Congress made demands on the states for recruits, and the states usually passed the responsibility on to the towns and counties. It was not until after 1781, when Robert Morris became superintendent of finance, that the army was better paid, equipped, and fed than in those first years of the war — years fittingly called by Thomas Paine "the times that try men's souls."

———— CHECK-UP ————

What were the relative advantages of the Americans and the British?

1. What different views on the Revolution existed in the colonies?
2. What advantages did the Patriots have over England?
3. How did the lack of a strong central government handicap the Americans?
4. Why were raising money and maintaining an army difficult problems?

3 British Military Blows Weaken the Patriots

The British move against New York. When General Howe's troops were forced to withdraw from Boston in March, 1776 (page 101), they sailed to Halifax, Nova Scotia. Within a few months, however, the British were ready to launch a large scale attack in a more vital locality. Anticipating the next British move, Washington had meanwhile shifted his troops from Boston to a strategic position at New York.

An army of about 30,000 British troops, under Sir William Howe, landed across the bay from Manhattan. This army was supported by a large fleet under Lord Howe (Sir William's brother), which blockaded the entrance to the harbor of New York. New York had been picked as the first big point of attack for good reasons. The excellent harbor made it easy for the British forces to obtain supplies. Also, if they won the fight here, they could cut off New England from the rest of the states. Thus, the English reasoned, they could divide the forces of rebellion and conquer them piecemeal.

Washington abandons New York and New Jersey. For a while, it looked as though this British plan would succeed. Over on Long Island, Washington faced the British with a much smaller army, made up largely of undisciplined recruits and raw militia. In August, 1776, Howe moved to drive the Americans from Brooklyn. He dealt a crushing blow, but failed to follow up his advantage. Washington skillfully avoided capture by ferrying his troops across the river to Manhattan during the night under cover of a helpful fog. Howe landed in Manhattan about three weeks later, but again Washington escaped him and retreated up the Hudson River. (See map, page 111.)

Matters went from bad to worse for the Patriots. Soon after a sharp skirmish at

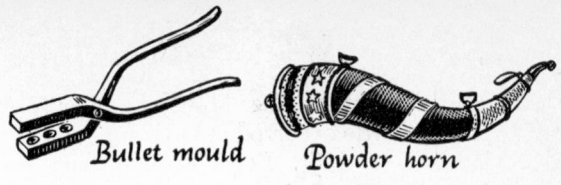
Bullet mould   Powder horn

White Plains, the Americans lost nearly 3000 men and large quantities of military stores when the British seized Fort Washington and Fort Lee on the Hudson. Again, Washington had to retreat to save what was left of his army. He moved hastily into New Jersey. Howe followed, but in no great hurry. Washington finally took refuge in Pennsylvania, across the Delaware River. "We have prevented them from crossing," Washington wrote in December, 1776, "but how long we shall be able to do it God only knows, as they are still hovering about the river."

The fact was that the Howe brothers were not eager to cause American bloodshed. As they pressed on with their forces, they held out the "olive branch" of peace as well as the sword. The king gave them authority to issue a proclamation pardoning all rebellious Americans who would remain "in peaceable obedience" to the king — an offer which was widely accepted in New York and New Jersey. Sir William Howe believed that the great majority of the American people were really loyal to the king. He was sure that the Patriot army would soon break up, and that the British empire would be restored to its former glory.

Patriot victories bolster morale. Howe's dreams of an easy victory were badly shattered when Washington won two brilliant victories over British troops on the New Jersey side of the Delaware. Quick action was needed because most of Washington's men had enlisted for short terms and many of them were due to leave for home at the end of 1776. In fact, on December 20, Washington wrote to Congress, "Ten days more will put an end to the existence of our army."

On Christmas night, his small force was ferried across the ice-clogged Delaware. Early the next morning, they attacked a detachment of Hessians stationed at Trenton. (See the route numbered 1 on the inset map, page 111.) The Hessians were caught off guard, partly from surprise and partly because of holiday celebration. The Americans won a complete victory and took nearly 1000 prisoners. Eight days later, when the British thought they had the "old fox" hemmed in at Trenton, Washington upset their calculations again. He left lines of campfires gleaming brightly to fool Lord Cornwallis. Then he flanked the main British force, and defeated three British regiments at Princeton. After that he led his army into winter quarters at Morristown, New Jersey. The Americans could face the future with new hope.

The British launch a threefold campaign. In 1777 the British opened a new offensive that again centered around New York. They still had a foothold there and could count upon a certain amount of support from the local Tories. Moreover, there was a British army in Canada all ready to fight the Continentals as soon as it could reach Howe on the lower Hudson. The British campaign had three parts. First, Lieutenant General Burgoyne was to proceed with almost 8000 men by way of Lake Champlain and the Hudson River. His goal was Albany, where his men were to be placed under Howe's command. At the same time, Lieutenant Colonel St. Leger was to bring other forces from Canada by way of Lake Ontario. St. Leger's men were to advance across upper New York State, and Howe was expected to send a detachment up the Hudson to co-operate with the other commanders.

These British plans failed to work out as expected. Instead of proceeding up the Hudson, Howe transported his troops to Chesapeake Bay to capture the "rebel capital," Philadelphia. (See map, page 111.) The advance of St. Leger and his men was stopped by General Herkimer and the Ger-

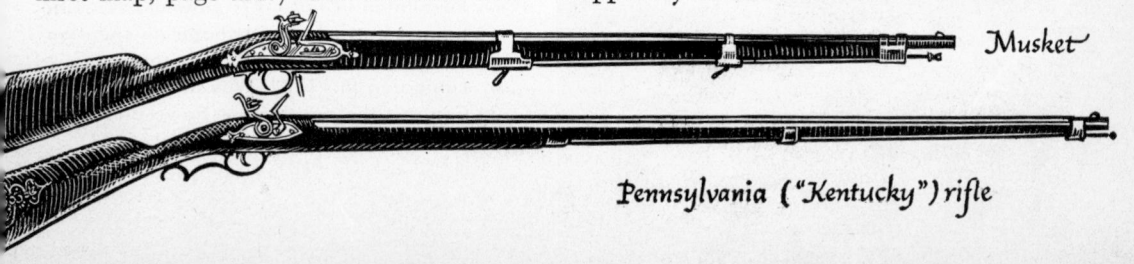
Musket

Pennsylvania ("Kentucky") rifle

man settlers of the Mohawk valley. A bloody battle occurred at Oriskany (or-riss'-kah-ne), and St. Leger turned back to Canada.

Burgoyne surrenders at Saratoga. With St. Leger in full retreat, and Howe on his way to Philadelphia, Burgoyne was the only British hope for conquering the state of New York. His forces moved down Lake Champlain and quickly captured Ticonderoga, but after that they were forced to proceed slowly. They were blocked at every step by the Continental army and the colonial militia. Moreover, every mile of Burgoyne's advance increased the problem of getting provisions. Every British soldier who fell was a soldier who could not be replaced. When Burgoyne sent a detachment of his German troops into Vermont to get supplies, it was defeated at Bennington and suffered heavy losses.

Burgoyne's situation grew steadily worse as he marched south. He was checked and then defeated at Freeman's Farm, or Stillwater, near Saratoga. He retreated to Saratoga. The American force, increased heavily by militia from nearby areas, surrounded him in bewildering numbers. On October

General Nicholas Herkimer, despite wounds which were to prove fatal, directed his German-American militia at Oriskany.

The influence of geography on military campaigns is shown in the map opposite. What were the American generals Montgomery and Arnold trying to achieve? In the campaign of 1777, why did the British follow the routes shown out of Montreal? What were they trying to accomplish? The cannon symbols represent forts.

17, 1777, he surrendered his entire army, about 5000 strong, to General Gates.

Howe takes Philadelphia. While Burgoyne had been crawling at a snail's pace toward Albany, Howe was carrying on a successful campaign against Philadelphia. Unwilling to let the colonial capital be taken without a fight, Washington faced the British at Brandywine, but he had to fall back with heavy losses. (See route 2, inset map, page 111.) Later, the Americans tried to surprise the British army at Germantown and were defeated again. By the end of 1777, Howe was in control not only of Philadelphia but also of the Delaware River and Delaware Bay.

Through the winter that followed (1777-78), Howe and his regiments led a life of comfort and luxury in Philadelphia. Washington and his ragged army, on the other hand, went into winter quarters at Valley Forge, where they suffered the worst hardships of the entire war. Many times during those bitter winter months, the American troops were entirely without provisions. At one time Washington wrote, "We had in camp not less than 2898 men unfit for duty by reason of their being barefoot and otherwise naked." The American camp was in the middle of a rich and fertile country, but the farmers chose to trade their produce to the British for gold rather than to the Americans for worthless Continental money.

––––––––– CHECK-UP –––––––––

How did the British harass the Americans?

1. Describe the opening campaign of the Revolution in 1776–77. How did Washington save an apparently hopeless situation?
2. What was the British threefold plan of campaign in 1777? Why did it fail?
3. Contrast the positions of Howe and Washington during the winter of 1777–78.

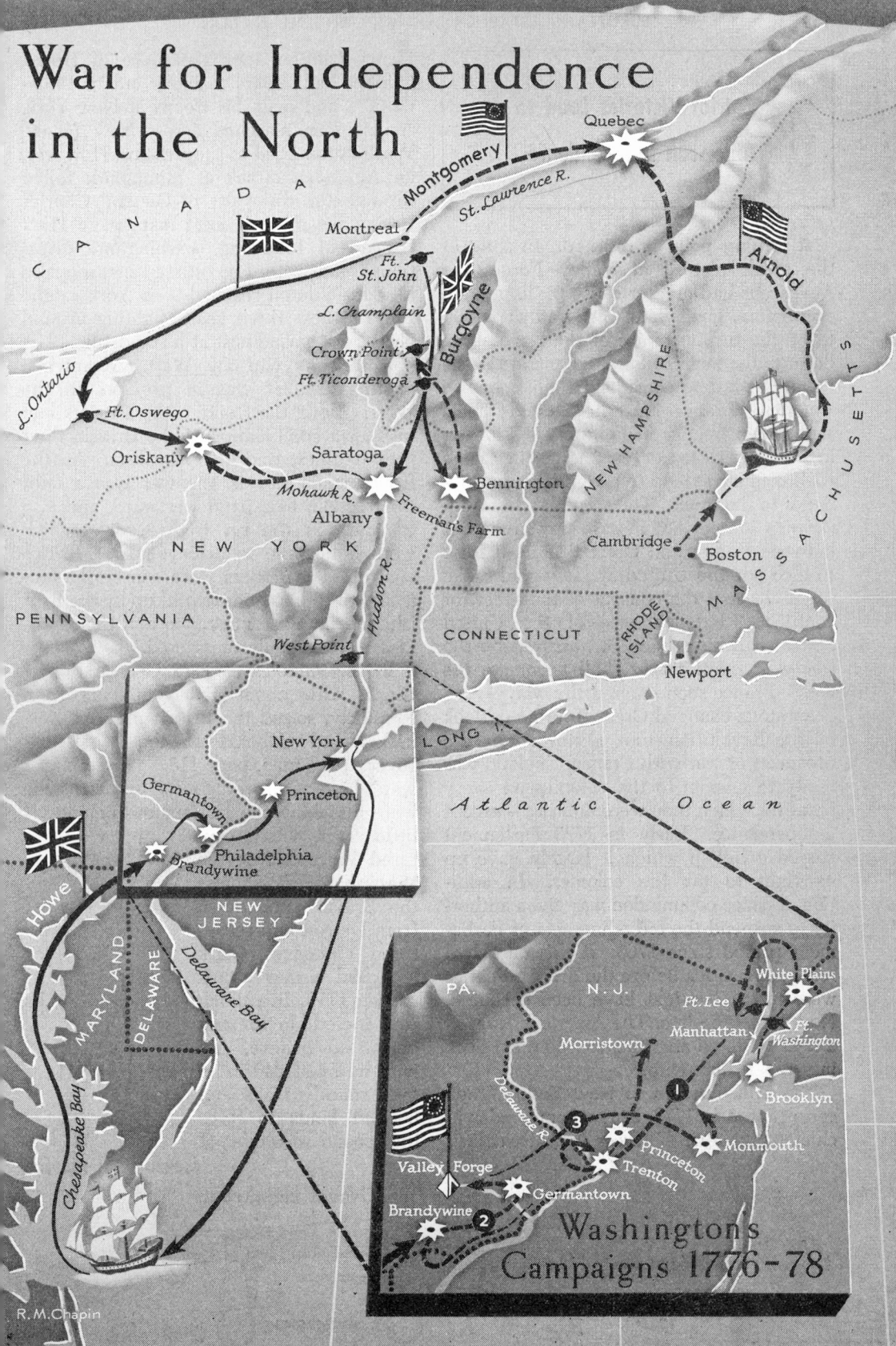

War for Independence in the North

CANADA

Montgomery

St. Lawrence R.

Quebec

Montreal

Ft. St. John

L. Champlain

Burgoyne

Crown Point

Ft. Ticonderoga

Arnold

NEW HAMPSHIRE

L. Ontario

Ft. Oswego

Oriskany

Saratoga

Mohawk R.

Freeman's Farm

Bennington

Albany

NEW YORK

Cambridge

Boston

MASSACHUSETTS

PENNSYLVANIA

Hudson R.

West Point

CONNECTICUT

RHODE ISLAND

Newport

New York

LONG I.

Atlantic   Ocean

Germantown

Princeton

Brandywine

Philadelphia

NEW JERSEY

Howe

MARYLAND

DELAWARE

Delaware Bay

Chesapeake Bay

PA.

N. J.

White Plains

Morristown

Ft. Lee

Manhattan

Ft. Washington

Delaware R.

①

Brooklyn

③

Princeton

Monmouth

Valley Forge

Trenton

Brandywine

②

Germantown

Washington's Campaigns 1776-78

R. M. Chapin

4 Patriot Victories Lead to American Independence

A turning point is reached. In spite of the bleak picture at Valley Forge, the Americans had greater cause for hope than ever before. Their victory at Saratoga proved to be the turning point of the Revolution, because the news of Saratoga made France willing at last to consider an alliance with America. France and the United States signed two treaties in February, 1778. The first was a treaty of commerce, in which each country agreed to give full trade privileges to the other. The second, a treaty of alliance, stated that in case war broke out between France and Great Britain, neither France nor the United States would make peace without the consent of the other, or "until the independence of the United States shall have been . . . assured by the treaty or treaties that shall terminate the war." France soon entered the war.

Saratoga changed Great Britain's outlook on the Revolution, too. Disturbed by the prospects of war with France, England was ready to give in to the colonies on every point for which they were fighting — except independence. Early in 1778 Parliament passed a bill in which it largely gave up its right to tax the colonies. In addition, a peace commission was given authority to suspend the offending acts of Parliament passed since 1763. If this offer had reached America before the French treaties were made, it might have been accepted. Now it was too late. The Americans turned a deaf ear to all attempts to woo them back into the British empire.

The British return to New York. When spring came in 1778, a new commander in chief of the British forces in America, Sir Henry Clinton, took the place of Howe. Clinton had orders to move out of Philadelphia and mass his troops at New York. As his men marched across New Jersey, Washington tried to stop them. However, an American attack at Monmouth failed through the disloyalty of General Charles Lee. (See route 3, inset map, page 111.) Instead of following Washington's directions to advance, Lee ordered his troops to retreat. Clinton reached New York safely. For the next three years, fighting around New York was almost at a standstill.

Americans win the West. Meanwhile another conflict was in progress in the West. Along the frontier, the Patriots had to fight a combination of the British, their Indian allies, and the Loyalists. As the frontiersmen saw it, the war was a fight for freedom to expand westward, and also to share in the fur trade — goals which were impossible to achieve under British control. The settlers were constantly subjected to Indian raids stirred up by the British, and many frontiersmen and their families were brutally massacred.

In the summer of 1778 George Rogers Clark, with about 150 volunteers from Kentucky, seized the British posts at Kaskaskia and Cahokia on the Mississippi River. (See map, page 113.) These places were havens of refuge for Indians who were attacking the frontier settlements. A little later, Clark captured Vincennes on the Wabash River. Though the British came down from Detroit and recaptured Vincennes, Clark launched a new attack early in 1779. In a march "too incredible for any person to believe," his men tramped 240 miles over muddy trails and flooded lands to force the second surrender of

Continental marine

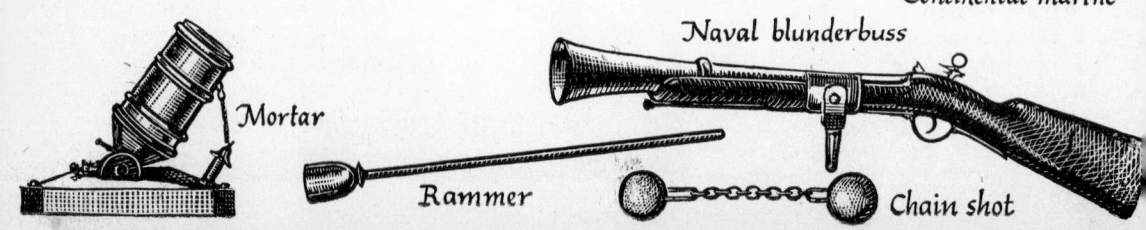

Mortar

Naval blunderbuss

Rammer

Chain shot

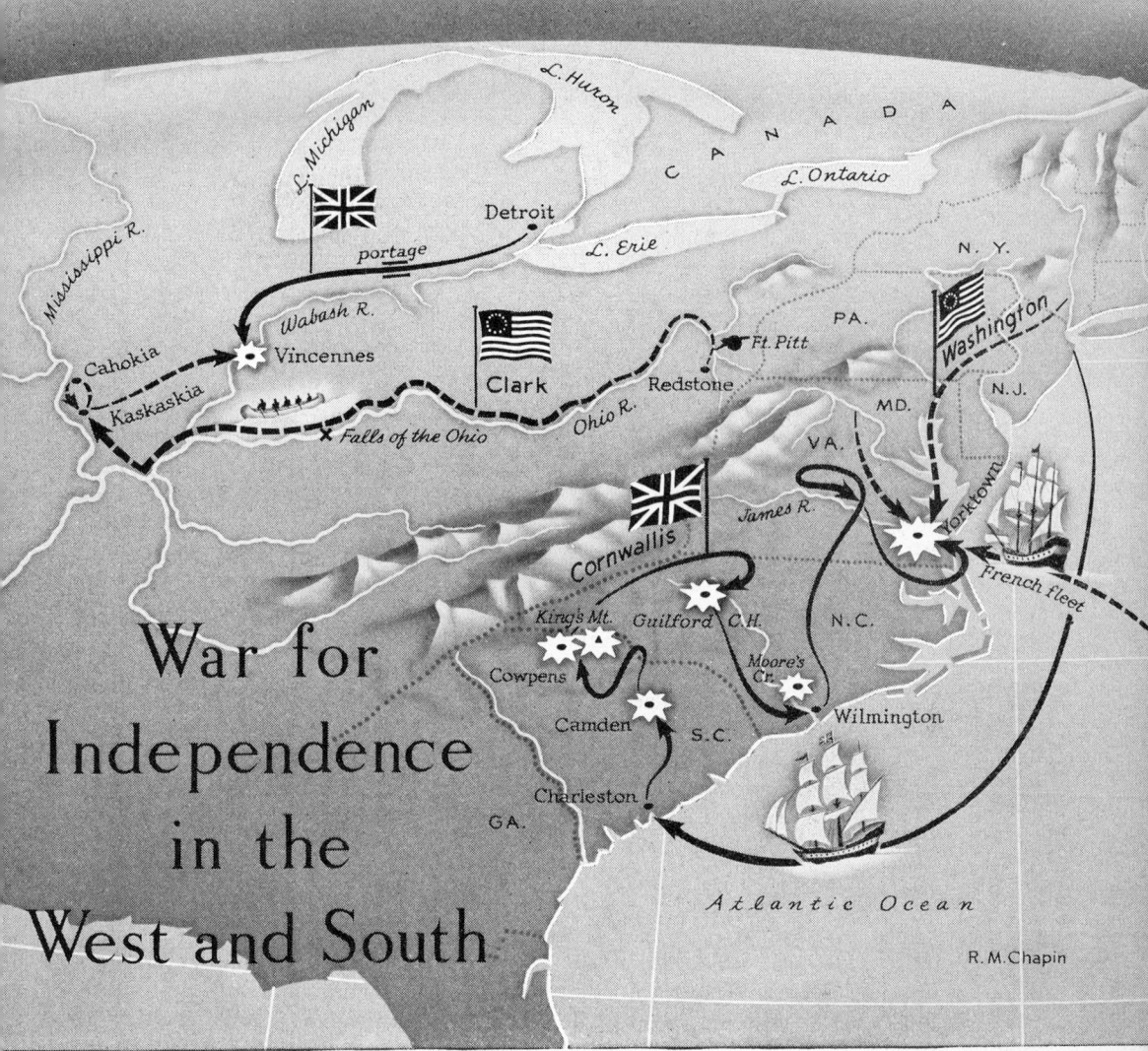

War for Independence in the West and South

R. M. Chapin

Clark's route to the West was selected for one main reason. What was it? What was the significance of the battle of Guilford Court House? Study the routes of the British and Americans in arriving at Yorktown. Why was the help of the French fleet important?

Vincennes. Although Clark failed to capture Detroit, his exploits saved the frontier settlements in Kentucky and may have influenced the British to give the region west of the Appalachians to the United States when the treaty of peace was signed. At the close of the war, Clark had a firm hold on a large part of the territory north of the Ohio River.

War is waged on the sea. The war was not fought entirely on land. Out of its slender funds, the Continental Congress managed to build a number of armed vessels. But they were too few, and often too

small, to be effective against the mighty British navy. The value of the American ships lay chiefly in their ability to attack the enemy's merchant ships. In this useful work, they were aided by American *privateers* — armed ships, privately owned but licensed by the government to make war on enemy ships. At least 2000 privateers were commissioned either by Congress or by the states. One privateer, the *Black Prince,* was reported to have "taken, ransomed, burnt, and destroyed" more than 30 British ships in less than three months. The privateers were of tremendous help to the American

113

cause. They captured military supplies, made the British trade routes unsafe, and forced marine insurance to unheard-of figures. They also obtained much-needed munitions and supplies for the American army. During the Revolution such famous naval captains as John Paul Jones, a native of Scotland, and John Barry, a native of Ireland, helped by their skill and courage to establish the traditions of the young American navy. In one of the greatest naval duels of all time, Jones — with an old French vessel renamed the *Bonhomme Richard* — won a desperate battle (September, 1779) with the British frigate *Serapis* (suh-ray'pis).

The British win victories in the South. In 1778 the British shifted their major attack from the middle states to the South. They expected less opposition because of the large number of Loyalists in that area. At first they were fairly successful. They captured Savannah in December, 1778, and within two months Georgia was cut off from the rest of the colonies. When the Continentals, with the help of the French, tried to recapture Savannah the next year, they met with disaster.

The British proceeded to take Charleston in May, 1780, capturing a large body of Continental troops and valuable stores. About this time, General Gates, who had undeservedly been given the credit for the victory at Saratoga, was sent to take command of the Continental forces in the South. He suffered a crushing defeat in a battle near Camden, South Carolina (August, 1780). (See map, page 113.) For a while, there was nothing left of American resistance in the South except guerrilla fighting under such daring leaders as Francis Marion, Thomas Sumter, and Andrew Pickens in South Carolina.

British successes are checked. The steady string of British victories in the South was finally broken by a band of mountaineers and backwoodsmen from frontier settlements in what is now eastern Tennessee and western North Carolina. These pioneers, feeling that their settlements were in danger, swarmed across the mountains. At the Battle of King's Mountain in October, 1780, they defeated the British and killed or captured the entire force. This important victory checked the British advance into North Carolina for the moment and lifted the morale of the Patriots.

General Nathanael Greene was sent to replace Gates. Greene failed to win any major battle, but he kept the British from making further advances in the South and forced them to abandon all their posts in the interior. One wing of his army, under the able Daniel Morgan, practically wiped out a British force at Cowpens near the boundary separating the Carolinas (January, 1781).

Lord Cornwallis then tried to strike Greene's forces while they were divided, but Greene lured the British into the interior of North Carolina far from Cornwallis' base of supplies. There the two sections of Greene's army united and fought Cornwallis at Guilford Court House (March, 1781). Although Cornwallis held the field at the end of the day, his losses were so great that another such victory would have ruined his army beyond repair. He retreated to the coast as quickly as he could, leaving Greene to recapture much of the ground which the Americans had lost.

The British position remains strong. In spite of Greene's successes, the future of the American cause looked discouraging in the early months of 1781. British forces still held New York and threatened the South. Benedict Arnold, who had fought brilliantly in the Quebec expedition and at Saratoga, had turned traitor to the American cause. He had tried to turn over West Point, and the control of the Hudson River with it, to Clinton (September, 1780). When the plot was discovered, Arnold escaped to the British, but Major André, his British accomplice, was captured and hanged. In addition, the war was going very badly in general for the Americans. Continental paper money was next to worthless. Few answered the calls for enlistment, and the troops already in service had started to mutiny for lack of food and pay. "We are at the end of our tether," commented Washington.

But this was the darkness before the dawn. Lafayette had gone back to France early in 1779 to persuade his government to give America more help. The following spring, Comte de Rochambeau (cont duh ro-shan-bo´) was sent over with a force of 5500 men. Rochambeau and his men remained for the most part at Newport, Rhode Island, until news came, in 1781, of the arrival of a powerful French fleet in the West Indies under Admiral de Grasse.

Cornwallis' surrender assures American victory. Early in the same year Cornwallis turned northward into Virginia. He tried to crush a small army under the "boy," as he contemptuously called the 24-year-old Lafayette. When this plan failed, Cornwallis settled down to fortify Yorktown. (See map, page 113.) The Americans and French now saw a chance for a surprise attack, and they made the most of their opportunity.

First, New York was threatened with attack to keep Clinton busy. Then a combined force under Washington and Rochambeau marched rapidly to Chesapeake Bay to embark for Yorktown. There, the French men-of-war under the command of de Grasse had already sailed into the bay in response to a request from Washington. The French and American armies closed in on Yorktown while de Grasse fought off a British squadron which tried to bring help to Cornwallis by sea. The combined assault on the British lines began during the last days of September. On October 19, 1781, Cornwallis' army of about 7000 men surrendered.

The war comes to a close. The surrender of Cornwallis really settled the issue of American independence, but the war went on for months before the British government was ready to make peace. There were still about 30,000 British troops in New York and the South, and the Continental Congress was almost at the end of its resources. At sea, however, the British were being harassed by French, Spanish, and Dutch fleets.

In England, the war was growing more unpopular all the time. A new ministry was appointed in March, 1782, which was more ready to yield to American demands.

A southern patriot, William Jasper, daringly raised the flag on a ramrod when the flagstaff was shot down during the British attack on Fort Moultrie, Charleston, in 1776. The South Carolina flag was blue with a white crescent. For his bravery Sergeant Jasper was given a sword by Governor Rutledge of South Carolina. He was killed in 1779 during the defense of Savannah.

Peace negotiations began at once, but they dragged on for over a year.

American independence is firmly established. The Treaty of Paris, which formally ended the war, gave the Americans just about everything they had fought for during the past eight years. (See map, page 116.) "His Britannic Majesty" acknowledged the thirteen states "to be free, sovereign, and independent States." He recognized their claim to territory as far west as the Mississippi River, as far north as

North America in 1783

Claimed by Great Britain and Spain

Hudson Bay

BRITISH TERRITORY

Disputed between U.S. and Great Britain

NEWFOUNDLAND

Grand Banks

LOUISIANA

Mississippi R.

NEW SPAIN

SPANISH TERRITORY

THE UNITED STATES

Disputed between U.S. and Spain

New Orleans

FLORIDA

WEST INDIES

CUBA

HISPANIOLA

PUERTO RICO

French

Pacific Ocean

Atlantic Ocean

R. M. Chapin

After the Revolution the United States had certain territorial disputes. With what countries did these disputes occur, and over what territories? Compare this map with the map on page 58. What territory had the British lost?

Canada, and as far south as Florida (which Great Britain had acquired from Spain in 1763). This area Great Britain agreed to evacuate. Fishermen of the new republic would keep the right to fish off the Grand Banks of Newfoundland.

On the other hand, the United States agreed that no legal obstacle should be placed in the way of British creditors in collecting from American merchants debts contracted before the Revolution. It also agreed that Congress should recommend to the states the return of property taken from the Loyalists, and that Loyalists would face no further persecution. The navigation of the Mississippi River should "for ever remain free and open to the subjects of Great Britain, and the citizens of the United States."

America was the only power in the war to make any real gains. France profited by weakening the power of Great Britain, but had to go heavily into debt to help the Americans. Spain regained Florida, without, however, obtaining an exact definition of its boundaries. She now faced a new rival in America. Expansion of the young republic might seriously threaten Spain's vast American empire.

So ends the first unit in this study of the birth and growth of a great nation. The people who had settled along the Atlantic seaboard had gained a new outlook on life, thanks to the courage of their leaders, to foreign aid, and to the indifference of the people of Great Britain. From now on, Americans were to seek their destiny, not as an offshoot of Europe, but as an independent nation, free to direct its own future. Whether or not this great privilege of independent action would be used wisely lay in the hands of future generations of Americans.

——————— CHECK-UP ———————

How did Patriot victories result in independence?

1. What effect did the battle of Saratoga have on the French view of the war? On the British?
2. Why was fighting in the West and on the sea important?
3. Why did the British transfer the war to the South? What events led to the surrender at Yorktown?
4. What were the chief provisions of the Treaty of Paris, 1783?

CHAPTER REVIEW

Terms to Understand

radicals   Continental currency
Loyalists   "sunshine patriots"
privateers   unalienable rights

People and Things to Know About

Bunker Hill   Burgoyne
Hessians   St. Leger
Benedict Arnold   Sir Henry Clinton
Thomas Paine   George Rogers Clark
Thomas Jefferson   John Paul Jones
Lafayette   Nathanael Greene
von Steuben   Lord Cornwallis
Robert Morris   Admiral de Grasse
Sir William Howe   Treaty of Paris (1783)

Historic Dates to Identify

1775   1777   1783
1776   1781

Questions to Discuss

1. The Patriots called them Tories and traitors. Today the British people speak of them as United Empire Loyalists. How do you think they should be regarded? Why?
2. What evidence is there that until 1775 the Americans, even the "radicals," were more interested in reform within the British empire than in independence? Why was the opening of American ports to world commerce of importance to independence?
3. What were the motives of the French in aiding the Americans? How was the Revolu-

Questions to Discuss (Cont.)

tion at once (a) a world war, (b) a war for independence, and (c) a civil war in America?
4. Every great cause has its slogans, as, for example, "make the world safe for democracy" during World War I. What might have been some of the slogans of the American Revolution?
5. After reading this chapter, would you favor the issuing of unlimited paper money today? Why or why not?
6. What were the important factors in the success of the American cause? Which of these factors do you consider most important?

Relating Geography and History

1. Explain the geographical significance of the threefold plan of campaign.
2. Locate on an outline map of the eastern part of the United States:
    (a) Ticonderoga, Trenton, Bennington, Oriskany, Saratoga, Kaskaskia, Vincennes, King's Mountain, Cowpens, Guilford, Yorktown.
    (b) The boundaries of the United States as established by the Treaty of Paris.

Other Things to Do

1. Prepare a blackboard "chalk talk" on one of the campaigns of the war. You might select the threefold campaign, the campaign in the West, the South, or the campaign around Yorktown.

2. Prepare a talk on the American efforts to secure aid before the treaty of alliance with France. This is a highly interesting story which brings in such persons as Franklin and the Frenchmen, Beaumarchais and Vergennes. For information see Bailey, Thomas A., *A Diplomatic History of the American People*, pp. 8–32.

3. Debate: *Resolved*, That French aid was the most vital factor in assuring an American victory in the Revolution.

4. What was the British government willing to concede to the Americans after Saratoga? How do these points compare with what the Americans had demanded before 1775? See Pease and Roberts, eds., *Selected Readings in American History*, No. 56, and summarize your conclusions briefly.

*5. Prepare a series of biographical clues to one of the important Revolutionary leaders. Read these to the class one at a time until someone determines who is being referred to.

*6. Imagine that you are a colonial newspaper editor. Write an editorial either for or against declaring American independence from England.

TO INCREASE YOUR UNDERSTANDING OF UNIT ONE

Unit Summary

1. Western Europe in the 1400's was ready for an era of discovery. Trade between Europe and the East had been built up as a result of the Crusades. As the feudal system declined, new national states emerged which were eager to share in the trade controlled by the Italian cities. Meanwhile, the revival of learning had aroused curiosity about the world outside Europe and had contributed to the improvement of navigation.

2. Stimulated by Prince Henry, Portuguese sea captains found their way around Africa to the East. Columbus, however, determined to seek the Indies by sailing westward. Following his example, other explorers not only proved that a new continent existed, but made extensive claims and conquests in the New World for their rulers. Spain carved out a huge empire in Central and South America, while France laid claim to the St. Lawrence and Mississippi regions.

3. England entered the race for colonies late, but made rapid strides after gaining mastery over Spain on the seas. Political, religious, and economic conditions led thousands of Englishmen to seek new homes along the Atlantic coast of North America. Between 1607 and 1733 thirteen English colonies were founded which later became the basis of the United States. Inevitably the English and the French became rivals in the New World, but by 1763 the British succeeded in bringing an end to French control in North America.

4. In the course of the 150 years following the first settlement, the English colonists built homes; developed farming, trade, and some industry; and constantly pushed back the frontier. After the earlier strenuous years, they had an opportunity to develop a definite colonial culture. Although settlers had come from many countries, their political institutions bore the stamp of the freer English form of government. This fact, coupled with loose control by the mother country and the influence of an unsettled continent, encouraged the beginning of self-government and nourished a spirit of independence.

5. The defeat of the French in North America brought increased burdens of empire to Great Britain. Feeling that the colonies should assume their share of these burdens, the British government embarked on a stricter policy of colonial control. This policy, however, ran counter to colonial ideas of representation, taxation, and individual liberty. From 1763 to 1776 relations between the colonies and the mother country became more strained and colonial resistance more bitter.

6. The vast majority of English colonists had hoped to preserve their rights as British subjects. The course of events finally led them to declare their independence, July 4, 1776. Thereafter, for seven years, the Americans carried on a military struggle against great odds. Foreign aid was an important factor in the final American victory. By the Treaty of 1783, the United States gained its independence from Great Britain, with possession of the territory north to Canada, south to Florida, and west to the Mississippi River. The first chapter in American history had been completed.

Summary of Important Dates*

1096 The first Crusade.
1271–95 Marco Polo visits the Far East.
1492 Columbus reaches the New World.
1497 Cabot explores North American coast.
1498 Vasco da Gama reaches India.
1513 Balboa discovers the Pacific ocean.
1519 Magellan starts around the world.
     Cortez begins his conquest of Mexico.
1534–35 Cartier explores the St. Lawrence.
1588 The Spanish Armada is defeated.
1607 Jamestown is founded.
1619 Virginia House of Burgesses meets.
1620 Pilgrims land at Plymouth.
1630 Boston is founded by the Puritans.
1634 St. Mary's, Maryland, is founded.
1636 Rhode Island and Connecticut founded.
     Harvard College is started.
1639 Connecticut draws up the Fundamental
     Orders.
1647 Massachusetts adopts its school law.
1649 Maryland Toleration Act is passed.
1660–63 Navigation Acts are passed.
1664 English take control of New Netherland.
1670 Charles Town, South Carolina, founded.
1682 La Salle reaches mouth of Mississippi.
     Philadelphia is founded.
1689 First war between the French and the
     English breaks out.
1733 Georgia is founded.
     Molasses Act is passed.
1735 Zenger trial establishes freedom of press.
1754 French and Indian war begins.
     Albany Plan of Union proposed.
**1763 Treaty of Paris; French driven out of
     America.**
1765 Stamp Act is passed.
1767 Townshend Acts are passed.
1770 Boston Massacre.
1773 Boston Tea Party.
1774 Intolerable Acts passed.
     First Continental Congress summoned.
1775 Battles of Concord and Lexington.
     Second Continental Congress meets.
1776 Declaration of Independence.
1777 Burgoyne surrenders at Saratoga.
1778 Treaty of alliance with France.
1781 Cornwallis surrenders at Yorktown.
1783 Treaty of Paris; United States wins its
     independence.

* Those dates printed in boldface type were recommended as most important in a report of the Committee on American History in Schools and Colleges of the American Historical Association, the Mississippi Valley Historical Association, and the National Council for the Social Studies.

Unit Activities

1. Make a further study of one of the thirteen original colonies. Discuss the development of its economic life, changes in its government, its population, and other significant factors.
2. It has been said that "geography is the maker of history." In a theme of not less than 150 words explain how geography influenced the development of (*a*) a particular English colony, (*b*) the English colonies as a whole, or (*c*) the French colonies.
3. Make a two-column chart headed "Democratic Institutions" and "Undemocratic Institutions." In one column list the democratic institutions and in the other the undemocratic institutions which were to be found in the English colonies. Be sure to note how widespread each was.
4. You have noted that the colonists had both an *economic* and a *political* argument against British policies before the Revolution. Write a summary of each. Remember that in a summary you concentrate on general points and do not give much attention to details.

For Further Reading

Original Sources

Commager, H. S., ed., *Documents of American History.* Crofts. Nos. 1–74. The most complete collection of important American historical documents in one volume. Useful for reference purposes.

Commager, H. S., and Nevins, Allan, eds., *The Heritage of America.* Little, Brown. Nos. 1–41. A highly useful collection of reading selections drawn from contemporary writers.

Pease, T. C., and Roberts, A. S., eds., *Selected Readings in American History.* Harcourt. Contains both readings and documents.

General References

Adams, J. T., *Epic of America.* Little, Brown. Pp. 3–96. A popular American history.

Bailey, Thomas A., *A Diplomatic History of the American People.* Crofts. Pp. 1–37. An interesting diplomatic history.

Faulkner, Harold U., *American Economic History.* Harper. Pp. 1–166. Devoted entirely to the economic aspects of our development.

Hicks, John D., *The Federal Union.* Houghton. Pp. 1–160. Good general discussion.

Riegel, Robert E., *America Moves West.* Holt. Pp. 1–30. Follows the frontier from the Appalachians to the Pacific. It makes the West come alive.

Special Accounts

Collier, John, *Indians of the Americas*. Mentor Books (formerly Penguin Books). Traces four centuries of American Indian history. Deals with the Indians of both North and South America.

Chronicles of American Series. Yale University Press. Richman, I. B., *The Spanish Conquerors*. Wood, William, *The Elizabethan Sea-dogs*. Munro, W. B., *Crusaders of New France*. Becker, Carl, *Eve of the Revolution*.

Earle, Alice Morse, *Home Life in Colonial Days*. Macmillan. Brings out the self-sufficiency of the colonial home.

History of American Life Series. Macmillan. Priestly, H. I., *The Coming of the White Man*. The non-English explorers and life in the Spanish and French colonies. Greene, E. B., *The Revolutionary Generation 1763–1790*. American society just before and during the Revolution.

Klingberg, Frank J., *Morning of America*. Appleton. A readable and informative narrative of the colonial and Revolutionary periods.

Langdon, W. C., *Everyday Things in American Life, 1607–1776*. Scribners. An illustrated history which deals with homes, cities, furniture, ships, roads, agriculture, and manufactures of colonial days.

Lucas, Mary S., *Vast Horizons*. Viking. The development of the trade routes to the Indies. Many maps and drawings.

Tebbel, John, ed., *The Battle for North America*. Viking. A good condensation of Francis Parkman's great works dealing with the wars between France and England.

Biography

Bakeless, John, *Daniel Boone, Master of the Wilderness*. Morrow. Follow Boone into Kentucky through the medium of this book.

Brockunier, S. H., *Irrepressible Democrat, Roger Williams*. Ronald. Williams is shown as one of the first Americans to have truly democratic qualities.

Carson, Julia M., *Patrick Henry*. Longmans. Boyhood and later career of Henry, with many scenes of the homelife of the times.

Forbes, Esther, *Paul Revere and the World He Lived In*. Houghton. The story of Boston before and during the Revolution, with Revere as its central character.

Franklin, Benjamin, *Autobiography*. Pocket Books. The boyhood and young manhood of the best known American of his age.

Gaither, Frances, *The Fatal River*. Holt. The life and explorations of La Salle.

Johnson, Gerald W., *The First Captain*. Coward. The life of John Paul Jones.

Morison, S. E., *Admiral of the Ocean Sea*. Little, Brown. The most authoritative and interesting biography of Columbus.

Robinson, H. M., *Stout Cortez*. Century. The conqueror of Mexico.

Woodward, W. E., *Tom Paine, American Godfather*. Dutton. Biography of the famous revolutionist.

Imaginative Writing

Boyce, Burke, *Perilous Night*. Viking. A novel which brings out the conflicting loyalties produced by the Revolution. Scenes laid in New York.

Boyd, James, *Drums*. Scribners. A carefully documented novel built around the career of John Paul Jones.

Byrne, Don, *Messer Marco Polo*. Century. Account of Marco Polo's fabulous travels, in fiction form.

Cather, Willa, *Shadows on the Rock*. Knopf. Life in Quebec under French rule.

Churchill, Winston, *The Crossing*. Grosset. George Rogers Clark's expedition to take the West from the British.

Forester, C. S., *To the Indies*. Little, Brown. A novel about Columbus by a great teller of sea stories.

Johnson, Mary, *To Have and to Hold*. Houghton (also Pocket Books). A romance of colonial Virginia.

Lancaster, B., *Trumpet to Arms*. Little, Brown. The change of local militia into the first American army.

Roberts, Kenneth, *Oliver Wiswell*. Doubleday. One of the finest novels about the Revolution; presents the Loyalist side.

Roberts, Kenneth, *Rabble in Arms*. Doubleday. The ill-fated invasion of the colonies by "Gentleman Johnny Burgoyne."

Poetry

Stevenson, Burton E., ed., *Poems of American History*. Houghton. Poems of a patriotic and historical nature arranged by themes.

Pictures

Adams, J. T., ed., *Album of American History*. Scribners. Vol. I. A recent and excellent pictorial history of America.

Pageant of America Series. Yale University Press. Wissler, C., Skinner, C. K., and Wood, W., *Adventurers in the Wilderness*. The exploration and early settlements. Wood, W., and Gabriel, R. H., *The Winning of Freedom*. The Revolution and the growth of Revolutionary sentiment.

Best-sellers in Colonial Days. What was the first book published by the English colonists? You might guess that it was the Bible, but you would be wrong. It was an almanac.

This book was published in 1639 by William Pierce of Cambridge, Massachusetts. Pierce must have been a keen judge of people's interests, for his almanac made an immediate hit. In fact, almanacs in the colonies became a publishing miracle. They hung in every chimney corner from Massachusetts Bay Colony to Oglethorpe's colony in Georgia. They were dog-eared by shipmasters, who used them to look up the rise of the tides for sailings. They were ruffled to tatters by farmers who wanted to plant their corn by the turn of the moon and by housewives in search of a remedy for colic.

In a way, almanacs were the comic books of the time. Besides giving "practical" information on the weather, astronomy, and "physick," they included jokes, amusing stories, and secrets for success. They also contained prophecies based on the stars and planets, as well as miracle tales that compare with the deeds of our most fantastic comic-book characters.

Seven almanacs were being published in Philadelphia alone in 1732, the year when Benjamin Franklin launched the most famous of them all. This was *Poor Richard's Almanack,* which eventually sold 10,000 copies a year — or one copy for every 100 colonists. Such a ratio today would mean 1,500,000 copies!

Witchcraft in Salem. One morning in the village of Salem, Massachusetts, two little girls were taken strangely ill. They frothed at the mouth and vomited pins. They yapped like dogs and screamed at a little yellow bird that nobody else could see. When the village doctor was called in, he solemnly announced that the girls were the victims of witchcraft. The children shrieked, "We are, we are . . ." and named the witches — a slavewoman in their family and two women of the village. The three women were put into chains, and so the famous witch panic of Salem began.

Others were accused of practicing witchcraft, and trials were held. Fantastic trials, they seem today. The two children sat as part of the court. If an accused person, when brought into court, caused them to scream, it was assumed that the person was guilty. If the accused confessed, he was believed innocent. Didn't all know that the Devil would let no witch confess? One stubborn citizen, 80 years old, snorted, "I'll neither confess nor plead Yes or No." For this he was pressed to death with weights on his stomach. In four months 19 persons were found guilty of witchcraft and hanged. Hundreds were under suspicion.

The witchcraft madness ended suddenly when the wife of the royal governor was accused of being a witch. Governor Phips promptly dismissed the court and freed all those who had been accused.

A Patriot Banker. If colonial newspapers had featured jail breaks in the fashion of American papers today, their headlines for August 11, 1778, might have screamed:

HAYM SALOMON ESCAPES
Patriot Banker Bribes British Army Jailer

Salomon had been condemned to death for a plot to burn the British fleet. His escape was of particular interest to the colonists because he and Robert Morris were the two most important bankers in the Revolutionary cause. Again and again, when the efforts of other people failed, Salomon raised money for the Continental Army.

Haym Salomon had been a refugee from Poland. There, when he joined the cause for Polish freedom, the Russians had forced him to flee for his life. In New York he had become a broker and banker. He had made a fortune, which he devoted without hesitation to the American fight for freedom.

If Salomon had not come to the rescue, the Americans would have lacked credits badly needed early in the struggle. Without credit there would have been no funds to pay troops or buy ammunition and supplies. Salomon was a master salesman. When things looked darkest for the Americans, he would still persuade other patriots to lend their money. And he was a man who practiced what he preached. He risked his own funds. By the end of the Revolutionary War, his country owed him more than $650,000 — a debt which was never paid. When his accounts were totaled after his death, it was learned that Haym Salomon had given every cent he possessed to the cause of freedom.

An early political rally

THE PLAN OF THE BOOK

PART ONE *Early America Develops*	1492 to 1783	**Unit One:** Discovery, Exploration, Development of the English colonies, American Revolution
	1783 to 1840	**Unit Two:** Framing of Constitution, The new republic, Rise of nationalism, sectionalism, and democracy
	1789 to 1865	**Unit Three:** Economic developments, Social change and reform, Rise of American culture
	1840 to 1865	**Unit Four:** Westward expansion, The slavery problem, War Between the States

PART TWO *Modern America Emerges*	1865 to the 1890's	**Unit Five** Foundations of the American economic system	**Unit Six** Social and cultural developments	**Unit Seven** Government, politics, and foreign affairs

PART THREE *Modern America Matures*	1890's to the Present	**Unit Eight** American economic system today	**Unit Nine** Social and cultural developments	**Unit Ten** The United States in world affairs	**Unit Eleven** Developments in government and politics

Unit Two

UNDER THE CONSTITUTION THE NEW NATION GROWS STRONG AT HOME AND ABROAD

When the thirteen colonies had won their independence from Great Britain, they faced many baffling problems. Not the least of these was the need for an efficient central government. A form of government, the Articles of Confederation, had been established in the closing years of the Revolutionary War, but it lacked power. This fact was partly responsible for the period of unrest that followed the war for independence.

In this crisis Americans showed that they had the ability to form institutions that would meet unusual conditions. A new Constitution, our present one, strengthened the central government, but gave it no powers that could be exercised better by the state governments. To protect the rights of citizens, amendments known as the Bill of Rights were added to the Constitution. During the first half-century of government under the Constitution, political democracy increased; that is, more people had a voice in the affairs of government. Nearly all white male citizens obtained the right to vote. As a result, more and more people took an interest in the way the government was run. Scenes like that in the picture, in which a political speaker addresses a group of ordinary citizens, became common.

The new nation tried to keep clear of "foreign entanglements" but nevertheless became involved in a war with England. This struggle, the War of 1812, freed the United States from its dependence on Europe and permitted the young republic to devote its full energies to national development. In the Monroe Doctrine of 1823 the United States made it clear that European powers must not interfere in, or seek to establish control over, lands in the Western Hemisphere.

Town crier

Chapter 6

A STRONG UNION REPLACES A WEAK

CONFEDERATION

Whilst the last members were signing, Dr. Franklin, looking towards the president's chair, at the back of which a rising sun happened to be painted, observed to a few members near him, that painters had found it difficult to distinguish, in their art, a rising from a setting sun. "I have," said he, "often and often, in the course of the session, and the vicissitudes of my hopes and fears as to its issue, looked at that behind the president, without being able to tell whether it was rising or setting; but now, at length, I have the happiness to know that it is a rising, and not a setting sun.

James Madison's notes on the signing of the Constitution

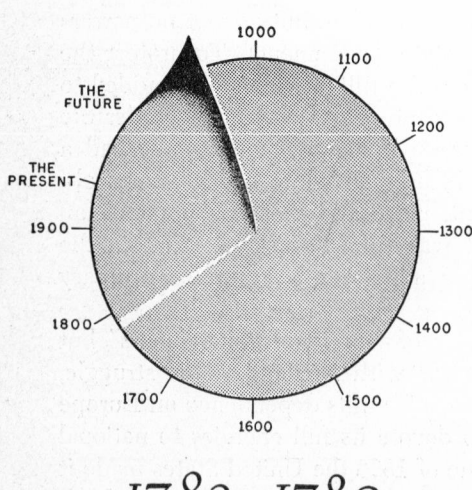

1783-1789

Since 1776 the Patriots had fought against discouraging odds to win independence. With the signing of the Treaty of Paris in 1783, that goal was won. Yet the end of the war did not bring an end to all difficulties. Fresh problems presented themselves. In the first place, the new nation had to maintain itself in a world of strong and jealous powers. Secondly, the fact that America was no longer a part of the British empire meant that new forms of government and new policies must replace those of the mother country. Finally, the American Revolution led to much greater changes than mere separation from Great Britain. In the words of the historians, Charles and Mary Beard, "It was in truth an economic, social, and intellectual transformation of prime significance — the first

124

of those modern world-shaking reconstructions in which mankind has sought to cut and fashion the tough and stubborn web of fact to fit the pattern of its dreams." The new-born republic faced conditions different from those of colonial America.

At first, the citizen of the new United States probably did not clearly sense the full importance of the changes that were taking place. But he was soon awakened to them. The first years of the new republic were so filled with problems and perils that they have been called the "critical period of American history." This chapter will trace these problems, as well as the steps taken to solve them. The major points are these:

1. The American people face changes and responsibilities.
2. The Articles of Confederation prove inadequate.
3. A new form of government is planned.
4. The Constitution is adopted by the states.
5. The Constitution provides a workable government.

1 The American People Face Changes and Responsibilities

The new nation is not closely-knit. In some respects the American citizen could see no striking change in his country after the war. He was, it is true, part of a larger population now. Between 1783 and 1790 the population increased from something over 2½ million (not counting Indians), to nearly 4 million. But at this time it was still thinly and unevenly distributed. Less than half the people were living in the states from Maryland southward. The frontier was not heavily settled; not much more than three per cent of the Americans lived beyond the Appalachian Mountains. Cities were small and few. Philadelphia,

the largest city in the country, had only 42,000 people. Travel and communication were still so difficult, and economic interests differed so much in the various parts of the country, that the American people were prevented from becoming a closely-knit nation.

Land ownership is changed. On the other hand, some features of American life showed the influence of the Revolution. Among them was a change in ownership of land. The Proclamation Line of 1763 no longer checked the pioneers. Men were free to push westward and to settle anywhere they wished. Lands that had belonged to the Crown and to the proprietors were now owned by the states. As a result, quitrents, which had been paid in former days to the king or to the proprietor, were abolished. Finally, small farmers had a chance to buy on easy terms parts of the large estates seized from wealthy Tories during the war.

Frontier land was easy to get but difficult to hold. Women sometimes fought off Indian raiders until their men could return from work in the woods and fields.

Social conditions are altered. The Revolution had not swept away all differences in social position, but class distinctions were less rigid than they had been in colonial America. British officials had returned to England, and many Loyalists had left the country, too. Thus the number of people in the aristocratic groups was much smaller. Moreover, it had become easier for a man to move from one level of society to another.

The middle class was still dominant in the North, while well-to-do planters held control in the South. The sharpest class distinction in America was that drawn between white persons and Negroes, but slavery was declining. In New England, where there were few slaves and slavery was unprofitable, the process of freeing the slaves had begun during the Revolution. In the middle states the freeing of slaves was well under way by the early 1800's. There were even many Southerners who looked upon slavery as a necessary evil. Important men in the South, like Patrick Henry, Thomas Jefferson, and George Washington, felt that slavery was not in harmony with their ideas of human rights.

State governments are developed. The Revolution changed the colonies into free republics and thus made it necessary to set up new governments. These new governments were founded upon state constitutions. Since the people had been governed in colonial times under charters, they wanted written documents drawn up which would define the new forms of government. In Rhode Island and Connecticut the task was simple. There, with slight changes, the colonial charters were made over into state constitutions. In the other states, new documents were approved. Many state constitutions included *bills of rights,* which were lists of personal rights definitely guaranteed to each citizen.

No matter what state he lived in, the citizen found that his government had certain features in common with other states. Most of the legislatures were made up of two houses and were granted broad powers. The governors, on the other hand, were given very little authority. Experience with royal governors had made the people cautious about allowing one man too much power. The proportion of people who had the right to vote would seem small today; only a few states gave the privilege of voting to as many as half of the adult males. Still, a citizen had a better chance of voting than was possible under the old colonial governments or in any of the European countries. If a man wished to become an officeholder, however, he still had to own a considerable amount of property.

The Articles of Confederation are established. Probably the greatest single change that took place when colonial America became an independent country was in the central government. Except for the supervision of the British government, there had been no central authority in colonial America. During the Revolution, the Second Continental Congress had taken over the thankless job of directing the colonies in their resistance to Great Britain. But the Congress had no formal authority to act as a central government. For that reason, one of the first things that the Congress did was to appoint a committee to plan a permanent confederation of the states. The committee reported to Congress not long after the adoption of the Declaration of Independence. Their recommendations were debated and revised for more than a year. Finally Congress accepted the revised recommendations (November, 1777), called them the Articles of Confederation, and turned them over to the states for their approval. Although most states ratified (approved) the Articles within a year, it was not until March, 1781, that Maryland ratified them and made it possible to put the new government into operation.

The delay in ratifying the Articles of Confederation was caused by a dispute among the states over the ownership of the region beyond the Alleghenies. (See map, page 127.) The states claiming this land, particularly Virginia, insisted that their claims be recognized. The states with no western claims demanded that the land be held for the benefit of the United States as a whole. Maryland, the leader of the second group, would not ratify the Articles

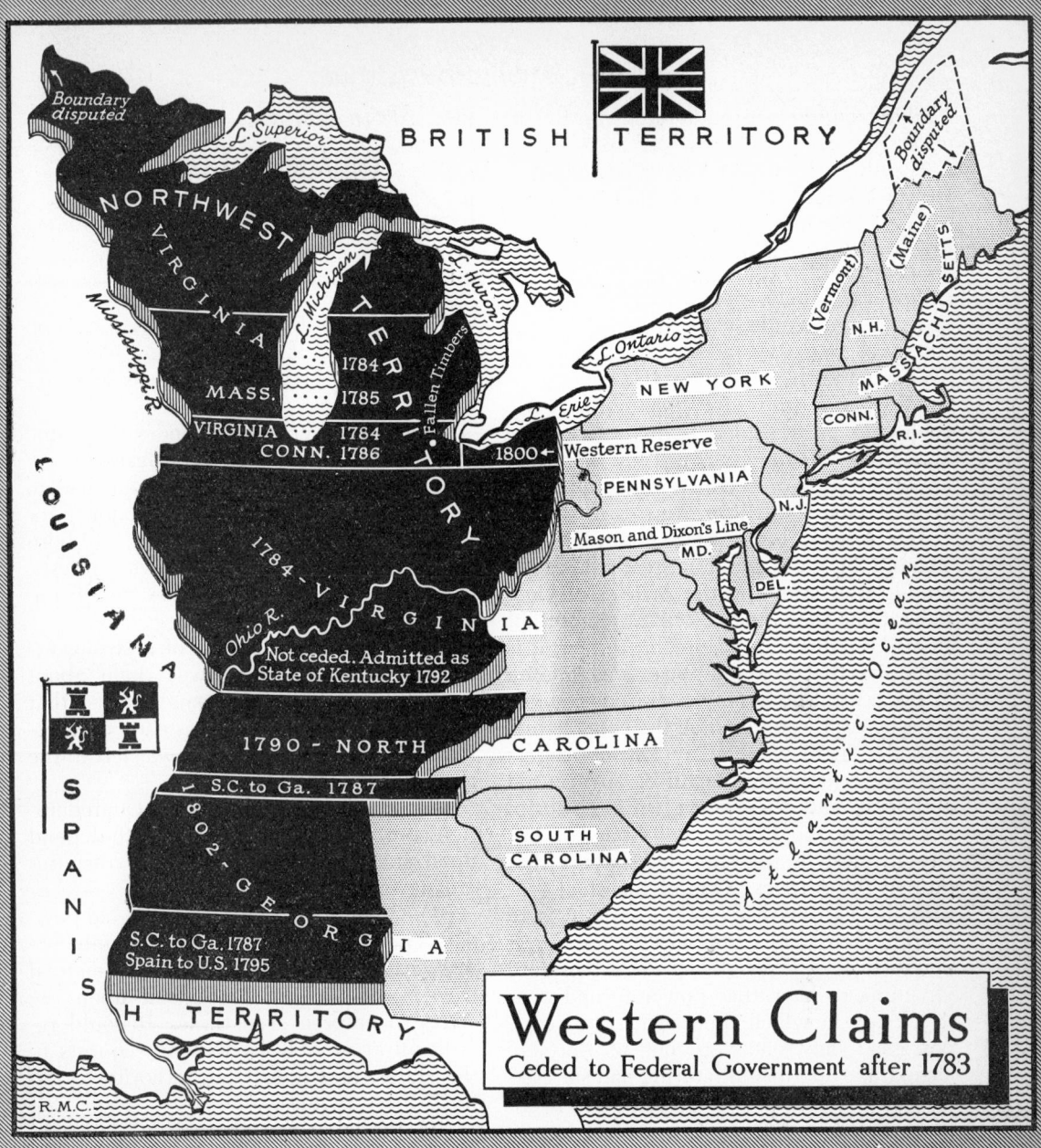

Boundary disputed

L. Superior

BRITISH TERRITORY

Boundary disputed

(Maine)

(Vermont)

N.H.

MASSACHUSETTS

NORTHWEST

VIRGINIA

L. Michigan

TERRITORY

Fallen Timbers

L. Ontario

L. Erie

NEW YORK

CONN.

R.I.

Mississippi R.

1784
MASS. 1785
VIRGINIA 1784
CONN. 1786

1800 ← Western Reserve

PENNSYLVANIA

N.J.

Mason and Dixon's Line
MD.

DEL.

1784 - VIRGINIA

Ohio R.

Not ceded. Admitted as
State of Kentucky 1792

1790 - NORTH

CAROLINA

S.C. to Ga. 1787

1802 - GEORGIA

SOUTH
CAROLINA

Atlantic Ocean

L O U I S I A N A

S P A N I S H

S.C. to Ga. 1787
Spain to U.S. 1795

T E R R I T O R Y

Western Claims
Ceded to Federal Government after 1783

R.M.C.

Not all of the states claimed land in the West. Why? Why were the claims of Virginia so extensive? Why was it fortunate for the nation that the states ceded their western claims to the federal government?

until Virginia agreed to give up her rights to the land north of the Ohio River. When Virginia agreed to do so, the outcome was a long stride toward national unity, since it prevented future quarrels among the states over possession of the West.

The Articles set up a league of states. The Articles of Confederation set up a "firm league of friendship" in which each state kept its sovereignty and independence, as well as all powers not specifically granted to the central government of the

United States. As for the central government, the Articles created a Congress which was given important powers. The new Congress had the legal authority to control foreign affairs, make war and peace, borrow money, regulate the value of coins, raise an army, and settle disputes between the states. Each state represented in the Congress had a single vote, so that a large state had no advantage over a smaller one. To make the rights of the states even safer, there was a provision that the Articles could not be amended unless every state agreed to the amendment, and no other important measure could be passed unless at least nine states approved.

The Articles are a step toward union. Though the states could not really be called united after adopting the Articles of Confederation, they had taken an important step in the direction of union. In fact, it is surprising that so much power was granted to the central government, considering the experiences through which the country had passed. There were many Patriot leaders who were naturally fearful of any central authority, and these men were powerful not only in the Continental Congress but also in most of the state legislatures that ratified the Articles. One of the chief reasons the Patriots had gone to war was to keep in their local assemblies the important power to levy taxes. They were therefore unwilling to have that power turned over to a body in which their own states each possessed only one vote out of thirteen. Since trade and manufacturing had suffered for years from outside regulation, they were in no mood to give up this control to any other power, even though it was American.

─────── CHECK-UP ───────

In what ways was America changed after the Revolution?

1. What changes in American society resulted from the Revolution?
2. How were the new state governments different from the colonial governments?
3. How were the Articles of Confederation established? What kind of central government did they provide?

The Articles of Confederation Prove Inadequate

The Articles show weaknesses. As soon as the Articles of Confederation were put into everyday use, certain defects were revealed.

(1) There were seldom more than nine or ten states represented in Congress at any one time. Almost everyone present had to agree if there was to be a legal majority for important business. One or two stubborn states, thinking only of their own interests, could therefore stop the passage of important legislation.

(2) Because of the fear of a strong executive power, nothing was done about setting up a separate department to see that laws were carried out. Instead, enforcement of the acts of Congress was left to the good will of the states.

(3) There were no regular Confederation courts, so that Congress had to depend upon state courts to settle legal disputes arising from its laws.

(4) Congress lacked other essential powers. The only control it had over commerce was its authority to make commercial treaties, and it had to depend upon the states to enforce even these. It could recruit an army only by making requests to the states, and it had no authority to enforce these requests.

(5) Probably the greatest weakness of the Articles of Confederation was the fact that Congress could raise money only by asking the states for it. For the years 1782–83, Congress asked the states for more than $11,000,000 but received less than $1,500,000. In 1781 Congress asked that the Articles be amended so that the central government could place a five per cent duty upon imports, but without success. Robert Morris, superintendent of finance, said that asking the states to tax their people for support of the Confederation was like "preaching to the dead." He resigned

rather than "increase our debts, while the prospect of paying them diminishes."

Congress deals with the Northwest Territory. Although there were quite a few things under the Articles of Confederation that the central government could *not* do, the picture was not all one-sided. Some worth-while business was accomplished under the Articles.

Probably most important, the Articles held the country together until it was evident that a closer union was necessary. It was under the Articles also that Congress settled the problem of the Northwest Territory — the area bounded by the Ohio and Mississippi rivers and the Great Lakes. (See map, page 127.) When Virginia gave up its claims to this land, other states with claims in the same area dropped theirs too. As pioneers pushed westward, the job of providing a land policy and a suitable government for the Northwest Territory was clearly up to Congress. It passed two important laws which settled these problems satisfactorily.

(1) Under the Land Ordinance of 1785, Congress authorized a survey of the Northwest Territory, which divided it into townships. Each township was to be six miles square and was to be subdivided into 36 sections. Each section included one square mile or 640 acres. The land was to be sold at public auction for not less than one dollar per acre. Out of each township, one section — or one square mile — was set aside for the support of public education. This plan resulted in a regular checkerboard division of the townships, which made it easy to locate any particular piece of property. Furthermore, the system set up by the Ordinance of 1785 was followed in most of the lands west of the Appalachians that were not already surveyed. It saved American landholders endless disputes over the boundaries of their property.

(2) Two years later (1787) Congress passed the Northwest Ordinance. This law set up a plan of government for the pioneers who moved into the Northwest Territory. Congress was to appoint a governor and three judges to carry on the government. When the number of adult, free males in

Costumes of the 18th century

the territory reached 5000, the voters would be permitted to elect a house of representatives. This body of representatives, together with a governor and legislative council appointed by Congress, would "make law in all cases for the good government of the district." In time, the Northwest Territory was to be divided into at least three, but not more than five, states. As soon as one of these had 60,000 people living in it, it would be admitted into the Union "on an equal footing with the original States in all respects whatever."

The Northwest Ordinance forbade the introduction of slavery, and guaranteed full liberty of conscience and religion to settlers within the territory. It also required that schools and the means of education should "forever be encouraged." Finally, the ordinance extended to the people of the territory important liberties such as trial by jury, the sacredness of contracts, and freedom from cruel and unusual punishments.

The new law starts a wise policy. The Northwest Ordinance was the beginning of a territorial policy of far-reaching importance. This policy helped make the advancing frontier a powerful influence for American liberty, democracy, and union. As new states were formed, not only in the Northwest Territory but westward to the Pacific, they received full rights and equality with the original states. Settlers who moved westward were guaranteed that they would not lose political rights nor be held subject to the original states. The territorial policy set up by this ordinance clearly indicated that Americans had profited by their unfortunate experiences as colonies of England. Forty years later, Daniel Webster expressed doubt "whether one single law of any lawgiver, ancient or modern, has produced effects of more distinct, marked, and lasting character than the ordinance of '87."

The Articles are blamed for hard times. The good accomplished under the Articles, however, was overshadowed by the growing feeling of dissatisfaction with them. Hard times followed the Revolution and were at their worst while the Articles were in effect. Many people blamed the government because it was unable to ease their misfortunes. Since the depression ended while the Articles were in force, it is unlikely that they were entirely responsible for the difficult conditions. Still, the idea that the government was at fault became firmly entrenched.

Businessmen find fault with the Articles. Various groups of businessmen were irritated by the Articles. Manufacturers had enjoyed boom times during the war, because imports from Great Britain were cut off and American goods were in demand. When peace came, war contracts ended and the demand for goods fell off. Conditions were made worse because Great Britain tried to win back its American trade by flooding our ports with goods which were generally better in quality and lower in price than American goods.

Shipping was also in a bad way. Great Britain refused to make a commercial treaty with the United States. She practically closed her doors to certain American products and cut off the United States from a share in the trade of the British West Indies. France and Spain also closed some of their colonial ports to American vessels. These were hard blows to the struggling nation and especially to those citizens engaged in shipping. And there was little relief in sight as long as Congress had no power to take stern measures against foreign governments.

The merchant was no better off than the manufacturer or the shipper. Currency was in a state of confusion. No coins were minted by the national government, and such coins as were in use had no uniform weight or value. So much paper money had come from the presses that it was almost without value. A few states passed laws requiring merchants to take worthless paper money in payment of debts. Some states put tariff duties or taxes on the products of other states. These tariffs were intended to produce revenue and protect local industries, but before long they were being used to take revenge upon neighboring states. New York, for example, put what amounted to a tax on garden produce from New Jersey. New Jersey promptly put a heavy tax upon Sandy Hook Lighthouse, which had been built by New Yorkers on the Jersey shore. Under such taxes and counter-taxes, healthy trade among the states was impossible.

Financiers and moneylenders were likewise discontented with government under the Articles of Confederation. By 1784 the debts of the states totaled more than $20,000,000, while the Confederation owed twice that amount. Much of this money had been advanced by American financiers. The interest on the national debt was not being paid, much less the principal. Holders of government bonds wanted a national government which could levy taxes to pay the public debt. Moneylenders suffered from those state laws which forced them to accept paper money in payment of debts and from other state legislation.

Shays' Rebellion reveals public discontent. The business class was not the only discontented group. The common people were complaining, particularly in those areas where property owners were in control. This unrest blazed up in Massachusetts when a personal tax was levied to pay off the Massachusetts war debt—a tax amounting to about $20 for a household of five people. This tax was a hardship for many because the cost of living was high after the war. Most debtors, who were already being hounded by creditors, favored issuing paper money in large quantities, since it would enable them to pay debts on easier terms. Property owners controlled the legislature, however, and demands for paper money were overruled.

There was an increase in the number of lawsuits and foreclosures (seizure of property for non-payment of debts) and the jails were soon filled with unfortunate debtors.

Unable to get help from the state legislature, the debtor class rebelled. Farmers, mechanics, and laborers marched into the courthouses to prevent the courts from handing down further judgments against people who owed money. They even released debtors who were already in jail.

The crisis came in Shays' Rebellion (1786). A group of angry Americans, led by Daniel Shays who had been a captain during the Revolution, forced several courts in western Massachusetts to close. Later, the same group tried to seize the arsenal at Springfield. Recruits poured in, and Shays' force swelled to almost 2000 before the rebellion was finally put down by state troops. Shays was taken prisoner, but later he and his followers were pardoned. Law and order ruled again in Massachusetts, but the uprising showed the extent of dissatisfaction among the mass of people.

Foreign respect is lacking. The government under the Articles of Confederation lacked prestige abroad as well as at home. European powers showed no confidence in the Articles, and were cool about welcoming the United States as an equal member of the family of nations. Franklin, writing from England in 1783, said "We should, I think, be constantly upon our guard, and impress strongly upon our minds, that though it [Great Britain] has made peace with us, it is not in truth reconciled either to us, or to its loss of us." Great Britain didn't even pay the United States the respect of sending a minister. In addition, Great Britain refused to give up fur-trading posts in territory that had been ceded to the United States by the treaty of 1783. In defense of its action, the British government charged that the United States had failed to make good its promises to allow British merchants to collect their American debts and to relieve Loyalists from persecution (page 116).

Spain was no friendlier. She wanted to make sure that the United States did not become her strong rival in America. She ignored articles of the Treaty of Paris which fixed the southern boundary of the United States and which guaranteed the free use of the Mississippi River. John Jay tried to smooth over the trouble between the two countries by working out a treaty with Spain in 1786. His treaty proposed that Spain grant the United States certain trade opportunities in return for which Spain would be allowed to close the Mississippi River to American boats for 25 years. The people of the South and of the western frontier angrily protested this plan because the Mississippi was their only outlet to the sea, and Jay's treaty with Spain was never ratified by Congress.

Relations were not much better with other governments. Even in Paris, Jefferson, the American minister to our former ally, was forced to admit, "We are the lowest and most obscure of the whole diplomatic tribe."

After four years, then, the United States was still trying without much success to push ahead. The nation was at the crossroads. Independence had been won, but dissatisfaction existed at home and contempt for the new country reigned abroad. The important question was whether the forces favoring strong national government would prove powerful enough to prevent disaster, or whether the Union would split up into thirteen rival states — an easy prey for European conquerors.

――――― CHECK-UP ―――――

Why did the Articles of Confederation prove inadequate?

1. What were the chief weaknesses of the new central government?
2. What were the provisions of the Land Ordinance of 1785? Of the Northwest Ordinance? Why were they important?
3. Why was each of the following dissatisfied with conditions: (a) the manufacturer, (b) the shipper, (c) the merchant, (d) the financier, (e) the common people?
4. What evidences were there in both domestic and foreign affairs that we needed a stronger central government?

3 A New Form of Government Is Planned

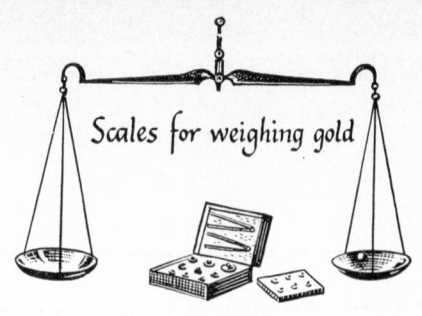

Scales for weighing gold

The need for stronger union becomes apparent. Even before the Articles of Confederation were ratified, their main weakness had been noted by the brilliant young Alexander Hamilton of New York. In 1780 he warned, "The fundamental defect is a want of power in Congress. . . . The idea of an uncontrollable sovereignty in each state, . . . will defeat the other powers given to Congress, and make our union feeble and precarious." Hamilton's criticism was echoed loudly and often during the next seven years. In a letter to the governors of all the states in 1783, George Washington stressed the need for a strong central power. Two years later he wrote: "We are either a united people under one head and for federal purposes, or we are thirteen independent sovereignties, eternally counteracting each other." In the same year (1785) the Massachusetts legislature passed a resolution suggesting that the Articles of Confederation be revised, especially by increasing the powers of Congress. Outbreaks like Shays' Rebellion made thoughtful people more certain than ever that something had to be done. But when it came to the point of exactly *what* should be done, there was little agreement.

Preliminary meetings lead to united action. The chain of events that led to the solution of the problem started in an argument between Virginia and Maryland over navigation rights on the Potomac River. The Virginia legislature appointed commissioners to discuss the situation with commissioners from Maryland. As an owner of western land, George Washington was interested in improving communication between the East and the West. At his invitation delegates of both states met at his home at Mount Vernon in 1785. As a result of this conference, Virginia sent an invitation to *all* the states for a second conference to be held the next year at Annapolis. Its purpose was to consider the advantages of a uniform system of trade regulations. Only five states were represented at Annapolis.

Alexander Hamilton influenced the delegates at Annapolis to adopt a report which suggested a third convention to meet in May, 1787, at Philadelphia. It was proposed that this convention take steps to form a government able to meet the needs of the country. Congress finally issued a formal call for the convention at Philadelphia — but only for the purpose of amending the Articles of Confederation.

The Constitutional Convention draws famous Americans. Although this meeting was originally called for the purpose of amending the Articles, it is now remembered as the Constitutional Convention. The 55 men who at one time or another attended the meetings at Philadelphia made up an assembly of notable persons. This famous group was led by George Washington, who was unanimously chosen president of the Convention, and Benjamin Franklin, who was in his eighties by that time. Also attending were the well-informed James Madison and the influential Edmund Randolph of Virginia; Robert and Gouverneur Morris and the brilliant James Wilson of Pennsylvania; the conservative Alexander Hamilton from New York; John Dickinson, now representing Delaware; the two Pinckneys and John Rutledge of South Carolina; Roger Sherman and Oliver Ellsworth of Connecticut; William Paterson from New Jersey; Luther Martin from Maryland; and Elbridge Gerry of Massachusetts. A majority of the delegates were, or had been, lawyers. Seven had been state governors and nearly 40 had served in Congress. About half of them were college graduates. George Mason, one of the Virginia delegates, wrote to his son: "America has certainly, upon this occasion, drawn forth her first characters. . . . The eyes of the United States are turned on this assembly, and their expectations raised to a very anxious degree. May God grant [that] we may be able to gratify them, by establishing a wise and just government."

With the exception of Franklin, this was an assembly of comparatively young men who represented the conservative wing of the old Revolutionary party. The more liberal Revolutionary leaders were not there. Jefferson, for example, was the American minister at Paris. John Adams and Thomas Paine were in England. Such outspoken defenders of liberty as Patrick Henry and Samuel Adams were absent.

The Convention reaches important decisions. Delegates to the Convention were aware of the great difficulties they faced. Times were too critical, they felt, to let the whole country know about their clashes of opinion, or to let the members fall under any outside influence or interference. For these reasons, the delegates agreed that none of the debates would be printed or published, except with special permission. Most of what we know today about the proceedings of the Convention comes from the very full notes of James Madison, which were published 50 years later, after his death. The Convention also decided to conduct business the way Congress did; votes would be cast by states, and each state would have one vote.

Almost at once, a vital issue came up. Should the delegates carry out their instructions and merely revise the unsatisfactory Articles of Confederation or should they disregard their orders and draft an entirely new constitution? The Convention decided to follow the latter course. Washington is reported to have made this statement while the members were assembling: "It is too probable that no plan we propose will be adopted. Perhaps another dreadful conflict is to be sustained. If to please the people, we offer what we ourselves disapprove, how can we afterwards defend our work? Let us raise a standard to which the wise and honest can repair. The event is in the hand of God."

One of the early acts of the Convention was to adopt a resolution "that a national government ought to be established consisting of a supreme Legislative, Executive, and Judiciary." Later the wording was changed by striking out "national," but the basic idea of a strong central government, and especially of the division of its powers, remained. Most of the delegates also believed that it was dangerous to place too much power in the hands of the people and were ready to prevent that possibility by putting certain "safeguards" into the new government. "The evils we experience," declared Elbridge Gerry, "flow from the ex-

Independence Hall in Philadelphia housed the Constitutional Convention, and is now one of our most important national monuments. The statue in the foreground is of John Barry, Irish-American naval hero of the Revolution.

cess of democracy." Edmund Randolph, too, linked the troubles of the past few years with "the turbulence and follies of democracy."

The Convention splits over opposing plans. Although the delegates generally favored a stronger central government, there was little agreement beyond that point. Madison's notes tell of heated debates and tense moments. The most threatening argument developed over the structure of the new government. A nationalist group in the Convention wanted to give the central government enough power so that it could enforce its decisions over the power of the states. They believed that such a government should rest upon the people, not upon the states. Another group, representing the smaller states, argued that the Articles of Confederation had been formed by sovereign states — independent republics, each of which was a law unto itself — and that this basic idea must be preserved at all costs.

The argument really came to this: was the national government to have more authority than any of the states? The nationalist view was offered to the Convention by Edmund Randolph as the Virginia Plan. It called for a Congress of two branches in which the total number of delegates would be divided among the states according to the number of free people living in each state. It proposed that these members of Congress, along with a President and judges, should represent the nation.

The Virginia Plan alarmed the smaller states. They were afraid that their smaller populations would entitle them to only a few delegates under such a system. William Paterson of New Jersey offered another proposal called the New Jersey Plan. This proposal provided for simply increasing the powers of the existing Congress, in which each state should have equal representation. Among Congress' new powers would be the authority to impose import duties and stamp taxes. The plan also provided for executive and judicial departments.

The Convention adopts the "Great Compromise." The Virginia Plan and the New Jersey Plan were debated so bitterly that several times the Convention was nearly broken up. "We were on the verge of dissolution," declared one delegate, "scarce held together by the strength of an hair." The most heated argument had to do with the method of representation in the new legislature. The large states were unwilling to have their interests overridden by the willfulness of a few small states. The small states were just as determined not to be swamped by the greater voting power of states with larger populations.

At last a compromise was reached and the crisis was over. By a close vote, the Convention agreed upon a legislature of two bodies or "houses." To satisfy those who supported the Virginia Plan, members of the lower house, or House of Representatives, were to be apportioned (divided) among the states on the basis of population, and were to vote individually, not as part of a state delegation. To satisfy followers of the New Jersey Plan, the states would have equal representation in the upper house, or Senate. Each state would elect two senators, who could vote individually. The legislative strength of the two bodies was equal except that all bills for raising revenue had to originate in the House. The "Great Compromise," as this settlement has come to be known, recognized the principle of nationalism in the House of Representatives but preserved equality of the states in the Senate.

The Convention reaches other compromises. Other compromises were worked out by the Convention. As Madison listened to the debates, he decided that the real division of interests "did not lie between the large and small states: it lay between the northern and southern." The commercial North was convinced that its best hope for prosperity lay in a government with complete control over commerce, both interstate and foreign. The agricultural South wanted to be free to buy goods and sell products in the most favorable markets to be found anywhere in the world. The South was afraid that Congress, under the influence of the North, might set up tariff duties that would block the

(Continued on page 136)

Result of Conn. Compromise

leg. bicameral — of 2 houses — Senate H. of Rep.

George Washington
(1732-1799)

Colonial Officer

GEORGE WASHINGTON's important accomplishments are well known to every American boy and girl. Born on a Virginia plantation, young Washington early became a surveyor. During the final French and Indian War he served with gallantry. Then, during the years when relations with Great Britain became more and more strained, Washington upheld the Patriot cause. Appointed commander in chief of the Continental forces, he led America successfully through the struggle for independence. In the dark days before final victory was achieved, his force of character and military skill proved a bulwark of strength to the American cause.

Though Washington retired to Mount Vernon, Virginia, at the end of the war, his interest in public affairs continued. He lent his support to the movement for a stronger central government. In the Constitutional Convention, where he served as the presiding officer, his influence was important. He was unanimously elected the first President of the United States. During his two terms the new nation was established on a firm financial basis and was able to steer clear of foreign entanglements. His "Farewell Address" has been considered one of America's most highly prized state papers.

President

George Washington, the man, is not so well known to the average American. The passing of a century and a half have helped to dim the outlines of his character

and personality. Biographers have praised him so highly that he seems scarcely human. But such is not a true picture of the father of our country. As a boy he delighted in physical prowess; as a man he took keen enjoyment in the supervision of his plantation. His reserve of manner was not born of a lack of spirit but of a self-control which caused him to restrain emotion. Kindly, thoughtful, and modest, he would have shrunk from being placed upon a pedestal. George Washington was a true American gentleman.

Virginia Planter

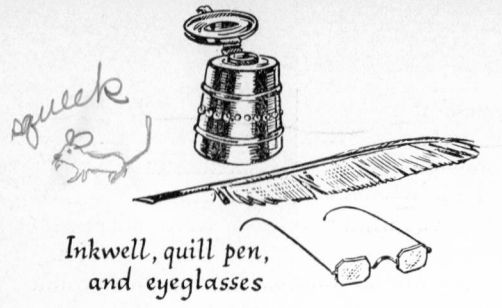

Inkwell, quill pen, and eyeglasses

free flow of goods to and from the country. It was also fearful that Congress might outlaw slavery. To avoid these threats to their way of life, the southern delegates wanted to increase the number of their representatives in the lower house. They proposed that the slaves should be counted in deciding the number of representatives per state. At the same time, they were unwilling to have slaves included when direct taxes were to be levied. Northern delegates to the Convention vigorously opposed this plan. A compromise was finally worked out, which provided that five slaves would count as three persons in figuring both the number of representatives and the amount of direct taxes.

The southern delegates were further troubled by the proposal to grant Congress the power to regulate foreign commerce. With this authority, plus the power to make foreign treaties, the new government would be able to prohibit slave trade or to make treaties unfavorable to the interests of southern planters. Again the delegates managed to reach a compromise. Congress was given the general power to regulate commerce among the states and with foreign nations. However, certain limitations on this power made Southerners feel safer: (1) Congress could not prevent before 1808 the importation of any persons, such as slaves, which the states might wish to admit. However, Congress could levy a tax of not more than ten dollars on each such person. (2) Congress could not impose duties on any exports. (3) A two-thirds vote was needed in the Senate to ratify a treaty. Thus the South, which held about half of the votes in the Senate, could defeat any treaty which might harm its interests. (4) Provision was made for the return of fugitive slaves to their lawful masters.

The Constitution is completed. Slowly the summer days of 1787 went by, and the new

Constitution gradually took final shape. The process was very difficult and often a middle ground had to be found between two extreme points of view. It is safe to say that hardly a delegate was entirely satisfied with the completed document. Even before the close of the Convention, several members walked out in disgust. When the last meeting was held on September 17, 1787, only 39 names were signed to the Constitution. Yet the document was a triumph of practical statesmanship and gave the country a form of government far stronger than the form the people had been living under.

The Constitution still had to be ratified by state conventions made up of elected delegates. Disregarding their instructions as well as the Articles of Confederation, which called for unanimous action, the delegates at Philadelphia provided that "ratification of the conventions of nine states shall be sufficient for the establishment of this Constitution between the states so ratifying the same."

--------- CHECK-UP ---------

How was a new government for the United States planned?

1. What events led to the calling of the Constitutional Convention?
2. Describe the membership of the Convention. What early decisions were made?
3. What basic differences in point of view came to light in the Convention? Over what matters did arguments arise? How were these differences compromised?
4. What was the attitude of the makers toward the completed Constitution?

4 The Constitution Is Adopted by the States

The country is divided over the Constitution. By the time the adoption of the Constitution was being discussed in the state conventions, the document and its provisions had become topics of daily conversation and argument all over the country. Those who wanted it adopted called themselves Federalists. Those who opposed it were known as Anti-Federalists. The Federalist group was made up of conservative property owners and businessmen. Among them were owners of government bonds, the commercial and manufacturing interests, the planter class, lawyers, and officers of the late army. The Federalists also were supported by most of the writers, newspapers, and clergymen, all of whom wanted a closer union of the states.

Most of the Anti-Federalists were people who did not own extensive property. Among them were the small farmers, the laborers in the cities, people who owed money, people who believed in issuing plenty of paper money, those who wanted a more democratic form of government, and those who did not want to see the states lose any of their power. Many people were dissatisfied because the Constitution had no "bill of rights" to protect individual liberty. Rufus King, a Federalist, said, "an apprehension that the liberties of the people are in danger, and a distrust of men of property or education, have a more powerful effect upon the minds of our opponents than any specific objections against the Constitution."

The Federalists have an advantage. If the Constitution had been put to the test of a popular vote, it might possibly have been rejected. The Federalists, however, had certain advantages which helped them win in the end. One of the greatest was the strong support given by Washington, the "Father of his Country," who was highly respected by the American people. Also the Federalists were better organized and more influential. They had a greater number of political leaders working with them and they carried on a more successful campaign. Of particular importance was the fact that, in practically all states, to be a voter a man had to own property. As a result the property-owning Federalist sympathizers were able to choose the delegates for the ratifying conventions.

Nine states ratify the Constitution. Four months after the Constitution was completed, it had been ratified by Delaware, Pennsylvania, New Jersey, Georgia, and Connecticut. In Massachusetts a bitter struggle developed. Men who represented the agricultural districts were not much interested in commerce. They were suspicious of the aims of the merchants and "aristocrats" of the seaboard. Only after such former Patriot leaders as John Hancock and Samuel Adams approved the Constitution were the scales tipped in favor of ratification. Next to fall in line were Maryland and South Carolina, in the spring of 1788. Then in June, New Hampshire, after a sharp struggle, became the ninth state to add approval. That was enough to put the Constitution into force for these nine states. Four others, the key states of Virginia and New York, along with North Carolina and Rhode Island, still held back.

Virginia makes it ten. In Virginia, the fight was a bitter one. James Madison, Governor Edmund Randolph, and John Marshall supported the Constitution, while Patrick Henry and George Mason led the Anti-Federalist forces. Angrily criticizing the work of the constitution-makers, Patrick Henry demanded, "Who authorized them to speak the language of *We, the People,* instead of *We, the States?*" Virginia finally ratified the Constitution, owing in large part to the favorable attitude of the planter class and representatives from the Shenandoah Valley.

New York makes it eleven. In New York, Federalist strength centered in and about the city of New York. Alexander Hamilton, with the assistance of Madison and Jay, wrote a series of letters to the newspapers which offered powerful arguments in favor of the Constitution. These 85 essays were later collected and published

Desk and stool

in book form as *The Federalist*. Their sound reasoning, expressed in simple words, won over many people not only in New York but elsewhere. The Anti-Federalists, led by Governor George Clinton, were at first in the majority at the convention. After ten other states had voted for the Constitution, however, the opposition gave way before the skillful arguments of Hamilton. New York became the eleventh state to ratify.

The new government is launched. In 1788 the Constitution went into effect for the eleven states which had already ratified it. A year later, North Carolina came into the Union after Congress had adopted a bill of rights. Rhode Island eventually had to follow suit or be treated as a foreign country in the tariff legislation of the new government.

Meanwhile, Congress asked the states to get the election of a President and members of the new Congress under way. Washington became the first President; John Adams was chosen Vice-President. On the whole, men of Federalist sympathies were elected to Congress.

When Washington was inaugurated in the spring of 1789, the new government actually started. It was none too soon. Since October 10, 1788, the old Congress had not been able to muster a quorum (the number required to be present in order to do business). For a year there had been no federal government worthy of the name in the United States. The new ship of state, however, was manned by a group of leaders who were determined to see it succeed. It was launched, like Columbus' small fleet of ships, upon an uncharted sea, and on all sides it was faced by unknown perils.

––––––––– CHECK-UP –––––––––

How was the Constitution ratified?

1. What groups favored the adoption of the Constitution? What groups opposed it? Why? Why did those in favor have an advantage?
2. In which states was the battle for adoption the hardest? Why?
3. What were the results of the first election under the Constitution?

5 The Constitution Provides a Workable Government

The Constitution has been widely admired. Before taking up the story of the new republic in the following chapters, it will be helpful to note some of the significant features of the Constitution. The form of government which it established has met the needs of the United States amazingly well. More than that, the Constitution has served as a model for constitutions in many other lands. World statesmen have been astonished that the men who framed this document could have finished such a tremendous task in only four months. The British statesman, Gladstone, called the Constitution "the most wonderful work ever struck off at a given time by the brain and purpose of man."

The document was not wholly original. When Gladstone made this remark, he put into one striking phrase what most Americans have felt about their most precious document. But the remark can be misleading in a way. It gives the idea that the Constitution was something brand new, something that was dashed off in a great burst of inspiration. That was not true. The delegates to the Constitutional Convention were far too practical to risk mere invention. They faced a grave crisis, and they realized it. They saw that they must work out a plan of government that would prevent a return to the conditions the country had endured under British rule and under the Articles of Confederation.

To find the right formula, the framers of the Constitution racked their brains. They dug soberly into their own experiences. They ferreted out those characteristics of other governments which they believed would be most helpful in building a firm and enduring political life for the nation. During the long, tiresome sessions of the Convention, they showed masterful skill in erecting a framework of government based largely on three elements: (1) British theories and customs; (2) colonial ways of doing things; and (3) the experiences of the states. The Constitution pulled these elements together and put them to work.

Seal and sealing wax

The Convention sets up a federal system. Probably the most tangled problem the Convention had to unsnarl dealt with the relations between the new central government and the states. Under the Articles of Confederation, the central government had no real authority over the states and no power to deal directly with the people. All of the delegates were agreed that the central government must have more power but not so much that the states were entirely subject to it.

Finally the Convention hit upon an unusual solution of the problem. It set up a *federal* government which would furnish a certain amount of centralized control and still preserve the benefits of state and local self-government. Under this plan, the states were to give up certain powers to the federal government. Within the range of these powers, the national government was to be supreme. In effect, it would receive those powers directly from the people and would be answerable to the people for the way it carried them out. But the states were still to exercise those powers that they did not hand over to the federal government. Thus, political authority was divided between the national government and the state governments.

The federal government receives specific powers. In working out this division of powers, the framers of the Constitution first listed or *enumerated* certain specific powers which the national government alone could exercise. All of these powers were nation-wide in scope and affected the people of all the states. Some of them had been granted to the central government by the Articles of Confederation, but many new powers were added by the Constitution in an attempt to clear up the confusion which threatened the country.

The "elastic clause" strengthens the federal government. The men who drew up the Constitution capped this list of enumerated powers with a statement giving Congress the authority to "make all laws which shall be necessary and proper for carrying into execution the foregoing powers, and all other powers vested by this Constitution in the government of the United States . . . ." This "necessary and proper" clause, or *elastic clause,* has been interpreted quite freely during the nation's history. It is safe to say that Congress has used the "necessary and proper" clause to pass legislation so far beyond the power originally planned that many members of the Constitutional Convention would gasp with astonishment at the results.

The Constitution becomes the supreme law. To make sure that no one could undermine the authority of the federal government, the framers of the Constitution also inserted this statement: "This Constitution, and the laws of the United States which shall be made in pursuance thereof; and all treaties made, or which shall be made, under the authority of the United States, shall be the *supreme law of the land.*" Thus, the Constitution was proclaimed the highest law in the United States. Everything else ranked below it in authority — state constitutions, state laws, and local ordinances. All judges, federal and state, had to abide by its provisions.

The States still retain much authority. Impressive though this list of congressional powers sounds, the states still held a fair amount of authority. They kept their control over voting qualifications, local governments, education, corporations, marriage and divorce, and the definition and punishment of all ordinary crimes. Through their "police power" the states also supervised the health, safety, and welfare of their citizens. To satisfy people who feared too great control by the federal government, the Tenth Amendment stated: "The powers not delegated to the United States by the Constitution, nor prohibited by it to the States, are reserved to the States respectively, or to the people." [1]

To safeguard the federal system still further, the Constitution directed the national government and the state governments to observe certain limits on their activities. It ordered the states not to interfere with powers of the federal government. At the same time, it ordered the federal government not to treat one state any differently from another. The Constitution also laid down certain rules which the states had to follow in dealing with one another.

The Bill of Rights is added. In working out the division of powers between the central authority and the states, the Convention was not unmindful of the liberties of the individual citizen. The Constitution gave some guarantee of individual rights, but not enough to suit many people. They were still afraid of tyranny, even after the Constitution was adopted. For that reason, ten amendments were added to it in 1791. These amendments have become known popularly as the *Bill of Rights*. Among other things the Bill of Rights guarantees to American citizens (1) freedom of religion, of speech, and of the press; (2) the right of assembly; (3) freedom from unwarranted search; (4) fair and impartial trial by jury; (5) protection of life, liberty, and property; and (6) protection from cruel and unusual punishments. (See diagram, page 141.) These guarantees of personal liberty were chiefly binding upon the national government, though similar safeguards have also been written into most of the state constitutions. The Bill of Rights has become one of the foundation stones of our American way of life.

The Constitution establishes three departments of government. Not only had the central government under the Articles of Confederation lacked sufficient power; it also lacked the machinery needed to operate the government of the country

smoothly. Congress, under the Articles, was the only governmental body. The new Constitution set up three departments of government:

(1) The making of laws was entrusted to Congress (the legislative branch), composed of the Senate and the House of Representatives. Senators, two from each state, were to serve six-year terms. Members of the House, apportioned according to population, were to serve for a term of two years.

(2) To carry out the broad powers entrusted to the federal government, the Constitution established an executive branch, with the President at its head. For the election of the chief executive, the Convention worked out an elaborate system which has become known as the *electoral college*. Instead of voting directly for a President, the voters of each state cast their ballots for a group of electors equal to the number of representatives and senators from that state. The electors in turn chose the President.

(3) To interpret and enforce the law, the Constitution created a Supreme Court (the judicial branch of the government), and gave Congress authority to set up any lower courts that might be necessary.

Separation of powers. The creation of three separate branches of the national government was intended not only to make the government efficient but to protect its citizens from tyranny. The framers of the Constitution had good reason to fear such a possibility. Their forefathers had suffered under the personal rule of Charles I, and they themselves had known tyranny under George III. They also wanted to avoid the English form of government, in which the same persons both made and enforced the laws. In England a powerful prime minister like Grenville had been able to plan legislation, push it through Parliament, and then have it enforced. To prevent such action, the Convention divided power between Congress, the President, and the courts. This three-way system in our government is called *separation of powers*.

The Convention sets up checks and balances. In their efforts to prevent tyranny, the delegates to the Constitutional Conven-

---

[1] Certain powers delegated to the federal government are not denied to the states. Known as concurrent powers, they can be exercised by the states as long as there is no conflict with the federal government. For example, both federal and state governments levy taxes.

Important Provisions of the Bill of

FREEDOM OF SPEECH AND PRESS

FREEDOM OF RELIGION

RIGHT TO ASSEMBLE

FREEDOM FROM UNREASONABLE
SEARCH

JUST COMPENSATION
FOR PRIVATE PROPERTY

RIGHT TO TRIAL BY JURY

Life, liberty, and the pursuit of happiness are guaranteed to individual Americans by the first ten amendments to the Constitution. Several which are very important to every American are pictured here. Turn to the first ten amendments to the Constitution beginning on page xliv to learn which have been omitted. Why were they important in 1791?

tion went even further. They worked out a careful, though complicated, system of *checks and balances.* Within the legislative, or lawmaking branch, each house was given certain checks on the other. For instance, the House of Representatives, which represented the people, shared its lawmaking power with the Senate, which represented the states. The fact that senators had to be older and could serve longer than members of the House of Representatives was expected to prevent hasty legislation.

Each department of the government was checked by the others. For example, the President could check Congress by rejecting, or vetoing, its legislation. But Congress could pass a law over the President's veto by majorities of two thirds in both houses. Following what was clearly in the mind of the nationalist group of the Convention, the Supreme Court has frequently declared laws passed by Congress and approved by the President to be unconstitutional. Both the President and members of the Supreme Court may be checked by Congress through its power to *impeach* (accuse) civil officers for "treason, bribery, or other high crimes and misdemeanors." These are but a few of the checks and balances written into the Constitution. Although this system has succeeded in preventing tyranny, it has slowed down the process of government. The delays that result could be serious, except that during wartime or other national emergencies Congress may grant special, temporary powers to the President.

141

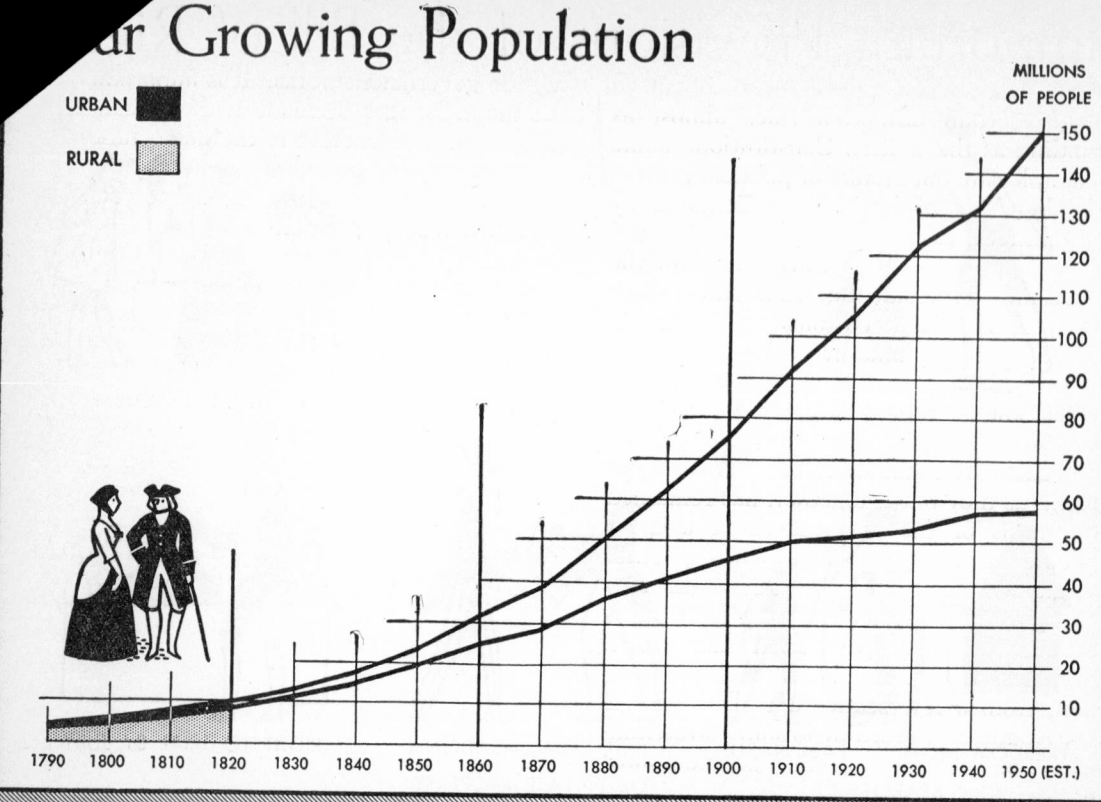

URBAN ■

RURAL ▢

MILLIONS OF PEOPLE

150 — 140 — 130 — 120 — 110 — 100 — 90 — 80 — 70 — 60 — 50 — 40 — 30 — 20 — 10

1790 1800 1810 1820 1830 1840 1850 1860 1870 1880 1890 1900 1910 1920 1930 1940 1950 (EST.)

The rapid growth of American population is dramatized in this chart. Trace it through, and notice the changing proportions of rural and urban population. (This chart will be repeated from time to time throughout this book, with emphasis on the period being studied. Here the period emphasized is from 1790 to 1820.)

The Constitution may be altered. The delegates to the Constitutional Convention tried to foresee all the problems that might arise. But they were practical men who knew that the Constitution might have to be changed to meet new conditions. Therefore they included a provision by which amendments might be added. "Is there not a constitutional door for alterations and amendments?" asked Washington, during the arguments over adoption, " . . . and will not our successors be as ready to apply the remedy as we ourselves if occasion should require it?" Yet in more than 150 years, only 22 amendments have been added to the Constitution.

The Constitution has expanded through court decisions. The framers of the Constitution also paved the way for further change through court decisions. They probably did not realize the full possibilities of the "elastic clause" when they included it. Because of this clause, Congress has been able to pass many laws needed to deal with the problems of our modern industrial civilization. These laws are not based upon any powers mentioned in so many words in the Constitution — they are based on *implied powers*. In other words, they have been considered "necessary and proper" to carry out the enumerated powers of the Constitution. The particular powers that have been easy to expand are those relating to war, taxation, and commerce. Expansion of the Constitution through the use of implied powers has been greatly strengthened by the fact that the Supreme Court, in its early years, interpreted quite liberally what was "necessary and proper."

The Constitution has grown through custom and usage. There is still another means by which the federal government has been able to meet the changing condi-

142

tions of the years. Custom and habit have made certain unwritten rules almost as binding as the written Constitution. Some examples are our system of political parties, the handling of business in Congress by committees, cabinet meetings, and the use of national nominating conventions for the choosing of presidential candidates. This body of important customs and usages is often called the *unwritten constitution*.

The Constitution has served the nation well. The changes that have been made in the original work of the Constitutional delegates are remarkably few. Their document, as they put it together, has remained the basis of the government of a great people for a longer time than any other single written document. Under the federal government established by the Constitution, America's population has grown from less than 4 million to over 150 million; from a few scattered settlements on the Atlantic seaboard to 48 states stretching from ocean to ocean; from a people almost entirely agricultural to a great farming, industrial, and commercial nation. It is a very great tribute to the Fathers of the Constitution that the system of government which they worked out, over a century and a half ago, has endured through the many startling changes which have taken place in this nation and in the world.

American citizens may quite properly take pride in their form of government, but they must not take it too much for granted. Each generation may make changes in the way the government works. It is important that those changes be made without damaging the basic structure of the democratic American way of life as it is outlined by the Constitution. To think, to talk, and to vote wisely when such questions of change arise demands that each citizen know the Constitution and how the government works.

This chapter has outlined the basic principles which guided the Fathers of the Constitution and the fundamental structure of the government they founded. Beginning on page xvii of this book is a section entitled "Your Government." Beginning on page xxxiii you will find the Constitution of the United States along with explanations of it. In these two sections you can learn more about how the government works today and how the Constitution has been changed through the years.

——— CHECK-UP ———

How does the Constitution provide a workable and successful government?

1. How does the federal system reconcile strong central government with the sovereignty of the states?
2. Why was the Bill of Rights added to the Constitution? What important guarantees does it contain?
3. What is meant by "separation of powers"? By "checks and balances"? Why does the Constitution include these? Give examples of each.
4. How has the Constitution been expanded to meet changing conditions?

CHAPTER REVIEW

Terms to Understand

sovereignty	debtor class
conservative	federal government
liberal	supreme law
compromise	police power
ratify	right of assembly
quorum	impeach
executive	separation of powers
legislative	checks and balances
judicial	enumerated powers
tariff	implied powers
unwritten constitution	amendment

People and Things to Know About

Articles of Confederation	Virginia Plan
Land Ordinance of 1785	New Jersey Plan
Northwest Ordinance	Constitutional Convention
township	Federalists
Shays' Rebellion	Anti-Federalists
Alexander Hamilton	*The Federalist*
Mount Vernon conference	Supreme Court
Annapolis conference	elastic clause
	Bill of Rights
	electoral college

Historic Dates to Identify

1781   1785   1787

Questions to Discuss

1. It has been said that the American Revolution was concerned not only with "home rule" but with "who should rule at home." Explain. In what respects was the Revolution more than just a separation from the British Empire?

2. Compare the following:

(a) The colonial governments with the new state governments.

(b) The Articles of Confederation with the United Nations.

(c) Powers of the states and powers of the federal government under the Constitution.

3. How did the plan for dealing with "colonial" areas in the Northwest Ordinance differ from the English view of the place of colonies in the Empire? Is this an evidence that people do learn something from history?

4. Relate each of the following in the new state governments to the experiences through which the Americans had passed: (a) a weak executive, (b) a written framework of government, (c) bills of rights, (d) two-house legislatures, (e) separation of executive and legislative functions.

5. The federal principle, by which a strong central government was created without destroying the state governments, is perhaps our greatest contribution to government, and it has been widely copied. Explain how the Constitution accomplished this.

6. In *Letters from A Farmer in Pennsylvania,* John Dickinson stated, ". . . for who are a free people? Not those over whom government is reasonably and equitably exercised, but those who live under a government so constitutionally checked and controlled, that proper provision is made against its being otherwise exercised." What did he mean? How did the Constitution provide for such a government? Do the benefits of such a system offset its defects? Why?

Questions to Discuss (Cont.)

7. Many of those who believed in states' rights came to object strenuously to the "implied powers" clause. Why do you think that this was true?

Relating Geography and History

Locate on an outline map of the United States:

(a) The frontier line of 1790.

(b) The boundaries of the Northwest Territory.

Other Things to Do

1. Prepare a more detailed report on the United States in 1790. You will find an excellent chapter on this topic in Morison and Commager, *Growth of the American Republic,* Vol. I.

*2. Make a list of the chief steps in the long effort to provide a central government in America. You might start with the New England Confederation. (Consult the index.)

3. Prepare a more detailed report on Shays' Rebellion, its causes, chief events, and results. Additional information can be found in McLaughlin's *The Confederation and the Constitution.*

4. Consult newspapers and news magazines for articles dealing with points of conflict between state and national authority today. Have these reached the Supreme Court? What other Supreme Court decisions have appeared in the news?

5. Debate:

(a) *Resolved,* That changing conditions make necessary a delegation to the national government of many powers previously exercised by the states.

(b) *Resolved,* That the President should be elected by a direct vote of the people.

6. Make a "before and after" cartoon contrasting the position and powers of the central government before and after the adoption of the Constitution.

Chapter 7

Surveyor

FEDERALISTS LAUNCH THE

NEW GOVERNMENT

The unity of government, which constitutes you one people, is . . . now dear to you. It is justly so; for it is a main pillar in the edifice of your real independence, the support of your tranquillity at home, your peace abroad; of your safety; of your prosperity; of that very liberty which you so highly prize.

George Washington, FAREWELL ADDRESS, 1796

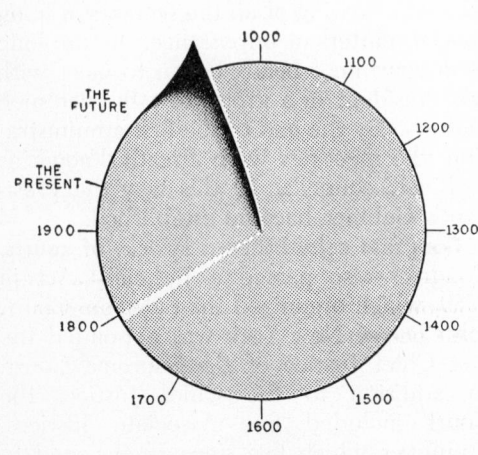

1789-1800

The day chosen for the official beginning of the new United States government was the fourth of March in 1789. By that date only a handful of senators and representatives had reached the city of New York, the temporary capital of the country. Bad roads and difficult traveling no doubt were responsible for the delay. But timid souls and others who thought ill of the new experiment in government saw in the delay a bad omen for the future. To the American of today such pessimism sounds strangely out of key. He considers the great strength and stirring accomplishments of his country and wonders how anyone in the 1700's could have doubted its future. But such uncertainties and fears were very real in those early days.

March of 1789 drifted into early April. Finally enough congressmen had reached New York to make a quorum for each house of Congress. It was not until the last day of April, however, that the formal inauguration of the President took place.

Even with the machinery of government at last in motion, the outlook was not encouraging. The Confederation had left unpaid salaries and a number of debts. The treasury was almost empty. At home, the government had to develop policies which would win the confidence of its citizens. Abroad, it had to win the respect of other nations. Much depended upon the wisdom of the new nation's leaders. This chapter will relate the steps which those leaders took to start the republic on its way and the extent to which they were successful. The story falls into four parts:

1. The new federal government is started.
2. Hamilton solves important financial problems.
3. The nation struggles with foreign problems.
4. The power of the Federalists is undermined.

1 The New Federal Government Is Started

Washington takes office. The first President's journey from his home at Mount Vernon to New York was a triumphal one, but Washington himself admitted that he was weighed down by serious doubts and fears. "My movements to the chair of government," he wrote, "will be accompanied by feelings not unlike those of a culprit who is going to the place of his execution; so unwilling am I, in the evening of a life nearly consumed in public cares, to quit a peaceful abode for an ocean of difficulties."

Nevertheless, the nation's strongest guarantee of success was its new President. No other man commanded so much respect and trust from the people. Few had worked as hard to unite the nation as Washington had. He had already shown his generalship in war, his determination, and his capacity to plan for distant goals. He did not display a flashing brilliance, but he did have the power to think things through.

When he made up his mind, nothing could turn him from the course he considered right and proper. His public acts had the stamp of dignity, justice, and courage. "Of all the great men in history, he was the most invariably judicious," commented a British historian.

Congress provides for executive departments. After its tardy opening, Congress settled down to work. One of its first actions was to set up executive departments to assist the President. It created the departments of Foreign Affairs (State), Treasury, and War, each department headed by a secretary. Two other important executive positions were created: that of attorney general to handle the legal business of the government, and postmaster general to take charge of post offices and post roads.

To fill these positions, Washington picked well-known Americans who had supported the Constitution. Thomas Jefferson became the Secretary of State. Alexander Hamilton, a lawyer of proven ability and a supporter of strong central government, was made Secretary of the Treasury. Henry Knox of Massachusetts was chosen Secretary of War and Edmund Randolph of Virginia became Attorney General. Washington soon adopted a policy of asking the advice in writing of all the secretaries upon special matters of importance. Before long the department heads began to meet with the President in a group to talk over such matters. By the end of the first administration, the meetings were already known as "cabinet" councils. In this way the President's Cabinet became established.

Congress establishes a system of courts. Congress also passed a Judiciary Act in 1789, which organized the Supreme Court. John Jay of New York was appointed the first Chief Justice of the Supreme Court. In addition to the Chief Justice, the Court included five Associate Justices, a number which has since been raised to eight. The act also created a series of federal courts in various parts of the country to deal with certain types of cases. One clause in the act was especially important in view of the tendency toward a stronger central government. It stated that the final judgment of any other court in the country — including the highest court of a state — might be re-examined in the Supreme Court if the case involved the Constitution, treaties, or federal laws.

——— CHECK-UP ———

How did the new federal government get started?

1. Why did the election of Washington help insure the success of the new government?
2. What executive departments were created by Congress? Who first filled these offices?
3. What were the provisions of the Judiciary Act of 1789?

2 Hamilton Solves Important Financial Problems

Hamilton tackles perplexing financial problems. The most urgent problem facing the first administration was the financial tangle the United States inherited from the Revolution and the Confederation. The credit for solving the problem belongs to the Secretary of the Treasury, Alexander Hamilton. Hamilton was only 32 years old, but he showed a boldness and a grasp of national affairs which rank him as one of our ablest financial leaders. He was of humble birth and was never a really wealthy man, but he had the viewpoint of businessmen and property owners who wanted the money matters of the nation handled with firmness. He aimed always to strengthen the central government. Hamilton drew up four reports (1790–91) which covered every angle of governmental finance. These reports painted a realistic picture of the nation's finances and made definite suggestions as to what to do about debts, banking, revenue, protection of manufactures, and coinage.

Hamilton proposes to settle the public debt. Hamilton's plan to pay off the public debt included three recommendations: (1) He proposed that the debt of the United

Washington's first Cabinet included Henry Knox (War), Thomas Jefferson (State), Alexander Hamilton (Treasury), and Edmund Randolph (Attorney General).

States to foreign creditors (nearly $12,000,000, including unpaid interest) be paid in full.

(2) He recommended full payment of the debt (over $40,000,000, with interest) which was owed by the government to the people of the United States. The certificates which represented these debts had been selling at prices considerably below their full value, owing to the government's weak financial condition. It would have been easy enough for the new government to make a settlement on these debts which was short of full payment. But Hamilton insisted that the certificates be redeemed in full. He pointed out that the United States had "repeatedly pledged" its word to pay. The only way in which government credit could be firmly established, he insisted, was by fulfilling this pledge.

(3) Hamilton recommended that the federal government assume the Revolutionary War debts owed by the states (over

$21,000,000). He said this would be "a measure of sound policy and substantial justice" both for the states and the Union.

Hamilton proposed that money to meet the entire federal and state debts should be raised by a single plan, rather than by many different plans. New bonds up to the full value of the state and Confederation certificates were to be issued by the federal government. Under such a plan, Hamilton argued, all public creditors would look to the federal government rather than to the states for the money owed them. Thus the strength and prestige of the Union would be increased.

Hamilton's proposals are adopted. One by one, the portions of Hamilton's program to build up the credit of the nation were adopted by Congress. The people who defended the program most strongly were, of course, those likely to profit by it, particularly the people who owned the debt certificates. Support also came from businessmen in general, who knew that conditions would improve as the state of public finances grew more settled. On the other hand, there were protests from the small farmers and the landowners. These people knew that most of the money to pay the debt would be raised by greatly increased taxes which they would have to pay, directly or indirectly. A loud outcry also rose from those who had sold debt certificates at a small fraction of their full value. Congress supported Hamilton's plan, however, and finally agreed to pay off the foreign and domestic debt of the United States at full value.

Hamilton's third recommendation — to take over state debts — caused a great turmoil. Some states had not contracted large debts during the war, and others had already paid a good part of theirs. Such states thought it was unfair for the federal government to pay the debts of states which had failed to keep their finances in order. Feeling ran high. The first formal vote in the House was against assuming the state debts. At this point Hamilton asked Thomas Jefferson for help. Some of the southern congressmen wanted to locate the capital city on the Potomac River rather than farther north. Jefferson obtained enough votes from southern congressmen to secure passage of Hamilton's bill. In return, an act was pushed through Congress which fixed the seat of the government for ten years at Philadelphia, then permanently on the banks of the Potomac.

Hamilton suggests a national bank. Hamilton urged the creation of a national bank. He believed that such a bank would provide a safe place to keep government funds. It would also help the government sell its bonds, and would issue a stable and uniform national currency, which would aid the country's business.

Congress approved Hamilton's suggestion. A bill was passed granting a charter to the Bank of the United States for a period of 20 years with a capital stock of $10,000,000. The bank was to be under private — not government — management, but the Secretary of the Treasury could demand weekly statements of the bank's condition. The government was to purchase one fifth of the stock; the balance would be in the hands of private individuals. The directors of the bank were given authority to establish branches in the states wherever they saw fit to do so. Furthermore, the bank had the right to issue bank notes (paper money) which could be used to pay taxes and debts to the government as long as the notes were "payable on demand, in gold and silver coin."

The national bank is started. The bank bill brought cries of protest even louder than those which had greeted Hamilton's earlier proposals. Southerners objected because a national bank would help the commercial North more than it would help the agricultural South. Others objected to what seemed another long stride in the direction of a stronger federal government. Thomas Jefferson attacked the bill so strongly that Washington asked three members of his cabinet for their opinions in writing.

Two documents of importance came out of this request. One, a protest written by Jefferson, challenged the bank bill on the ground that it was not constitutional. Jefferson argued for a *strict* interpretation

(Continued on page 150)

Alexander Hamilton
(1757-1804)

College Student

DURING THE REVOLUTIONARY WAR and the critical years that followed, America profited greatly from the talented services and patriotism of Alexander Hamilton. At King's College (Columbia) Hamilton's brilliance and his ability to learn attracted attention. When relations between the colonies and Great Britain became strained, the young student threw himself wholeheartedly into the patriot cause. During the Revolutionary War he served with distinction as Washington's aide and as an officer in the Continental army.

Hamilton constantly urged the need for a stronger government in the critical years that followed the Revolution. He was influential in issuing the call to the Constitutional Convention and worked hard to secure the ratification of the Constitution. With Madison and Jay he wrote the essays of *The Federalist*, which proved a strong force in bringing about the acceptance of the Constitution.

Continental Officer

Hamilton's crowning achievement was the establishment of a strong financial basis for the new republic. In a series of masterly reports, distinguished for their clear reasoning and grasp of financial principles, he set forth his ideas. Congress accepted his proposals, and the financial chaos which had threatened the nation was averted. Hamilton was also responsible for popularizing the idea of a strong federal authority. To achieve this he supported a broad interpretation of the powers granted to the federal government in the Constitution. Though born in lowly circumstances, he was aristocratic in sympathies and had little faith in the ability of the people to govern themselves efficiently.

Hamilton's friends were devoted to him, but his enemies feared him. One of the latter, Aaron Burr, challenged him to a duel. The two men met on the dueling field one beautiful July morning in 1804. Burr's first shot mortally wounded Hamilton, and thus death cut short a promising career in the prime of life.

Secretary of the Treasury

of the Constitution. To take one step beyond the powers clearly expressed in the fundamental law, he believed, was "to take possession of a boundless field of power, no longer susceptible of any definition." The other document, prepared by Hamilton, championed a *loose* interpretation of the Constitution. Hamilton insisted that the creation of a bank was constitutional because certain definite powers of Congress (those of borrowing money and regulating currency) contained in the Constitution itself could not be carried out without the aid of a bank.

Washington was convinced by Hamilton's reasoning. Believing that the idea of a national bank was economically sound, he signed the bill (February, 1791). Arguments for and against the bank sharpened the feeling between Americans who wanted to increase the central authority, and those who wanted to limit it. The debate also brought into the open the economic differences between the commercial North and the agricultural South.

Congress levies tariff duties. The next problem was to raise money to pay the government's expenses and reduce its debt. One of the first laws passed by Congress (1789) placed tariff duties on certain imported goods. This tariff was levied chiefly for revenue, rather than to encourage home industry. Two years later Hamilton ably presented the case for a system of protective duties aimed at encouraging home manufacturing. In 1792, when the need for more revenue made a change in the tariff rates necessary, Congress raised many rates

First Bank of the United States, Philadelphia

enough to protect home industries. The tariff measures of 1789 and 1792 were passed in spite of the protests of the merchants and farmers, who felt they were being taxed unfairly to help American manufacturing interests.

Congress levies an excise tax. When Hamilton found that the first tariff measure did not bring in enough money to the government, he turned to an *excise tax* (tax levied on goods manufactured, sold, and consumed within the country). He wanted an excise tax put on whisky distilled within the United States. Hamilton believed that an excise tax would accustom people to the taxing power of the central government. Congress once more followed his recommendations.

The whisky tax was a severe blow to the western farmers. They were in the habit of converting their surplus grain into whisky because bad roads and high transportation costs made anything as bulky as grain expensive to ship. What the sale of butter and eggs became to farmers later on, the sale of whisky was then. There was hardly a farmer in the western counties of Pennsylvania, Maryland, Virginia, or North Carolina who did not have a whisky still. These farmers protested vigorously that the whisky tax was a direct blow at their way of making a living. The matter came to a crisis in western Pennsylvania, where whisky was frequently used in place of money in business transactions. In the Whisky Rebellion of 1794 many farmers refused to pay the tax and government agents were attacked or forced to flee.

The Whisky Rebellion is put down. The federal government decided to meet this first open defiance of its authority with firmness. Hamilton led a force of militia across the mountains, accompanied part of the way by Washington. The army was unnecessarily large, partly because Hamilton wished to overawe the rebels. Opposition melted when the army drew near. Some leaders of the rebellion were arrested. Two of them were convicted but they were pardoned by the President. Although the firmness with which the Whisky Rebellion was put down gave new strength to the government, it increased the number of Americans who were against Hamilton's program.

Hamilton plans for sounder currency. Another part of Hamilton's financial program had to do with regulating and standardizing metal currency. There were too few coins in circulation, and among these were foreign coins of all kinds and denominations. The government, under the Articles of Confederation, had laid plans for a complete American coinage system, but had not actually issued many coins. To Hamilton the solution seemed to be the use of a decimal system of coinage. This system was to be based upon both silver and gold. Fifteen ounces of silver were to be equal in value to one ounce of gold.

The Mint Act of 1792 followed Hamilton's suggestion closely. A mint was established to coin the gold eagle ($10), half eagle, and quarter eagle. Silver was to be coined into dollars, half dollars, quarter dollars, dimes, and half dimes. Copper would be used for cents and half cents. These new coins, together with paper money issued by the national bank, provided a dependable currency.

The financial program aids prosperity. An upswing in American prosperity had started even before the inauguration of the new government. But there is no doubt that Hamilton's program did much to encourage better times. Paying the foreign debts strengthened the government's position abroad. In European markets the new bonds of the United States brought prices well above their face value. The stock of the United States Bank was selling at high prices. Trade between the states flourished now that it was no longer blocked by tariff walls. Before long, 90 per cent of the ships entering American ports were of American ownership, thanks to encouragement given American shippers by acts of Congress. Exports doubled between 1791 and 1794, as American vessels nosed their way into distant ports. Foreign wealth was eagerly invested in America. The outbreak of wars in Europe created lively markets for American manufacturing and commerce. The infant republic, nearly bankrupt a short time earlier, was already building up an

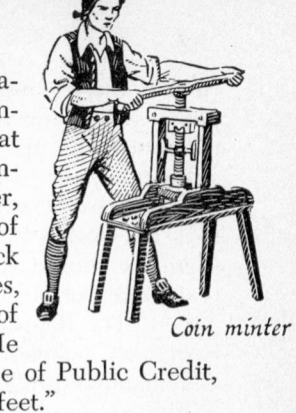

Coin minter

enviable financial reputation. All these accomplishments reflected great credit on Alexander Hamilton. Forty years later, Daniel Webster said of him, "He smote the rock of the national resources, and abundant streams of revenue gushed forth. He touched the dead corpse of Public Credit, and it sprang upon its feet."

Political parties are started. In spite of the general air of prosperity, many Americans were opposed to Hamilton's policies. The division of public opinion on these matters was so sharp that it led to the formation of political parties. The people supporting Hamilton were generally those who had wanted the Constitution in the first place, and now wanted a strong, centralized government under the guidance of a few leaders. They came to be called *Federalists,* and their ranks included great landowners, merchants and manufacturers, holders of government bonds, lawyers, and the clergy. Although they were a minority of the population, they were wealthy, influential, and well organized. Indeed, they were already so powerful that they controlled the government and its most important offices. A broad interpretation of the powers granted to the federal government in the Constitution was necessary to carry out their ideas. For that reason the Federalists became the party of *loose construction.* Federalist strength was centered largely in New England and the middle states.

As Hamilton rounded out his program he increased the number of his enemies. Nearly every move he made — paying the national debt in full, taking over state debts, starting the national bank, promoting tariffs and excise taxes — hurt some group. At last these groups united under the banner of Thomas Jefferson and took the name of *Democratic-Republicans,* or simply *Republicans.*[1] From their point of view, Hamilton was making a few people

[1] This party is not to be confused with the present Republican Party which was organized in the 1850's.

rich at the expense of the great mass of people. They did not think it right for one class to run the government — a class which, they felt, was using the government for its own advantage. Jefferson believed that the people as a whole — not just a small, privileged part of them — were the real source of authority and power in the nation. The Republicans also charged that Federalist policies helped the mercantile and manufacturing interests of the North at the expense of the agricultural South and the frontier regions. The Republicans saw that a narrow interpretation of the Constitution would check the plans of the Federalists. Thus the Republicans became the party of *strict construction*.

The parties test their strength. The two opposing parties had their first trial of strength in the election of 1792. Washington had not wanted to run for President again, but Jefferson and Hamilton persuaded him to do so. Washington received the vote of every elector. The real contest rose in the fight for the Vice-Presidency. The Federalists supported John Adams, who won the election, but the Republicans gained control of the House of Representatives. In spite of Washington's hatred of party strife, the differences between the Federalists and the Republicans grew steadily. When Washington finally retired in 1797, the two parties faced each other in open opposition. (See chart, page 215.)

——— CHECK-UP ———

How did Hamilton solve important financial problems?

1. What was the nature and purpose of each of these parts of Hamilton's program? (a) Full payment of the domestic and foreign debt, (b) Assumption of state debts, (c) Creation of a national bank, (d) Levying an excise tax and a tariff.
2. What parts of Hamilton's program aroused differences of opinion? Why?
3. How did Hamilton's program affect our national credit? the creation of political parties?
4. What part did political parties play in the election of 1792?

3 **The Nation Struggles With Foreign Problems**

The French Revolution arouses enthusiasm in America. Barely had the new government solved its financial troubles when it faced serious problems in its foreign relations. In 1789, the year that Washington was inaugurated, the French Revolution broke out. Because it was a revolt of the French people against the divine-right monarchy of Louis XVI and the privileged position of the upper classes, it aroused a great deal of sympathy among Americans in all parts of the country. When French revolutionists stormed the Bastille, a gloomy fortress in Paris, Americans applauded the event almost as loudly as they had cheered the blows struck at Lexington and Concord. "In no part of the globe," John Marshall wrote, "was this revolution hailed with more joy than in America." Americans were so enthusiastic that they adopted French mannerisms and ideas. They stopped using the titles of Sir and Mister, and substituted the "social and soul-warming term Citizen." They adopted the French slogan, "Liberty, Equality, Fraternity." In Boston pro-French enthusiasts changed the name of Royal Exchange Alley to Equality Lane, while in New York Crown Street was renamed Liberty Street. A popular enthusiasm for celebrations, including songs, pageants, and "civic feasts," was expressed on all sides.

Federalists and Republicans disagree over France. As it gathered strength, control of the French Revolution passed from moderate leaders to extremists. Certain Americans then began to have a change of heart about the French cause. Many followers of Hamilton distrusted the great emphasis placed by French revolutionists upon democracy and the rights of the common man, and were alarmed by the hostility shown to religion and social position. When America heard that the liberal La-

inter hood   Linen cap   Hood   Linen cap

WOMEN'S HATS REFLECTING FOREIGN INFLUENCE

fayette had been forced to flee for his life (1792), that Louis XVI had been beheaded (1793), and that France had been plunged into the Reign of Terror, even the more liberal Federalists lost all sympathy with the revolutionists.

The same could not be said of the Republicans. Jefferson did not approve of the violence, but he thought it a temporary stage of the Revolution which could not be avoided. All over the United States democratic societies sprang up, modeled after French political clubs. Extreme Republicans hoped that the equalizing process which had swept through France would take place also in America.

Washington issues a neutrality proclamation. It should be remembered that the United States was still under certain obligations to the French government by the treaties of 1778 (page 112). In these treaties it had agreed to help France in case her West Indian possessions were attacked, and to give French ships special privileges in American ports. Now it became necessary for the United States government to announce a policy toward the new French republic. A decision was forced in 1793 by the news that a minister, "Citizen" Genêt, was to arrive from the new French republic, and that war had broken out between France and Great Britain.[2]

Washington hurriedly called his cabinet together to decide how the new French government should be treated. Hamilton was firmly opposed to the French democratic ideas. He favored setting aside the treaties with France until the form of government in France should be settled. He

[2] The persecution of the French nobility and the attempts to spread the doctrines of the French Revolution all through Europe involved France in a war with the leading European countries, including Great Britain and Spain. The revolutionists, indeed, proclaimed their struggle as one of "all the peoples against all Kings."

wanted America to be neutral for the time being.

Jefferson, on the other hand, felt that the treaties were still binding, even though the French government had been completely changed. He wanted to keep the United States out of the European war, but he thought that a declaration of neutrality would aid Great Britain. If the United States declared neutrality, said Jefferson, it ought to receive something in return from Great Britain. But Washington opposed any bargaining. He issued a proclamation on April 22, 1793, announcing a friendly and neutral policy toward all the warring powers of Europe and warning American citizens to avoid all hostile acts.

Genêt arouses resentment. The President found that neutrality was not as easy to carry out as to announce. Citizen Genêt had landed in the South, where he was given a rousing welcome. He made plans at once to dispatch an expedition from American soil against Spanish-held territory in North America. Even before presenting himself to President Washington, he armed and outfitted a number of privateers, manned in part by American citizens, to prey on British commerce.

Genêt was hailed enthusiastically by Republicans all the way from Charleston to Philadelphia, but the President gave him a chilly reception. The French minister decided that Washington did not truly reflect the feelings of the American nation. He also felt that the people would support the French cause in case there was an open break with the government. In this Genêt was quite wrong. When he boldly tried to appeal to the American people over the President's head, he found he had gone too far. Even Jefferson joined Hamilton in urging Washington to request that France recall Genêt. Genêt's mission was over. Owing to a shift in the control of the

French government, however, he feared to return to France and was granted permission to remain in the United States as a private individual.

Relations with Great Britain grow critical. Meanwhile, there had been strained feelings between the United States and Great Britain ever since the close of the American Revolution. The British had broken the Treaty of 1783 by not removing their garrisons from the fur-trading posts on the Great Lakes, and by failing to pay for slaves carried off by their army. Moreover, Great Britain would not allow American shippers to trade with British colonies.

Another cause for resentment was the fact that the British government disregarded American rights on the high seas. France had been almost completely cut off from her colonies by the British fleet. As a result the French government threw open its West Indian ports to commerce with neutral countries. American merchants were quick to increase their profitable trade with the West Indies. But their joy over this situation turned to dismay when the British government ordered the seizure of all vessels carrying provisions or other supplies bound either to or from France or the French colonies (1793). As a result of this order, hundreds of American ships and their cargoes were seized. In many cases, too, American seamen were forced, or "impressed," into British service on the ground that they were Englishmen or deserters from the royal navy.

The parties disagree over war with Great Britain. These British actions drew an official protest from Thomas Jefferson, the Secretary of State. Many of Jefferson's followers, the Republicans, wanted even stronger measures taken against Great Britain. The Federalists, on the other hand, did not favor war with England. They felt that the United States was too young a nation to engage in a dangerous and costly struggle. Nor were they forgetting that British investors had bought American bonds, and furnished the credit for American trade and industry. An even more important reason for avoiding trouble with England was the fact that nearly 90 per cent of American imports came from Eng-

land. Duties on those imports furnished almost the entire federal income. Finally, Great Britain was fighting France, whose doctrines were hateful to the Federalists.

Now, added to all their other disagreements, the Federalists and the Republicans had a new difference of opinion over foreign affairs. Jefferson found himself out of sympathy with the administration and unable to serve any longer with Hamilton. He resigned as Secretary of State and was succeeded by Edmund Randolph.

Jay negotiates with Great Britain. In his anxiety to keep peace, Washington sent John Jay to England to settle the disputed matters. The treaty which Jay finally signed with Great Britain was unpleasant proof that the United States was a weak member in the family of nations. In Jay's Treaty, Great Britain agreed to withdraw from the northwestern frontier by June 1, 1796. She also agreed to submit to arbitration (settlement by a joint commission) certain disputed boundaries, as well as damages to American shippers for "illegal captures or condemnations." The British gave the Americans some trade privileges in the British Empire, but these fell far short of expectations, especially with reference to the West Indies. On its part the United States was to pay British creditors for losses caused by interference with the collection of Revolutionary debts. British vessels were to be admitted to American ports on favorable terms. But nothing was said about the British paying for the slaves carried off by the British army or about the way the British had forced American sailors into their service.

Jay's Treaty is approved despite protests. When the American people learned what was in Jay's Treaty — and what was not — they protested vigorously. Jay was accused of selling his country to Great Britain and was burned in effigy in many cities and towns. Hamilton was stoned in New York when he tried to speak in favor of the hated treaty. Even Washington was a target for criticism. Through the President's influence, however, the treaty was ratified by a bare two-thirds majority of the Senate in the summer of 1795. The terms were far from what Americans wanted, but to make any kind of treaty just then seemed a wise move. Peace was thus kept between the United States and Great Britain at a critical period in the history of the new republic.

The Pinckney Treaty is concluded. Another advantage of Jay's Treaty was that it cleared the way for a settlement of America's long-standing dispute with Spain. The Spanish government was afraid that the United States, with her British troubles settled, might threaten the safety of the Spanish empire in America. Late in 1795, therefore, Thomas Pinckney was able to conclude a treaty with Spain. The Pinckney Treaty fixed the boundary between the United States and West Florida, and it guaranteed to American citizens the right to navigate the Mississippi. Spain also granted the use of New Orleans as a "port of deposit," where American goods could be transferred from river boats to ocean-going vessels without payment of regular duties. This treaty went a long way toward satisfying the frontiersmen, although they were not too pleased to have New Orleans remain in the possession of a foreign power.

More Americans move to the frontier. The Jay and Pinckney treaties, coming soon after the Northwest Ordinance (page 129), helped to encourage settlement in the land beyond the Alleghenies. Previously the American urge to push westward had been blocked by the hostility of the Indians and the presence of the British and Spanish along the frontier. Congress tried to improve Indian relations by passing an act in 1790 to protect the natives from greedy traders and land speculators. However, when Indians attacked white settlers to stop their advance, the government used military force against them. The frontier militia under Governor Arthur St. Clair was badly defeated by the Indians in 1791, but Anthony Wayne won a decisive victory at Fallen Timbers in 1794. (See map, page 127.) Indian leaders later signed treaties which opened new frontier areas to white settlers. The Jay Treaty (which was made possible in part by Wayne's victory) and the Pinckney Treaty added further gains. The

John Jay, first Chief Justice of the Supreme Court and envoy to England, was honest, patriotic, but unpopular. An aristocrat, he once said, "Those who own the country ought to govern it."

withdrawal of the British from their frontier trading posts and the opening of the Mississippi to American navigation encouraged westward expansion.

More settlers now pushed their way into the wilderness. The wandering trapper and fur trader came first, then the squatter who settled on land to which he had no title, and finally the land-owning settler. The frontier offered them all the freedom of opportunity and equality among men which were vital traditions of American liberty. By 1800 Vermont, Kentucky, and Tennessee had been admitted to the Union on terms of complete equality with the original states.[3] By that time also the white population of the Northwest Territory had passed 45,000. Settlement of the Northwest Territory was also encouraged by an act (1800) which authorized the sale of public

[3] Vermont was admitted to the Union in 1791. Kentucky was accepted in the following year, and Tennessee became a state in 1796.

lands in half-section lots (320 acres) instead of section lots. A man who bought a half-section was allowed to pay for it at the rate of $160 per year, and could take four years to pay for the whole piece of land. Later (1820) the amount of land which must be purchased was reduced to as little as 80 acres, and the price was lowered as well.

Washington retires. Washington had been saddened by attacks upon his administration and by quarreling between the Federalists and Republicans. He made up his mind to retire at the end of his second term of office. He would then be 65 years old, and he could look back upon nearly half a century of devoted service to his state and country. His decision to retire was announced in a Farewell Address which has since become one of America's treasured public documents. In it he gravely warned the country of the evils of sectional jealousy and of "the baneful effects of the spirit of party." He stressed the need of continuing the policy of neutrality to avoid entanglements with foreign nations. His decision not to serve for a third term led to a custom in American government that a President should hold office no longer than two terms. That custom was not broken until 1940.

——— CHECK-UP ———

How did foreign problems affect the new nation?

1. How did the French Revolution further divide Americans?
2. Why did the neutrality proclamation cause controversy? What was the Genêt affair?
3. What grievances did the United States have against Great Britain? To what extent were these settled by Jay's Treaty? What was the effect of the treaty upon Americans?
4. What was the Pinckney Treaty? Why was it important?
5. What factors speeded up the settlement of the frontier? On what terms might settlers purchase western land?
6. What advice was contained in Washington's Farewell Address?

4 The Power of the Federalists Is Undermined

The Federalists elect John Adams. As the election of 1796 drew near, rivalry between the Federalists and Republicans grew more intense. The Federalists in Congress held a private conference and made clear their approval of John Adams for the Presidency and Thomas Pinckney (who had drawn up the Spanish treaty) for the Vice-Presidency. The Republicans held a meeting and recommended Jefferson for President and Aaron Burr for Vice-President.[4] Then Hamilton, who was not on the best of terms with Adams, worked out a scheme to make Pinckney the new President, instead of Adams. He tried to secure for Pinckney more electoral votes than Adams would get, and thus automatically elect Pinckney. But Adams' supporters discovered the trick. The result was that Adams, a Federalist, was elected President, while Thomas Jefferson, leader of the Republicans, became Vice-President.[5]

John Adams is not popular. John Adams did not have the qualities which make for popularity. His honesty and patriotism were beyond question, and he was studious, upright, and sincere. At the same time, Adams was vain and tactless and was out of tune with the democratic trend of the

[4] These congressional conferences, or *caucuses,* as they later were called, were not provided for in the Constitution. In theory, the electors were still to use their own judgment in the choice of candidates, but the caucus tended to concentrate votes on men who were satisfactory to the party leaders.

[5] Hamilton urged all the Federalist electors to vote for Adams and Pinckney. He expected, however, that certain southern Federalists would vote for Pinckney but not for Adams. In this way he thought Pinckney might secure more electoral votes than Adams and thus become President. As it happened, enough New England electors withheld their votes from Pinckney to make sure he would not slip in ahead of Adams. The result was the elimination of Pinckney altogether and the election of Jefferson to the Vice-Presidency.

Post rider

times. He found it hard to grasp the point of view of the mass of American people. Adams felt that the government should protect the poor from being exploited by the rich. But he also felt that the rich needed protection against those who tried to break down the special privileges which went with wealth and social position. He went on record as favoring control by "the rich, the well-born, and the able."

The XYZ Affair leads to a state of war. Foreign affairs kept troubling the government during Adams' administration. The French were angry over Jay's Treaty with Great Britain. They also charged that the United States was violating the French-American treaties of 1778. For these reasons the French government authorized seizure of American ships carrying British goods. French cruisers and privateers began to attack American ships.

But that was not all. At this time, the government of France was headed by a group of leaders known as the Directory. When the United States sent a minister, Charles C. Pinckney, to France, the Directory not only refused to receive him but practically forced him out of the country.

The extreme Federalists demanded war with France, just as the more extreme Republicans had called for action against England before Jay's Treaty. Instead, Adams sent John Marshall and Elbridge Gerry to join Pinckney in making terms with France. The French government did not officially recognize these envoys, but certain persons, claiming to speak for the Directory, talked with them. These French agents made outrageous demands, including a large sum of money for the "pocket of the Directory" before they would get down to the business of a settlement.

After much useless quarreling the Americans put an end to these underhanded dealings, and Marshall returned to America to report the whole story to Adams. Meanwhile Adams sent the reports of his envoys to Congress. In these reports the American envoys referred to the French agents as X, Y, and Z. News of the way the French had insulted the American commission was too much even for the Republicans. Many of them joined the Federalists in such slogans as "Millions for defense, but not one cent for tribute." The country swiftly grew war-conscious. Military preparations were made, and Washington was called upon to take command of a volunteer army. Though war was not actually declared, fighting took place between Frenchmen and Americans on the high seas.

A settlement is reached with France. When France saw that the United States could not be frightened into submission, she let it be known indirectly that a minister from the United States would now be received and treated with respect. Adams felt it his duty to make the most of the French offer, even though any step toward peace was contrary to the feeling of the Federalists. Adams sent commissioners to France in the autumn of 1799. Before their arrival, Napoleon Bonaparte had overthrown the corrupt Directory and made himself the head of a new government. Napoleon was easier to deal with than the Directory had been, and in 1800 an agreement was signed. Under that agreement France gave up the treaties of 1778 and trade was regulated between the two nations.

The Alien and Sedition laws are adopted. Out of the quarrel with France flared a new and more intense fight between the Federalists and the Republicans. The Federalists saw the advantage of using anti-French sentiment to make their party stronger. Under the claim of a national emergency, they forced measures through Congress that were aimed at weakening the Republicans:

(1) They passed a Naturalization Act which stated that to become a citizen a person had to live in the United States for fourteen years, instead of for five years,

the previous minimum. This meant that it would take Republican sympathizers (most immigrants were Republicans) nine more years to become citizens.

(2) An Alien Act gave the President power to order aliens whom he judged "dangerous to the peace and safety of the United States" to leave the country. This move was aimed at checking French influence.

(3) An additional alien law was passed which provided that in case of war or invasion the President could imprison or remove all alien enemies whose presence was a danger to public safety.

(4) Finally, a Sedition Act provided a fine and imprisonment for anyone who tried to hinder the operation of the government. There was a special section of the Sedition Act which was aimed especially at the Republican press. It called for punishment of anyone who made or published "false, scandalous, and malicious" statements against the government, Congress, or the President, or which tended "to stir up sedition within the United States."

People all over the country protested against the Alien and Sedition Acts. Although no persons were prosecuted under the Alien Acts, they stirred deep resentment among foreign-born citizens and noncitizens in the country. Under the Sedition Act, however, ten Republican editors or printers were tried and convicted. A Republican congressman from Vermont was actually fined and put in prison merely for stating that Adams had turned men out of office for party reasons, and for criticizing the President's "continual grasp for power" and his "unbounded thirst for ridiculous

pomp, foolish adulation, and selfish avarice."

Republicans protest the Alien and Sedition Acts. The Republicans made good use of the Alien and Sedition Acts to denounce the Federalists. They attacked the Acts as violations of the First Amendment to the Constitution, which guaranteed freedom of speech and the press to all Americans. Protests from Kentucky and Virginia carried the most weight. The Kentucky legislature adopted a set of resolutions opposing the Acts (autumn, 1798). These resolutions had been drawn up in part by Thomas Jefferson, and they emphasized the *compact* theory of union. This theory held that the Constitution was a compact, or agreement, among sovereign states which granted to the federal government certain definite powers. Since no power had been granted which permitted Congress to pass the Alien and Sedition acts, these acts were not legal. Other resolutions drawn up by James Madison were passed by the Virginia legislature. These resolutions called upon the states to defend their rights.

Some of the northern states criticized the Kentucky resolutions. The new, democratic, frontier state responded by having its legislature go even further the next year. It declared that 'the several states" had the right to pass upon acts of Congress. If the states decided that an act of Congress was unconstitutional, they did not have to obey it. Here was the puzzling problem of *states' rights* — a problem that was to appear again and again in the future.

Republicans win in the election of 1800. As the Adams administration drew to its end, feeling between the two parties ran high. Opposing the Federalists was the large body of small farmers, skilled workers, and small traders, under the leadership of Jefferson. During the campaign, the Republicans attacked the whole Federalist program: Hamilton's financial policy, loose interpretation of the Constitution, the growing centralization of government, the increase of taxes, failure to reduce the debt, and an increase in the number of public offices. The Alien and Sedition Acts were a special target because Jefferson had

Trapper

The Philadelphia Mint, for the manufacture of lawful coins, was the first building erected by the government for public use. It maintains an air of stability even in a modern setting. That stability probably helped persuade early citizens that their government was sound. A statue of William Penn is on top of the building in the background.

sworn "eternal hostility against every form of tyranny over the mind of man." Federalist difficulties were increased by disputes within the party, and by the fact that Adams' efforts toward peace with France took away their strongest issue — that of war.

As election time approached, it was clear that Jefferson would run for the Presidency on the Republican ticket. At the congressional caucus, Aaron Burr was chosen as his running mate. The Federalists again supported John Adams for President and Charles C. Pinckney for Vice-President.

Hamilton's dislike for Adams led him once more, as it had in 1796, to try to get the Federalist vice-presidential candidate elected President. But when the electoral votes were counted, Adams had 65, Pinckney 64, while Jefferson and Burr each had 73.

Thomas Jefferson becomes President. The tie vote meant that the House of Representatives had to choose between Jefferson and Burr for the Presidency.[6] The Federalists, by presenting a united front, could

[6] See Article II, Section 1, of the Constitution, page xxxix.

throw the Presidency to either Jefferson or Burr, or they could hold up the choice of a President indefinitely. Everyone knew that the Republicans wanted Jefferson for the Presidency. But most of the Federalists liked Burr better; he was young and brilliant, though undependable. Besides, his election would greatly embarrass the Republicans. At this point Hamilton stepped in and made his political weight felt. Though he disagreed sharply with Jefferson on many matters, he liked Jefferson better than Burr, whom he regarded as a man without principles. The contest in the House was bitter. On the thirty-sixth ballot, Jefferson was finally chosen. This election led to the adoption, in 1804, of the Twelfth Amendment, which provided that the electors should vote on separate ballots for President and Vice-President.

The Federalists keep their control of the courts. The bitterness between the parties grew even sharper just before Jefferson took office. During the closing days of the Federalist rule, Congress passed a Judiciary Act. This act established new positions for sixteen judges, as well as a number of marshals, clerks, and prosecuting attorneys. The Republicans naturally regarded this act as a trick of the Federalists to keep control of the one department of the federal government which was not controlled by popular vote. Because Adams was still at work signing commissions for the new officials on the night before Jefferson's inauguration, the men who received these commissions became known as "midnight judges." The Federalists may have considered the creation of new judges an act of great importance in preserving their principles, but of even greater importance was Adams' selection of John Marshall of Virginia as Chief Justice of the Supreme Court several weeks earlier (page 164).

The Federalists are credited with important contributions. The Federalists were defeated in 1800, but they could look back with satisfaction upon their achievements during the first twelve years of the republic. They had set the machinery of government in motion. They had established the United States upon the solid rock of sound finance. They had avoided serious trouble with other nations. They had firmly fixed the principle of adequate power in the federal government. They had served their purpose, but they no longer represented the popular will. The bankers, the merchants, and the manufacturers who controlled the Federalist party were only a small part of the population. Their insistence on the control of government by the well-born, the well educated, and the well-to-do seemed unfair and unreasonable to the small farmers and working people in the towns who made up the mass of the American people. Besides, the Federalist emphasis on nationalism had a great number of opponents who felt strongly about local patriotism and states' rights. It was the turn of the Republicans to take up the reins of government.

——————— CHECK-UP ———————

What developments contributed to the downfall of the Federalists?

1. What reasons did we have for going to war with France? How was war averted?
2. What were the provisions of (a) the Naturalization Act, (b) the Alien Acts, (c) the Sedition Act? Why were they passed? Why did they create ill feeling? How did the resolutions of the Virginia and Kentucky legislatures answer them?
3. What were the chief features of the election of 1800? What is meant by the term "midnight judges"?
4. What were the accomplishments of the Federalists?

CHAPTER REVIEW

Terms to Understand

executive departments
cabinet
debt certificates

excise tax
political parties
neutrality

Terms to Understand (Cont.)

loose interpretation
strict interpretation
assumption of debts

arbitration
compact theory of union
caucus

People and Things to Know About

Alexander Hamilton	Anthony Wayne
Thomas Jefferson	Thomas Pinckney
Judiciary Act of 1789	Charles C. Pinckney
John Jay	Washington's Farewell
Bank of the United	Address
States	XYZ Affair
Whisky Rebellion	Naturalization Act
Federalists	Sedition Act
Democratic-Republi-	Alien Act
cans	"midnight judges"
French Revolution	"Citizen" Genêt

Historic Dates to Identify

1789	1793	1800
1791	1795	

Questions to Discuss

1. In 1790 the United States was something new in the world. It was a triple experiment in *republicanism, federalism,* and *independence.* Explain each of these terms, and tell why each was an experiment to prove something to a skeptical world.

2. Why was it probably fortunate that the new government came into the hands of the Federalists in 1789, but that it passed out of those hands in 1800? One author says that "the downfall of the Federalists came because they had outlived their usefulness." Do you agree?

3. Compare the following:

   (*a*) The attitude towards the Whisky excise tax with that towards the Stamp tax.

   (*b*) The doctrines of loose and strict construction of the Constitution.

   (*c*) The problems of the Federalists with those of Parliament before the Revolution.

4. Why is an "opposition party" necessary in a democracy? Do you think that the Federal-

Questions to Discuss (Cont.)

ists and Democratic-Republicans understood the importance of an opposition party? Why or why not?

5. Before John Adams died, he requested as an epitaph, "Here lies John Adams who took upon himself the responsibility of peace with France in the year 1800." Can you explain his request?

6. The Sedition Act highlights the very serious problem of how far a democracy should go in allowing criticism of itself. How would you evaluate the Sedition Act?

7. Why might isolation from European politics have been the best policy for the United States in 1790 but not today?

Other Things to Do

1. Read the amusing and interesting story of the first days of the first Congress, in Bassett, *The Federalist System,* Chapter 1.

2. "Citizen" Genêt married an American woman and settled down in America. Prepare a more detailed report on his hectic career.

3. Debate: *Resolved,* That the Sedition Act was a violation of the First Amendment.

*4. Make a list of the chief parts of Hamilton's program and give the provisions of each.

*5. Prepare a two-column chart headed "Federalists" and "Democratic-Republicans." Compare the two groups as to foreign policy, financial policy, attitude towards the central government, and supporting groups.

6. Imagine that you are a cartoonist for either a Federalist or a Democratic-Republican newspaper. Draw a cartoon to sway public opinion on one of these issues: (*a*) the creation of a national bank, (*b*) relations with France and England, or (*c*) enactment of a tariff.

Trapper

Chapter 8

REPUBLICANS STRENGTHEN THE

NATION AT HOME AND ABROAD

Still one more thing, fellow citizens — a wise and frugal government, which shall restrain men from injuring one another, shall leave them otherwise free to regulate their own pursuits of industry and improvement, and shall not take from the mouth of labor the bread it has earned. This is the sum of good government, and this is necessary to close the circle of our felicities.

Thomas Jefferson, FIRST INAUGURAL ADDRESS, 1801

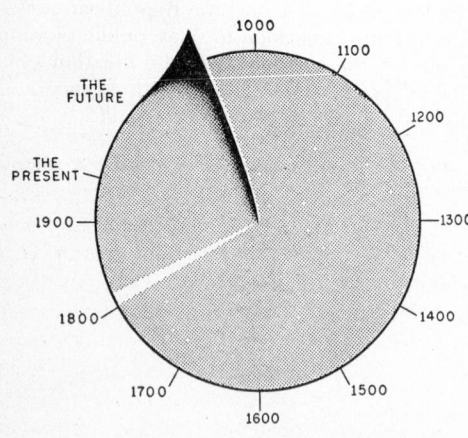

1801-1815

There were some noticeable differences between the first presidential inauguration and the one which took place on March 4, 1801. One difference grew out of the increasing importance of political parties. When Washington went into office, there were many problems to be solved, but at least there was no tug of war between parties. Now Republicans under Jefferson moved eagerly into the government while Federalists moved grudgingly out.

Another difference arose from the circumstances of the inauguration itself. Washington had taken the oath of office in New York City, but Jefferson took over the reins of power in the new and permanent United States capital on the Potomac River. The city of Washington then was a far cry from thriving New York and nothing at all like the capital of today. Situated

162

in a wilderness, it contained only a few shops and boarding houses scattered around the rising public buildings. It was described in this sarcastic way by Gouverneur Morris: "We want [lack] nothing here but houses, cellars, kitchens, well-informed men, amiable women, and other little trifles of this kind, to make our city perfect." To make the difference between this inauguration and the first one even sharper, the pomp and show of the earlier administrations were completely absent. Instead, the keynote of this first Republican inauguration was simplicity, in keeping with the ideals of the new President. Thomas Jefferson, looking very much like a "tall, large-boned farmer," walked from his lodging to the still-unfinished Capitol with as little ceremony as a businessman going to work.

This inauguration marked the beginning of a long period of Republican control. Jefferson and his successor, James Madison, each served for two administrations. During that time, new policies were put into action. The United States doubled in size, strengthened its industry, and fought a war to protect its rights. This chapter recounts, under the following major headings, what happened to the nation when the Republicans took charge:

1. The Republicans introduce new policies.
2. The Louisiana Purchase doubles United States territory.
3. Jefferson struggles to protect American rights.
4. The United States is drawn toward war.
5. The War of 1812 increases the prestige of the United States.

1 The Republicans Introduce New Policies

Jefferson brings about a peaceful revolution. The change from Federalist to Republican control promised such drastic changes that Jefferson and other Republicans called it the "Revolution of 1800." The beliefs of Hamilton and Jefferson differed quite sharply. For example, Jefferson believed that the federal government should be limited in its activities to the defense of the nation, to foreign relations, and to matters of national concern. Other duties of government, he felt, should be left to the states. Again, Jefferson was far too democratic in his principles to agree with the Federalist doctrine of government by the rich and the well-born. For Jefferson, government was not something above or beyond the people; it was the people themselves, speaking and acting through their chosen representatives. Thus, in theory at least, Jeffersonian democracy meant the use of political power by the majority of American citizens.

President Jefferson's ideas of government, as well as his liberal points of view concerning popular education and religious freedom, made the Federalists decidedly uneasy. Actually, when the Republican administration got under way, it proved to be surprisingly moderate. The gloomy warnings of revolution sounded by some Federalists proved to be false. For all his lofty idealism, Jefferson was a practical politician. He saw that by winning Federalists to the Republican Party, rather than by offending them, he could gain more in the long run. He was supported in his policies by James Madison as Secretary of State, and by Albert Gallatin, one of the best informed and ablest financiers of America, as Secretary of the Treasury.

Jefferson introduces democratic customs. Jefferson disliked some of the customs that had been started by the Federalists, customs which he felt were not democratic. He promptly dropped them. For instance, the custom which Washington had started of delivering his message to Congress in person made Republicans think of the king of England speaking to Parliament. Since Jefferson was not a good speaker anyway, he changed this custom by sending his recommendations to Congress in writing. All succeeding Presidents did the same until the days of Woodrow Wilson (1913–

John Marshall, Chief Justice of the Supreme Court for 34 years, wrote many decisions which increased the power of the national government.

1921). Jefferson likewise put an end to many of the social customs of the Federalist period. He dropped the stately receptions and the formal atmosphere which had been part of Washington's administration. In their place, Jefferson offered the generous hospitality of a Virginia planter, at whose table everyone was welcome.

Republicans become officeholders. Jefferson also made changes among the federal officeholders. He found government positions almost entirely in the hands of Federalists. While he did not make wholesale removals, he filled whatever vacancies occurred with members of his own party. The process was a slow one at best; as Jefferson expressed it, "Few government officials die and none resign." By the end of his first term, about half the offices at his disposal were held by Republicans.

Congress reverses Federalist policies. Congress followed Jefferson's lead in its program of legislation. The keynote of this program was simplicity and economy in government. Steps were taken to save money and to reduce the public debt, which Jefferson and Gallatin believed should be paid off as quickly as possible. Expenses of government were sharply cut and government funds were appropriated only for definite purposes. Many government jobs were eliminated, and the number of officials in foreign service was reduced. The army, already small, was cut down to about 3000 men.

The unpopular Alien and Sedition Acts had expired before Jefferson became President. Now Congress reduced to five years the term of residence needed to become a citizen. No changes were made in the tariff and the national bank, but Congress did repeal the excise taxes, including the one on whisky. This move greatly pleased the Westerners. Congress also passed legislation which established the Congressional Library and authorized a military academy at West Point.

Federalists remain strong in the courts. One of the early acts of Congress under Jefferson was to repeal the Judiciary Act of 1801. This threw out of office some judges who would otherwise have served as long as their conduct was suitable. The Federalists protested bitterly that the repeal of the act was not constitutional. Even after these judges were removed, however, the courts were still controlled almost entirely by Federalists. The Republicans therefore planned to weaken the Federalist hold by impeaching several Federalist judges. One Federalist judge was removed by impeachment, but when the Republicans impeached Justice Chase of the Supreme Court, they could not muster enough votes in the Senate to convict him. After that failure, they gave up their attack upon the courts.

Marshall strengthens the federal government. So far, the activities of Jefferson and the Republicans could hardly be called dangerous or destructive. Indeed, it seemed unlikely that any attack on the powers of the federal government would succeed while John Marshall remained Chief Justice of the Supreme Court.

Marshall had grown up among the hardships of the Virginia frontier. He had had

(Continued on page 166)

Thomas Jefferson
(1743-1826)

Political Writer

THOMAS JEFFERSON, like George Washington and Alexander Hamilton, made important contributions to his country during its formative years. Growing up amid comfortable circumstances in Virginia, Jefferson attended William and Mary College, and then studied law. Events interrupted his legal career, however, and he became active in the patriot cause. A member of the Continental Congresses, he was chiefly responsible for the ideas and style of the Declaration of Independence. From 1776 to 1781 Jefferson served Virginia as a member of the legislature and as its governor.

For the next 25 years or so public service of one kind or another claimed Jefferson almost continuously. He helped in the movement to persuade the states to surrender their claims to western lands. He drafted the plan of government for the Northwest Territory. From 1784 to 1789 he served as minister to France. When the federal government got under way in 1789, he became its first Secretary of State, but he resigned four years later because of sharp differences of opinion with Hamilton. Jefferson drew up the Kentucky Resolutions in protest to the Alien and Sedition Acts. In 1800 he was elected President. During his two terms the outstanding events were the purchase of

President

Louisiana and growing tension with Great Britain over violations of American rights. In 1809 he retired to his home at Monticello. His advice was sought by both Madison and Monroe on important public questions.

Two of Jefferson's outstanding characteristics were his strong belief in democracy and in freedom of thought. His democratic feelings led him to be inaugurated without pomp or ceremony and to receive the dignified representative of Great Britain in informal dress and heelless slippers. His freedom of thought was evident in his theories of education and religion, which were advanced for his times. Though his enthusiasm often carried him, as one biographer says, "to the edge of personal imprudence, . . . he always stopped short of that line." In practice, Jefferson tempered his theories to meet the cold facts of reality.

Architect

little opportunity for schooling, and had studied law for only a few months at William and Mary College. He served in the army during the Revolution. Later he fought for the adoption of the Constitution in his native state, and then held government offices both at home and abroad under the Federalist administrations (pages 137 and 157).

As Chief Justice, Marshall showed keen intellect, as well as ease and forcefulness in expressing himself. Thanks to these qualities, his legal opinions have become landmarks in the development of the Supreme Court. At the very time when the Republican program was getting under way, Marshall laid down the important principle that the Supreme Court had the power to declare an act of Congress unconstitutional (Marbury *vs.* Madison, 1803). Jefferson and his followers read the opinion with dismay, because they felt that it gave the courts too much power over the other branches of government.

——— CHECK-UP ———

What new policies were adopted by the Republicans?

1. What important changes did the inauguration of Thomas Jefferson bring?
2. What policies of the Federalists did the Republicans drop or change? What policies did they keep?
3. How did the Federalists continue to exercise some power in Jefferson's administration? How did John Marshall's decisions influence government policy?

2 **The Louisiana Purchase Doubles United States Territory**

Napoleon alarms the United States. The Republicans were interrupted in carrying out their program by the turn of events in Europe and the threat of foreign interference along the Mississippi. In 1800, the day after France signed the treaty that restored peaceful relations with the United States (page 157), Napoleon made a secret treaty with Spain. By it, he secured for France the territory known as Louisiana, west of the Mississippi River. Two years later our right of deposit at New Orleans (page 155) was withdrawn. This action stopped the Mississippi-overseas trade, which made up almost 40 per cent of American exports.

The news was a bombshell to Americans. The West was bitterly indignant, and the government was alarmed. It was easy enough to see what Napoleon planned. Now that he owned Louisiana, he was surely going to re-establish a French colonial empire in America. Jefferson was fully aware of the significance of the move. In 1802 he wrote a message to the United States representative in France, Robert R. Livingston, in which he said:

There is on the globe one single spot, the possessor of which is our natural and habitual enemy. It is New Orleans, through which the produce of three eighths of our territory must pass to market. . . . The day that France takes possession of N. Orleans . . . we must marry ourselves to the British fleet and nation.

Jefferson tries to buy New Orleans. From beyond the mountains came an urgent call for war, and the government was flooded with demands for immediate action. Jefferson instructed Livingston to sound out Napoleon on the possibility of buying New Orleans and the Florida region east of the Mississippi. Congress voted $2,000,000 to pay any unusual expenses that might be needed in negotiations between the United States and foreign nations. James Monroe was sent to help Livingston in his talks with the French government.

Napoleon sells all of Louisiana. Luckily the chain of events played into the hands of these American commissioners. First, a stubborn revolt had previously broken out in the rich French island of Santo Domingo, formerly called Hispaniola. (See map, page 116.) A French expedition sent to put it down had met with disaster. Moreover, an uneasy peace between France and England seemed about to end. Napoleon, realizing that France was headed for another war, knew that he would need money. With Great Britain in control of the seas, he was not anxious to undertake the defense of Louisiana. For these important reasons, Napoleon suddenly dropped his colonial project. Through his minister of foreign affairs, he offered to sell to the United States the entire territory of Louisiana.

Castle, French Island of Santo Domingo

Though the astonished Livingston had no instructions to buy this huge empire, he accepted the French offer. When Monroe arrived, he helped draw up the terms of the sale. In 1803 the vast Louisiana region became the possession of the United States for approximately $15,000,000. (See map, page 169.) Three fourths of this sum was to be paid in the form of United States bonds. The remainder was to be kept in the United States to pay claims that American citizens held against France for damages to trade.

Livingston realized the future importance of Louisiana. After they had finished the treaty of purchase, he is said to have told the men who worked with him: "We have lived long, but this is the noblest work of our whole lives . . . From this day the United States take their place among the powers of the first rank."

The purchase violates Republican principles. When the news of the Louisiana Purchase reached America, Jefferson found himself in an embarrassing position. He had been one of the strongest enemies of the Hamilton program because it increased the national debt. As a cornerstone of his own program, he had promised to reduce that debt. Now suddenly he was called upon to add $15,000,000 to the debt at one stroke. Jefferson had also bitterly attacked the Federalists for interpreting the Constitution freely. Yet to justify the purchase of Louisiana he would have to interpret the Constitution loosely himself; there was not a word in it which definitely gave the United States the right to buy a single foot of land. To make his position even more embarrassing, the purchase of Louisiana would place under the control of the

federal government an area larger than all the states put together. Yet Jefferson had always believed that the federal government should be limited to as few activities as possible.

Jefferson thought of recommending that Congress propose an amendment to the Constitution to make the purchase of Louisiana legal. An amendment was a slow process, however, and reports from Livingston warned that Napoleon might change his mind. For those reasons, Jefferson took the advice of men around him who said that the purchase of Louisiana could be justified under the treaty-making power of the Constitution. Jefferson admitted that the government had probably gone beyond its authority, but he felt that a majority of the people would approve of what was being done.

The Louisiana Purchase is ratified. In the debate over ratifying the purchase treaty in the Senate, the Republicans and the Federalists switched their usual positions. Now it was the Federalists who challenged the constitutional right of the President or Senate to add Louisiana to the Union, and who objected to spending so much money. Behind these Federalist objections was the fact that the commercial and industrial interests, the backbone of the Federalist party, saw little to be gained from western expansion. Besides, they were afraid the purchase would hasten the time when congressmen from beyond the mountains would be able to outvote the senators and representatives of the seaboard states. But the purchase treaty was ratified over Federalist protests. In December, 1803,

Lewis and Clark are shown here at the end of a portage around a falls in the Columbia River, which now forms the boundary between the states of Oregon and Washington. Sacajawea, an Indian woman guide, appears at the right. In their journals, Lewis and Clark gave her credit for being of great assistance to the expedition.

the Stars and Stripes were hoisted over government buildings in New Orleans. At one stroke, the size of the United States was doubled. The new territory proved to be one of the richest areas in the world. An immediate outcome of the purchase was the strong loyalty which the western frontier showed the national administration which had so effectively met its needs.[1]

Spain and America argue over West Florida. Another outcome of the purchase was a dispute between the United States and Spain as to who owned western Florida. The treaty with France set the same boundary for Louisiana as the territory had under the French before 1763, and later in the hands of Spain. (See map, page 116.)

[1] In 1804 Louisiana was divided into two parts, the District of Louisiana and the Territory of Orleans. (See map, page 169.) The Territory of Orleans, in which most of the inhabitants were to be found, was placed under the complete control of the President. This situation was changed the next year to permit an elected territorial assembly and a delegate to Congress. It was not, however, until the Territory of Orleans was admitted to the Union as the state of Louisiana in 1812 that its residents received the full rights and privileges of American citizens guaranteed by the treaty of purchase. The Federalists found in this whole course of action further unjustified stretching of the Constitution.

Actually this description did not make clear whether West Florida was part of the purchase. Napoleon did not consider it so, but Jefferson became convinced that the United States *had* bought West Florida as part of the Louisiana Purchase. The long drawn-out quarrel was still going on when Madison, Jefferson's successor, was President. When a revolt broke out inside the disputed area, President Madison seized the chance to take possession of West Florida by proclamation (1810). About half the disputed area was taken and made a part of the Territory of Orleans, and two years later of the state of Louisiana. The rest was attached to Mississippi Territory in 1813.

Lewis and Clark reach the Pacific. President Jefferson had long been curious about the territory of Louisiana and its possibilities. Authorized by Congress, Jefferson's secretary, Meriwether Lewis, and Lieutenant William Clark (a younger brother of George Rogers Clark) made preparations to lead a group of nearly 50 soldiers to explore the western lands. In May of 1804 they struck west from a point near St. Louis, and followed the Missouri River to the vicinity of what is now Bismarck, North Dakota. Here they spent their first winter among the Mandan Indians. Then they crossed the Continental (or "Great") Divide which separates the Mississippi valley from the Pacific watershed. (See map below.) In August, 1805, the expedition came to a branch of the Columbia River and three months later they reached the "roreing" ocean. After spending the second winter near the mouth of the Columbia, the group returned to St. Louis, arriving in September, 1806.

The members of the expedition gave valuable reports about their experiences. Their reports described the strange wonders of nature that they had seen, and the resources and opportunities for trade which this new country had to offer. The explorations by Lewis and Clark opened the gate to the Far West. Later on, it gave the United States a stronger claim to the Oregon Country.

Pike explores the Southwest. The Lewis and Clark expedition was not the only one to explore the new territory. In 1805–06 Lieutenant Zebulon Pike explored the headwaters of the Mississippi River. He was then commissioned to lead an expedition into the Southwest. Starting from St. Louis, Pike headed west to the Arkansas River. He followed this river until he reached the region near the peak which is named after him in what is now Colorado. Then Pike and some of his men turned south to find the source of the Red River, and soon found themselves in Spanish territory. (See map below.) As they fol-

The expeditions of Lewis and Clark and of Pike generally followed rivers. Why? Why did they cross mountain ranges when they did? What were the practical results of these expeditions? Compare the boundaries of the Louisiana Purchase as shown on this map with the settlement agreed upon in the Treaty of 1819 (see map on page 280).

Americans Explore the Far West

R. M. Chapin

lowed the course of the Rio Grande — by mistake, Pike said — they were arrested by Spanish authorities for trespassing. When Pike was released, he came back through Texas and reached American territory in the summer of 1807. Although the Spaniards had taken his papers from him, Pike remembered a great deal of what he had seen, and brought back much useful information about the Southwest.

Jefferson is re-elected. The Republicans approached the election of 1804 in a strong position. Under their four-year administration, the country had become prosperous, and the national debt had been considerably reduced in spite of the Louisiana purchase. Jefferson's policies were generally approved, while the Federalists had made themselves unpopular by their actions. Jefferson was easily re-elected over the Federalist candidate, Charles C. Pinckney. That democratic ideas were gaining headway was shown by the increased number of states in which presidential electors were chosen by popular vote. The "Revolution of 1800" may have disappointed some of its critics because it was peaceful, but it was a real revolution just the same. Jefferson had tempered some of his beliefs in order

to solve the practical problems, but his dream of the common man as the ruler of the country was taking firm hold in America.

——————— CHECK-UP ———————

How did the United States secure the Louisiana Territory?

1. How did the transfer of Louisiana to France threaten United States interests?
2. What developments led to the sale of Louisiana to the United States?
3. On what grounds was the purchase opposed? What were Jefferson's views?
4. What regions were explored by Lewis and Clark? By Zebulon Pike?

3 **Jefferson Struggles to Protect American Rights**

The Barbary States, in North Africa, take their name from the Berbers, their chief inhabitants. How did they interfere with the commerce of other nations? How did the United States end their interference? Which state was the first to make peace?

Jefferson opposes Mediterranean pirates. Almost from the time he became President, Jefferson was plagued by foreign troubles just as Washington and Adams had been. Jefferson found that American shipping had to be protected from pirates in the Mediterranean Sea. For years, the Mohammedan rulers of Tripoli, Tunisia, Algeria, Fez, and Morocco (the Barbary states) in northern Africa had been seizing the ships of Christian nations and holding their crews for ransom. (See map, this page.) Washington and Adams, with no navy strong enough to fight back, had done as European powers did — they had bought peace by paying annual tribute to these North African states. To Jefferson, this was throwing money away. Even though he was opposed to a warlike policy, he believed that a show of force was the only way to deal with the Barbary pirates.

Therefore Jefferson sent a small squadron of American ships to the Mediterranean in 1801. When the news came back that the ruler of Tripoli had practically declared war by cutting down the flagstaff of the

Barbary States

SPAIN

PORTUGAL

Cape Trafalgar

Elba

Mediterranean Sea

ALGERIA

TUNISIA

TRIPOLI

FEZ

MOROCCO

A F R I C A

■ Barbary States   R.M.C.

American consulate there, more ships were sent over. The American fleet, operating thousands of miles from home, gave a fine account of itself. However, hostilities dragged on for four years before Tripoli made peace. Many more years passed before the United States was able to get guarantees of safety for American ships from the other North African rulers.

American neutrality rights are threatened. The trouble with the Barbary pirates was unimportant compared with a new situation which arose in 1803. When war broke out between France and Great Britain in that year, the problem of protecting American rights became very difficult. By a series of masterly strokes, Napoleon managed to gain control of a large part of Europe. Great Britain, however, kept control of the sea as a result of Admiral Nelson's smashing victory at Trafalgar in 1805. After that, "the tiger and the shark" (Napoleon and England) were locked in a struggle so bitter that neither one thought or cared much about the neutral rights of the United States.

France and England seize American ships. The pressure on American shipping and trade came from both sides. In order to starve Napoleon and his allies into surrender, Great Britain issued what were called *orders in council*. These orders said that neutral ships would not be neutral in British eyes if they went into European ports controlled by Napoleon.[2] Napoleon, on the other hand, issued a number of decrees, the most important of which were the Berlin and Milan decrees. These warned that any neutral ships which traded with the British Isles or let themselves be searched by British cruisers were liable to seizure by France. Caught in this crossfire of orders and decrees, American trade was badly crippled.

[2] The plight of American shippers had been made worse by the British decision in the *Essex* case (1805). A British court held that this American vessel engaged in carrying enemy goods to an enemy port was subject to seizure even though it stopped en route in an American port. Scores of American vessels engaged in such broken voyages were captured by the British.

British seaman

Actually Napoleon didn't have the naval power to do serious damage to neutral shipping, but Great Britain did. British men-of-war were often stationed outside American harbors to keep a watchful eye on ships that came in and went out. American vessels had to "look sharp" to escape the British net. Even so, many American captains ran the blockades. High merchandise prices and rising freight rates brought such fantastic profits that a merchant made money if only one out of three of his ships dodged the British cruisers and landed its cargo. The export trade of the United States in 1807 — even when ship after ship was being seized by the British — was the highest in its history until 1835. Customs revenues for 1807 were nearly twice those of any year before 1800.

American sailors seized by Great Britain. The British blockade was only one of several serious difficulties that America faced during the Napoleonic Wars in Europe. A second was the hateful practice of *impressment*, which resulted in the forcing of American sailors into British naval service. The rapid growth of American commerce created a demand for more and more sailors on American merchant vessels. To get them, American shippers paid seamen high wages, gave them good food and fair treatment. These working conditions were so much better than Great Britain's that thousands of British sailors deserted their country's merchant marine and navy for American service. Soon Great Britain was in serious need of seamen and to meet this need she resorted to impressment on a wide scale.[3] For instance, when an American ship reached a British port, it was searched. It might even be stopped on the

[3] Impressment was not practiced merely in the case of American sailors. It was the usual way of recruiting man power for the British navy. British sailors were regularly impressed from British merchant ships to serve on British warships.

British naval officer

high seas by British cruisers. British officers inspected the crew and if they decided that an American sailor was a British deserter, they seized him. The fact that a sailor carried American naturalization papers made no difference to the British; their answer was "once an Englishman, always an Englishman." Mistakes were often made, accidentally or purposely, and many native-born Americans were carried off to serve on British men-of-war.

The "Chesapeake Affair" outrages America. Impressment was bad enough when it was used against American merchantmen. When it touched the American navy, it became a direct insult. In June, 1807, the American frigate *Chesapeake* set out from Hampton Roads for the Mediterranean. Only a short distance off the Virginia shore, within the three-mile limit,[4] it was overhauled by the British ship-of-war *Leopard,* which sent an officer to search the *Chesapeake* for deserters. The American commander, Commodore Barron, told the British officer he had no deserters aboard and that he would not let his men "be mustered by any other but their own officers."

The British officer left. Then, without warning, the *Leopard* opened fire. Three American sailors were killed and eighteen wounded. Commodore Barron had not been ready for a sudden attack, and he struck his colors. The British searched the ship and took away four men they said were deserters, three of whom proved to be Americans. The unlucky *Chesapeake* was then left to limp back to her home port. The United States protested vigorously to Great Britain, and the British foreign secretary agreed to make payment for the attack of the *Leopard.* But he refused even to discuss the impressment of American seamen. The British went right on with this practice.

Jefferson tries an embargo on trade. Americans were outraged by such happenings, but instead of using force to defend neutral rights Jefferson attempted to find

[4] According to international law, a nation's authority extends over the area three miles off its shores.

"peaceable means of repressing injustice." Actually there was little else for him to do because the policy of economy adopted during his first term had left the army and navy in no condition to fight a war.

Jefferson hoped to force England and France to recognize American rights by depriving them of American trade. He thought that American trade was so important to France and England that they could not run the risk of having it cut off. To apply economic pressure, he had signed a bill in 1806 that stopped many articles of British manufacture from being imported into the United States. He increased the pressure near the end of 1807 when he recommended — and Congress passed — an Embargo Act. The Embargo Act stated that no American ship carrying cargo would be allowed to leave for a foreign port. The embargo went into effect at once and remained a law for nearly fifteen months.

The embargo fails. The embargo turned out to be a boomerang. Not only did it fail to bring France and England to terms; it nearly ruined American commercial and financial interests. Exports fell alarmingly — in 1808 they were only a fifth of the previous year's exports. Government income, most of which came from duties on imports, fell during the time of the embargo to less than half of its former level.

Of course the manufacture of goods in America picked up because there were no foreign goods for sale. But every port along the Atlantic was crowded with idle and rotting ships. Warehouses were soon filled to bursting with products waiting for export. A traveler observed of New York: "The streets near the water-side were almost deserted, the *grass had begun to grow* upon the wharfs." Carpenters, sailmakers, and seamen were thrown out of work.

Shipbuilding stopped almost entirely. Merchants went into bankruptcy. Farmers lost a large part of the market for the crops they raised.

In New England and along the Canadian frontier there was widespread smuggling to avoid the embargo. The smuggling led to the passage of strict enforcement acts, and these acts in turn aroused further bitterness. In the commercial Northeast there were threats of *secession* (withdrawal from the Union). Finally, just before Jefferson left the presidency (March, 1809), Federalists working with discontented Republicans forced repeal of the hated Embargo Act.

----------- CHECK-UP -----------

How did Jefferson try to protect American neutral rights?

1. What steps did Jefferson take against the Barbary states?
2. How did both France and England violate our neutral rights? What was the "Chesapeake Affair"?
3. How did Jefferson hope to bring France and England to terms? Why did this method fail?

4 The United States Is Drawn Toward War

Madison tries a new trade policy. In the election of 1808, the Republican party under James Madison won an easy victory, though the Northeast voted solidly against the Republican ticket. Now it was Madison's turn to look for a safe path through the tangle of foreign affairs. On the whole, Madison leaned toward Jefferson's policy of economic pressure. The act which repealed the embargo in 1809 substituted a policy of non-intercourse. "Nonintercourse" meant that while trade with Great Britain, France, and their colonies was strictly forbidden, trade with the rest of the world was permitted. The Non-Intercourse Act also stated that, if either France or Great Britain called off its restrictions on American shipping, America would trade once more with that country. Under the Non-Intercourse Act, American trade improved somewhat, but relations with Great Britain and Napoleon remained unsatisfactory.

The Macon Act changes American policy. In the spring of 1810 America tried a new way to escape from its commercial straitjacket. A new law, the Macon Bill, reopened trade with all countries for one year. The law added, however, that if either Great Britain or France withdrew its trade decrees — and the other did not follow suit within three months — then the Non-Intercourse Act would go back into effect against the other country. Although such bargaining did not add to American prestige, American shipping improved. In the year after the Macon Bill was passed, exports from the United States rose to more than $60,000,000 in value.

Napoleon springs a trap. The person most displeased by the Macon Bill was Napoleon, who up to this time had found America's commercial policy very satisfactory. The embargo had fitted in perfectly with his plans to stifle British trade, and the Non-Intercourse Act had served almost as well. The Macon Bill he did not like at all. It gave the British a market in the United States which would help make up for their loss of trade on the European continent. Besides, the British fleet was able to block American trade with France and with French territory.

Nevertheless, Napoleon saw in the Macon Act a chance to trap America into ending trade relations with Britain. He might even be able to use it to drag the United States into open conflict with England. He first announced through his minister of foreign affairs that the Berlin and Milan decrees were revoked by France, "it being under-

American seaman

stood that, in consequence of this declaration, the English shall revoke their orders in council . . . ; or that the United States . . . shall cause their rights to be respected by the English." The note added: "His Majesty loves the Americans. Their prosperity and their commerce are within the scope of his policy."

President Madison fell right into the trap, a trap which, as one statesman predicted, "would catch us in an English war." Madison gave Great Britain three months' notice that non-intercourse would be used against her again unless the English orders in council were repealed. America soon found that Napoleon's Berlin and Milan decrees actually remained in force, since France kept on seizing American ships. Nevertheless Congress, in support of Madison, passed the bill that stopped trade with Great Britain. Napoleon's purpose was now accomplished — he had tricked the United States into joining his blockade of the British.

A demand for war arises. By this time the American people saw that "peaceable coercion" was a failure, and demands for more vigorous action arose. The loudest outcry for war did not come from the commercial Northeast, as might have been expected, but from the South and the frontier regions. New England merchants were still making money, despite the seizure of American shipping, the impressment of American seamen, and the trickery of Napoleon. They did not want to start a war which would ruin their trade. But the South and the West had little interest in the welfare of the Northeast shipping industry. The West had a greedy eye on Canada, while the South looked with great interest at Florida. Both were willing to go to war to add to their territories. Canada belonged to Great Britain, and Florida belonged to Great Britain's ally, Spain. The people in favor of war in the South and along the frontier, therefore, were inclined to overlook Napoleon's scheming and to stress the injustices America was suffering at the hands of Great Britain.

The "War Hawks" scream for action. The war fever was clearly seen in Congress.

Many of the members who had passed the Macon Act were defeated at the mid-term election of 1810, and a new and younger group of representatives had taken their places. Among this new, younger group were Henry Clay of Kentucky, Richard M. Johnson of Kentucky, and John C. Calhoun of South Carolina. They were intensely patriotic and were called "War Hawks" because they were against taking any more insults from foreign nations. They were heartily in favor of extending the frontier. "I shall never die contented," declared Johnson, "until I see her [Great Britain's] expulsion from North America, and her territories incorporated with the United States." These men also had unlimited faith in their country's destiny, and they were not afraid even to lead the nation into war. "In four weeks from the time that a declaration of war is heard on our frontier," Calhoun assured fellow members of Congress, "the whole of Upper and a part of Lower Canada will be in our possession."

Indian trouble adds to the uproar. Bitter feeling toward Great Britain was increased by news that came out of the West. For some time past, the steady advance of the white men had threatened to deprive the Indians of the Northwest Territory of their hunting grounds. The Indians tried to strengthen their position by setting up an Indian confederacy, with its center at the point where Tippecanoe Creek flows into the Wabash River. (See map, page 178.) The leaders of the confederacy were Tecumseh and his brother, the Prophet. Tecumseh, wishing to make this Indian union even stronger, went southward to make alliances with the Creeks and other tribes. Taking advantage of his absence, a force of about 1000 men marched against the center of the Indian confederacy on the Tippecanoe. They were led by William Henry Harrison,

American naval officer

American infantryman

governor of the Indiana Territory. While the Americans camped along the Tippecanoe, the Indians suddenly attacked them before dawn (November, 1811). In the desperate struggle which followed, Harrison lost many men but held possession of the field of battle. Whether or not it was true, frontier people believed that "British intrigue and British gold" were behind the confederacy of Tecumseh. Harrison reported that it was the British who supplied every Indian "with a gun . . . and an abundance of ammunition." At any rate, the battle at Tippecanoe was one more proof to the "War Hawks" that war had to come. They said the safety of Americans on the frontier depended on driving the British out of North America.

War is declared. War clouds grew darker during the early months of 1812. The British government stated firmly that it would not repeal the orders in council until it was clear that the French decrees had been "absolutely and unconditionally" repealed. Finally Madison submitted to Congress the vital question of war or continued peace. Among the grievances against Great Britain, he listed (1) impressment of American seamen, (2) violation of America's rights within the three-mile limit, (3) the orders in council, and (4) stirring up the Indians on the frontier. Congress responded with a declaration of war (June 18, 1812). In the final vote, the commercial Northeast showed stubborn opposition to the war. The frontier states of Vermont, Ohio, Kentucky, and Tennessee, on the other hand, were almost one hundred per cent in favor of it.

By a twist of fate, war came at the very time when one of the main reasons for it was removed. At about the time that Congress declared war — but before the news could reach London — England revoked the orders in council as far as they affected American ships and cargoes. Unfortu-

nately, the American minister, William Pinkney, had given up hope of reaching a satisfactory settlement with the British government and had come back to America in 1811. Otherwise, the United States might have known that Great Britain was likely to make concessions in order to avoid war.

Madison wins re-election. The presidential election of 1812 was fought over the war issue, and again reflected the feelings in different sections of the country. Madison was supported by Henry Clay and the "War Hawks." De Witt Clinton of New York became the northern "peace candidate." The electoral votes showed that New England favored peace, the middle states were divided, but the southern and frontier states voted solidly for Madison and the war policy.

––––––––– CHECK-UP –––––––––

What developments led to the War of 1812?

1. How did non-intercourse differ from the embargo? The Macon Bill from non-intercourse?
2. How did Napoleon try to make use of Madison against the British?
3. Why was the demand for war greater in the frontier region than in New England?
4. In what sense was the War of 1812 an unnecessary war?

---

5 The War of 1812 Increases the Prestige of the United States

The United States is poorly prepared. Although the "War Hawks" had talked with great confidence about the military resources of the nation, the United States in 1812 was sadly unprepared to carry on a war. It had a regular army of fewer than 7000 men, poorly trained, and commanded by veterans who had seen little active service since the Revolution. When Congress tried to increase the size of the army, the results were disappointing. Massachusetts and Connecticut would not even let their militias be ordered out for service. On the ocean, American frigates were few and they were no match for the huge navy of Great Britain, except in duels between individual ships.

Money to carry on the war effort was difficult to obtain, in part because Congress in 1811 had refused to recharter the national bank (page 182). The financial problem was made worse by the opposition of the wealthy New England states to the war and their refusal to lend money to the national government. Fortunately, in the early part of the war Great Britain was locked in a death struggle with Napoleon and was unable to pay much attention to the war in America.

The invasion of Canada fails. American forces made a poor showing when they tried to invade Canada, and the attempt ended in dismal failure. The British had only a small army there, but instead of launching one major attack, the Americans tried a series of minor ones. In August, 1812, General William Hull, who had been ordered to invade Canada, surrendered Detroit to the British almost without firing a shot. Then Fort Dearborn (on the present site of Chicago) fell to the Indians, who later massacred the prisoners they had taken. These setbacks meant the loss of the greater part of the Northwest. American forces tried twice more to invade Canada — once by way of the Niagara River and once by way of Lake Champlain. Both efforts ended in humiliating defeat. One of the main reasons for these early disasters was inefficiency and jealousy among the commanding officers.

The Northwest Territory is regained. The year 1813, however, brought a ray of hope. The Northwest Territory was recovered through the energy and ability of Captain Oliver Hazard Perry. After overcoming many obstacles, Perry launched a tiny fleet on Lake Erie and defeated a superior British squadron in a sharp engagement. He described the battle to his superior, General Harrison, in these brief words: "We have met the enemy and they are ours: Two Ships, two Brigs, one Schooner and one Sloop." Perry's victory gave him control of Lake Erie and threatened the position of the British at Detroit. They

started to retreat into Canada, followed closely by an American army under General Harrison. The two armies clashed at the Thames River, where furious attacks by the Americans defeated the British. (See map, page 178.) The death in this battle of the dread Indian leader, Tecumseh, marked the end of the Indian confederacy.

Fighting in the North ends in a deadlock. The Americans made a final attempt to invade Canada in the summer of 1814. They were led by able commanders, but this invasion ended in an indecisive battle at Lundy's Lane, near the Niagara River. Meanwhile the defeat of Napoleon in Europe meant that fresh British troops were available for the American war. A force of about 11,000 of them advanced down the Lake Champlain route in the fall of 1814. The British fleet on the lake, however, was defeated by the youthful Captain Thomas Macdonough, and the British troops had to retreat. After three years of war neither side had made any great gains along the northern frontier.

Americans fight bravely on the seas. On the seas, the early success of American ships was more encouraging and proved a distinct surprise to the British. Soon after General Hull surrendered Detroit to the British, his nephew, Captain Isaac Hull, scored a great naval victory. Captain Hull, in command of the *Constitution* ("Old Ironsides"), met the British frigate *Guerriere*. In brief but furious action, the aim of the Yankee gunners proved deadly. The British ship was quickly turned into a helpless hulk.

Before the end of 1812, the Americans had won three other important duels at sea. The American sloop *Wasp* defeated the British sloop *Frolic*. The *United States*, captained by Stephen Decatur, forced the *Macedonian* to strike her colors. The *Constitution* defeated the *Java* off the coast of Brazil.

Privateering was also successful. Over 500 American privateers left home ports during the war to prey upon British commerce. They seized more than 1300 British vessels of various kinds. In time, however, nearly all the American ships were either captured or blockaded. American trade

The U.S.S. Constitution, often called "Old Ironsides," thoroughly wrecked H.M.S. Java when they battled in December, 1812. The American frigate mounted 44 guns.

was all but driven from the sea. As the British blockade tightened, American exports fell to little more than a tenth of their prewar value.

The British attack Washington and Baltimore. Along the Atlantic coast, the British had their own way. They took possession of a part of Maine and used it as a base for raids upon small villages and seaports. They also carried out a successful attack upon Washington. The capital was far from ready to face attack. Five miles outside the city about 6000 raw militiamen were hastily brought together, but they broke and ran before the British advance, leaving Washington at the mercy of the invaders. The city was in wild disorder as President Madison and his cabinet took what records they could put their hands on and fled. The British set fire to the White House, the Capitol, and several other government buildings.[5] The British fleet then attacked Baltimore. Here they met determined resistance which forced them to give up their attack. It was the sight of the American flag still flying after the all-night bombardment of Fort McHenry at Baltimore that inspired Francis Scott Key to write "The Star Spangled Banner."

Andrew Jackson wins at New Orleans. In addition to the attacks on Washington and Baltimore, the British launched an ex-

pedition against New Orleans. This large-scale southern operation gave the Americans their greatest land victory. It also brought into prominence one of the most striking figures in American history, Andrew Jackson.

Jackson had already gained something of a reputation as a military leader. He had broken the power of the Creek Indians at Horseshoe Bend, in Mississippi Territory, forcing them to sign a treaty (1814) by which they surrendered the larger part of their territory. When the British established a military base at Pensacola, Florida, Jackson made a daring invasion of Spanish Florida and drove them away. (See map, page 178.) Now as the year 1814 drew to a close, he went to New Orleans to defend the city against a strong British fleet and army. He ordered the construction of breastworks of earth and bales of cotton, and then settled down to wait. The main British assault opened up on January 8, 1815. As the English veterans advanced, Jackson's men poured a withering fire at them which, a British officer said, "mowed us down by whole sections." The invaders lost their commander, Sir Edward Pakenham, and more than 2000 were killed, wounded, or missing. There were only 71 American casualties. The new British commander refused to press the attack and gradually withdrew his battered forces. The most tragic side of the Battle of New Orleans was that, with modern means of communication, these losses could have

---

[5] This action was in revenge for American destruction of the Parliament House at York (Toronto) during an American invasion of Canada the preceding year.

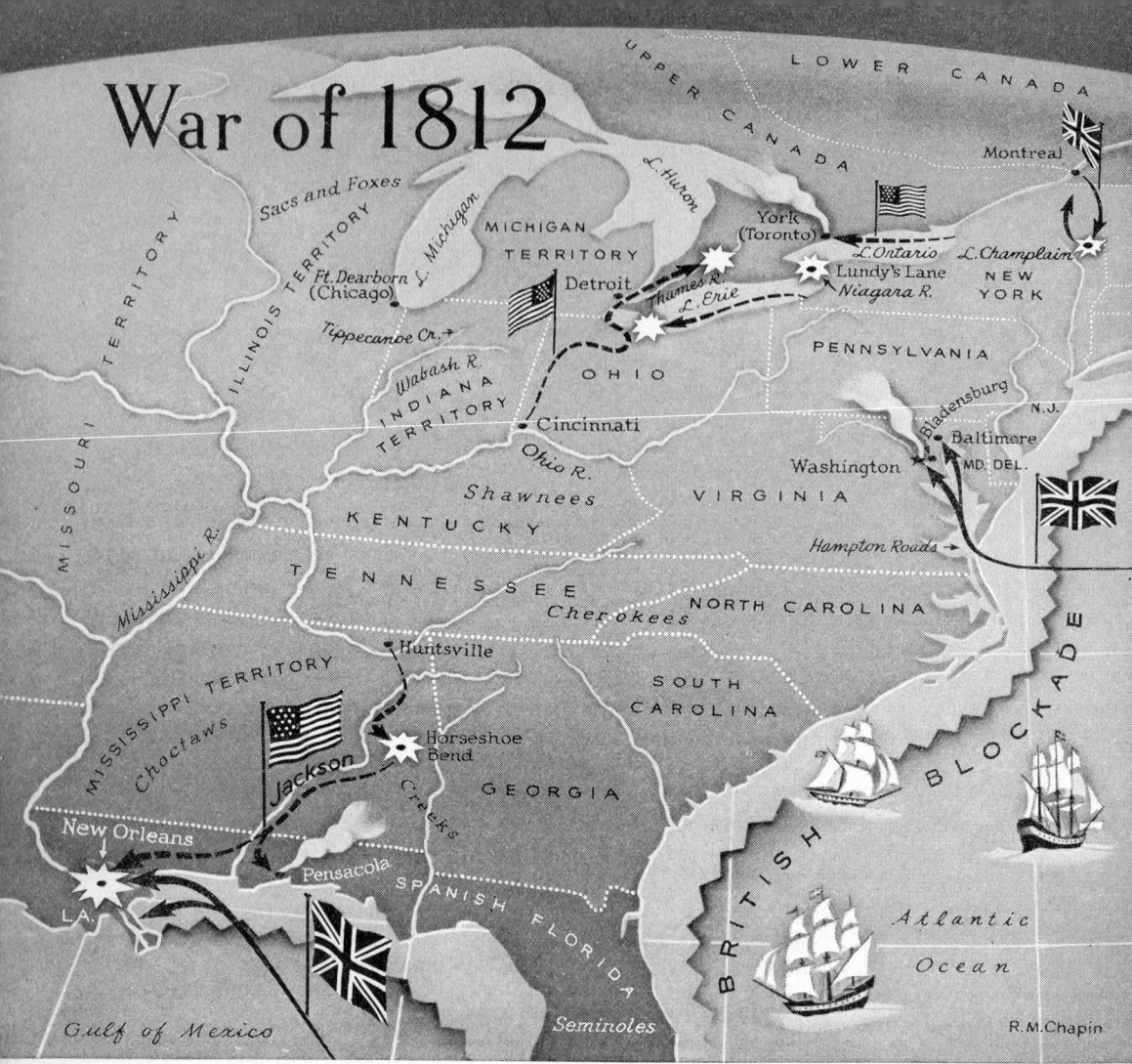

War of 1812

The importance of naval power in the War of 1812 is shown in a number of places on this map. Identify each and explain its importance.

been avoided. A treaty of peace between the United States and Great Britain had already been signed in Europe, on December 24, 1814. The American victory at New Orleans, therefore, played no part in bringing the war to an end.

New England protests the war. Throughout the war the government had had to face opposition at home as well as battle with a foreign enemy. The New England Federalists were the core of this opposition. They refused to fight a war which they claimed was being waged for the benefit of those who favored expansion of the frontier. The wealthy New England states pledged only $3,000,000 of the $80,000,000

that the government raised from loans. Moreover, food kept moving from New England across the Canadian border to supply British troops.

The Hartford Convention meets. New England discontent over the war grew so strong that the Massachusetts legislature finally invited the other New England states to meet in a convention. Its purpose was "to deliberate upon the dangers to which the eastern section of the Union is exposed by the course of the war." During December, 1814, Federalist delegates met at Hartford for a three-week secret session. Their report sharply condemned the war but admitted that secession could be justified only in case of absolute necessity. The right of a state to nullify (repeal or cancel) acts of Congress was clearly set forth, however, in almost the same language as the Virginia Resolutions of 1798. "In cases of deliberate, dangerous, and palpable infractions of the Constitution, affecting the sovereignty of a State, . . . it is not only the right but the duty of such a State to interpose its authority." This was a far cry from the Federalist beliefs of Alexander Hamilton! Seven amendments to the Constitution were also proposed, and the aim of all seven was to strengthen the commercial Northeast at the expense of the agricultural South and West.

The Convention weakens the Federalists. The sudden end of the war changed the Hartford Convention from a serious threat to a harmless gesture. When three Federalist envoys, sent to negotiate with the administration, finally reached Washington, news had already been received of the victory at New Orleans and of the peace treaty. While the city was celebrating happily, the envoys slipped quietly out of the capital, and not much more was heard from New England on the subject of states' rights. At the same time, because of its support of such a program, the Federalist Party suffered a deathblow.

Peace ends a futile war. By 1814 both sides badly wanted peace. Great Britain was staggering under a burden of debts and heavy taxes. There was danger, too, that war would start again in Europe, even though Napoleon had been exiled to the island of Elba. The United States was on the verge of collapse. Its military schemes had failed, its commerce and its income had been hard hit, and New England was threatening nullification.

In the summer of 1814 American commissioners met British representatives at Ghent, Belgium. The five American commissioners were John Quincy Adams, Albert Gallatin, Henry Clay, James A. Bayard, and Jonathan Russell. After long, drawn-out negotiations, a treaty was finally signed on Christmas Eve. It was based on a return of "all territory, places, and possessions whatsoever taken by either party from the other during the war." Nothing was said about the impressment of American seamen or of the violation of American rights on the seas. But these were dead issues now. Since Napoleon's downfall, Great Britain had no need to impress American sailors or to seize American ships. John Quincy Adams' comment sums up the treaty well: "We have obtained nothing but peace." Nevertheless the way was paved for Great Britain and the United States to settle their differences peaceably in the future.

The war earns respect for America abroad. All through the administrations of Washington, Adams, and Jefferson, events abroad had shaped the course of American politics. This dependence upon Europe came to an end with the Treaty of Ghent. After the war the countries of Europe looked with new respect at the United States, the young nation which had dared to cross swords with the leading naval power of the day.

Of even more importance was the fact that the United States now turned its back on Europe and poured all its energies into developing its resources and settling problems within the country. With the defeat of the Indians along the frontier the way to the west was open as never before. John Quincy Adams sounded the keynote of the new era when he wrote: "May we persevere in the system of keeping aloof from all their [Europe's] broils, and in that of consolidating and perpetuating our own Union."

——————— CHECK-UP ———————

How did the War of 1812 increase American prestige?

1. Why was the United States unprepared for war?
2. Why was the United States unable to invade Canada successfully? How were British invasions of the United States stopped? What success and failures did the United States experience on the sea?
3. Why was the Hartford Convention called? What did it demand? Why did it fail?
4. On what terms was the War of 1812 ended? What was the importance of the war?

CHAPTER REVIEW

Terms to Understand

"Revolution of 1800"   blockade
negotiations   embargo
treaty-making power   secession
tribute   frigate
impressment   nullification
economic pressure

People and Things to Know About

Albert Gallatin   Non-Intercourse Act
Judiciary Act of 1801   Macon Bill
John Marshall   Henry Clay
Napoleon Bonaparte   Tecumseh
James Madison   Oliver Hazard Perry
Lewis and Clark   William Hull
Zebulon Pike   Thomas Macdonough
Berlin and Milan de-   "War Hawks"
   crees   Andrew Jackson
"Chesapeake Affair"   Hartford Convention
Embargo Act   orders in council
John Marshall

Historic Dates to Identify

1801	1807	1812
1803	1809	1814
1804–06		

Questions to Discuss

1. Can you explain these apparent contradictions?

(*a*) Jefferson, who had always favored France, considered an alliance with England in 1803.

(*b*) Westerners, rather than New Englanders, demanded a war to defend our rights on the sea.

(*c*) Jefferson disliked a national debt yet greatly increased it.

(*d*) Jefferson believed in "strict construction" yet used the implied power clause.

(*e*) The apparent reasons for the War of 1812 were removed before the war began, and the greatest battles were fought after the war was over.

2. Which Federalist policies did Jefferson retain? Why? Which did he reject? Why? What policies did the Federalists follow after 1800? Why? What does all this reveal about the policies of parties when in and when out of power?

3. What similarities do you see between Jefferson's embargo and the methods used by the colonists to bring England to terms before the Revolution? Some of its enemies stated that

Questions to Discuss (Cont.)

the embargo had "all the disadvantages of war with none of the advantages." Do you agree?

4. It has been said of the War of 1812 that "free land rather than free seas" was its basic cause. Is there any truth in this quip?

5. The Louisiana Purchase is justifiably one of the great events of our history. Why was it important for (*a*) national unity, (*b*) national prosperity, (*c*) future expansion, (*d*) national safety in foreign relations?

Relating Geography and History

1. Why was the acquisition of control over the Mississippi River of great importance to our future as a nation?

2. Why was each of the following a strategic point in the War of 1812? (*a*) Detroit, (*b*) New Orleans, (*c*) Lake Champlain, (*d*) Lake Erie.

3. Locate on an outline map of the United States:

   (*a*) The region of the Louisiana Purchase.

   (*b*) The routes of Lewis and Clark and of Zebulon Pike.

Other Things to Do

1. Jefferson's First Inaugural Address is one of the great American documents. Read it in Commager, *Documents of American History*, No. 106. What does the address reveal about Jefferson's philosophy?

2. Jefferson accomplished much, but he wished to be remembered for founding the University of Virginia, for the Declaration of Independence, and for the Virginia Statute of Religious Liberty. Read and study the latter in Commager, *Documents*, No. 8. Why did Jefferson consider the Statute so important?

3. Prepare a report on the experiences of the Lewis and Clark expedition. Indicate the scene of each important event on a map. There are numerous editions of the original journals of Lewis and Clark.

4. Prepare a talk on one of the military phases of the War of 1812. Paine, *The Fight for a Free Sea* has highly interesting chapters on these.

5. Write a theme pointing out the contrast in social atmosphere surrounding the Washington and Jefferson administrations. Consult Ford, *Washington and His Colleagues* and Bassett, *The Federalist System* for Washington; Johnson, *Jefferson and His Colleagues* and Channing, *The Jeffersonian System* for Jefferson.

Orator

Chapter 9

GROWING NATIONAL UNITY IS

CHECKED BY SECTIONAL DIFFERENCES

In war we are one people. In making peace we are one people. In all commercial regulations we are one and the same people. In many other respects the American people are one, and the government which is alone capable of controlling and managing their interests in all these respects is the government of the Union . . . America has chosen to be, in many respects and to many purposes, a nation.

John Marshall, 1821

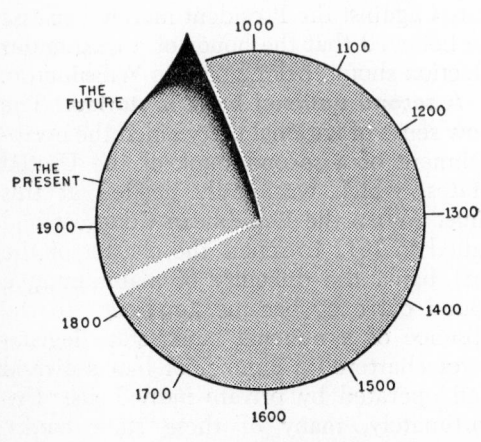

1816-1833

Probably the most important result of the War of 1812 was the growth of a strong sense of national unity. Today we take such a feeling as a matter of course. The American of today feels a special loyalty to his local community, to his state, and to the section of the country in which he lives. But whether he comes from Maine, Florida, Arizona, or Oregon, he places his loyalty to the nation above his local and sectional interests.

This has not always been true. In colonial times, as we have seen, local ties were of primary importance. A man thought of himself first and foremost as a Pennsylvanian, a Virginian, or a New Englander. Even the bitter experiences of the Revolution and the troubled era of the early republic failed to weaken local ties to any great extent. The War of 1812 created in the average American a new awareness of the common bond he had with his fellow Americans. On the one hand, the War of 1812 aroused pride in the position which the United States had achieved among the nations of the world; on the other hand, it revealed national weaknesses which could be overcome only by united effort.

In the surge of nationalism following the war, new policies were undertaken which gained support from the various sections of the country. The special interests of the Northeast, the South, and the West were by no means entirely wiped out, but the current of nationalism ran strong. As the 1820's and 1830's wore on, sectional differences stood out more clearly and the wave of strong national feeling receded. This chapter relates the influence of strong nationalism in party politics, in financial policies, in court rulings, in western expansion, and in foreign relations. In these pages also are the shadows of disaster that lurked in sectional differences over slavery and the tariff. The story will be told under the following headings:

1. National enthusiasm affects politics and policies.
2. The expanding frontier strengthens the nation.
3. American foreign policy reflects national strength.
4. Sectional differences become more pronounced.
5. The tariff question leads to a crisis.

1 **National Enthusiasm Affects Politics and Policies**

Party strife disappears. From the time that the Federalist and Republican parties were formed in the early 1790's, sharp struggles had taken place between them. By 1812 not even the peril of war could soften the bitterness of party feeling. For about ten years after the Treaty of Ghent, however, party strife declined. In the election of 1816, James Monroe, a Republican,

won an easy victory over the Federalist candidate, Rufus King. From that time on, the Federalists as a party practically disappeared, for they never again nominated a presidential candidate. The truth was that the Republicans had borrowed many Federalist principles, and the Federalists in turn had been swallowed up by the converted Republicans. Moreover, Federalist policies during the war had discredited that party in the eyes of the nation.

Not long after President Monroe was inaugurated in 1817, he made a tour of the Northeast and the West. Wherever Monroe went, he was given an enthusiastic welcome. He was applauded not so much because he was highly popular but rather because he was the President of a country in which there was a new spirit of unity. A Federalist paper in Boston suggested that Monroe's term of office should be called the "era of good feelings." That phrase won the approval of the American people. Monroe sensed the new national feeling even in his first annual message. He rejoiced, he said, that "local jealousies are rapidly yielding to more generous, enlarged, and enlightened views of national policy." The absence of party feeling was clearly marked in the election of 1820. Monroe received every electoral vote except one. One elector is said to have voted against the President merely because he believed that the honor of a unanimous election should belong only to Washington.

A second national bank is started. The new sense of national unity aided the establishment of a second Bank of the United States, which was badly needed at this time. When the Republican Congress had failed in 1811 to renew the charter of the first bank, the difficulty of maintaining a sound currency became apparent. In the absence of a national bank, state legislatures chartered a number of banks owned and operated by private individuals. Unfortunately, many of these state banks, especially in the West, had the right to issue as much paper money as they saw fit. Some of them took risks and issued much more paper money than they could back up with gold or silver. As a result,

Hat making

such paper money became almost worthless. During the five years following the end of the first national bank, the number of state banks tripled, and the amount of bank notes more than doubled. The Treasury of the United States suffered a direct loss because the bank notes it accepted for taxes were in many cases nearly worthless.

To remedy the situation, Congress chartered a second Bank of the United States in 1816. This action was taken in spite of the previous distrust which Republicans had felt for a national bank. Henry Clay, who had opposed rechartering the first bank, explained that he was now willing to sacrifice "the pride of consistency" rather than the interests of the country. President Madison had also been prejudiced against the bank, but he finally overcame his fears and signed the bill in April, 1816. The bank was required to pay the government a bonus of $1,500,000 in return for certain favors granted in its 20-year charter.

Manufacturing suffers from foreign competition. Another problem which the government had to face after the War of 1812 was the protection of new industries from foreign competition. Such measures as the Embargo and Non-Intercourse Acts had effectively cut down the flow of manufactured goods from England, and America had been almost forced into supplying more and more of its own industrial needs. Even before the War of 1812 the United States was making its own woolen and leather goods, soap, and earthenware. It was also able to supply a large part of the country's need for iron goods, textiles, hats, paper, liquors, gunpowder, and window glass. The war stopped foreign trade almost entirely, and the demand for American-made products increased. Much American wealth formerly invested in shipping and trade was invested in manufacturing.

When peace returned, the warehouses of English merchants were bulging with goods piled up during the war. Determined to regain their former trade with America, these merchants flooded the American market with a huge supply of manufactured articles, which they sold at prices far below those of American products. Many American manufacturers were driven out of business. In the area around Providence, Rhode Island, for instance, there had been more than 150 textile mills. Fewer than a dozen survived the flooding of American markets with English goods.

Congress passes a protective tariff. Under these circumstances, American manufacturers demanded help from Congress. Even Thomas Jefferson, who had formerly urged that "our work-shops remain in Europe," now wrote, "Experience has taught me that manufactures are now as necessary to our independence as to our comfort." At President Madison's suggestion, Congress passed a new tariff act in the spring of 1816, which placed higher duties on many imported articles. Prices on foreign goods rose in this country as a result of the tariff, and thus American manufacturers were protected from foreign competition. This "protective tariff" was opposed by shipowners of the North, who wanted to haul cargoes from England, and to some degree by the agricultural South, which had no desire to pay higher prices to protect northern industry. In general, however, the tariff was supported by representatives from all sections of the country. John C. Calhoun of South Carolina, who in later years became a bitter enemy of the protective tariff, approved the tariff of 1816 as a national need. He said, "It is the duty of this country, as a means of defense, to encourage the domestic industry of the country."

The Panic of 1819 sweeps the country. In 1819 an economic crisis crippled the nation. This depression was caused partly by the rapid expansion of new industries at a time when British merchants were flooding American markets with cheap goods. It was also a result of poor management of the Bank of the United States. In the western areas, settlers were eagerly scrambling for land. These land deals were financed by "wildcat banks," which lent money too freely and thus encouraged speculation (buying with the hope of selling at a profit

Periods of Prosperity and Depression

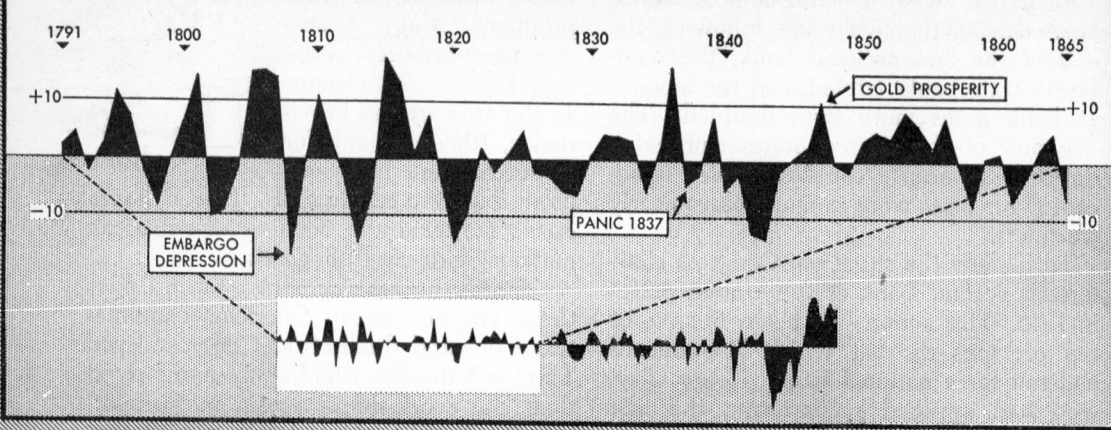

The rise and fall of American business activity are shown in the center portion of this chart. (The small inset at the bottom of the chart suggests how the rise and fall have continued throughout our history. See also pages 375 and 535.) Where the chart rises, the country was enjoying prosperity. Where it falls, a depression was going on. The lines labeled +10 and −10 help to show the relative degree of prosperity or depression. The chart singles out three events which were related to the rise and fall of business activity. What were they? What were the causes and effects of the Embargo depression?

when the price rises). The Bank of the United States, instead of restraining the "wildcat banks," at first encouraged their risky dealings. In the latter half of 1818, however, the directors of the Bank of the United States began to make it more difficult to obtain loans. A panic broke out. Prices of goods fell sharply, factories were closed, and great numbers of people were thrown out of work. A depression followed the panic, and hard times continued until about 1824.

The Supreme Court confirms the bank. The Panic of 1819 helped to arouse hard feelings against the Bank of the United States. Even before 1819 some states, especially in the West and South, had tried to prevent the establishment of local branches of the bank. One means of discouraging such branches was to put heavy state taxes upon their business transactions. Opposition came to a head when the cashier of the Baltimore branch refused to pay a tax levied by the state of Maryland. A suit was brought in the state courts which upheld the tax, and the case was appealed to the Supreme Court.

In this case (McCulloch *vs.* Maryland), John Marshall wrote one of the most important opinions in the history of American courts. He made it clear that Congress had only the powers given to it in the Constitution. He pointed out, however, that the very grant of power implied the right to use it in any necessary and proper way and no state could limit this right. Congress had decided that a national bank was "necessary and proper" in order to carry out its financial powers — the powers of levying and collecting taxes and of borrowing money. "Let the end be legitimate," Marshall said, "let it be within the scope of the Constitution, and all means which are appropriate, which are plainly adapted to that end, which are not prohibited, but consist [agree] with the letter and spirit of the Constitution, are constitutional." Furthermore, the states had no right to tax the national bank, for the taxation of federal agencies by the states "would defeat all the ends of government." The decision of the Supreme Court confirmed Marshall's opinion that the Bank of the United States could not be taxed by the states.

Marshall's opinions strengthen the government. Dominated by Marshall, the Supreme Court handed down other decisions about this time which gave the federal government new strength against interference by the states. A famous group of these decisions, as in the McCulloch *vs.* Maryland case, set aside state laws which conflicted with the Constitution. In the Dartmouth College Case (1819), Marshall stated that the New Hampshire legislature could not change the old royal charter of Dartmouth College. The charter, he explained, was a contract establishing obligations which the state was forbidden by the Constitution to tamper with. In another case (Gibbons *vs.* Ogden, 1824), Marshall smashed a monopoly of the navigable waters of New York State — a monopoly granted by the New York legislature to Robert R. Livingston and Robert Fulton. He pointed out that navigation of the Hudson River involved interstate commerce, which, by the provisions of the Constitution, Congress alone was permitted to regulate.

Republicans put up strong protests against these and other decisions, but without success. Over a period of 34 years (1801–35), John Marshall by means of forceful opinions wrote his nationalistic ideas into law. To him the Supreme Court was more than a court; it was a platform from which he could proclaim to the nation those principles which gave real life to the Constitution. Marshall accomplished two important things. First, he strengthened the federal government at the expense of the states by a broad interpretation of the Constitution. Secondly, through his energy and vigor, the Supreme Court gained an importance in the federal government which it has held to this day.

Saddlebags

What evidences of stronger national feeling appeared after the War of 1812?

1. Why was there only one political party for a time?
2. Why was a second Bank of the United States chartered?
3. What conditions led to the passage of the tariff of 1816?
4. What were the causes of the Panic of 1819?
5. What were the decisions of John Marshall in each of the following? (a) McCulloch vs. Maryland, (b) Dartmouth College Case, (c) Gibbons vs. Ogden. Why were Marshall's opinions significant?

2 The Expanding Frontier Strengthens the Nation

Pioneers move beyond the mountains. Another force which strengthened national feeling was westward expansion. In the years between the Revolution and the War of 1812, a stream of pioneers kept flowing into the new western areas. After the War of 1812, the stream became a flood. This great movement was caused by: (1) the emigration of more people from Europe, (2) hard times in the East, (3) the lessening of Indian troubles on the frontier, (4) the rapid extension of cotton planting in the new South, and (5) a keen thirst for land.

The trip westward was a hard one, but the hopeful pioneers pushed steadily on. They followed winding river valleys through the mountain barrier of the Appalachians, then pushed on through the foothills and across the flatlands. Some made their way on horseback, others in large canvas-covered wagons, and still others walked, carrying everything they owned. Flatboats and "arks" floated down the larger rivers, transporting excited land-hunters and their possessions. A tremendous volume of traffic moved down the

Ohio River, which fortunately flowed the "right way" — into the West.

Band box Some idea of the extent of this westward movement is brought to us by an English traveler in 1817. "Old America," he reported, "seems to be breaking up and moving westward. We are seldom out of sight, as we travel on this grand track toward the Ohio, of family groups, behind and before us, some with a view to a particular spot, close to a brother, perhaps, or a friend who has gone before and reported well of the country. Many, like ourselves, when they arrive in the wilderness, will find no lodge prepared for them. . . . This is a land of plenty, and we are proceeding to a land of abundance."

New states are created. This westward surge was so great that the population beyond the Appalachians more than doubled between 1810 and 1820. In fact, by 1820 it was greater than 2¼ million. Within five years after the Treaty of Ghent, four new states were admitted to the Union: Indiana (1816), Mississippi (1817), Illinois (1818), and Alabama (1819). These new states had been created from national territory, and the people there owed both their land and their privileges to the federal government. It was not surprising that loyalty to the nation was stronger there than in the older states along the Atlantic seaboard.

Better transportation is demanded. The opening of the frontier made transportation far more necessary than it had ever been before. Almost every man who pushed across the mountain barrier became a farmer. He and his fellow pioneers soon raised far more farm products than they could use and were eager to market them in the East. Better transportation, therefore, became an urgent need. As long as the pioneer farmer had to haul his produce over crude roads or ship it down the Mississippi and around Florida to the East coast, he could not hope to make much profit. Even in sections nearer the coast, transportation was a problem. For example, a Virginia congressman estimated in 1818 that it cost "the farmer one

Hat Box

bushel of wheat to pay the expense of carrying two to a seaport town" less than 80 miles away. East-west transportation was even worse. Since there was not yet any practical way to ship goods up the Mississippi River, manufactured goods from the East had to be hauled by wagon through the mountain barrier at high cost. The new western areas were not able to finance any large-scale schemes for roads or canals. Consequently, western congressmen asked for better transportation and other improvements at national expense. Their demands were seconded by the seaboard cities which wanted a larger trade with the interior.

Clay proposes economic independence. The new western states could not hope to carry out their program alone — they did not have that much power in Congress. But Henry Clay of Kentucky in his *American System* tied up the western demand for internal improvements at national expense with the eastern desire for a protective tariff. A tariff would not only provide revenue for financing internal improvements but would protect the American manufacturer from European competition. Such protection would make it possible to sell eastern manufactured goods in the growing markets of the West and South. In turn, these areas could give the workers of the North and the East the foodstuffs and raw materials that they needed. Thus the system would bind the different sections in an economic unit that would be almost independent of Europe. "I hope," Clay declared in Congress in 1824, "that it will yet be said, America is America's best customer."

The National Road is constructed. Actually, a start toward federal aid for internal improvements had been made even before the War of 1812. In 1802 the act which formed the state of Ohio had provided that Congress set aside a small part of the receipts from public land sales and use it to build a road to the new state.[1] The route for that road led from Cumberland, on the Maryland side of the Potomac River, to

[1] Similar provisions were made later in admitting Indiana, Illinois, and Missouri.

Wheeling, on the Virginia side of the Ohio River. Construction was started in 1811. Seven years later a stretch of 130 miles was completed. The new road was called the Cumberland (or National) Road. Still later this road was carried as far west as Vandalia, Illinois. (See map, page 231.) Over the Cumberland Road, in ever-increasing numbers, lumbered heavy Conestoga wagons — broad-wheeled, canvas-covered, and heavy-laden — usually drawn by six horses. The new West looked at this road as a symbol of national power, and it did a great deal to bind together the West and the East.

A plan for internal improvement fails. People were beginning to realize that a system of roads and canals would not only aid the development of the country but would help to reduce jealousy between the different sections. Toward the end of Madison's administration a plan was suggested for a permanent program of internal improvements at national expense. John C. Calhoun of South Carolina presented the plan to Congress. He proposed to set aside for internal improvements the bonus of $1,500,000 which the government received from the second Bank of the United States for its charter (page 183). To this sum he suggested adding the annual dividends on the bank stock held by the government. Calhoun's plan, called the Bonus Bill, won the approval of Congress in 1817, but it was vetoed by the President on his last day in office. Madison agreed that the country needed roads and canals. But he was convinced that the Constitution did not give the federal government the power to spend money for this purpose. The burden and expense of improvements were thus shifted to the states or to private citizens.

——— CHECK-UP ———

How did the expanding frontier strengthen the nation?

1. What factors encouraged the westward movement after the war? What new states were added?
2. Why was transportation a serious problem in the West? How did the National Road help solve this problem?
3. Why was Clay's American System a national program? What happened to the part of the program having to do with internal improvements?

3 American Foreign Policy Reflects National Strength

American-British relations improve. In the capable hands of John Quincy Adams, Secretary of State under President Monroe, our relations with other countries were so well conducted that Americans had a growing feeling of pride in their nation. Relations with Great Britain were noticeably improved. In 1817, by a treaty called the Rush-Bagot Agreement the United States agreed to a policy of disarmament on the Great Lakes and Lake Champlain, except for a few gunboats for police purposes. This disarmament agreement has lasted to this day. Not only has it saved millions of dollars that would have been spent in fortifying our boundaries, but it has helped to preserve permanent peace between Canada and the United States.

In 1818, by another treaty, Great Britain gave Americans permanent fishing privileges along certain parts of the Labrador and Newfoundland coasts. Also a northern boundary was fixed between the United States and Canada — from the Lake of the Woods west to the Rocky Mountains along the forty-ninth parallel. (See map, page 278.) The Oregon Country was to be "free and open" to the citizens of both the United States and Great Britain for ten years. At

Conestoga wagon

the end of the ten years, this arrangement was continued indefinitely, but it was understood that the agreement could be brought to an end by either country upon one year's notice.

Trouble arises with Spain. Our relations with Spain were more difficult to handle. Trouble first arose over the Floridas. (See map below.) Claiming West Florida under the terms of the Louisiana Purchase, the United States had occupied that area in 1810 and 1813. In East Florida, meanwhile, Spanish authority was very weak. Only a few posts such as Pensacola and St. Augustine were fortified, and the peninsula had become a refuge for roving Indians, runaway slaves, pirates, and smugglers. In the Pinckney Treaty of 1795 (page 155), Spain had agreed to keep Florida Indians from attacking American citizens and property, but she was powerless to control these lawless bands.

When new Indian outbreaks occurred (1817), the United States government decided to force a showdown. Andrew Jackson, the hero of New Orleans, was sent to the Florida border with orders to "adopt the necessary measures" to end Indian resistance. Jackson and his men swept across the border into Spanish territory, claiming to have the approval of the President. They not only took possession of the whole

Boundary disputes between Spain and the United States went back to the close of the Revolution, when the Floridas were returned to Spain without a clear northern boundary for the area west of Georgia. Spain claimed the area even as far north as the Tennessee River, owing to actions against the British during the Revolution. But the British, in 1783, had secretly granted the area between 31° and 32°28′ to the United States. The United States had still another claim to this area. What was it? Why was West Florida especially important to the United States? How did the United States finally acquire a clear claim to both East and West Florida?

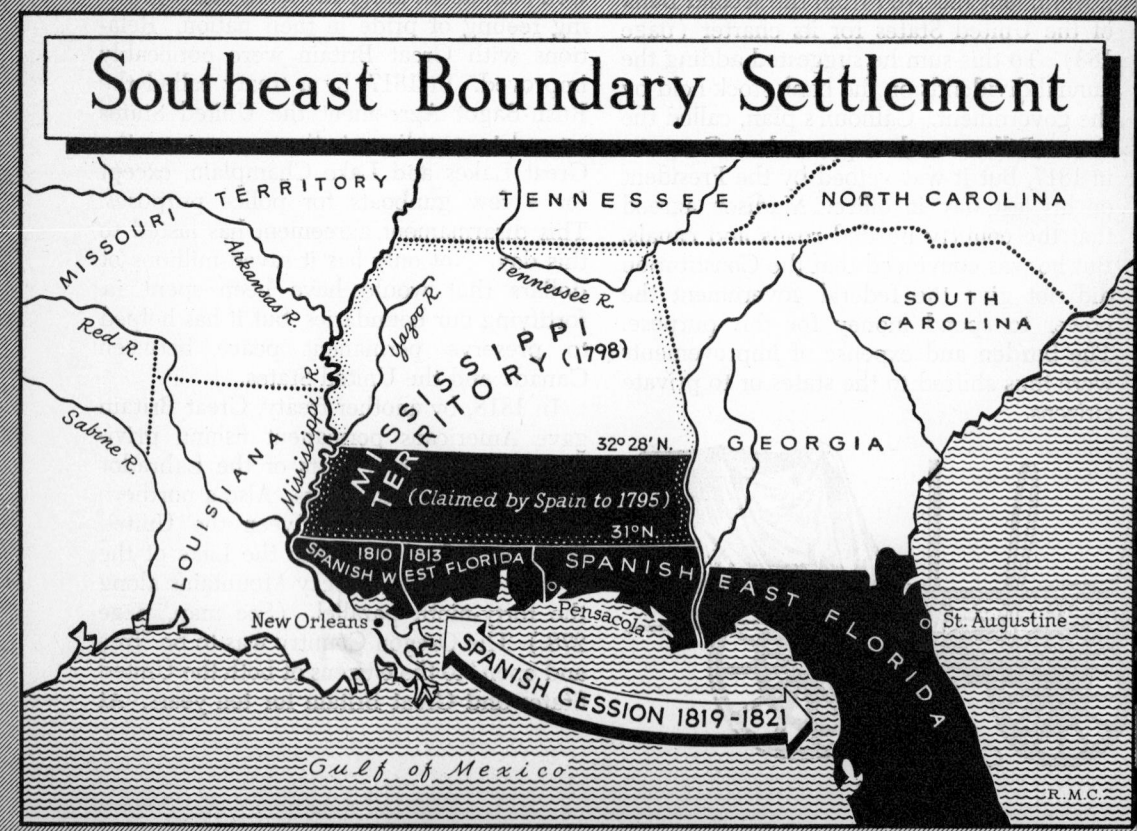

Southeast Boundary Settlement

MISSOURI TERRITORY

TENNESSEE

NORTH CAROLINA

Arkansas R.

Red R.

Sabine R.

Yazoo R.

Tennessee R.

MISSISSIPPI TERRITORY (1798)

32°28′ N.

(Claimed by Spain to 1795)

31°N.

SOUTH CAROLINA

GEORGIA

L O U I S I A N A

Mississippi R.

1810   1813
SPANISH WEST FLORIDA

SPANISH EAST FLORIDA

New Orleans •

Pensacola

St. Augustine

SPANISH CESSION 1819-1821

Gulf of Mexico

R.M.C.

western part of the province but executed two British subjects for stirring up Indian warfare against the United States.

For a while Jackson's action threatened trouble with Great Britain. Fortunately, the British foreign minister decided that the two men had been carrying on "unauthorized practices" and did not make a formal protest. Spanish resentment, however, was a real problem. At first the President and most of the cabinet refused to accept responsibility for Jackson's invasion of Spanish territory, but Secretary Adams succeeded in persuading them to adopt a firm policy. A blunt note was delivered to the American minister at Madrid. This note demanded that the Spanish government "either . . . place a force in Florida adequate . . . to the protection of her territory . . . or cede to the United States a province, of which she [Spain] retains nothing but the nominal possession."

Florida is ceded to the United States. Spain was having trouble at home and in her colonies, and was in no position to build up a military force in Florida. She therefore decided to withdraw but at the same time to get the best possible terms from the United States. A treaty, drawn up in 1819, ceded Florida to the United States. In return, America agreed to pay the claims that its own citizens held against Spain to an amount not over $5,000,000. By the same treaty, the United States accepted a new line for its western boundary. This line proceeded in a stairlike formation from the Sabine River, alternately north and west to the forty-second parallel and along that line to the Pacific. (See also map, page 280.) Thus the United States gave up its claim to Texas as part of the Louisiana territory.[2] The Senate promptly approved the treaty, but Spain delayed the actual transfer of Florida until 1821.

Spain loses her American colonies. Relations between Spain and her colonies in

[2] The surrender of Texas was a great disappointment to many, including John Quincy Adams himself. At the time, however, few Americans were settling in Texas, and the region was regarded as of doubtful value. To give up a questionable right to this undeveloped region seemed a fair exchange for the immediate possession of Florida.

Simón Bolívar, called The Liberator, led the movements for independence in the present-day countries of Colombia, Venezuela, and Peru. This portrait hangs in the office of the President of the United States.

Central and South America provided still another chance for the United States to show her new national strength and pride. Starting with Columbus' discovery, Spain had built a rich and vast colonial empire in Central and South America and in the Caribbean. Many people in the Spanish colonies, however, resented Spain's strict control of their government, commerce, and daily life. Feeling was especially bitter among the Indians and Creoles (people of Spanish or French blood born in the New World). These sparks of discontent were fanned into flame by the liberal ideas of the American and French Revolutions. A few leaders in the Spanish colonies began to preach independence from Spain.

During the troubled years of the Napoleonic Wars, unsettled conditions in Spain offered the Spanish colonies a chance for successful revolt. Starting in 1810, one Spanish colony after another declared its

Early transportation, Brazil

independence and took up the sword to defend it. Such men as Father Hidalgo (ee-dahl' goh), Simón Bolívar (see-mohn' boh-lee' var), and José de San Martín (ho-zay' day sahn mahr-teen') became heroic figures in the history of Latin American freedom. (See map, page 191.) Many Americans were intensely interested in seeing their neighbors to the south throw off Old World controls. The United States gave moral support to their cause in 1822 by officially recognizing the independence of Mexico, Great Colombia, the Argentine Confederation, Peru, and Chile.

Europe threatens Latin America. The monarchs of Europe disliked and feared the revolutionary ideas and movements in Europe and the New World. After Napoleon was defeated, the leading European powers held a series of international congresses in which the main purpose was to unite and fight such ideas. At one of these meetings, in 1822, Austria, Prussia, Russia, and France decided to put down a revolutionary uprising in Spain. The next spring, a French army crossed the Pyrenees Mountains and soon had most of Spain under its control. Would their next move be to put down the new independent governments in Latin America?

Great Britain was opposed to such a move. British merchants had already developed a profitable trade with the new republics. They could expect to lose much of that trade if the new republics were overthrown. Moreover, the British government was troubled by the possibility that France might gain territory in the Americas as a result of helping to suppress the revolts. The British foreign secretary,

George Canning, suggested that the United States and Great Britain go "hand in hand" in stopping Europeans from seizing any part of Latin America.

Russia threatens the Pacific Coast. Fear over the seizure of parts of the American continent by foreign powers was further heightened by Russia's advances on the Pacific coast of North America. In 1821 the Czar (ruler) of Russia had issued a decree that extended the boundary of Alaska (which belonged to Russia) as far south as the fifty-first parallel, well within the Oregon country. This decree, furthermore, warned the ships of other countries not to approach within 100 miles of the Alaskan coast.

Adams favors independent action. For three reasons Secretary of State Adams was opposed to co-operation with Great Britain. (1) He did not think the European nations would actually invade South America. (2) It seemed likely that Canning wanted the United States to promise not to take any of the Spanish-American possessions for itself. Such a promise would be embarrassing if the United States had a chance to annex Cuba. (3) It might become necessary for the United States to take independent action against territorial claims by European countries because of the Russian advance on the Pacific coast.

With these things in mind, Adams felt that America should act alone, rather than come in as "a cock-boat in the wake of the British man-of-war."

Monroe makes a famous proclamation. Therefore President Monroe, in his annual message to Congress in December, 1823, included a statement of American foreign policy which has come to be known as the *Monroe Doctrine*. It consisted of two main parts. The first stated American intentions toward Europe and European colonies in

San Martín's conquests took him as far north as Lima, Peru. Later he voluntarily retired, and his armies fought under Bolívar. How did the physical features of South America affect their campaigns? What relation did the Monroe Doctrine have to the work of Bolívar and San Martín?

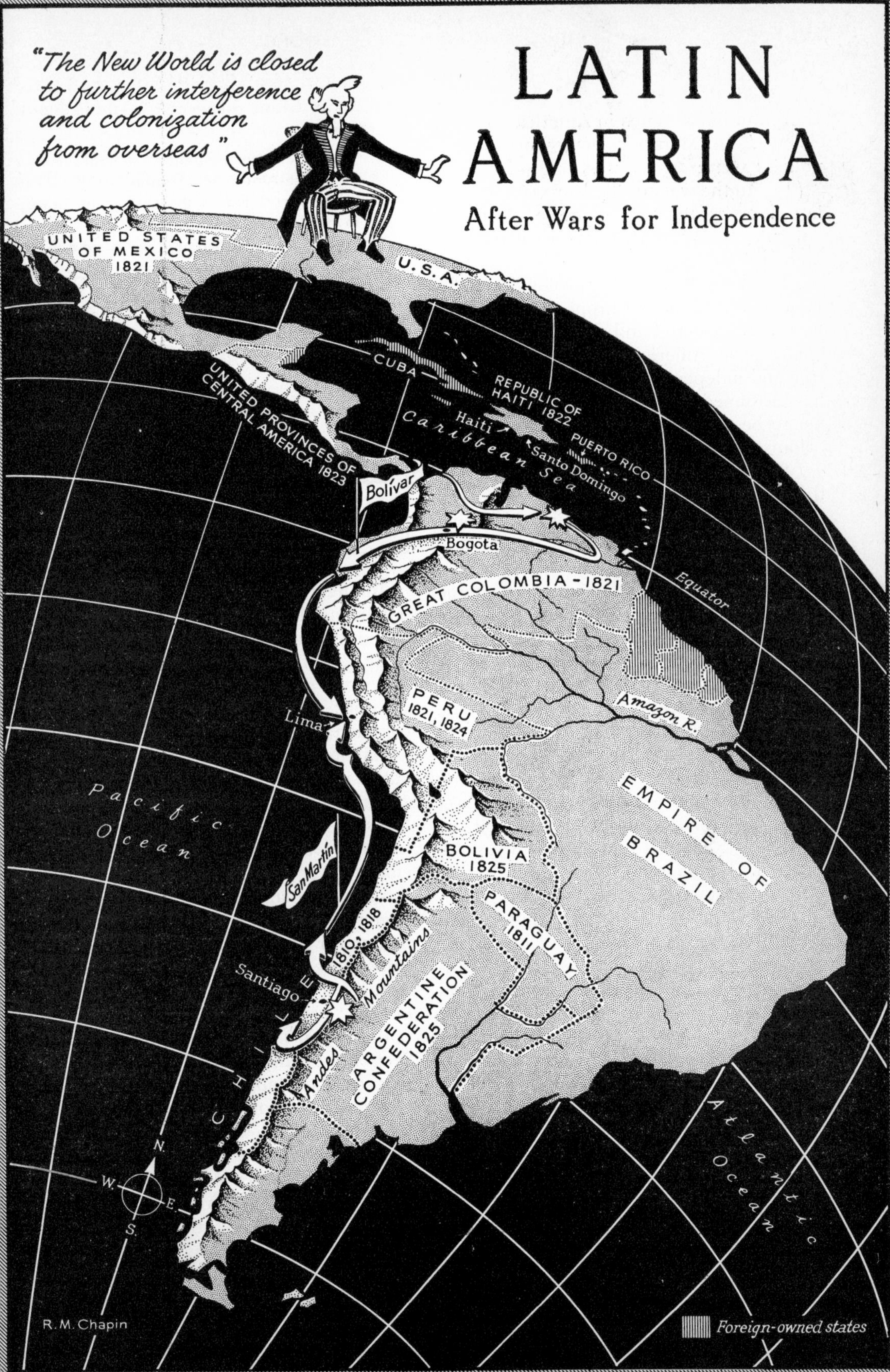

"The New World is closed to further interference and colonization from overseas"

LATIN AMERICA

After Wars for Independence

UNITED STATES OF MEXICO 1821

U.S.A.

CUBA

REPUBLIC OF HAITI 1822

Haiti

PUERTO RICO

Santo Domingo

UNITED PROVINCES OF CENTRAL AMERICA 1823

Caribbean Sea

Bolivar

Bogota

GREAT COLOMBIA — 1821

Equator

PERU 1821, 1824

Amazon R.

Lima

Pacific Ocean

San Martin

EMPIRE OF BRAZIL

BOLIVIA 1825

PARAGUAY 1811

1810-1818

Santiago

Andes Mountains

ARGENTINE CONFEDERATION 1825

Atlantic Ocean

N. W. E. S.

R. M. Chapin

Foreign-owned states

America (1 and 2 below). The second expressed the American attitude toward European interference in America (3 and 4 below). In Monroe's own words, these policies were:

(1) "In the wars of the European powers in matters relating to themselves we have never taken any part, nor does it comport [agree] with our policy so to do."

(2) "With the existing colonies or dependencies of any European power we have not interfered and shall not interfere."

(3) "The American continents, by the free and independent condition which they have assumed and maintain, are henceforth not to be considered as subjects for future colonization by any European powers."

(4) "We should consider any attempt on their [European powers'] part to extend their system to any portion of this hemisphere as dangerous to our peace and safety."

The Monroe Doctrine defines our foreign policy. The Monroe Doctrine was published at just the right time. At home, this statement of American foreign policy was in tune with the national feeling and met with the approval of the people. Abroad, thanks to the support of the British government and to the fact that the other European powers were in no position to oppose it vigorously anyway, it did what it had set out to do — it kept European hands off the Americas. Spanish America was not touched. Russia soon agreed to a settlement that established 54° 40′ as the southern boundary of Alaska. In time, Spain recognized the independence of her American colonies. The United States, fortunately, was not called upon to face any real attack upon the Monroe Doctrine until she was powerful enough to do so successfully.

The real importance of the Monroe Doctrine lay in the future. It became one of those principles in the development of the American nation which grew more meaningful and more important as the years went by. For almost a century it was the cornerstone of American foreign policy. When conditions changed, the policy was given a broad interpretation to meet the needs of an energetic and ambitious America.

How did American foreign policy reflect national strength?

1. What were the evidences of improvement in British-American relations after 1814?
2. What events led to the cession of Florida to the United States?
3. Why didn't the United States co-operate with Great Britain in pursuing a joint policy toward Latin America?
4. What were the provisions of the Monroe Doctrine? For what reasons was it important?

4 Sectional Differences Become More Pronounced

The new nationalism is short-lived. What has been told so far in this chapter reflects the growth of national unity after the War of 1812. Freed from the problems of war and from dependence upon Europe, the vigorous young nation became aware of a common background, a common need, and a common destiny. The display of national enthusiasm, which left a permanent impression on the life of the nation, led Marshall to declare that Monroe's administration "was not darkened by a single cloud." Yet the seeds of future discord were being planted even then. Rivalry between the sections of the country, which had never entirely disappeared, soon became more intense than ever and presented disturbing problems to the American people.

The sections develop conflicting interests. Sectional rivalry developed because each part of the country wanted the national government to follow a policy which would benefit its own people. For instance, many people living in the Northeast would profit by a national policy which protected home industry (the tariff) and kept the currency under sound control (the national bank). On the other hand, New England did not favor westward expansion. One reason for this attitude was that as new states sent congressmen to Washington, New England's power in Congress would decrease. Manufacturers saw, too, that westward migration would draw away their labor supply as discontented New England workers set out for the frontier. New Englanders were willing to back up the West in its demand for better means of transportation, but only because they would benefit from the increased trade in manufactured goods.

The southern planter had very different needs. His life had been greatly changed after Eli Whitney invented the cotton gin in 1793. This machine, which quickly separated the seeds from the cotton fibers (page 226), made it possible for the Southerner to produce large and profitable cotton crops. By the 1820's cotton growing had become his chief occupation. Naturally, the Southerner was in favor of any government action which helped the cotton trade, and he was opposed to any policy which hurt it. For instance, since there were almost no factories in the South, the Southerner had to buy most of his clothing and other manufactured goods elsewhere. He preferred to buy these things in England, because that country was the best market for his cotton. He was therefore opposed to any tariff on manufactured articles. He was not interested in the building of roads and canals at national expense, since the market for his products was not in the West. Over slavery also there was wide disagreement between the South and the other sections. As cotton growing increased, Southerners more than ever needed slaves to help with the crops. In the issue of slavery lay the germ of a serious conflict, especially because Southerners moving into new territory demanded the right to bring their slaves with them.

The West had still a third point of view. It was a farming area, in need of a market for surplus products. The Westerner therefore favored a government policy that made land available on easy terms and took care of road building and other internal improvements at national expense. He generally supported New England in its demand for tariff protection. On the other hand, he was strongly opposed to the financiers of the Northeast, especially those who controlled the Bank of the United States, because their influence in tightening bank credit made it harder for the Western farmer to make ends meet.

Admission of Missouri raises a dispute. The first real struggle among the different sections of the country took place during Monroe's first administration. The trouble arose over the territory of Missouri, which had been formed in 1812. Six years later, Missouri asked to be admitted to the Union as a state. The Missouri Bill started a lively debate in the House of Representatives. James Tallmadge of New York offered an amendment: "That the further introduction of slavery or involuntary servitude be prohibited, except for the punishment of crimes . . . ; and that all children of slaves, born within the said state, after the admission thereof into the Union, shall be free, but may be held to service until the age of twenty-five years." The Tallmadge amendment barely passed in the House by a close vote that was divided according to sectional interests. It was defeated in the Senate after a long and heated debate. When Congress adjourned in March, 1819, the Missouri Bill was still deadlocked. Whether Missouri should be admitted as a slave state or should become a free state was a topic for angry discussion all over the country.

Why was the Missouri dispute important? The battle over admitting Missouri was of special importance because the even balance between free and slave states would be upset. In the early years of the republic, the populations of the North and the South had been about even, and the southern representatives in the House were not greatly outnumbered by the Northerners. By 1820, however, the picture had changed. The population north of Mason and Dixon's line and of the Ohio River was over 5 million, compared with less than 4½ million to the south, including slaves. This difference in population meant that the North had a larger number of representatives in the House than the South had. The sections were evenly balanced in the Senate,

John Quincy Adams, the sixth President, was the son of John Adams. He served his country long and well in many capacities. Adams' forbidding manner and stern sense of duty, however, made him unpopular with many citizens.

however, because there were eleven free and eleven slave states in 1819. The North now feared the voting power of another slave state in the Senate. At the same time, Southerners realized that unless Missouri came into the Union on their side, they would be outvoted in the Senate as well as the House.

Feeling over Missouri becomes tense. Arguments over the Tallmadge amendment grew bitter. In the North, state legislatures and mass meetings passed resolutions against admitting Missouri as a slave state. In the South, people felt that the amendment interfered with states' rights under the Constitution and denied the Southerner his right to move into new territories with his property, including slaves. Southern members of Congress argued that the Union was made up of states with equal rights, and that when Congress admitted a state it

had no power to restrict that state's freedom of action. The crisis was serious. Thomas W. Cobb of Georgia warned that if the amendment were passed, it would mean the breaking up of the Union. "We have kindled a fire," he is reported to have said, "which all the waters of the ocean cannot put out, which seas of blood can only extinguish."

The Missouri Compromise is accepted. Fortunately, while the debate was going on, the northeastern counties of Massachusetts asked to be admitted to the Union as a separate state, to be called Maine. Here was an opportunity to end the deadlock over Missouri. The Senate proposed to admit Missouri as a slave state and Maine as a free state. At the same time, the Senate proposed that in the rest of the Louisiana Purchase territory north of the parallel 36°30′, slavery should be prohibited. (See map, page 195.) Early in 1820 the House accepted this compromise, and bitterness among the sections was checked. But John Quincy Adams predicted, "the present question is a mere preamble — a title-page to a great tragic volume."

"Favorite sons" compete for the Presidency. The hidden forces of sectionalism again rose to the surface as the election of 1824 drew near. James Monroe was the last of the group of prominent Republicans in Virginia. There was no two-party system and there were no clear-cut issues. As a result, the campaign narrowed down to a struggle among several outstanding political leaders. Since the congressional caucus (see footnote, page 156) gave the voters little chance to express themselves, it was already losing popularity as a way to nominate candidates. For that reason, a number of state legislatures boosted their own "favorite sons."

New England gave grudging support to the stern and unbending John Quincy Adams, most promising of the northern candidates. Southern hopes were centered on William H. Crawford of Georgia, Secretary of the Treasury and the choice of a weak congressional caucus. Out of the West came two favorite sons — Henry Clay

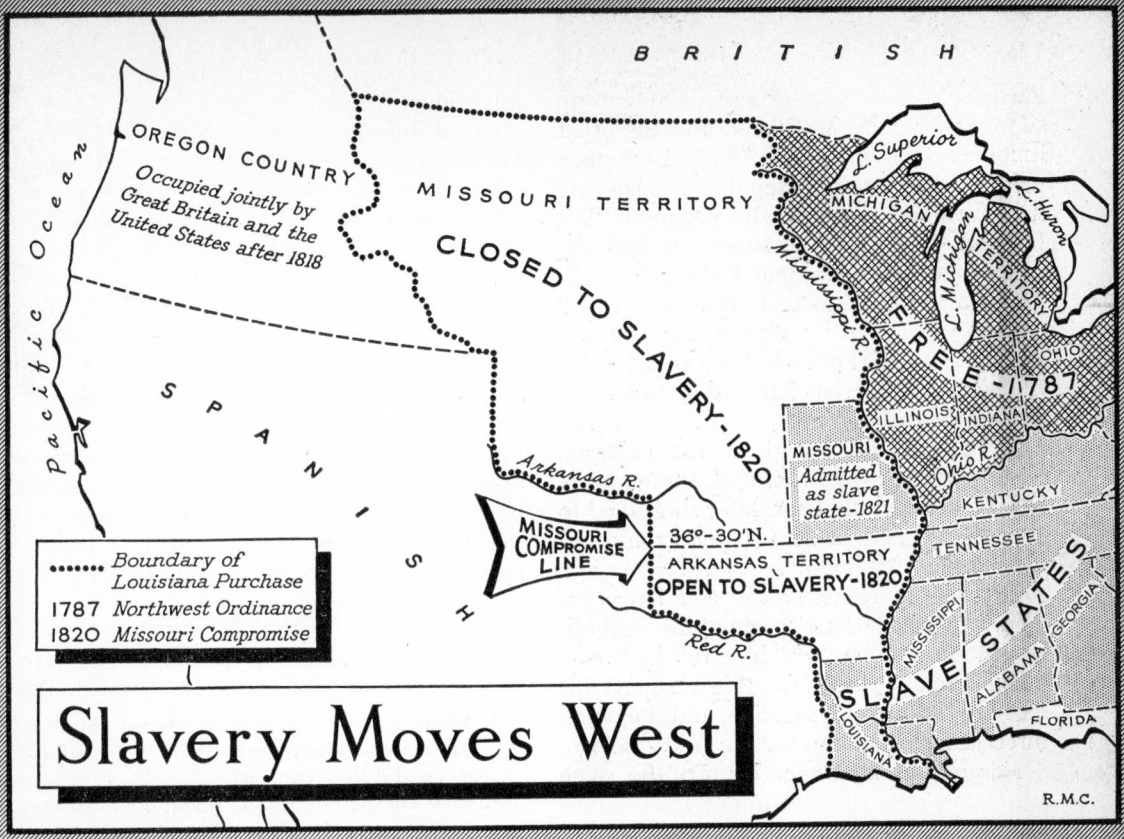

Legend:
•••••• Boundary of Louisiana Purchase
1787 *Northwest Ordinance*
1820 *Missouri Compromise*

Slavery Moves West

The Missouri Compromise settled the slavery question in the territory of the Louisiana Purchase. Can you see why the South favored further territorial expansion?

of Kentucky, champion of nationalism, and Andrew Jackson of Tennessee, Indian fighter, hero of New Orleans, and idol of the frontier.

When the electoral votes were counted, Jackson led with 99 votes. Adams ran second with 84, mostly from New England and New York. Crawford, handicapped by serious illness, came in third with 41, while Clay got only 37. Since no candidate had a majority of the electoral votes, the final choice for President rested with the House of Representatives. As provided in the Twelfth Amendment, house members were to vote by states on the three highest candidates.

Clay had no chance of election, but his powerful influence in the House enabled him to aid or defeat any candidate. He was opposed to Jackson because Jackson was his own rival in the West and because he was a "military chieftain." Clay gave his support to Adams, with whom he most

nearly agreed on the important questions of the day. Adams won on the first ballot. Two days later he announced the appointment of Clay as Secretary of State.

The Republican Party splits. Even before this announcement, there had been rumors of a "deal" between Adams and Clay. Clay's appointment now struck Jackson and his followers as proof of "the disgraceful traffic of Congressional votes for executive office." Adams was the soul of honesty. He was not the type of person to take part in a corrupt deal. But many people believed the charge against him, especially people in the West. The election of Adams was also attacked on the ground that it went against the wishes of the people. Since Jackson had received more electoral and popular votes than any other candidate, his managers claimed that the House was under obligation to elect him.

Two important developments resulted from the dispute. First, the Republican

195

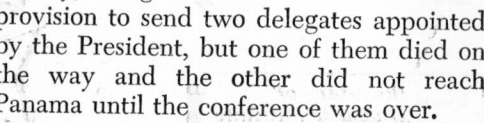

Party split into two groups. One group supported Adams and Clay, and the other followed Jackson. The Adams-Clay men were called National Republicans because they favored a nationalistic program. The Jackson wing was a mixture. It had the support of Vice-President Calhoun, Crawford, Jackson's regular followers, and all people who for any reason disliked the administration. For example, support for Jackson came even from the Northeast where factory workers and farmers felt Jackson was the friend of the common man. Jackson's followers took the name of Democratic-Republicans, later shortened to Democrats, and took up Jefferson's old ideas of states' rights.

The second result of the election argument was that Jackson made up his mind to win the Presidency, which he felt had been taken from him unjustly. He resigned his seat in the Senate in 1825 and began a three year's campaign for the next election.

Adams' administration is unfruitful. The arguments over the election of 1824 handicapped the Adams administration from the start. Nor did Adams' personality help matters. Though John Quincy Adams was one of the best equipped of American Presidents, he lacked the winning charm of Henry Clay and the glamour of Andrew Jackson. Cold and forbidding, he set a rigid standard of conduct for himself and others. He refused to use his control over government positions as a means of rewarding his friends or punishing his enemies.

Adams also stood firm on his program of nationalism, an attitude which made enemies among the representatives of the different sections. For example, he recommended a broad program of internal improvements to a Congress which was hostile to the idea. Again, when he tried to uphold the treaty rights of the Creek and Cherokee Indians, he was drawn into a quarrel with the governor of Georgia. That argument lost Adams the friendship of the people of Georgia and of other Southerners. He emerged with

Cherokee Indian

little glory in the conduct of foreign affairs. He wanted to send delegates to a meeting of American republics at Panama to consider problems affecting "the prosperity of the American hemisphere." Though this proposal was violently attacked, he would not give in. Finally, Congress made provision to send two delegates appointed by the President, but one of them died on the way and the other did not reach Panama until the conference was over.

Creek Indian

——————— CHECK-UP ———————

How did the Missouri question and political rivalry contribute to the rise of sectionalism?

1. What were the economic interests of the Northeast, West, and South? In what ways did they conflict?

2. How did the question of admitting Missouri bring sectional feeling to a head? How was the issue settled?

3. How did the election of 1824 lead to a split in the Republican Party? Why was Adams not a successful President?

5. The Tariff Question Leads to a Crisis

Tariff disputes arise. The tariff question finally brought out all the bitterness that existed among the different sections of the country. When the tariff bill of 1816 was passed, national feeling had been so strong that there had been no real fight over the bill. By the end of Monroe's second administration that national feeling had largely disappeared. In spite of strong protests from southern planters and New England shippers, a new tariff bill was passed in 1824 which offered more protection for manufacturers. Encouraged by this success, factory owners grew more insistent every year in their demands for tariff protection. Since manufacturing was taking the place of shipping as New England's leading activity, the Northeast as a whole became favorable to a protective tariff. At the same time, opposition increased in the South. "There is not a petty manufacturer in the union," charged Doctor Thomas Cooper, president of South Carolina College, "from the owner of a spinning factory to the maker of a hobnail . . . , who is not pressing forward to the plunder; and who may not be expected to worry Congress with petitions, memorials, and querulous statements for permission to put his hand into the planter's pocket."

The "Tariff of Abominations" pleases nobody. As the election of 1828 drew near, Jackson's backers looked around for some way to discredit Adams. The tariff issue offered a good opportunity. They proposed a tariff measure which gave a high degree of protection to manufacturers. The advantages, however, were offset by the fact that the measure also raised duties on raw materials, such as wool, that New England manufacturers needed to import. The Jackson supporters hoped that many northern votes would be cast against the bill because

the price for protection would be too high to pay. They further expected that these northern votes, combined with a solid southern opposition, would defeat the tariff bill. The blame for this defeat could then be placed upon the New Englanders and their leader, Adams.

The scheme failed. Distasteful as the bill was to New Englanders, enough of their congressmen voted for it to pass the so-called "Tariff of Abominations" in both houses. As Daniel Webster later put it: "Its enemies spiced it with whatsoever they thought would make it distasteful; its friends took it, drugged as it was."

The South protests the new tariff. The "Tariff of Abominations" raised violent objections in the South. In Charleston, flags were flown at half-mast. Southerners talked openly about refusing to obey the tariff law, and a boycott was urged against the products of the North. The most impressive protest against the new tariff was written by Vice-President John C. Calhoun. In his famous *Exposition and Protest*, approved by a committee of the South Carolina legislature, the southern statesman attacked the tariff as "unconstitutional, unequal, and oppressive." It was unconstitu-

Duties on imports from 1790 to the 1860's are emphasized in this chart. (See also pages 383 and 544.) What was the tariff policy of the United States until 1816? Why were rates increased after 1816? Why were they reduced after 1833?

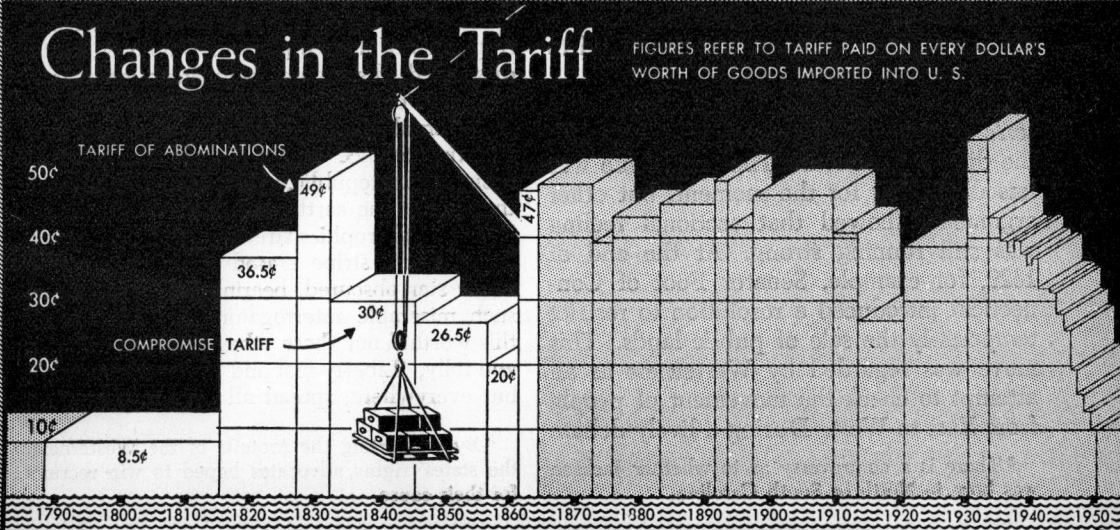

Changes in the Tariff

FIGURES REFER TO TARIFF PAID ON EVERY DOLLAR'S WORTH OF GOODS IMPORTED INTO U. S.

tional, he said, because it was not meant to raise revenue but to protect one field of industry at the expense of the others. It was unequal and oppressive because the South, which usually purchased its manufactured articles from Europe, was the chief victim. Then Calhoun went on to say that the remedy for such a situation lay in state action. He argued that the Union was a compact, or agreement, among sovereign states, and that the states had the right to judge whether the compact had been broken by the federal government. If any state decided that acts of Congress were unconstitutional, a convention representing the people of that state could decide how the acts should be declared null and void [of no effect] inside its borders.

Jackson wins the election of 1828. The South put off any definite action on the protective tariff until after the election of 1828. Jackson, a native Carolinian,[3] had not gone on record in favor of protection. It was hoped that, if elected, he might be able to solve the tariff problem. The election campaign between Adams and Jackson was one of bitter personal attacks on both sides. Each party waged a vigorous campaign of mud-slinging and slander. In the election, Adams carried only New England, Delaware, New Jersey, and parts of Maryland and New York. Jackson won the solid vote of Pennsylvania and the states west of the Alleghenies and south of the Potomac. In the largest popular vote yet cast, he received nearly 650,000 as against about 500,-000 for Adams. Calhoun was re-elected to the Vice-Presidency.

Hayne and Webster debate. After Jackson's election, tension continued between the different sections. The tariff issue was less disturbing for the moment, but other arguments showed that sectional feeling was still running strong. At the end of 1829, for example, Senator Foot of Connecticut introduced a resolution to restrict temporarily the sale of public lands. This move was regarded by Westerners as an attempt to check the movement of people from East to West. During a lively debate

on the resolution, Senator Robert Y. Hayne [4] of South Carolina made a brilliant speech. He accused the North of an "unprovoked attack upon the South," and condemned the increase of federal power as "the worst of evils." His speech made a strong case for the doctrine of states' rights and *nullification*, as expressed in the South Carolina *Exposition and Protest.*

His argument was answered by Daniel Webster. Before a packed Senate, Webster delivered what is generally regarded as the greatest oration heard in Congress during the 1800's. His speech was a powerful plea for the defense of the Union against the advancing tide of sectionalism. He said it was absurd to regard the federal government as a mere instrument for carrying out the will of the states. "It is, sir," declared Webster, "the people's constitution, the people's government; made for the people; made by the people; and answerable to the people." Within the limits of the powers granted in the Constitution, the federal government should be the supreme authority. No state should be allowed to set aside a law of Congress, or the Union would be no more than "a rope of sand." Whether a law was constitutional was not a decision for states to make, but one that should be left to the federal courts or the people. Webster ended his speech with this eloquent plea for union:

When mine eyes shall be turned to behold for the last time the sun in heaven, may I not see him shining on the broken and dishonored fragments of a once glorious Union; on States dissevered, discordant, belligerent; on a land rent with civil feuds, or drenched, it may be, in fraternal blood! Let their last feeble and lingering glance rather behold the glorious ensign of the republic, now known and honored throughout the earth, still full high advanced, its arms and trophies streaming in their original lustre, not a stripe erased or polluted, nor a single star obscured, bearing for its motto, no such miserable interrogatory as "What is all this worth?" nor those other words of delusion and folly, "Liberty first and Union afterwards"; but everywhere, spread all over in characters

---

[3] There is a controversy as to whether Jackson was born in North or South Carolina.

[4] By supporting the protests of the Westerners, the states' rights advocates hoped to win recruits for their cause.

of living light, blazing on all its ample folds, as they float over the sea and over the land, and in every wind under the whole heavens, that other sentiment, dear to every true American heart — Liberty *and* Union, now and forever, one and inseparable!

The conflict between states' rights and a strong union had never before been expressed with such drama and vividness as they were in the debate between Hayne and Webster.

Jackson toasts the Union. The political group favoring states' rights wanted very much to draw President Jackson over to their side. They tried to do it several months after the Webster-Hayne debate at a banquet on the anniversary of Jefferson's birthday. On this occasion, states' rights and nullification were referred to as true Democratic principles. Then Jackson smashed the hopes of the states' rights group. Called upon to give a toast, he rose to his full height and said, deliberately: "Our *Federal* Union: *It must be preserved.*" All eyes turned to Vice-President Calhoun. He waited until everyone sat down. Then he slowly offered a second toast: "The Union: Next to our liberty, the most dear." After a slight pause he went on: "May we all remember that it can only be preserved by respecting the rights of the States." This dramatic incident lasted only a moment, but those present knew just how important it was. Soon afterward there was an open break between Jackson and Calhoun. Jackson then reorganized his cabinet to get rid of Calhoun's political friends.[5]

The tariff quarrel breaks out again. Meanwhile, anger over the tariff was increasing in South Carolina. Although some

[5] The breach between Jackson and Calhoun was widened by the President's discovery that Calhoun, as a member of Monroe's cabinet in 1818, had urged the recall and censure of Jackson for his rash invasion of Florida. This fact, long harbored as a secret, was revealed to the President by Calhoun's enemies just at the moment Jackson's ire against Calhoun had been aroused. Furthermore, Jackson wished Peggy Eaton, the wife of one of the cabinet members, to be accepted by Washington society, but Calhoun's wife was one of the leaders in the movement to snub her because of her lowly background and unconventional past.

John C. Calhoun of South Carolina, sometimes called the Great Nullificator, was a brilliant political thinker. He fought unceasingly against the increasing power of the federal government.

of the worst features of the "Tariff of Abominations" were modified by a new tariff act in 1832, a protective tariff had clearly become the settled policy of the government. South Carolina decided to take action.

A state convention declared, in the name of the sovereign people of South Carolina, that the tariff acts of 1828 and 1832 and all other protective acts were null and void and of no effect upon the state and its citizens. Federal or state officials were forbidden to collect customs duties in the state after February 1, 1833. Finally, immediate secession from the Union was threatened if the federal government tried to use force "to reduce this State to obedience."

Jackson meets the threat of nullification. President Jackson met the defiance of South Carolina at once. The tariff might be good or bad, but in his opinion there was only one answer to the action South Carolina had taken: the laws must be enforced and the Union preserved. He issued a proclamation denying any state the right to nullify acts of Congress. Meanwhile, orders had been given to strengthen the garrisons of the forts in Charleston Harbor, and revenue cutters had been sent with orders to be ready for instant action.

It is not certain whether either side was prepared to push the issue to an open break. South Carolina expected aid from the other southern states, but though the other southern states were more or less in sympathy with states' rights doctrines, none of them openly supported her stand. On the other hand, Jackson's followers were afraid of an open split in Democratic ranks and they suggested an adjustment of the tariff. Calhoun, who had resigned the Vice-Presidency to take a seat in the Senate and lead in the debates, was willing to give way if some of the southern demands were met.

A compromise tariff is proposed. In the end Clay, who had no desire to furnish his old rival, Jackson, with the chance to lead an army into South Carolina, worked out a compromise tariff. This measure won the approval of Calhoun and was adopted by Congress. The rates were essentially the same as in the act of 1832. However, all duties above 20 per cent were to be gradually scaled down until, in 1842, none of them would be over 20 per cent. At the same time, Congress passed a Force Bill, which gave the President power to use the army and navy to collect customs duties if necessary. The South Carolina convention assembled again, repealed its ordinance nullifying the tariff acts but in turn nullified the Force Bill. The last gesture was harmless since the President no longer had any reason to use force.

The nullification quarrel had subsided at last, and both sides claimed they had won. In South Carolina, people felt that Congress had been obliged to back down on its tariff policy. On the other hand, nationalists were cheered by Jackson's firm stand and by the passage of the Force Bill, which received large majorities in both houses. For the moment, compromise had been successful, but the depth and intensity of sectional feeling stood revealed in sharp and fearful outlines.

——————— CHECK-UP ———————

How did the tariff question lead to a crisis?

1. Why was the tariff a sectional issue? What was the Tariff of Abominations?
2. What was Calhoun's plan for state action against a national law?
3. How did the question of public lands lead to a debate on states' rights? How was Jackson's attitude shown on this issue?
4. How did the tariff of 1832 lead to a showdown between South Carolina and Jackson? How was the issue finally compromised?

CHAPTER REVIEW

Terms to Understand

sectionalism
state banks
bonus
protective tariff
"wildcat banks"
internal improvements
Creoles

"favorite sons"
nationalism
compact
resolution
nullification
states' rights
secession

People and Things to Know About

"era of good feelings"
second Bank of the
  United States

Rush-Bagot Agreement
ment
Simón Bolívar

People and Things to Know About (Cont.)

James Monroe
John C. Calhoun
Panic of 1819
McCulloch vs. Maryland
Dartmouth College Case
National Road
Henry Clay
American System
John Quincy Adams
José de San Martín

Monroe Doctrine
Tallmadge amendment
Missouri Compromise
William H. Crawford
"Tariff of Abominations"
Exposition and Protest
Webster-Hayne Debate
Compromise Tariff
Force Bill

Historic Dates to Identify

1811	1819	1828
1816	1820	1832
1817	1823	1833
	1824	

Questions to Discuss

1. What policies would you have wanted the national government to adopt in 1815 had you been (a) a New England manufacturer, (b) a New England merchant, (c) a southern planter, (d) a frontier farmer?

2. Frederick Jackson Turner, a great American historian, has defined a *section* of the country as "any part of the national domain which is geographically and socially sufficiently unified to have a true consciousness of its own ideals and customs and to possess a sense of its distinction from other parts of the country." How would you compare sectionalism and nationalism? Why do you suppose that states' rights became closely linked with sectionalism? Do we still have sectionalism?

3. What progress was made in removing foreign influence from the Western Hemisphere during the period covered by this chapter? Why was the Monroe Doctrine the climax to this development?

4. To what extent was Adams' lack of success as a President due to his personal qualities and to what extent to factors outside of his control?

5. Why could we say of the Missouri question that "coming events cast their shadows before"? What other compromises have you noted in your study of American history? What are the advantages and disadvantages of compromises as solutions to problems? Are compromises necessary in a democracy?

6. If the United States and Canada have been able to get along peaceably for such a long time, why cannot European nations do the same?

7. Are we in as much need of a protective tariff today as we were in 1815?

Relating Geography and History

On an outline map of the United States locate:

(a) The frontier lines of 1790 and 1830.

(b) Our northern boundary as established by the agreement with England in 1818.

(c) Our western boundary as established by the treaty of 1819.

(d) The states which were added to the union between 1790 and 1830.

(e) The divisions made by the Missouri Compromise.

(f) The route of the National Road.

When dealing with historical map data you should learn to use an historical atlas. Paullin, C. O., *Atlas of the Historical Geography of the United States* is the most complete, but Lord, Clifford and Elizabeth, *Historical Atlas of the United States* is very good. All of the information for the questions above can be located in these atlases.

Other Things to Do

1. Read Jackson's famous reply to the South Carolina nullifiers in Commager's *Documents,* No. 144. Sum up Jackson's arguments against the right of a state to nullify a national law.

2. Debate: *Resolved,* That the states rather than the Supreme Court should have the final authority to pass on the constitutionality of a national law.

3. Prepare a talk on the building of the National Road and the travel on it. You will find information in Riegel's *America Moves West,* and Hulbert's *The Cumberland Road.* Numerous stories are associated with the road. Be sure to bring some of these into your talk.

*4. The Monroe Doctrine was the first great declaration of foreign policy principles by the United States, and we had been building consistently towards it. List in chronological order the chief steps which resulted in the Monroe Doctrine. (Washington's proclamation of neutrality, the recognition of the Latin-American Republics, and the purchase of Florida were some of the steps.)

Election parader

Chapter 10

ANDREW JACKSON DOMINATES THE

POLITICAL SCENE

Under our free institutions, I am sure the people in every part of the United States are too enlightened not to understand their own rights and interests, and to detect and defeat every effort to gain undue advantages over them . . .

Andrew Jackson's Farewell Address

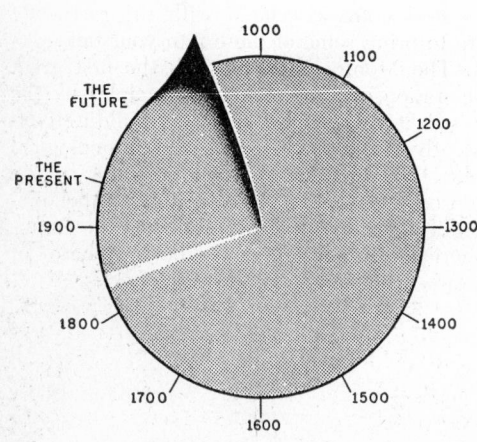

1828-1842

We have seen two conflicting tendencies in American life after the War of 1812. For ten years or so there was a strong growth of national feeling. In time, however, this unity was checked by sectional rivalry as the various parts of the country sought to advance their own particular interests. In the 1820's — and more strongly in the 1830's — still a third force made itself felt. Led by frontiersmen, common people everywhere began to demand a voice in the government. This trend toward *democracy* was to affect profoundly the life of the Republic.

The spread of democracy in the United States is closely linked with the name of Andrew Jackson, vigorous American champion of the common man. In the words of one historian, however, "Jackson himself was a product, rather than the creator, of the new democratic spirit, for he rode into power on a tide of forces that had been gathering strength for more than a decade . . . " This growth of democracy had its beginnings in the westward surge of the American people. Out of the hardships of frontier living grew a feeling of equality among men, that led the frontier people to live and act in more democratic ways. During the "Jacksonian Era," which included not only Jackson's two terms but that of his successor, Van Buren, these tendencies came to affect the entire nation.

This chapter tells how democratic attitudes increased. It reports the colorful behavior of Jackson in the White House. It tells how the forces of opposition finally brought an end to the Jacksonian era in 1840, although they failed to put into effect any real program of their own. The highlights of the chapter are these:

1. Democracy spreads during the Jacksonian Era.
2. Andrew Jackson favors nationalism and the West.
3. The Whigs bring an end to the Jacksonian Era.
4. The opponents of Jackson win a hollow victory.

---

1 Democracy Spreads During the Jacksonian Era

Voting is limited in the early republic. Andrew Jackson's election, like Jefferson's in 1800, reflected the demands of a growing nation. As the population of the country expanded, the cry for a greater share in the government became louder. The framers of the Constitution, you will recall, had looked with grave doubts upon the idea of allowing the common people to direct their government. Instead, they left the decisions concerning *suffrage*, or *franchise* — that is, the right to vote — to the individual states. In most states during the first 25 years of the republic, an American could not vote or hold office unless he owned property. When Washington was President, hardly more than six per cent of the total white population was able or bothered to vote. The "revolution of 1800," when Jefferson became President, did not greatly change the suffrage. Jefferson believed in the rule of the common people, but the early Republicans made few efforts to remove the restrictions which prevented most people from voting or holding office. Many political leaders still did not believe that the common people could be expected to vote wisely. As late as 1820 Daniel Webster declared that "it would seem, then, to be the part of political wisdom to found government on property."

Democracy gets a start in the West. The movement to let more people vote and hold office came chiefly out of the rapidly growing West. The frontiersman lived under rugged conditions, in which common sense and hard work were important. His rank among his fellows was determined by what he could do — not by wealth, birth, or social position. By 1828, in the eleven

Women could vote in New Jersey in the early years, but the right was removed in 1807. It was 113 years before all eligible women in the United States were permitted to vote.

new frontier states which had been admitted to the Union, nearly all free, white males were allowed to vote. One after another, the older states followed the example of the West. During Jackson's administration a movement was also begun to lower or do away with the property qualifications for holding office.

Workingmen vote for better conditions. The East quickly felt the effect of extending the suffrage. Now the laborer and the mechanic of the city, though they owned no land, had the right to vote side by side with the cultured clergyman and the wealthy merchant or manufacturer. Workers began to use this political strength to improve living and working conditions. In 1828 they formed a Workingmen's Party in Philadelphia. Among other things, this new party demanded: (1) public education, (2) equal taxation, (3) election of all public officials by the voters, and (4) an end to the practice of imprisoning debtors. In New York another Workingmen's Party with a similar platform elected a candidate for the legislature in an exciting campaign in 1829. These early political efforts brought some results. Laws were passed which forbade sending a man to jail because he was unable to pay a debt. A beginning was made in free public education. Some laws were passed to make factory work safer for employees. Such changes alarmed property owners, who began to make gloomy predictions about the future. But these early labor parties did not last long. Labor leaders lacked political experience, and there were many disagreements within the parties. The people who owned property opposed the labor parties at every turn.

Party politics brings the spoils system. The extension of the right to vote was accompanied by important developments in party politics. Political leaders of the older parties now had to attract and hold the loyalty of the new voters. Year after year these leaders were expected to deliver a certain number of votes for the party ticket. Such leaders, or "bosses," often held no government positions themselves, but they were frequently able to dictate the choice

of candidates for office as well as the policies of the party. The leaders built up political organizations to carry on their work. Some organizations worked so smoothly and efficiently that they earned the name of *machines*. In order to hold the political workers in line, it became the custom to reward them by appointments to office. This custom was summed up by Senator Marcy of New York when he said, "To the victor belong the spoils." The *spoils system* was first used in state politics, notably in New York and Pennsylvania. During the Jacksonian era it was introduced into national politics on a fairly wide scale.

Nominating conventions come into use. The rising democratic spirit of the nation was also indicated by the growing use of conventions for nominating candidates for federal office. The selection of candidates by caucuses of legislators (page 156), who were out of touch with the voters, was not in keeping with the democratic trends of the day. It became customary for local groups to choose delegates to county conventions which, in turn, nominated county officers. This convention system soon was used in state and national politics. A minor party, called the Anti-Masons,[1] held a national convention at Baltimore in 1831, at which they nominated a candidate for President and adopted a sort of platform. Near the end of the year, the National Republicans nominated Henry Clay for President in a convention of eighteen states at Baltimore. A few months later in May, 1832, a convention of the Democratic Party, also meeting in Baltimore, nominated Jackson for President. To secure the Democratic nomination, a candidate had to get a two-thirds vote, a rule which the party generally followed until 1936.

Jackson's inauguration shows democratic trends. The lively democratic spirit of the nation was on parade when Andrew Jack-

(Continued on page 206)

---

[1] The Anti-Masons were organized to oppose secret societies. They were angered by the alleged murder of a man who had disclosed the secrets of Freemasonry. The Anti-Masons were later largely absorbed by the new Whig Party.

Andrew Jackson
(1767-1845)

Frontier Lawyer

WHEN ANDREW JACKSON became President in 1829, his opponents were uneasy — and with good cause. In background, personality, and political views he differed greatly from the line of Virginia Presidents and the New England Adamses who had preceded him.

Jackson's early life was spent amid the hardships of the frontier, where, as a lad, he was forced to shift for himself. Acquiring some knowledge of law, he moved to Tennessee to practice the profession. Soon after Tennessee was organized as a state, Jackson was sent as a representative to Congress. Though in later life he was a commanding figure, he was described at this time as "a tall, lank, uncouth looking personage, with long locks hanging over his face, and a cue down his back tied in an eel-skin; his dress singular, his manners and deportment that of a rough backwoodsman." He won fame and popularity, however, particularly in the West, because of his record as an Indian fighter and a soldier. Though unsuccessful in the presidential election of 1824, he redoubled his efforts and was swept into office four years later.

Soldier

Jackson's character aroused either loyalty or hatred. He possessed a strong will and a violent temper. To cross him was to make him a personal enemy. In his younger days he fought more than one duel. Such character traits, however, were offset by rugged honesty and fearlessness. In point of view he represented the rising democracy of the West. He believed wholeheartedly in the rule of the people and considered himself as their direct representative. As a result he expanded the influence of the Presidency and stamped it with his own personality as few other Presidents have done. His two terms were filled with strife over the tariff, nullification by South Carolina, and a battle over the Bank of the United States; yet at their close he retired to Tennessee, still popular with the great mass of people and leaving his chosen successor in the White House. Few periods in our national development stand out so clearly as the Jacksonian era.

President

son took his first oath of office as President in 1829. "Today we have had the inauguration," wrote Webster. "A monstrous crowd of people is in the city. I never saw anything like it before. Persons have come five hundred miles to see General Jackson, and they really seem to think that the country is rescued from some dreadful danger." At the reception held afterwards at the White House, no social distinctions were made. The mansion swarmed with frontiersmen, farmers, and laborers, both colored and white, who had come to shake hands with the new President. No arrangements had been made to handle such a crowd. For a better view of their idol, men climbed with muddy boots on the damask-covered chairs and sofas. They broke china and glassware in a mad scramble for refreshments. In this crush, the President might have been injured if he had not escaped through a back door. After several thousand dollars' damage had been done, the noisy crowd was lured out of the building by tubs of punch placed on the lawn. "It was the People's day, and the People's President," declared an observer. To a startled justice of the Supreme Court, however, "the reign of King 'Mob' seemed triumphant."

Jackson dominates the government. Andrew Jackson was one of the most forceful characters among American Presidents. He was tall and rugged, full of fierce energy, a man able to grip the imagination of the people. Jackson was a true son of the frontier. Though he had only a very little schooling, he was by no means illiterate, and he could express himself in clear, forceful English. When he had made a decision, he clung to it stubbornly. His temper was violent and he had strong prejudices, but there was never a doubt about his sincerity, honesty, and courage. He was a born leader of men, and his military glory made him the hero of the people.

Jackson had a firm faith in the principles of democracy. When he became President, political power passed from the few to the many. A favorite phrase which crops up again and again in his writings was "the will of the people," although he usually took it upon himself to interpret their will in his own way. Jackson's energetic personality and his deep-seated belief that he spoke for the people helped to make the office of President a much stronger influence in national affairs than it had been up to that time. His enemies liked to picture him as a tyrant, but actually Jackson used his powers with moderation.

Jackson consults his "kitchen cabinet." "Old Hickory," as Jackson was affectionately nicknamed, appointed Martin Van Buren as his Secretary of State. This choice was a good one, but Jackson filled other cabinet offices with politicians, instead of with men of outstanding ability. The truth was that Jackson paid little attention to the advice of his cabinet. Instead, he liked to consult old and tried political friends, like Amos Kendall of Kentucky and William B. Lewis of Tennessee. These men held only minor federal offices, but the "people's President" listened to them when he wanted to find out what the people were really thinking. Jackson's enemies scornfully called this little group the "kitchen cabinet."

Jackson uses the spoils system. Soon after Jackson became President, he turned his attention to the problem of officeholding. Up to that time a man appointed to federal office could usually expect to hold that job for life. As a result, many government officials were old. Most of them had been appointed from the well-to-do classes. Jackson felt that such a situation was neither sound nor democratic. "The duties of all public officers," he said, "are, or at least admit of being made, so plain and simple that men of intelligence may readily qualify themselves for their performance; and I cannot but believe that more is lost by the long continuance of men in office than is generally to be gained by their experience." Jackson and his advisers also felt that federal positions should be in the hands of their friends, who should "rotate" in office (hold a job for a time and then make room for another).

Jackson did not make a clean sweep of the officeholders. Some of them, indeed, were among his supporters. But over 900 were removed during the first eighteen months of Jackson's Presidency. There followed a "general scramble for plunder." To qualify for an appointment, loyalty to the party or a promise of future service became an important requirement. Jackson's use of the "spoils system" was bitterly attacked by his enemies but was not as bad as they charged. What made it appear so was that Jackson, in contrast to Jefferson, made many of his removals all at once, rather than over a period of time. Actually, out of the total number of federal office-holders, the percentage of Jackson's removals was about the same as Jefferson's, and was not so high as the percentage under some later Presidents.

Building a frontier road

─────── CHECK-UP ───────

How did democracy spread during the Jacksonian era?

1. What changes were made in suffrage requirements? How else did our country become more democratic?

2. What was the spoils system? The nominating convention? How were they evidence of the growing democratic spirit?

3. What were Jackson's ideas about the Presidency? What political means did he use to insure his power?

2 Andrew Jackson Favors Nationalism and the West

Jackson supports nationalism. Jackson was a firm champion of nationalism. He had made that clear in his famous toast to the Union, and in his sharp answer to South Carolina's threat of nullification (pages 199 and 200). After those two incidents, no one doubted that Jackson put national welfare above sectional interests.

Jackson strengthens the nation abroad. Jackson's foreign policy strengthened the position of the United States. Trade with the British West Indies had been restricted since the Revolution and had almost died out during the Adams administration. Jackson succeeded in reopening it by getting Congress to withdraw certain restrictions on British vessels. England then agreed to permit full freedom of trade for American vessels in the British West Indies.

Jackson likewise succeeded in working out agreements with several European nations, which settled claims of the United States for damages suffered by American merchants during the Napoleonic wars. One of these agreements was made with France in 1831. But when France failed to make her payments, the President lashed out in a message to Congress which offended the French legislature. The French demanded an apology before they would pay what they owed. Jackson refused to back down. For a short time, relations between France and the United States were strained, but finally the matter was settled to the satisfaction of both sides. America's position abroad was now stronger, and Jackson became even more popular at home for the successful way he had handled foreign affairs. His forthright methods of dealing with foreign countries became known as "shirt-sleeve diplomacy."

Jackson opposes internal improvements. Although Jackson, as a son of the frontier, had been solidly supported by the new western states, he clearly considered the national welfare more important than their special interests. The western states were eager for internal improvements, especially roads at national expense. Their hopes received a definite setback when "Old Hickory" vetoed a bill calling for federal aid in the building of the Maysville Road in Kentucky. Jackson explained his veto on the ground that the road was "of purely local character." He believed it would not be wise to pour federal money into private undertakings before federal taxes were cut down and the national debt was paid. The Democrats accepted Jackson's firm stand as party policy, and for the time being there were no more internal improvements at federal expense.

Jackson favors a liberal land policy. With western demands for a more liberal land policy and the removal of Indians, Jackson was much more sympathetic. It is true that the selling price of public lands was not reduced, as the frontier states had hoped it would be. A beginning was made, however, in improving the position of "squatters," or those pioneers who were living on land they had cleared but to which they had no legal title. Laws were passed permitting squatters to buy, for the actual cost of a survey, the lands they were actually living on and cultivating. Jackson himself believed that the public lands should cease to be a source of government income as soon as the government could get along without the money they brought in.

Indians are moved westward. The problem of cheap land was closely connected with the problem of Indian tribes living east of the Mississippi. When available land in this area grew scarce, the white men turned greedy eyes toward fertile land held by the Indians. As a former Indian fighter and frontiersman, Jackson agreed with the point of view that the Indians should give way to the white settlers. When Georgia tried to extend its authority over Indian lands within its border, the Supreme Court decreed that the state had no legal basis for its action. Georgia refused to obey the Supreme Court, and President Jackson sympathized with the state's stand. In fact, Jackson is reported to have said, "John Marshall has made his decision [in the Georgia case]: *now let him enforce it!*"

In an attempt to solve the Indian problem, Jackson recommended to Congress that the government should give the Indians land farther

Seminole Indian

west in return for their land east of the Mississippi. Congress accepted the suggestion and appropriated $500,000 to help transfer those Indians who were willing to accept the government's offer.

The removal of the Indians went on all through the Jacksonian Era. States passed laws extending their authority over Indian lands within their boundaries and more or less forced the Indians to pick up and go west. The Indians, especially the Sac and Fox tribes under Black Hawk, and the Seminoles in Florida, resisted stubbornly, but without success. (These tribes may be located on the map on page 178.)

Jackson attacks the national bank. In his vigorous attack upon the United States Bank, Jackson was very positively fighting for the interests of the West. The average settler in the West had to borrow money from time to time to buy land, put up buildings, or market his crop. For that reason, he favored a cheap and plentiful currency which would make it easier for him to pay his debts.[2] But the giant Bank of the United States kept the currency on a sound basis. Its bank notes (paper money) were freely accepted by creditors everywhere. State banks were thus forced to keep their notes on a solid footing. So long as the Bank of the United States was in existence, the chances for cheaper currency were slim.

Westerners had still other reasons for disliking the United States Bank. Most of its stock was owned in the East and abroad, but its profits came from loans made in the West and South. "All the flourishing cities of the West are mortgaged to this moneyed power," charged Thomas H. Benton in the Senate. Westerners also believed that the bank had used its influence against Jackson in the election of 1828. It was rumored that some of Jackson's chief foes, notably Clay and Webster, had received financial favors from the bank. Jackson supported

[2] A cheap or depreciated currency would make prices rise. The western farmers thus expected to get more dollars for their crops. Since debts, unlike prices, were fixed in terms of dollars, a cheap and plentiful currency would give the farmers more dollars to meet their debts than a sound currency would.

Prairie fires were one of the many hazards of pioneer life in America. In this old print, settlers are hastily building a backfire while trying to control their terrified horses.

the western point of view toward the bank in various messages to Congress. He attacked the bank's constitutionality, questioned the soundness of its currency, and urged a thorough investigation of its activities.

Congress favors recharter of the bank. The battle over the second Bank of the United States came to a climax in 1832, the very year in which Jackson was a candidate for re-election. The bank's charter still had four years to run. But if Jackson were re-elected, the fight over renewing the charter would come up during his second term — at a time when a decision against the bank would not do any harm to his political career. Jackson was by no means anxious to make an issue of the recharter of the bank in the election of 1832, because a split in the ranks of the Democratic Party might result. But Henry Clay, a strong supporter of the bank and a probable candidate for the Presidency, thought he could help his own cause by forcing the bank issue on Jackson before the election. For that reason, he and other National Republican leaders put pressure upon Nicholas Biddle, the president of the bank, to apply for a new charter in 1832. In July, 1832, Congress passed a bill to recharter the bank.

Jackson vetoes the bank bill. Jackson met the challenge squarely. He sent the bill back to the Senate with a stinging veto message which had "all the fury of a chained panther biting the bars of his cage." In his veto, Jackson condemned the bank as aristocratic and un-American, a tool of the eastern financiers and the foreigners who held its stock. He also charged that the bank increased sectional jealousy. The West, which held only $140,000 in bank stock, was paying more than $1,500,-000 yearly in interest on its loans. Such a payment, Jackson maintained, was a heavy tax upon western enterprise. In Jackson's opinion, the charter of the bank created nothing less than a monopoly which worked "to make the rich richer and the potent more powerful." Yet the duty of the government, he pointed out, was to give equal protection and privileges to all. The

Frontier bank

fact that the Supreme Court had declared the bank constitutional was of small importance to the aroused Jackson. His veto message was so worded that it inflamed the frontier against the East, the poor against the wealthy, and supporters of the new democracy against representatives of the established classes. Neither the House nor the Senate could muster a two-thirds majority to override the presidential veto.

Jackson is re-elected. By his veto, Jackson made certain that the election would turn mainly upon the question of "bank or no bank." Clay and Biddle thought the veto would split the Jacksonian forces. They soon discovered their mistake. The great mass of eastern workers and western farmers hardly ever came into personal contact with the bank, either as borrowers or depositors. When Jackson, their champion, lashed at it as a "monster" which beat down the poor, they rallied to his banner. The election became a smashing triumph for the President. Clay carried only three states in New England, along with Delaware, Kentucky, and part of Maryland. In the electoral college, Jackson polled 219 votes, against Clay's 49. Swept into office with Jackson, Martin Van Buren became Vice-President.

Government funds are removed from the Bank. If the supporters of the bank thought that the President would now let up in his attacks, they were greatly mistaken. Jackson regarded his victory at the polls as a complete endorsement of his anti-bank policy. He was more determined than ever to break all ties between the government and the bank. Early in 1833 he wrote, "Until I can strangle the hydra of corruption, the Bank, I will not shrink from my duty, or my part."

Jackson determined upon two steps to carry out this purpose. He decided (1) to stop depositing government funds in the

Bank of the United States or its branches and (2) to draw out the federal deposits already in the bank until nothing was left. This plan did not work out as easily as expected. Jackson had trouble getting a Secretary of the Treasury who would carry out his orders. He promoted one secretary to the State Department and dismissed another before he finally found one, Roger B. Taney, who would go along with his scheme. After that, government deposits were placed in selected state banks, or "pet banks" as they were popularly called, instead of in the Bank of the United States. This action had been ordered while Congress was not in session, and a storm of protest broke loose when the Senate met again. Under the guidance of Clay, the Senate condemned the President's whole course of action, and refused to confirm the appointment of Taney as Secretary of the Treasury.

Financial conditions become unstable. Jackson's policy toward the bank added to his great popularity in the West, but it clouded the final years of his administration with financial troubles. The nation's currency, formerly kept sound by the Bank of the United States, was soon in a chaotic condition. The number of state banks more than doubled between 1829 and 1837, while their circulation of bank notes tripled. Moreover, government revenue from the tariff and the sale of public lands was sufficient to pay off the public debt by 1835. In 1837 the United States passed on to the states a surplus of more than $28,000,000. Legally this sum was a loan, but in reality it was a gift. The surplus was used by some of the states for public improvements or for education, but in some states it was squandered on wasteful projects. The cheap and plentiful bank note currency, along with distribution of the surplus, brought on a period of speculation, especially in the purchase of western lands.

Jackson issues the Specie Circular. Outwardly, the country seemed to be riding a wave of prosperity. In 1836 the acreage of land sold was ten times the average of the previous ten years. But these lands were being bought with paper currency of doubtful value and often for speculation rather than use. Besides, the government's funds were on deposit in banks that were shaky because they had given too much credit. In order to correct this dangerous situation, Jackson issued the Specie Circular (1836) ordering that in the future public lands were to be sold only for gold and silver. The Specie Circular pricked the bubble of speculation. Soon after Jackson left office, a financial panic swept over the country (page 213).

And so Jackson's eight strenuous years in office drew to a close. Right or wrong, he had won every major contest of his administration. He was still the idol of the West. Even in the East, his popularity was so great that Harvard College, much to the disgust of John Quincy Adams, conferred an honorary degree upon him. His friends worshiped him and his enemies attacked him bitterly. Jackson's importance lay chiefly in the fact that he had caught the democratic spirit of the frontier, stamped it with his own vigorous personality, and made it a vital part of national life. Enemies might scorn the Jacksonian administration as the "reign of King Andrew," but it was actually the "day of the people."

——————— CHECK-UP ———————

How did Jackson favor nationalism and the West?

1. What were Jackson's policies in regard to (a) the Indians, (b) land sales, (c) road building? Why?
2. Why was the Bank of the United States unpopular in the West? What reasons did Jackson have for opposing it?
3. What events led to Jackson's veto of the bank bill? Why was the veto of political significance?
4. How did Jackson destroy the bank's power. What results followed?

An attempted assassination took place in 1835 when a madman named Lawrence fired two pistols at President Jackson. The caps exploded but the charges failed to go off. Political enemies claimed that the event was staged to arouse public sympathy for Jackson.

3 The Whigs Bring an End to the Jacksonian Era

The Whig Party is formed. As Jackson's second term wore on, opposition to the President grew stronger and brought about the formation of a new political organization called the Whig Party. Various groups of people joined the Whigs, and their only point of agreement was their hostility to "King Andrew" and his policies: (1) The largest group among the Whigs was the National Republican Party. This group came to control the Whig political beliefs, and their leader, Henry Clay, became the party's master mind. Clay favored a system of internal improvements, a protective tariff, and re-establishment of the Bank of the United States. (2) Other political groups within the Whig Party made it a peculiar hodgepodge. There were outspoken states' rights and anti-tariff men from the South, who were normally Democrats but had been drawn into the party because of Jackson's stand against nullification in South Carolina. Other recruits to the party included (3) merchants, bankers, and anyone else who was aroused over the President's attack upon the national bank, (4) Anti-Masons, and (5) personal enemies of Jackson.

The Whigs fail at the polls. In the election of 1836, the Whigs were handicapped by the lack of a national organization. They did not hold a national convention, issue a platform, or even agree upon a single candidate. They could not, therefore, put up a united front against the Democrats. Their plan was to take advantage of local feeling against Jackson and thus gain enough anti-Democratic votes in the electoral college to throw the choice of the President into the House of Representatives. For example, the Anti-Masons of Pennsylvania tried to snare western votes by backing General William Henry Harrison, Indian fighter and former Gov-

ernor of Indiana Territory. The Massachusetts Whigs supported Daniel Webster in an effort to hold the Northeast. In the South, anti-Jackson men supported Senator Hugh Lawson White of Tennessee.

To stand off these scattered attacks, the Democrats needed to hold a majority of their party together. Jackson was able to accomplish this because of his great popularity with the common people and his willingness to reward the faithful with appointments. Everyone knew that "Old Hickory" wanted Vice-President Van Buren to follow him in office, and this knowledge was enough to give Van Buren the unanimous nomination at a convention held in Baltimore. No platform was adopted. In fact, no platform was needed. Jackson had clearly identified the Democratic Party with certain principles: (1) the preservation of the Union at any cost, (2) the use of silver and gold instead of paper money, (3) the power of the common people, (4) opposition to internal improvements at national expense, and (5) opposition to the United States Bank. In the election of 1836, Van Buren received a substantial majority of 46 votes in the electoral college, even though he polled only 25,000 more popular votes than the combined total received by his opponents. Jackson retired to his home in Tennessee (1837), pleased that the people had approved his policies and that the presidential chair was now occupied by his closest adviser.

Van Buren proves unpopular. It was soon clear that the people as a whole did not share "Old Hickory's" enthusiasm for Van Buren. Van Buren had accepted the nomination with the promise "to tread generally in the footsteps" of Jackson. Many people doubted his ability to do so. Van Buren was smooth and polished in manner, one of the shrewdest politicians of his day, but he had few of the personal traits which had caused the common man to idolize Jackson. Stories about his snobbish habits were heard everywhere. He was accused of turning the White House into a "royal establishment," of using expensive silver and eating from gold plate, and of having "an ardent love for the horse race." Later generations, however, have come to believe that such rumors were exaggerated and that much of Van Buren's unpopularity came from circumstances over which he had no control.

A severe panic grips the nation. Van Buren had scarcely taken office before he was faced with a major business depression. The easy credit made possible by the "pet banks" and "wildcat banks" had resulted in wasteful spending for internal improvements and had encouraged reckless speculation. The Specie Circular, the tightening of bank credit, a crop shortage, pressure from foreign investors, and the scarcity of sound money — all these contributed to the crash in 1837 (page 211). Jackson's financial policy had helped to create the conditions of "boom and bust" but cannot be held entirely responsible for a depression into which England as well as the United States was plunged.

Once the panic had begun, it picked up speed rapidly. Some banks had to close their doors. Most of the others stopped payments in gold and silver. Prices and real estate values dropped everywhere. Land sales fell off sharply, and projects for internal improvements were suspended or given up entirely. By autumn, nine tenths of the factories in the East were closed, and thousands of people were out of work. Financial ruin stalked the country, but the weight of the depression fell most heavily upon the laboring people. During the winter of 1837–38, there was widespread suffering from hunger and exposure. Several bitter years went by before the country recovered from the panic and depression.

The independent treasury is established. The panic forced Van Buren's administration to spend most of its time wrestling with problems of finance and currency. To meet the emergency, Van Buren called a special session of Congress in September, 1837. The special session authorized an issue of $10,000,000 in treasury notes to pay current expenses. The Congress then turned to the problem of the banks. It seemed clear that there must be some federal financial institution to replace the

Henry Clay, from the backwoods of Virginia, became a great statesman. Because of his continual efforts to reconcile conflicting national interests he came to be called the Great Compromiser.

Bank of the United States. Van Buren recommended a treasury system which would be entirely independent of the nation's banks. According to this plan, as money was paid in to the government, it was to be stored in the Treasury at Washington, in the vaults of the mint, or in branch treasuries (sub-treasuries) to be built in the principal cities. The plan did not go through at once, because the Whigs — and some Democrats — preferred a new national bank. However, the independent treasury system was approved in 1840. Congress then set up the sub-treasuries and ordered treasury officials to use them to store public funds. Thus the United States government was completely separated from the banking business.

The Whigs organize for victory. The Whigs saw a real chance for victory in the election of 1840. The Panic of 1837, with the resulting depression and unemployment, gave them a long-awaited opportunity. As the campaign drew near, they loudly blamed the country's troubles upon the Democratic Party. As far back as the year of the panic, Henry Clay had written that the only true remedy for the calamity was a change in the administration. Daniel Webster entered the fight, attacking the Democrats for the "mal-administration of the government in currency, finance, and revenue."

When the Whigs met at their national convention in December, 1839, it seemed only logical that Clay should be chosen as the standard-bearer of the party. He was the outstanding Whig leader. But Clay had many enemies among the anti-Jackson forces that made up the Whig party. To his great disappointment, he was passed over by the convention, which his political enemies controlled. Instead, they secured the nomination for William Henry Harrison. Harrison was popular in the West and was widely known for his military career. (See page 175 for battle at Tippecanoe.) In addition, Harrison's political opinions were so vague that they could not be held against him by any of the anti-Jackson people. To make doubly sure of the support of the anti-Jackson group in the South, the convention nominated John Tyler of Virginia for the Vice-Presidency. Tyler found himself among the Whigs mainly because he was so violently opposed to the methods of Andrew Jackson. The convention adopted no platform at all. Avoiding any positive statement of principles, they planned to win with the cry, "Down with Van Buren," for Van Buren was running again as the Democratic nominee.

A Whig triumph ends the Jacksonian era. The Whigs tried all sorts of ballyhoo to stir up enthusiasm for their candidate. Somebody scornfully said of Harrison, "Give him A BARREL OF HARD CIDER, and settle a pension of two thousand a year on him, and . . . he will sit the remainder of his days in his log cabin by the side of a sea-coal fire, and study moral philosophy." The Democrats published this statement as an attack on Harrison, but the Whigs picked it up and used it in their campaign. Harrison was praised for his supposedly simple tastes and honest virtues, while Van Buren was denounced for luxurious living.

Uniformed Whigs paraded through the streets, great mass meetings were held, and campaign songs were lustily sung. Everywhere, the log cabin and the cider barrel became symbols of political simplicity and honesty. Such campaign slogans as "Tippecanoe and Tyler too" and "Van is a used-up man," were heard on all sides. Thus, the methods of the new democracy were used to defeat the very party which had introduced them. In the election of 1840, 2,400,000 people voted as compared with 1,500,000 in the previous election. Harrison won 234 electoral votes, while Van Buren received only 60. The Whigs also gained control of both houses of Congress.

Costumes of the 1840's

––––––– CHECK-UP –––––––

How did the Whigs bring an end to the Jacksonian Era?

1. Why was the Whig Party such a hodgepodge? Why was it unsuccessful in 1836?
2. What developments made Van Buren unpopular? What was his independent treasury plan?
3. How did the Whigs try to insure success in 1840? What were the results of the election?

4 The Opponents of Jackson Win a Hollow Victory

The Whigs make a poor start. The triumph of the Whigs did not last long. Only their hatred of Andrew Jackson had held them together during the campaign. As soon as they tried to carry out a legislative program, their lack of unity became clear. They were also embarrassed in making government appointments. The Whig leaders had loudly attacked the spoils system of the Democrats. When they moved into office, however, pressure for appointments became so great that the new administration had to "clean house" just as Jackson had. Many officeholders were removed, and the positions filled by people on the Whig side of the political fence.

Tyler succeeds Harrison. The Whigs had hardly tasted power before they were hit by a real calamity. President Harrison, weakened by age and over-exertion, was worn out by the clamor of office seekers. His health failed, and he died only one month after taking the oath of office. For the first time since the republic had been founded, a Vice-President was raised to the presidential chair. This turn of events was unfortunate for the Whig leaders, who favored a strong national government. Tyler had been nominated Vice-President merely to get the good will of a minority in the South. He was a confirmed believer in states' rights and in a strict interpretation of the Constitution. He was against a national bank and the protective tariff, and had little in common with Clay, Webster, and Adams. Once in office, President Tyler demonstrated a firmness in his beliefs that widened the gulf between him and a large part of the Whig Party.

Tyler and the Whig Congress fail to agree. The leader of the Whigs, Henry Clay, took over the direction of the administration. In a special session of Congress in 1841, Clay mapped out a complete

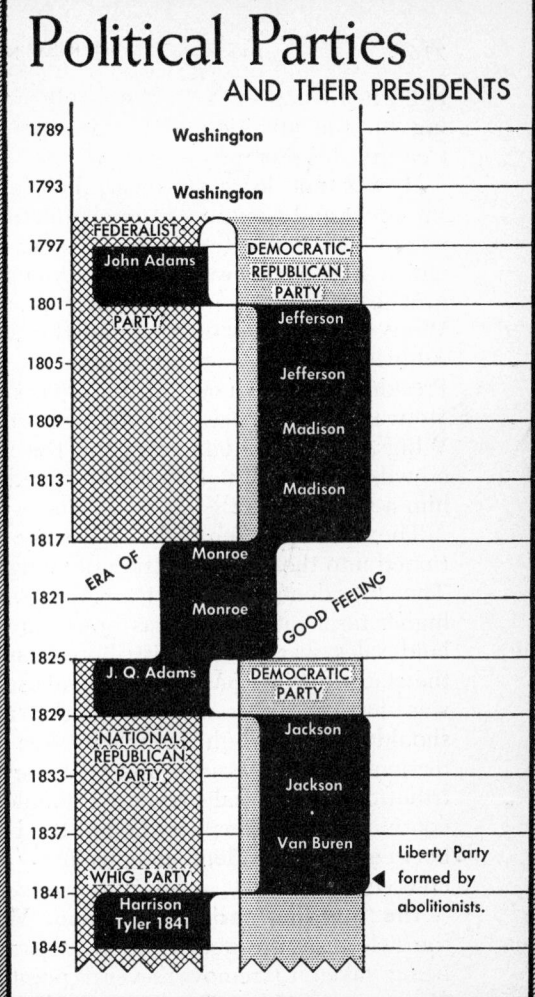

Political Parties
AND THEIR PRESIDENTS

1789	Washington
1793	Washington
1797	FEDERALIST — John Adams / DEMOCRATIC-REPUBLICAN PARTY
1801	PARTY / Jefferson
1805	Jefferson
1809	Madison
1813	Madison
1817	ERA OF / Monroe
1821	Monroe / GOOD FEELING
1825	J. Q. Adams / DEMOCRATIC PARTY
1829	Jackson
1833	NATIONAL REPUBLICAN PARTY / Jackson
1837	Van Buren / Liberty Party formed by abolitionists.
1841	WHIG PARTY — Harrison Tyler 1841
1845	

Political party development in the early years of our history is summarized here. Party affiliations of the Presidents are also shown. What does the chart show about President Washington's relation to political parties? What does it show about party politics during the administration of President Monroe? (For continuations of this chart, see pages 327, 466, and 775.)

legislative program in keeping with his nationalistic ideas. He proposed to abolish the independent treasury and to charter a new United States Bank. He also suggested a return to his "American system" (page 186) which called for a higher tariff measure and a bill for distributing among the states the profits from public land sales. Tyler no doubt resented Clay's leadership,

215

but when Congress sent him a bill providing for the abolition of the independent treasury, he promptly signed it.

It was not long, however, before the President and Congress were completely at odds. Twice Congress passed bank bills which it believed would meet Tyler's approval. Twice Tyler vetoed the bills. The Whig leaders were furious, and the whole cabinet except Webster resigned. The President was "read out" of the Whig Party. He was denounced as a traitor by northern Whigs, and burned in effigy by the same crowds that had noisily campaigned for him a year earlier.

The clash between Tyler and Clay continued into the regular session of Congress. The President opposed the adoption of higher tariff rates so long as revenues from land sales were being distributed among the states for internal improvements. Clay was just as determined that the tariff should be made high enough to give protection to manufactures, and that the distribution of land sale revenues should be continued. Tyler finally won, but the break between the President and his party was now complete.

The "Caroline" incident is settled. While the Tyler-Clay struggle went on, steps were being taken to remove several points of disagreement between the United States and Great Britain. One of these sprang from a rebellion which had broken out in Canada in 1837. The *Caroline*, an American steamboat used to transport supplies and men to the Canadian rebels, was seized by the British at its wharf in American waters and sent blazing over Niagara Falls. During this trouble an American was killed. Relations between the United States and Great Britain became strained, and there was a public demand for war. The crisis was averted by tactful diplomacy and by concessions on both sides.

The Northeast boundary is fixed. There were other difficulties which caused friction between the United States and Great Britain. One was a dispute over an area of about 12,000 square miles on the boundary between Maine and Canada. People who lived in the disputed area were greatly aroused, and at one time American and Canadian forces almost came to blows in the Aroostook valley. But in 1841 a change of government leaders in England opened the way for settlement of the dispute. Negotiations resulted in the Webster-Ashburton Treaty of 1842. That agreement gave the United States more than half the disputed area between Maine and Canada and settled the boundary west of Lake Superior. (See map, page 647.) Getting the Webster-Ashburton Treaty ratified was one of Webster's greatest services to the country. Soon after the treaty was completed, he resigned from the cabinet to make room for someone who could agree more fully with President Tyler.

The American scene changes. The Whigs, then, had won an empty victory. They had managed to force the Democrats out of office, but they failed to undo the work of Jackson or to carry out any real program of their own. Now that the right to vote had spread to almost every free adult male, democracy was firmly entrenched. At the same time, the forces of nationalism were nearly exhausted. The old issues of the bank, the tariff, and internal improvements no longer excited public interest. Instead, attention shifted to territorial expansion in the Far West and to a struggle over the extension of slavery into newly acquired areas. Meanwhile, however, life in America was being deeply affected by certain social, economic, and cultural forces. Before tracing westward expansion and the struggle over slavery, it will be well to pause for a brief survey of the ways the American people lived and worked during the first half of the 1800's.

────── CHECK-UP ──────

Why was the Whig victory a hollow one?

1. Why did Tyler and the Whigs fail to get along? With what results?
2. What was the Caroline Affair? The Webster-Ashburton Treaty?
3. In the 1840's what new issues and new problems were attracting the attention of the American people?

CHAPTER REVIEW

Terms to Understand

franchise
nominating
  convention
"bosses"
"wildcat banks"
easy credit
democracy
party machine

Jacksonian Era
shirt-sleeve diplomacy
squatters
cheap currency
removal of deposits
"pet banks"
surplus
independent treasury

People and Things to Know About

Workingmen's Party
spoils system
"Old Hickory"
"kitchen cabinet"
Maysville Road
Specie Circular
Anti-Masons
Whigs

William Henry Harrison
Martin Van Buren
"Tippecanoe and Tyler
  too"
John Tyler
Caroline Affair
"King" Andrew
Webster-Ashburton Treaty

Historic Dates to Identify

1832   1837   1842
1836   1840

Questions to Discuss

1. You have noted that Jackson was in almost continuous conflict with Congress. Is such a conflict absolutely necessary under the separation of powers and checks and balances system? Why or why not? How is our present President getting along with Congress?

2. Do you approve or disapprove of Jackson's policies toward (*a*) the bank, (*b*) the Indians, (*c*) road building, (*d*) nullification? Give your reasons.

3. Jackson has been called the first modern President in that he was the first to see the power which a President might exercise. How did he make different use of the Presidency

Questions to Discuss (Cont.)

than previous Presidents? How did the growth of democracy give him a greater opportunity to wield power?

4. Compare John Quincy Adams and Andrew Jackson. What conclusions can you draw about the qualities which the American people admire in a President?

5. We speak of "King" Andrew and also of Jacksonian democracy. How is this seeming inconsistency to be explained?

6. Why was the extension of the suffrage a momentous and revolutionary step? Why did some people fear this widening of the right to vote?

Other Things to Do

1. Prepare a chart on the public land acts of the United States before 1860. Begin with the Ordinance of 1785. Give the names of the acts, their chief provisions, their advantages and defects. Riegel's *America Moves West* will be helpful.

*2. In a two-column chart headed "Controversial Issues" and "Jackson's Position," list the chief issues of Jackson's administrations and the courses of action which Jackson took towards them. This activity should cover both Chapters 9 and 10.

3. Debate: *Resolved,* That voting in national elections should be made compulsory for all citizens.

*4. Show by means of a diagram the development of political parties from 1789 to 1845. Indicate the party platforms, leaders, and relationships between parties.

5. Assume that you are a cartoonist for either a Democratic or Whig newspaper. Draw a cartoon for or against one of Jackson's policies.

TO INCREASE YOUR UNDERSTANDING OF UNIT TWO

Unit Summary

1. At the close of the Revolutionary War, the independence of the United States was undisputed, but serious problems confronted the new nation. Many of these problems resulted from the absence of a strong central government. The Articles of Confederation, which

were adopted during the Revolution, provided for little more than a weak league of states. Dissatisfaction with conditions under the Articles finally led to the Philadelphia Convention and the adoption of the Constitution.

2. The new Constitution granted new powers to the central authority without destroying the authority of the states. The organization

of government machinery under three departments, each of which had checks and balances
over the others, was designed to prevent
tyranny. The fact that the Constitution did
not offer full protection of individual liberties
led to the addition of the Bill of Rights shortly
afterwards.

3. George Washington, who was inaugurated
as first President in 1789, faced many difficult
problems. Under his wise leadership, however,
the new republic made a good start. The
program proposed by the brilliant Alexander
Hamilton put the country on a firm financial
basis. Serious trouble with foreign powers was
averted. Differences of opinion over these
various policies led to the formation of two
political parties, the Federalists and the Republicans. Under Washington and John
Adams, the Federalists were in control of the
government; but a rising tide of popular feeling swept Thomas Jefferson and the Republicans into office in 1800.

4. Although Jefferson was a firm believer in
government by the people, he made only
moderate changes in government policies. The
greatest accomplishment during his administration was the Louisiana Purchase. Interference
with American rights at sea clouded the closing years of Jefferson's administration. His
policy of trying to force recognition of American rights by peaceful means was carried on
by his successor, James Madison, but did not
succeed. This fact, plus an insistent frontier
cry for territorial expansion, led to war with
England in 1812.

5. The War of 1812 gained the United States
little but peace, although foreign powers found
no further need to interfere with our rights.
At home the war ushered in a period of growing national pride and unity. This tendency
was evidenced by a lack of party strife, by the
acceptance of policies that had formerly been
opposed in certain sections of the country, and
by a vigorous foreign policy. Already visible,
however, was the shadow of sectional disagreement, as indicated by the quarrel over
the admission of Missouri and by disputes over
the tariff in the 1820's and 1830's. Out of the
tariff quarrels came a clear statement of states'
rights and the doctrine of nullification.

6. Still a third tendency, one toward greater
democracy, swept the country during the
Presidency of Andrew Jackson. As the movement toward universal manhood suffrage made
great headway, the political power of the common man increased. Andrew Jackson, vigorous son of the frontier, did much to popularize

this tendency. Though his outspoken attitude
on various public questions earned him many
enemies, he was able to pass on the Presidency
to Van Buren, his chosen candidate. The
Panic of 1837 gave the opponents of Jacksonian democracy, the Whigs, their opportunity. They won the election of 1840, but
they were unable, because of division within
their own party, to carry out a constructive
program. By the 1840's the old problems
ceased to hold public interest, and gave way
to new ones — the problem of territorial expansion and the spread of slavery into the
newly acquired regions.

Summary of Important Dates

1781 Articles of Confederation effective.
1785 Land Ordinance passed.
     Mount Vernon Conference.
**1787 Philadelphia Convention draws up the
     Constitution.**
     Northwest Ordinance adopted.
1789 Washington inaugurated first President.
1791 Bill of Rights adopted.
1793 Invention of the cotton gin.
     Washington's Neutrality Proclamation.
     Genêt affair.
1795 Completion of Jay and Pinckney treaties.
1800 Jefferson elected in "revolution of 1800."
1803 Purchase of Louisiana.
1807 Embargo Act.
1808 Madison elected.
**1812 War breaks out between Great Britain
     and the United States.**
1814 Treaty of Ghent.
     Hartford Convention.
1816 Protective tariff adopted.
     Second United States Bank established.
1817 Rush-Bagot Agreement.
     Monroe inaugurated; "era of good feel-
     ings" begins.
1818 Canadian boundary settled.
1819 Spain cedes Florida to the United States.
1820 Missouri Compromise.
1823 Monroe Doctrine.
1828 Tariff of Abominations.
     Election of Jackson.
1832 South Carolina nullifies the tariff.
     Jackson vetoes Bank Bill.
1836 Specie Circular.
     Van Buren elected.
1837 Panic of 1837 sweeps country.
1840 Triumph of Whigs; end of Jacksonian
     Era.
1842 Webster-Ashburton Treaty.

Unit Activities

1. In your study of American history you will discover that there are certain "constants" or problems which continue to recur. Among these are (a) public land policy, (b) Indian relations, (c) foreign relations, (d) territorial expansion, (e) settlement of the West, (f) sectional conflict, (g) banking and currency, (h) the tariff. You may be able to add others. Using these problems or topics as headings, make chronological lists of the chief developments which occurred in Unit Two.

2. Summarize the unit by (a) making a list of important summarizing points, and (b) making a list of conclusions or generalizations which you think may be derived from these points. For example, after studying the election of 1800 and its results, you may state as a summarizing point that "although Jefferson dropped some of the Federalists' policies, he retained many of them." A possible tentative conclusion which might be drawn from this is that "political parties are less likely to be critical of the policies of their opponents when in office than when out of office." As you can see, there is less danger of error in making the first, more factual type of statement than there is in making the conclusion.

The process just described is known as generalizing, or deriving broad principles from many particular facts. Generalizing is something which we do all the time, although often in a faulty fashion because our conclusions do not square with the facts. In generalizing remember to (a) regard all conclusions as temporary, (b) continue to test your conclusions against new facts, (c) look for exceptions to your generalization, (d) ask yourself whether or not any of your prejudices have entered into your reasoning.

For Further Reading

Original Sources

Commager, H. S., ed., *Documents of American History*. Crofts. Nos. 75–161.

Commager, H. S., and Nevins, A., eds., *The Heritage of America*. Little Brown. Nos. 42–60.

Nevins, Allan, ed., *The Diary of Philip Hone*. Dodd. The very interesting diary of a Whig man of affairs who was "in" on many great events.

Padover, Saul K., ed., *Thomas Jefferson on Democracy*. Mentor Books (formerly Penguin Books). A collection of the writings of the great democrat.

Pease, T. C., and Roberts, A. S., eds., *Selected Readings in American History*. Harcourt. Nos. 60–132.

General References

Adams, J. T., *Epic of America*. Little, Brown. Pp. 96–175.

Bailey, Thomas A., A *Diplomatic History of the American People*. Crofts. Pp. 53–228.

Faulkner, Harold U., *American Economic History*. Harper. Pp. 166–240.

Hicks, J. D., *The Federal Union*. Houghton. Pp. 161–458.

Morison, S. E., and Commager, H. S., *The Growth of the American Republic*. Oxford. Vol. I, pp. 231–493.

Riegel, Robert E., *America Moves West*. Holt. Chapters 5–7, 9, 10, 12–16.

Special Accounts

Adams, Henry, *History of the United States During the Administrations of Jefferson and Madison*. Scribners. The outstanding history of the period covered.

American Nation Series. Harper. Babcock, K. C., *Rise of American Nationality*. Bassett, J. S., *The Federalist System*. McLaughlin, A. C., *The Confederation and the Constitution*. Turner, F. J., *Rise of the New West*.

Bowers, Claude, *Jefferson and Hamilton*. Houghton. Deals with the conflict between these two great men but is sympathetic to Jefferson.

Bowers, Claude, *Jefferson in Power*. Houghton. Deals with Jefferson's administrations.

Bowers, Claude, *Party Battles of the Jacksonian Period*. Houghton. Jackson's conflicts with Clay, Calhoun, and others of his "enemies."

Chronicles of America Series. Yale University Press. Corwin, E. S., *John Marshall and the Constitution*. Farrand, Max, *Fathers of the Constitution*. Johnson, Allen, *Jefferson and His Colleagues*. Paine, Ralph D., *The Fight for a Free Sea*.

Crow, John A., *The Epic of Latin America*. Viking. A history of the origin and progress of Latin America from the time of the Incas to the present.

Havighurst, Walter, *Land of Promise: The Story of the North West Territory*. Macmillan. Contains interesting chapters on the chief developments in the "laboratory" of American statehood.

Hendrick, Burton J., *Bulwark of the Republic*.

Little, Brown. A "biography" of the Constitution from its establishment to the present.

History of American Life Series. Macmillan. Fish, C. R., *Rise of the Common Man.* Krout, J. A., and Fox, D. R., *The Completion of Independence 1790 to 1830.* The volumes in this series deal with American social and economic life.

Minnigerode, Meade, *The Fabulous Forties.* Garden City. Provides many interesting sidelights on the society of the 1840's.

Peck, A. M., *The Pageant of Latin America.* Longmans. An interesting history of the Latin American republics.

Schlesinger, Arthur M., Jr., *The Age of Jackson.* Little, Brown. One of the most important books on the Jackson era. Emphasizes the rise of cities and industry.

Van Doren, Carl, *The Great Rehearsal.* Viking. A recent study of the making and ratifying of the Constitution.

Biography

Hutchins, Frank, *Thomas Jefferson.* Longmans. A biography in the popular manner but accurate.

James, Marquis, *Andrew Jackson: Portrait of a President.* Bobbs. A biography of Jackson covering the presidential years.

Morgan, Helen, *Mistress of the White House.* Westminster Press. A portrait of one of the most interesting of First Ladies, Dolly Madison.

Schachner, Nathan, *Alexander Hamilton.* Appleton-Century-Crofts. A biography of Hamilton written in an easy-to-read style.

Van Loon, H. W., *Thomas Jefferson.* Simon & Schuster. Highly illustrated and easy-to-read story of Jefferson.

Whitney, Janet, *Abigail Adams.* Little, Brown. A story of the wife of John Adams.

Imaginative Writing

Forester, C. S., *Captain from Connecticut.* Bantam Books. A story of the War of 1812.

Hawthorne, Hildegarde, *Westward the Course.* Longmans. A novel based on the Lewis and Clark expedition.

Jennings, J. E., *Salem Frigate.* Doubleday. The scene of much of this novel is the frigate *Essex.*

Mudgett, H. P., *The Seas Stand Watch.* Knopf. The eastern seaboard between the Revolution and the War of 1812.

Page, Elizabeth, *Tree of Liberty.* Farrar. A novel which traces the growth of the United States, with Thomas Jefferson as a central character.

Roberts, Kenneth, *The Lively Lady.* Doubleday. Epic of an American privateersman in the War of 1812.

Shepard, Odell, *Holdfast Gaines.* Macmillan. A novel which brings in such personages as Jackson, Tecumseh, and the pirate, Jean Lafitte.

Sperry, A., *Storm Canvas.* Winston. Adventures of a fifteen-year-old boy on an American vessel during the War of 1812.

Van Every, Dale, *Westward the River.* Putnam. The turbulent days of 1794 on the western frontier.

Pictures

Adams, J. T., *Album of American History.* Scribner. Vol. II, pp. 1–338.

Nevins, Allan, and Weitenkampf, Frank, eds., *A Century of Political Cartoons.* Pp. 20–62. Famous cartoons with annotations.

Pageant of America Series. Yale University Press. Gabriel, Ralph, *Lure of the Frontier.* Ogg, F. A., *Builders of the Republic.* Wood, William, and Gabriel, Ralph, *The Winning of Freedom.*

 *Sidelights on American History*

A City Is His Monument. In Arlington National Cemetery, which contains the famous Tomb of the Unknown Soldier, there is a grave with a strange marker. A map of the city of Washington is cut on a great slab of stone. Here is buried the man to whom all Americans are indebted for perhaps the most beautiful

capital city in the world – a Frenchman named Pierre Charles L'Enfant.

In the early years of our republic, Congress gave President Washington the authority to choose a site for our country's capital. The land which he selected along the Potomac River was donated by the states of Virginia and Maryland for federal use. In 1791, when Washington and Jefferson wanted a plan drawn for the "new federal town," they called on L'Enfant. He had come to America with Lafayette, and he had served in our Revolution as a Major of Engineers.

The Frenchman designed a city which for that period was breathtaking. It was to have great avenues named after the states, vast parks with fountains, and large pools to reflect the clouds and the sky. There would be hundreds of miles of tree-lined streets and scores of wide vistas to give the city "breadth" and "sweep." It was a plan of genius, at least a hundred years ahead of its time.

L'Enfant's design took much time and money to carry out, and it could be followed only in a general way. Many details of his planning, however, are part of Washington as we know it — the Capitol, broad Pennsylvania Avenue, the White House, and the Washington Monument, for example. Above all, there is a feeling of space and openness not generally found in cities today.

Dream of Empire? To this day historians are uncertain whether the brilliant Aaron Burr really planned a revolt against the United States. The truth may never be known, but the story will always remain a fascinating one. According to those who believe that Burr planned an "Empire of the West" beyond the Mississippi, the conspiracy was launched in the spring of 1805. Aaron Burr had been Vice-President of the United States. Unpopular in the East after his duel with Alexander Hamilton, Burr departed mysteriously for the frontier regions of the Ohio and the Mississippi rivers. Here he conferred with government officials and military commanders. Burr's accusers say that he was sounding them out to find possible allies for his cause. They also tell us that he talked with French and Spanish agents in New Orleans.

Midway in his western trip, Aaron Burr stopped to visit a character almost as strange and baffling as himself. Harmon Blennerhasset was a rich, wild, and romantic Irishman who lived in splendor on an island in the Ohio River. He had built a home like a palace and furnished it with luxuries from Europe — paintings, rich draperies, silks, satins, and priceless silver. Burr easily won over the simple-minded Blennerhassett. "Colonel Burr," declared the lord of the island, "will then, after setting up the Empire, advance on Mexico and make himself king. I am so sure that I am staking my property on the expedition. And I am to be the first Minister to England."

The following year (1806) an expedition was in preparation at Blennerhasset Island. Boats were built; recruits enlisted from the river towns. In December, Burr headed downriver from the island with 60 men, 9 boats, arms, and supplies. His "invasion" — if he intended invasion — was on. But the American army commander at New Orleans had reported to authorities that Burr had tried to interest him in the conspiracy. Burr was placed on parole and requested to report to the authorities regularly.

The high-spirited Burr refused to submit to such supervision. He disguised himself and fled, only to be arrested by American agents near the border of Spanish territory. The charge against him was treason, but the evidence was too slight to convict him. From that moment he disappeared from public life, and the public heard no more of his dream of an "Empire of the West."

Pirate Lafitte. On the Louisiana shore not far from New Orleans is a region of brackish lagoons and many islands, called Barataria Bay. Here, where the oaks are hung with Spanish moss and the islands form a protecting maze among lagoons and bayous, the pirate king Jean Lafitte once had his hideaway. On an autumn day in 1814 three British officers made a surprise visit to Lafitte. They had come to ask for his help in an attack soon to be made on New Orleans. In return they promised him great tracts of land and a captaincy in the British navy.

The pirate king listened carefully and seemed to be agreeable to the British proposal. Actually he gave all his information about the planned attack to the American authorities in Louisiana. Three weeks before the British opened the attack on New Orleans, Louisiana's governor, in a formal proclamation, "invited" Lafitte and his Baratarian pirates to join in the defense. Lafitte and many of his men fought gallantly with General Andrew Jackson's army in the Battle of New Orleans.

For this aid President Madison pardoned the pirate leader and all his men for their past crimes. But the adventurous pirate life was so tempting to Lafitte that he returned to his outlaw existence. "Of his death no facts are established," say the historians, but you may visit today the Lafitte Cemetery in the little settlement of Barataria, where local legend says that Jean Lafitte is buried.

Along the Erie Canal

THE PLAN OF THE BOOK

PART ONE Early America Develops	1492 to 1783	**Unit One:** Discovery, Exploration, Development of the English colonies, American Revolution			
	1783 to 1840	**Unit Two:** Framing of Constitution, The new republic, Rise of nationalism, sectionalism, and democracy			
	1789 to 1865	**Unit Three:** Economic developments, Social change and reform, Rise of American culture			
	1840 to 1865	**Unit Four:** Westward expansion, The slavery problem, War Between the States			
PART TWO Modern America Emerges	1865 to the 1890's	**Unit Five** Foundations of the American economic system	**Unit Six** Social and cultural developments	**Unit Seven** Government, politics, and foreign affairs	
PART THREE Modern America Matures	1890's to the Present	**Unit Eight** American economic system today	**Unit Nine** Social and cultural developments	**Unit Ten** The United States in world affairs	**Unit Eleven** Developments in government and politics

Unit Three

IMPORTANT CHANGES OCCUR IN

THE AMERICAN WAY OF LIFE

In 1850 everyday life in the United States was more like what it had been a century earlier than what it is today. Nevertheless important changes had taken place, and new forces were shaping life in America.

Unrest in Europe and the promise of better living in the New World attracted millions of immigrants. Some of them settled on farm lands in the West. Others went to work in the factories of the eastern cities. Most of them became naturalized citizens of the United States.

The Industrial Revolution introduced new machines and new types of power. Steamboats were plying the rivers and the inland waterways; steam locomotives were puffing along the iron rails; steam engines were providing power for machinery. Improved roads, canals, and the telegraph tied the nation closer together. Americans were demonstrating their inventiveness in the field of applied science.

Americans have always been dissatisfied with things as they are. A constant stream of restless men and women were moving westward. Northern businessmen were expanding their commerce and factory output. Southern planters were enlarging their lands and their production of cotton. Reformers were urging social change — temperance, emancipation for the Negro, better opportunities for women, humane treatment for the insane.

A new interest in literature, science, and the arts also was making its appearance. America was throwing off European influence in these fields and beginning a culture of its own.

Finally, there was a growing demand for more and better free public schools. The extension of the right to vote, the influx of immigrants, the concern of workers for better opportunities for their children, the growth of cities — all pointed the need for increased educational opportunity. Americans have a deep conviction of the worth of education. They know that the destiny of a democracy is determined by the quality of thinking done by its citizens.

Chapter 11

Early train

CHANGES OCCUR IN AMERICAN

ECONOMIC LIFE

Under the spur of the Industrial Revolution, the making of machines that would do the work of many men, American industry rose and hummed. Americans bought, borrowed, copied, stole, invented, improved, the designs of lathes, looms, engines, all power-driven appliances. They were used to ingenious tinkering . . . They had water power, coal, iron, all the metals. They had first-class craftsmen . . . They labored under no restrictions, not even wise ones — ingenuity and invention had full play.

From AMERICA by Stephen Vincent Benét *

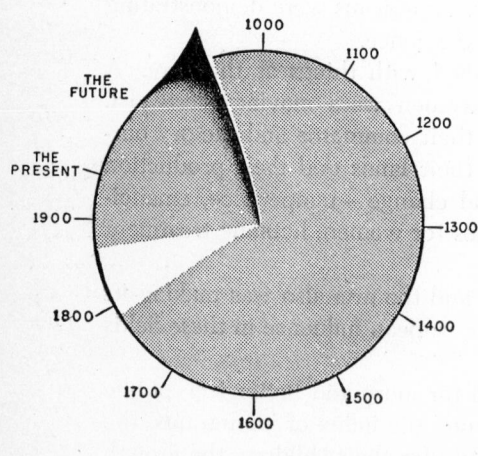

1789-1865

If Benjamin Franklin had still been alive in the early 1800's, he would not have seen much change in the way American people lived and carried on their business. Travel by horseback, stagecoach, or sailing ship was still slow and difficult. Most of the people still earned their living by farming, using the crude tools of colonial days, and cooking over big open fireplaces the food they raised themselves. Living conditions in cities were far more simple and easy-going than they are today, and there were almost none of the labor-saving devices which we now take for granted. But Franklin, if he had lived as late as 1817, might have noticed certain signs which showed that the American people were about to make striking changes in their ways of working and living. In 1817, for example,

* From *America*, published by Rinehart & Co., Inc. Copyright, 1944, by Rosemary Carr Benét.

the Cumberland Road was opened for travel, work was started on the Erie Canal, and a successful round trip was made by steamboat between the upper Ohio River and the mouth of the Mississippi. This was the eve of revolutionary changes in farming, industry, transportation, and communication — changes which cleared a path for the swift economic life of our own day. It is the purpose of this chapter to show what some of these far-reaching developments were. There are four main points in the chapter:

1. Important changes occur on farms and plantations.
2. An Industrial Revolution begins in the United States.
3. The factory system brings new economic groups.
4. Transportation and communication are improved.

1 Important Changes Occur on Farms and Plantations

Farmers adopt new methods. When Thomas Jefferson became President, farmers in America were still using much the same methods and tools that they had used in colonial days. With these crude tools farming was a back-breaking task. Plows were made largely of wood and at best did a poor job. For a long time farmers refused to use metal plows because they claimed that the metal poisoned the soil. They still cut grain with the sickle or scythe, then threshed it with a flail or by the trampling of horses. They were just starting to use the cradle, a device which made it easier to gather the grain in bunches. There was plenty of land to be had, and it was cheap. Under such conditions of production many farmers kept moving westward to new soil rather than staying where they were and improving their old land by drainage, crop rotation, and the use of fertilizers.

A revolution began to take place in agricultural methods between 1825 and 1850. By 1825 the farmer had started to use a plow made at least in part of metal; it had a cast iron tip. Next he learned that there was a new machine that would cut his grain more easily and cheaply — the McCormick reaper, which was brought out in the early 1830's. Later came the threshing machine for separating the kernels of grain from the straw. The farmer soon realized that he could produce more food with less hard work by using these "newfangled" farm tools and others like the horse-drawn rake, the mowing machine, and the seed drill. He also became interested in methods which would improve his livestock and his harvests, such as controlled breeding, crop rotation, and fertilizers. He could read about these new agricultural ideas in farm journals which were now being published, and he could look over the new machinery at county fairs.

Whitney invents the cotton gin. The most dramatic change in American agriculture had begun in 1793 when a young teacher with an interest in mechanics invented the *cotton gin*. This invention made cotton-raising the principal occupation of the southern states. To understand the far-reaching effect of the cotton gin, it is necessary to look back a little. During the late 1700's, a series of important inventions in England completely changed the means by which many goods were produced. This change, called the Industrial Revolution,

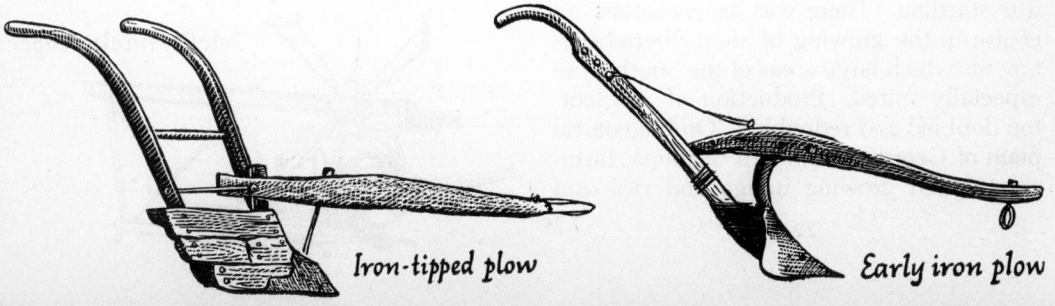

Iron-tipped plow   *Early iron plow*

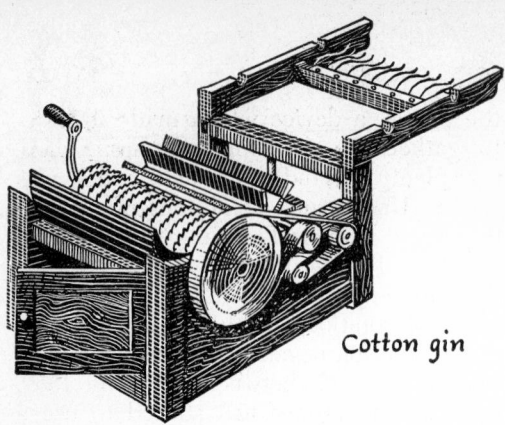

Cotton gin

was most noticeable in the cloth, or textile, industry. Previously the spinning of thread and the weaving of cloth had been done at home on spinning wheels and hand looms. Now it was done in factories by power-driven machinery. These new machines could make cloth very rapidly, so that English factory owners had to look around for greater supplies of flax, wool, and especially cotton.

Eli Whitney, a young graduate of Yale, helped to meet the demand for more cotton by inventing the cotton gin. As a youth, Whitney had been an expert with tools. A carpenter at Yale once said to him, "There was a good mechanic spoiled when you came to college." Young Whitney, however, went to the South to become a teacher. Soon after he arrived there, he noticed the slow, expensive way in which slaves picked the seeds from the cotton fibers by hand. By this tedious method, the average slave could produce only about one pound of cotton a day. Interest in this process led Whitney to invent a machine which would separate the seeds from the fibers. A slave using this machine could turn out about 50 pounds of cotton a day. Later, when the cotton gin was improved and run by water power or steam, one operator's daily output rose to 1000 pounds.

The cotton gin makes cotton "king." The effect of Whitney's cotton gin on the South was startling. There was an enormous increase in the growing of short-fibered cotton, for which large areas of the South were especially suited. Production of raw cotton doubled and redoubled. On the coastal plain of Georgia and South Carolina, farmers stopped growing indigo and rice and

started to grow cotton instead. Many Virginia plantation owners gave up tobacco raising and turned to cotton. Cotton growing also spread into North Carolina and Tennessee. By 1845 the United States was producing seven eighths of the world's cotton; by 1860 cotton made up 60 per cent of the total exports of the country and cotton exports were valued at nearly $200,000,000 a year. Southerners hailed cotton as king, and claimed that it was the backbone of the country's wealth.

But "King Cotton" was hard on the soil. After some years of cotton growing, large areas in the older sections of the South became less productive, and planters began to look for new lands. By the middle 1800's the production of cotton had shifted noticeably to the west and south so that the three states which led in cotton growing were Mississippi, Alabama, and Georgia. The seaboard cities of Charleston and Savannah grew less important, while New Orleans, Memphis, and Mobile became the commercial centers of the South. Slavery, which had been on the decline just before 1800, now became firmly lodged in the South because it seemed necessary for producing huge quantities of cotton.

Many crops are raised in the South. Although cotton was king, the South raised many other crops which added to her prosperity. The broad tobacco fields of Virginia and Kentucky made the South the world's leading producer of tobacco. Sugar cane, rice, and hemp were other products that regularly poured into the world's markets from the South. The more general kinds of farming were also important, particularly in the Shenandoah Valley and the blue-grass region of Kentucky. In 1850 the South was raising over half of the corn, a third of the oats, and more than a fourth of the wheat grown in the United States.

McCormick reaper

Early threshing machine

──────── CHECK-UP ────────

What important changes occurred in agriculture?

1. What inventions or developments were to have a revolutionary effect on agriculture?
2. What circumstances led to the invention of the cotton gin?
3. How did this invention affect the production of cotton?
4. What products other than cotton were raised in the South?

---

2 An Industrial Revolution Begins in the United States

The Industrial Revolution transforms industry. While farming had come a long way in the United States by the 1850's, the headway made in manufacturing was even more striking. It was due chiefly to the growth of the Industrial Revolution in the United States. Originating in England, the Industrial Revolution involved a change from handwork to machine production, from industry in the home to manufacturing in factories.

New industries struggle, then flourish. The industrial progress in the early nineteenth century was all the more remarkable because American manufacturers had a hard time getting started. When English manufacturers began to make many products by machinery — especially textiles — they jealously guarded the secrets of their new machines. To help them keep their secrets, Parliament passed laws which strictly forbade the export of any machine or the emigration of any skilled machine workers. One English textile worker broke through the emigration restrictions, however. He was Samuel Slater, who has become known as the father of the American factory system. When he arrived in New York in 1789, Slater wrote a letter to Moses Brown, a prosperous Quaker farmer and merchant in Rhode Island. He told Brown

that he thought he could build from memory the machinery needed to set up a successful cotton factory. Brown replied, "If thou canst do what thou sayest, I invite thee to come to Rhode Island."

Slater went to Rhode Island, and within a year the first American textile factory was in operation beside a waterfall at Pawtucket. Other factories were soon built, but the struggle to keep them busy was discouraging because of the competition of cheap English goods. There were only eight such mills in the whole nation at the beginning of the 1800's.

Business began to improve, however, about the time of the War of 1812, when trade relations with Great Britain were broken. As time passed, American industry expanded with increasing speed. The Lowell loom, which made possible the spinning and weaving of cotton in the same factory, came into general use before 1820. Elias Howe's improved sewing machine (1846) helped to revolutionize the making of clothing, shoes, and other leather goods. Iron was successfully smelted with the aid of anthracite coal about 1830, and by the 1850's better methods of making steel were developed.

Steam aids the rise of industry. The progress of industry was greatly aided by the increased use of steam for driving machinery. Until steam engines were available, mills were run by water power and had to be located where there were swift-running streams, notably in New England and the middle states. Then toward the end of the 1700's, a high-pressure steam engine was developed by Oliver Evans of Philadelphia.[1] As mechanical improvements were made, more and more industries made use of steam power. This trend

[1] The invention of the first practical steam engine is credited to a Scotsman, James Watt.

Eli Whitney earned little from his cotton gin, but became wealthy manufacturing firearms. He was the first manufacturer to make standard parts which could be assembled or interchanged later.

was speeded up when bituminous, and later anthracite, coal became available as fuel. A factory no longer had to be built beside a stream — it could be built wherever supplies of coal and raw materials were near at hand. Most factories and foundries were still clustered in the New England and middle states, however. Into them flowed the ever-increasing raw materials of the growing country — cotton from the South, wool from the West, apparently limitless supplies of timber, coal, iron, and other minerals from various parts of the country.

Industry becomes firmly established. As the hum of industry grew louder in the northeastern and middle states, more and more people gave up farming to work in factories. Factories multiplied, and under the *factory system* (the production of goods in factories, as opposed to home industry) towns and cities grew rapidly too. The urban (city and town) population of Rhode Island increased from less than ten per cent in 1810 to nearly 40 per cent in 1840. New England led the country's industrial development, especially in the manufacture of textiles. In 1860 the value of cotton goods produced there was nearly $80,000,000, as compared with a third of that amount in the middle states and only $8,000,000 in the South. The Northeast also led in the manufacture of

textile machinery, ships, steam engines, clothing, and shoes. But by the middle of the century industrial activity had begun to spread. The middle states were giving New England a race for leadership, especially in the production of iron and steel. By this time, too, the western regions were pushing forward in the production of farm machinery, lumber, meat products, and flour. The South, however, did not build up industries on a large scale until after the War Between the States.

——————— CHECK-UP ———————

What developments marked the beginning of the Industrial Revolution in America?

1. How were the first factories started in America?
2. What evidence is there of the rapid development of the factory system after 1812?
3. Name several inventions which contributed to the rise of American industry. What were the advantages of steam over water power?
4. In 1860 what was the position of the various sections in manufacturing?

---

3 The Factory System Brings New Economic Groups

Capitalism grows strong in America. In the early 1800's factories were small. Usually there was only a little money invested in the equipment of any one plant. Goods were turned out slowly and in small quantities, for a limited number of buyers.

As industry grew, however, it offered golden opportunities to men with keen business insight who had enough *capital* (money or property) to put their ideas into action. As the factory system took root in America, a capitalist class began to develop. By the middle of the century, a group of industrial leaders were in control of many business ventures. They were aided by the growing popularity of the *corporation* as a form of business organization.

A corporation was permitted by law to sell shares of stock (certificates of ownership) to the general public, and to use the money gained by the sale to carry on its business.[2] By this means, men who wanted to start new industries could get together much larger amounts of capital than any one, or a few of them, might have been able to manage alone. With this capital, they built larger factories, put in more expensive machinery, bought greater amounts of raw materials, and developed wider markets for the goods they produced. The profits from the business were then split up among the stockholders, according to the number of shares of stock owned by each. Investors who owned a large number of shares of stock became increasingly wealthy.

A laboring class emerges. Money and machines played an important part in the growth of American industry, but without a large enough number of workers, the industrialists could never have carried out their plans. Luckily, enough good workers could be found. Sons and daughters of farmers, eager to escape the hard work and long hours on the farms, joined with an ever-increasing stream of immigrants to operate the mines, run the machines, and do other work in industry. Among the immigrants, 1½ million Irish had found their way to America by 1860. Most of them went to work in the factories of the industrial centers, or with the gangs of workmen building canals and railroads. About the same time, a million German immigrants arrived, many of whom were skilled factory workers.

The life of the industrial worker changed greatly from what it had been. As factories grew larger and corporation managers took charge, the worker had less and less personal contact with his "boss." Managers simply carried out the orders of owners or stockholders, who in turn were more concerned with expenses and profits than with

[2] For a fuller explanation of the corporation, turn to pages 369–70.

the personal problems of the workers. This state of affairs did not harm the skilled worker much, for he was always in demand and as a rule made good wages. But the unskilled worker had a hard time making both ends meet. His average pay in Massachusetts until 1860 was about five dollars a week. Women received less than half that much, while children were even more poorly paid. All workers labored from twelve to fifteen hours a day. In some places they started to work as early as four thirty in the morning. Women and children made up a large part of the factory labor supply. It was estimated in 1832 that two fifths of the workers in New England textile mills were children from four to sixteen years of age, who were "brought up as ignorant as the Arabs of the desert."

Labor makes demands. Laboring people, separated from their employers by an ever-widening gulf, began a struggle for more decent conditions early in the century. They formed unions and demanded shorter hours, higher wages, better working conditions, more chances for education, political rights, and social improvement. The early unions in the United States were limited largely to skilled workers. Progress in labor organization was slow because it had been regarded as illegal for work-

The **sewing factory** of an early New York department store shows that workers were beginning to be supervised by alert foremen.

ers to band together for the purpose of raising wages. This legal attitude was strengthened by public opinion, which condemned labor organizations as un-American and unpatriotic. Public opinion also opposed strikes for higher wages on the ground that higher wages meant that consumers must pay higher prices for the goods produced.

Yet, in spite of these obstacles, unionization went on. Under the influence of Jacksonian democracy, workers in every important craft or trade formed unions. In the large industrial centers, these unions joined forces in common action. A movement was also started in the 1830's "to unite and harmonize the efforts of all the producing classes of the country" by means of a federation of all labor unions. This scheme was halted by the Panic of 1837, and during the succeeding years the labor movement largely disappeared. It was revived in the 1850's, and by the close of that decade the printers, machinists, iron molders, and many other groups of workers were organized locally, and were joined to some extent in national groups. Bitter and prolonged strikes took place between 1850 and 1860.

--------- CHECK-UP ---------

What new economic groups were established by the factory system?

1. What is meant by the capitalist class? How did corporations stimulate the development of capitalism?
2. What were the sources of labor in the early factories? Describe the pattern of life of an early factory worker.
3. What progress was made in unionization? What were the conditions that worked against unionization?

Collecting a toll

4 Transportation and Communication Are Improved

Modern transportation begins. The remarkable changes in farming and industry during the first half of the 1800's would have been impossible if improvements had not also been made in travel and transportation. In the early 1800's, people traveled just about as they had in early colonial days. Ocean and river traffic were still slow and undependable. Overland routes were next to impassable. Some stagecoach lines were running, but trips by stage coach were tiring and expensive. Stage travel cost about ten cents a mile, including inn charges. South of the Potomac, the roads were especially bad, and, in most cases, horseback was the only means of travel. "Of eight rivers between here [Monticello] and Washington," wrote Jefferson, "five have neither bridges nor boats." But these poor traveling conditions were soon to change. As the country expanded and wealth piled up from farms and factories, the nation began to develop better means of transportation and travel.

Roads are improved. Today we are so used to fine, hard-surfaced highways that it is almost impossible for us to imagine how poor American roads were in the years that followed the Revolution. Often they were mere paths cut through the wilderness, following the narrow trails blazed by Indians, jagged with ruts in dry weather and swimming with mud in the rainy seasons. At the muddiest places, logs were laid side by side across the width of the road to make a "corduroy" over which horses stumbled and carriages jounced. Breakdowns and serious accidents happened often, frequently holding up other traffic for hours at a time. But even before the end of the 1700's, some improvements began to be made. For example, the Lancaster Turnpike, running about 65 miles from Lancaster, Pennsylvania, to Philadel-

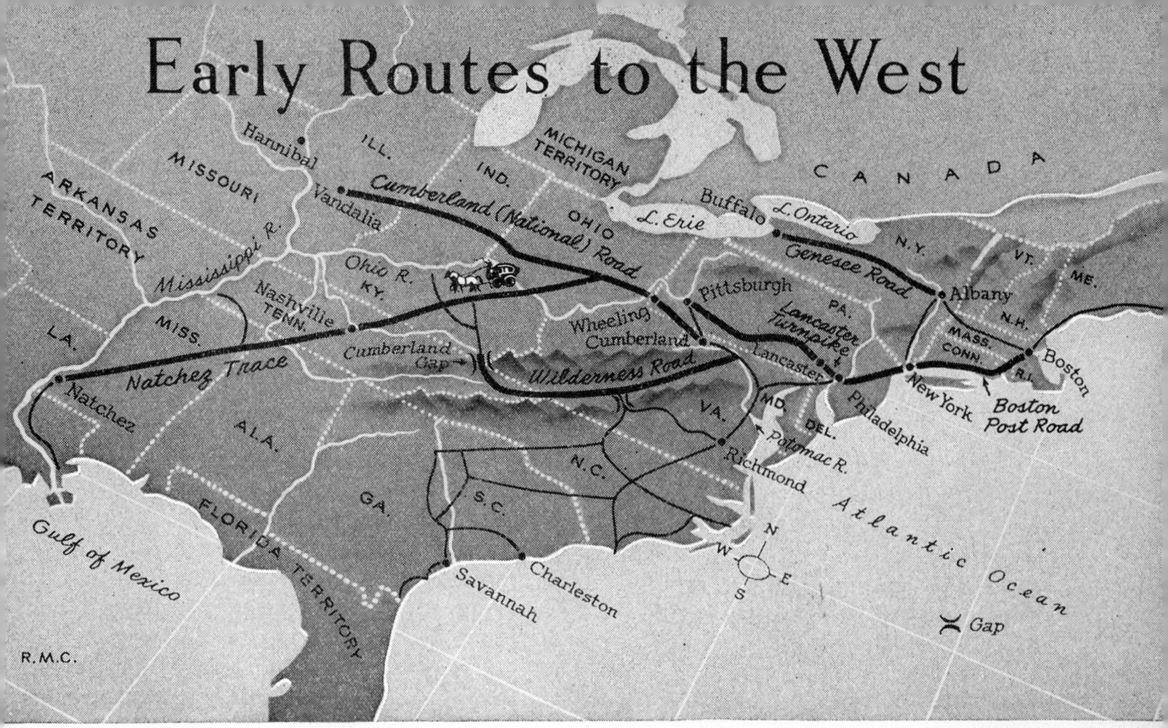

Early Routes to the West

Eastern roads, like the Boston Post Road, were heavily traveled, but roads to the West became especially important as the nation grew. If an Ohio farmer took produce to the lower Mississippi River by flatboat, how might he return home?

phia, was started in 1792 and finished two years later at a cost of nearly $500,000. Other roads and turnpikes (toll roads), some better and some not so good, were soon being built to link all the states, especially in the East. (See map above.) Most of these were built by private companies and paid for by toll charges to travelers. Over them flowed much of the freight and passenger travel which helped farming and industry to expand rapidly.

The Cumberland Road, later called the National Road, captured the popular imagination. People who traveled over it wrote many descriptions of life along this road. These descriptions give a picture of great herds of cattle and hogs being driven from the West to feed the people along the eastern seaboard. They also tell about long lines of slow, heavy-wheeled, six-horse Conestoga wagons lumbering along and being passed by rattling express wagons, "making the highway look more like a leading avenue of a great city than a road through rural districts."

Flatboats carry cargoes downstream. Settlers moving to the land west of the

Allegheny Mountains but east of the Mississippi always used flatboats, or keelboats, on the rivers when they could, for it was much easier to float their families and furnishings downstream than to haul them overland. It was natural that these settlers should use the same kind of boats to haul their produce to markets. Crude as they were, flatboats in the early years of the 1800's were carrying large cargoes of salt, iron, and farm products from towns like Marietta, Ohio, and Louisville, Kentucky, down the Ohio and Mississippi rivers to New Orleans. But flatboats were not suited to upstream navigation.

Steamboats ply the rivers. The invention of the steamboat made it possible to develop river traffic fully. The first successful steamboat in America was the *Clermont*, built by Robert Fulton.[3] In

[3] As early as 1787, John Fitch experimented with a crude steamboat on the Delaware River. Two years later William Longstreet ran a steamboat on the Savannah River at Augusta, Georgia.

Keelboat

The **"Clermont,"** first fully successful steamboat in America, is shown in this modern painting as she might have looked steaming past a scornful sailing ship in the lower Hudson River. Inventors in several states, as well as in Europe, had been experimenting with steam-propelled boats almost from the time the steam engine was invented in Scotland by James Watt. Historians recognize the importance of their efforts, but consider that Fulton deserves first honors for developing a practical model.

1807 the *Clermont* chugged 150 miles up the Hudson River from New York to Albany in about 30 hours. Fulton wrote, "The power of propelling boats by steam is fully proved." And he added, "The morning I left New York, there were not perhaps thirty persons in the city who believed that the boat would move one mile an hour or be of the least utility." Crowds turned out along the river to marvel at the new steamboat. One spectator wrote, " . . . fishermen became terrified, and rode homewards, and they saw nothing but destruction devasting their fishing grounds, whilst the wreaths of black vapor and rushing noise

of the paddle wheels, foaming with the stirred up water, produced great excitement." [4]

Four years later, in 1811, Nicholas Roosevelt launched the *New Orleans* at Pittsburgh. It reached the city of New Orleans the next spring, but it could not return against the current. In 1816, however, a more powerful steamboat made the trip from New Orleans up to Louisville in 25 days. By 1820, 60 steamboats were operating on the Mississippi and its tributaries. From this time until the War Between the States, steamboats on the western rivers hauled the largest part of American freight. They carried grain, iron, and many other products southward, and they brought back sugar, rice, and cotton.

It was dangerous to navigate the western rivers. They were full of hidden rocks, fallen trees, shoals, swift currents, and shifting channels. Bursting boilers and blown cylinder heads took a heavy toll of life and property. Sparks from the wood fuel started disastrous fires, and there were bad collisions resulting from carelessness or the difficulties of navigation. But these perils were offset by the advantages of swifter and cheaper transportation. The steamboat reduced travel time between New Orleans and Pittsburgh from 100 days to 30, and cut the cost of transportation in half. Both the farmer and the manufacturer profited from the new markets that improved transportation made available.

The canal era begins. Turnpike and river travel did not solve all the transportation problems. Shipping goods by wagon was expensive. River transportation was no help to people who did not happen to live near large rivers. Many areas were therefore shut off from cheap transportation, and through water travel between the East and West was impossible. One means of solving these problems was the construction of canals. The canal made it possible for four horses to pull 100 tons a distance of 24 miles in a day, while on a good turnpike those same four horses could haul only one and a half tons 18 miles a day.

[4] From *The Paths of Inland Commerce*, volume 21, THE CHRONICLES OF AMERICA. Copyright Yale University Press.

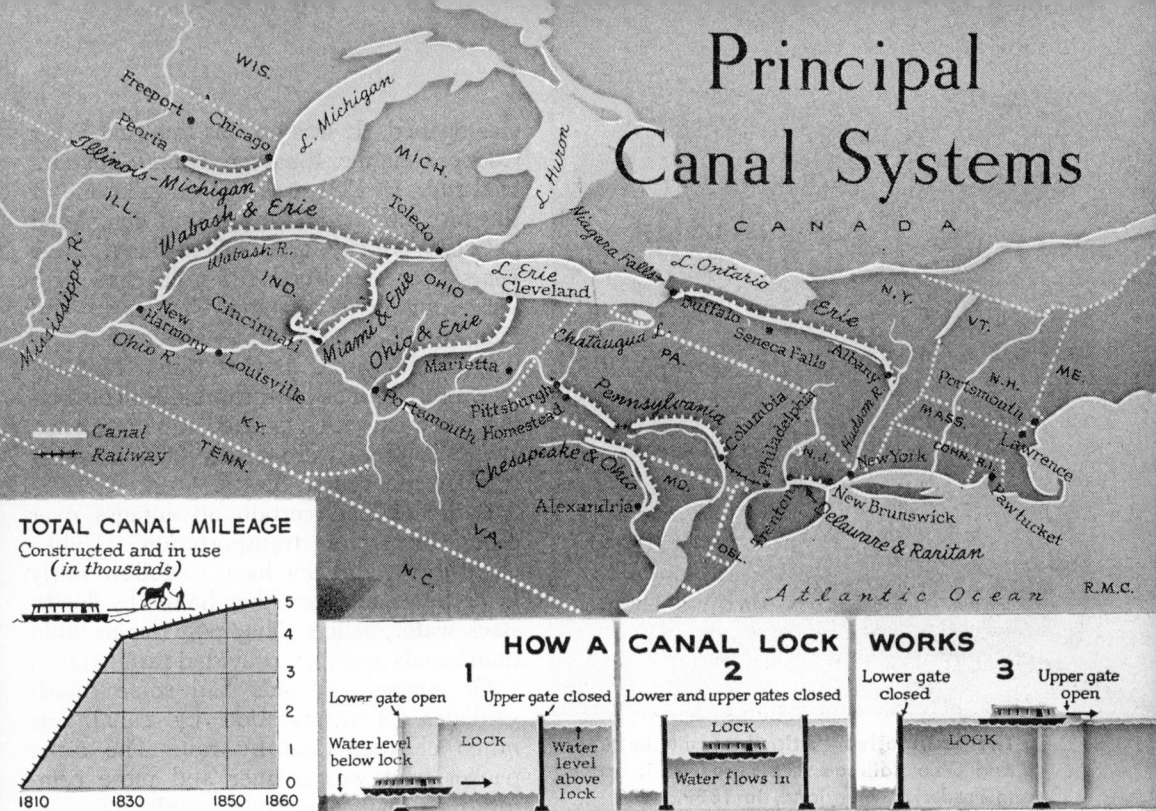

Principal Canal Systems

TOTAL CANAL MILEAGE
Constructed and in use
(*in thousands*)

HOW A CANAL LOCK WORKS

1 Lower gate open   Upper gate closed   Water level below lock   LOCK   Water level above lock

2 Lower and upper gates closed   LOCK   Water flows in

3 Lower gate closed   Upper gate open   LOCK

Canal boats, carrying a few passengers but mostly freight, were vital in the development of industry and agriculture. How many miles of canals were in use in 1810? in 1860? What was the special importance of the Erie Canal? What three canals connected Lake Erie with the Ohio and Mississippi Rivers? Why were they important? The Pennsylvania Canal was expensive to build. Why was it worth the cost?

Travelers also found the canal boat a more comfortable and interesting way to travel than the stagecoach. Charles Dickens, the English writer, described a trip on a canal boat: " . . . The fast, brisk walk upon the towing-path, between [arising] and breakfast, when every vein and artery seemed to tingle with health . . . the lazy motion of the boat, when one lay idly on the deck . . . the gliding on at night, so noiselessly . . . the shining out of the bright stars, undisturbed by noise of wheels or steam, or any other sound than the liquid rippling of the water as the boat went on; all these were pure delights." [5]

The Erie Canal leads the way. A few short canals had been built in early America to get around falls or rapids in rivers; but the canal era really started when the Erie Canal was finished in 1825. (See

[5] From *The Paths of Inland Commerce,* volume 21, THE CHRONICLES OF AMERICA. Copyright Yale University Press.

map above.) This canal was built mainly through the efforts of Governor DeWitt Clinton of New York. It stretched 363 miles, from the Hudson River to Lake Erie. Between the two ends, a series of locks raised or lowered the canal boats about 600 feet. The Erie Canal cost about $8,000,000, but toll charges in the first nine years paid the entire cost of building the canal.

The Erie Canal greatly influenced the growth of American industry and agriculture. It was also important because it bound the Middle West to the East by a commercial tie that was profitable to both sections. Grain, lumber, and other products from the Great Lakes region traveled by way of the canal to New York. Freight could now be shipped from Buffalo to New York in eight days instead of twenty, and the cost of hauling it was cut from $100 to $10 per ton. Manufactured goods also could be shipped to the West at a small cost. Towns along the canal route grew

The locomotive "Atlas" of the Baltimore and Ohio Railroad is pictured as it arrived in Frederick, Maryland, in 1839.

was opened. It was on this line that Peter Cooper's engine, the *Tom Thumb*, made a trial run. In 1831 a seventeen-mile line of the Mohawk and Hudson was completed between Albany and Schenectady. Two years later a railroad 137 miles in length was completed between Charleston and Hamburg, South Carolina — the longest railway in the world at that time. Railroad construction, mostly of short lines connecting principal cities, pushed rapidly ahead. By 1840, there were nearly 3000 miles of track in the United States.

Railroads had certain advantages over other forms of transportation. Unlike canals, they did not have to follow fairly level routes, nor were they halted by floods, slack water, or ice. They cost less to build than canals and they provided faster travel.

Of course, railroads had some disadvantages. Transportation by canal was much cheaper than by rail. The canal packet boat was cleaner and more comfortable than the train, with its soot, cinders, and dirt. The wood-burning locomotive, belching forth showers of sparks, was a real danger to the passengers and the countryside. A passenger who rode the first train between Albany and Schenectady later recalled: "They used dry pitch for fuel, and there being no smoke or spark catcher to the chimney or smoke stack, a volume of black smoke strongly impregnated with sparks, coals, and cinders, came pouring back the whole length of the train. Each of the passengers who had an umbrella raised it as a protection against the smoke and fire. They were found to be but momentary protection, for I think in the first mile the last umbrella went overboard, all having their covers burnt off from the frames, when a general mêlée took place among the deck passengers, each whipping his neighbor to put out the fire." [6]

There were dangers of collisions and fatal accidents, in addition to those of fire and smoke, for the early railroads had few safety devices. The rails, made of wooden beams covered with iron strips, often

into thriving cities, and New York became one of the leading commercial centers of the world. Many New England farmers, finding it hard to compete with the products of the mid-western fertile lands, left their farms to work in the factories of the growing mill towns. Others moved west, and many of them used the "packet boats" on the canal to move their families and possessions.

The success of the Erie Canal led to similar projects in other locations. Canals were built to join the Great Lakes with the Ohio and the Mississippi rivers. In Pennsylvania a canal was dug to connect Philadelphia and Pittsburgh, building a portage railway to carry the boats over the mountains. This portage railway, finished in 1834, was looked upon as the engineering marvel of its day. It ran for about 35 miles and included several inclined planes which carried loaded canal boats over a crest about 1000 feet high.

Railroads are built. About the time that canal building reached its peak, the railroad began to compete with other means of transportation. In 1830 a fourteen-mile stretch of the Baltimore and Ohio Railroad

[6] From *The Railroad Builders*, volume 38, THE CHRONICLES OF AMERICA. Copyright Yale University Press.

caused trouble when the strips came loose and wound around the wheels. Again, the distance between the rails (called the gauge) varied on different railroads, so that it was impossible for the trains of one line to run on the tracks of another. The railroads also had to overcome the ignorance and distrust of the public as well as the opposition of the canal and turnpike companies. Many people felt that it was folly to risk their necks on this new contrivance which traveled at such "terrific" speed.

Railroads increase rapidly. The railroads continued to grow in spite of handicaps and opposition. (See map, and chart below.) By 1860 there were more than 30,000 miles of railroad in the nation, of which about two thirds were north of Mason and Dixon's line. During the 1850's many of the short lines were united. Through shipments of freight could now be made between the Atlantic coast and the Middle West.

Railroads, of course, were very expensive to build. That problem was overcome by help from the government and private agencies. State governments helped by lending money, buying railroad stock, or

Railroad construction increased sharply after 1850 (see graph in upper left-hand corner). Can you explain why? Why did the railroads before about 1860 end at the Mississippi River? Why did most railroads run east and west rather than north and south?

Early Railroad Systems and Overland Mail Routes

Total railroad mileage constructed and in use (in thousands)

guaranteeing the railroad's securities. After 1850 the federal government helped too. It turned over public lands to the states to be regranted to railroad companies. The government hoped that the land it retained nearby would rise so much in value that it would make up for the cost of the gift. As soon as it was seen that railroads offered a chance for rich profits, bankers and investors — both at home and abroad — poured capital into this new investment field.

Early communication is poor. Poor transportation in the years following the Revolution was matched by equally poor communication. There was, of course, no telegraph or telephone. If a man wanted to get in touch with a friend some distance away, he had to make a journey or write a letter. Congress was given the power to improve the postal service, but for a long time not much was done. In fact, not much could be done until the means of travel were improved.

The postal service grows. A letter sent from Maine to Georgia in the early 1800's took 20 days in transit. Postal rates were graded according to distance. It cost, for example, eight cents to send a letter of one sheet within a distance of 30 miles. At this

Flying Cloud was the most famous of many clipper ships designed by Donald McKay of Boston, leading naval architect.

time, the postal service carried an average of only one letter per year for each adult in the country. As new methods of transportation came into use, however, improvement in the postal service became possible. Postal rates were cut, in 1845, to five cents per half-ounce for a distance of not over 300 miles. Six years later a rate of three cents per half-ounce for 3000 miles was set up, and at the same time a three-cent postage stamp was authorized. Under these conditions the volume of mail increased.

The telegraph comes into use. The invention and development of the telegraph was the most notable advance in communication during the first half of the 1800's. Samuel F. B. Morse, after many attempts, perfected an electrical instrument by which combinations of dots and dashes could be transmitted along a metallic wire. He appealed to Congress for a grant of $30,000 to build an experimental line between Baltimore, Maryland and Washington, D.C. Congress finally approved the grant, and in 1844 the line was completed. Morse set up his telegraph instrument in a room of the Supreme Court in Washington, while a friend waited at the other end of the line in Baltimore. While curious and unbelieving spectators stood around, Morse tapped out the first telegraph message, a quotation from the Bible: "What hath God wrought!"

Soon telegraph lines stretched between the important cities of the Northeast. By 1850, New York was connected by telegraph with Chicago and Milwaukee, while Washington had a direct link with New Orleans. Ten years later there were 50,000 miles of telegraph lines east of the Rockies, and the Western Union, with federal help, was extending its lines to the Pacific. In fact, the telegraph grew so fast that it put the famous Pony Express out of business only about a year after it was founded. (See page 368.)

Packet ships sail the Atlantic. Ocean travel was improved as greatly as land travel during this period of economic expansion. By the 1820's sailing ships called "packets" carried passengers and high-grade freight across the stormy Atlantic on regular schedules. The trip took about 18 or 20 days. The packets were soundly built and strongly rigged to withstand the Atlantic gales. Their crews were usually a hard-living, hard-fighting lot, but their skippers were sober, responsible, strong-willed men who kept the boats on schedule. For that reason they were trusted to handle mail, money, and important documents. These ships were the best means of communication between the United States and Europe until the 1850's when they were driven out of business by the ocean-going steamship.

Clippers lead the world. The swift and stately clipper ship, first built around the shores of Chesapeake Bay and later in New England, was the greatest contribution of American shipbuilders to the history of sailing ships. Built for speed rather than for maximum carrying capacity, they sailed the seven seas and outstripped everything else afloat at a time when fantastic profits came to the ship which reached port first. An Englishman explained in this way why American shipping led the world: "The reason will be evident to any one who will walk through the docks at Liverpool. He will see the American ships, long, sharp built, beautifully painted and rigged, and remarkable for their fine appearance and white canvas. He will see the English vessels, short, round, and dirty, resembling great black tubs."

The American clipper ship reached the peak of its development soon after the middle of the century. The *Great Republic*, built in 1853, was twice the size of the average modern freighter. The *James Baines*, built about the same time, maintained a speed of 21 knots for several hours and sailed from Boston Light to Liverpool in twelve days, six hours. The clipper ship could not only outstrip any other sailing vessel, but with a fair breeze it could even outdistance a steamship. The trip around Cape Horn from New York to San Francisco was twice made by the *Flying Cloud* in 89 days.

Steamships outdistance sails. English shipbuilders tried to win back the sailing trade from the Americans, especially with their tea clippers, which brought valuable tea cargoes from the Orient. They were never quite able to outsail the Americans. The English regained their mastery of the seas, however, with the ocean-going steamship. Although steamships had been crossing the Atlantic since about 1820, they did not seriously threaten the supremacy of the Yankee packets and clippers until the middle of the century, when the English introduced the screw propeller and the iron hull. The improved steamship was able to cut the time of passage across the Atlantic to a little over nine days, but the Americans went on using their energies to improve the clippers. Partly as a result of this situation they lost out to the iron steamships of the British. American shipbuilding declined in the late '50's, and investors became more interested in railroads and factories.

The modern day is foreshadowed. The improvements which had taken place in American agriculture, industry, transportation, and communication by the middle of the 1800's were very remarkable indeed, and they laid the foundation for the economic and industrial society in which we live. But it would be a mistake to overestimate them. The daily life of the people was still closer to the 1700's than to the 1900's. Even so, the atmosphere had changed. The leisure of former days had gone, and in its place was the throb and hustle of a new age. A traveler in New York in 1840 observed that "in the streets all is hurry and bustle; the very carts, instead of being drawn by horses at a walking pace, are often met at a gallop, and always at a brisk trot; [while the people themselves] seem to enjoy this bustle, and add to it by their own rapid pace . . . as if under the apprehension of being too late." Expansion to the Far West and the sinister shadow of a coming battle over slavery held the center of the American stage for a time. But the foundation for a new economic era was already laid.

——— CHECK-UP ———

How were the means of transportation and communication improved?

1. Describe land transportation before improvements were made. How were roads improved?
2. How did steamboats revolutionize river travel?

3. What were the effects of the completion of the Erie Canal?
4. What were the advantages of railroads? What improvements had been made in railroads by 1860?
5. How were the means of communication improved before 1860?
6. Why was American overseas shipping largely lost to British shippers by 1860?

CHAPTER REVIEW

Terms to Understand

factory system
capitalist class
corporation
labor union
flatboat
packet boat
clipper ship

Conestoga wagon
toll road
land grants
cotton gin
canal lock
Industrial Revolution
"King Cotton"

People and Things to Know About

McCormick reaper
the canal era
Baltimore and Ohio
  Railroad
the *Flying Cloud*
the Erie Canal

Eli Whitney
Samuel Slater
Elias Howe
Robert Fulton
DeWitt Clinton
Samuel F. B. Morse

Historic Dates to Identify

1793   1825   1844
1807   1830

Questions to Discuss

1. If you had been a New England farmer of the early 1800's, what factors might you have considered in deciding (a) to remain on your farm, (b) to move to the West, (c) to move to a factory city?
2. Compare the following:
 (a) The life of an early factory worker with that of a modern factory worker.
 (b) The relative advantages of the steamboat and the railroad.
 (c) The effects of the cotton gin and the McCormick reaper.
 (d) Modern roads and early nineteenth century roads.
3. Give a brief definition of the Industrial Revolution. Why would the development of the factory system be highly dependent on (a) a revolution in transportation and communication, and (b) a revolution in agricultural methods?

Questions to Discuss (Cont.)

4. How might you have traveled from New York to Buffalo in 1810? In 1830? In 1860?
5. What effects upon the growth of America resulted from the improvements in transportation and communication? See how extensive a list you can make.

Relating Geography and History

1. After consulting a physical map, explain (a) why New York was better situated than Boston or Philadelphia to establish trading connections with the West, (b) why Chicago was potentially a great railroad center, and (c) why New Orleans became a great port.
2. Why would early settlements tend to cluster in the Ohio valley? How did the completion of the Erie Canal affect the location of new settlements?
3. Locate on an outline map of the eastern part of the United States: the Cumberland Road, the Erie Canal, the Pennsylvania Canal.

Other Things to Do

*1. The coming of the first railroad was an event of importance for many American towns. Find information on this event for your community by consulting your local library or writing to your state historical association.
2. Write an imaginative newspaper account of the events connected with (a) the opening of the Erie Canal, or (b) the voyage of the *Clermont*. Hulbert, A. B., *The Paths of Inland Commerce* and Carmer, Carl, *The Hudson* are possible sources of information.
3. Construct a pictorial map showing the chief routes of transportation in 1850 with the modes of travel used on them.
4. Contribute to a collection of pictures for the class bulletin board illustrating the development of transportation from 1850 to the present.

Chapter 12

Policeman, 1840

A GROWING POPULATION CALLS FOR

SOCIAL REFORMS

The absence of the prejudices of the old world leaves us here the opportunity of consulting independent truth; and man is left to apply the instinct of freedom to every social relation and public interest.

From "The Oracle of the People," by George Bancroft, 1835

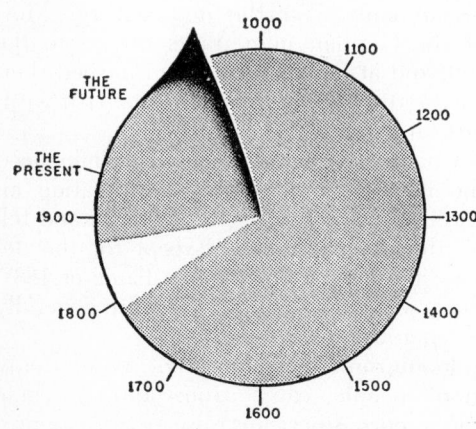

1789–1865

Developments in farming, industry, transportation, and communication were not the only important changes in the United States during the first half of the nineteenth century. The very character of the nation was changing. The population was growing, building up cities and towns, and spilling over the mountains into the West. As a result of the democratic spirit of the time, certain movements for social improvement were in the air. There was increased emphasis on the rights of the common man in the young nation. The country was throbbing with strength and vigor, and everywhere there were opportunities for getting ahead. There seemed less excuse than ever for the existence of distress or inequality. For that reason, in the 1830's and '40's many reformers led crusades to help the average man, woman, and child live a better life.

239

The story of the growing nation and the movements for reform will be told in three parts:

1. The population of the country increases.
2. Some northerners crusade against slavery.
3. Reformers try to improve American life.

1 **The Population of the Country Increases**

Important population changes occur. One of the important social developments taking place in the United States during the first half of the 1800's was the rapid growth in population. (See chart, page 242.) By 1840 the inhabitants of the United States numbered 17 million people, and in the next 20 years the total in the states and territories increased to nearly 31½ million. The western areas grew faster than the other parts of the country; by the middle of the century, almost half the population lived west of the Alleghenies. Another important trend was the growth of larger centers of population. In 1840, for instance, there were 44 communities with a population of 8000 or more, making up one twelfth of the country's total population. Twenty years later there were over three times as many cities and towns of that size or larger, making up about a sixth of the total population. By 1860 more than a million people lived in the combined areas of New York City and Brooklyn, New York.

Immigration increases. A large part of this population increase was caused by waves of immigration to American shores. From the beginning, of course, the United States had been a nation of immigrants. The flow had started during the colonial period, as English, Scotch, Irish, Scotch-Irish, Germans, Swedes, Dutch, and others came in search of homes, freedom, and fortunes in the New World. After the new republic was formed, new waves of immigration occurred: for example, during the ten-year period from 1821 to 1831, about 150,000 immigrants arrived. From 1841 to 1851 the total immigration figure was nearly 1¾ million, and from 1851 to 1861 it rose to more than 2½ million. (See chart, page 243.)

Many immigrants come from Ireland and Germany. Most of the immigrants in the first half of the 1800's came from the British Isles and northern and western Europe. In the years between 1820 and 1850 the greatest number of immigrants came from Ireland. Many Irishmen emigrated to America because they were unhappy under British rule. Then in 1845 Ireland's potato crop failed, and a severe famine swept the country. During the next few years, hundreds of thousands of Irishmen were literally starved into leaving their native land. To them America was the land of promise. Nearly all the Irish settled in the East, especially in the cities.

The next largest group of immigrants to America during these years were the Germans. Many Germans came because of poor crops and hard times at home. Others left their country because of persecutions after the failure of a revolutionary uprising in Germany near the mid-century. Most of the German immigrants turned to the soil, and at least half of them pushed their way across the mountains to the rich western farm lands.

Conditions in America also influenced the flow of immigrants. Immigration always rose during prosperous times and fell off during bad times. Except for the depression years following the Panic of 1837, the years from 1820 to 1850 were generally prosperous.

Immigrants meet hostility. As more and more people came from abroad, some native-born Americans raised a storm of protest. Most of the newcomers from across the ocean became laborers, farmers, or mechanics and were willing to work long hours for low wages. Employers were more than willing to hire them. Immigrants who

(Continued on page 242)

NEW SALEM ON
THE FRONTIER

Log construction of houses and other buildings throughout the wooded frontier is shown in this detail. This building served as a general store in Lincoln's day.

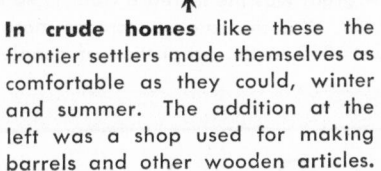

A portrait of Lincoln hangs over the stone fireplace of the postoffice where Lincoln once served as postmaster.

In crude homes like these the frontier settlers made themselves as comfortable as they could, winter and summer. The addition at the left was a shop used for making barrels and other wooden articles.

A frontier store looked like this in early days. It stocked only such foods and articles as could not be grown or made at home.

The blacksmith was one of the most important citizens in early communities. In addition to shoeing horses, he repaired tools and wagons.

New Salem, Illinois, became a frontier community like thousands of others when pioneers were pushing westward toward the Mississippi River. Most traces of such communities have vanished, but New Salem has been restored and is visited by many people each year because it was here that Abraham Lincoln grew to manhood. Simple scenes like these were everyday sights to thousands of American citizens only 100 years ago.

settled in the cities were likely to make their homes in wretched tenements and shanties, because they could afford nothing better. Since low wage scales tend to lower the standards of living, native-born workers resented the threat to their own higher standards of living.

Opponents of the Democratic Party also were disturbed because so many of the new Americans added voting strength to Democratic political machines, such as the Tammany Hall machine in New York City. Some religious groups also objected to the newcomers because many of the immigrants, particularly among the Irish and Germans, were Roman Catholics. Protestants were alarmed by the increase of Catholic churches, convents, and parochial schools.

In the early 1850's the scattered groups which opposed the immigrants formed a semi-secret political organization which called itself the American Party. When asked about the name and purpose of the party, its members replied: "I know nothing." Soon the party came to be called the "Know-Nothing" Party.

——————— CHECK-UP ———————

Why did the population of the United States increase rapidly in the second quarter of the nineteenth century?

1. What evidences were there that our population was rapidly increasing?
2. Why did the Irish migrate to America? the Germans? Where did these two nationalities tend to settle?
3. Why were some Americans hostile to the immigrants? How did they show their hostility?

The growth of population in the United States from 1790 to 1950 is shown in charts on this page, on page 423, and on page 584. About how large was the population in 1820? About how great was the increase from 1790 to 1820? What was the approximate population in 1860? Was the rate of increase more rapid before or after 1820? What was happening by 1860 to the proportion of people living in urban places?

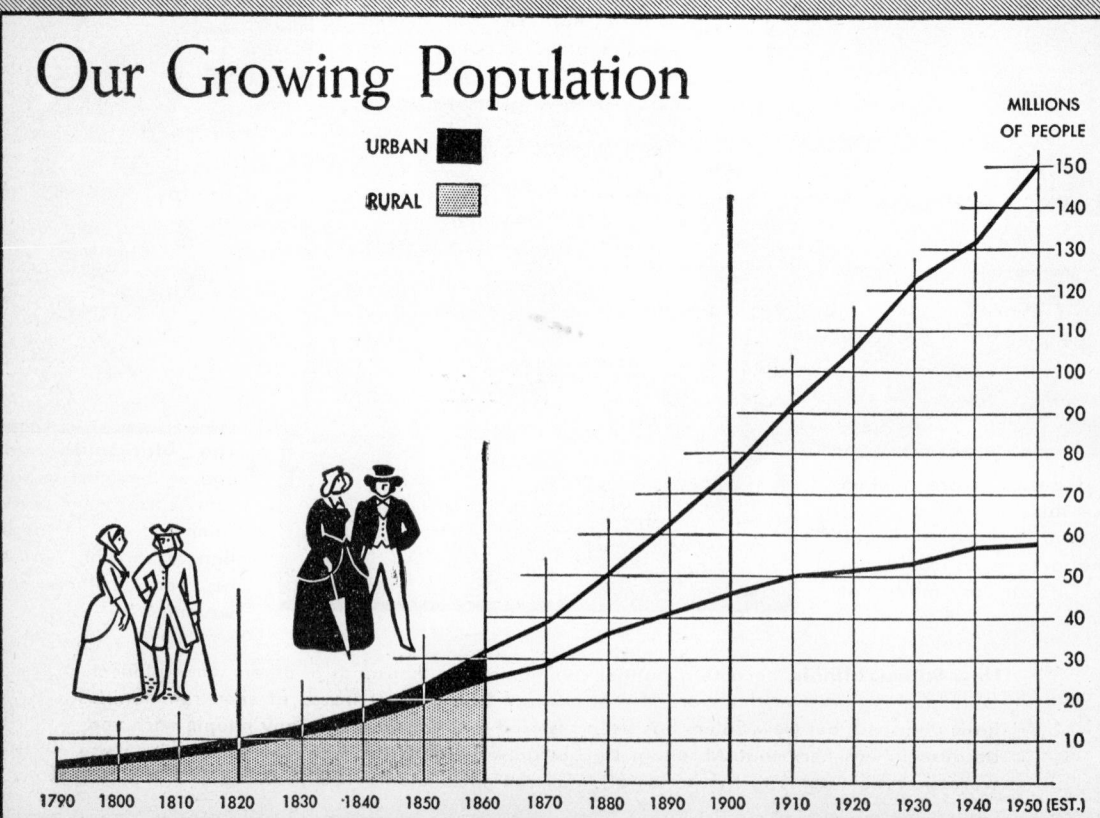

Our Growing Population

URBAN ■

RURAL ▒

MILLIONS OF PEOPLE

150
140
130
120
110
100
90
80
70
60
50
40
30
20
10

1790 1800 1810 1820 1830 1840 1850 1860 1870 1880 1890 1900 1910 1920 1930 1940 1950 (EST.)

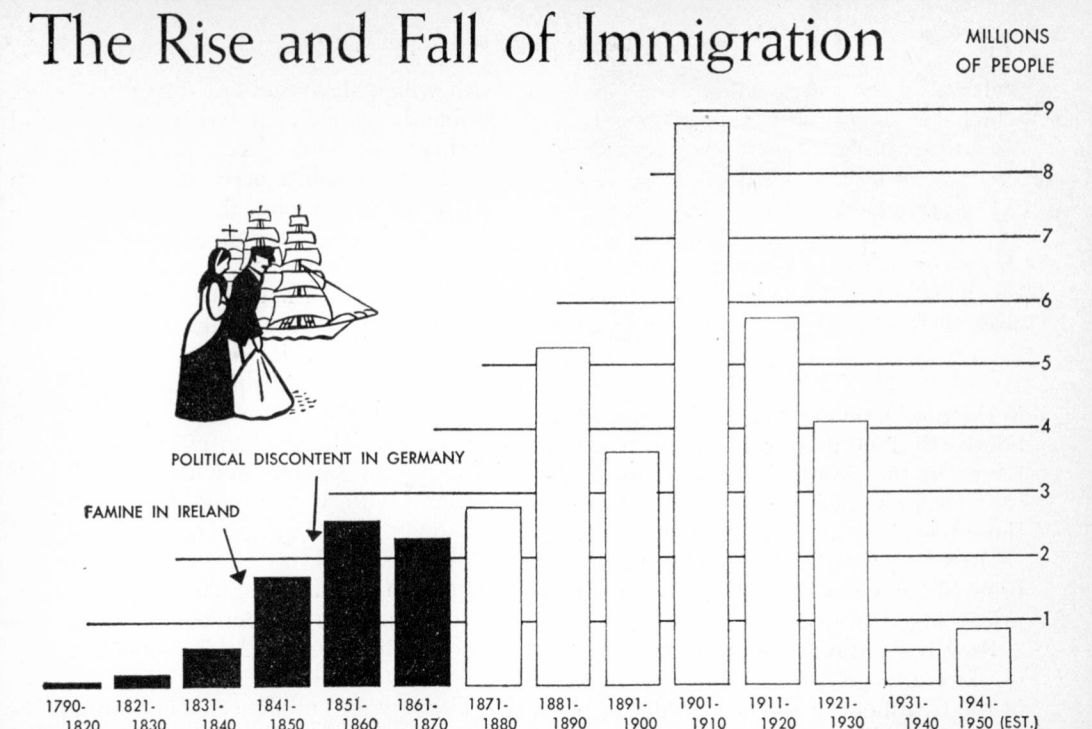

The Rise and Fall of Immigration

MILLIONS OF PEOPLE

POLITICAL DISCONTENT IN GERMANY

FAMINE IN IRELAND

| 1790-1820 | 1821-1830 | 1831-1840 | 1841-1850 | 1851-1860 | 1861-1870 | 1871-1880 | 1881-1890 | 1891-1900 | 1901-1910 | 1911-1920 | 1921-1930 | 1931-1940 | 1941-1950 (EST.) |

Immigration was an important reason for the rise of our population from 1820 to 1860. About how many million immigrants arrived during this time? Why did so many come from Ireland and Germany?

2 Some Northerners Crusade Against Slavery

Slavery retards southern population growth. Most immigrants were attracted to the North and West rather than to the South. There was little manufacturing in the South at this time, largely because the chief economic interest in this area was the growing of cotton. Mechanics and other skilled factory workers, therefore, had little reason to look southward. Nor were there many attractions for laborers and farmers, who would have to compete with slave labor in the cultivation of cotton. An immigrant who wanted to become an independent farmer was also discouraged by the prospect of competing with the great planters who owned large numbers of slaves. Few immigrants, therefore, were attracted to the slave states, and the South gradually lost ground in population in comparison with the North and West.

The South develops social groups. Slavery also helped to create more distinct social classes in the South than were to be found in other parts of the country. In 1860 the aristocracy at the top of the social ladder included about 6000 great planters and their families, out of a total southern white population of about 6 million. Then there were the well-to-do townsmen, the small independent farmers, and mechanics and tradesmen, which together made up the middle class. Still lower were the "poor whites" of the sand hills, the pine barrens, and the secluded mountain regions. Living in isolation on poor land and lacking opportunities for education, the "poor whites" endured poverty and hardship. At the bottom of the social scale were the slaves, who were believed to be absolutely necessary

243

Plantation house

in the production of the staple crops of the South. By 1860 there were nearly 4 million slaves in the South, but the demand for slaves kept growing, and their value continued to increase. At the start of the century, a "prime" (or excellent) field hand brought from $400 to $500 but by 1860 the price ranged from $1200 to $1500.

How were slaves treated? Descriptions of slave life give quite different versions of the treatment of slaves. No doubt there were individual plantation owners and overseers who were as cruel as Simon Legree in *Uncle Tom's Cabin*, but such cases were unusual. Many relationships between members of the two races were as happy as the one pictured by Joel Chandler Harris in his stories about Uncle Remus and the little white lad who listened entranced to the tales of "Brer Rabbit."

On the whole, the slaves of the South received fairly good treatment. In fact, it was against an owner's best interests to abuse his slaves, for they were valuable property and represented a heavy investment. They were adequately fed in most cases and given the proper care. Most of them submitted to their lot without protest. They probably worked no harder than the northern "hired man," and at least they had fewer worries about unemployment and old age. House servants were treated better than field hands, though conditions varied in different localities and even on neighboring plantations. Flogging was the usual form of punishment for slaves, since imprisonment would have meant the loss of their labor, and reduced food allowances would have cut down their ability to work. Probably the worst side of slavery was the frequency

244

with which slave families were broken up, husbands being separated from wives and mothers from children.

Slavery presents economic risks. From a business standpoint, the practice of slavery was open to question. Its disadvantages were likely to outweigh its advantages. Unlike the northern manufacturer, the southern planter had to invest heavily in his labor supply. Having done so, he had to struggle constantly to earn a fair profit on this investment. Sometimes his crops were poor. Then, when crops were good, there might be too much cotton on the market, with a resulting drop in price. Whatever happened, the cotton planter had to take care of his slaves and keep the plantation going. Unlike the northern manufacturer, a planter could not reduce expenses in bad times by laying off his help and closing his doors.

There were other economic disadvantages in slavery. When a planter wanted to enlarge his plantation he had to buy not only more land but also more slaves. Furthermore, a slave was a perishable piece of property. When he became sick or old, or when he escaped or died, the planter suffered real financial loss. Finally, the slave usually was not a willing worker. His work called for constant expensive supervision.

The emancipation movement begins. It is possible that slavery might eventually have come to an end in the United States because of its disadvantages. Before this could happen, however, a movement to do away with slavery sprang from a growing interest in the slave as a human being. From the American and French Revolutions had risen a belief that all human beings had certain rights. Slavery could

Slave dwelling

New Orleans, major port for shipment of southern cotton to the world's markets, was already a large and busy city when this old print was made in the 1850's. Notice the busy river traffic. Compare this picture with the one on page 330.

not be made to harmonize with that belief. As a result, a number of societies were formed between 1775 and 1830 to carry on a campaign of educating the country to the gradual *emancipation* (or freeing) of slaves. Another step in the same direction was the founding of the American Colonization Society in 1816 for the purpose of sending emancipated Negroes to Liberia, Africa. But the emancipation movement made little progress in these years because it would have brought economic losses and created social problems in the South.

Garrison demands abolition of slavery. Suddenly, the nature of the anti-slavery movement changed. New voices demanded the *abolition* of slavery. The most influential abolitionist was William Lloyd Garrison. A fiery New Englander still in his twenties, Garrison demanded the immediate and unconditional freeing of the slaves. He believed that slavery was a "national sin" which could not be excused on the grounds of economic profit. He even went so far as to say that if the Constitution protected slavery, then the fundamental law of the land was nothing better than "an agreement with HELL."

Garrison's newspaper, *The Liberator,* first appeared on January 1, 1831. In this issue, Garrison hurled defiance at people who wanted gradual emancipation. He wrote: "I *will be* as harsh as truth, and as uncompromising as justice. On this subject I do not wish to think, or speak, or write, with moderation. . . I am in earnest — I will not equivocate — I will not excuse — I will not retreat a single inch — AND I WILL BE HEARD."

Garrison arouses Northerners. Garrison soon found that he had stirred up a hornet's nest. His bold language shocked conservative anti-slavery people in the North. He also made enemies among northern financiers and merchants who were interested in the manufacture of cotton and in protecting their trade with the South. Abolitionist meetings were broken up, their speakers howled down and stoned, and their printing presses and assembly halls torn down or burned. Garrison himself was mobbed in the streets of Boston and barely escaped with his life.

Garrison angers Southerners. In the South the abolitionists made even more violent enemies. Southerners bitterly resented Garrison's calling slavery the "sum of all villainies," and his attack on slaveholders as "greedy and relentless tyrants." Anger turned to alarm when the worst slave uprising the South had ever known took place in 1831, the same year *The Liberator* appeared. Led by Nat Turner, an uneducated Negro preacher, slaves in Virginia massacred about 60 white people, most of whom were women and children. Southerners blamed Garrison and abolitionist propaganda for the destruction of property and loss of life.

The South quickly took steps to prevent further rebellions and to safeguard fully its institutions. State militias were reorganized. Laws were passed to prevent uprisings and to stop literature on the slavery question from being circulated. Attempts were also made to close the mails to abolitionist attacks, while the abolitionists themselves were challenged to go into the South and meet the punishment promised them.

The South defends slavery. The abolitionist attacks changed the southern point of view toward the institution of slavery. Before this time, the South had looked upon slavery as a "necessary evil." Now it was defended as a "positive good." Southerners argued that the slave was better off than the worker in a northern factory and that slavery was a natural relationship between the two races, a way of life with benefits for Negroes as well as for whites. Thus the abolitionists made the differences between the North and the South even more pronounced than before.

Sentiment against slavery grows. Abolition efforts seemed to thrive on opposition and persecution. Anti-slavery organizations increased by the hundreds. The number of

their publications multiplied, and their petitions for action against slavery flooded Congress. The House of Representatives tried to prevent these petitions by passing a resolution in 1836 which would have freed the House from even considering them. John Quincy Adams, who had been elected to the House, began a determined fight against this resolution. He was no abolitionist, but he believed that such a "gag rule" was contrary to the right of petition granted to the people by the Bill of Rights. After an eight-year struggle Adams was successful. The resolution was repealed.

The abolitionists also organized the Liberty Party, which supported James Birney, a former slaveholder, as its candidate for the Presidency in 1840 and again in 1844. But the most dramatic activity of the abolitionists was the "underground railroad." Along this network of secret, zigzag routes, fugitive slaves were helped in escaping to Canada or to places of safety in the North. The runaway was hidden by day, and whisked by night from one safe place to another. The number of slaves who were led to freedom was small, but the "underground" made the North and South even more hostile to each other. To offset the escape of slaves, Negroes in the North were sometimes kidnapped and taken to the South. In turn, Pennsylvania and other northern states passed "personal liberty laws" to prevent this practice, and to protect their free Negro population.

––––––– CHECK-UP –––––––

How did opposition to slavery grow?

1. How did cotton planting and slavery affect the growth of population in the South? social classes in the South?
2. What were the advantages and disadvantages of slavery to the plantation owner?
3. How did Garrison affect the anti-slavery movement? How did the North react to his work? the South?
4. What arguments and methods were used by the abolitionists? by the pro-slavery group?

3 Reformers Try to Improve American Life

"Ideal" communities fail. Abolition was the most talked-about reform movement in the first half of the 1800's, but there were many other ways in which the spirit of reform showed itself. Some people felt that the most satisfying conditions of living could be realized only in brand-new settlements established under ideal conditions. An English reformer, Robert Owen, came to America in 1824 and tried to set up such an ideal community at New Harmony, Indiana. A number of famous writers started a co-operative community at Brook Farm, near Boston, where they meant to support themselves without outside help and to lead lives of high moral and spiritual value. Many other ideal communities were set up, but most of them failed. There were other reform movements, however, which met with a greater measure of success.

The temperance movement starts. An important crusade was waged during the first half of the 1800's against the use of intoxicating liquor. At first, the reformers campaigned only for temperance in drinking, and by 1831 there were more than 2000 local temperance societies. Later more extreme groups developed, which were opposed to any use of liquor. These groups worked to pass laws which would prohibit the liquor business entirely. Among other things, they argued that drinking made workers inefficient and that liquor was harmful to anyone who used it. A convention of their delegates from 21 states met at Philadelphia in 1833 and formed an organization which soon became the American Temperance Union.

In 1846 Maine stopped the retail sale of intoxicating liquors for drinking purposes — liquors could be sold only when needed as medicine. Ohio and Illinois passed similar laws. By 1856 thirteen states of the

The demand of women for a larger part in the economic life of the country was dramatized in Lynn, Massachusetts, in 1860, when 800 women shoe workers led 4000 workmen in a strike parade. The Lynn city guard went along to keep order.

North and West had passed laws intended to stop the sale of distilled spirits. But prohibition remained a subject of debate. Its opponents pointed out that these laws were hard to enforce and that to make laws which could not be enforced was bad for the country. Prohibitionists argued that their efforts had led the people of the United States to become more moderate in their drinking.

Women seek to improve their position. Another reform sought to give the American woman greater freedom and an improved position. In the early 1800's, a woman's place was believed to be entirely in the home. Careers for the "weaker sex" were frowned upon. Girls were not given much schooling, even in the wealthier families. They seldom had a chance to study more than the three R's — reading, 'riting, and 'rithmetic. Women had no right to vote, and under the common law a

Fire bucket

woman's property became her husband's property upon marriage.

The employment of women in factories was an opening wedge in enabling them to become active outside the home. When women tried to take part in such reform movements as abolition and temperance, however, the propriety of their conduct was challenged. As a result, certain outstanding women, notably Elizabeth Cady Stanton and Lucretia Mott, began a real struggle for the intellectual, economic, and political freedom of their sex.

Their efforts resulted in some progress. During the 1830's and '40's, women were given a better chance for education. A few seminaries and normal schools were founded that admitted girls only. Oberlin College took the lead in admitting women on practically equal terms with men. At the same time, women began to enter more freely into the occupation of teaching. Before the mid-century had passed, seven states had passed laws allowing women to keep control of their property after marriage. In 1848 a Women's Rights convention was held at Seneca Falls, New York, at which a declaration of women's rights was drawn up. But a long and unpopular campaign lay ahead before women were to obtain any real equality with men.

Reformers promote the public welfare. Interest in helping the common man brought about various improvements in the public welfare. For example, there was an increase in the number of public and private charitable institutions. Inability to pay a debt was no longer the grave offense which earlier in the century had put tens of thousands of people in prison every year. In most states the whipping post was abolished. In 1850 Congress outlawed flogging in the navy. Fewer crimes brought the death penalty, and life in prison was improved to a point where it was more bearable. State prisoners were put into individual cells instead of being herded into

Fireman

a common room. Youthful lawbreakers were treated more intelligently. More humane ways were found to take care of the insane, largely through the investigations and efforts of Dorothea L. Dix. Massachusetts opened the door on still another field of reform by passing laws to protect children who worked in factories.

City life is improved. Improvements in city life were also made during these years. Formerly, people who lived in cities had to draw their water from springs, wells, or rain barrels — all of them possible sources of disease. Now, Philadelphia, New York, and other cities introduced the piped-water system. City streets, which had always been dark at night, were lighted by gas in Boston and New York before the year 1830. Horse-drawn omnibuses came into use about the same time. Soon the rattle of traffic was reduced in many cities by pav-

Early fire engine

ing the streets with wooden or granite blocks instead of cobblestones. Greater order and safety came to American cities after uniformed police and paid fire companies were introduced near the middle of the century. Shortly afterward, the first public sewerage system based on scientific principles was begun in Chicago. Improvements like these brought more comfort and convenience into the homes of city dwellers.

Interest in religion increases. This was a time, too, when interest in religion was high. Frequent religious revivals were held in the more settled communities. Along the frontier, circuit riders or wandering preachers brought the word of God to the pioneers. The number of religious groups, or denominations, increased greatly. Many new sects appeared, like the Mormons and the Adventists.

The Mormon movement owed its origin to Joseph Smith, who claimed to have received divine revelations. These he translated into the "Book of Mormon" and established the "Church of Jesus Christ of the Latter-Day Saints" (1830). Within a few years the new faith attracted thousands of converts. However, the activity of the church in business and the later rumors of polygamy, made the Mormons unpopular in a number of states in the Mississippi valley where they attempted to settle. In 1847, after the murder of Smith by an angry mob, several thousand settlers, under the leadership of Brigham Young, moved far beyond the reach of civilization to the basin of the Great Salt Lake in Mexican territory. From the start the new venture in the "promised land" prospered.

Older bodies — Baptists, Methodists, Presbyterians — split into smaller groups. It has been estimated that three fourths of the people in the United States in 1850 belonged to some Christian organization or at least considered themselves Christians.

The Roman Catholic Church was larger than any of the others, claiming over 1½ million members. The Methodists came next with about 1¼ million. All denominations were equal before the law and none had special approval from the government. No single group could dominate the others,

Circuit rider

and this fact built greater tolerance. Except for the persecution of Mormons for their unusual teachings, and except for anti-Roman Catholic activities by some native Americans, the middle of the century was free from religious persecution. Most of the new state constitutions drawn up in the first half of the 1800's showed that discrimination against Roman Catholics, Jews, and atheists was decreasing. These constitutions provided that no religious tests should be required when a man wanted the right to vote or hold public office, and that a person's religious views should not affect his civil rights and privileges.

The chief emphasis in religion was still upon personal salvation rather than social service. The various movements for improvements in human welfare show clearly, however, that a stronger social consciousness was springing to life in America.

———— CHECK-UP ————

How did reformers try to improve American life?

1. What was the temperance movement? What success did it have?
2. How did women try to improve their position in society?
3. In what ways were the public welfare and general living conditions improved?
4. What were the chief developments in religion?

CHAPTER REVIEW

Terms to Understand

parochial schools	right of petition
aristocracy	fugitive slaves
"poor whites"	temperance
emancipation	religious denomination

People and Things to Know About

"Know-Nothings"	Liberty Party
abolitionists	"underground railroad"
The Liberator	Robert Owen
William L. Garrison	"personal liberty laws"
Nat Turner's rebellion	Elizabeth Cady Stanton
"gag rule"	Lucretia Mott
Mormons	Dorothea L. Dix
Brigham Young	

Questions to Discuss

1. In what ways was the United States in 1860 a better place to live in than it had been in 1790?

2. What is your reaction to each of the following generalizations?

 (*a*) All Negro slaves were treated badly.

 (*b*) Most of the South was divided into large, slave-tilled plantations.

 (*c*) All southern plantation owners were wealthy and lived in large mansions.

3. Compare the following:

 (*a*) Economic and social conditions in the North and South in 1860.

 (*b*) Advantages and disadvantages of slave labor.

 (*c*) Abolitionism with the other reform movements.

 (*d*) Position of women in society in 1830 and today.

4. What would your attitude towards slavery have been had you been (*a*) a southern "poor

Questions to Discuss (Cont.)

white," (*b*) a southern plantation owner, (*c*) a northern merchant, (*d*) a northern minister?

5. Why do you suppose that John Quincy Adams fought against the "gag rule" even though he was not an abolitionist? Is such a viewpoint and policy necessary to maintain a democracy?

6. Slavery was criticized on both economic and moral grounds. Distinguish between them.

Relating Geography and History

1. Why were there fewer large cities in the South than in the North? Which were the largest southern cities? Why did they grow?

2. In which areas of the South were the plantation system and slavery most concentrated? What were the geographical characteristics of these areas? (See an historical atlas.)

Other Things to Do

1. Prepare a biographical report on one of the important reformers of the period. What did he or she advocate? What methods did he or she use? What was accomplished?

°2. Prepare a two-column chart in which you contrast the North and the South in 1860 in as many ways as possible.

3. Write an editorial either condemning or praising the abolitionist movement.

4. Prepare a talk on the "underground railroad." Macy, *The Anti-Slavery Crusade* has additional material on this topic.

5. As an active participant in the early movement for women's rights, compose a series of effective slogans to popularize your point of view. You may wish to draw ideas from the women's "Declaration of Independence" given in Commager and Nevins's *The Heritage of America*.

Chapter 13

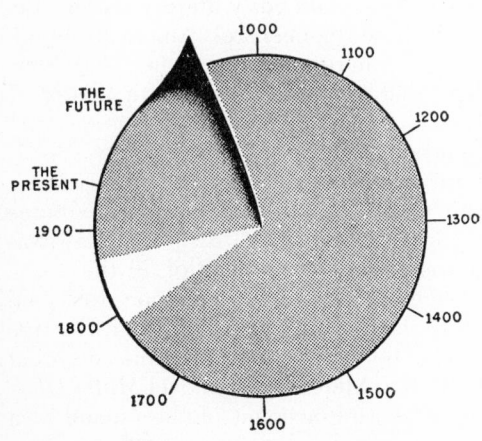

Banjo player

AMERICANS CREATE AN AMERICAN

CULTURE

Our day of dependence, our long apprenticeship to the learning of other lands, draws to a close. The millions that around us are rushing into life cannot always be fed on the sere remains of foreign harvests.

Ralph Waldo Emerson, 1837

THE
FUTURE

1000
1100
1200

THE
PRESENT

1900

1300

1800

1400

1700
1500

1600

1789-1865

A nation's progress must not be judged only by its government and its military victories, its farms and factories. Sometimes the growth of a nation can be seen as clearly in its cultural progress — its contributions to literature, music, art, and science.

At the beginning of the 1800's, the American people had done little to create a truly American culture. There were many stirring subjects to write about, but the American reading public was so small that literary effort did not seem worth while. The drama was just beginning to break free from earlier restrictions. American verse was mostly patterned after English models. Of the American painters who flourished before the Revolution (page 78), only one — Charles W. Peale — stayed on in America to portray through his art the spirit of the new American republic. Except for Benjamin Franklin and a few others, Americans paid little attention to important scientific discoveries then being made in Europe.

Medical practice was still crude, and the sciences allied with it — dentistry, surgery, and pharmacy — were still in their infancy.

By the middle of the 1800's, however, the situation was greatly changed. Americans could then boast a culture that was really their own. This chapter tells how this change came about and what persons were responsible for it. These are the major points:

1. American writers create a distinctive literature.
2. Progress is slower in drama, fine arts, and music.
3. Science and education move forward.

1 American Writers Create a Distinctive Literature

New developments encourage cultural efforts. There were three important reasons for the growth of American culture in the first half of the 1800's: (1) The breaking of our ties with Europe encouraged pride in American achievement. (2) The Jacksonian era, with its vigorous democratic spirit and its keen interest in human welfare, offered a challenge to the best minds in the country. (3) Important changes brought by the Industrial Revolution aided the growth of American culture in many ways. For example, the growth of towns and cities made it easier for people to share their cultural interests. Men who made money in the new industrial ventures had the means as well as the leisure to promote and enjoy the arts. Inventions in transportation, communication, and printing speeded up the exchange of ideas between people in different sections of the country.

A truly American literature appears. As late as 1820 an English critic asked scornfully, "Who reads an American book?" Within a very few years there was a defiant answer to this question. A distinctive American literature began to flourish with the writings of James Fenimore Cooper,

Washington Irving, William Cullen Bryant, and Edgar Allan Poe.

Cooper wrote romances of American life, most of them dealing with the frontiersman and the American Indian. His *Leatherstocking Tales* were eagerly read in England as well as America. Irving, writing on both American and European subjects, delighted Americans with his impressions of Europe and gave the Old World a more accurate picture of trends in American life.

Bryant was distinguished both as a poet and as an editor. His poem, *Thanatopsis*, written before he was twenty, was at first rejected by Richard H. Dana, of the *North American Review*, on the ground that poetry of such beauty and perfection could not have been written by an American. As editor of the New York *Evening Post* for a half century, Bryant was the first of a number of distinguished American editors and journalists.

Poe's literary contributions were varied and important. (1) He was the first American to develop standards for judging the merits of literature. (2) He experimented freely and successfully with a new form of literature, the short story. (3) He did much to develop the mystery, or detective, story. (4) His weird and mystical poetry was noteworthy for its style and rhythm.

New York is an early literary center. Because these pioneers of American literature were more or less identified with New York, that city early became a center of literary activity. Somewhat later, two other important names added to New York's literary fame. Just after the mid-century, Walt Whitman published his first volume of poems, *Leaves of Grass*. Whitman was the most vitally American of all the poets. Writing mainly about common folk and nature, he expressed himself boldly in free verse. The other important name was that of Herman Melville. His novel *Moby Dick*, the fascinating account of the pursuit of a white whale, is rated as one of the masterpieces of American literature.

New England writers take the lead. It was in New England, especially in and around Boston, that the new movement in

(Continued on page 254)

Washington Irving
(1783-1859)

Boyhood

WASHINGTON IRVING was born in New York City in the year the Revolutionary War came to an end. New York resembled a country town, rich in the traditions of its Dutch and colonial background. Young Irving absorbed much of this atmosphere. A summer's hunting in the Sleepy Hollow country at fifteen, and a later voyage up the Hudson, further enriched his knowledge of the region.

Irving was trained for the law but never practiced it seriously. Although not fully decided on a career of writing, in 1809 he finished *Diedrich Knickerbocker's History of New York*. In this delightful mixture of fact, sentiment, and humor, Irving caught the true atmosphere of New York under the Dutch rule.

In 1815 Irving went to Europe and remained for seventeen years. During this time he turned to writing as a life work and produced most of his books. The *Sketch Book* marked him as a master of the short tale or sketch. Thoroughly American in their atmosphere, two of the sketches — "Rip Van Winkle" and "The Legend of Sleepy Hollow" — have earned a permanent place in American literature. Irving also went to Madrid, Spain, where he wrote several books which have preserved the charm of old Spain as effectively as his earlier works did the Dutch influence in America.

In Spain

When Irving returned to America, he accompanied an Indian commission to Fort Gibson on the Arkansas River. This trip led him to write *A Tour of the Prairies*. The rest of his life, except for four years when he was ambassador to Spain, was spent at "Sunnyside," his home near Tarrytown on the Hudson.

People of Irving's day enjoyed his writings both for the pleasure they gave and for the clear understanding they offered of American and European backgrounds. His work was noteworthy for its charm, feeling, and humor, expressed in smooth, clear prose. The great English writer Thackeray called him "The first ambassador whom the New World of Letters sent to the Old."

In the West

Sport and fashions, as well as the arts, had begun to interest New Yorkers before the mid-1800's, as this old painting shows.

literature blossomed most richly. An amazing group of important literary figures appeared there, including Longfellow, Whittier, Lowell, Holmes, Hawthorne, Emerson, and Thoreau. Henry Wadsworth Longfellow was probably the best known and most widely loved of all American poets of that day. He sketched human nature in charming and simple verse. The popularity of *Paul Revere's Ride, Hiawatha, The Courtship of Miles Standish,* and *Evangeline* continues to this day.

Most of the New England literary figures were brilliant thinkers who championed certain causes or challenged some features of American life. In his poems of New England and the White Mountains, John Greenleaf Whittier described the attractions of nature and the simplicity of country life. Although he was an active pacifist, his poems often ring with defiance of slavery. James Russell Lowell was regarded abroad as the leading spokesman of American ideals. He opposed war in general and war with Mexico in particular (page 274). He was hostile to slavery and to intemperance. His vigorous writings on these subjects mark him as a reformer as well as poet and teacher.

Oliver Wendell Holmes was a writer who pointed out some of the failings of human nature. Holmes was a physician, poet, and novelist, as well as a humorist whose wit was tempered with kindliness. His poems include *The Chambered Nautilus,* and the amusing tale of the deacon and his "wonderful one-hoss shay." Nathaniel Hawthorne, for a long time considered America's leading novelist, was a staunch supporter of democracy. "The truth is," Hawthorne wrote in *The House of the Seven Gables,* "that once in every half-century, at longest, a family should be merged in the great obscure mass of humanity, and forget all about its ancestors."

Another New England name which stands high in the history of American letters is that of Ralph Waldo Emerson. He was a poet, a philosopher, and a writer of essays. Outstanding among his ideas was his belief that the individual should be self-sufficient, and he protested sharply against the growing industrialism which he felt made it difficult for people to keep their individuality.

The most extreme of the New England group was Henry David Thoreau. Like his friend Emerson, Thoreau felt that individuals should be free from the restraints of society, the church, and the state. "Let every one mind his own business and endeavor to be what he was made," was his teaching. Thoreau was a nature lover and an excellent literary stylist. In *Walden, or Life in the Woods,* which told about his own simple and retiring life at Walden Pond in Concord, Massachusetts, Thoreau wrote as a critic of the life and manners of his time.

Southern writers describe southern life. In addition to Poe, who grew up in Virginia, the chief southern poets before The War Between the States were William Gilmore Simms, Henry Timrod, and Paul Hamilton Hayne of South Carolina. Many Southern writers of this time, such as Simms and Nathaniel Beverly Tucker defended slavery in their books. Yet they also took time both to describe life around them, often in a humorous vein, and to write romantic stories about the past. Simms' best-known novels are *The Yemassee* and *The*

Partisan. William Tappan Thompson is remembered for *Major Jones's Courtship*, an amusing novel told in letters, which passed through seventeen editions within a dozen years after its publication in 1844. John Pendleton Kennedy, a friend of Poe, portrayed in his novels the plantation aristocracy.

Historical writing increases. American literature of this period was enriched by the works of several talented historians. Americans felt that their country's history deserved attention, and historians appeared who could do it justice. Especially prominent was Francis Parkman, who wrote an excellent history of English and French activities in the New World. Though handicapped by poor health and failing eyesight, Parkman wrote several volumes that are still read not only for their sound scholarship but also for their fine literary style. George Bancroft, another historian, produced an extensive *History of the United States.* John L. Motley and William H. Prescott turned their attention to aspects of European history. Prescott has also thrown much light upon the history of the Spanish empire in the Americas.

Modern newspapers begin. A new era developed in journalism which was in keeping with the growing spirit of nationalism and democracy. Before the Jacksonian period, newspapers were published in limited quantities. Readers subscribed for a whole year, usually at a rate of six cents a copy. In the early 1830's, however, the New York *Sun* began to be sold daily at the street corners for a penny a copy. It dealt with current happenings which interested the man in the street. Within a few years, quite a number of dailies — including James Gordon Bennett's New York *Herald* and Horace Greeley's New York *Tribune* — were bringing the news to the great mass of the people. Such editors usually owned their own newspapers and were free to write exactly what they thought. Thus they were probably able to exert a greater personal influence upon the opinions of their readers than any editors before or since.

Certain inventions of the day also aided the progress of journalism. After the telegraph was invented, a publisher was able to print the news of the day with unheard-of speed. "You are going to turn the newspaper office upside down with your invention," Horace Greeley remarked to Samuel Morse. The Hoe cylinder press, along with other improvements in printing and paper-making, made large-scale newspaper production possible. Circulation increased rapidly. By 1860 every big city had one or more inexpensive daily papers. As a result, the newspaper became one of the leading means of molding public opinion and shaping political, social, and economic movements.

Magazines help spread ideas. The growth of American magazines helped to spread knowledge and opinion. Many lasted only a short time, and some served only special interests. Still, there were magazines which appealed to practically every group of society, and which contained every desired form of writing. Among the best known magazines were the *North American Review*, the *Atlantic Monthly*, *Harper's New Monthly Magazine*, the *Southern Literary Messenger*, and the popular *Godey's Lady's Book*.

——— CHECK-UP ———

How did a distinctive literature develop in America?

1. What influences encouraged the development of an American culture?
2. Who were some of the outstanding American writers of the period? What did they take as their subjects?
3. How did newspapers change? How can these changes be accounted for?

Hoe press

Bed and
trundle bed

2 Progress Is Slower in Drama, Fine Arts, and Music

Plays gain in popularity. Before the Jacksonian Era, the drama had held only a small place in American life. Now theaters began to appear in most of the cities. Thanks to better transportation, such American actors as Edwin Forrest, Joseph Jefferson, and James H. Hackett toured the eastern cities and presented American as well as English plays. As ocean travel improved, English actors appeared on the American stage. By the close of the War Between the States, such American dramas as *Francesca da Rimini, Rip Van Winkle, Uncle Tom's Cabin,* and *The Gladiator* had been presented to enthusiastic audiences. The outspoken attacks on slavery in the last two plays undoubtedly were partly responsible for their popularity in the northern states.

Sculpture, painting, and architecture develop slowly. While literature and drama were making lively progress, the field of art lagged far behind. Americans were too busy with the practical affairs of life to give much time to art.

256

Sculpture failed to attract much interest in America, painting declined, and little was accomplished in architecture. French architectural influence continued strong in Louisiana. In other parts of the country, building generally followed the European revival of Greek forms of architecture. Contributions to the Greek revival were made by Thomas Jefferson, who designed the capitol at Richmond in the classical style, and by Benjamin Latrobe, one of the designers of the Capitol at Washington. But this style was merely a borrowed form. It had nothing to do with American needs, and it was in no way an expression of American creative talent. By the 1850's, the classical style was giving way to new tastes in architecture. There followed a jumble of almost every known style, made worse by a clutter of machine-made trimmings.

American interest in music grows. The growth of American interest in music resulted largely from the influence of certain immigrants, especially the Germans. Around the mid-century, they were leaders in organizing musical societies and orchestras which did much to acquaint America with the music of the Old World. American composers tried writing operas and symphonies, but their works had no lasting success. Appreciation of music, however, continued to spread, and schools and colleges began to offer courses in music. Boston started to give musical instruction in its public schools, largely through the efforts of Lowell Mason, an American composer of sacred music. Minstrel shows popularized American tunes like Stephen Foster's "My Old Kentucky Home," "Oh!

Duncan Phyfe
side chair

Pembroke table

Susannah," and "Old Folks at Home," and Dan Emmett's "Dixie." The Chickering piano won world-wide reputation for its excellent construction. Piano playing and composition became distinctive American accomplishments.

──────── CHECK-UP ────────

What progress was made in the fine arts?
1. What were the chief developments in the theater?
2. What styles of architecture succeeded one another in America?
3. To what extent did Americans become more interested in music?

3 Science and Education Move Forward

The Greek revival in American architecture is shown by the columns and other features of this old State Capitol in Iowa City. The sugar urn (lower left) also shows classical influence.

American science begins to be important. Science at this time moved ahead much faster than the arts. Among the Americans who won fame for important scientific contributions were Louis Agassiz (ag' uh-see), Benjamin Silliman, Asa Gray, and John Audubon. Agassiz and Silliman made contributions to the knowledge of geology (the study of the earth), and Agassiz is remembered as well for his work on zoology (study of animals). Gray was America's leading botanist (botany is the science of plant life), and Audubon is known for his observation and description of bird life. The public was able to learn about recent discoveries through new periodicals, scientific publications, museums, and scientific associations. The Smithsonian Institution in Washington was of particular importance. It was found-

Silver sugar urn

ed in 1846 through the generosity of an Englishman, James Smithson, "for the increase and diffusion of knowledge among men."

Americans excel in applied science. Americans took the lead at this time in the practical use of scientific knowledge to meet human needs. As one foreign observer put it, "These very Americans who have not discovered one of the general laws of mechanics have introduced into navigation an engine that changes the aspect of the world." He went on to say that the "social conditions and institutions of democracy" peculiarly fitted men "to seek the immediate and useful practical results of the sciences." By actually putting science to work in transportation, communication, building, manufacturing, and the production of the material comforts of everyday life, Americans started along the road to leadership in the industrial world. They borrowed freely from the Old World. England's mechanical devices — textile and other machines, the steam engine, and the

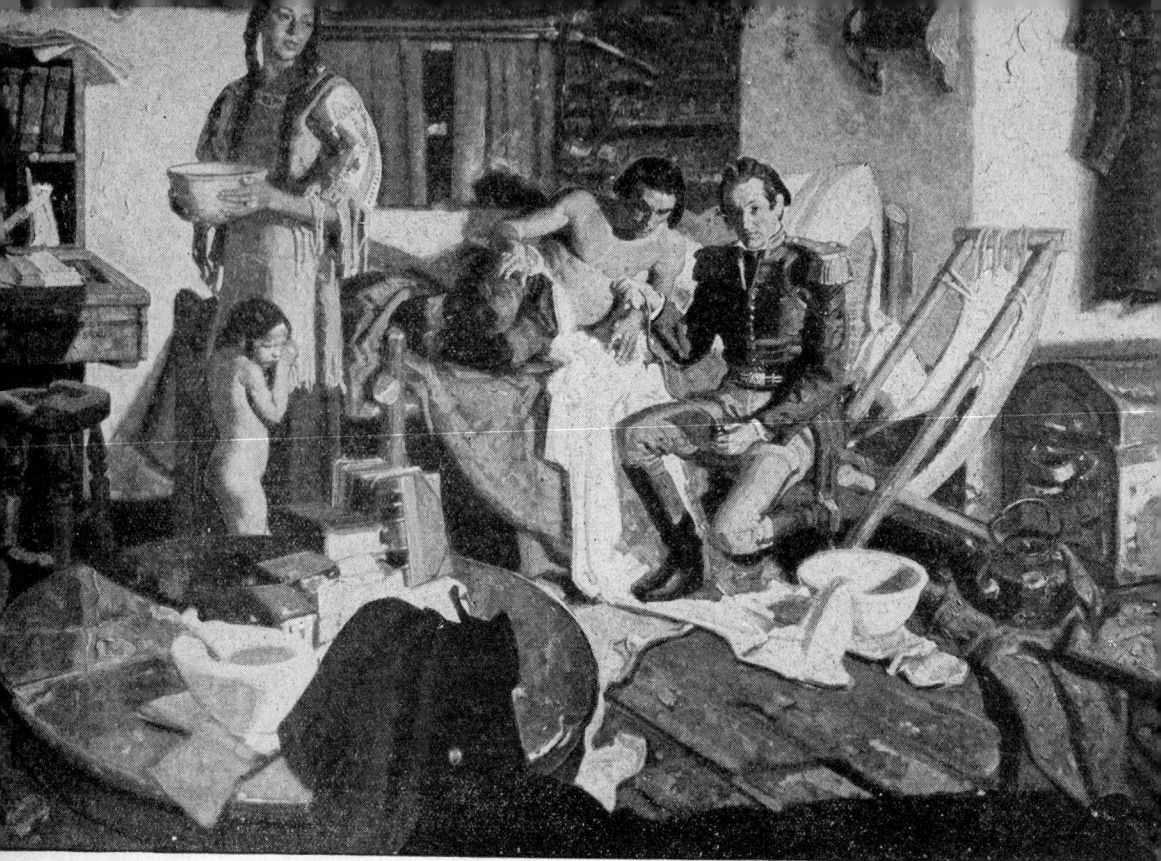

American medical science was making forward strides in 1825 when an army surgeon, William Beaumont, made a study of digestive processes. His observations were made on a French-Canadian named St. Martin who had an unhealed gunshot wound in his stomach.

locomotive — were skillfully improved to fit American needs.

American doctors develop anesthetics. The greatest accomplishment of American medical science was the development of anesthetics to prevent pain in surgical operations. Like many of the world-shaking advances in human history, this great blessing was discovered by several men at about the same time. In 1844, Dr. Horace Wells, of Hartford, Connecticut, demonstrated the value of nitrous oxide in pulling teeth without pain. Two years earlier, Dr. Crawford W. Long of Georgia performed an operation in which he used ether to deaden pain, while in 1846 Dr. W. T. G. Morton successfully used ether in an operation at a Boston hospital. "Within a few years," wrote Charles and Mary Beard, "practitioners in the United States had done more for the relief of human pain and suffering than all the soothsayers . . . of ten thousand preceding generations."

Public education strides ahead. Toward the mid-century no field showed more striking progress than public education. School attendance in the United States had tended to decline during the first quarter of the century, principally because of the steady expansion westward. Settlers of the frontier communities which were growing up in virgin forests and fields had little time for education. They were far too busy struggling with nature and fighting Indians. Arts and letters were out of the question, and many people on the border grew up without even learning to read and write.

But a startling change took place in education during the second quarter of the century. The chief reasons for educational progress were (1) the spread of political rights, (2) the growth of city population, (3) the demands of the working classes, now given the right to vote, and (4) the endowment of education by grants of land from the government. The United States took the lead among the nations of the world in establishing a system of free democratic education and in broadening educational privileges, along with voting rights.

Horace Mann and others promote free primary schools. Establishing free democratic education was a real struggle. It involved, first of all, the building and operation of public schools to be paid for by taxation. Some influential people fought the idea of tax-supported education. Among the opponents were (1) many large taxpayers, (2) religious groups which had their own church schools and did not want to pay increased taxes for the support of public schools, and (3) people who ran private schools and who had valuable property rights at stake. On the other side were such leaders of the educational movement as Thomas Jefferson, DeWitt Clinton, Henry Barnard, and Horace Mann. By 1850, most children in the thickly settled parts of the North had the chance to get a free elementary education.

The most important figure in the growth of public education was Horace Mann. As secretary of the Board of Education in Massachusetts, he was tireless in his efforts to spread the gospel of free public schools, to widen the list of subjects taught in school, and to improve the training and professional standing of school teachers. He also played an important part in founding the first normal school for the training of teachers (Massachusetts, 1839). Henry Barnard carried on similar efforts in Rhode Island and Connecticut.

Public high schools are started. The democratic ideals of public education were also extended into the upper grades of school. During the first half of the 1800's, private academies had sprung up all through the North. These academies taught more practical subjects than the older Latin schools, but not all families could afford to give their children this type of education. Less prosperous parents wanted the same kind of school privileges for their own children, and their demands led to the establishment of free public high schools. Massachusetts led the way by founding the first public high school in Boston in 1821. Except in New England, however, public high schools were not generally started until after the War Between the States.

Higher education moves ahead. The new enthusiasm for education naturally affected the field of higher education. The older colleges became universities as they added departments of law, medicine, and

Public schools in our early history were often small and dilapidated, but they offered the beginnings of education to many children who later became historical figures.

In the new age of the common man in America, the traveling peddler was an important figure. To the pioneer settlements he brought the household furnishings, clothing, and books now being produced by American arts and industries. In this picture, a modern artist has visualized a typical Yankee peddler showing dress goods to eager housewives. A little girl is excited by a new spice handmill, while her older brother is interested in a new book, perhaps one of the new encyclopedias which at this time were bringing all kinds of information to people who were eager to learn.

science. The number of small colleges — controlled and supported for the most part by religious groups — increased rapidly. Michigan started the first free state university in 1837, and Wisconsin founded one ten years later. The opportunity to receive higher education was also given to women. In Ohio, Antioch College followed the example of Oberlin and opened its doors to women as well as men. Wesleyan College, established in Macon, Georgia, in 1836, was the first college for women only. Holyoke Female Seminary, founded in Massachusetts in 1837 under the influence of Mary Lyon, later became Mt. Holyoke College. However, higher education for

women was generally delayed until after the mid-century.

America's schools crown American achievement. Thus in the 70 years since the republic was launched under the leadership of George Washington, the United States had made remarkable progress. A stable government had been established, and European domination thrown off. American nationalism sprouted and grew, and democracy advanced steadily. At the same time, agriculture progressed, industry took giant strides, an interest in social problems developed, and a beginning was made in national literature, music, and science. Not many nations could show as much progress during a similar period.

The crowning achievement of American life, however, was its growing school system. A democratic school system was a guaranty that the benefits of national progress did not belong to a privileged class, but were to be shared by all the American people. In the new age of the common man, the Americans whose toil was building the nation knew that they would have a share in its triumphs.

CHAPTER REVIEW

Terms to Understand

culture   free public education
drama   academies
anesthetic   philosopher

People and Things to Know About

James Fenimore   Henry David Thoreau
  Cooper   William Gilmore Simms
Washington Irving   Horace Greeley
William Cullen Bryant Francis Parkman
Edgar Allan Poe   George Bancroft
Walt Whitman   Hoe cylinder press
Herman Melville   Stephen Foster
Henry W. Longfellow   Louis Agassiz
James Russell Lowell   John Audubon
Oliver Wendell Holmes Dr. Crawford W. Long
Nathaniel Hawthorne   Dr. W. T. G. Morton
John G. Whittier   Horace Mann
Ralph W. Emerson   Smithsonian Institution

Questions to Discuss

1. How was the question "Who reads an American book?" answered?
2. The United States has often been called a nation of gadget-makers. Do you agree?
3. Why was free public education a revolutionary idea? Why would you expect the United States to take the leadership in the development of free public education?
4. You are probably now in a tax-supported school. Try to explain why the community at

———— CHECK-UP ————

How did science and education move forward?

1. Why could it be said that Americans generally "used" rather than "originated" scientific principles?
2. What conditions encouraged free tax-supported public education? Why did this movement involve a struggle?
3. What changes occurred in secondary education? In higher education? In education for women?

Questions to Discuss (Cont.)

large should pay for your personal education. What obligations do you assume in return?
5. Compare the following:
   (a) Applied science and pure science.
   (b) Education in colonial times and in 1860.
   (c) Education in 1860 and today.
   (d) A newspaper of 1860 and today.

Other Things to Do

1. Debate: Resolved, That free, tax-supported education should be extended to the college level.
2. Prepare a talk on one of the important scientists of the period. Audubon and Agassiz make interesting subjects.
3. Listen to recordings of some of the works of Stephen Foster. Do they reflect his times in any way?
4. Prepare a book review on one of the literary works mentioned in this chapter. In preparing a book review, remember to (a) give background information about the author and subject, (b) try to interest the audience in reading the book, (c) give your reactions to the work, telling why you liked it or disliked it, (d) tell something about the style of the author.
5. Appoint a committee to visit a newspaper office in your community. Have it report back on the important steps in the preparation of a modern newspaper and, if possible, on the mechanical devices used.

TO INCREASE YOUR UNDERSTANDING OF UNIT THREE

Unit Summary

1. Between 1789 and 1860 the United States made great progress in farming and industry. Farming was improved by the introduction of new tools and by the use of new processes. Cotton became "King" in the South as the result of the invention of the cotton gin and the extension of cotton growing. Manufacturing spread rapidly as machines were introduced and factories were built. The Northeast became the most active industrial center of the country.

2. These changes in farming and industry were accompanied by remarkable progress in transportation and communication. Travel was improved as better roads were built, steamboats came into use, canals were constructed, and railroads were developed. The invention of the telegraph did much to speed up communication. American shippers, after leading the world with their clipper ships, lost out to British steamships.

3. Progress in farming, industry, transportation, and communication produced certain social changes. The factory system helped to divide owners and workers into different groups. The widespread cultivation of cotton by slave labor helped to sharpen the lines between social classes in the South. Waves of immigrants, drawn by the opportunities that existed in the energetic new nation, helped to swell the population. Towns and cities grew in size and number.

4. During the Jacksonian Era, with its emphasis on the common man, various reform movements were launched. The abolitionists undertook an energetic fight to abolish slavery. A temperance movement got under way. Some progress was achieved in improving the position of women. The treatment of prisoners and the insane, formerly very severe, became more humane.

5. During the same span of years, 1789–1860, cultural progress took place. By the middle of the 1800's, America was producing a distinctive literature of its own. Greater interest was shown in the theater, in music, and in science. America's greatest cultural achievement in this period was the growth of tax-supported public schools.

Summary of Important Dates

1789 Slater starts United States factory system.
1793 Whitney invents the cotton gin.
1807 Fulton's steamboat makes a successful run.
1811 The Cumberland Road is begun.
1821 First public high school in Boston.
1825 Completion of the Erie Canal.
1830 Cooper's locomotive makes successful run.
1831 McCormick invents the reaper.
     Garrison's *Liberator* first published.
1837 Horace Mann starts educational reforms.
1844 Morse successfully uses the telegraph.
1845 Famine in Ireland results in great wave of immigrants to United States.
1846 Elias Howe invents the sewing machine.
     Hoe cylinder printing press invented.
     Dr. Morton uses ether as anesthetic.
1848 Women's Rights Convention is held.

Unit Activities

1. Compare social and economic conditions in the United States in 1790 with those about 1860. Select your subtopics carefully so that only those of greatest importance will be included.
2. One way of gaining a picture of the United States as it was before the War Between the States is to try to see ourselves as others saw us. During the period covered by this unit many prominent Europeans traveled in our country and wrote about their experiences. You will find such accounts in Nevins's *American Social History as Recorded by British Travellers*; and Commager's *America in Perspective* (Mentor-Pelican Books); Dickens's *American Notes*; Commager and Nevins's *The Heritage of America*; and de Tocqueville's *Democracy in America*. How did these visitors feel about the United States? About its future?

Reading such accounts will also provide a valuable exercise in judging the value of different sources. While reading, ask yourself such questions as these about the author: (1) What was his background? Would it influence his views? (2) Does he make broad generalizations without adequate facts to support them? (3) Does he betray the use of "implied standards," that is, does he measure America in terms of the country from which he came? (4) Does he show prejudices for or against certain institutions, or is he open-minded?

For Further Reading

Original Sources

Commager, H. S., ed., *America in Perspective.* Mentor-Penguin. An inexpensive but excellent collection of writings on the United States by foreigners.

Commager, H. S., ed., *Documents of American History.* Crofts. Nos. 149–51, 163, 172, 182.

Commager, H. S., and Nevins, Allan, eds., *The Heritage of America.* Little, Brown. Nos. 65–112.

de Tocqueville, Alexis, *Democracy in America.* Knopf (also an abridgement by Oxford). One of the best studies of America by a foreigner.

Nevins, Allan, ed., *American Social History as Recorded by British Travellers.* Holt. The reactions of English travelers in the United States.

Nevins, Allan, ed., *Philip Hone's Diary.* Dodd.

Pease, T. C., and Roberts, A. S., eds., *Selected Readings in American History.* Harcourt. Nos. 118, 120, 130, 133.

General References

Adams, J. T., *Epic of America.* Little, Brown. Pp. 147–205.

Dick, Everett, *Vanguards of the Frontier.* Appleton-Century-Crofts. Chapter 7. A valuable book with chapters devoted to special topics connected with the frontier.

Faulkner, Harold U., *American Economic History.* Harper. Pp. 240–355.

Hicks, J. D., *The Federal Union.* Houghton. Pp. 459–492.

Morison, S. E., and Commager, H. S., *The Growth of the American Republic.* Oxford. Vol. I, pp. 493–551.

Riegel, Robert E., *America Moves West.* Holt. Pp. 205–304.

Special Accounts

American Nation Series. Harper. Hart, A. B., *Slavery and Abolition.*

Brooks, Van Wyck, *The Flowering of New England.* Dutton (also Garden City). The age of the great New England writers, for more advanced readers.

Buckmaster, Henrietta, *Let My People Go.* Harper. Tells of the "underground railroad."

Chronicles of America Series. Yale University Press. Dodd, W. E., *The Cotton Kingdom.* Hulbert, A. B., *Paths of Inland Commerce.* Macy, Jesse, *The Anti-Slavery Crusade.*

Orth, S. P., *The Armies of Labor.* Paine, R. D., *The Old Merchant Marine.* Perry, Bliss, *The American Spirit in Literature.* Slosson, E. E., *The American Spirit in Education.* Thompson, H., *The Age of Invention.*

Cubberley, E. P., *Public Education in the United States.* Houghton. A well-written history of American education.

Harlow, A. F., *Old Towpaths.* Appleton-Century-Crofts. The canal era in the United States.

History of American Life Series. Macmillan. Cole, A. C., *The Irrepressible Conflict.* Fish, C. R., *The Rise of the Common Man.*

Kaempffert, W. D., *A Popular History of American Invention.* Scribner. Tells of inventions and inventors; well illustrated.

Langdon, W. C., *Everyday Things in American Life 1776–1876.* Scribner. Deals with such subjects as roads, canals, newspapers, home life, manufactures.

Minnegerode, Meade, *The Fabulous Forties.* Garden City. American social life in the 1840's.

Phillips, U. B., *Life and Labor in the Old South.* Little, Brown. The best account of slavery and the plantation system.

Rivers of America Series. Rinehart. Cramer, Carl, *The Hudson.*

Wittke, Carl, *We Who Built America.* Prentice-Hall. The story of the immigrant.

Biography

Baker, Rachel M., *Elizabeth Blackwell.* Messner. A woman's battle against prejudice to become a woman doctor in the 1840's.

Fuess, Claude, *Carl Schurz.* Dodd. The life of one of the greatest of the German "forty-eighters."

Rourke, Constance, *Audubon.* Harcourt. The life of the great naturalist, illustrated with his famous drawings.

Wade, Macon, *Margaret Fuller.* Viking. A biography of one of the prominent leaders in the reform movement.

Imaginative Writings

Adams, S. H., *Canal Town.* World. A novel about the Erie Canal.

Dana, R. H., *Two Years Before the Mast.* P. F. Collier. One of the great American sea stories.

Edmonds, W. D., *Rome Haul.* Modern Library. *Erie Water.* Little, Brown. Excellent novels dealing with the canal era.

Ferber, Edna, *Showboat.* Doubleday (also Grosset and Penguin Books). A story taking place on a floating theater that attracted audiences up and down the Mississippi.

Fisher, Vardis, *Children of God.* Harper. The epic of the Mormons.

Melville, Herman, *Moby Dick.* Modern Library. Life aboard an American whaler whose captain has dedicated his life to killing a great white whale.

Stern, Philip Van Doren, *Drums of Morning.* Doubleday. Records the excitement of antislavery days.

Twain, Mark, *Life on the Mississippi.* Harper. (also Bantam Books). Mark Twain recounts his experiences as a river steamboat pilot.

Poetry

Barnes, Ruth A., *I Hear America Singing.* Winston. American folk music.

Colcord, Joanna, *Roll and Go.* Bobbs. Songs of American sailors with music.

Pictures

Adams, J. T., ed., *Album of American History.* Scribners. Vol. II.

Pageant of America Series. Yale University Press. Hamlin, T. F., *The American Spirit in Architecture.* Keir, M., *The March of Commerce.* Weigle, L. A., *American Idealism.* Williams, S. T., *The American Spirit in Letters.*

 # Sidelights on American History

Johnny Appleseed. The undeveloped lands west of the Alleghenies were a strong lure to early Americans. Day after day on his farm near Pittsburgh, Jonathan Chapman watched travelers pass by, their faces hopefully looking westward to the wilderness of the Ohio Valley. Chapman couldn't resist speeding the travelers along with a small gift — a little packet of apple seeds from the orchard on his farm. The travelers were grateful, too. With the seeds they started their own orchards when they arrived at their new wilderness homes.

When Chapman had given away all the seeds he could spare, he picked over his neighbors' cider mash to obtain more. At last he answered the call of the West himself. Selling his farm, he loaded two canoes with sacks of cider mash and set out on an adventure that lasted the rest of his life. From 1801 until his death in 1847 he wandered across 100,000 miles of the Middle West. Everywhere he went, he took apple seeds, planted them in forest clearings, and tended the young trees. When his shoes wore out, he went barefoot. When his clothes became ragged, he wore an old sack with holes cut in it for his neck and arms.

It is hardly surprising that Chapman earned the name of Johnny Appleseed. He was known all over Ohio, and years later in Indiana, Michigan, and Illinois. He asked for little — a share in the supper of a frontier family, per-

haps, but seldom for shelter, because he liked to sleep outdoors. Wild animals were his friends. Indians respected him for his knowledge of woodcraft and for his peaceful, friendly ways. Everywhere he was welcome as a bringer of news, as a storyteller, as a reader of the Bible. But above all Johnny Appleseed was loved and remembered on farms where apple orchards, grown from his little gift of seed, were a constant reminder that he had passed that way.

Camp Meeting Time. The frontier family in the cabin in the lonely clearing had seen no more than half a dozen outsiders all winter and spring. Monotony and loneliness were gnawing at their hearts. Then a chance hunter, or perhaps a passing peddler, brought the news.

"Camp meetin' over to Cane Ridge Grove this July. Hunnerts of folks is goin'."

Cane Ridge was fifty miles away. No matter. The family planned to go, on horseback or afoot. On the frontier in the early 1800's there were few churches and few ministers. Traveling preachers went from one community to another, seeking to revive interest in religion. A preacher would hold a "sacramental meeting," and since most of his congregation had to come from great distances, they found it necessary to camp and stay a long week end. In the frontier areas the summer camp meetings, or religious "revivals," were often the most exciting events of the whole year.

Usually camp meetings were held in a setting of great natural beauty — near a running stream perhaps, or in a wood of cathedral-tall pines. In the dim-green grove a platform would be raised, from which the preacher would speak. At night the great trees would arch upward in the ruddy light of pine knot fires. Fireflies would flit through the aisles of the forest, and from the outer darkness would sound the haunting cry of the whippoorwill.

Some of the camp meeting preachers were masters of psychology and could almost hypnotize a crowd. "Are you cleansed of sin?" the preacher's voice would boom through the forest. "Are you washed in the blood of the Lamb?" The frontier folk were often lifted to great heights of emotion, which they expressed by weeping or joining heartily in the hymns.

When neighbors became more numerous and loneliness was no longer an important aspect of frontier life, the camp meetings declined and eventually ceased entirely. Gradually they were replaced by summer lectures, such as were sponsored by the Chautauqua movement during the later 1800's.

Never a Royal Road. Does your school day seem long? Consider the schedule in the early years of Transylvania College, Lexington, Kentucky, the oldest college west of the Alleghenies. Students at Transylvania were required to be in their rooms and at their books from eight in the morning to eight at night, with time out only for recitations and meals.

Or the next time you grumble, "What's the use of studying this?" think of the students in an early Missouri school at the time when Missouri became a state in 1821. The trustees called in a young man to examine him on his fitness to teach. "Mr. Jones," they asked him, "is the world round or flat?"

"I don't know for sure," replied Jones, "but I'm prepared to teach it either way." He got the job and was ordered to teach it flat.

The Discovery of Ether. Dr. Crawford Williamson Long was a "doctor on horseback." He practiced in the tiny village of Jefferson, in Jackson County, Georgia. In 1842 Jefferson could boast fewer than a thousand inhabitants,

but in this small town was made one of medicine's greatest discoveries.

In those days a popular party stunt in many American towns was the "nitrous oxide frolic." Nitrous oxide is the gas a dentist sometimes uses when he wants to pull out a tooth. People had just discovered that it was a "laughing gas" and that a few whiffs made a person hilarious — and very funny to others watching him. So at parties people liked to try it on one another, and they doubled up with laughter at the antics that resulted.

One evening at a "frolic" in Jefferson, Dr. Long suggested that the guests try another kind of gas. This was a mixture of alcohol and sulphuric acid, he said, and a perfectly harmless gas to inhale. The gentlemen present found that it had much the same effect as nitrous oxide. Those who inhaled the gas hilariously hit against chairs and bumped into walls as though walking in their sleep. And Dr. Long noticed a peculiar thing: When they struck against a table or a door — even when they hit it hard — they did not seem to feel the blows. Was it possible that they really felt no pain? Then the full possibility occurred to him: could sulphuric-ether gas be used to deaden pain that was even more acute — the pain of surgery?

On March 30, 1842, Dr. Long tried an experiment. A patient had a tumor in the back of his neck. Dr. Long removed the tumor after the man had inhaled the new ether gas. Miraculously the patient felt no pain. During the next five months the experiment was attempted again in eight operations. In each case it was successful.

But Dr. Long is not usually credited with the discovery of ether. That honor goes more often to William Thomas Green Morton, a New England dentist who hit upon the same discovery four years after Long's experiments. It was in October, 1846, that a surgical patient was etherized in a Boston hospital, and a few days later Dr. Morton applied for a patent on the gas, which he called "letheon." The Georgia physician's earlier use of ether was not generally known until 1849, when he published an account of it in a medical journal. Dr. Long explained his delay in making his experiments known. He wanted to be sure, he said, that the effects of the ether were not the result of imagination or of a patient's particular inability to feel pain.

Stagecoach for the West

JOHN CORNELL

THE PLAN OF THE BOOK

Unit Four

THE EXPANDING NATION IS TORN

APART, THEN REUNITED

During the 1800's many Americans were as determined to cross the continent as early explorers had been to seek a waterway through North America. They felt that this country was destined to extend from ocean to ocean. They were willing to go to war to make the dream come true.

The fact that the farm land along the eastern seaboard was "wearing out," the desire for free land and a better living, and the wish to have "elbow-room" were among the reasons for the westward march of the pioneers. Because of their desire to develop new cotton lands, southern plantation owners were among the leading advocates of expansion.

Territorial expansion became linked with the question of slavery and led to conflict between the North and the South. For a long time this great issue between the two sections was settled by compromise. But when those who opposed the extension of slavery in the territories organized a political party which won the presidential election of 1860, eleven southern states seceded from the Union. The Republican Party and most leaders in the North denied that states had the right to secede.

The War Between the States decided the issue of whether the Union should be preserved, and led to Constitutional amendments freeing the slaves and giving them citizenship. Industrialization in the North made great gains during the war, but the war caused terrible damage in the South. The harsh policy adopted by Congress for restoring the seceded states to the Union had important effects on southern progress and attitudes.

Chapter **14**

Panning gold

THE NATION EXPANDS

TO THE PACIFIC

Gentlemen are talking of natural boundaries. Sir, our natural boundary is the Pacific Ocean. The tide of our population must roll on until that mighty ocean interposes its waters, and limits our territorial empire.

Representative Francis Baylies of Massachusetts, 1823

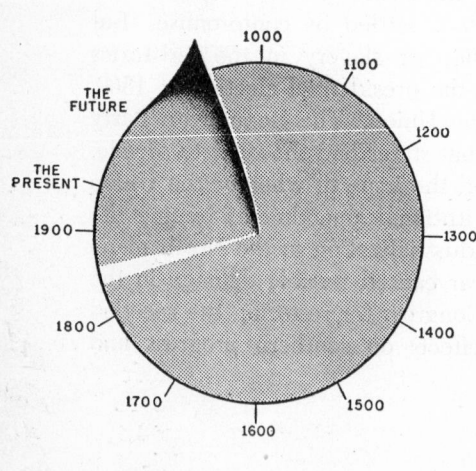

1836–1853

In the years following the Jacksonian era the eyes of Americans turned more and more to the lands toward the setting sun. From the beginnings of American history the frontier had been an ever-shifting line, moving farther westward with each new cabin in the wilderness. At the end of the Revolution, Americans had thought of the Mississippi River as the natural western boundary of their new republic. Men of Monroe's day had more ambitious ideas. Fired by the stories of Lewis and Clark, Zebulon Pike, fur traders, and ship captains who had touched the Pacific Coast, they began to dream of a country that would stretch from the Atlantic to the Pacific. As industry developed and transportation was improved, adventurous Americans could not escape the lure of the West. Was it not written in the stars, they asked — was it not "manifest destiny" — that the United States should own and develop the land as far west as the Pacific and as far south as the Rio Grande?

This chapter will tell a story of which Americans never tire — the story of expansion to the Far West. It will show restless pioneers pressing into distant Oregon, California, and the land to the south known as Texas. It will explain how the drive to the Far West became so important by the 1840's that it was the most powerful single force in American politics and in the development of the nation. This story of growth to the West is told in three parts:

1. Americans establish the Lone Star Republic.
2. The United States acquires Texas and Oregon.
3. The United States stretches from sea to sea.

1 Americans Establish the Lone Star Republic

The westward movement is continuous. Interest in moving westward had been an ever-present factor in the nation's history. Whether it was the early colonist venturing into the wilderness beyond the thin line of coastal settlements, or the later pioneer moving into the fertile lands opened up by the purchase of Louisiana, the motives had been much the same. Men sought adventure, new lands, or the freedom of frontier living.

Expansion is influenced by slavery. Early in the 1800's a new interest in western expansion developed. This interest grew out of the needs of southern planters engaged in growing cotton. Like most Americans, the planters preferred to seek new and better land rather than attempt to enrich the old soil. They wanted fertile land, of course, suitable for growing the staple products of the South: cotton, tobacco, rice, sugar cane, wheat, and corn. They also desired land that was open to slavery, since slave labor seemed essential to their prosperity.

Within the existing limits of the United States, these requirements gave southern planters little opportunity to expand. After the Missouri Compromise (page 194) and the admission of Arkansas as a state in 1836, only Florida Territory was eligible for admission to the Union as a slave state. Southerners were also upset because the non-slave area north of the Ohio River and the 36°30′ line was filling in rapidly. Michigan was accepted as a free state in 1837. By 1840 it seemed likely that Iowa and Wisconsin would soon be admitted as free states. Southerners could foresee an early breakdown in the balance of free and slave states, resulting in a decline in southern power in the Senate. They now realized that the Missouri Compromise had been a mistake. The only solution to their problem, they believed, was to acquire more territory suited to slavery.

Texas attracts attention. Southern planters therefore looked eagerly toward the vast area known as Texas. This land was twelve times as large as South Carolina, with millions of acres of fertile land well-suited to the growing of southern crops. Whatever shadowy claims the United States had to this territory had been given up by the treaty with Spain in 1819 (page 189) over the loud protests of spokesmen for the South and West. Nevertheless, American interest in Texas continued.

Texas, along with the New Mexico and California regions, had become the possession of the Mexican government in 1821, when Mexico won its independence from Spain. But Mexico was in a very unsettled condition. One leader after another had been overthrown by revolution. Just a few scattered people lived in the outlying provinces, and only a thread of loyalty bound them to the central government at Mexico City.

Americans settle in Texas. About the same time that

Pioneer Texas settlers

At the Alamo, a fortified mission at San Antonio, fewer than 200 Texans held out for 12 days against 3000 Mexicans. Finally all the Texans were killed, including Davy Crockett, famous scout and Indian hunter, who left a diary describing this heroic battle. In the battles which followed, Texans shouted the war cry, "Remember the Alamo!"

Mexico won its independence from Spain, American settlers started to move into Texas. Moses Austin, a Connecticut Yankee, had received a huge grant of land from the Spanish governor of Texas. He died before carrying out his plans, but his son, Stephen F. Austin, was able to have the grant confirmed by the new Mexican government. Stephen F. Austin succeeded in planting a thriving American settlement in Texas. The Mexican government also made grants to other promoters, chiefly Americans. Settlers from the United States, many of them slave owners, began to stream across the border into Texas. By the early 1830's the 20,000 Americans in Texas greatly outnumbered the Mexicans. Every section of the United States was represented, but most of the pioneers came from Louisiana, Alabama, Tennessee and other southern states.

Texas becomes independent. The Mexican government, realizing too late that its control of Texas was threatened by the coming of so many Americans, took steps to check further immigration. Severe restrictions were imposed on the Texans, including a check on the further importation of slaves. These restrictions so inflamed the American settlers that they finally broke into open rebellion. Blood was shed on both sides, and by 1836 Texas was fighting for independence from Mexico.

The struggle was short but desperate. Mexican forces were led by Santa Anna. The Texans followed Sam Houston, who had once been governor of Tennessee and was a friend of Andrew Jackson. The settlers in Texas were thoroughly aroused by a battle that took place at the Alamo (al'uh-mo), a fortified mission in San Antonio that was under the command of Colonel William Barrett Travis. (See map, page 275.) There the Mexican army of about 3000 besieged a band of fewer than 200 heroic Texans and mercilessly destroyed them. "Remember the Alamo" became the avenging war cry of the Texans. A few weeks later (April 21, 1836) they had their revenge at the Battle of San Jacinto (ja-sin'toe). Here Houston and his men inflicted a crushing defeat on the Mexicans that practically ended the war. Santa Anna, who was taken prisoner, signed an agreement promising that the Mexicans would retreat beyond the Rio Grande (ree'oh grahn'day) River, and that he would obtain his government's recognition of Texan independence. Although Mexico refused to recognize this agreement, the "Lone Star Republic" was organized with Sam Houston as its first elected president.

Some Americans favor annexation. Freed from the rule of Mexico, Texas sought admission into the Union as a new state. Texans found considerable support for this project within the United States. Southern planters felt that the annexation of Texas was necessary for their continued prosperity. Southern political leaders believed that annexation was the only way of maintaining a balance of political power between the North and the South. Four or five large states could be carved out of the vast area, enough to offset the states that were likely to be admitted to the Union from the free territories to the north. In addition there were Americans known as "expansionists," who felt that the United States was clearly destined, sooner or later, to extend to the Pacific.

The expansionists argued that the annexation of Texas would increase the nation's wealth and power.

Northerners oppose annexation. Many Northerners, however, argued strenuously against annexing Texas. The loudest protests came from people who opposed the extension of slavery, or who feared the power of the South. Abolitionists shouted that the expansion program was a slaveholders' plot to extend the slave territory, and that it might draw the United States into a war with Mexico. In the midst of the clamor, Jackson retired from the Presidency in 1837 without taking any steps beyond giving delayed recognition to the independence of Texas. Mexico, however, continued its refusal to recognize the Lone Star Republic.

The Texas question remains unsettled. The Texas annexation question remained unsettled until the administration of President Tyler. Tyler, who favored adding Texas to the Union, submitted a treaty of annexation to the Senate in 1844. While the Senate was considering the treaty, speculators in Texan bonds and land, who would make large profits from annexation, made up a powerful lobby [1] in Congress. But the anti-annexation group in the Senate was too strong, and the treaty was decisively defeated. The annexation of Texas then became a leading issue in the election campaign of 1844.

––––––––– CHECK-UP –––––––––

How did Americans establish the Lone Star Republic?

1. Why were Southerners eager for territorial expansion? Why did Texas attract their attention?

2. Who were the early American settlers in Texas? What developments led to Texas independence?

3. What were the arguments for and against the annexation of Texas? Why was annexation postponed?

[1] A lobby is a group of people who try to influence the votes of members of a lawmaking body. This activity is carried on *outside* the legislative chambers, hence the origin of the term "lobby."

2 The United States Acquires Texas and Oregon

Americans and British occupy Oregon. While the Texas question was being debated, the issue of expansion also arose in far-off Oregon. Spain and Russia had surrendered their rights to this desirable territory in 1819 and 1824, respectively (pages 189 and 192). Both the United States and Great Britain, however, presented strong arguments to support their claims to the region. The United States offered as proof of its rights: (1) the discovery of the Columbia River by Captain Robert Gray in 1792, (2) the Lewis and Clark expedition (page 169), and (3) the establishment of a fur-trading post near the mouth of the Columbia River by John Jacob Astor in 1811. (See map, page 278.)

Great Britain, in turn, offered equally convincing proofs of her title to the land. (1) In 1778 Captain Cook had mapped the northwest shore line as far as Bering Strait. (2) In 1792 Captain Vancouver had discovered and named Puget Sound, and sailed around Vancouver Island. (3) British fur traders from Canada had pushed into the Oregon territory and set up profitable trading posts. The United States and Great Britain had been unable to reach a satisfactory settlement, and in 1818 they agreed that they should occupy Oregon jointly (page 187).

Americans settle in Oregon. At first, the joint occupation of Oregon benefited Great Britain more than the United States. The British Hudson's Bay Company, extending its operations in all directions, gained control of most of the fur trade. Back east, American people knew very little about the possibilities of Oregon. Only a daring person would undertake the perilous six months' trip from Independence, Missouri, across plain and mountain to the Columbia River valley.

But American settlers finally did start moving into Oregon. Credit for attracting them belongs chiefly to the expansionist, H. J. Kelley, and to missionaries like Jason Lee and Dr. Marcus Whitman. Kelley aroused interest in the settlement of Oregon, while Whitman and Lee made the long trip west, braving its hardships in order to bring Christianity to the savage Indians. Although their main object was to spread Christianity, they also laid the basis for the agricultural development of Oregon. They wrote home glowing descriptions of the climate and soil of the Oregon region. As a result, more and more pioneers found their way to Oregon. Most of them crossed the plains by wagon train, but a few went by ship around Cape Horn. By 1843 enough American emigrants had settled in Oregon to set up and maintain a provisional government "until such time as the United States of America extend their jurisdiction . . . " As the election of 1844 drew near, therefore, the problem of Oregon as well as that of Texas demanded public attention.

Expansion becomes an election issue. It seemed likely at first that the question of expansion might be ignored in the election of 1844. In a public letter the Whig candidate, Henry Clay, opposed the annexation of Texas, and the Whig platform made no mention of the issue. The most likely Democratic candidate, Van Buren, also opposed annexation. But the expansionists were unwilling to let the matter drop so easily. Obtaining control of the Democratic Convention, they managed to nominate James K. Polk of Tennessee, who was strongly in favor of annexation and expansion. The Democrats forced the issue in the election by launching a vigorous campaign for the extension of both free and slave territory. They made the most of such slogans as "Fifty-four forty or fight" [2] and "The re-occupation of Oregon and the re-annexation of Texas."

Clay suddenly found himself in a tight

[2] This slogan refers to the latitude which marked the limits of the Russian-held Alaska. By the slogan the Democrats indicated that they wanted the whole Oregon territory and were willing to go to war in order to obtain it.

spot because of these effective campaign tactics. He tried to straddle the issue of annexation by stating that he would be glad to see Texas come into the Union upon "just and fair terms." This last-minute attempt was useless. In the election Polk received only about 40,000 more votes than Clay, but he received 170 electoral votes to Clay's 105.

Texas is annexed. The election was regarded as proof that the people of the country were, on the whole, in favor of territorial expansion. When Congress met in December, President Tyler pointed out that a large majority of the states had expressed themselves in favor of "immediate annexation." A long, drawn-out debate followed, but in February of 1845 Congress passed a joint resolution annexing Texas. President Tyler signed it just three days before his term of office ended. With the consent of Texas, according to the resolution, four other states might be made from the territory. If this were done, slavery was to be prohibited north of 36°30′. The United States government was to take over the dispute between Texas and Mexico over the Texas boundary, but Texas was to keep her public lands and pay her own debts. A Texan convention voted almost unanimously to accept the American terms. In late December of 1845 Texas became a state of the Union.[3]

President Polk encourages expansion. President Polk's attitude toward the Mexicans was friendly enough, but his keen interest in expansion pointed to trouble between the United States and Mexico. He had missed the glory of annexing Texas when Tyler signed the Texas resolution just before leaving office. Now he turned longing eyes toward the regions of New Mexico and California. He felt that these provinces, where Mexican authority was weak, should be added to the United States — peacefully, if possible.

The advance guard of the pioneers had

<hr>

[3] The balance between free and slave states was soon restored. Florida also entered the Union as a slave state in 1845, but Iowa was admitted as a free state in 1846, and two years later Wisconsin joined the Union.

Throughout our westward expansion, great wagons like these carried the belongings of settlers. Borrowing a word from the sea, people called them "prairie schooners."

already reached these distant regions. American traders, struggling along the Santa Fe Trail, had made their way into New Mexico and established a prosperous trade. Farther west lay California, described as "the richest, the most beautiful and the healthiest country in the world." Early in the century American fur traders and whalers had reached California by sea. Then over the mountains came adventurers and trappers. By 1840 there were nearly 400 Americans in California out of a white population of about 6000. Mexico tried to check the growing American influence in New Mexico and California. The restrictive laws which Mexico imposed were not enforced, however, and served only to irritate the Americans.

The Oregon question is settled. Growing American interest in California helped bring about a settlement of the Oregon question. The United States and Great Britain still held Oregon jointly, and Polk had been elected on a platform demanding the whole of this territory. However, since relations with Mexico were strained, this seemed a bad time to break openly with Great Britain. Therefore Polk was willing to back down a little from the extreme demand of his election platform. When Great

Britain indicated that she was willing to compromise by extending the boundary to the Pacific at the forty-ninth parallel, the President submitted the terms to the Senate for advice. The Senate advised acceptance, and a treaty was completed in 1846. The forty-ninth parallel became the fixed boundary, although Great Britain kept all of Vancouver Island as well as the right to navigate the Columbia River. Thus, a serious quarrel was avoided, and all were satisfied except the most extreme expansionists.

——————— CHECK-UP ———————

How did the United States acquire Texas and Oregon?

1. What were the claims of the United States and Britain to the Oregon country? Why did Americans settle in Oregon? How did this settlement affect our claims to Oregon?

2. How did the question of expansion get into politics? With what results?

3. How was Texas annexed? On what terms? How was the Oregon question solved?

4. In what other areas were Americans beginning to settle?

3 **The United States Stretches from Sea to Sea**

Trouble with Mexico looms. While the treaty with Great Britain was being worked out, an open break with Mexico developed. A few days after Congress had passed the resolution annexing Texas, Mexico had broken off diplomatic relations with the United States. She protested the annexation and refused to recognize the Rio Grande as the southern boundary of Texas. When Mexico started active preparations for war, the United States War Department ordered a detachment of the regular army to take up a position on "or near the Rio Grande." The commander in charge of this detachment, Gen-

eral Zachary Taylor, was told to protect Texas against possible invasion by Mexican troops. At the same time, secret orders were sent to Commodore J. D. Sloat of the United States Navy in the Pacific. Under these orders, Sloat was to seize California if he should learn definitely that Mexico had declared war against the United States.

U.S. infantryman

The Secretary of State also notified the American representative in California that "whilst the President will make no effort and use no influence to induce California to become one of the free and independent States of this Union, yet if the people should desire to unite their destiny with ours, they would be received as brethren, whenever this can be done without affording Mexico just cause for complaint."

Attempts at settlement fail. In a final attempt to settle peaceably the grievances dividing the two countries, Polk sent John Slidell as special envoy to Mexico in November, 1845. Slidell was instructed to obtain agreement, if possible, on the following points: (1) The independence of Texas was to be considered a "settled fact," not open to discussion. (2) The United States government would agree to assume $2,000,000 worth of unpaid claims held by American citizens against Mexico. In return, Mexico was to recognize the Rio Grande as the southern boundary of Texas. (3) The United States would pay $5,000,000 for New Mexico. (4) If Mexico would cede California, the United States would pay up to $25,000,000 for the territory.

By this time the Mexican people were so hostile toward the United States that the Mexican government refused to receive Slidell. Meanwhile General Taylor — affectionately called "Old Rough and Ready" — was ordered early in 1846 to march southward from Corpus Christi to occupy the north bank of the Rio Grande. To do this, Taylor had to enter territory claimed by both Texas and Mexico since the capture of Santa Anna at San Jacinto.

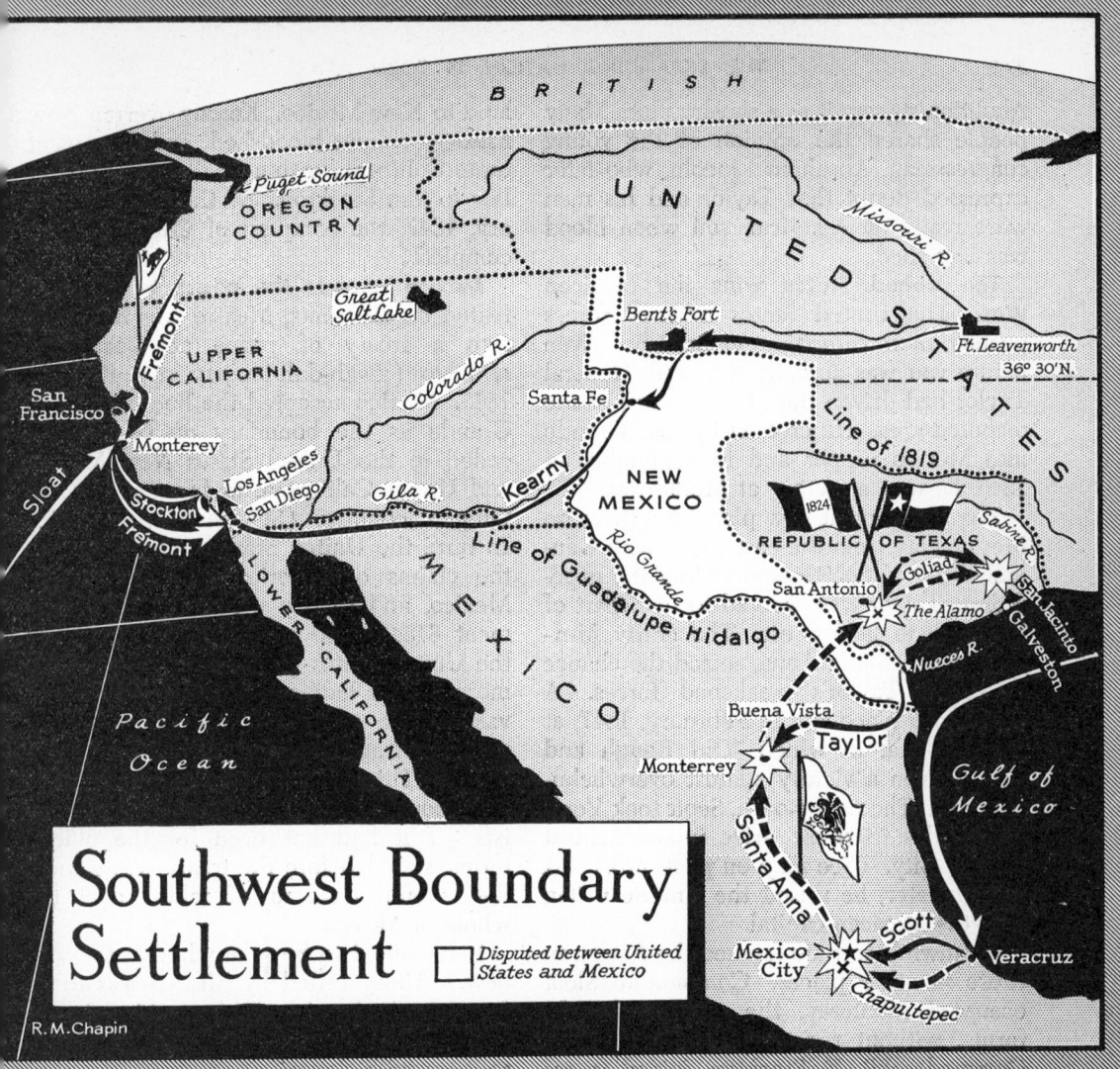

Southwest Boundary Settlement

☐ Disputed between United States and Mexico

R. M. Chapin

Important campaigns and battles of the War for Texan Independence and the Mexican War are shown on this map. Why were the boundaries of Texas disputed after the republic was established? Identify the flags shown on this map.

War with Mexico breaks out. The trend of events convinced President Polk and most of his cabinet that war with Mexico could not be avoided. All that was needed now was a spark to kindle the flame of war. That spark was not long delayed. Taylor's advance from the Nueces (nu-ay′-sees) River toward the Rio Grande was considered by President Polk a defensive movement. To the Mexican government, however, it was an act of aggression, and the Mexicans

"defended" themselves by entering the disputed area. On May 9,1846, news reached Washington that American troops had been attacked in a cavalry skirmish on the Texas side of the Rio Grande. Two days later, the President sent a message to Congress stating that "war exists, and, notwithstanding all our efforts to avoid it, exists by the act of Mexico herself . . ." Congress then declared war on Mexico.

This clash with Mexico was popular with Americans in almost every section except New England. There the Whig Party was openly critical. Massachusetts went so far as to call the conflict a war of conquest.

U.S. officer

Abolitionists saw it as a slavery plot. Many people shared the opinion of the young congressman, Abraham Lincoln, who later expressed doubt that Taylor and his men were really on American soil when blood was first shed.

The United States wins the Mexican War. The United States military forces pushed their campaign vigorously. Even before war was actually declared, General Taylor had driven the Mexicans out of the disputed area. He crossed the Rio Grande into Mexico proper and in September of 1846, he won a victory at Monterrey.

The government now planned a drive on Mexico City from the east coast, with General Winfield Scott commanding the expedition. Taylor was ordered to send part of his army to help Scott. The crafty Mexican leader, Santa Anna, seized the chance to attack Taylor's weakened forces. A battle took place late in February, 1847, at Buena Vista, in which "Old Rough and Ready" won a victory against overwhelming odds. The next month, Scott took Veracruz and started his drive inland against Mexico City. (See map on page 275.) Six months later, he raised the American flag over the Mexican capital.

Meanwhile fortune favored the American cause in other places. Commodore Sloat occupied Monterey, the capital of California, without resistance. His successor, Commodore R. F. Stockton, joined forces with Captain John C. Frémont. Frémont had already stirred up a revolt in California which had resulted in the proclamation of the "California Republic" under the "Bear Flag."

During this time Colonel Stephen W. Kearny (car'nih) had recruited an army in Missouri and was starting a march overland to New Mexico. Kearny overran New Mexico without bloodshed, and then went on to California with a small force of regulars to join Stockton. By the end of January, 1847, the conquest of California was complete.

Mexico accepts the peace terms. Defeated on all fronts, Mexico was forced to sign a treaty of peace at Guadalupe Hidalgo (gwah-dah-loo'pay ee-dal'go) in 1848. Mexico accepted the line of the Rio Grande as the boundary of Texas. She ceded to the United States New Mexico and Upper California, as far north as the Oregon country. (See map, page 275.) In turn, the United States agreed to settle the claims of American citizens against Mexico, and to pay the defeated government $15,000,000 in cash. By this treaty the United States gained on its own terms more than a half million square miles — a vast stretch of land greater in area than modern France, Italy, and Germany put together. This great territory, however, was not enough to satisfy extreme expansionists. If it had not been for the official terms, stated before the treaty was signed, they would have urged taking over the whole of Mexico.

It remained to be seen whether the vast new territory ceded by Mexico was to be free, or whether it would provide — in the words of the abolitionists — "bigger pens to cram with slaves."

Gold brings California into the Union. California was the first of the former Mexican territories to gain a large enough population to be able to request statehood. In January of 1848 gold was discovered in Sutter's mill stream in the Sacramento valley. During the year, the news spread like wildfire along the Pacific coast, across the United States, and apparently to all corners of the earth. What followed was one of the most remarkable movements in history — the Gold Rush of '49.

Like bees to honey, the "forty-niners" swarmed into California, lured by visions of untold wealth. Farmers mortgaged their farms, clerks left their desks, ministers their pulpits, and workmen their tools, to seek

(Continued on page 278)

Prospector

MONTEREY IN THE FAR WEST

A fine mission was built at Monterey in 1779, four years after the King of Spain made this town the capital of ◄ California. When the mission was later moved, this building became the Royal Chapel of the Presidio, a military post for Spanish soldiers.

During festivals in modern Monterey, descendants of Spanish and Mexican inhabitants dress as their ancestors did many years ago.

▼

Colton Hall was built immediately after the Mexican War by the Reverend Walter Colton, first American alcalde (municipal officer and judge) of Monterey. It was the meeting place for California's Constitutional Convention in 1849, when plans for admission to the Union were drawn up. Now, as then, it houses municipal offices.

An American settler built this building in 1847. It was used, among other things, for → California's first theater. Revivals of old plays are still presented there.

The Old Custom House, started in 1814, has flown the flags of Spain, Mexico, and the United States. It is now a museum.

Monterey, California, was settled by Spaniards and Mexicans. It became the capital of California while the American Revolution was being fought 2500 miles away. Within 70 years, during the Mexican War, Americans captured this far-western town. The Americans, however, chose Sacramento as their capital. Partly for this reason Monterey has remained a small city and has been able to keep many of its Spanish-Mexican traditions and landmarks. These historic attractions bring many visitors to Monterey.

"that golden land." Tens of thousands came by wagon across the plains and mountains, braving hardships and intense suffering. Those who could afford to pay for a six months' ocean trip made the easier but tedious trip around Cape Horn. Large numbers crossed the disease-ridden Isthmus of Panama, and fought for passage on the few unseaworthy and crowded vessels which sailed along the Pacific coast. Mexicans, South Americans, Europeans, and Chinese joined the Americans in the struggle for gold claims. The forty-niners drank, gambled, and fought in a country that was practically without law and order.

Before the end of 1849, the population of California was about 80,000. To set up a government for this booming region, a convention was held at Monterey. It drafted a state constitution that prohibited slavery. This constitution was ratified by a large popular majority, and California was ready to enter the Union immediately as a free state.

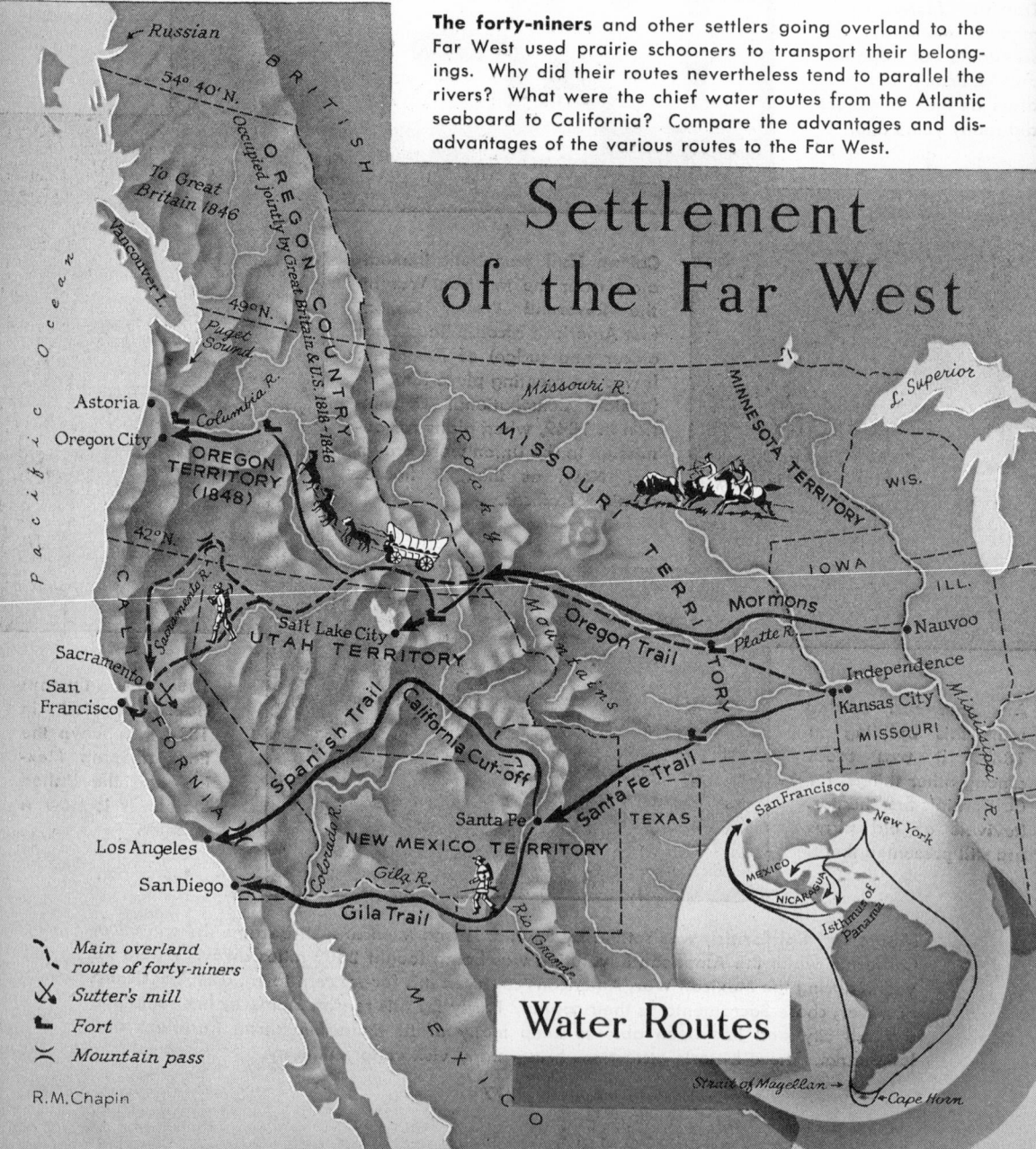

The forty-niners and other settlers going overland to the Far West used prairie schooners to transport their belongings. Why did their routes nevertheless tend to parallel the rivers? What were the chief water routes from the Atlantic seaboard to California? Compare the advantages and disadvantages of the various routes to the Far West.

Settlement of the Far West

Main overland route of forty-niners
Sutter's mill
Fort
Mountain pass

Water Routes

R. M. Chapin

Manifest destiny is fulfilled. In 1853, five years after the Mexican War, the United States paid Mexico $10,000,000 for a strip of land along the southern border of the New Mexican cession. This land, called the Gadsden Purchase after the man who had arranged for the purchase, was bought to insure a direct line across American territory for the building of a southern railway to the Pacific. With this purchase the clamor for American expansion ceased. For the time being, at least, the United States had achieved its "manifest destiny."

--------- CHECK-UP ---------

How was American continental expansion completed?

1. What were the terms by which the United States tried to reach a settlement with Mexico? Why were we unable to secure a peaceable solution?
2. How did war with Mexico come about? Who favored it? Who opposed it? Why?
3. What events led to American victory? What were the peace terms?
4. What were the effects of the discovery of gold in California?
5. What area did the United States acquire between 1845 and 1853?

CHAPTER REVIEW

Terms to Understand

staple products   joint resolution
annexation   special envoy
plurality   provisional government

People and Things to Know About

Stephen F. Austin
Sam Houston
Santa Anna
"Remember the Alamo"
Lone Star Republic
Robert Gray
Hudson's Bay Company
Marcus Whitman
"manifest destiny"
Santa Fe Trail

"Fifty-four forty or fight"
James K. Polk
Zachary Taylor
Winfield Scott
John C. Frémont
"Bear Flag Republic"
Treaty of Guadalupe Hidalgo
"forty-niners"
Gadsden Purchase

Historic Dates to Identify

1792	1845	1849
1836	1846	1853
1844	1848	

Questions to Discuss

1. Compare the following:
   (a) The Federalists and the War of 1812 with the Whigs and the Mexican War.
   (b) The claims of the United States and Great Britain to the Oregon Country.
   (c) The terms offered by Slidell and the actual peace terms.
   (d) The acquisition of Texas with the acquisition of Oregon.
2. How would you have felt about annexing Texas had you been (a) a Mexican, (b) a southern planter, (c) a northern abolitionist, (d) a citizen of Texas, (e) a frontier farmer?

Questions to Discuss (Cont.)

3. What characteristics of the American people did our territorial expansion illustrate? Do you think they were all commendable? Why?
4. What were the immediate causes of the war with Mexico? What were the underlying causes? Do most wars have both immediate and underlying causes? Give illustrations.
5. Texas has lived under six flags. How many can you name?
6. Texas would probably have been annexed earlier had it not been for sectionalism. What are some other sectional controversies that you have studied?

Relating Geography and History

On an outline map of the United States:
   (a) Draw in the Oregon Trail, the Santa Fe Trail, and the Gila Trail.
   (b) Show the chief areas which we acquired between 1845 and 1853.
   (c) Locate Independence, Missouri; the forty-ninth parallel; Santa Fe, New Mexico; the Nueces River; the Rio Grande River; the Columbia River.

Other Things to Do

*1. Construct a chart showing the territorial acquisitions of the United States. Use as headings the area, date of acquisition, how acquired, and significance.
2. Debate: *Resolved,* That the United States was justified in going to war with Mexico.
3. Texans have a lot of "tall" stories about their state, but many of them can be backed up with fact. Make a collection of such stories and facts and present them to your class. Gunther's *Inside U.S.A.* and Perry's *Texas, A World in Itself* have many of these.

Other Things to Do (Cont.)

4. The ill-fated Donner Party furnishes one of the most tragic tales in the history of the West. The story is told in many places. Use Monaghan's *The Overland Trail* (Trails of America Series), Morgan's *The Humboldt* (Rivers of America Series), and De Voto's *The Year of Decision* for a report on this subject. Try also to find other books on the subject.

5. Prepare a report on the discovery of gold in California and the Gold Rush. White's *The Forty-Niners* (Chronicles of America Series), Dana's *The Sacramento* (Rivers of America Series), and Cleland's *From Wilderness to Empire* have helpful information.

6. The Pacific Northwest has some of the last great comparatively undeveloped areas in the United States. Tell the class of the great potential resources of this region and what is being done to develop them. Gunther's *Inside U.S.A.* has some interesting data.

Our nation grew to its present size through a series of territorial acquisitions and adjustments. For review, see if you can explain how each segment shown on this map was added. Our vast country is more closely tied together today than the thirteen colonies were in 1776. What do you find in this map that helps explain that fact?

Territorial Growth of The United States

WASH.
MONT.
OREGON COUNTRY from Great Britain 1846
ORE.
Line of 1819
IDAHO
WYO.
from Great Britain 1818
N.D.
MINN.
MICH.
WIS.
S.D.
LOUISIANA PURCHASE from France 1803
IOWA
NEB.
THE UNITED STATES 1783
ILL. IND. OHIO W.VA.
ME.
VT. N.H.
MASS.
N.Y. CONN. R.I.
PA.
N.J.
MD.
DEL.
ORIGINAL THIRTEEN COLONIES
CALIF.
NEV.
UTAH
COLO.
KAN.
MO.
KY.
VA.
N.C.
MEXICAN CESSION 1848
ARIZ.
N.M.
Ceded by Texas-1850
OKLA.
Line of 1819
ARK.
TENN.
S.C.
GADSDEN PURCHASE 1853
TEXAS ANNEXATION 1845-1848
TEXAS
LA.
MISS. ALA. GA.
FLA.
SPANISH CESSION 1819-21

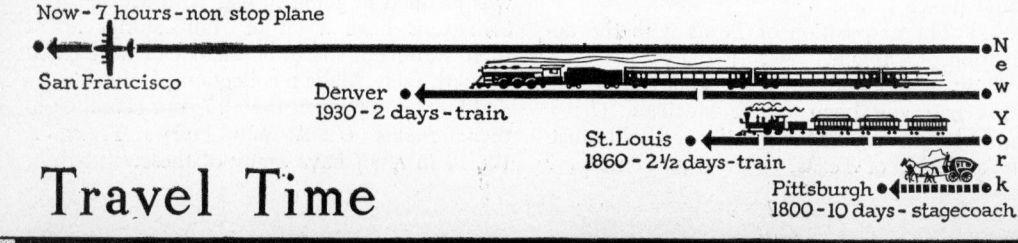

Travel Time

Now - 7 hours - non stop plane
San Francisco
Denver 1930 - 2 days - train
St. Louis 1860 - 2½ days - train
Pittsburgh 1800 - 10 days - stagecoach
New York

Chapter 15

John Brown

THE SLAVERY ISSUE LEADS TO

SOUTHERN SECESSION

"A house divided against itself cannot stand." I believe this government cannot endure permanently half slave and half free. I do not expect the Union to be dissolved, I do not expect the house to fall, but I do expect it will cease to be divided. It will become all one thing, or all the other.

Abraham Lincoln, 1858

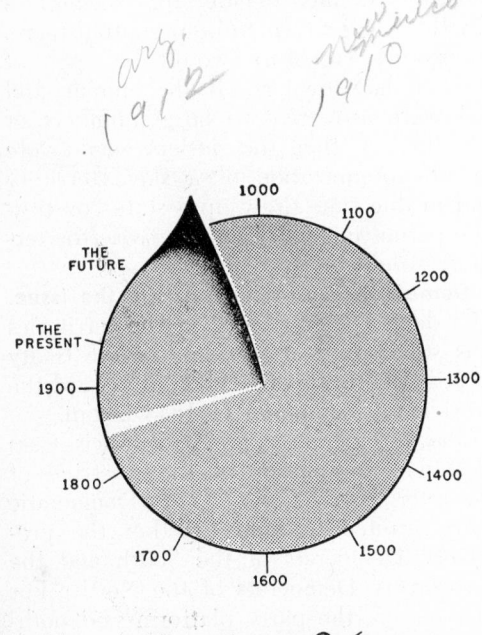

1846-1861

Hardly had the Mexican War begun when the possibility of adding to the nation's territory stirred up a heated contest in Congress over the extension of slavery. Many Americans had hoped, when the Missouri Compromise took place back in 1820, that the rivalry of the North and South over slavery would come to an end. But in the years which followed that famous settlement, the economic interests of the two sections moved further and further apart. To protect these interests, both the industrial North and the agricultural South sensed the need of maintaining power in Congress. When new territories were added to the country, each side tried to win control over them. Meanwhile the efforts of the abolitionists to stamp out slavery were widening the gap between the North and South.

This chapter shows the dark clouds of sectional hostility growing more threatening. It shows the desperate attempts at

281

compromise, the death of existing political parties and the birth of new ones. It describes how bitter words led to bloody action until, with the election of Abraham Lincoln in 1860, the smoldering passions of both North and South burst into flame. The story is outlined under these headings:

1. The Compromise of 1850 postpones a break over slavery.
2. The Kansas-Nebraska Act has far-reaching consequences.
3. Sectional differences become more intense.
4. The North and the South are split apart.

1 The Compromise of 1850 Postpones a Break over Slavery

The slavery issue is reopened. The question of slavery in the territories, which seemed to have been settled by the Missouri Compromise of 1820 (page 195), became a bitter issue again soon after the Mexican War began. In 1846 a bill authorizing funds for the purchase of territory from Mexico was introduced into the House. David Wilmot of Pennsylvania proposed a fateful amendment to this bill. It provided that in territory gained from Mexico "neither slavery nor involuntary servitude shall ever exist in any part of said territory . . ." Instantly fierce sectional bitterness flared up, not only in the halls of Congress, but all over the country. The Wilmot Proviso was generally approved in the North, but mass meetings and conventions in the slave states passed resolutions vigorously condemning it. The proviso passed the House twice but was defeated both times in the Senate.

Other solutions are suggested. The Wilmot Proviso expressed very well what anti-slavery people in the North felt about extending slavery into the new territories. In the South, on the other hand, the doctrine of *non-interference* rapidly gained favor. John C. Calhoun, the author of this doctrine, maintained that since the territories belonged to all the states, they must be supervised for the benefit of all. He argued further that the Constitution guaranteed property rights, and that its provisions applied to the territories as well as to the states. Since slaves were a form of property, it was the privilege of a citizen to take his slaves into any territory, and it was the duty of the government to protect them there.

Other more moderate proposals were made to settle the problem of slavery in the territories. One proposal was based on the theory that Congress had the right to make laws for the territories. It called for the extension of the Missouri Compromise line (36°30') to the Pacific, with slave states permitted only south of the line. (See map, page 195.) Another scheme rested upon the principle of *popular sovereignty*, or *squatter sovereignty*. Under this plan the people who lived in each territory should decide for themselves whether slavery was to be permitted there. Thus every territory would be open at first to slave owners. If the climate and soil were attractive to large numbers of slaveholders, then the settlers would vote for the organization of a slave territory and in due time draw up a state constitution permitting slavery. Otherwise the territory would be free.

Democrats and Whigs dodge the issue. The debate over slavery in the territories was still raging at the time of the treaty of peace with Mexico. Soon afterward the presidential campaign of 1848 began.

The Democrats nominated Lewis Cass of Michigan, author of the doctrine of "squatter sovereignty." The Democratic Party wanted to hold together the pro-slavery Democrats of the South and the anti-slavery Democrats of the North. For that reason, the party platform said nothing about the issue of slavery in the territory just ceded by Mexico. The Whigs also dodged the slavery question; in fact, in the hope of getting the vote of both the northern and southern wings of their party, they did not issue any platform at all. Remembering General Harrison's smashing victory in 1840, the Whigs nominated another military leader, Zachary Taylor. Taylor was new to politics. Although he owned many slaves, his opinions upon the political questions of the day were unknown. Actually there was no clear dividing line between the Whig and Democratic parties, even on the question of the Mexican War. The Democrats claimed credit for winning the war, while the Whigs nominated the outstanding war hero.

The Free Soil Party insures a Whig victory. Dissatisfaction with the way both major parties dodged the deep-seated slavery question led to the formation of a third party — the Free-Soil Party. (See chart, page 327.) The Free-Soilers made their stand on slavery very clear. Unlike the Liberty Party, which had favored abolition (page 246), this new third party merely opposed the extension of slavery into the territories. The Free-Soilers included (1) Martin Van Buren's followers in New York, called "Barnburners,"[1] (2) former members of the Liberty Party, and (3) free-soil Democrats and Whigs. With "Free Soil, Free Speech, Free Labor, and Free Men" as their slogan, the Free-Soilers nominated Van Buren for the Presidency.

In the election, Van Buren did not carry a single state, but he managed to split the Democratic vote in a number of states, notably in New York. As a result, the election went to Taylor, the Whig candidate. However, the Free-Soilers elected thirteen members to the House of Representatives. Since the House was almost evenly divided between Democrats and Whigs, the Free-Soilers held the balance of power. For this reason, their power in Congress was much greater than their voting strength would suggest.

Congress splits over slavery in the territories. When Congress assembled in De-

[1] This reform wing of the Democratic Party in New York favored the Wilmot Proviso. Members of this wing had the reputation of stopping at nothing to overcome opposition; their opponents called them Barnburners to compare them with the stupid farmer who burned his barn to rid it of rats.

Mormons created their own civilization in the wilderness of Utah. In this old photograph, huge stones are being cut for their Tabernacle.

cember, 1849, it had to grapple with the problem of slavery in the regions added to the nation by the Mexican War. Specifically, it had to settle the admission of California as a state in the Union and the organization of Utah and New Mexico as territories.[2] Bitterness was widespread and intense, despite President Taylor's warning to avoid "exciting topics of a sectional character." The South made threats of disunion which were answered by defiance in the North. Southern statesmen argued that if California were admitted as a free state, the political balance between the free and slave states would be upset. The South also demanded an effective fugitive slave law to meet the threat from the "underground railroad" and the personal liberty acts passed by the legislatures of some of the northern states (page 246). The North not only opposed these arguments but further demanded that slavery and the slave trade be prohibited in the District of Columbia.

[2] In 1849, after Utah had come into the possession of the United States, the Mormons drew up a constitution for the state of Deseret, but the American government was not willing to admit this state into the Union.

Clay offers a compromise. In the Congress which faced these conflicting sectional demands was an impressive group of statesmen. It included Henry Clay, the persuasive author of the compromise tariff of 1833, John C. Calhoun, now the ablest defender of southern rights, and Daniel Webster, champion of free soil and most powerful orator of his day. But these three distinguished leaders were nearing the end of their careers in the service of the Union. Ambitious new political leaders were also making themselves heard. Among them were William H. Seward, Jefferson Davis, Salmon P. Chase, and Stephen A. Douglas.

Amid the strained atmosphere of the Senate, the aged Henry Clay, bent with the weight of his 73 years, came forward with a proposal to harmonize the conflicting demands of the North and South. Laying aside his presidential hopes, Clay labored to save his country by introducing into the Senate in January, 1850, a series of compromise measures. The important provisions of Clay's resolution, included in the so-called Omnibus Bill, were:

(1) That California be admitted as a state without slavery.

(2) That territorial governments be established in New Mexico and Utah without provisions either for or against slavery.

(3) That the boundary between Texas and New Mexico be fixed. In return for the surrender of territory by Texas to New Mexico, the United States was to pay Texas the sum of $10,000,000.

(4) That the slave trade, but not slavery, be prohibited in the District of Columbia.

(5) That a more effective fugitive slave law be passed.

(6) That Congress have no power to interfere with the slave trade among the slave-holding states.

Congress debates the compromise. The debate on these proposals was one of the most stirring ever heard in the halls of Congress. Clay threw all his powers of persuasion into a passionate appeal for harmony. Could not both sections be satisfied, he pleaded, with the gains they would make under his proposals? The South's answer came from Calhoun. Too weak to deliver his speech, Calhoun heard it read in the Senate by one of his colleagues. Through it rang a note of despair. The ties that bound the states together, Calhoun had written, were slowly but surely breaking. The South could make no compromise. In fact, unity could be preserved only by assuring the South that it could remain in the Union with safety.

Much depended upon the attitude of Webster. If he opposed the compromise, it was doomed to failure. If he supported it, its chances were good. The atmosphere of the crowded Senate chamber was tense as Webster rose on the seventh of March to make his last great oration. Though strongly opposed to the extension of slavery, he put aside that feeling out of devotion to the Union and gave full support to the compromise. He made his address "not as a Massachusetts man, nor as a Northern man, but as an American." Warning that "peaceable secession" was impossible, he appealed to his colleagues to preserve the Union and the Constitution. Webster's courageous speech saved the compromise, but it brought down upon his head the bitter criticism of anti-slavery groups in the North. The abolitionists called Webster a second Benedict Arnold and a "fallen angel," who was giving up his principles in an effort to win the support of the southern Whigs in the coming presidential election.

The Compromise of 1850 is adopted. Though younger and more extreme leaders such as William H. Seward and Salmon P. Chase opposed the compromise, circumstances worked in its favor. Vice-President Millard Fillmore of New York succeeded to the Presidency on the death of President Taylor (July, 1850). Fillmore was in favor of the compromise and used all his influence to push it through Congress. Even so, the provisions had to be voted on separately. Only four senators voted in favor of all the provisions. As finally adopted, they were practically the same as what Clay had originally proposed.

The compromise benefits both North and South. The Compromise of 1850

The Capitol at Washington, begun in 1793, was nearing completion as we know it when Millard Fillmore was President. Notice, however, that the dome was not yet finished.

seemed to benefit both sections of the country. (See map, page 287.) The North made an important gain by the admission of California as a free state. The balance between the free and slave states was now shifted in favor of the North. The North was also pleased by the abolition of the slave trade in the District of Columbia, even though it was of little practical importance. In addition, although the fact was not apparent at the time, the compromise delayed an open break between the two sections for ten years. The importance of this delay lay in the fact that the North, as each year went by, outstripped the South more and more in population and resources.

But the South made important gains too. The territory given up by Texas as part of New Mexico was still open to slavery. With the $10,000,000 from the government, Texas paid the war debt it had incurred before being admitted to the Union, and was thus helped to become a powerful state. The Wilmot Proviso had been definitely defeated. The South was also pleased by a strict fugitive slave law which bound federal authorities to help in the return of escaped slaves. Unfortunately this last measure kept bitter feeling alive between the two sections. Anti-slavery forces looked upon its provisions as so extreme that many northern states passed laws to hinder its operation.

The nation enjoys a four-year truce. Nevertheless, the dangerous quarreling over the slavery issue appeared to be at an end. The status of slavery was now fixed in nearly every part of the nation. Talk of secession in the South died down and Americans were glad to turn their attention to other things. The first few years after the passage of the compromise were prosperous. Immigrants poured into the country to swell the supply of laborers and increase the number of western pioneers. Industry expanded, factories increased, railroad construction leaped ahead, and cities grew rapidly. The election of 1852 seemed to prove that the Compromise of 1850 had settled the slavery issue. Both the Democrats and the Whigs approved the compromise in their campaign platforms. The Democratic candidate for President, Franklin Pierce of New Hampshire, won an overwhelming victory over his Whig opponent, General Winfield Scott. At his inauguration, President Pierce made an earnest plea for national harmony.

Desire for Cuba leads to the Ostend Manifesto. During President Pierce's administration the idea of annexing Cuba became popular. Southern slaveholders saw the advantage of adding another slave state to the Union, and the President himself seemed to think that such a move would add glory to his administration. Interest in Cuba caused several embarrassing episodes between the United States and Spain. The climax came in 1854, when three American ministers in Europe were given authority to clarify the position of the United States on the matter. At Ostend, Belgium, they issued what became known as the Ostend Manifesto. In this document they stated that if Spain refused to sell Cuba, we were justified in seizing the island by force. But Spain still refused to sell, and the United States government wisely rejected the action of its ministers.

Commodore Perry opens Japan. Another important event of Pierce's administration broadened the horizon of American commerce. In 1853 Commodore Matthew C. Perry boldly sailed into Japanese waters, which had previously been closed to Americans. He obtained a treaty from Japan (1854) which (1) protected seamen shipwrecked in that area, (2) furnished a port of entry for American goods, and (3) permitted an American consul to reside in Japan. The importance of this treaty was scarcely appreciated at this time. It not only opened a profitable avenue of trade to the United States and other nations of the world, but it marked the beginning of Japan as a modern industrial nation.

――――― CHECK-UP ―――――

How did the Compromise of 1850 postpone the break over slavery?

1. Why did the ending of the Mexican War re-open the slavery question? What different proposals were made for solving it?
2. What part did the issue play in the election of 1848? Why were the results significant?
3. What was the South demanding in 1850? The North? How did Henry Clay try to harmonize these demands?
4. How was the Compromise of 1850 passed? What were its immediate results?
5. What important foreign relations attracted attention in the early 1850's?

2 The Kansas-Nebraska Act Has Far-Reaching Consequences

The slavery quarrel starts again. Despite the hopes aroused by the Compromise of 1850, it provided no more than a lull in the battle over slavery. In 1854, a new and more menacing crisis arose with little warning. During the rest of the 1850's, events carried the United States with relentless force toward the brink of disunion and open warfare.

The sudden shattering of the truce between the North and the South came as a result of the proposal to organize the vast region between the Missouri River and the Rockies, known as Nebraska. Nebraska had remained unorganized territory for more than 30 years after the Missouri Compromise, but by the middle of the century this undeveloped stretch of fertile land had attracted many settlers. Adventurers became familiar with its resources as they passed through on the way to the valleys of Oregon or the gold fields of California. Schemes for spanning the continent by railroad also increased the value of the territory.

The Kansas-Nebraska Bill is introduced. Nebraska became front-page news early in 1854. As chairman of the Senate committee on territories, Senator Stephen A. Douglas of Illinois sponsored a bill to organize the territory. In its final form this bill divided the territory at the fortieth parallel into Kansas and Nebraska. (See map, page 287.) It further declared that the Missouri Compromise was "inoperative and void," and that the people of the territories were "perfectly free to form and regulate their domestic institutions in their own way." In other words, the principle of "squatter sovereignty" was to be followed in determining whether these territories would be slave or free. Douglas assumed that Nebraska would be admitted as a free state and Kansas as a slave state.[3]

The Kansas-Nebraska Bill is passed. The bill was political dynamite, both in and out of Congress. The voices of Clay, Calhoun, and Webster had been silenced by death, and the slavery debate was now carried on by a younger and more fiery generation. Prominent anti-slavery congressmen in both houses attacked the bill as "a gross violation of a sacred pledge." The North was greatly alarmed by the

[3] The motives of Douglas in sponsoring the Kansas-Nebraska Bill have been the subject of much debate. For one thing, he is known to have been interested in western lands, whose value would be increased by the construction of a transcontinental railroad westward from Chicago. In the second place, Douglas was acting, no doubt sincerely, on a belief that, as a result of the Compromise of 1850, the principle of popular sovereignty had replaced the idea of a line drawn by Congress to separate free from slave territory. A third motive was charged by his opponents — that he hoped by the passage of this bill to get southern support in the next presidential election. Finally, Douglas believed that many Missourians, fearful of what might happen to slavery in Missouri if their state should be almost surrounded by free territory, wanted a new slave state west of them.

A vast area was opened to slavery by the Compromise of 1850 and the Kansas-Nebraska Act. Was it likely that slavery actually could be extended into this area? Why was the North especially opposed to the Kansas-Nebraska Act? (See also map on page 195.)

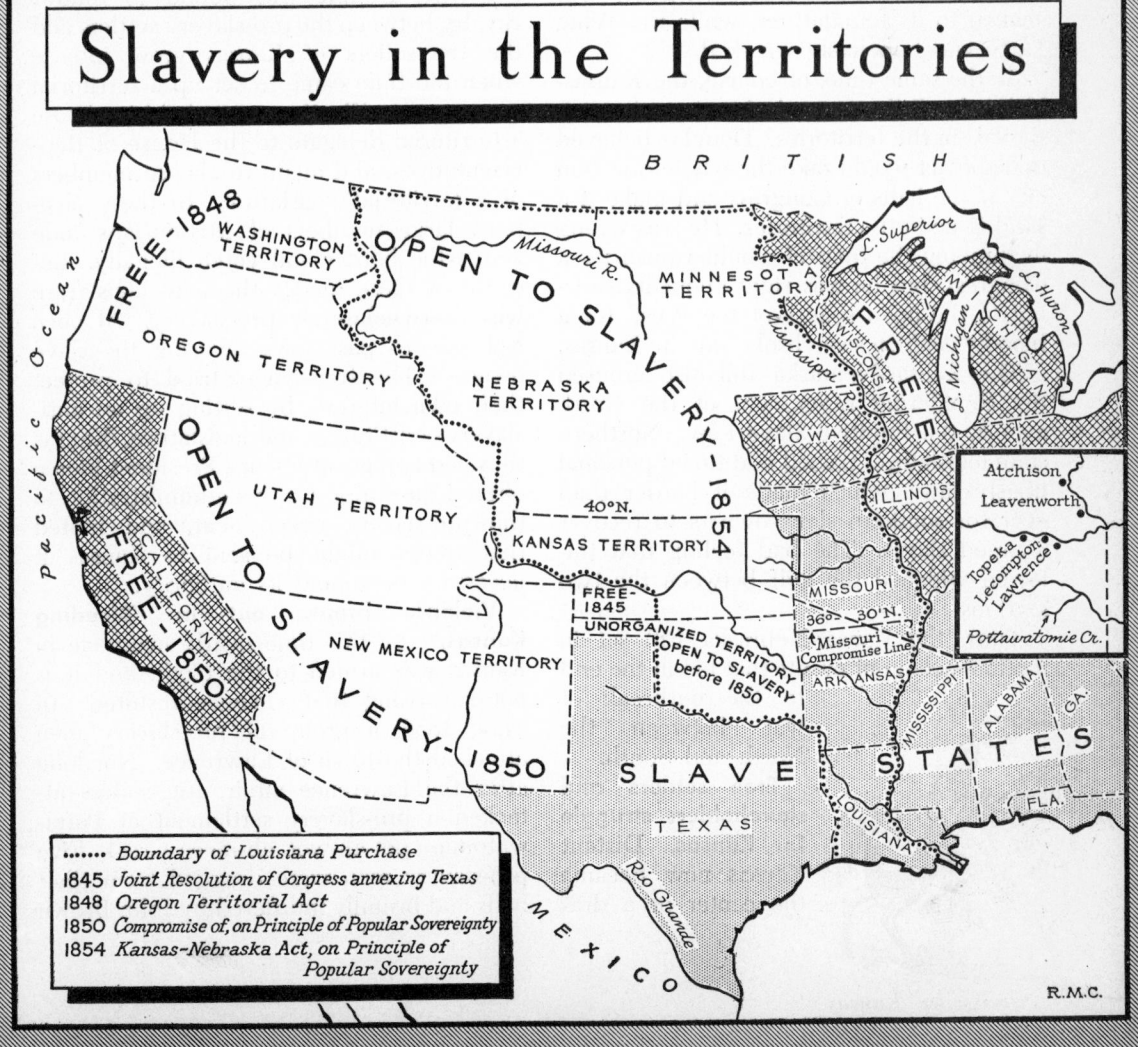

Slavery in the Territories

Legend:

...... Boundary of Louisiana Purchase
1845 *Joint Resolution of Congress annexing Texas*
1848 *Oregon Territorial Act*
1850 *Compromise of, on Principle of Popular Sovereignty*
1854 *Kansas-Nebraska Act, on Principle of Popular Sovereignty*

R.M.C.

threat of repealing a compromise more than 30 years old and of breaking the truce reached by the compromise of 1850. Southerners, though they had not been responsible for re-opening the argument over slavery in the territories, felt that southern honor required them to carry it to a finish. Douglas, short in stature but towering in intellect, fought for the bill almost single-handed. Under his masterful leadership, it was pushed through both houses of Congress.

The Kansas-Nebraska Bill brings fateful results. Passage of the Kansas-Nebraska Bill had several important results. First, the vote for and against the bill showed deep splits in both major political parties. Southern Whigs and Democrats both voted for the bill. Northern Whigs voted solidly against it, while northern Democrats were divided. Thus the Democratic Party was shaken to its foundations, while the Whig Party was hopelessly wrecked.

At the same time, of course, the Kansas-Nebraska Bill renewed the struggle over slavery in the territories. Douglas believed that the act would take the whole question out of the halls of Congress and make it a local issue in the territories. He was wrong in thinking the quarrel would vanish from Congress, but he was right about its shifting to the open spaces of the West, for a bloody conflict soon broke out in Kansas.

The Kansas-Nebraska Bill also aroused the smoldering resentment of the North against the Fugitive Slave Law. Northern state legislatures passed additional personal liberty laws, which made it harder than ever for southern slave owners to recover escaped slaves. The bad feeling that followed widened the gulf between the two sections.

Thus, the Kansas-Nebraska Bill set in motion a chain of events that led in the end to the outbreak of war between the North and South.

Free settlers and slaveholders struggle for Kansas. Distant Kansas now became the center of a dra-

matic struggle. The abolitionists regarded the Kansas-Nebraska Act as a challenge. They started a crusade to encourage "freedom-loving settlers" to move in and colonize Kansas. Headquarters for the anti-slavery group were established in the town of Lawrence. Meantime, in a thin stream, pro-slavery settlers from Missouri were crossing the border too. They settled near the Missouri River and founded the towns of Atchison, Leavenworth, and Lecompton. Few slave owners as yet wanted to risk valuable property by moving their slaves into Kansas. Nevertheless, the pro-slavery men boldly declared in their paper called *The Squatter Sovereign* that they were ready "to lynch and hang, tar and feather and drown, every white-livered abolitionist who dares to pollute our soil."

Serious trouble was bound to follow. Rivalry between the pro-slavery settlers and the free-soilers of Kansas grew intense when the time came to set up a territorial government. Elections were held to choose a territorial delegate to the House of Representatives, and again to choose members of a territorial legislature. In these elections large numbers of Missourians rode across the border and voted illegally. Because of these tactics the new legislature was overwhelmingly pro-slavery. At once it began to pass laws favoring the slave owners. The free-soilers tried to protect their own interests by setting up an anti-slavery constitution and legislature. Kansas thus had two governments. President Pierce offered the support of his administration to the pro-slavery government, and hinted that troops might be sent to Kansas if necessary to uphold its authority.

Violence breaks out in "Bleeding Kansas." By this time nearly everyone in Kansas was armed to the teeth, and it is not surprising that violence resulted. In May, 1856, a group of pro-slavery men attacked the town of Lawrence. Not long after the Lawrence affair, free-soilers attacked a pro-slavery settlement at Pottawatomie (pot-ah-wot' ah-mee) Creek. Five pro-slavery men were dragged from their beds and brutally murdered by John Brown

Free-soiler-Kansas

and seven others, including four of Brown's sons and his son-in-law. Men in Kansas began to carry guns as they went about their business. Terror stalked on all sides. United States troops were sent in to put down the disorders, and the free-soil legislature at Topeka was broken up. But unorganized warfare went right on. Nearly 200 lives were lost, and property to the value of $2,000,000 was destroyed. The grim struggle for control of Kansas went on for another five years. In 1861 Kansas was admitted to the Union as a free state.

The fight for control of Kansas echoed loudly in the halls of Congress. In 1856, while pro-slavery and anti-slavery groups strove to control Kansas, Senator Charles Sumner of Massachusetts addressed the Senate on "The Crime Against Kansas." Bitterly attacking the South, Sumner went out of his way to slander Senator Butler of South Carolina, who was absent. A few days later Preston S. Brooks, a member of the House of Representatives and a relative of Butler, entered the almost deserted Senate chamber, where Sumner was working. With a heavy cane, Brooks beat Sumner unconscious. While the North condemned the attack, the South defended it. Brooks resigned his seat in the House, but the voters in his district defiantly re-elected him.

A new political party appears. In the meantime, the effect of the Kansas-Nebraska Act upon the political parties was becoming evident. The Whig Party, split into a northern faction and southern faction, collapsed completely. Its break-up paved the way for a new party firmly opposed to the extension of slavery. This new party was started in Wisconsin early in 1854 while the Kansas-Nebraska Act was still being argued in Congress. It spread rapidly to other states. Its membership included anti-slavery Democrats, northern Whigs, Free-Soilers, and Know-Nothings. Later in the same year, a large body of men met in an oak grove at Jackson, Michigan, and formally laid the foundation of the party. This meeting drew up a clear-cut platform which called for (1) the repeal of the Kansas-Nebraska Act, (2) the

Pro-slavery men are shown in this old picture as they move into Kansas during the struggle over the Kansas-Nebraska Act.

repeal of the Fugitive Slave Law of 1850, and (3) the abolition of slavery in the District of Columbia. It also recommended nation-wide measures to stop the extension of slavery. Its members agreed to "co-operate and be known as *Republicans* until the contest be terminated." (See chart, page 327.)

The Republicans show political strength. By 1856 the Republican Party was strong enough to give the Democrats a real race in the presidential election. It held its first national convention in Philadelphia and chose John C. Frémont of California as the party candidate. Frémont was not an experienced politician, but his various expeditions and his part in the war with Mexico had given him a romantic appeal, and his name was well known to people all over the country. Because there were no delegates from the cotton states, the Republican Party was a purely sectional group. In fact, leading Southerners threatened that the South would not remain in the Union if a "Black Republican" were elected President.

The Democrats selected James Buchanan to run against Frémont. In the election, the first major test for the new party, the Republicans showed a surprising amount of strength. Buchanan won the election with 174 electoral votes, but Frémont managed

Fashions of the 1850's

to secure 114 and carried more northern states than Buchanan. This strong showing encouraged Republicans to redouble their efforts for the election of 1860.

——— CHECK-UP ———

What were the effects of the Kansas-Nebraska Bill?

1. How did Douglas' bill renew the slavery controversy? What were the provisions of the bill?
2. What were the consequences of the Kansas-Nebraska Bill? What did civil war in Kansas show about "squatter sovereignty"?
3. Account for the founding of the Republican Party. What did it stand for? How did it fare in the election of 1856?

3 Sectional Differences Become More Intense

The Dred Scott case stirs the nation. The satisfaction which the Republicans felt over the election of 1856 turned to dismay as the result of a famous decision made by the United States Supreme Court in March of 1857 — the Dred Scott decision.

The case of Dred Scott was unimportant in its beginnings. Scott was a slave who belonged to an army surgeon. His master had taken him from Missouri to Illinois, a free state, and later to a part of the Louisiana territory which had been declared free un-

der the Missouri Compromise. A few years after his return to Missouri, Dred Scott was persuaded to sue for liberation on the ground that living in a free state and in free territory had given him the right to freedom. A lower court in Missouri decided the case in Scott's favor, but when the case was appealed to the Supreme Court of Missouri, the decision of the lower court was set aside.

Dred Scott was then sold to a New Yorker. His anti-slavery supporters were anxious to bring a test case before the federal courts. Claiming to be a citizen of Missouri, Scott brought suit for freedom against his owner (a citizen of another state) in the United States Circuit Court at St. Louis. The court agreed to hear the case, and in so doing practically recognized Scott's claim that he was a citizen. But the jury refused to grant him his freedom. The case was appealed to the Supreme Court of the United States. In due time, the Supreme Court decided that the federal circuit court had made an error in letting Dred Scott sue, because he was not a citizen of Missouri. According to Chief Justice Taney, Negroes had not been considered citizens by the framers of the Constitution.

The Missouri Compromise is declared unconstitutional. If the Dred Scott decision had stopped there, the case probably would have attracted little attention. But Chief Justice Taney went on to deliver an opinion on Dred Scott's claim to freedom because of having lived in free territory. The Chief Justice declared that the Constitution distinctly recognized that slaves were property, and that it pledged the federal government to protect owners in possession of this property in all the territories of the United States. Therefore the Missouri Compromise was unconstitutional. Congress

Evening dress - 1850's

had no power to regulate slavery in the territories. Only when a territory became a state of the Union could it decide for or against slavery. In the opinion of the highest court in the land, therefore, slavery was now legal in every part of the country where it was not forbidden by state laws.

The Dred Scott decision increases the tension. The Dred Scott decision aroused deep resentment in the North. To the new Republican Party, founded on the idea that Congress had the right to regulate slavery in the territories, it was a serious threat. Abraham Lincoln, then a rising Republican leader in Illinois, said that while the Republicans would not fight the decision of the Court, they would do their best to have the Court reverse the decision. William H. Seward went further — he denounced the decision as unconstitutional and hateful. The South, of course, rejoiced that the most extreme of its demands had been recognized by the highest court in the land.

The Lincoln-Douglas debates attract attention. One event after another fanned the flames of sectional bitterness. In 1858 public interest was drawn to a contest in Illinois for the United States Senate. Stephen A. Douglas was a candidate for re-election on the Democratic ticket. His Republican challenger was Abraham Lincoln. Lincoln had lived in the poverty and hardship of the frontier. He had had few opportunities for schooling. His simplicity, honesty, intelligence, and keen sense of humor, however, had helped him advance in public life. Four times in succession, he had been elected a member of the state legislature. He had also served one term in Congress and was a leading member of the Illinois bar. As a campaign speaker, he was respected even by Douglas, a famous orator.

During the campaign a series of public debates was arranged between Lincoln and Douglas, which became more important than the election itself. At first glance, Douglas seemed to have distinct advantages over Lincoln. The "Little Giant" was handsome and self-assured, and he was at the peak of his career. He was recognized as the greatest debater in public life, able to

Roger Taney succeeded John Marshall as Chief Justice of the Supreme Court in 1836. He often favored the rights of the states.

hold his audiences spellbound for hours by his eloquence. In contrast, Lincoln was little known outside of Illinois. He was awkward, ungainly, and ill-at-ease. His thin, high-pitched voice compared unfavorably with the deep tones of Douglas. But to the thousands who came from miles around to listen to the debates, "Honest Abe" had other qualities which made him a worthy opponent of Douglas. He did not engage in flowery oratory, but he struck at the very heart of a question with a logic that was crystal clear.

Lincoln sharpens the slavery issue. It was with the weapon of clear thinking that Lincoln delivered his sharpest thrust at Douglas in the second debate, at Freeport. Douglas had won the support of many people because he preached the doctrine of popular sovereignty. But Lincoln based his attack on the fact that Douglas also accepted the Dred Scott decision, with its verdict that slavery was legal in all territories. Lincoln asked his opponent whether the people of a territory could lawfully keep slavery out before they set up a state constitution. Douglas attempted to justify the stand he had taken, but it was like walking a tightrope. "The people have the lawful means to introduce it [slavery] or exclude it as they please," declared Douglas, "for the reason that slavery cannot exist a day or an hour anywhere, unless it is supported by local police regulations." In other words, the people of a territory could refuse to pass such "police regulations," and thus, according to Lincoln, could legally exclude slavery from a place where the Supreme Court said slavery had a legal right to be! Forced by Lincoln into this *Freeport Doctrine*, Douglas either was contradicting himself or was stating that the Dred Scott decision meant nothing at all.

Douglas' reply satisfied the supporters of popular sovereignty, and he won the senatorship. At the same time he definitely lost popularity in the South by his attitude toward the Dred Scott decision. Lincoln, on the other hand, emerged from the debates a national figure and a promising candidate for the presidential nomination in the coming campaign of 1860. Throughout the debates, he had made his listeners realize that the extension or limitation of slavery was the vital question before the country.

John Brown's raid increases bitter feeling. In October, 1859, the country was startled by the news that a force of men had seized the United States Arsenal at Harper's Ferry in Virginia. The person responsible for this act was none other than John Brown, leader of the Pottawatomie massacre in Kansas. Brown believed with fierce determination that he had been chosen by God to destroy slavery. He planned to establish military posts in the Virginia mountains, swoop down upon the near-by plantations, and free the slaves. He hoped in time to extend his operations all through the South and put an end to slavery.

Brown opened his campaign at Harper's Ferry. He seized the bridge, the town, and the arsenal. He took several prominent persons in the vicinity as prisoners, and carried off bewildered slaves from a neighboring plantation to join his "army." But his retreat was cut off by the local militia, and soon afterward Colonel Robert E. Lee arrived with a company of United States marines. Brown was taken prisoner, together with all his followers who had not escaped or been killed. He was tried almost immediately, declared guilty of treason, and hanged. The raid was of little practical importance, but it increased sectional hatred. Southerners believed it was a deliberate plot, supported by Republican leaders, to encourage slave rebellion. In the North, Brown's raid was widely criticized as the act of an extremist, but at the same time he had many sympathizers. Ralph Waldo Emerson referred to him as "the rarest of heroes, a pure idealist."

The crisis grows deeper. During these critical years, the feelings of people in the North toward slavery were being greatly influenced by speakers and writers. Henry Ward Beecher, one of the outstanding preachers of his day, poured out his wrath upon the slaveholding South. Whittier wrote poem after poem in defense of the oppressed Negro. Even greater numbers of people were inflamed by Harriet Beecher Stowe and her book, *Uncle Tom's Cabin*, which appeared in 1852. The novel vividly pictured the abuses of slave life and was a powerful influence in molding anti-slavery feeling in the North. It was particularly effective among the rising generation that was to take part in the election of 1860. A play based on the novel was presented by wandering players all over the North, and reached hundreds of thousands who never would have read the book. In the South, on the other hand, the story was denounced as a dreadful distortion of the truth.

From the South itself there also came a protest against the slave system. In 1857 a volume appeared entitled *The Impending Crisis of the South: How to Meet It*. Written by a nonslaveholding North Carolinian named Hinton R. Helper, the book attacked slavery on economic grounds. It demanded justice not for the Negro but for the poor whites of the South who were forced to compete with slave labor. Helper argued that if these "white victims of slavery" were to prosper and if the South were ever to develop its agriculture, commerce, and industry, then slavery must end. The book had little effect in the South because

(Continued on page 294)

Abraham Lincoln
(1809-1865)

Frontiersman

ABRAHAM LINCOLN's life has a unique appeal for the American people. Part of this springs from the prominent role he played in our country's history. His election to the Presidency in 1860 helped to bring on the crisis of secession. With him lay the weighty responsibilities of guiding the North through the grim war years. Furthermore, the tragic circumstances of his death struck at the heart of the American people.

However, Lincoln's appeal rests largely on other grounds. For example, his life illustrates in an unusual way the American ideal of unlimited opportunity. Born under conditions of poverty and hardship, Lincoln rose from the log cabin to the White House through his own worth and achievements. Though deprived of any real educational opportunities, he became a master of the English language. His inaugural addresses and his Gettysburg speech (page 317) display not only clear thinking but rare simplicity and beauty of expression.

Storyteller

Lincoln's appeal also rests on his great human qualities. A commoner himself, Lincoln never lost contact with the common people. His sense of humor and his gift for storytelling have resulted in a wealth of Lincoln anecdotes. He was kindly and tolerant toward all. Though the responsibilities of the war rested more heavily upon him than upon anyone else in the North, he never displayed the hatred and bitterness toward the South that men of lesser character did. No matter how pressing the affairs of state might be, he always found time to listen to the plea of some heartbroken wife or mother. The tragedy is that, despite these great human qualities Lincoln was a lonely man, often misunderstood and frequently unjustly criticized. Through it all, as the poet Edwin Markham wrote,

President

He held his place —
Held the long purpose like a growing tree —
Held on through blame and faltered not at praise.
And when he fell in whirlwind, he went down
As when a kingly cedar green with boughs
Goes down with a great shout upon the hills,
And leaves a lonesome place against the sky.

few of the poor whites were able to understand it. The book was banned in several southern states, but it soon became a Republican campaign document in the North.

——— CHECK-UP ———

Why did sectional differences become still more intense?

1. What were the facts of the Dred Scott Case? What did the Supreme Court decide?
2. What were the Lincoln-Douglas debates? What was John Brown's raid? How did these events contribute to the growing tension between the North and the South?
3. How did "Uncle Tom's Cabin" and "The Impending Crisis" affect the slavery issue?

4 The North and the South Are Split Apart

The Democratic Party is divided. As the election of 1860 drew near, feeling became more strained. The South took seriously the threats of the northern abolitionists, and southern leaders spoke more and more violently. The Democratic Party was the first to hold its convention — at Charleston, South Carolina. Douglas was the choice of the northern wing of the party, but many southern Democrats opposed him because of his Freeport Doctrine. The platform committee took the southern point of view. It attacked the doctrine of popular sovereignty and upheld the right of anyone to settle in the territories with his slaves, under federal protection if necessary.

When the pro-southern report of the platform committee was submitted to the convention as a whole, however, the majority of the delegates turned it

Convention delegates

down and backed Douglas. Unwilling to accept the decision of the convention, the Alabama delegation, led by William L. Yancey, walked out of the hall. Most of the delegates from seven other southern states followed. The two Democratic groups then held separate conventions in Baltimore. Douglas was chosen as the candidate of the northern Democratic Party, while the southern Democrats nominated John C. Breckenridge of Kentucky.

The Republicans nominate Lincoln. This split in Democratic ranks was a "break" for the Republican Party. Excited Republican delegates from the northern, western, and border states poured into Chicago in May. Ten thousand people crowded the vast hall called the Wigwam as the convention started to ballot for a presidential nominee. Other thousands milled about outside.

Seward hoped for the nomination, but his extreme anti-slavery views and his connection with party politics in New York made him unacceptable to many delegates. Also, it was commonly believed that a western candidate was needed to beat Douglas, "the Little Giant" from Illinois. On the first ballot Seward led the field by more than 70 votes. On the second, a movement toward Lincoln began. Lincoln received the nomination on the third ballot. "There was a moment's silence," reported an eyewitness. "The nerves of the thousands, which through the hours of suspense had been subjected to terrible tension, relaxed, and as deep breaths of relief were taken, there was a noise in the wigwam like the rush of a great wind, in the van of a storm — and in another breath, the storm was there. There were thousands cheering with the energy of insanity." The Republican platform opposed slavery in the territories. It also called for protection of industries, free homesteads in the West, and federal aid for a transcontinental railroad.

The Constitutional Union party favors moderation. Out of the political confusion sprang still another party, the Constitutional Union Party. Delegates meeting at Baltimore in the spring of 1860 nominated John Bell of Tennessee. This group included mainly what was left of the old

Whig and Know-Nothing parties, and announced that it stood for "the Constitution of the country, the union of the States, and the enforcement of the laws." On slavery, the burning issue of the day, it remained silent.

Lincoln wins the election of 1860. In the bitter campaign of 1860, then, the voters had a choice among four different candidates and platforms. In the South, the campaign became a three-cornered struggle among Breckenridge, Bell, and Douglas. In the North and West, Lincoln competed against Bell and Douglas. When the battle of ballots was ended, Lincoln had won with an electoral vote of 180 against a total of 123 for the other three candidates. The two states of the Far West and the entire North gave their votes to Lincoln. But the Republicans failed to receive a majority in either house of Congress.

The issue is clearcut. As the year 1860 ended, the Union was at a crossroads. In less than a century of national existence, two conflicting civilizations had grown up — one largely commercial and industrial, and the other basically agricultural. Southerners believed that the existence and spread of slavery was essential to their well-being. At first, southern leaders had been willing to have Congress legislate upon slavery in the West. They gave up this position for the more favorable theory of squatter sovereignty. Still later they demanded even more — the full protection of their property in the western territory. When it seemed possible that a "Black Republican" candidate might be elected, the South had threatened to secede from the Union. That possibility had now become a fact. The country awaited anxiously the decision of the states below Mason and Dixon's line.

The southern states secede. The news of Lincoln's election in 1860 was received in the South with intense alarm. The legislature of South Carolina, which had decided to remain in session until the results of the election were known, passed a bill calling for a convention to consider the relations of that state to the Union. This convention met on December 17, 1860. Attended by booming cannon, pealing bells, and general rejoicing in the streets of Charleston, the South Carolina convention unanimously passed an Ordinance of Secession. It declared that the Union "subsisting between South Carolina and other States, under the name of 'The United States of America,'" was at an end. Commissioners were sent to Washington "empowered to treat . . . for the delivery of the forts . . . and other real estate" held by the federal government within the limits of South Carolina.

The other cotton states at once took up the question of secession. In Georgia, Alexander H. Stephens expressed doubt about the wisdom of seceding just because the Republicans had won an election. He pleaded with his fellow citizens to wait for some really hostile action by the federal government before taking this fateful step. In Mississippi, Jefferson Davis at first advised delay, while in Texas, Sam Houston argued the cause of the Union. The action of South Carolina, however, had brought matters to a head, and the feeling in favor of secession was overwhelming. By February 1, 1861, conventions in Mississippi, Florida, Alabama, Georgia, Louisiana, and Texas had followed South Carolina's example.

The Southern Confederacy is formed. In February, also, a convention of delegates from all the seceded states except Texas met at Montgomery, Alabama, to organize a temporary southern government. They chose Jefferson Davis for President. Davis had served as Secretary of War in Pierce's cabinet and as senator from Mississippi. He had succeeded Calhoun as spokesman for the South. Alexander H. Stephens of Georgia became Vice-President. Soon afterwards a permanent constitution for the Confederate States of America was adopted.

This constitution was similar in many ways to the Constitution of the United States, but it openly accepted the doctrine of state sovereignty. The foreign slave trade was prohibited, but slavery was definitely approved, and the Confederate Congress could not pass any law denying or interfering with the right of property in slaves. The Confederate constitution also forbade its Congress to levy a protective tariff, but duties could be placed upon exports by a two-thirds vote of both houses. A simple method for amending the constitution was included, but no arrangement was made for secession.

By the time Lincoln was inaugurated on March 4, 1861, a powerful and well-organized government existed below Mason and Dixon's line. It had taken steps to raise an army and to secure funds. It had also sent commissioners to Washington to work out a treaty and to arrange for the division of the common property of the states.

Why did the southern states secede? When the cotton states seceded, they acted on the belief that the Union was merely a compact, or agreement, among sovereign states. But their action was influenced as much by emotion as by constitutional reasoning. Decade by decade, Southerners had become increasingly disturbed by their lessening influence in the government. The election of 1860 appeared to them to be the last straw. After 40 years of compromise,

the South had become convinced that the Union no longer cared about southern interests and well-being.

The strength of such feeling in the cotton states can easily be explained. For one thing, the political balance between the free and slave states had been definitely destroyed. The South might have put up with this situation as long as the Democratic Party — in which southern sentiment held the upper hand — kept control of the Presidency, both branches of Congress, and the Supreme Court. But the election of Lincoln, a candidate who had received almost no support from slave territory, was a deadly blow to southern prestige. Southerners now feared that their loss of political power would place the agricultural South permanently under the thumb of the industrial and commercial interests of the North. From an economic standpoint, the Republicans stood for everything that the South opposed. They would undoubtedly bar slavery and the southern way of life from the territories that would in time become states. They favored a tariff to protect northern industrialists. They called for free homesteads and internal improvements at federal expense, both of which were contrary to the interests of the South. All through the South, therefore, people felt that the southern states would be better off economically if free from the North. Finally, the dispute over slavery had brought about a deep-seated hostility between the North and the South. Abolitionists made extreme attacks upon the institution of slavery and upon the Southerners who supported it. It was as impossible for a northern abolitionist to grasp the point of view of the South as it was for a southern gentleman to give up the belief that "every Yankee had hated every Southern citizen from the day of his birth."

Buchanan fails to take action. The four months between Lincoln's election and his inauguration proved a trying period for the Union. Bewildered by the speed with which events had moved, President Buchanan wavered in his course of action. In his annual message, he stated that the southern states had no right to secede but

Southerners in 1860 had a prosperous society, as this old picture of Mobile, Alabama, reveals. Notice the large church, broad streets, fine carriages, and spirited horses.

that, on the other hand, Congress had no power to make them stay in the Union. Buchanan wanted only to keep the crisis within bounds until he could turn it over to Lincoln.

Compromises are tried and fail. Northerners were by no means in agreement over how the South should be treated. Many favored a peaceful withdrawal of the South. Horace Greeley's *New York Tribune* said that if the cotton states felt they would be better off outside of the Union, they should be permitted to go peacefully. But others claimed the South had no right to secede and were determined to hold the Union together. The number of those who believed this increased daily.

The outlook was so gloomy that statesmen fell back on the time-honored practice of compromise. The aged Senator Crittenden of Kentucky proposed several amendments to the Constitution, but Republican opposition was strong and the Crittenden proposals failed in Congress. Another compromise was tried, this time by the border states, led by Virginia. A peace convention, representing 21 states, opened at Washington on February 4, 1861. But its proposals received little consideration in the Senate. The nearest approach to compromise came with an amendment to the Constitution which made slavery secure in the states where it existed by law. The amendment was approved by both houses, but it was ratified by only two states. It was clear by now that the day for compromise had passed. The country waited uneasily for the inauguration of the new administration and a direct statement of policy.

Lincoln takes office. On March 4, 1861, the city of Washington was full of excitement. Thousands jammed the capital to watch the inauguration ceremonies. Unusual steps were taken to guard the life of the incoming President. His inaugural address was firm but kindly in its sentiment toward the South. Lincoln denied any intention of interfering with slavery in the states where it legally existed. On the other hand, he made clear his determina-

Jefferson Davis, president of the Confederate States of America, is shown with his wife in this old picture. Like Lincoln, Davis was born in Kentucky. He grew up in Mississippi, graduated from West Point, and served in the United States Army, fighting in the Mexican War. He was Secretary of War in President Pierce's cabinet. Davis's birthday, June 3, is now a holiday in most of the southern states.

tion to enforce the laws of the Union in all the states, to keep possession of government property, and to collect the duties and taxes due the United States. He made a strong appeal to the sentiment for union in the South. "In your hands, my dissatisfied fellow countrymen, and not in mine, is the momentous issue of civil war. The government will not assail you. You can have no conflict without being yourselves the aggressors."

_____ CHECK-UP _____

How did North and South split apart?

1. Account for the existence of four important parties in 1860. Who were their candidates and what were their platforms?
2. Why did South Carolina secede? By what process? How was a southern confederacy formed?
3. What were the immediate reasons for secession? The more basic reasons?
4. What last minute efforts toward compromise were made? Why did they fail?
5. How did Abraham Lincoln regard the issue of secession?

CHAPTER REVIEW

Terms to Understand

balance of power   popular sovereignty
test case

People and Things to Know About

Wilmot Proviso   John Brown
Zachary Taylor   John C. Frémont
Free Soil Party   James Buchanan
Stephen A. Douglas   Dred Scott decision
Jefferson Davis   *Uncle Tom's Cabin*
William H. Seward   *The Impending Crisis*
Compromise of 1850   Constitutional Union
Kansas-Nebraska Bill   Party
Franklin Pierce   Ordinance of Secession
Republican Party   Commodore Matthew
Charles Sumner   C. Perry
Ostend Manifesto

Historic Dates to Identify

1850	1857	1859
1854	1858	1860
1856		

Questions to Discuss

1. The Kansas-Nebraska Bill has been called the most "fateful" bill ever passed by Congress. Do you agree? Compare the bill with the pre-Revolutionary Tea Act in its effects.

2. What evidence does this chapter give to show that the slavery controversy had ceased to be a matter of reasonable discussion and had become emotional? Can democracy function properly under such conditions?

3. Compare the following:

(a) Calhoun's doctrine of non-interference and the Dred Scott decision.

(b) The Free Soil Party and the Republican Party.

(c) The gains of North and South in the Compromise of 1850.

(d) The platform of the Republican Party and the demands of the abolitionists.

(e) The South Carolina Ordinance of Nullification and the Ordinance of Secession.

(f) The reasons for southern secession with the reasons for American separation from England.

4. Can you explain these seeming contradictions?

(a) Northerners accepted squatter sovereignty in the Compromise of 1850 but opposed it in the Kansas-Nebraska Bill.

Questions to Discuss (Cont.)

(b) Southerners had not demanded the Kansas-Nebraska Bill, yet they fought bitterly for it.

(c) Douglas appeared to say that slavery could be excluded from a place where it had a legal right to be.

(d) Both pro-slavery Southerners and abolitionists opposed the Compromise of 1850.

5. The slavery question is probably the most bitterly debated issue which ever arose in the United States. What was there about it that made it different from other issues? The slavery controversy affected nearly every other question before 1860. Show how this was the case (take railroad building, for example).

Relating Geography and History

On an outline map of the United States:

(a) Show by appropriate lines the various areas affected by the Compromise of 1850 and the Kansas-Nebraska Act.

(b) Locate Lawrence, Harper's Ferry, Montgomery. (See maps, pages 287, 309.)

Other Things to Do

1. Try to find information on any events connected with the slavery controversy which occurred in your state during the period under consideration. Your state may have had a personal liberty law or an ordinance of secession, or it may have participated in the underground railway.

*2. Prepare a five-column chart headed "Missouri Compromise," "Compromise of 1850," "Wilmot Proviso," "Kansas-Nebraska Act," and "Dred Scott decision." For each of these list (a) their basic provisions for regulating slavery, (b) their other provisions, if any, (c) the areas which they affected, and (d) their important consequences.

*3. Jot down at random the important events of this chapter, then rearrange them in correct chronological order by renumbering.

4. Read an account of the great scenes in Congress during the passage of the Compromise of 1850. Hendrick's *Bulwark of the Republic* is particularly good for this purpose.

*5. Make a four-column chart headed by the four parties of 1860. Compare them with regard to (a) candidates, (b) platforms, (c) membership, (d) position in election returns.

6. Debate: *Resolved,* That the southern states were justified in seceding from the Union in 1860.

Chapter **16**

Army recruit

NORTH AND SOUTH FIGHT

A BITTER WAR

We are not enemies, but friends. We must not be enemies. Though passion may have strained, it must not break our bonds of affection. The mystic chords of memory, stretching from every battlefield and patriot grave to every living heart and hearthstone all over this broad land, will yet swell the chorus of the Union, when again touched, as they surely will be, by the better angels of our nature.

Abraham Lincoln, 1861

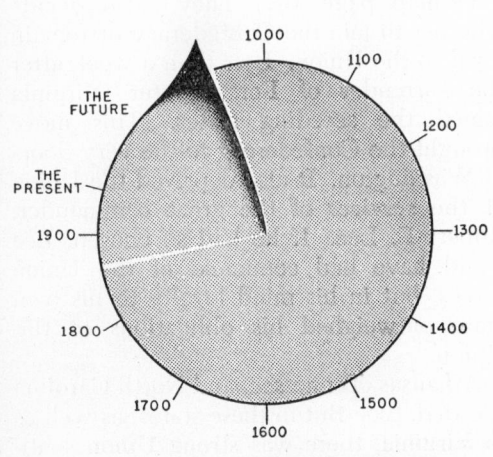

1861-1865

We have seen how all attempts to settle the differences between the North and the South had resulted in failure. Efforts at compromise had been made. President Lincoln had spoken firmly though calmly at his inauguration, but the issue had not been solved. Only an incident was needed now to bring the two sides to blows. That incident came with the Confederate attack on Fort Sumter. For four terrible years, from 1861 to 1865, the country rocked with the thunder of guns.

This mighty conflict, often called the War Between the States, was an important turning point in American history. At its conclusion such questions as slavery and whether the Union could be broken — questions which had held the spotlight for so long — seemed to be settled for all time. National attention shifted to new interests and trends — such as the settlement of the West, the speeding up of transportation, and the amazing growth of industry. In time these developments were to create a new America and to raise new problems.

The story of the War Between the States is told under these headings:

1. The North and South take up arms.
2. The early years of the war bring no decision.
3. Northern victory preserves the Union.
4. Both sections face serious problems during the war.

1 The North and South Take Up Arms

The Confederates attack Fort Sumter. Abraham Lincoln had hardly taken office (March, 1861) when he had to face a critical situation at Fort Sumter in Charleston Harbor. Every fort south of Virginia, except Sumter and three others, was already in Confederate hands. Major Anderson, in command of Fort Sumter, found that he could not hold his position much longer without supplies and more troops.

On April 6 Lincoln dispatched a messenger to the governor of South Carolina, announcing his intention to send relief to Fort Sumter. The Confederate cabinet then met to discuss what they should do. Robert Toombs, the Confederate Secretary of State and a strong secessionist, warned against an attack upon the fort. He said, "The firing upon that fort will inaugurate a civil war greater than any the world has yet seen." Nevertheless the Confederate government sent orders to their General Beauregard at Charleston, giving him authority to move against Sumter at once. Anderson refused to surrender, and shells from Confederate shore batteries began to

Shore cannon

drop on Fort Sumter on April 12, 1861. After a fierce bombardment for 34 hours, Anderson gave up. The war for Confederate independence had begun.

The North rallies to Lincoln's support. The news from Fort Sumter abruptly ended all talk in the North about the peaceful secession of the South. Men from all walks of life and from all parties rallied to the support of the government. Douglas, the leader of the northern Democrats, announced his intention to support the President in his efforts to preserve the Union. "There are only two sides to the question," he declared. "Every man must be for the United States or against it."

On April 15 Lincoln issued a proclamation calling for 75,000 volunteers for three months' militia service to put down "combinations too powerful to be suppressed by the ordinary course of judicial proceedings" in the southern states. The response was overwhelming. Lincoln also proclaimed a blockade of the southern coast from South Carolina to Texas. The blockade was later extended to cover the ports of North Carolina and Virginia.

The border states choose sides. When Lincoln called for volunteers, a crisis developed in the eight slave states which lay between the North and the cotton states. (See map, page 301.) They had to decide whether to join the Confederacy or remain loyal to the Union. Less than a week after the surrender of Fort Sumter, Virginia joined the seceding states. This move brought the Confederacy to the very doors of Washington. It also deprived the Union of the services of the great commander, Robert E. Lee. If he had so chosen, Lee could have had command of the Union forces, but in his mind loyalty to his own state outweighed his obligations to the Union.

Arkansas, Tennessee, and North Carolina seceded, too. But in these states, as well as in Virginia, there was strong Union sentiment. The feeling in Virginia was so intense that the northwestern counties split off from the mother state. They drew up a constitution, asked for admission as a separate state, and came into the Union in 1863 as the state of West Virginia.

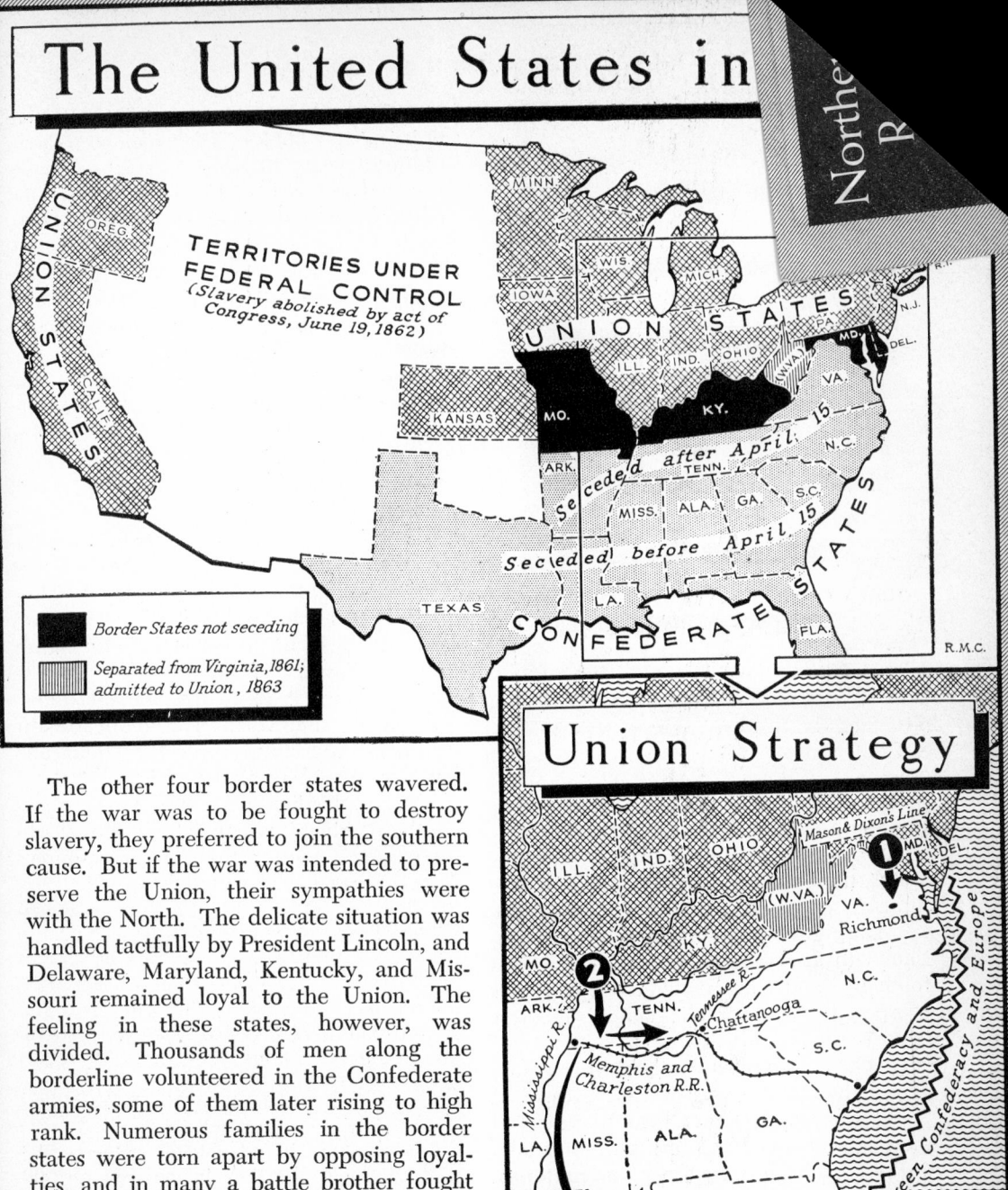

Northe...
R...

TERRITORIES UNDER
FEDERAL CONTROL
*(Slavery abolished by act of
Congress, June 19, 1862)*

UNION STATES

OREG.

CALIF.

MINN

IOWA

WIS. MICH

ILL. IND. OHIO

MO. KY.

KANSAS

ARK.

TEXAS

LA.

Seceded after April 15

Seceded before April 15

CONFEDERATE STATES

VA.

N.C.

TENN.

MISS. ALA. GA. S.C.

FLA.

N.J.
MD. DEL.

R.M.C.

	Border States not seceding
	Separated from Virginia, 1861; admitted to Union, 1863

Union Strategy

ILL. IND. OHIO

Mason & Dixon's Line

(W.VA.) VA.

Richmond

MO. KY.

ARK. TENN.

N.C.

Chattanooga

Tennessee R.

Mississippi R.

Memphis and
Charleston R.R.

S.C.

LA. MISS. ALA. GA.

New Orleans FLA.

Blockade of shipping

between Confederacy and Europe

The other four border states wavered. If the war was to be fought to destroy slavery, they preferred to join the southern cause. But if the war was intended to preserve the Union, their sympathies were with the North. The delicate situation was handled tactfully by President Lincoln, and Delaware, Maryland, Kentucky, and Missouri remained loyal to the Union. The feeling in these states, however, was divided. Thousands of men along the borderline volunteered in the Confederate armies, some of them later rising to high rank. Numerous families in the border states were torn apart by opposing loyalties, and in many a battle brother fought against brother.

The North has greater resources. Thus in the spring of 1861 the two sections stood poised for battle. It was clear that the North had distinct advantages in men and resources. (See chart, page 302.)

(1) On the northern side were 23 states, with a population of more than 22 million. The eleven states of the Confederacy had a population of only 9 million — of whom 3½ million were slaves. Army enrollments

The line-up of the states as war started is shown in the map at the top. The lower map shows the main points of Union strategy: (1) to capture Richmond, (2) to cut the Confederacy in two along the Mississippi River and again across Georgia, and (3) to blockade the Confederacy.

...rn and Southern
...esources in 1860

	NORTH	SOUTH
POPULATION	70%	30%
AREA	76%	24%
RAILROAD MILEAGE	71%	29%
FACTORIES	86%	14
INDUSTRIAL WORKERS	92%	8
VALUE OF FARMLAND	72%	28%
VALUE OF LIVE STOCK	65%	35%

in the North were greater than those in the South by at least three to two.

(2) In the North were nearly all the mines, the iron, steel, textile, and munition industries, and most of the banking capital. During the war northern industry continued to grow. New industries gained a foothold, and the manufacturing cities prospered. Most of the skilled laborers lived in the North.

(3) Over two thirds of the railroad mileage of the country was in the North.

(4) Most of the merchant marine and the navy remained in northern hands.

The South has military advantages. Strong as the North was, the South had advantages, most of them military.

(1) Many of the country's experienced and talented commanders defended the southern cause. Jefferson Davis was a West Point graduate, a veteran of the Mexican War, and a former Secretary of War. Robert E. Lee, likewise a West Point graduate, was the ablest commander of the war. "Stonewall" Jackson and Joseph E. Johnston also showed great military skill.

(2) Southerners were used to outdoor

life, physical exertion, and the handling of firearms and horses. They took to military life more easily than many Northerners.

(3) The South had a head start in preparing for war. They had been making ready for several months, and had control of military property which the federal government had stored in that section.

(4) The slaves were also assets to the South in waging the war. The North had expected slave rebellions to break out, but none did. Instead, most of the Negroes went on working in the fields, leaving the white manpower free to join the army.

(5) The South had good prospects of foreign help.

(6) One of the most important advantages to southern forces was the fact that they were fighting on their own soil. They were battling to defend their homes and property, and for a cause in which they firmly believed. The South asked only to be left alone. It could fight on the defensive, while the North had to invade the South in order to preserve the Union and recover federal property.

During the first part of the war, these southern advantages weighed heavily. In later years, however, the superior resources of the North began to tell.

--------- CHECK-UP ---------

What was the military situation as the war began?

1. Why was Fort Sumter important to both North and South? What were the effects of its surrender?
2. Why was it difficult for the border states to choose sides? What did they do?
3. What were the advantages of the North? Of the South? Why in the long run did the North have greater advantages?

2 The Early Years of the War Bring No Decision

The strategy of the war unfolds. With the important exception of the Battle of

Gettysburg (Pennsylvania) the war was fought below Mason and Dixon's line. Union forces took the offensive from the start, but they could not make a solid, unified advance because of the Appalachian mountain barrier. Therefore the war broke up into eastern and western military campaigns. In the East, the Union campaign centered on efforts to seize Richmond, Virginia, which had become the permanent capital of the Confederacy. The war in the West was based upon driving a wedge between the Confederate territory east and west of the Mississippi River, and opening the Missisippi to northern commerce.

Union forces lose at Manassas Junction. Many Northerners believed that the war would be short, and there was great clamor for a battle to end it speedily. Union leaders made the error of giving in to popular demand for an immediate advance upon Richmond. Most of the Union forces were men who had signed up for three months' duty and whose enlistment period was about to end. They were poorly trained and without experience. Nevertheless General McDowell, early in the summer of 1861, agreed to lead them against General Beauregard, who had taken up a position at Manassas Junction. This was a railway center in Virginia about 35 miles south of Washington, near a stream called Bull Run. (See map, page 309.) At first, fortune favored the Union troops, but at a critical point of the battle, Beauregard was reinforced by the Confederate troops of General Joseph E. Johnston.

Congressmen and sightseers, who had come out from Washington to witness the n o r t h e r n triumph, found that what had looked like victory was suddenly turned into a panic. In McDowell's words, the northern army became "a confused mob, entirely demoralized." All the next day, exhausted Union soldiers poured into Washington to place themselves behind the defences of the capital. Luckily for the North, the Confederate forces were too weary and disorganized to follow up their victory. The defeat at the Battle of Bull Run was a rude shock to the overconfident North. Talk of a 90-day war ended. Steps were taken to raise an army of 500,000 three-year volunteers.

Confederate cavalryman, officer

McClellan takes Union command in the East. President Lincoln now called Major General George B. McClellan to Washington and put him in command of the troops in the vicinity of the capital. McClellan was a graduate of West Point, and had seen active service in the Mexican War. He was popular with his men and showed great skill in the organization and disciplining of his troops. But he was over-cautious and constantly in disagreement with the government at Washington. He always gave the enemy credit for more strength than it had, and at the same time tended to underestimate his own forces. At the very time that the North was demanding action, all was "quiet along the Potomac."

The War in the West opens. Although the western campaign did not get started until the opening months of 1862, it proved much more encouraging for the North. The first step was to pierce the Confederate line of defense, running from the Kentucky shore of the Mississippi River eastward into central southern Kentucky. (See map on page 309.) The chief command in Missouri and western Kentucky had been given to Major General Henry W. Halleck, but the real credit for breaking through the Confederate line belongs to a man who served under him, General Ulysses S. Grant.

Grant's career, until the war opened, had not been distinguished. He was a graduate of West Point and a veteran of the Mexican War, but he had resigned from the army. Afterwards he had failed both as a farmer and as a businessman. Grant offered his services when the war broke out, and his

Confederate infantryman

reputation grew as he successfully carried out the tasks assigned him. He rose at last to the position of the outstanding leader of the Union forces.

Grant opens the attack in Tennessee. Grant opened an offensive early in 1862. He moved first against Forts Henry and Donelson, which were important because they guarded the interior of Tennessee. Grant was supported by Commodore Foote, in command of a fleet of river gunboats.

Fort Henry fell quickly before the attack of Foote's gunboats. But Fort Donelson put up stubborn resistance. Foote's fleet was disabled, but Grant threw his forces around the fort and got ready to attack it or starve its defenders into surrender. The Confederates tried to break through the Union lines but were thrown back. When asked for his terms of surrender, Grant made his famous reply: "No terms except unconditional and immediate surrender can be accepted. I propose to move immediately upon your works." On February 16, 1862, about 14,000 men and 40 cannon passed into the hands of "Unconditional Surrender" Grant, as he was known from that time.

The conquest of western Tennessee is completed. During the weeks that followed the capture of Fort Donelson, Grant moved his forces southward along the Tennessee River. At the same time, Confederate forces were gathering at Corinth, Mississippi, an important point on the Memphis and Charleston Railway, near the border of Tennessee. The Confederates did not wait for Grant to reach Corinth. Commanded by General Albert S. Johnston, they attacked Grant in a surprise move at Shiloh (Pittsburg Landing), Tennessee. A terrific battle took place on April 6 and 7 of 1862. The gallant Confederate commander was mortally wounded, and both armies suffered heavy losses. At the end of May the occupation of Corinth by the Union armies completed the conquest of the western part of Tennessee.

Union forces struggle for the Mississippi. While Grant was pushing down the Tennessee River, a parallel drive was moving south on the Mississippi River. Commanded by General Pope and Commodore Foote, Union forces advanced to Memphis in southwestern Tennessee. After Memphis fell (June, 1862), the Union held the Mississippi River as far south as Vicksburg, Mississippi.

Meanwhile, a naval expedition under David G. Farragut paved the way for the capture of the important city of New Orleans on the lower Mississippi River. Two forts guarded the lower river, but the Union fleet, under Farragut, ran past their blazing guns and headed up the river to New Orleans.

New Orleans lacked adequate defenses, and the city became a scene of wild disorder. Thousands of bales of burning cotton along the waterfront and in ships cast adrift turned night into day. The streets were jammed with milling crowds of panic-stricken people. Confederate forces retreated, and the city was occupied by Union forces. Thus, by the summer of 1862, the Mississippi was lost to the Confederacy except for a narrow strip between Vicksburg and Port Hudson.

The capture of Vicksburg reopens the Mississippi. Union forces in the West now moved against Vicksburg. The South needed this city desperately, for it was the last point through which she could get sugar, grain, and beef from the regions west of the Mississippi, as well as munitions shipped from Europe by way of Texas and Mexico. Lodged upon a high bluff, Vicksburg was a natural fortress. It could easily fight off any attack from the river, and the approach from the land side was almost as difficult.

Grant started his campaign against Vicksburg in the fall of 1862 but met with repeated failure. Lincoln was urged to remove him from command, but the President replied, "I can't spare this man: he fights."

The next spring, Grant carried out a brilliant piece of strategy. By twice crossing the Mississippi River, he maneuvered his forces to a position south of Vicksburg. He defeated a body of Confederate re-enforcements near by, and then turned on the city.

Field gun

A direct attack failed, and the Union army settled down for a long siege. For six weeks, shells from the Union guns spread destruction all through the city. Starvation stalked the streets. The Confederates held out valiantly until finally, on July 4, 1863, Vicksburg fell. A large quantity of arms and 29,000 men were taken. Within a week, Port Hudson surrendered, and on July 16 a cargo from St. Louis was landed at New Orleans. Lincoln remarked with deep satisfaction, "The Father of Waters again goes unvexed to the sea."

Union forces move slowly in the East. During these years, 1861-63, Union forces in the East had little success. They not only failed to take Richmond, but were forced to turn back two invasions of Union territory. After months of delay and inaction, Lincoln ordered McClellan to advance (February, 1862). Instead of moving directly against Richmond, McClellan transported his forces by sea to Fortress Monroe. Then he started up the peninsula between the York and James Rivers. (See map, page 309.) With maddening caution, he approached the Confederate capital, always overestimating the size of the Confederate forces. By May 16, McClellan was only a single day's march from Richmond, and the southern capital seemed doomed. Still McClellan failed to strike.

Richmond is successfully defended. In late June, McClellan was still waiting for reinforcements and had not yet attacked. Meanwhile, "Stonewall" Jackson had slipped out of the Shenandoah Valley and joined the Confederate army at Richmond, under the command of Robert E. Lee. Now it was the Confederates who took the offensive. They hammered away at McClellan in a series of engagements known as the Seven Days' Battles. McClellan dropped back to the James River. Here he had the protection of the fleet and could wait for the expected reinforcements.

This Peninsular Campaign showed disappointing results for the Union but it was not an out-and-out failure. Lee had paid a heavy price for his success, for he had lost more men than McClellan. The latter had retreated in an orderly fashion, without injury to his baggage trains. The spirit of his army was good. But McClellan had lost the confidence of the administration. His forces were ordered back to the Potomac, and by this move the North lost all the gains of the Peninsular Campaign.

Pope is defeated at Bull Run. Most of McClellan's forces were now added to the command of General Pope. In contrast to McClellan, Pope was overconfident, and this failing led to his downfall. He was drawn into the second Battle of Bull Run by Lee, who was ably assisted by Jackson. Completely baffled by Lee's rapid marches and brilliant moves, Pope suffered a severe defeat. By now Washington was again under threat of attack, and the administration turned once more to McClellan. McClellan took charge of Pope's retreating army, and again restored order out of confusion.

Lee's invasion is checked at Antietam. Early in September, Lee began an invasion of Maryland. He hoped that the Marylanders, many of whom were sympathetic to the South, would join his forces. It was also believed that a Confederate victory in the North would cause Great Britain to recognize the independence of the South and force a satisfactory peace.

Lee started north with his army. McClellan followed, but with his usual caution, he failed to strike hard when Lee's forces were divided. Finally the Union and Confederate armies clashed at Antietam (an-tee'tum) Creek on September 17. This was the bloodiest single day's combat of the war. Although neither side was victorious, the next night Lee decided to give up his drive.

McClellan disappointed the federal government by not only failing to renew the battle but even letting the Confederate forces retire leisurely beyond the Potomac. The administration, once again discour-

Confederate cavalrymen fought with brilliant daring during the War Between the States. General "Jeb" Stuart is shown above leading a cavalry charge.

aged with McClellan, removed him from command. But the battle of Antietam was important. Lee's invasion of the North had been checked, and European recognition of southern independence was put off.

Union forces suffer new defeats. During the next nine months the outlook for the Union was grim. Northern generals could not match the skill and daring of Lee and Jackson. After Antietam, General A. E. Burnside took McClellan's place. Burnside proved as overbold as McClellan had been overcautious. He made a terrific attack upon Fredericksburg, Virginia (December, 1862) in which more than 12,000 Union soldiers were sacrificed, while the South lost fewer than 5400.

Burnside was replaced by "Fighting Joe" Hooker, who prepared for a direct advance upon Richmond. But Hooker, in early May of 1863, was completely outclassed by Lee and Jackson at Chancellorsville, Virginia. Confederate joy over the victory at Chancellorsville was quickly changed to grief, however, when it was learned that "Stonewall" Jackson, mistaken by his own men for one of the enemy, had been mortally wounded. His death was a terrible loss to the South.

Gettysburg marks a turning point. In the North, feeling against the war was rising steadily. Lee felt that the time had come for a bold stroke to end the conflict. He made up his mind to invade the North and threaten Philadelphia, Baltimore, and Washington.

With over 70,000 men, Lee crossed the Potomac in June, 1863, and made his way across Maryland into Pennsylvania. Panic swept the cities of the North. Hooker rushed his army northward in a line parallel with the southern forces. Then Hooker was removed from command, and General George G. Meade took his place. Meade had the full confidence of the officers and men in the army. With larger forces and better equipment, he joined battle with Lee at Gettysburg on July 1 in the most decisive battle of the war.

The fighting raged for three days. On the third day, Lee made a desperate bid for victory. He ordered Pickett, with 15,000 of the finest Confederate troops, to charge against the strong Union center on Cemetery Ridge. Pickett's men smashed into the Union lines with superb courage. They never faltered, though they were being mowed down by the murderous fire of Union batteries. On and on they went, until about 100 of them managed to reach the crest of Cemetery Ridge. For a dramatic moment of hand-to-hand fighting, the Confederate flag fluttered at the crest. But the odds against the Southerners were too great. The Union lines closed in, and the remnants of Pickett's shattered force fell back.

The next day Lee did not renew the attack. Meade, apparently satisfied, let the Confederate forces march southward and recross the Potomac. "We had them within our grasp," mourned Lincoln; "we had only to stretch forth our hands and they were ours." "Still," he added later, "I am very grateful to Meade for the great service he did at Gettysburg."

Union cavalryman

Why did the early years of the war bring no decision?

1. What did the first battle at Manassas Junction show?
2. What were the North's objectives for the war in the West? What were the steps in achieving them?
3. Why did the war in the East move slowly? What was the importance of Antietam?
4. Why may Gettysburg be considered a turning point of the war?

3 Northern Victory Preserves the Union

General Ulysses S. Grant distinguished himself by planning and carrying out the northern victories which ended the war.

Fighting centers around Chattanooga. The Union victory at Gettysburg and the fall of Vicksburg in the West were only one day apart. Union forces in the West were now free for a new campaign in Tennessee. The first step was to take Chattanooga, an important railroad center in the southeastern corner of the state.

A Union army under General Rosecrans moved into Chattanooga and occupied it without resistance in September, 1863. Thinking the Confederate withdrawal from Chattanooga was part of a general retreat into Georgia, Rosecrans set out in pursuit. The Confederate leader, General Bragg, unexpectedly turned on the Union troops on the banks of Chickamauga Creek. A bloody battle was fought there. Rosecrans was saved from total defeat only by the stubborn stand of the Union left wing, under General Thomas. Thomas came to be called the "Rock of Chickamauga."

The Union Army then retreated to Chattanooga. Meanwhile, Bragg fortified two ridges, Lookout Mountain and Missionary Ridge, to the south and east of the city, and laid siege. The Union army was all but cut off from supplies and was in a desperate position. Disaster was avoided by the arrival of Grant and the Union forces that had taken Vicksburg. Late in November, 1863, a three-day battle raged. In a bloody but brilliant victory, Grant finally drove the Confederates from Lookout Mountain and Missionary Ridge.

Grant plans Union strategy. Grant's superb generalship was now fully recognized. In March, 1864, Lincoln made him commander of the United States armies, with the rank of lieutenant general. For the spring of 1864, Grant planned three major campaigns. (1) Meade, still in command of the eastern forces, was to operate against Lee before Richmond. (2) The armies in the West were to move southeastward so that the Confederacy would be crushed as if by the jaws of a huge nutcracker. (3) A combined land and naval force was to attack Mobile, Alabama.

Sherman takes Atlanta. Grant went to Virginia early in the spring of 1864, leaving General William T. Sherman in command in the West. With Chattanooga occupied by Union forces, and the Confederates in retreat, the way was now open for a Union advance into Georgia. Atlanta was the first objective.

Sherman started his drive to the South in May. He was opposed by a much smaller Confederate army under Joseph E. Johnston, who had taken Bragg's place.

By a series of flanking movements, Sherman forced Johnston back to Atlanta. At this critical moment, President Davis, who did not fully appreciate Johnston's splendid defense, gave the command to General J. B. Hood. Hood was badly defeated on three occasions and driven back into Atlanta. Sherman then closed in upon the city. Early in September, 1864, Hood was forced to withdraw.

Sherman marches to the sea. After destroying Atlanta, Sherman set out upon one of the most daring campaigns of the entire war. He made up his mind to abandon his line of communication and strike out boldly for Savannah on the Atlantic coast, more than 300 miles to the southeast. Sherman began his march in November, 1864, right through "the garden spot of the Confederacy." Sweeping across an area 60 miles wide, Sherman's army took what it wanted and then deliberately destroyed everything that could be of possible military use to the Confederacy, and many things that could not.

Harvested crops were carried off. Cattle and horses were slaughtered or taken away. Railways were torn up, factories wrecked, warehouses and public buildings burned. The railway connections from Virginia and the Carolinas to the far southern states were cut beyond repair, so that the hard-pressed southern armies had a worse time than ever to keep themselves in supplies. The morale of the South was deeply shaken. Savannah was besieged in December, and on Christmas Eve, Lincoln received this brief message from Sherman: "I beg to present you as a Christmas-gift the city of Savannah, with one hundred and fifty heavy guns and plenty of ammunition, also about twenty-five thousand bales of cotton."

Sherman pushes northward. As the year 1865 opened, Sherman turned northward into the Carolinas to help Grant crush the Confederacy. Even more destruction was carried on here. Both Columbia, the capital of South Carolina, and Charleston fell into Union hands. Sherman faced bad weather and other obstacles, but he pushed forward so effectively that Johnston, who had been given the task of trying to block

him, said that "there had been no such army since the days of Julius Caesar." Sherman pushed his way on into North Carolina. On April 26, 1865, he forced Johnston to surrender near Durham.

Grant launches the Wilderness Campaign. About the time that Sherman started his march through Georgia, Grant was directing the Army of the Potomac in a final drive upon Richmond. Grant's forces moved directly toward Richmond through a tangled, marshy wood known as the Wilderness. Lee put up strong resistance and checked the Union forces. Grant then issued the following characteristic dispatch: "We have now ended the sixth day of very heavy fighting . . . I . . . propose to fight it out on this line if it takes all summer." This policy of hammering at the enemy until they would have to give up involved frightful human losses. Before Grant reached Richmond, the so-called Wilderness Campaign cost him 55,000 men. Still he could not pierce Lee's defenses. His generalship was widely criticized, but with bulldog determination he kept pounding the Confederate lines.

Gradually the superior resources of the North began to tell. In the early days of April, 1865, Petersburg, the back door to Richmond, was captured. Then Richmond fell. Lee's army set off southwestward, with Grant in pursuit. With his retreat blocked by other Union forces, his supplies gone, and his army weakened by desertions and sickness, Lee asked Grant for terms of surrender at Appomattox Court House, Virginia, on April 9, 1865.

Lee and Grant meet. The meeting of Grant and Lee to work out the terms of surrender was one of the most dramatic events of the entire war. The two men presented a decided contrast in appearance. Grant was still in his forties. He had a short, stocky figure, round shoulders, and a shabby uniform. In appearance, he was not impressive. Lee, in contrast, looked the part of a great officer. His erect bearing, white hair and beard, and a splendid new uniform combined to make him a striking figure.

When the terms of surrender were under discussion, the unassuming Grant showed

The main points of Union strategy were carried out after long effort. What were they? (See map, page 301.) What was the special importance of Chattanooga? The northern navy blockaded the Confederacy and captured southern ports. How else did it help to carry out Union strategy? What was the Peninsular Campaign? What was its outcome? When Grant circled Richmond and took Petersburg, a railway center, Lee had to withdraw from Richmond. Why? What was Lee attempting to do when he retreated from Richmond?

Two Confederate flags are shown here. The Stars and Bars (shown at Montgomery) was official but was little used in battle because of its similarity to the Stars and Stripes. The Battle Flag (shown at Richmond and elsewhere) was commonly flown in the field.

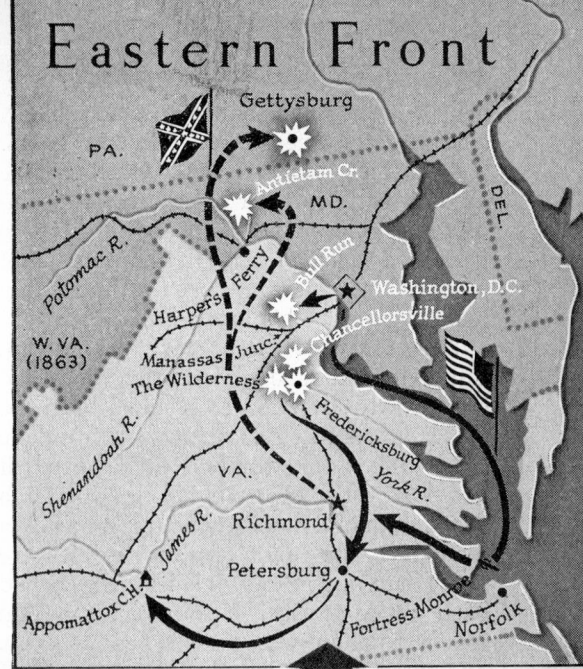

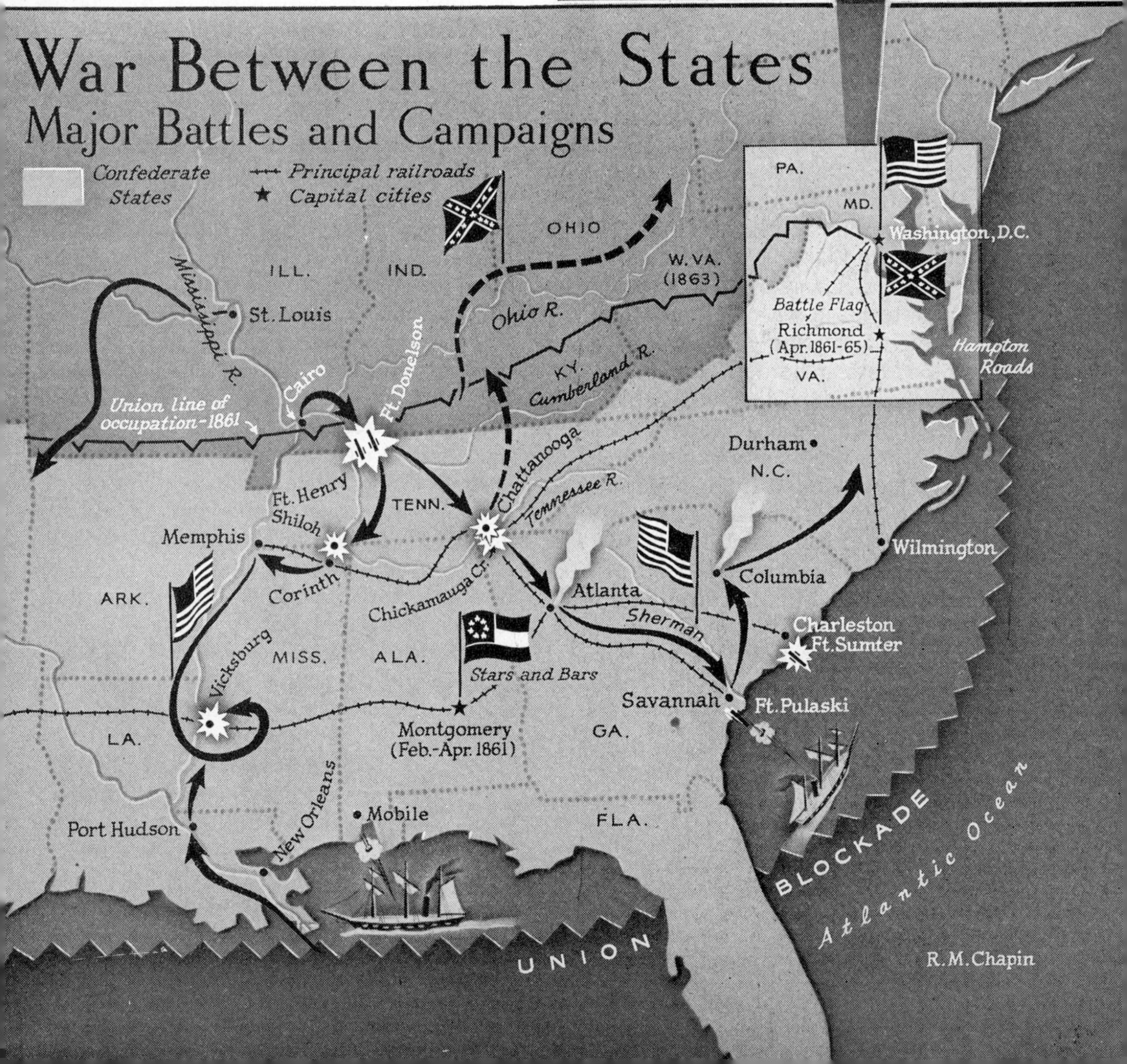

Eastern Front

War Between the States
Major Battles and Campaigns

R. M. Chapin

generosity and consideration which deeply affected Lee. The Confederate officers and enlisted men were paroled. Officers were allowed to keep their side arms, and officers and men who owned horses were permitted to keep them. In addition, Grant promised Lee 25,000 rations for the scantily fed remnants of his army.

The blockade strangles the South. Throughout four long years the South had been slowly strangled by a naval blockade along the southern coast. (See map, page 309.) When the war had first started, it had been just a "paper" blockade — that is, a declaration of a blockade not enforced by a real navy. The Union's sailing vessels were out of date, and in 1861 only 24 steamers had been put in service. However, a program of construction was undertaken at once. The government bought steamers, side-wheelers, clipper ships, tugboats, and even ferryboats. To make the blockade effective was a tremendous task, for it had to cover more than 3000 miles of coast line, with nearly 200 harbors. Nevertheless, after May, 1862, the Confederacy held only the ports of Wilmington (North Carolina), Charleston (South Carolina), Mobile (Alabama), and Galveston (Texas). From these points a few swift blockade runners were able to trade with Bermuda and the West Indies, and some goods were slipped in over the Mexican border. This contraband trade, however, grew less as the blockade tightened during the last years of the war.

The first ironclads appear. The need to break the blockade led the Confederacy to experiment with ironclad ships. When the South seized Norfolk, Virginia, in 1861, a 40-gun steam frigate called the *Merrimac,* which had been partly destroyed and sunk, came into the hands of the Confederates. They floated this crippled vessel, covered it with four-inch iron plating, fastened a large cast-iron ram to the bow, and re-christened it the *Virginia.* It was a queer-looking craft when it steamed out of Norfolk Harbor on the afternoon of March 8, 1862, to break the blockade. Before sundown, it had destroyed two Union frigates.

The next morning, however, an even stranger vessel appeared off Norfolk. This was the newly-built *Monitor,* a Union ironclad. The deck of this "Yankee cheesebox on a raft" was nearly level with the water, and it was equipped with a revolving turret that carried two heavy guns. The duel between the *Monitor* and the *Merrimac* was the first between ironclad men-of-war. Neither ship could seriously damage the other, however, and finally both withdrew. The battle proved the superiority of ironclads and foreshadowed the end of wooden vessels in warfare.

The blockade contributes to the collapse of the Confederacy. The noose of the blockade was drawn even tighter in the closing years of the war. In August, 1864, Admiral Farragut entered Mobile Bay and succeeded in overcoming the Confederate vessels stationed there and in silencing the land defenses. In the end the northern blockade proved to be one of the most effective forces in overpowering the South.

The war ends. The spring of 1865 brought an end to the bloody conflict. Early in the year an attempt was made to negotiate peace in a conference at Hampton Roads, Virginia. Lincoln and Secretary of State Seward met representatives of the Confederate government, but no agreement was reached. However, when Lee and Johnston surrendered in April, the southern government had no choice but to accept the northern terms.

The surprising fact is not that the Confederacy finally gave way in 1865, but that the collapse had not occurred sooner. The Confederate states had battled against heavy odds. With their gallant fight they had written new chapters of courage into the record of the American people.

(Continued on page 312)

Monitor and Merrimac

Robert E. Lee
(1807-1870)

West Point Cadet

GREAT CRISES often breed great men. The War Between the States produced Robert E. Lee as well as Abraham Lincoln. Born of a family that had rendered outstanding service to Virginia and the nation, Lee represented the full flowering of southern civilization. He possessed those physical graces which Lincoln so notably lacked — perfection of figure, erectness of carriage, and a pleasing countenance. Another great southerner, Alexander H. Stephens of Georgia, described him as "the most manly and entire gentleman I ever saw."

Lee decided to follow a military career. He attended West Point and served with distinction in the Mexican War. With the opening of the War Between the States, however, the most important chapter of Lee's life began. Though a splendid career undoubtedly awaited him in the Union army, Lee chose to defend the southern cause. During the four years of combat, he became the outstanding military figure in the Confederate forces. Some of his success was due to his military skill, but it arose as well from his power over his men. His grip over his soldiers is best appreciated when one remembers their affection for him in defeat as well as in victory. Northern and foreign critics have been generous in their praise of Lee's military achievements. One military expert has described him as "one of the most famous of the world's great generals."

Confederate General

College President

With the return of peace, Lee sought quiet and relief from the cares of public service. He expressed loyalty toward the United States government. Though saddened by the misrule of the reconstruction governments, Lee did not give way to pessimism nor bitter criticism. He became president of the college now known as Washington and Lee, where he displayed the same qualities of leadership that he had shown on the field of battle. Thoughtful, kindly, greathearted, Lee had a lofty understanding of obligation to duty.

———— CHECK-UP ————

How did the North finally achieve victory?

1. What were the three campaigns planned by Grant to end the war?
2. What were the objectives of Sherman's march? What were its chief features?
3. What were the objectives of the Wilderness Campaign? How did it bring the war to an end?
4. Why was the blockade important? What did the battle between the "Merrimac" and the "Monitor" show?

---

4 Both Sections Face Serious Problems During the War

Both sides use a military draft. One of the most pressing problems faced by both the North and the South during the War Between the States was the job of raising armed forces. In the early months, when enthusiasm ran high, volunteers enlisted faster than they could be armed and equipped. "After a time I had cut down my uniform so that I could see out of it and had conquered the drill sufficiently to see through it," wrote one Union private. "Then the word came: On to Washington!" But when it was evident that the war would be long, enlistments started to fall off. Both governments then used *bounties* to attract recruits. State and local governments added their own bounties, so that a volunteer in the North might get as much as $1000 in cash for joining up. But local bounties led to the abuse known as *bounty-jumping*. Volunteers would desert as soon as they had received their bounty in one place, enlist again in a different place under a different name and collect another bounty.

Both sides also found it necessary to draft men for armed service. The Confederacy issued a draft which, before 1862 ended, made every able-bodied white male between the ages of 18 and 45 liable for service. The North imposed a draft early in 1863, making all able-bodied male citizens between 20 and 45 liable for service. The real purpose of the northern draft was to encourage enlistments by the threat of draft. In both sections, however, certain groups were exempted. Furthermore, a drafted man could hire a substitute to take his place, and in the North he could also get exemption from service by paying the government $300.

Such provisions aroused opposition to the draft. People in both sections charged that the conflict was "a rich man's war and a poor man's fight." Resistance to the draft in the North reached a peak in New York City in July, 1863, where, for several days, draft riots swept the city. Nearly 1000 people were killed or wounded, and large-scale property damage resulted.

Heavy taxes are levied in the North. Obtaining the funds needed for carrying on the war was a major problem for both sides. On the whole the North, with its greater resources and larger population, had an advantage. First, the federal government established a program of heavy taxation. As the war continued, tariff duties were raised until the average rate reached 47 per cent — the highest in American history up to that time. In addition, high internal revenue taxes were also put into force, a direct tax was laid upon the states, and income taxes were levied.

The federal government sells war bonds. The money received from these sources was still not enough to pay for the war, and the federal government began to borrow money through the sale of bonds. To encourage people to buy bonds, a national banking system was organized in 1863. Any group of five or more persons who met certain requirements could obtain a national bank charter. Such a bank had to invest at least one third of its capital in United States bonds. Upon deposit of these bonds with

N.Y. volunteer ("Zouave")

the Treasurer of the United States, the bank received national bank currency equal to 90 per cent of the value of the bonds. This National Banking Act served two purposes: it created a market for government bonds, and it helped set up a firm and reliable national currency which eventually took the place of state bank notes.

Additional currency is issued. The Union government adopted still another means of raising money. It issued paper money with nothing to back it up except the government's promise to redeem it at some future date. These United States notes, or *greenbacks* as they were called, could be used to pay all debts, public or private, except customs duties and interest upon the public debt. Since the value of the greenback depended entirely upon the government's ability to pay, greenbacks rose and fell in value with the fortunes of war. The greenbacks hit bottom in the dreary summer days of 1864, when they were worth only 39 cents on the dollar. Even when the war ended, they were worth only about 67 cents in terms of gold.

As the purchasing power of the greenback went down, gold and silver became more valuable, and the prices of goods rose. People then started to hoard their gold and silver, and paid their bills in greenbacks. Soon even small silver coins disappeared. Then people turned to makeshift paper currency, popularly known as *shin-plasters,* for fractional parts of a dollar. The government met this need for fractional money by issuing paper money in denominations as low as three cents.

The South has trouble financing the war. The South found it even harder than the North to finance the war. There was little available capital in the cotton states, so that the amount that could be raised from loans at home was limited. As for foreign loans, the Confederacy was much less successful than was expected, although one foreign loan of $15,000,000 was arranged. A direct tax on property was also tried, but the results were disappointing.

The South, therefore, was left to finance the war chiefly by means of paper money

Drawing lots for the draft

with no security but the Confederate government's promise to redeem it. This currency was issued in almost unlimited amounts, and its value fell as the fortunes of the Confederacy declined. By the end of the war, a Confederate dollar was worth only a cent and a half in gold or silver. Prices skyrocketed. Flour sold at $1000 a barrel, while a pair of shoes cost as much as $200. As the southern cause became more and more hopeless, bonds also fell in value.

Europe's attitude is important. From the outbreak of the war, both the North and the South realized that the attitude of European powers could make or break them. The South had a powerful weapon in its monopoly of cotton and its promise of a free-trade policy. If Great Britain and France recognized the Confederacy, its outlook for victory would be bright. But if the North could blockade southern ports effectively and at the same time keep European powers from recognizing the Confederacy, it could feel confident of final victory.

France and England at first favor the South. In Great Britain and France there was much sympathy for the southern cause. The upper classes of England did not approve American efforts to achieve individual equality. They would have welcomed a southern victory as a blow to democracy. Further, British manufacturers would benefit from an independent southern confederacy, which could supply them with cotton but which would place no tariff on British manufactures. British shippers looked forward to the ruin of their chief competitors, the New England and Middle Atlantic states. Even those Englishmen

313

who might have favored the Union in a struggle against slavery were discouraged by the early statements of Lincoln and Secretary of State Seward that the war was being fought entirely to preserve the Union. Only among labor leaders and the working classes of England was there strong interest in a victory by the North. Those groups viewed the conflict across the Atlantic as a crusade for the cause of free labor.

Sympathy for the Confederacy was also strong among the French governing classes. Napoleon III, the ruler of France, believed that if the South won, the Monroe Doctrine would be weakened and that he could extend French influence in the Americas. He would have been glad to recognize the independence of the Confederacy if he had been able to get England to do the same.

Trouble brews between England and the North. With European sympathies leaning so strongly toward the South, it took skill and tact on President Lincoln's part to maintain friendly relations between the United States and Great Britain. Before the close of 1861, an incident occurred which threatened to bring an open break between the two powers. Two Confederate commissioners to England and France — James M. Mason and John Slidell — were taken from the British steamer *Trent* by Captain Wilkes, who was in command of a Union warship. This highhanded act violated a principle for which the United States had fought in the War of 1812, but Wilkes was hailed as a hero in the North. In England, there was quite a different reaction. Indignation reached such a pitch that the British began military and naval preparations, and even sent 8000 troops to Canada. Fortunately for the Union cause, Lincoln realized the importance of

disclaiming responsibility for Wilkes' highhanded action. He ordered the release of Mason and Slidell, and war with Britain was avoided.

Nevertheless, strained relations between the North and Great Britain continued. The Union blockade of the South was hurting England seriously. Her cotton imports from the South fell off sharply. British commercial interests were suffering, textile mills were closing down, and laborers were being thrown out of work. The North, on the other hand, was irritated with England. Vessels were being built in British shipyards for use by the Confederates as commerce destroyers. These destroyers, of which the most famous was the *Alabama,* inflicted heavy losses on northern merchantmen. Matters came to a head in 1863 when the North learned that two powerful ironclad rams were being built in England by a private company for the use of the Confederacy. The United States minister to England protested sharply, whereupon the British government issued an order against the release of the ironclads.

The South loses European support. As the war went on, relations between the North and Europe improved. The British textile industry began to import cotton from other countries. In addition, Lincoln's Emancipation Proclamation on January 1, 1863 (page 315) reassured Great Britain that the war was being fought to abolish slavery and not simply to conquer the South. Finally, Union victories made the recognition of the Confederacy a bad risk for European countries. Except for Napoleon III's attempt to set up a puppet ruler in Mexico in defiance of the Monroe Doctrine (page 473), relations between the North and Europe remained friendly during the rest of the war. When France and

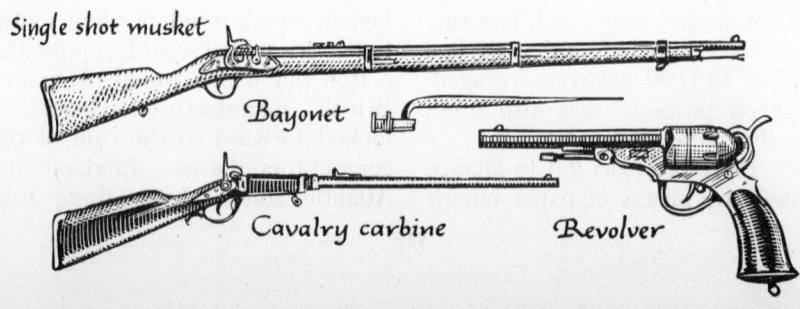

Single shot musket

Bayonet

Cavalry carbine

Revolver

Great Britain failed to recognize the Confederacy formally, southern hopes were crushed.

The slavery problem troubles Lincoln. Another thorny problem for the North grew out of the position of the slaves. When the war started, both Lincoln and Congress made it clear that the war was being fought to preserve the Union, and not to conquer the South or to interfere with its established institutions. But the North soon had to face the fact that slavery was a big advantage to the South in waging war. Slaves tilled the soil and left the white manpower free to fight. Slaves also drove munition wagons, cooked in the army camps, dug trenches, and built fortifications. Meanwhile, the extreme abolitionists in the North demanded immediate and complete emancipation of slaves and bitterly attacked the government for failing to do anything about it.

Still the government moved slowly. In April, 1862, Congress abolished slavery in the District of Columbia, and paid the loyal owners of the emancipated slaves. Two months later, slavery was abolished forever in the territories of the United States. In addition, Congress passed a resolution which offered financial help to any state which would make provision for gradual emancipation. Lincoln did his best to get the border states to accept this plan of "compensated emancipation," and was bitterly disappointed when they rejected it.

Beyond this point Lincoln was not yet ready to go. He could do only what military necessity demanded. He could not afford to antagonize the border states, nor to lose the support of those people of the North who were willing to fight to preserve the Union but not to free the Negro. Early in 1862, when the northern radicals grew too insistent, he declared his position in positive terms: "My paramount object in this struggle is to save the Union, and is not either to save or to destroy slavery. . . . What I do about slavery and the colored race, I do because I believe it helps to save the Union; and what I forbear, I forbear because I do not believe it would help to save the Union."

Women of North and South relieved the suffering of the wounded. Among them were these nurses of the United States Sanitary Commission, forerunner of the Red Cross.

The Emancipation Proclamation is issued. In the summer of 1862, Lincoln finally became convinced that the emancipation of the slaves "was a military necessity absolutely essential for the salvation of the Union." He laid before the cabinet a draft of the Emancipation Proclamation. Then he put it aside to wait until a Union victory should give a favorable moment for publication. The battle of Antietam gave him the opportunity. Late in September, Lincoln announced that, at the beginning of the next year, he would declare "forever free" the slaves in any states or parts of states which were then in arms against the authority of the federal government.[1] The famous proclamation was signed and issued on January 1, 1863. It indicated which states, and parts of states, it applied to, and declared that all slaves in those sections were now legally free.

Steps are taken to abolish slavery. The Emancipation Proclamation did not offer a

[1] Lincoln's right to issue the Emancipation Proclamation lay in his authority as commander in chief of the northern forces. As a matter of fact, both Lincoln and Davis were severely criticized for exercising broad powers under the emergency of war, which interfered with personal liberties.

complete and final solution to the slavery problem. For example, it did not apply to the loyal border states, but only to the regions still in arms against the government. There, it was treated with scorn. The effectiveness of the proclamation depended entirely upon which side won the war. If the South won, the proclamation would be meaningless. Even if the North won, the proclamation could do little more than pave the way for a change in the Constitution that would legally abolish slavery.

An amendment to the Constitution for this purpose was introduced into Congress at the beginning of 1864. The amendment prohibited slavery in the United States or in any place which was subject to the jurisdiction of the United States. Nearly a year passed before the measure received the necessary two-thirds vote in both houses of Congress. By December of 1865, enough states had ratified the amendment to make it a part of the Constitution.

Lincoln is re-elected. Union politics during the war went hand in hand with military successes and failures. In the congressional elections of 1862, which took place while Union armed forces were doing badly, Democratic strength increased in the House of Representatives. Two years later the country was called upon to elect a President. The Republicans took the name of the Union Party and renominated Lincoln, with Andrew Johnson — a Unionist Democrat from Tennessee — as his running mate. The northern Democrats chose General McClellan as their standard-bearer. They called the war a failure and urged immediate efforts to end it. The most outspoken of this group were the extreme Democrats known as Copperheads. During the campaign, the Unionists had some anxious moments. As late as August, 1864, Lincoln admitted that his re-election was not likely. Just before the election, however, Union victories again brightened the outlook for the North. Farragut's attack at Mobile was successful, and Sherman occupied Atlanta. Opposition to the war died down, and Lincoln was re-elected by 212 electoral votes to McClellan's 21.

The Gettysburg Address was delivered by President Lincoln on November 19, 1863, at the dedication of the National Cemetery on the battlefield of Gettysburg. It is one of the most famous and most often quoted speeches of all time. In the midst of the troubles and bitterness of war, Lincoln was able to express in a few unforgettable words the highest ideals of our democracy.

War welfare work is developed. During the war, great advances were made in caring for the soldiers and their widows and orphans. Noteworthy was the work done by the United States Sanitary Commission, which foreshadowed the American Red Cross. The Sanitary Commission organized hospital units, sent men and women to nurse the wounded, and supplied the soldiers with clothing, comforts, and luxuries. The women of the North took a leading part in the work of this commission.

Equally active, and even more self-sacrificing, were the women of the South. Mrs. Jefferson Davis, in writing of these southern women war-workers, said, "they fed the hungry, cared for the orphans, deprived themselves of every wonted luxury to give it to the soldiers, and were amid their deprivations so cheerful as to animate even the men with hope." Many southern women devotedly nursed the wounded in hospitals or in their homes.

Industry increases in the North. Industry boomed in the North under the pressure of war needs. Factories grew in number and production increased because of improved machinery. The sewing machine advanced the efficiency of the needle-trade workers, while a similar machine increased the production of shoes about 100 per cent. Greater amounts of coal, iron, copper, and lumber were produced than ever before. Transportation facilities were greatly improved. On the farms, wider use of labor-saving machinery made up for the loss of men to the army.

Some Northerners become rich. Enormous profits were reaped in the North. These were made possible by high prices which resulted from the high protective tariff and from the lowered value of the

(Continued on page 318)

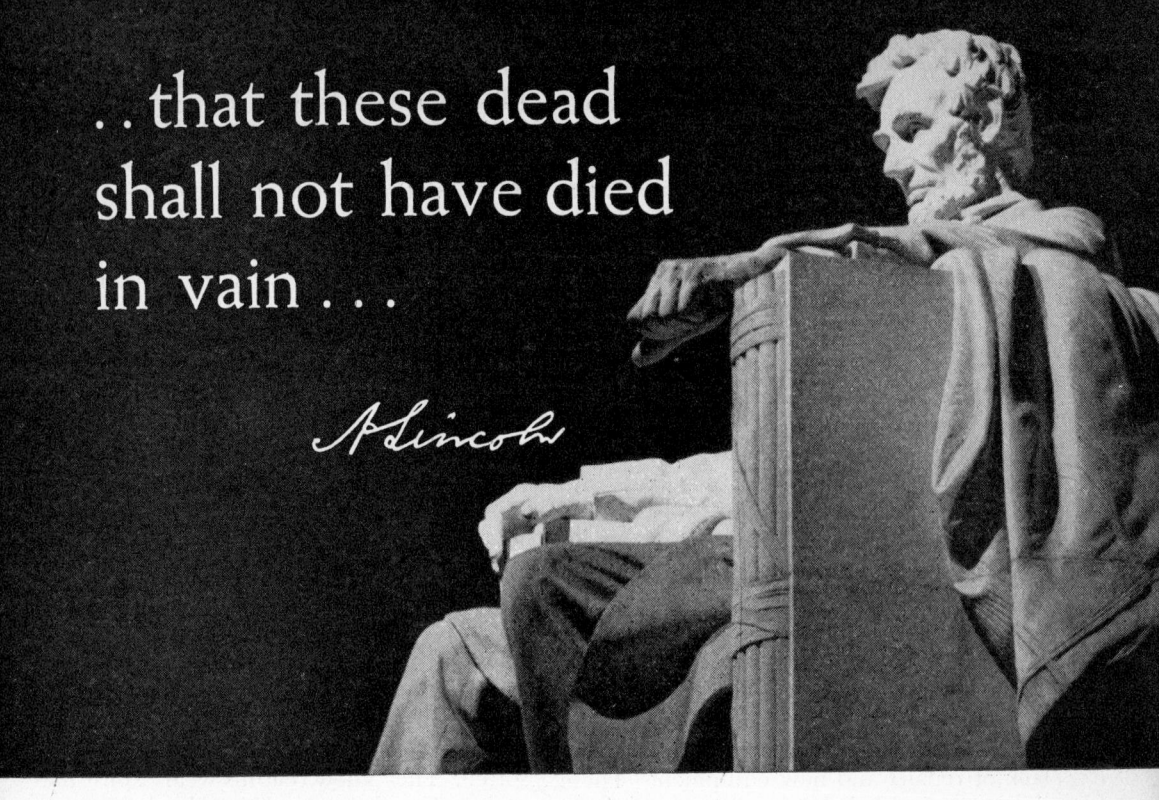

.. that these dead
shall not have died
in vain ...

A. Lincoln

THE GETTYSBURG ADDRESS

FOURSCORE and seven years ago our fathers brought forth on this continent a new nation, conceived in liberty, and dedicated to the proposition that all men are created equal.

Now we are engaged in a great civil war, testing whether that nation, or any nation so conceived and so dedicated, can long endure. We are met on a great battlefield of that war. We have come to dedicate a portion of that field as a final resting place for those who here gave their lives that that nation might live. It is altogether fitting and proper that we should do this.

But, in a larger sense, we cannot dedicate—we cannot consecrate—we cannot hallow—this ground. The brave men, living and dead, who struggled here, have consecrated it far above our poor power to add or detract. The world will little note nor long remember what we say here, but it can never forget what they did here. It is for us, the living, rather, to be dedicated here to the unfinished work which they who fought here have thus far so nobly advanced. It is rather for us to be here dedicated to the great task remaining before us — that from these honored dead we take increased devotion to that cause for which they gave the last full measure of devotion; that we here highly resolve that these dead shall not have died in vain; that this nation, under God, shall have a new birth of freedom; and that government of the people, by the people, for the people, shall not perish from the earth.

currency. Some profiteers took advantage of the government's need. They sold at high prices blankets, "paper-soled" shoes, and clothing made from cloth of poor quality called "shoddy." Such unfair dealing laid the groundwork for some of the swollen fortunes of the postwar period. On the other hand, the rising industrialism was not kind to the laborers, for prices rose faster than wages.

The South suffers hard times. In the South no such industrial boom took place. Strenuous efforts were made to manufacture war materials and clothing, but with only a limited amount of success. Many factories were set up, but they were handicapped by the lack of capital, machinery, and skilled workers. Transportation facilities broke down under the strain and stress of war. Some of the railroads fell into Union hands. Parts of others were destroyed by the invading or retreating armies, and the rest went to pieces from lack of repairs and new equipment. These conditions added heavy burdens to the hardships of the southern people. Foodstuffs might be plentiful in one section, but there was no way to ship them where they were needed. There were profiteers in the South, as there were in the North. During the latter years of the war, many parts of the South were in desperate need of food, clothing, and other essentials. It was almost impossible to get such articles as tea, coffee, and soap.

The war exacts a terrible price. The war preserved the Union and it abolished Negro slavery, but at what a price! Brother had fought against brother. Families had been torn apart. A whole section of the country lay destroyed and helpless. To fight the war 5 billion dollars had been spent and over 2 billion dollars in slave property had been wiped out. About 600,-000 men had lost their lives, and as many more had been wounded or maimed.

A great deal now depended upon the spirit in which the nation turned to bind up its wounds. President Lincoln urged a charitable and humane policy. He told his cabinet that "he hoped there would be no persecution, no bloody work, after the war was over. None need expect he would take any part in hanging or killing these men, even the worst of them. . . . Enough lives have been sacrificed. We must extinguish our resentments if we expect harmony and union."

Lincoln is assassinated. It was as unfortunate for the South as for the North that Lincoln was not spared to put these humane principles into action. On the night of April 14, 1865, free at last from the cares of war, the President sat in the presidential box at Ford's Theater in Washington. A half-crazed actor named John Wilkes Booth stole silently up behind the Chief Executive. Thinking that he was avenging the South, Booth shot Lincoln in the back of the head.[2] Throughout that anxious night, Lincoln hovered between life and death. In the morning those who stood by his bedside saw the lines of care in his face soften. They knew that his weary spirit had at last found peace. "Now he belongs to the ages," Secretary of War Stanton said solemnly, when Lincoln breathed his last.

[2] The assassination of Lincoln was part of a general plot to kill a number of Union leaders. Seward was stabbed, and his son was injured in defending him. Grant escaped attack.

——————— CHECK-UP ———————

What serious problems were faced by both North and South during the war?

1. Why was raising troops a problem? How did each side attempt to solve it?
2. What methods were used to finance the war? Why was the North better off than the South in this matter?
3. Why did many Southerners believe that Great Britain would recognize the Confederacy? Why were they disappointed? What events strained the relations between Great Britain and the United States?
4. Why was the question of emancipation a difficult one for Lincoln? What did he finally do? What were the effects of his action?
5. What were the economic effects of the war on both North and South?

CHAPTER REVIEW

Terms to Understand

merchant marine
"paper" blockade
contraband trade
ironclads
bounty-jumping

draft
war bonds
commerce destroyers
emancipate
profiteers

People and Things to Know About

Fort Sumter
Robert E. Lee
"Stonewall" Jackson
Ulysses S. Grant
David G. Farragut
George B. McClellan
"Pickett's Charge"
"Rock of Chicka-
mauga"
William T. Sherman
Wilderness Campaign

Monitor and *Merrimac*
National Banking Sys-
tem
shin-plasters
greenbacks
Trent affair
Emancipation Procla-
mation
Sanitary Commission
Copperheads
John Wilkes Booth

Historic Dates to Identify

1861   1862   1863   1865

Questions to Discuss

1. Southern leaders debated whether or not Fort Sumter should be taken forcibly. Do you think the decision to take it was a serious mistake? Give your reasons.
2. What qualities exhibited by Lincoln during the period of the war show that he was truly a great President?
3. Why is it difficult for a democracy to fight a war and still maintain democratic procedures? What difficult problems of this kind did Lincoln have to solve during the war?
4. Compare the following:
   (a) Grant and McClellan as generals.
   (b) The blockade and the British Orders in Council during the War of 1812.
   (c) The War Between the States draft and the World War II draft.
   (d) The effects on industry of the War Between the States and the War of 1812.
5. The South hoped that (a) the North would not fight, (b) all the border states would secede, and (c) foreign nations would inter-

Questions to Discuss (Cont.)

vene if a war did start. Did the South have good reasons for these hopes? Why didn't they materialize?
6. It has been said that the Emancipation Proclamation freed hardly a single slave. Can you explain why?
7. Do you feel that Sherman's destructive march through Georgia was justified? Why?

Relating Geography and History

1. On an outline map of the United States:
   (a) Show the sites of the chief battles. Give dates and indicate whether they were northern or southern victories.
   (b) Show the original seceding states, the border states which seceded, the border states which remained loyal.
2. Explain the importance of each of these in the War Between the States: the Appalachian Mountains, the Mississippi River, western Tennessee, Georgia. It will be necessary to consult a physical map for some of these.

Other Things to Do

1. Read Lincoln's great second inaugural address. Why do you suppose that it is among our treasured state papers? What can we still learn from it?
2. Prepare a biographical report on one of the outstanding military leaders or statesmen of the War Between the States. Most persons know little about Southern statesmen other than Jefferson Davis. You will find information about some of these men in Hendrick's *Statesmen of the Lost Cause*.
*3. Prepare a two-column chart in which you compare the relative advantages of North and South in fighting the war.
4. Photography was new, but the War Between the States was well covered by the great war photographer, Mathew Brady. See if your library has copies of the *Photographic History of the Civil War*.
5. Try to find information on the part played by the troops of your community or state in the War Between the States.

Carpetbagger

Chapter 17

THE SOUTHERN STATES ARE RESTORED

TO THE UNION

The war being at an end, the Southern states having laid down their arms, and the questions at issue between them and the Northern states having been decided, I believe it to be the duty of everyone to unite in the restoration of the country and the re-establishment of peace and harmony.

General Robert E. Lee, 1865

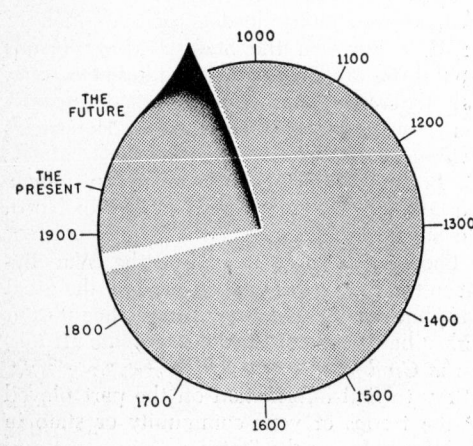

1865-1877

War, even when it does not last long, upsets the normal life of a people. A severe and long-drawn-out war throws a nation completely off stride. Men have to leave their ordinary occupations to fight and to speed the production of war materials. Wealth and natural resources are wasted, and property is destroyed. Families are broken up. Emotions are roused to a high pitch.

After the war is ended, tremendous readjustments must take place. Armies have to be disbanded, and the industrial activities of the nation must be changed from a wartime to a peacetime basis. The ordinary operations of the government must be resumed, and conditions gradually brought back to normal. The desire to destroy must be transformed into a spirit of rebuilding or *reconstruction*.

The United States faced such gigantic problems in the spring of 1865. They were not problems which could be solved quickly; in fact, they vexed the nation for the next ten or twelve years. The task of solving them was made even more difficult by the untimely death of President Lincoln. Later, when conditions began to approach normal, scars of bitterness still remained — scars which have lasted even until today. The Reconstruction Era, as this post-war period is called, was a tragic time in American history. This chapter gives an account of the Reconstruction Era under three headings:

1. The administration favors lenient reconstruction.
2. Congress adopts a harsh program.
3. The South suffers from misrule.

Nearly a ton of shot and shell was found in this Atlanta house after the siege ended.

1 The Administration Favors Lenient Reconstruction

The South is badly crippled. In the North, reconstruction was not too great a task. There had been little fighting on northern soil. Northern business had not been hurt; in fact, many businesses had actually been helped by the war. The South, however, was not so fortunate. Marching armies had ruined plantations, railroads, and buildings, leaving a trail of desolation and destruction. Government in

the greater part of the South was disorganized. Confederate bonds and currency, representing billions of dollars, were worthless. Under these conditions, the reconstruction of the South was certain to offer serious difficulties.

The freedmen face problems. Southern reconstruction was made even more difficult since over 3½ million Negroes had suddenly been set free by the war. What was to be their political, social, and economic future? Many Negroes, of course, did not know how to use their newly gained freedom. Most of them were uneducated and

Scenes of devastation awaited Southerners when they returned to their homes after the war. The destruction was especially severe along the railways. This picture shows tracks torn up, the wheels of burned cars, and a factory completely destroyed near Atlanta.

without property. The plantation system had given them little experience in learning how to support themselves or face the responsibilities of citizenship. Some of these freedmen continued to live in their old cabins and hired themselves out to their former masters for wages. Many others left the plantations, roamed the countryside, and waited for the government to help them. A rumor was widespread that the government intended to seize a large part of the land of former slaveowners and give "forty acres and a mule" to each freedman. When the rumor proved false, the freedmen were disappointed.

"Black codes" anger the North. The wandering and unemployed freedmen became a problem to the state governments organized in the South after the war. To deal with the problem, state laws were passed known as the "black codes." These put limitations on the civil rights of "persons of color." They included laws which provided that certain Negro children might be made to serve as apprentices. Other laws imposed fines and imprisonment on freedmen who did not have lawful business or employment. A freedman so convicted and unable to pay his fine could be hired out by the local authorities — in many cases to his former owner. Many Northerners considered these black codes a clear attempt to make the Negro a slave in everything but name. From the Southerner's viewpoint, however, these laws were needed to keep the freedmen at work and to maintain stable conditions in the South.

Lincoln plans a generous southern policy. Still another problem of reconstruction — and probably the most important of all — was the position of the former Confederate states in the Union. Eleven states had tried to secede. Had they lost their statehood by this action? If so, how could it be restored to them?

Lincoln had given much thought to this question. As early as December, 1863, he had issued a proclamation based upon his pardoning power. The proclamation granted a full pardon to every southern citizen who would take an oath of allegiance, with the exception of the civil and

military leaders of the Confederacy. The proclamation also provided that when ten per cent of the people who had been voters in any state in 1860 had taken the oath to support the Constitution, the laws of Congress, and the proclamations of the President on slavery, they could organize a government. The President would then recognize this government as the true government of the state. Lincoln cautiously added, however, that "whether members sent to Congress from any state shall be admitted to seats, constitutionally rests exclusively with the respective houses." Before the end of the war Louisiana, Arkansas, and Tennessee had set up loyal governments under this generous plan.

Congress tries to stiffen the plan. Lincoln's plan made it so easy for a southern state to get back into the Union that many Northern leaders opposed it. The Republicans in Congress had split into two groups — the so-called radicals and the conservatives. The radical Republicans wanted to punish the Southerners, especially the planter class which had controlled the cotton states. To them Lincoln's plan was completely unacceptable. The conservatives backed Lincoln, but even they wanted a plan which would adequately protect the rights of the Negroes.

In 1864 Congress proposed the Wade-Davis Bill as a substitute for the Lincoln plan. The Wade-Davis Bill would have given Congress, not the President, the right to control reconstruction. It required a *majority,* rather than ten per cent, of the white male citizens in a seceded state to take the oath of allegiance before a legal state government could be organized. The Wade-Davis Bill passed both Houses of Congress and came to Lincoln for his signature at the close of the congressional session. Taking advantage of that fact, Lincoln killed the bill by taking no action upon it.

Lincoln's death upsets the reconstruction program. Lincoln hoped to carry out his program of reconstruction during the summer of 1865 while Congress was not in session. His death changed the whole course of southern restoration. There is a good chance that Lincoln — generous, patient, and with kindly feelings toward the southern states — might have been able to guide the country safely through the difficult task of reconstruction. No doubt he would have had to struggle with the radical leaders in Congress. Nevertheless, with his tact and understanding of human nature, he probably would have avoided many of the mistakes made by his successor. If Lincoln had lived to take charge of reconstruction, the South might have been spared the misgovernment forced upon it by congressional leaders.

Andrew Johnson becomes President. The new President, Andrew Johnson, had risen from poverty through sheer force of character. He came from a poor, nonslaveholding family in North Carolina, and had started adult life as a tailor in eastern Tennessee. He had little or no chance to get an education; in fact, it is said he was unable to write until his wife taught him. As a member of the poorer class in the South, he had inherited a bitter hatred of the planter aristocracy.

Johnson entered politics early in his life and worked his way up to the position of United States senator. He had opposed the secession of his state, and when Tennessee finally left the Union, Johnson did not resign from the Senate. Later, when the northern forces occupied Tennessee, he was appointed military governor by Lincoln, and he performed his duties with real ability. His nomination for the Vice-Presidency came about partly because the Republicans, in 1864, wanted to show that their party was not sectional, and partly because they wanted a man who could help win the support of the war Democrats. Johnson was honest, sincere, self-reliant, and courageous. On the other hand, he was narrow-minded and obstinate. Unfortunately he failed to show the statesmanship, the tact, and the generous understanding which were so sorely needed in the period of adjustment that followed the war.

Johnson tries to carry out Lincoln's program. At first the radical Republicans hailed Johnson as an ally. The radicals knew that

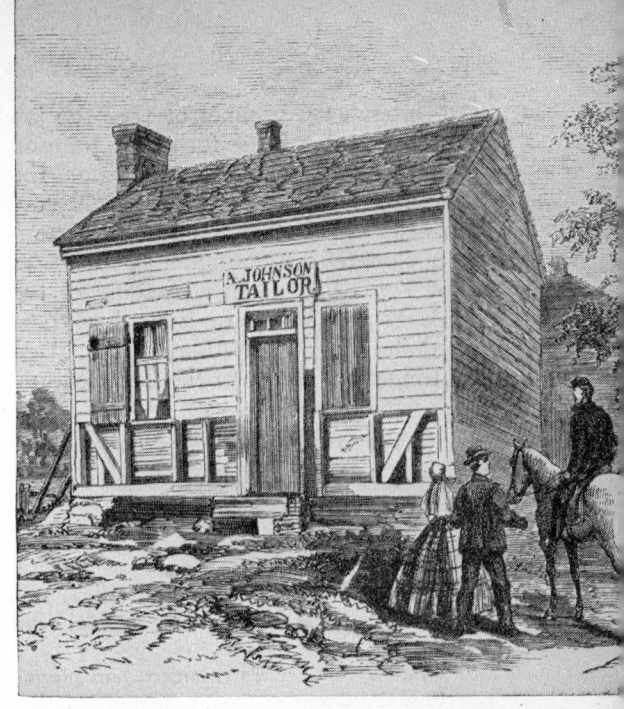

President Andrew Johnson began his career in this simple shop in eastern Tennessee. Of humble origin like Lincoln, Johnson tried to carry out Lincoln's humanitarian plan of reconstruction. He was blocked, however, by revengeful politicians.

he hated the southern planter class and thought he would adopt a harsh attitude toward the South and its leaders. They soon discovered their mistake.

Johnson was deeply impressed by the task he faced. He started to follow a policy toward the South that was almost as generous as Lincoln's had been. He gave full official recognition to the state governments that had been sponsored by Lincoln in Louisiana, Arkansas, and Tennessee — as well as to a shadowy loyal government that Lincoln had encouraged in Virginia. Beginning in May, 1865, he also issued proclamations which mapped a plan of reconstruction for the other seven states of the Confederacy. In only two ways did his plan differ from Lincoln's. First, Southerners who owned property valued at more than $20,000 were barred from taking the oath if they had voluntarily taken part in the war. Second, Johnson did not make clear what percentage of voters had to take an oath of allegiance before a state government could be started.

All through the summer of 1865 the job of reconstruction went forward. Johnson appointed temporary governors for the southern states. The states organized governments, elected officials, and chose members of Congress. By autumn, all the states except Texas had taken advantage of the President's proclamations. Enough of them ratified the Thirteenth Amendment (page 316) to make it a part of the Constitution.

─────── CHECK-UP ───────

What were the administration's plans for reconstruction?

1. What conditions existed in the South following the war?
2. What problems did the freed Negroes present? How did the South try to deal with them?
3. What were Lincoln's reconstruction plans? How did Congress react to them?
4. What was Andrew Johnson's background? What were his reconstruction plans? What progress was made in putting them into effect?

2 Congress Adopts a Harsh Program

Radical Republicans favor a harsh program. When Congress finally met in December, 1865, it turned immediately to the problem of southern reconstruction. The radical Republican leaders were in an angry mood. They disagreed with Lincoln's and Johnson's theory that the war was a rebellion of individuals, and that reconstruction could be accomplished through the President's pardoning powers. In place of the presidential program, Senator Sumner set forth his "state suicide" theory. According to this theory, the seceding states had lost all their rights and could no longer operate as states. Instead, they had slipped back to the condition of territories, and their return to the Union depended upon the will of Congress. Sumner also called for full civil and political rights for the Negro.

Sumner's proposals were strong, but less harsh than those of Thaddeus Stevens, the grim leader of the radical Republicans in the House. Stevens insisted that the southern states were no better than "conquered provinces," subject to the laws of war. He would not even grant the former southern states the standing of territories, since they had renounced the Constitution. In his opinion they were completely outside the Union.

Southern congressmen refused admittance. The mood of the new Congress was shown in its first act. Both houses refused to admit the newly elected members from the southern states. There were several reason for this action.

(1) The southern congressmen had been elected under governments declared legal by the President, but Congress was not willing to recognize those governments. The war had upset the normal relations between the President and the legislative department. As commander in chief of the army and navy, the President had possessed broad emergency powers, and Congress had been pushed aside. Now that the war was over, Congress was ready to insist upon its old authority.

(2) The congressmen whom the South had sent to Washington included Confederate leaders. The radical Republicans believed that this action indicated a defiant attitude on the part of the South. Also, they regarded the black codes as further defiant attempts to re-enslave the Negroes and rob them of equal civil rights.

(3) The Republicans felt that their political control was at stake. Before the war

Mississippi steam packet

five Negroes had been counted as three to determine the number of representatives for a state. Now, as freedmen, the Negroes were on the same basis as the whites. Thus, when congressional seats were determined the next time, the South would have thirteen more representatives in the House than it had before the war. Since the Johnson governments were controlled by white Southerners violently opposed to the Republican Party, they were certain to send Democrats to Congress. Something must be done, the Republicans felt, either to hold down Southern representation or to secure Republican congressmen from the South by giving Negroes the right to vote.

For these reasons, Congress rejected the work of Johnson. Instead, it appointed a joint committee on reconstruction. The fifteen members of the committee were to study the problem of the seceded states, then report on whether they had a right to representation.

Congress protects the rights of Negroes. While it waited for the report of the committee, Congress took steps to protect the Negro. Its first move was to extend the life and powers of the Freedmen's Bureau. This bureau had been set up by Congress in March of 1865 to provide food, clothing, and fuel to freedmen. President Johnson vetoed this bill,[1] as well as a Civil Rights Bill which declared that the Negroes were citizens of the United States, entitled to equal civil rights with the whites. The Civil Rights Bill carried out part of the program of the conservative Republicans; therefore Johnson's veto cost him their support. Thoroughly angry, Congress passed the Civil Rights Bill over the President's veto and forced the enactment of a new Freedmen's Bureau Bill in spite of his protest and his veto.

Congress approves the Fourteenth Amendment. Until the summer of 1866, then, the radicals spent most of their energy blocking the presidential program. After that they set out upon a definite

[1] Johnson's action was based on the belief that there was no need to expand the activities of the Bureau in peace time, and that some of the provisions of the bill were unconstitutional.

Andrew Johnson as President is shown in this early daguerreotype. Compare the furniture with that shown on page 194.

policy of punishing the South and protecting the rights of the Negroes. The joint committee on reconstruction proposed a constitutional amendment. After some changes, it was passed in both houses (June, 1866) and sent to the states for ratification as the Fourteenth Amendment. The amendment had four main parts:

(1) It opened with the statement that "all persons born or naturalized in the United States, and subject to the jurisdiction thereof, are citizens of the United States and of the state wherein they reside." Thus citizenship was given to the freedmen. The amendment then proceeded to safeguard the civil and political rights of citizens. It forbade any state to make or enforce "any law which shall abridge the privileges or immunities of citizens of the United States." It also provided that no state shall "deprive any person of life, liberty, or property, without due process of law," nor "deny to any person within its jurisdiction · the equal protection of the laws."

(2) The second section of the amend-

ment declared a penalty for any state which denied the right to vote to any adult male citizen except for "participation in rebellion or other crime." Such a state was to have its representation in the House of Representatives cut down. This clause was intended to force the southern states either to give freedmen the right to vote, or lose part of their representation in the House.

(3) The third section of the amendment was aimed at southern leaders who had taken an active part in the war. It barred from public office anyone who by taking part in the war against the union had violated his oath to support the Constitution. Such a person was to be barred from office until pardoned by a two-thirds vote of Congress.

(4) The fourth section of the amendment forbade the United States or any state to pay any part of the Confederate debt, or any claim for the loss or emancipation of any slave.

The South resists the program of Congress. The amendment was submitted to all the states, including those of the former Confederacy. In July, 1866, Tennessee ratified the amendment, and was promptly restored with full rights to the Union. The other Confederate states, however, rejected the amendment by overwhelming votes. They especially disliked the clause barring former southern leaders from office because of their part in the war. Having the support of the President, the southern states still hoped for a more generous plan of reconstruction.

Congress passes the Reconstruction Act. In the elections of 1866 the radicals greatly

A former
Southern
leader
returns
to Congress

increased their strength in Congress. They became bolder. Riots at Memphis and New Orleans in which several hundred Negroes were killed or wounded strengthened their belief that severe measures were needed. Since the southern states had rejected the Fourteenth Amendment, the joint congressional committee drew up a reconstruction act aimed at forcing the South to terms. When it was finally passed, this first Reconstruction Act grouped the ten states that were still out of the Union into five military districts. Each district was under a high ranking officer of the army. These officers had the power to preserve order and to enforce martial law if necessary.

The Reconstruction Act also outlined the steps by which the states could be freed from military control. Each state was to hold a convention of delegates chosen by all adult male citizens, without regard to race or color (except those deprived of the vote for taking part in the war). Each convention was required to adopt a state constitution that gave Negroes the right to vote. This constitution was to be approved by a majority of these same voters in the state and by Congress. The Fourteenth Amendment must then be ratified by the legislature elected under the new state constitution. When the amendment became a part of the Constitution of the United States, the state that had taken each of these steps would be allowed to return to its former position in the Union.

Through this plan, the Negro received the right to vote and enough whites were deprived of it to make sure that the South would be controlled by the radical Republicans. Johnson rejected the bill, but Congress immediately passed it over his veto (March 2, 1867).

Congress impeaches President Johnson. The feud between President Johnson and the radical Republicans was approaching a climax. The crisis came after Congress passed the Tenure of Office Act over Johnson's veto. Under this law the President could not dismiss any civil officer without consent of the Senate. When Johnson dismissed Secretary of War Stanton, who was co-operating with the radical Republicans, the House impeached the President for "high crimes and misdemeanors." The trial was held before the Senate, with Chief Justice Chase presiding.

The radical leaders were determined to get rid of Johnson and make room for one of their own group in the Presidency. As a result, their handling of the case was marked by political hostility rather than open-minded justice. However, every effort to prove Johnson guilty of "high crimes and misdemeanors" failed. In spite of strong pressure, seven Republican senators defied their leaders and voted with the Democrats for acquittal. The final vote was 35 to 19, one less than the two thirds required for conviction. The margin was slim, but it spared the country the disgrace of having a President removed from office for purely political reasons. Johnson reorganized his cabinet and finished his term in comparative quiet.

The southern states are readmitted. While the capital was stirred up by the impeachment trial, reconstruction was proceeding in the South along the lines laid down by the Reconstruction Act. Many of the civil officers of the Johnson state governments were removed. Delegates to constitutional conventions were elected, largely by Negro voters. New constitutions were drawn up under the provisions of the Reconstruction Act. New state legislatures, controlled by the radicals, ratified the Fourteenth Amendment. During the year 1868, most of the southern states were admitted to full standing in the Union — in time for the freedmen to vote for the Republican ticket in the presidential election of that year. The military governors turned the administration of the governments over to the new state and local officials, though federal troops were kept at hand.

The Fifteenth Amendment is ratified. The election of 1868 showed the radical Republicans the need of protecting the Negro votes in the South. The Republican candidate, General Grant, received 214 electoral votes to 80 for Horatio Seymour, the Democratic nominee, but the popular vote was close in many states. Without the

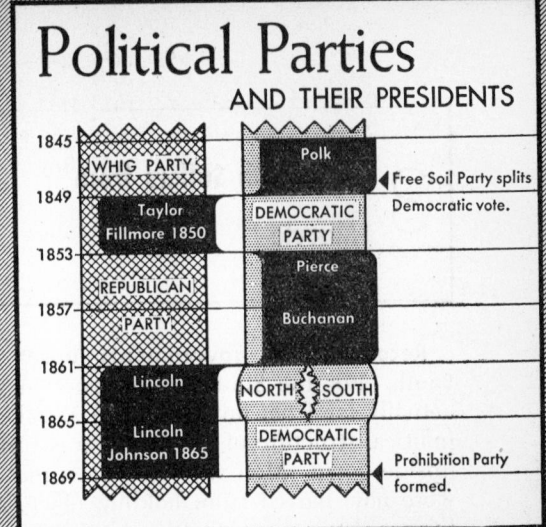

The Whig Party disappeared from national politics after 1854. Why? What important new party was formed about that time? Why were the Democrats defeated in 1848? In 1860?

Negro vote in the South, Grant would have received a minority of the popular vote and probably of the electoral vote too.

The radicals promptly made use of their control in Congress and in the southern states by adding the Fifteenth Amendment to the Constitution. This amendment provided that the right to vote should not be restricted in any way because of "race, color, or previous condition of servitude." The last three southern states to be restored to the Union — Virginia, Mississippi, and Texas — were required to ratify this amendment. It became a part of the Constitution in 1870. So far as the radicals were concerned, the political reconstruction of the southern states was just about complete.

———— CHECK-UP ————

How and why did Congress take charge of reconstruction?

1. Why did the President and Congress come into conflict? What were the Congressional theories of reconstruction?
2. What were the various provisions of the Fourteenth Amendment? Of the Reconstruction Act?
3. Why did Congress impeach Johnson? With what results? What were the results of the election of 1868?

3 The South Suffers from Misrule

Reconstruction governments upset the South. For the South, reconstruction was actually far from finished. The social and political structure of the South was turned upside down. Men who had been masters were now barred from holding office, and former slaves were given an active part in the government. In South Carolina, for instance, in 1868 about two thirds of the members of the lower house of the legislature were ex-slaves. The freedmen in turn were under the control of *carpetbaggers* and *scalawags*. Carpetbaggers were northern politicians who came into the South, carrying everything they owned in a carpetbag, to take advantage of the freedmen's new political power. Scalawags were white Southerners who helped the carpetbaggers with their schemes. The freedmen representatives, since they had little or no education, were easy victims for the carpetbaggers.

The program of carpetbag government which the radicals forced upon the southern states introduced a period of shameful dishonesty and misrule. This political corruption continued in the various states anywhere from two to nine years.

Reconstruction governments squander public funds. Though the members of the reconstruction legislatures owned little or no property and paid practically no taxes, they took advantage of their power to appropriate large sums of money and spend them recklessly. For example, the South Carolina legislature poured out large sums for unnecessary and expensive furnishings at the state capitol. In Arkansas, the expenses of the government increased 1500 per cent, and in Louisiana the state debt was increased by nearly $34,000,000 in three and one-half years. Millions of dollars were granted to railroads in North Carolina — but not a mile of track was laid.

Teacher, Freedmen's Bureau School

Not all of the legislation by the reconstruction governments was bad. Money was spent on roads, bridges, and public buildings, and on encouraging the education of both whites and freedmen. On the whole, however, the money and credit of the southern states were wasted in graft and wild spending at a time when wise financial policies were vitally needed to rebuild the stricken South. Most of the debts created by the reconstruction governments were later outlawed.

Southern whites resort to violence. Some southern whites, unable to improve conditions in a lawful and orderly way, decided to go outside the law. Their most effective weapons were secret organizations, such as the Ku Klux Klan and the Knights of the White Camellia. The Ku Klux Klan started as a social club in a small Tennessee town in 1866. Gradually it spread all through the South. The main purpose of the order was to drive out the carpetbag governments and to bring back southern white supremacy. Its methods were very effective.

Riding forth at night dressed in white, with their horses' hoofs muffled, the klansmen were an awesome sight to the Negroes and to the whites who worked with the Negroes. The first step was usually to give warnings against political activity in some way that would arouse the superstitions of the uneducated Negroes. If these warnings were not heeded, the victims were flogged, their cabins were burned, or they were maimed or even murdered. The state and federal governments tried to check the lawless raids of the klansmen. Federal troops were sent into the South to watch over federal elections. But the Negroes, the carpetbaggers, and the scalawags were thoroughly frightened. Finally, to enforce obedience to the Fourteenth and Fifteenth Amendments, Congress passed acts (1870-1871) which gave the President power to use force to put down "unlawful combinations."

White control is restored in the South. The Ku Klux Klan and similar societies, however, obtained the results they wanted. By terrifying the freedmen, they kept great numbers from voting and prepared the way for the return of white control in the South. As each year went by, more and more young whites, to whom the disqualifying clause of the Fourteenth Amendment did not apply, reached voting age. At the same time, people in the North gave less and less support to the rule of force which the radicals had imposed upon the South.

By 1871, Tennessee, North Carolina, and Georgia were under white control. Congress helped restore home rule in the other southern states by passing the Amnesty Act in 1872. This act did away with the political limitations of the Fourteenth Amendment for all but a few hundred Southerners. Some of the carpetbag governments, however, went on for several more years. Home rule did not come to South Carolina, Florida, and Louisiana until after the election of 1876. In 1877 the last federal troops were withdrawn from the South.

Southern Negroes are barred from voting. For a long time, southern Democrats held down the Negro vote by terrorism, or offset it by ballot-box stuffing and other illegal means. Finally, beginning about 1890, the same results began to be achieved by law. Southern legislatures passed laws which prevented a person from voting unless he paid a poll tax and could read and interpret passages from the state constitution. The laws were aimed, of course, at the Negroes, most of whom had no property or education and little chance of getting either. There were many poor, illiterate whites who could not pass such tests, but some southern states put into their laws what was called the *grandfather clause*. This clause provided that if a man could not meet the property and educa-

tional tests, he still had the right to vote if he had been eligible to do so on January 1, 1867, or if he was the son or grandson of such a voter. Under such laws, large numbers of Negroes were barred from voting, but the representation of the southern states in Congress was not reduced in accordance with the provisions of the Fourteenth Amendment.

The South experiences further changes. War and reconstruction brought important social and economic changes in the South. The planter class was ruined. "God only knows the full tide of misery which has set in on these people," an observer wrote of the planters around Charleston. The plantation owner's money and his Confederate bonds were worthless. His slaves were gone. He had nothing left but his ravaged lands, which were of little value without workers to cultivate them. On the other hand, the middle-class farmer was now better off because he could increase his holdings of land without much expense.

The freedmen, of course, faced severe handicaps. But they started to make progress. Some remained in their cabins, worked as free laborers on the plantation, and settled down to a normal farm life. Others became *sharecroppers* on estates

A classroom at Atlanta University in the late 1800's shows one of many efforts to provide education for the freedmen.

The success of the South in solving the problems of reconstruction are reflected in this spectacular modern photograph, which shows the public cotton warehouse and grain elevator at New Orleans. Compare this picture with the one on page 245.

which were cut up into small plots and leased on shares to former slaves or poor whites. Under this system, the man who owned the land furnished the seed, tools, and domestic animals, while the local storekeeper furnished supplies on credit until the sharecropper could harvest his crop.

General interest in education grew. Southern states, helped by the Freedmen's Bureau and by private individuals and organizations, slowly provided public education for the Negroes. By 1880, 20 per cent of the Negroes had learned to read and write, and by 1900 more than half were classed as literate. Institutions of higher learning were established for them too, such as Howard, Fisk, and Atlanta universities, and Hampton and Tuskegee institutes.

The reconstruction program delays recovery. Looking back at the years which followed the War Between the States, we can see clearly that the policy which Congress followed did not speed reconstruction in the South. Instead of helping the southern states return to normal conditions, it held back their recovery for at least a generation. The misgovernment forced on the South aroused a feeling of hatred toward the North, traces of which still exist. The radical Republican leaders had thought their program would build a strong Republican organization among the southern freedmen. Instead, the Democratic Party grew stronger. For some time, in fact, we have used the term "the Solid South" to mean that the whole South usually votes Democratic. The attempt to force Negro rule upon the South also delayed settlement of the economic and social problems existing between the two races. Finally, the "crime of reconstruction" left as its chief effect a strong sectional feeling among many Americans.

——— CHECK-UP ———

Why did the South suffer misrule during the reconstruction period?

1. What was the nature of the southern reconstruction governments? In what ways were they bad?

2. What was the Ku Klux Klan? Its purpose?
3. How was white rule restored to the South? How did the whites bar the Negroes from voting?
4. What economic problems faced both whites and Negroes in the South after reconstruction?

CHAPTER REVIEW

Terms to Understand

freedmen
civil rights
apprentices
military governor

martial law
home rule
poll tax
sharecropper

People and Things to Know About

"the black codes"
ten per cent plan
Wade-Davis Bill
radical Republicans
Thaddeus Stevens
Fourteenth Amendment
Freedmen's Bureau
"Solid South"

Civil Rights Bill
Tenure of Office Act
Andrew Johnson
Carpetbaggers
Scalawags
Ku Klux Klan
Amnesty Act
grandfather clause

Historic Dates to Identify

1865   1867   1877

Questions to Discuss

1. On what grounds did both Congress and the President claim the right to reconstruct the South? What earlier instances can you recall in which Congress and the President had come into conflict?
2. Compare the following:
   (a) The Lincoln-Johnson and the radical plans of reconstruction.
   (b) The use of the terms "radical" and "conservative" in 1866 and today.
   (c) The Thirteenth, Fourteenth, and Fifteenth Amendments.
   (d) The statements in the Fourteenth Amendment and in the Dred Scott decision on citizenship.
   (e) The relations of Johnson with the Republicans and Tyler with the Whigs.

Questions to Discuss (Cont.)

3. Why did the radicals finally have to set up military governments to carry out their program?
4. Do you think that the radical Republicans went too far in identifying the interests of their party with the interests of the country? Why was it important to the radicals that Negroes have full political and civil rights?
5. Would you have voted for the conviction of Johnson had you been a member of the United States Senate? Why or why not?

Other Things to Do

1. Debate: *Resolved*, That the southern states were justified in passing their "black codes." (You can find examples of the "black codes" in Commager's *Documents of American History*.)
2. Until fairly recently Johnson has been one of the most criticized of our Presidents. Prepare a report on more recent views of him. One reference to use in this connection is Claude Bowers' *The Tragic Era*.
3. Prepare a talk on the nature and activities of the Ku Klux Klan. See Fleming's *The Sequel of Appomattox*.
4. Prepare a report on the position of Negroes with regard to civil and political rights in the United States today. In this connection, try to find out what gains the Negroes have made as a result of Supreme Court decisions and congressional and state legislation. Use the *Readers' Guide to Periodical Literature*.
*5. Make a chronological list of the chief steps in reconstruction from the ten per cent plan to the readmission of the southern states.

TO INCREASE YOUR UNDERSTANDING OF UNIT FOUR

Unit Summary

1. During the 1840's territorial expansion became a burning public issue. To the ever-present restlessness of adventurous Americans were added an interest in achieving America's "manifest destiny" and a desire on the part of Southerners to acquire territory open to slavery. Texas was annexed, a treaty with Great Britain gave the United States Oregon as far north as the forty-ninth parallel, and the Mexican Cession was obtained as a result of the Mexican War. The Gadsden Purchase in 1853 rounded out the nation's continental boundaries.

2. Expansion, however, brought up the troublesome question as to whether the newly acquired territories should be open to slaveholders. Various solutions were advanced but brought no agreement. The Compromise of 1850 resulted in gains for both the North and the South and postponed serious trouble but offered no final solution to the problem.

3. Four years later, with the adoption of the Kansas-Nebraska Act, the quarrel flared up once more. Bitterness over the issue not only was present in "bleeding Kansas," but was reflected in Congress and throughout the nation. Year by year the gulf between the industrial North and the agricultural South grew deeper. When the new Republican Party elected Lincoln on a platform opposing the extension of slavery in the territories, many Southerners became convinced that their way of life was threatened if they remained in the Union. Following the lead of South Carolina, eleven states in all seceded from the Union and formed the Confederacy.

4. Last minute attempts at compromise proved useless. The Confederate attack on Fort Sumter in 1861 signaled the beginning of armed conflict. By 1863 the North had succeeded in opening up the Mississippi River, but had been unable to capture the Confederate capital of Richmond. Superb leadership and gallant fighting on the part of the Confederates kept the war going until 1865. Eventually the superior resources of the North, together with an effective blockade of the southern coast line and the failure of European powers to aid the Confederacy, turned the tide in favor of the North. The bitter struggle strained the resources of both sections but left its deepest scars upon the South, where most of the fighting occurred.

5. Once the struggle was ended, the nation faced the difficult task of reconstruction. President Lincoln introduced a generous plan for reinstating the seceded states. Following his untimely death, President Johnson attempted to carry out a similar plan but was checked by Congress, under the control of the radical Republicans. Instead, Congress insisted upon a much harsher program of reconstruction, which would punish southern whites and protect the political rights of the freedmen. Eventually all the seceded states were readmitted to the Union, but not before the South had suffered deeply from misgovernment under the reconstruction governments supported by federal troops. Politically, the Reconstruction Era resulted in a solid Democratic South.

Summary of Important Dates

1836 Texas wins independence.
1845 Texas annexed by United States.
1846 Settlement of Oregon boundaries.
 Mexican War breaks out.
1848 United States obtains Mexican Cession following the end of the Mexican War.
1849 California Gold Rush.
1850 Compromise of 1850.
1853 Gadsden Purchase completes "manifest destiny."
1854 Kansas-Nebraska Act passed.
 Beginnings of Republican Party.
1857 Dred Scott decision.
1858 Lincoln-Douglas debates.
1859 John Brown's raid on Harper's Ferry.
1860 Election of Abraham Lincoln.
 South Carolina secedes.
1861 Firing on Fort Sumter begins the War Between the States.
1862 Battle between the *Monitor* and the *Merrimac.*
1863 Emancipation Proclamation.
 Battle of Gettysburg.
 Surrender of Vicksburg.
1865 End of the War Between the States.
 Assassination of Lincoln.
 Thirteenth Amendment adopted.
1866 Fourteenth Amendment proposed by Congress.
1867 Reconstruction Act passed.
1870 Fifteenth Amendment adopted.
1877 Final withdrawal of troops from the South.

Unit Activities

1. Make a list of the chief personalities who were involved in the controversy between the North and the South from 1850 to 1861. Write a brief explanation of how each was concerned with the issue.

2. Write an essay on the subject "The causes of the War Between the States." You should do further research on this, for it is still a topic over which there is much disagreement.

3. Write a short paragraph commenting upon the statement that the War Between the States marked the end of an era in American history.

4. Choose some activity dealing with Lincoln. Read one of the many novels based on his life and work, read or write a poem about him, prepare an imaginary interview with him with regard to one of the great decisions he was forced to make, write a newspaper editorial upon his life and services for publication after his assassination. Perhaps you can suggest some other activity on this great democratic leader.

For Further Reading

Original Sources

Angle, Paul, *The Lincoln Reader*. Rutgers University Press. The life of Lincoln as told through source accounts and important secondary accounts.

Commager, H. S., ed., *Documents of American History*. Crofts. Nos. 165–69, 174–267.

Hulbert, A. B., *The Forty Niners*. Little, Brown. Migration over the Oregon Trail as told in the authentic diaries of actual forty-niners.

Nevins, A., and Commager, H. S., eds., *The Heritage of America*. Little, Brown. Nos. 107–32, 139–90.

Parkman, Francis, *The Oregon Trail*. Longmans. The classic which tells of Parkman's adventures in the West.

Pease, T. C., and Roberts, A. S., eds., *Selected Readings in American History*. Harcourt. Nos. 134–95.

General References

Adams, J. T., *The Epic of America*. Little, Brown. Chapters 8 and 9.

Bailey, Thomas A., *A Diplomatic History of the United States*. Appleton-Century-Crofts. Chapters 15, 16, 17, 21, 22, 23.

Faulkner, H. U., *American Economic History*. Harper. Chapters 16 and 17.

Hicks, J. D., *The American Nation*. Houghton. Chapters 1 and 2.

Morison, S. E., and Commager, H. S., *The Growth of the American Republic*. Oxford. Vol. I, Chapters 29 to 37. Vol. II, Chapters 1 and 2.

Riegel, Robert E., *America Moves West*. Holt. Chapters 22 to 30.

Special Accounts

Adams, J. T., *America's Tragedy*. Scribner. A critical interpretation of the War Between the States and its aftermath.

American Guide Series. Writers Program of the W.P.A., *Texas* and *The Oregon Trail*. Hastings House.

American Nation Series. Harper. Chadwick, F. E., *Causes of the Civil War*. Dunning, W. A., *Reconstruction, Political and Economic*. Garrison, G. P., *Westward Extension*. Hosmer, J. K., *The Appeal to Arms*. Smith, T. C., *Parties and Slavery*.

Bill, A. H., *Rehearsal for Conflict*. Knopf. Deals with Mexican War as a training ground for the men who were to fight the War Between the States.

Bowers, Claude, *The Tragic Era*. Houghton. An analysis of the reconstruction period which is highly critical of the radical Republicans.

Chronicles of America Series. Yale University Press. Bolton, H. E., *The Spanish Borderlands*. Fleming, W. L., *The Sequel of Appomattox*. Macy, J., *The Anti-Slavery Crusade*. Stephenson, N. W., *Abraham Lincoln and the Union, The Day of the Confederacy*, and *Texas and the Mexican War*. Thompson, H., *The New South*. White, S. E., *The Forty-Niners*. Wood, W., *Captains of the Civil War*.

Cleland, R. G., *From Wilderness to Empire*. Knopf. A history of California from 1542 to 1900.

De Voto, Bernard, *The Year of Decision: 1846*. Little, Brown. A narrative history of one of the most eventful years in American history.

Dick, Everett, *Vanguards of the Frontier*, Appleton-Century-Crofts. Contains chapters on the Mormon migration and the Santa Fe trail.

Dowdey, Clifford, *Experiment in Rebellion*. Doubleday. Behind-the-scenes stories of the personalities who figured in the War Between the States.

Gunther, John, *Inside U.S.A.* Harper. The historical backgrounds and present-day descriptions of many of the areas and states you have been studying.

Hendrick, Burton J., *Bulwark of the Republic.* Little, Brown. Devotes much attention to the struggle over slavery and reconstruction as they affected the Constitution.

Hendrick, Burton J., *Statesmen of the Lost Cause.* Little, Brown. Deals with the non-military problems of the South and the men who handled them.

Horn, Stanley F., *The Gallant Rebel.* Rutgers University Press. The fabulous cruise of the Confederate commerce raider, the *Shenandoah.*

Leech, Margaret, *Reveille in Washington.* Harper. Interesting sidelights on life in the northern capital during the war.

McCaleb, W. F., *The Conquest of the West.* Prentice-Hall. Gives attention to Texas and the Mexican War.

Milton, G. F., *Age of Hate.* Coward. A history which attempts to re-evaluate Johnson.

Milton, G. F., *Eve of Conflict.* Houghton. A history of the slavery controversy which is sympathetic to Stephen A. Douglas.

Minnegerode, Meade, *The Fabulous Forties.* Garden City. Contains an interesting chapter on the California gold rush.

Mirsky, Jeannette, *The Westward Crossings.* Knopf. Stories of the great transcontinental explorers.

Monaghan, Jay, *The Overland Trail.* Trails of America Series. Bobbs. Events and developments growing out of the use of the Oregon Trail.

Perry, George E., *Texas, A World in Itself.* McGraw. Interesting stories about Texas.

Rivers of America Series. Rinehart. Dana, Julian, *The Sacramento: River of Gold.* Davidson, Donald, *The Tennessee.* Morgan, Daniel L., *The Humboldt: Highroad to the West.*

Imaginative Writing

Benét, S. V., *John Brown's Body.* Doubleday. A book-length narrative poem of the War Between the States.

Crane, Stephen, *The Red Badge of Courage.* Appleton-Century-Crofts (also Modern Library). The War Between the States as it appeared to a private who was torn between pride and fear.

Dowdey, C., *Where My Love Sleeps.* Little, Brown. The last year of fighting around Petersburg and Richmond.

Garth, David, *Gray Canaan.* Putnam. A story of the fortunes of the Confederacy during the summer of 1862.

Glasgow, Ellen, *The Battleground.* Doubleday. Life in the South before and during the war.

Gorman, H. S., *The Wine of San Lorenzo.* Farrar. A lively account of the battles of the Mexican War.

Henkle, H. B., *Deep River.* Harcourt. The story of a Georgian who is opposed to slavery and secession.

Hough, Emerson, *The Covered Wagon.* Grosset (also Pocket Books). Adventures of a party making the trip to California on the Overland Trail.

Jackson, Helen H., *Ramona.* Little, Brown. The effect on the Indians of California of the coming of the Americans.

Lynn, Margaret, *Land of Promise.* Little, Brown. Kansas settlement during the slave-free struggle in that state.

Mitchell, Margaret, *Gone with the Wind.* Macmillan. A novel which has now become a classic on the War Between the States.

Morrow, Mrs. H. W., *We Must March.* Grosset. An historical novel of the American settlement of Oregon.

Robertson, C. N., *Fire Bell in the Night.* Holt. A novel about the underground railroad.

Stone, I., *Immortal Wife.* Doubleday. A novel about Jessie Benton Frémont, the wife of the explorer.

Street, J. H., *By Valor and Arms.* Sun Dial Press. An ironclad vessel destroys part of Farragut's fleet and delays the capture of Vicksburg.

White, L. T., *Look Away, Look Away.* Random. A story about southerners who went to South America after the war.

White, S. E., *Gold.* Doubleday. A tale of the forty-niners.

Williams, Ben Ames, *A House Divided.* Houghton. A lengthy but highly interesting novel of the War Between the States.

Young, Stark, *So Red the Rose.* Scribner. A moving novel of the War Between the States.

Biography

Bradford, Gamaliel, *Lee, the American.* Houghton. A short biography and study of Robert E. Lee.

Bradford, Gamaliel, *Union Portraits* and *Confederate Portraits.* Houghton. Political and military figures of the war.

Charnwood, Lord, *Abraham Lincoln.* Holt

(also Pocket Books). A biography of Lincoln by an Englishman.

Daugherty, James, *Abraham Lincoln*. Viking. An easy-to-read biography of Lincoln.

Daugherty, James, *Their Weight in Wildcats*. Houghton. Biographies of great American frontiersmen.

Freeman, Douglas S., *R. E. Lee*. Scribner. The finest biography of the great southerner.

James, Marquis, *The Raven*. Bobbs. The life story of Sam Houston.

Mayo, Barbara, *Henry Clay*. Rinehart. Stresses the public life of Clay.

Rourke, Constance, *Davy Crockett*. Harcourt. The story of an almost legendary character.

Sandburg, Carl, *Abe Lincoln Grows up*. Harcourt. A biography of Abe Lincoln the boy that makes him seem an intimate friend.

Thomason, J. W., *J. E. B. Stuart*. Scribners. The great Confederate cavalry leader.

Todd, Helen, *A Man Named Grant*. Hough-

ton. An intimate portrait of the man who rose from failure to lead the Union armies.

Wiley, B. I., *The Life of Johnny Reb*. Bobbs. The life of the common soldier in the Confederate armies.

Pictures

Adams, J. T., ed., *Album of American History*. Scribner. Vols. II and III.

Butterfield, Roger, *The American Past*. Simon and Schuster. A pictorial and textual history of the United States "from Concord to Hiroshima."

Meredith, Roy, *Mr. Lincoln's Cameraman*. Scribner. The famous photographs of the War Between the States taken by Mathew Brady.

Pageant of American Series. Yale University Press. Bassett, J. S., *Makers of a New Nation*. Gabriel, R. H., *Lure of the Frontier*.

Ogg, F. A., *Builders of the Republic*.

 # Sidelights on American History

Founder of Texas. Though Stephen Fuller Austin was a less spectacular figure than Sam Houston or Davy Crockett, he would probably be rated by historians as Texas' most useful citizen. His father, Moses Austin, had obtained from the Spanish government in Texas a vast tract of land, with the right to establish on it a colony of 300 families. But Moses Austin died before he could carry out his plan. Stephen, schooled in Connecticut and trained in the law of both Louisiana and Arkansas, negotiated with the Spaniards for the right to complete his father's project. There had been squatters and border-jumpers on the Texas territory, but Stephen F. Austin's American settlement was the first legal one. Though probably nobody suspected it at the time, the little colony of 300 American families was the beginning of the end of Spanish rule north of the Rio Grande.

When Mexico established her independence from Spain (1821), Austin gained almost unlimited powers and influence from the rather weak Mexican government. Mexico put its stamp of approval on his rights to the lands in Texas. He was also made a military commander, chief justice, lawmaker, and chief

civil executive. With absolute power over immigration, he could open the door to as many new settlers as he pleased.

Austin was in charge of everything. He planned the system of land holdings, mapped the country, and promoted the building of schools, sawmills, and cotton gins. In return for bringing in more families of settlers, he received additional land for his own use. The settlers, on the other hand, paid him fees for his services to them.

Austin was slow to adopt the idea that Texas should be independent from Mexico. In fact, he is said to have favored a policy of remaining under Mexican authority and supporting the forward-thinking Mexican Liberal Party. But when the Texas revolution did come, Austin gave it his active backing, even arranging loans and credit in Washington for the newborn state. He stood for election as its first president, but was defeated by the more colorful General Sam Houston. Austin died soon afterward, at the early age of forty-three.

Stephen F. Austin worked sincerely for the development of Texas under Mexican rule. When the break with Mexico came, he urged that Texas remain independent of the United

States. His life is sometimes called a contradiction in results, for it was Austin's colonization of Texas that made it possible for that great territory to become a part of the Union. Texas honored him by giving his name to the capital of the state.

The Bounty Jumping Game. Soldiers in World War II sometimes spoke of desertion as "going over the hill." In the War Between the States the troops called a certain kind of desertion "jumping the bounty." The bounty was a cash reward for voluntary enlistment. Early in the war, the North offered $100 to every man who enlisted. Later the amount ran as high as $400. To this sum, states and counties often added more. Sometimes a man could fatten his wallet by $900 to $1000 almost overnight.

To many a war-weary and penniless soldier the bounty suggested a scheme for easy money. "Tomorrow," he thought, "instead of falling in again on the march, why don't I just fade into the bushes? I can get civilian clothes, travel at night, and take a new name. Then I'll re-enlist in another regiment — and collect another bounty." One bounty jumper collected bounty money 32 times. In some regiments over half the enlisted men jumped the bounty.

The first draft laws of the war permitted a certain undemocratic procedure. If a drafted man could find a substitute to take his place in the army, he did not have to go to war. This practice gave rise to "substitute brokers," enlistment agents who made a living by finding substitutes for draftees. If you were drafted, you might pay a broker to find someone who would take your place in the army. The substitute enlisted, accepted the bounty, and gave the broker a percentage. Then he deserted as soon as he could, and reported to the broker for another enlistment and another chance to jump the bounty.

The bounty system was one of the principal causes of the high rate of desertions in the War Between the States. In the Union army alone there were over 260,000 cases of desertion.

Old Git-there-fustest. During World War II it was often said that the way to win battles was to "git there fustest with the mostest." This quotation goes back to the time of the War Between the States, and the man to whom the statement is attributed was Nathan Bedford Forrest of Tennessee. Forrest was a famous cavalry general of the Confederacy, who developed raiding to a high art. He led what in World War II would have been called commando raids.

His raids pierced the Union lines and raised havoc with communications and supply depots in the rear. Forrest's specialty was to use horses to "git there" but then to "fit" on foot. Often no "fitting" was necessary, because the Confederate commander had a habit of terrifying a garrison by insisting on immediate surrender, with the threat that he would grant no quarter after the raid had begun.

Forrest was as daring in personal conduct as he was in military tactics. In the heat of battle he would forget himself and rush in to fight at the head of his troopers. Twenty-nine horses were shot from under him. In one fight, after being wounded so severely that he couldn't sit in the saddle, he led his mounted raiders in a buggy. His courage was the kind that did not need the excitement of battle to spur it on, however. The general was once threatened with lynching by a mob. He had no weapon on him but a knife. By sheer force of will and the power of his words he over-awed the mob, until at last it broke up and slunk away. Moral courage, so much rarer than physical courage, was also his. On a certain occasion he was challenged to a duel over a matter in which he knew himself to be in the wrong. He did the unheard-of thing — he apologized.

GLANCING BACK OVER PART ONE

CHRISTOPHER COLUMBUS, sailing for Asia, discovered the New World in 1492. Spain, France, England, and other European nations began to colonize this vast area. Spain became strong in Central and South America, while England at length became the dominant power in North America.

Between the settlement of Jamestown, Virginia, in 1607 and the inauguration of George Washington as their first President in 1789, the American people increased to nearly four million in number. Their experience in government, starting with the House of Burgesses in Virginia, had continued through the establishment of their independence, the formation of state governments, and the adoption of the Constitution. Nine out of ten Americans had established a good standard of living based on farming. The rest earned livelihoods from fishing, trade, shipbuilding, and small but thriving industries. Meantime, new ideas of social equality were stirring in people's minds.

Important developments — political, economic, social and cultural — from the founding of the government through the War between the States are summarized below and on page 338.

	POLITICAL	ECONOMIC	SOCIAL AND CULTURAL
	George Washington (1789-1797: Federalist) started the federal government under the Constitution. Courts were set up, department heads appointed, and the Cabinet developed. Through a period of troubled foreign affairs, neutrality was preserved.	Public debt funded. A national bank begun. The tariff levied. A sound currency established. Cotton gin invented.	The rich, well-born, and talented made up the Federalists. Farmers and workers in towns and cities joined the Republicans.
	John Adams (1797-1801: Federalist), in spite of his merits, was not a popular President. In the face of threats of war, he managed to preserve peace. Passage of the Alien and Sedition Acts by the government aroused violent protests.	The financial policies of Hamilton continued. Excise taxes and tariff brought high revenue. Bank stock rose. Prosperity continued.	National capital permanently established in Washington. Naturalization for citizenship made more difficult.
	Thomas Jefferson (1801-1809: Republican), became President as political power shifted from the rich and well-born to the small farmers and workers. Louisiana was purchased and explored. Efforts to protect American neutral rights failed.	Economy stressed in government. Excise taxes repealed. National debt reduced. Tariff continued. Prosperity declined.	Democratic practices introduced at capital. Former naturalization law restored. *Clermont* points way to improved travel.
	James Madison (1809-1817: Republican) became President in the midst of the struggle over American neutral rights. He was no match in diplomacy for the wily Napoleon, who enticed the United States into the War of 1812 with England.	Loss of English trade promoted industry. War finances difficult. A second bank begun. A protective tariff enacted.	Westerners eager to expand into Canada and Florida. Irving published *Knickerbocker's History of New York*.
	James Monroe (1817-1825: Republican) was President during the Era of Good Feelings, when party politics disappeared. It was a period of national growth and enthusiasm. At this time, also, the Monroe Doctrine was proclaimed.	Panic of 1819. The bank upheld by the Supreme Court. Clay proposed the American System. National road opened.	Westward migration increased after war. New states admitted. Slavery an issue in Missouri. First high school begun.
	John Quincy Adams (1825-1829: National Republican) was chosen by the House when no candidate received a majority of the electoral vote. Conflicting sectional interests and Adams' own personality made his administration difficult.	Tariff of Abominations enacted. Erie Canal opened. Baltimore and Ohio Railroad Company organized.	20,000 immigrants arrived yearly. Workingmen formed political parties.

	POLITICAL	ECONOMIC	SOCIAL AND CULTURAL
	**Andrew Jackson** (1829-1837: Democratic) was the most colorful of American Presidents. Though referred to as "King Andrew," he was the champion of democracy. The nation was strengthened at home, and American prestige increased abroad.	Internal improvements checked. South Carolina raised nullification issue over the tariff. National bank crippled.	Garrison forced the Abolitionist issue. Early labor unions organized. Penny newspapers appeared.
	**Martin Van Buren** (1837-1841: Democratic), a shrewd politician, was elected with the understanding that he would tread in Jackson's footsteps. But the Panic of 1837 troubled his administration. His defeat in 1840 ended the Jacksonian era.	Panic of 1837 swept the country. Depression and unemployment spread. Independent treasury established.	Population reached 17 million. Horace Mann improved public schools. Schools of higher education increased.
	**William H. Harrison** (1841: Whig) became the candidate in 1840 because Henry Clay had too many political enemies and his views were too well known. Harrison was elected after a spirited campaign, but he died a month after inauguration. **John Tyler** (1841-1845: Whig) succeeded to the Presidency. He was a states-rights Democrat, but hostility to Jackson made him a Whig. He soon broke with his cabinet and was read out of the party. At this time the Maine boundary was fixed.	Plantation system extended westward. Better tools and machines aided farming. Industrial revolution made progress. Independent treasury ended. Tyler opposed bank and protective tariff. Over 85% of world's cotton grown in U.S.	Immigration increased to 100,000 per year. Rhode Island became 40% urban. Emerson's *Essays* published. Telegraph introduced. Sewage and water systems started. Social reforms began.
	**James K. Polk** (1845-1849: Democratic) became President on the issue of territorial expansion. Tyler stole his thunder by annexing Texas, but Polk acquired Oregon to the 49th parallel, and, after the Mexican War, added the Mexican Cession Territory.	Howe's sewing machine appeared. Hoe press in use. Gold rush of 1849. Wilmot Proviso proposed.	Anesthetics introduced. Smithsonian Institution founded. Women's rights convention held. Temperance reform.
	**Zachary Taylor** (1849-1850: Whig) was also chosen because his views on important questions of the day were not too well known. Both major parties dodged the leading issue, which was the extension of slavery into the territories. **Millard Fillmore** (1850-1853: Whig) became President when Taylor died in the midst of the struggle over the Compromise of 1850. The quarrel over slavery seemed to be ended. California was added to the Union as a free state.	Cotton established as "king" in the South. Texas received payment of ten million dollars. Factory system developed rapidly. Period of business prosperity. Railroad mileage expanded. Federal land grants aided railroads.	Unskilled workers got low pay for long hours. Irish immigration increased. New styles in art and architecture. Mail service improved. Immigration opposed. *Uncle Tom's Cabin* published. Labor unions revived.
	**Franklin Pierce** (1853-1857: Democratic) favored the continuation of the terms of the Compromise of 1850. Yet his administration was soon disturbed by the fateful Kansas-Nebraska Bill and by civil war in Kansas.	Bessemer steel-making process developed. Golden era of clipper ships. Trade opened with Japan.	400,000 immigrants per year. Longfellow's *Hiawatha*, Whitman's *Leaves of Grass*, Thoreau's *Walden* published.
	**James Buchanan** (1857-1861: Democratic) was President when the crisis of secession confronted the nation. The Supreme Court held that all territories were open to slavery. Buchanan tried to maintain existing conditions until he was out of office.	New England ahead in production of textiles. Middle States increased iron and steel output. West produced farm machinery and food.	American population reached 30 million. Helper's *Impending Crisis* published.
	**Abraham Lincoln** (1861-1865: Republican) faced an open break with the Confederacy. It took four years of war to show that the Union was not a compact of states from which a state could secede. Relations with England and France were strained.	Tariff, taxes raised. Homestead Act passed. Greenbacks issued. Industry grew in North. Southern economy crippled.	Slavery abolished. Telegraph supplanted Pony Express. Sanitary Commission cared for wounded. Morrill Act passed.
	**Andrew Johnson** (1865-1869: Unionist) succeeded to the Presidency after Lincoln's assassination. He started to follow Lincoln's lenient plan of reconstruction, but ran into a hostile Congress which favored the freedmen but was harsh to the South.	Planter aristocracy ruined in South. Position of middle class farmers improved. Freedmen made a living as sharecroppers.	Status of freedmen became a problem. Educational facilities set up for freedmen. Vassar, college for women, opened.

Part Two

MODERN AMERICA EMERGES

LOOKING AHEAD IN PART TWO

Before you begin to read Part Two of this book, you have an opportunity in this page and the next to look ahead to the more important events which took place in American history from the close of the War Between the States to the late 1800's. First there is a general statement about the importance of the larger developments in this period. Then follows a listing of specific events which took place during the various presidential administrations. These have been put in separate columns according to whether they were political, economic, or social and cultural events, just as they were in "Glancing Back Over Part One," pages 337 and 338. If you will study these columns before reading Part Two, you will be better able to keep in mind important interlocking developments during this period.

THE PERIOD in American history from 1865 to the late nineteenth century was an important one, particularly in economic development. It was in this period that our great industries began to grow — steel, oil, meat-packing, milling, and others. This industrial development went hand in hand with great strides in transportation and communication. As businesses grew until they became national in scope, labor struggled to protect its interest by building up its bargaining power. Farmers were losing their place of first importance in the American economy, and were discontented because of falling prices for agricultural products. On the political scene, the Republican Party had successfully accomplished the purpose for which it had been formed — resisting the extension of slavery. It was now struggling to keep the control it had won. In general, it had the upper hand over the Democratic Party, which had to overcome the charge that it had been the party of those who tried to break the Union. In foreign affairs the United States upheld the Monroe Doctrine and generally kept free of foreign entanglements. Relations between the United States and Great Britain, not too good at the close of the war, became more friendly. During this period also, American culture was rounding out, and some progress was made in helping the poor and oppressed.

POLITICAL	ECONOMIC	SOCIAL AND CULTURAL
1869-1877 (*Republican*)		

POLITICAL

Ulysses S. Grant, a great general, was far less successful as President. He had been generous to the Confederates at Appomattox, but in the White House he became a willing tool of those who wished to deal harshly with the South. Surrounded by cunning politicians, Grant seemed unable to make sound judgments either on policies or on men to advise him. Political scandals rocked the federal government. In New York, extensive graft carried on by a notorious political group called the Tweed Ring emphasized the low level to which public morality had fallen.

ECONOMIC

Important transportation developments:
 Completion of transcontinental railroad,
 Granger laws passed to regulate railroads,
 Westinghouse air-brake patented,
 Refrigerator car built by Swift.
Knights of Labor founded.
Panic of 1873 started.
Telephone and duplex telegraph invented.

SOCIAL AND CULTURAL

Graduate schools began.
Chautauqua movement aided adult education.
Women's Christian Temperance Union and National Woman's Suffrage Association founded.
Museums started in several large cities.
National League of Professional Baseball Players founded.
Centennial Exposition held at Philadelphia.

POLITICAL	ECONOMIC	SOCIAL AND CULTURAL

1877-1881 (*Republican*)

Rutherford B. Hayes, a man of high political principles, was elected President in a disputed election. Neither the Congress nor the public gave him the support he needed. Nevertheless, federal troops were withdrawn from the South during his administration, and the South was free again to manage its own affairs. Hayes also pushed forward a program of civil service reform to improve the efficiency of government service.

Important currency developments:
  Redemption of greenbacks in gold,
  Bland-Allison Act for silver coinage.
Railroad strike of 1877 showed labor unrest.
Beginning of the labor federation which became the A.F. of L.
Cattle raising boomed.

Treaty with China modified to exclude Chinese labor.
Beginning of the New York and Boston symphony orchestras.
Important inventions: Phonograph, Incandescent lamp.
Great gains made in movement for co-education.

1881-1885 (*Republican*)

James A. Garfield, minister, college president, and Union general, was assassinated within a few months after his inauguration. Vice-President **Chester A. Arthur** succeeded him and completed a creditable administration. During his term the Pendleton Act was passed, which firmly established the principles of civil service reform and weakened the hold of the spoils system in the federal government. The modern navy began at this time.

The trust — a new form of organization for big business—created by Standard Oil.
Basis laid for development of steel industry when Andrew Carnegie and H. C. Frick combined their steel and coke interests.
Growth of unrest among the farmers.
Extravagant appropriation bills rejected by President Arthur.

New high level of immigration, but Chinese laborers were excluded, and importation of contract laborers prohibited.
Journalistic events: New York *World* taken over by Joseph Pulitzer, *Ladies Home Journal* and *Good Housekeeping* started.
Metropolitan Opera opened.

1885-1889 (*Democratic*)

Grover Cleveland, the first Democratic President after the War Between the States, was blocked by a Republican Senate during his entire four years of office. However, non-partisan measures like the Presidential Succession Act and Electoral Count Act were passed. Cleveland outraged war veterans by vetoing pension bills. He favored civil service reform, reduction of tariffs, and conservation of resources.

Labor unrest and radical labor leadership shown in the Haymarket affair.
Efforts of the states to regulate railroads upset by Wabash case.
Interstate Commerce Act passed, the first federal attempt to regulate business.
Surplus in treasury.

Dispossessed Indians taken under government protection by the Dawes Act.
Printing speeded up by Mergenthaler linotype machine.
Appearance of first skyscraper — a ten-story building in Chicago.
Modern bicycle introduced.

1889-1893 (*Republican*)

Benjamin Harrison was not a leader but was content to let members of Congress carry out their own policies. The first Pan-American conference was held. Theodore Roosevelt was appointed to the Civil Service Commission. Six new states from the plains and mountain area were admitted to the Union, and the frontier disappeared. The formation of the Populist Party was proof of widespread discontent in the West and South.

Oklahoma opened for settlement.
Purchase of more silver provided for by Sherman Silver Act.
New high level of protection established by McKinley Tariff.
Sherman Antitrust Act advanced regulation of private enterprise.
Homestead strike.

Hull House founded by Jane Addams.
Timber conservation act passed.
Significant publications:
  Whitman's complete *Leaves of Grass,*
  Riis' *How the Other Half Lives,*
  Garland's *Main-Traveled Roads.*

1893-1897 (*Democratic*)

Grover Cleveland became President a second time in the midst of a financial panic, which was followed by a long depression. Although he was in no way responsible, Cleveland was blamed. He plodded courageously through four "luckless years," attempting again to reduce the tariff and to stimulate business recovery. Upholding the Monroe Doctrine, he narrowly avoided war with Great Britain over a Venezuelan boundary dispute.

Panic of 1893.
Sherman Silver Purchase Act repealed.
J. P. Morgan's purchase of bonds relieved gold scarcity.
President disappointed by Wilson - Gorman Tariff.
Pullman strike broken.
Free Silver defeated in election of 1896.

Chicago's Columbian Exposition showed American progress.
Developments in transportation:
  Henry Ford's first automobile tested,
  Electric trolley cars changed city life.
Motion pictures began.
Rural Free Delivery established.

A steel mill of the 1890's

THE PLAN OF THE BOOK

PART ONE Early America Develops	1492 to 1783	**Unit One:** Discovery, Exploration, Development of the English colonies, American Revolution			
	1783 to 1840	**Unit Two:** Framing of Constitution, The new republic, Rise of nationalism, sectionalism, and democracy			
	1789 to 1865	**Unit Three:** Economic developments, Social change and reform, Rise of American culture			
	1840 to 1865	**Unit Four:** Westward expansion, The slavery problem, War Between the States			
PART TWO Modern America Emerges	1865 to the 1890's	**Unit Five** Foundations of the American economic system	**Unit Six** Social and cultural developments	**Unit Seven** Government, politics, and foreign affairs	
PART THREE Modern America Matures	1890's to the Present	**Unit Eight** American economic system today	**Unit Nine** Social and cultural developments	**Unit Ten** The United States in world affairs	**Unit Eleven** Developments in government and politics

Unit Five

FOUNDATIONS ARE LAID FOR THE

MODERN ECONOMIC SYSTEM

Following the close of the War Between the States, America went through an era of transition. At the beginning of the period from 1865 to the mid-90's the United States was a land such as you have known only through books and moving pictures. Near its close, however, this country was taking on many characteristics which you would recognize today.

At the beginning of the period more Americans earned their living from the soil than otherwise. There was a frontier to which adventurous persons might journey — to search for precious metals, to graze cattle on the open range, or to locate a free homestead. By the mid-90's however, the Indians were on reservations, the open range was shrinking, and the frontier was a thing of the past. Scientific agriculture and increased use of farm machinery had transformed the life of the once-independent farmer. He had become a businessman dependent upon world prices.

Even more startling changes took place in industry. Inventions and increased use of machinery, large-scale production, and business consolidation brought great industrial growth. Machine production created more goods for the average American to enjoy. On the other hand, craftsmanship became less important, and the master-worker had less opportunity to go into business for himself. The time was near when job-skill was to be learned not through long apprenticeship but through a brief period of on-the-job training.

These rapidly changing conditions brought problems which Americans tackled energetically. Farm groups fought for higher farm prices and labor organizations for better working conditions. Through new laws the federal government made a beginning in regulating big business and railroads.

Chapter 18

Pioneer woman

PIONEERS SETTLE THE LAST FRONTIER

We've broken land and cleared it, but we're tired of where we are.
They say that wild Nebraska is a better place by far.
There's gold in far Wyoming, there's black earth in Ioway,
So pack up the kids and blankets, for we're moving out today! . . .

We're going West tomorrow, where the promises can't fail.
O'er the hills in legions, boys, and crowd the dusty trail!
We shall starve and freeze and suffer. We shall die, and tame the lands.
But we're going West tomorrow, with our fortune in our hands.

Stephen Vincent Benét *

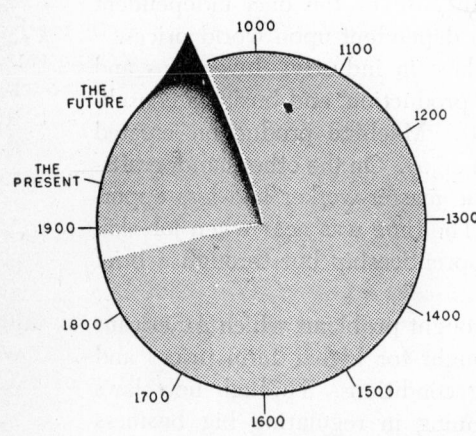

1860-1890

The news of Abraham Lincoln's election was sped from St. Joseph, Missouri, to Sacramento, California, by "Pony Express." The time required for carrying the message was nearly two weeks. The vast western country over which the Pony Express riders spurred their horses in 1860 was still the Wild West of Kit Carson and the frontier scouts. It was a land of mountains which white men had not yet climbed, streams over which they had not built bridges, and valleys which they had not explored. Millions of buffaloes roamed and stampeded on the plains. Between the Mississippi River and the western slope of the Rockies, more than 200,000 Indians — such as the fierce and warlike Sioux, Cheyenne, and Comanche — lived and fought. Near the Great Salt Lake

* From "Western Wagons" in *A Book of Americans*, published by Rinehart & Company, Inc. Copyright, 1933, by Rosemary and Stephen Vincent Benét.

in Utah, the Mormon settlement planted thirteen years before was growing strong and prosperous. Otherwise there was little to show that the white man was about to take over the far-reaching wilderness. Small bands of fur-traders, miners, and soldiers seemed lost on its endless horizons.

Yet within 30 years the frontier had vanished. By 1890, a solid row of states stretched from the Atlantic to the Pacific. There were 17 million white people living west of the Mississippi. Large areas that had been marked "Indian territory" or "Great American Desert" on the maps were now dotted with towns, villages, and homesteads. Transcontinental railways had replaced hurtling stage-coaches and lumbering wagon trains. Telegraph lines had long since driven the Pony Express out of business.

The settlement of the great American West is an endlessly exciting story — as any movie-goer knows. The highlights of the story are told in this chapter under these headings:

1. Miners seek their fortunes in the mountains.
2. Cowboys herd cattle over the open range.
3. Farmers settle the great prairies.
4. The Indians of the West are placed on reservations.
5. The West gives new strength to the nation.

1 Miners Seek Their Fortunes in the Mountains

A new mining boom begins. The cry that had electrified the nation in '49 went up again in the spring of '59. Rich deposits of gold and silver had been found again — this time on the eastern slopes of the Sierra Nevada near Lake Tahoe. (See map, page 4.) As the news spread, miners rushed to the mountains to stake their claims, some

of which became immensely profitable. From a single mine, the Comstock Lode, more than 300 million dollars' worth of silver was taken in its first 20 years. Soon a territorial government was established in this region, and by 1864 Nevada entered the Union as a full-fledged state.

It was in 1859 also that gold was discovered in the foothills of the Colorado Rockies, near Pike's Peak. Remembering the stories of the first "forty-niners," "fifty-niners" from all parts of the country raced to Colorado in prairie schooners bearing the slogan, "Pike's Peak or Bust!" Before long, many of these fortune hunters changed their motto to "Busted, by gosh!" — and headed back home. A few struck it rich, however, and others went to work for wages in the mines. During the '70's, the population grew as ranchers and farmers moved in. In 1876, just a century after the Declaration of Independence, Colorado entered the Union as the "Centennial State."

Lured on by the rich strikes in Nevada and Colorado, grizzled prospectors began to comb the slopes of the Rockies. Soon, the ore-bearing hills of Arizona, Idaho, Montana, and Wyoming were giving up gold and silver far beyond the wildest dreams of John Smith and his Virginia "gentlemen." Between 1870 and 1890, about 1½ billion dollars worth of gold and silver alone came out of the western mines.

Mining towns are rough and ready. Hundreds of thousands of prospectors, miners, and other workers tackled the back-breaking job of getting all this wealth to the surface. They were a brawny, hard-living crowd, who quickly built towns to meet their rough-and-ready needs.

There are many "tall tales" about how quickly these western towns grew. An early settler of Cheyenne, Wyoming, was once asked if he could remember who built the first house there. He said, "Well, one fine day, early in July, 1867, four or five

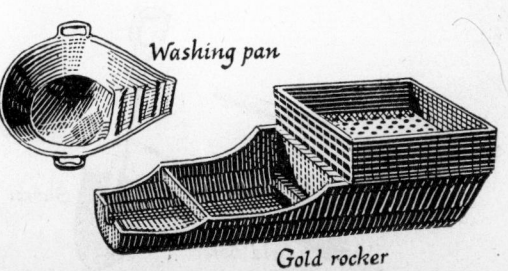

Washing pan

Gold rocker

hundred of us pitched our tents here, where there wasn't a sign of civilization, and about half of us woke up at daylight the next morning to find that the other half were living in board shanties!"

The rugged life in a mining town was described in this way by a man who lived for a time in Virginia City, Montana:

This human hive, numbering at least ten thousand people, was the product of ninety days. Into it were crowded all the elements of a rough and active civilization. Thousands of cabins and tents and brush wikiups [rough huts] . . . were seen on every hand. Every foot of the gulch, under the active manipulations of the miners, was undergoing displacement . . . Gold was abundant, and every possible device was employed by the gamblers, the traders, the vile men and women . . . to obtain it. Nearly every third cabin in the town was a saloon where vile whiskey was peddled out for fifty cents a drink in gold dust. Many of these places were filled with gambling tables and gamblers, and the miner who was bold enough to enter one of them with his day's earnings in his pocket, seldom left until thoroughly fleeced . . . Not a day or night passed which did not yield its . . . fights, quarrels, wounds, or murders. The crack of the revolver was often heard above the merry notes of the violin.

Miners make their own laws. The same observer added, however, "Underneath this exterior of recklessness, there was in the minds and hearts of the miners and business men of this society a strong and abiding sense of justice — and that saved the Territory." In the struggle to keep a sense of law and order, private citizens sometimes organized themselves into vigilance committees to handle outlaws. The members of these groups were known as "Vigilantes" (vih-jil-an'teez). During the winter of 1863–64, for instance, the Montana Vigilantes caught and hanged 24 desperadoes who had robbed and murdered dozens of persons in the territory.

The miners often set up their own local governments and made their own laws. They held meetings, elected officials, and made regulations limiting the size and type of claim a man could stake out. To keep a claim, a miner usually had to work it several days a week. These self-organized, self-governing mining districts grew fast in the Far West; there were more than 1100 by 1866. The mining law developed at that time underlies the mining codes of our western states today.

After a while the easy strikes of gold and silver gave out. To burrow deeper and deeper into the mountainsides for the ore called for expensive machinery. Thus mining became a business that could be carried on best by large companies. Many prospectors moved on, or settled down to other work. Except for a few "ghost towns" there is little left in the mountain regions to remind us of the early mining rush.

——— CHECK-UP ———

What were the characteristics of the miners' frontier?

1. Where were important mineral deposits discovered during 1859 and the years following?
2. How did these discoveries affect our national wealth and the admission of new states?
3. What were the chief features of life in the mining camps? How did the miners establish law and order?

2 Cowboys Herd Cattle Over the Open Range

The East needs more beef. Another dramatic chapter in the development of the West was written by the cattlemen. Over the vast Texas plains roamed great herds of lanky longhorn cattle. Under a loose form of ownership, they ran "wild as Texas steers." Before 1865 they were raised
(Continued on page 348)

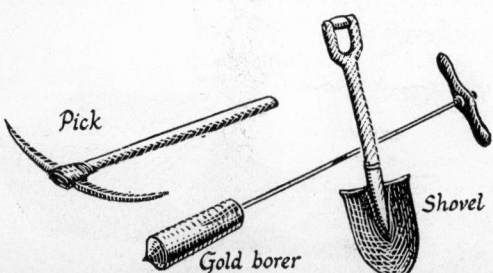

Pick

Shovel

Gold borer

CENTRAL CITY IN THE MOUNTAINS

The Opera House, where famous actors and actresses of the 1870's once played, is opened for a series of plays each year. Travelers attend the plays and then stroll through the streets in order to get a sample of what life was like on the mining frontier.

An early locomotive and cars, relics of the rich past, are displayed for travelers today.

The slopes of a gulch bearing fabulous deposits of gold and silver became the site of Central City. Rugged miners and their wives made homes on these steep and barren slopes.

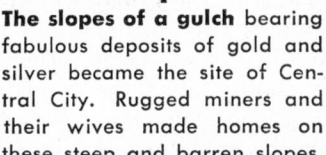

The Teller House, "queen of frontier hostelries," became famous for its elegance amid frontier ruggedness. It was built in 1872 and was host the following year to President Ulysses S. Grant.

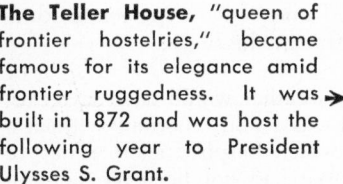

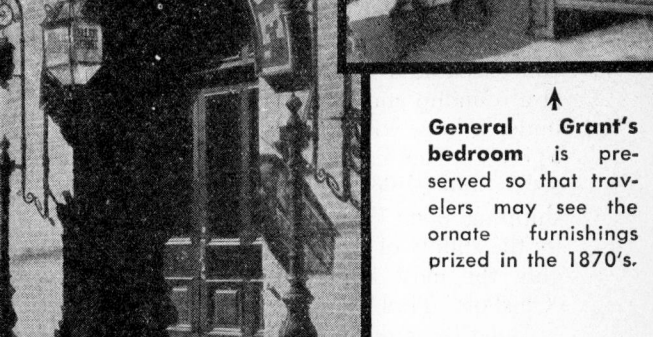

General Grant's bedroom is preserved so that travelers may see the ornate furnishings prized in the 1870's.

Central City, Colorado, once called "the richest square mile on earth," is visited each year by travelers in search of some of the flavor of the West in its great mining days. Since a prospector made the first strike here in 1859, more than 70 million dollars' worth of gold and silver have been taken from this area.

Stampeding longhorns, pictured here by a modern Texan artist, were one of many hazards faced by cowboys on the "long drive." Strange sights and sounds on the plains would sometimes startle the yearlings and drive them into wild, terrified flight.

chiefly for their hides. Northern and eastern city-dwellers, however, began demanding more beef. Because a steer that could be bought for three or four dollars in Texas was worth ten times as much in New York, Texas cattlemen started to look for some way to get their cattle to market.

The "long drive" is organized. From the settled farm lands of the Middle West to the Rockies, and from Texas to the Canadian border, stretched endless miles of unfenced plains. Before they had been slaughtered by hunters shortly after the War Between the States, enormous buffalo herds had thrived on the wild grass of this region. Even in winter, the buffaloes pawed away the snow and ate the dried grass underneath. The cattlemen reasoned that if the buffaloes could fatten on the plains, cattle could, too. Therefore, the cattlemen moved their herds in on these great open spaces.

Each spring, cattle ready for market were separated from the rest of the herd at a roundup and started north from Texas under a boss, with a gang of cowboys and a cook. The cattle were driven slowly across unoccupied lands toward a railroad shipping point. Routes were determined by the supply of water and of grass. Probably the most famous of them was the "Chisholm Trail."

Along the railway lines which were now pushing steadily west, towns like Abilene and Dodge City in Kansas, Ogallala in Nebraska and Miles City in Montana became noted "cow-towns." (See map, page 365.) From 1866 to 1885, an average

of 300,000 cattle a year were driven from Texas to the northern plains. Some were sold at the "cow-towns" for shipment to the stockyards; others were sold to the cattlemen in the new "cow country" for breeding purposes. Easterners and Europeans invested millions of dollars in the cattle business, and made huge profits. By the '80's cattle raising centered in Wyoming, Montana, western Nebraska, and western Dakota. Cattle bred from both Texas and eastern stock were raised by the hundreds of thousands and shipped to market. Meat packing became a great industry in Chicago and Kansas City, especially after the refrigerator car made it possible to ship fresh beef eastward.

The "long drive" is a hard one. The roundup and the "long drive" furnished much of the romance in the story of the vanishing frontier. The unique costumes and the free and adventurous life of the cowboy caught the imagination of the people. But the cowboy's life was not all fun, for the "long drive" also meant hardship. Andy Adams, a famous Texas cattleman, described one of his experiences during a dry season in this way:

Good cloudy weather would have saved us, but in its stead was a sultry morning without a breath of air, which bespoke another day of sizzling heat. We had not been on the trail over two hours before the heat became almost unbearable to man and beast . . . Over three days had now elapsed without water for the cattle, and they became feverish and ungovernable . . . They finally turned back over the trail, and the utmost efforts of every man in the outfit failed to check them. We threw our ropes in their faces, and when this failed, we resorted to shooting . . . They disregarded this and every other device to turn them and passed wholly out of our control. In a number of instances wild steers deliberately walked against our horses, and then for the first time a fact dawned on us that chilled the marrow of our bones — *the herd was going blind.*

The bones of men and animals that lie bleaching along the trails abundantly testify that this was not the first instance in which the plain had baffled the determination of man. It was now evident that nothing short of water would stop the herd, and we rode aside to let them pass. . .

The open range disappears. The open range and the roving cowboy made an exciting and important contribution to the taming of the West, but their days were numbered. Railroads crept nearer and nearer to the home ranches. When contagious cattle diseases broke out, cattlemen were prevented by quarantine laws from moving their herds from one section to another. Sheep raisers and homesteaders, who followed the railways into the plains, fenced in feeding areas and waterholes so that the cattle could no longer graze at will. Public demand for more tender meat led to the breeding of better beef cattle than the long-legged, open-range steer — but such animals were too valuable to risk to the hazards of the hard winters. Great fenced-in ranches, operated as big businesses, began to supply the meat-packing companies. In the 1890's few cattlemen depended entirely on the open range, but instead grew winter feed for their cattle. Cowboys that were mere ranch hands lost much of their glamor.

——— CHECK-UP ———

What were the characteristics of the cattlemen's frontier?

1. What was the "long drive"? What factors made it possible and profitable?
2. What were some of the problems of the long drive?
3. How did cattle raising change in the '80's and the '90's?

3 Farmers Settle the Great Prairies

Farmers move West again. The westward march of the homesteaders was less dramatic than the mining boom or the cattle drives, but in the end it was more important. An Easterner crossing the plains on horseback in 1866 reported that he was hardly ever out of sight of ox or mule teams hauling wagons. In a week's ride west of Leavenworth, Kansas, he passed 680 wagons loaded with the families and belongings of farmers who had sold out their holding and were trekking west. These people were urged on in part by the desire to try something new, but there were three more important reasons why so many of them were seeking new homes:

(1) *The Homestead Act passed by Congress in 1862.* Under this act, any head of a family or any adult who had not borne arms against the government could become owner of 160 acres of public land. All he had to do was live on it, cultivate it for five years, and pay a small fee to have his ownership recorded.

The cowboy of story and song is shown here amid familiar surroundings: cattle, corral, windmill, and water tanks.

The sod house of the prairie looks crude, but was practical where no trees grew. This one, in Nebraska, was photographed in 1892.

(2) *The influence of the war.* During the War Between the States the army needed food which new western farms might supply. At the same time many men chose to go west rather than stay at home and take their chances with the draft. Then, as the war came to an end, many veterans decided to start their own farms in the West, instead of taking factory jobs in the East.

(3) *The extension of the railroads.* Railroads, pushing steadily westward, made the Great Plains easier to reach. The railroads also advertised the West in the East and in Europe. The railroads needed settlers on the great plains in order to make money. The settlers would pay freight charges on their produce which they shipped east, and they would also order eastern goods to be shipped to them.

Some settlers live in dugouts. The early pioneer on the prairies faced many problems. Once he had struggled to the West and staked out his homestead, he had to build a place in which to live. Except along river bottoms and creeks, there was no timber on the prairies, so that few pioneers were able to build the usual log cabins. But they did what they could with the materials available. The typical prairie homes were dugouts and sod houses. Here

350

is a description that gives a picture of how an early dugout was made, and what it was like to live in one:

The dugout was a room dug in the side of a hill or ravine. A few rails or posts were used to make a door frame and possibly a window. The door, of course, opened out into the ravine. The front wall was made of square cut turf, or logs if they were available. A roof sloping back on the hill was made of poles or logs covered over with brush, a layer of prairie grass thick enough to hold dirt, and finally a layer of dirt over the grass. It was by no means ideal, however, for after a rain the high water often drove the occupants from their home. It was necessary to dig a trench from the house to the drainage level to carry water off the floor. Then, too, a frog pond for a front yard meant mosquitoes in summer and a very unhealthful environment. Even in dry weather the place was dirty. Occasionally cattle wandered over the housetop — shaking dirt down onto the dining table.*

Other settlers live in sod houses. A sod house was harder to build than a dugout, but it was a better place in which to live. The first step was to plow a strip of thick sod with a moldboard plow. With a spade, the upturned sod was cut into bricks about three feet long. Then the sod bricks were laid in place and held together with adobe mud [1] to make walls, just as ordinary bricks are laid and held together with mortar. Door frames and window frames were set in the walls. In the best sodhouses, roofs were made of wood rafters covered with boards, tar paper, and a layer of sod over all. In a short time, weeds and grass and

[1] Adobe mud was a mixture of earth, water, and grass or straw.
* Appleton-Century-Crofts. Everett Dick, *The Sodhouse Frontier.*

Wild turkey

Prairie
chicken

even sunflowers would flourish on the roof.

The worst feature of most sodhouses was the roof. It usually leaked during a heavy rain, and muddy water dripped over food, beds, and people. But the sodhouse had its good points too. It was insulation against the bitter cold and the scorching heat of the Great Plains. It was practically fireproof, and it could withstand windstorms.

Fuel and water are hard to find. The first settlers, who made homes along the streams, found firewood nearby. Latecomers sometimes had to haul wood for 30 or 40 miles, or burn dried cornstalks, corncobs, sunflower stems, and twisted hay. Away from the streams, wells for water had to be dug at tremendous effort, sometimes to a depth of 200 feet.

Food is abundant but simple. Early pioneer families usually ate corn for breakfast, dinner, and supper. A Nebraska paper printed 33 ways of cooking corn, including corn bread, corn cake, corn muffins, corn dumplings, corn pudding, and, of course, corn meal mush. Mush was served even at parties, and in 1873 one Nebraska town had a "mush and milk festival" to raise funds for its brass band. "Coffee substitutes" were made from dried pumpkin, squash, carrots, peas, molasses, parched barley or rye, and other unlikely ingredients. Canning had not been perfected, but housewives dried everything they could for winter use. Corn, squash, and rhubarb hung from the rafters. Tomatoes were preserved in barrels of strong salt brine. For sweetening, there was usually sorghum molasses, with occasional wild honey or maple sugar. Watermelons were easy to grow, and along the streams there were wild nuts and berries of many kinds. In the early years, there was plenty of wild game to give a change to the diet.

Barbed wire and windmills fill needs. Homesteaders often found that the "free land" which they were offered was far from being a farm. It needed fencing, to keep out roving herds of cattle, and it needed a water supply. Since the plains were almost without trees, rail or post fences were out of the question. But in 1874 cheap barbed-wire fencing was patented and put on the market. Six years later, its yearly sales had risen to more than 80 million pounds, and western farmers were "fencing out" the cattlemen.

Another simple invention, the windmill, solved the problem of water supply. On the semi-dry Great Plains, water often lay 50 to 200 feet below the surface. To draw bucketfuls from a well by hand to water the stock was an impossible task. The American-type windmill, developed in the 1850's, came into general use in the '70's to furnish a steady and cheap source of pumping power. From Texas to North Dakota it became the flag of civilization.

School houses are primitive. As soon as the homesteaders had their houses and farms in running order, they began to build schools for their children. For a long time, most of the schoolhouses in the western prairie states were dugouts or sod houses. In the eastern section of the prairie they were built of logs. Log schools were described in this way:

The roof was often made of branches and sod and the whole structure built as a community enterprise. The logs were chinked with blocks and pointed up with clay in lieu of mortar. A long board rested on pegs inserted in the logs along two sides of the room. This formed a steep desk. The seats were rough slabs of wood from the sawmill or hewn logs with pegs put in for legs. These seats and desks around the room were for the older pupils. The little ones had benches in the center of the room. There were no backs to any of the benches. The teacher was fortunate to have a rude desk and chair. The dirt floor was dusty in dry weather and mussy with pools of water from the leaking roof for three days following a rain. *Windmill* There was a recitation

351

The Apaches were among the most difficult Indians to subdue, but the army hired some of them as scouts to help round up the others. This picture shows one of the scouts.

bench in front of the teacher. At one end of the room was a large fireplace or stove, and at the other end were the door and window . . . In these first schools there was not the faintest suggestion of a blackboard. There were no maps, no globe, and the nearest dictionary was often miles away.*

New states replace wide open spaces. Every year the frontier line of settlement moved westward. After the War Between the States, the population of the western states and territories doubled and redoubled and then doubled again. Nebraska became a state in 1867, Colorado in 1876. In 1889–1890 six new states were admitted to the Union: North and South Dakota, Montana, Washington, Idaho, and Wyoming. Six years later Utah became the forty-fifth state. Only in the Southwest was the solid belt of states from Atlantic to Pacific broken.

The states are completed from coast to coast. The settlement of Oklahoma, "the beautiful land," was a dramatic episode in

---

* Appleton-Century-Crofts. Everett Dick, *The Sodhouse Frontier.*

the homesteader's conquest of the western territory. The government had secured thousands of square miles of Oklahoma land from the Indians, and in 1889 this area was opened to settlement. At noon on April 22, a signal was given. Thousands of eager "boomers," in all kinds of wagons or on horseback, poured helter-skelter across the boundary and raced madly to stake out homesteads and town lots. Cities and towns literally sprang up overnight. By the end of the year, Oklahoma boasted a population of 60,000. Ten years later this number had increased to 400,000. Organized as a territory in 1890, Oklahoma was combined with Indian Territory and was admitted as a state in 1907. In the same year New Mexico and Arizona turned down admission as a single state, but five years later they were admitted separately as the forty-seventh and forty-eighth states of the Union.

––––––– CHECK-UP –––––––

How did farmers settle the great prairies and plains?

1. Why did each of the following stimulate western settlement? (a) The Homestead Act, (b) The War Between the States, (c) The extension of railroads.
2. What were the problems of living and making a living on the great prairies and plains? What solutions were found?
3. What efforts were made to provide schools?
4. How did settlement speed up the admission of new states?

---

4 **The Indians of the West Are Placed on Reservations**

Whites and Indians are rivals for the West. For every forward step taken by the white men, the red men had to step back-

Indian peace pipe

ward — at the cost of their lands and often their lives. The retreat of the Indians may be looked at from two points of view: that of the pioneer and that of the Indian himself.

(1) The miner, the cattleman, and the homesteader looked upon the destruction of the "savages" as natural, inevitable, and even desirable. They argued that the Indian, during the centuries that he had lived in the land, had done little to develop the country and its resources. Now, they believed, he threatened to be a dangerous obstacle to progress. The settler saw nothing good in the Indians; he saw only their cunning, their ferocity, and their shocking cruelty. Along the whole frontier white settlers cried angrily, "There are no good Indians except dead Indians!"

(2) The red men, on the other hand, saw only that they were losing their land and their lives through the dishonesty or greed of white men. Homes and hunting grounds granted to them by solemn treaties were overrun by fortune seekers. Corrupt government agents and dishonest traders and settlers added to their troubles. From the Indians' point of view, there was no choice but to fight for their right to live in the homeland of their ancestors.

The Indians lose their means of support. The Plains Indians depended chiefly on hunting for their food supply. Before the coming of white settlers the region teemed with wildlife — wild geese and ducks, prairie chickens, turkeys, deer, antelope, and many other kinds of game. But by far the most important game was buffalo. Each year the Indians killed tens of thousands of buffaloes for meat, clothing, bowstrings, harnesses, and tents. Even so, the buffaloes lived on in such great numbers that a train on the Kansas Pacific as late as 1868 ran for 120 miles through "an almost unbroken herd."

But with rifle and pistol the white man slaughtered the buffaloes in short order — and most of the other game too. William F. Cody was called "Buffalo Bill" because he claimed to have killed over 4000 buffaloes in eighteen months to feed the builders of the Kansas Pacific Railroad. Professional hunters, out to get buffalo robes for the eastern market, slaughtered over 3 million of the animals in three years. Other hunters killed hundreds of thousands of them just for sport, leaving their carcasses to rot on the plains. By 1887 only a few hundred buffaloes were left in the United States. The Plains Indians had been stripped of their chief means of support.

The Indians fight a losing battle. For about 25 years after the War Between the States, the western Indians fought a desperate but losing battle against the advancing settlers and the United States Army. The tribes which gave the most trouble were the Sioux, who lived around the upper Mississippi and westward to Wyoming, and the Apaches (ah-patch'eez) in the Southwest. The Sioux, under such leaders as Little Crow, Red Cloud, and Crazy Horse, took a heavy toll of settlers, travelers, and soldiers. The Bozeman Trail, which led through the Sioux hunting grounds in what is now Wyoming and Montana, was stained with the blood of both white men and Indians.

The most famous fight in all the Indian

From native settings like this pueblo the government at first tried to entice the Indians. Now native customs are encouraged.

wars took place in 1876. In a campaign against the Sioux and their allies, General George A. Custer, with about 600 cavalrymen, was sent into the valley of the Little Big Horn River. A detachment of some 200 men under Custer's personal command was ambushed and wiped out. But in spite of such successes, the Indians had no chance of permanent victory. In one region after another they lost out and were herded together on reservations. Among the last to be defeated were the Apaches, who fought on under their leader, Geronimo (jeh-ron'ih-mo), until 1886.

The Indians become citizens. By the late '80's the Indians, once lords of all the West, had been forced to live on steadily shrinking "reservations" whose boundaries were set by the United States government. When the Indian wars ended, Congress took steps to help the Indian take part in the common life of the country. For instance, by the Dawes Act of 1887 a piece of land and United States citizenship were offered to any Indian who would give up allegiance to his tribe. To guard him against land speculators, the law forbade the Indian to sell or mortgage his land

for a period of 25 years. (The Burke Act of 1906 modified this provision by giving the Secretary of the Interior the authority to reduce the 25-year period in any case where he thought the Indian capable of managing his own affairs.) In 1887 the annual appropriation for Indian education passed the million-dollar mark. Soon afterward, compulsory education for Indian children was provided by law. In 1924 full citizenship was granted to all Indians.

Indian community life is encouraged. This plan of "turning Indians into red-skinned whites" was not very successful. In the twentieth century, oil was found on some Indian lands, such as that of the Osages in Oklahoma, and they became rich by accident. Most of the Indians, however, barely managed to exist under the government's guardianship. Their former way of life had not prepared them — and often their land was too poor — for individual farming. Government-sponsored education was often impractical. Patterned very largely on the ideas and methods of white schools, it ignored many attractive and important characteristics of Indian life.

The Wheeler-Howard Act of 1934 marked a shift in this attitude. This act tried to revive community life on the reservations. It provided for more self-government and for the holding of land by the tribe rather than by individuals. John Collier, Commissioner of Indian Affairs at that time, vigorously promoted the new policy. The Indians were given lessons in soil conservation and in improved methods of raising livestock. Schools were made a part of community life, and one of the goals of instruction was to help solve practical local problems. There was a new respect for Indian culture.

For a long time it looked as though the American Indians were a vanishing race. That is no longer so. In 1940 there were about 330,000 Indians in the United States, as compared with 240,000 in 1920. Today there are Indians living in all the states, and they own extensive lands in more than half of them. Their holdings amount to about 53 million acres, an area a fourth larger than all of New England.

"Yellowstone" Kelly, one of the scouts who inspired hair-raising fiction, fought in the last battle against the Indians.

cut

What happened to the Indians of the West, and how were they treated?

1. How did the Indians and the whites regard one another?
2. How did the destruction of the buffalo herds affect the Indians?
3. What were the provisions of the Dawes Act? What is our present Indian policy?

5 The West Gives New Strength to the Nation

The West influences business and government. The settlement of the West was a vital step in the progress of the nation. Western resources, such as gold, silver, iron, copper, timber, and other products, were essential to America's great industrial advance in the period following the War Between the States. A constant flow of western wheat and corn was available to feed our growing cities.

The conquest of this last frontier — like the earlier westward movement of Andrew Jackson's time — favored certain political trends. The newly-created states sent a group of more than 20 senators and many more representatives to Congress to look after the agricultural and mining interests of the West. They also helped restore a balance between the agricultural and industrial interests of the nation, a balance which had been upset by the ruin of the agricultural class in the South. From the West also came many progressive political ideas, such as the initiative and referendum, the recall, the direct election of United States senators, and woman suffrage. These will be discussed in Chapters 32 and 41.

The frontier West believed in social equality. For this reason, movements aimed at social reform gained force from the West. Also, as long as desirable lands in the West could be had, poor farmers from the East could go to them. In good times and in bad, discouraged men went west to look for a fresh start in life. When the best of the land was gone, however, this opportunity decreased, and at the same time people in the West were forced to introduce many aspects of eastern industrial life.

The West inspires writers. The filling-in of the frontier also had a far-reaching effect upon American literature. The roundup, the cattle trail, Indians and Indian wars, and the transformation of the Wild West into farms and ranches and cities, have furnished material for many glamorous chapters. Generations of youthful Americans have been thrilled by books, movies, and radio programs dealing with the romantic exploits of Buffalo Bill, Diamond Dick, Jesse James, the Lone Ranger, and other frontiersmen in fact or fiction. Less romantic, more realistic, but just as absorbing to older readers are the stories of Mark Twain, Bret Harte, Hamlin Garland, and Willa Cather. Such books as Edna Ferber's *Cimarron*, describing life in Oklahoma, Ole Rölvaag's *Giants in the Earth*, with its setting in North Dakota, and Owen Wister's *The Virginian*, a story of Wyoming, portray the widely differing economic conditions which developed in the West. The cowboy's way of life, which he sang about in his ballads, has been preserved for us in song collections by John A. Lomax: *Cowboy Songs* and *Songs of the Cattle Trail and Cow Camp*.

American history up to the twentieth century may well be interpreted in terms of westward expansion. It was a vital force. In a little over 100 years, the country had grown from thirteen sparsely settled states to a mighty nation of 76 million people, spread from the Atlantic to the Pacific.

How did the West give new strength to the nation?

1. In what way did the West influence the nation as a whole?
2. What was the significance of the disappearance of the frontier?

CHAPTER REVIEW

Terms to Understand

prospector
claim
sod house
roundup

dugout
"long drive"
reservation

People and Things to Know About

Comstock Lode
George A. Custer
"fifty-niners"
Wheeler-Howard Act

William F. Cody
Homestead Act
Dawes Act

Historic Dates to Identify

1859   1862   1887   1890

Questions to Discuss

1. Do you feel that miners were justified in making their own laws and enforcing them? Compare the activities and objectives of the Vigilantes with those of the Ku Klux Klan.

2. Why would farmers and cattle raisers have conflicting interests? Was it fortunate or unfortunate that the farmers' interests prevailed?

3. Explain how the railroads could help bring the "long drive" into existence and also help bring it to an end.

4. It has been said of the Homestead Act that the government was willing to bet the farmer 160 acres of land that he couldn't live on it for five years. What truth is there in this jest?

5. Why was it to the advantage of western railroads to promote settlement of the regions through which they were constructed?

6. Why are we of the present likely to take a different view of the Indians than did the pioneers? Do you feel that our former ruthless policy was necessary?

7. Emerson Hough, a writer about the West, has stated that the axe, the rifle, the boat, and the horse were the instruments for conquering the frontier. Do you believe that the list can be applied to the conquest of the great plains

Questions to Discuss (Cont.)

and prairies? If not, what additions or changes would you make?

Relating Geography and History

On an outline map of the western half of the United States show:

(a) The areas known as the great prairies and great plains.

(b) The important cattle trails.

(c) The cattle towns of Ogallala (Neb.), Dodge City and Abilene (Kansas), and Miles City (Mont.).

(d) The mining towns of Virginia City and Carson City (Nevada), Boise and Silver City (Idaho), Central City, Cripple Creek and Colorado Springs (Colorado), Helena, Anaconda, Butte, and Virginia City (Montana).

Other Things to Do

*1. Try to define the word "frontier." Does one definition cover all the justifiable uses of the term?

*2. Imagine that you are (a) a homesteader, (b) a miner in the silver rush, or (c) a cattleman. Write a letter to a friend back East and tell about some of your experiences and problems.

3. Read Mark Twain's description of some sharp mining practices in Chapter Three of *Roughing It*. You may also wish to read Twain's stories about frontier crime and justice in Chapters Six to Eight of the same book.

4. Debate: *Resolved,* That the continuous existence of a "West" has been the most important factor in shaping American character and American life.

5. Prepare a report on (a) the extinction of the buffalo, (b) the long drive, or (c) life on the sod house frontier. Webb's *The Great Plains* or Riegel's *America Moves West* will be useful references.

Early steelworkers

Chapter 19

OUR MODERN BUSINESS AND

INDUSTRIAL SYSTEM IS BORN

No other generation in American history witnessed changes as swift or as revolutionary as those which transformed the rural republic of Lincoln and Lee into the urban industrial empire of McKinley and Roosevelt.

AMERICA: THE STORY OF A FREE PEOPLE, Nevins and Commager

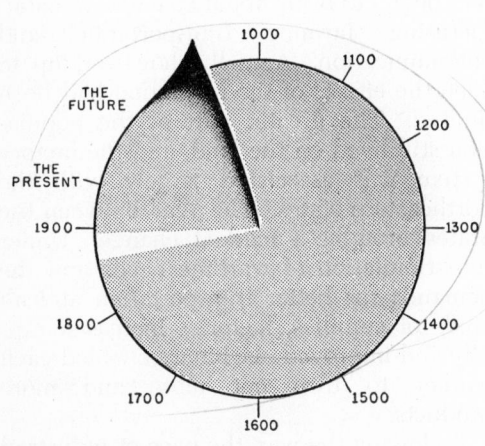

1865-1896

In many ways the United States of Abraham Lincoln was not very different from that of George Washington. In 1865, within even such a great city as New York, horsedrawn vehicles furnished the fastest transportation. Since there were no transcontinental railroads, the traveler who wanted the quickest trip from the Missouri River to California bought a seat in a horsedrawn stagecoach. His freight followed more slowly in a wagon train drawn by oxen or mules. Telegraph lines were in operation in many parts of the country, but there were no trans-Atlantic cables, no electric lights, no typewriters, and no telephones. Steel was produced only in very small quantities, and even the largest buildings were made of wood and stone with only a little brick and iron. The United States was still predominantly a land of farming. Business concerns and industries operated on a small scale and generally served only the local communities in which they were located.

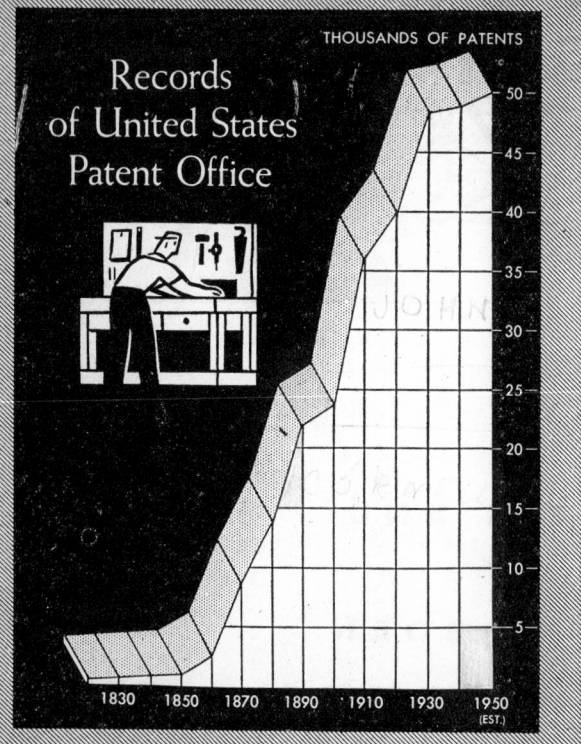

THOUSANDS OF PATENTS

Records
of United States
Patent Office

50
45
40
35
30
25
20
15
10
5

1830 1850 1870 1890 1910 1930 1950
(EST.)

The new technology in American industry is reflected in this chart. Notice that the granting of patents turned sharply upward in 1860 and kept climbing very rapidly.

By 1900 a startling change had taken place. The very years that witnessed the filling in of the West and the passing of the frontier also saw a revolution in the business and economic life of America. From a country which was not well developed industrially, the United States had grown into a land of big business — business which was no longer local but nation-wide in scope. Improved forms of communication and railroads which spanned the continent bound the nation together. In the quantity and value of its products it had become the leading manufacturing country of the world. Its population was shifting rapidly to the cities, centers alike of wealth and grinding poverty. Unheard-of quantities of capital had been collected in single enterprises, and a new chapter was being written in the relations between business and labor.

In the following pages, we shall consider some of the factors which brought about the growth of big business. We shall

also note some of the results of the development of modern industrial America in the period from the War Between the States to the close of the century. The story will be organized under these topics:

1. Technology helps transform the United States into a great industrial nation.
2. Railroads spread across the country.
3. Electricity brings instant communication.
4. The corporation becomes the dominant form of business organization.
5. Steel and oil illustrate the growth of American industry.
6. Panics and depressions become more severe.

1 Technology Helps Transform the United States into a Great Industrial Nation

The Industrial Revolution gains speed. You have already read (in Chapter 11) how the Industrial Revolution gained a foothold in the United States and how it had begun to bring about changes in manufacturing, farming, transportation, and communication. Actually, however, up to 1860 the effects of the revolution had been limited. The greater part of the population still lived on the land, and the factory system was associated largely with the northeastern states. The War Between the States brought a marked change. Under the stimulation of wartime needs and the demands for better transportation and all kinds of supplies, factories increased rapidly and improved machinery enabled each worker to turn out more and more products.

Following the war, the pace of industrial change grew still faster and faster. The great prosperity and business activity brought about by the war continued and even increased in the North after the war. The years from 1865 to 1873 saw new inventions and processes multiply, new manufacturing and business enterprises develop, and old industries expand. This industrial growth was checked in the 1870's by depression following the Panic of 1873 (page 375). But in the 1880's and in the first part of the 1890's, business and manufacturing boomed at an unheard-of rate.[1] Whereas the value of the manufactured goods produced in 1860 amounted to 2 billion dollars, by 1900 it amounted to more than 13 billion dollars a year. In 1860 the industrial output of the United States was small compared with that of Great Britain. By 1900 the United States had passed Britain in the quantity and value of its manufactured products and had become the world's foremost industrial nation.

Technology and invention alter the American scene. This new and different America was brought about chiefly by *technology* — the practical application of science to industry. Technological advances made possible the large-scale manufacturing of steel, which is the foundation of our modern industrial age. And in the latter part of the 1800's technology gave us a new and important form of power — electric power geared to machines. Through the application of technology, all sorts of machines, labor-saving devices, and scientific processes were invented or perfected.

The vast sweep of this new technology is indicated by the records of the United States Patent Office. The chart on page 358 shows how the number of patents granted by the Patent Office began to rise about 1860. To put it another way, during the seventy years from its establishment in 1790 up to 1860, the Patent Office granted only 36,000 patents. In the thirty years from 1860 to 1890, it issued 440,000.

Edison's achievements illustrate the new technology. Between 1868 and his death in 1931, Thomas A. Edison's keen mind produced hundreds of inventions which influenced every walk of American life. His name is linked — either by inventions or

[1] In 1893 a depression began which lasted for four years. But at the end of the century prosperity was once more in full swing, and business and industry were booming again.

improvements — with the electric light, generators and power stations, electric street cars, the automatic telegraph, the telephone, the phonograph, motion pictures, and the microphone. Edison laid no claim to being a great scientist. But he was an expert at technology; that is, he had unusual skill in taking a scientific principle and making it serve a practical purpose.

Changes in one field affect other fields. The new technology affected all aspects of American economic life — farming, transportation and communication, and industry. Furthermore, developments in one field brought about changes and growth in others. For example, the infant steel industry was stimulated by the railroads, which needed steel rails for the lines being built in the West. In turn, the business of the railroads was expanded by the need of the growing steel mills for the transportation of iron ore, coal, and other materials. Similarly, the building of railroads encouraged the settlement of the West. Then, bumper crops from this fertile area had to be hauled to market, and this further stimulated railroad building. At the same time, industry produced farm machinery which made it possible for America's farms to raise huge crops with fewer farm work-

Output of steel, a key to industrial progress, began to climb in the 1860's. By 1900 it had passed 10 million tons yearly.

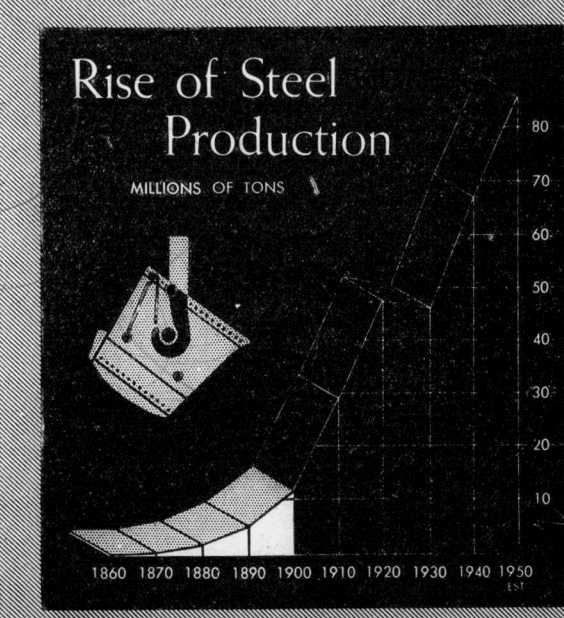

Rise of Steel Production

MILLIONS OF TONS

1860 1870 1880 1890 1900 1910 1920 1930 1940 1950

Thomas A. Edison, shown at work on the phonograph, made important contributions to many great industries.

ers. As a result, many farm workers were released to take jobs in mines and factories. In the same way, new methods of communication promoted the growth of all kinds of business and, in turn, were themselves stimulated by that growth.

The new industrialism has a solid foundation. New technological processes and inventions created modern industrial America. But, without certain other favorable factors, this outburst of industrial activity in the last half of the 1800's would not have been possible. Here is a brief summary of the many advantages which the United States possessed in this era and which combined to produce a large-scale development of business and industry:

(1) The United States had vast natural resources, including fertile land, coal, oil, iron ore, and other minerals, as well as timber and water power.

(2) There was a large and growing labor supply. This was caused partly by immigration and partly by the large numbers of farm workers who were thrown out of jobs by labor-saving farm machinery.

(3) Many Americans and Europeans had surplus capital (more money than they needed to live on) which they wished to invest in promising businesses.

(4) The War Between the States created an urgent demand for more manufactured goods, and this demand encouraged the growth of factories and mills. After the war, the settlement of the West and the rapidly growing population maintained a lively market for manufactured goods.

(5) An amazing number of new labor-saving machines were invented and produced in large quantities. These machines greatly reduced the costs of production. The manufacture of these machines also created great new industries.

(6) Cheap transportation by the expanding network of railroads (as well as by water) brought raw materials, factories, and markets within easy reach of each other.

(7) The government was friendly to business. It adopted a hands-off policy toward the growth of business, and at the same time kept high tariffs to protect American manufacturers from European competition.

(8) Within the United States itself there were no tariff walls or other barriers to prevent trade from moving freely from state to state and from section to section.

These factors in the development of industrial America reveal the solid foundations on which our industrial society was built. Some of them will be discussed at greater length later in this chapter; others will be treated more fully in succeeding chapters.

Industrial development becomes nationwide. The spectacular growth of industry was not confined to any one section of the country. Before 1860, as was pointed out earlier (Chapter 11), manufacturing had been largely centered in New England and the Middle Atlantic states (New York, Pennsylvania, and New Jersey). By the close of the century industry and manufacturing had found their way into all parts of the country. In 1850 the center of manufacturing in the United States was near Harrisburg, Pennsylvania; by 1890 it was in mid-Ohio.

Industry continues strong in the East.
Although the East no longer had a near-monopoly on manufacturing, the industrial development of this section leaped forward rapidly. For one thing, there was an ample supply of capital and skilled labor for industrial development. The Northeast, too, was rich in water power, which operated nearly all machines before steam and internal-combustion engines came into use.[2] New England was especially noted for the manufacture of textiles, shoes, and paper. The industrial development of the Middle Atlantic states was more varied. In this area, metal working and the manufacture of clothing were of special importance.

Industry moves westward. Particularly noteworthy was the movement of industry westward. Wherever the railroads went, there industry developed. Of special importance was the growth of brand-new industries. For example, the new meat-packing industry developed in Chicago and Kansas City. Minneapolis, in the midst of the famous Minnesota wheat fields, became the flour-milling capital of the nation. The East North Central states (Illinois, Indiana, Ohio, and Michigan) took the lead in manufacturing farm machinery and vehicles. As the eastern forests were cut down, lumbering and woodworking also moved westward.

[2] Water power became important again when electricity and the hydro-electric generating plants were developed.

Industry moves into the South. After the southern states recovered from the first shock of reconstruction, they, too, began to share in the industrial development of the country. The South was rich in water power and was able to produce in abundance such raw materials as cotton, tobacco, lumber, coal, oil, and iron ore. There were also large numbers of workers, who generally were willing to work for lower wages than those in the North. All of these advantages plus low taxes attracted northern industry, especially cotton manufacturing, into the South. By the turn of the century nearly half of the cotton goods manufactured in the United States came from southern mills. By-products of cotton ginning, such as cotton-seed cakes and oil, also became important in southern industry.

In Alabama there were rich deposits of coal, iron ore, and limestone — the main resources needed in the manufacture of iron and steel. Soon Birmingham, the "Pittsburgh of the South," became the center of the southern iron and steel industry. Southerners also began logging their huge forests, thereby increasing the importance of the South in the production of lumber. Manufacturing was by no means confined to a few industries. Furniture plants, tobacco factories, and almost all other forms of industry also sprang up in the South.

Industries no longer serve merely a local market. Before 1860 the great majority of business enterprises were small and found

The great packing houses of today had their beginnings in packing houses like the one shown in this old print. Butchered hogs are being moved along cutting blocks and trimming tables on their way to large-city markets.

a market for their products almost entirely in the communities in which they were located. In fact, the typical community looked to its local craftsmen for the making of the products it needed and did not expect them to be brought in from outside. For example, shoes for the family were handmade by the village cobbler. The suits worn by the men of the family were handmade by the local tailor. The village butcher bought livestock from local farmers, slaughtered it, and then sold the meat to customers living in his community. Grain was ground into flour by the local gristmill. Local craftsmen made furniture, wagons and carriages, and most of the other products which the family did not make for itself.

Inventions and other technological developments brought rapid changes in the period after 1860. During the war, the McKay sole-sewing machine helped revolutionize the making of shoes. Soon almost all footwear was being made in factories, and the local cobbler became a repairer rather than a maker of shoes. Likewise, a machine for cutting cloth in the 1870's led to the manufacture of ready-made clothing. New processes for milling flour made it increasingly difficult for the local grist mill to compete with the mills which installed the new machinery. Similar developments, particularly the use of refrigerator cars, gradually put the local butcher out of business and helped the development of the new meat packing business of the Middle West.

The many new industries that developed as a result of these changes sought a national rather than a local market. In a short time, the same products made by the same companies were being sold everywhere throughout the country. This change from local to national business would not have been possible without the tremendous expansion of the railroads and the improved means of communication which followed the War Between the States. To these developments in transportation and communication we shall turn our attention in the next two sections of this chapter.

——— CHECK-UP ———

How did technology help transform the United States into a great industrial nation?

1. What was the effect of the War Between the States on industrial development? By 1900 what changes had taken place in the position of the United States as an industrial power?
2. What is meant by "technology"? How did technological developments in one field affect other fields?
3. What are some of the basic factors that made possible American industrial development?
4. Explain how industrial development became nation-wide. Why did the East remain strong industrially? What industries developed in the West? What industries became important in the South?
5. Why did business and industries no longer serve merely a local market? What were some of the new nation-wide industries which developed?

2 Railroads Spread Across the Country

Railroad traffic reaches a new high during the war. Even before the War Between the States, railroads had become the most important means of American transportation. (See page 235.) They carried about two thirds of the internal trade of the country, most of it east of the Mississippi River. One road, however, pushed as far west as St. Joseph, Misouri, close to the frontier line of settlement. During the war the need for transporting supplies for the armies forced railroad traffic to a new high, and the railroads became prosperous. By the close of the war, the railroads had clearly proved how important they were to the welfare of the country. Nevertheless, few people at that time would have predicted that an even more startling period of railroad development lay ahead. There was some talk of a transcontinental rail-

The transcontinental railroads were built by men who had to be ready to drop their tools and grab rifles to fight off Indians. Here workmen are being helped by soldiers.

road, but not many took it seriously. In fact, General Sherman in 1865 said that he would not be able to buy a railroad ticket to the Pacific Coast "for his youngest grandchild."

The government encourages railroad building. Yet in less than five years Sherman was proved wrong and the East and the Far West were joined by iron rails. Even before the war, surveys had been made to find "the most practicable and economic route" across the continent. Jealousy between the sections of the country, however, blocked the adoption of any of four routes that were suggested. In 1862, with southern opposition gone, Congress finally decided upon a central route which would eventually connect Chicago with San Francisco. The Central Pacific Railroad was licensed to build eastward from Sacramento, California, while the Union

Pacific was to push westward from Omaha, Nebraska. Somewhere between these points they would meet.

To encourage the huge cross-country construction job, Congress promised generous terms to the two railroad companies. In addition to getting a free right of way through the public lands, they were given liberal grants of land also. For each mile of track they laid, the railroad company received ten square miles of land, in alternate sections, along the right of way. In other words, they were given half the land that bordered the railroad.[3] The government also offered to lend the railroads $16,000,

[3] The sections of land owned by the railroads alternated with sections owned by the government. Because this checkerboard pattern cannot be drawn to scale, the map on page 365 shows that all the area along the railroad routes belonged to the railroads.

Chinese laborers were hired by the Central Pacific as it drove tunnels, built bridges, and laid tracks eastward.

$32,000, or $48,000 for each mile of road they built. The size of the loan depended on the nature of the territory to be crossed — prairie, plateau, or mountain area.

The "iron horse" crosses the continent. The Central Pacific and the Union Pacific, eager to make the most out of these tempting government subsidies, began to build rapidly. They faced great difficulties, however. The Central Pacific had to transport many of its materials by sea from the East Coast. When the Union Pacific began construction in 1865, Omaha was not connected by rail with Chicago. Rails and equipment had to be shipped up the Missouri River or by wagon-train from the nearest railroad. Even when Chicago was connected by rail with Council Bluffs, Iowa, in 1867, there was no bridge across the river connecting Council Bluffs with Omaha.

During the winter of 1868–1869, the construction race became intense. Thousands of men — Chinese coolies on the Central Pacific, and Irish immigrants on the Union Pacific — battled time, nature, and the Indians. Finally, on May 10, 1869, the two lines came together at Promontory Point near Ogden, Utah. A spike of gold was driven into the final tie. News of this event was instantly telegraphed to all parts of the country, and noisy celebrations were held in the principal cities.

More transcontinental roads are built. Even before the joining of the Union Pacific with the Central Pacific, new lines were started over other western routes. Construction was interrupted, however, by the Panic of 1873, and it was not until about ten years later that the new railroads were opened to transcontinental traffic. The Northern Pacific stretched from Duluth, Minnesota, across the fertile prairies of Dakota and Montana to Portland, Oregon, and Tacoma, Washington. The Southern Pacific, running from New Orleans across Texas and through the Gadsden Purchase to California, tapped the wealth of the Southwest. At about the same time the Atchison, Topeka, and Santa Fe pierced the Arkansas valley and put the scenic canyons and deserts of Arizona and New Mexico within reach of tourists from the East.

Railroads and settlers help each other. As the railroads fanned out over the prairies, they encouraged more settlers to go West. Homesteaders in territory through which railroads ran could easily ship their goods to the markets of the East, and they avoided many of the dangers and hardships of the earlier pioneers. At the same time, the railroads depended for their prosperity upon a growing western population to provide freight and passengers for them to haul.

The close relationship between railroad prosperity and the growth of the West was clearly understood by the outstanding railroad promoter, James J. Hill. Hill built the Great Northern railway system, the lines of which were completed from the Great Lakes to Seattle, Washington, early in 1893. He came on the scene too late to share in the generous government land grants. He realized that the success of his railroad would depend upon the development of the vast resources of the Northwest. Therefore Hill organized excursions and conducted trainloads of prospective settlers to see for themselves what possibilities the lands in this region offered them.

Even after the settlers arrived, Hill con-

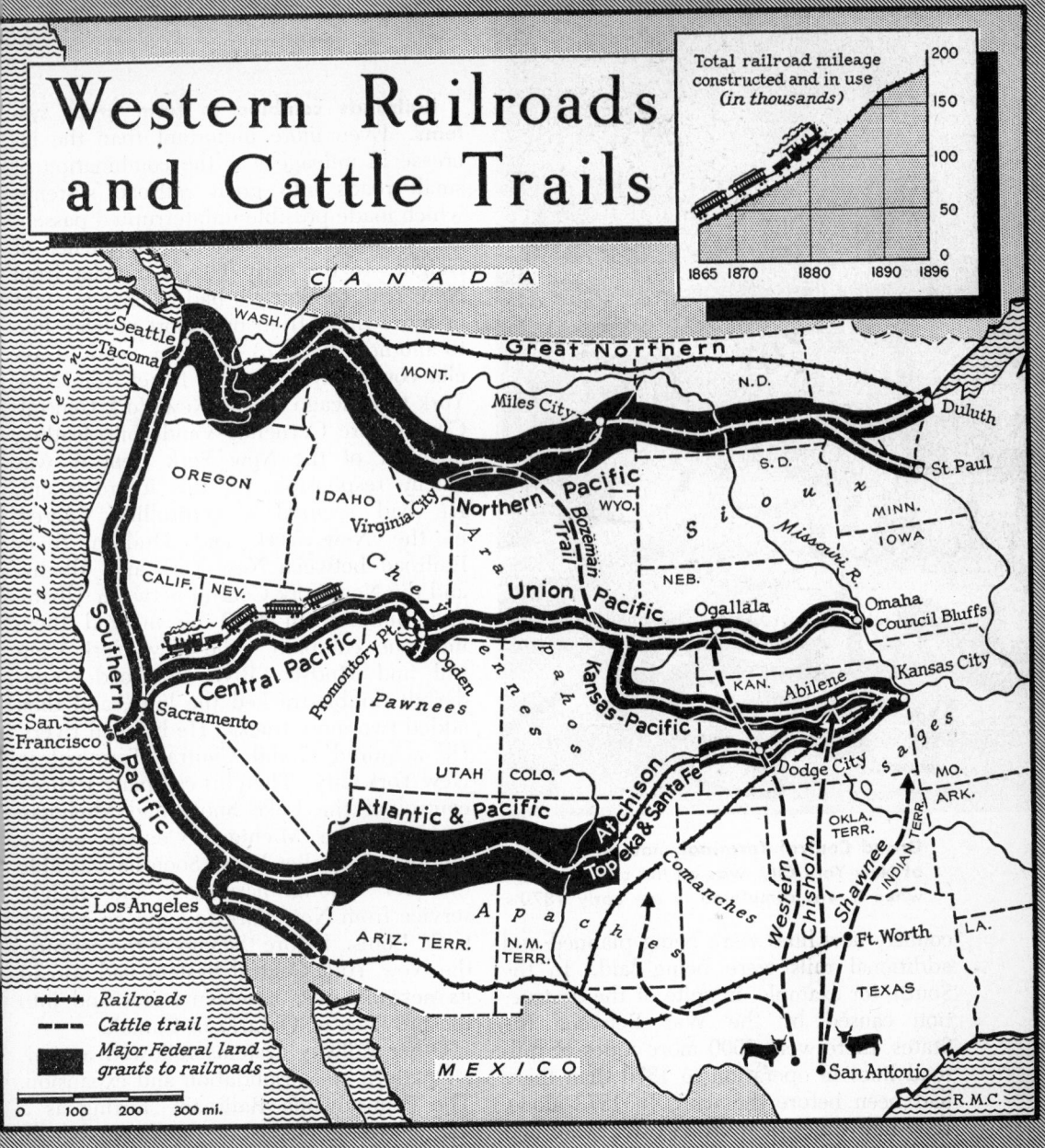

Western Railroads and Cattle Trails

Total railroad mileage constructed and in use (in thousands)

Railroad mileage multiplied about five times between 1865 and 1896. Included in the increase were five lines to the Far West. Notice how cattle trails joined them. Notice also that there was no rail connection with the East when western railroads were started (see page 364).

Railroads

Cattle trail

Major Federal land grants to railroads

0   100   200   300 mi.

tinued to take an interest in their welfare. To create a new market for what they produced, he arranged for steamship service between the Orient and the Pacific terminals of his railroad. Soon American food, as well as raw materials and manufactured goods, were flowing in a steady stream to the ports of China and Japan. Hill's foresight and boldness helped to establish prosperous ranches and thriving towns from Minnesota through the Dakotas, Montana, and Idaho to the west coast.

Railroad mileage increases throughout the country. The most spectacular growth of railroads in the era after 1865 took place in the West. Yet it would be a mistake to assume that railroad expansion was confined to any one section. Throughout the

Grand Central Terminal, now in the heart of New York City, was on the city's outskirts when it was completed in the early 1870's.

Railroads combine to form great systems.

Even more important than the increase in mileage was the combination of small roads into great railroad systems, which made possible uninterrupted passenger journeys and through shipments of freight. In the early '60's, a traveler from New York to Chicago had to change eight or more times from one short railway line to another. By 1873, however, such a traveler could buy a through ticket from New York to Chicago on the New York Central. Commodore Cornelius Vanderbilt, leading financier of the New York Central, was chiefly responsible for this improvement. He had secured a controlling interest in the New York and Hudson River Railroad between New York and Albany, and the New York Central between Albany and Buffalo. In 1869 he merged them into one company — the New York Central and Hudson River Railroad. Vanderbilt double-tracked the lines, and then added two more tracks. He bridged rivers. He acquired Grand Central Terminal in New York City. Then his company secured control of the Lake Shore and Michigan Southern, the Michigan Central, and a number of smaller lines. Soon he was able to offer through-passenger and freight service from New York to Chicago and on to St. Louis. Before the end of the century, the New York Central System had spread its network over nineteen states and into the province of Ontario in Canada.

country new lines were being planned and additional rails were being laid. In the South, for example, in spite of the destruction caused by the War Between the States, there were 2500 more miles of railroad lines in operation in 1870 than there had been before the war. In 1873 alone, 1300 new miles of railroad track were laid in the South.

In the entire country in 1860 there had been 30,000 miles of railroad lines. This mileage was more than doubled in the eight years after the War Between the States, when 35,000 additional miles of track were laid. The rate of railroad expansion was slowed down after the Panic of 1873, but in the 1880's an even more dramatic advance was made. In the ten years from 1880 to 1890, over 70,000 miles of new track were added by the railroads.

Other railway systems followed a similar pattern of consolidation and expansion. The Pennsylvania Railroad, starting as a line between Harrisburg and Pittsburgh, expanded until by 1900 it connected such widely separated points as Washington, Cleveland, Chicago, and St. Louis. The crowning achievement of the Pennsylvania Railroad, however, came some years later when it reached the heart of New York City by tunneling under the Hudson River. Meanwhile, the Baltimore and Ohio had reached Chicago in 1875. The Erie Railroad, after some shady financial dealings, was reorganized and became a leading freight-carrying road between New York and Chicago. Similar consolidations took place in the railroad systems of the South. Of special importance was the Richmond and West Point Railway, which became the basis for the development of the Southern Railway System.

Railroads become safe and more comfortable. At the same time that railroads were being expanded and combined, the new technology was providing greater safety, comfort, and service to the public. George M. Pullman introduced the sleeping-car in 1864 and followed it a few years later with "restaurant cars," or diners. Old wooden-and-iron or iron rails were discarded in favor of all-steel tracks which could carry heavier trains. The roads adopted a standard gauge, or width, between their rails so that the locomotives and cars of one company could roll along the tracks of another. Steel bridges did away with slow ferry-crossings. Greater safety at higher speeds was made possible in 1869 by the Westinghouse automatic air brake, which enabled the engineer to apply brakes to all cars at the same time. Automatic block signals reduced the danger of collisions, and the safety coupler saved the lives of many trainmen. The United States government took over some responsibility for railway safety in 1893, when Congress passed a law requiring railroads to use power brakes and automatic couplers.

Railway construction slows down. While the railroads continued to grow after 1890, they never again matched the tremendous construction of the 1880's. Toward the end of the century, the country boasted nearly 200,000 miles of railroad. This was more than in all of Europe combined, and nearly 40 per cent of the total railway mileage of the world. But the great age of railroad building was near an end. Railroad mileage in the United States reached its greatest extent, about 250,000 miles, just before the outbreak of World War I. After that, old roadbeds were abandoned faster than new ones were built.

Railroads influence all aspects of American life. It would be difficult to overestimate the importance of the railroads in the period from 1865 to the end of the century. They were the common element that influenced and stimulated all of the tremendous economic activity that took place at that time. The building of transcontinental lines brought about the settling of the West and had an important effect on the growth of agricultural production. Without the railroads to transport raw materials to the factories and to move the manufactured products from mill to consumer, big business and industries — nation-wide in scope — would not have come into being.

----------- CHECK-UP -----------

How did railroads spread over the country?

1. By what means did the government encourage railroad building?
2. What was the route of the first transcontinental railroad? What other transcontinental railroads were built?
3. How did the settler and the railroad help one another? How did technology improve railroad transportation?
4. What are some significant facts about the growth of railroads after 1865? How were railroad lines combined into large systems? What parts did Cornelius Vanderbilt and James J. Hill play in railroad building and operation?

Before the modern Pullman car, sleeping cars like this were available, but little sleep could be had. Passengers reclined, but were alert for sudden stops or lurches. They usually kept their boots on for quick changes of train in the night. Notice the conductor's ornate uniform and kerosene lantern.

The transcontinental telegraph, another heroic construction job, put the Pony Express out of business soon after it began.

3 Electricity Brings Instant Communication

An improved telegraph speeds messages. The Pony Express made its fastest time in 1861 when it carried Lincoln's *First Inaugural Address* from Nebraska to the end of the western telegraph line in Nevada in seven days and seventeen hours. Within a year, however, the first transcontinental telegraph had driven the Pony Express into bankruptcy. The transcontinental telegraph was successful in spite of everybody's expectation that Indians or buffaloes would destroy the poles. Rates at first were very high — a dollar a word for a message from Missouri to California. When the first burst of enthusiasm for sending messages died down, the cost was cut to five dollars for a ten-word telegram. After the War Between the States, new telegraph lines were built and the rates were lowered. The invention of the duplex telegraph (1872) meant lower costs and greater efficiency, for a message could be sent in both directions over the same wire at the same time. Later, the invention of the multiplex telegraph made it possible to send a number of messages over the same wire at the same time. Gradually most of the telegraph lines came under the control of the Western Union Telegraph Company, which provided a unified service over most of the country.

Cyrus W. Field lays the first cable. Meanwhile, attempts were being made to speed up communication between America and Europe. As early as 1854, Cyrus W. Field was laying a cable to carry electrical impulses under the Atlantic Ocean from Newfoundland to Ireland. In August, 1858, Queen Victoria and President Buchanan sent messages to each other along the completed cable, and Field was showered with congratulations. But these congratulations turned to ridicule when the cable broke down. Undiscouraged, Field kept working to remove technical difficulties. In 1866 he finally succeeded in setting up a permanent cable service. The time for sending trans-Atlantic messages, which formerly took ten days by steamship, was now cut to practically nothing.

The telephone revolutionizes communication. The success of the cable was remarkable enough, but people were really astonished ten years later by the invention of the telephone. At the Centennial Exposition in Philadelphia in 1876, a young teacher of the deaf, Alexander Graham Bell, exhibited a queer-looking instrument which, he claimed, would transmit the human voice by electricity. It attracted little attention until the Emperor of Brazil, a visitor at the exposition, consented to listen to it. "It speaks! It speaks!" he is said to have exclaimed in amazement. From that moment Bell's "talking box" was the sensation of the exposition.

Although at first most people thought of the telephone as a sort of mechanical toy, by 1890 there were more than 400,000 subscribers. As with the telegraph, it was soon found that service became more reliable and satisfactory when it was unified. For that reason, at about the turn of the century, the American Telephone and Telegraph Company took over the American Bell Telephone and gradually gained control of the most important telephone lines of the country.

Like the railroads, the telephone and other new forms of communication played a part in stimulating the growth of big, nation-wide business and industry. Now the business leader could keep in constant touch with the sources of raw materials and with the salesmen selling his products far from the factories where they were produced.

——————— CHECK-UP ———————

What new means of communication did electricity make possible?

1. How did the telegraph change communication? What improvements were made in the telegraph?
2. Why is the date 1866 important in the development of the cable?
3. Who invented the telephone? What effects did it have on business and industry?

This telephone exchange, photographed in New York in the 1890's, served telephones like those shown below.

4 The Corporation Becomes the Dominant Form of Business Organization

Corporations increase in importance. In order to operate successfully, every business must have some form of organization. Before 1860 the most common forms of business organization were the *partnership*, owned by two or more individuals, and the *proprietorship*, in which a single individual owned the entire concern. But a partnership or a proprietorship was generally unable to raise the huge sums needed to finance large-scale business. Few men had enough money to build a railroad or a steel mill or a large shoe factory. A form of business organization was needed in which the small savings of many investors could be combined to provide the neces-

sary funds. As you have learned (page 229), for this purpose the *corporation* proved ideal. Already well established by 1860 in the cotton-mill and railroad industries, corporations were soon organized in many other kinds of business.

What is a corporation? Any group of people who wish to form a corporation can apply to the proper state official for a *charter*. The charter gives them the legal right to conduct a certain kind of business in a certain way under a corporation name (the United States Steel Corporation, for example). They may then raise funds, or *capital*, by selling shares of *stock*, or certificates of ownership. The initial price of

Transmitter

Receiver

Receiver

Receiver

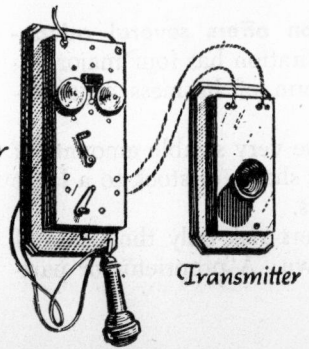

Transmitter

EARLY TELEPHONES

a share of stock may be set at $100, or at some other figure such as a mere five dollars, and an individual may buy as many shares as he desires. He hopes, of course, that the business will prosper so that he will receive *dividends* (that is, his share of the profits), and so that his stock will increase in value.

Stockholders' meetings are commonly held once a year. At these meetings stockholders elect the *directors* and *officers* of the corporation. A stockholder votes in proportion to the number of shares he owns — for example, a man who owns 1000 shares will cast 1000 votes, while the owner of a single share will cast only one vote. Corporations may also borrow money by issuing *bonds*. Bondholders are entitled to a fixed rate of *interest* before any dividends are paid, but they do not share in the ownership of the corporation.

Stocks of a corporation are usually widely owned. Stock ownership in some well-known American corporations has been restricted to a very few persons or even to members of a single family. For example, the meat-packing firm of Armour and Company was family-owned for 50 years, while the Ford industries were family-owned and operated until the death of Henry Ford, their founder, in 1947. More common, however, is the corporation with large numbers of stockholders. The control of these corporations is supposedly shared by all stockholders. Actually, decisions are usually left to the officers, or *management*, of the corporation and to the major stockholders. For example, the annual meeting of the United States Steel Corporation is held in one small room — which is, at that, quite large enough for as many of its 200,000 shareholders as care to attend.

The corporation offers several advantages. The corporation has four major advantages as a form of business organization:

(1) It can raise very sizable amounts of money by selling shares of stock to a large number of buyers.

(2) Stockholders risk only the value of the stock they own. A proprietor or part-ner who fails in business may have to sell his private possessions and give up all his savings in order to pay his debts. Also, any partner is liable for all the debts of the partnership. The owner of a $100 share of stock in a bankrupt corporation may lose his $100, but that is all.

(3) Stocks can be more easily sold or transferred than a partnership or an individually-owned business.

(4) A corporation continues indefinitely. If a proprietor or partner dies, a business has to be reorganized or cease operation. If a stockholder, even a very large stockholder, dies, corporation affairs usually go on as before.

Corporations grow rapidly after 1865. Before the War Between the States, business and industry were largely concerned with a small local market (pages 361–2). To supply these local markets there were hundreds and even thousands of small businesses, mostly run by individual proprietors or partnerships. In the outburst of manufacturing after 1865, production on a large scale for a larger national market seemed to offer the best hopes of good profits. Keen competition between rival companies led to price-cutting, and made low costs of production necessary if a company was to stay in business. The new labor-saving machines and technological processes lowered production costs, but these machines were usually too expensive for the small local businessman to buy. Consequently, many small businessmen were forced to join with other businessmen to form corporations, or they were driven out of business. As time went on, a larger and larger share of business and industry was conducted by corporations. By the 1890's corporations produced nearly three fourths of the total value of manufactured products in the United States.

As business became national in scope, another interesting change took place. The number of manufacturing companies actually became smaller, while each corporation became larger and larger. In the 1860's, for example, more than 2000 factories made agricultural implements. By 1890 this number had been cut in half, and after the turn of the century one company alone produced a large majority of all the plows, reapers, and cultivators.

Pools try to share the market. Sometimes the new corporations, with their labor-saving machinery and efficient organization, produced too much for their own good. Such a crisis occurred in the 1870's in the cordage business, for example, when so much twine and rope was manufactured that it was impossible to sell it all. Trying to unload their products, manufacturers cut prices until many firms could no longer meet their costs and were forced to close their doors. The cordage manufacturers met the crisis by organizing a *pool.* They divided the business of the country among themselves, and each member of the pool agreed to limit his sales to a certain volume. In other industries, too, pools were formed to fix prices, divide profits, or parcel out markets. The practice of pooling was especially common among rival railroads. But pooling had one drawback: it was outside the law. A firm which violated its pooling agreement could not be sued in the courts. Many firms signed agreements and then acted as though they hadn't. Pools, therefore, proved an unreliable method of controlling sales and markets.

Trusts prove more effective than pools. Realizing that the pool could not regulate sales and markets, the officers and directors of the Standard Oil Company decided to seek a new form of business organization — a "super corporation." The controlling shares of stock in about 40 separate oil companies were turned over to a single board of nine *trustees.* The stockholders received in exchange *trust certificates* which entitled them to a share in the profits of the *trust.* The entire management of all these 40 companies was then centralized in the hands of the trustees. Competition among the companies was, of course, eliminated.

The Standard Oil trust served as the model for many others, including the sugar trust, the whisky trust, and the lead trust. In time, the term "trust" came to mean any business organization which secured a *monopoly* — that is, the exclusive, or almost

"**Modern Colossus of (Rail) Roads,**" a cartoon of the times, criticizes the railroad monopoly of Vanderbilt and others. The title was a pun. Can you figure it out? As a hint, look up the "Colossus of R . . ." in an encyclopedia.

exclusive, control of an industry. Since trusts conducted business on a huge scale, they were able to reduce their costs in many ways: by using specialized machinery, by controlling their own raw materials, and by transforming "waste material" into salable by-products.[4] Instead of giving the consumer the benefit of their lower costs, however, the trusts frequently raised the

[4] The ability of the great packing houses to use by-products was described by "Mr. Dooley" (Finley Peter Dunne) as follows: "A cow goes lowin' softly into Armours an' comes out glue, beef, gelatine, fertylizer, celooloid, joolry, sofy cushions, hair restorer, washin' sody, soap, lithrachoor an' bed springs so quick that while aft she's still cow, for'ard she may be anything fr'm buttons to Pannyma hats."

prices of articles under their control. Where a real monopoly existed, the consumer had no choice but to pay the price or do without.

Corporations help the growth of the American industrial system. Like the expansion of the railroads, the growth of the corporation as a form of business organization was stimulated by the widespread economic changes taking place in the country. And at the same time, also like the railroads, corporations helped to speed up those changes.

——————— CHECK-UP ———————

Why did corporations become the dominant form of business organization?

1. What are the chief features of the corporation? What are its advantages over other forms of business organization?
2. How does the ownership of a corporation differ from its control and management?
3. Why did corporations grow rapidly after 1865? What happened to many small businesses? Why did the number of companies manufacturing a particular product decrease?
4. What advantages did corporations secure by combining? Distinguish between the pool and the trust. Why did the trust supplant the pool?

5   **Steel and Oil Illustrate the Growth of American Industry**

Steel becomes a great industry. The steel industry is an outstanding example of the growth of large-scale production and business consolidation which are characteristic of modern American business. Before 1860 steel was costly and was used only for the manufacture of fine tools and cutlery. The annual national production was only a few thousand tons. At the turn of the century, however, not only had the United States become the world's leading producer of steel, but its output equaled that of the next two producers, England

and Germany, combined. Railroads, steamships, bridges, skyscrapers, and a thousand other familiar items depended upon steel for their important roles in the development of modern America. (See chart, page 359.)

The dramatic growth of the steel industry took place for several reasons:

(1) Important technological advances in the manufacture of steel, notably the introduction of the Bessemer and open hearth processes, made possible the production of high grade steel at low cost. In the 1850's an Englishman, Henry Bessemer, and an American, William Kelly, discovered a way to make large quantities of steel cheaply. Experimenting separately, they discovered that a blast of air directed at molten iron would remove its impurities.

(2) Abundant deposits of iron ore in the region of Lake Superior, particularly in the Mesabi Range in Minnesota, provided what seemed to be an inexhaustible supply of raw material.

(3) Men of vision, daring, great energy, and resourcefulness were attracted to the industry.

(4) Producers of steel were aided by high tariff rates on foreign steel.

Andrew Carnegie builds an empire in steel. During its early years, the steel industry was dominated by Andrew Carnegie. At the age of thirteen, Carnegie, the son of poor Scotch immigrants, went to work as bobbin boy in a cotton mill at $1.20 a week. He possessed certain remarkable qualities that carried him rapidly up the ladder of success. By the time he was 30, he resigned as a district superintendent of the Pennsylvania Railroad to go into business for himself. His first venture was in the building of iron bridges, which led him into the manufacture of iron and steel. Soon he was buying out one competitor after another. After he joined forces in 1882 with Henry C. Frick, who controlled the coke industry,[5] Carnegie's position as king of the steelmakers was unquestioned.

Carnegie had seen businessmen ruined because their rivals controlled the sources

[5] Coke, a product made by baking coal, was essential in "firing" the great blast furnaces of the steel industry.

of raw materials, or because railroads favored their competitors with lower rates and better service. The only safe way to run his own business, he believed, was to buy up everything needed for the manufacture and sale of steel. Frick's coke ovens were only part of the long-range plan. The Carnegie Steel Company acquired its own coal and iron mines, its own steamships and barges, its own railroads. Through its control over these resources, it achieved very efficient production. "The ore which is lying in the wilds of Minnesota on Monday morning," comments a writer on the romance of steel, "is dug up, transported a thousand miles, and made into steel rails by Saturday night."

The U. S. Steel Corporation is formed. Carnegie's business ventures continued to prosper. In 1900 they made annual profits of nearly $40,000,000, of which Carnegie's personal share was $25,000,000. But Carnegie was getting old and wanted to retire. It was no easy matter to find a purchaser for such valuable properties. By threatening to extend his activities and to start a destructive price war, however, Carnegie convinced his rivals that they must buy him out or be ruined. In 1901, the great investment firm of J. P. Morgan and Company organized the United States Steel Corporation to take over the Carnegie properties as well as other holdings. This new industrial giant was founded on a capital investment of about $1,400,000,000, and controlled over half of the iron and steel production of the United States — from the mining of the ore to the distribution of the finished steel products.

Oil becomes big business. The development of the petroleum or oil industry is another dramatic story in the growth of American industry. Before 1859 seepages of oil on farms were looked upon as nuisances, since the oil made streams impure and ruined wells. Sometimes small quantities of petroleum were sold as medicine — Kier's "rock oil," for example, was recommended as a "natural remedy" for a wide variety of human ills. But when chemists discovered that kerosene, distilled from pe-

troleum, was a better fuel for lamps than expensive whale-oil, oil lands suddenly became valuable.

The first oil well was drilled by Edwin L. Drake in 1859. Northwestern Pennsylvania, where Drake's well was situated, immediately became the center of the first oil boom. Gaunt, wooden oil derricks sprang up everywhere on the farms and town lots in northwestern Pennsylvania. Fortunes were suddenly made, and often suddenly lost. The price of oil rose and fell violently. At the close of 1859, crude oil brought $20 for a barrel of 42 gallons; two years later, because of overproduction, it was worth at one time only 10 cents. Again in 1864 it was worth $12. The annual production of crude oil grew steadily until by the end of the century the United States was producing a large part of the world supply. Most important of the petroleum products in the early days were kerosene, naphtha, lubricating oils, and wax. In later years gasoline, fuel oil, and asphalt became more and more important.

Rockefeller organizes the Standard Oil Company. John D. Rockefeller's career in the oil industry parallels that of Carnegie in steel. At the age of sixteen, Rockefeller was earning 50 cents a day as a clerk in

The first oil well, as pictured by a modern artist, is being "brought in" by workmen. Edwin L. Drake and a friend are directing the operation.

Cleveland. He was steadily promoted to better jobs in the wholesale produce business, went into business for himself, and saved enough money to set himself up in the oil-refining industry (1862). Eight years later Rockefeller, with his brother and other associates, formed a million-dollar corporation called the Standard Oil Company of Ohio. The company's refinery, which could produce 600 barrels a day, was one of the largest of some 250 refineries which had sprung up since the Pennsylvania oil boom. The new corporation met with startling success, partly because of Rockefeller's extraordinary business ability, and partly because of business methods which, if not always praiseworthy, were at least remarkably effective.

Standard Oil secures favors from railroads. One way to outsmart competition was to get special privileges from the railroads over which oil had to be shipped. Standard Oil joined with some lesser refineries in 1871 to form the South Improvement Company, a Pennsylvania corporation organized for the special purpose of

Early oil wells had crude wooden derricks and sheds. This one was photographed in Pennsylvania in the late 1860's.

bargaining with the railroads. The railroads were anxious to secure the South Improvement Company's tremendous business, and for that reason they agreed to *rebate* (refund) part of the established freight charge on every barrel of oil shipped. Since rebates lowered operating costs for the favored refineries, they could make larger profits or sell oil more cheaply than their competitors.

But the South Improvement Company went even further. It actually persuaded the railroads to pay it rebates not only on its own oil but on oil shipped by competing companies! Public discovery of these agreements brought loud protests, and the charter of the South Improvement Company was repealed by the Pennsylvania legislature. Nevertheless Rockefeller went on to arrange secret rebates with railroads on Standard's shipments of crude oil.

Standard Oil builds a monopoly. By 1878 the Standard Oil Company controlled 90 per cent of the country's petroleum business. Rockefeller bought out competing refineries at his own price. If competitors hesitated to sell, the company was ruthless in crushing them. Prices were cut below cost in the competitor's district, so that the competitor had the choice of closing his business at once or of selling at a loss. Standard, on the other hand, with its great resources and large marketing area, could make up its losses in one district by raising prices in another. Or the company could carry a loss for a long time, knowing that when its rivals had been bought out or ruined, it could raise prices at will.

The selling organization of the Standard Oil Company was particularly efficient. The country was mapped out into divisions, and the Standard sales manager in each division was expected to get *all* the business in his territory. In return, the company set out to give the consumer good service and high quality products. Before 1900 the Standard Oil Company dominated the production, transportation, and refining of crude petroleum in the United States, as well as the distribution of the refined products throughout the world.

In 1882 this gigantic business was consolidated into the Standard Oil Trust. (See page 371.) After the trust was dissolved by a decree of the Ohio courts in 1892, the nine men who had been trustees continued to hold the controlling stock of the 20 corporations which had composed it.

——————— CHECK-UP ———————

How do steel and oil illustrate the growth of big business?

1. What were the reasons for the spectacular growth of the steel industry?
2. What part did Carnegie play in the development of steel? Why was the United States Steel Corporation formed?
3. How did oil become big business? What devices did the Standard Oil Company use to reduce competition?

6 **Panics and Depressions Become More Severe**

Earlier in this chapter, references have been made to the periods of depression in the latter part of the 1800's. Ever since the Industrial Revolution began in America, periods of prosperity and expansion have been followed by panics and depressions — and in turn, by recovery.[6] This pattern of rising and falling business activity is known as the *business cycle.* After 1865, as industry grew stronger and as more and more people began to work in factories, boom times became more pronounced and depressions more severe.

The Panic of 1873 ends a period of prosperity. The period of prosperity which gained momentum during and after the War Between the States came to an abrupt end with the Panic of 1873. This panic, and the depression which followed, were caused (1) by overproduction on farms and in factories, (2) by the building of too many railroads, and (3) by too much

[6] For the panics of 1819 and 1837, see pages 183 and 213. Another panic occurred in 1857.

Periods of Prosperity and Depression

Rapid economic growth occurred between 1865 and 1897. Still, periods of prosperity were followed by panics and depressions. Can you explain why?

speculation, or gambling, on the stock and commodity exchanges. When the great banking house of Jay Cooke and Company failed, banks and corporations toppled like bowling pins. Hundreds of thousands of wage earners were thrown out of work. Six years elapsed before the country shook off this depression.

1893 brings another crisis. With the exception of a minor set-back in 1884–86, the period from 1879 to 1893 was a time of tremendous business activity and prosperity.[7] The Panic of 1893 was caused (1) by too much speculation, (2) by too heavy investments in railroads and other ventures, and (3) by lack of confidence that a sound currency would be maintained. Hundreds of banks failed. Over 15,000 business concerns closed their doors in 1893, and a number of railroads went bankrupt. Financial ruin, unemployment, discontent, and labor disorders resulted. Another four-year period of depression followed before conditions returned to normal.

Industrialization brings problems as well as benefits. By the 1890's it was becoming fairly clear that the boom-depression cycle was a definite characteristic of the

[7] Farming was in a state of depression after 1887, but hard times did not hit city workers until after 1893.

modern industrial age. It was associated with the process of industrialization — the use of machines, large-scale production, and business consolidation — which had come to dominate American life. To be sure, industrialization had brought many benefits. Higher standards of living were attained by a larger number of people. New methods of travel and communication enlarged the horizons of many communities. Much of the drudgery of labor was removed, and the hours of toil were reduced without loss of production. On the other hand, with the growing concentration of population in cities and manufacturing centers, slums and poverty-stricken areas appeared. The replacement of men by machines created a serious condition of unemployment. The monotonous and wearisome repetition of mechanical work and the fact that little or no skill was required for the ordinary machine job raised problems for the workingman. And to all these there was added the constant rise and fall of business activity, which created grave economic and social problems. The industrialized America of the 1890's was indeed a far cry from the nation of small independent farmers of which Thomas Jefferson dreamed.

———— CHECK-UP ————

Why did panics and depressions become more severe?

1. What is meant by the business cycle? Distinguish between a panic and a depression.
2. What were the causes of the Panic of 1873? The Panic of 1893?
3. What were some of the problems and benefits which the new industrial age produced?

CHAPTER REVIEW

Terms to Understand

technology	management
patent	pool
standard gauge	trust
investment	by-product
corporation	monopoly
stock	rebate
directors	business cycle
dividend	industrialization

People and Things to Know About

Thomas A. Edison
Union Pacific Railroad
Central Pacific Railroad
James J. Hill
Cornelius Vanderbilt
Alexander Graham Bell
Cyrus W. Field

Andrew Carnegie
John D. Rockefeller
United States Steel Corporation
Edwin L. Drake
Standard Oil Company
Panic of 1873
Panic of 1893

Historic Dates to Identify

1859	1869	1876
1866	1873	1893

Questions to Discuss

1. How did the railroads contribute to the

Questions to Discuss (Cont.)

rapid disappearance of the frontier after the War Between the States?

2. Should James J. Hill be considered as more than just a railroad builder? Should his accomplishments be discounted because they were profitable to him?

3. How might you be affected by the introduction of the mechanical cotton picker (a technological advance) if you were (a) a sharecropper, (b) a large southern plantation owner, (c) a consumer of goods made of cotton, (d) a manufacturer of cotton textiles?

4. Compare the following:

(a) The chief methods of producing goods in 1790 and in 1890.

(b) The advantages and disadvantages of a specialized factory worker with a handicraft worker of 100 years ago.

(c) The problems of railroad building east and west of the Mississippi.

5. It is true of many corporations that the people who own them do not run them, and the people who run them do not own them. Explain. Is this condition of any significance?

6. Name several kinds of business that are well-adapted to the proprietorship or partnership, and several which are best adapted to the corporate form.

Relating Geography and History

Show on an outline map of the United States:

(*a*) The routes of the chief transcontinental railroads.

(*b*) The chief industrial cities of the United States with appropriate symbols to indicate the chief products of these cities.

(*c*) The chief sources of our most important raw materials.

Other Things to Do

*1. Make a list of what you consider to be the most important inventions in American history. Be ready to defend your choices.

2. George Westinghouse and C. F. Kettering are like Edison in having made numerous important inventions. Prepare a report on the life and work of one of these two men.

3. Contribute to a collection of pictures taken from magazines which show recent advances in technology. Arrange to have these placed on a bulletin board.

4. If there is some large manufacturing plant

Other Things to Do (Cont.)

in your community, visit it and report your observations. Look particularly for evidences of labor-saving devices.

5. Prepare a talk on stagecoach operation and travel before the transcontinental railroads were built. Mark Twain's *Roughing It*, Riegel's *America Moves West*, and Dick's *Vanguards of the Frontier* have excellent accounts.

6. Secure further information on the meaning of such important terms connected with our economic development as "corporation" and "trust." You will find others in the lists of *Terms to Understand* and *People and Things to Know About*. This activity provides a good opportunity to become acquainted with the useful set of references known as *The Encyclopedia of the Social Sciences*. In these volumes you will find comparatively brief but authoritative discussions of the above terms and many others. Use this encyclopedia as you would any other. Be sure to note the cross references given at the beginning of each article.

Chapter **20**

Railroad striker

EXPANDING INDUSTRY PRESENTS

PROBLEMS TO BOTH GOVERNMENT

AND LABOR

Corporations, which should be the carefully restrained creatures of the law and servants of the people, are fast becoming the people's masters.

Grover Cleveland

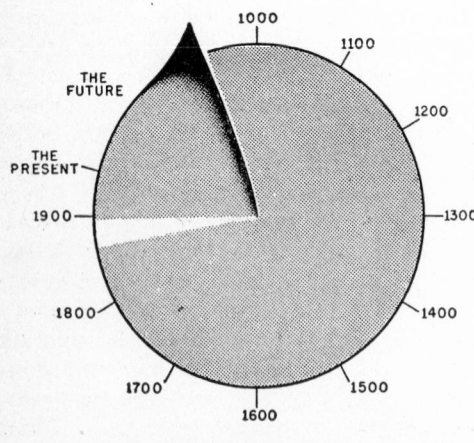

1865-1896

One of the early laws passed in 1789 by the first Congress of the United States was a measure providing for a tariff on imports. According to the preamble of this law, the purpose of the tariff was not only to raise money for running the government but also to provide "encouragement and protection of manufacturers." Thus, from the very beginning of the United States there was acceptance of the idea that the government should encourage national economic development. Although various laws were passed during the 1800's to improve the economic well-being of Americans, the tariff was the government's chief means of protecting and aiding the development of American business and industry.

At the same time that the United States government had encouraged eco-

378

nomic development, and manufacturing in particular, it had just as strongly frowned on government interference with the actual operation of business. This "hands-off" policy toward business was stated as early as 1789 by James Madison when he said:

[I declare myself] the friend to a very free system of commerce . . . It is . . . a truth that if industry and labor are left to take their own course they will generally be directed to those objects which are most productive, and this in a more certain and direct manner than the wisdom of the most enlightened legislature could point out.

By the end of the 1800's, however, the rapid development of industry and the growth of larger and larger corporations had produced a significant change in the organization and workings of our economic system. What, now, should the government's attitude toward business be? Should the government, as Madison had urged, leave business and labor "to take their own course"?

The industrialization of the country had also brought serious problems to the workingman. Gone was the close friendly relation between the worker and the owner in the small shop or factory. In place of scattered groups of workingmen in small towns, there had arisen in our cities a multitude of laboring men and women who were entirely dependent on impersonal giant corporations for their livelihood. It was inevitable that these workers should consider their common problems and attempt to find ways to solve them.

First of all, this chapter will carry the story of government's protection of manufacturing down to the late 1800's and indicate why government raised tariffs to an even higher level. It will then discuss the relations of government and business and of business and labor, as well as some of the many pressing problems which growing industry brought to government and labor during the last half of the 1800's. These problems will be presented under the following topics:

1. High tariffs encourage the growth of business and industry.
2. The government begins to change its

policy concerning the regulation of business.
3. The government tries to regulate the railroads.
4. The government's attempt to curb monopolies meets with little success.
5. Labor begins to organize to meet the growing power of industry.
6. Labor and capital battle for position.

1 High Tariffs Encourage the Growth of Business and Industry

Differences arise over the tariff. Almost from the beginning of the new republic, the tariff aroused differences among various groups within the country. But it was not until after 1828 and the high "Tariff of Abominations" that objections became violent. Congressmen who represented agricultural states, especially those in the South, fought vigorously against what they considered to be a means of enriching one element in the population — manufacturing — at the expense of the rest of the country. Thereafter, from the early 1830's until 1860, tariff rates were steadily reduced. The War Between the States abruptly checked the downard trend of tariff duties and ushered in an era of much higher tariffs. After 1860, rates on imports mounted rapidly until in 1864 the average duty was nearly two and a half times that of the prewar period.

Industrialists demand continued protection. The boost in tariff rates, or duties, during the War Between the States was caused by the government's need for money to carry on the war. When the fighting ended, however, northern manufacturers, whose business had expanded to meet wartime demands, wanted the high duties maintained. These industrialists argued that even if high tariff duties were not needed for government revenue, they were required to protect American industry from foreign competition. Three major reasons were given for keeping tariff rates high:

(1) *A high tariff encouraged the development of new industries.* This is known as the "infant-industries" argument. Americans who were just beginning to produce steel, for example, could not make it as efficiently and as cheaply as their English competitors who had the advantages of experience, well-established plants, and a supply of skilled labor. A duty on imported steel was necessary to raise its price to a level at which American manufacturers could afford to sell their steel.

(2) *The United States could become self-sufficient behind a tariff wall.* It was better for the country, industrialists said, to provide for its own needs than to satisfy them with foreign goods which might be cut off in case of war.

(3) *High tariffs meant high wages.* American manufacturers argued that if they had to price their goods to compete with those of Europe and Asia, American workers could not continue to receive wages higher than those in foreign countries.

Republicans sponsor protection. These demands by manufacturers for high tariffs were supported in Congress by the radical Republicans (page 322), who controlled Congress for a number of years after 1865. As a matter of fact, the tariff question was one important reason why the radical Republicans were opposed to admitting southern representatives to Congress after the war. They were afraid that the agricultural South would join with the agricultural West in an effort to reduce the tariff.

In the early 1870's, those who opposed high tariffs forced through some slight reduction in import duties. After the Panic of 1873, however, when government revenue dropped, higher tariff rates were restored. In 1882 a tariff commission recommended a cut of 20 per cent in rates. But Congress was not convinced, and a year later it passed a tariff law which lowered the general level of rates by only 5 per cent. At this time, the Republican Party seemed generally in favor of high tariffs for the protection of industry. The Democrats, for their part, remained cautiously silent.

High tariffs fill the Treasury to overflowing. During the War Between the States, the chief argument for higher tariffs had been the government's need for funds. By the mid-eighties, however, this need no longer existed. Thanks mainly to high tariff rates, the United States Treasury was actually collecting about 100 million dollars a year more than it paid out.

Strange as it may seem, this condition was not desirable. It meant that the supply of money in circulation was cut down, because the surplus was simply stored away by the Treasury. Meanwhile, the country's growing population and expanding industry needed more money — not less — with which to carry on its business. It was clear that the government ought to whittle down its surplus. But, to do that was not as easy as it might seem.

How could the surplus be reduced? There were three ways in which the surplus could be reduced: (1) The government could lower the tariff. (2) The government could spend more money. Internal improvements, veterans' pensions, and an expanded navy could consume huge sums. (3) The government could use the surplus to pay off the national debt.

At first glance, paying the national debt seemed like good common sense. The debt, however, was in the form of bonds which were owned by individuals and institutions all over the country. The bonds were not yet due. In order to repay the debt ahead of schedule, the government would have to buy up the bonds from their owners. Some bondholders might not wish to sell; others would sell only at an increased price (at a *premium*). But there was a more serious objection to buying up the bonds. They formed the basis for the type of paper money known as national banknotes (page 313). If the bonds were retired, this paper money would also have to be recalled. In brief, if the surplus were used to pay the government debt, the United States Treasury would be putting the surplus into circulation with one hand while it removed the national banknotes from circulation with the other. Such a procedure would not put into circulation the amount of currency which the nation's expanding business needed.

Cleveland urges tariff reduction. In 1885 Grover Cleveland became the first Democratic President since the War Between the States. President Cleveland was willing to approve liberal expenditures for the new steel navy, but he balked at heavy appropriations for veterans' pensions and internal improvements. The more he considered the problem of the surplus, the more he became convinced that tariff reduction was the only solution.

Cleveland's annual message to Congress in 1887 was given over entirely to the subject of the tariff. He denounced the surplus because it made the Treasury "a hoarding place for money needlessly withdrawn from trade and the people's use, thus crippling our national energies . . ." The solution was clear to him: "Our present tariff laws ought to be at once revised and amended."

Cleveland pointed out that, besides bringing in too much money, these tariffs raised the cost of living for everyone. People who bought foreign-made articles were paying for the duty in the price they paid for the articles; people who bought American-made articles that were "protected" from foreign competition paid this same high price. Everything from the farmer's plow to the housewife's kitchen stove, from the children's clothing to the blankets on the bed, was more expensive because of the duties on iron and steel and wool. Cleveland also objected to the argument that high tariffs meant high wages. He pointed out that only 15 per cent of all American workers were employed in "protected" industries. For the other 85 per cent, he said, the tariff raised prices without bringing about a wage increase to pay for them.

Cleveland did not favor _free trade_ (the removal of all tariff duties). He insisted, in fact, that the lowering of tariffs must be done "without imperiling the existence of our manufacturing interests." But he thought that American industry should not demand "immense profits instead of moderately profitable returns." He declared, "It is a condition, and not a theory, that confronts us."

A Republican cartoon of 1888 pictures a Democratic congressman destroying American factories with a flood of foreign goods.

Cleveland's recommendations fail. A tariff bill which met Cleveland's demands was introduced into the House of Representatives and was passed after a warm debate. The Republican Senate, on the other hand, tried to substitute a law providing for high tariffs. The issue was deadlocked until after the election of 1888. In that campaign the Republicans declared themselves definitely in favor of protection, while the Democratic platform pledged support for the President. After a heated contest in which the tariff was a leading issue, the Republicans carried both branches of Congress and elected their presidential candidate, Benjamin Harrison.[1]

Congress enacts the McKinley Tariff. The Republicans interpreted their victory as an endorsement of their stand on the tariff, and promptly used their strength in Congress to raise tariff walls to new heights. William McKinley of Ohio, chairman of the House Ways and Means Committee, introduced a bill which raised the level of rates high enough to satisfy even the most

[1] Cleveland, however, had more popular votes. See page 464.

thoroughgoing protectionists. The McKinley Tariff was adopted in 1890. In an effort to gain the good will of western farmers, the McKinley Act laid import duties upon certain foreign farm products such as wheat, corn, and potatoes. The act also included a *reciprocity* clause — an idea which became increasingly important later on. The reciprocity clause, in effect, said to foreign countries, "I'll treat you as you treat me." This is how it worked: Under the McKinley Act, certain commodities, like raw sugar, molasses, tea, coffee, and hides, were placed on the "free list" — that is, they could be sent into the United States without tariff duties. This provision was intended particularly to increase our trade with Latin American nations. But the reciprocity clause gave the President authority to impose duties upon these commodities whenever the countries exporting them to us placed "unjust and unreasonable" duties on American products being shipped into their territory.

Another new feature of the McKinley Act was a provision that the government pay a *bounty* of two cents a pound to American sugar growers for all the sugar they grew in this country. This provision was an attempt to reduce the government's revenue. At the same time, it was intended to please (1) American sugar refiners, who wanted raw foreign sugar on the free list,[2] and (2) American sugar growers, who wanted protection for their "infant industry."

In general, the McKinley Act gave a higher degree of protection to industry than any tariff measure passed up to that time.

The McKinley Tariff proves unpopular. To the discomfort of the Republicans, the McKinley Act failed to win popular approval. The new tariff, which went into effect a month before the congressional elections of 1890, brought a sharp rise in retail prices. The Democrats naturally called this fact to the attention of the voters. Moreover, farmers failed to receive the benefits which they had been led to

expect from the new duties on agricultural products.[3] As a result, the elections reflected widespread discontent. An overwhelmingly Democratic majority was elected to the House. McKinley, "the guardian angel of protection," was one of several Republican representatives who failed to be re-elected. The Senate, however, remained Republican and was therefore able to block any attempts of the House to lower the tariff.

The tariff is an issue in the presidential campaign of 1892. In the elections of 1892 the Democrats made the most of popular discontent and pledged the party to a reduction of the tariff. After being out of the White House for four years, Grover Cleveland was elected to a second term and the Democrats gained control of both houses of Congress. But Cleveland faced a different situation from the one that confronted him in his first term; he no longer needed to worry about a surplus. The rates of the McKinley Tariff were so high that they prevented entirely the importations of many foreign-made articles. This was exactly what the supporters of a high tariff wanted. But of course it cut down government revenue, for income from duties on imported goods was greatly reduced. At the same time, lavish appropriations for pensions, sugar bounties, and other purposes had raised government expenditures to a new high. When Cleveland re-entered the White House, there was a deficit in the treasury.

Democrats plan tariff reduction. Nevertheless, when the new Congress met, the House of Representatives proceeded to fulfill the low tariff pledge of the Democratic platform. Sponsored by William Wilson of West Virginia, a bill which provided for numerous reductions passed the House without much difficulty. In the Senate, though, where the Democrats had only a narrow majority, the Wilson bill met determined resistance.

[2] Refined sugar continued to carry a substantial duty.

[3] The United States produces such large quantities of agricultural products (like wheat, corn, or cotton) that it does not need to import them. Therefore there is no point in trying to raise the prices of such products by a tariff on imports.

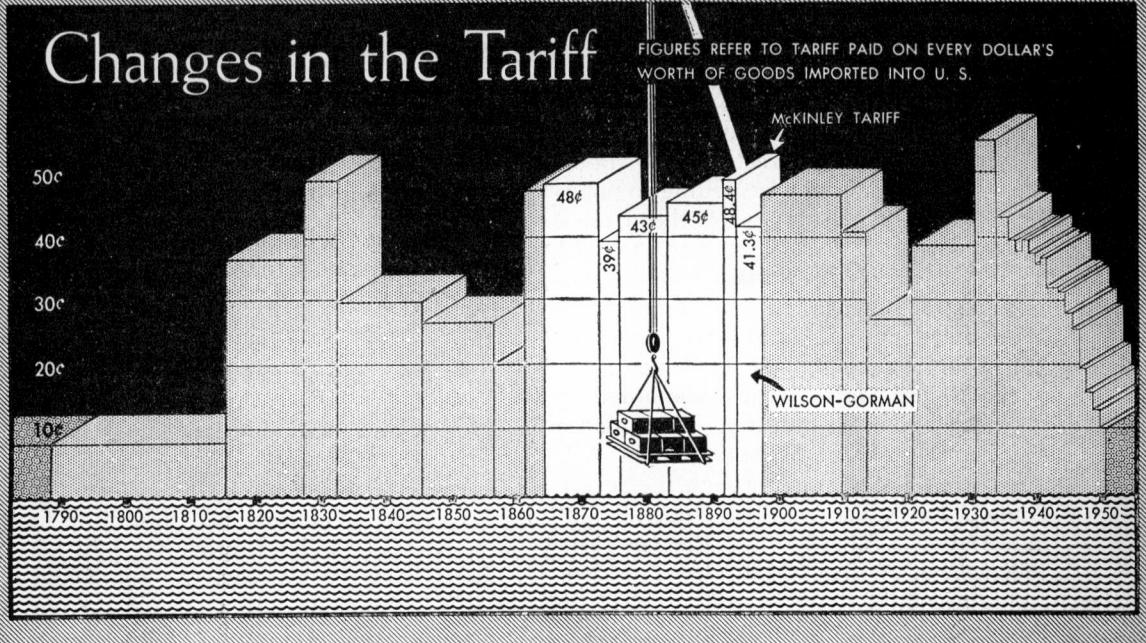

Changes in the Tariff

FIGURES REFER TO TARIFF PAID ON EVERY DOLLAR'S WORTH OF GOODS IMPORTED INTO U. S.

McKINLEY TARIFF

50¢
40¢
30¢
20¢
10¢

48¢   43¢   45¢   48.4¢   39¢   41.3¢

WILSON-GORMAN

1790 1800 1810 1820 1830 1840 1850 1860 1870 1880 1890 1900 1910 1920 1930 1940 1950

Tariff rates, which were raised during the War Between the States in order to increase government revenue, continued high after the war for other reasons. What were the arguments in favor of a high tariff at this time? (Look back to the chart on page 197 to recall details of the tariff prior to this time.)

The Wilson-Gorman Tariff is passed. Republican senators, of course, opposed reduction in the tariff. And there were Democrats, too, who were determined that the industrial or farming interests of their own states should not suffer from lowered tariff rates. The Louisiana senators, for example, demanded protection for sugar, while those from Maryland and Alabama wanted protection for coal and iron ore. Under the leadership of Senator Gorman of Maryland, the Senate completely revised the Wilson bill. More than 600 amendments were added, so that the final measure, known as the Wilson-Gorman Act, was scarcely less protective than the McKinley Act.

All through the debates, representatives of the steel, wool, sugar, and other protected industries had been very active in Washington. They did everything they could to persuade congressmen to pass the kind of tariff law they wanted. These pressure groups, which came to be known as lobbies, began to alarm many citizens. "The question is now," Representative Wilson declared, "whether this is a government by the American people for the American people, or a government of the sugar trust for the benefit of the sugar trust."

President Cleveland found himself in a difficult spot. To sign the Wilson-Gorman Act would put his stamp of approval upon a measure which he considered a piece of "party perfidy and dishonor." To veto it would sacrifice the slight advantages it possessed over the existing law. As there was little prospect of securing a law more to his liking, Cleveland let the bill become law without his signature.[4]

An income tax is declared unconstitutional. To make up for an expected loss of revenue, the Wilson-Gorman Act included a tax of two per cent on incomes of more than $4000 a year. The eastern financial interests, upon whom this tax fell most heavily, fought against it bitterly. When they failed to defeat it in Congress, they carried the issue to the Supreme Court. After lengthy deliberation, the Court decided, by

[4] An act passed by both houses of Congress goes to the President for his signature before it can become a law. If he does not sign or veto the measure within ten days (Sundays excepted), the bill becomes a law if Congress is still in session.

the narrow margin of five to four, that the income tax was contrary to the Constitution because it was a direct tax, not apportioned among the states according to population. (See Constitution of the United States, Article I, Section 8a, page xxxvii.) This decision of the Supreme Court was unexpected because an income tax had been levied during the War Between the States and had not been challenged.

The United States stands committed to tariff protection for industry. Even before the passage of the Wilson-Gorman Act, the United States went through the severe Panic of 1893. Blaming the Democratic administration for hard times, the voters in 1896 elected William McKinley President and returned the Republicans to power. By this time business had become strongly allied with the Republican Party. It contributed to Republican campaign funds and looked for Republican support of such programs as the high protective tariff. Increasingly, critics and economists began to point out the growing dangers of a high tariff. Nevertheless, as the 1800's drew to a close, the majority of the people believed firmly that the prosperity of the United States depended on the government's providing a high tariff for the benefit of business and industry. And, likewise, there is no doubt that the protective tariff had encouraged and aided the amazing growth of business and industry.

———— CHECK-UP ————

Why did the United States maintain a high tariff after the War Between the States?

1. What were the arguments for maintaining high tariff rates? What position did the Republican Party take?

2. What was the problem of the treasury surplus? How was the tariff related to it?

3. What were Cleveland's arguments in favor of tariff reduction? What happened to his recommendations?

4. What were the chief features of the McKinley Act? What were its effects?

5. Why was an income tax included in the Wilson-Gorman Act? What happened to it?

2 The Government Begins to Change Its Policy Concerning the Regulation of Business

The growth of business gives cause for alarm. The achievements of business and industry in the latter half of the nineteenth century were remarkable indeed. Because of railroad, telegraph, and telephone, all parts of the country were within easier reach of each other. Factories had sprung up in many parts of the land, providing jobs for millions of wage earners. As more and more back-breaking jobs were taken from human shoulders and given to the machine, the life of the farmer, as well as the city worker, became more pleasant and comfortable.

But the American public of the late 1800's began to view the activities of rapidly growing trusts and monopolies with alarm as well as admiration. Andrew Carnegie once described the millionaire as "the toiling bee laying up the honey in the industrial hive, which all the inmates of that hive, the community in general, will certainly enjoy." But the popular cartoonist more often pictured him as a tyrant exacting tribute from the farmer, the laborer, the consumer, and the small businessman.

It was true enough that the growth of industry and the rise of big business had poured immense power and wealth into the hands of a few men and that this condition was not always in the interests of the general welfare. Many workers became less secure in their jobs because their skills were no longer needed. The lower costs of large-scale production frequently did not bring lower prices to the public. From many sides came demands that the government "do something."

Government follows a policy of non-interference with business. Yet the government and the people were reluctant to regulate the operations of business. From colonial days, when the British Parliament tried to regulate our commerce and industry, the American people had cherished strong feelings against "government interference in business." The framers of the Constitution, with these memories fresh in their minds, limited the power of the central government over business to the regulation of foreign and interstate commerce. So, until the 1880's and '90's, with few exceptions, the national economic policy was dominated by the theory of *laissez faire*. According to this theory, government should not tamper with the economic system; it should let business do what it wished. If business were free to act without interference from the government, the theory implied, conditions in the long run would work out for the benefit of the greatest number of people.

State control of corporations is limited. The state governments, of course, had some control over corporations through their power to grant charters. Their right to revoke charters once they had been granted, however, was limited by the Dartmouth College decision (page 185). Also, a corporation having a charter in one state was free to do business in all the other states. Hundreds of corporations chartered in Delaware and New Jersey, where tax laws were especially favorable to them, carried on nation-wide activities.

Government policy begins to change. In addition to a policy of *laissez faire* the American people had long cherished another economic ideal — a belief in free competition and equality of opportunity for all.

Costumes of the 1870's

The development of giant corporations and trusts rapidly began to restrict competition and to limit opportunities for the small businessman and other groups. As the 1800's drew to a close, many people felt that the old theory of *laissez faire* was not working very well for the best interests of all Americans. The government, therefore, began to change its policy and to regulate certain business practices. First to feel the effects of government regulation were the railroads.

─────── CHECK-UP ───────

Why did the government begin to change its policy concerning the regulation of business?

1. What is "laissez faire"? Why did Americans believe in it?
2. Why did the government begin to abandon its policy of "laissez faire"?

┌─────────────────────────────────────┐
│   │
│ 3   **The Government Tries to**   │
│   **Regulate the Railroads**   │
│   │
└─────────────────────────────────────┘

Railroads engage in unfair practices. As the railroads expanded their network throughout the country after 1865, they brought many benefits to the American people. But they also brought some problems:

(1) *Dishonest stock practices.* Some railroads were overcapitalized — that is, the value of their properties was stated to be higher than it actually was. This practice made it look, on their records, as though these railroads were losing money. Thus, they were able to charge the public with excessive freight and passenger rates, and to pay lower stock dividends than they should have paid. The worst result was heavy loss to people who bought their stocks. Promoters like Jay Gould and Jim Fisk influenced thousands of people to buy stocks that were overvalued. When the stocks fell in value on the stock market, the promoters would buy them back at the lower figure. In this way, many an investor lost savings that he had taken years to accumulate.

(2) *Influence over government.* Those in control of railroads resorted to politics to get what they wanted. They used their money and power to determine who should and who should not be chosen for public office. By issuing free passes to legislators and influential officeholders, the railroads obtained special favors from those who made or enforced the laws. Some railroad leaders believed that their power put them above the law. When the great railroad magnate, Cornelius Vanderbilt, was once reminded that certain transactions violated New York laws, he is said to have burst out, "Law! What do I care about law? Hain't I got the power?"

(3) *Unequal freight rates.* You have seen (page 374) how the Standard Oil Company undermined its competitors by getting special rates or rebates from the railroads. Large shippers of steel, cattle, and other commodities received similar favors which were unfair to the average businessman. Equally unfair were the favorable rates given to certain cities and sections of the country. Where there was strong competition between railroads, or where inexpensive water transportation was available to shippers, freight rates might be ridiculously low. For example, cattle at one time could be shipped from Chicago to New York for $1.00 per carload. On the other hand, where there was no competition, the railroads tried to make up what they were losing elsewhere. During the middle '70's, it cost more to send freight directly from Rochester, New York, to St. Louis, Missouri, than to send it by way of New York City. In 1886 it cost $3.25 to send a bale of cotton 275 miles by rail from Winona, Mississippi to New Orleans, but only $1.00 to send it 450 miles by rail from Memphis, Tennessee, to New Orleans. Even over the same route the railroads often charged more for a "short haul" than for a "long haul."

(4) *Pooling agreements.* Where several railroads served the same territory, pooling agreements were formed. (See page 371.) In defense of their pooling agreements, the railroads argued that only by some such means could they put a stop to price cuts that would drive them all out of business. But the public feared that so much power in a few hands was dangerous, especially when anything as important as transportation was at stake.

State attempts at regulation fail. Of all the unfair practices that came with the growth of the railroads, unequal freight rates directly affected the greatest number of people. The farmers — especially in the Middle West and West — suffered most of all. Finally, they decided to act. Through farmers' organizations, known as Granges (pages 402–403), they persuaded state legislatures to aid them. The Illinois legislature, for example, set up a commission to fix maximum freight rates, and outlawed favoritism in rates or service between persons and places (1871). When these so-called "Granger laws" were first brought before the United States Supreme Court (1876), the Court ruled that they were constitutional. Later, however, in the case of the Wabash, St. Louis, and Pacific Railroad vs. Illinois (1886), the Court modified its earlier decision. It now held that the states had no right to regulate interstate commerce or to interfere with traffic moving across state borders, because this power was conferred by the Constitution upon Congress. Since nearly all important shipments were between states, the operation of the "Granger laws" were for practical purposes made valueless by this decision.

Congress is asked to take action. From the Supreme Court's ruling, it appeared that only the national government could regulate the railroads. Farmers and other shippers therefore demanded that Congress take action. They denied the claim of the railroad operators that railroads were private businesses and therefore not subject to interference by the government. The railroads, they argued, had profited by public grants of land, and the public depended on them as truly as on the public highways. It was insufferable, they said, that the railroads should carry on their business without regard for the public welfare. So ran the argument which was presented to Congress.

The Interstate Commerce Act is passed.
After long investigation and debate, Congress passed the Interstate Commerce Act in 1887. This important law forbade (1) pooling, (2) favoritism in rates among persons, places, or commodities, (3) rebates, (4) higher charges "for a shorter than for a longer distance over the same line, in the same direction," and (5) unreasonable or unjust rates. The Interstate Commerce Commission (ICC), made up of five men appointed by the President and confirmed by the Senate, was created to administer the law.

The Interstate Commerce Act proves ineffective. The Interstate Commerce Commission, however, could enforce its orders only through the courts, and in seeking the aid of the courts, it met with difficulties. There were endless delays. In one case damages which the commission ordered paid were still uncollected six years later. Judges insisted on re-hearing cases which the commission had settled, and often overruled the commission. When, in 1897, the Supreme Court declared that the commission had no power to prescribe rates, there was little left for the commission to do but gather and publish information about railroad rates and how they operated. Still, the Interstate Commerce Act had established the principle that railroads were subject to regulation by the national government. The public knew more than it had known before about railroad practices, and a basis had been laid for more effective legislation in later years.

─────── CHECK-UP ───────

Why did the government begin to regulate railroads?

1. What unfair practices did railroads engage in? With what effects?
2. How did regulation begin? Why was it necessary for the national government to take over the job?
3. What were the provisions of the Interstate Commerce Act? Why was the act ineffective at first?

"The New Central Power" was the title of this sarcastic cartoon by Thomas Nast. Uncle Sam is talking to Jay Gould, the financial promoter. He says, "Wall, really! So you're the fellow that's to run all the railroads and telegraphs and things! Wall, there's no accountin' for tastes. Our folks was dreadful 'fraid I was goin' to do it, and now they've pitched on you."

4 The Government's Attempt to Curb Monopolies Meets with Little Success

Decisions of the Supreme Court make the states powerless to control big business. During the latter half of the 1800's many people became suspicious of the growing power of industrial trusts and monopolies, just as they had of the railroads. But early efforts by state governments to restrict the industrial giants were even less successful than the "Granger laws." Corporations found a strong defense in the Fourteenth Amendment to the Constitution, which provides that no state may deprive any *person* of life, liberty, or property *without due process of law,* nor deny to any *person* the *equal protection of the laws.*

The words in italics caused endless arguments in the courts, and their meaning has shifted with changes in the membership of the Supreme Court. At first, the Court held that the Fourteenth Amendment applied only to individuals and not to corporations. But in 1886 the Court reversed its previous position and declared that a corporation was a *person* within the meaning of the amendment. In a number of cases the Court set aside the actions of state legislatures or commissions on the ground that they interfered with the liberty or property of corporations. In this way, the Supreme Court made the states as powerless to control big business as they were to regulate the railroads.

Congress attempts to curb the trusts. In response to public demand, Congress turned its attention to the problem of large corporations. A congressional investigation revealed the great power and ruthless methods of the Standard Oil trust, the beef trust, and the sugar trust. It also influenced President Benjamin Harrison to recommend legislation restricting the activities of corporations. No clause in the Constitution gave the government specific power to control business, but Congress used its authority over foreign and interstate commerce to enact the Sherman Antitrust Act in 1890. This law forbade (1) "every contract, combination in the form of trust or otherwise, or conspiracy in *restraint of trade or commerce* among the several States, or with foreign nations" and (2) attempts to monopolize any part of such trade.

The Sherman Antitrust Act proves ineffective. The immediate results of the Sherman Act were meager. The government made no determined attempt to enforce the act, while big business employed the best legal talents to evade it. Court decisions also weakened the law. The Supreme Court's decision in the Knight Company Case (1895) illustrates the government's handicaps in enforcing the Sherman Act. The American Sugar Refining Company had purchased refineries in Philadelphia which, with its other holdings, gave it control of more than 95 per cent of the sugar refining business of the country. The government asked the courts to cancel the purchase.

The Supreme Court, however, refused. It asserted that the mere purchase of sugar refineries "bore no direct relation to commerce between the States or with foreign nations."

Four labor unions and a half-dozen small business associations were successfully prosecuted under the Sherman Act, but no large trust was broken up. By the end of the 1890's the Sherman Antitrust Act was considered dead, and more and more new trusts were being formed. In spite of their ineffectiveness, however, the Interstate Commerce Act and the Sherman Antitrust Act were significant. They marked the beginning of a change in the national attitude toward the relations of government and business.

——————— CHECK-UP ———————

How did the government attempt to curb monopolies?

1. How did the Fourteenth Amendment protect the growth of trusts?
2. What were the provisions of the Sherman Antitrust Act? Why was it ineffective?

---

5 | Labor Begins to Organize to Meet the Growing Power of Industry

Industrialization brings new problems for the workingman. The swift growth of industry in the United States brought numerous benefits to working men and women. More and more people came to be employed in the factories. With their wages they were able to buy many of the comforts and conveniences which poured out of the factories. Also, thanks to the new technology, many back-breaking jobs were taken off of human shoulders and assigned to the tough steel and tireless power of machines.

But, as it did to all other groups of people, industrialization brought some very real problems to laboring men and women.

Balanced against the great benefits of the factory system was the subordination of a worker's personality to his machine. The worker found that he was becoming a cog on a huge, industrial driving wheel. The skilled shoemaker, for instance, who had once taken personal pride in making a good pair of shoes, found little satisfaction in punching eyelets in thousands of pairs of shoes a day. The security that skill gives to a worker began to disappear. A man who had done the same work on a machine for ten years might be little better at the job than a newly-hired boy.

These revolutionary changes in the nature of work put the laboring man in a difficult spot. Machinery — not labor — became the center of industrial plants, for labor could be hired or fired, while machinery represented a large and permanent investment. Working people owned no land and no machinery — they had only their labor to depend upon. In good times, they worked ten or twelve hours a day, often for wages so low that it was impossible to save for old age and hard times. When depressions came, they lost their jobs and suffered hardships. In theory they were free to bargain with their employers for better wages, hours, and working conditions. Actually, as Theodore Roosevelt later put it, there was "a crass inequality in the bargaining relation between the employer and the individual employee standing alone. [For example] the great coal-mining and coal-carrying companies, which employed their tens of thousands, could easily dispense with the services of any particular miner. The miner on the other hand, could not dispense with the companies. He needed a job; his wife and children would starve if he did not get one."

Caught in this predicament, many working men and women believed there was only one way to protect themselves and their families — to organize. Organized workers, standing together and bargaining as a group, they argued, would have power enough to stand up to their employers. Their struggle "to organize labor" began before the War Between the States, and it is still going on.

Locomotive engineers were among the first to 'organize. This old photograph shows an early roundhouse and old-style engines.

Trade unions secure a foothold. Though labor unions came into existence during the early 1800's (page 229), it was the War Between the States which marked the real beginning of a strong labor movement. Workers were in demand in war industries. At the same time, prices were advancing more rapidly than wages, and working people grew discontented. Wage earners began to rely more and more upon group action to improve their circumstances. By 1870, about 30 important crafts [5] with nearly 200,000 members were organized on a national scale. Among the most powerful of these were the printers, the hatters, the iron molders, the machinists and blacksmiths, the locomotive engineers, the shoemakers, and the cigar makers.

The National Labor Union attempts to unite all unions under one leadership. Alongside this development of craft unions ran a movement to unite all industrial workers into a single great industrial union.

[5] Groups of workers in a particular skilled trade.

In 1866, there appeared a loose federation of local unions, national unions, and other labor organizations, known as the National Labor Union. At its peak it represented some 600,000 workingmen. It favored an eight-hour day, arbitration [6] of labor disputes, and co-operative factories run by craftsmen without the aid of capitalists. The National Labor Union's existence, however, was rather brief; its venture into politics proved its undoing. After its failure in 1872 to secure the election of its favored candidates for public office, the organization fell to pieces.

The Knights of Labor form one big union. Meanwhile, a movement to unite labor on a different basis was in progress. In 1869, the garment workers of Philadelphia, led by Uriah S. Stephens, founded the Noble Order of the Knights of Labor. It was a secret society, complete with ritual, oath, and fraternal handshake. Instead of organizing only skilled workmen into separate unions for each trade, the Knights of Labor invited all workers to join its local lodges. Skilled and unskilled, male and female, white and Negro, citizens and alien — the door was open to all except professional gamblers, liquor dealers, bankers, and lawyers. By 1886 the Knights of Labor had more than 700,000 members.

The aims of the Knights of Labor were idealistic. To bring "the greatest good to the greatest number" they proposed "to secure to the toilers a proper share of the wealth that they create; more of the leisure that rightfully belongs to them." Specifically, they supported (1) the use of arbitration in labor disputes, (2) the prohibition of child labor, (3) the eight-hour day, (4) equal pay for both sexes, and (5) laws to protect the safety and health of workers.

Among other things the Knights of Labor helped to secure legislation restricting the immigration of foreign labor. Under the leadership of Grand Master Terence V. Powderly, they also won a number of strikes. However, a series of poorly managed strikes, along with popular feeling against "radicals," injured their cause. The Knights also had difficulty keeping skilled and unskilled labor working together. Many skilled workmen, resenting the domination of the unskilled — who were in the majority — went back to their craft unions. By 1890 the membership of the Knights of Labor had dwindled to 100,000.

The A. F. of L. assumes leadership. The craft unions were meanwhile forming a federation destined for much greater success than the old National Labor Union. In New York a young English immigrant, Samuel Gompers, had found work in a cigar-making shop. His ability and energy brought him into office and influence in the Cigarmakers' Union. Soon, his experiences in leading strikes and his study of labor's handicaps gave him firm convictions about how labor should be organized. Gompers led in a reorganization of the International Cigarmakers' Union, and helped form the national federation of trade unions which became known as the American Federation of Labor (A. F. of L.). As President of the A. F. of L. for every year but one from the time it was organized in 1886 until his death in 1924, Samuel Gompers controlled its policies.

The principles upon which the American Federation of Labor was based were five in number:

(1) Workers were organized on a craft basis — electricians in the Electrical Workers' Union, cigarmakers in the Cigarmakers' Union, and so on. Membership was therefore limited mainly to skilled workers.[7]

(2) Local craft unions combined to form state and national unions of each craft. Officers of each national union issued charters to local unions, made contracts, and called strikes in its own field. In turn, national unions were allied in the Federation, which worked out over-all policies, handled public relations, influenced lawmaking, and helped to organize new units.

(3) Membership dues were set high enough to build up substantial funds. These funds were used in part to carry on

(Continued on page 392)

---

[6] Arbitration means that a dispute is submitted to an impartial committee or board for decision.

[7] Later, the A. F. of L. organized a number of industrial unions as well as unions of unskilled labor.

Samuel Gompers
(1850-1924)

Cigarmaker

SAMUEL GOMPERS, sometimes called the "Labor Statesman of the World," occupies a unique position in the history of the American labor movement. Gompers was born in a London tenement, the son of a cigar maker. His early boyhood surroundings impressed upon him vividly the problems of the workingman. Obliged to go to work at the age of ten, he was first apprenticed to a shoemaker but soon changed to the cigarmaking trade. Lured by the hope of a better life across the sea, the Gompers family landed in America in 1863 and settled in New York's East Side.

Samuel Gompers was ambitious for learning. He spent spare hours at Cooper Union, attending lectures and taking part in debates. In the cigar shop where he worked it was the practice for one man to read while the others worked. Gompers was frequently called upon to read and thus had a further opportunity to increase his knowledge and test his ideas.

Labor Organizer

Gompers' first real achievement in the labor field was to help reorganize the Cigarmakers' Union. This union was the "kindergarten and preparatory school" in his labor training. Gompers also took an active part in the formation of the American Federation of Labor. Except for one year he served as its President from 1886 until his death.

The A. F. of L. owed so much to Gompers in its formative years that it could well be said, "The Federation was Gompers and Gompers was the Federation." Some of the basic principles of the A. F. of L., such as the power reserved to member unions and the insistence on immediate goals like better pay and shorter hours, stemmed from Gompers. Gompers also believed in persuasion rather than violence, and in democratic methods in reaching Federation decisions.

During World War I Gompers was a member of the National Council for Defense, and he bent every effort toward victory. He was appointed at the Peace Conference to the Committee on International Labor Legislation. He gloried in his physical endurance and kept up his efforts in behalf of labor till his very death.

Labor Statesman

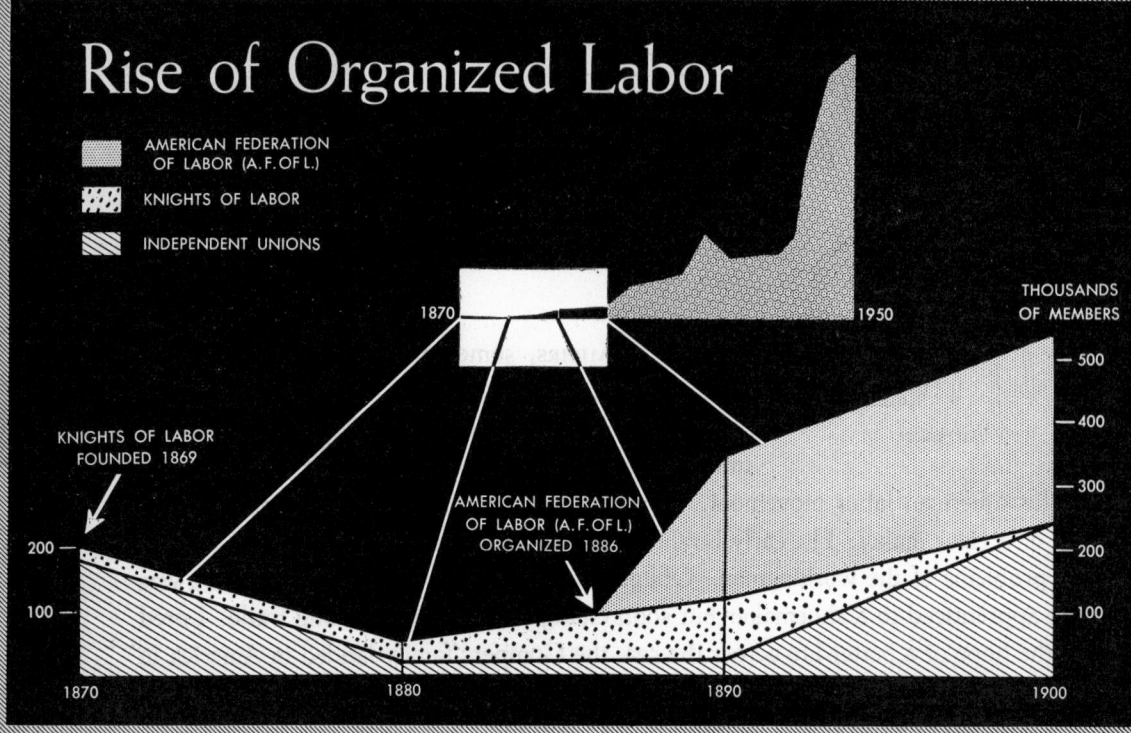

Rise of Organized Labor

- AMERICAN FEDERATION OF LABOR (A.F.OF L.)
- KNIGHTS OF LABOR
- INDEPENDENT UNIONS

KNIGHTS OF LABOR FOUNDED 1869

AMERICAN FEDERATION OF LABOR (A.F.OF L.) ORGANIZED 1886.

1870   1950   THOUSANDS OF MEMBERS

— 500
— 400
— 300
200 —   — 200
100 —   — 100

1870   1880   1890   1900

The rise of organized labor from 1870 to 1950 is silhouetted in the small chart at the top, above. From the highlighted portion, lines lead down to an enlargement of the period from 1870 to 1900. The number of workers belonging to unions in 1870 was about 200,000. By 1880 there were only about 50,000. Why? In 1886 their ranks began to increase, until by 1900 there were well over half a million members enrolled in organized labor. What was the main reason for the increase? Glance ahead now to the chart on page 526 to see in more detail how organized labor has grown from these beginnings.

the work of the organization, in part to build up reserves for the benefit of members in case of old age, sickness, death, strikes, or depressions.

(4) The aims of the A. F. of L. were practical and immediate. Instead of setting remote ideals, as the Knights of Labor did, the A. F. of L. worked for such goals as higher wages, shorter hours, the six-day week, and the abolition of child labor. As one leader declared, "We have no ultimate ends. We are going on from day to day. We are fighting only for immediate objects — objects that can be realized in a few years."

(5) The political power of the Federation was used to support candidates of established political parties who favored labor, rather than to run candidates on a special labor ticket.

From its first headquarters in "a little

office, which was about ten by eight, had a door, a small window, and a brick floor," the A. F. of L. expanded until in 1900 it had a membership of more than half a million. Avoiding the pitfalls of earlier organizations, the A. F. of L. has continued through the years to be a powerful "spokesman for labor."

——— CHECK-UP ———

How did labor meet the growing power of industry?

1. What problems did industrialization bring the workingman?
2. What progress had been made in trade union organization by 1870? What did the National Labor Union advocate?
3. What were the aims of the Knights of Labor? Why did this organization fail?
4. What were the underlying principles of the American Federation of Labor?

6 Labor and Capital Battle for Position

Ideas differ on labor's rights. Behind the industrial warfare of the late 1800's were conflicting ideas as to the rights of labor. To the average employer, his workmen were a part of his business, and he insisted that he had the right to run his business as he pleased. If one of his workers was dissatisfied, let him go elsewhere. He did not intend to have "outside agitators," as he called the union leaders, telling him what wages he should pay or what conditions he should offer.

The worker, on the other hand, felt that he had a "right to his job" which no strikebreaker[8] had a right to take from him. Labor leaders objected to the treatment of labor as a mere means of production, to be discarded when it was outworn. Instead, they believed that labor was entitled to a larger share of the wealth it helped to create, and to a voice in controlling working conditions.

Between 1881 and 1900 there were about 23,000 strikes in American industry, involving more than 6½ million workers. Approximately one third of the strikes were successful in obtaining their objectives; the rest of them ended in compromise or failure. In most cases, workers struck for higher wages, shorter hours, or for recognition of the right of their unions to bargain for them.

Both sides have weapons. In this industrial conflict, labor's most powerful weapons during the '80's and '90's were the *strike* and the *boycott*. During a strike, the striking employees would quit their jobs and stay away from the factory or mine in an attempt to force the employer to meet their demands. Workers also boycotted a struck factory by refusing to buy its product. Sometimes a boycott was carried a step

[8] A non-striker hired by the employer to do the work of the striker.

further. Employees of companies which had any dealings with a struck plant refused to handle that plant's product. In effect, this forced their employers to boycott the struck plant.

To combat the strike, employers used the *lockout*. The lockout meant that an employer closed the door of his plant and refused to deal with his employees until they accepted his terms. Another weapon was the *blacklist*. Names of union leaders or others taking an active part in labor organization were placed on this list, which was made available to all members of an employers' association. A person whose name appeared on the list would then find it practically impossible to secure employment. In most major industrial conflicts, employers also had money resources much greater than those of labor.

Violence enters labor disputes. Strikes, lockouts, boycotts, and blacklists were, in theory, "peaceful" methods for settling disputes between capital and labor. Actually, industrial conflict took place in an atmosphere so charged with feeling that the line between" peaceful" and "non-peaceful" was hard to draw. In many cases, both sides resorted to violence. On the labor side, an extreme example of violence was the "Molly Maguires," a secret society of coal miners which flourished in the Pennsylvania coal fields during the early '70's. The Molly Maguires not only destroyed mine property but injured or murdered mine owners and others who opposed them. Finally, a private detective worked his way into the inner circle of the society and exposed its leaders. Some of the culprits were sent to the gallows, others to prison. Such incidents received widespread publicity and increased popular hostility to labor organizations, especially to secret ones.

Violence was also used by employers on some occasions. Labor organizers were often beaten by hired thugs, thrown into jail on flimsy pretexts, or ridden out of town on a rail. Bloody, unequal battles occurred when strikers were set

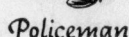

Policeman

upon by armed police, militia, or private detectives under the orders of employers. The force of public opinion also was generally on the side of the employers.

Federal troops break a railroad strike. Several major strikes in the closing years of the nineteenth century added to the excitement aroused by the Molly Maguires. One was a railroad strike in 1877 which paralyzed most of the lines east of the Mississippi and then spread as far west as San Francisco. There had been several wage cuts on the railroads. When another ten per cent cut was announced, workmen on the Baltimore and Ohio Railroad walked out. The strike spread rapidly to other lines, and at its height 100,000 men in fourteen states were involved. Several thousand miles of railroad were tied up, affecting many allied industries as well. In large railroad terminal cities, clashes occurred between strikers and the state militia. Workers were killed or wounded. The strikers retaliated by destroying millions of dollars' worth of property. At Pittsburgh alone, the loss was estimated at $10,000,000. The backbone of the strike was broken by the use of federal troops sent in by order of President Rutherford B. Hayes. The men sullenly returned to work at reduced wages, angry over the use of federal troops to break their strike and at the lack of public sympathy for their cause.

The Haymarket affair discredits labor. Anti-labor and anti-radical feeling reached a peak after the so-called Haymarket affair. On May 4, 1886, a meeting was called in Haymarket Square, Chicago, to protest an attack by police on strikers. The gathering was orderly until near its close, when a force of police appeared and ordered what remained of the crowd to break up. Suddenly a bomb was hurled into the midst of the police, killing one and fatally wounding several others. The bomb-thrower could not be identified, but eight "radicals" who at one time or another had advocated the use of violence were rounded up and charged with murder. All eight were con-

Private detective

victed as "instigators." Four were hanged, one committed suicide, and the remaining three were imprisoned. The Knights of Labor had not been associated with the Haymarket affair, but it never recovered from the wave of anti-labor sentiment which swept the country. Feelings ran so strong that several years later, when Governor Altgeld of Illinois pardoned the three surviving convicts, he was severely criticized throughout the country and was ruined politically.

Labor loses in the Homestead strike. A strike in the Carnegie Steel Company plant at Homestead, Pennsylvania, in 1892, was one of the bitterest in the history of capital and labor conflict. When the strike started, officials of the company brought in armed detectives to protect the plant. Strikers and detectives met in a pitched battle which ended in victory for the strikers. It was a short-lived victory, however, for the state militia was called out and the strike was crushed. After a five months' struggle, the men went back to work on the company's terms. The Carnegie Steel Company and other corporations now refused to deal further with the Amalgamated Association of Iron and Steel Workers, and the power of that union was broken. For many years after the strike, labor in the steel mills remained unorganized.

Government helps break the Pullman strike. Two years after the Homestead strike, a workers' committee in the Pullman Palace Car Company, near Chicago, protested a sharp reduction in wages. When three members of the committee were promptly discharged, the employees went out on strike. The General Managers' Association, representing 24 railroads entering Chicago, upheld the Pullman Company. The American Railway Union, a newly-organized industrial union with 150,000 members, backed up the strikers by refusing to handle Pullman cars. The walkout spread from Chicago to 23 railroads, affecting railway operation in 27 states and territories. Violence and destruction of a large amount of property followed.

The United States Attorney General persuaded President Cleveland to intervene. In spite of Illinois Governor Altgeld's protests that local police and state militia were able to maintain order, Cleveland sent federal troops to Chicago for the declared purpose of protecting the mails. Protecting the mails meant that the trains had to go through. The strike was broken.

The injunction and the Sherman Antitrust Act are used against labor. A legal device which helped break the Pullman strike was the *injunction* (a court order forbidding the performance of some stated act or acts). The injunction handed down by the courts in the Pullman strike ordered the officers and members of the union to cease (1) obstructing the transportation of the mails, (2) damaging the property of the railroads, and (3) forcing or persuading employees to refuse to perform their duties. When Eugene V. Debs and other leaders continued their strike activities, they were arrested and charged with contempt of court for violating the injunction. In such a case there is no jury — the same judge who issues the injunction may sentence violators. Debs and six others were sentenced to six months' imprisonment. To the disappointment of organized labor, their appeal to the Supreme Court failed. The Court upheld the sentence largely on the ground that the union was engaged in a "conspiracy to hinder and obstruct interstate commerce." According to the Court, the injunction was a proper means for preventing violation of the Sherman Antitrust Act.

The injunction was not a new device. It was well established in English and American law, and had previously been used in labor disputes, including the great railway strike of 1877. The Sherman Antitrust Act, combined with the use of the injunction, became a more effective legal weapon with which to break strikes than to curb monopoly. It was ironic that the very same law which had proved ineffective in its intended purpose of curbing corporations and trusts should be used with success against labor.

The advantage rests with management. Thus, at the end of the century, labor seemed to be at a disadvantage in its

The **Homestead strike** began with a victory for the workmen when they fought off squads of armed detectives. The detectives are shown here as they leave the scene after their surrender. The strike was lost some months later when Pennsylvania state militia were ordered to stop it.

struggle with management. Business was well organized and getting bigger. Efforts of the government to check its growing power were halting and ineffective. On the other hand, labor had made but little progress in its efforts to build up bargaining power. To make matters worse for labor, the legislative departments of the government, the executive departments, even the courts, seemed to be on the side of the owners of property, rather than favorable to the working classes.

───────── CHECK-UP ─────────

How did capital and labor compete for power?

1. How did capital and labor differ on labor's

role in industry? What weapons were used by capital? By labor?

2. What were the chief features of (a) the Railroad Strike of 1877, (b) the Haymarket Affair, (c) the Homestead Strike, and (d) the Pullman Strike?

3. What is an injunction? How was the injunction used against labor?

CHAPTER REVIEW

Terms to Understand

"infant industries"
laissez faire
treasury surplus
bounty
reciprocity
lobbies
income tax
free trade
over-capitalization
combination in restraint of trade
injunction

due process of law
promoter
public welfare
commission
government regulation
craft union
lockout
blacklist
arbitration
local union
strike-breaker

People and Things to Know About

McKinley Tariff
Wilson-Gorman Tariff
"Granger Laws"
Wabash, St. Louis, and Pacific Railroad vs. Illinois
Interstate Commerce Act
Sherman Antitrust Act
Fourteenth Amendment
National Labor Union
Knights of Labor
Grover Cleveland

Uriah S. Stephens
Terrence V. Powderly
American Federation of Labor
Eugene V. Debs
Haymarket Affair
"Molly Maguires"
Homestead Strike
American Railway Union
Pullman Strike
Samuel Gompers
William McKinley

Historic Dates to Identify

1886   1887   1890   1894

Questions to Discuss

1. How would you react to each of these statements connected with the tariff?

(a) Foreign trade is unimportant to the United States. It accounts for only a small per cent of our total trade.

(b) Tariffs protect American workers against the competition of cheap foreign laborers.

Questions to Discuss (Cont.)

(c) We cannot expect to export unless we import.

(d) Tariffs aid some producers but at the same time hinder others.

2. Explain in your own words the meaning and purpose of each of the provisions of the Interstate Commerce Act.

3. What was the original purpose of the Fourteenth Amendment? Explain how it could be interpreted to protect corporations.

4. What were the weaknesses of the Knights of Labor? How were these eliminated in the A.F. of L.?

5. Manufacturers attempt to buy machinery and raw materials at the lowest possible prices to bring down costs of production. Why should they not regard labor in the same manner?

6. The government is more likely to intervene in a railroad strike than in many other kinds of strikes. Why is this true?

Other Things to Do

*1. Make a chart listing the chief tariff acts enacted after the War Between the States and before 1896. Give a brief summary of the features of each.

2. Debate: Resolved, That the United States government was justified in intervening in the Pullman Strike.

*3. List the weapons used by labor in one column and those used by management in a parallel column. Give the meanings of each.

4. Draw a "before and after" cartoon showing the condition or position of workers before and after labor unions were organized.

5. Examine current newspapers or magazines for some labor-management dispute now in progress. Report to the class on (a) the cause of the dispute, (b) the contentions of each side, (c) the methods used by each side and (d) the efforts towards settlement.

Chapter 21

Farmer

THE FARMER INCREASES PRODUCTION

BUT SUFFERS HARD TIMES

When we've wood and prairie land,
Won by our toil,
We'll reign like kings in fairy land,
Lords of the soil.

Song, after Hamlin Garland

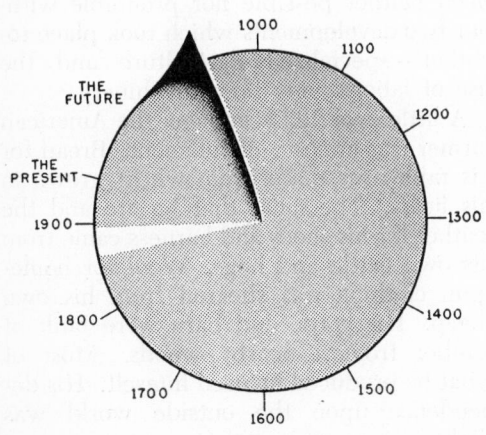

1865-1896

If you had been riding over the western prairies in the latter half of the nineteenth century, you might have heard homesteaders singing the song quoted above as they plowed the tough prairie sod, struggled to build homes and schools for their families, and endured the hardships of pioneer life. The song expressed their hope of a better future for themselves and their children, and their determination to make that hope come true.

The future looked bright, indeed, for the thousands of homesteaders who, beginning early in the 1860's, made the long trek westward. Endless stretches of fertile land were theirs for the taking. The new technology (page 359) was having an effect on farming, as it was on transportation, communication, and manufacturing. Farm machinery and scientific methods pointed to prosperous times for the farmer. But the farmer's dream was to take a long time in coming true. Although he doubled production and then doubled it again, his income kept shrinking.

397

The farmer's troubles were caused in part by important changes in the way farming was carried on. As long as the farmer had been content to raise only enough crops for his own use, and as long as the farmer's wife made most of the family's clothing, they and their children were not greatly affected by what went on in the factories and the cities. But more and more farmers, especially in the South and Middle West, began to make farming a business. They became specialists in the raising of cotton, wheat, corn, or livestock. They sold their products at prices established in great markets like Chicago or New Orleans. In turn, they bought clothing, all kinds of farm equipment, and even food that had been produced by others. For better or worse, farming was now tied up with industrial activity, financial speculation, problems of money and prices, and the ups and downs of the business cycle. The farmer, however, usually suffered more from the "downs" than he profited from the "ups."

Despite the huge crops he raised, the era after the War Between the States was generally a period of hard times for the farmer. Caught in the grip of powerful economic forces and perplexing financial problems, the farmer was restless and discontented. He was beset by many problems — drought, heavily mortgaged farms, and high freight rates. But low prices for his farm products plagued him worst of all. The problem of prices was closely related to the problems of money, finance, and government control of the currency.

This chapter will trace the farmer's efforts to adjust himself to his new position in the national scene and in particular his attempts to solve the problem of low prices. The main points are these:

1. Machinery and science increase farm production.
2. Faced by hard times, farmers begin to organize.
3. Western farmers and debtors lose the battle over greenbacks.
4. The West and the South seek relief from low prices through free silver.

1 Machinery and Science Increase Farm Production

Fewer farmers produce more food. During the latter half of the 1800's, there was a sharp drop in the percentage of farm workers needed to produce America's food. In the early years of the republic about 90 per cent of the working people in the United States were farmers or farm workers. By the end of the nineteenth century that figure had fallen, so that 40 per cent of the population was engaged in farming. Yet this lower percentage of agricultural workers raised more food for each person in the country than the 90 per cent at the beginning of the century. "Large-scale" farming was responsible.

Machinery and specialization transform agriculture. The settlement of the western plains paved the way for large-scale farming. But large-scale farming would have been neither possible nor profitable without two developments which took place together — specialized agriculture and the use of labor-saving farm machinery.

A little over 100 years ago, the American farmer was almost self-sufficient. Bread for his table was made from wheat grown in his fields. The meat that he ate and the leather for his shoes and harness came from his own cattle and hogs. Wool for homespun clothing was sheared from his own sheep. His house and barn were built of lumber from a nearby woods. Most of what he produced he used himself. His dependence upon the outside world was slight.

The introduction of farm machinery altered this situation, and the self-sufficiency of the farmer began to diminish. Even before the War Between the States, widespread use of the steel plow, the reaper, the mower, and other machinery encouraged the farmer to grow crops for market as well as for home use. Then, during the 1870's and 1880's, more and better farm

Steam engines on wheels were among the most important contributions of industry to agriculture. Above, such engines are being assembled; at the right, one is providing power for a threshing machine. Usually several farmers would co-operate in buying an engine, then follow its lumbering course from farm to farm and help each other at threshing time. Farm wives went along to cook huge meals for the crews.

machinery was introduced. This new machinery included improved plows and cultivators, corn-planters, hay-loaders, new mowing machines, the combined reaper and binder, the steam threshing machine, and later the "combine" or complete harvester and thresher. The changes which occurred in farming as a result of this labor-saving machinery and other developments have been called an agricultural revolution.

The producing power of the farmer was now greatly increased. Government experts have figured that the amount of human labor needed to turn out a bushel of wheat dropped from a little over three hours in 1830 to about ten minutes in 1896. The amount of farm land in active use was doubled between 1860 and 1900, but the wheat harvest increased nearly four times, and corn production about three times. In some sections, large specialized farms produced a single crop, such as cotton, wheat, or corn, for sale in the world's markets.

The government encourages scientific farming. The output of farms was also increased by the application of scientific methods to agriculture. Scientific farming is a fairly recent development. For a long time, farming was mostly a father-to-son, learn-by-doing art. In the early days a few progressive farmers, such as Thomas Jefferson, experimented with methods for conserving the fertility of the soil. But for a long time the typical American attitude was that if your land didn't suit you, you could find better land farther West.

Increasing Output of Farm Workers

YEARLY OUTPUT PER FARM WORKER IN 1870 = 100

400
300
200
100

1870 1880 1890 1900 1910 1920 1930 1940 1950 (EST.)

Output per farm worker increased about 50 per cent between 1870 and 1900. Why?

Agencies established or encouraged by the government have helped to promote scientific progress in agriculture. In 1862 a Department of Agriculture was established in Washington, though its head did not become a member of the Cabinet until 1889. In 1862, also, Congress passed the Morrill Act. Under this law a generous grant of public land was allotted to each state if it would establish a college chiefly devoted to the teaching of "such branches of learning as are related to agriculture and the mechanic arts." Nearly 70 "land-grant" colleges, scattered through most of the states, were founded or assisted under the Morrill Act. The Hatch Act, 1887, set up an agricultural experiment station wherever a land-grant college was located.

——— CHECK-UP ———

How did machinery and science increase farm production?

1. How did machinery and specialization change agricultural production?
2. How did the agricultural revolution reduce the self-sufficiency of farmers?
3. What is meant by scientific farming? Give examples. How has government promoted scientific farming?

2 Faced by Hard Times, Farmers Begin to Organize

Nature balks the western farmer. For some time after 1865, many farmers were still pretty much "on their own." The Department of Agriculture was not yet in stride, and scientific farming was just getting started. The farmer of the Great Plains [1] found that methods which had worked fairly well east of the Mississippi River and four or five hundred miles west of it were not adaptable to the wide-open spaces of western Kansas, Nebraska, and the Dakotas. Here the farmer had to battle not only against bitterly cold winters, scorching summers, plagues, and high winds, but especially against a scanty water supply. Nature often dealt crushing blows to his hopes for profitable harvests. And there was no one to tell him that his methods of plowing and farming often increased the harshness of nature's blows. During a series of wet years, homesteaders pushed into lands that were normally too dry to support their crops. They prospered for a while. Then their hopes were dashed when periods of drought or plagues of grasshoppers came along.

One farmer who lived through such discouragements on the Great Plains wrote:

In 1874 came a gigantic calamity in the form of a raid of grasshoppers which ate up every bit of green vegetation from the Rocky Mountains to and beyond the Missouri River. I recall that when coming home late one afternoon for supper I stepped back surprised to see what became known as Rocky Mountain locusts covering the side of the house. Clouds of them promptly settled down on the whole countryside — everywhere, unavoidable. People set about killing them to save gardens, but this soon proved ridiculous. Specially contrived machines, pushed by horses, scooped up the hoppers in grain fields by the barrelful to

[1] The Great Plains began west of the 98th to the 100th meridian. East of that point were found the prairies, where there was usually plenty of rain.

burn them. This, too, was then nonsensical. Vast hordes, myriads. In a week grain fields, gardens, shrubs, vines, had been eaten down to the ground or to the bark. Nothing could be done. You sat by and saw everything go. . . .

To add to the terror of the locust invasion was the general accompaniment of weather tending always to be dry. A steady hot current of air brought the dreaded dry times. How one hated to see the heavens seal their cisterns and the plains to be sear! In a hot droughty summer most of the wells and springs gave out early. Water in creeks trickled so shallowly that dogs lay panting in them while hardly able to immerse more than their paws. The southwest wind blew, sweeping the land with a flinty dust. Husbands hated to go home to meals, for they must meet the appeals of their wives to climb on wagons and strike out for back home.

"Sell for what you can get, John — give it away — leave it — only let's get out. I don't have to ride on a railroad. A schooner [covered wagon] headed east looks awfully good to me."[2]

Farm prices drop. When a good year came and grain stood high as a man's shoulders, the farmer's troubles still were not over. Prices, upon which most western farmers depended because they were raising crops to sell, rose and fell for reasons beyond the farmer's control. After the War Between the States, farm prices fell so much that a bushel of wheat selling for $1.45 in 1866 brought only 76 cents in 1869 and 49 cents in 1894. Corn dropped from 75 cents a bushel in 1869 to 28 cents in 1889. In some sections it was cheaper to burn corn than to sell it and buy fuel. To increase his income, the farmer plowed more land, planted more seed, bought more machinery, and produced more grain. But the fact that more grain was on the market merely drove prices lower. Trains and steamships had created a world market, but it was uncertain. The farmer could not estimate the demand for his crop. A drought in the Russian Ukraine

might force wheat prices up, but a bumper crop in the Argentine might drive them down.

What was true of grain and the western farmer was also true of other crops and of farmers in other sections of the country. For example, in 1873 the southern cotton growers received 17 cents a pound for cotton. In 1893 the price was only 9 cents a pound.

Farm costs stay high. While his income fell, the farmer's costs stayed high. As a specialized farmer, he had to purchase machinery, fertilizer, and barbed wire. Often these necessities were controlled by monopolies that kept their prices high. The tariff on manufactured products also added dollars to the cost of household necessities and clothing.

For some of his most burdensome expenses the farmer blamed the railroads. Freight rates were high. In 1869 it cost 52½ cents to send a bushel of grain from the Mississippi River to the eastern sea-

The struggle of a farmer to win a living from the soil is symbolized in this modern mural painting in Washington, D.C.

[2] This account in the main describes the farmer's problem on the Great Plains — western Kansas, Nebraska, and the Dakotas; it does not apply to Minnesota, Iowa, Missouri, and the eastern portions of Kansas, Nebraska, and the Dakotas.

board. Freight rates on cattle were so high that many Illinois farmers drove stock overland to Chicago rather than pay railroad charges. Railroad companies often owned grain elevators, warehouses, stock pens, and other storage facilities and charged unreasonable sums for their use. Middlemen and grain speculators, too, got a share of the price of farm products.

The hard-working and hard-pressed farmer deeply resented all of these charges. And if the farmer could not meet his expenses and had to borrow, the interest he had to pay for the use of money was usually high. He was rarely charged less than 10 per cent interest, often more. "There are three great crops raised in Nebraska," wrote a disgruntled observer. "One is a crop of corn, one a crop of freight rates, and one a crop of interest. One is produced by farmers who by sweat and toil farm the land. The other two are produced by men who sit in their offices and behind their bank counters and farm the farmer."

Farm tenancy increases as prices fall. A collapse of prices was a real disaster for the farmer who was in debt. During good years, many farmers mortgaged their farms to buy more land or equipment. Toward the end of the 1800's, nearly half of the farms in the West were mortgaged. Altogether, these mortgages amounted to more than a billion dollars. But mortgages and interest had to be paid in money, and the farmer's ability to pay depended on what he could get for his crops. If prices fell, he was in trouble. A $1000 mortgage was worth 690 bushels of wheat in 1866, but it took 1315 bushels to repay it three years later. If he could not meet his debts when they fell due, the farmer had to give up his land and go to work as a laborer or tenant on someone else's land. Before the War Between the States, nearly every farmer owned his own land. After 1865 more and more farmers began to give up their land until, by the turn of the century, one third of American farm families no longer owned their farms but paid some form of rent.

Farmers begin to organize. There wasn't much the farmer could do about droughts or grasshoppers. But he did think his position in the economic life of the nation was unfair, and he began to hope that he could better it by joining with other farmers. His chance to "join something" came in a simple way. Oliver H. Kelley, an energetic clerk in the Department of Agriculture, became concerned about the loneliness and isolation of farm life. He therefore organized the Patrons of Husbandry, a secret fraternal order, to bring groups of farmers together for social gatherings and entertainment. The local unit was called the Grange, and the members were known as Grangers.

Getting the farmers together was not easy. They were often separated by long distances, and on the frontier especially they were noted for their sturdy individualism. Nevertheless, the idea caught on and the organization grew rapidly, especially in the Midwest and the West. By 1874, the Granges had about 750,000 members. The benefits of the Grange were once described in this way: "Crabbed men came out of their shells and grew genial; disheartened women became cheerful; repressed children delighted in the chance to play with other boys and girls of their own age."

Grangers work to improve the lot of the farmer. While the Patrons of Husbandry was founded originally as a social organization, it provided the farmers with occasions to discuss their grievances. Soon the Patrons of Husbandry became active in improving the economic and political position of the farmer. Through their Granges, farmers began to buy their supplies and equipment together, getting the benefit of wholesale

Small town
grain elevator

The Rise and Fall of Farm Prices

BASE PRICES FOR 1926=100

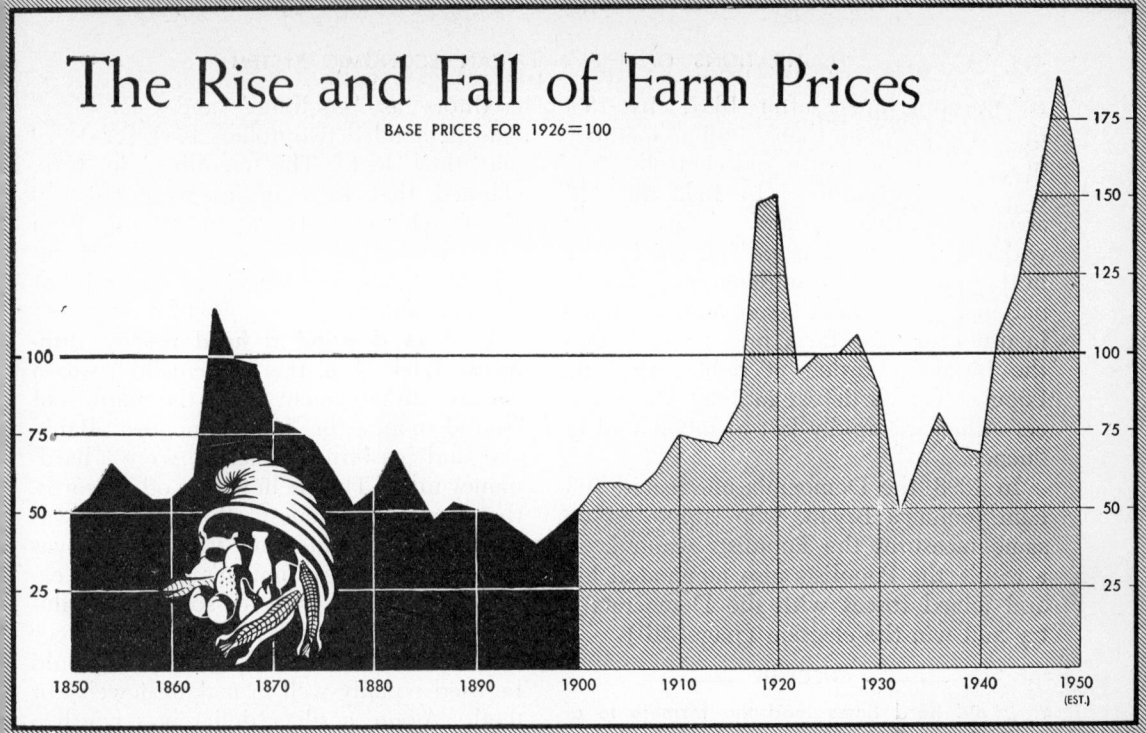

Prices for farm products rose during the War Between the States. Then they started to fall and kept falling, with minor exceptions, until 1896. Can you explain the decline?

prices. Some Granges built their own factories to manufacture reapers, plows, and other expensive equipment. Others operated banks, creameries, elevators, warehouses, insurance companies, and retail stores. These co-operative efforts were not very successful, however, partly because of the inexperience of the farmers and partly because their projects were opposed by bankers and other businessmen with greater resources and managerial skill.

In politics, however — especially in the matter of railroad regulation — the Granges made their influence felt. The most glaring grievances of the western farmers were against the railroads. At first the farmers had welcomed the railroads as an indispensable aid in the opening of the West. There were many reasons, however, why the farmers began to change their attitude and to blame the railroads for many of their economic ills. Chief among these reasons was the fact that the farmer was the principal victim of the abuses — high rates, pooling, discrimination, and rebating — in which the railroads indulged. By

electing their members to state legislatures, the Grangers were able to obtain the passage of laws restricting railroad rates and setting up state railroad commissions. The so-called "Granger laws" (page 386), which were first passed in Illinois, were taken up by other states. Throughout the depression years of the 1870's the Grangers made their political influence felt in most of the middle western States.

After 1876, largely because of the failure of the co-operative ventures and the rising tide of prosperity, the Granger movement declined and lost its influence. It continued, however, as a social organization.

Farmers enter national politics. During the 1880's the farmers discovered that state regulation of the railroads was not too effective. They therefore turned their attention to national politics as well. The farmers' influence was responsible in part for the passage of the Interstate Commerce Act in 1887 (page 387).

During the 1880's the Grange's place in politics was taken by Farmers' Alliances, which grew rapidly when depression hit the farming areas after 1887. By 1890 they enrolled more than a million members in the West and South and controlled several state legislatures. In 1892 the Alliances and other farmers' groups merged with the Populist Party. The chief plank in that party's platform demanded that the national government issue more currency in order to raise farm prices and lighten the farmer's burden of debt. After the Populist Party's defeat in 1892, the Farmers' Alliances rapidly lost members and influence.

In 1896, the Democrats nominated William Jennings Bryan, who supported the same measures the Populists wanted. As a result, the Populists also nominated him and joined forces with the Democrats to try and win the election (page 410).

─────── CHECK-UP ───────

How did hard times lead the farmers to organize?

1. Why was farming difficult on the Great Plains?
2. Why did the size of his crops make little difference in the farmer's income?
3. Why did the farmer feel that he was being exploited by industry and railroads?
4. How did the Grange try to help the farmer?
5. What were the Farmers' Alliances? The Populist Party? Why did the farmer enter national politics?

---

3 | **Western Farmers and Debtors Lose the Battle over Greenbacks**

A money dispute gets started. A steady squabble over the question of money went on in the United States for 30 years after the War Between the States. On one side was the *creditor* group — bankers and eastern financiers who had money to lend at interest. On the other side was the *debtor* group — mostly farmers and small businessmen who often had to borrow money to carry on their affairs. They attacked their

creditors as "goldbugs" and "gamblers" who demanded two dollars back for every one they lent. The creditors, in turn, claimed that their critics were shiftless cheats who were trying to get out from under lawful debts. They thought of themselves as the defenders of "sound" or "honest money."

Bankers demand a hard money standard. Back of all this name-calling was a sincere disagreement over the nature of "sound money" or "honest money." Bankers and eastern financiers were "hard-money men." They believed, in other words, that money had honest value only if it was made out of something valuable or was backed by the government's promise to exchange it at any time for something valuable. For instance, a $10 gold piece was valuable because the gold in it could be used equally well in making jewelry or teeth. Again, a silver dollar was worth a dollar only if it could be melted down into a dollar's worth of silver for knives, forks, or spoons. According to this argument, paper money was "worth no more than the paper it was printed on" unless people trusted the government's promise to exchange it for *specie* (gold or silver). When hard-money men spoke of sound money or honest money, then, they meant (1) gold, (2) silver worth its face value in gold, or (3) paper money backed up dollar-for-dollar by precious metals stored in the vaults of banks or of the United States Treasury.

Farmers and other debtors demand stable purchasing power. The hard-money argument sounded like simple common sense, but the problem was not so simple as it sounded. Gold is itself a commodity whose purchasing power changes from time to time. Suppose that in a certain year, ten bushels of wheat could be exchanged for a $10 gold piece. Then, suppose that for five years the supply of gold in the nation remains unchanged but the wheat supply doubles. It might take 20 bushels of wheat to buy a $10 gold piece. What has happened? Has the price of wheat fallen, or has the price of gold risen? The answer to that question would make

In country stores and Grange halls all over the nation, farmers came together to discuss their common problems and to apply united political effort to their solution.

little difference if no one had lent or borrowed money. To a debtor or creditor, however, the way that question is answered may mean the difference between prosperity and ruin. For example, a farmer borrows $1000 from a lending company when $1000 in gold equals 1000 bushels of wheat. Five years later he must pay it back. When he offers 1000 bushels of wheat, he learns that 1000 bushels are now worth only $500 in gold. The lending company claims that the farmer is paying only half his debt. To pay $1000 in gold, he must produce 2000 bushels of wheat. The farmer now claims that he is repaying twice as much as he borrowed. The lending company — the creditor — feels that repayment in gold is the only "honest" course. On the other hand the farmer — the debtor — is as firmly convinced that such a settlement is unreasonable and "dishonest."

The chief problem here is the purchasing power of money at different times — that is, how much can be bought with a given amount of money at a given time. When the value of money is low, prices are high and each dollar will buy less. When the value of money is greater, prices are lower and a dollar will purchase much more.

Money grows scarcer. The late nineteenth century was a time of scarce money, and therefore prices were low and the pur-

chasing power of each dollar was high. In 1865 the amount of currency [3] in circulation for each person in the United States was $31.18. By 1872 the figure had dropped to $20.43; by 1878 to $16.95. As money grew scarcer, it was harder to get and its purchasing value rose. In other words, commodity prices — especially farm prices — dropped. The farmer who happened to be in debt was "up against it." He felt that it would be simple justice as well as sound business for the government to expand the currency by issuing more money. He insisted that it was the government's business to issue enough money to keep prices stable. If there were not enough gold for this, he believed that money must be based on something else.

Greenbacks expand the currency. You recall that one way in which the government financed the War Between the States was by printing paper money (page 313). These "greenbacks" were not backed by gold or silver, but only by the government's promise to pay at some future date. Their value rose and fell with the fortunes of war. When the struggle ended, there were about 400 million dollars' worth of greenbacks in circulation.

Retirement of greenbacks is halted. After the war, the government began

[3] Currency means the money of all kinds that are "current" as a medium of exchange.

gradually to *retire* the greenbacks. That is, as the greenbacks came into the Treasury, the government kept them out of circulation and cancelled them. This action quickly aroused opposition. The farmers, particularly those in the West, had borrowed these paper dollars when they were worth as little as 50 cents in gold or silver. If the greenbacks were retired, and the currency restored to a gold basis, they would have to pay back their loans (both interest and principal) in dollars worth 100 cents in specie. Because of the increase in the purchasing power of the dollar, commodity prices would fall and the farmer would get fewer dollars for his products. Protests by farmers and others were strong enough by 1868 to stop further retirement of the greenbacks.

Greenbacks are an issue in the campaign of 1868. The money question became one of the issues in the campaign of 1868. Many members of the Democratic Party were friendly to the idea that the government pay off the national debt in greenbacks.[4] In other words, the Democrats in general stood for (inflation) — they believed that the government should increase the supply of money fast enough to keep pace with, or perhaps even outstrip, the production of goods. They argued that prices would then rise and that the repayment of debts, both public and private, would become easier. The Republicans, however, with some exceptions, were generally opposed to this plan.

The government promises to redeem greenbacks in gold. The Republicans won the election, and early in 1869 Congress passed a resolution pledging the United States Government to repay its debts in specie or its equivalent. Congress, in 1875, went a step further and adopted a Resumption Act. By this measure the United States Government promised to redeem in specie all greenbacks presented to the Treasury on or after January 1, 1879. The Secretary of the Treasury was authorized to build up

a gold reserve sufficient for this purpose. Since the government had now promised to redeem them in specie, the value of the greenbacks increased and before January 1, 1879, they were worth their full value in gold. As a result, there was no rush to redeem them. Congress then decided that about 346 million dollars' worth of greenbacks should stay in circulation as a permanent part of the United States currency.

This return to specie payment was a victory for the people who wanted "hard-money" — that is, the creditor group which held most of the government bonds and had money out on loan to farmers and others. But it was a serious blow to the people who backed inflation — the farmer and debtor group — for money was still scarce and expensive. Some of them banded together to organize a new political party, the Greenback Party. "We demand a government," its platform declared, "of the people, by the people, and for the people, instead of a government of the bondholders, by the bondholders, and for the bondholders." The Greenback Party ran presidential candidates in 1876, 1880, and 1884, but never polled as much as four per cent of the popular vote.

A "hard money" cartoon of the time spoke in favor of return to specie payment. Brother Jonathan, supposed to represent the average American, is saying: Ah, Specie! Glad to see you, Specie! Been looking for you for some time. Your substitute, Greenback, was very well in his day; but, fact is, I wanted some "Change"!

---

[4] The stand of the parties was not entirely clear-cut. Although the Democratic platform called for paying off the debt in greenbacks, the Democratic candidate for the Presidency was a "sound-money" man. On the contrary, a few prominent Republicans were "soft-money" men.

Why did farmers and other debtors battle creditors over greenbacks?

1. How did debtor and creditor groups differ in their attitudes toward currency?
2. What were the effects of the growing scarcity of money following 1865 on western farmers and other debtors?
3. What were the greenbacks? Why was there a controversy over their retirement? How was it settled?

4 | **The West and the South Seek Relief from Low Prices Through Free Silver**

The silver supply increases. During the last quarter of the 1800's, farmers and others who backed the idea of expanding the currency shifted their attention from paper currency to silver. Before 1860, silver bullion [5] had been scarce and silver coins still scarcer. A law of 1834 provided for the coinage of both gold and silver at a ratio of about sixteen to one. Under this arrangement the United States mint offered the same price for sixteen ounces of silver as for one ounce of gold. This ratio slightly undervalued silver — that is, at that time sixteen ounces of silver were actually worth more than one ounce of gold when bought on the market. Since producers of silver could get more from a silversmith than they could get from the government, they took little or no silver to the United States mint to be coined into dollars. On the contrary, silver dollars were sometimes melted for use in industry.[6]

During the 1870's, however, the supply of silver increased tremendously. Because of the discovery of rich deposits in Colo-

rado and Nevada (page 345), the value of United States silver production rose from $165,800 in 1860 to $40,401,000 in 1878. This increase in production came at the same time that silver was being used less and less as money in Europe.

The mint stops coining silver. As the supply of silver increased and the demand for it decreased, its price fell. In 1874 — for the first time in 37 years — silver which was sold to private concerns or individuals brought less than 1/16th of its weight in gold. Silver producers rushed to the mint to get their silver coined into money, only to find the doors of the mint closed to them. A coinage law of 1873 had omitted silver dollars from the list of standard coins. Ignored at the time because no one wanted to sell silver at sixteen to one anyhow, this law was now denounced as a deliberate trick of the "goldbugs," and was called the "Crime of 1873."

Congress passes the Bland-Allison Act. From the West and South came the loudest demands for a change in the silver laws. In 1877 Richard P. Bland of Missouri ("Silver Dollar Dick"), who had once been a Nevada miner, introduced into the House of Representatives a bill providing for the free and unlimited coinage of silver at the ratio of sixteen to one.[7] Under the leadership of Senator Allison of Iowa, the Senate modified the bill. It became the Bland-Allison Act, and, as such, it required the Treasury to buy, every month, not less than 2 million dollars nor more than 4 million dollars in silver bullion at the market price. The bullion was to be coined into dollars which were to be acceptable for the payment of all debts. For convenience, silver certificates (certificates are paper money) were to be issued to circulate in place of some of the heavy "cart wheels" (a common term for silver dollars). The Bland-Allison Act became law in 1878 over the veto of President Hayes. The vote in Congress broke across party lines and reflected the economic in-

---

[5] Bullion is the uncoined metal.

[6] Smaller silver coins contained less silver than their face value indicated; ten silver dimes, for example, did not contain as much silver as one silver dollar. This policy was (and still is) followed in order to keep small change in circulation and to prevent such coins from being melted.

[7] *Free* coinage means the acceptance of unlimited amounts of the metal for coinage. Coinage by the government without charge is called *gratuitous* coinage.

terests of the different sections. The West and South, as debtor sections, favored the bill while the Northeast, or creditor, section of the country opposed it.

The Bland-Allison Act fails to help the farmer or silver producers. During the twelve years that the Bland-Allison Act remained in force, it turned out to be a disappointment both to the farmers who wanted cheap money and to the silver miners and producers. The cheap-money people were dissatisfied because the purchasing value of the dollar kept on rising and the price of farm commodities continued to decline. The situation of the silver miners also grew worse instead of better. Silver production increased faster than the Treasury was allowed to buy it, and the price of the metal kept on dropping.

The Sherman Silver Purchase Act is passed. The demand for further action increased during the 1880's. Farmers' Alliances (page 403), favoring cheap money, elected senators and representatives to Congress. Furthermore, when six new western states [8] were admitted to the Union in 1889–1890, twelve new senators, many of whom were free-silverites, entered Congress to fight for cheap money and the silver interests. These new western senators traded their support of the McKinley Tariff for eastern support of the Sherman Silver Purchase Act (1890). This law authorized the government to buy 4½ million ounces of silver a month at the market price, to be paid for by legal-tender treasury certificates. The Secretary of the Treasury was instructed to redeem these certificates in

[8] North Dakota, South Dakota, Wyoming, Montana, Idaho, Washington.

either gold or silver. Actually, the new act let the government buy practically the entire output of the American silver mines. But to the disappointment of the western silver producers, the price of silver continued its downward trend. By 1893 the bullion in a silver dollar was worth only 60 cents and after the panic of that year it fell to 49 cents. But the value of the dollar did not drop, for the Treasury continued to redeem all silver and paper money with gold. As a result, western and southern farmers were not helped, and the price of farm commodities remained low.

The Sherman Silver Purchase Act is repealed. During the financial panic of 1893, many banks closed and many firms went bankrupt. Although there were a number of reasons for the crisis, President Cleveland declared that it was "principally chargeable to congressional legislation touching the purchase and coinage of silver." Banks that stayed open were hoarding their gold and getting rid of their legal-tender treasury certificates. People who had both silver and gold were spending the silver and saving the gold. The situation was made even worse by the fact that foreign debts had to be paid in gold,[9] so that there was a constant flow of the yellow metal out of the country. Under these circumstances, the government's gold reserve dwindled. Bankers and eastern financiers feared that the government would soon be out of gold, and that the much cheaper silver dollars would take the place of gold dollars as the standard of monetary value. The effect would be a tremendous rise in prices. This was, of course, what the western and southern farmers wanted, but it would probably have meant disaster for many businesses and the eastern creditors.

Cleveland, who believed sincerely in a currency backed by gold, called Congress in special session to consider the repeal of the Sherman Silver Purchase Act. The representatives of the debtor farmers of the West and South, together with the "silverites" of the Far West, waged a hard battle,

[9] Gold was the international medium of exchange.

Coining press

particularly in the Senate where the western states had their greatest voting strength. Nevertheless Cleveland succeeded in securing repeal of the act, though his victory cost him his party leadership.

The gold reserve keeps shrinking. The repeal of the Sherman Silver Purchase Act checked the flow of silver into the Treasury, but the gold reserve kept right on shrinking. This further decline was caused mainly by the fact that the Treasury *kept on redeeming silver certificates and treasury notes in gold.* Attempts to build up the shrinking reserves ended in failure. Twice in 1894 the Secretary of the Treasury sold gold bonds to bring new supplies of gold into the Treasury, but that method did not work. Purchasers who paid gold to the Treasury for the bonds got the gold back by presenting greenbacks, silver certificates, or treasury notes for redemption. By 1895 the reserve had fallen to $41,000,000. It was a question how much longer the government could continue redeeming its paper currency with gold — in other words, how long the country could remain on the gold standard.

Cleveland gets help from Wall Street. Faced with this problem, Cleveland turned a willing ear to a practical plan of relief suggested by the financial leader, J. P. Morgan. A banking group, headed by Morgan, agreed to supply gold in return for government bonds. It further agreed (1) to secure half of this gold abroad, (2) not to take any of the precious metal from the Treasury by redeeming legal-tender notes, and (3) to cut down its exports of gold to other countries. Morgan drove a shrewd bargain, yet at the same time he performed a distinct service for his country. His action restored confidence in the currency and banking system and the ability of the United States to meet its obligations. Cleveland was severely criticized for his "deal with Wall Street," but he was satisfied that he had saved the credit of the United States Government and had kept the country from going from a gold to a silver standard.

Free silver is defeated in 1896. The nation-wide hubbub over silver reached a

William Jennings Bryan had an immense following throughout his political career but failed to be elected President.

climax in the presidential campaign of 1896. The discontented Democrats of the West and South found a dramatic standard-bearer in young William Jennings Bryan of Nebraska. Bryan made a speech which ranks as a masterpiece of political oratory and swept the Democratic convention into a frenzy of enthusiasm. He attacked the backers of the gold standard in the Republican Party, as he thundered, "Having behind us the producing masses of this nation and the world, supported by the commercial interests, the laboring interests, and the toilers everywhere, we will answer their demand for a gold standard by saying to them: You shall not press down upon the brow of labor this crown of thorns, you shall not crucify mankind upon a cross of gold!" Bryan was nominated for the Presidency. Free and unlimited coinage of silver at a ratio of sixteen to one was made the central plank in the Democratic platform. The Republicans had already chosen McKinley and pledged themselves to maintain the gold standard.

This campaign marked the first clear-cut division on the money issue. It drove many "gold" Democrats, like Cleveland, out of the Democratic Party, while "silver" Republicans, like McKinley, either changed their minds, or went over to the Democrats. Bryan's appeal satisfied the Populists, who also nominated him and who thereafter were merged in the Democratic Party.

During Bryan's campaign (page 469), the ideas expressed in his "Cross of Gold" speech echoed across the nation. Bryan traveled through cities and farmlands, speaking day and night. His followers idolized him for his devotion to the cause of the common people. His opponents were equally emotional in their opposition to him. The *New York Tribune* labelled him "that wretched rattle-pated boy [he was 36] posing in vapid vanity and mouthing resounding rottenness." Bryan carried the farmers of the South and most of the West, but he failed to sway the working classes or the conservative farmers in the North Central States and the East. After one of the bitterest campaigns in our history, the Republicans carried the election.

The advantage lies with business and industry. As the election returns came in, the western and southern farmers could see that they had lost again. For the most part, the 30 years that had elapsed since the War Between the States had been big booming years for business and industry. But the farmers could look back on 30 years of hardship. In a word, modern industrialism was transforming the nation into the world's industrial leader, but it had also set its mark upon one of the oldest of occupations, the tilling of the soil. In the race with business and industry, the farmers by the mid-1890's had come out only second best.

Although they did not know it at the time, new forces were even then taking shape which would shortly bring new prosperity to farmers and to industry as well. And, in the twentieth century, the farmers would see most, if not all, the measures they had favored enacted into law.

——— CHECK-UP ———

Why did the West and South seek relief from low prices through free silver?

1. Why was there a sudden interest in silver as currency following 1873?
2. What were the provisions of the Bland-Allison Act? The Sherman Silver Purchase Act? Why were they unsatisfactory?
3. Why was it difficult to keep gold in the Treasury? How did Cleveland solve the problem?
4. What part did silver play in the election of 1896? Why did farmers of the West and South believe that the free coinage of silver would help them?

CHAPTER REVIEW

Terms to Understand

agricultural
   revolution
scientific farming
tenancy
mortgage
co-operatives
creditor
debtor
specie

middleman
inflation
"hard money"
"cheap money"
gold standard
free silver
gold reserve
silver certificate
"sixteen to one"

People and Things to Know About

Department of Agri-
   culture
Morrill Act
Hatch Act
Oliver H. Kelley
Patrons of Husbandry
Grange
Farmers' Alliances
Resumption Act

Greenback Party
Bland-Allison Act
Sherman Silver Pur-
   chase Act
"Crime of 1873"
Grover Cleveland
William McKinley
J. P. Morgan
William Jennings Bryan

Historic Dates to Identify

1862   1879   1890   1896

Questions to Discuss

1. Compare the advantages and disadvantages to the farmer of self-sufficient and large-scale farming.
2. Why was the farmer at a disadvantage in relation to labor and industry? How would the farmer be affected by tariffs?
3. Why did the controversy between debtors and creditors take on a sectional flavor? On what other issues had the East and West been divided in our history?
4. Do you feel that Cleveland was right or wrong in making his bargain with J. P. Morgan? Why?
5. The power of the national government over currency can affect the distribution of wealth. Explain how this can be the case. How might

Questions to Discuss (Cont.)

your attitude toward inflation differ if you were (*a*) a widow living on life insurance, (*b*) a day laborer, (*c*) a "white collar" worker, (*d*) a farmer, (*e*) a banker?

6. Compare the following:

(*a*) The resumption of specie payments with Hamilton's funding of the national debt.

(*b*) The Bland-Allison Act with the Sherman Silver Purchase Act.

Relating Geography and History

Show on an outline map of the United States the principal areas where the important "cash-crops" are produced.

Other Things to Do

1. Examine your newspapers and magazines for significant activities on (*a*) developments in scientific agriculture, and (*b*) developments in agricultural technology. Be prepared to report on them in class.

Other Things to Do (Cont.)

2. Read the description of the great locust plagues in the Dakotas in O. E. Rölvaag's *Giants of the Earth,* pp. 339–353.

*3. Assume that you are a newspaper editor during the last quarter of the nineteenth century. Write an editorial either attacking or supporting the idea of cheap money.

4. Read William Jennings Bryan's famous "Cross of Gold" speech. Do you think that his arguments were sound? Compare his arguments with those of Cleveland in his message on the repeal of the Sherman Silver Purchase Act. You will find both statements in Commager's *Documents of American History.*

5. Read one of the many good works of historical fiction on the life of the pioneer farmer in the latter part of the nineteenth century. Those by O. E. Rölvaag, Bess Streeter Aldrich, and Hamlin Garland are especially interesting.

6. Find out whether or not there is a Grange organized in your community. If so, report on its present activities.

TO INCREASE YOUR UNDERSTANDING OF UNIT FIVE

Unit Summary

1. During the three decades following the close of the War Between the States, striking developments took place which laid the foundations for present-day America. One of these, the filling in of the West, was clearly evident to the growing nation. Leading this movement had been the prospectors or "fifty-niners" in search of gold and silver, and the cowboys who rode the open range. Then, lured by the promise of free public lands, pioneer farmers in large numbers settled the Great Plains. These pioneers had many difficulties to overcome, including the hardships of Nature and the attacks of Indians who resisted their advance. Nevertheless, so many people settled in the West that by 1890 the frontier had ceased to exist. An unhappy legacy of the filling in of the West was the Indian problem, which continued to vex the government for many years.

2. Other changes, having to do with the growth of our business and industrial system, were equally important but less well understood. The practical application of science to industry (technology), tremendous natural resources, and an ample supply of labor made possible large-scale production. Although industry continued to be active in New England and the Middle Atlantic states, it also spread westward and into the South. The growth of industry and business was greatly stimulated by the spread and consolidation of railroad lines, and by such communication aids as the telegraph, the Atlantic cable, and the telephone. To reap the benefits of large-scale production, corporations multiplied. Presently large trusts and holding companies appeared. The stories of Carnegie and Rockefeller aptly illustrate the growth of large business and industrial concerns. As the country became more and more industrialized, boom and depression periods became more pronounced.

3. Although our early government had accepted responsibility for encouraging manufactures through tariff protection, it had adhered strictly to a policy of non-interference with business since its start in 1789. Now as railroad and industrial combinations became so powerful that they threatened the welfare of the people, there were demands to abandon a *laissez faire* policy in favor of government regulation. The early attempts at regulation of railroads (the Interstate Commerce Act) and industrial monopolies (the Sherman Antitrust Act) were generally ineffective, but marked a significant change in point of view. At the same time, despite the attempts of Cleveland and the Democrats to lower the tariff, the tariff acts passed in these years indicated that the country at large still accepted the idea of tariff protection.

4. Two groups, labor and the farmer, were especially affected by the changing industrial picture. Various attempts at unionization, of which the A. F. of L. was the most successful, were made to increase labor's power to bargain with giant industrial combinations. Organized labor carried on numerous strikes, some of them bitter and bloody, to gain their ends. Meanwhile the farmer, because he now raised farm products for sale rather than for his own use, became increasingly affected by railroad rates, world prices, and the ups and downs of the business cycle. To overcome their difficulties farmers joined the Grange movement and sought relief through state legislation. Because of falling prices, western farmers also took part in two movements (the greenback movement and the free silver movement) in an effort to improve their financial condition, but neither effort was successful.

Summary of Important Dates

1859 First oil well drilled by Drake.
  Fifty-niners prospect for precious metals in Nevada and Colorado.
1862 Homestead Act passed.
  Morrill Act paves way for land-grant colleges.
1866 Atlantic cable successfully laid.
1869 First transcontinental railroad completed.
  Knights of Labor founded.
1873 Panic.
  "Crime of '73" demonetizes silver.
1876 Bell invents the telephone.
  Custer's force wiped out.
1878 Bland-Allison Act passed.
1879 Edison invents incandescent light.
1882 Organization of Standard Oil trust.
1886 Haymarket riot in Chicago.
  American Federation of Labor organized.
  Supreme Court rules against Granger laws.
1887 Interstate Commerce Act passed.
  Dawes Act passed.
1890 Sherman Antitrust Act passed.
  Sherman Silver Purchase Act passed.

McKinley Tariff Act passed.
  Frontier ceases to exist.
1893 Panic.
1894 Wilson-Gorman Tariff Act becomes law.
  Pullman strike.
1896 Bryan defeated in free silver campaign.
1901 United States Steel Corporation formed.

Unit Activities

1. Make as extensive a list as you can of the ways in which the United States of 1890 differed *economically* from the United States of 1790.

2. Make a three-column chart headed "Labor," "Capital" and "Agriculture." Compare these three interests in respect to "problems," "aims and desires," "methods adopted," and "achievements by 1896." Summarize in a few paragraphs the position of each of these groups in relation to one another in the latter years of the nineteenth century.

3. Trace the development of industry in your community during the last third of the 1800's. Consider such topics as (1) industries established, products produced, prices, (2) hours, wages, working conditions, (3) labor-management relations, (4) relations with competing industries. Possible sources of information are: town, county, and state histories; old newspapers; anniversary issues of contemporary newspapers; diaries; old letters; company records; accounts of old settlers. Write a feature article based on what you have learned.

4. If there is an Indian reservation near your community, learn what you can about its manner of living. Try to find out how this Indian community has been affected by the federal government's shifting Indian policy. What you learn may be included in the script for a pageant or an assembly program.

For Further Reading

Original Sources

Commager, H. S., ed., *Documents of American History*. Crofts. Nos. 298–300, 311–328, 341–343.

Commager, H. S., and Nevins, Allan, eds., *The Heritage of America*. Little, Brown. Nos. 191–200, 213–219.

Pease, T. C., and Roberts, A. S., eds., *Selected Readings in American History*. Harcourt. Nos. 199–200, 202, 205–209, 212–215.

General References

Adams, J. T., *Epic of America*. Little, Brown. Chapters 10 and 12.

Faulkner, H. U., *American Economic History*. Harper. Chapters 17 and 18.

Hicks, J. D., *The American Nation*. Houghton. Chapters 4, 6, 8, 11, 12.

Morison, S. E., and Commager, H. S., *The Growth of the American Republic*. Oxford. Vol. II, Chapters 4, 5, 6, 7, 9, 11.

Riegel, Robert. *America Moves West*. Holt. Chapters 29 to 40.

Special Accounts

American Nation Series. Harper. Sparks, E. E., *National Development*.

Beard, Mary R., *A Short History of the American Labor Movement*. Macmillan. A standard history of the growth of organized labor.

Chase, Stewart, *Men and Machines*. Macmillan. How machines have transformed American life.

Chronicles of America Series. Yale University Press. Buck, S. J., *The Agrarian Crusade*. Ford, H. J., *The Cleveland Era*. Hendrick, B. J., *The Age of Big Business*. Hough, E., *The Passing of the Frontier*. Moody, J., *The Masters of Capital* and *The Railroad Builders*. Thompson, H., *The Age of Invention*.

Collier, John, *Indians of the Americas*. Mentor Books. An inexpensive yet authoritative book on our Indian policy.

Dick, Everett, *The Sod-House Frontier*. Appleton-Century-Crofts. Deals with frontier life on the Great Plains.

Dick, Everett, *Vanguards of the Frontier*. Appleton-Century-Crofts. Has topical chapters on important developments in our Far West.

Hicks, J. D., *The Populist Revolt*. University of Minnesota Press. Covers the history of the Farmers' Alliances and the Populist Party.

History of American Life Series. Macmillan. Nevins, Allan, *Emergence of Modern America, 1865–1878*. Chapters 2–7, 11, 13, and 14. Tarbell, Ida, *The Nationalizing of Business, 1878–1898*.

Langdon, W. C., *Everyday Things in American Life*. Scribner. Contains interesting information on the development of railroads and manufactures.

Marshall, James, *The Sante Fe*. Random House. The story of a railroad which built an empire.

Rivers of America Series. Rinehart. Streeter, Floyd B., *The Kaw*. Tells of the Kansas cow towns and the farmers' invasion. Burt, Struthers, *Powder River*. Deals with the conquest of the northern Great Plains.

Taussig, F. W., *Tariff History of the United States*. Putnam. A standard history of American tariffs.

Webb, W. P., *The Great Plains*. Ginn. The best discussion of how the white man conquered the Great Plains and of how the Indians lived there.

Biography

Adams, Andy, *Log of a Cowboy*. Houghton. Adventures on the "long drive" as told by a participant.

Garst, Doris S., *The Story of Buffalo Bill*. Bobbs. A good picture of the West, centered around William Cody.

Nevins, Allan, *Grover Cleveland: A Study in Courage*. Dodd. The best biography of Cleveland.

Nevins, Allan, *John D. Rockefeller: the Heroic Age of American Enterprise*. Scribner. A biography of the founder of the Standard Oil Company.

Stevenson, Orlando, *Alexander Graham Bell*. Messner. An easy-to-read biography of the inventor of the telephone.

Werner, M. R., *Bryan*. Harcourt. The champion of the embattled western farmers.

Winkler, J. K., *Morgan the Magnificent*. Vanguard. A biography of John Pierpont Morgan, Sr. *John D.: A Portrait in Oils*. Vanguard. A biography of John D. Rockefeller. *Incredible Carnegie*. Vanguard. A biography of Andrew Carnegie.

Poetry

Barnes, Ruth A., *I Hear America Singing*. Winston. American folk poetry.

Lindsay, Vachel, *Collected Poems*. Macmillan. "The Eagle That is Forgotten," "Bryan, Bryan, Bryan, Bryan," "The Ghost of the Buffalo."

Lomax, John A., *Cowboy Songs*. Macmillan. Contains many famous cowboy songs.

Sandburg, Carl, *The American Songbag*. Harcourt. Folk songs, contains music.

Pictures

Adams, J. T., *The Album of American History*. Scribner. Vol. III, 1853–1893.

Building America Series. National Education Association. Vol. III, No. 2., *Our Farmers*. Vol. IX, No. 6, *Labor and Management*.

Butterfield, Roger, *The American Past*. Simon and Schuster.

Dick, Everett, *The Sod-House Frontier*. Appleton-Century-Crofts. Contains numerous photographs of pioneer ways of life.

Nevins, Allan, and Weitenkampf, Frank, *A Century of Political Cartoons*. Scribner.

Pageant of America Series. Yale University Press. Gabriel, Ralph H., *The Lure of the Frontier*. Keir, Malcolm, *The March of Commerce* and *The Epic of Industry*.

 # Sidelights on American History

Flying Pine and Crooked Arrow. Ever since cattle were first pastured on open ranges, it has been necessary to mark the cattle to show ownership. An early way of marking was to notch the ears in a certain manner. A more satisfactory method is to brand the cattle by burning the owner's mark into their hides. The first branding was done with a straight poker heated red hot. Called a "running rod," it was used by the cattleman to draw his mark on the hide of his steer. Because it was burnt in, the mark was permanent.

Some brands, particularly those drawn on with a "running rod," can be altered and made to look like other brands. Cattle thieves have resorted to this dishonest practice when stealing, or "rustling," cattle. To check the activities of "rustlers," branding irons were fashioned that would burn the whole brand pattern on at one time. Such a brand is much harder to change.

Cattle brands are registered, just like trade marks or designs, and are the exclusive property of their particular owners. Many of them are very picturesque in their appearance and in their origins. The 6666 brand, for instance, was adopted by a cattleman who won tremendous stakes at poker with a hand that held four sixes. A fisherman turned cattle rancher used a symbol of crossed fishhooks.

Like the heraldry of the knights of medieval times, cattle brands have a language of their own. You can hardly understand it sometimes unless you have worked in cattle country on the range. For example, someone's reference to "lazy H under rail" may describe a brand with a symbol like the letter H lying on its side under a straight line. Such a brand may also be called "lazy H under dash" or "lazy H under bar." "Rocking H," on the other hand, may refer to a brand that looks like an H held up by a section of a circle. "Flying pine" and "crooked arrow" describe two other famous brands.

Although we usually think of cattle brands as particularly American, they are almost as old as history. The Egyptians used them before the Christian era. Brands were brought into the New World by the Spaniards of Mexico, when they introduced cattle raising into Texas and California.

Southpaw Outlaw. The most famous outlaw of the old Southwest was a quiet-spoken, left-handed killer whom the frontier people knew as Billy the Kid. Born William H. Bonney in New York City, the Kid began the life of a desperado at an early age. When he was six, his family moved west to Santa Fe. At the age of twelve the Kid stabbed a man and killed him. Four years later, three peaceful Indians who were taking furs to market near Fort Bowie in Arizona were set upon by three or four white men. The Indians were killed and their furs stolen. The leader of the white men was Billy the Kid.

Wherever there was fighting and shooting, it seemed, the Kid could be found. He went to work for a cattle rancher and was soon involved in a "cattle war." Two factions — the McSweens and the Murphys — were trying to drive each other out of the range country. They were stopping at nothing in their warfare, from cattle stealing to homicide. Billy the Kid became the leader of the McSweens, and when a sheriff turned up to stop the fighting, the Kid and his men shot him down.

Even the United States government in Washington had to take a hand in Billy the Kid's desperate career. An army general was sent to urge the Kid to give himself up, and thereby end the cattle war. "Even if I were tried, convicted, pardoned, and then set free," the Kid is said to have replied, "it would be the end of me. My enemies would murder me within a day."

The desperado's end, however, was not far away. Sheriff Pat Garrett tracked the Kid down and captured him. At Mesilla, New Mexico, the outlaw of outlaws was tried, convicted, and sentenced. "To be hanged by the neck until dead," pronounced the judge, "at the town of Lincoln, upon the 13th day of May." The Kid was locked in the Lincoln jail with his handcuffs and leg irons still on. Law-abiding folk of the frontier breathed more easily.

But Billy the Kid got away again. Two weeks before the day set for his hanging, he somehow managed to kill his two guards and escape. Sheriff Garrett — a man as cool and fearless as the Kid — was soon on his trail. Ten weeks later the Kid was discovered in his hiding place. In the battle that followed the Kid was killed. He died in 1881, when he was only 22 years old.

The Trusty Six-shooter. Indians attacking a wagon train on the Great Plains used tactics that worked successfully again and again. Riding swift horses, they would gallop rapidly toward the prairie schooners, which had been drawn up in a circle for protection. As the riders drew near the wagons, they would be fired upon — but only once, for they would close in fast, before their enemies had time to reload. Many a band of white settlers was wiped out because of these tactics. A day came, however, when the settlers were able to refire immediately, and to refire again and again, until the Indians toppled from their horses by the score.

The new weapon that saved the lives of so many pioneers was the repeating Colt revolver. Its inventor, Samuel Colt, had taken out patents for the new firearm in February, 1836, and had then manufactured a few of the six-shooters at a factory in Paterson, New Jersey. Though the new weapon was the first repeating firearm that really worked, it was not an immediate success. In fact, six years later Samuel Colt's company failed.

But American army regulars used the Colt during the war with the Seminole Indians. The Texas Rangers tried it out at the time when they figured prominently in border trouble with the Mexicans. Both fighting units reported that there had never before been such a "shooting iron." Samuel Colt suddenly found himself in business again. The government ordered several thousand Colts. To get them made, the inventor had to have Eli

Whitney's factory in New Haven do the job. Later Colt made the weapon in Hartford, Connecticut, and by the end of the War Between the States had turned out over half a million.

The Colt revolvers of that time had no metal cartridges like those of today. Each of the six chambers was loaded with loose powder and a lead bullet. The spark to fire each charge came from a percussion cap struck by the hammer of the revolver when the trigger was pulled. But the weapon was deadly accurate. The parts were precision made, and the barrel of the weapon was rifled so that the gun would shoot true.

Stop That Train! In 1948 the Freedom Train, displaying famous documents and mementoes of American history, attracted attention all over the country. It visited hundreds of towns and cities in all parts of the United States, and it covered 33,000 miles. This was not the first American train to make a nation-wide tour, however. In President Grover Cleveland's first term of office, there was a railroad tour that excited all Americans, particularly the railroading people. A train of 50 freight cars was not only showing off a remarkable new invention but also proving that it really worked.

The invention was George Westinghouse's air brake. It had been patented in 1869 but did not work perfectly until 19 years later. When improvements had been made and the device perfected, the country-wide demonstration trip was planned. Before the Westinghouse invention, whenever brakes were applied to a train of railroad cars, there had been a time gap between the moment when the first car was braked and the moment that the brakes were effective on the last car. For a train of 50 cars this time lag would have been 18 seconds, and sometimes that brief time was responsible for serious collisions. On the demonstration train, however, the 50th car could be braked only two seconds after the first car.

The only brakes on early trains were found on the locomotives. These brakes were practically the same as the ones on stage coaches: wooden blocks applied to the wheel rims by the force of a lever operated by the engineer's strong right arm. Today all trains use air brakes, and they operate almost instantaneously on every car of the train.

Outing of a bicycle club

THE PLAN OF THE BOOK

Unit Six

A GROWING POPULATION FACES

PROBLEMS AND ENRICHES

ITS WAY OF LIFE

In the years after 1865 the expanding economy of the United States attracted millions of immigrants interested in achieving a better living for themselves and their children. To them America was a land of opportunity. Many of them settled on fertile farmland, particularly the land west of the Mississippi. Even more found work in the mines, the forests, and the huge factories. Population growth in cities was particularly rapid.

City life provided contrasts of great wealth and grinding poverty, of added conveniences and problems of health and housing. Reformers sought to relieve conditions in the slums, to promote temperance, and to achieve political equality for women. The need for Americanizing the foreign-born and for making useful members of society out of all citizens in a democracy led to increased emphasis on public education.

The public library, theatrical and musical presentations in the city, and the Chautauqua movement for adult education in rural areas also helped increase the general level of knowledge and taste. Sports such as baseball, football, and boxing were finding a place both in amateur and professional circles. Books written by "local color" writers served to acquaint each region with the folkways of other areas. The increasing sale of newspapers and magazines showed that Americans were eager for information about happenings in the United States and in the outside world.

Such topics as these — all bearing on the way people lived — are discussed in Unit Six.

Suffragette, 1800's

NEW AMERICANS JOIN WITH OLD TO

MEET NEW PROBLEMS

So at last I was going to America! The boundaries burst. The arch of heaven soared. A million suns shone out for every star. The winds rushed in from outer space, roaring in my ears, "America! America!"

Mary Antin, THE PROMISED LAND

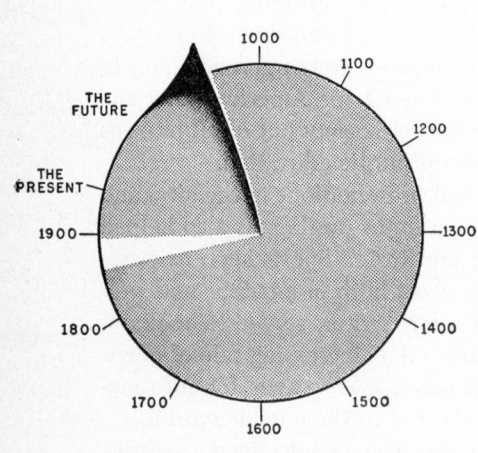

1865-1896

The first United States census, completed in 1790, was taken by 217 men. Riding through the thinly settled countryside, carrying their inkhorns and quill pens in their saddlebags, they made census records on odds and ends of paper, for the government was too poor to furnish regular forms. Their totals showed that the population of the country was less than 4 million.

Many more census takers were needed in the year 1860, for by that time the population had increased to more than 31 million. This figure had doubled 30 years later — to almost 63 million. With such swift growth came a number of problems. The population of the 1890's did not resemble that of 1860 in the way that an enlargement resembles a snapshot — in everything but size. The pattern had changed. The proportions of the groups within our population had shifted. Some groups were relatively larger, or had gained in prestige and power. Others, important 30 years before, had lost importance. Population centers had shifted, and living conditions had changed greatly.

This chapter tells the story of changing elements in our fast-growing population and of certain conditions that resulted. The following topics cover this story:

1. An increase in immigration brings many changes.
2. Extremes of wealth and poverty develop in America.
3. Social problems demand consideration.

Health officer vaccinating immigrant

1 An Increase in Immigration Brings Many Changes

America continues to attract foreigners. The remarkable growth in our population between 1860 and 1890 resulted partly from a high birth rate and partly from the fact that immigrants from foreign countries were coming to America in larger numbers than ever. Over 9 million came from Europe alone during this period. By 1890 there were more than 12½ million foreign-born people in the country. (See chart, page 421.)

Immigrants come for many reasons. Conditions in Europe were partly responsible for the migrations. A few persons were still leaving the lands of their birth to escape religious persecution. There was also political unrest; some men came to this country to escape army service in European wars. By far the largest number came in the hope of making a better living here. Some of them had suffered from the crop failures in parts of Europe between 1870 and 1880. Men who were thrown out of work during periods of economic unrest looked eagerly to America as a land of opportunity, especially those who were hearing glowing reports of America from relatives. The efforts of steamship companies to fill their steerage (lowest class) accommodations led to lower fares for the ocean voyage. As a result, more and more immigrants found it possible to break home ties and to establish new homes across the sea.

More immigrants arrive in good times. The number of immigrants arriving in a single year depended upon economic conditions in America as well as in Europe. With the growth of American industry, some manufacturers attempted to recruit laborers abroad. There was much work to be done in this country, and there were not enough workers to do it. Factories had to be built, forests cut down, railroads constructed. Immigrants were more than welcome, particularly those who were willing to work for low wages and to live with few comforts and no luxuries.

In hard times fewer immigrants came. During the depression which followed our Panic of 1873, for example, the number decreased until in 1878 less than 140,000 foreign-born came into this country. This total was the smallest since 1862. But with the return of good times the flood of newcomers grew until in 1882 the number was nearly 800,000 a year.

Northern Europe sends the most immigrants. In the period following the War Between the States, as before the war, a larger number of new arrivals to this country came from the British Isles than from any other part of Europe. More came from Germany, however, than from any other single country. During the '70's and '80's there was a marked increase in the group from Norway, Sweden, and Denmark, most of them hard-working farmers, who found homes in Illinois, Wisconsin, Minnesota, and the Dakotas. Large numbers of people continued to come from Ireland, though the totals never equaled those resulting from famine during the '40's and the '50's.

By the early 1890's there was already a noticeable rise in the rate of immigration from southern and eastern Europe — Italy, Russia, Poland, and the Balkan countries. This increase in the number of southern and eastern Europeans was only the beginning of a mighty wave that reached a peak in the early 1900's (see pages 586 and 587).

Immigrants are blamed for social evils. Beginning in the 1870's there were objections raised in this country against the immigrants. Patriotic societies began to protest the admission of so many foreign elements to the "melting pot." They urged restriction of immigration to America. The foreign-born were blamed for the increase in crime in their sections of the great cities. If the newcomers were at fault, it was owing in part to their ignorance of American laws and ways of life, in part to the fact that bad housing and poverty often lead to crime.

Labor and industry favor restriction. Organized labor was a second group that favored restrictions on immigration. Its leaders were afraid that an unlimited number of people coming to these shores would mean ever-lower wages and that immigrants would furnish a constant supply of strike-breakers. Captains of industry made up a third group which began to want limits put on the number of newcomers. They had once favored free immigration because it gave them cheap labor. Now they began to blame the foreign-born for increasing labor unrest and growing violence in strikes. Foreigners were labeled "radicals." "The ranks of anarchy and riots number no Americans," stated Chauncey M. Depew in 1887. "The leaders boldly proclaim that they come here not to enjoy the blessings of our liberty and to sustain our institutions but to destroy our government, cut our throats, and divide our property."

The Chinese are excluded. The first important attempt to restrict immigration affected the Chinese. In 1868 the United States had drawn up the Burlingame Treaty with China. This agreement allowed special privileges to Americans in China and gave Chinese citizens the right to travel and live in the United States. While the first transcontinental railroad was being constructed (page 364), the Chinese were welcomed to this country because they provided cheap labor. By 1879, however, American labor complained that it could not compete with the Chinese coolies who worked for starvation wages and lived under conditions that Americans would not endure. Because of such protests, President Hayes succeeded in modifying the Burlingame Treaty so that the United States had the right to "regulate, limit, or suspend" the entry of Chinese laborers.

When even more drastic measures than this were demanded, a law was passed in 1882 which excluded Chinese laborers for a period of ten years and denied American citizenship to all Chinese nationals. In 1892 the period was extended for another ten years. This restriction continued in force until World War II. During this time only students and certain specified classes of Chinese were admitted to the United States.

Special groups are barred. In 1882, another law was passed which reflected the tightening immigration policy of the United States. Objectionable persons like paupers, convicts, and the insane were forbidden to land on our shores, and the steamship companies were required to return to their homelands those who were not admitted. Three years later (1885) the door was closed to aliens who arrived under contract to work for an American employer. Restrictions were extended in 1891 to exclude those suffering from contagious and loathsome diseases. Then a bill requiring all new arrivals to prove their ability to read and write was passed by Congress, but it was vetoed by President Cleveland. Cleveland insisted that it was better to "admit a hundred thousand immigrants who, though unable to read and write, seek among us a home and opportunity to work, than to admit one of those unruly agitators and

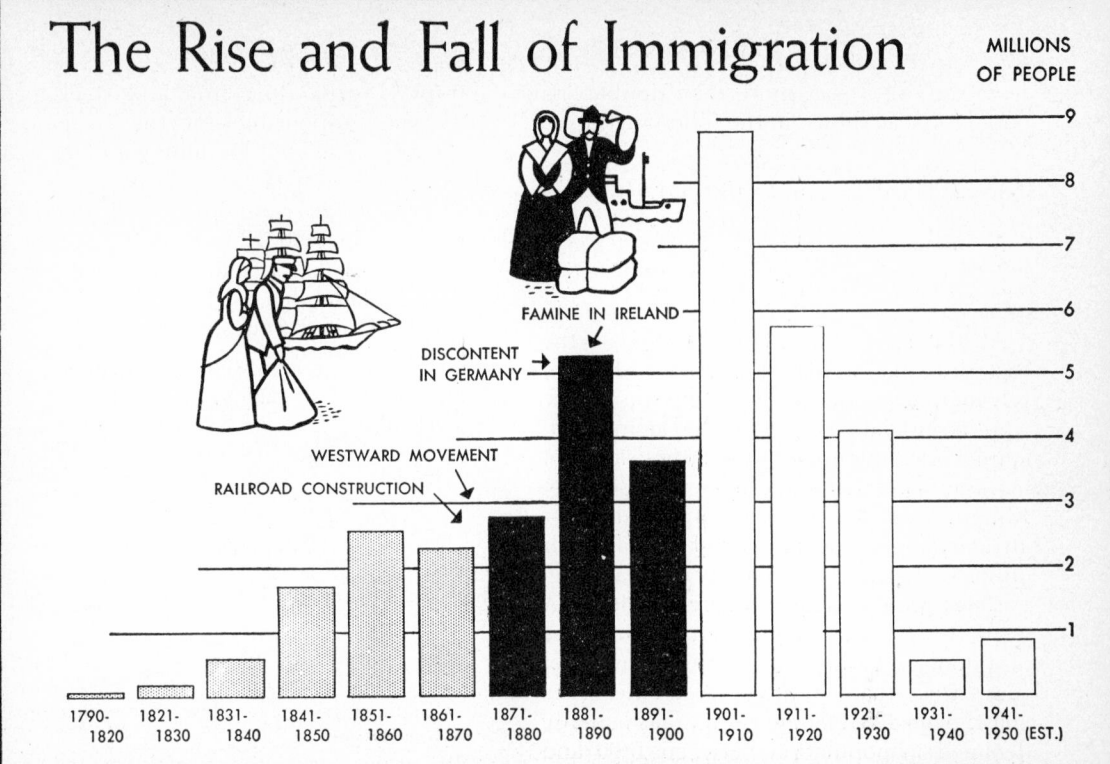

The Rise and Fall of Immigration

MILLIONS OF PEOPLE

FAMINE IN IRELAND

DISCONTENT IN GERMANY →

WESTWARD MOVEMENT

RAILROAD CONSTRUCTION

| 1790- | 1821- | 1831- | 1841- | 1851- | 1861- | 1871- | 1881- | 1891- | 1901- | 1911- | 1921- | 1931- | 1941- |
| 1820 | 1830 | 1840 | 1850 | 1860 | 1870 | 1880 | 1890 | 1900 | 1910 | 1920 | 1930 | 1940 | 1950 (EST.) |

Many more immigrants came to America from 1881 to 1890 than came from 1871 to 1880. Can you explain why? Why did immigration decline after 1890? Compare this chart with the one on page 243. What new reasons for immigration appeared after the War Between the States?

enemies of governmental control who can not only read and write, but delight in arousing by inflammatory speech the illiterate and peacefully inclined to discontent and tumult."

The center of population shifts. As millions were added to our population, certain important changes took place along with the increase. In the first place, the center of population shifted 150 miles westward from 20 miles southeast of Chillicothe, Ohio (1860), to 20 miles east of Columbus, Indiana (1890). The shift westward had been taking place gradually for many years, but during this postwar period the rate of change was very rapid. To be sure, the most densely populated section was still the one that included New England and the Middle Atlantic states of New York, New Jersey, and Pennsylvania. By 1890 this eastern section had an average of nearly 103 persons per square mile. The Mountain and Pacific regions (map, pages

12–13), by way of contrast, had an average of about 3 persons per square mile.

Some states grow faster than others. A second trend was that some states grew very slowly in comparison with others. When we remember that the population of the country doubled between 1860 and 1890, the increase in some states may seem surprisingly low. For example:

	1860	1890
Maine	628,279	661,086
Vermont	315,098	332,422
Virginia	1,596,318	1,655,980

The slow growth of such states is evidence of two facts: (1) they did not attract large numbers of immigrants; (2) some of their people moved to industrial centers and to areas where fertile land was cheap and plentiful.

Some of the agricultural states of the Middle West, especially those not far removed from frontier conditions, and the huge state of Texas, more than doubled in population, as shown in the following table:

	1860	1890
Iowa	674,913	1,912,297
Kansas	107,206	1,428,108
Minnesota	172,023	1,310,283
Nebraska	28,841	1,062,656
Texas	604,215	2,235,527

At the same time, some states of the eastern seaboard, like New York and Pennsylvania, expanded rapidly because they were industrial. They provided homes and employment for hundreds of thousands of immigrants. Some middle western states — Illinois, Michigan, and Ohio, for example — attracted new people because of their opportunities in both industry and farming.

Cities grow faster than rural sections. A third trend that accompanied the increase in population was the slower growth of rural areas than of towns and cities (see chart, page 423). Some rural areas actually declined in population between 1860 and 1890. Such a decline took place particularly in Pennsylvania, New Jersey, New York, and New England, chiefly because the farmers living in these areas were unable to market crops in competition with the farmers of the Middle West. For one thing, the middle western farmers had the advantage of more fertile land. For another, the level open countryside made it possible for each farmer to cultivate more extensive areas. Large numbers of rural folk in the East migrated westward, and even larger numbers moved to the city.

Western cities grow faster than eastern. By 1880 about half the people in the region from Maryland northward to Maine lived in towns and cities having 4000 or more inhabitants. The following figures show the growth of some of the larger cities of the East:

	1870	1890
New York	1,478,103	2,507,414
Philadelphia	674,022	1,046,964
Boston	250,526	448,477
Pittsburgh	139,256	343,904
Providence	68,904	132,146

The growth of middle western cities was much more striking. In some of them

the rapidly expanding iron and steel industry was responsible for the increase. Others were benefited by milling and meat-packing. Still others were active trading centers for large rural areas. Of the 50 largest cities in 1890, 12 were in the Middle West. By 1880 Chicago had taken the place of Philadelphia as the second largest city in the United States.

	1870	1890
Chicago	298,977	1,099,850
Cleveland	92,829	261,353
Detroit	79,577	205,876
St. Paul	20,030	133,156
Denver	4,759	106,713

——————— CHECK-UP ———————

What changes resulted from increased immigration after 1865?

1. What areas of Europe contributed large numbers of immigrants, 1865–1895? Why was there an uneven flow of immigration, year by year?
2. What were the attitudes of labor and industry on the immigration question? Why?
3. What restrictions were placed on immigration during this period?
4. What were the trends in population growth, 1865–1895?

2 Extremes of Wealth and Poverty Develop in America

Prosperity follows the war. As you have already seen, the War Between the States stimulated American industry. During the years that followed, it grew by leaps and bounds. Among the important new industries which developed during this period were those centering around steel production, petroleum, and meat-packing. Other older industries, such as the manufacture of shoes and clothing, adopted machine methods and large-scale production. Between 1860 and 1870 the number of manufacturing establishments in the country as a whole increased about 80 per cent.

Our Growing Population

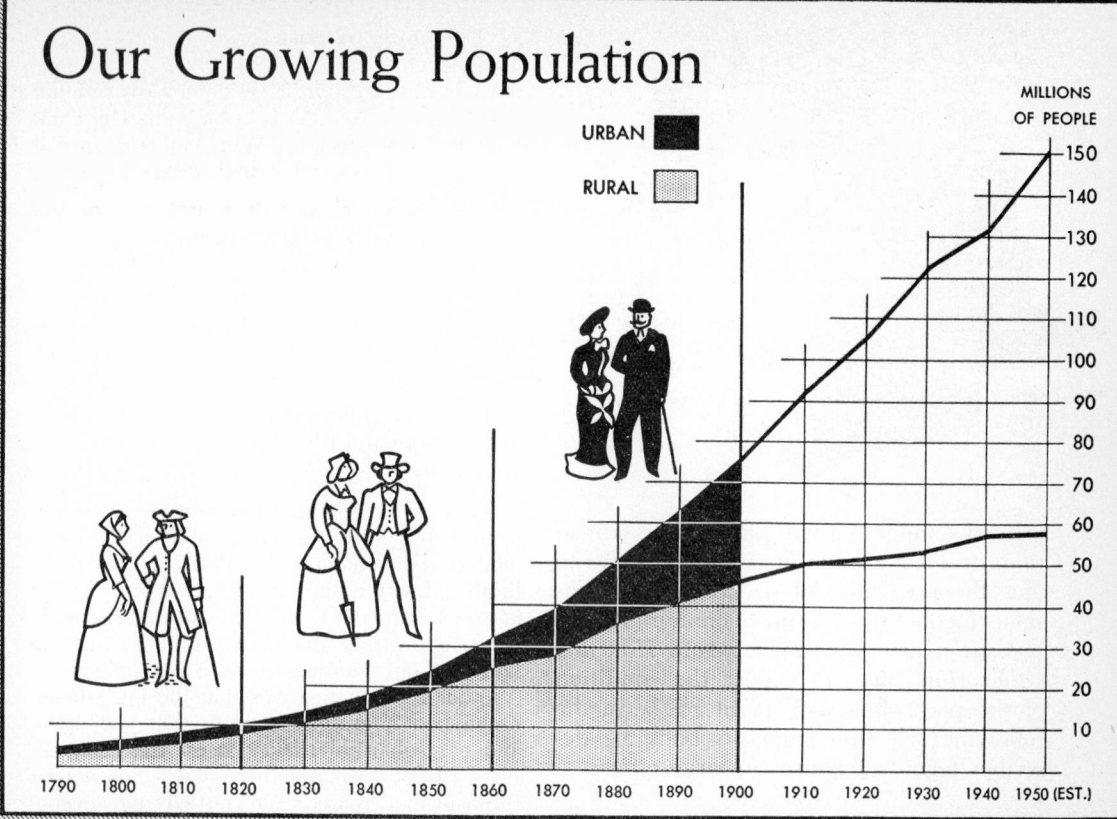

The population of the United States was about how large in 1900? About how many people lived in rural areas at that time? In urban areas? Why did the proportion of people living in urban areas begin to increase so rapidly after 1860?

This tremendous growth offered a golden opportunity to business leaders with vision, boldness, and executive ability.

The wealthy class grows. It is not strange, therefore, that the number of wealthy persons increased greatly in this period. It has been estimated that in 1861 there were only three millionaires in the country. Before the turn of the century this number had increased to at least 3800, and about nine tenths of the country's wealth was controlled by one tenth of the population. Interest on bonds and dividends on stocks made it unnecessary for members of this top-income group to work. If they wished, they could spend their time in summer and winter resorts, European travel, and their palatial city residences. The period, called by Mark Twain the "Gilded Age," was one in which ability and success were measured very largely by wealth.

Under such conditions it is not surprising to find that many of the newly rich were spending money in showy ways. They lived in elaborate, over-ornamented homes and had many servants to wait on them. One such man was the financier Jim Fisk, who lived perhaps more extravagantly than anyone else in his day. In New York City he occupied a great marble home that contained his own opera house. Hundreds of canary birds in gilded cages sang in the rooms. He loved showy clothes, and once he arranged to meet President Grant while dressed in an admiral's uniform, decorated with gold lace.

The poor live in misery. While a handful of the rich lived in luxury, millions of the very poor were filling the slums of the great cities. They lived in wretched tenement houses under crowded conditions that fostered disease and encouraged crime. Most of them were unskilled laborers, working for low wages. Many were newly-

Home of the 1870's

arrived immigrants without money, education, or a knowledge of American ways to give them a choice of occupation or location. Jacob Riis, a Danish immigrant who became a newspaperman, wrote *How the Other Half Lives* to expose the condition of the poor of New York in 1890. In the following selection from his book he describes tenement houses in large cities:

Suppose we look into one . . . Be a little careful, please! The hall is dark, and you might stumble over the children pitching pennies back there. Not that it would hurt them; kicks and cuffs are their daily diet. They have little else. Here where the hall turns and dives into utter darkness is a step, and another, another. A flight of stairs. You can feel your way if you cannot see it. Close? Yes! What would you have? All the fresh air that ever enters these stairs comes from the hall door that is forever slamming and from the windows of dark bedrooms that in turn receive from the stairs their sole supply of the elements God meant to be free but man deals out with such niggardly hand. That was a woman filling her pail by the hydrant you just bumped against. The sinks are in the hallway, that all the tenants may have access — and all be poisoned alike by their summer stenches. Hear the pump squeak? It is the lullaby of tenement house babes. In summer, when a thousand thirsty throats pant for a cooling drink in this block, it is worked in vain. But the saloon, whose open door you passed in the hall, is always there. The smell of it has followed you up. Here is a door. Listen! That short, hacking cough, that tiny, helpless wail — what do they mean? They mean that the soiled bow of white you saw on the door downstairs will

have another story to tell — oh! a sadly familiar story — before the day is at an end. The child is dying with measles. With half a chance it might have lived, but it had none.

The middle class sets a pattern for the "American way of life." Between the very rich and the very poor was the large middle class. It included most persons engaged in professional, business, and white-collar jobs as well as many skilled workers. Clarence Day, the author of *Life With Father*, described his childhood home in a comfortable upper-middle-class section of New York City:

Our new home was a four-story brownstone-front house with a stoop, and it had all the modern conveniences of 1879. It had gaslights in every room, even the cook's. We used kerosene lamps in the parlor, but that was only because the gas chandelier was too high to light without climbing up on a step-ladder . . . Another convenience was that the big kitchen range had a grating in front that slid open, and a mechanical shaker to let the cook stir the coal fire . . . And there was a fine hot-air furnace that roared and rattled and misbehaved itself wildly. Most of the rooms had fireplaces, too . . . On every floor except the fourth of the new house we had running water, and there were two shining tin bathtubs . . . The cook and waitress didn't have a bathtub, but there was a white china water-pitcher and bowl in their bedroom, the same as in mine.

Middle-class homes of the late 1800's had their sewing machines and pianos as well as their gas lights and bathrooms. Middle-class standards of taste, comfort, and morality were idealized as "the American way of life," and were imitated or envied by those who could not afford them.

Stove

How did extremes of wealth and poverty develop in America after 1865?

1. What conditions led to the development of a wealthy class? What were the marks of the "Gilded Age"?
2. What are slums? Why did slum areas develop in American cities?
3. What is the middle class? Why is their way of life thought of as characteristically American?

3 Social Problems Demand Consideration

The use of child labor in factories was not uncommon in the late 1800's. Long hours and poor sanitation menaced the children.

Slum living requires correction. The slums were one of the major social problems in the last quarter of the nineteenth century. Many immigrants found their dreams of a land of opportunity shattered by miserable living conditions which they had to endure in America. Slum living was even more glaring because it existed side by side with the luxurious comfort of the rich.

The slum problem became even more serious when 2 or 3 million people found themselves out of work following the Panic of 1873. "In New York City," wrote one historian, "out of a hundred thousand slum dwellers, twenty thousand lived in cellars; in Boston one fifth of the total population lived in flimsy, overcrowded tenements." These people were unable to feed or clothe their families properly. Diseases like smallpox and typhoid, which could have been prevented, spread easily in the filth of the slums. In America, the land of plenty, some slum dwellers actually died of starvation.

The "battle against the slum" was a long, uphill fight in which many people took part. Reformers appealed to city governments, to state legislatures, to federal authorities to do away with the unhealthful conditions in which the unfortunate poor were living. Sanitation and building laws were passed that provided better sewage disposal and for at least a minimum amount of light and air in the construction of new houses. Fire laws forbade flimsy construction and required fire escapes where they were necessary.

Jane Addams befriends the poor. But there were some people who attacked the slum problem by going themselves among slum dwellers and trying to make their lives easier. Outstanding among these was Jane Addams. Even as a young girl she had the dream of owning a large house among the "horrid, dirty houses" so that poor people could come to her for aid. The daughter of a banker who owned mills in Illinois, Jane Addams as a girl observed living conditions among the mill workers and resolved to devote her life to helping the poor. After preparing herself for her life work in this country and in Europe, she founded Hull House in Chicago in 1889 with the intention of serving the community where it was located. Starting with a nursery for children whose mothers worked, Miss Addams soon discovered countless other needs in the community. Before the end of her useful life she had influenced the regulation of child labor, the improvement of factory conditions, and the establishment of playgrounds and parks.

Chicago's "greatest citizen" was an inspiration throughout the nation. Settlement houses like Hull House were organized in other cities where devoted helpers pushed forward the work of social service in which Miss Addams had pioneered.

The liquor problem continues. A second important problem that concerned many of the people during this period was that of intoxicating liquor. We have seen in Chapter 12 that during the first half of the 1800's many temperance societies had been formed. As the temperance movement gained strength, large numbers of men "signed the pledge," promising never to touch strong drink. After 1865, however, the movement lost ground.

The rapid growth of the cities after the war probably helped to make the problem of liquor more serious. In the cities and towns liquor was sold in places called saloons, some of which tried to create the atmosphere of clubs. There were saloons of all grades, those for the rich as well as those for the less well-to-do and the poor, just as there were all grades of restaurants. Some evidence of the popularity of saloons is shown by the fact that in 1880 there was a total of $193,000,000 invested in the liquor business.

Reformers grow more active. But as intemperance grew, more effort was put into the prohibition movement by those who wanted to do away with the poverty and crime that often go hand in hand with the sale of liquor. Certain church groups waged an active campaign against "the demon rum," fighting for state laws that would prohibit the sale of strong drink. A new political party called the Prohibition Party was formed in 1869. The party did not attract a particularly large number of votes, but it nominated a presidential candidate in every election from 1872 on, and it kept the liquor question constantly before the public. The Women's Christian Temperance Union (W.C.T.U.) was particularly active in educating the public through speeches and pamphlets on the evils of intemperance.

One of the most active women in the cause of prohibition was Frances E. Willard, who resigned from the teaching staff of Northwestern University in 1874 to become corresponding secretary of the W.C.T.U. Later she became its president, and her influence was felt for many years in that organization and in the Prohibition Party.

Women are handicapped. The position of women in the business and political life of the country must be considered as one of the social problems of the period. Women, who normally make up half the adult population, still had to suffer some of the handicaps of a minority group. Like the immigrants, women occupied an unfavorable position in American economic life of the 1800's. They were barred from many medical and law schools and from most divinity and engineering schools. Thus their opportunities in the professions were more or less restricted to nursing and public school teaching. When women worked in industry, their wages for the same labor were lower than men's. In many states a married woman's earnings, as well as her property, belonged to her husband. In fact, as late as 1930 there was still one state in which a wife's earnings were legally her husband's property, and one in which a father could assign the custody of his child to another person than its mother.

Women struggle for political equality. Women seemed more eager than men to ban the sale of liquor and do away with the evils for which it was responsible. Therefore most of the people who fought for prohibition also favored giving women equal rights and opportunities with men. Though women were active in various reform movements, they were limited in what they could accomplish by the fact that they did not enjoy the right to vote.

In 1869 the fight for woman suffrage made a real advance when the territory of Wyoming allowed women the right to vote. In the same year the National Woman Suffrage Association was organized under the leadership of Susan B. Anthony. Her forceful personality and ceaseless energy helped the association to gain great strength and influence. She worked closely with her

(Continued on page 428)

Jane Addams
(1860-1935)

A Visit to the Slums

FEW AMERICAN WOMEN have led lives of greater usefulness than Jane Addams. The daughter of a well-to-do mill owner in a small Illinois town, she lacked for nothing. Even at an early age, however, Jane showed a concern for those less fortunate than herself.

Jane Addams attended Rockford Seminary and then decided to study medicine. Because of a childhood spinal difficulty, she was not strong enough to complete the course. She went to Europe, where she enjoyed the culture of the Old World but was saddened by the misery of its poor. Visiting the slums of London's East End on a Saturday night, she saw greedy hands stretched out for rotting vegetables and fish too decayed to be saved for the Monday market. The suffering she observed in other cities strengthened her girlhood determination to do something for those who had to endure poverty and unhappiness.

Sewing Class at Hull House

After studying at Toynbee Hall, London's social service center, Jane Addams developed the plan that was to become her life work. She purchased Hull House, a large mansion in the heart of Chicago's slum area, and opened its doors in 1889. At first the people of the neighborhood regarded Hull House with suspicion but were soon won over by the atmosphere of friendly service. There were classes and healthful recreation for boys and girls, daylong kindergartens for the children of working mothers, rooms for working girls, and a helping hand for all who were in distress.

Jane Addams's influence spread far beyond Hull House. Volunteer workers who trained there carried its philosophy and methods to other cities. Miss Addams also became a pioneer in getting laws passed in Illinois for better working conditions, protection of children, cleaner streets, and more parks. Active in the movement for women's rights, she vigorously supported Theodore Roosevelt in the Progressive campaign in 1911. She was a devoted worker in the cause of world peace and was awarded the Nobel Peace Prize in 1931. Sometimes called America's Joan of Arc, she is best remembered as Jane Addams of Hull House.

Champion of Reform

good friend Elizabeth Cady Stanton in many reform causes, among them the drive to secure federal legislation which would give political rights to women. Mrs. Stanton, a brilliant writer and speaker, was president of the National Woman Suffrage Association for many years.

The women's movement makes progress. Meanwhile, the fact that some of the states gave women a voice in school elections was another step toward complete political equality. At last in 1890 Wyoming was admitted to the Union with the distinction of being the first state to grant full political rights to women. By 1896 three other states — Colorado, Utah, and Idaho — had also adopted woman suffrage.

During the years following the War Between the States, in spite of their handicaps, the number of women active in business and industry had noticeably increased. In 1870 there had been one woman employed in industry to every eight men, but before the end of the century this proportion was one to five. More and more women were engaging in social welfare work,

teaching school, attending college, and, where they could, even entering the professions of law, medicine, and the ministry. An outstanding example of woman leadership was Clara Barton. After devoting her services to establishing nursing care for the wounded in the War Between the States, she struggled almost without assistance to organize the American Red Cross. The organization was founded in 1881, and for 23 years she was its head.

––––––––– CHECK-UP –––––––––

What social problems demanded attention in the period 1865–1895?

1. What efforts were made to eliminate slums and to relieve slum conditions? What did Jane Addams do about this problem?
2. What was the liquor problem? What groups were active in the temperance movement?
3. What rights were denied women in the period after 1865? What women and what groups led the fight for women's rights?

CHAPTER REVIEW

Terms to Understand

immigrants
"melting pot"
coolies
center of population
millionaire

middle class
"American way of life"
slum dwellers
tenements
woman suffrage

People and Things to Know About

Burlingame Treaty
"Gilded Age"
Jacob Riis
Jane Addams
Hull House
W.C.T.U.

Frances E. Willard
Prohibition Party
Susan B. Anthony
Elizabeth Cady Stanton
Clara Barton

Historic Dates to Identify

1869   1882   1890

Questions to Discuss

1. Why were restrictions placed on immigration after 1865? Are immigration restrictions today more strict or less strict?
2. How do you account for the rapid growth of certain states and cities between 1870 and

Questions to Discuss (Cont.)

1890? Are any states and cities today going through a period of rapid growth? Why?
3. How was it that some people seemed to be getting poorer at a time when the country was in a period of rapid industrial expansion?
4. Why did the women's rights movement grow rapidly in strength after 1865? Is there such a movement today?

Other Things to Do

1. Make a line graph to show the annual immigration, 1865–1895. Explain the rises and drops in your graph.
*2. Study the population growth of your city or state, 1865–1895. Explain the trends you find.
3. Report on efforts to relieve slum conditions in your community or a neighboring area. Remember that there are rural "slum" areas as well as urban slums.
4. Report to the class on one of the following: Jane Addams, Jacob Riis, Elizabeth Cady Stanton, Frances E. Willard, Susan B. Anthony, Clara Barton.

Baseball player, 1800's

Chapter 23

AMERICAN CULTURE DEVELOPS

RAPIDLY

This is our land, this is our ancient ground —
The raw earth, the mixed books and the strangers,
The different eyes, the wind, and the heart's change.
These we will not leave though the old call us.
This is our country-earth, our blood, our kind.

Archibald MacLeish

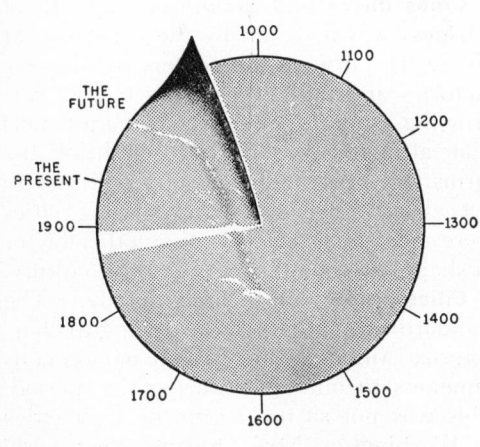

1865-1896

"Sell the cook stove if necessary and come," wrote the novelist Hamlin Garland in 1893 to his aged parents on their Dakota farm. "You *must* see this fair." Millions of other Americans who visited the World's Columbian Exposition in Chicago felt the same way. To celebrate the four-hundredth anniversary of the discovery of America, a gleaming "White City" had been erected on a stretch of lake front not far from Chicago's business district. Hamlin Garland's parents did come. The contrast between the rude, barren life on their farm and the beautiful buildings, splashing fountains, placid lagoons, and lovely parks of the Exposition brought tears to their eyes.

The Columbian Exposition was more than just another fair. In its buildings were displayed the developments in industry, transportation, communication, and agriculture that had brought the United States to the foremost rank among the nations of the world. A Palace of Fine Arts contained outstanding works of American painters and sculptors. Scholars and scientists from all over the world came to exchange views with American thinkers. Even the Exposition's famous Midway, with its huge ferris wheel and "Streets of Cairo," was to set the pattern for future amusement centers.

The strength of the rich culture reflected in the Columbian Exposition had been drawn from every section of the Union. The Palace of Fine Arts may have been a strange contrast to the ferris wheel and the amusements of the Midway, but this growing American culture was marked by sharp contrasts. Although many of the 12 million visitors may have missed the finer points of the architecture and the paintings and the sculpture on display, they were altogether American in their enthusiasm for these "good things of life." They went home determined to beautify their own towns and to give encouragement to the artists and musicians who lived next door.

The development of American culture in the latter half of the nineteenth century is the subject of this chapter. You will see how people lived, what they learned in school, how they amused themselves, what they wrote and read. The important steps are these:

1. An American way of life develops.
2. Americans enjoy better education.
3. Literature and science advance.
4. Artistic and musical tastes improve.

1 An American Way of Life Develops

Economic life changes rapidly. As you have seen, changes in American economic life were rapid in the years following the War Between the States. The nation was swiftly interlaced with railroad tracks from coast to coast, and over the new transportation lines thousands of people poured across the Mississippi River every year. Telegraph wires brought New York into close touch with San Francisco, and

Horse drawn omnibus

Chicago with New Orleans. Bell's invention of the telephone (1876) led the way to even more rapid communication. Swiftly the frontier came to an end.

Immigrants and settlers were not alone in traveling on the new trains into the western lands. Mail cars brought catalogues from mail-order houses in the East and Midwest. The freight cars carried stoves, churns, wagons, and farm machinery from eastern factories. As every section of the country was brought into increasingly closer touch with every other, an American way of life developed that was similar in all parts of the United States. In standardizing life for all Americans — at work, at home, and at play — the businessman led the way. As the editor of the Atlanta *Constitution* told his readers on January 8, 1890, "After all, business is the biggest thing in this country. Politicians may talk, but businessmen will act, control, and dominate the destinies of this common-sense country."

Cities thrive and grow. The growth of business was matched by the rapid rise of cities. These were the centers of the new factories and mills, the homes of an ever-growing army of workers, and the magnets that attracted the restless youth of the farms to bright lights and opportunities to get ahead. The swiftly expanding cities were more important than any other factor in shaping the pattern of American culture.

Cities show little individuality. The standardization that was beginning to characterize American life gave a monotonous sameness to our cities during this period. This was not so much true of such cities as Washington, New Orleans, New York, San Francisco, and Boston, but the majority of both cities and towns were very much alike in appearance. There was nothing particularly beautiful about their architecture or their general appearance. Their streets, lined with unsightly telephone poles, were usually unattractive and drab;

their skylines were made ugly by belching chimneys and dirty factories.

These cities would have looked strange to our eyes. Their streets were generally narrow and often unpaved. Instead of automobiles and service stations, horses and wagons and livery stables and blacksmith shops were to be seen. No electric or neon signs called attention to stores and theaters. For that matter, there were few theaters; the motion picture projector was not invented until 1894. City streets were dark at night by modern standards, but methods of lighting were improving. After 1879 the feeble gas lamps were replaced with brilliant electric arc lamps. Inside the home the incandescent lamp, which we now call a "light bulb," was just coming into use. Patented by Edison in 1880, it gave off a cooler and brighter light than the old kerosene lamp or the open-flame gas jet.

Cities still had a "huddled" appearance, because of the limited transportation of the times. Horse-drawn streetcars and carriages could not carry large numbers of people quickly over any great distances. Not until the days of the electric streetcar, the elevated train, and the subway was city life changed so that the residential districts could be removed from the industrial area.

Health conditions improve. During the later 1800's a number of steps were taken to reduce disease and cut down the death rate. Cities installed better water and sewage disposal systems. Better plumbing was introduced into homes. Laws were passed to insure the cleanliness and quality of milk and other foodstuffs. There was one source of uncleanliness, however, which could be found in every city. Despite attempts to improve housing conditions, tenements and slums persisted. The crime, disease, and vice which existed in

New York docks in the 1880's showed bowsprits far over the streets, where horse-drawn wagons pounded over cobblestones.

these districts tended to offset the advantages which city life offered.

Homes are cluttered with furnishings. If there was a sameness in the cities of America, the standardized way of life was just as evident inside the home. The middle-class city home of the '70's and '80's was cluttered with such objects as bamboo stands, glass domes sheltering wax flowers, and furniture with horsehair upholstery. The houses were poorly heated, and the interiors were gloomy. Often the gloomiest room in the house was the parlor, which was little used except for entertaining "company." The parlor, like the other rooms, contained furnishings which were considered ornamental. Often there was a "whatnot" (a set of shelves used to display bric-a-brac), and on the parlor table rested a photograph album of family pictures, bound in plush. Some statuary or an ornamental bowl of alabaster called a "tazza" might be seen on a pedestal.

Popular taste gradually improves. At the same time efforts were being made to increase the attractiveness of homes and home furnishings. Newspapers and such new magazines as the *Ladies' Home Journal* (founded in 1883) and *Good Housekeeping* (1885) had great influence on homemakers. High schools and colleges, moreover, began to introduce courses in domestic science.

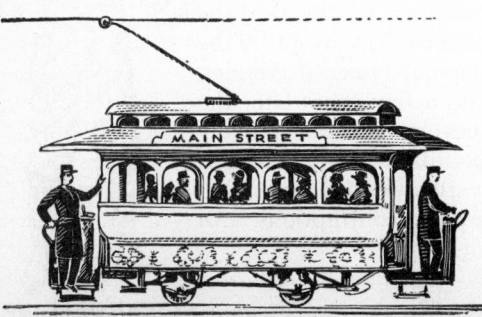

MAIN STREET

Electric streetcar

These courses taught the use of the new home appliances then coming on the market and urged homemakers to get rid of useless furnishings that only added to the housework. The drudgery of household tasks was thus decreased considerably, and American women began to devote leisure time to social activities and to "improving their minds."

Rural life is not easy. As American cities grew, they proved more and more inviting to large numbers of farmers' sons and daughters, who left their homes in search of fame, fortune, and fun. Most of these people were forced to live the rest of their days as wage earners or as housewives in rented houses, but they usually preferred to stay in the cities rather than go back to the farms.

In those days there were many drawbacks to life on the farm. Modern machines to lighten the farmer's labor were just appearing on the market. His wife had to get along without most household conveniences available to city dwellers. Many a farm was far from any other habitation and had no mail delivery. The farm family, therefore, was cut off from the stimulating ideas and life of the larger communities.

On the other hand, though farm life may have been strenuous, it was not entirely drab. On Saturdays the farmer and his family went to town to trade, or buy finery so that they could attend church in their "Sunday best." And rural life offered many amusements. In the summer the boys could be found at the "old swimmin' hole" while their parents enjoyed occasional picnics. The fall found them organizing nutting and hunting expeditions. Sleigh parties were popular in the winter wherever snow was plentiful, and country dances were held all the year round.

Baseball becomes the national sport. Whether they lived in villages, small towns, or the rapidly growing cities, Americans began to enjoy the same sports and amusements. Even "the pursuit of happiness" was becoming standardized. During the '70's and '80's, baseball became the national pastime. The first professional team, the Cincinnati Red Stockings, was organized in 1869. Its superiority over amateur teams soon led to the organization of other professional groups, and in 1876 the National League of Professional Baseball Players was founded. Meanwhile the rules of the game were being perfected, a ball not too lively and not too "dead" was agreed upon, and gloves and masks were introduced. In 1888 a series of exhibition matches was played in England before the Prince of Wales, and another in Egypt, where one of the pyramids served as a backstop.

Football and boxing gain national favor. In the '70's the game of football, modified from English rugby, was enthusiastically taken up by the colleges. Rivalry between the colleges became so heated, especially in the East, that one college president in the '90's feared that the degree of B.A. would soon stand for "Bachelor of Athletics." Another rugged sport, but one rather looked down upon by respectable people, was professional boxing. Boxers usually fought with bare fists, and often for 40 or 50 rounds. In 1889 the famous John L. Sullivan fought 75 rounds with Jake Kilrain in New Orleans, in what proved to be the last bare-knuckle championship fight. Sullivan won $20,000 and a diamond belt. Three years later, however, Sullivan lost to "Gentleman Jim" Corbett, whose victory began a new era in which scientific boxing counted for more than brute strength.

Other sports become popular. When sports and amusements like roller-skating, basketball, horseracing, rowing, tennis, archery, and golf are added to the list of national pastimes, the importance of sports of all kinds in the latter half of the 1800's becomes evident. In the 60's the country was swept by the popular craze of croquet, and a few years later the bicycle became equally popular. Early bicycles were awkward if not dangerous contraptions. An

Football player

enormous front wheel was fitted with pedals, and the tires were solid. The rider's seat was placed over the front wheel, a position from which he was often pitched without warning over the handlebars. In the '80's, however, the "safety" bicycle, with low wheels of equal size equipped with pneumatic tires, was introduced. There was even a woman's model, which assured the ladies of a modest appearance. It permitted a folding screen to be attached to the front of the bicycle "to protect the feet and ankles from view when mounting or riding." By the '90's millions of persons of both sexes and all classes were riding bicycles.

Crowds of Americans attend amusements. Americans were already showing their fondness for spectator sports and amusements. For example, more than 50,000 persons watched the annual Yale-Princeton football game on Thanksgiving Day in 1893. Likewise thousands of people gladly turned out whenever that typical American institution, the circus, came to town. The most famous showman of this period was P. T. Barnum, who, in 1871, formed a traveling tent circus which he claimed was "the greatest show on earth." His circus displayed dwarfs, waxworks, Swiss bell ringers, and an assortment of animals including the giraffe, which was still a rare sight in those days. The next year Barnum's circus began to travel by railway. This achievement involved very careful planning of details, but it made the show a national institution.

More people go to the theater. The black-face minstrel show was now declining in favor, and musical comedy and vaudeville grew in popularity. Theater audiences also enjoyed melodramas, which often had for a theme the story of the innocent country girl's trip to the wicked city, where she is rescued — but only in the nick of time — from the clutches of the wily city slicker!

The theater also provided serious drama. Both European and American plays were popular. Audiences warmly received such famous stage personalities as Sir Henry Irving and Sarah Bernhardt from overseas,

Travel as a pastime began attracting Americans in the late 1800's, even at risk of a cinder in the eye or a lost hat.

and they applauded Edwin Booth and other notable American actors. During the '80's a large number of traveling companies, headed by one or more stars, began to tour the cities in the interior. Thus it was possible for audiences in various parts of the country to enjoy the same standards of acting and taste that New York enjoyed. One of the best of the road companies was headed by John Drew and Maurice Barrymore. The latter's three children — John, Lionel, and Ethel -- were later to become famous on the American stage and in films.

Americans enjoy popular music. The Metropolitan Opera opened in New York in 1883, and some of the famous symphony orchestras came into existence at about this time. But the great majority of people were less concerned with classical than with popular music. Most of the popular songs died a quick death but others lived on, including "After the Ball," "The Sidewalks of New York," "A Bicycle Built for Two," "On the Banks of the Wabash," and "Oh Promise Me." Popular songs were played everywhere – by the Italian organ grinder, by the German street band, and by Edison's phonograph, invented in the '70's and sold by the tens of thousands in the '90's.

The soda fountain makes its appearance. This period also saw a great demand for "pop" and other "soft" drinks. Soda fountains with their marble and onyx counters mushroomed. This era is also responsible for the appearance of another American habit – chewing gum.

——————— CHECK-UP ———————

How did an American way of life develop?

1. What were the chief characteristics of cities in the late nineteenth century? What is meant by standardization of life?
2. How did homes reflect American tastes?
3. What were the chief features of rural life?
4. How did Americans spend their leisure time in the late 1800's?

---

2 Americans Enjoy Better Education

Public school attendance increases. One of the most wholesome developments in American life of this period was the improvement of the educational system. In 1878 there were about 9½ million children in public schools; before the end of the century about 15 million children were attending public schools, and more than 30 states had laws which made attendance compulsory. Even more rapid was the growth of high schools. In 1878 fewer than 100,000 students were enrolled in less than 800 high schools. But 20 years later the country could boast of 5500 high schools and an attendance of more than 500,000 students (see chart, page 600).

Standards of education vary. Of course, educational standards were not the same in all sections of the country. The cities, with concentrated populations and greater wealth, were able to provide longer school terms, better school buildings, and higher

salaries for teachers. The country districts had to get along with the "little red schoolhouse." In these schools, pupils of all grades met in one room and received their instruction from a single teacher. Rural schoolteachers were nearly always overworked and underpaid. Yet they were probably the most important single force in spreading the ideals of American democracy.

Americans could be proud of the decrease in illiteracy. Though in 1850, 28 per cent of the population could not read or write, illiteracy had dropped to less than 11 per cent by the end of the century (see chart, page 435). Even in 1898, however, the average American had received only five years of schooling – or, in other words, had not gone beyond the fifth grade of elementary school.

The South makes educational strides. A valiant chapter in the history of American public school education was written by the people of the South. They had come out of the War Between the States with their economy ruined and their social system completely changed. But the southerners made magnificent attempts to improve educational conditions and to wipe out widespread illiteracy. Many housewives who could read and write volunteered to teach.

Medicine and pharmacy, like other sciences, began making rapid strides in the late 1800's. This picture by a modern artist recreates a scene in which William Proctor, Jr., father of American pharmacy, reads to his student-apprentice the results of a recent experiment.

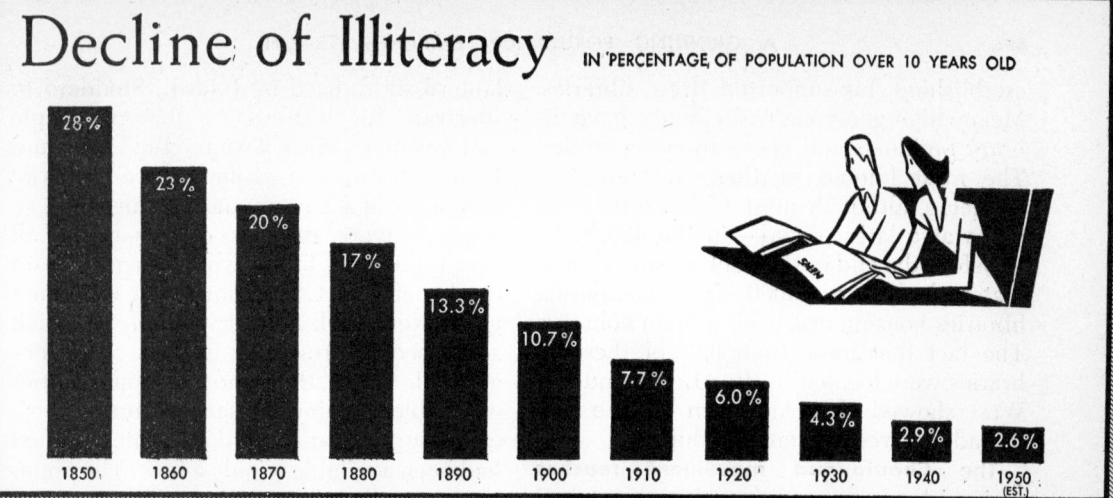

Decline of Illiteracy IN PERCENTAGE OF POPULATION OVER 10 YEARS OLD

1850	1860	1870	1880	1890	1900	1910	1920	1930	1940	1950 (EST.)
28%	23%	20%	17%	13.3%	10.7%	7.7%	6.0%	4.3%	2.9%	2.6%

Nearly nine out of ten Americans could read and write by 1900. Few, however, had gone beyond the elementary grades in school. Glance ahead to the chart on page 600 to see how opportunities for high school education increased after 1900.

In many country districts these teachers had to work in schoolhouses that were only log shacks and that lacked desks, blackboards, or even windows. Yet school attendance increased in the South from 2,700,000 in 1878 to almost 4,500,000 ten years later. The 1890 annual report of the United States Commissioner of Education stated that "the schools of the South, taken as a whole, enroll a larger percentage of the population than those of the older states of the North . . ."

Colleges grow in influence. During this period, colleges were increasing in numbers and raising their standards. But there was great room for improvement. In 1874 an educator claimed that a visitor to a college town would find the railway station and the county jail better built, better heated, and better equipped than the college buildings. Faculty members worked hard to earn their rather small salaries. Libraries and laboratories were not satisfactory.

The colleges emphasized Greek, Latin, logic, mathematics, and a little science, without the benefit of laboratories. By the 1890's, however, some of them had begun to offer courses in modern history, the social sciences, and modern foreign languages. Better professional education was also provided in medicine, engineering, and law. Some universities were, of course, in advance of the times. Graduate schools

were established at Yale and Harvard in the '70's. There and at John Hopkins University which opened in Baltimore in 1876, college graduates could continue with advanced studies and research without having to travel to European universities. Columbia followed in the next decade, and each of these universities conferred the Ph. D. as its highest degree.

State colleges and universities are founded. To this period also belongs the rise of great state universities in the Middle West and other regions. By the Morrill Act of 1862 the federal government granted land to the states to encourage the establishment of colleges of agriculture and the mechanical arts. As a result, there was increased emphasis on scientific agriculture and engineering. Co-education became the rule in the new land-grant colleges, though this movement at first met much opposition.

Libraries enrich all sections. American culture was broadened also by the growth of libraries. In 1870 there was no library in the country that had as many as 200,000 books, although there were 20 such in Europe. As a matter of fact, there were only six libraries in the United States with as many as 100,000 volumes, the largest being the Library of Congress in Washington.

This situation rapidly improved as city after city answered public demand by establishing tax-supported free libraries. Meanwhile generous individuals gave library buildings and books to communities. The most famous of these was Andrew Carnegie, although most of his gifts were made at a later period — in the 1900's.

Before the end of the century, the United States had over 9000 free circulating libraries housing nearly 47 million volumes. The fact that more than half of these libraries were located in the Middle and Far West showed that American culture was spreading over the entire country.

The Chautauqua movement reaches thousands of communities. An educational enterprise called the Chautauqua movement, founded in 1874, grew in influence and in its effect on the intellectual life of the country. Thousands of persons journeyed to the summer sessions at Chautauqua Lake in New York State. They came from every state in the Union, eager to combine the pleasures of summer camp life with stimulating lectures and round table discussions.

Prominent educators came to talk at the Chautauqua sessions. The audiences were also delighted with the famous colored

Paul Bunyan, massive lumberman, became a favorite subject of folklore as Americans began choosing local themes for their art.

lantern slides used by John L. Stoddard to illustrate his lectures on foreign people and customs. Mark Twain, "Bill" Nye, and James Whitcomb Riley were favorite humorists at Chautauqua meetings.

There were millions of Americans all over the United States who wished to share the benefits of Chautauqua, but could not go to New York State to do so. To reach such people, traveling groups were organized. Thus thousands of communities were able to enjoy the same lectures, musical programs, and readings which at first had been available to only a few. The popularity of the Chautauqua movement has been partly explained as the worthy ambition of middle-class Americans to make up for the educational lack which they had suffered through no fault of their own.

——— CHECK-UP ———

How did Americans secure a more democratic educational system?

1. What were some of the characteristics of education in (a) cities, (b) rural areas, (c) the South?
2. In what respects were colleges changing?
3. How did libraries and the Chautauqua help to enrich American life?

3 **Literature and Science Advance**

A new phase in writing begins. For some years following the War Between the States, the most famous literary figures in America were those writers — found mostly in New England — who had made their reputations earlier. Longfellow, Whittier, Bryant, and Holmes were still writing poetry, while Emerson was the most respected figure in American philosophy. All of these men, however, belonged to an age that was passing, and the great New England school of writers was now in the twilight of its existence.

Fresh voices were heralding a new maturity in American literature. American writers followed European standards less and less, and were beginning to write in new ways which reflected the American scene.

Whitman sings truly American themes. One voice which had first been raised just before the War Between the States continued to sing a new fresh theme. Walt Whitman, one of the great poets of the world, was perhaps the most typically American. In strong contrast to the polished style of the writers of the New England school, Whitman's verse struck out along new paths. Passionately he praised the American heritage, its beauty and its strength, its belief in the worth and dignity of the common people. He rejoiced because America promised a better life for all men, regardless of differences of creed, race, and social rank. Nothing was too unimportant for Whitman to write about: tramps, the Brooklyn ferry, a blade of grass, or the changing landscapes.

> The varied and ample land, the South and
> the North in the light, Ohio's shores
> and flashing Missouri,
> And ever the far-spreading prairies covered with grass and corn.

Whitman's subjects were unusual, but the style of his verse was more unusual still. Much of it does not rhyme but is in the form of "free verse" (like the lines above). Whitman dared at all times to be frank and "earthy," and this quality made it difficult for some to accept his poetry. But even if he shocked the readers of his day, Whitman had a deep influence upon the course of American thought, for he was its most glowing champion of democracy. (See page 439.)

"Local color" writers interpret America. During the first half of the 1800's nearly all American writers lived on the Atlantic seaboard, most of them around Boston, New York, and Philadelphia. It was after 1850 that the Middle West emerged as a major region. The admission of California into the Union and the opening of the Northwest called attention to areas of the country still further distant from New England.

Towns, mountains, and deserts of the Far West attracted writers and readers. This picture shows San Jose, California, about 1860.

Now Americans became conscious — as they had never been in the past — of the size of their country and the variety within it. They were eager to read about its different regions. Fortunately this era was rich in writers who could faithfully and vividly portray the sections from which they came. We call such authors local color writers.

Harte and Miller describe the West. California was interpreted with rare humor and sympathy by Bret Harte, a New Yorker who moved to the Far West and wrote tales of what he found there. He won fame in his writings of the ranches, the lawless mining camps, stage coaches and western barrooms, gamblers and robbers, and the Chinese laborers who were brought over to help build the railroads. Two of his stories, "The Luck of Roaring Camp" and "The Outcasts of Poker Flat," portrayed the rough yet sentimental characters of the mining camps. They gave eastern readers a new insight into frontier life in the Far West.

The more picturesque side of this region, as well as the grandeur of its natural scenery, was described by the poet Joaquin (wah' keen) Miller. His experiences as a miner, soldier, lawyer, and judge are reflected in his *Songs of the Sierras*.

Southern writers portray their section. The South also produced a number of local color writers. The life of the old Virginia

Mark Twain, shown here toward the end of his life, became one of the most famous Americans at home and abroad. He was in great demand as an amusing lecturer as well as a writer. His books are still sold by the thousands every year.

gentry was portrayed by Thomas Nelson Page and F. Hopkinson Smith, while George W. Cable of New Orleans wrote some outstanding sketches called *Old Creole Days.* Vigorous tales of the people living in the mountains of Tennessee were told by a frail little woman who wrote under the name of Charles Egbert Craddock. Meanwhile a Georgia reporter on the Atlanta *Constitution* named Joel Chandler Harris published in 1880 his first book of Uncle Remus tales, a series of charming Negro animal legends filled with humor and pathos.

Other local color writers appear. The struggles of the pioneering families in the Middle West were graphically described in *Main-Traveled Roads* by Hamlin Garland. Country life in southern Indiana was the subject of a famous novel, *The Hoosier Schoolmaster,* written by Edward Eggleston and published in 1871. Another Middle Westerner, William Dean Howells, went to live in the East, where for years he was a distinguished editor and critic. A keen observer of human nature, Howells examined the problems of middle-class life in Boston in such novels as *A Modern Instance* and *The Rise of Silas Lapham.*

Mark Twain wins lasting fame. The greatest local color writer of his generation and probably the finest humorist in American literature was Samuel Langhorne Clemens, known to the world by his pen name, Mark Twain. Clemens spent his boyhood in Missouri, where he often watched the great sidewheelers churning the muddy waters of the Mississippi River. In time Clemens became a river pilot himself, until that career was cut short by the War Between the States. He then journeyed to Nevada and the mining West.

Mark Twain put his early experiences to wonderful use. The scenes of his childhood have been made immortal in *Tom Sawyer* — which Howells called "the best boy story ever written" — and in that other favorite of young and old Americans, *Huckleberry Finn.* The railroads and rising cities of post-war America had destroyed the river civilization that had flourished when the Mississippi had been so important to American life. In *Life on the Mississippi* Mark Twain wrote an unforgettable picture of that fast-dying culture. The East was treated to a vivid and entertaining account of Far Western life in *Roughing It.* The typically western form of humor expressed in obvious exaggeration set the whole nation to laughing in *The Celebrated Jumping Frog of Calaveras County.*

New magazines are founded. The increase in new literary works at this time was matched by the establishment of numerous monthly magazines. Three magazines of excellent literary standards were *Harper's Monthly,* the *Atlantic Monthly,* and *Scribner's Monthly* (which became the *Century* in 1881). These periodicals printed the writings of many new authors, both American and foreign, who later became famous. Other magazines, less "high-brow" in content and popularly priced, were also founded. They contained attractive illustrations and striking advertisements, short stories and articles on personalities of the

(Continued on page 440)

Walt Whitman
(1819-1892)

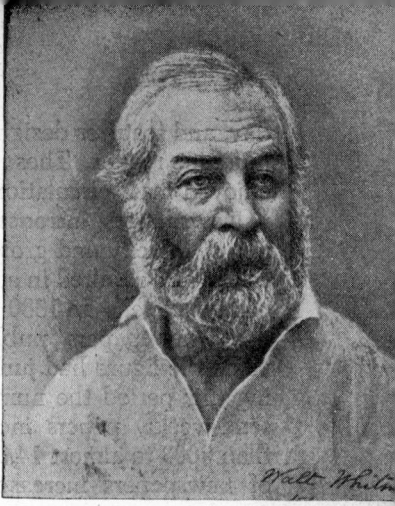

Reporter

WALT WHITMAN, the poet of democracy, still remains to many of his countrymen a shadowy figure. Born on Long Island, young Walt attended school, learned the printer's trade, and took up newspaper work. Whitman spent much of his time in apparently aimless wandering, but actually learning what he could about all kinds of people. A trip to New Orleans, where he worked briefly on a newspaper, offered a chance for further glimpses of the young and throbbing country.

Shortly after his return to New York, Whitman gave up his newspaper work. He spent his days carpentering and his nights writing poetry. Then, in a little Brooklyn printing shop, he set the type for the first edition of his most important volume of poetry, *Leaves of Grass* (1855). The book was severely criticized.

Whitman's writing was interrupted by the War Between the States. His brother was wounded, and Whitman went to take care of him. Stirred by the anguish of the great conflict, he remained in Washington nursing the wounded, writing their letters, and providing them with tobacco and books. After the war he served as a government clerk and continued writing until 1873,

Typesetter

when he was stricken ill. Whitman never fully recovered his health. He lived out his days in Camden, New Jersey.

Whitman's poetry was expressed in free verse, at that time a new and disturbing form. His work had a far-reaching effect on American verse. As one writer says, "The old poetry was a house with a set number of rooms out of which the poets dared not wander. Whitman inspired the building of new rooms." Equally important was the message his poetry contained. Whitman was proud of America's past but was far more impressed with its promise for the future. He had a passionate faith in his native land, in its people, and in democracy. This faith he sang in grand and lusty tones. Though in his own day his greatness was appreciated by few, he was "an inspired interpreter of the soul of the republic."

Nurse

day, and features designed to appeal to the feminine reader. These popular magazines enjoyed mass circulations.

Newspapers increase in number. The rise of the city and growth of popular education also resulted in a tremendous growth of newspapers. In 1880 there were only 971 daily newspapers published. Within 20 years the figure had jumped to 2226. During this period the number of weekly and semi-weekly papers increased from fewer than 9000 to almost 14,000. As the number of newspapers increased, so did the demand for a wider news coverage. There had been local press associations even before the War Between the States, but to meet the new demand, these various associations began to unify in the '80's, relaying news stories to each other. As a result, identical stories appeared in hundreds of newspapers scattered throughout the country. In this way not only was news standardized, but public taste and attitudes tended to become standardized, too. Meanwhile to boost circulation — and incidentally advertising rates — the editors of many newspapers deliberately made their news stories popular and sensational.

Americans excel in applied science. The period between 1865 and 1896 was marked by important advances in the use of science in daily affairs. Inventor after inventor began to patent new labor-saving machines, new devices to speed communication, new forms of transportation, new means of setting type for newspapers. In short, American inventors were revolutionizing American business and daily living, laying foundations for the physical environment in which we find ourselves today.

There is space to mention only a few of the important inventions of the period in a quotation from the historians Charles and Mary Beard:

In 1868, the Sholes typewriter was put to commercial use. In 1869, Westinghouse took out the initial patent for his railway air brake. . . . In 1872, Edison announced his duplex telegraph which made it possible to send two messages over the same wire at the same time. In 1875, G. F. Swift built his first refrigerator car. In 1876, Alexander Bell sent his historical telephone message by wire. In 1877, Edison heard "Mary had a little lamb" on his phonograph. . . . In 1886, Mergenthaler's linotype machine rang out the coming doom of typesetting by hand in the great newspaper offices. . . . In 1892, Bell opened telephonic communication between New York and Chicago. In 1893, Henry Ford tested his first automobile on the road. In 1894, Jenkins gave a motion picture show . . . [in] Indiana.

─────── CHECK-UP ───────

What advances were made in literature and science?

1. What were the characteristics of Whitman's poetry?
2. What writers interpreted particular regions of America? What were their chief works?
3. How did newspapers change during the latter part of the nineteenth century?
4. What were some important inventions?

┌─────────────────────────────────────┐
│ 4 │ **Artistic and Musical Tastes Improve** │
└─────────────────────────────────────┘

Famous painters follow European trends. The artists of this period had little of the originality shown by writers and inventors. Nevertheless, Americans developed higher standards of taste in the latter half of the 1800's. American painters continued to follow the lead of Europe, and it was not until the twentieth century that artists found in regional subject-matter the inspiration that Mark Twain and other local color writers had found. George Inness, however, achieved some fine effects with his

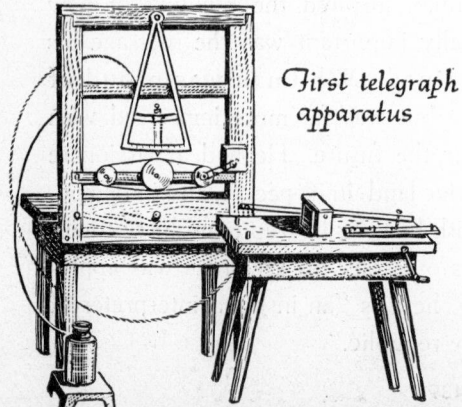

First telegraph apparatus

landscapes. Likewise the striking sea paintings of Winslow Homer, some of which show life in tropical waters filled with man-eating sharks, are valued highly today.

The two outstanding portrait painters were James A. McNeill Whistler and John S. Sargent, both of whom were popular in England. Sargent showed brilliance in his paintings of elegant ladies and gentlemen; prominent social figures of his day commissioned him to do their portraits. Whistler is probably best known for his "Portrait of the Artist's Mother."

The period produces some famous caricatures. Caricature is a form of art that makes no pretense at being enduring, but it requires a definite skill. Americans have always excelled in caricature. The political graft and corruption of this period gave rich opportunities to cartoonists like Thomas Nast, who aroused the public against the corrupt politician, Boss Tweed, and his Ring. Likewise, magazine illustrating began to pay well as more and more periodicals came into existence. One popular illustrator was Charles Dana Gibson, who sketched the "smart set" in the '90's.

Good and poor sculpture is created. In the years after the War Between the States most communities erected monuments to local citizens or national heroes who had taken part in the struggle. The statuary that resulted was often less worthy than the feelings which called it forth. The average American household of this period was usually decorated with little plaster statuettes; these, too, were poor in workmanship and sentimental in subject matter.

American sculpture improved, however, with the return of young artists from schooling in Europe, who brought with them new standards of taste and craftsmanship. Outstanding among these sculptors was Augustus Saint-Gaudens, many of whose works can be seen today. Among these are his statue of Admiral Farragut in New York, the statue of Lincoln in Lincoln Park, Chicago, and the "Peace of God" in Rock Creek Cemetery, Washington, D.C.

An appreciation of art was fostered by art courses in the schools and by the appearance of excellent art galleries. Three of these were particularly important: the

The linotype machine helped newspapers to print up-to-the-minute news. In this mural an editor is examining the first newspaper in which the letters were set by linotype.

Corcoran Gallery in Washington, the Metropolitan Museum of Art in New York, and the Museum of Fine Arts in Boston.

America contributes to architecture. The 1800's, both in Europe and in the United States, were notorious for an imitation Gothic style in building. This style featured towers, castle-like walls, and too much ornamentation, which to modern eyes seem pointless and tasteless.

Toward the end of the century, however, both private and public buildings came to have greater simplicity of design. Meanwhile there was need for economizing space in the business districts of great cities. In new buildings the emphasis was on height. The invention of the hydraulic (and afterwards the electric) elevator made possible the construction of skyscrapers. As a result, a ten-story building was erected in Chicago in 1885, followed by higher buildings as the years passed by. At the close of the century, New York could boast of a building 29 stories high. The skyscraper with its steel frame remains perhaps the most important American contribution to architecture. Louis Sullivan, who championed simplicity of design, is called "father of the modern skyscraper."

The ranks of music-lovers increase. If America produced no first-rank composer during these years, at least its people grew tremendously in their appreciation of good music. A number of famous orchestras were formed, including the New York Symphony in 1878 and the Boston Symphony three years later. Famous conductors from Europe were invited to lead them, and outstanding foreign singers began to appear at the Metropolitan Opera House.

Many cities established conservatories where young musicians could develop their talent, and an increasing number of colleges made music a part of the curriculum. The first important American composer was Edward A. MacDowell. Some of his *Woodland Sketches,* published in 1896, are still popular, especially "To A Wild Rose" and "To a Water Lily."

If America had little to show in the way of serious music, it had a rich heritage in other musical fields. The haunting Negro spirituals are among the most precious possessions of American culture. Another American contribution was ragtime, which was the rage at the turn of the century, and which, with certain changes in style, is the popular music of today.

——————— CHECK-UP ———•———

To what extent did artistic and musical tastes improve?

1. Who were some important late nineteenth century American painters?
2. What is caricature? For what purposes was it used?
3. What were the American achievements in sculpture? In architecture?
4. What evidences were there that the appreciation of good music was increasing?

CHAPTER REVIEW

Terms to Understand

standardized life
incandescent lamp
melodrama
vaudeville
illiteracy

co-education
"free verse"
local color
conservatories of music
ragtime

People and Things to Know About

John L. Sullivan
P. T. Barnum
Metropolitan Opera
land-grant college
Morrill Act of 1862
Chautauqua
Walt Whitman
Bret Harte
George W. Cable
Joel Chandler Harris

Hamlin Garland
Mark Twain
duplex telegraph
James Whistler
John S. Sargent
Augustus Saint-Gaudens
Corcoran Gallery
imitation Gothic
Edward A. MacDowell

Questions to Discuss

1. In Europe people living a few miles apart often have different customs and ways of life. American life is quite standardized over thousands of miles. How do you account for this?

2. Compare the following:

(a) The large city of the late nineteenth century with the present-day large city.

(b) Urban and rural life in the late 1800's.

(c) Artistic tastes of the late nineteenth century and today.

(d) Colleges 75 years ago and colleges today.

3. Why was transportation an important factor in making modern urban centers possible?

4. The leisure time activities of a people are often considered the best key to its character. It this is true, what would you say are some of the chief characteristics of the American people?

5. It has been said that American education has greatly reduced illiteracy but has not significantly raised the level of reading tastes. What evidences are there that this charge is or is not true?

Other Things to Do

1. Read one or more of Walt Whitman's poems. Do you feel that Whitman had a true feeling for American democracy? Why?

2. Investigate to determine whether your area has produced any regional writers and artists. If so, report on one of their works.

3. Prepare a brief report on the history of some popular American sport. Dulles, F. R., *Americans Learn to Play*, Appleton-Century-Crofts, is an excellent reference for this purpose.

4. Prepare a report on some aspect of the growth of cities in the United States. See A. M. Schlesinger's *The Rise of the City* in the History of American Life Series.

5. Make a list of the ways in which you think that your community is a typical American community, and also a list of the ways in which you think that it is not typical. Compare your lists with those of other class members.

TO INCREASE YOUR UNDERSTANDING OF UNIT SIX

Unit Summary

1. During the 30 years after 1865 a high birthrate plus growing immigration led to a great increase in the population of this country. The New England and Middle Atlantic states continued to be the most densely populated, but states in the Middle West made unusual population gains. Cities increased much more rapidly in population than did rural areas.

2. Among the factors which brought about slums there were three important ones: the influx of foreign-born, the rapid growth of cities, and unsatisfactory working conditions. To improve living conditions among the poor, American cities adopted stricter building regulations and made more adequate provisions for sanitation. Many reformers crusaded against liquor and for women's rights.

3. The proportion of children and youth enrolled in school increased, as did the quality of their education. The states also established tax-supported colleges and universities. Public libraries, the Chautauqua movement, magazines with a nation-wide circulation, and an improved daily newspaper service also made important contributions to the national culture.

4. Living in even an upper middle class home of the late 1800's was (by present-day standards) drab and uncomfortable. In the country, living was much less comfortable than in the city. Spectator sports (baseball, football, boxing), the theater, and music were steadily growing in popularity.

5. Many of the important authors of this period were so-called "local color" writers who rendered an important service by helping Americans understand the various sections of their great country. Two writers of this period have achieved a high and lasting place in American literature — Walt Whitman, the poet who hailed the American heritage, and Mark Twain.

Summary of Important Dates

1862 Morrill Act grants land for establishing state colleges of agricultural and mechanical arts.

1868 Burlingame Treaty gives Chinese right to travel and live in the United States.

1869 Territory of Wyoming gives women the right to vote.

1874 Chautauqua movement founded. W.C.T.U. founded.

1880 Edison patents the incandescent lamp.

1881 American Red Cross organized.

1882 Chinese labor excluded; Chinese denied citizenship. Immigration law excludes paupers, convicts, and insane persons.

1885 Contract labor excluded from the United States.

1889 Hull House founded by Jane Addams.

1890 Wyoming becomes first state to grant full political rights to women.

1891 Persons suffering from contagious and loathsome diseases excluded from the United States.

Unit Activities

1. Try to get an idea of what life was like in your community or state in the '80's or early '90's. Consider (1) homes and furnishings, (2) clothing, (3) ways of earning a living, (4) popular sports and forms of recreation, and (5) methods of local transportation. If possible, use old newspaper and magazine files, consider furnishings in old homes or museums, and interview old settlers. What, in

your opinion, are the most important ways in which life has changed?

2. What evidences are there that "art forms" and "ways of doing things" long ago are treasured today? Consider furniture, jewelry, music, literature, sports, customs. Can you explain why these things are cherished? Do you yourself ever enjoy old things and old ways?

3. List the restrictions imposed on immigration to this country between 1865 and 1895. Try to explain why each law was passed. See what you can learn about the immigration policies of other countries.

For Further Reading

Original Sources

Adams, H., *The Education of Henry Adams*. Houghton. A searching examination and criticism of American life and culture, written as a kind of autobiography.

Bok, E. W., *The Americanization of Edward Bok*. Scribner. A Dutch immigrant who became a journalist of great influence tells his own success story in this autobiography.

Commager, H. S., ed., *Documents of American History*. Appleton-Century-Crofts. Nos. 306, 307.

Commager, H. S., and Nevins, A., eds., *The Heritage of America*. Little, Brown. Nos. 201–212.

Pease, T. C., and Roberts, A. S., eds., *Selected Readings in American History*. Harcourt. No. 203.

General References

Adams, J. T., *Epic of America*. Little, Brown. Chapter 11.

Hicks, J. D., *The American Nation*. Houghton. Chapters 5 and 13.

Morison, S. E., and Commager, H. S., *The Growth of the American Republic*. Oxford. Vol. II, Chapters 7, 12, and 15.

Special Accounts

American Nation Series. Harper. Dewey, D. R., *National Problems*. Sparks, E. E., *National Development*.

Chronicles of America Series. Yale University Press. Orth, S. P., *Our Foreigners*. Perry, B., *The American Spirit in Literature*. Slosson, E. E., *The American Spirit in Education*. Thompson, H., *The Age of Invention*.

History of American Life Series. Macmillan. Nevins, A., *The Emergence of Modern America, 1865–1878*. Chapters 3, 5, 8, 9, 10, and 12. Schlesinger, A. M., *The Rise of the City, 1878–1898*.

Brooks, Van Wyck, *New England-Indian Summer*. Dutton. Cultural development in New England after 1865.

Commons, J. R., *Races and Immigrants in America*. Macmillan.

Cubberley, E. P., *Public Education in the United States*. Houghton. The rise of education to meet the needs of all children and young people.

Jaffe, B., *Men of Science in America*. Simon and Schuster.

MacLaren, G., *Morally We Roll Along*. Little, Brown. Story of the Chautauqua movement.

Riis, J. A., *How the Other Half Lives*. Scribner. A foreign-born citizen writes about slums.

Stephenson, G. M., *History of American Immigration*. Ginn.

Sullivan, M., *Our Times*. Scribner. Volumes I and II contain material about America just before the turn of the century.

Train, A., *The Story of Everyday Things*. Harper.

Biography

Brown, H. G., *Grandmother Brown's Hundred Years*. Little, Brown.

Dorr, R. C., *Susan B. Anthony*. Stokes. A partisan biography of a leader in the movement for woman suffrage.

Drew, J., *My Years on the Stage*. Dutton. Stories about three generations of Barrymores and Drews.

Epler, P. H., *Life of Clara Barton*. Macmillan. The story is based on material left by Miss Barton for her biographers.

Harlow, A. F., *Joel Chandler Harris: Plantation Story Teller*. Messner.

Nolan, J. C., *O. Henry: the story of William Sidney Porter*. Messner.

Paine, A. B., *Boy's Life of Mark Twain*. Harper. Based on the official three-volume biography.

Rogers, C., *The Magnificent Idler*. Doubleday. A readable biography of Walt Whitman.

Seitz, D. C., *The James Gordon Bennetts*. Bobbs. For 83 years father and son controlled the New York *Herald*.

Imaginative Writing

Cather, W., *My Ántonia*. Houghton. Immigrant life in Nebraska.

Harte, B., *The Luck of Roaring Camp*. Houghton. Life in the California mining camps.

Marquand, J., *The Late George Apley*. Little, Brown. Upper middle class life in New England.

Rölvaag, O., *Giants in the Earth*. Harper. Norwegian immigrants settle in South Dakota.

Sandoz, M., *Old Jules*. Little, Brown. The story of a hardy pioneer.

Tarkington, B., *The Magnificent Ambersons*. Grosset. City life in the Middle West.

Wharton, E., *The Age of Innocence*. Appleton-Century-Crofts. Pictures New York City in the 1870's.

Pictures

Adams, J. T., ed., *Album of American History*. Scribner. Vol. III.

Butterfield, R., *The American Past*. Simon and Schuster.

Kouwenhoven, J. A., *Adventures in America*, 1857–1900. Harper. The pictures are from *Harper's Weekly*.

Pageant of America Series. Yale University Press. Coad, O. S., and Mims, E., *The American Stage*. Gabriel, R. H., *Toilers of Land and Sea*. Hamlin, T. F., *The American Spirit in Architecture*. Krout, J. A., *Annals of American Sport*. Mather, F. J., Morey, C. R., and Henderson, W. J., *The American Spirit in Art*. Weigle, L. A., *American Idealism*. Williams, S. T., *The American Spirit in Letters*.

Peters, H. T., *Currier and Ives: Printmakers to the American People*. Doubleday. Though many of these prints picture events prior to 1865, the prints enjoyed a great popularity in the period after that date.

Rogers, A., and Allen, F. L., *The American Procession*. Harper. The social scene after 1860.

 Sidelights on American History

"A Friendlie Kind of Fyghte." The early English settlers brought some rugged British sports to this country, among them wrestling, fisticuffs with bare knuckles, and cudgel play. There was nothing that resembled football as we know it today, but here and there in the colonies men and boys sometimes gathered to toss around and pass back and forth what they were pleased to call a "ball." This was usually a leather sack stuffed with sawdust, or a pig's bladder blown up, tied at the neck, and dried. But the ball was seldom kicked, and play was less like a football game of our time than "a friendlie kind of fyghte," as one Englishman had referred to a similar sport many years before.

It wasn't until more than 50 years after the Revolution that this rather haphazard sport began to show signs of being a real game. The pig's bladder was encased in a calfskin cover, and a custom arose of limiting each side to 15 or 20 players. The ball was round, and goals were scored by passing, hitting, throwing, and even kicking over the opponents' fence. But there was little team play, and players used nothing like the co-ordinated tactics of today.

Then in 1867 the first organized football team was formed. (Andrew Johnson was in the White House and the United States was negotiating the purchase of Alaska from Russia.) The members of the Oneida Football Club of Boston were the boys of a Latin school in Boston, who had played together as a team for a number of years. No longer was the football a pig's bladder. It was a round rubber ball.

A football game between two colleges was not played until after the War Between the States. In the first intercollegiate match the opposing teams were from two colleges in New Jersey, Princeton and Rutgers. These colleges had had a long-standing feud over which was to get and keep a certain cannon that had been used in the Revolutionary War. One day in 1869 it was decided that instead of the annual fight over the cannon, the two colleges would battle out their high spirits in a football game.

The contest must have looked something like a small mob scene. Fifty players arrived at the field, pulled off their coats and vests, and entered the battle. Rutgers' system of short kicks and fast dribbling won the match. A little about how the game was played is revealed in a sentence from a report published in the Princeton newspaper: "We bat with hands, feet, head, sideways, backward, any way to get the ball along." Obviously football in those days was more like what we call soccer today.

In England, meantime, football was developing into a running game with the player carrying the ball. This new development originated at Rugby, the famous English school. It was picked up by visiting Americans and brought back to the United States.

Finally "the father of American football" appeared, and he made certain important improvements in the game. Walter Camp had been a star football player while a student at Yale. After college his interest in the sport continued. It was he who was responsible for changing the English Rugby type of game into something distinctively American. Camp suggested the following improvements: there should be eleven players on a side instead of fifteen; the ball should be put into play by kicking or snapping it back (instead of putting it on the ground between rush lines and letting both teams go after it); a new player, who would receive the snap-back, should be called the "quarterback."

When Yale played Princeton in 1881, the game was played with these innovations, and American football, as we know it, was on its way.

"Home, Sweet Home." During the period after the War Between the States, popular songs became nation-wide favorites just the way certain catchy tunes do now. If there had been a way to rate the popularity of such songs, "Home, Sweet Home" would undoubtedly have stood high on the list. Though it brought very little money to its composer, "Home, Sweet Home" grew in popularity from the year it was written (1823), and it is still an old favorite today.

The song was composed, appropriately, by a homesick American abroad. John Howard Payne was born in New York City, and he had spent memorable childhood years in the village of Easthampton, on Long Island. "Home, Sweet Home" speaks of roaming abroad "'mid pleasures and palaces," and the words give a fairly good description of Payne's own life. He became an actor at the age of 16, turned playwright later, and was always a wanderer. He lived and acted abroad during much of his life, and he knew many great people, but he was constantly homesick for America.

His most famous work was written for his opera *Clari, the Maid of Milan,* while Payne was staying in Paris at the Palais Royal Hotel. It became popular immediately, but *Clari* was the only work of this playwright that enjoyed any success. Payne later became United States Consul at Tunis, North Africa, and there he died, far from his beloved country. But in 1883 his body was brought home, and he was buried in Washington, D.C. At the burial service a choir of a thousand voices sang "Home, Sweet Home."

The Kalamazoo Case. Today Americans take it as a matter of course that the state and local governments have the right to establish any kind of public educational institution. Citizens may be taxed for the support of such institutions, whether they are elementary schools or state universities. But Americans did not always take such things for granted. There was a time when citizens disputed the wisdom and legal right of the government to use the taxpayer's money for founding and supporting any school higher than an elementary school.

During Grant's second term as President, the town of Kalamazoo, Michigan, then a mere village, wanted to collect taxes for the support of a public high school. But one of the citizens of Kalamazoo, Charles E. Stuart, raised strong objections. Higher education, he said, was not the business of government. As far as education was concerned, the money of the taxpayers should be restricted to the support of elementary schools. Stuart and other Kalamazoo residents finally brought a court action to restrain the school authorities from collecting taxes to support the high school.

In 1874 the Michigan Supreme Court decided the case against Stuart. It was right and constitutional, declared the court, that a state establish at public expense a complete system of education, right up through the university. This case, with its historic decision, is known as the Kalamazoo Case. It set a legal precedent for other states in the matter of taxing the citizens for the support of secondary and higher education.

Into the Peach Basket. Most sports had their origins far back in history. No one knows when the first polo game was played or when the first goal kicker booted a football. But there is one sport whose birthday is known exactly — the game of basketball. Basketball didn't "just grow." It was deliberately invented.

In 1890 in the YMCA Training College at Springfield, Massachusetts, a certain Dr. James Naismith was an instructor in physical education. Dr. Naismith had pondered for a long time on how to devise an indoor ball game which would be as fast and as exciting as outdoor games. One day he took a peach basket and nailed it high up on the wall of the gymnasium. He practiced tossing a soccer ball so that it dropped into the basket. Dr. Naismith then sat down and thought up rules and procedure for the new game of basketball. They appeared in January, 1892, in the paper of the YMCA college.

The new game caught on like wildfire. Now the routine gymnasium exercises, which many considered dull and monotonous, could be replaced with an indoor sport in which there were competition and suspense, two things which Americans have always loved. Because the YMCA had international branches, basketball was soon known all over the world.

A torchlight parade

THE PLAN OF THE BOOK

	1492 to 1783	**Unit One:** Discovery, Exploration, Development of the English colonies, American Revolution			
PART ONE *Early America Develops*	1783 to 1840	**Unit Two:** Framing of Constitution, The new republic, Rise of nationalism, sectionalism, and democracy			
	1789 to 1865	**Unit Three:** Economic developments, Social change and reform, Rise of American culture			
	1840 to 1865	**Unit Four:** Westward expansion, The slavery problem, War Between the States			
PART TWO *Modern America Emerges*	1865 to the 1890's	**Unit Five** Foundations of the American economic system	**Unit Six** Social and cultural developments	**Unit Seven** Government, politics, and foreign affairs	
PART THREE *Modern America Matures*	1890's to the Present	**Unit Eight** American economic system today	**Unit Nine** Social and cultural developments	**Unit Ten** The United States in world affairs	**Unit Eleven** Developments in government and politics

Unit Seven

POLITICAL PARTIES STRUGGLE

FOR CONTROL

During the period from 1865 to the 1890's, politics in the United States was largely a battle for power between the two major parties. Both the Democrats and the Republicans fought to gain power and — when in office — to hold it. In this political tug of war the Republicans enjoyed the advantage, keeping control of the Presidency for all but two terms from 1865 to 1897.

In their ambitions for political office both major parties frequently ignored vital public issues. This fact led from time to time to the organization of third party movements. The most successful of these was the Populist Party, which definitely influenced national policies in the early '90's.

One of the important developments of this period was the growth of the merit system, designed to do away with many evils of the spoils system. Perhaps the greatest testimonial to the basic strength and stability of America was the calm acceptance of the outcome of the disputed election of 1876. Although one half the voters doubted the fairness of the election returns, there was no disorder or violence.

The Presidents of this period, both Democratic and Republican, in general maintained the traditional policy of isolation in foreign affairs. On at least two occasions the United States clearly demonstrated its determination and ability to defend the Monroe Doctrine. There were some signs, however, that changes were in the making. Though expansionist sentiment was not strong, the United States annexed territory outside its boundaries, notably Alaska and Hawaii. It also increased its influence in Latin America. Both these tendencies were evidence that the rapid growth of American industry was producing an interest in overseas trade and possessions. It was not until the turn of the century, however, that these trends appeared in definite form.

Chapter **24**

Political paraders

POLITICAL ABUSES DEMAND REFORM

AS PARTY STRIFE INTENSIFIES

It is my wish that the collection of revenue should be free from partisan control and organized on a strictly business basis with the same guarantees for efficiency and fidelity in the selection of the chief and subordinate officers that would be required by a prudent merchant. Party leaders should have no more influence in appointments than other equally respectable citizens.

Rutherford B. Hayes

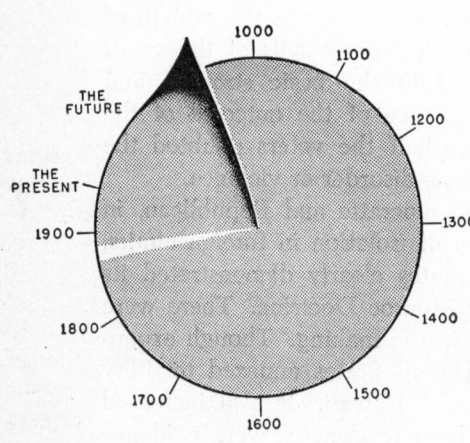

1869–1884

The industrialization of America had far-reaching effects upon the whole country. As you have seen, it brought perplexing economic and social problems. It also helped in time to stimulate America's participation in world affairs, as you will read later (Unit 10). Finally, industrialization had a great influence on politics and political parties.

Politicians were slow at first to grasp the significance of the changes through which the nation was passing. But when various groups began to put pressure on them for legislative favors, and when these politicians saw the need to protect the public welfare, they were forced to think and plan along new and unfamiliar lines. Statesmen of the early republic had aimed chiefly at achieving and keeping *political* democracy. Statesmen from 1865 to the present have been faced also with the need of bringing about *social and industrial* democracy. Progress has been made in this direction, but many of the vexing economic and social questions of the last century still exist today. A basic change in our idea of government has resulted from the fact that the government of an industrialized state must provide an increased number of services. Consequently our federal, state, and local governments employ many more workers and spend much greater sums of money than formerly.

This chapter tells the story of politics and parties for the first two decades following the War Between the States. The material is developed under these topics:

1. Corruption follows the War Between the States.
2. The Republicans retain control.
3. Hayes and Arthur bring about reforms.
4. The Democrats are returned to power.

1 Corruption Follows the War Between the States

The major parties battle for power. For a quarter-century after Lincoln was elected in 1860, the Republican Party remained in power. During the first four years, the party's efforts were entirely concerned with the war effort. Since the Republicans drew their strength largely from the North and the West, the defeat of the Southern Confederacy was more or less a Republican party triumph. But when slavery was abolished and the North and South were reunited, the Republican Party had to search for new issues if it was to survive.

For a time, the problem of reconstructing the South filled this need. As this problem faded into the background of public interest, however, the Republican Party continued "waving the bloody shirt." In other words, its spokesmen reminded the nation of how the Republican Party had preserved the Union, and at the same time they branded the Democratic Party as the party of rebellion. The voters were thus asked to show their gratitude by keeping the Republicans in power. The issues that were really important were often ignored; the Republican leaders were concerned chiefly with improving the party's political fortunes.

Grant is disappointing as President. Ulysses S. Grant, successful as the commander of the Union armies, was honored with the highest political office in the land. In the Presidency, however, Grant showed few of the sterling qualities of leadership which had distinguished him upon the field of battle. He was upright, honest, and loyal to his friends — to a fault. But being a man of little political experience, he was confused by the obligations of his office. His understanding of human nature was slight, and he took advice from people who were interested only in furthering their own interests. Perhaps because he had been so poor in his early years, he had great respect for men of wealth. Some of them made friends with him and then used their association with the President to further their own corrupt schemes.

Because of his trusting nature, Grant became the easy victim of crafty political leaders. He had a real sympathy for the South, and had ended his acceptance of the presidential nomination with the words, "Let us have peace." Yet at the request of radical Republican leaders he supported the tottering carpetbag governments, and "for the good of the party" flooded the South with federal troops.

Grant's poor judgment leads to Black Friday. President Grant's over-trusting nature was also revealed in the gold conspiracy of 1869. Two financial adventurers, Jay Gould and James Fisk, Jr., were scheming to corner the gold supply of the country, that is, to buy all or at least most of the gold in the country, and then to make a huge profit by forcing up the price of gold. The one obstacle to their scheme was the fact that the United States Treasury, which re-

Fashions in men's hats

ceived large amounts of gold, released several million dollars' worth in the course of every month in exchange for government bonds. A conspiracy for cornering the gold supply would never succeed unless the government sale of gold could be stopped. The two promoters persuaded the President to issue the necessary order. As a result, during the week of September 20, the price of gold mounted from 140 to 163; that is, it took $163 in greenbacks to buy $100 in gold. In other words, greenbacks dropped in value. Business was badly upset, and frantic appeals were made to Grant to lift the ban on the Treasury's sale of gold. Finally orders were issued to sell government gold, and the corner on the market was broken.

Meanwhile, Gould had been warned by the President's brother-in-law that the Secretary of the Treasury was going to start selling gold again. Gould quietly began to sell out his holdings while Fisk was still feverishly buying. The crash came on "Black Friday," September 24, 1869. The price of gold dropped to 135, and chaos filled the stock exchange. In the panic which followed, hundreds of business firms

News of the crash on "Black Friday" caused intense excitement in financial circles throughout the country. This old print shows a scene of turmoil in the "Gold Room" of the New York Stock Exchange, as quotations show the price of gold going down.

were ruined, but Gould had managed to sell his gold, while Fisk escaped by refusing to admit his obligations and letting his brokers fail. A congressional committee of investigation freed Grant from any suspicion of conspiracy. His blindness to the real purpose of Gould and Fisk, however, and his association with them during the entire affair, left a bad impression upon the public.

The Crédit Mobilier scandal involves high officials. During Grant's term as President, so many political scandals came to light that many people began to believe that corruption among government officials was common. One scandal, which had its beginnings before Grant became President, centered about the construction of the first transcontinental railroad (page 363). Some leading stockholders of the Union Pacific Railroad had formed a finance and construction company called the Crédit Mobilier. Because of their influence as stockholders in the railroad, they were able to vote enormous contracts to the construction company, which brought them fat profits. One of the members of the Crédit Mobilier was Oakes Ames, a congressman from Massachusetts. It was his task to distribute shares of the company stock among members of Congress where they would "do the most good" in securing legislative favors and preventing interference with the Crédit Mobilier. In these transactions, Ames lent congressmen the purchase price of the stock until enough dividends were earned to pay the cost. Many prominent politicians were involved. When the affair became known, Ames was censured by the House for selling stock below its face value. Vice-President Colfax and several others were so deeply involved in the scandal that they were forced to retire from public life.

Scandals increase. Other scandals came into the open and disgusted the public. In the Middle West a "whisky ring" which had been evading the internal revenue tax was exposed. Investigation showed that one of the prominent members of the ring was a revenue officer who had given Grant a team of beautiful horses. From the same man the President's private secretary, O. E. Babcock, also received a piece of jewelry valued at $2400. Babcock was tried and acquitted, and though several members of the ring were sent to prison, they were later pardoned by Grant. In another scandal, Grant's Secretary of War, Belknap, was found to have accepted bribes from an employee in the Indian service. By unanimous vote the House impeached Belknap, and he was saved from conviction only because the President accepted his resignation.

Just at the end of Grant's first term (March 3, 1873) Congress took a step which lowered public confidence still further. It passed an act which not only raised congressional salaries but made the increases effective for the previous two years. By this "salary grab," each member of Congress would pocket $5000 in addition to the salary he had already received. Faced by a storm of protest, Congress at the next session repealed the act, except as it applied to the President and the justices of the Supreme Court.

The Tweed Ring robs New York City. These unpleasant scandals which disgraced national politics were paralleled in local governments. Almost every large American city has at one time or another fallen into the hands of some political ring which made itself rich at the expense of the taxpayers. Perhaps the most notorious was the Tweed Ring which dominated New York City during the Grant period. Its leader was William M. ("Boss") Tweed, head of Tammany Hall, an organization which controlled the Democratic political machinery of New York City. Tweed controlled not only New York City but the governor and the state legislature as well. The Tweed Ring's methods of grafting were so expert that, though members of the ring were stealing millions of dollars from the city, direct evidence against them could not be found. For example, a contract might call for a payment of $110,000. Of that amount, the ring would pocket $100,000 while the contractor, also connected with the ring, would get $10,000. So far as the city accounts were concerned, there seemed to be no dishonesty. Under this system, one plas-

"Boss" Tweed of New York, leader of the Tammany Hall political machine, became immensely wealthy but died in jail.

terer received nearly $3,000,000 for nine months' work. Finally a member of the Tweed Ring, who thought he was not receiving his share of the graft, revealed to the New York *Times* how the ring operated. At the same time a series of skillful cartoons by Thomas Nast in *Harper's Weekly* inflamed public opinion against the ring. (A Nast cartoon on another subject appears on page 387.) Samuel J. Tilden, a prominent New York attorney, aided greatly in the prosecution of the grafters. Tweed himself was convicted and spent his last days in jail.

--------- CHECK-UP ---------

Why did corruption follow the War Between the States?

1. What problem did the Republican Party face with the ending of the War? What was the attempted solution?

2. What were Grant's weaknesses as President?

3. How do each of these illustrate the corruption which followed the war? (a) The corner on gold, (b) The Crédit Mobilier, (c) The Whisky Ring, (d) The "salary grab."

4. What was the Tweed Ring? How was it broken?

2 The Republicans Retain Control

Grant is re-elected in 1872. As Grant's first administration drew to a close, voters were expressing considerable dissatisfaction with conditions in the South and with the low tone of public morality. A vigorous reform movement developed into a new Liberal Republican Party. Its delegates held a convention in Cincinnati in May, 1872. They drew up a platform condemning the administration of Grant, demanding an end to restrictions on the South, and urging civil service reform (making appointments to public office on merit rather than as a reward for political service). Unfortunately, the Liberal Republicans passed over their leading candidates and nominated Horace Greeley, the eccentric editor of the New York *Tribune*. The convention could hardly have made a worse choice. Greeley was against civil service reform. Moreover, he was opposed to the Democratic Party, whose support was necessary if the Liberal Republicans were to win the election.

Greeley was a bitter pill for the Democrats to swallow. They knew, however, that their only chance of winning the election and of bringing to a close the military occupation of the South, lay in backing the Liberal Republican candidate. Although they chose him as their standard-bearer, they gave him only lukewarm support during the campaign. In the election, Grant, nominated on the regular Republican ticket, polled 286 electoral votes to 66 for Greeley. Before a month had passed, Greeley died. He was broken by the abusive campaign and his decisive defeat, as well as by financial troubles and the death of his wife.

The hold of the Republican Party weakens. During Grant's second term several notable events took place. The Resumption Act was passed (page 406), the telephone was invented (page 368), and the Centen-

nial Exposition was held at Philadelphia in 1876. On the whole, however, this was a discouraging period. Corrupt carpetbag governments still controlled parts of the South. Shocking scandals in public life continued to be uncovered. Finally, the failure of the banking house of Jay Cooke and Company began the Panic of 1873 (page 375). Business failures and unemployment increased, but the government made practically no attempt to provide relief. Public dissatisfaction and resentment were reflected in the Democratic landslide in 1874. Such strong Republican states as New York, Massachusetts, Pennsylvania, and Ohio elected Democratic governors. A Democratic House was chosen for the first time since the war, and the Senate was saved for the Republicans by the fact that only one third of its members were up for election. It was clear that the GOP ("Grand Old Party,") was losing power.

Hayes opposes Tilden for the Presidency. The Republicans were worried about the coming presidential election (1876). Their best chance to win seemed to lie in repeating the old charge that the Democratic party had been disloyal to the Union, and in insisting that the party which had saved the Union must continue in power. But who would be its candidate? A third-term movement for Grant was checked by a resolution of the House of Representatives that it would be "unwise, unpatriotic, and fraught with peril to our free institutions." A logical choice would have been James G. Blaine of Maine, a brilliant leader in the quarter-century following the war. Blaine's candidacy, however, was made doubtful by the fact that certain Republican leaders were his enemies. The Republican convention finally nominated Rutherford B. Hayes of Ohio. Hayes had a good war record. He was known to be in favor of reform, and he had announced that he wanted to wipe out forever "the distinction between North and South in our common country." The Republican platform stressed the services of the party during the war, called for civil service reform, and urged a protective tariff. Hopeful of victory, the Democrats nominated Samuel J. Tilden, the reform governor of New York, who had smashed the Tweed Ring. Their platform emphasized the need for reform in state and national government, in the currency system, in the tariff, and in the civil service.

Election returns are disputed. On the morning after the election, it seemed certain that Tilden had won. The Republican campaign managers and almost every Republican newspaper conceded defeat. Tilden had carried the important doubtful states. He had a plurality of 250,000 and had 184 undisputed electoral votes to 165 for Hayes. But the electoral returns from Florida, Louisiana, and South Carolina — three states still under carpetbag rule — as well as one vote from Oregon, were in dispute. In order to win, Hayes must have every one of the 20 electoral votes in question. The dispute in Oregon was easily settled in favor of Hayes. From the three southern states, however, double sets of returns were forwarded to Washington. The Republicans claimed all three states for Hayes, but the Democrats protested that under carpetbag rule the will of the majority had not been represented. In Louisiana, in particular, enough so-called "fraudulent votes" had been thrown out by Republican officials to turn a Democratic majority of over 6000 into a Republican victory.

The election dispute is settled. The Constitution provided for the opening and counting of the electoral votes before the combined houses of Congress, but it failed to state exactly *by whom* the votes should be counted. This situation led to much violent argument, but ended peacefully enough when Congress passed the Electoral Commission Act. This act set up a commission of fifteen — five from the House, five from the Senate, and five justices of the Supreme Court — to consider the electoral returns. Their decision was to be final, unless turned down by both houses voting separately. By previous arrangement the Democratic House chose three Democrats and two Republicans, and the Republican Senate chose three Republicans and two Democrats. The act designated four of the justices — two Repub-

The Panic of 1873, stimulated by the failure of Jay Cooke and Company, was a shock to banks and other businesses throughout the country. This old print shows a run on a bank at the peak of the excitement.

licans and two Democrats — and provided that these four were to choose a fifth. It was understood that Justice David Davis of Illinois, an independent, would be the fifteenth member of the commission, but at this time Davis was elected to the Senate. With Davis out of the picture, only Republicans were left on the Supreme Court bench, and Justice Bradley was chosen. The commission divided along party lines, and by a vote of eight to seven Hayes was given every disputed electoral vote. Two days before Grant's term expired, Hayes was declared elected by a vote of 185 to 184. The Democrats were bitterly disappointed, but Tilden took the decision in sportsmanlike fashion. The fact that the country accepted the election verdict without any disturbances and that Hayes was peacefully inaugurated on Monday, March 5, 1877, was a victory for American democracy and sense of order.

The question as to who was actually

elected is a difficult one. Had there been a free election — without fraud or attempts to frighten the voters — the Republicans, under the Fourteenth and Fifteenth Amendments, no doubt would have carried the three states. On the other hand, without the aid of federal troops the Republican organizations in those states did not have a chance. In fact, as soon as the troops were withdrawn, the three states went back into the Democratic ranks.

———— CHECK-UP ————

How were the Republicans able to retain control of the government?

1. What groups supported Greeley in the election of 1872? Why? What was the outcome of the election? Why?
2. What were some of the important events of Grant's second term?
3. What factors dictated the choice of presidential candidates in 1876?
4. Why did the election of 1876 result in a dispute? How was the dispute settled?

3 **Hayes and Arthur Bring About Reforms**

President Hayes urges reform. President Hayes faced a difficult situation when he went into office. More than half the country questioned his right to the Presidency. Democratic newspapers spoke of him as "His Fraudulency" and "Old Eight to Seven," and pictured him with the word "Fraud" printed across his brow. During the first half of his term, the House of Representatives was controlled by the Democrats, and during the latter half the Democrats had a majority in both houses. To make matters worse, Hayes was unable to command the loyalty of his own party leaders. After 1876 the Republicans were split into two groups, known as the "Stalwarts" and the "Half-breeds." The Stalwarts were led by Roscoe Conkling of New York, "Don" Cameron of Pennsylvania, and John A. Logan of Illinois. They included most of those prominent in the ranks of the radical Republicans during the time of President Grant. The Stalwarts were conservatives; they had great contempt for the Half-breeds, led by Blaine and John Sherman, a group which showed a moderate interest in reform. The Stalwarts called the new President an "old woman" and "granny Hayes," and spoke slightingly of his reform program as a "milk-and-water diet."

Despite the hostility of the Democrats and the opposition of the Stalwart Republicans, Hayes went forward with his policies. He was conscientious, industrious, and courageous. In an inaugural address of unusual excellence, he spoke in favor of self-government and material development for the South, reform in the civil service, and a return to specie payment as provided by the Resumption Act (page 406).

Hayes withdraws troops from the South. A problem upon which the new President acted immediately concerned the South. Before his election, Hayes had indicated that if he won, he would withdraw federal

Carl Schurz, an immigrant from Germany, performed many valuable services for his adopted country. As a member of Hayes' cabinet, he strongly advocated civil service reform.

troops from Louisiana and South Carolina. Even though the Republican governments in these states were expected to collapse if military support was taken away, Hayes made good his promise. The Republican reconstruction governments promptly gave way to the Democrats, and President Hayes was bitterly condemned for his "surrender." The Democrats in Congress at this time managed to bring about the repeal of that part of the "Force Acts" which provided for the use of federal troops in supervising southern elections. From that time, the South was free to manage its own political affairs. The final remains of the radical reconstruction program were being swept away.

Hayes faces new problems. Hayes' administration was less remarkable for its accomplishments than for certain events which forecast the problems that were to be front page news in administrations to come. For instance, the railroad strike of 1877 (page 394) pointed to the rising unrest in the ranks of organized labor, smarting under the injustices of the new industrial system. When Hayes sought to have modified the treaty permitting the unlimited immigration of Chinese, his action marked the beginning of a new policy of immigration restriction (page 420). The passage of the Bland-Allison Act (page 407) was the opening gun in the campaign for free silver.

The President supports civil service reform. An important part of the post-war reform movement was aimed at abuses in the civil service. The purpose of these reforms was to do away with the practice of appointing officials to reward them for past political services, and of forcing officeholders to give part of their salaries to the campaign chest of the party in power. Civil service reform had the ardent support of certain members of Congress, such as Thomas A. Jenckes and Carl Schurz. Largely as a result of their efforts, President Grant had recommended — as early as 1870 — competitive examinations for federal offices. The next year Congress passed an act setting up a civil service commission, but the law soon became a dead letter be-

Chun Lan Pin, first Chinese Minister to the United States, is greeted by President Hayes.

cause no funds were provided for financing it.

President Hayes was in complete sympathy with civil service reform. He laid down a number of general principles for appointment to office. For instance, no sweeping changes of officials were to be made. Persons recommended for office by congressmen were to be investigated. No relatives of the President or the President's wife were to be appointed, however good their qualifications. In addition, the Department of the Interior and the New York Post Office were placed on a merit basis. An investigation of conditions in the New York Customhouse led to the removal of Chester A. Arthur, Collector of the Port of New York, and Alonzo B. Cornell, naval officer of the port. President Hayes went even further by issuing an order denying United States officials the privilege of taking part in the management of political organizations and forbidding assessments of federal workers for campaign purposes. This order, unfortunately, was so drastic that Hayes was unable to put it into effect. Likewise, when he tried to persuade Congress to provide funds for the Civil Service

Commission, his request was not granted.

Republicans win in 1880. The election of 1880 was noteworthy for noisy conventions, lavish spending, and a Republican deadlock which ended in the nomination of a "dark horse." After four years of a reform President, the Republican Stalwart leaders favored another term for Grant, whom they had found easy to manage. When the Republican convention opened, Grant had over 300 votes. His supporters, the "old guard," stuck with him to the end. The other leading candidates were Blaine and John Sherman, but neither was strong enough to get the required majority. On the thirty-fifth ballot, a stampede started in favor of General James A. Garfield of Ohio. On the following ballot a union of the Blaine and Sherman forces made his nomination possible. To reconcile Conkling and the Stalwarts, the convention chose for the Vice-Presidency Chester A. Arthur, former Collector of the Port of New York.

The Democrats, weakened by the retirement of Tilden, turned to General Winfield S. Hancock of Pennsylvania, an officer of the Union Army who had a good war record. The platforms of the two major parties were almost the same, as far as actual issues were concerned. The only really positive platform was offered by a third party — the Greenback Party. Their platform called for an increase in the volume of money, labor legislation, regulation of interstate commerce, an income tax, and wider suffrage. Garfield and Arthur, helped by a large campaign fund and by the general prosperity of the country — for which the Republicans claimed credit — got a solid majority in the electoral college. But the popular vote was almost evenly divided. The Republicans won the House by only a narrow margin, while two independents held the balance of power in the Senate.

President Garfield antagonizes the Stalwarts. Garfield's rise to the Presidency is an inspiring example of the opportunities a poor boy enjoys in America. He had been born in lowly circumstances in a log cabin, and as a young man, he had driven mules along the towpath of the Ohio Canal. He managed to get a college education, and then became a clergyman, college president, major general in the Union forces, representative in Congress, and senator-elect from Ohio.

Unfortunately, his brief administration was darkened by disclosures of corruption, from which he did not escape entirely untouched.[1] His term of office was disturbed even further by the hostility of the Stalwart branch of the Republicans. Although the Stalwarts had helped elect him, he failed to reward them as they had expected. Roscoe Conkling was angered by the appointment of his bitter enemy, Blaine, as Secretary of State. Garfield also named another opponent of Conkling's, W. H. Robertson, to the influential position of Collector of the Port of New York. The gap between the President and the Stalwarts widened as many hungry office seekers failed to win appointments. One of these, a half-insane man, Charles Guiteau, fired the fatal shot which brought the President's life to an untimely end. After a lingering illness, the President died in mid-September, 1881.

Chester A. Arthur succeeds to the Presidency. When Chester A. Arthur became President the hopes of the reformers sank, because Arthur was a Stalwart leader. But the dignity and responsibilities of the office brought out the best qualities in Arthur.

[1] On certain routes in the Far West and the South mail was carried by stage lines. A political ring raised the rates on these routes to unreasonable amounts, and then pocketed the proceeds. The ring was broken up, but the leaders managed to escape without punishment. Certain letters of Garfield's were also uncovered which encouraged one of the worst features of the spoils system, the levying of assessments upon government officials.

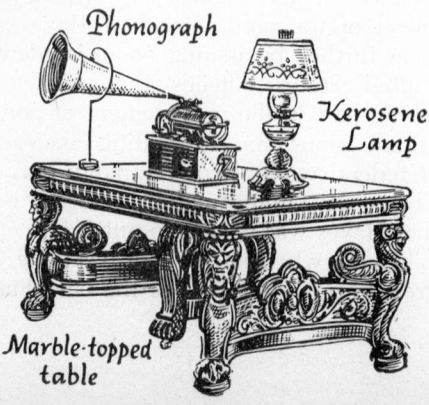

Phonograph

Kerosene Lamp

Marble-topped table

His administration, in fact, turned out to be one of real achievement. He refused to approve a Chinese exclusion act which he felt violated our treaty with China, but instead signed a bill that limited Chinese immigration temporarily (page 420). Arthur also showed his independence of Congress by vetoing an extravagant rivers and harbors bill. His administration marked the beginning of the modern United States Navy. The crowning achievement of his term, however, was a reform of the civil service.

The Pendleton Act is passed. As sometimes happens, it took a dramatic incident to awaken the American people to the need for civil service reform. That incident was the assassination of President Garfield. Because Garfield's death had stemmed from the spoils system, President Arthur became interested in civil service reform. He discouraged the levying of assessments upon federal office holders and urged Congress to legislate civil service reform. Congress responded by passing the Pendleton Act (1883), sometimes called the "Magna Carta" of civil service reform. This act forbade the assessment of federal officials for political contributions. It also provided for the appointment of a Civil Service Commission which was to conduct competitive examinations in the different states for the "classified service," that is, those offices classified for appointment on merit. Appointments to office and promotions inside the federal service were to be made from a list of eligible candidates prepared as a result of the examinations. The system was to start in the customs districts and the larger post offices, but the President was given wide powers to extend the list of offices to be filled by examinations.

The Merit System grows in spite of opposition. The professional politicians bitterly opposed the Pendleton Act. Spoilsmen contemptuously referred to the "snivel service," and spoke of the people who backed it as "goody-goodies." They changed the well-known slogan to read, "To the vanquished belong the spoils." Nevertheless, civil service reform had come to stay. The Presidents who followed Arthur varied in their feelings toward it, but in little more

Fashions of the 1880's

than a half-century they increased the number of positions filled by competitive examination from some 16,000 to a million. Even this progress, however, left much to be desired. Many of the more important offices were still filled on the basis of political favoritism, rather than on grounds of fitness for the office.

——— CHECK-UP ———

What reforms were begun during the administrations of Hayes and Arthur?

1. Why was Hayes in a weak position as President?
2. What policies did Hayes follow with regard to (a) reconstruction, and (b) civil service reform? What were his accomplishments?
3. What were the chief features of the election of 1880?
4. Why was civil service reform needed? What groups opposed it? What was accomplished during Arthur's administration?

---

4 **The Democrats Are Returned to Power**

Republicans nominate Blaine in 1884. The contest between the parties in 1884 was unusually bitter. An open split in the

Children's dress, 1880's

Republican ranks gave the Democrats a real advantage. Arthur's excellent record entitled him to renomination, but he had made enemies among the Stalwarts and he had only lukewarm support from the reform element of the party. On the first ballot of the nominating convention, Blaine polled some 50 votes more than Arthur, and on the fourth ballot he obtained the needed majority. John A. Logan, Stalwart leader of Illinois, was named the candidate for Vice-President. The reformers did not like either of these selections. Some of the independent Republicans, like Theodore Roosevelt, reluctantly accepted their party's choice. But a group nicknamed "Mugwumps" refused to fall into line.

Cleveland leads the Democrats. These Mugwumps applauded the choice of Grover Cleveland, governor of New York, as the standard-bearer of the Democratic Party. Cleveland was scrupulously honest, absolutely fearless, and left no doubt about where he stood on the debatable questions of the day. As county sheriff, and later as mayor of Buffalo and as governor of New York, Cleveland had shown political uprightness and independence. In contrast to the brilliant and magnetic Blaine, Cleveland was plodding and unimaginative. But once he had reached a conclusion, he could not be moved.

Cleveland wins. The campaign became a battle of personalities instead of issues. Blaine's early political record was criticized. Cleveland, on the other hand, was not only accused of being a drunkard but was also denounced for having hired a substitute in the War Between the States. One editor characterized the campaign as "worthy the stairways of a tenement house." The Mugwumps, along with many independent Republican newspapers, gave their support to Cleveland. On the other hand, although victory in the campaign hinged chiefly upon New York, the Stalwart Conkling refused to take the stump for Blaine in that state, declaring that he did not engage in "criminal practice." The vote in New York was so close that the outcome was in doubt for several days. It finally went to Cleveland by the narrow margin of 1149 votes — and with New York went the election. The Democrats also succeeded in carrying the House, but the Senate remained Republican.[2]

---

[2] On the eve of the election, Blaine was tendered a reception in New York by a delegation of clergymen. During the reception the Reverend Dr. Burchard referred to the Democrats as the party of "rum, Romanism, and rebellion." The Republican nominee failed to comment on this slur upon the Catholics. Though Blaine's mother was Irish, and though he had been popular among the Irish Catholics, it was believed by many that this incident cost him the election. The Prohibition vote in New York State that year was more than 25,000, another factor in Blaine's defeat. If this party had not had its own candidates, doubtless most of the votes would have gone to Blaine.

--------- CHECK-UP ---------

How did the Democrats finally return to power?

1. Who supported Cleveland in the election of 1884? Why?
2. What were the chief features of the campaign?

CHAPTER REVIEW

Terms to Understand

civil service
"dark horse"
"corner"
bankruptcy

censure
political ring
plurality
merit system

People and Things to Know About

"waving the bloody shirt"
Black Friday
Crédit Mobilier

Samuel J. Tilden
Electoral Commission
"Stalwarts" and "Half-breeds"

People and Things to Know About (Cont.)

"whisky ring"   Chester A. Arthur
"salary grab"   Winfield S. Hancock
Tweed Ring   Greenback Party
Thomas Nast   James A. Garfield
Liberal Republicans   Pendleton Act
Horace Greeley   "Mugwumps"
James G. Blaine   Grover Cleveland
Rutherford B. Hayes   Carl Schurz

Historic Dates to Identify

1876   1883

Questions to Discuss

1. Compare the following:
(a) Grant as a general and as President.
(b) The Liberal and regular Republicans.
(c) The disputes involved in the elections of 1800, 1824, and 1876.
(d) "Stalwarts" and "Half-breeds."
(e) The Merit System and the Spoils System.
2. Nearly all government policies of an economic nature are of more direct benefit to some groups than to others. Can you give examples from our history which illustrate this? How would you distinguish between legitimate government assistance and such corrupt assistance to private groups as are discussed in the text?
3. Which other Presidents that you have studied were like Hayes in that they lacked support both within and outside their parties? Why can such situations occur under the American system of government?
4. What abuses are eliminated by the method of securing public officials through competitive examinations? What might be some of the disadvantages of this method?

Questions to Discuss (Cont.)

5. The American system has sometimes been criticized on the ground that it does not raise the most able men to the Presidency. Do you agree with this observation? Give examples. Do you think that this point was particularly true of the period we have been studying? What factors entered into the selection of candidates? What qualifications do you think that a President should have, taking into consideration all of the duties he must perform?

Other Things to Do

°1. Make a four column chart in which you compare the presidential elections from 1872 to 1884. Your headings should be "Candidates," "Platforms," "Chief Features," and "Results."
°2. Imagine that you were a "reform" newspaper editor in 1882. Write an editorial demanding civil service reform legislation.
3. Investigate and report on present-day legislation to help eliminate dishonest practices from politics. A textbook on government will be of help in this connection.
4. The Centennial Exposition of 1876 in Philadelphia was devoted to the progress which the United States had made during the preceding 100 years. Draw up a list of the evidences of progress which you would have wanted displayed. Make an additional list of developments of which you would not have been so proud.
5. The cartoonist's art is still important in molding public opinion. Make a collection of cartoons, both pro and con, on some important modern issue.

Politicians

Chapter 25

POLITICAL CONTROL SHIFTS FROM

PARTY TO PARTY

Public officers are the servants and agents of the people, to execute the laws which the people have made.

Grover Cleveland

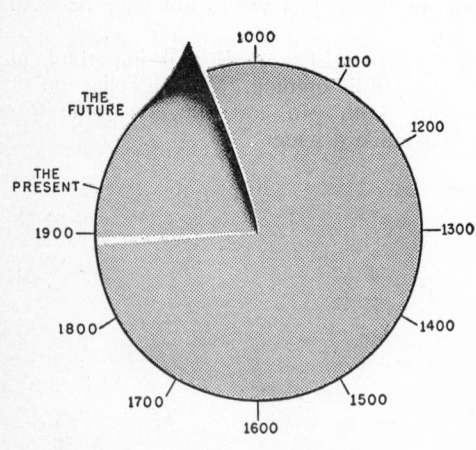

1885-1896

In the years between Lincoln's election in 1860 and Cleveland's election in 1884 the Republican Party held continuous control of the Presidency. For the balance of the 1880's and during the early 1890's a seesaw struggle developed in which neither party was able to obtain a clear-cut advantage. Thus, after four years as President, Grover Cleveland lost the election of 1888 to a Republican, Benjamin Harrison, chiefly on the tariff issue. Harrison, in turn, permitted leaders of the Republican Party to dominate his administration, and widespread discontent paved the way for Cleveland's return to the White House in 1893. Whatever plans Cleveland had were seriously affected by the panic which swept the country in that year. Economic conditions went from bad to worse during his second term, and Cleveland, though unfairly, was held responsible. After an exciting campaign the Republicans regained control in the election of 1896, a control they managed to retain until 1913.

This chapter will relate the political ups and downs of the 1880's and 1890's under the following headings:

1. Cleveland makes progress despite opposition.
2. Republican control gives way to Democratic.
3. Feeling runs high in the election of 1896.

1 Cleveland Makes Progress Despite Opposition

Cleveland faces opposition. Grover Cleveland was the first Democrat to occupy the White House after the fall of Fort Sumter. The Republicans greeted his inauguration in 1885 with dismal prophecies for the future. They predicted hard times, payment of the southern debt, and even a restoration of slavery. None of these calamities took place, but Cleveland suffered from the opposition of various groups. For four years a hostile Republican Senate fought his every move. War veterans opposed his attempts to cut down government spending. Business interests interfered with his program to reduce the tariff. To make matters worse, growing labor agitation disturbed the country during his term.

Cleveland makes civil service reforms. From the time of his inaugural address, President Cleveland indicated his desire for civil service reform. Government jobs, he declared, should be distributed on the basis of merit and ability rather than party loyalty. Toward the end of his administration, he had nearly doubled the classified list. Cleveland also stood firm against the practice of collecting a tax "for the party" from officeholders. The stand that he took toward civil service keenly disappointed the hungry Democratic spoilsmen who had been eagerly awaiting the change in administration that would sweep some

120,000 Republicans out of office. Such heavy pressure was put on Cleveland by his own party, however, that by the end of his term few Republicans, except for those on the classified list, were still in office.

He antagonizes the war veterans. By his position on the question of pension legislation, Cleveland made enemies among the war veterans. Although the Pension Bureau was fairly liberal toward the veterans, many claims for pensions were turned down. Disappointed claimants, spurred on by pension agents looking for a fee, were often able to influence Congress to pass private bills which would provide for their relief. Some individuals not entitled to pensions under any general rule managed to secure them through these private bills. Many of the claims were dishonest and ridiculous. Cleveland gave careful attention to each bill. Although he signed more of these pension bills than Grant, Hayes, Garfield, and Arthur combined, he vetoed more than 200. Moreover, he took the trouble to explain each veto. In one case, he objected because a widow's "soldier husband" had been shot by a neighbor while hunting. In another the widow's husband, who had been captured by the Confederates, finished the war fighting for the South. Cleveland also vetoed a dependent pension bill. This would have given twelve dollars a month to any veterans who had served three months and who were now disabled and dependent upon their own labor or upon others for support. Cleveland's enemies unfairly claimed that his vetoes were due to his "rebel sympathies."

Important laws are passed. Although many of Cleveland's moves were blocked, important laws were passed during his administration.

(1) The most outstanding was the Interstate Commerce Act, which marked the beginning of government regulation of transportation (page 387).

(2) The Presidential Succession Act (1886) stated that, in case both the President and Vice-President should die or be dis-

Postman

abled, the members of the cabinet should succeed to the Presidency in the order of the creation of their offices by Congress.[1]

(3) An Electoral Count Act was also approved (1887), which was aimed at preventing another such disputed election as the one of 1876 (page 455). It provided that a single electoral return from a state had to be accepted unless turned down by both houses of Congress. If more than one set of returns were sent in, and the two houses could not agree as to which should be approved, Congress must accept the returns approved by the executive of the state.

The building up of the navy, which had been started in the preceding administration, was vigorously pushed forward. President Cleveland also sought to develop a policy for conserving natural resources. About 80 million acres of public land, illegally held by individuals or corporations, were restored to public control. In the President's annual message he also urged the nation to take great care of its natural resources, but this advice fell on deaf ears. Resources were too abundant for the public to see any need for conservation. It was several years before Congress took effective action in this direction. (Chapter 31.)

Harrison carries the election of 1888. There was much opposition to the renomination of Cleveland, especially among the leaders of his party. But as the election of 1888 drew near, his position became stronger and he was chosen to lead the Democrats without the formality of a ballot. The Republicans nominated General Benjamin Harrison, an able lawyer and a grandson of President William H. Harrison.

Cleveland had made persistent efforts to reduce the government surplus by lowering tariff rates (page 381). Now the tariff question became the leading issue of the campaign. The Republicans stoutly argued that tariff protection was essential to American prosperity. During the campaign there was

[1] In July, 1947, this succession act was amended at the request of President Truman. In the absence of a Vice-President, the Speaker of the House and then the Senate President *pro tempore* would succeed the President. The President argued that these were elected rather than appointive officers.

a wide discussion of the tariff issue, and campaign literature was distributed everywhere. Cleveland's plurality was more than 100,000 votes, but the votes were so distributed that Harrison, who carried some of the larger states by small majorities, had a greater number of votes in the electoral college. Although the election gave no proof that the country had rejected Cleveland's policies, the new administration began to reverse them as though elected by an overwhelming vote.

———— CHECK-UP ————

How did Cleveland make progress despite opposition?

1. What policy did Cleveland follow with regard to (a) civil service reform, and (b) veterans pensions? Why?
2. What legislation of a non-partisan nature was passed during Cleveland's first term?
3. Who were the candidates and what were the issues in the election of 1888? What were the results?

2 Republican Control Gives Way to Democratic

The House adopts the Reed rules. The new House of Representatives was almost evenly divided between the two parties, and it was only after a struggle that the Republicans gained the upper hand. The Democrats, by remaining away, or by refusing to answer the roll call, could prevent a quorum and the transaction of business. This strategy was upset by Thomas B. Reed, Speaker of the House. One day, when the roll call resulted in no quorum, Reed looked over the House and saw that a number of Democrats who had not answered the roll call were present. Directing the clerk to mark them present, he declared that a quorum existed. This was a new procedure, and the Democrats protested bitterly. "The Chair is making a statement of fact that the gentleman . . . is present," drawled Reed. "Does he deny it?" This episode led to the adoption of two rules. One prohibited motions made simply to obstruct action. The other permitted the Speaker to count as present those members who were actually there, even though they did not answer the roll call. Reed was called a "Czar" for his high-handed rulings, but when the Democrats again gained control of the House they found the same regulation desirable.

Congress assumes leadership. Harrison was not an outstanding leader. Unlike Cleveland, who had assumed a vigorous leadership of the nation, Harrison believed that the President's powers should not go beyond those definitely given him by the Constitution. He looked upon the members of Congress as the real representatives of the people and considered it his duty to carry out the measures enacted by Congress, rather than to try to influence that body.

The result was that Harrison's administration was dominated by such party leaders as Secretary of State Blaine, Speaker Reed, and Senators Sherman of Ohio and Quay of Pennsylvania. Party workers benefited when Harrison made a clean sweep of Democratic officeholders outside the classified list. To his credit, however, was the appointment to the Civil Service Commission of Theodore Roosevelt — an enthusiastic supporter of civil service reform.

Congress passes important legislation. Under Republican control, Congress proceeded to pass a number of important acts. These included the McKinley Tariff Act (page 381), the Sherman Silver Purchase Act (page 408), and the Sherman Antitrust Act (page 388). Congress also started a program of liberal spending. A dependent pension bill was approved, similar to the measure vetoed by Cleveland. A direct tax, which had been levied upon the states during the war, was repaid to the states. Money spent on rivers and harbors reached a new high, while money spent for the navy increased from less than $14,000,000 in 1880 to more than $22,000,000 in 1890.[2]

2 As a result of the naval program the number of modern steel war vessels in the navy increased

Election night, in 1888 as now, called out large crowds. An early projection screen shows election returns to New Yorkers.

In fact, the appropriations of Harrison's first Congress reached the billion-dollar mark. Democratic protests at such extravagant spending were met by the Republican boast that this was a "billion-dollar country."

Dissatisfaction arises. Toward the end of the term, the Harrison administration ran into some serious difficulties. Prices had risen, and the Democrats were quick to blame the McKinley Tariff. Our relations with other countries were strained; in fact, incidents that involved the Samoan Islands, the Bering Sea, Chile, and the Hawaiian Islands brought us at times nearly to the brink of war (Chapter 26). The silver legislation had failed to relieve the hard-pressed farmers and miners as predicted. The discontent in the West made the immediate future of the Republican Party look black.

from 3 to 22 in four years. By 1893 the U.S. Navy had advanced from twelfth to fifth place among the navies of the world. At the start of the twentieth century, only the navies of Great Britain and France outranked that of the United States.

Political Parties
AND THEIR PRESIDENTS

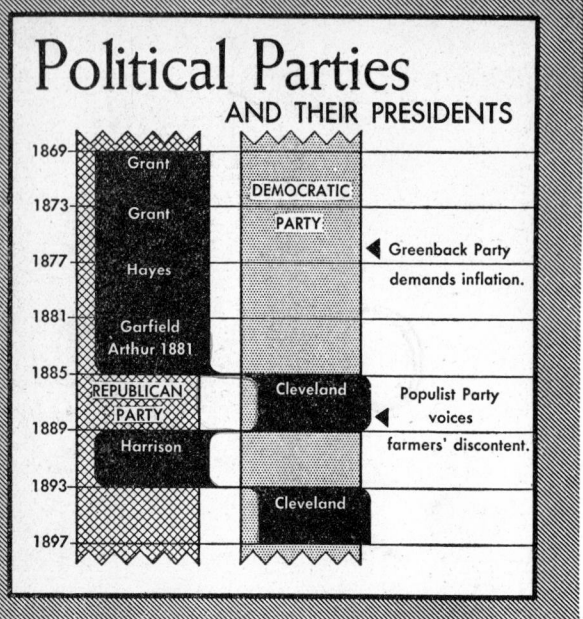

1869	Grant
1873	Grant
1877	Hayes
1881	Garfield / Arthur 1881
1885	REPUBLICAN PARTY / Cleveland
1889	Harrison
1893	Cleveland
1897	

DEMOCRATIC PARTY

◀ Greenback Party demands inflation.

◀ Populist Party voices farmers' discontent.

The Republican Party elected its candidates to the Presidency for all but eight years from 1869 to 1897. Can you explain why?

A new third party is organized. As the election of 1892 loomed ahead, it became clear that new forces were entering the political scene. There were many discontented voters, chiefly among the farmers of the West and South, but also among the silver miners of the West (page 404). In the early '90's, wheat, largely because of overproduction, was selling at less than 50 cents a bushel. Corn was worth so little that the farmers were burning it for fuel. Cattle on the hoof brought only two or three cents a pound. In the South, the price of cotton had fallen to nine cents a pound, or even less at times. In the words of Hamlin Garland, "As ten-cent corn and ten per cent interest were troubling Kansas, so six-cent cotton was inflaming Georgia — and both were frankly sympathetic with Montana and Colorado whose miners were suffering from a drop in the price of silver."

The upshot of all this discontent was a gathering at Cincinnati in May, 1891. Delegates representing many agricultural and a few labor organizations formed a new party called the People's Party, which became known as the Populist Party. They held their first national convention at Omaha the next year. Here they drew up a platform which called for the free and unlimited coinage of silver and gold "at the present legal ratio of sixteen to one." They demanded also: (1) an increase in the supply of money to not less than $50 per person in the country; (2) an income tax, graduated so that those with higher incomes paid a proportionally higher tax; (3) postal savings banks; and (4) government ownership of railroads, the telegraph, and the telephone. In addition, there were supplementary resolutions. These proposed the introduction of the secret ballot, the use of the initiative and referendum (page 744), the eight-hour day for government workers, restriction of undesirable immigration, a single term for the President, and direct election of United States senators. These demands sounded radical in 1892, but it is interesting to note that most of the suggested reforms have since been accepted as part of our political and economic system. The Populist convention chose James B. Weaver as its presidential candidate.

Cleveland returns as President in 1892. The logical Republican candidate was President Harrison, who was nominated on the first ballot. The Republican platform favored the protective tariff. It tried to straddle the silver issue, however, because the western Republicans demanded the free and unlimited coinage of silver, while the eastern Republicans insisted upon the gold standard.

As for the Democrats, Grover Cleveland, who had returned to private life, was the outstanding man of the party. Certain Democratic leaders were against nominating him, but the Democratic convention chose him on the first ballot. In the election, the Democrats won a sweeping victory. Cleveland had a popular plurality of 380,000 votes, and an electoral vote of 277 to 145 for Harrison and 22 for Weaver. For the first time since the election of Lincoln, the Democrats were in control of both houses of Congress as well as the Presidency. The Populists had made an impressive showing, nevertheless. Altogether, they polled more than a million votes, carried a number of western states, and in Kansas elected the entire Populist ticket. Ten Populist representatives and five senators were sent to Washington. The Populists added solidly to their vote in the congressional elections of 1894, and before the next presidential contest, people who believed in Populist principles succeeded in winning control of the Democratic Party.

Cleveland experiences his "luckless years." Cleveland had to face one difficulty after another during this second administration. Liberal spending by the Republicans had exhausted the surplus, and the Treasury was empty. On important measures such as currency and the tariff, the country — and the Democratic Party — were sharply divided along sectional lines. Before Cleveland was inaugurated, a panic had taken place on the stock market, and during his entire administration the country was in the grip of a depression (page 375). Banks closed their doors and business houses were ruined. The unemployed walked the streets of the cities, and under "General" Jacob Coxey even marched on the capital to demand relief.[3] As the party in power, the Democrats were held responsible for the depression.

The President is criticized everywhere. Everything that Cleveland did seemed to antagonize some group or some section of the country. When he took steps to bolster up the dwindling government reserves and to maintain the gold standard (page 409), the South and West heaped abuse upon his head. Though his party controlled both houses of Congress, he could not carry out the pledge of tariff reform (page 381). The labor groups were antagonized when the Pullman strike was put down by federal injunction backed by federal troops (page 394). Cleveland's foreign policy, which almost involved the nation in war with Great Britain over the Venezuelan boundary, also drew heavy criticism (page 473).

[3] Coxey led a group of unemployed from Ohio to Washington to get government relief. When he and two others were arrested for trespassing on the Capitol lawn, his "army" broke up.

"General" Jacob Coxey is here being led away from the Capitol steps by police. His "army" of about 500 unemployed Ohioans, weary and hungry after their march to Washington, mingled with the crowd and dispersed.

Conditions were bad enough to try even the greatest of leaders, and Cleveland fell short of belonging to this select group. He lacked the personal charm that appealed to the masses. He was blunt and tactless. After reaching a decision, he was impatient with people who disagreed with him. His determination often amounted to stubbornness. On the other hand, he earned the right to a place among the great Presidents of the United States by his honesty, his sound judgment on public questions, and his courage in carrying out policies in spite of their effect upon his political fortunes.

——————— CHECK-UP ———————

How did Republican control give way to Democratic?

1. What new rules were adopted in the House of Representatives? Why?
2. What view of the presidency was taken by Harrison? Why was Harrison's Congress called the "billion dollar" Congress?
3. Who were the Populists? What was their program?
4. Who were the candidates and what were the results of the election of 1892?
5. Why was Cleveland's second term called his "luckless years"?

3 Feeling Runs High in the Election of 1896

The election of 1896 approaches. As the campaign of 1896 approached, the Democratic party was in a sorry state. Cleveland was denounced in strong terms on all sides. The Atlanta *Constitution*, a Democratic paper, said, "Grover Cleveland will go out under a greater burden of popular contempt than has ever been excited by a public man since the formation of the government." In fact, the Democrats were so thoroughly discredited that the Republicans boasted that their party could nominate a "rag baby" for the Presidency and still win the election. Such statements were too enthusiastic, however, for the Republican Party itself was divided along sectional lines. Republicans in the West urged the free coinage of silver, while eastern Republicans favored the gold standard. On the other hand, the Republicans had one big advantage; they had been out of power during the years of economic distress after 1893.

Free silver agitation increases. In the West, the free coinage of silver was more and more associated with the welfare of the discontented classes. Gold became the symbol of the wealthy, while silver was the coinage of the poor and toiling masses.

A writer for the *Arena* magazine said, "It is a question of entrusting Federal power to men in hearty sympathy with the great common people or to men in sympathy with Wall Street." The chief arguments in favor of an increased coinage of silver were given in *Coin's Financial School*, a handbook on free coinage, which played an important part in the free-silver agitation. Western enthusiasm for the free and unlimited coinage of silver reached the point of frenzy. As one historian expresses it, "With the enthusiasm and the sincerity of the early crusaders, the people assembled in ten thousand schoolhouses to debate the absorbing subject of the currency . . . Low prices, the stagnation of industry, empty and idle stores, workshops and factories, the increase of crime and bankruptcy — all were laid at the door of the gold standard."

"Mark" Hanna leads the Republicans. For this election of 1896, the fortunes of the Republican Party were in the hands of a capable leader — Marcus A. Hanna of Ohio. "Mark" Hanna, a typical successful businessman in politics, became interested in William McKinley. He had been grooming McKinley for the Presidency long before the Republican convention, and he lined up delegates who were pledged to support his candidate as the "advance agent of prosperity." Thanks to Hanna's efforts, McKinley was nominated by the convention on the first ballot. In its final form the Republican platform opposed the free coinage of silver except by international agreement (which the party pledged itself to promote). It also insisted that silver and paper currency be maintained at parity with gold, that is, that the government stand ready at all times to redeem silver and paper money in gold.

Bryan sweeps the Democratic Convention. Before the Democrats gathered at Chicago for their convention, it was clear that those who supported free silver would be in control. When the convention met, the silverites managed to elect one of their men as temporary chairman and to seat a contested silver delegation from Nebraska over the opposition of the gold Democrats.

"Gibson Girl"

College student

Costumes of the 1890's

They also wrote the majority report of the resolutions committee which took a firm stand for the immediate free and unlimited coinage of silver. The final speaker to support the majority report in the debate before the convention was William Jennings Bryan of Nebraska. Bryan at this time was only 36 years old. He had served two terms in the House of Representatives, where he had taken an active part in tariff and currency discussions. Nevertheless, he was comparatively unknown to the members of the convention. He had a splendid voice which carried without apparent effort through the convention hall, and he commanded the immediate attention of his tired and noisy audience. The convention hung breathlessly on the words of the silver-tongued orator as he proclaimed that while "[tariff] protection has slain its thousands, the gold standard has slain its tens of thousands." He brought his speech to a dramatic conclusion by lashing out at the supporters of the gold standard: "If they dare to come out in the open field and defend the gold standard as a good thing, we will fight them to the uttermost."

In Bryan, radical democracy had found its spokesman. The convention was carried away on a wave of enthusiasm. By the end of his speech, Bryan was the new leader of the Democratic Party. The amendments of the conservatives were voted down in a hurry, and the majority platform was adopted. Bryan was nominated for the Presidency on the fifth ballot.

The Populists fuse with the Democrats. Since the Democratic platform had adopted the Populists' chief issue, the Populists were uncertain what to do. One of their leaders wrote, "If we fuse, we are sunk. If we don't fuse, all the silver men will leave us for the more powerful Democrats." The majority of the Populist Convention endorsed the nomination of Bryan. They drew up a platform which called for "the free and unlimited coinage of silver and gold at the present legal ratio of sixteen to one." They also demanded an increase in the volume of money until there was enough in circulation to meet the demands of business and the general public

and to restore a just price level for both labor and business. The Populists and Democrats fused in 26 states.

Bryan campaigns brilliantly. In a whirlwind campaign, Bryan traveled 18,000 miles. He claimed to represent the farmers and the workers everywhere, and he skillfully tried to link the free coinage of silver with the welfare of the toiling masses. He pictured the Republican Party as the party of the bloated plutocrats, the holders of great wealth who controlled the government in their own interests. His appeal to the common people aroused the forces of social unrest, and no one could tell how deeply this might affect the final vote in November.

The Republicans are cautious. The Republicans under Hanna's direction carried on an effective but safe campaign. From his front porch in Canton, Ohio, McKinley delivered prepared speeches and answered questions raised by friendly delegations which visited him. In this way he was carefully guarded against making statements which might be used against him. Nevertheless, the Republicans were thoroughly alarmed. Powerful interests gave liberally to the Republican campaign fund, and money was spent lavishly to instruct the voters on the subject of the currency. In the closing days of the campaign, economic pressure was added to persuasion. Contracts and orders for the delivery of goods were made dependent upon the election of McKinley. Farmers were warned that if Bryan were elected, their mortgages would not be renewed. Workingmen were paid off before the election and told not to return to work in the event of Bryan's election. As one magazine observed, "Probably no man in civil life has succeeded in inspiring so much terror, without taking life, as Bryan."

The election goes to McKinley. When the final test of strength came, the Republicans won — though the shifting of a few thousand votes at critical points would have reversed the result of the election. McKinley received 7 million votes, a plurality of more than 600,000 in the largest vote that had ever been cast. The electoral vote was

SINCE JULY
WHEAT
HAS RISEN
30 CENTS PER
BUSHEL
AND IS RISING
STEADILY

AND THE WHEAT GOES TUMBLING DOWN!

"The Last Straw" for Bryan, according to this Republican cartoon, was the fact that farm prices were rising without the help of his campaign promises to farmers.

271 to 176. Bryan carried the South and West, but was unable to win a single industrial state or any of the industrial cities. McKinley, on the other hand, carried the entire Northeast. The extent of the discontent was shown by the fact that Bryan received a greater popular vote than any previous presidential candidate. Not until the re-election of Wilson in 1916 did a Democratic candidate poll more votes than Bryan in 1896.

Business enterprise is triumphant. This election of 1896 was a victory for people who owned property and for the doctrine of *laissez faire* in business. Big business, including the railroads, now had nothing to fear in the way of unfriendly legislation. In fact, as a result of the friendly attitude of McKinley and a return to high-tariff rates under a new tariff act in 1897 (page 539), business consolidation grew by leaps and bounds. Bondholders had no further

cause for alarm at the possibility of a cheapened currency. Even before the inauguration of McKinley, economic recovery had started — not only in America but in the world at large. An increased gold supply reversed the downward trend of prices, and after 1896 they began to go up. As agricultural prices rose, discontent among the farmers died down.

——— CHECK-UP ———

Why was the election of 1896 significant in American history?

1. How did "cheap" money become a sectional issue? How did the issue affect political parties?
2. Who were the candidates and what were the platforms of the two major parties in 1896? What happened to the Populists?
3. What campaign methods were used by the Democrats and the Republicans? What were the results of the election?

CHAPTER REVIEW

Terms to Understand

classified list   graduated tax
pensions   plutocrats
quorum   spoilsmen

People and Things to Know About

Presidential Succes-   Populist Party
  sion Act   Jacob Coxey
Electoral Count Act   *Coin's Financial School*
Thomas B. Reed   "Mark" Hanna
"billion-dollar country"   William McKinley
James B. Weaver   William J. Bryan
Grover Cleveland

Historic Dates to Identify

1892   1896

Questions to Discuss

1. Compare the following:

  (*a*) Cleveland's first and second terms.

  (*b*) Harrison's and Cleveland's views of the Presidency.

  (*c*) Republican and Democratic campaign methods and platforms in 1896.

2. Explain how the Electoral Count Act would prevent a repetition of the disputed election of 1876.

3. Why did the tariff play such an important role in the elections following the War Between the States? Do you think that it was given too much attention in relation to other problems?

4. Explain how Cleveland could win a plurality of the popular votes and yet lose an election.

5. Why should the Populists be in favor of (*a*) a graduated income tax, (*b*) the direct election of senators, (*c*) government ownership of railroads, (*d*) an increase in the supply of money?

Other Things to Do

1. Show graphically the popular and electoral votes received by the major candidates in the elections following the War Between the States. The *World Almanac* will be of assistance in preparing such graphs.

By this time you have probably found out how useful the *World Almanac* is as a source of statistical and other factual information. This reference is but one of several such sources. You should also become acquainted with *The Statistical Abstract of the United States* published by the Bureau of the Census. It contains much useful data on such things as population, crime, education, the labor force, and our social and economic systems generally. *The Statesman's Yearbook* is useful when you wish to look up information on foreign countries. *The Commerce Yearbook*, published annually by the United States Department of Commerce, contains much helpful material on such matters as exports and imports, wages, cost of living and other things of an economic nature. Now that we are beginning the study of recent American history, try to get into the habit of making use of these references.

2. Make a list of the most important problems which you think faced the American people during the last quarter of the nineteenth century. Make a similar list for the present day. Compare your lists with those of your classmates.

3. This chapter tells about the budget of our first "billion dollar" Congress. Try to find information on the size of our present national budget and how it is apportioned.

4. Prepare a talk on the Populist movement. Buck's *The Agrarian Crusade* will provide additional information.

Chapter 26

Pacific islanders

Row, Row, Row Your Boat

THE UNITED STATES CONTINUES ITS

POLICY OF ISOLATION

No European power or combination of powers shall forcibly deprive an American state of the right and power of self-government and of shaping its own political fortunes and destinies.

Richard Olney, 1895

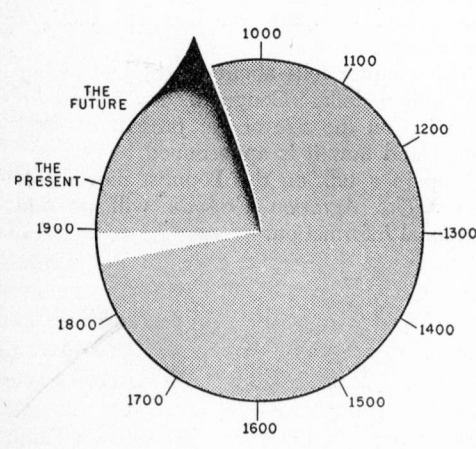

1860-1898

During the latter part of the nineteenth century, the United States seemed to lack a definite and continuous policy in foreign affairs. Indeed, American foreign policy was largely determined by the President and the Secretary of State who happened to be in office at the time.

In general, however, there appear to have been two main trends in foreign policy during this period. In the first place, the United States continued to follow a policy of isolation by avoiding alliances with other nations and by keeping foreign powers out of the Western Hemisphere. The second trend was a gradual and somewhat reluctant extension of United States influence outside the boundaries of the continent. This trend was one outcome of the growth of American industry. Though not fully understood at the time, it was a response to increasing demands for new markets for our exports, new sources of raw materials, new opportunities for investment, and protection for our growing trade.

472

In addition to these two main trends, there was a change in our relations with Great Britain. In the last half of the 1800's, the United States was involved in a number of disputes with Great Britain, arising in part from our nearness to Canada and other British possessions in the New World. Out of the peaceful settlement of these disputes and the growing realization of our common interests there grew a friendlier feeling between Great Britain and the United States.

The story of our foreign policy during the latter part of the 1800's will be told in this chapter under three headings:

1. The United States upholds the Monroe Doctrine and extends its influence in Latin America.
2. The United States acquires new territories overseas.
3. The relations of the United States with Great Britain improve.

---

1 The United States Upholds the Monroe Doctrine and Extends Its Influence in Latin America

---

The United States uses the Monroe Doctrine against the French in Mexico. The Monroe Doctrine, thanks to the support given it by Great Britain, was not directly challenged in the period before the War Between the States (page 192). It was in Mexico during and after that war that the doctrine was first seriously threatened. Because the government of Mexico was in a state of confusion, Great Britain, France, and Spain in 1861 sent vessels to Mexican ports to force the payment of debts owed to them. Great Britain and Spain soon reached an agreement with Mexico and withdrew. But Napoleon III of France thought he saw a chance to revive the great Napoleon's scheme of extending French colonial influence in the New World. He therefore proceeded to set up Archduke Maximilian, brother of the Emperor of Austria, as ruler of Mexico. At that time the United States had its hands tied by the War Between the States. Consequently, for the duration of the war, this country was able to do no more than to protest France's action and refuse to recognize the government of Maximilian.

At the close of the war, however, the United States took more vigorous action. An army was sent to the border. Secretary of State William H. Seward notified France that the continuation of Maximilian's empire, supported by French forces, endangered friendly relations between France and the United States. He demanded that the French troops be withdrawn immediately. Gathering war clouds in Europe gave Napoleon III a good reason for recalling the French troops. Maximilian tried to retain his throne without Napoleon's support, but his empire was soon overthrown. Maximilian himself was captured and put to death. Though Seward had not mentioned the Monroe Doctrine by name, its principles had been upheld, and the doctrine was greatly strengthened.

A dispute between Venezuela and Great Britain involves the United States. During the last ten years of the 1800's, a question over Venezuela's boundary involved the United States and Great Britain in a dispute which proved to be a test of the Monroe Doctrine. Between Venezuela and British Guiana lay a trackless wilderness, and Venezuela had long disagreed with Great Britain over the boundary line between the countries. When gold was discovered in this area, Venezuela insisted that Great Britain was enlarging her claims. But the British government refused to submit the dispute to arbitration, and Venezuela broke off diplomatic relations (1887). Again and again the United States vainly offered to act as arbitrator. In 1895 the American Secretary of State, Richard Olney, in a sharp communication to the British government, set forth the interest of the United States in the Venezuelan dispute. Olney claimed that when Great Britain enlarged her territorial claims and then refused to submit the dispute to arbi-

Ill-equipped Mexican Indians defeated French troops at Puebla in 1862. Their victory is still celebrated in Mexico.

tration, she had challenged the Monroe Doctrine. He further declared that the "controversy is one in which both its [the United States'] honor and its interests are involved and the continuance of which it cannot regard with indifference. . . . The United States is practically sovereign on this continent. . . ."

President Cleveland upholds the Monroe Doctrine. The British Prime Minister replied to Olney four months later. He stated that in his opinion the Monroe Doctrine was not a part of international law and that the boundary dispute had no relation to the dangers which had caused President Monroe to issue the doctrine. He insisted, therefore, that the United States had no "apparent practical concern" in the controversy. Being unwilling to let the matter rest, President Cleveland laid the situation before Congress.

Cleveland repeated his belief in the soundness of the Monroe Doctrine, stated

that it applied to this disagreement, and claimed a place for the doctrine in international law. He therefore asked Congress to vote funds for a commission to determine the true boundary line between British Guiana and Venezuela. After this commission had reported its findings, he said it would be the duty of the United States to support them "by every means in its power." Cleveland evidently meant that the United States should proceed to establish a boundary even though Great Britain had refused to submit the question to arbitration and that the United States should then compel Great Britain to accept that boundary.

The Venezuelan boundary dispute is settled by arbitration. The strong stand taken by President Cleveland aroused grave concern on both sides of the Atlantic. His warlike message was followed by a panic on the New York Stock Exchange and many business failures. Public opinion in the United States generally supported Cleveland's position, but leaders in both countries strongly expressed their desire to keep the peace. Congress promptly passed the legislation requested by Cleveland. An able and fair-minded boundary commission was appointed, which asked the co-operation of both Great Britain and Venezuela in the settlement of the dispute. Both countries agreed, but in 1897 they made the work of the commission unnecessary by drawing up a treaty which created a special tribunal, or court, to settle the boundary line. Although most of the disputed territory was awarded to Great Britain, the affair had turned out well for Cleveland and the United States.

The Venezuela dispute shows the strength of the United States. Until the end of the 1800's, the United States by itself had never really enforced the Monroe Doctrine. European powers had usually respected the doctrine, in part because they knew that it was supported by Great Britain and British naval power. It was to the advantage of Great Britain to uphold the Monroe Doctrine because her trade with Latin America was profitable and benefited from the independence of the Latin

American countries. In the dispute over the Venezuelan boundary, however, the United States showed the world not only that this country was now strong enough by itself to uphold the Monroe Doctrine, but also that we were prepared to use the doctrine even against Great Britain.

The first Pan-American Conference promotes friendship with Latin America. At the same time that the United States was displaying its growing strength, an attempt was being made to foster friendly relations and to promote American influence with our neighbors to the south. An enthusiastic supporter of closer relations with Latin America was James G. Blaine, who twice served as Secretary of State. Largely as a result of Blaine's efforts, in 1889 the first of several Pan-American conferences was held at Washington by the delegates of the United States and Latin American countries. Many topics were discussed, such as the settlement of disputes by arbitration, the establishment of a uniform system of weights and measures, and the adoption of a uniform silver coin. One important outcome of the conference was the organization of the International Bureau of American Republics. Later this became the Pan-American Union with permanent headquarters in Washington. The purpose of the Union was to collect and distribute information about the products, laws, and customs of the various Pan-American states. It has proved an important factor in encouraging friendly relations among the American republics.

Trouble with Chile creates ill-will. Unfortunately the effects of the Pan-American Conference at Washington and the friendly services of the United States in settling several Latin American quarrels were largely offset by a dispute which arose between the United States and Chile. During a revolt against the President of Chile in 1891, the American minister stationed in Chile was accused by the rebels of favoring the government in power. That same year the United States also detained the *Itata*, a vessel carrying arms from San Diego, California, to the Chilean revolutionists. Resentment against the United States flared

up. When some of the sailors from the United States cruiser *Baltimore* were on shore leave at Valparaiso, they were attacked by Chilean citizens. In the riot which followed, a number of American sailors were killed or wounded. Secretary Blaine immediately demanded an apology and the payment of an indemnity, both of which were refused. For a time the relations between the two countries were strained, but Chile finally met Blaine's demands and the incident was closed. However, the belief that the United States had interfered in the internal affairs of Chile and had used its superior power to force acceptance of Blaine's conditions created an unfavorable impression among the republics of Latin America.

——— CHECK-UP ———

How did the United States strengthen the Monroe Doctrine and extend her influence in Latin America?

1. Who was Maximilian? What happened to him? Why did French backing for Maximilian threaten the Monroe Doctrine?
2. What position did Cleveland take in the boundary dispute between Great Britain and Venezuela? How was the dispute settled? What was the significance of the Venezuelan dispute?
3. What was James G. Blaine's policy toward Latin America? What did the first Pan-American conference accomplish?
4. How did a dispute with Chile develop? What was the result of this dispute?

2 **The United States Acquires New Territories Overseas**

Alaska is purchased from Russia. Even after the era of great national expansion in the 1840's, some Americans hoped that the United States would extend its possessions still further. One such American was William H. Seward, Secretary of State under Lincoln and Johnson. When he learned that Russia wanted to sell its pos-

OUT-HOUSE)

Russian blockhouse, Alaska

sessions to the northwest of Canada, Seward hastened to draw up a treaty providing for the purchase of Alaska at a cost of $7,200,000. Instead of being received with enthusiasm, however, this proposal by Seward aroused opposition and ridicule. People called Alaska "Seward's Folly," and "Johnson's Polar Bear Garden," and one jokester suggested that it be called "Walrussia." But Seward persisted. In 1867 the Senate ratified the treaty, partly to show this country's appreciation for Russian friendliness during the War Between the States, and partly to "cage the British lion on the Pacific coast." The purchase of Alaska removed the influence of another European power from the western hemisphere. It also gave the United States possession of nearly 600,000 square miles of territory which turned out to be rich in fish, furs, timber, coal and other minerals. Even today Alaska's resources have been developed only to a small extent.

The Senate rejects expansion in the West Indies. Secretary Seward also tried to push his policy of expansion to the south. He wanted to secure coaling stations for the growing American navy and to check European influence in the Caribbean region. Therefore, in the same year that the United States acquired Alaska, Seward concluded a treaty with Denmark for the purchase of St. Thomas and St. John, two islands in the Danish West Indies. The price was to be $7,500,000. After a long delay, however, the Senate rejected the treaty. Not only did the price seem much too high, but the radical Republicans were determined to block any action which might reflect credit upon President Johnson and his administration.

Shortly afterward, an unsuccessful attempt to annex Santo Domingo was also made. A treaty for this annexation was worked out by President Grant's private secretary with the President of the Dominican Republic, but Grant could not convince the Senate that it was wise to acquire this territory. The treaty was finally rejected (1870).

A break with Spain is avoided. If the American public had been more eager to expand the nation's possessions, the United States might well have interfered in a rebellion which broke out in Cuba in 1868 and continued for ten years. President Grant wanted to back Cuba against Spain, but through the foresight of Secretary of State Hamilton Fish, a policy of neutrality was adopted. Nevertheless, American sympathy for the downtrodden Cubans was keen. In spite of official neutrality, money and munitions for the rebels continued to flow from American ports. This situation led to trouble. In 1873 a Spanish gunboat on the high seas captured a ship called the *Virginius,* which was flying the American flag and transporting men and supplies to the Cuban rebels. The *Virginius* was taken to Santiago, where 53 of those on board, including 8 American citizens, were shot. Feeling ran high in the United States, but serious trouble was avoided when it was found that the ship had obtained American registry by fraud and therefore was not entitled to fly the Stars and Stripes. The incident was closed when Spain agreed to surrender the *Virginius,* to pay damages for having seized it, and to make payments to the families of the men who had been executed.

The United States acquires Tutuila. Late in the century the United States began to show an interest in the distant Pacific. American attention was first focused on the island of Tutuila (too-too-ee'lah) in the Samoan group, about 5000 miles southwest of California. Arrangements were made in 1872 for a coaling station at Pago Pago (pongo pongo) on this island, but it was not until 1878 that the treaty was ratified by the Senate. Germany and Great Britain were also interested in Samoa, and an informal agreement to supervise the islands was made by representatives of the three countries.

A few years later Germany tried to seize complete control of these islands. In order to protect its interests, each country sent armed vessels to the harbor of Apia in Samoa. Trouble was brewing in 1889, when a sudden hurricane destroyed all the war vessels anchored in Apia except one British boat which steamed out to sea in the teeth of the gale. The tension was relieved by this disaster, and the three powers drew up a treaty providing for a joint protectorate. Later, this three-power protectorate was given up; Great Britain withdrew entirely, and received in exchange territory in Africa and part of the Solomon Islands. The United States was given Tutuila and some smaller islands. Germany retained the rest of the group until World War I, when they were taken over by New Zealand. Thus for the first time the United States departed from its well-established policy of isolation by entering into an agreement with foreign powers for the annexation of territory outside the American continent.

The United States becomes interested in the Hawaiian Islands. During this period the United States also became interested in the Hawaiian Islands, located about 2400 miles off our Pacific coast. This interest stemmed partly from the zeal of American missionaries and partly from American commercial ambitions. A move toward closer relationship with Hawaii took place in the 1870's, when the influence of American settlers in Hawaii brought about a *reciprocal trade* agreement (an agreement on tariff duties, by which both countries profit).

Baron de Stoeckel, Russian minister, stands at globe talking to Seward (seated at left) during negotiations for purchase of Alaska.

Through this agreement, sugar and other products from the islands were to be admitted to the United States without duty. Several years later, when this treaty was renewed, Pearl Harbor was ceded to the United States as a coaling station. When Queen Liliuokalani (lee-lee-oo-oh-kah-lah' nee), who was hostile to the white settlers, came to the throne, a crisis resulted. In 1893 Americans whose interests had been damaged by the McKinley tariff (page 381) used their influence to depose the queen and to set up a provisional government. The American minister to Hawaii, J. L. Stevens, aptly described American sentiment in Hawaii at this time when he wrote to the State Department: "The Hawaiian pear is now fully ripe, and this is the golden hour for the United States to pluck it."

The Hawaiian Islands are annexed. A treaty providing for the annexation of the islands was actually before the Senate for ratification when President Cleveland began his second term (1893). Cleveland, suspicious of the activities of American officials in Hawaii, withdrew the treaty and sent a commissioner to investigate the whole situation. This commissioner ordered the American flag hauled down from the government building at Honolulu. He re-

Pacific islander's home

Brigantine, Hawaiian Islands trade

ported that the native government had been overturned through fear of the armed naval forces of the United States. Matters were allowed to drift for several years. During that time, the provisional government, which was supported by the influential and property-owning class in Hawaii, was able to maintain itself until the return of the Republicans to power in the United States. In 1898, after the outbreak of the Spanish-American War (Chapter 34), the islands were annexed to the United States by joint resolution of the two houses of Congress.

As the twentieth century opened, Hawaii was organized as an American territory, and American citizenship was conferred upon all the citizens of the islands. Unlike other territories, Hawaii kept the control of its public lands and the revenue that came from those lands. Since then, under American administration, Hawaii has prospered.

––––––––– CHECK-UP –––––––––

How did the United States begin to acquire territories overseas?

1. What territories did Secretary of State Seward wish to acquire? Why? How successful was he?
2. What happened to the attempt to annex Santo Domingo? What was the *Virginius* affair? How was it settled?
3. Why has the annexation of Tutuila been called the "first departure of the United States from its policy of isolation"? What happened in Samoa?
4. What were the chief events leading to the annexation of Hawaii? What status did Hawaii acquire?

3 **The Relations of the United States with Great Britain Improve**

The Alabama claims are settled. Throughout the later 1800's the problem of American expansion was not the only one that troubled those who were responsible for this country's foreign policy. During this period the United States was often at odds with Great Britain.

The first controversy grew out of British relations with the South during the War Between the States. The *Alabama* and other Confederate commerce destroyers that had dealt American shipping a crippling blow (page 314) had been built in England and then had been allowed to "escape" into Confederate hands. After the war ended, the United States demanded that Great Britain pay for the losses inflicted by these raiders. The direct damages were estimated at about $15,000,000. Chairman Charles Sumner of the Senate Foreign Relations Committee demanded that Great Britain also pay indirect damages of more than $2,000,000,000 by turning over to the United States her possessions in the Americas. This claim was based upon the theory that Britain's failure to observe neutrality was responsible for prolonging the struggle. Great Britain, realizing that war was about to break out in Europe (1870), and fearing that commerce destroyers might be released from American ports, was willing to settle this country's *Alabama* claims.

As a result, the Treaty of Washington was signed and ratified in 1871. According to its terms, Great Britain expressed regret for the escape of the Confederate raiders, and agreed to submit the question of damages to arbitration. The court of arbitration met at Geneva, Switzerland, during the next year. The issue of indirect damages, raised by Sumner, was ruled out by the tribunal when Secretary of State Hamilton Fish was unwilling to press those demands.

The court awarded the United States the sum of $15,500,000, but awards to British claimants growing out of other parts of the treaty totaled nearly half this amount.[1] Like the Webster-Ashburton Treaty (page 216), this incident was an important step in the settlement of international disputes by arbitration.

The Bering Sea seal herd is threatened. Other disputes with Great Britain arose from the purchase of Alaska. Along with this territory, the United States obtained possession of the Aleutian Islands and acquired certain rights over the Bering Sea.

[1] The Treaty of Washington also asked the German Emperor to settle the Puget Sound boundary dispute between the United States and British Columbia. His award in 1872 upheld the American claims. In addition, the treaty set up a commission to determine the rights of American fishermen in Canadian waters. The commission's decision was unsatisfactory to the United States, and the troublesome fisheries question continued to be a source of friction between Great Britain and the United States. In 1909 the question was again submitted to arbitration and a satisfactory settlement was reached.

The first difficulty arose over the authority of the United States to protect the Bering Sea seal herd. Every year, about the first of June, these seals returned from the Pacific to the Pribilof Islands in the Bering Sea to rear their young. A great many male seals could be killed each year without endangering the herd, but the victims could be selected only on land. The privilege of hunting the seals was granted by the United States government to a single corporation. Other hunters, attracted by the profits in the valuable seal skins, came from all sides — particularly from Canada — to kill the seals in the open waters of Bering Sea and in the straits between the islands. These unlicensed hunters slaughtered the female seals as well as the males and threatened to wipe out the herd completely.

The Bering Sea controversy is settled by arbitration. The United States was interested not only in the protection of the seal herd but also in maintaining its monopoly of the seal fisheries. In the late 1880's, therefore, American revenue cutters seized

To protect seals from extermination, United States Marines were sent to Alaska in 1891. Here, a group of poachers are surprised in the act of butchering a herd of seals.

a number of Canadian sealing vessels. The British ministry protested these seizures on the ground that they took place outside the three-mile limit — the usual extent of a nation's authority under international law. The United States argued that in this special case, the Bering Sea was a "closed sea" entirely under its control. A long and somewhat heated diplomatic correspondence followed between Secretary of State James G. Blaine and the Prime Minister of England. Finally, the dispute was turned over to a court of arbitration. The chief question at issue was whether the United States had the right to protect the fur-bearing seals outside the three-mile limit. The court decided against the United States (1893), and awarded Great Britain damages of nearly half a million dollars. To protect the seal herd, however, regulations were drawn up under which the seals might be hunted. These regulations did not prove effective. Greedy hunters nearly wiped out the herd before Great Britain, Russia, Japan, and the United States in 1911 finally reached an agreement for its protection.

The Venezuelan boundary dispute marks a change in Britain's attitude. As you have read (page 473), the Venezuelan boundary dispute revealed that the United States was conscious of its growing strength and determined to enforce the Monroe Doctrine even against Great Britain. When Great Britain agreed to arbitrate the dispute, there were several reasons for her change in attitude. Her new policy was caused in part by the rise of Germany as a sea power in the 1890's. The British realized that their navy might have to be concentrated in European waters. In that case, they would need a friendly United States navy to protect their possessions and interests in the Western Hemisphere. Equally important in changing the British government's attitude was the feeling of horror which swept over the British people at the thought of war with the United States.

The Alaskan boundary is fixed. After the Venezuelan boundary incident, relations between Great Britain and the United States improved. Proof of this fact is found in the way the two countries at the end of the century reached an agreement over the disputed boundary between Canada and Alaska. The United States had acquired Alaska with the limits established by a treaty between Russia and Great Britain in 1825. Unfortunately, the language of this treaty was indefinite, especially in regard to the southeastern boundary. The discovery of gold in the Klondike in 1897 (map, page 627) made the fixing of this boundary important, because entrance to the region was gained through the Alaskan panhandle. Canada now claimed a number of bays and towns in this region. In 1903 the dispute was put into the hands of a tribunal made up of three representatives from the United States, two from Canada, and Lord Alverstone, the Lord Chief Justice of England. Lord Alverstone voted with the Americans, and the boundary was fixed in accordance with the American claims. Many Canadians felt that Lord Alverstone had sacrificed their interests to promote friendly relations with the United States. As in the case of the Venezuelan boundary dispute, the desire of the British government to cultivate the good will of the United States was present in this settlement. It is also true that the Canadian claims ran counter to the original purpose of the treaty — which was to keep Canada from deep water along the Alaskan coast.

The United States preserves its policy of isolation. The United States, then, made no striking changes in its foreign policy until near the end of the nineteenth century. It still held generally to the policy of isolation, accepting the principle stated by Washington that we should not "entangle our peace and prosperity in the toils of European ambition, rivalship, interest, humor or caprice." Even the preliminary steps to extend American influence into the Pacific failed to arouse any degree of public enthusiasm. On the contrary, our interest in Samoa caused a great deal of worry in the minds of President Cleveland and many others. Even as late as 1897 it was impossible to get the two-thirds vote of the Senate needed for the ratification of the treaty to annex Hawaii. The United States had yet to show any real interest in the scramble for empire which involved most of the great European powers.

─────── CHECK-UP ───────

How did relations between the United States and Great Britain improve despite a series of conflicts?

1. What were the points in dispute in connection with the following controversies: (a) the "Alabama" claims, (b) the Bering Sea seals, (c) the Venezuela boundary, (d) the Alaska boundary?

2. What method of settlement was used in each case? What were the terms of each settlement?

3. Summarize American foreign policy during the last quarter of the nineteenth century.

CHAPTER REVIEW

Terms to Understand

arbitration
protectorate
mediation
provisional government

"closed sea"
three-mile limit
entangling alliance

People and Things to Know About

Napoleon III
Maximilian
"Seward's Folly"
the *Virginius*
William H. Seward

Alabama claims
Treaty of Washington
Pan-American Conference
James G. Blaine

Historic Dates to Identify

1867   1871   1889   1898

Questions to Discuss

1. Compare the following:

(*a*) The original purpose of the Monroe Doctrine and the purpose for which it was applied in the Venezuela dispute.

(*b*) American territorial expansion before and after the War Between the States.

(*c*) The strengths and weaknesses of arbitration as a means of settling international disputes.

2. What circumstances which made a policy of isolation practicable in the nineteenth century have changed in our day?

3. In the disputes with foreign countries discussed in this chapter, do you feel that the United States was in the right? Give reasons.

4. Why was it that the United States was more frequently at odds with Great Britain

Questions to Discuss (Cont.)

than with other nations? How do you regard these disputes in the light of the present-day world situation?

Relating Geography and History

1. Locate on an outline map: Santo Domingo, Virgin Islands, Samoan group, Bering Sea, Aleutian Islands, Venezuela.

2. Try to account for the lack of interest in acquiring overseas territory on the part of Americans during the last quarter of the nineteenth century.

3. Explain why the United States is interested in the West Indies.

4. Compare the relationship of Alaska to Europe on a polar map projection and on a Mercator projection. What are your conclusions about the strategic importance of Alaska?

Other Things to Do

1. Debate: *Resolved,* That Alaska (or Hawaii) should be granted statehood.

2. Make a list of the chief commodities produced in Alaska. Arrange them in the order of their importance.

3. Explain to the class the chief steps in the settlement of a dispute by arbitration. Use a textbook on international relations for reference if possible.

4. The type of international agreement which was signed to protect the seal herds is known as a *convention.* What other such agreements does the United States have with foreign nations? Consult an international relations text.

TO INCREASE YOUR UNDERSTANDING OF UNIT SEVEN

Unit Summary

1. For twenty years after the War Between the States the Republican Party maintained itself in power and elected its candidates (Grant, Hayes, Garfield) to the Presidency. This supremacy was made possible in part by the military occupation of the South (until 1877). The period after the war was characterized by corruption in government.

2. Several Presidents (Hayes, Arthur, Cleveland) were interested in reforming the civil service. The Pendleton Act (1883) established a Civil Service commission and forbade the assessment of federal workers for political contributions.

3. Hard times in the late 1880's caused serious unrest in the West and South, and led to the organization of the Populist Party (1891). The 1892 Populist platform called for an increased supply of money, a federal income tax, and government ownership of railroads and telegraph and telephone lines. In 1896 the Populists joined with the free-silver Democrats to support the presidential candidacy of William Jennings Bryan. Bryan was defeated.

4. Until near the end of the 1800's the United States maintained its policy of isolation. Nevertheless the country acquired such outlying territories as Alaska, Tutuila (Samoan Islands), and Hawaii. The increased power of the United States was reflected in its application of the Monroe Doctrine to disputes over Mexico and the Venezuelan boundary. In the former, the French government was told to withdraw its troops from Mexico. In the latter, Great Britain was told that its failure to submit the Venezuelan boundary dispute to arbitration was in the nature of a challenge to the Monroe Doctrine.

5. Despite the tension resulting from the Venezuelan boundary dispute, relations between Great Britain and the United States steadily improved. Such outstanding problems as the *Alabama* Claims, control over the Bering Sea seal herd, and the Alaskan Boundary dispute were settled by arbitration.

Summary of Important Dates

1867 Alaska purchased from Russia.
1871 Treaty of Washington allows settlement of *Alabama* Claims by arbitration.

1872 The United States acquires a coaling station on Tutuila.
1876 Famous dispute over presidential election.
1877 Federal troops withdrawn from the South.
1883 Pendleton Act provides for civil service reform.
1886 Presidential Succession Act.
1887 Electoral Count Act.
1889 First Pan-American Conference held in Washington.
1891 Populist Party organized.
1893 Bering Sea controversy settled by arbitration.
1896 William Jennings Bryan defeated in the "free silver election."
1898 Hawaii annexed.
1903 Alaskan boundary dispute settled by arbitration.

Unit Activities

1. Prepare a three-column chart with the headings "Administration," "Important Events in Domestic Affairs," and "Important Events in Foreign Affairs." Summarize on this chart the chief developments by administrations between 1864 and 1896.

2. Make a four-column chart and head the columns "Controversy," "Significance," "Means of Settlement" and "Terms of Settlement." Summarize on this chart our important disputes with Great Britain.

3. Prepare brief statements on the parties, candidates, issues and results of the elections between 1868 and 1896.

For Further Reading

Original Sources

Commager, H. S., ed., *Documents of American History.* Appleton-Century-Crofts. Nos. 268, 274, 279, 281, 283, 308, 312, 317, 322, 323, 329, 332, 338, 340, 341, 342.

Commager, H. S., and Nevins, Allan, eds., *The Heritage of America.* Little, Brown. Nos. 230–232.

Pease, T. C., and Roberts, A. S., eds., *Selected Readings in American History.* Harcourt. Nos. 188, 191, 198, 201, 204, 205, 211, 213, 214, 215.

General References

Adams, J. T., *The Epic of America.* Scribner. Chapters 10 and 11.

Bailey, Thomas A., *A Diplomatic History of the American People.* Appleton-Century-Crofts. Chapters 23–30.

Faulkner, Harold U., *American Economic History.* Harper. Chapter 19.

Morison and Commager, *The Growth of the American Republic.* Oxford. Vol. II, Chapters 3, 10, 11, 13.

Special Accounts

American Nation Series. Harper. Dewey, D. R., *National Problems.* Dunning, W. A. *Reconstruction, Political and Economic.* Sparks, E. E., *National Development.*

Chronicles of America Series. Yale University Press. Buck, S. J., *The Agrarian Crusade.* Fish, C. R., *The Path of Empire.* Ford, H. J., *The Cleveland Era.* Orth, S. P., *The Boss and the Machine.*

Colby, Merle, ed., *A Guide to Alaska, Last American Frontier.* Macmillan. One of the series in the Federal Writers Project of the WPA.

Fish, C. R., *The Civil Service and the Patronage.* Harvard University Press. The standard work on the beginnings and progress of civil service reform.

History of American Life Series. Macmillan. Nevins, Allan, *The Emergence of Modern America, 1865–1878.* Tarbell, Ida, *The Nationalizing of Business, 1878–1898.*

Peck, Harry T., *Twenty Years of the Republic.* Dodd. An interesting history of the period from 1885 to 1905.

Perkins, Dexter, *Hands Off: A History of the Monroe Doctrine.* Little, Brown. The best general work on the Monroe Doctrine.

Stanwood, E., *A History of the Presidency.* Houghton. Tells of presidential administrations from 1788 to 1928.

Stone, Irving, *They Also Ran.* Doubleday. The dramatic story of the men who were defeated for the Presidency.

Biography

Bradford, G., *American Portraits.* Houghton.

Brief sketches of Blaine, Cleveland, and other public figures.

Fuess, C. M., *Carl Schurz, Reformer.* Dodd. A German immigrant who became an American political leader and crusader for reform.

Muzzey, D. S., *James G. Blaine, A Political Idol of Other Days.* Dodd. The life and career of an important Republican leader.

Nevins, Allan, *Grover Cleveland, A Study in Courage.* Dodd. The best biography of Cleveland, and a valuable reference for a study of the times.

Seitz, D. C., *Horace Greeley.* Bobbs. The life of one of the most interesting of Americans.

Werner, M. R., *Bryan.* Harcourt. The story of the western political idol.

White, W. A., *Masks in a Pageant.* Macmillan. Tells about many of the political leaders of the last quarter of the nineteenth century.

Imaginative Writing

Atherton, Gertrude, *Senator North.* Lane. Washington politics after the War Between the States.

Churchill, Winston, *Coniston.* Macmillan. Political machines during the Grant administration.

Churchill, Winston, *Mr. Crewe's Career.* Macmillan. The influence of railroad interests on an eastern government.

Ford, P. L., *The Honorable Peter Stirling.* Stitt. A novel which brings in Grover Cleveland.

Garland, Hamlin, *A Spoil of Office.* Appleton-Century-Crofts. Deals with the corruption in the major political parties and praises Populism.

Pictures

Adams, J. T., *The Album of American History.* Scribner. Vols. III and IV.

Butterfield, Roger, *The American Past.* Simon and Schuster.

Nevins and Weitenkampf, *A Century of Political Cartoons.* Scribner.

 # Sidelights on American History

How Memorial Day Began. Three years after the close of the War Between the States, an unusual request was made of the members of the Grand Army of the Republic, which was the veterans' organization of the Union forces. Their commander in chief, General John A. Logan, asked the veterans to do honor to their dead comrades by decorating the graves of those who had fallen in the war. He named May 30 as the special Memorial Day (it is also called Decoration Day), and in the northern states that date has been a legal holiday ever since.

Yet even before General Logan set the date, the custom of decorating the graves of soldier dead had been started. During the war, the women of the South were accustomed to put spring flowers on the graves of soldiers — Union soldiers as well as those of the Confederacy. Southern states also observe Memorial Day, but on dates that range from late April to early June.

After World War I the responsibility for Memorial Day exercises passed from the Grand Army of the Republic to the American Legion. The holiday honors those who fought in the Spanish-American War and in World Wars I and II as well as the soldiers of the War Between the States. In addition to the decoration of graves with flowers and flags, Memorial Day exercises may include military parades and speeches and often the reading of Lincoln's Gettysburg Address.

Log-rolling. Have you ever come across references, particularly in newspaper editorials, to "Congressional log-rolling"? The expression dates back to the days of our pioneer ancestors, but with a slightly different meaning. Settlers on the frontier could not afford to hire help when particularly heavy tasks had to be done, and besides there was little labor for hire. Many a pioneer was faced with a difficult problem of getting rid of trees that had been felled to make a clearing. Fireplace wood was plentiful; the settler had more than he needed. There were no sawmills to convert the logs into lumber and no means of shipping them to a sawmill. The easiest way to dispose of the big trees was to burn them on the spot.

Even burning was not easy. The logs had to be piled in some fashion to make a gigantic bonfire, and one man could not roll the logs into place by himself. He needed the help of at least one other man, and usually of more. So the frontiersman would call on his neighbors for assistance with his log-rolling. The neighbors were willing enough to oblige, for in another season they, too, might need help, and the favor would be returned. Two, or three, or four men working together could accomplish a task that would be impossible for one man alone.

Today log-rolling in Congress refers to another kind of mutual help. Congressmen sometimes agree to swap votes. "I want a certain bill passed. If you agree to vote for it, I'll vote for the measure that you are proposing." By helping each other, Congressmen can accomplish something that might be impossible for one man.

Sometimes log-rolling results in wasteful legislation, but it has a long, and, on the whole, respectable history in this country. A famous early example of log-rolling took place when Alexander Hamilton was urging that the federal government assume payment of the states' debts. Knowing that he would need southern support to accomplish this aim, he promised northern votes for one of Thomas Jefferson's proposals — that the nation's capital be located on the site chosen by George Washington on the Potomac River. Jefferson, in turn, promised southern votes for Hamilton's proposal. By log-rolling for each other, both men were able to secure the legislation they wished.

Death of an Empress. In January, 1927, the world in general took little notice when an old woman, over 85, died in a chateau in Belgium. But the people working in the fields round about the chateau, on hearing the news, looked at one another and said, "The empress is dead."

Yes, at one time the little old woman had been an empress — the Empress of Mexico. She was Marie Carlota Amelie, a daughter of King Leopold I of Belgium. At the age of 17 she had married Maximilian, the Archduke of Austria. A few years later, at the suggestion of Napoleon III of France, the Mexicans had invited Maximilian to come to Mexico City and be their ruler. He was given the title of emperor.

But the reign of Maximilian and Carlota turned out to be neither long nor happy. Napoleon III had tricked Maximilian into believing that the Mexicans really wanted him for their ruler. Within three years Mexico was in a turmoil of civil war, and Napoleon III withdrew his support of the young emperor. Carlota fled to France and tried again to obtain Napoleon's aid for her luckless husband. She pleaded in vain. She then visited the Pope, hoping for his help because the Holy Father had been one of the leading sponsors of Maximilian's emperorship.

Carlota was still in Italy when the bad news came from Mexico. Maximilian's affairs had gone from bad to worse. Unable to hold out against the forces of the Mexican Republic, Maximilian had been offered a chance to escape. He had refused it because he would have had to desert two faithful friends, capable generals in his little army. A trusted officer had betrayed him into the hands of his enemies, and he had been executed as a traitor before a firing squad.

The Empress Carlota — only 27 at this time — almost immediately went insane. From then on she dragged out her life in obscurity, cared for at various chateaus, and scarcely remembering that at one time she had been empress in a land across the sea.

Juarez, President of Mexico. A man of pure Indian blood is regarded by the Mexicans as one of their country's great leaders. He was Benito Juarez, who established the first really stable government in Mexico after that country had freed itself from the Spanish rule. Under his presidency Mexico enjoyed the most liberal government it had had up to that time. Juarez worked hard to improve the economic conditions of his people.

Juarez was educated as a lawyer, and he was elected governor of one of the states of Mexico. In 1858 he was president of the Mexican Supreme Court of Justice at the time that the president of Mexico was forced to flee the country during a revolt. Juarez took his place as acting president until an election could be held. At that election the Mexicans voted him into office.

Mexico had borrowed money from other countries, and one of the decisions of the new president was that no interest should be paid on this money for two years. Great Britain, France, and Spain, angered at this move, decided to collect the debts by force. Together they planned an armed expedition to Mexico. England and Spain came to an agreement with the Mexican government, but Napoleon III of France intended to do more than simply collect debts. He planned to obtain control of Mexico, throw out Juarez, and put a puppet ruler in his place. His plan was a direct violation of the Monroe Doctrine, but the United States was then engaged in its own war and could raise no effective opposition. The French armed forces were able to overthrow Juarez's government, and Maximilian of Austria was set up as Emperor of Mexico.

But the Empire lasted only three years, from 1864 to 1867. At the close of the War Between the States, Napoleon was told firmly to get his army out of Mexico, and he prudently decided to do so. After Maximilian's death, Juarez returned to the presidency, but he held it only a few years until his death.

He Sold Civil Service to America. Today an American wishing to have a government job — like letter carrier, or tax collector, or stenographer in a government agency — expects as a matter of course to take and to pass an examination which will make him eligible for the position he wants. "I have to pass my Civil Service," he will say. Chances are very good that he has never heard of George William Curtis, the man who, more than anyone else, "sold" the worth of civil service reform to Americans.

Curtis worked for reform in civil service through the administrations of five Presidents (Grant through Cleveland). He was the guiding genius of the National Civil Service Reform League. This organization of civic-minded private citizens educated the country in the value of and the need for the work of a Civil Service Commission. President Grant had created the Civil Service Commission in 1871, though actually Grant himself was not much interested in civil service reform. The commission was created to make rules for the reform of civil service, but it could not operate because no money was appropriated to keep it going. Later, when the commission received the backing of Congress, the commissioners' duty was to see that the provisions of the Civil Service Act were followed; that government officials awarded civil service jobs only under civil service regulations; that examinations were properly held; and that the names of those who passed the examinations were publicly announced.

At first both the members of Congress and the people of the country were unsympathetic with the work of the commission — or completely indifferent to it. Americans in general were inclined to scoff at the civil service examinations, saying that they were so general in subject-matter that they were no test of a candidate's fitness for a specific government position. Commission officials, it was charged, often juggled the rank of the candidates who passed examinations, in order to give their favorites an advantage.

It was George William Curtis and his National Civil Service Reform League that combatted these criticisms and finally convinced Americans that the civil service procedure was a vast improvement on the old spoils system.

Part Three

MODERN AMERICA MATURES

LOOKING AHEAD IN PART THREE

Part Three covers the events of American history from about 1897 to the present. Before you begin to read Part Three, study pages 488-491. Your understanding of the period will be greater if you know the inter-relationships among the most important events — political, economic, social and cultural.

As THE 1800's drew to a close, a Progressive Movement started. It was based on ideas voiced in part by the Populist Party and in part by liberal thinkers and labor leaders. Between the Spanish-American War and World War I, these ideas were the keynotes of American life. Politically, the object of the Progressive Movement was to take power from political bosses and captains of industry and restore this power to the people. Economically, the aim was to curb big business and give the small businessman and the workers a chance. Socially, the Progressive Movement was intended to correct some abuses which had crept into the American way of life. Presidents Theodore Roosevelt and Woodrow Wilson, and to a lesser degree President Taft, were spokesmen for these progressive ideas. Foreign affairs moved into a place of first importance. The Monroe Doctrine was given a new meaning, and our Far Eastern policy began to take shape. The period was one of economic growth and social reform.

POLITICAL	ECONOMIC	SOCIAL AND CULTURAL
1897-1901 (*Republican*)		
 **William McKinley** headed an administration which was notable for a change in American foreign policy. We acquired Tutuila, annexed Hawaii, and, as a result of the Spanish-American War, added the Philippines, Guam, and Puerto Rico. The American people approved this policy of imperialism by re-electing McKinley in 1900, but McKinley was shot by an anarchist shortly after his inauguration. The election of McKinley in 1896 had been a triumph for the businessman. A period of prosperity followed. For the time, at least, antitrust legislation and railroad regulation were very largely forgotten.	High tariff rates restored. Currency placed on a gold basis by Gold Standard Act. Gold from the Klondike region increased supply. Open Door Policy prevented commercial restrictions in China. Rising farm prices decreased farmers' discontent. "Full dinner pail" promised for workers.	Yellow fever eliminated in Cuba by Dr. Walter Reed. Associated Press formed. Extremes of wealth and poverty shown by the gilded age for the rich and slums for the poor. Population of United States reached 76 million. Two thirds of people still lived on farms or in villages.
1901-1909 (*Republican*)		
 **Theodore Roosevelt,** who became President after McKinley's death, was such a colorful and forceful figure that he dominated national politics for the seven and a half years that he was President. His popularity was shown by his triumph in the election of 1904 and by his ability to dictate the nomination of Taft for President in 1908. Roosevelt's aggressive conduct of foreign affairs increased the influence and prestige of the United States abroad. The beginning of the Panama Canal, extension of the Monroe Doctrine, and promotion of the peace movement are associated with the Roosevelt era.	Over 40 suits started to curb big business. Power to regulate railroad rates given Interstate Commerce Commission (ICC). U.S. Steel Corporation organized. Dept. of Commerce and Labor started. A "square deal" advocated for labor. Conservation program advanced. Newlands Act encouraged irrigation.	Books written protesting certain conditions: Tarbell's *Standard Oil,* Phillips' *Treason of the Senate.* Legislation promoted public welfare. Graduate School of Business Administration established at Harvard. Immigration reached highest level. Wrights flew first airplane at Kitty Hawk.

POLITICAL	ECONOMIC	SOCIAL AND CULTURAL

1909-1913 (*Republican*)

William Howard Taft, chosen by Roosevelt as his successor, proved disappointing to the supporters of Roosevelt's progressive policies. To them it seemed that Taft had allied himself with the conservatives. Yet some important progressive measures were adopted during his administration. Taft's foreign policy has been designated as "dollar diplomacy." Unable to reconcile the progressives and conservatives in the Republican Party, Taft was defeated in the election of 1912 because the Progressives formed a new party.

Tariff rates increased.
Power of ICC further increased.
Standard Oil and American Tobacco trusts dissolved.
Income tax made possible by Sixteenth Amendment.
Parcel post and Postal Savings Banks started.
Conservation program further advanced.

Bureau of Mines started to protect miners.
Legislation to protect workers, especially women and children.
Education rapidly developed. Junior high schools and junior colleges established.
Sixty-story Woolworth Building completed.
First Charlie Chaplin movies became popular.

1913-1921 (*Democratic*)

Woodrow Wilson immediately launched a program to lower the tariff, reform the currency and banking system, curb big business, and improve working conditions. Reform efforts and troubles with Mexico were forced into the background by the war in Europe. Despite efforts to remain neutral, the United States became involved in World War I, and Congress gave vast emergency powers to the President. After the defeat of Germany, Wilson persuaded the peace conference to organize the League of Nations, intended to prevent future wars. The United States Senate, however, refused to approve the treaty.

Tariff lowered.
Adequate, flexible currency provided by Federal Reserve Act.
Business further regulated by Clayton Act.
Government and business relations improved by Federal Trade Commission.
Panama Canal opened.
Government operated the railroads.
United States became a creditor nation.
Labor laws passed.

National prohibition provided for in Eighteenth Amendment.
Nineteenth Amendment established national women's suffrage.
Government encouraged vocational education.
Over a million immigrants came yearly, most from southern and eastern Europe.
First radio station, KDKA, began.
Long-distance telephone perfected.

WITH THE INAUGURATION of Warren G. Harding as President, the era of reform came to an end. The keynote now became a return to "normalcy" — to the "good old days." After a mild postwar depression, the country, during the Coolidge era, entered upon a period of great prosperity called the "golden twenties." All groups, except the farm population, shared this prosperity. Shortly after the inauguration of Herbert Hoover, this period came to an abrupt end with the gigantic crash of 1929. This, in turn, was followed by a long and disastrous depression. Meantime, we remained out of the League of Nations and of the World Court. To make sure that peace would continue, however, we drew up a series of treaties at the Washington Conference and also agreed to the Paris Peace Pact.

POLITICAL	ECONOMIC	SOCIAL AND CULTURAL

1921-1923 (*Republican*)

Warren G. Harding stood for a return to "normalcy." Much was accomplished in solving the problems of readjustment to peacetime conditions. To advance world peace and encourage disarmament, Harding called the Washington Conference. The public was shocked by revelations of corruption in the administration which reflected a low tone of public morality. On his way back from a trip to Alaska, suspecting that he had been betrayed by his advisers, Harding died.

Industrial warfare occurred between labor and management.
Farmers hurt by low prices for farm goods.
Federal budget system established.
Tax reduction adopted.
War debts funded.
Tariff revised upward, first by emergency tariff, then by Fordney-McCumber Act.

Veterans' Bureau set up.
Veterans' bonus bill vetoed by the President.
Prohibition found difficult to enforce.
Increase in gangsterism and lack of respect for law.
New flood of immigrants restricted.

POLITICAL	ECONOMIC	SOCIAL AND CULTURAL

1923-1929 (*Republican*)

Calvin Coolidge, after succeeding Harding to the Presidency, was re-elected in his own right in 1924. He stood for economy in government and noninterference in industry and agriculture. The Coolidge era is associated with the prosperity of the "golden twenties." With other nations we signed the Paris Peace Pact, agreeing not to resort to war to settle international differences. Coolidge did not "choose to run" for re-election in 1928.

Taxes and the national debt reduced.
Period of prosperity — for all but farmers.
Farm-relief bill vetoed.
Development of the merchant marine fostered.
Speculation in stocks reached high level.
Bonus bill passed over President's veto.

Immigration further restricted by quotas.
Supreme Court decisions failed to protect labor.
Great increase of automobiles and radios.
Lindbergh flew solo to Paris.
Sound movies started with *The Jazz Singer*.
Age of racketeering.

1929-1933 (*Republican*)

Herbert Hoover was a firm believer in the policy of *laissez-faire*. His good-will policy toward Latin America foreshadowed the Good Neighbor policy of the next administration. When Japan inaugurated an aggressive policy in Manchuria, a doctrine of non-recognition was announced. The domestic and foreign accomplishments of the administration were overshadowed by the stock market crash of 1929 and the depression which followed.

New high level of tariff protection under Hawley-Smoot Act.
Efforts at marketing relief for farmers were unsuccessful.
Stock market crash and depression.
War debts defaulted.
Reconstruction Finance Corporation set up to aid banks, railroads, etc.

Unemployment rose.
National income unevenly distributed.
Bonus army demanded relief for veterans.
Reports from Research Committee on Social Trends and Wickersham Committee on law enforcement.
Lewis, Mencken, and others wrote cynical books.

THE PERIOD AFTER the election of 1932 includes the vast sweep of New Deal policies, World War II, and, again, reconstruction and postwar readjustment. President Franklin D. Roosevelt was inaugurated in the midst of unparalleled depression, unemployment, and discouragement. Our whole economic system seemed about to fall apart. The President's early program was devoted to relief and domestic recovery. At the President's urging, Congress passed many laws intended to stimulate economic activity, and to prevent in the future certain business practices which it was believed had helped bring on the depression. Emergency measures were taken to help the unemployed and their families until there were enough jobs to go around. All of these efforts, and others, represented a sharp and dramatic departure from the earlier policy of *laissez faire*.

With the rise of Hitler in Germany, and the growth of a policy of aggression in Italy and Japan, the fear that we might be dragged into another war led to the passage of neutrality legislation. These laws were intended to prevent those conditions which might involve us in war. Foreign affairs grew in importance. The President recognized the Russian government, and developed a Good Neighbor policy toward Latin America. The nations of the Western Hemisphere united in a determination to resist aggression. Step by step the United States moved closer to war, in spite of its desire for neutrality, and it became involved when Japan attacked Pearl Harbor. Once again, every effort of the nation was devoted to winning the war. While the military services carried on complicated global operations, American factories and farms produced goods at unheard-of rates. As the war went on, plans were made for postwar international co-operation. This time the United States joined the United Nations. But even after the war was won, it was clear that the road to peace would be long and difficult.

POLITICAL	ECONOMIC	SOCIAL AND CULTURAL

1933-1945 (*Democratic*)

Franklin Delano Roosevelt promised the country a "New Deal." During his administration, legislation of far-reaching importance was passed. Permanent reforms and planning involved drastic changes in our traditional social and economic system. Roosevelt was re-elected for a second, a third, and a fourth term, thus breaking the two-term tradition. Foreign affairs, at first somewhat neglected because of the domestic emergency, grew in importance. In spite of the President's efforts to preserve our neutrality, we were obliged to go to war again. The President died suddenly, shortly after his inauguration for a fourth term, on the eve of final victory, but not until after plans for world co-operation had been adopted.

Gold standard abandoned and dollar devalued to raise prices. Banking system reformed. Money spent for relief. Farm relief program brought rise of farm prices. NRA set up to stimulate business. SEC designed to protect investors. Tariffs lowered. Labor aided by Wagner Act and other laws. Price control started during war.

End of national prohibition. Program adopted for relief of unemployed; CCC, PWA, and WPA established. Conservation advanced. Conservative Supreme Court transformed into a liberal one. Food, drug, and cosmetics act passed. Program of social security adopted. Fairs in San Francisco, Chicago, and New York showed modern progress.

1945- (*Democratic*)

Harry S. Truman succeeded President Roosevelt at a time when the country faced many problems, both foreign and domestic. Problems of demobilization, labor-management relations, and inflation had to be solved at home, while foreign relations, especially our relations with Russia, presented new issues. In 1946 the election of a Republican Congress widened a breach between the President and Congress. Contrary to expectations, President Truman was re-elected in 1948, and the Democrats regained control of Congress. The threat of Communist aggression led to the North Atlantic Pact and United Nations intervention in Korea.

Widespread strikes followed by wage increases. Taft-Hartley Act designed to restore balance between labor and management. Public debt very high. Removal of price controls followed by price increases. Marshall Plan adopted for European recovery. Inflation became a major problem.

Juvenile delinquency increased by war conditions. American standard of living at highest level in history. National income more equally distributed. Television perfected. More than 40 million automobiles in use. Civil rights an issue. Statement of human rights by UN.

491

A modern conservation project

THE PLAN OF THE BOOK

PART ONE *Early America Develops*	1492 to 1783	**Unit One:** Discovery, Exploration, Development of the English colonies, American Revolution			
	1783 to 1840	**Unit Two:** Framing of Constitution, The new republic, Rise of nationalism, sectionalism, and democracy			
	1789 to 1865	**Unit Three:** Economic developments, Social change and reform, Rise of American culture			
	1840 to 1865	**Unit Four:** Westward expansion, The slavery problem, War Between the States			
PART TWO *Modern America Emerges*	1865 to the 1890's	**Unit Five** Foundations of the American economic system	**Unit Six** Social and cultural developments		**Unit Seven** Government, politics, and foreign affairs
PART THREE *Modern America Matures*	1890's to the Present	**Unit Eight** American economic system today	**Unit Nine** Social and cultural developments	**Unit Ten** The United States in world affairs	**Unit Eleven** Developments in government and politics

Unit Eight

MIGHTY ECONOMIC FORCES

COMPETE FOR MASTERY IN

MODERN AMERICA

The trends in industry, transportation and communication, and agriculture which emerged after the War Between the States gathered greater force and speed during the 1900's. To such factors as rich natural resources, plentiful labor, inventive skill, and business leadership were added the methods of mass production and mass merchandising. New forms of power (electricity and the gas engine) developed new industries and speeded up old. Transportation and communication were revolutionized. More powerful business combinations appeared. Aided by machine methods of crop production, scientific research, and a broad program of education, farm output was stepped up. The United States thus became the industrial and agricultural leader of the world.

The United States has now become a country closely knit by lines of communication and transportation. The development of industry and agriculture has given Americans good jobs, the highest standard of living in the world, large surpluses for export — and the heavy responsibilities of a world power. But this same economic expansion has resulted in serious problems, too: periodic over-production, low prices at some times and inflation at others, unemployment, labor-management conflicts, questions relating to a sound currency and a wise regulation of foreign trade, and the growing need for the conservation of natural resources.

This unit tells about the forces that have made our economic growth possible, some of the problems resulting from it, and the part played by the government in insuring "the greatest good for the greatest number."

Chapter **27**

Early automobile

THE UNITED STATES BECOMES AN

INDUSTRIAL GIANT

As the United States of America entered the twentieth century there was a general feeling that the country had reached maturity. . . A dynamic America stood confidently on the threshold of an epochal period in its own and the world's history.

Foster Rhea Dulles

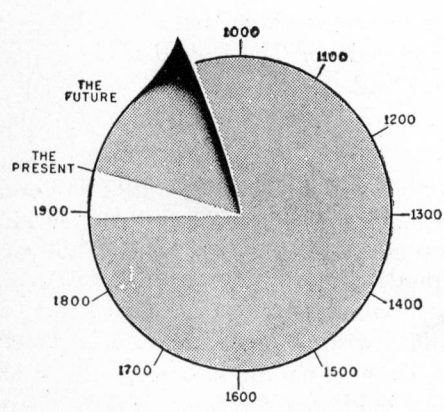

1897–The Present

During the twentieth century, the tempo of American economic development increased. Once more, transportation and communication were revolutionized. Production of farm and factory boomed. Tremendous sums of money were concentrated in certain great industries, and big business organizations continued to grow larger as they spread to new fields. Manufacturers learned the techniques of mass production and mass merchandising. By these methods businessmen were able to put countless new conveniences and comforts in the hands of the American people, generally at prices they could afford to pay. But this pell-mell growth of business also raised urgent economic problems. Some businessmen tried to corner markets for themselves and thus created serious problems for small business concerns and the general public. Panics and depressions, which had long plagued the country, became more acute and more disastrous.

This chapter tells the story of the rise of business during the twentieth century — especially the rise of big business. The highlights of that dramatic story are:

1. New forms of transportation and communication revolutionize American life.
2. Big business grows bigger as factory production booms.
3. Bad times alternate with good.

---

1 New Forms of Transportation and Communication Revolutionize American Life

---

The automobile starts rolling. Startling changes occurred in American transportation early in the twentieth century. Ever since the 1880's, such men as George B. Selden, Charles E. Duryea, Elwood Haynes, and Henry Ford had been tinkering with gasoline-driven, internal-combustion engines. Since these did not require large steam boilers and furnaces, they were particularly suitable for light vehicles designed for road travel. During the 1890's several models were tried out in Europe and America. In 1895 there were four registered automobiles in the United States. By 1900 their number had grown to 8000, by 1915 to 2½ million and by 1949 to 41 million.

Automobiles could be produced in such huge quantities because of (1) the use of standardized parts which could be interchanged, (2) the creation of many specialized jobs on a long assembly line, and (3) the inventive genius and business ability of American automobile manufacturers. These factors made it possible for American industry to turn out automobiles within the price range of the average man's income. Henry Ford did more to make the motor car popular in America than any other single individual. During the 1920's he sold a car ready for the road at a price well under $400, payable in easy installments. The Model T Ford does not seem a thing of beauty today, but it was dependable,

easy to drive, and cheap to operate. Since the 1920's constant efforts have been made to beautify the motor car and to make it a more efficient and more comfortable means of travel.

The automobile changes the American scene. The effect of the automobile on American life was so great that it is impossible to overestimate it. It created a totally new industry involving billions of dollars in capital and employing millions of workers. It stimulated the construction of hundreds of thousands of miles of expensive roads by federal, state, and local governments. Moreover, the automobile industry encouraged the growth of many industries and occupations which were related to automobile production. For instance, the prosperity of the oil, rubber, steel, and other industries depended to a large extent upon the automobile. Garages, filling stations, roadside stands, tourist camps and hotels, and other developments along the highways were only a few of the by-products of the motor age.

Motor buses gradually took the place of most of the electric railways between cities, and the buses crowded many electric cars off the city and suburban streets. They ended the loneliness of many farm families, and caused suburbs to expand rapidly as outlying areas became easier to reach. Since the buses could make use of the public highways, they were able to charge lower fares for passenger travel than the railroads, even for long journeys. Finally, motor trucks cut deeply into the freight business of the railroads, especially for short hauls or where speed and door-to-door pick-up and delivery were important.

The automobile creates social problems. The automobile actually changed American life in 150 different ways, according to a report in 1933 by the President's Research Committee on Social Trends. Not all of these changes were for the better. Probably the worst outcome was slaughter on the highways. From 1930 to 1949, deaths from automobile accidents in the United States averaged more than 30,000 in a year. Crime increased as professional criminals used the automobile in expanding their

(Continued on page 498)

THE AUTOMOBILE—
THEN AND NOW

Automobiles looked like this soon after men like Duryea, Haynes, and Ford began to tinker with them. Their changing appearance is shown by other pictures on this page. ➤

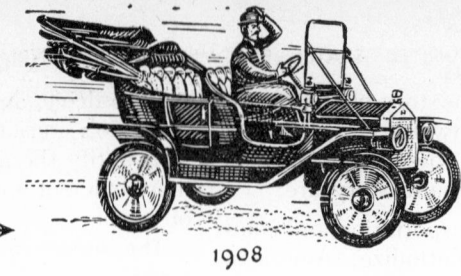

1908

INCREASE OF
AUTOMOBILE
REGISTRATIONS
(in round numbers)

1900	8 thousand
1920	9 million
1930	27 million
1950	40 million

◄ **Dusty or muddy roads** plagued auto drivers until early efforts at road maintenance began. Here, oil is being spread to keep down the dust. Compare the modern highway shown below.

Go! Go! Go!

In American communities, large and small automobiles have become indispensable. This picture shows the busy main street of Cushing, Oklahoma. ➤

1924

Highway is ↗↗

◄ GOSHEN Ha!

Fine highways, like this one in Connecticut, have speeded up traffic and increased safety. Still, congested traffic and highway accidents are constant American problems.

1931

The automobile, once a luxury, has become a necessity in the personal as well as business lives of many Americans. The chart at the top of this page shows how the number of automobiles in America has increased in the 1900's, providing jobs for hundreds of thousands of people and bringing many important changes in the American way of life.

THE AIRPLANE— THEN AND NOW

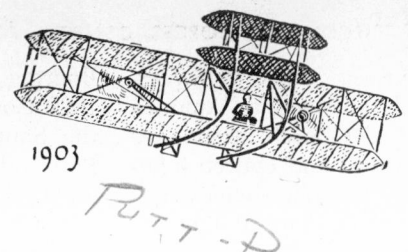

1903

Putt-Putt !

Airplanes resembled box kites in the years immediately after the flight of the Wright brothers at Kitty Hawk, North Carolina. Drawings and other pictures below show progress of aircraft design.

AIRPLANE PASSENGER MILEAGE	
(in round numbers)	
1930	103 million
1940	1 billion
1950	7 billion

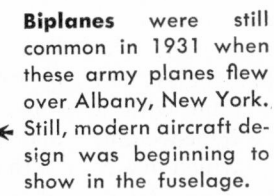

Biplanes were still common in 1931 when these army planes flew over Albany, New York. Still, modern aircraft design was beginning to show in the fuselage.

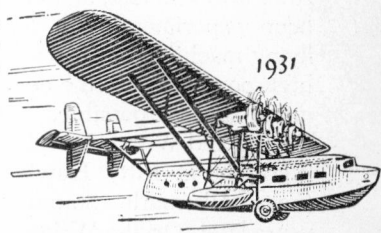

1931

Huge aircraft like the Constellation were on drawing boards when World War II broke out. They were soon produced in large numbers, and later used for peacetime travel.

484043

ET
OUR
REAR
N THERE
BUDDY!

© 1948, General Electric Co.

Military uses of aircraft became immensely important after development of the atom bomb. This picture shows the tail assembly of a large bomber.

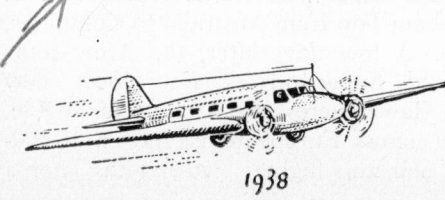

1938

The airplane by the mid-1900's had not directly affected the lives of the American people as the automobile had. Its influence in both war and peace, however, was very great. Early fears of flying were quieted in many people as American airlines ran up an impressive number of safe passenger miles (see chart above). American participation in global flight also became very important as our part in world affairs increased.

operations and making their getaways. Manners and morals changed as America took to the highways. Church attendance on Sundays was lowered and church influence was weakened. Juvenile delinquency increased when parents and social agencies lost control of the whereabouts of boys and girls.

Man conquers the air. The internal-combustion engine which sped man over the highways also lifted him into the air. The American scientist, Samuel P. Langley, had been experimenting a long time with a flying machine, but it was the light-weight, high-powered gasoline engine which finally made success possible. After many trials, Orville and Wilbur Wright made a successful flight at Kitty Hawk, North Carolina (near Albemarle Sound), in 1903. Six years later, Orville Wright flew over Washington, D.C., for more than an hour, carrying a passenger with him. Still the man in the street scoffed at the vision of the poet who

Saw the heavens fill with commerce, argosies
    of magic sails,
Pilots of the purple twilight, dropping down
    with costly bales.

But the miracle really came to pass in the first half of the century. Airplanes were used effectively in World War I, at first for scouting but later in actual combat. During the early '20's aircraft were constantly improved in design and in construction. Airports were built and regular passenger, mail, and express lines were established. The federal government helped develop air service by giving profitable mail contracts to private air transport companies.

Sensational flights stimulate interest. The interest of the American people in air travel was further aroused by a series of spectacular flights in the 1920's and 1930's. On a cold dawn in May, 1927, a 25-year-old youth, Charles A. Lindbergh, took off from Roosevelt Field, New York, on the first solo flight across the Atlantic. Thirty-three and a half hours later, after a perfectly navigated flight, he brought his plane down amidst shouting crowds that thronged Le

Bourget Field outside Paris, France. In 1929 Commander Richard Byrd flew over the South Pole. Two years later, Wiley Post and Harold Gatty circled the globe in eight days, fifteen hours, and fifty-one minutes. In the summer of 1933, Post circled the globe alone and cut 21 hours off that record. On the fifth anniversary of Lindbergh's flight, his feat was duplicated by a fearless woman, Amelia Earhart. Planes kept getting faster. In the summer of 1938, Howard Hughes, with a crew of four, flew around the world in three days and a little more than nineteen hours.

The airplane comes of age. Regular airplane service was established across the Atlantic before World War II. Commercial airlines encircled the globe, and air transportation began to rival railroads and steamships in both popularity and safety.

The airplane had become important in peace, but in war it was decisive. Germany's superior air power gave her a great advantage early in World War II. But America's all-out airplane production, together with great forward strides in construction and equipment, was vital in the defeat of the Axis. The airplane pounded Germany's cities and factories to rubble and dropped the atomic bombs which brought about Japan's surrender.

Airplane developments continue. After World War II, American planes were capable of reaching almost any spot in the world on a non-stop flight. Ocean crossings became an everyday ferry service. Transport planes reached a cruising speed of 350 miles an hour, while rocket planes equaled and passed the speed of sound — with promise of more speed to come. The speed and reliability of American planes was convincingly demonstrated by a number of outstanding flights. For example, in 1946 a Navy twin-engine patrol bomber called the *Truculent Turtle* established a non-stop record of 11,236 miles in a 55-hour hop from Australia to Columbus, Ohio. A few days later, the Army four-engined Super-fortress *Dreamboat* flew from Hawaii across the Arctic polar region, south across Europe to Egypt — a 10,000-mile non-stop flight. Two months later a commercial airliner made the trip from New York to London, over 3000 miles, in ten hours and twelve minutes.

Passenger planes were now equipped with automatic pilots and with electronic devices which made landings possible when weather was bad and visibility poor. Because of soundproofed "pressurized" cabins, flights at 30,000 feet were as comfortable as low-altitude flying. American airline operators, safety-conscious, were able to claim that a person might make a trans-Atlantic or trans-continental trip every day for a life span of 80 years without normal expectation of a fatal accident. To millions of air-minded Americans the airplane meant speed, comfort, and safety at reasonable cost.

Railroads try to meet the new competition. For some time the railroads did little about this new competition, but in the 1930's and 1940's they met the challenge by improving both their service and their equipment. They introduced luxury passenger trains — fast, streamlined, air-conditioned, and moderate in their charges. Cleanliness and comfort were increased by electrifying some of the lines and by the use of Diesel-electric engines on others. Through passenger service from the Atlantic to the Pacific was established. Freight shipments were speeded, and pick-up and delivery service was offered. In the early 1940's, largely because of war conditions, the railroads were carrying a greater tonnage of freight than ever before. After the war, fewer passengers were carried than in the 1920's, but the average trip was longer so that, actually, more passenger-miles were covered.

Wireless communication is developed. Improvements in communication kept pace with developments in transportation during the twentieth century. In 1901 the Italian scientist Guglielmo Marconi showed the possibility of telegraphy without the use of wires. Signals transmitted from England were snatched out of the ether in Newfoundland, 1800 miles away. Within a few years, wireless telegraphy was carrying messages to all parts of the globe. It was especially welcome to ships in distress,

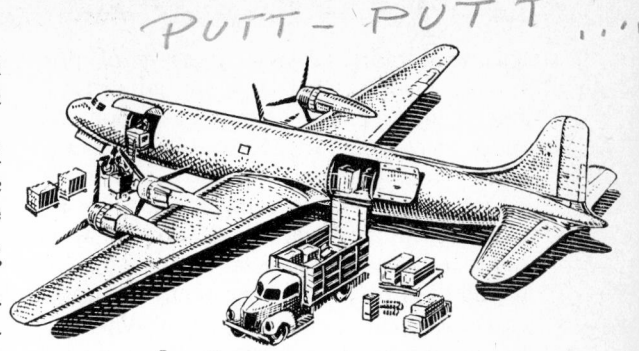

Loading an air freighter

which were now able to call other ships to help them.

The next big step was the transmission of the human voice without wires — wireless telephoning. The American scientists R. A. Fessenden and Lee De Forest played important roles in this development, particularly as it involved the use of the vacuum tube. Speech was transmitted across the ocean without wires in a successful experiment in 1915. During World War I further progress was made, and it was possible to communicate to and from airplanes by wireless telephones. Improvements followed rapidly, and by the end of World War II wireless telephone communication was a commonplace. It connected business offices with ships at sea or with speeding trains and airplanes. Even private automobiles could be equipped with two-way radio telephones. By teletype, messages could be written on a typewriter, automatically transmitted, and retyped at the receiving end of a circuit.

Radio moves into the American home. To the average person the most notable result of wireless telephony was the radio. The radio was mainly a toy for amateur scientists until about 1920, when Station KDKA in Pittsburgh became the first broadcasting station in the United States. Then the new industry grew by leaps and bounds. Other broadcasting stations were established and broadcasting systems developed. During the 1920's, radio sets were installed in nearly half the homes throughout the country. As the middle of the century approached, some 37 million homes — almost every home in the land — had at least one radio. A wide variety of programs, chiefly supported by advertisers, was available to the listener at all hours of the day and night. Music and entertainment, from operas, symphony orchestras, and serious drama to comedy and play-by-play accounts of sporting events, were ready at the touch of a button. In the hectic days of World War II, news broadcasts "scooped" the newspapers. A powerful instrument, able to reach more than 100 million Americans, was placed in the hands of churchmen, educators, politicians, and propagandists.

Television contributes to American life. Before the mid-century, television sets had made their way into many American homes. Now it was possible to see as well as hear events which were taking place miles away. Disagreements among manufacturers and broadcasters, however, temporarily held back the expansion of the television industry. Some wished to continue black and white reproduction, already well established. Others wanted to concentrate on developing color television. However, by the mid-century nearly a million new television sets a year were being put into operation around the broadcasting stations in the metropolitan areas, adding a new enrichment to American life.

Telephone service is increased and improved. The amazing development of new forms of communication was matched by a spectacular growth of telephone service and subscribers. In 1895 there were 339,500 telephones in use. By 1900, this number had grown to 1,355,900 — nearly four times the number of subscribers five years earlier. The twentieth century saw this dramatic growth continued. It was estimated in 1948 that there were 35,000,000 telephones in operation. At that time, with less than 7 per cent of the world's population the United States had over 57 per cent of the world's telephones. The telephone had become a necessity for home and business.

At the same time, telephone service was improved and new services were provided. In 1915 New York and San Francisco were linked in the first coast-to-coast long-distance telephone service. Important improvements were made in telephone equipment which speeded up and improved service. In large cities the telephone companies began supplying many special services such as information on the weather or the correct time. Dial telephones were introduced in many cities, and rates for long distance calls were reduced.

Postal services are extended. Postal service kept pace with the growing needs of the country as new means of transportation were developed. In 1896 rural free delivery (RFD) was made available on an experimental basis, and soon farmers practically everywhere were receiving mail delivery daily. During President Taft's administration Postal Savings Banks were started (1910), and post offices began to handle the delivery of packages through parcel post (1913). In 1918 air-mail service was inaugurated.

Transportation and communication contribute to the growth of business. The new means of transportation and communication and the improved older services bound the United States even closer together. They also provided a tremendous stimulus to the growth of business and industry. Without them the gigantic increase in industrial output in the twentieth century would have been out of the question.

——————— CHECK-UP ———————

How were transportation and communication revolutionized in the twentieth century?

1. Trace the development of the automobile. Why was it possible to produce automobiles in large quantities? What effect has the automobile had on American life and business?

2. Who developed the airplane? What famous flights stimulated interest in air travel? List some recent developments that have taken place in the airplane and in airplane travel?

3. In what ways did railroads meet the competition of new forms of transportation?

4. How did wireless telegraphy, radio, and television develop? What influence has each had?

5. How have telephone and postal services been increased and improved?

2 Big Business Grows Bigger as Factory Production Booms

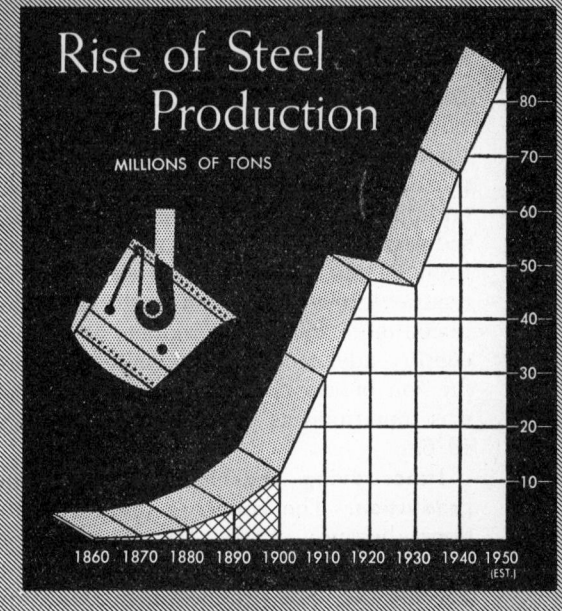

Rise of Steel Production

MILLIONS OF TONS

80
70
60
50
40
30
20
10

1860 1870 1880 1890 1900 1910 1920 1930 1940 1950
(EST.)

Output of steel, essential to industry, has reached record heights in America.

Technology expands industrial production. By the close of the 1890's (see page 359), the United States had become the world's leading industrial nation. Yet the industrial output for 1900 was small indeed compared with that of the twentieth century. The value of manufactured goods produced in 1900 was about 13 billion dollars. By 1929 this figure had increased more than five times, as over 68 billion dollars' worth of products were manufactured. In 1943, at the peak of production in World War II, manufactured products amounted to the staggering total of about 125 billion dollars. Manufacturing remained high even after the war ended; in 1947 over 97 billion dollars' worth of products were manufactured.

Another way to grasp the tremendous growth of industry is to study the figures for the production of steel, the backbone of our industrial society, as shown in the chart on this page. As you can see, the production of steel by 1950 was about 17 times what it had been in 1890.

The spectacular growth of manufacturing owed much to the effectiveness of machines and new technological processes. After the War Between the States, as you read in Chapter 19, the number of patents issued to inventors showed a marked increase. Inventions mushroomed even faster during the twentieth century. From 1900 to 1930 the Patent Office issued 1,119,000 patents — nearly three times as many as in the 30-year period from 1860 to 1890.

Perhaps the most significant technological changes in the twentieth century were brought about by the perfection of two new kinds of power — electricity and the internal combustion engine.

Great new industries promote industrial growth. The internal-combustion engine and electricity not only supplied new kinds of power; they also led to the development of great new industries. You have already seen (page 495) the tremendous changes resulting from the development of the automobile and airplane. By the 1930's automobile manufacturers ranked first among the country's industries in the number of workers employed and in the value of their total product.

Electricity was also a powerful force for revolutionizing life and industry in the twentieth century. An electric generator at the Columbian Exposition in Chicago in 1893 attracted great attention, and, in the years following, electric power was to become increasingly important. During the 1920's alone the production of electric power for use in factories and homes doubled. In 1944 the electric power produced was more than five times what it had been in 1920. Electricity turned the wheels of industry and lighted homes. It also led to the production of new manufactured products. Radios, motion pictures, electric refrigerators, electric stoves, and a thousand other new appliances were all dependent upon electricity. The total value of the electrical appliances and machinery produced in 1930 amounted to more than 2 billion dollars.

Older businesses like horseshoeing and

carriage making declined during the 1900's, but a vast variety of new industries more than took their place. The production of plastics, chemicals, and photographic equipment are just a few of the many new industries which science and technology brought into being. Each of these new industries grew larger and larger and produced more and more products as the new century advanced. For example, the production of the chemical industry in 1945 was four times as great as it had been in 1926.

Labor-saving machinery brings mass production. The country's great corporations, because of the huge amounts of money which they controlled, were able to develop the mass production methods and mass sales which are the fundamentals of big business. To attain mass production, they bought large quantities of expensive labor-saving machines. Or if they couldn't find a machine to do a certain job, they spent whatever money was necessary to have one designed. The results were remarkable. As early as the 1920's, for example, workmen using new machinery could make four times as many tires as they could have made before World War I, and the tires were better. The dial telephone system made it possible for one or two highly trained technicians to do work that had formerly called for hundreds of switchboard operators. One steam shovel took the place of the muscles of 500 men; in fact, it did jobs that could not have been done by hand at all.

Ford sets up an assembly line. One of the first companies to bring together men, money, and machines in the combination called mass production was the Ford Motor

(Continued on page 504)

HE'S HAD HIS WHEATIES
THIS MORNING !
↙ HAVE YOU ?

The manufacture of steel, backbone of any industrial nation, is symbolized (left) in a painting by William Gropper of Joe Magarac. Magarac is the legendary hero of American steel-workers, as Paul Bunyan is of the loggers. Steel-workers must still exert great strength and endurance, but more and more operations are being handled by machines. At the lower left, molten steel is being cast in ingot molds. At the lower right, a beam is being shaped by a mechanical rolling mill.

Henry Ford
(1863-1947)

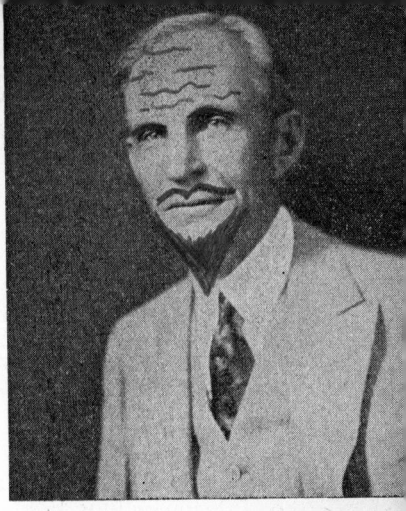

Inventor

SCREW - BALL

HENRY FORD, outstanding American industrialist, was born on a farm in Dearborn, Michigan, not far from Detroit. In his boyhood he lived a wholesome outdoor life with plenty of chores, and attended a one-room schoolhouse.

Three characteristics account in large part for Ford's success. The first was his attitude toward work. A firm believer in hard work, Henry Ford practised what he preached. When he went to Detroit at seventeen to learn the machinist's trade, he not only put in a full day at the shop but spent his evenings doing watch repairing. Even as an old man of nearly eighty, Ford shouldered the direction of the huge Ford business when his son Edsel died. But Ford had little patience with drudgery and unnecessary labor. He constantly sought to do things more efficiently.

Equally important was his interest in mechanics. Much of his boyhood was spent observing the village blacksmith, repairing farm machinery, and tinkering with engines. The sight of a portable steam engine rumbling down the road when he was a lad had much to do with his interest in automobiles.

A third characteristic was his urge to try new materials and to test new ideas. The gas engine was said to be impractical, but that did not discourage the experiments that led to the first sputtering Ford in 1893. His associates frowned on the idea of mass production of a single model at a low price, but the 15 million Model T Fords that rolled off the assembly lines between 1908 and 1929 put "America on wheels."

Industrialist

I'LL TAKE 'O OF THEM', SIR

Henry Ford opposed war and sponsored a peace ship which sailed to Europe in 1915 to "get the boys out of the trenches by Christmas." Yet the Ford plants performed marvels in the production of war materials. Ford spent much time and money in later years collecting antiques and restoring places of historical interest. But his genius lay in his chosen field. By developing the assembly line technique and by building up an industrial empire which controlled all stages of production, Ford pointed the way for America's industrial supremacy.

~~*Philanthropist*~~

EGOTIST

503

Company. Ford installed expensive machinery to make the hundreds of parts that go into an automobile. These parts were moved up to their proper places alongside an *assembly line*. A bare automobile frame started at one end of the line and came off the other end a completed automobile ready for the road. Along this assembly line, each of the many workers performed a single, specialized operation again and again. Under this system the Ford factories in the early 1920's were able to turn out 8000 motor cars each day. "By 1926," writes one commentator, "it was a matter of thirty-three hours from the time iron ore left the bottom of a Great Lakes freighter until a new Ford honked for clearance on the open road."

Mass production demands mass markets. Mass production allowed manufacturers to lower prices and still make good profits. Thus millions of Americans could afford to buy automobiles, radios, refrigerators, and vacuum cleaners. But unless millions kept on buying, these products could not be made in such great quantities or be sold at such low prices or bring in such attractive profits. To hold and extend their markets, manufacturers began to spend tremendous sums on nation-wide advertis-

Output of workers in industry has more than doubled since 1900. Why? What does this mean for our standard of living?

Increasing Output of Industrial Workers
YEARLY OUTPUT PER INDUSTRIAL WORKER IN 1900 100

| | | | | | 225 |
| 1900 | 1910 | 1920 | 1930 | 1940 | 1950 (EST.) |

ing and skillful salesmanship. Installment buying, made respectable by the phrase "buying out of future income," was widely encouraged. Then, when the home market was unable to absorb the endless output of the factories, manufacturers went after foreign markets. All over the world there were people eager to buy the products of American factories. International trade soon became vital to American industry.

Merchandising becomes big business. While manufacturers were quick to adopt big-business organization, merchandisers were slower. Marshall Field and Company, the largest department store in the world by 1940, did not become a corporation until 1901. John C. Wanamaker was the sole proprietor of the Wanamaker Stores until they were incorporated in 1907. The independent grocery, the home-owned drug-store, and the small-town variety store are still features of American life. They are pushed hard, however, by the competition of such giant corporations as the Atlantic and Pacific Tea Company, the Walgreen drug chain, Sears Roebuck and Company, and the F. W. Woolworth Company. The United States Department of Commerce estimated in 1946 that nearly 22 per cent of the nation's retail sales were handled by chains and mail-order houses. Such firms enjoy the usual advantages of big business. They can employ expert management, buy in large quantities or even build factories to manufacture the goods they sell, and cut costs on such necessities as advertising and accounting. Some of these savings may be passed on to customers in the form of lower prices. For these reasons, the small, independent merchant often can compete successfully only if he (1) cooperates with other independents to cut his costs (as in the Independent Grocers' Association, for example), (2) sells goods of exceptional appeal — as in an exclusive dress shop, or (3) gives better and more personal service than the chain stores can offer.

Industry reaches the Far West. American industry was not only growing in size; it was also reaching out to all sections of the country. In 1940 California stood seventh among the states in the value of its industrial products. The Los Angeles, San Francisco, and Seattle areas ranked high among the industrial centers of the country. The rapid growth of the aircraft and other industries in the Far West during World War II had much to do with the fact that this section increased in population faster than any other part of the country during the 1940's.

In 1890, as you saw (page 360), the center of manufacturing in the country was in the middle of Ohio. By 1930 it had reached Chicago, and in the 1940's the midpoint moved still farther westward.

Industry continues to increase in the South. The expansion of industry in the South which began in the last part of the 1800's continued increasingly in the twentieth century. By 1912 more cotton products were being manufactured by southern mills than by those in New England. The iron and steel industry, which was centered in Birmingham, Alabama, continued to grow in importance. During the first third of the twentieth century the South led the nation in the production of lumber.

A new phase of southern economic development began just after the turn of the century, when rich oil fields were discovered along the Gulf Coast of Louisiana and Texas. In time, the oil fields were found to extend into the interior. First Oklahoma, and later Texas, took the lead among the states of the Union in the production of crude petroleum.

Big business forms new combinations. The enormous growth and spread of industry led to the development of bigger and bigger corporations. It also led businessmen to seek new forms of business organization which would cut down competition and enable them to get a larger share of the market. After trusts "that restrained trade" were declared illegal (page 388), a favorite form of business organization was the *holding company.* The holding company is a corporation which does not operate a business of its own, but exists only to buy and "hold" shares of stock in other corporations. The stock makes the holding company part owner of the other corpora-

The Far West was converted from a land of raw frontiers to a complex industrial society. This picture shows Tacoma, Washington.

tions and brings all of them under the same control. A prominent illustration of a holding company is the American Telephone and Telegraph Company, which owns the stock of the Bell System and other operating companies. Holding companies became especially popular as a method of controlling prices, reducing competition, and securing the most economical type of operation among railroads, mines, and public utility companies. [1]

Another method of cutting down competition within a field of industry was the system of *interlocking directorates,* in which the same men acted as directors of different corporations. In the late 1920's, for example, the directors of the New York Central Railroad were said to hold more than 300 directorships in other corporations.

Business consolidation continues. The government passed laws to break up monopolies and to prevent big business combina-

[1] A public utility company is one which performs an important public service, such as supplying gas, electricity, or transportation.

505

tions (pages 388, 514). Nevertheless, the attempts to slow down the pace of business consolidation were not really successful. During the '20's there were mergers of automobile manufacturers, power companies, banking firms, food producers, motion picture makers, and other businesses. In 1941, a list of 30 corporations with assets[2] of more than one billion dollars included a number of railroads, banks and life insurance companies, together with General Motors, United States Steel, Standard Oil of New Jersey, and the American Telephone and Telegraph Company. The American Telephone and Telegraph Company had grown from a $100,000 concern in 1885 to be one of the largest business organizations in the world, with assets of 4 billion dollars. World War II resulted in the further growth of great corporations and a further consolidation of industry. But, even the figures in this paragraph underestimate the real concentration of financial and industrial power. Through holding companies and interlocking directorates, a few financiers were able to control a very large proportion of the nation's industrial resources.

Small manufacturers are still important. Despite the growth of big business in the United States, the small manufacturer was still an important figure. In 1940, for example, about 20 per cent of our manufacturing establishments had no more than 20 employees. All these plants put together, however, produced only about 5 per cent of the manufactured products, and employed less than 10 per cent of the nation's wage earners. At the other extreme, less than one per cent of the factories turned out 40 per cent of the country's goods and employed nearly a third of the wage earners. Thus, in volume of production big business was far ahead of small manufacturers.

Cartels control international trade. Big business combinations were not confined to a single nation. Sometimes, all the large

[2] The term *assets* refers to all the resources of a company: cash, real estate, buildings, machinery, inventories on hand, money owed to the company, and so on.

firms in the world which were selling such a product as rubber, aluminum, or sugar made an agreement to divide up sales territories and thus control prices in a large part of the world. Such an agreement was called an international *cartel*. Before World War II, it was estimated that cartels dominated nearly 90 per cent of the mineral products, 60 per cent of the agricultural products, and more than 40 per cent of the manufactured goods in international trade.

——— CHECK-UP ———

Why did big business grow bigger?

1. What changes took place in the value of manufactured goods in the twentieth century? What effect did inventions have on the growth of industry?
2. What new forms of power were perfected in the 1900's? What new industries did they help develop? How did other new industries help increase production?
3. How did labor-saving machinery affect production? What is an assembly line?
4. How did mass production help develop mass markets? What changes took place in merchandising?
5. What developments took place in industry in the Far West? In the South?
6. What new business organizations were formed? What happened to the size of business in the 1900's? What place did cartels have in international trade?

3 **Bad Times Alternate with Good**

Business activity rises and falls. American business went through the same kind of ups and downs during the twentieth century that it had experienced in the nineteenth. After McKinley took office as President in 1897, the depression of the early '90's lifted. For the next ten years the whole country enjoyed great prosperity. Then, late in 1907, there was a short financial panic. Beginning with the failure of the Knickerbocker Trust Company and several other banks in New York City, the crisis spread rapidly to other parts of the nation. Since the business of the country was essentially sound, however, unemployment was temporary and did not spread far outside a few great industrial centers. Business prospects were not good in 1914, but the outbreak of World War I brought a heavy demand for supplies, and a period of war prosperity followed. After the demand for war supplies had fallen off, a minor depression followed in 1920–1921. Prices fell off, unemployment increased, and an epidemic of strikes broke out. No financial panic accompanied this depression, however, and in a short time business adjusted itself again.

Prosperity creates the "golden twenties." Then came the greatest outburst of prosperity that the country had ever experienced. During the so-called "golden twenties," industrial activity expanded enormously, while incomes and profits rose to new heights. Many people predicted that this new era of prosperity would never end. The business boom was accompanied by a wave of fantastic speculation. Prices of stocks kept going up and up. Dazzled by hopes of easy riches, more and more people began to dabble in the stock market. Many a purchaser hardly stopped to think about the true value — the earning power — of the company whose stock he bought. He was sure that stock prices would continue to go higher and higher, and that whenever he bought stock he would be able to resell it at a profit.

Panic and depression grip the nation. This boom of the '20's ended in a panic "of unexampled violence." It was caused chiefly by overproduction and too much speculation. Late in October, 1929, the prices of even high-grade stocks on the New York Stock Exchange went plunging downward from 20 to 40 points (dollars per share) in a single day. Within two weeks, the market value of stocks on the Exchange decreased by 25 billion dollars. But this was only the beginning. The value of the stocks listed on the Exchange was nearly 90 billion dollars in September, 1929.

Galloway

Business and industry continued to grow in the South in the 1900's. This picture shows part of Birmingham, Alabama, heart of the southern steel industry.

By July, 1932, it had melted to 15½ billion.

A long and tragic depression followed this financial collapse. There were several reasons why it lasted so long and became so severe:

(1) Constant improvements in labor-saving machinery had thrown many people out of work. This state of affairs is called *technological unemployment.* When people are without jobs, they are unable to buy their normal share of the goods produced by industry.

(2) Workers were receiving a small share of the total national income. *Real wages,* that is, wages measured in terms of what they will buy, were low. For that reason, wage earners could not buy enough manufactured goods to keep the factories busy. Moreover, many people went far into debt by purchasing anything and everything on installments. When they couldn't meet their payments, their goods were taken away and put back on the market.

(3) The purchasing power of the farmer was sharply restricted, even during the prosperous years following 1921 (page 555). He, too, was unable to buy his share of factory-made goods.

Once started, the depression kept whirl-

Industry began humming again as orders for war supplies began coming in during the latter years of the 1930's. This machine and operator are performing a "drawing" operation in the textile industry, one of the largest in the United States.

ing in a vicious circle. A decline in business activity resulted in further unemployment; unemployment meant a further reduction in purchasing power; a decline in purchasing power caused a further slump in industrial production; and so on.

The New Deal "primes the pump." After the inauguration of the New Deal [3] by President Franklin D. Roosevelt in 1933, business activity again started slowly on an upward spiral. This recovery was brought about in part because Congress appropriated billions of dollars to "prime the pump" of industry — that is, to get purchasing power back to work. By 1937 business was approaching normal. Then the reduction of government expenditures and labor difficulties helped cause a "recession" which began in the summer of 1937. Private industry, alarmed by the New Deal program, hesitated to push ahead. Unemployment figures again began to rise. The government was disturbed because it had not accomplished the recovery which had

[3] When Franklin D. Roosevelt became President in the midst of the great depression, he declared that the country needed a "new deal." The legislation which was passed under his leadership during the next few years is called the "New Deal."

seemed to be "just around the corner," and it began once more to pour out money in an effort to stimulate industry. The curve of business activity again swung upward, but in an irregular fashion.

World War II revives industry. The outbreak of World War II in Europe brought an end to the New Deal's efforts to overcome the depression. As war industries speeded up, unemployment was gradually replaced by a sharp shortage of manpower. After the United States entered the war, industrial production reached unheard-of heights. Wages and profits rose. The national income, which had fallen below 40 billion dollars in 1932, reached 180 billions a year at the height of the war.

Postwar business thrives. The end of the war was followed by another great burst of industrial activity. Labor held, and even improved, the high level of wages won during the war. Employment reached the high figure of over sixty million jobs. As a result, labor was getting a larger share of the national income than ever before. Workers could now buy the products of industry in large quantities, and factories were kept humming. During the war, the production of houses, automobiles, electric appliances, and other consumer goods had been halted or greatly restricted. Thus so great a backlog of demand was built up that industry seemed unable to meet it. The result was that industrial production reached new peacetime levels. Prices were high, some of them twice what they had been before the war, but many workers had the money to pay the prices. So did many farmers, for the farm income was four times what it had been before the war. Also, some of the weaknesses of the boom period of 1929 were absent. Speculation was not in evidence. The high inventories (stocks of goods) of the earlier period were avoided. In the late 1940's, the national income reached a mark well above 200 billion dollars. At this time, the American people were able to enjoy a higher standard of living than ever before — higher, in fact, than any people had enjoyed at any previous time.

——— CHECK-UP ———

How prosperous has American business been in the 1900's?

1. Trace the rise and fall of prosperity in the United States from 1897 to 1950.
2. What effect did World War I have on business? What important trends in busi-

ness activity occurred during the "golden twenties"?

3. What were some of the chief causes of the great depression after 1929?
4. What was the New Deal program for stimulating industry? What finally brought about business recovery?
5. Why did business thrive after World War II?

CHAPTER REVIEW

Terms to Understand

internal-combustion engine
assembly line
non-stop flight
rocket plane
wireless telegraphy
two-way radio
teletype
mass production
merchandising

holding company
interlocking direc-
   torates
cartels
"golden twenties"
technological unem-
   ployment
real wages
overproduction
"priming the pump"

People and Things to Know About

Henry Ford
Samuel P. Langley
Orville and Wilbur
   Wright
Charles A. Lindbergh
Amelia Earhart
Guglielmo Marconi

KDKA
RFD
Postal Savings Banks
parcel post
Panic of 1907
Panic of 1929
New Deal

Historic Dates to Identify

1903   1907   1920
1927   1929

Questions to Discuss

1. Name several technological developments which were the result of our need for mass-production during World War II. Were any new industries brought into existence?
2. Compare the following:
   (a) Rural life before and after production of the Model T Ford.
   (b) Transcontinental passenger transpor-

Questions to Discuss (Cont.)

tation before and after establishment of major airlines.
   (c) Outstanding passenger trains before World War I and today.
3. Which of these forms of transportation has done most to change ways of living in the United States? (a) The railroad, (b) The automobile, (c) The airplane.
4. How is television affecting other forms of recreation — attending sports events, going to the movies, listening to the radio, reading.
5. How has the telephone changed everyday living in the United States? How has it changed business practices?
6. What conditions make the United States a leader in mass production?

Other Things to Do

1. Find in the library a copy of the report made by the President's Research Committee on Social Trends. Tell the class about some interesting statements made by this committee.
*2. Report to the class on the achievements of some pioneer or present-day leader in aviation. If you live near an airport you may be able to make arrangements with the manager so that your class may visit the airport.
3. Find someone in your community who has worked on an assembly line. Ask him to report his experiences to the class. What questions will you want to ask him?
4. Debate: Resolved, That big business has eliminated competition from industrial production and the distribution of products.

Railroad switchman

Chapter 28

THE GOVERNMENT RESTRAINS BIG

BUSINESS BUT AIDS LABOR

The biggest corporation, like the humblest citizen, should be held to strict compliance with the will of the people as expressed in the fundamental law.

Theodore Roosevelt

When I am fighting monopolistic control . . . I am fighting for the liberty of every man in America, and I am fighting for the liberty of American industry.

Woodrow Wilson

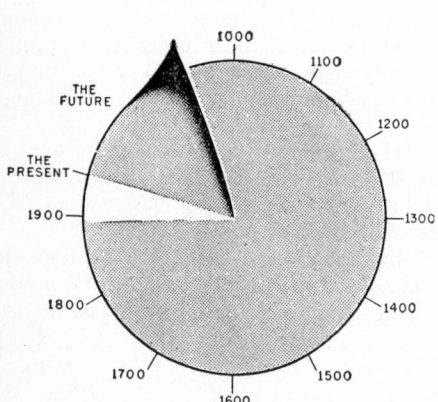

1897–The Present

In the early twentieth century, a powerful reform movement gained popular support that was not limited to either the Democratic or Republican Party. This reform movement was directed chiefly toward curbing the power of big business. It sprang from the widespread belief that for the good of the general public something must be done to (1) curb the power of the growing trusts and (2) correct the abuses which existed in our great transportation system (page 385).

Reform leaders found a ready champion in Theodore Roosevelt, the vigorous Republican President who held office from 1901 until 1909. Some of Roosevelt's enemies painted him as an enemy of big business. Actually, he was not. But he favored a control and supervision of big business "within reasonable limits." President Taft's attitude toward big business was similar to that of Theodore Roosevelt. But Taft's successor, President Wilson, modified their program somewhat. Wilson's aim was to bring about reform through a better understanding between government and business. During the Republican administrations of the "golden twenties" there was a lull in the attempts to bring big business under control, but under the New Deal, during the thirties, the government seemed to reach into every phase of business.

Meanwhile, organized labor was showing increased strength. In the early years of the century, the working man was at a disadvantage in bargaining power. By the middle of the century, however, the picture had changed so much that some people thought that the forces of labor were in the driver's seat. At this time 15 million or more Americans were numbered among the ranks of organized labor.

The story of the tug-of-war during the 1900's between big business and the American public as well as the struggle between labor and big business will be told under the following headings:

1. President Theodore Roosevelt vigorously attacks big business.
2. Government changes its policy toward big business.
3. The New Deal extends government control.
4. Government effectively regulates transportation and communication.
5. The needs of labor receive government consideration.
6. Labor grows strong under the New Deal.
7. New labor problems follow World War II.

President Theodore Roosevelt Vigorously Attacks Big Business

Big business grows bigger and stronger than ever. The last years of the nineteenth century and the first of the twentieth were favorable times for big business. Big business had been afraid that radical or reform ideas might control the national government, but the defeat of Bryan and the election of McKinley completely removed this fear. Under McKinley, the depression of the early 90's gave way to a rush of prosperity. The Spanish-American War in 1898 led to a still greater increase in business activity.

Under these favorable conditions business not only prospered, but grew bigger and bigger. The Sherman Antitrust Act had not proved effective (page 388), and the McKinley administration made no great effort to enforce it. As a result, a tremendous number of new business combinations and trusts were formed. In 1896 there were only 12 big business combinations, with a total capital of one billion dollars. By 1904, more than 300 big business combinations had been brought into being with a combined capital of nearly 7 billion dollars.

As big business grew bigger, the small businessman found it increasingly difficult to compete, particularly when the giant corporations used their power — often unfairly — to create monopolies and to drive small manufacturers out of business.

The "muckrakers" arouse public opinion. Within a short time, however, the attacks on big business combinations and trusts were renewed with increasing vigor. A number of writers early in the twentieth century used the magazines to help arouse the indignation of the American public. These writers exposed the vast power and the selfish policies of certain businessmen, as well as corrupt scheming between business and government officials. Ida M. Tarbell's "History of the Standard Oil Company" began to appear in *McClure's Magazine* in 1902. In this work Miss Tarbell exposed the company's methods in killing competition and in dealing with the public and the government. *McClure's* also published Lincoln Steffens' "Shame of the Cities." A first-rate reporter, Steffens gave names and places as he described the shocking way in which local governments had been corrupted by big business. In a

"Trust-Buster" Theodore Roosevelt beams from the window in this cartoon as the head of his Bureau of Corporations squeezes alleged excessive profits out of the trusts.

magazine called *Everybody's*, Thomas Lawson's "Frenzied Finance" laid bare to the public the dishonest workings of the stock market. *Cosmopolitan Magazine* printed a series of articles called "The Treason of the Senate" by David Graham Phillips, in which he claimed that the great majority of United States Senators were favoring railways, the beef or sugar trusts, the oil or steel combinations, or other special interests.

This "literature of exposure" also included several outstanding novels. *The Jungle*, by Upton Sinclair, revealed shocking conditions in the meat-packing business. Frank Norris's *The Octopus* brought to public attention the control the railroads held over rural political and economic life. Another effective book was Winston Churchill's [1] *Coniston*, which described corrupt relationships between business and the political machines of large cities.

All these writings were based upon facts, but many others less truthful were published in an effort to create a sensation. Because some of these authors went too far

[1] This Winston Churchill was an American novelist, not the British statesman.

in their enthusiasm to reveal greed and corruption, the label of "muckraking" was applied to the whole movement. Nevertheless, the "muckrakers" performed a real service in drawing public attention to some sore spots in American life.

President Theodore Roosevelt earns the title of "trust-buster." The literature of exposure accomplished another important result. It helped win the support of President Theodore Roosevelt, who was quick to sense the development of a popular movement. Early in 1902, he shocked the business world by instructing his Attorney General to bring suit against the Northern Securities Company as an illegal monopoly. This powerful holding company had been organized by James J. Hill, with the help of J. P. Morgan and E. H. Harriman, in order to get control of three rival railroads in the Northwest. The case ended two years later, when the Supreme Court decided by a five to four vote that the company was a "combination in restraint of trade," and that it should be broken up.

This decision greatly increased the President's prestige among the people, though not among the leaders of industry. It also encouraged the Attorney General to continue prosecuting the trusts. Congress cooperated by appropriating money to enforce the interstate commerce and antitrust laws. It also speeded the breaking of trusts by passing the Expedition Act (1903), which gave antitrust suits the right of way in the federal courts. By another measure, a Department of Commerce and Labor was created, with a secretary in the President's Cabinet. The Department included a Bureau of Corporations to investigate the affairs of large industrial combinations. For his activities in fighting big business, Roosevelt earned the nickname of "trust-buster."

"Trust-busting" continues. Encouraged by his overwhelming victory in the election of 1904, Theodore Roosevelt continued the battle against what he called the "malefactors of great wealth." A case against the beef trust was carried to a successful finish. As a result of facts uncovered by the Bureau of Corporations, proceedings were also started against the Standard Oil Company of New Jersey and the American Tobacco Company. Eventually both companies, as they existed at that time, were broken up by the Supreme Court. Altogether, over 40 court actions against big business organizations were begun during Theodore Roosevelt's term of office.

Public health is protected. Closely connected with "trust-busting" was the passing of laws to protect the public from harmful products. As a result of Upton Sinclair's disclosures in *The Jungle*, Congress appointed a commission to investigate the stockyards and meat-packing houses of Chicago. This led to the passage of the Meat Inspection Act (1906). This law authorized federal authorities to see that meat shipped in interstate commerce came from healthy animals and was packed under sanitary conditions.

In the same year, a Pure Food and Drugs Act prohibited the "manufacture, sale, or transportation of adulterated or misbranded or poisonous . . . foods, drugs, medicines, and liquors." Makers of patent medicines were required to put a label on containers, stating the true character of the contents. Moreover, the manufacturers were prohibited from using in their products any harmful substance.[2]

Big business opposes Roosevelt. While Theodore Roosevelt's efforts to control big business brought praise from the public, they aroused hostility among business leaders. When the Panic of 1907 occurred, the President's critics were quick to put the blame on his policies. "We who are about to bust salute thee!" cried the New York *Sun*. But Roosevelt refused to change his stand. He compared the attitude of his opponents to that "of a man who, having a cancer which can be cured by the use of the knife, nevertheless screams and refuses to submit to an operation because he knows there will be temporary pain and discomfort."

President Taft continues Roosevelt's antitrust policy. William Howard Taft, who

[2] In 1939 federal food and drug control was extended to include cosmetics and to prevent "false and misleading" advertising of such products.

succeeded Theodore Roosevelt as President in 1909, continued the policy of trying to break up and regulate giant industrial combinations. In fact, Taft's Attorney General started nearly twice as many antitrust suits as had been begun during the Roosevelt administration. Taft also prosecuted vigorously the antitrust suits that had already been undertaken by President Roosevelt. It was during Taft's term in office (1911) that the important cases against the Standard Oil Company and the American Tobacco Company were brought to a successful conclusion and the trusts dissolved.

--------- CHECK-UP ---------

What did President Theodore Roosevelt do about big business?

1. What developments took place in big business in the late 1890's and early 1900's?
2. How did writers help to arouse public opinion against trusts?
3. What action against trusts was taken under Theodore Roosevelt?
4. What laws were passed to safeguard public health?
5. What policy toward business did President Taft follow?

2 Government Changes Its Policy Toward Big Business

"Trust-busting" fails to stop monopolies. There were several reasons why legal prosecution of big business and monopolies was unsatisfactory. For one thing, prosecuting trusts in the courts was like locking the barn door after the horse had been stolen. At best, it punished rather than prevented activities that hurt the public welfare. Very often, too, illegal practices could not be proved to the satisfaction of the courts. Moreover, even if the government won its case and the trust was dissolved, the monopoly might continue in other forms. For example — as we have seen — both the Standard Oil Company and the American Tobacco Company were dissolved by Supreme Court decision. But the separate units into which they were divided went right on managing their affairs through a "community of interest" in such a way that competitors still found it very difficult to hold their own against them.

The government begins to distinguish between good and bad combinations. In the early years of the century, the muckrakers had aroused public opinion against the abuses of big business in general. Many people became opposed to all business combinations and wanted the "malefactors of great wealth" punished. Although Theodore Roosevelt vigorously attacked big business and business combinations, more and more he began to make a distinction between those combinations which were merely big, and those which were actually harmful to the general public. He asked Congress to pass laws telling which business practices were fair and which unfair, but Congress took no action.

In 1911, during President Taft's administration, however, the Supreme Court made two significant decisions which bore out the distinction that Roosevelt had tried to make. Although in these decisions the Court ruled against the Standard Oil and American Tobacco companies, it laid down an important principle — the "rule of reason" — which it said should be used in judging business combinations. The "rule of reason" declared that only those combinations were illegal which were "unreasonable" and "which would constitute an interference that is an undue restraint" of trade. Nine years later (1920), the Supreme Court went even further. It refused to dissolve the United States Steel Corporation, declaring that it did not use any unfair methods of competition, and that size alone was no reason for dissolving a corporation.

President Wilson secures the passage of two new laws. By the time Woodrow Wilson became President (1913), the muckraking days were past and it was more clearly recognized that not all big business was bad. People began to see that large-scale production and efficient transportation and communication could result from business combinations which would be in the interest of the public.

President Wilson was honestly opposed to monopolies and the evils which they often brought. He felt, however, that the way to eliminate the bad features of big business was not just to prosecute the trusts in the courts and to break them up. Instead, he believed that government should define unfair practices and regulate big business so that such practices would not develop. Under the existing law, however, neither the corporations nor the government knew which business practices the courts would consider "reasonable" and which unfair. In 1914, therefore, President Wilson asked for and secured the passage of two new laws — the Federal Trade Commission Act and the Clayton Antitrust Act.

Both of these laws were intended to prevent unfair competition and unlawful combinations from developing rather than to break up monopolies and trusts after they had been formed.

The Federal Trade Commission is created. The Federal Trade Commission, which was created by Congress in 1914, was authorized to advise and regulate corporations engaged in interstate or foreign commerce. It could order a corporation to stop unfair methods of competition. If the order was not obeyed, the commission could apply to a court for aid in enforcing the ruling. The commission was designed to bring the knowledge and advice of economic experts to the aid of both the corporations and the courts. These methods were intended to prevent the growth of monopolies which the Attorney General might later have to prosecute. They brought about better understanding between big business and government and reduced the number of antitrust suits.

The Clayton Antitrust Act lists unfair practices. The Clayton Antitrust Act, also passed in 1914, aimed at plugging the loopholes in the Sherman Antitrust Act and at

THE BANKS

POLITICS

STICKY FINGERS

POL[I]TICS

THE BANKS

A continuing problem in recent American history is represented here by a cartoonist of the early 1900's. To what extent should government interfere with banks and other business; to what extent should banks and other business interfere in government? The cartoonist chose not to favor either point of view, but merely to suggest that the whole question was an important one for the American people to think about.

making the law more specific. It carefully listed the illegal methods of competition which were forbidden. Here are some of the provisions of the act:

(1) Price discriminations which would "lessen competition or tend to create a monopoly" were declared unlawful.

(2) A corporation was not allowed to acquire the stock of another company for the purpose of creating a monopoly.

(3) Interlocking directorates were made illegal for the larger banks and for industrial corporations capitalized at a million dollars or over, which were or had been competitors.

In addition to these provisions, the act contained clauses favorable to organized labor (page 522).

During President Wilson's first administration the Federal Trade Commission and the Clayton Antitrust Act were generally successful in accomplishing their objectives. When the United States entered World War I, however, President Wilson had to devote all his efforts to the war, and

it was not possible to pay much attention to enforcing the antitrust laws.

Trust regulation relaxes after World War I. During the years that followed World War I, federal control of business was relaxed. Business was prosperous and large combinations were growing larger.[3] They also became more popular with the public, because millions of Americans had bought stock in giant concerns and were sharing their huge earnings. Presidents Harding, Coolidge, and Hoover believed that the economic welfare of the country depended upon the prosperity of industry. For that reason they took no steps that would interfere with big business. The Department of Justice no longer worried about the size of business combinations. When industrial activity slowed down after 1929, the government's problem was how to encourage business rather than how to restrict it.

[3] The Webb-Pomerene Act of 1918 exempted from the provisions of the antitrust laws combinations engaged solely in the export trade.

——— CHECK-UP ———

What changes took place in the policy of the government toward big business?

1. Why was "busting a trust" an unsatisfactory method of controlling business?
2. What led the government to make a distinction between "good" and "bad" big business? What was the "rule of reason?"
3. What was President Wilson's attitude toward big business? What were the purposes of the Federal Trade Commission and the Clayton Act?
4. What happened to trust regulation after World War I?

3 The New Deal Extends Government Control

President Hoover uses the power of government to fight the depression. When hard times had hit the country in depressions like those of 1837, 1873, and 1893, the Presidents who were in office had felt that such problems did not concern government, but should be left to business to solve. Then in 1929 the greatest depression of all engulfed the country. Herbert Hoover was the first President to recognize that government should use its power to fight hard times and to improve business conditions in the interests of all the people. At the request of President Hoover, Congress passed a number of measures intended to bring about a revival of business activity. Chief among these was a bill setting up the Reconstruction Finance Corporation (RFC), which had the job of lending money to hard-pressed business concerns. But many people felt that Hoover was not doing enough to overcome the depression, and in 1932 he was defeated by Franklin D. Roosevelt.

Business welcomes government aid. When Franklin D. Roosevelt became President in 1933, business was practically at a standstill. Barns were bursting with food

which the farmers could not sell, yet the cities were full of hungry people. Farmers needed manufactured goods but could not buy them because they had no money. Factory workers were unemployed because there was no market for their products. The problem seemed to be mainly one of distribution. The products of the farm needed to be placed in the hands of city folk at prices which they could afford, but those prices had to be high enough to enable the farmer to buy the products of the city. American industry needed to be revived to the point where it could employ workingmen at wages which would enable them to purchase their share of the necessities and luxuries of life. The situation was so critical in 1933 that even big business welcomed efforts by the government to start the wheels turning again.

Congress sets up the NRA. Faced with this black picture, Congress in June, 1933, established the National Recovery Administration (NRA). In the words of President Roosevelt, the law establishing the NRA aimed to set up "the machinery necessary for a great co-operative movement throughout all industry. . . . " Antitrust laws were discarded to the extent that private industries were permitted to make agreements among themselves insuring fair competition. Codes of fair competition were drawn up for almost every industry in the country. These codes (1) provided for the elimination of child labor, (2) established maximum hours of labor, (3) fixed minimum wage rates, (4) gave labor the right of collective bargaining, and (5) aimed at setting the prices of merchandise by agreements among businessmen, which before this had been illegal. Most businessmen at first welcomed the NRA, but when conditions became better, they vigorously opposed it. At length in May, 1935, the NRA was declared unconstitutional by a unanimous decision of the Supreme Court on the ground that it delegated too much legislative power to the President.

The New Deal affects all economic life. During this period of national emergency, Congress had approved a tremendous number of measures which affected every part of the nation's economic life. In other parts of this book you will read about New Deal measures affecting workingmen (pages 525–526), farmers (pages 557–560), the unemployed (page 761), the aged (page 593), banking (page 535), and housing (page 585). The Reconstruction Finance Corporation (RFC), established during the last year of President Hoover's administration, was continued. It saved large numbers of banks, railroads, and industrial concerns from bankruptcy. Through the Export-Import Bank, loans were provided to finance American foreign trade.

The Securities and Exchange Commission (SEC), created in 1934, gave the average investor better protection for his investments. All stock exchanges, and later all commodity exchanges [4] had to be licensed by the SEC and had to follow certain rules in their operation. (In 1940, investment trusts were also brought under the control of the SEC.) Speculation was restricted, while dealers and brokers who made false and misleading statements about their securities faced severe penalties. To the old advice, "Let the buyer beware," was added the warning, "Let the seller also beware."

Control is extended to power companies. Steps were also taken to bring giant power companies under government control. It was felt that the power industry, like railroads, was so essential to the public welfare that it could not be allowed to operate as independently as non-essential industries. The Wheeler-Rayburn Act of 1935 was passed over the bitter opposition of the power interests. This act forced all public utility holding companies to register with the SEC and get its permission before they acquired new properties or issued stock. A "death sentence" clause ordered

[4] Examples of commodity exchanges are the Chicago Board of Trade (wheat), the New York Coffee Exchange and the Merchants' Exchange of St. Louis (furs). Transactions in such exchanges are on paper only; the actual goods are not present. Much buying is done in terms of future delivery. Wheat that will ripen in May, for example, is commonly bought and sold during previous March.

As depression waned, the New York Stock Exchange became busy again.

the SEC gradually to break up many of these holding companies.

The government made another effort to check public utility monopolies — this time by going into the business itself and competing with the monopolies. The result was the Tennessee Valley Authority (TVA) and others like it, by means of which the government undertook to supply consumers with cheap electric power (page 570). Two other agencies, the Public Works Administration (PWA) and the Rural Electrification Administration (REA), created in 1935, came to the aid of cities, co-operatives, and other local units which wanted to provide their own power.

Big Business opposes the New Deal. Big Business accepted many of the new government agencies as temporary measures to meet a great emergency. As the country pulled out of the depression, however, the demand for less government interference became strong once more. Leading industrialists urged that New Deal policies be almost completely reversed. Point by point, they demanded removal of restrictions on stock and commodity exchanges, a sharp reduction in government expenditures, and modification of the government's pro-labor policies. Although the administration of Franklin D. Roosevelt recognized "fair business profits as an essential for increasing employment and private investment," it insisted that there could be no compromise in the basic aims and measures of the New Deal. The arguments between industrial leaders and New Dealers were often bitter, each side insisting that its program offered the best chance to maintain the American way of life. The argument was still raging when another emergency — World War II — pushed it into the background.

President Truman tries to return to trust-busting. President Truman, especially after his re-election in 1948, seemed eager to return to the trust-busting policies of the first Roosevelt. The Department of Justice started many suits to break up monopolistic practices. Price-fixing, pooling, division of territories among business concerns, even cartel agreements were objects of attack by Attorney General Tom Clark. Some notable decisions were reached in the courts, particularly in preventing motion picture producers from operating theaters and in the control of color films.

——————— CHECK-UP ———————

How did the New Deal extend government control of business?

1. Who was the first President to use the power of the federal government to fight business depressions? What was the Reconstruction Finance Corporation?

2. What were the provisions of the law setting up the National Recovery Administration?

3. What are some of the other measures which were taken by the government under the New Deal and which affected business?

4. Account for the changes in the attitude of business toward the New Deal. What attitude did President Truman take toward business?

Locomotive - 1917

4 Government Effectively Regulates Transportation and Communication

As you have seen (page 387), railroad regulation in the late 1800's was not very effective. Although the Interstate Commerce Commission had been established, it had little real power. Unfair practices continued to be used, and illegal rebates still flourished. During the twentieth century all this was to change. Not only was effective railroad regulation to become an accomplished fact, but other forms of transportation and communication were also to come under the control of government.

The ICC gains strength. When Theodore Roosevelt became President, he energetically renewed the drive to regulate the railroads. Under his leadership, Congress passed two measures which strengthened the hands of the Interstate Commerce Commission. The first of these was the Elkins Act (1903), which made it illegal for a shipper to accept a rebate, just as it was already illegal for a railroad to grant one. In addition, under Roosevelt's urging, Congress passed a measure of even greater importance — the Hepburn Act (1906). This act assigned seven members to the Interstate Commerce Commission and gave it added strength so that it became a really effective means of regulating the railroads. The most important provisions of the Hepburn Act were these:

(1) The commission's authority was broadened to include control over express and sleeping-car companies, pipe lines, and railroad terminals.

(2) With certain unimportant exceptions, free passes were forbidden.

(3) The commission was specifically given the power to "determine and prescribe what will be the just and reasonable rate," subject to approval by the federal courts.

In 1910, during President Taft's administration, Congress went a step further.

It passed the Mann-Elkins Act which extended the authority of the commission to include supervision of telephone, telegraph, and cable companies.

World War I brings government operation of the railroads. World War I began a new era in the relations between the federal government and transportation companies. When the United States entered the war, the railroads were faced with a tremendous job of transporting troops and freight. Because they worked as separate companies, they were unable to co-operate as efficiently as the government thought they should. Consequently, as a war measure, the government took over control of the railroads in December of 1917. The government also took control of the Pullman and express companies and the internal waterways. Owners were guaranteed a fair income from their investment during the emergency, as well as the return of their business to private management after the war.

A Director General of all the railroads was appointed — William G. McAdoo, Secretary of the Treasury. He merged the railroads into a single system, with common ticket offices, terminals, and equipment. With the roads under government operation, supply and troop trains moved more rapidly. Wages were raised, but so were freight and passenger rates. Even so, government management was costly. The operating loss for about two years amounted to nearly a billon dollars.

The railroads are returned to private ownership. When the war ended, Congress was ready to return the railroads to their owners. In doing so, however, the legislators wanted to guard against conditions which in the past had prevented the railroads from operating efficiently and in the best interests of the public. After much debate, they passed the Esch-Cummins Act, or Transportation Act of 1920, which included these provisions:

(1) The Interstate Commerce Commission was reorganized with increased powers and eleven members.

(2) The commission was authorized to establish and maintain rates that would

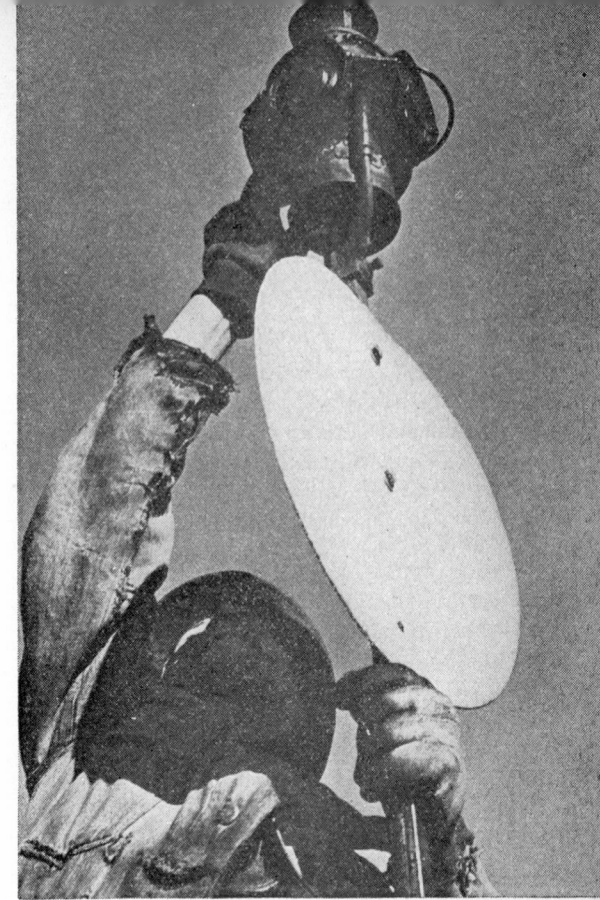

Railroad equipment had to be kept in working order during the 1920's in spite of vexing problems concerning railroad management. In this picture a workman is shown tending an old-style, kerosene signal lamp.

yield "a fair return" upon the total value of the railroad property of the country.

(3) To assist weak roads and to prevent strong ones from earning too high profits, all roads earning more than six per cent of their property valuation were to set aside one-half of the excess in a reserve fund of their own. The other half was to be turned over to the commission.[5] By this means, the commission acquired a fund which could be used in making loans to less prosperous roads.

(4) The commission was authorized to work out plans under which the nation's railroads could combine, if they voted to do so, into a limited number of systems.

[5] This provision of the Esch-Cummins Act is known as the "recapture clause."

Diesel freight locomotive

(5) A Railroad Labor Board was created to settle labor disputes between the roads and their employees.

Railroads battle the great depression. After the railroads returned to private ownership, however, they did not prosper. One reason was that attempts to combine the many roads into a few great systems did not work out. Also, the railroads were meeting competition from new forms of transportation (page 495). Motor buses, airplanes, and private automobiles took much of their passenger traffic. Motor trucks, pipe lines, and water transportation, especially through the Panama Canal, cut deeply into the volume of freight shipments. For these reasons, the railroads shared only moderately in the prosperity of the 1920's, and they keenly felt the effects of the depression which followed.

By 1932, passenger and freight business had dropped alarmingly, and the number of railroad employees had been cut in half since 1920. Losses kept mounting until companies owning nearly a third of the railway mileage of the country were in financial difficulties. Yet every attempt by the railroad operators to solve their problems met with determined protests. When they tried to reduce manpower or wages, the powerful railroad brotherhoods (unions of railroad employees) prevented them. When they tried to increase rates, the shippers protested loudly, and the Interstate Commerce Commission sided with the shippers. When they tried to consolidate or abandon unprofitable lines, strong opposition came from shippers and from local governments which were afraid of losing taxes.

The railroad crisis becomes a national threat. The railroad situation affected the lives of millions of Americans. The railroad systems represented a capital investment of 25 billion dollars. For a long time rail-road bonds had been regarded as a type of investment almost as safe as United States government bonds. For this reason, insurance companies, savings banks, and similar organizations had bought large quantities of them. If the railroads failed, the hard-earned savings of millions of people would be threatened. The railroads also gave work to a large number of employees, and were America's greatest taxpayers. They simply could not be allowed to fail. The Reconstruction Finance Corporation (RFC), created in 1932, lent the railroads huge sums of money to meet taxes and bond payments.

The New Deal helps the railroads. The serious difficulty in which the railroads found themselves was given additional attention when Franklin D. Roosevelt became President. One of the first measures of the new Congress was the Emergency Railroad Transportation Act (1933), which had several important features:

(1) It provided for mergers and for the consolidation of railroad facilities under the direction of a Federal Co-ordinator of Transportation (FCT), to hold office until June, 1936.

(2) It set aside the operation of all anti-trust laws (pages 388, 514) which hindered the solution of railroad problems.

(3) It repealed the "recapture clause" of the Esch-Cummins Act of 1920, and adopted a more flexible rule for the making of rates.

(4) It protected the essential rights of employees.

World War II brings prosperity to railroads. Improved service on the railroads, and the increase in business which came with World War II, brought prosperity again to the railroads. When the war ended, however, increased costs and higher wages again raised serious problems and led the Interstate Commerce Commission to grant the railroads the right to charge higher rates.

Trucks and buses are regulated. With the Motor Carrier Act of 1935, Congress extended the authority of the Interstate Commerce Commission to cover the rates and services of interstate highway carriers such as trucks and buses. The commission now followed the theory that "each type of carrier can do certain things better than any of the others," and that none of them should be regulated out of existence. Five years later (1940), the Wheeler-Lea Act enlarged the commission's power over all interstate commerce except air traffic.

Air transportation is brought under control. Meantime, air traffic control was set up by the Civil Aeronautics Act of 1938. The Civil Aeronautics Authority, established by this act, was later (1940) reorganized to consist of the Civil Aeronautics Board (CAB) and the Civil Aeronautics Administration (CAA). The CAA supervises air-carrier operation and sees that safety standards are met. One purpose of the CAB is to promote the development of air transport, and to encourage foreign and domestic air commerce.

Shipping, radio, and television are regulated. The Merchant Marine Act of 1936, which established the United States Maritime Commission (USMC), moved far in the direction of providing a government-owned shipping fleet. Likewise, a Federal Communications Commission (FCC) was set up in 1934 to regulate interstate and foreign communication by wire and radio. The FCC grants licenses to radio and television broadcasting stations and regulates some phases of their operation. It also licenses operators, and regulates telegraph, cable, telephone, and radio companies engaged in interstate and overseas service.

——— CHECK-UP ———

How did government regulation of transportation and communication become more effective?

1. How was the Interstate Commerce Commission strengthened?
2. Why did World War I bring changes in railroad operation? How were railroads restored to private owners?
3. How did the depression following 1929 affect the railroads? How did the New Deal try to help the railroads? What happened to the railroads in World War II?
4. How did the government regulate other types of transportation and communication?

┌───┐
│ 5   **The Needs of Labor Receive**   │
│   **Government Consideration**   │
└───┘

Labor is at a disadvantage as the 1900's begin. Working people in the late 1890's (as you have already seen, pages 393–395) had good reason to feel that government as a whole was more friendly toward business than toward labor. As the new century got under way, the Sherman Antitrust Act continued to be used against labor organizations. In 1902, for example, the hatters' union attempted a nation-wide boycott of the products of a hat manufacturer of Danbury, Connecticut. The company brought suit for damages under the Sherman Antitrust Act. The Supreme Court, after a long delay, held that this boycott was a combination in restraint of trade. Members of the Danbury Hatters Union were ordered to pay three times the amount of damages suffered by the manufacturer.

The twentieth century was to see a tremendous change in the attitude of the government, and even of business itself, toward labor. This change came about slowly, but the age of reform which produced more effective regulation of business also brought greater protection for workers and their organizations under the law.

Theodore Roosevelt settles a coal strike. Theodore Roosevelt stood for a "square deal" for labor as well as business. In 1902, soon after he became President, he was faced with a test of his policy during a coal strike. Under the leadership of John Mitchell, the United Mine Workers demanded a nine-hour day, an increase in wages, and recognition of the union. Mitchell offered to submit the miners' demands to arbitration. But George F. Baer, who was president of the Philadelphia and Reading Company and a leading

Miner, early 1900's

coal operator, refused to arbitrate. He declared stubbornly that "the rights and interests of the laboring man will be protected and cared for, not by the labor agitators, but by the Christian men to whom God, in His infinite wisdom, has given control of the property interests of the country."

As the strike continued into the autumn, Eastern cities faced a winter without fuel. Roosevelt then took action. He asked both sides to accept arbitration. When the mine owners still refused, he threatened to operate the mines with federal troops. Under this threat the owners gave in. An arbitration commission awarded the miners a ten per cent wage increase, a shorter work day, and a guarantee that future disputes would be referred to a board of conciliation.

More important than the immediate gains of labor in the coal strike was the new principle introduced as a result of the President's interference. The doctrine of *laissez faire* was already giving way to a new theory in which the welfare of the people at large was to be of primary consideration. President Roosevelt was untroubled by the fact that he had no definite constitutional authority to step into the middle of labor disputes. He declared that the "public interest" justified his action. Most of the public agreed with him. His settlement of the strike greatly increased his popularity.

There was a still further gain for labor under Theodore Roosevelt when the railway brotherhoods secured passage of a law that made interstate railroads liable for injuries received by employees while at work. Also President Roosevelt's stand on the "square deal" encouraged many states to pass laws improving working conditions.

The IWW tries to organize unskilled workers. During Theodore Roosevelt's administration there developed a new and radical labor organization called the Industrial Workers of the World (IWW). Founded in 1905, the IWW made a special effort to organize unskilled industrial workers, the group that had been left almost entirely outside the American Federation of Labor. It appealed particularly to the unskilled and "floating" workers of the northwestern mining and lumber camps and the northeastern textile mills.

The IWW platform declared, "The working class and the employing class have nothing in common. A struggle must go on until the workers of the world organize as a class, take possession of the earth and the machinery of production, and abolish the wage system." One of the founders of the IWW was Eugene V. Debs, later the Socialist candidate for President. Its fiery leader for many years was "Big Bill" Haywood. The IWW's radical program and its belief in sabotage — the destruction of machinery and other property used in production [6] — were as distasteful to conservative laboring people as to business leaders.

The IWW carried out some successful strikes in its time. One of them was a particularly bitter strike among the textile workers of Lawrence, Massachusetts, in 1912. During World War I, however, the organization angered many citizens who felt it was unpatriotic to promote strikes in copper mines and lumber camps when their output was essential to the war effort. After 1917 the movement rapidly declined, largely as a result of strong legislation in the states against it.

The Clayton Act and Wilson's policies help labor. The Clayton Act, passed in 1914 under President Woodrow Wilson (page 514), contained provisions favorable to labor. As you have seen, in the Pullman strike (page 394) and in the Danbury Hatters Case, the injunction and the Sherman Antitrust Act were used successfully against labor unions. The Clayton Act exempted labor unions from prosecution under the antitrust laws on the ground that "the labor of human beings is not a commodity or article of commerce." It also permitted peaceful strikes or boycotts. It prohibited the granting of an injunction in any industrial dispute "unless necessary to prevent irreparable injury to property." The Clayton Act was hailed as a victory and a great forward step for labor, and

[6] The term *sabotage* is also, but less frequently, used to mean a deliberate, concerted slowing-down of work.

Theodore Roosevelt's attack on the doctrine of "laissez faire" brought business leaders to Washington to plead with him. J. P. Morgan, financier, is shown here presenting an argument.

during Wilson's Presidency it was successfully used to help labor. Later, it proved a disappointment to its sponsors. Conservative courts interpreted it in such a way that injunctions continued to be a powerful weapon against strikes.[7]

President Wilson did more than sponsor the Clayton Act. Throughout his administration he maintained a friendly attitude toward labor. At the end of President Taft's administration, Congress had created a separate Department of Labor. President Wilson selected as the first Secretary of Labor a union man who was sponsored by the American Federation of Labor. The new Department of Labor made studies of such subjects as wages and living costs, employment and unemployment, and strikes. These studies proved of great value to the government.

World War I benefits labor. When World War I broke out in Europe, American business benefited from the demands for supplies and war materials. Since the railroads played a vital role in transporting war materials, their workers were in a position to press for advantages. In 1916, they threatened a nation-wide strike unless they were granted the same pay for an eight-hour day that they had been getting for a ten-hour day. President Wilson asked Congress for a law to that effect, and Congress responded at once by passing the Adamson Act. The President was severely criticized by his political opponents for this "surrender" to labor.

World War I marked a high point in the history of American labor. The tremendous demand for goods, along with the shortage of workers caused by the enlargement of our military forces, pushed wages higher than ever before. The eight-hour day and the six-day week were accepted as normal in many industries, and the standard of living of the American workingman rose to a new level.

Strikes break out after World War I. When peace came, industrial activity slowed down and wages were seriously cut. The unions during the war had enlarged their membership lists and filled their treasuries. Now, they declared they would hold onto their wartime gains. The result was that in the year 1919 nearly 4000 strikes took place, involving one fifth of America's workers.

One of the most important of these strikes involved a third of a million steel workers. The steel workers protested against the twelve-hour day in the steel mills, and they went on strike in an effort to unionize the mills and obtain an eight-hour day. The strike, under the radical leadership of William Z. Foster,[8] ended in complete failure. Four years later, the steel industry granted the eight-hour day, but

---

[7] There was no real change in attitude until the Norris-La Guardia Anti-Injunction Act was passed in 1932. This act forbade federal courts to issue injunctions in cases where workers exercised their rights peaceably and without fraud.

[8] Foster later became the leader of the Communist Party in America.

the unions were not recognized until the late 1930's.

Near the end of 1919, 400,000 soft-coal miners went out on strike. They demanded an increase in wages and a 30-hour week, intended to spread employment over the entire year. Since the country was technically still at war, Attorney General Palmer took advantage of the fact to secure injunctions against the strike leaders. With the remark "We can't fight our government," John L. Lewis, the union leader, admitted defeat. But the miners finally got a wage increase of 27 per cent when the government took the side of the miners.

Labor discontent decreases during the "Golden Twenties." Labor shared the prosperity of the 1920's. High wages, bonuses, and ownership of stock in their companies made many workers feel that industry's welfare was linked with their own. Some employers also fostered "company unions," that is, unions sponsored by management with membership limited to their own plants. The National Association of Manufacturers conducted an active campaign for what it called the "American plan." This plan included the *open shop,* employing both union and non-union labor, as opposed to the *closed shop,* where only union members may work. During the "Golden Twenties," strikes steadily decreased in number and importance, and membership in the A. F. of L. fell 25 per cent.

Only one important piece of labor legislation was passed during the 1920's. This was the Railway Labor Act of 1926, supported by both management and union. This law set up a permanent Mediation Board to adjust disputes and encourage collective bargaining (the right of workers to organize and to bargain with their employers through their organizations).

A modern coal mine, as it may look from the outside, is shown in this painting. Notice that small electric locomotives are used for hauling mine cars. Formerly small donkeys, or even human labor, were used to move the cars.

© 1948, General Electric

——— CHECK-UP ———

Why did the needs of labor begin to receive government consideration?

1. What was the condition of labor and labor organizations at the turn of the century?
2. What were the causes of the 1902 coal strike? What part did Theodore Roosevelt play in its settlement?
3. What was the IWW? What program did it have?
4. What gains were made by labor in the Wilson era? How did World War I affect labor?
5. Why did strikes break out after World War I? Why did labor discontent decrease?

6 Labor Grows Strong Under the New Deal

Operators and unions have co-operated to make mining safer. Here, below ground, a squad of miners receives safety instruction.

Congress tries to help labor. In the depression which followed the financial crash of 1929, the position of labor was threatened. The spread of unemployment and the inability of many union men to pay their dues resulted in a further shrinkage in A. F. of L. membership. It dropped to less than 2 million at the beginning of 1933, the lowest figure since 1915. Unemployment also weakened the effectiveness of labor's chief weapon, the strike. Wages, even for those who kept jobs, dropped far below their former levels.

As part of its program to restore purchasing power, the first Congress in President Franklin D. Roosevelt's administration tried to put "a floor under wages and a ceiling over hours." The law setting up the National Recovery Administration (NRA) included labor standards which were considered essential to "fair competition" (page 516). The act also set up a National Labor Board (later the National Labor Relations Board or NLRB) to settle disputes.

Congress encourages collective bargaining. When the NRA was declared unconstitutional, Congress tried to rescue its labor program by passing a new law — the National Labor Relations Act (1935). This act, also called the Wagner-Connery Act after its sponsors, was known more commonly as the Wagner Act. Under this measure, the National Labor Relations Board (NLRB) received broad powers. It was in-

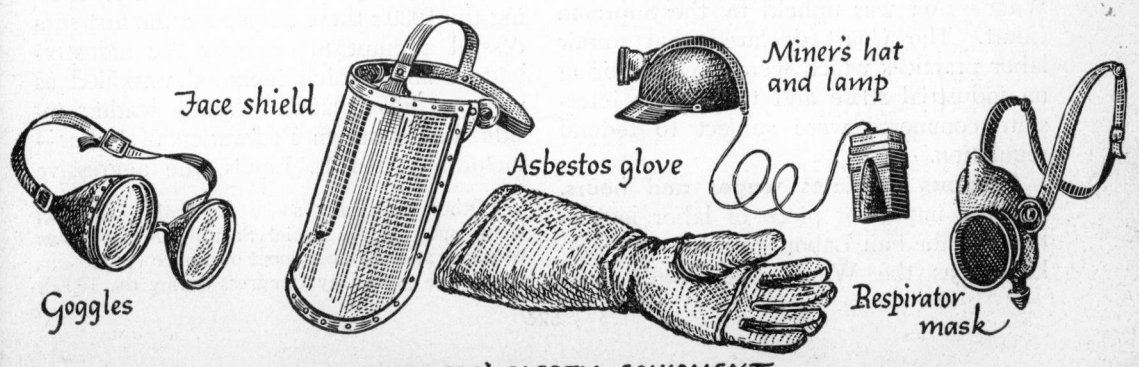

Goggles · *Face shield* · *Asbestos glove* · *Miner's hat and lamp* · *Respirator mask*

WORKERS' SAFETY EQUIPMENT

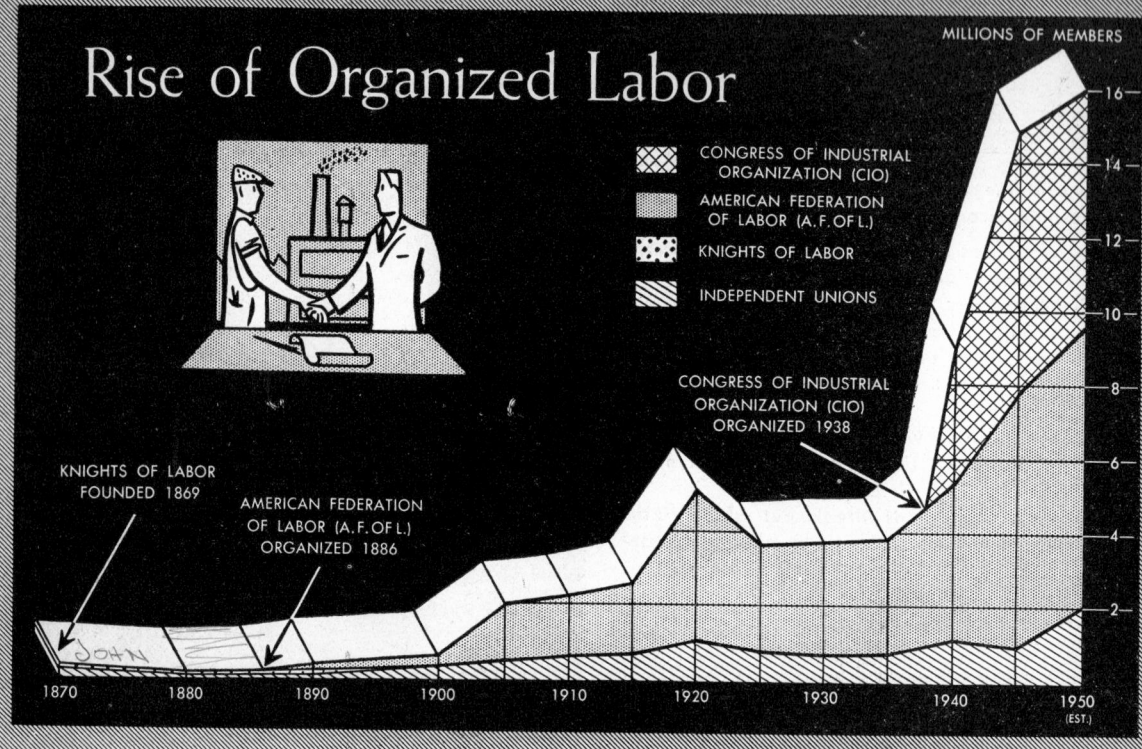

Rise of Organized Labor

MILLIONS OF MEMBERS

CONGRESS OF INDUSTRIAL
ORGANIZATION (CIO)

AMERICAN FEDERATION
OF LABOR (A.F. OF L.)

KNIGHTS OF LABOR

INDEPENDENT UNIONS

CONGRESS OF INDUSTRIAL
ORGANIZATION (CIO)
ORGANIZED 1938

KNIGHTS OF LABOR
FOUNDED 1869

AMERICAN FEDERATION
OF LABOR (A.F. OF L.)
ORGANIZED 1886

JOHN

1870 1880 1890 1900 1910 1920 1930 1940 1950 (EST.)

The ranks of organized labor increased rapidly after 1900, but the movement had a setback after World War I. Why? Why did a still more powerful period of growth set in after 1933? What are the two most powerful labor organizations today?

structed to remove "the inequality of bargaining power" between workers and employers, and to prevent employers "from engaging in any unfair labor practices." Among the unfair practices listed in this act were (1) domination of labor organizations by employers, (2) the hiring or firing of workers to discourage union membership, and (3) the refusal to bargain collectively with properly selected delegates of the workers. The board was given authority to conduct elections among workers to decide which union should represent them in dealing with employers. In 1937 the Wagner Act was upheld by the Supreme Court. The Court declared that unfair labor practices which were likely to bring on industrial strife and thus affect interstate commerce were subject to federal regulation.

Congress regulates wages and hours. Another important piece of labor legislation was the Fair Labor Standards Act, also known as the Wages and Hours Law

(1938). Under this law hours and wages for industrial workers engaged in interstate industries were to be adjusted, over a period of years, to a standard week of 40 hours and a minimum wage of 40 cents an hour. Products made in violation of these provisions could not cross state lines. Goods manufactured with "oppressive child labor" were banned in the same way. The constitutionality of the Wages and Hours Law, including its child-labor provisions, was upheld early in 1941 by a unanimous decision of the Supreme Court.[9]

The CIO organizes mass industry. During the 1930's there developed the first successful attempt to organize big industry-wide unions which included unskilled as well as skilled labor. Certain leaders inside the American Federation of Labor — including John L. Lewis, the aggressive

[9] Other important social legislation affecting labor, such as the Social Security Act, old age pensions, and unemployment insurance (pages 592, 593) were passed by Congress during the 1930's

chief of the United Mine Workers (UMW) — had become more and more critical of the A. F. of L.'s failure to organize workers in the mass-production industries. These leaders formed a Committee for Industrial Organization to unionize workers in the automotive, steel, rubber, textile, electrical, radio and other industries on a *vertical* basis. All workers in the Ford plant, for example, could join the United Automobile Workers instead of being separated into the electrical workers' union, the metal workers' union, the welders' union, and so forth.[10] Soon the Committee for Industrial Organization had enrolled 4 million members. Those industrial unions which had joined the CIO were expelled from the A. F. of L. They held their own convention at Pittsburgh in 1938 and adopted the CIO, or Congress of Industrial Organizations, as the permanent name. John L. Lewis was elected their president.[11]

The CIO succeeded in organizing industrial workers who had not been in unions before. Its membership increased to about 6 million by 1948. At that time the A. F. of L. had grown to 7 million members, and there were also about 2 million enrolled in independent unions. All efforts to reunite the A. F. of L. and the CIO failed. Rivalry between the two organizations was especially bitter when representatives of both the A. F. of L. and the CIO tried to enroll the same group of workers. Sometimes this led to *jurisdictional strikes*. An example of a jurisdictional strike would be a strike by an A. F. of L. union because the employer was doing business with a CIO union.

Labor disputes continue under the New Deal. Organized labor made great gains under the New Deal, but labor disputes continued. At the start of Franklin D. Roosevelt's second term, CIO unions introduced a new weapon — the *sit-down strike*.[12] This type of strike meant that instead of

[10] Contrasted with this vertical organization is the *horizontal* organization of the A. F. of L., which may have many separate craft unions in a single great plant.

[11] In 1946 Lewis and the United Mine Workers returned for a time to the A. F. of L.

[12] In 1939 the Supreme Court declared sit-down strikes illegal.

leaving a plant and setting up picket lines, striking workers stayed at their posts and refused to leave, thus preventing employers from using strike-breakers. General Motors and Chrysler gave in to sit-down strikes, and United States Steel recognized the CIO steel-workers' union without their having to resort to a strike. In 1941, three or four hundred new strikes each month involved more than 2 million workers. Many of these were jurisdictional strikes arising from the rivalry between the A. F. of L. and the CIO unions. World War II was raging in Europe, and some of these strikes tied up important defense industries. Legislation to prevent strikes was proposed in and out of Congress, and federal troops were used as a last resort to keep some of the defense plants working.

Labor supports World War II. When the United States entered World War II, labor and management agreed that there should be no strikes or lockouts for the duration, and that all disputes should be settled by peaceful means. Such disputes, if they arose, were to come under the authority of the National War Labor Board (WLB), which was set up by the President in 1942. In general, labor gave its full support to the war effort, and days lost in labor disputes were kept at a minimum. In the spring and summer of 1943, however, John L. Lewis took half a million mine workers out on strike, defying the President, the WLB, and the public. Steel production, the most important industrial work of the war, was seriously affected. Congress in-

Labor leaders argue a point during a public hearing. William Green, President of the A. F. of L. (left) states his case, while John L. Lewis (right) listens intently.

dignantly passed the Connally-Smith Anti-Strike Act over the President's veto. Effective until six months after the war ended, this law provided fine and imprisonment for anyone encouraging a strike or lockout in any plant under government operation. Workers in privately-operated plants might vote to strike only after a 30-day notice to their employers.

─────── CHECK-UP ───────

What caused labor to grow strong under the New Deal?

1. How did the depression of 1929 affect labor?
2. What were the provisions of the Wagner Act? The Fair Labor Standard Act? How did each of these help labor?
3. Trace the development of the CIO. How did it differ from the A. F. of L.? Did labor unions grow or decrease in size during the 1930's? Why?
4. What is a sit-down strike? A jurisdictional strike?
5. What was the position of organized labor during World War II?

7 New Labor Problems Follow World War II

Major strikes occur in 1946. During the war, workers had been earning unusually high wages, partly because of overtime pay. When the war ended in 1945, they were faced with the end of overtime work and the possibility of a cut in "take-home pay." Labor leaders were determined to hold the advantages they had gained during the war, and they demanded an increase in hourly wages that would keep their purchasing power at war levels. Management declared, on the other hand, that increased wages meant higher prices and would result in inflation. For a time, the whole program of reconversion — getting industry back to a peacetime basis — was threatened by strikes in the automobile, petroleum, meat-packing, mining, steel and other key industries. Early in 1946 a million and a half workers were out on strike. During that first post-war year, six times as many man-days of work were lost through strikes as had been lost in the average of the years from 1934 to 1939. Early in 1946, strikes in steel, General Motors, and General Electric were settled by wage increases. Then in April, John L. Lewis again called out the soft-coal miners. Since soft coal was burned by a large percentage of the railroad locomotives and was used to generate well over half the mechanical and electrical power of the country, all industry soon felt the effects of the coal strike. After about six weeks, the government took over the mines, and in June a settlement granting most of the miners' demands was reached. But in November of the same year, Lewis grew dissatisfied with government operation of the mines and announced the end of the union contract. The government then secured an injunction restraining Lewis and the UMW from breaking the contract. When the injunction was ignored, the miners' union was fined $3,500,000 (reduced to $700,000 by the Supreme Court) and Lewis $10,000. After that, Lewis called the men back to work.

Wages and prices spiral upward. These first post-war labor disputes led to wage increases which averaged about 18.5 cents an hour above wartime wages. Price increases followed, and soon these higher wages bought no more than the lower wages had earlier. Organized labor then argued for a second round of wage increases. It insisted that corporation profits could be cut down to make up this wage increase without raising prices. Businessmen argued that this was impossible. A second and a third round of wage increases were followed by corresponding increases in prices. Nevertheless, *real wages*, wages measured by their purchasing power, were high, unemployment was at a minimum, and the standard of living of the American workingman was higher than ever before.

The Taft-Hartley Act revises labor policy.
Meanwhile, most employers had become dissatisfied with the Wagner Act (page 525). While the Wagner Act guaranteed important rights to labor, they felt that it set unfair limits on an employer's freedom. For example, if an employer wrote a letter to an employee urging him to return to work when a strike was in progress, he committed an "unfair labor practice." He might be accused of another "unfair labor practice" if he negotiated with any group of workers other than the majority authorized by the NLRB. But the freedom of the unions, employers argued, was not limited to a similar degree. If, for instance, a CIO industrial union was the authorized bargaining agency in his plant, the employer was forbidden to bargain with an A. F. of L. group. But the A. F. of L. group was free to strike against him — perhaps even stopping all plant operations — because he did not bargain with them. Added to the dissatisfaction of employers was the growing impatience of the public in general when labor disputes interfered with delivery of important goods and services.

The Wagner Act was finally replaced in 1947 by the Taft-Hartley Act (Labor-Management Relations Act). This law restated labor's right to organize and to bargain collectively. It also retained the National Labor Relations Board. But it changed labor policy in several important respects:

(1) It required at least a 60-day notice (a cooling off period) before a contract could be ended by either employer or union. If the national health or safety was threatened, the Attorney General could secure an injunction postponing a threatened strike or lockout for 80 days.

(2) The closed shop was outlawed, but the *union shop,* in which non-union workers may be hired on condition that they join the union at once, was permitted if the majority of employees voted for it.

(3) The NLRB might secure injunctions against either employers or unions engaging in illegal labor-relations practices.

(4) Unions were forbidden to establish secondary boycotts,[13] to call jurisdictional strikes, to refuse to bargain collectively with an employer, to put pressure on non-members, or to charge unusually high initiation and membership fees.

(5) Both employers and unions might sue for damages for breach of contract.

(6) Both employers and unions were forbidden to contribute to political campaigns.

(7) Unions were ordered to file copies of their constitutions and by-laws, schedules of fees, lists of officers, and other information with the Secretary of Labor.

(8) Officers of unions were required to swear that they were not Communists and did not support any organization advocating the overthrow of the United States government by illegal methods.

The Taft-Hartley Act became law over the veto of President Truman and in spite of the strenuous opposition of organized labor. For a time, the number of strikes decreased, in part because of uncertainties over the interpretation of provisions in the act. The act, however, was unpopular with labor, and particularly with labor leaders. In the campaign of 1948, President Truman urged its repeal and the re-enactment of the Wagner Act. After the re-election of President Truman the repeal of the Taft-Hartley Act became an important part of Truman's "Fair Deal" program. At the same time, it became increasingly doubtful whether Congress would restore the Wagner Act in its entirety. Neither the efforts to repeal the Taft-Hartley Act nor attempts to amend it met with success.

[13] A secondary boycott is an attempt to force the public or a third party to refuse to deal with a business concern against which the employees have a grievance.

——— CHECK-UP ———

What new labor problems followed World War II?

1. Why did major strikes occur after the end of the war?
2. What happened to wages and prices?
3. Why was the Taft-Hartley Act passed? What were its provisions?

CHAPTER REVIEW

Terms to Understand

"trust-busting"
price discrimination
"combination in restraint of trade"
injunction
collective bargaining
open shop
closed shop
minimum wage
unskilled worker
secondary boycott

sabotage
industrial union
"golden twenties"
"public interest"
union shop
sit-down strike
jurisdictional strike
"take-home pay"
"unfair labor practice"
cooling off period

People and Things to Know About

"muckrakers"
Northern Securities Company
Hepburn Act
Pure Food and Drugs Act
"community of interest"
"rule of reason"
Clayton Antitrust Act
Esch-Cummins Act
"recapture clause"
Reconstruction Finance Corporation
Wheeler-Lea Act
National Recovery Act
Securities and Exchange Commission
Danbury Hatters case
Fair Labor Standards Act

Industrial Workers of the World
Committee for Industrial Organization
National War Labor Board
Connally-Smith Anti-Strike Act
Federal Trade Commission
Taft-Hartley Act
Theodore Roosevelt
Mann-Elkins Act
Wheeler-Rayburn Act
John L. Lewis
Federal Communications Commission
Civil Aeronautics Board
Wagner Act

Historic Dates to Identify

1902	1920	1935
1906	1929	1938
1914	1933	1947

Questions to Discuss

1. Why is it necessary that consumers have greater protection by the government today than 100 years ago?
2. Do you feel that labor unions are too strong

Questions to Discuss (Cont.)

or too weak at present? Give reasons for your answer.
3. Distinguish between (a) the closed shop and the open shop, (b) a company union and a national union, (c) a craft and an industrial union, (d) a jurisdictional strike and a strike for better working conditions.
4. Do you feel that in most cases a settlement reached by free bargaining between employers and employees is more desirable than a settlement enforced by government? Why?
5. Why would the creation of the Federal Trade Commission have the tendency to cut down the number of antitrust suits?
6. How did each of the following improve the position of organized labor:
(a) the Clayton Antitrust Act, (b) the National Recovery Administration, (c) the Fair Labor Standards Act (d) the Wagner Act?

Other Things to Do

1. Prepare a book report on Upton Sinclair's *The Jungle* or one of the other "muckraking" books.
2. Debate: *Resolved,* That the government should own and operate the railroads.
*3. Make a list of the important milestones in the government regulation of business. Give the provisions of each.
4. Debate: *Resolved,* That all issues leading to strikes should be settled through compulsory arbitration by government.
5. Write to your state department of labor and/or to the American Association for Labor Legislation, 131 East 23d Street, New York City, for information concerning the labor laws in force in your state. Find out about specific provisions pertaining to (a) safety and sanitation, (b) hours of labor, (c) special protection for women and children, and (d) compensation for industrial injuries. Report your finding to the class.
6. There are evidences all around you when you go shopping that the government is protecting you as a consumer. Submit a list of such evidences (inspected scales would be one).

Listing prices of stocks

Chapter 29

FINANCE AND FOREIGN TRADE AFFECT

THE NATION'S PROSPERITY

Full, stable, and durable business recovery can only be effected by the restoration of international trade and finance.

Cordell Hull

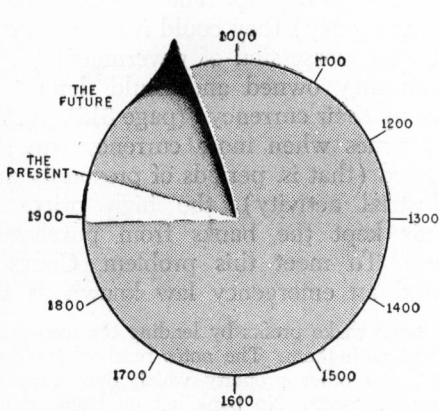

1897 – The Present

Two of the less spectacular but none-the-less important problems that faced the United States during the twentieth century were those dealing with (1) currency and banking, and (2) the tariff and foreign trade. Both of these problems aroused differences of opinion, for their solution directly affected the prosperity, or lack of it, of many people in the United States.

Of course, neither of these problems was new. They had troubled Congress and Presidents throughout the 1800's. Farmers had battled unsuccessfully for currency expansion after the War Between the States. (See Chapter 21.) At almost any time in our history, mention of the tariff had usually provoked an argument.

But new conditions in the 1900's brought new attitudes and new solutions for persistent problems. One panic (1907) resulted in a much-needed change in our currency system. Another panic (1929), and the great depression that followed, produced profound changes in our money system and

531

banking laws. The traditional American practice of a high protective tariff faced new attacks when the United States changed from a debtor to a creditor nation after World War I. President Woodrow Wilson aptly summarized the new problem facing the United States when he said, "If we want to sell, we must be prepared to buy."

The two troublesome problems of finance and international trade and their effect on our prosperity will be considered under these headings:

1. The Federal Reserve System provides a more flexible currency.
2. The New Deal meets a financial crisis.
3. Inflation and national debt become major problems.
4. The era of reform brings a reduction in tariffs.
5. World War I alters the problems of trade and tariffs.
6. World-wide depression brings a new tariff policy.

1 The Federal Reserve System Provides a More Flexible Currency

Gold becomes the single standard. When Bryan was defeated for the Presidency in 1896, the country was deep in depression. The farmers and debtors who had pinned their hopes on higher prices through currency inflation and the free coinage of silver (page 409) seemed doomed to disappointment. Yet shortly after President McKinley's election prosperity began to return — for both the farmer and the businessman. One of the reasons why prosperity returned, strangely enough, was an increase in the amount of currency in circulation, the very thing that Bryan and the farmers had wanted. But it was brought about, not by an increase in the amount of silver, but rather by an expansion in the supply of gold. The discovery of vast gold

deposits in Alaska and South Africa increased the world's supply enormously.

With gold more plentiful, many of the arguments against the gold standard disappeared, and "free silver" became a dead issue. In 1900 Congress passed the Gold Standard Act, which established gold as the single standard of value and provided that all other forms of currency should be redeemable in gold.

The need for a more flexible currency develops. More than ten years went by after the Gold Standard Act was passed before further important changes were made in our currency system. The financial crisis of 1907, however, made clear the need for a flexible currency — that is, the need to have more currency in circulation at times when business needed more, and less when the demands of business were not so great. When the Panic of 1907 was at its height, a number of sound banks failed because they could not quickly change their assets into currency to meet the heavy demands of their depositors who wanted to draw out funds.[1] Besides, there was no means for quickly transferring currency from a bank with plentiful resources to another which needed temporary relief during a "run." The national banks could not do much to help. The volume of notes (paper money) they could issue depended upon the possession of government bonds which they owned and could deposit to back up their currency [2] (page 312). At the very times when more currency was demanded (that is, periods of prosperity and industrial activity), the high prices of bonds kept the banks from purchasing more. To meet this problem, Congress passed an emergency law known as the

[1] Banks make profits by lending the money deposited with them. The notes received for these loans, and other property which they own, are known as assets. No bank has on hand, at any given moment, sufficient funds to pay back all of its depositors. A "run" on a bank develops when a large number of depositors become panicky and demand their money immediately.

[2] The national banks were permitted by the Gold Standard Act to increase their issue of paper money from 90 per cent to the full value of the United States bonds which they had deposited with the Treasury.

Aldrich-Vreeland Act (1908). This measure allowed national banks, in times of need, to issue a limited amount of bank notes on the basis of certain securities other than United States bonds. Still, the need for a thorough reform of the banking and currency system remained.

The Federal Reserve System is created. The Federal Reserve Act was passed by Congress in 1913, upon the recommendation of President Woodrow Wilson and under the guidance of Senator Carter Glass of Virginia. By the terms of this act the country was divided into twelve districts, each with a Federal Reserve Bank. Every national bank was required to join the Federal Reserve System, and state banks were invited to join. Each regional Federal Reserve Bank had its own board of directors. The whole system was directed by the central Federal Reserve Board, whose members at first included the Secretary of the Treasury, the Comptroller of the Currency, and other members appointed by the President.[3]

The currency becomes elastic. The Federal Reserve System made it possible to expand or contract the currency (put more currency into circulation or withdraw some from circulation) according to the needs of business. Federal Reserve Banks were bankers' banks — they served only their member banks and had no direct dealings with individuals or business concerns. They granted loans based upon government bonds. They were also authorized to "rediscount," or make loans upon, certain *promissory notes* held by member banks. In times of industrial activity or crop movements, for example, businessmen and farmers go to banks for loans. In return for these loans they give the banks promissory notes — promises of repayment. Instead of holding these promissory notes until they become due, a member bank could use them as security to borrow more money from the Federal Reserve Bank and in this way build up the reserve which they were required to keep at the reserve bank. Upon

[3] The Secretary of the Treasury and the Comptroller were removed from the reorganized Board of Directors by the Banking Act of 1935.

The Federal Reserve System was created to prevent runs like this, which occurred in New York during the Panic of 1907.

the basis of these rediscounted promissory notes the Federal Reserve Bank could put more Federal Reserve Notes into circulation.

When businessmen and farmers no longer needed heavy credit, the member bank could repay its loans to the Federal Reserve Bank and recover its promissory notes. Federal Reserve notes up to the value of the loans were then retired from circulation, and in this way the amount of currency in circulation was reduced.

The Federal Reserve Board might also require its regional banks to rediscount notes for each other. In this way, funds that were not immediately needed in one section of the country could be transferred to another where there were pressing demands for credit. The Federal Reserve Board could also raise or lower the rediscount rate (the interest rate for loans to member banks), and in this way encourage or discourage credit expansion. During World War I and again during the period of prosperity of the 1920's, the Federal Reserve System proved its ability to provide a flexible currency to keep the banking reserves of the country in action.

——————— CHECK-UP ———————

What measures were taken from 1900 to 1929 to improve the currency system?

1. What connection did currency and money have with the return of prosperity after 1897? Why was "free silver" no longer an issue? What was the Gold Standard Act of 1900?
2. How did the Panic of 1907 reveal the need for a more flexible currency?
3. What were the provisions of the Federal Reserve Act? How did the Federal Reserve System make currency more elastic?

2 The New Deal Meets a Financial Crisis

Bank failures create panic. The Panic of 1929 put a burden upon the banks of this country which they were not able to carry. As the depression deepened, bank failures increased. In the year 1931 alone, nearly 2300 banks locked their doors. Ugly rumors resulted in "runs" on banks, and ruin overtook many basically sound institutions which could not on the instant satisfy the demands of their depositors. People doubted the stability of banks and started to hoard currency. Thus money became scarce. Congress tried to meet the problem by the first Glass-Steagall Act (1932), which provided for more liberal expansion of the Federal Reserve currency and credit. Despite frantic efforts, however, the financial outlook grew blacker.

Foreign debtors default. International finance was also involved in the crisis. The whole world was the victim of economic distress, and the United States found that the Allied Powers were unable to meet their World War I obligations (page 542). For that reason, President Hoover, in the summer of 1931, proclaimed a one-year *moratorium,* or suspension of payments, on intergovernmental debts. But conditions grew worse instead of better. Because world prices were falling and world trade kept shrinking in volume, the Allies became

less able to pay their war debts. Reparation payments from Germany stopped entirely.[4]

The first installment on war debts after the Hoover moratorium fell due in December, 1932. Great Britain paid in gold, and Italy paid in government bonds. But France, Belgium, Hungary and Poland defaulted (made no payments). Two years later Congress passed the Johnson Act, which prevented governments in default from receiving further loans in the United States. In June of 1934, Finland was the only country to pay in full.. Great Britain, owing a payment of more than a quarter-billion dollars, gave notice that she would "suspend all . . . payments pending a final revision of the settlement." Except for Finland, default was now general. The war debts became more and more a closed chapter.

Banking takes a "holiday." In the days just before President Franklin D. Roosevelt was inaugurated on March 4, 1933, the United States found itself in the grip of the worst financial paralysis in its history. In an effort to save banks that had not already closed, governors in almost all states declared a "bank holiday." Hardly a bank in the country was still open by the time of the inauguration. Business was at a standstill, while people found themselves with no money to spend except the few dollars in their pockets. The country waited, breathless, for the new President to act.

In his inaugural address President Franklin D. Roosevelt declared: "We require two safeguards against a return of the evils of the old order: there must be a strict supervision of all banking and credits and investments, so that there will be an end to speculation with other people's money, and

---

[4] Reparations were goods and money which Germany had to give to the Allies to repay them in part for losses suffered in World War I. The United States, first by the Dawes Plan, sponsored by Charles G. Dawes, and later by the Young Plan, suggested by a conference headed by Owen D. Young, had played a leading role in fixing German reparations. During the depression, Germany claimed that she was unable to make these payments to the Allies. In fact, the sums borrowed by Germans but never repaid were larger than Germany's reparations payments.

Periods of Prosperity and Depression

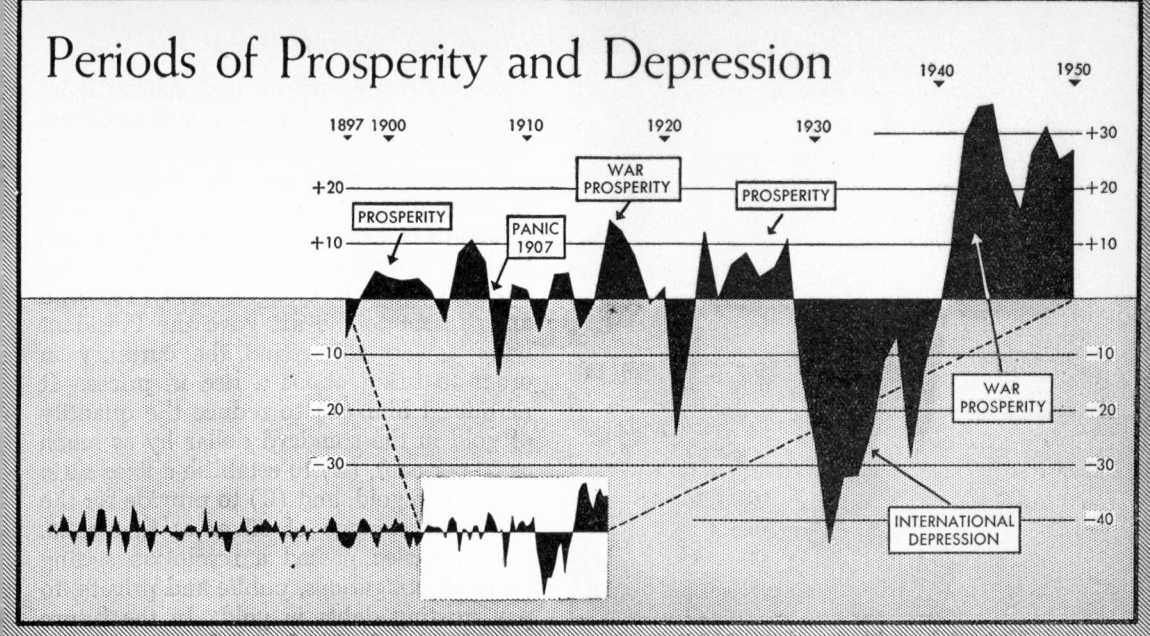

Periods of prosperity and depression have been more pronounced in the 1900's than ever before, as the small inset shows at the bottom of this chart. Can you explain why? To trace details throughout our history, look back to the charts on pages 184 and 375.

there must be provision for an adequate but sound currency." His first official act was to proclaim a national bank holiday. Further shipment of gold out of the country was prohibited. Paper currency could not be turned in for gold. A special session of Congress was called for March 9 to deal with the crisis.

The banks reopen. On the first day of this special session Congress passed an emergency banking measure. It gave the President power to extend the bank holiday, to control the movement of gold, and to supervise the banks of the country. Sound banks were to be reopened or reorganized. Emergency Federal Reserve currency was to be issued to meet the unusual demands. On the following Sunday evening, in the first of several radio "fireside chats" to the American people, the President announced the gradual reopening of sound banks and added: "Let me make it clear that the banks will take care of all needs . . . I can assure you that it is safer to keep your money in a reopened bank than under the mattress." When the banks began to reopen, it was evident that the panic had died down. The banks took in more money in deposits than they paid

out in currency. Within a month, two thirds of a billion dollars in gold coin or gold certificates were returned to the Federal Reserve Banks. The New York Stock Exchange, closed during the bank holiday, reopened with a record rise in stock values. By the end of March, two thirds of the banks were operating on an unrestricted basis.

Congress increases banking security. As the emergency lifted, Congress proceeded to put into law the reforms proposed in the President's inaugural address. The Banking Acts of 1933 and 1935 provided stricter regulation of banks and credit by the Federal Reserve Board. These laws also required the commercial banks to give up all "security affiliates" — organizations controlled by banks for trading in stocks and bonds for purposes of speculation. Small depositors were given renewed faith in banks when the Federal Deposit Insurance Corporation (FDIC) was created. The FDIC insured every deposit up to $5000 in member banks.[5] Bank failures stopped

[5] All banks belonging to the Federal Reserve System were automatically members of the FDIC. Others were eligible if they met requirements. Soon, 90 per cent of the banks were members.

Financial problems of the 1930's were aggravated by the country's need to spend vast sums for relief to those out of jobs. This picture shows part of a "bread line" in New York.

almost entirely, and in the cases of the few banks which did close their doors, losses to depositors were negligible.

The SEC regulates stocks and bonds. Congress also tried to prevent the kind of wild speculation in securities (stocks and bonds) that had taken place in the late 1920's (page 507). An act passed in May, 1933 — and amended by the Securities and Exchange Act of 1934 — gave the government the power to regulate all security sales. The law required that stocks and bonds offered for public sale be registered with the Securities and Exchange Commission (SEC). Public utility holding companies were brought under SEC control by the Wheeler-Rayburn Act of 1935 (page 517).

The New Deal abandons the gold standard. The President's proclamation of March 5, 1933, stopping the export of gold and the redemption of paper currency in gold, meant that the gold standard had, in actual practice, been abandoned. The fact was officially announced in April. In place of the gold standard, the President and his advisers planned a currency which they believed to be better suited to the country's

needs. Because prices had fallen to an abnormally low level during the depression, a plan was adopted for raising them by reducing immediately the purchasing value of the dollar.

Congress expands the currency. When the first Agricultural Adjustment Act (page 557) was passed by Congress (May, 1933), an amendment to the act gave the President wide powers to expand the currency in order to bring about a rise in prices. It permitted him (1) to reduce the quantity of gold in the standard dollar by as much as 50 per cent, (2) to establish a fixed ratio of silver to gold, and (3) to provide for the unlimited coinage of silver at that ratio. Congress also passed a resolution setting aside all obligations, public and private, to pay existing debts in gold. In the future no obligation had to be paid in any specific type of currency.

In October, 1933, the President announced that the Treasury would purchase foreign and newly mined gold at a price far above the old standard of $20.67 an ounce. Early in 1934, Congress adopted a measure which (1) fixed the value of the dollar at 50 to 60 per cent of its former gold content, and (2) authorized the President to "manage" the currency within these limits. The President then fixed the gold value of the dollar at 59.06 cents in terms of its old gold value. In other words, it would take 35 of the new dollars, instead of $20.67 of the old, to buy one ounce of gold.

Still, prices did not rise rapidly enough to suit the Administration. So, in June of 1934, Congress passed a Silver Purchase Act, which it was hoped would raise prices. This measure declared that it was the policy of the United States to maintain one fourth of the monetary stock which backed up its paper currency in silver and three fourths of its value in gold. The President was authorized to buy silver up to the specified amount and to issue silver certificates against it.

The Supreme Court upholds the devaluation of the dollar. Did the government have the right to abandon gold payments? The answer was "no," said holders of gold certificates, Liberty Bonds, and other bonds payable in gold. Owners of such securities were supposed to be able to redeem them for dollars of the old gold content. Some people demanded $1.69 in New Deal currency for each dollar's worth of their securities. But the Supreme Court, by a five to four vote (1935), decided that neither the government nor private debtors could be compelled to pay their obligations in dollars of the old gold content.

——————— CHECK-UP ———————

How did the government try to solve the financial crisis following 1929?

1. Why did bank failures increase greatly after 1929? What happened to the payment of debts owed by foreign countries?
2. Why were bank holidays declared early in 1933? What did President Roosevelt do to reopen the banks?
3. How did the government try to protect bank depositors? To protect the buyers of stocks and bonds?
4. Why did the government abandon the gold standard? How did it try to raise prices? What was the decision of the Supreme Court concerning the devaluation of the dollar?

3 Inflation and National Debt Become Major Problems

President Franklin D. Roosevelt tries to check inflation. During most of Franklin D. Roosevelt's first two terms, he was trying to lower the value of the dollar in order to bring about a rise in prices. Then for the balance of his administration, he had to fight inflation. During and after World War II, conditions favored price rises. Wages and other incomes were high, but the amount of goods available for purchase by consumers was limited by the war. People were willing to pay more and more for scarce consumer goods.

In addition, there was a large increase in the amount of currency in circulation be-

cause of the sale of billions of dollars of government bonds to banks. In 1937 the per capita money in circulation was $50.07; by 1941 it had reached $72.16, and by 1946 it was $200.00. The effect was inflationary, since the greater the amount of money in circulation, the less the dollar (the unit of value) will buy. Still another force causing inflation was the fact that the dollar had actually been reduced in value. The people were using dollars that were worth only 59 cents by previous standards.

In an attempt to check inflation and the skyrocketing of prices, the President in 1942 mapped out a seven-point wartime program. With the approval of Congress, the following program was put into effect:

(1) Wage and salary increases were limited by the War Labor Board (WLB).

(2) An Office of Price Administration (OPA) was established to fix ceilings (top limits) on retail and wholesale prices and to control rents in industrial areas. Prices for many articles were limited to those prices charged in March, 1942. The OPA was also authorized to ration (limit the sale of) certain products, of which there were not enough to go around because of the demands of war. A long list of articles — sugar, meat, fats, coffee, canned goods, shoes, gasoline, fuel oil, tires, and other products — were rationed for civilians.

(3) The Department of Agriculture and the OPA were to co-operate in holding down farm prices.

(4) Taxes were increased.

(5) People were urged to put their money into war bonds instead of goods.

(6) Easy credit and installment buying were discouraged, and the payment of debts was encouraged.

(7) An Office of Economic Stabilization (OES) was created to administer the program. Justice James F. Byrnes resigned from the Supreme Court to head this agency.

Prices rise despite control. These anti-inflation moves did much to hold prices in line during the war years, yet some price rises did occur. Some businessmen believed, rightly or wrongly, that they were entitled to higher prices for the goods or services they sold. Many working men and women insisted on higher wages and, since there was a shortage of labor, industry was willing to increase them. Wage and price ceilings were attacked and often evaded. At the end of the war, for example, prices of some goods were higher by 20 to 50 per cent than they had been in 1942.

Inflation controls are relaxed. After the war ended, price control became increasingly difficult. In 1946, labor was able to break through wage ceilings for hourly increases of nearly 20 per cent (page 528). After that, demands for increased prices became more insistent. Producers would refuse to put an article on the market at an OPA price of $4.00 when, because of the higher cost of labor, it might actually cost $5.00 to manufacture and sell. Acute shortages of many products developed. Some of these were justified by increased costs or insufficient raw materials. Others were brought about artificially in order to put pressure on ceiling prices. Business leaders claimed that the way to solve the problem was to remove price controls. They declared that such a step would result in increased production and, in time, in lower prices.

When the price-control act expired in June, 1946, President Truman and Congress were unable to agree upon terms for extending it. Each tried to shift responsibility upon the other, but wage and price controls — except for rent control in certain areas — were permitted to expire. A sharp rise in prices followed the return to normal conditions of supply and demand. In a single month, food prices rose nearly 14 per cent. By 1949 the purchasing value of the dollar in general had been cut to about half its value in 1939.

National debt, taxes, and inflation are related. The government's attempt to fight inflation was complicated because of the fantastically large national debt. One way to combat inflation, for example, would be to raise taxes in order to pay off this debt. Such a move would take bonds out of circulation and at the same time leave less money in people's pockets — money which was being used to bid for scarce items and

which was thus forcing prices up. On the other hand, if taxes were raised too high, people would stop buying, businessmen would slow down production, and a depression might set in. The beginning of this problem goes back to 1917–1919, for the national debt of 1947 was in part handed down from World War I.

A national budget system is organized. The national debt at the close of World War I was about 25½ billion dollars. On this debt the United States was paying interest of about one billion dollars a year. To encourage economy in government and thus make possible a reduction both of the national debt and of taxes, a National Budget Act was adopted by Congress in 1921. This act created a Bureau of the Budget in the Treasury Department. Up to this time Congress had made appropriations with little thought of balancing expenditures and income — of "balancing the budget." Now, however, the Director of the Budget was to receive requests for funds from all government departments and agencies. He was then to prepare a budget containing an estimate of receipts and expenditures for the coming year. The President, in turn, would submit the budget to Congress. Congress might raise or lower the Director's estimates, and then finally grant the necessary appropriations. Under the capable control of Charles G. Dawes, the first Director of the Budget, the process of organizing and spending public funds was made more efficient. The new budget system made it possible to use surplus revenue to reduce the national debt. During the 1920's, the debt was cut down by one third. But it still amounted to some 16 billion dollars when the great depression set in.

The debt rises during the depression. The reduction of the national debt came to an end when the national income declined sharply after the Panic of 1929. The Congress which assembled in December, 1931, was faced by the largest peacetime deficit in the country's history up to that time. To help meet this deficit, Congress raised income taxes and levied a wide variety of other taxes. Nevertheless, the public debt again began to rise. As the New Deal program got under way, President Roosevelt divided the budget into two parts: the ordinary budget for regular government expenditures, and an emergency budget to "prime the pump" for industry and agriculture. No attempt was made to balance the emergency budget. The money borrowed and spent to relieve unemployment and bring about recovery pushed the national debt to a new high of about 50 billion dollars before the United States entered World War II.

Debt reduction is slow. The daily expenditures of the United States government during World War II were about a quarter billion dollars — about ten times as great as during World War I. By 1946, when the war was over, the national debt amounted to nearly 270 billion dollars, or over $1900 for every man, woman, and child in the United States. Federal taxes for 1947 were around 40 billion dollars a year on a national income of over 200 billions — by far the highest in our history. For this reason, it was possible to make a substantial reduction in the debt. But it was obvious that if deflation set in and the national income dropped sharply, debt reduction would be impossible.

In 1947, for the first year since 1930, the national debt was reduced, by more than 10 billion dollars. President Truman urged that taxes be kept high in order to continue retiring the debt while times were good, and also to decrease the amount of money which consumers could spend on scarce, high-priced goods. He argued that high taxes would help bring prices down to stable levels. Republican leaders in Congress, on the other hand, claimed that high taxes worked a hardship on the average citizen and discouraged investments in business. In 1948 they passed a tax-reduction law over the President's veto. Prospects for cutting down the public debt were dimmed, but many found consolation in the fact that the debt was owed to the American people themselves and not to outside nations or investors. The government bonds, which represented loans to the government, were held by the American

people or by American banks which had used the deposits of their customers to buy them.

——— CHECK-UP ———

Why did inflation and the national debt become major problems?

1. Why did inflation become a serious problem in World War II? How did the government try to check the rise in prices? With what success?
2. What happened to price control and prices after the war ended?
3. How does the Bureau of the Budget help to systematize federal taxing and spending?
4. Why did the national debt increase during World Wars I and II and the depression? Why is reduction of the debt difficult to achieve?

4 The Era of Reform Brings a Reduction in Tariffs

The Dingley Tariff raises duties to a new high. So far this chapter has traced the story of currency and banking reforms as well as the problems of inflation and debt reduction. The years since the opening of the twentieth century have also brought changes in tariff policy. As we have seen, Cleveland's attempts at tariff reduction failed to bear fruit (Chapter 20). The election of 1896, which brought William McKinley to the White House (page 469), was interpreted by the Republican leaders as an order to proceed full speed ahead with all of the measures which had become identified with the Republican Party. First and foremost of these was a high tariff to protect business and industry. A tariff bill, introduced at a special session of Congress by Nelson Dingley of Maine, went swiftly through Congress and became law in 1897. The Dingley Tariff reduced the number of items on the free list and in general set a new high for tariff protection.

The Rise and Fall of American Exports

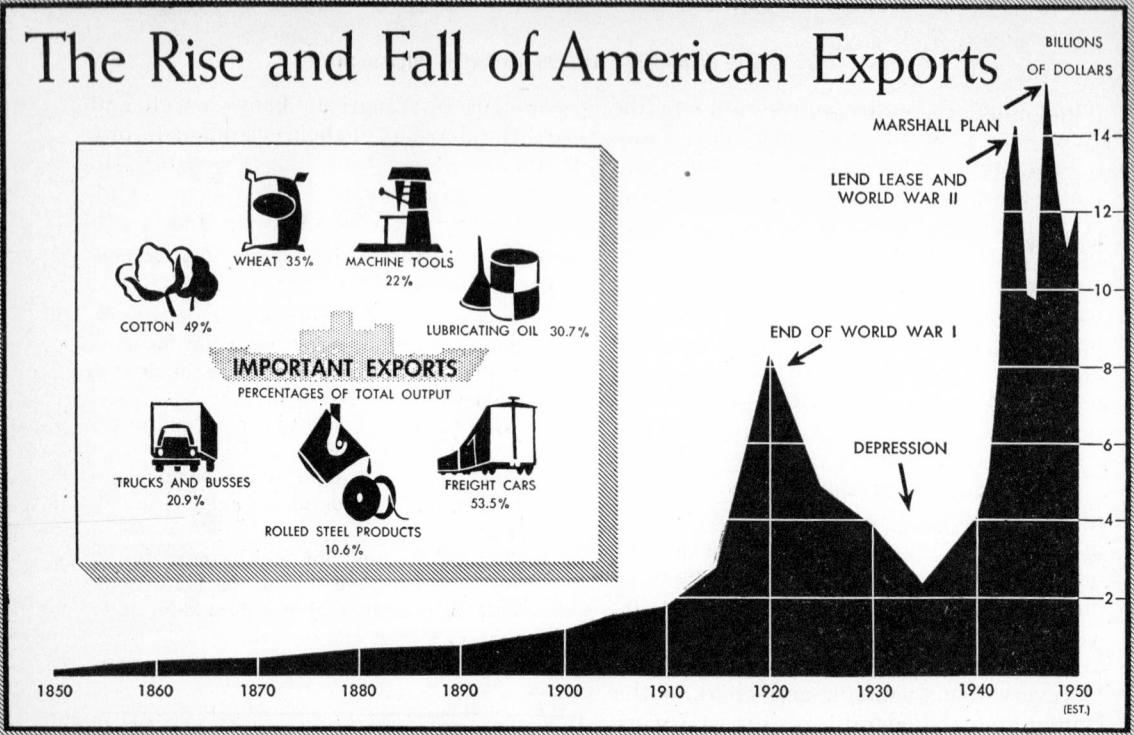

BILLIONS OF DOLLARS

MARSHALL PLAN

LEND LEASE AND WORLD WAR II

END OF WORLD WAR I

DEPRESSION

IMPORTANT EXPORTS
PERCENTAGES OF TOTAL OUTPUT

WHEAT 35%
MACHINE TOOLS 22%
COTTON 49%
LUBRICATING OIL 30.7%
TRUCKS AND BUSSES 20.9%
ROLLED STEEL PRODUCTS 10.6%
FREIGHT CARS 53.5%

1850 1860 1870 1880 1890 1900 1910 1920 1930 1940 1950 (EST.)

Exports to foreign countries account for a relatively small percentage of our total output, but that percentage is vital to certain industrial and agricultural enterprises. What do you find in this chart that proves this? What effect may high tariff rates have on the volume of exports? What else may have effect on foreign trade?

Doubts about tariff protection grow. The Dingley Tariff remained in force for a dozen years. Since this was for the most part a period of prosperity, the Republicans — particularly the Republicans from the industrial East — pointed with pride to the tariff as one cause of good times.

Yet many people began to question seriously whether the public at large was the gainer or the loser from a policy of high protection. Farmers came to realize that the duties contained in the Dingley Tariff did not increase the price of the produce they sold, but instead raised the price of articles they had to buy. The farmers in the Middle West, particularly, began to object more and more to the high tariff. The argument that infant-industry must be protected was under suspicion, too. Some "infants" had grown into giant trusts (pages 370–375). In addition, many economists denied the claim that "high tariffs make high wages." They pointed out that wages, generally speaking, were as high in industries that were unprotected by tariff as in those that were protected. Wage rates, they declared, depended much more upon the efficiency of labor than on tariff rates. Even President McKinley had come to doubt the merits of a high tariff. The day before he was shot he said, "We must not repose in fancied security that we can forever sell everything and buy little or nothing. . . . The period of exclusion is past."

As the era of reform got under way during the early years of the twentieth century (page 511) and as reformers and muckrakers vigorously attacked various problems in American life, criticism of the tariff became stronger and stronger. The country was enjoying good times, but the price of manufactured articles was relatively higher than the price of other commodities. As prices rose, the general public began to suspect that perhaps the high cost of living was the fault of the "wicked trusts" and big businesses which were protected by the tariff. There developed a widespread and persistent demand on the part of the public that the tariff be lowered.

Republicans promise tariff revision. In the election of 1908 the Republicans took into account the change in public opinion and declared themselves "unequivocally for a revision of the tariff." They now stated that the purpose of revision should be to set "such duties as will equal the difference between the cost of production at home and abroad, together with a reasonable profit to American industries." Since the Democratic Party favored tariff revision even more strongly, the tariff was not an important issue in the campaign. The Republican presidential candidate, William Howard Taft, was elected. In his inaugural address he promised that tariffs would be revised downwards.

The Payne-Aldrich Tariff emerges. However, just the reverse came about. A new tariff bill sponsored by Representative Sereno E. Payne began, like the Wilson-Gorman Act (page 383), as a fair attempt to carry out the party pledge. Many raw materials were to be admitted without duty, while other articles were to come in under reduced rates. But when the bill emerged from the Senate Finance Committee, under the chairmanship of Nelson W. Aldrich, it was very different from the original measure. The committee had added nearly 850 amendments, some three quarters of which represented increases. Instead of providing for a general reduction from the levels of the Dingley Act, the Senate bill actually kept many tariff rates as they had been, and authorized a sharp increase in still others.

The Payne-Aldrich bill arouses heated argument. There followed a bitter debate on the Senate floor. Senator Aldrich, a leader of the high tariff group, defended his bill in these words: "If it costs ten cents to produce a razor in Germany and twenty cents in the United States, it will require one hundred per cent duty to equalize the conditions in the two countries. . . . As far as I am concerned, I shall have no hesitancy in voting for a duty which will equalize conditions."

A small group of "insurgent," progressive Republican senators from the Middle West opposed the Senate bill. Led by Robert M. La Follette of Wisconsin, A. J. Beveridge of Indiana, Joseph L. Bristow of Kansas, and A. B. Cummins of Iowa, they waged a hard struggle against regular Republicans who were trying to "steam-roller" the bill through Congress. They denounced every tariff increase. They advertised to the country at large the injustice of many of the rates. At first President Taft encouraged these insurgents, but finally he gave his support to the Senate bill. He did prevail upon the Senate to make a few slight reductions in rates. He also persuaded the Senate to add a small tax on the net earnings of corporations, and to prepare a constitutional amendment enabling Congress to levy a tax on incomes.[6] But the bill which finally came from Congress, and which Taft signed, was substantially the same as that recommended by Senator Aldrich.

The debate over the Payne-Aldrich Tariff splits the Republican Party. The fact that twenty Republicans in the House and seven in the Senate voted against the final bill caused an open split in the Republican Party. When President Taft publicly defended the measure, declaring that it was the "best tariff ever passed by the Republican Party," he injured his own personal prestige, especially in the West. Throughout the nation there was an undercurrent of resentment, a feeling that the interests of the public had been betrayed.

The Democrats plan to lower the tariff. The victory of the Democrats under Woodrow Wilson in 1912 opened the way for a change in tariff policy. A month after his inauguration, President Wilson broke a century-old custom and appeared in person before Congress to ask for a downward revision of the tariff. A bill designed to carry out the President's wishes was promptly introduced into the House by Oscar Underwood, a Congressman from

6 The Sixteenth Amendment to the Constitution, which enabled Congress to levy a tax on incomes, was ratified by the required number of states and was declared a part of the Constitution by the Secretary of State on February 25, 1913, just before President Taft left office. The first income tax levy, however, was made by Congress during President Wilson's administration.

Alabama. When the supporters of a high tariff in the Senate threatened to amend the House Bill, as they had done in the past, Wilson publicly denounced those who were lobbying for special interests and prevented any serious changes in the proposed bill.

The Underwood Act reduces tariff rates. The Underwood Tariff, passed in 1913, was the first thoroughgoing reduction in tariff rates since the War Between the States. The free list was greatly enlarged. It included foodstuff, raw materials, and daily necessities like meats, iron ore, and agricultural implements. On the other hand, luxuries, raw materials not produced in the United States, and chemicals were heavily taxed for purposes of revenue. Altogether there were nearly 1000 decreases in rates and fewer than 90 increases. The average level of duties dropped from about 37 to 27 per cent.

To make up for the expected loss of revenue, the Underwood Act included provisions for a personal income tax. This tax was to be "graduated," that is, persons with higher incomes were to pay at a higher tax rate — up to six per cent on incomes over $500,000. The Underwood Act, including the income tax provision, brought some increase in government revenue during the first year it operated. But before its full effect on government and business could take place, World War I seriously upset the conditions of international trade.

─────── CHECK-UP ───────

What changes did the era of reform bring in tariff policy?

1. What did the Dingley Tariff do to the level of tariff rates?
2. Why did many citizens in the early 1900's come to question the arguments in favor of high tariff protection?
3. What stand did William Howard Taft take on the tariff? Why did the Payne-Aldrich Tariff fail to achieve its original purpose — reduction of tariff rates?
4. What was President Wilson's attitude toward the tariff? What changes were made by the Underwood Tariff Act?

5 World War I Alters the Problems of Trade and Tariffs

Before 1914 we were a debtor nation. From the 1880's to World War I the United States had enjoyed what is known as a "favorable" balance of trade; in other words, we exported more than we imported. This was as it should be, because we were a debtor country. Throughout our national existence, and especially after the War Between the States, European money had been attracted to our shores. America's fast-growing industries and railroads, together with its vast natural resources and undeveloped West, invited the investment of foreign capital. As a result of such investments, by 1914 between 5 and 6 billion dollars in American stocks and bonds were held abroad. Each year their owners received hundreds of millions of dollars in interest and dividends. Furthermore, American goods were shipped in foreign vessels, and much of our insurance was handled by foreign companies. For these services also, payments were due to European countries.

The United States did not actually ship gold to Europe to meet these payments. We shipped goods which were bought by Europeans, and their payments found their way to our European creditors instead of coming to this country. Shipping large quantities of goods to Europe not only helped pay our debts but furnished an outlet for the surplus products of American farms and factories. Under these circumstances and in spite of the tariff, American exports to foreign countries averaged some 2 billion dollars a year during the period that preceded World War I.

The United States becomes a creditor nation. World War I changed the United States from a debtor to a creditor country. The Allied Powers made huge purchases of war supplies in this country during the years 1914–1917, before the United States entered the war. The principal purchasers were Great Britain and France. Money to pay for these materials was raised in three ways: (1) gold was shipped to the United States in direct payment; (2) American stocks and bonds owned by foreign investors were sold to Americans; (3) bonds of European governments were sold to American investors.

Modern freighter

After the United States declared war, this process continued. Furthermore, the United States Treasury extended large loans to the Allied governments to help them pay for their purchases in this country. After the war, the Allies owed the United States government about 10 billion dollars. This was in addition to large sums of money owed by Europeans and European governments to private individuals and corporations in the United States.

The war debts are funded. To arrange for the payment of these war debts to the United States, Congress set up a World War Foreign Debt Commission early in 1922. This commission declared that no nation could be expected to pay "sums in excess of its capacity to pay." It said, further, that no settlement which slowed up the recovery and development of debtor nations could serve the best interests of the United States. The commission refused to cut down the amount owed to us, but it did arrange for payment over a long period (62 years), and reduced interest rates in accordance with the ability of the debtor country to pay.

Our new wealth creates new trade problems. The fact that European countries owed the United States and its citizens more than we owed them had an effect on foreign trade. European purchases of American goods could no longer be financed by interest paid to Europeans. Moreover, during the war great numbers of American merchant vessels were built which were now prepared to carry cargoes formerly carried in foreign vessels. This change, of course, reduced Europe's ability to earn dollars with which to buy our goods. Could they pay for our goods in gold? The United States already had more than its share of

the gold supply of the world. If European governments exported much more of their gold, their paper money, which was backed by their gold, would drop in value.

How, then, could Europeans pay for the goods that we wanted to sell them? There was only one way — by selling goods to us. And if they were to repay their war debts as well as buy our goods, they would have to sell us more than we sold them.

Americans balk at a surplus of imports. But this was a condition that was not acceptable to the American people. They were unwilling to buy more than they sold overseas. American farms were producing more than the American people could consume, and farmers looked abroad for a market for their surplus. In addition, American factories were geared for the production of a surplus for export. To enable the United States to sell surplus goods and products abroad, American bankers and investors lent Europeans another 4 billion dollars. Our foreign trade consequently doubled during the 20's, and the same was true of the excess of exports over imports. This situation could hardly continue forever. When Americans not only stopped lending but tried to collect some of their loans (1929), an international financial crisis resulted which helped bring on the world-wide depression.

Congress fails to face the realities of international trade. Meanwhile our tariff policy only made matters worse. The Republican Congress which came in with President Harding in 1921 failed to take into consideration the fact that we had become a creditor nation. New industries, like the dye and toy industries, were clamoring for tariff protection, and the farmers were in distress because of the collapse of world farm prices (page 555). The solution seemed clear enough to President Harding and Congress: restore "the good old times when the Republican

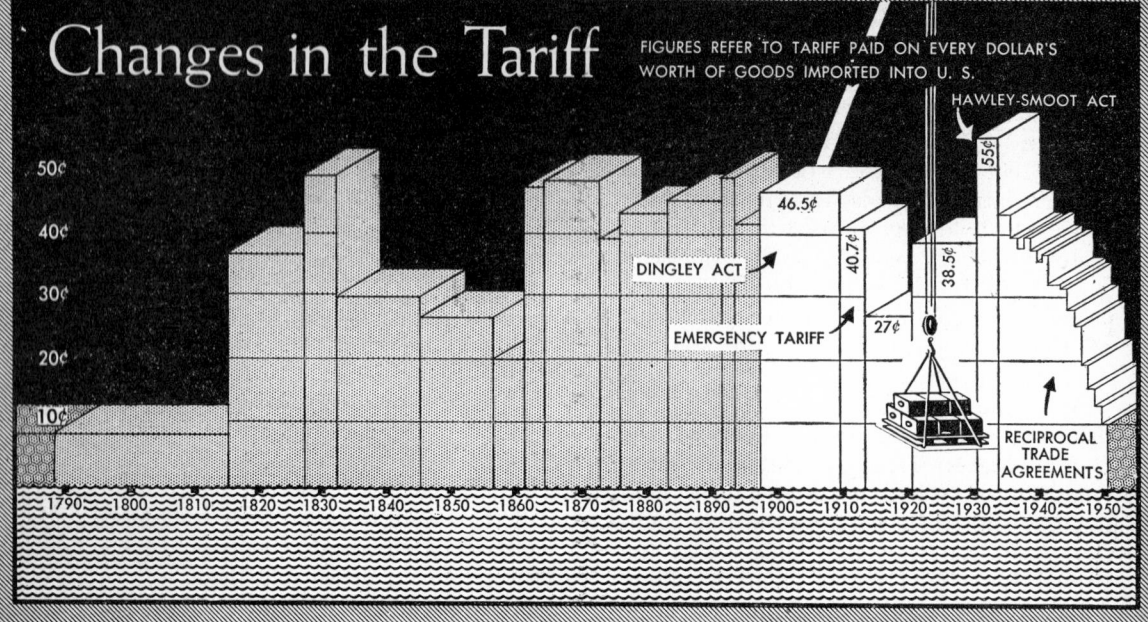

Changes in the Tariff

FIGURES REFER TO TARIFF PAID ON EVERY DOLLAR'S WORTH OF GOODS IMPORTED INTO U. S.

HAWLEY-SMOOT ACT

55¢

46.5¢

40.7¢

38.5¢

DINGLEY ACT

EMERGENCY TARIFF

27¢

RECIPROCAL TRADE AGREEMENTS

50¢
40¢
30¢
20¢
10¢

1790 1800 1810 1820 1830 1840 1850 1860 1870 1880 1890 1900 1910 1920 1930 1940 1950

Tariff rates reached the highest point in our history under the Hawley-Smoot Act of 1930. Then, after 1933, they began to go steadily downward. Can you explain why?

protective tariff filled the treasury and at the same time gave protection to American industry."

The Fordney-McCumber Act raises tariffs again. An emergency tariff act, intended to help the farmers, was passed by a special session of Congress in the spring of 1921. The next year, Congress passed the Fordney-McCumber Act, which reduced the free list and established a new high level of tariff rates. The Fordney-McCumber Act also authorized the President to raise or lower the rates by as much as 50 per cent whenever investigation by a Tariff Commission showed that existing duties did not equalize costs of production at home and abroad. In actual practice this provision resulted in many more increases than decreases.

The Hawley-Smoot Tariff hits a new high. Those who favored extremely high tariff duties, however, were not yet satisfied. Congress, called into special session in 1929 by President Hoover to make a "limited revision" of certain duties, started another thorough revision. Many groups now opposed a rise in tariffs. The farmers were badly in need of help, but they were now convinced that high tariffs on agricultural products would not solve their problems. Bankers and importers vigorously objected

to a general rise in rates. Manufacturers who sold much of their produce abroad were worried by the possibility that other countries might strike back. Despite all these protests, Congress raised the duties on farm commodities, raw materials, minerals, textiles, and dyestuffs. The Hawley-Smoot Tariff, sometimes known as the Grundy Tariff,[7] raised the rates of the Fordney-McCumber Tariff by an average of 7 per cent. The Tariff Commission was retained to investigate production costs and to recommend the raising or lowering of rates.

President Hoover approves the Hawley-Smoot Tariff. In the spring of 1930, nearly a thousand leading American economists issued a statement calling upon President Hoover to veto the tariff bill. They warned him that it would result in higher prices to the consumer. They also predicted that other nations would seek revenge by raising their tariff on our goods or by restricting our exports in other ways. Nevertheless, President Hoover approved the bill. Within two years some 40 countries had adopted measures to cut down their imports of American goods.

[7] Joseph Grundy, a Pennsylvania tariff lobbyist who was appointed to fill a vacancy in the Senate, played a leading role in the writing of this law.

Why did the United States as a creditor nation need to reconsider its tariff policies?

1. How did the international economic position of the United States change during World War I? Why?

2. What rules did the United States set up for funding the debts owed by European countries? How were European countries able to buy goods from us during the 1920's? What happened when we tried to collect the money owed us?

3. What was the American tariff policy under Presidents Harding, Coolidge, and Hoover? What effect did the Hawley-Smoot Tariff have on European countries?

4. Why was the United States unwilling to adopt a low tariff policy?

6 World-Wide Depression Brings a New Tariff Policy

Revival of foreign trade is needed. When Franklin D. Roosevelt became President in 1933, the country was in the depths of the great depression. Our foreign trade had dropped to less than a third of its 1929 value. Producers of such goods as cotton, copper, tobacco, and light machinery normally sold a considerable proportion of their products abroad. Unless they could recapture foreign markets, they could not hope to get back on a profitable basis. The revival of foreign trade was an essential part of the Roosevelt program for pulling the United States out of the depression.

But how could this be done? To reduce the tariff was tricky business at a time when thousands of concerns were on the verge of bankruptcy and a slight shift in prices might push them over the edge. The rest of the world was in a depression, too, and lower tariffs might give them a chance to dump surplus products in this country.

Congress passes the Trade Agreements Act. Faced with this situation, Secretary of State Cordell Hull turned to *reciprocity* (page 382), a principle which had been a part of many tariff laws since 1890. At

Hull's urging, Congress passed the Trade Agreements Act in 1934. This act gave the President authority for three years to make reciprocal trade agreements without the approval of the Senate. But increases and decreases were not to go higher than 50 per cent of the established rates, and goods on the free list were not to be removed from it. As one three-year-period after another expired, Congress each time renewed the grant of authority for another term of years.

Nearly 30 reciprocal trade agreements were soon signed under the vigorous leadership of Secretary Hull. By 1949, agreements had been made with 42 countries. The outstanding ones were with Great Britain, Canada, France, Cuba, the Argentine Republic, and Brazil. By the 1936 agreement with France, for example, the United States lowered duties on 71 items, including lace, Roquefort cheese, and champagne. The French in return agreed to lower the rates on American automobiles, timber, metal machinery, radio apparatus, typewriters, and fresh apples and pears.

The most-favored nation clause benefits everyone. Many of our commercial treaties provided that when we reduced the tariff on a product imported from one country, we should automatically give the same reduction on the same product to any other nation that did not discriminate against the United States. For example, when we reduced duties on French lace under the Franco-American agreement of 1936, our duties on lace from Belgium were automatically reduced. This is known as the "most-favored nation" principle. In other words, Belgium, which did not discriminate against the United States, had a right to be treated as well as the nation apparently "most favored" in our trade policy. The policy worked in both directions. When Belgium made an agreement with France, lowering the duty on French automobiles, this also lowered Belgian duties on American automobiles. In this way, every reciprocal trade agreement started a chain-reaction of tariff reductions throughout the world.

Our foreign trade revives. Before the outbreak of World War II, American foreign trade was twice as great as it had been at the low point of the depression. Although the Roosevelt administration did not take full credit for this increase, it did claim that the trade agreements acted as a "powerful force" in reviving the nation's foreign commerce.

War interrupts the trade agreement program. The outbreak of World War II and the spread of hostilities throughout the world affected many countries with whom we had trade agreements, and seriously interfered with American trade. Yet American exports, stimulated by demands for war materials by our allies abroad, soared to new high levels. And they remained high after the war ended. Countries shattered by the war needed thousands of commodities from the United States, and especially foodstuffs for their hungry citizens. Their only problem was how to pay for these purchases in American dollars.

Trade agreements continue into the postwar period. The Democratic administration still believed after World War II that the principle underlying the reciprocal trade agreements offered "the only possible basis on which the economic life of the world [could] be successfully rebuilt." In 1945 Congress therefore extended the Trade Agreements Act for another three-year period. At this time the President was authorized to lower rates again by 50 per cent in return for similar reductions from other nations. In June, 1948, when the Trade Agreeements Act was about to expire, the Republicans were in control of both houses of Congress. Many of the Republicans, like Senator Vandenberg, were internationally minded and saw a close connection between world trade and world peace. "Peace and economics," said Vandenberg, "are inseparably akin." Other senators were eager for a return to the days of high protection. Senator Hugh Butler of Nebraska, for instance, denounced the trade pacts as "a gigantic hoax on the American people . . . solely for the benefit of other nations."

The Republican Congress voted to renew the act for one year, instead of the usual three. At the same time, modifications were introduced which weakened the power of the President to negotiate trade agreements and increased the importance of the Tariff Commission. In case the President made reductions greater than those recommended by the Commission, he was required under the new act to explain his reasons to Congress. President Truman, who was re-elected in November, 1948, urged a return to the full reciprocal trade agreements program.

America leads the way toward freer trade. Under American leadership several steps were taken to encourage world trade during the postwar period. In April, 1947, representatives of the leading commercial nations — not including Russia — met at Geneva, Switzerland, with a double purpose: (1) to remove trade barriers, such as tariff and cartel arrangements, and (2) to draw up a charter for an International Trade Organization (ITO) as an agency under the United Nations. More than 100 trade agreements were drawn up among 23 nations, affecting about two thirds of the world's trade. Under the Trade Agreements Act the United States was able to negotiate these agreements without waiting for the approval of the Senate, and they went into effect generally on January 1, 1948. Every treaty provided that an advantage given any one country should be granted to all other nations taking part in these pacts (the most-favored nation principle). One result of these agreements was an increase in American imports and a decline in exports, thus lessening our huge surplus of exports over imports.

In addition to the trade agreements arranged for at the Geneva meeting, a draft of an ITO charter was drawn up for submission to a World Trade Conference to meet at Havana in November, 1947. In April, 1948, 56 nations — representing 90 per cent of the world's trade — completed the ITO charter. The charter was signed by 53 nations, including only Czechoslovakia of the eastern bloc, and was to go into effect as soon as 20 nations ratified it. Its main purpose was to reduce not only tariffs, but also import quotas, trade preferences, and other stumbling-blocks to international trade. The new charter, however, faced strong opposition on the part of protectionists in the United States.

——— CHECK-UP ———

What tariff policy was adopted by the United States during and after the great depression?
1. What was the basic purpose of the Trade

Agreements Act? What provisions of this act served to increase international trade?
2. What happened to reciprocal trade agreements after World War II?
3. What did the United States do in the postwar period to encourage international trade? What was the fundamental purpose behind the International Trade Organization?

CHAPTER REVIEW

Terms to Understand

"run" on a bank
"bank holiday"
gold content
creditor nation
gold standard
rediscount
moratorium
devaluation
inflation

free trade
"prime the pump"
flexible currency
reparation payment
balancing the budget
favorable balance of
   trade
most-favored nation
   principle

People and Things to Know About

Gold Standard Act
Federal Reserve
   System
National Budget Act
New Deal
Carter Glass
Cordell Hull
Federal Deposit Insurance Corporation
Securities and Exchange Commission
Dingley Tariff

Office of Price Administration
Payne-Aldrich Tariff
   Act
Underwood Tariff Act
Fordney-McCumber
   Tariff
Hawley-Smoot Tariff
   Act
Trade Agreements Act
International Trade
   Organization

Historic Dates to Identify

1897	1913	1933
1900	1930	1934
1909	1931	

Questions to Discuss

1. Why was the standard gold dollar devalued in 1933? What groups are helped and hurt, respectively, by inflation? Why would deflation today be an even more serious problem than in the years after 1929?
2. What groups urge a return to higher tariffs? Why?
3. The Marshall Plan has helped western European nations purchase needed goods and machinery in the United States. How will these nations be able to pay for such purchases?
4. How was the problem of repayment of war debts handled after World War I? World War II?

Questions to Discuss (Cont.)

5. Compare the following:
   (a) The currency before and after the Federal Reserve System was established.
   (b) The foreign trade problems of a debtor and a creditor nation.
   (c) The currency before and after March, 1933.
   (d) Efforts of the New Deal to fight deflation and inflation.
6. Do you feel that our tariff policy has contributed to the well-being of the United States? Why?
7. Do you approve or disapprove (a) President Taft's signing of the Payne-Aldrich Tariff, (b) President Hoover's approval of the Hawley-Smoot Tariff? Give reasons for your answers.

Other Things to Do

1. Make a graph to show the size of the national debt in 1915, 1920, 1925, 1930, 1935, 1940, 1945, and last year. Explain increases and decreases.
2. Use the *Readers' Guide* to find articles about the International Trade Organization. Report your findings to the class.
3. Look in files of magazines for the 1930's to find articles suggesting that the United States should reduce its purchasing from abroad as much as possible, and try to become self-sufficient. Evaluate the arguments used and report to the class.
*4. Make a chart showing the tariffs and other measures affecting international trade which have become law since 1897. Indicate the chief provisions of each.
5. Look in the files of your local newspaper to discover changes in commodity prices since 1900. Make a graph to show changes for one or more commodities (like eggs, wheat, corn, or potatoes). Plot the prices for the same date each year, or at regular intervals. Can you explain the reasons for rises and declines in prices? What do you conclude about the purchasing power of the dollar?

County agent and farmer

Chapter 30

FARMERS SEEK AID FROM

THE GOVERNMENT

The great cities rest upon our broad and fertile prairies. Burn down your cities and leave our farms, and your cities will spring up again as if by magic; but destroy our farms, and the grass will grow in the streets of every city in the country.

William Jennings Bryan

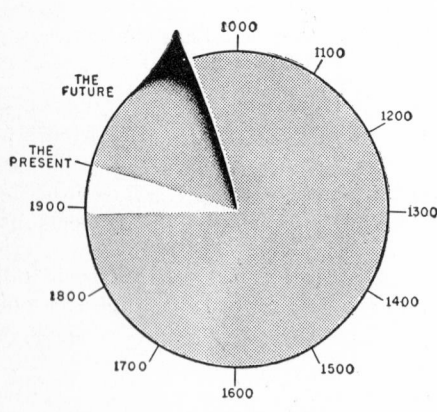

1897 – The Present

Agriculture in the United States during the first half of the twentieth century had two main characteristics: (1) Although the number of farmers decreased, the production of America's farms multiplied by leaps and bounds. This increased production resulted largely from the rapid development of farm machinery, the growth of scientific research, and better education. (2) The problems which had been troubling the farmers of the United States in the last half of the 1800's continued to vex them. For a time in the early 1900's they enjoyed moderate prosperity. But after World War I hard times set in again. While the rest of the country prospered during the "golden twenties," farmers suffered a steadily increasing depression. Hard times lasted until another war stimulated demands for farm products.

As in the agricultural depressions of the 1800's, the low price that the farmer re-

548

ceived for his products remained his chief headache. In the 1800's he had tried without success to solve his problem by asking the government for currency expansion and cheap money. In the 1900's he turned again to government — but for a different kind of aid — and this time succeeded in getting the government's help in raising prices. Support of agricultural prices by the government became to many farmers what tariff protection had been to the businessman.

The story of the farmer in the twentieth century is told in this chapter under the following topics:

1. Machines, science, and education increase farm production.
2. The government tries to help the farmer.
3. New government policies and another war bring farm prosperity.

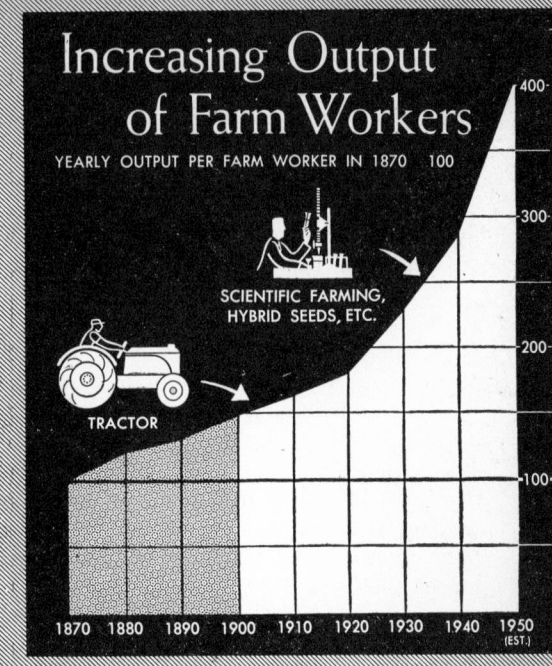

Increasing Output of Farm Workers

YEARLY OUTPUT PER FARM WORKER IN 1870   100

SCIENTIFIC FARMING, HYBRID SEEDS, ETC.

TRACTOR

400-

300-

200-

100-

1870 1880 1890 1900 1910 1920 1930 1940 1950 (EST.)

Output per farm worker has more than doubled in the 1900's. What does this mean in relation to the population chart on page 584?

1 Machines, Science, and Education Increase Farm Production

Farm production soars in the twentieth century. The amazing increase in the production of farm products which took place in the last half of the 1800's continued undiminished in the twentieth century. The production of corn, for example, nearly doubled from 1890 to 1945. In 1945 nearly three times as many bushels of wheat were produced as in 1890. Likewise, in the same period the annual production of cotton increased 50 per cent. Remarkable increases also took place in the production of other farm commodities.

At the same time, a smaller and smaller percentage of the country's population was engaged in farming. In 1870 over one half of the nation's workers were on farms. By 1890 this figure had dropped to 42 per cent, and in 1940 only a little over 18 per cent of America's workers were farmers.

The increased productivity of the farms was the result of many factors — new machines and technological improvements, new scientific methods of farming, and better education of farmers.

Machines and technology help step up farm production. Improved farm machinery continued to help farmers produce more products. In particular, new forms of power — the gasoline engine and electricity — were harnessed to do the work of the farm. Motor-driven tractors replaced horses, and millions of acres formerly needed for pasturage or for raising feed for horses could thus be released for cultivation. Motor-driven trucks carried produce easily to distant markets, while the automobile, the telephone, and the radio made farm life easier and more efficient. At the same time, the extension of electricity to farm areas not only improved lighting but also made possible the use of electric milking machines, cream separators, water pumps, refrigeration, and many other labor-saving devices.

In 1890, machines in use on farms were valued at 500 million dollars. By 1930, the value of farm machinery had risen to 3½ billion dollars.

Science improves farming methods. Perhaps even more important than farm machinery in increasing production was the development of scientific agriculture. The accomplishments of farm specialists and scientists in laboratories and on experimental farms make an exciting chapter in the history of American agriculture. Hardly any aspect of farming has escaped their attention. Among their many achievements, the following were particularly important in increasing farm production: (1) They succeeded in protecting plants from many diseases and insects which destroyed whole crops. (2) They developed new and better varieties of plants which produced larger yields. (3) They bred better livestock which yielded more meat, milk, and other food products. (4) They enriched and improved the soil so that it would produce bigger and better crops. (5) They discovered new and better methods of plowing, planting, and cultivating.

In planting and cultivating alone many new methods were developed or perfected. For example, *contour plowing,* in which the furrows follow the curves of a hill rather than a straight line, has helped prevent the wearing away (erosion) of soil. In the dry plains area, a new method called *dry farming* preserves the moisture in the soil. *Crop rotation,* which interested George Washington and Thomas Jefferson, has been perfected so that now farmers know just what crops to raise each year on a piece of land in order to preserve the richness of the soil.

Luther Burbank pioneers in the development of new varieties of plants. One of the first agricultural specialists to achieve fame was Luther Burbank. In the latter part of the 1800's, Burbank became known as the "plant wizard" because of his success in producing new and better varieties of vegetables, fruits, and flowers. These new varieties gave a bigger yield, or produced bigger fruit, or both.

Burbank's first success was in growing a new variety of potato. One of his most spectacular achievements was the production of a variety of cactus without thorns, which provided a rich food for cattle in the dry western areas. Although Burbank's fame was well established by 1900, he continued to produce new and better plants and fruits up to the time of his death in 1926.

Luther Burbank, like Thomas A. Edison, was not a theoretical scientist but a genius at practical experimentation. Without a thorough knowledge of the scientific principles of cross-breeding and selection, he produced hundreds of new varieties of plants which made a significant contribution to American agriculture.

Mark Carleton helps revolutionize wheat production. After 1887, when the Hatch Act established agricultural experiment stations (page 400), government workers made more and more of the significant contributions to scientific farming. Typical of the thrilling achievements of these hardworking, but often unknown, agricultural scientists is the story of Mark Carleton.

In the late 1890's drought held the Mid-West in its grip. Wheat shriveled and died on the dry lands of the Great Plains. At the state experimentation station in Kansas, Mark Carleton, a quiet research worker, made up his mind to find a wheat that would grow and produce with little rainfall. For five years Carleton searched in vain. But at last in the dry upland regions

(Continued on page 552)

Two-row corn picker

Hay mower

Tractor

MODERN FARM MACHINERY

Luther Burbank
(1849-1926)

Factory Worker

"I SHALL BE contented if, because of me, there shall be better fruits and fairer flowers." Many men seek wealth or power, but Luther Burbank won fame by pursuing the goal which he set forth so simply in these words.

Burbank was born in Lancaster, Massachusetts. He attended public schools and a local academy. He did not go on to college but was a wide reader of books dealing with botany and plant life. As a boy, he worked during several summers in a plow factory in a nearby city. He showed such inventive skill that his friends predicted a successful future along these lines. But young Burbank clung to his interest in growing things. He began market gardening and seed raising in a small way. His first triumph was an improved potato, the Burbank potato. In 1875 he set out for California. There he passed discouraging days at odd and distasteful jobs until he became established in his chosen field.

Seed Raiser

Burbank's words are a key to his purpose as well as an explanation of his fame. His experiments with hundreds of thousands of plants, extending over many plant generations, were undertaken to make possible better varieties of fruits, vegetables, and flowers rather than merely to increase scientific knowledge. Burbank devoted almost forty years to developing new and better varieties of plums and prunes, and, during most of the same period, worked on the improvement of berries. The thornless cactus, developed after painstaking care, provided new sources of food for livestock. Many of the flowers in the florist's window or in the home garden are outcomes of Burbank's magic skill.

Tree Grafter

As the years passed, Luther Burbank's fame spread beyond our borders. Visitors from other countries came to talk with the best known plant originator in the world. He not only produced better fruits and fairer flowers himself, but he also stimulated others to seek the same goals. In his chosen field, Burbank is another example of the American genius for practical research.

551

of Russia he found what he was looking for — a drought-proof wheat that would flourish on the American plains. Later he brought back from Russia still another variety of wheat that increased the farmer's yield.

The new varieties of wheat which Mark Carleton introduced into the United States not only would grow on dry soil; they proved to be immune to rust, a plant disease that was ruinous to farm crops. By World War I a large proportion of the hard, winter wheat grown in this country was descended from the Russian varieties that Mark Carleton had discovered. By cross-breeding different kinds of wheat and selecting the best varieties, Department of Agriculture specialists improved wheat yields still further.

Government scientists lead the way to better farming. Mark Carleton is only one of many scientists who, working alone or in groups through the Department of Agriculture, the land-grant colleges, or the agricultural experiment stations, have wrought miracles in increasing farm production and in overcoming serious obstacles. Corn production was boosted by the development of hybrid corn, which yields larger

Dusting cotton with insecticide from an airplane is an important way of combating the boll weevil and other insects.

ears and better resists drought, disease, and pests. California orchards were able to escape a crushing blight when certain Australian insects — natural enemies of the blight — were turned loose by the Department of Agriculture. A long-staple cotton that would grow on the upland regions was developed in South Carolina, and increased tremendously the cotton production of the South. Southern cotton growers also learned to combat the boll weevil effectively by new methods of cultivation and by dusting the plants in the infected areas with new insecticides. Millions of cattle have been saved by scientific battles against Texas tick fever, hoof-and-mouth disease, and tuberculosis. A scientist at the University of Wisconsin laid the basis for the modern dairy industry by devising a test for the butter-fat content of milk.

Most of the scientists who were responsible for these discoveries are little known to the general public, but their achievements have meant much to the American farmer. In recent years, scientific advances in farming have been made less frequently by individual scientists working alone in their laboratories. More often they have come from teams of agricultural specialists at the government experimental stations, in the agricultural colleges, and in the Department of Agriculture.

The Smith-Lever Act provides "on-the-spot" education for farmers. It is of little value to develop new scientific methods of farming if these remain in the laboratory or are used only on experimental farms. Farmers must learn about the new developments and use them on their own farms if more abundant crops and better livestock are to result.

Perhaps the greatest single influence in educating the farmer to use the findings of scientific agriculture has been the *extension service* of the United States Department of Agriculture. This service had its beginnings in the early 1900's when the Department of Agriculture sent agents into the southern states to help the farmers fight the boll weevil, which was destroying the cotton plants. The work of these agents proved so successful that Congress in 1914 passed the important Smith-Lever Act, which put the extension service on a permanent basis.

The Smith-Lever Act provided that an agent of the extension service should be placed in each farm county to help and advise farmers. The *county agent,* as he is called, has been of tremendous value to the farmer. He has kept the farmer in touch with the findings of research and has helped him use the latest scientific methods. The extension service and the work of the county agent are paid for partly by the federal government and partly by the state and county.

The Smith-Hughes Act encourages agricultural and vocational education in high schools. In 1917, Congress passed the Smith-Hughes Act, which has aided the development of agricultural and other vocational education in secondary schools. According to this act, part of the cost of providing instruction in agriculture, home economics, and other vocational fields in the public schools is paid for by the federal government.

4-H Clubs and the Future Farmers of America encourage better farming. Just before World War I the Department of Agriculture and the land-grant agricultural colleges sponsored the development of 4-H Clubs ("head, heart, hand, and health"). In these clubs young people learn to use the newest methods in farming and homemaking. They compete with each other to see who can raise the best corn or the fattest hogs or put up the best jellies. The work of the clubs is usually supervised by the county agent. By 1946 the clubs had over 1,700,000 members.

The Future Farmers of America was organized on a national basis in 1928 by the United States Office of Education. Its purpose is to provide citizenship and farm leadership training, as well as social activities, for boys studying vocational agriculture in high schools. Soon after the Smith-Hughes Act went into effect (1917), groups of boys who were enrolled in the Smith-Hughes courses began to organize local clubs. The local clubs joined to form state organizations, and finally a national organi-

A young farmer receives expert instruction in corn raising. Good farming today calls for a real knowledge of science.

zation was developed. The activities of the Future Farmers of America supplement the work given in agriculture courses. Teachers of vocational agriculture in the high schools act as advisers to local clubs.

In 1945 the United States Office of Education sponsored a similar organization for girls called the Future Homemakers of America. Its activities are related to the courses in home economics which are given in high schools under the Smith-Hughes Act.

All of these organizations are helpful in bringing home to rural young people the importance of agriculture and their part in improving farming and home living.

Industry finds increasing use for farm products. As farming became more scientific and as government experiment stations developed new and better ways of doing old jobs, farm production increased. Farm production was also stimulated by the new uses which have been found for farm products in industry. At Tuskegee Institute in Alabama, George Washington Carver showed that literally hundreds of industrial products could be made from peanuts. The development of plastics has opened a whole new field for the products of the farm. The soybean, for example, is now being grown for many industrial uses, such as paint and various kinds of plastics. Corncobs have

"Rice Harvest" by Thomas Benton shows a tractor driving a threshing machine on a southern farm. Benton's pictures of American farms and farm life are famous.

found a number of uses in industry, including the making of synthetic rubber.

In 1938 Congress authorized the Department of Agriculture to establish a number of regional laboratories for the purpose of discovering industrial uses for farm products. In the future, as our supplies of oil and coal and other natural resources become smaller, industry will undoubtedly rely more and more on farm commodities for the raw materials from which to manufacture its products.

Farmers' organizations stress education and co-operative marketing. During the twentieth century farmers formed new organizations and continued some older ones. The Grange became active again and was particularly strong in the Northeast. The Farmers' Union, which was founded in Texas, became a national organization with its greatest strength in the West North Central States. One of the largest of the new organizations and perhaps the most national in character was the American Farm Bureau Federation. The formation of the American Farm Bureau Federation was an indirect result of the

Smith-Lever Act. The county agents were to work through county farm bureaus. The county bureaus united to form state bureaus, and finally in 1920 the national organization was formed.

Although all of these organizations were active supporters of laws which would help the farmer, their chief interest was in education and in fostering co-operative marketing. An exception was the Non-Partisan League, which was primarily a political organization.

——————— CHECK-UP ———————

What factors helped increase farm production?

1. Explain what happened to farm production and the number of farm employees from 1890 to the 1940's. What technological improvements helped the farmer?

2. In what ways did science increase farm production? What contributions did Luther Burbank make? Mark Carleton?

3. What did the Smith-Lever Act provide? The Smith-Hughes Act? Why are they important?

4. How do 4-H Clubs and the Future Farmers of America encourage better farming?

5. What new uses are being found for farm products?

6. What purposes did the new farm organizations serve?

---

2 The Government Tries to Help the Farmer

Farmers enjoy a period of prosperity. The farmers shared in the upturn in prosperity at the turn of the century (page 506), and from 1900 to 1920 the farmer was fairly well off. The prices of agricultural products increased nearly 50 per cent, and the value of farm property doubled.

World War I was particularly beneficial to the farmer, because the increased demand for food products caused prices to soar. Wheat, which before the war sold for 93 cents per bushel, jumped to the unheard-of price of $2.75. Corn and cotton were correspondingly high. Under these circumstances the average farmer increased the size of his farm, frequently tilling soil that was unprofitable under normal conditions. At the same time he bought more machinery, purchased an automobile or a truck, had a telephone put in his house, and in many cases electrified his house and barn. In most cases, however, the farmer did not have the cash to pay for these things and had to borrow to make the necessary payments. As a result, farm mortgages greatly increased.

Hard times follow World War I. Conditions abruptly changed soon after World War I ended. With the return of peace the demand for farm and factory products declined. Industry recovered quickly from this postwar depression, but agriculture did not. Land values, which had boomed during the war, went down until they reached their prewar level. Farm prices tumbled.

There were two chief reasons why farm prices stayed low after World War I:

(1) Between 1910 and 1925 new machinery, tractors, trucks, and scientific farming increased farm output by 30 per cent. Likewise, they increased the output of the agricultural worker by 50 per cent. As a result, the supply of farm products increased until there was a surplus — and a surplus meant lower prices.

(2) World conditions held down farm prices. In the world market America's food products had to compete with those of Canada, Australia, Argentina, and Soviet Russia. Farms in European countries ravaged by war began to produce again. On the other hand, countries like China and Japan, which had a real need for our farm surplus, were unable to pay for it. The southern cotton grower faced competition both from new textiles, such as rayon and celanese, and from cotton growers in Russia, India, and Egypt. The American tariff, too, cut down the foreign demand for American farm products. Nations which could not sell their goods in this country could not pay for American-grown food.

The farmer's situation becomes desperate. For these reasons, the prosperity of the 1920's passed the farmer by. As the industrial depression deepened after 1929, conditions on the farm became more and more desperate. In 1932 wheat sold for 38 cents a bushel, corn for 32 cents, and cotton for 6 cents a pound — which in each case was less than it cost to grow the product. The farmers' annual cash income dropped from about 15 billion dollars in 1919 to less than 5 billion in 1932. On the other hand, the prices of goods which farmers bought were still above the prewar level, while taxes and interest on mortgages amounted to nearly twice the amount paid out in 1914. The average farmer could not meet his obligations. Mortgages were foreclosed, farms were sold for taxes, and farmers became tenants on land they formerly owned. Meanwhile the farmer was unable to buy machinery, automobiles, furniture and other manufactured articles. Consequently more factories had to shut down, and the general depression was deepened.

The government makes farm credit easier. The great depression after 1929

Poverty-stricken by depression and by catastrophes of nature, many farmers of the midwest trekked to the Pacific Coast in the 1930's.

Congress tries to fix farm prices. When liberal credit alone failed to bring prosperity to the farmer in the 1920's, Congress turned its attention to the problem of low farm prices. Though about 80 per cent of the American wheat crop was consumed in this country, its price was determined in the world market. Producers of wheat and other food products proposed a number of ways by which the price of food products in the United States might be raised above the level of the world price. To carry through their plans, congressmen from the agricultural states formed a *farm bloc* in Congress — a group of both Democratic and Republican congressmen who had certain interests in common and who were willing to combine their voting strength in order to help the farmer.

The farm bloc sponsored the McNary-Haugen bill, which provided that the surpluses of such commodities as wheat, instead of being exported for sale, should be bought by a government agency. This agency was then to sell the surplus abroad at a loss.[1] It was expected that such a move would increase the price of farm products consumed in this country. The bill passed Congress in 1927 and again — with some details changed — in 1928. But each time it was vetoed by President Coolidge. He objected to the bill on the grounds that it involved government price-fixing, that it was unconstitutional, and that it would not — he believed — be of any real help to farmers. He declared that if wheat brought a higher price, the farmers would only produce more than could be consumed, and people would buy less anyway because the price was higher.

The Agricultural Marketing Act is passed but proves a failure. In the campaign of 1928 both political parties promised relief to the farmers. Soon after his inauguration President Hoover called Congress into special session to consider the farmers' plight. Congress responded by passing the Agricultural Marketing Act (1929). This

really drove home the lesson that the prosperity of all the people was closely linked with the farmer's prosperity. Long before that time, however, there had been many people who realized the need of helping the farmer. Even before World War I, Congress came to the aid of farmers who needed to borrow money. The Federal Reserve Act (1913) helped farmers get short term loans at reasonable interest rates. In 1916, Congress made a more thorough attack on the farm credit problem with the Federal Farm Loan Act. By this bill twelve federal land banks were set up to finance loans for farmers through co-operative loan associations. Farmers could borrow up to 50 per cent of the value of their land and 20 per cent of the value of permanent improvements at interest not higher than 6 per cent. This plan made it possible for farmers to borrow money at a rate much lower than the interest they had previously had to pay private bankers. Loans could be repaid gradually over a period of 33 years. During the 1920's, when the farmer was suffering hard times, other measures were also passed by Congress to make credit still easier for farmers and farm co-operatives.

[1] The government would be repaid for this loss by charging each farmer an "equalization fee" of about ten cents a bushel on all the wheat he produced.

measure set up a Federal Farm Board to handle a special fund of 500 million dollars. From it, co-operative farm groups could borrow money to pay for the costs of storing their produce until the price was right. The Farm Board also tried to raise prices by buying up farm surpluses. It created a Grain Stabilization Corporation which bought up surplus wheat in 1930 and again in 1931. For a while these operations kept the price of wheat in the United States from 20 to 30 cents a bushel above the world figure. But when the Grain Stabilization Corporation ran out of money and stopped buying, the price dropped below what it had been before the Corporation was started. A Cotton Stabilization Corporation experienced the same sort of failure. Thus the government's effort to establish stable farm prices ended in disaster. It not only failed to maintain prices, but it also lost large sums of money through the Farm Board. Furthermore, it left the government holding 250 million bushels of wheat and more than a million bales of cotton bought at prices far above current market levels.

——————— CHECK-UP ———————

How did the government try to help the farmer?

1. Why was the farmer prosperous during World War I? What happened to him after 1920? Why?
2. What did the government do to make credit easier for the farmer?
3. What was the farm bloc? How did it try to help the farmer? What was the Mc-Nary-Haugen bill? What happened to it?
4. What were the provisions of the Agricultural Marketing Act? How successful was it?

<table>
<tr><td>3</td><td>**New Government Policies and Another War Bring Farm Prosperity**</td></tr>
</table>

The farmer's plight remains desperate. The farmer's condition was at its worst in the early 1930's. The grain-growing states of the Middle West suffered a devastating drought, which in some areas brought crop yields down to next to nothing. Frightful "dust storms" carried the loose soil hundreds of miles, and made many farmsteads virtually uninhabitable. But low prices for his products still remained the worst of the farmer's troubles.

The AAA tries to limit production. In the campaign of 1932, Franklin D. Roosevelt, the Democratic presidential candidate, argued in favor of a form of farm relief known as the *voluntary allotment* plan. This plan proposed that farmers should agree to limit their output of certain products in order to avoid the surpluses which were holding down prices.

Soon after Roosevelt's inauguration in 1933, this "voluntary allotment" plan was enacted into law as part of the Agricultural Adjustment Act, which set up the Agricultural Adjustment Administration (AAA). Farmers were encouraged to cut down their production of such staple crops as wheat, corn, rice, and tobacco. Each farmer who co-operated in this plan received a check from the government, the size of the check depending upon how many fewer acres he planted than he normally would have planted. Money for these gov-

After the dust storms, many formerly prosperous farms were left like this one, barren, desolate, and uninhabitable.

"Storm in Kansas," painted by a modern artist, shows a wheat field about to be drenched by rain. In addition to wheat and other grains, Kansas raises livestock of all kinds.

ernment payments was raised by a tax on the processing of basic farm products (meat-packing, flour-milling, and so forth). The *processing taxes* were, of course, passed on to the consumer in the form of higher prices. But in arguing for the plan, Secretary of Agriculture Henry Wallace declared that "the slight contribution the consumer will make through retail prices will be more than compensated for by the revived power of farmers to buy the goods and services the city has to sell."

Farm income rises, but the AAA is declared unconstitutional. Farm income increased more than 50 per cent from 1933 to 1936. Producers of basic farm products received about a billion dollars in benefit payments, and the prices of farm products rose. In 1936, however, the United States Supreme Court ruled that the Agricultural Adjustment Act was unconstitutional. According to a majority of the judges, farming was a strictly local business, and the

AAA interfered with states' rights by putting limits on production. The Court held also that Congress had made an improper use of its taxing power in levying the processing tax.

After the AAA was declared unconstitutional the federal government tried to achieve its goals by other means. Farmers were offered benefit payments for building up the soil — for example, by shifting production from wheat, corn, tobacco, and cotton, which exhaust the soil, to crops like clover, alfalfa, and beans, which enrich the soil. The purpose of this policy was declared to be soil conservation, but it was hoped that such a policy would also result in smaller harvests of wheat, corn, tobacco and cotton. If smaller harvests resulted, these staple crops would bring the farmer higher prices.

Farm credit is eased again. The New Deal also attacked the problem of farm mortgages and farm credit. This was an old problem, but it was getting worse. Between 1927 and 1932, ten per cent of American farm property was sold at auction to meet unpaid mortgages. In some sections farmers even banded together to frighten purchasers away from auctions and to threaten officers of the law.

The Farm Credit Administration (FCA), created in 1933, took over the administration of all types of credit for farmers. Federal land banks as well as other credit banks were placed under its supervision. The Land Bank Commissioner was authorized to make emergency loans to carry farm mortgages undertaken before January 1, 1933, and to provide the farmers who had mortgaged their lands with funds for general agricultural purposes.

Farm ownership is promoted. Fewer and fewer farmers had been able to retain ownership of their farms. By 1935, in fact, 42 per cent of them had become tenants. The New Deal set out to correct this situation through another agency, the Federal Security Administration (FSA), created for the purpose of increasing farm ownership. The Federal Security Administration made long-term loans at low interest rates to tenants or sharecroppers or farm laborers who wished to buy farms. In addition, it made short-term loans for the purchase of seed, feed, farm implements, or other necessities. After World War II, the Federal Security Administration also extended loans and guidance to war veterans who wanted to establish themselves on farms. By the mid-forties a million families had borrowed more than a billion dollars from the FSA, and many thousands were on the road to ownership of family-size farms.

Congress creates a second AAA. A second Agricultural Adjustment Administration was set up by Congress in 1938, two years after the Supreme Court overthrew the first one. This second AAA made marketing rather than production the point of control. Its chief provisions were these:

(1) The Secretary of Agriculture was authorized to decide, if necessary, what amount of each of the five major crops (cotton, corn, wheat, tobacco, and rice)

Farm prices reached a peak in 1920 and then declined. Why? In 1933 they were only one third of the 1920 level. Why? Why did they reach an all-time high in the late 1940's?

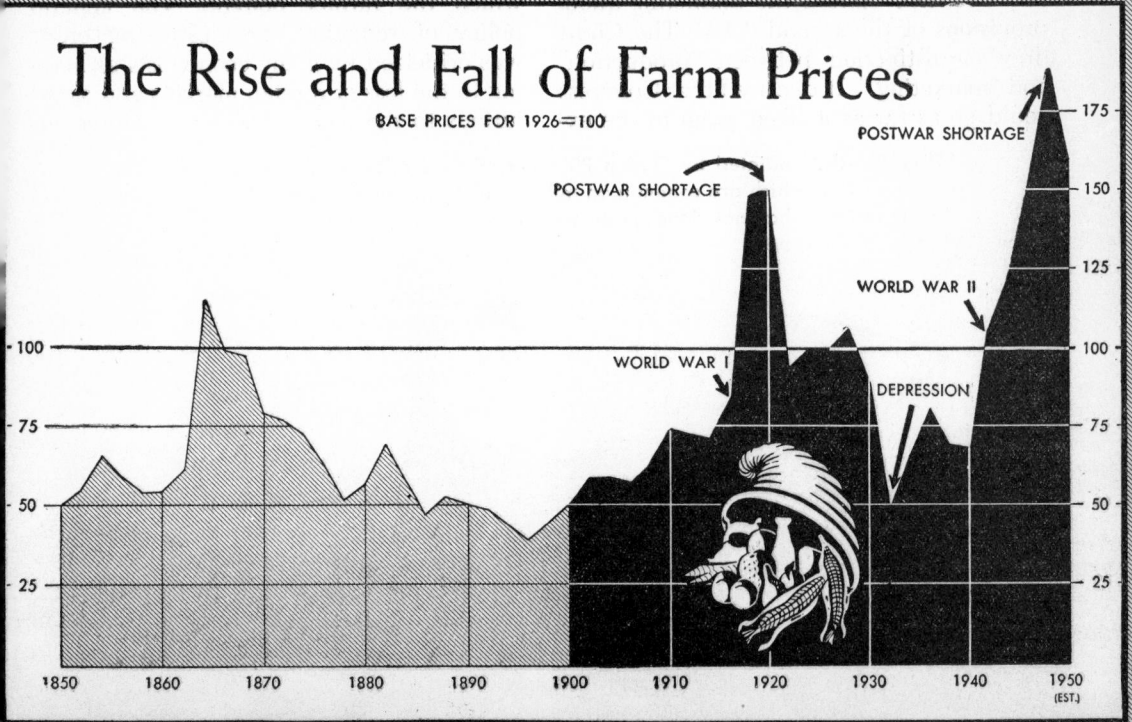

The Rise and Fall of Farm Prices

BASE PRICES FOR 1926=100

POSTWAR SHORTAGE

POSTWAR SHORTAGE

WORLD WAR II

WORLD WAR I

DEPRESSION

175
150
125
100
75
50
25

100
75
50
25

'1850   1860   1870   1880   1890   1900   1910   1920   1930   1940   1950 (EST.)

could be marketed in any year. With the approval of two thirds of the producers of each commodity in certain designated local areas, each producer would then be assigned a certain allotment. He would have to pay a tax on all his sales that exceeded his allotment.

(2) Subject to congressional appropriations, payments might be made to farmers who agreed to limit their crops. These were called *parity payments* because they were intended to restore farm purchasing power to parity (equality) with the purchasing power of the years before World War I.

(3) Farmers could also obtain *commodity loans* on surpluses. The surpluses were to be stored and finally marketed when prices were right or when crops were poor. In this way, the farmers would get the benefit of the higher prices and could then repay the loans.

(4) Provision was also made to continue benefit payments to farmers who planted soil-building crops and improved the fertility of their lands. Those farmers who did not co-operate with the AAA program were to be denied parity and conservation payments and commodity loans.

In 1939, the Supreme Court, in a six to two decision, upheld the marketing-quota provisions of the second AAA. The Court drew a distinction between "production" and "marketing." It declared that Congress could go as far as it liked, even to the ex-tent of completely blocking the flow of trade, in its regulation of interstate and foreign commerce.

The New Deal program is praised for aiding the farmer. The farm policies of the New Deal provoked widespread differences of opinion. They were praised for helping to bring about a rise in commodity prices and an improvement of the farmer's condition. The credit position of farmers had been strengthened, and the purchase of farms by people in the low-income groups had been encouraged. In years when there were crop surpluses, the Federal Surplus Commodities Corporation (FSCC) found new uses for some crops and helped dispose of them. The farmers' cash income rose from less than 5 billion dollars in 1932 to about 9 billion dollars in 1940.

The New Deal farm policy is criticized. Despite these benefits, many thoughtful critics of the New Deal found flaws in the government farm program. They charged that the cost of the program was too high, that AAA funds had not been spent to the best advantage, and that the interests of the small farmer had been neglected. They pointed out that gains from higher agricultural prices had been offset in part by a corresponding rise in the prices of goods which the farmer bought. The general policy of reducing and destroying crops was criticized by many economists as leading to the loss of foreign markets and as injurious to the national welfare. Moreover,

"Hay Ranch," painted by Ogden Pleissner, shows a farmer building a hay stack. Such scenes as this, which are common on millions of farms year in and year out, are reminders that machinery has not done away with hard work on farms.

alarm was expressed over increasing government control of production and the tendency of farmers to look to the federal government for grants and subsidies. The farmers themselves were not entirely satisfied. Farmers by tradition have been "individualists" who have wanted to "stand on their own feet." Although government farm policies aided them, they were troubled by the problem of government control. In the elections of the early 1940's, some agricultural regions stopped voting for Democratic candidates and returned to their traditional allegiance to the Republican Party.

War and reconstruction bring farm prosperity. World War II and the period of adjustment which followed brought abounding prosperity to the American farmer. He received high prices for grains, meat, cotton, tobacco — in fact for everything he had to sell. Before the mid-century, farm income had soared to nearly four times what it had been in 1939. Of course, the farmer paid more for the things which he bought, but in general, he was better off than ever before. He could

Modern farm buildings

well afford to pay twice as much for a new automobile or pay high prices for new machinery, because he was getting four times as much for the things he had to sell — and he had money in the bank. In many cases, he was able to pay off all or part of the farm mortgage. The high prices which he received were backed up by the government, which guaranteed minimum prices for many of his products. After the war, the export market for farm products was threatened by lack of dollars in Europe with which to buy American products. However, the farmer was helped by the Marshall Plan (page 719), which was intended primarily for the relief of Europe. Farm prosperity was reflected in the economic welfare of the country as a whole, for now the farmer was able to buy his share, and more, of the products of the cities.

Modern grain elevator

--------- CHECK-UP ---------

How did the New Deal and World War II affect the farmer's prosperity?

1. How did the first AAA try to help the farmer? What were the results?
2. How did the New Deal try to improve farm credit and promote farm ownership?
3. What were the provisions of the second AAA? How did it differ from the first AAA?
4. Why was the New Deal farm program praised? Why was it criticized?
5. What happened to the farmer's economic condition during and after World War II?

CHAPTER REVIEW

Terms to Understand

contour plowing
crop rotation
dry farming
cross-breeding
selection

hybrid corn
blight
boll weevil
extension service
vocational agriculture

Terms to Understand (Cont.)

plastics
soybean
world market
mortgage
parity payment

bloc
"voluntary allotment"
   plan
soil building crop
marketing quota

People and Things to Know About

Luther Burbank	George Washington
Mark Carleton	Carver
agricultural experi-	Federal Farm Loan
ment station	Act
Smith-Lever Act	Agricultural Marketing
county agent	Act
Smith-Hughes Act	Farm Credit Admin-
4-H Clubs	istration
Future Farmers of	Agricultural Adjust-
America	ment Administration
Future Homemakers of America	

Historic Dates to Identify

1914   1917   1933   1938

Questions to Discuss

1. Other conditions remaining the same, how would each of the following affect the relationship between the demand and supply of farm products? (a) War in Europe, (b) A declining birth rate, (c) Unemployment in industry, (d) The introduction of hybrid corn, (e) New irrigation projects, (f) Increased use of tractors, (g) An increase in the farm to city movement of labor.

2. Compare the following:

(a) The farmer of today with the nineteenth century frontier farmer.

(b) The first and second Agricultural Adjustment Administrations.

(c) The economic problems of the farmer, the wage-laborer, and the manufacturer.

3. What is the relationship between soil conservation and a more prosperous agriculture?

4. Do you see any similarities between tariffs, minimum wage laws, and "parity" prices?

5. What were the arguments for and against the Agricultural Adjustment Acts?

Other Things to Do

1. Organize a panel to discuss the pros and cons of government assistance to maintain agricultural prices.

2. Debate: *Resolved,* That the government should continue to support agricultural prices through the use of the parity principle.

In the determination of "parity" prices for agriculture, use is made of a device known as *index numbers.* Index numbers provide us with a means of measuring, in terms of percentages which can be directly compared with one another, the relative changes in a number of variables (different prices, for example)

Other Things to Do (Cont.)

over a period of years. Insofar as agriculture is concerned, the problem is to see what prices the farmer should receive for a bushel of corn, wheat, etc., to give him the same purchasing power per unit (bushel, bale, etc.) as he had in some previous good year. When index numbers are used, this previous year is called the *base year,* and the prices which the farmer paid and the prices which he received at that time are each given a value of 100. Now, if the farmer got $.75 per bushel for wheat in the base year and gets $1.50 today, the index number for wheat today would be 200. But the prices which the farmer pays for manufactured goods may have gone up three times, giving them a present index number of 300. As you can readily see, although the farmer is getting higher prices he is worse off than he was in the base year in terms of purchasing power. To determine what the farmer would have to receive for his wheat to have *parity* (equality) with the base year, we would multiply $.75 by 300 per cent. This gives us $2.25 per bushel as the "parity" price of wheat. (It should be noted here that agricultural prices are not supported at full parity but usually at some lesser percentage of full parity.)

Index numbers have a variety of uses other than the one discussed above. Try to find other examples of their use in newspapers and magazines. Bring these to class. Other examples can be found in several of the charts in this book.

*3. Consult newspapers and magazines for articles on the present policy of the government with regard to aid to agriculture. Be prepared to report on such articles in class.

*4. Compose two editorials, one for a farm magazine and the other for a city newspaper on the Supreme Court's decision invalidating the first Agricultural Adjustment Administration.

5. Organize a committee to interview a farmer with regard to the present problems of agriculture and the relationship of government to agriculture. Prepare the questions to be used co-operatively in class.

6. Look up and report to the class the contributions of one or more of these agricultural scientists: (a) Marion Dorset, hog cholera; (b) George Mohler, hoof and mouth disease; (c) David R. Coker, cotton; (d) Seaman Knapp, rice; (e) Stephen M. Babcock, milk and butter-fat; (f) Theobald Smith, tick fever.

Chapter **31**

Civil engineer

CONSERVATION BECOMES A

NATIONAL PROBLEM

With riches has come inexcusable waste. We have squandered a great part of what we might have used, and have not stopped to conserve the exceeding bounty of nature . . . scorning to be careful, shamefully prodigal as well as admirably efficient.

Woodrow Wilson, 1913

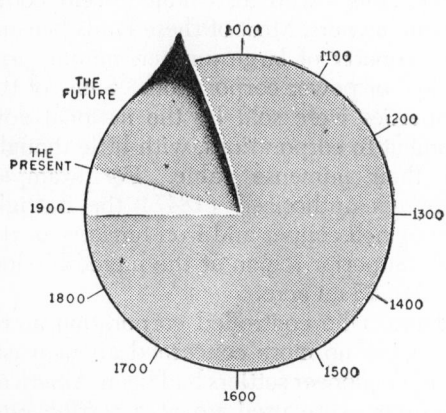

1897 – The Present

The prosperity of the United States rests largely upon its natural resources. Our fertile farmlands feed a growing population; our energy resources — water, coal, and petroleum — make it possible to multiply human effort many times; our rich stores of iron ore are the basis of the age of steel in which we live; our forests are among the most magnificent on earth. We have deposits of nearly all important industrial minerals: copper, iron, coal, aluminum, magnesium, lead, zinc, gypsum, phosphates, petroleum, potash, silver, sulphur. No people on earth has been more richly endowed by nature than the people of the United States.

But neither has any people on earth been so wasteful of nature's bounty. The woodlands pioneer considered trees a nuisance; he destroyed them so that he might have a field. The plantation owner and farmer wasted topsoil that had taken centuries to accumulate. The miner dug frantically for

A forest fire has left this hillside useless. Before the 1900's, little was done to prevent such expensive losses.

ore, and when easy surface pickings were gone, he moved on without bothering himself about the desolation that he left behind. To the pioneer, natural resources were something to use up as fast as possible, and people spoke with pride of "developing" resources and "conquering" nature. This pioneer attitude became even more dangerous with the swift growth of technology and big-business organization. Great lumber companies reduced millions of acres of fine timber to desolate stretches of stumps. Mining companies equipped with modern machinery tore down whole mountains to get out the ore, and speeded the exhaustion of minerals. Oil wells, operating day and night, recklessly pumped out petroleum which had been accumulating for millions of years.

A few American citizens began to protest such recklessness, predicting that some day there would be shortages of our so-called inexhaustible resources. At first their efforts to conserve resources were an uphill fight against selfish interests and public indifference. At last, however, in the twen-

tieth century enough people became sufficiently worried so that the government started a systematic program of conservation. This program, which has had both successes and failures, is of vital concern to America's future. This chapter traces the development of our program of conservation under the following topics:

1. Theodore Roosevelt awakens the American people to the need for conservation.
2. Conservation moves haltingly forward.
3. The New Deal sponsors conservation.
4. Conservation is a continuing problem.

1 **Theodore Roosevelt Awakens the American People to the Need for Conservation**

Exhaustion of resources becomes alarming. At the same time that pioneers were turning the fertile farm lands of the West into homesteads, another kind of development was going forward on a larger scale. Great tracts of land — rich in timber or minerals, or valuable for irrigation or power sites — were also being developed by private owners. Most of these lands became the property of large lumber, mining, irrigation, or power corporations. Some of the properties were sold by the national government to corporations, with little thought for their immense value. For example, Congress authorized (1847) the outright sale of rich copper and iron territory of the Lake Superior region at the incredibly low price of $5 an acre.

Those who controlled corporation activities were no more concerned about waste than the pioneer settlers had been. America's resources were used up at a terrific rate. At the beginning of the twentieth century, 80 per cent of the forests had been cut over with no thought of replanting, protection from fire, or preservation of young trees. Oil and natural gas were allowed to gush out unused. In the coal fields, only the choice veins, which could be worked cheaply, were mined. Poorer veins were sealed off.

Informed people became alarmed. The American Association for the Advancement of Science urged Congress to do something about the forests as early as 1873, but the scientists were shouted down. They were considered "cranks." Most people still believed that our resources were inexhaustible.

Conservation makes a beginning. But the scientists kept writing letters to Congressmen and urging citizens to support their stand. At last, in 1891, Congress passed a law authorizing the President to withdraw timber lands from public sale. President Harrison set aside a national forest reserve of more than 17 million acres. Presidents Cleveland and McKinley more than doubled this area during their administrations. This was a beginning, but only a beginning. The national forest reserves were still a very small part of the total forest land, and other conservation problems were untouched.

Theodore Roosevelt fights for conservation. It was President Theodore Roosevelt who, more than any other single individual, awakened the American people to the urgent need for conservation. He had three qualities which combined to make him the outstanding champion of conservation: his love of the outdoors, his concern for future generations, and his genius for making himself heard. "The forest and water problems are perhaps the most vital internal problems of the United States," he shouted in 1901. In a special message to Congress, he said, "The mineral wealth of this country, the coal, iron, oil, gas, and the like, does not reproduce itself, and . . . wastefulness in dealing with it today means that our descendants will feel the exhaustion a generation or two before they otherwise would. . . . There must be the look ahead, there must be a realization of the fact that to waste, to destroy, our natural resources . . . will result in undermining in the days of our children the very prosperity which we ought by right to hand down to them. . . ." Meanwhile, Roosevelt's Chief

Forester, Gifford Pinchot (pin'show), was writing articles for the *National Geographic,* the *Outlook,* and other magazines. His articles were filled with facts and figures to drive home his statement, "Nearly every one of our wonderful resources we have used without reasonable foresight and reasonable care."

Roosevelt further dramatized the need for conservation by calling a series of conferences. The Conservation Conference, which met at the White House in 1908, included governors of states and territories, congressmen, cabinet members, scientists, businessmen, and experts on conservation. It passed resolutions calling for (1) control of forest fires, (2) improvement of inland waterways, (3) conservation of water resources for irrigation and power, and (4) elimination of waste in mining. It also urged the appointment of a national conservation commission as well as of state commissions.[1] In 1909 Roosevelt sponsored

[1] State conservation commissions later were set up in 41 states.

Thoughtless waste of oil is illustrated by this painting of a boom town some 30 years ago. Profits alone were important.

Bighorn

a second conference at which representatives of Canada, Newfoundland, and Mexico joined those of the United States in discussing the conservation problems of all North America. He even proposed a World Conservation Conference to consider the natural resource problems of the entire planet. Probably the most important outcome of these conferences and proposals was to drive home to the public the need for greater care in the use of natural resources.

Roosevelt rescues part of the public domain. Theodore Roosevelt needed all the popular support he could arouse, because Congress turned a deaf ear to his requests for conservation laws. It even refused to appropriate $25,000 for the expenses of his National Conservation Commission, of which Gifford Pinchot was chairman. Even without new legislation, however, Roosevelt accomplished a great deal by enthusiastic administration of the timber law of 1891. He added about 150 million acres to the national forest reserve. Forests were protected from thieves and destructive fires. Only timber that was ready to market was cut, and millions of young trees were planted. Ranchers had to pay the government for grazing privileges on public lands. The President also withdrew from public sale 80 million acres of coal lands, nearly 5 million acres of phosphate lands, and land that bordered on water-power sites. Certain areas in which wild life would be protected were set aside, and a number of new national parks were created. Roosevelt accomplished all this over the protests of lumber, mining, power, and livestock interests.

Irrigation creates new farmlands. When President Theodore Roosevelt urged that the government provide money for irrigation projects, he found greater support. In the Southwest, in sections where the rainfall was insufficient to grow regular crops, there were vast expanses of potentially fertile land. Western congressmen enthusias-

tically supported the proposal that the United States Government supply water to irrigate this land. In 1902, early in Roosevelt's first administration, the Newlands Reclamation Act was passed. Under this act, money from the sale of public lands in sixteen western states was put into a "reclamation fund" for the construction of irrigation works which would make lands suitable for farming. Also, money received from the sale of water to settlers on the irrigated lands was put back into the fund for the reclamation of more land. During the next four years, 28 projects were started for the irrigation of 3 million acres, enough for 60,000 farms. The Roosevelt Dam on the Salt River in Arizona — put in operation in 1907 — created a reservoir which covered an area of nearly 18,000 acres and irrigated over 200,000 acres. On lands formerly unfit for cultivation were grown alfalfa, grain, sugar beets, and fruit — "the desert's response to the intelligent application of water to her sunburned valleys."

--------- CHECK-UP ---------

How did the conservation movement get its start?

1. Why was it necessary to begin a conservation program? What were the first steps in the program?
2. How did Theodore Roosevelt regard our natural resources? What was recommended by his Conservation Conference?
3. What did Theodore Roosevelt do (a) to save our forest and coal resources, and (b) to reclaim arid lands?

2 Conservation Moves Haltingly Forward

Taft promotes conservation. The conservation movement suffered a setback during the early part of President Taft's administration. Certain public lands valuable for their water power were to be withdrawn from sale, but the order was stopped by

Taft's Secretary of the Interior, Richard A. Ballinger. He claimed that the order was illegal because the President's authority extended only to timber lands. Gifford Pinchot, who had remained in the government as Chief Forester, protested this action and also accused Ballinger of permitting valuable coal lands in Alaska to fall into private hands. The House of Representatives supported Ballinger, and the President removed Pinchot from his job. People who favored the conservation movement indignantly charged that Taft had allied himself with private interests which were making themselves rich on natural resources that belonged to the public.

Actually, Taft did much to promote conservation. Because he questioned whether Theodore Roosevelt had had legal authority to withdraw from sale anything but timber lands, he persuaded Congress to give the President greater authority. By the end of the Taft administration, nearly 59 million additional acres of coal lands had been withdrawn from sale. Taft also signed the Appalachian Forest Reserve Act. This measure made it possible for the government to buy over 1¼ million acres of land in the White Mountains and the southern part of the Appalachian chain, where the sources of important streams were to be found.

Conservation goes forward under President Wilson. Two laws which promised a great deal for the future of conservation were enacted by Congress during Woodrow Wilson's Presidency. The Mineral Leasing Act of 1920 provided that mineral-bearing public lands should not be sold outright. Instead, they were to be leased on a long-time basis, and the government would receive royalties based on the value of the minerals taken from them. The leasing system was widely used for coal, petroleum, phosphates, and potassium and sodium salts. When well administered, it had many advantages for the public: (1) It produced a substantial revenue. (2) Waste in mining could be controlled by the terms of leases. (3) Safety standards could be required. (4) Reserves of essential minerals could be maintained.

The same Congress set up the Federal Water-Power Commission. This commission had authority to give or deny to private companies the right to build dams on navigable streams or their tributaries.

Conservation is retarded during the 1920's. President Warren G. Harding, who followed Wilson in the White House, was not particularly interested in promoting conservation. He appointed Albert B. Fall, a spokesman for the oil interests, as Secretary of the Interior. Fall's former associates, Sinclair and Doheny, were improperly granted leases to immensely valuable naval oil reserves at Teapot Dome in Wyoming and at Elk Hills in California. When news leaked out that Fall had received "loans" or gifts amounting to thousands of dollars from the two men who had been granted the leases, the "Teapot Dome scandal" broke. The leases were cancelled, Fall was forced to resign, and later he was sentenced to prison.

The Federal Water-Power Commission, too, found itself handicapped by lack of presidential support. Short of funds and

Salt River valley in Arizona, once a desert, began to produce such crops as these when irrigation brought water.

Mountain goat

workers, it failed to accomplish what its backers had hoped.

During World War I, the United States Government had built a dam and power-house at Muscle Shoals on the Tennessee River. Conservation enthusiasts, led by Senator George W. Norris of Nebraska, urged that the project be extended and publicly operated. Norris twice managed to get Congress to pass bills authorizing such action, but they were vetoed by Presidents Coolidge and Hoover.

Hoover Dam is a victory for conservation. Conservation had one important and dramatic development in the late 1920's. This was the beginning of Hoover (or Boulder) Dam on the Colorado River. Hoover Dam was authorized by Congress in 1928 and completed in 1936. More than 700 feet high and nearly 1000 feet across the top, it created the largest artificial reservoir in the world. This reservoir, known as Lake Mead, is 115 miles long. It supplies water for irrigation and other uses to seven states of the Southwest. Its power plant supplies about half the power consumed in southern California, including current for the city of Los Angeles. At the same time, the dam regulates the flow of the Colorado River so as to protect the nearby lands from floods. It is expected that most of the construction cost — about $150,000,000 — will eventually be repaid to the government by users of water and power.

─────── CHECK-UP ───────

What progress was made in conservation from 1909 to 1930?

1. What was the Ballinger-Pinchot controversy? How did Taft promote conservation?
2. What was the mineral leasing system and what were its advantages?
3. What happened to conservation during the 1920's? What was the "Teapot Dome scandal"?
4. Why was the building of Hoover Dam a great achievement?

─────────────────────────

3 The New Deal Sponsors Conservation

The CCC saves forests and soil. Conservation went forward swiftly when Franklin D. Roosevelt entered the White House in 1933. The great depression was on, and young men as well as older ones were out of jobs. Within a month after Roosevelt's inauguration, Congress established the Civilian Conservation Corps (CCC). The CCC served a double purpose — it employed, all told, about 2½ million young men who would otherwise have been idle, and it did a valuable job of salvaging forests and soil. CCC boys built dams, cut fire-breaks, fought plant diseases, and planted trees by the billion. The CCC, planned as an emergency measure for the relief of unemployment, proved so valuable that it was continued until the manpower demands of World War II brought it to an end.

The National Resources Board makes an inventory of the nation's resources. Meanwhile, President Roosevelt was planning a far-reaching conservation program. Early in 1934 he appointed a National Resources Board to prepare an inventory of the nation's resources. The *Report* of this board brought together for the first time an expert analysis of our land, water, and mineral problems and showed their relation to each other. Some of the findings of its various sub-committees were as follows:

(1) *The Land Planning Sub-Committee* reported that more than two thirds of the

Moose

nation's 1900 million acres of land had been damaged by erosion — the washing away or the blowing away of topsoil. Erosion goes on very slowly under normal conditions because the roots of trees and grasses hold the earth firm against the wash of rain water and the force of wind. The loss by erosion is then just about balanced by the natural formation of new topsoil. When land is plowed, however, rain and wind are much more likely to carry away the loose earth. The National Resources Board *Report* revealed that 35 million acres of American farmland had been "essentially destroyed" by erosion — reduced to gullies or dustbowls. The topsoil had been practically washed off from another 125 million acres. Fewer than 536 million acres were listed as having practically no erosion. "From a country with a large proportional area of rich agricultural land we are plunging almost heedlessly in the direction of a nation of predominantly poor agricultural land," said the *Report*.

Another part of the Land Planning section of the *Report* dealt with forest resources. It pointed out that destruction of forests was partly responsible for widespread erosion. Nearly 445 million out of 615 million acres of forest land were still in private hands, and in these forests "with relatively few exceptions, management continues . . . a process of destructive exploitation." Nearly half this privately held forest land had no fire protection and suffered an annual average loss by fire of 20.75 per cent of its acreage. This figure was contrasted with a fire loss of less than one fourth of one per cent in the national forests.

(2) *The Water Planning Sub-Committee* pointed out that erosion and forest loss were part of the explanation for both floods and drought. Rainwater runs down gullied surfaces to swell the small streams that together make up the big floods. Without grass and roots to hold the water, the reserves of sub-surface water are reduced. Then, when a dry season comes along, wells give out and vegetation dies. The *Report* also pointed out that streams and harbors were being poisoned by sewage and industrial wastes.

(3) *The Mineral Planning Sub-Committee* found that while we still had large reserves of most ores, we had used up many of the best and easiest deposits. Many mines had been allowed to cave in or to flood after their best veins were exhausted. "The long-time outlook in the field of mining . . . is for increasing costs through the exhaustion of the rich and more accessible deposits. . . . Depletion is much further advanced than is generally realized. . . . In oil and gas, the wastes are proverbial. At the present time in one field, enough gas is being blown into the air to supply all domestic consumers in the United States. In bituminous [soft] coal mining the avoidable loss is placed at 20 per cent."

Science and government combat erosion. The menace of erosion became a disastrous reality on May 12, 1934. On that day the sun was darkened from the Rocky Mountains to the Atlantic Ocean by clouds of dust whirled up by high winds from the wheat fields of the Great Plains. Parts of Kansas, Nebraska, Texas, Oklahoma, New Mexico, and Colorado were literally deposited in the Gulf of Mexico and the Atlantic Ocean. People spoke of this region as the "dust bowl." Throughout the 1930's, violent floods and killing droughts

Hoover Dam controls the Colorado River, produces power, and irrigates a vast area.

brought home the need for conservation of our fundamental resources — land and rainfall.

The Department of Agriculture had been studying soil erosion on a small scale for several years, but finally Congress set up the Soil Conservation Service as a permanent, major agency of the government. With the co-operation of state governments, which established soil conservation districts, the Soil Conservation Service helped farmers to use their land wisely. They were taught to keep steep hillsides in pasture or woodland instead of plowing them, to terrace gentle slopes, and to rotate crops in their fields. Farmers were also taught to protect their woodlands from fire, insects, and disease, and to cut lumber in such a way as to improve, not exhaust, the timber. The Agricultural Adjustment Administration (AAA) gave billions of dollars in soil-conservation payments to farmers who co-operated. The Chief of the Soil Conservation Service declared in 1941, "Erosion has been controlled, for all practical purposes, on 20 million acres of land in private

Cattle once grazed on this hillside. Erosion ruined it after poisonous fumes from a copper smelter killed the vegetation.

ownership. We have found a solution, or at least a partial solution, for every type of erosion that occurs on American agricultural land." He added, however, "Despite all this encouraging progress, the country as a whole is not moving fast enough in the direction of conservation. . . . Although we now know how to save our land, the real job of soil conservation in this country has only just begun."

TVA demonstrates a unified program. An important development in conservation during the 1930's was a long-term program for the Tennessee River valley. What to do with the government-owned dam and power plant at Muscle Shoals, Alabama, had still not been decided when Franklin D. Roosevelt became President. Roosevelt wanted the power plant to be government-owned and operated — but he wanted much more than that. On his recommendation Congress created (1933) an agency to plan the development of the entire Tennessee River valley in order to: (1) relieve unemployment, (2) restore the forests, (3) halt erosion, (4) reduce flood damage, (5) improve navigation, (6) supply cheap power, and (7) better the living conditions of families who had been able merely to "eke out a precarious existence."

The Tennessee Valley Authority (TVA), was given all the powers of a private corporation, together with the right of eminent domain.[2] It started a broad program for promoting the social and economic welfare of citizens in an area comprising 40,000 square miles in seven states. It built dams and power plants, sold electricity at low rates, taught farmers to save their land, encouraged co-operatives and small local industries, promoted public health, built low-cost housing, and provided facilities for recreation. After ten years, one of TVA's early directors summarized its accomplishments in these words:

This is the story of a great change. It is a tale of a wandering and inconstant river now become a chain of broad and lovely lakes which people enjoy, and on which they can depend, in all seasons, for the movement of

[2] This is the power to take private property for public use, provided that the owners are given reasonable compensation.

the barges of commerce that now nourish their business enterprises. It is a story of how waters once wasted and destructive have been controlled and now work, night and day, creating electric energy to lighten the burden of human drudgery. Here is a tale of fields grown old and barren with the years, which now are vigorous with new fertility, lying green to the sun; of forests that were hacked and despoiled, now protected and refreshed with strong young trees just starting on their slow road to maturity. It is a story of the people and how they have worked to create a new valley.

Private industry objects to TVA. The direct competition of TVA, a government agency, with private power companies naturally brought protests from businessmen. TVA's low charges for electricity could be explained, they maintained, only by its accounting methods. Because part of the costs of running TVA were charged to flood control and improvement of navigation, they argued that TVA's rates were not a fair "yardstick" for measuring the reasonableness of private charges. Wendell L. Willkie, President of the Commonwealth and Southern Corporation, led a vigorous legal battle against TVA. In 1936 and again in 1939, however, the United States Supreme Court upheld TVA.

TVA engages in war production. During World War II, TVA produced great quantities of war materials, including explosives, aluminum for airplane construction, and synthetic rubber. In 1940 twelve dams were being operated by TVA. Under the pressure of war demands, nine more dams were placed in operation by 1945. At that time, the total capacity of the power plants was 2¼ million kilowatts. Nearly 600,000 customers — 100,000 of them farmers — were being provided with cheap electric current.

A Columbia River project proves profitable. Second in importance only to the development of the Tennessee Valley was the project for the Columbia River valley in Oregon and Washington. Its twofold purpose was the production of cheap power and the reclamation of arid lands. In 1933 construction was started on Grand Coulee Dam in Washington, some 70 miles west of Spokane. Eight years later it was placed in operation. The dam created a

Galloway

Young orange trees are growing on the terraces of this California ranch. Terraces protect rich topsoil from erosion.

reservoir about 150 miles long to furnish water for irrigation of more than a million acres. The power units were designed for a capacity of nearly 2 million kilowatts.

Still other great dams, like Bonneville near Portland, Oregon, and Shasta in northern California, were also started under the administration of Franklin D. Roosevelt. By 1945 over 20 million acres of land in the seventeen western states were being irrigated. About one fourth of this area was dependent in whole or in part upon federal irrigation systems. These systems had cost the taxpayers a quarter of a billion dollars, but the value of the reclaimed land was several times this amount.

Mineral conservation lags. New Deal achievements in the conservation of minerals were far less effective than were those in the conservation of water and land. The Guffey Coal Act — passed in 1935 to apply controls to the soft coal industry — was declared unconstitutional by the Supreme Court on the ground that coal mining was a state activity and therefore not subject to control by Congress. This interpretation hampered any attempt at controlling the production of minerals. Congress had no authority. The states had legal authority but lacked real power, for the prices of oil and ores are set in a national and international market.

The Connally Law of 1935 was an attempt to halt excessive production of petroleum. It prohibited interstate and foreign shipments of oil produced in excess of the amounts permitted by state laws. In 1945, about 40 per cent of the nation's petroleum output was subject to some degree of regulation by the Interior Department under the Connally Law.

——————— CHECK-UP ———————

How did the New Deal promote conservation?

1. How did the CCC combine conservation with the relief of unemployment?
2. What chief facts were brought out in the report of the National Resources Board?
3. How has the Soil Conservation Service taught farmers to save the soil?
4. What were the objectives of the TVA? Why did private industry object to the TVA? How did the TVA help win the war?
5. What developments have taken place in the Columbia River valley?

Rich deposits of iron ore in Minnesota and Michigan will soon be exhausted. Steel companies are looking for other supplies.

4 Conservation Is a Continuing Problem

World War II interrupts conservation. During World War II the government had to shift, of course, from conservation of natural resources to immediate use of them. Production of essential minerals reached an all-time high in 1944 and did not fall until the war was over. But the government saw to it that the resources were used for necessary purposes. Lumber, coal, and petroleum, as well as iron, copper, and other metal ores, could be sold only with the approval of some government agency which divided them among essential industries.

When the war ended, most Americans were anxious to relax restrictions. They wanted to forget caution and return to peacetime business conditions. To be sure, dangerous shortages of critical war materials caused Congress to pass the Strategic and Critical Materials Stock-Piling Act (1946). This measure gave the Secretaries of War, Navy, and the Interior authority to buy and store essential minerals. Even before the war ended, however, Congress had abolished the National Resources Planning Board.

Those who argued against the need for continued conservation were able to support their arguments with facts. Now 68 per cent of the nation's cropland was included in the soil conservation program. Government and private industry had made progress in conserving and replenishing timber. New forest growth each year just about supplied the nation's need for pulpwood and fuelwood. Fresh oil fields were being brought in about as rapidly as old fields became exhausted. Improved methods made it practicable to extract motor fuels from our tremendous deposits of oil shale. Geologists had located undeveloped mineral resources estimated at the value of 6 trillion dollars. Predictions were made that atomic energy would furnish the power of the future.

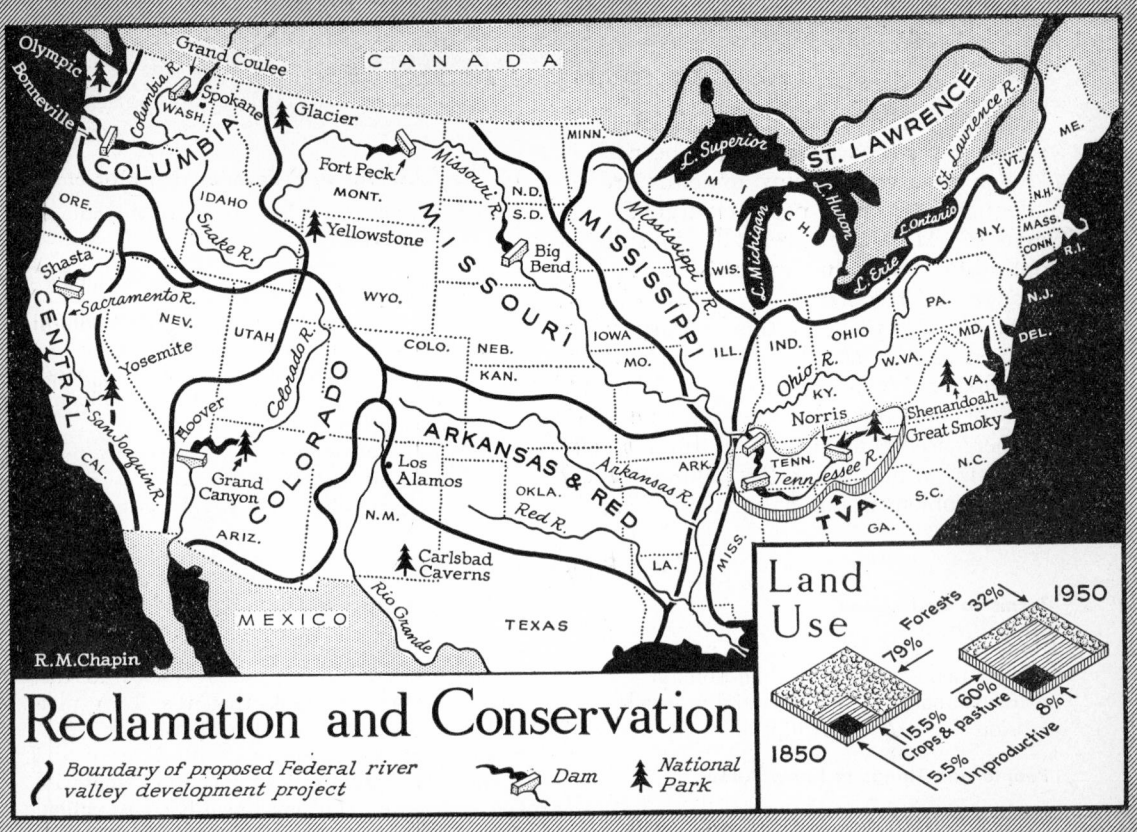

Reclamation and Conservation

) Boundary of proposed Federal river
valley development project

Dam

National Park

Land Use

Forests 79% 32% 1950

15.5% Crops & pasture 60%

5.5% Unproductive 8%

1850

R.M.Chapin

The area served by the Tennessee Valley Authority is highlighted on this map. Can you locate it? Find several dams elsewhere throughout the country. This map also shows the areas that would be affected by river valley projects which have been proposed for the future. Now look at the small inset at the lower right. What does it tell you about land use during the past 100 years?

The conservation problem remains acute. On the other hand, people who urged continued conservation came forward with facts which suggested that the outlook was not so promising. A survey by the United States Forest Service (1945–1946) found only 1601 billion board feet of saw timber (suitable for sawing into boards), compared with 2826 billion board feet in Theodore Roosevelt's survey of 1909. This was a reduction of 44 per cent in 36 years. The Chief Forester declared: "The plain fact is that our supply of readily accessible, merchantable, standing timber is running low. The present shortage of timber products therefore will not be of short duration. It will last until we grow a great deal more saw timber, and you can't grow trees of saw timber size overnight."

The Chief of the Soil Conservation Service pointed out that the exhausting of our topsoil was still critical. "What makes the problem especially serious," he stated, "is the tremendous speed at which our soil resources are going out. When we consider the country as a whole, we find that most of our land has been under cultivation less than a hundred years; and there is a considerable acreage in the West that was not broken out of native sod until the present century. Yet in this remarkably short time — a mere tick of the clock over the span of centuries — we have lost 14 per cent of our land and put another 35 per cent on the move, not by any natural catastrophe but by carelessness and outright abuse. . . . The United States has wasted its precious soil resources faster than any other nation or race that ever attempted to practice agriculture on an extensive scale."

As for minerals, 80 per cent of our fantastic reserves were coal, and much of it was low grade. There were actual shortages of such essential minerals as copper and lead. The Secretary of the Interior stated in his report for 1945, "The nation's known reserves of many minerals are inadequate to meet peak emergency demands." Minerals were still — in spite of optimistic talk — an "exhaustible, non-reproducible" resource.

At the mid-point of this century, it remained as true as when Theodore Roosevelt first said it in 1907, that "the conservation of our natural resources and their proper use constitute the fundamental problem which underlies almost every other problem in our national life."

———— CHECK-UP ————

Why is conservation a never-ending problem?

1. How did World War II affect our natural resources?
2. What is the purpose of the Strategic and Critical Materials Stock-Piling Act?
3. To what extent have our natural resources been depleted?
4. What arguments are presented by those who believe that conservation is no longer an important problem?
5. What arguments are presented by those who believe that conservation is a continuing problem of great importance?

CHAPTER REVIEW

Terms to Understand

forest reserve
reclamation
conservation
erosion

natural resources
public domain
essential minerals
topsoil

People and Things to Know About

Gifford Pinchot
Newlands Reclamation Act
National Conservation Commission
Richard A. Ballinger
Appalachian Forest Reserve Act
Federal Power Commission
George W. Norris
Civilian Conservation Corps

Tennessee Valley Authority
"reclamation fund"
"Teapot Dome scandal"
"Dust Bowl"
Soil Conservation Service
Grand Coulee Dam
Guffey Coal Act
Connally Law
Stock-Piling Act
Theodore Roosevelt
Franklin D. Roosevelt

Historic Dates to Identify

1891   1908   1935
1902   1933   1946

Questions to Discuss

1. Is government intervention necessary to promote conservation? Why or why not?
2. Do you agree with Theodore Roosevelt that "the conservation of our natural resources and their proper use constitute the fundamental problem which underlies almost every other problem in our national life"? Why or why not?
3. What resources do we utilize today which were little used 100 years ago? How does this illustrate man's ability to adapt environment to his use?

Questions to Discuss (Cont.)

4. The TVA has sometimes been termed socialistic. What are your reactions to this charge? Do you think that the TVA plan should be extended to other areas?
5. Compare the following:
   (a) The attitudes of Theodore Roosevelt and Warren G. Harding towards conservation.
   (b) The conservation policies of Theodore and Franklin D. Roosevelt.

Other Things to Do

1. Make a poster which contains a plea for the conservation of our natural resources.
2. Prepare a report on the work of the TVA. Illustrate your report with a map of the Tennessee Valley area and any pictures which you can secure. Consult David E. Lilienthal's *T.V.A., Democracy on the March.*
*3. Make a list of the ways in which you see our resources being wasted in everday living.
*4. In two columns headed "Acts" and "Provisions," list the chief legislative enactments which have promoted the conservation movement.
5. Write to your state planning commission for literature on its work and its recommendations for the more efficient use of your state's resources.
6. Find out if a soil conservation project is in progress or has been completed in your area. A committee of the class might be sent to visit and then report on the project.
7. Debate: *Resolved,* That the problem of conservation has been overestimated in the light of probable future scientific progress.
8. Try to secure the famous documentary films "The River" and "The Plow That Broke the Plains" for class showing.

TO INCREASE YOUR UNDERSTANDING OF UNIT EIGHT

Unit Summary

1. In the 1900's all parts of the United States and the world were bound closer together by new forms of communication and transportation — and improvements in old forms. Business and industry were stimulated for the same reason. The use of power and the development of labor-saving machinery led to mass production and created a need for mass markets. To cut down on competition, big business experimented with new forms of business organization like holding companies and interlocking directorates.

2. The monopolistic practices of big business at the turn of the century caused the federal government to impose regulations in the public interest. The government undertook not only to break up trusts, but also to prevent unfair competition (Federal Trade Commission Act and Clayton Antitrust Act). Controls were relaxed after World War I, but became stricter than ever under the New Deal.

3. In the early 1900's American workers were handicapped, because court injunctions and the "restraint of trade" clause of the Sherman Antitrust Act were used against labor organizations. The rights of labor to organize and to bargain collectively were greatly strengthened during the administrations of Woodrow Wilson and F. D. Roosevelt. After World War II the respective rights of labor and management were somewhat modified by the Taft-Hartley Act.

4. The great expansion of American industry and agriculture strained the monetary system and led to the creation of the Federal Reserve System. The falling prices and the bank failures of the great depression brought about still further reforms. The gold standard was abandoned, the gold value of the dollar was reduced, and bank deposits were guaranteed. During World War II government spending was so heavy and production of civilian goods was cut so greatly that great inflationary pressures resulted. These were fairly well controlled during the war. When peace came, however, controls were relaxed and wages rose, with the result that there was a sharp rise in prices. In the fall of 1948 employment, production, and prices began to "level off."

5. The great expansion of American industry was in part made possible by a high tariff policy. As United States production increased, and especially as the United States became a creditor nation during World War I, this policy came to interfere with our foreign trade. Nevertheless, tariffs were raised to a new high during the 1920's and early 1930's. Since 1933 a policy of reciprocal trade agreements has led to a great reduction in rates and has helped to expand foreign trade.

6. During the first twenty years of this century American farmers were prosperous. Improved farming methods and increased use of machinery made possible a great increase in agricultural production. After World War I, farm income slumped despite the increased use of farm products by industry. Crop surpluses and the loss of foreign markets led to falling prices and foreclosures on farm property. The New Deal eased farm credit and sought to increase farm income, first by limiting production and later by controlling marketing. The greatly increased demand for agricultural products during and after World War II had made the period since 1939 a prosperous one for United States farmers.

7. Before the turn of the century neither the government nor American industry and agriculture were concerned about conservation. From the time of Theodore Roosevelt, however, most Presidents have been interested in conserving timber and other natural resources, controlling erosion, and furthering land reclamation. After 1933 the reports of the National Resources Board, the work of the CCC, the soil-building policies furthered under AAA, and the example of broad-scale planning set by TVA called attention to the importance of conservation. During World War II wartime demands seriously depleted American resources, and today the need for conservation is greater than ever.

Summary of Important Dates

1891 Forest Reserve Act provides for conserving timber lands.
1896 Rural free delivery established.
1900 Congress passes Gold Standard Act.

1903 Wright Brothers make first successful flight in an airplane.

1906 Meat Inspection Act; Pure Food and Drugs Act.
Hepburn Act strengthens Interstate Commerce Commission.

1913 Federal Reserve System established.
Underwood Tariff makes a general reduction in rates.

1914 Clayton Antitrust Act.

1917 Smith-Hughes Act.

1921 National Budget Act passed by Congress.

1929 Beginnings of the great depression.

1932 Reconstruction Finance Corporation established.

1933 United States abandons gold standard.
T.V.A. created.
First AAA established.
Farm Credit Administration established.
Civilian Conservation Corps established.

1934 Trade Agreements Act makes possible tariff reduction through reciprocal agreements.
Securities and Exchange Commission established.

1935 National Labor Relations Act.

1938 Fair Labor Standards Act passed.
Second AAA established.

1947 Taft-Hartley Act.

Unit Activities

1. Make a list of the great improvements in communication and transportation since 1900. Indicate briefly: (1) how each has affected everyday life, and (2) how each has affected American business and industry.

2. Make a list of important efforts to regulate business in the public interest, made by the federal government since 1900. For each, (1) state the title and date of the act, (2) give the chief provisions of the act, and (3) tell to what extent the regulation was effective.

3. Make a list of important efforts to strengthen the position of labor, which have been made by the federal government since 1900. For each, (1) state the title and date of the act, (2) give the chief provisions, and (3) evaluate its effectiveness. What is the trend today?

4. Make a list of important efforts to help the American farmer made by the federal government since 1900. For each, (1) state the title and date of the act, (2) give the chief provisions, and (3) evaluate its effectiveness.

5. Turn to the "Balance of Trade under Tariff Acts" table in *The World Almanac*. For each of the tariff acts since 1897 calculate (1) the average dollar value of exports, and (2) the average dollar value of imports for each year the act was in effect. Do you see any connection between tariff rates and foreign trade? What other factors affect the volume of foreign trade? Why is the last tariff act listed as 1930? How have tariff rates been modified since 1933 despite the fact that no general revision has been made?

For Further Reading

Original Sources

Commager, H. S., ed., *Documents of American History*. Appleton-Century-Crofts. Nos. 356, 363, 369, 370, 402, 403, 414, 424, 438, 461, 462, 474, 477, 484, 500, 517.

Commager, H. S., and Nevins, Allan, eds., *The Heritage of America*. Little, Brown. Nos. 227, 228, 250, 251.

Pease, T. C., and Roberts, A. S., eds., *Selected Readings in American History*. Harcourt. Nos. 227, 228, 243, 244, 249, 257, 262, 263, 267, 271, 272.

General References

Adams, J .T., *Epic of America*. Little, Brown. Chapter 12.

Faulkner, Harold U., *American Economic History*. Harper. Chapters 16–18, 21–23.

Morison, S. E., and Commager, H. S., *The Growth of the American Republic*. Oxford. Vol. II, Chapters 7, 9, 15, 16, 17, 18, 22, 24.

Parkes, H. B., *Recent America*. Crowell. A history of the United States since 1900.

Special Accounts

Allen, F. L., *Only Yesterday*. Harper (also Bantam Books). An informal and lively history of the nineteen twenties.

American Nation Series. Harper. Dewey, D. R., *National Problems*. Sparks, E. E., *National Development*.

Beard, Mary R., *A Short History of the American Labor Movement*. Macmillan.

Brooks, Robert R., *When Labor Organizes*. Yale University Press. The methods used by labor unions.

Chase, Stuart, *The Tragedy of Waste*. Macmillan. Tells of the recklessness with which the United States has used its resources.

Chronicles of America Series. Yale University Press. Hendrick, B. F., *The Age of Big Business*. Moody, J., *The Masters of Capital*. Orth, S. P., *The Armies of Labor*.

Coleman, McAllister, *Men and Coal.* Farrar and Rinehart. Coal miners and coal mining in the United States.

History of American Life Series. Macmillan. Faulkner, H. U., *The Quest for Social Justice* (1878–1898). Slosson, P. W., *The Great Crusade and After* (1914–1928). Tarbell, Ida, *The Nationalizing of Business* (1878–1898).

Lilienthal, David E., *T.V.A.: Democracy on the March.* Pocket Books. The story of the T.V.A. as told by its director.

McWilliams, Carey, *Ill Fares the Land.* Little, Brown. The story of migratory agricultural labor.

Public Affairs Pamphlets. No. 76. Carskadon, T. R., *Workers and Bosses are Human.* No. 117. Carskadon, T. R., *Your Stake in Collective Bargaining.* No. 100. McWilliams, Carey, *Small Farm, Big Farm.* No. 84. Stewart, M. S., *Jobs and Security for Tomorrow.* No. 105. Stewart, M. S., *There Can Be Jobs for All.*

United States Department of Agriculture. U. S. Government Printing Office. *Farmers in a Changing World.* The 1940 yearbook of agriculture, contains authoritative information on almost every phase of American agriculture, including conservation.

United States Department of Agriculture. U. S. Government Printing Office. *To Hold This Soil.* Miscellaneous publication No. 321.

Biography

Merz, C., *And Then Came Ford.* Doubleday. The contributions of Ford to American production.

Minton, B., and Stuart, J., *The Men Who Lead Labor.* Modern Age. Brief sketches of contemporary labor leaders.

Winkler, J. K., *John D.: A Portrait in Oils* and *Morgan, the Magnificent.* Vanguard. These are biographies of John D. Rockefeller and of J. P. Morgan, the powerful financier.

Imaginative Writing

Benson, Ramsey, *Hill Country.* Stokes. Pioneer life in Minnesota, and the Farmers' Alliance movement.

Bromfield, Louis, *The Farm.* Harper. Traces four generations of a family living on an Ohio farm.

Burke, Fielding, *Call Home the Heart.* Longmans. Industrial conflict in a small North Carolina mill town.

Cantwell, R., *The Land of Plenty.* Farrar. Story of labor conflict in a lumber mill in the west.

Duffus, R. L., *Night Between the Rivers.* Macmillan. The crisis which would arise with a general strike in New York City.

Hergesheimer, Joseph, *The Three Black Pennys.* Knopf. Background is the development of the iron and steel industry in the United States.

Lumpkin, Grace, *To Make My Bread.* Macauley. The New South and the transformation of mountaineers into mill hands.

Pauls, E. H., *The Stars and Stripes Forever.* Putnam. Conflict between a factory owner's paternalism and labor's power to organize.

Poole, Ernest, *The Harbor.* Macmillan. Labor unrest early in the 1900's, developed against the background of New York harbor.

Scarborough, Dorothy, *Can't Get a Red Bird.* Harper. Hardships of a tenant farmer in the cotton belt.

Winther, S. K., *Take All to Nebraska.* Macmillan. The difficulties and problems of a tenant farmer in Nebraska shortly after 1900.

Pictures

Adams, J. T., ed., *Album of American History.* Scribner. Vol. IV, (1893–1918).

Butterfield, Roger, *The American Past.* Simon and Schuster.

Caldwell, Erskine and Bourke-White, Margaret, *You Have Seen Their Faces.* Modern Age. Photographs with commentaries on poor white and Negro farmers in the South.

Lange, Dorothea, and Taylor, Paul S., *An American Exodus.* Reynal. Photographs showing the hardships of evicted tenant farmers.

Pageant of America Series. Yale University Press. Keir, Malcolm, *The Epic of Industry* and *The March of Commerce.*

 Sidelights on American History

Out of a Woodshed, Aluminum! Everyone is familiar with the uses of aluminum — in cooking pans, for instance, or in wrappers for candy bars and chewing gum. It is hard to believe that this common metal was once scarcer and more valuable than gold. Until about 1825, in fact, aluminum was a mystery metal. Chemists were sure it existed, but it was locked away in compounds with other elements. Nobody had ever actually seen any aluminum.

Then a Danish chemist by the name of Oersted "isolated" aluminum and became the first person to see the metal. Later another scientist found a way to produce larger quantities of aluminum outside the laboratories. Its cost, however, was still very high — about $17 a pound — and therefore aluminum had few practical uses. It was so dear, in fact, that it was used for jewelry.

It was an American only 22 years old who first discovered how to make aluminum so cheaply that it could be used for everything from pans to airplanes. Charles Martin Hall was a student at Oberlin College in Ohio in 1885. His professor of chemistry said one day to the class, "If anyone could invent a process to make aluminum on a commercial scale, he would be a world benefactor. He would also make a fortune." Hall turned to his nearest classmate. "I'm going after that metal," he said.

Behind the home of Hall's parents stood an old woodshed, in which Hall set up a laboratory. The neighbors snickered a little over young Charlie Hall's simple laboratory equipment: a plumber's torch, a carbon-lined crucible, some carbon sticks for electrodes, and some electric batteries. But Hall knew, as did any chemist, that aluminum could be made by passing a current through a mixture of the white powder called aluminum oxide and the icelike mineral known as fused cryolite, which came from Greenland. Hall intended to improve on this inefficient and expensive method by dissolving aluminum oxide powder in *melted* cryolite and passing an electric current through the solution.

Hall proceeded to put the mixture into his crucible and to heat the crucible with his blowtorch. Suspended in the solution were sticks of carbon, to which were attached wires leading to the electric batteries. The young inventor really was using the simplest of electric furnaces, and the result of his experiment was a deposit of pure aluminum in the bottom of the crucible. The experiment in the woodshed laid the foundation for the vast aluminum industry of today. In a few years the price of the metal whose costliness had once rivaled gold was only 18 cents a pound.

Nobody Drives a Selden. Most American automobiles keep alive the names of early inventors and makers of cars. There is one notable exception. Nobody drives a Selden today, in spite of the fact that a man named George Baldwin Selden made the first practical American car.

Selden never had to live on a crust of bread, nor struggle with poverty, nor perform experiments in a rat-ridden garret. His father was a successful lawyer, judge, and lieutenant-governor of New York State. Selden attended the University of Rochester and Yale University, but he was so mechanically minded that college courses did not interest him. While still in his 20's, he had invented a new kind of engine that burned a mixture of kerosene and nitrous oxide (laughing gas). This invention was unsuccessful, so Selden turned to an engine that had been invented four or five years earlier and experimented with running it on petroleum fuels.

By attaching this engine to a vehicle that would run on the roads, Selden became the father of the American automobile. He called his contraption a "road locomotive." He designed the vehicle himself, including the running gears, the clutch, the propeller shaft, and the cooling system. The body did not differ much from the carriages of that day.

The new conveyance became known to scoffers as the "explosion buggy." It cut a sorry figure beside the fast-moving surreys and gigs that raced by. "Get a horse!" shouted the little boys on the sidewalks. But in a few years there were several companies interested in making "explosion buggies." The firm that had bought Selden's patents was suing the others for wrongfully using the inventor's designs and ideas. The most famous of these suits was the one brought against Henry Ford's company. The courts upheld Ford's claim that his engine was quite different from Selden's.

Selden later tried to build and sell automobiles himself, but, like many inventors, he was a poor business man. His company was not a success. Today you cannot step on the accelerator of a Selden Eight.

Hormel Tries "Straight-time." Joe Fredericks, who works in a big woolen mill in New England, seems to have a pretty good job. He operates one of the looms, and some weeks his pay will be as much as $85. But Joe is often uneasy.

"It's good pay and a good company," he says, "but you never can tell how long the work will last. You can't be sure how many weeks will go by before business is bad and there has to be a lay-off. I'd rather work for less money and be sure of 52 weeks' work a year."

Joe's worry is a common one among Americans who work for a weekly wage. And common too is Joe's preference: a guaranteed job — maybe even at less pay — for an entire year. But for a long time the very idea has been considered an impossible dream. No one is going to guarantee a certain amount of annual business to the company Joe Fredericks works for. How then can Joe's company guarantee wages to its employees?

But all through history certain men have been fascinated by impossible dreams. One such was an American named Jay C. Hormel, head of a butchering and meat packing company in Austin, Minnesota. The Hormel Company was one of the most successful of its kind in the United States, and much of its success was founded on ideas. Mr. Hormel was interested in the idea of giving his employees "straight-time" (another name for the guaranteed annual wage).

In 1931 Mr. Hormel proposed a plan to the company workers. The company would contract with the men of any department for a year's work at pay based on the production average over a period of ten years. Whether there was little work, or much, or none, each employee in that department would receive a guaranteed amount each week for 52 weeks of the year. This offer was a surprise and a sensation. Many people said it would never work — because it never had. But the workmen in the smokehouse division of the Hormel firm — the department that handles the curing and smoking of hams and other meats — wanted to try the plan and voted to do so.

"Straight-time" worked so well, and the employees liked it so much, that all other departments at Hormel took it on. For the first time the "impossible dream" of millions of wage earners was realized. Other American companies have tried it, and more are finding it successful every year. Joe Fredericks and other wage earners like him are eager for the day when "straight-time" will be general in American business and industry.

The automobile brings recreation

THE PLAN OF THE BOOK

Unit Nine

THE AMERICAN PEOPLE DEVELOP

A MODERN WAY OF LIFE

From the beginning of their country's history, Americans were conscious of differences among themselves — sectional, social, and racial. Sharp differences in customs and manners divided foreign-born groups from each other and from native-born Americans. The interests of urban and rural areas were in conflict. Such differences have grown steadily less, and the people of the United States are becoming increasingly unified. Many of the reasons for this transformation will be discussed in Unit Nine.

Restrictions on immigration have greatly reduced the number of foreign-born. There are other reasons why Americans have grown more and more alike in their values and desires: instantaneous communication (telephone, radio, television); the increased mobility of population (made possible by improved public transportation and the passenger automobile); the development of a national press, literature, and music; and the common experience which results from viewing the same motion pictures and sports. The steady flow of population from country to city, the movement of city dwellers out to suburban and rural areas, and the availability of all kinds of comforts and luxuries have also helped standardize American culture.

Throughout their history Americans have put a premium on education. It has been a powerful force for passing on the American heritage. Today secondary education is accepted as the right of all youth, and a larger number of young men and women are going to college than ever before. Emphasis in education is being placed increasingly on the achievement of such fundamental goals as loyal and intelligent citizenship, worthy membership in home and family, and the ability to get and hold a job.

Suffragettes

Chapter 32

SOCIAL CHANGES HELP TO MAKE A

NEW AMERICA

I am the people — the mob — the crowd — the mass.
Do you know that all the great work of the world is done through me?
I am the workingman, the inventor, the maker of the world's food and clothes.
I am the audience that. witnesses history.

Carl Sandburg

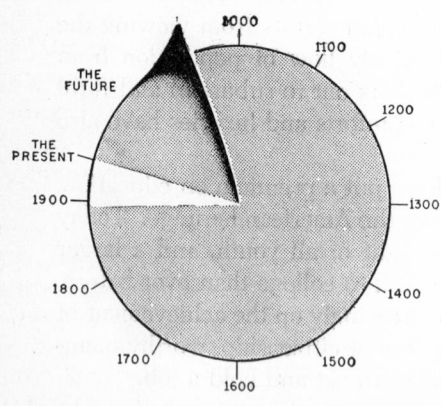

1897 – The Present

It is often said that Americans are the world's greatest "joiners." We join social clubs, business associations, improvement societies, church groups. But whether an individual "joins" these particular organizations or not, he belongs to a number of groups, for Americans can be grouped in many ways. There are countless shades of differences among us, because we come from many different backgrounds and have been affected by various kinds of conditions.. Groupings may be made, for example, on the basis of geographical location, national origin, occupation, or race. To follow social change in the United States since the 1890's, it is necessary to group Americans in several ways so that the people can be seen from more than one

582

point of view. This chapter will discuss social change under the following headings:

1. Changes continue within our population groups.
2. The tide of immigration turns.
3. Immigrants and their descendants make valuable contributions.
4. Social reforms affect American life.

1 Changes Continue Within Our Population Groups

The average age has increased. One big difference between the American people of today and those of a century ago is a difference in average age. In 1820 sixteen years was the "median age"; that is, there were just as many Americans younger than sixteen as there were Americans who were older. By 1900 the median age was 22.9 years, and by 1940 it was 29. To put the same story in a different way, in the 1840's less than half of all Americans were over 20, but in the 1940's two thirds were over 20.

The main reasons for the increase in the average age are:

(1) The advances in medical science, public health, and sanitation. In 1901 the average American could expect to live until he was 49. In 1927 he was likely to live until 59. In 1949 the average life expectancy for white males in the United States was about 65 years and for white females about 70 years.

(2) The declining birth rate. In 1860 it was estimated that the average American family had five children. In 1900 the average was three to a family and in 1946, two.

(3) Most immigrants were young people, and immigration has been very greatly reduced.

The shift in age groups has influenced our social and economic life in many ways. One important result has been the greater need for old-age pensions (see page 593).

Another result has been a smaller enrollment in the primary schools in proportion to the population, though a sharp rise in the birth rate during and after World War II temporarily stopped this trend.

The population is increasing more slowly. In spite of longer average lives, the combination of falling birth rates and reduced immigration has slowed down the general rate of population increase. Between 1870 and 1880, for example, the population of the United States increased more than 30 per cent. Between 1930 and 1940, on the other hand, it increased only seven per cent. In the 1940's statisticians were predicting a population peak of over 161 million in 1985, but the 1950 census indicated that this estimate would be low.

There have been regional shifts in population. America is a nation of restless people. It was a restless, courageous disposition that brought people here originally. If such people had been content with life in the lands from which they came, they would never have traveled thousands of miles to make new homes on a new continent.

This restlessness continued long after the frontier days had passed. During the five years between 1935 and 1940 twelve per cent of the people moved their place of residence from one county to another. The story of population growth shows no even distribution but a shift from section to section. From 1820 to 1870, for example, the population of the North increased more rapidly than that of the South. Between 1890 and 1930 just the opposite was true, and from 1930 to 1940 the southern states made a gain of 10.1 per cent while the northern population increased only 4.2 per cent.

The Far West, which first appeared in the census in 1850, has gained faster than either South or North ever since. During the '40's alone the population increase in the Far West was about 40 per cent. On the other hand, during the "dust bowl" period of the '30's some of the West Central states — Oklahoma, Kansas, Nebraska, and the Dakotas — actually decreased in population.

Our Growing Population

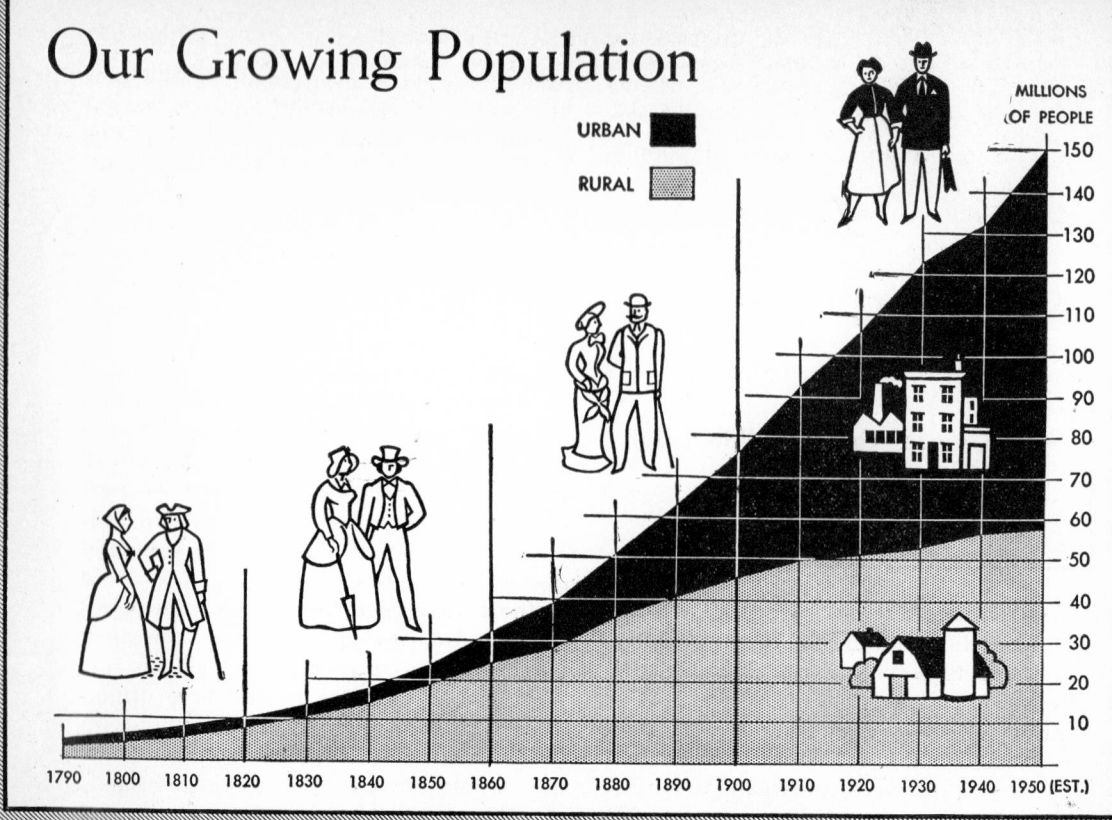

URBAN ■

RURAL ▨

MILLIONS OF PEOPLE

150 — 140 — 130 — 120 — 110 — 100 — 90 — 80 — 70 — 60 — 50 — 40 — 30 — 20 — 10

1790 1800 1810 1820 1830 1840 1850 1860 1870 1880 1890 1900 1910 1920 1930 1940 1950 (EST.)

What former characteristic of our population has been altered in this century? About how many people now live in urban areas? How has this been made possible?

There has been a shift from farm to city. As you have already seen, another important population change was the shift from farm to city. In 1790 there were only 24 "urban places" — communities of more than 2500 people — in the United States. They contained only five per cent of the people. By 1890 about 35 per cent of the people lived in cities or towns, and by 1950 this proportion was more than 60 per cent. Not only did people live in cities, but they lived in bigger cities (page 422). The 1940 census showed 38 million people living in cities of 100,000 or more.

Incomes and occupations are related. One way of grouping the American people is by incomes. Incomes and occupations are closely related. People in certain professions and high-salaried managers of business receive the highest incomes, while unskilled laborers receive the lowest. A very important trend during the twentieth century has been the decrease in the proportion of unskilled workers. In 1910 un-

skilled workers numbered 36 per cent of all persons employed. In 1940 the number had dropped to 25.9 per cent. During the same period the proportion of low-paid farm laborers dropped from 14.5 to 7.1 per cent of all workers. Machines were doing more and more of the work of unskilled laborers. At the same time, there were gains in the groups of semi-skilled and professional workers.

After 1900, the wealth of the highest income group continued to increase. It has been pointed out (page 423) that before 1900 there were about 3800 millionaires in the United States. During the 1920's, the number of millionaires grew to 50,000. At present, as for a number of years in the past, twelve per cent of the total net income of this country is received by one per cent of all the persons receiving incomes. Since the 1930's, this concentration of wealth has been slowed down, however, by increases in the amount of individual income taken by federal and state governments through income taxes. Income tax rates have gone up, particularly on the larger incomes. The greater amounts of money received by the government through income taxes are used for larger state and federal expenditures on public projects of various sorts.

Rich men are not necessarily "idle rich." Their fortunes have been used to benefit the community and the nation. John D. Rockefeller, for example, gave millions to educational and charitable institutions. The Rockefeller Foundation and the Rockefeller Institute for Medical Research have been of tremendous value to the nation and to the world in the field of public health. John D. Rockefeller, Jr., who took the chief responsibility for administering the family gifts, probably put in an average working day longer and harder than that of most men working for wages or salaries.

The condition of the less fortunate improves. During our century more and more people have taken an interest in the welfare of the less fortunate. The condition of the low-income groups has steadily improved. With the construction of sewerage systems, the extension of water supply systems, and the establishment of street-cleaning departments, much of the filth and litter of the slums has been eliminated. Housing laws have been passed by both city and state governments to make the worst kind of tenements illegal. In more recent times there have been public housing programs which have provided models for low-cost city homes. Low-income groups have also benefited by public health services, improved education, public parks, and various relief projects.

Organized charity also has done much to assist the poor. Many rich men followed the examples of Rockefeller and Carnegie in making gifts to build libraries, encourage education, promote family and child welfare, give hospital and medical care, and perform other social services. In recent times gifts from people of various income levels have swollen "community chests," which provide funds for hospitals, Boy Scouts and Girl Scouts, handicapped children, and the like.

——— CHECK-UP ———

What important changes affecting population groups have taken place in this country?

1. What has happened to the median age of people in this country? Why?
2. What are some important population shifts in the 1900's?
3. What are the trends with respect to the number of unskilled workers in the nation's labor force? The concentration of wealth? The condition of the less fortunate?

Light, air, and cleanliness in housing, as shown at the right below, have begun to replace the dinginess and squalor of earlier low-cost houses (left below).

The Rise and Fall of Immigration

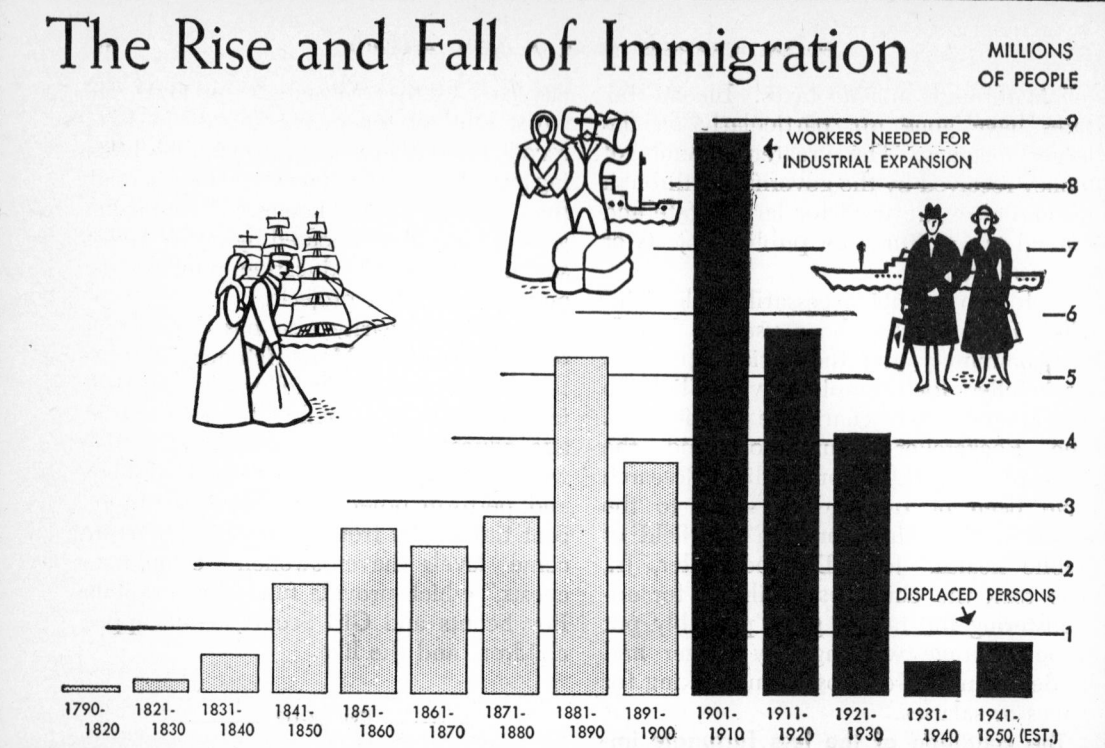

MILLIONS OF PEOPLE

WORKERS NEEDED FOR INDUSTRIAL EXPANSION

DISPLACED PERSONS

1790-1820 | 1821-1830 | 1831-1840 | 1841-1850 | 1851-1860 | 1861-1870 | 1871-1880 | 1881-1890 | 1891-1900 | 1901-1910 | 1911-1920 | 1921-1930 | 1931-1940 | 1941-1950 (EST.)

More people came to America between 1901 and 1910 than at any other time. Why? What caused the sharp drop in immigration after 1930? The slight increase in the '40's?

2 The Tide of Immigration Turns

Immigration from southern Europe increases. In the years just before 1900 a noticeable change began to take place in the stream of immigrants to the United States. You will recall (page 419) that up to about 1890 most of our immigrants had been coming from northern Europe — Great Britain, Germany, and the Scandinavian countries. But now the stream shifted to southern and eastern Europe. It was made up of Poles, Italians, Slovaks, Rumanians, Czechs, Jews, and Greeks, whose backgrounds made it more difficult for them than for the northern Europeans to adjust to American life. Cheap, fertile land was no longer available after the passing of the frontier, and most of the new immigrants flocked to industrial jobs in large cities. They accepted work at low pay. Within the cities they collected into little national groups, clinging to the language and customs of the countries from which they had come. Native-born Americans were suspicious of the immigrants' strange customs. Jacob Riis as early as 1890 described New York as composed of an Irish West Side, a German East Side, a "Little Italy," a Chinatown, and sections that were mostly Russian, Polish, or Greek. Under these conditions the process of Americanization became more difficult.

Immigration reaches a peak. In the first ten years of our century immigration reached an all-time high with a total of 8.8 million, and was responsible for more than half the total increase in population. In those days the invitation inscribed on the Statue of Liberty could be taken literally:

Give me your tired, your poor,
Your huddled masses yearning to breathe free...
Send these, the homeless, tempest-tossed, to me;
I lift my lamp beside the golden door!

Nevertheless, it is important to note that until 1910 the number of foreign-born in proportion to the total population remained at about one seventh.

The Japanese are restricted. You have seen in Chapter 22 that in the latter half of the 1800's there was a loud outcry in favor of restriction of immigration. This attitude gained strength after 1900. Early in the century people began to protest against the number of Japanese along the Pacific coast. In 1906 the Japanese became indignant at a decree of the San Francisco school board which barred children of Japanese parentage from the public schools. President Theodore Roosevelt persuaded the school board to withdraw its decree. Because of the strong anti-Japanese feeling, however, Roosevelt arranged an informal understanding with Japan known as the "Gentlemen's Agreement" (1907). Oriental pupils under sixteen were to be admitted to the regular public schools, but Japan in turn agreed to refuse passports to Japanese laborers who wanted to enter the United States. An immigration act in 1907 denied admission to all Japanese who did not possess proper passports. This law was interpreted to exclude Japanese who came from island possessions of the United States or from any country other than Japan.

Although Japan observed the terms of the Gentlemen's Agreement, the Pacific Coast states continued to make restrictions on the Japanese. California denied Chinese and Japanese the right to buy farms or to lease them for more than three years (1913). Other states followed California's example. Japan found it difficult to understand the powers of the states with which the federal government could not interfere. The United States was accused of not keeping its part of the bargain. The Japanese were well aware that immigrants of European background were being given privileges that were denied to Asiatics. They considered these restrictions an insult to their national honor.

The sons and daughters of many lands have come to live in America. Once here, after a period of adjustment, they have added their skills and customs to those of other Americans. This is one reason why the United States has become a great power.

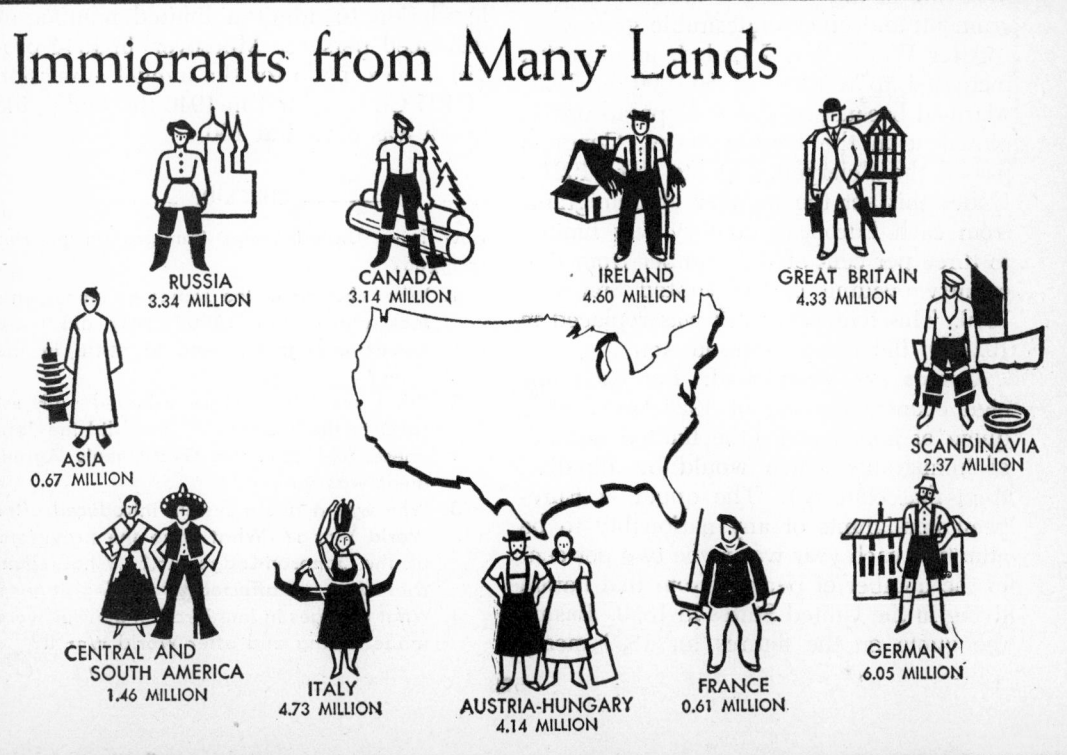

Immigrants from Many Lands

RUSSIA
3.34 MILLION

CANADA
3.14 MILLION

IRELAND
4.60 MILLION

GREAT BRITAIN
4.33 MILLION

ASIA
0.67 MILLION

SCANDINAVIA
2.37 MILLION

CENTRAL AND
SOUTH AMERICA
1.46 MILLION

ITALY
4.73 MILLION

AUSTRIA-HUNGARY
4.14 MILLION

FRANCE
0.61 MILLION

GERMANY
6.05 MILLION

© 1948, General Electric Co.

Charles Steinmetz, son of German-Polish parents, came to America in 1889. He gained fame for research in electricity.

Immigration is further restricted. In spite of restrictions against Asiatics and a few others, immigration continued at an average of nearly a million persons a year until World War I broke out. In 1917 an important change in our immigration policy took place. Over President Wilson's veto Congress passed an act which barred illiterates, vagrants, chronic alcoholics, persons believing in the violent overthrow of government, and other undesirable groups.

After World War I ended, immigration increased to a total of 800,000 in 1921. Alarmed because of the widespread unemployment in the United States, Congress passed the Emergency Quota Act (1921). Under this act the number of immigrants from each European country was limited to three per cent of the number from that country residing in the United States in 1910. This temporary bill was replaced in 1924 by the Lodge-Johnson Act.

Quotas are established. For each foreign country the act of 1924 provided a quota of immigrants (the limited number of immigrants which would be admitted from that country). The quota of European immigrants of any nationality to be admitted each year was to be two per cent of the number of persons from that nation living in the United States in 1890. Basing the quota on the figures for 1890 meant favoring northwestern Europe. Certain groups — students, for example, or wives and children of resident American citizens — were not subject to quota restrictions. Neither were citizens of Canada, Mexico, and the independent republics of Central and South America. Immigrants barred from citizenship, including Japanese, were totally excluded.

Total immigration is limited. After 1929 the total number of quota immigrants was limited to about 150,000 a year. At that time each European country was given a quota based upon the percentage of the people of that national origin in the American population in 1920. During the depression of the 1930's immigration dropped far below quota limits, partly because many people who in normal times would have found employment were rejected on the grounds that they were "likely to become public charges." From 1931 to 1945, with the single exception of 1939, less than one third of the quota was filled each year.

After World War II many people urged that the immigration laws be modified. They felt that this country should admit more people who had lost their homes and their means of making a living during the great struggle. Congress therefore passed legislation to admit a limited number of displaced persons. Moreover, in 1944 provision was made for the annual admission of 105 Chinese, and in 1946 the Philippine quota was placed at 100.

——— CHECK-UP ———

How have United States immigration policies changed?

1. What change in the source of immigrants took place after 1890? Why did these newer immigrants tend to settle in the cities?
2. What restrictions were adopted with respect to the Japanese? Why did the Japanese feel that the Gentlemen's Agreement was violated?
3. Why was a quota system introduced after World War I? What were the provisions of the Johnson-Lodge Act? What countries were not affected by this legislation?
4. What changes in immigration policies were made during and after World War II?

<table>
<tr><td>3</td><td>

Immigrants and Their Descendants Make Valuable Contributions

</td></tr>
</table>

We are all immigrants or their descendants. The word *immigrant* is sometimes used in an uncomplimentary way by those whose ancestors arrived in this country many years ago. We should remember, however, that everyone in this country except the American Indian is either an immigrant or the descendant of an immigrant. Those aboard the *Mayflower* were immigrants. They came to America under conditions that do not exist today, but they too knew what it was to leave home and friends in order to start a new life in a strange land.

Immigrants have developed our resources. The United States would not be a leading nation today if it had not become a melting pot of all nationalities. Merely to possess natural resources is of little benefit to a country. They must be developed, and such development calls not only for business management and inventive skill but also for much patient, tiring, and often low-paid work. Much of that kind of heavy labor has been done by the foreign-born. They dug canals, mined coal, and worked

Louis Brandeis, liberal member of the Supreme Court, was one of many Jews who have made lasting contributions to American life.

in the steel mills. Foreign-born plowed the prairie lands, felled the forest giants, mixed and poured the concrete for the skyscrapers. They mined the iron ore and the silver, and drove the spikes in the heavy railroad ties.

Immigrants become leaders in many fields. The foreign-born have also contributed leadership in politics, business, and the arts. Some of the famous immigrants who have left a lasting impression on American life are Carl Schurz and John P. Altgeld (both born in Germany) in politics, Joseph Pulitzer (Hungary) and Jacob Riis (Denmark) in journalism, James J. Hill (Canada) in business, Samuel Gompers (England) in labor organization, Alexander Bell (Scotland) in invention. Augustus Saint-Gaudens, perhaps the outstanding American sculptor, was born in Ireland. The great majority of first-rank American musicians, including the directors of practically all our great symphony orchestras, have been immigrants.

Immigrants have settled in many parts of the country. On nearly every part of the country the immigrants have left an indelible stamp. In southern Pennsylvania,

Serge Koussevitzky, who left Russia for America in 1924, was for 25 years conductor of the Boston Symphony Orchestra.

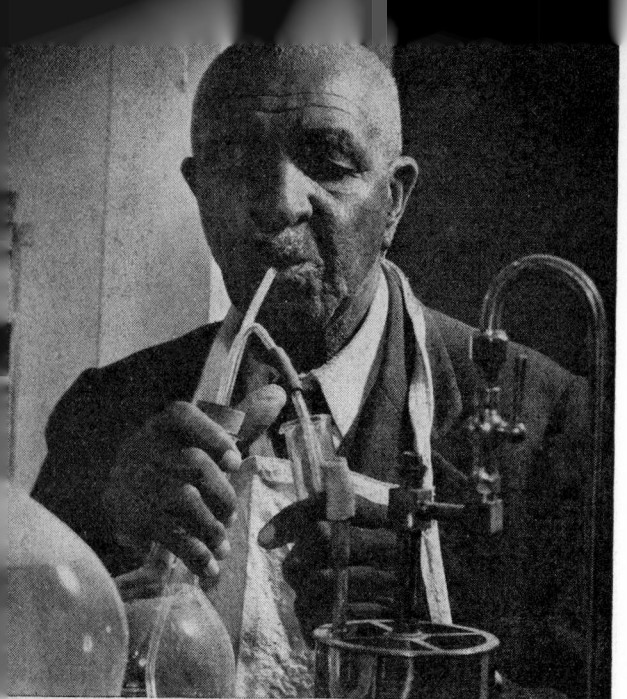

George Washington Carver, botanist and chemist, studied and taught better farming methods which have aided southern agriculture.

for example, may be found customs and even a little of the language of the Germans who settled there before the Revolutionary War. The descendants of these settlers are still sometimes called "Pennsylvania Germans" or "Pennsylvania Dutch." A later German migration sent colonists to the Middle West in the mid 1800's; cities like Milwaukee and St. Louis have profited from the love of these Germans for freedom and their interest in democratic government. Certain communities in the northern Middle West have been enriched by the inflow of thrifty, hard-working Scandinavians, many of whom have become prosperous farmers and dairymen. Many cities, particularly industrial ones, have become the homes of immigrants from southern and eastern Europe.

French influence is very strong in Louisiana, where French, in addition to English, continues to be spoken. French law has had a distinct influence on the legislation of that state, and French customs and cooking attract many visitors to Louisiana every year. A wide use of the Spanish language persists in certain states of the Southwest, where historic mission buildings, Spanish architecture, and many customs survive to remind us that Spain once controlled this vast region. Spanish has contributed many words to our own language.

The Negro population changes. There is one group of "descendants of immigrants" that is different from the others in the fact that many of their ancestors came here from a foreign land unwillingly and were sold into slavery. In 1790 about 15 per cent of the population of the United States was classified as Negro. By 1940 the percentage had decreased to 9.8, not because the Negroes have decreased in number but because of the more rapid increase of white population brought about by immigration. Formerly the Negro population was concentrated in the South, and most of the southern Negroes were employed on farms. During World War I, however, when jobs were plentiful, millions of Negroes went north and west, in search of better opportunities. By 1940 eleven of our large cities had more than 100,000 Negroes each. New York's Negro population was nearly half a million. Almost half the Negro population in 1940 was living in cities, while about a third, almost entirely in the South, lived on farms.

Negroes make great progress. Following the War Between the States and for many years thereafter, Negroes were handicapped by a lack of economic opportunities. They had to overcome great obstacles, but by the 1940's there was evidence that their economic position was improving. More and more Negroes were employed in professions and in business. Amateur and professional sports were increasingly open to them, and in 1947 Negroes played for the first time on major league baseball teams. Joe Louis, the heavyweight fighter, and Jesse Owens, the runner, have been acclaimed as all-American athletes.

In no field has the Negro made more progress than in education. In 1865 a very large majority of Negroes were illiterate. By 1880, however, 30 per cent were classed as literate; by 1930, 84 per cent. By 1940 there were over 150,000 Negro college graduates. Booker T. Washington, founder of the Tuskegee Institute in Alabama, favored vocational education for Negroes, and this was also stressed at Hampton Institute, in Virginia. Negro educators, who desired the same higher education for Negroes as for whites, saw their ideas carried out at Howard, Atlanta, Fisk, and other Negro universities. Educational opportunities for the Negro are steadily improving at both the public school and college level.

Negroes contribute to the arts and sciences. Some of the important developments in American culture include Negro contributions. Negro spirituals are America's most distinctive contribution to religious music. Negroes have contributed outstanding concert and entertainment artists, including the singers, Marian Anderson and Roland Hayes, and the band leader, Duke Ellington. Countee Cullen, Langston Hughes, and Richard Wright have been among the successful Negro authors, and George Washington Carver and Ernest E. Just have been outstanding scientists.

——————— CHECK-UP ———————

What contributions have immigrants and their descendants made to American culture?

1. Why can it be said that nearly all Americans are immigrants or the descendants of immigrants?
2. What are some areas in which the influence of certain national groups is especially strong? How have immigrants contributed to the development of America?
3. What handicaps have Negroes had to overcome? What contributions have they made to American culture?

---

4 **Social Reforms Affect American Life**

Women become active outside the home. An important characteristic of American life in this century is that an increasing number of women are taking part in activities outside the home. More and more young women have found employment in the business world. In 1900 the number of female breadwinners in the United States

was over 5 million. By 1930 the number had risen to about 11 million, and 253 out of every 1000 women were at work for pay. In 1940 nearly 30 per cent of the women between the ages of 18 and 64 were employed outside their homes. Two thirds of all the single women were earning money. Most employed women worked in domestic and personal service, factories, clerical occupations, and the professions.

Woman suffrage becomes nation-wide. It was inevitable under these circumstances that women should demand full political equality with men. The fight for woman suffrage was a hard struggle; many of its bitterest opponents were women themselves. In the first years of suffrage parades in New York, the marchers would be met with cries of "Go home and wash the dishes!" But after 1910, under the leadership of such women as Anna Howard Shaw and Carrie Chapman Catt, active campaigning began to meet with real success. In that year Washington became the fifth state to give women full political rights. In 1911 California followed this example. Then

How many women were employed in 1870? In 1950? Can you explain the increase?

Women at Work

MILLIONS

1870 1880 1890 1900 1910 1920 1930 1940 1950 (EST.)

Sexy!

1900

1920

TENNIS COSTUMES

Kansas, Oregon, and Arizona came into line in 1912, and by 1914 equal suffrage existed in eleven states. Beginning in 1919, one state after another ratified the Nineteenth Amendment to extend the vote to women, and in August, 1920, it became part of the Constitution.

By 1940 women were to be found in practically all branches of public life. There had been women governors, senators, representatives, judges, and a woman member of the President's Cabinet. Growing numbers of women exerted their influence through activities in political parties and in non-partisan organizations like the League of Women Voters.

Some people condemn equality of women. The historian Francis Parkman condemned feminism in the 1800's as an attempt "to overleap Nature's limitations," disrupt the home, and give women excitement that was "too much for their strength." Women were criticized for being restless, dissatisfied, and — worst of all! — "strong-minded." Even in the 1940's best-selling books and popular magazine articles blamed the new freedom of women for the high divorce rate, juvenile delinquency, mental illness, and the general decline in manners, morals, and religion. Whether this charge contained elements of truth or not, it seemed evident that women would never step back willingly into the minor role they played in the middle 1800's. Having become accustomed to freedom and equality with men, they would probably never be content with less.

Americans experiment with prohibition. During the early years of our century women continued to be as active in the cause of temperance as they had been in the late 1800's. Many had donned the white ribbon of the W.C.T.U., and a few even burst into the saloons to pray and sing hymns in an effort to reform the drunkards. Both men and women gave increasing support to the Anti-Saloon League, which had been formed in 1893, and which within ten years became financially and politically powerful. Many states went "dry," and by 1917 two thirds of the states had passed prohibition laws. In 1919 the Eighteenth Amendment was added to the Constitution, forbidding the manufacture, transportation, and sale of intoxicating liquor. The Volstead Act was passed by Congress to carry this amendment into effect.

Prohibition had merits and brought problems. National prohibition of liquor was one of the most unusual experiments in the history of the American people. The net value of this experiment can probably never be accurately determined. There seems to have been a reduction in arrests for drunkenness and in the poverty caused by drunkenness. Prohibition had a real effect on diet, too, for the consumption of milk, soft drinks, ice cream, and candy increased in the '20's, and the soda fountain became the convenient community social center.

On the other hand, the enforcement of prohibition turned out to be almost impossible. "Anyone who has watched whole families happily picnicking around a keep-off-the-grass notice or riding in automobiles at forty miles an hour past fifteen-miles-an-hour-speed-limit signs," wrote one historian, "could hardly expect the thirsty minority to accept the new regime." Illegal drinking also led to gangsterism and racketeering, for the manufacture and sale of whisky and beer were immensely profitable.

After fourteen years of "bootleggers" and "speakeasies" and "moonshine," the prohibition experiment was brought to an end when the Twenty-First Amendment was added to the Constitution (1933) to repeal the Eighteenth.

The Social Security Act provides benefits. One of the most far-reaching programs of social reform grew out of depression conditions in the 1930's. As part of the New Deal program, Congress passed the Social

Security Act in 1935. The provisions of the act fell into three main parts:

(1) *Old-age insurance.* The law set up a compulsory old-age insurance system, which provides benefits for workers who retire at 65 years of age. The old-age insurance plan is administered by the federal government. Funds to finance the plan are raised by a compulsory pay roll tax on both employers and employees.

(2) *Unemployment insurance.* This part of the plan was intended to relieve workers of the worries and hardships caused by unemployment. In order to take part in this scheme states had to set up approved unemployment insurance plans. Funds are raised by a pay roll tax on employers and are administered by the state governments.

(3) *General welfare.* The federal government agreed to match funds established by the states to assist dependent mothers, to aid crippled and dependent children,

and to provide pensions to needy persons over 65 years of age.

The old-age pension and unemployment sections of the act, together with auxiliary state laws, were upheld by the Supreme Court in May, 1937. Although the old-age insurance system was a wide departure from previous activities of the federal government, it proved popular and led to a widespread demand that its benefits be extended to workers who were not covered by the original Social Security Act.

——————— CHECK-UP ———————

How did social reforms affect American life?

1. What has happened to the proportion of women working for wages? Why?
2. How did women secure political equality?
3. Why did the United State experiment with prohibition? Why was the Prohibition Amendment repealed?
4. What benefits did the Social Security Act bring to the American people?

CHAPTER REVIEW

Terms to Understand

median age
W.C.T.U.
prohibition
"speakeasies"
rate of population increase

old-age pensions
"Pennsylvania Dutch"
domestic service
"bootleggers"

People and Things to Know About

Booker T. Washington
Marian Anderson
George Washington Carver
Gentlemen's Agreement
Twenty-first Amendment

Carrie Chapman Catt
Lodge-Johnson Act
Eighteenth Amendment
Nineteenth Amendment
Social Security Act

Historic Dates to Identify

1907   1919   1920   1933   1935

Questions to Discuss

1. Why can Americans born today be expected to live to a greater age than those born in 1900? What difference does this fact make?
2. Why is there a population movement from country to city? From some states to others?
3. Compare the following:
   (a) The distribution of income in the

Questions to Discuss (Cont.)

1920's and the 1930's; in colonial times and today.
   (b) The immigration policy of the United States before and after 1914.
4. Why was it difficult to enforce national prohibition? Are there any "dry" communities today?

Other Things to Do

1. Make graphs, using data from *The World Almanac*, to show the United States birth and death rates over a period of at least 50 years. What conclusions do these statistics support?
*2. Make a chart showing the restriction of immigration. List (a) the name of the act, (b) the date of the act, and (c) the chief provisions of the act.
3. Help your class make a survey of the members to determine the "national origin" of each student. Compare the results with the proportion of people from various countries in the nation as a whole. (Use *The World Almanac*.)
4. Report to the class on how an immigrant group in your community has contributed to American culture. Consider literature, art, music, sports, cookery, and so on.

Chapter 33

Microscope

MODERN TIMES BRING CULTURAL

CHANGES IN AMERICAN LIFE

This country is, I once heard it put, absolutely "lousy with greatness" — with not only the greatest responsibilities but with the greatest opportunities ever known to man.

John Gunther

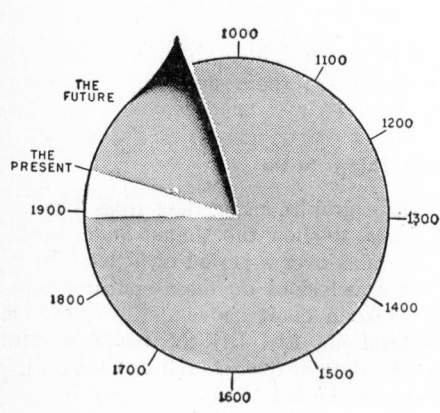

1897–The Present

In 1933, forty years after its famous Columbian Exposition, Chicago opened the Century of Progress Exposition. Hamlin Garland had advised his parents to "sell the cook stove if necessary" to see the fair in 1893, but at the Century of Progress Exposition the exhibits encouraged visitors to sell the old stove and buy a new one. On display in the huge buildings were the latest household appliances, shiny automobiles, streamlined locomotives — to name a few items at random. Everything on view proclaimed that the United States had become the most powerful industrial nation on earth and that her people enjoyed the highest standard of living.

Yet if we try to describe twentieth century civilization in the United States, we must consider more than the high standard of living. We point with pride to the fact that we have 80 per cent of the world's automobiles and at least half of the telephones, but we should take even greater satisfaction in evidences of intellectual and cultural maturity. In this exciting century there has been an almost unbelievable record of ballyhoo. On the other hand, there is a deeper, more permanent side to American life — a record of universal education, breathtaking scientific discoveries, projects for slum clearance and conservation. Painters have shown the world how beautiful the Iowa or Kansas countryside can be. Playwrights, novelists, and poets have won national and international recognition.

This chapter will show twentieth century America in good times and bad. It will describe periods of irresponsible gaiety and years of sober maturity. It will review some of the achievements in education, science, literature, art, and music. The discussion will be presented under the following headings:

1. Important developments bring changes in American life.
2. Education becomes universal.
3. Science achieves new successes.
4. Many writers contribute to American literature.
5. Art, music, and drama develop and mature.

1 Important Developments Bring Changes in American Life

The keynote of the new century is optimism. By 1900 the United States was a world power, with great influence in the Caribbean and the Pacific. The population had more than doubled since 1865. The frontier had disappeared before a torrent of settlers who had penetrated every corner of the Union to take advantage of its apparently endless resources. The American people looked forward to good times in a land of opportunity.

To be sure, every class and group did not share this optimism to the same degree.

Thousands of immigrants, living in city slums, had to work long hours for poor wages in unhealthful factories. Certain racial and religious groups suffered from unfair treatment, and millions of people were illiterate. But Americans in general believed that such conditions would soon be corrected by applying the principles of democracy, for in 1900 Americans were just as "sold" on the democratic way of life as they are today. They believed in their form of government. They admired a social system that gave dignity to the individual. They relied on their own initiative and energy, and they were confident of their country's future.

The population was still mostly rural. In 1900 about two thirds of the people still lived on farms or in villages. Although the farmer was making increased use of his new machinery, he and his family were out of touch with life in the larger communities. In fact, many farmers could not even have their mail delivered; less than 200,000 persons were served by rural free delivery in 1900. Except for the traveling Chautauqua, the county fair, and an annual visit of the circus, rural communities had to rely largely on their own resources.

Improved transportation and communication bring changes in American life. In the years before World War I a revolution in transportation and communication brought sweeping changes in the lives of both city and country dwellers (see Chapters 19 and 27). The first automobiles developed by Ford, Olds, and others were crude affairs, but these were soon replaced by efficient four-cylinder models and later by smooth "sixes." Competition in the new auto industry was keen and progress was rapid. More and more automobiles appeared on the road as Henry Ford astonished the world by his efficiency in mass-production. By 1915 there were about 2½ million cars registered. The popularity of the automobile encouraged the construction of better roads, making it easier for farmers to come to the city and for city dwellers to enjoy the countryside. Equally important in making it possible for workers to live farther from the industrial and

Horsedrawn fire engines were exciting to watch in the early 1900's, but their days were numbered because of the new gasoline engine.

business sections of the city was the widespread operation of street-car lines.

American life was also influenced by advances in communication. By 1915 most middle class homes in the cities had telephones, and the telephone was already helping to break down the isolation of rural life. In January of that same year Alexander Bell spoke into a phone at New York and was heard in San Francisco. The man who received his message was the same one who, 39 years earlier, had listened to Bell's first message from one room to another.

Americans enjoy unusual prosperity after World War I. The United States emerged from World War I with many new attitudes. A wave of feeling that it was a mistake to take part in Europe's affairs swept the country. Along with this isolationist attitude there was a swing to conservative politics. A brief depression was followed by the greatest wave of prosperity that the country had ever known. At the same time the high ideals with which Americans had taken part in the "war to end wars" gave way in the '20's to an almost wholesale desire to "get rich quick." Eagerly Americans bought as many of the "good things in life" as they could afford — vacuum cleaners, cars, refrigerators, radios. If a family lacked the necessary cash to pay for these products, they could be bought on the installment plan. The important thing was to have as much as everyone else — to "keep up with the Joneses."

"Spectator sports" attract huge crowds. In the '20's even sports became largely commercialized. Giant stadiums were erected in cities and on college campuses, and every year millions of spectators flocked to see college football games. Hundreds of millions of dollars were spent annually by Americans who did not take part in sports themselves, but who paid admission to see their idols in action: Babe Ruth in baseball, Red Grange in football, Dempsey and Tunney in boxing, Tilden and Helen Wills in tennis, Hagen and Bobby Jones in golf, Man o' War in horseracing.

Entertainment flourishes. The '20's offered many other amusements, too. Jazz music had become popular, and there were many nightclubs. Until Al Jolson appeared in *The Jazz Singer* (1927), moving pictures were silent, but the whole nation took delight in the comedies of Charlie Chaplin, the swashbuckling deeds of Douglas Fairbanks, the girlish appeal of Mary Pickford, and the romantic roles of Rudolph Valentino. The radio was just getting started, but already millions of listeners were clamping earphones to their heads and listening to programs whose chief merit was their novelty.

The '20's have been termed "the era of wonderful nonsense." Newspapers gave great publicity to Shipwreck Kelly, who perched for days on a flagpole. The public followed the antics of a cross-continent "Bunion Derby" promoted by C. C. Pyle. They took a keen interest in Atlantic City's bathing-beauty contests. They gladly paid admission to watch "dance marathons," in which for days the contestants alternated brief periods of dancing and resting, with the hope of winning a substantial prize for endurance.

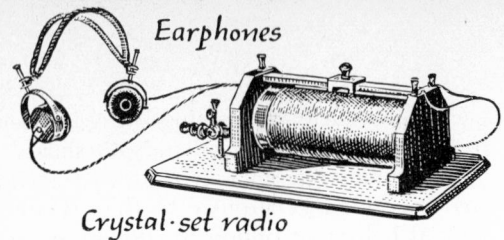

Earphones

Crystal·set radio

Standards and values change. And finally, there was a revolution in manners and values during the '20's. An ever-increasing number of women took up smoking. Short skirts and the use of cosmetics became fashionable. Divorces increased. There was a growing tendency on the part of the younger generation to rebel against the authority and the attitudes of their elders. More and more young women debated whether they should put a career before marriage.

The market crash begins a new era. In September, 1929, stocks on the New York Stock Exchange crashed from the dizzy peaks to which speculation and false prosperity had pushed them. The effect of the crash upon American life marked the end of a glittering but unhealthy era.

The early '30's were a bitter shock. Millions of people suddenly found themselves unemployed. In the words of President Roosevelt, one third of the nation was ill-housed, ill-clad, and ill-nourished. High school and college graduates looked desperately for jobs; men, old and young, turned to government projects for employment. Banks closed by the thousands, and millions of people lost their savings.

Americans overcome misfortune. There was much less ballyhoo in the '30's, but Americans kept their sense of humor and their love of amusement. On their 52 million radio sets they tuned in on variety programs and radio comedians. They continued to go to moving pictures, which were not entirely "talkies." They putted their way around vacant lots which had been transformed into miniature golf courses. Times were bad, but Americans used their 27 million passenger cars to relax on drives into the country. They laughed at Donald Duck and the pictures of themselves snapped by a candid camera photographer on Main Street. They listened to the President's fireside chats. They gradually worked themselves out of the depression.

597

Despite the depression, new household comforts kept appearing on the market, and Americans were made conscious of plastics, cellophane, zippers, nylon stockings, air-conditioning, and streamlined day coaches with reclining seats. The day of commercial aviation was at hand, offering the public adequate safety standards, speed of travel, and pretty hostesses!

Americans assume social responsibility. The depression, which greatly influenced the American way of life during the '30's, made Americans aware of their obligations to society. The federal government sponsored projects which not only provided jobs but also developed and conserved the nation's resources. The people watched the construction of mighty dams, new highways, broad parkways, soaring bridges such as those spanning the Golden Gate and the Hudson River. They were concerned with soil conservation, reforestation, and the economic and social development of entire regions, such as took place under the Tennessee Valley Authority.

Babe Ruth, home-run king of the '20's and '30's, had two strikes against him in the World Series of 1932. At that point, as an artist has shown here, he faced the stands and pointed to the spot where he planned to hit a home run. Then he did just that!

Early school desk and chair

Another war changes American life. The period of the '40's was completely overshadowed by World War II and the world-wide dislocation and unrest that followed. Fortunately the muscles and moral qualities of the American people had been strengthened by their difficulties during the '30's. They stood up magnificently under the trials of one of the fiercest struggles in history.

This war completely changed the American way of living. Young men left schools, colleges, and their jobs to fight in distant places: Guadalcanal, Anzio, Germany, Kasserine Pass, and the Burma Road. On the home front, the sisters and mothers of those men worked in factories to turn out shells, airplanes, and other implements for waging modern warfare. Living was regulated by rent controls, rationing of food and clothing, allocation of scarce materials, high taxes, and compulsory savings.

The United States becomes the most powerful nation. At the end of World War II, the nation began to reconvert its industry and agriculture to peacetime conditions. Many people were eager to throw off wartime restrictions, but the majority of Americans knew that postwar United States could never be the same as in the days before Pearl Harbor. For one thing, America had become the most powerful nation in the world. It was the only big power which had escaped without serious wartime damage. In fact, its economy was greatly expanded. The rest of the world was looking to us for the material assistance which would allow the war-devastated peoples to get back on their feet. It looked to us also for leadership in the modern world.

The United States answered this challenge by leading the way in organizing the United Nations. This international organization had for its objectives maintaining

peace and security, improving living standards, and ensuring that all persons should enjoy fundamental human rights. Americans responded generously to the cry for material help, and billions of dollars were devoted to relief and reconstruction abroad. The postwar years brought many difficult problems, but Americans approached them with a new maturity born of their own experiences.

——————— CHECK-UP ———————

How did important developments after 1900 change American life?

1. Why did optimism characterize American life in the early 1900's?
2. How was American life affected by the automobile, the streetcar, and the telephone?
3. What were the trends in entertainment after World War I? How did standards and values change?
4. How did the depression help Americans develop a sense of social responsibility?
5. How did World War II change life in the United States and the role of this country in world affairs?

2 Education Becomes Universal

Education continues to improve. Americans have long believed that democracy will fail unless the citizens are educated to their responsibilities. During the present century the school has greatly increased in importance, because it has been given the responsibility of preparing citizens to face problems which grow more and more com-

Combination school desk and chair - 1900's

plex. By the school year of 1925–26 the United States was spending nearly 3 billion dollars every year on education, almost as much as the rest of the world combined.

Between 1898 and 1914 the number of children in elementary schools increased from 15 million to more than 20. The "little red schoolhouse" was giving way to the consolidated school, partly because bus transportation became available to pupils in rural areas. Even greater gains were made in the number of boys and girls attending high school. Only about one out of ten went to high school in 1900. By 1950 about three out of four were enrolled. (See chart, page 600.)

Enrollments in the South increase. During the early 1900's the southern states continued to make rapid educational progress. In 1902 North Carolina started an active campaign for better schools. Virginia took similar steps the following year, and all the states of the South took up the movement. As a result, school revenues doubled or trebled within ten years, and the number of white children attending school increased by almost a third between 1898 and 1914.

John Dewey influences education. Teachers and school administrators, however, were giving thought to other matters than increasing enrollments and providing facilities for more pupils. They considered also whether the courses of study, the methods of teaching, and the books and other teaching materials were preparing youth to live in a rapidly changing world. A man whose philosophy of education has greatly influenced the schools of our day is John Dewey, a member of the staff at the University of Chicago who later became professor of philosophy at Columbia University.

Until the time of Dewey, the schools of this country had aimed at giving the pupils little except factual knowledge. Dewey argued that a school should be a place where the student learns about life by actually living it. Thus a school had to offer more than book learning. It must include opportunities for play, and give the student contact with nature and with community life. It must attempt to develop the child's personality.

The aims of education change. Influ-

Fine new schools reflected the increasing attention of Americans to education. This attractive high school is in California.

enced by Dewey's philosophy, the American elementary school has tried to do more than merely to develop the child's intellectual knowledge. The secondary school continues to prepare numbers of young people for college, but it also gives others a chance to acquire vocational education. For the great majority of high school youth, the emphasis is on meeting life's needs — preparing for home and family life, citizenship, and choosing and holding a job.

Thus the high school has developed into a center for providing as broad an education as possible for all American youth. In many communities the junior high school has been introduced to smooth the change from elementary to secondary schools. The junior college, in many ways an extension of the high school, provides vocational classes as well as general education.

Colleges grow larger. During our century American colleges and universities have increased both in enrollment and in community influence. In 1914 they enrolled about 300,000 students, but by the end of the '20's the figure had risen to nearly a million. To take care of so many students, the colleges had to expand their "plants" — erect new lecture halls and laboratories, add to their libraries, and construct new dormitories. The taxpayers contributed larger sums of money for state universities; private institutions relied on gifts from wealthy benefactors as well as income from tuition. The University of Chicago, for example, received large sums from Rockefeller; the University of Rochester was given millions by George Eastman, inventor of the Kodak; while James B. Duke, the tobacco manufacturer, expanded Trinity College in North Carolina into Duke University, the wealthiest institution in the South.

Modern life demands specialization and professional training for youth. Universities have met this challenge by offering a wider range of subjects. Graduate schools in medicine, dentistry, and education, for example, have sprung up in increasing numbers. Harvard founded its famous Graduate School of Business Administration in 1908. Four years later a bequest of a million dollars from the famous publisher, Joseph Pulitzer, enabled Columbia

University to open a school of journalism.

College enrollments reach a peak after World War II. In 1948 college enrollments reached an all-time high of about 2½ million students. This record was made possible in part by the fact that hundreds of thousands of veterans were getting financial assistance under the "G.I. Bill of Rights." [1] The number of ex-servicemen on campuses began to decline in 1949, but there was every indication that college attendance would remain far above the pre-war average.

Education is available to adults. It is also possible for adults and out-of-school youth to receive further education. Such opportunities are made available in a number of ways — through libraries, forums, and various "mass media" like newspapers, magazines, radio, television, and motion pictures. But more and more schools and colleges are also providing instruction in any subject for which there is a demand in the

[1] G.I. is an abbreviation for *government issue*. Applied to anything that the government provides for the enlisted man (G.I. shoes, G.I. hat), it is also used to refer to the enlisted serviceman himself.

High school enrollment has increased steadily since 1900. Why? In what ways are high schools different today from high schools before World War I? Explain why.

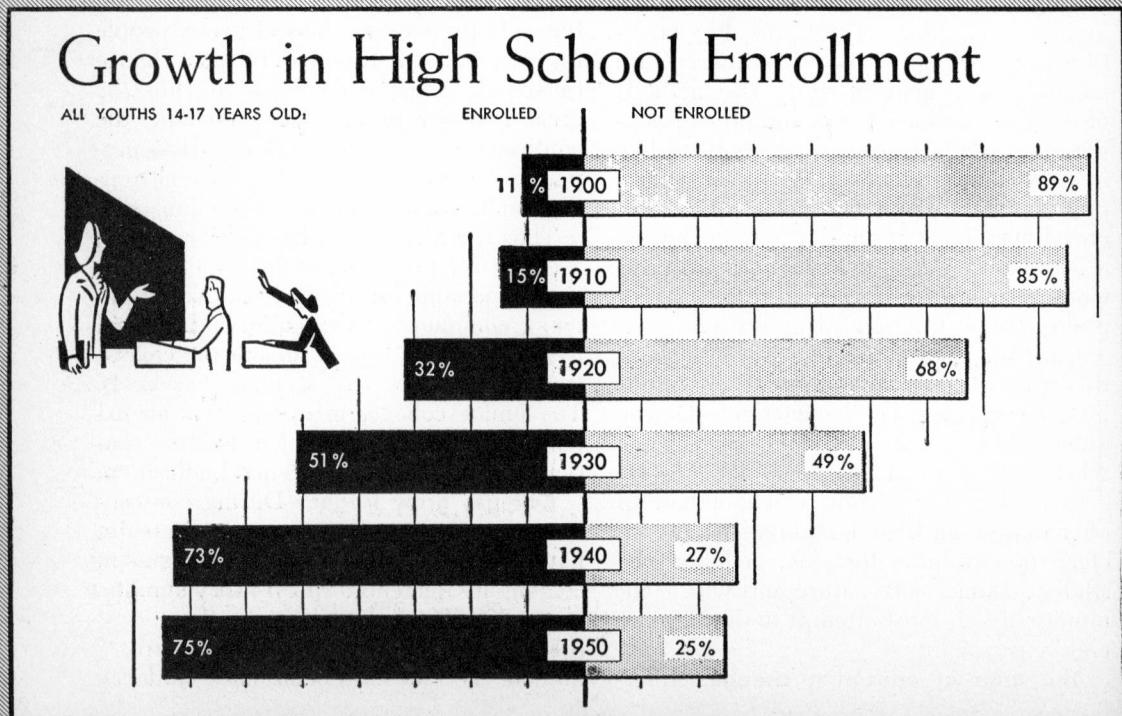

Growth in High School Enrollment

ALL YOUTHS 14-17 YEARS OLD: ENROLLED   NOT ENROLLED

	ENROLLED	NOT ENROLLED
1900	11%	89%
1910	15%	85%
1920	32%	68%
1930	51%	49%
1940	73%	27%
1950	75%	25%

community. Such instruction is given free or at low cost. Classes meet in the late afternoon or evening, or on Saturdays. Among the goals sought through adult education are (1) increased vocational skill, (2) rewarding ways of using leisure time, and (3) increased understanding of current problems.

Libraries aid education. Although there were libraries in this country as early as colonial times, the growth of public libraries and their influence upon American education reached their height in our own century. Since the early 1900's, when the gifts of Andrew Carnegie encouraged the growth of libraries, they have spread so widely that today a library is to be found in nearly every town of any size. From his fortune amassed in the steel industry, Carnegie made generous gifts designed to further the causes of world peace, scientific research, and public enlightenment. Before he died, Carnegie had erected over 2500 libraries in the United States, Canada, and other lands. Today more books are published than ever before, and many of these are circulated by means of traveling libraries and "bookmobiles" to rural districts that do not have the benefit of local public libraries.

——————— CHECK-UP ———————

How has education changed during the twentieth century?

1. What are the trends in education at these levels: elementary, secondary, college and university, adult?
2. What agencies other than the schools and colleges share responsibility for the education of Americans?

---

3 Science Achieves New Successes

America seeks scientific knowledge. Not only in education have there been great developments in this century; science, too,

The world's largest telescope, on Mt. Palomar, California, brings in light from stars a billion light years away.

has made tremendous strides. Vast sums have been spent in scientific research by universities, foundations, industrial organizations, and the government, with amazing results. Great medical laboratories have been built. Institutes of technology have carried on advanced research in chemistry, physics, and other fields. To seek out the mysteries of the universe, mammoth telescopes have been erected, notably on Mt. Wilson and Mt. Palomar in California and Mt. Locke in Texas.

The life span is longer. Striking progress has been made in medicine. Even before World War I such dread diseases as scarlet fever, typhoid fever, and diphtheria were being checked through the use of inoculations. We have learned to control tuberculosis, if it is discovered at an early stage. Smallpox has all but disappeared. Knowledge of vitamins and the discovery of penicillin and the sulfa drugs have further reduced the dangers of infection and disease. Modern sanitation, improved public health, rising standards in medical attention, and increased services from hospitals and clinics

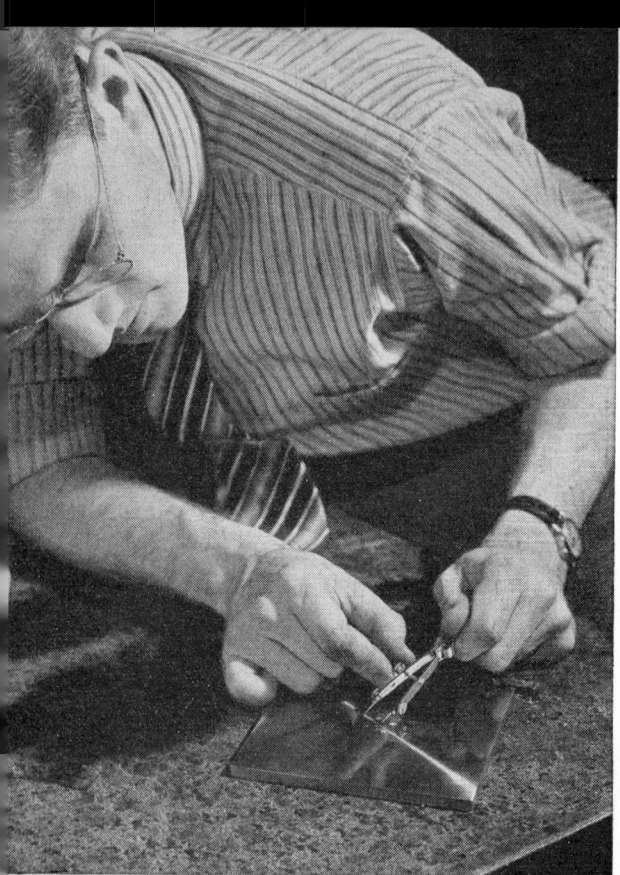

Scientific experts, measuring, probing, analyzing, became more and more important in American life during the 20th century.

have increased life expectancy. Scientists now are struggling for victory over cancer and heart disease. The fact that these two diseases are taking a heavier toll than ever before only proves that people are living long enough to die from diseases that usually come with old age.

Yellow fever is eliminated. One of the finest chapters in the history of medicine was written during the American occupation of Cuba (page 622). Before that time yellow fever had been a scourge in Cuba. A group of doctors, headed by Dr. Walter Reed, studied the problem. They tested the theory of a Cuban doctor, Carlos J. Finlay, that the disease was spread, not by contact, but by the female mosquito of a certain variety. Two of the doctors allowed themselves to be bitten by mosquitoes that had fed on patients who had yellow fever. These doctors contracted the disease, but their experiments served a great cause. Understanding how yellow fever was trans-

mitted, public health officials soon were able to rid Havana of the disease. During the many years required to build the Panama Canal, not a single case of yellow fever originated in the Canal Zone.

Science makes life easier. Science research affects our daily living in countless ways. It has brought us such building aids as plywood and new kinds of concrete. Fewer servants were available, but science stepped in to make life easier with modernized kitchens, improved dishwashers and washing machines, garbage disposal units, a variety of electric appliances, and air-conditioning. Chemistry gave us a wealth of new materials — cellophane, rayon, nylon, synthetic rubber. Plastics had many and varied uses.

Atomic energy is released. World War II and the post-war period brought into common use amphibious vehicles, radar, and jet-propelled aircraft. These inventions have peacetime uses fully as important as their value in war. But the greatest scientific achievement of the '40's was the atomic energy project. Working against time and under the handicap of strict secrecy, scientists and engineers combined their knowledge and ability to make the atomic bomb possible. Huge plants were built by the government at Oak Ridge, Tennessee, and at Hanford, Washington — plants containing revolutionary machinery and apparatus. Technicians had to work behind walls which shielded them from the deadly atomic rays. Some idea of the size of the atomic energy project can be obtained from the fact that at Hanford the entire Columbia River is employed as part of the cooling process in obtaining plutonium, an essential ingredient in the release of atomic energy.

Our ability to smash the atom and thus to release some of the energy which it contains may change the power sources in common use. The destruction of the Japanese cities of Hiroshima and Nagasaki heralded a new age of warfare. The use of atomic energy for warfare could mean the destruction of mankind. We must have faith that atomic power will create instead a new and better world of peace.

——— CHECK-UP ———

How has modern science changed American life?

1. Why has the life span grown longer in the twentieth century?
2. How has science made life easier?
3. Why is the discovery of the secret of how to release atomic energy of outstanding importance to mankind?

---

4 Many Writers Contribute to American Literature

The novel grows in popularity. The 1800's had made some distinguished contributions to American literature, particularly in poetry, the short story, and humorous prose. While poets and humorists continued to enrich our literature after 1900, modern American literature was even more successful in the fields of the novel and drama.

In the early years of this century the public enjoyed a variety of romantic novels. For a while there was a craze for historical fiction, including Charles Major's *When Knighthood Was in Flower*, S. Weir Mitchell's *Hugh Wynne*, and that popular romance of the legendary kingdom, *Graustark*, by George B. McCutcheon. The romantic nature of the popular novel reflected the longing of many people for an escape from the social problems and the monotony of everyday life.

Novelists attack social evils. At the same time, these very problems were being attacked by a group of brilliant authors, as you have seen in Chapter 28. Some of them wrote novels which were realistic — even brutal — in attacking various evils in American life. But by exposing these evils to their thousands of readers, "muckrakers" like Frank Norris and Upton Sinclair helped bring about much needed reform.

The problems of society also concerned Jack London, a writer who himself had led a picturesque life as a rancher, sealer, and oyster-pirate, and who in the winter of 1897 reached the goldfields of the Klondike. The harshness of life among the pioneers was described in Hamlin Garland's *A Son of the Middle Border*. The brilliant Willa Cather, in *My Ántonia* and other novels, also did much to strip away the false glamor surrounding the frontier.

"Debunkers" ridicule life in the '20's. The writers just after World War I would more properly be called "debunkers" than "muckrakers." Like the era in which they lived, they were disillusioned and cynical. They took delight in exposing the hypocrisy and the folly they saw around them and in ridiculing many of the accepted attitudes and ideals. The most influential literary critic of this day was Henry L. Mencken, editor of the *American Mercury*.

Many people had long believed that the large city was wicked and that the small town held everything that was good and virtuous. Sinclair Lewis, in his famous *Main Street* (1920), did much to explode this view. In *Babbitt* he attacked with biting sarcasm the smug "boosters" in American town life and the shallowness of his "hero," a prosperous real estate dealer. The residents of "Main Streets" all over the country bought Lewis' books eagerly and helped increase his reputation. Eventually he received international recognition and the Nobel Prize for literature.

Constructive fiction appears in the '30's. The 1930's meant depression and hard times for most Americans, but that very suffering seemed to awaken in writers a new social responsibility. Their novels became more sympathetic and constructive. The tragedy of the "Okies" who trekked westward from the Dust Bowl to California is described in John Steinbeck's *The Grapes of Wrath*. Margaret Mitchell's *Gone with the Wind* gave a graphic description of life in the South during and after the War Between the States.

Among other excellent writers of this era was Ernest Hemingway, who had probably the greatest single influence upon younger American writers. One of his best known novels, published in 1940, was *For Whom the Bell Tolls*. This study of life and death

Robert Frost, the poet, is shown here in the New England countryside which is the setting for most of his poems.

Sandburg. In *John Brown's Body* Stephen Vincent Benét gives us a moving account of the War Between the States. His love of the American scene is shown by such poems as "American Names," part of which follows:

> I have fallen in love with American names,
> The sharp names that never get fat,
> The snakeskin titles of mining claims,
> The plumed war-bonnet of Medicine Hat,
> Tucson and Deadwood and Lost Mule Flat.
>
> I will remember Carquinez Straits,
> Little French Lick and Lundy's Lane,
> The Yankee ships and the Yankee dates
> And the bullet towns of Calamity Jane.
> I will remember Skunktown Plain.*

Newspapers influence vast numbers of people. Probably the greatest influence in shaping adult attitudes and opinions of this century has been the newspaper. The linotype machine and the printing presses have been perfected so that it is now possible to turn out huge daily editions. News-gathering agencies like the Associated Press and the United Press increased the efficiency of their service and the number of newspapers they served. Features were added that would appeal to every member of the family and every group in the community: foreign dispatches, sports stories, financial news, puzzles, so-called comic strips, theater news, and items of interest to women.

By the beginning of the century certain publishers and editors were already emphasizing sensational news. Their "yellow journalism" was responsible for cheapening tastes and standards. However, the majority of newspaper editors maintained fairly high standards. Each section of the country could boast of newspapers that offered good news coverage and exerted a constructive influence on local and national thought.

Magazines become more attractive. Periodical literature has also grown in popularity during this century. The great weekly magazines, with their attractive make-up,

in the Spanish civil war helped make Americans conscious of the struggles taking place overseas, in which they were soon to be involved. Another novelist, Pearl Buck, gave her readers a dramatic account of Chinese rural life in *The Good Earth* and other books.

Poets interpret America for us. If the 1900's have not yet produced any American poet equal to Walt Whitman, at least there have been many of genuine excellence. Robert Frost has portrayed the New England scene. Poems of lyrical beauty have been written by Edna St. Vincent Millay. In his *Spoon River Anthology*, a best seller in 1915, Edgar Lee Masters attacked the drabness and pettiness of the lives of people we meet every day. The bursting vigor of industrial Chicago and a real belief in the basic worth of the common people are themes in the rhymeless verse of Carl

* From "American Names" in *Selected Works of Stephen Vincent Benét*, published by Rinehart & Co., Inc. Copyright 1927 by Stephen Vincent Benét.

short stories, feature articles, and lavish advertisements, are bought by millions of families. News magazines and picture magazines have become increasingly popular. There are likewise literary and political periodicals, which have a smaller circulation but exert a great influence among their readers. Almost every major business and industry in the country now boasts its own trade journal.

Many of the finest literary productions of our day are to be found in the pages of the weekly and monthly magazines. Thoughtful social and political essays appear monthly in such periodicals as *Harper's* and the *Atlantic Monthly.* That unique publication *The New Yorker* deserves mention, for it combines with its wit and satire a keen analysis of American society, written in a lively and sophisticated style. Regular contributors to this magazine include our foremost humorists and essayists. E. B. White's editorials on the relationship of our democracy to the nations of the world have provoked much thought among his readers. Here is a quotation from one of his *New Yorker* articles:

We received a letter from the Writer's War Board the other day asking for a statement on "The Meaning of Democracy." It presumably is our duty to comply with such a request, and it is certainly our pleasure.

Surely the Board knows what democracy is. It is the line that forms on the right. It is the *don't* in *don't shove.* It is the hole in the stuffed shirt through which the sawdust slowly trickles; it is the dent in the high hat. Democracy is the recurrent suspicion that more than half of the people are right more than half of the time. It is the feeling of privacy in the voting booths, the feeling of communion in the libraries, the feeling of vitality everywhere. Democracy is a letter to the editor. Democracy is the score at the beginning of the ninth. It is an idea which hasn't been disproved yet, a song the words of which have not gone bad. It's the mustard on the hot dog and the cream in the rationed coffee. Democracy is a request from a War Board, in the middle of a morning in the middle of a war, wanting to know what democracy is.*

* Copyright 1943 E. B. White. Originally published in *The New Yorker.*

--- CHECK-UP ---

What are some important directions in which American literature has developed?

1. Why are romantic novels popular? How have muckraking and debunking writers affected life in this country?
2. What are recent trends in the development of prose and poetry?
3. How have American newspapers and magazines changed in the twentieth century?

Deadwood, South Dakota, and other frontier towns have inspired much forceful American writing. Deadwood, for example, is mentioned in the verses by Stephen Vincent Benét on page 604. This photograph, taken in 1876, shows Deadwood soon after gold was discovered in the surrounding Black Hills.

The American skyscraper is dramatized in this aerial view of lower Manhattan. Seen from the water level, these towering buildings help form the famous New York skyline.

5 Art, Music, and Drama Develop and Mature

Architecture has a functional beauty. A soaring suspension bridge or a 700-feet-high concrete dam is not alone a monument to engineering skill. It may also be a marvel of simplicity, grace, and artistic proportion. Likewise, many of our buildings constructed since 1900 are magnificent both for their construction and as examples of projects that may be beautiful as well as functional (useful).

Most distinctive of the American contributions to architectural design is the skyscraper. As you have seen earlier (Chapter 23), this type of building was introduced in the closing years of the 1800's. The tallest and finest examples of the steel skyscraper, however, have been built in our times. For many years the tallest building in the world was the Woolworth Tower in New York City. Today the Empire State Building is the tallest and the Chrysler Building next. The R.C.A. Building in Rockefeller Center has also achieved a distinction because of its soaring beauty and because it is part of a larger, planned group of buildings of modern design. There are other cities that have fine skyscrapers, too. Los Angeles has built its city hall in this style, while the University of Pittsburgh is housed in a 40-story building.

Distinctively American art develops. In the early years of this century Whistler and Sargent continued to gain fame for their excellent canvases. American painters in general, however, were content to imitate the techniques of European artists.

After World War I, the younger American painters struck out along more original paths. Many of them had studied in Europe, but they saw that the American scene offered exciting subject matter. Grant Wood, for example, came back from Paris and started to paint the farmlands, the people, and the natural beauties of his native state, Iowa. Thomas Benton, another brilliant regional painter, had an imagination "which Sinclair Lewis described as displaying in paint the humor of a Mark Twain. Benton portrayed frontier scenes on canvas as humorously as *Roughing It* did in print, and small-town folk amused him enormously. Like the mature

Twain, he also worried over the sufferings and follies of the American people." *

The government finances art projects. During the depression of the '30's many writers, musicians, and artists were out of work and had no opportunity to give full expression to their talents. The Roosevelt administration established federal projects that gave employment to these artists, and encouraged creative expression. The results were not all of equal excellence, but much of permanent value was produced. Some artists decorated new public buildings with murals. Others hunted out the handicraft and folk arts still flourishing in many regions. More Americans of all classes came to appreciate art. Painting and sculpture were no longer considered either "quaint" or "highbrow," but an important part of a well-rounded life.

Popular music is more popular than ever. Americans have always loved popular songs, and there has never been a lack of composers to write them. Each year has its full quota of "hits," running from such ballads as "After the Ball" and "The Sidewalks of New York" at the turn of the century to "Chattanooga Choo-choo" and "White Christmas," both popular with the armed forces during World War II. There was

* Charles A. and Mary R. Beard, *America in Mid-Passage*, Macmillan, vol. 2, p. 803.

little doubt that popular music would continue to keep the American people humming so long as the entertainment world could produce its Bing Crosbys, Frank Sinatras, and an endless procession of "name bands."

Musical taste improves. At the same time, Americans have become more appreciative of fine music. Symphonies and concerts are no longer something for only the "long-hairs" to enjoy. All ages and groups are broadening their musical education through formal schooling, radio programs, and the concerts of the great symphony orchestras in large cities. America has bought many millions of phonograph albums recorded by the world's outstanding concert artists and has reached the same maturity in music that it achieved in art.

America has its own music. Moreover, America has been composing music which is excellent in its own right. Earlier in this century, the most popular of the composers was the Irish-American Victor Herbert. His romantic and melodic music, if not great, was an improvement over the popular ballads of his day. Since World War II, composers of symphonic and operatic music have come to the fore; some of them, like Roy Harris, Aaron Copland, and Deems Taylor, have been recognized abroad as well as in this country. Taylor

Striking home designs, like this one by Frank Lloyd Wright, have attracted many Americans. Most people, however, continue to prefer traditional home architecture.

George Gershwin was first attracted to music at the age of 6, when he stopped to hear a mechanical piano in a penny arcade.

is known both for his opera *Peter Ibbetson* and for his work as a radio commentator on musical subjects.

During the '30's Americans developed a strong interest in the spirituals and folk ballads which are a part of our rich heritage. We began to understand as never before how much the Negro, the southern mountaineer, the plainsman, the rancher, and the railroader have contributed to our folk music. The poet Carl Sandburg gathered many of their classics in his *American Songbag,* and a number of ballad singers like Burl Ives have made them popular.

Musical comedy is a typically American musical form. The spirit of our age has been captured in this field by such gifted composers as Jerome Kern, Cole Porter, and Richard Rodgers. Rodgers' *Oklahoma!* has already become a classic. Before George Gershwin's untimely death at the age of 39, he enriched American music by proving that jazz could be an art of lasting value.

Interest in drama increases. The growth of cities in our century has increased the demand for city amusements, among them theatrical entertainment. In the early 1900's the public continued to be interested in stage plays dealing with historical and romantic subject matter. Vaudeville became very popular at this time. On the other hand, the melodramas that had attracted large crowds in the 1890's became less appealing as audiences grew more sophisticated. At the same time that literature became more realistic, the "problem play" began to attract keen audiences.

The American theater was fortunate before World War I in having a number of outstanding producers, actors, and actresses, among them David Belasco, Mrs. Fiske, Maude Adams, John and Lionel Barrymore, David Warfield, and Otis Skinner.

Important playwrights appear. Some outstanding playwrights began to excite admiration, particularly after World War I. The most powerful of these was Eugene O'Neill. This dramatist concerned himself with themes of complex human behavior. In his plays may be found a sense of tragedy not unrelated to the dramas of ancient Greece. Some of his many successful plays have been made into movies, including "The Emperor Jones," "Anna Christie," "Mourning Becomes Electra," and "The Long Voyage Home."

Among important dramatists of recent years are Maxwell Anderson and Elmer Rice. Anderson caused a sensation in 1924 when audiences first saw his *What Price Glory,* a play written in collaboration with Lawrence Stallings. Filled with soldier slang and swearing, this play presented the grim facts of war with a realism that jolted many playgoers. Elmer Rice examined legal problems in several of his plays, as well as some of the reasons for international conflict in his *Judgment Day* (1934).

Motion pictures revolutionize the field of drama. It was during our century that a new art form developed which broke all records for popularity. Before the turn of the century, motion pictures were shown largely as a curiosity, but by 1910 there were movie houses in nearly every town in the country. The first pictures were crudely made. It was in 1915 that the brilliant producer D. W. Griffith made "The Birth of a Nation." This picture revealed new film techniques and proved that motion pictures had unusual dramatic possibilities.

The motion picture industry grew rapidly. A new chapter in the story of films was written in 1927 when sound was added. Successful experiments with sound movies made silent pictures entirely out of date. In the '30's came color films, which increased enjoyment and added to the artistry of the movies. The motion pictures have shown their ability to portray every dramatic theme and mood, from those found in the lightest comedy and farce to the somber tragedies of William Shakespeare.

Television brings entertainment to the home. Radio audiences have long taken delight in broadcast drama, from serial "soap operas" to short adaptations of the finest dramatic writing. Some excellent dramatic writing has been done especially for radio by some of our most important authors. Now, as television continues to be perfected, the drama is brought right into the home, along with other types of stage entertainment.

How television will affect radio entertainment as well as the theater is not yet clear. Its present appeal is greater than that of any other of the "mass media" of communication.

——————— CHECK-UP ———————

What are important trends in the development of art, music, and drama during the twentieth century?

1. What are some of the characteristics of distinctly American art? How did the federal government contribute to the development of the arts during the depression?
2. What are some American contributions in the field of music? What evidence is there that taste in music is improving?
3. What are some important steps in the evolution of the motion picture?
4. How have the radio and television contributed to the spread of culture?

CHAPTER REVIEW

Terms to Understand

cultural maturity
rural free delivery
"horseless carriage"
isolationist
spectator sports
debunker

social responsibiiity
adult education
penicillin
plastics
atomic energy

People and Things to Know About

John Dewey
Andrew Carnegie
Dr. Walter Reed
Carlos J. Finlay
Margaret Mitchell
Sinclair Lewis
Eugene O'Neill

Carl Sandburg
Stephen Vincent Benét
Ernest Hemingway
Grant Wood
Thomas Benton
Victor Herbert

Questions to Discuss

1. How have American standards and values changed in the twentieth century? Why? Can you give a personal example of such a change?
2. Why have Americans always attached great importance to education? Do you think that all youth of high school age should attend high school? Why?
3. How has science changed life during your lifetime? Why is it said that science "creates problems as well as solves them"? Give some examples.

Questions to Discuss (Cont.)

4. Compare the following:
   (a) A painting by Grant Wood and one by Whistler.
   (b) The style of writing of Ernest Hemingway and George B. McCutcheon.
   (c) The music of Victor Herbert and Cole Porter.
5. What type of literature, music, art, and drama do you like best? Explain why.

Other Things to Do

1. Debate: *Resolved,* That the automobile has made a greater change in American life than the radio.
2. Report to the class on one of the great doctors, authors, actors, or artists mentioned in this chapter. Try to locate recent material in *Readers' Guide.*
*3. Make a chart showing differences in American life before 1900 and after 1945. Use such headings as "Sources of Information," "Means of Communication," "Means of Transportation," "Sports," "Music and Drama."
4. Report to the class on the evolution of the motion pictures, radio, or television.
5. Plan a musical program to illustrate trends in American music. You may wish to use recorded music.

TO INCREASE YOUR UNDERSTANDING OF UNIT NINE

Unit Summary

1. Immigration has played an important role in modern America. Immigrants have made many valuable contributions to our culture. In the early 1900's the tide of immigration reached a peak with the large numbers coming from southern and eastern Europe. After World War I, due to increasing restrictions and unsettled conditions, the influx of immigrants was very sharply reduced.

2. Because of reduced immigration and a lower birth rate, the population today is growing less rapidly than during the 1800's. Increased life expectancy is resulting in a higher average age. For economic reasons there is a flow of population from some regions to others, especially from rural areas to the cities. Since World War I, Negroes have moved north in great numbers and have moved from rural areas to urban centers. They are making important contributions to American culture and progress in their efforts to achieve economic equality with other groups.

3. The Nineteenth Amendment provided for woman suffrage, and women have achieved equality with men in most occupations. Women were active in working for temperance. National prohibition was adopted in 1919 and repealed 14 years later.

4. Improved transportation (automobile, airplane) and communication (telephone, radio, television) have revolutionized living. Although Americans have a great fondness for spectator sports and commercial recreation, they also have had the stamina to conquer depressions and to win wars.

5. The proportion of children and youth attending school is much higher than during the 1800's, and the goals of education are becoming increasingly practical. After World War II the number of college students reached a peak. Americans have made great progress in both pure and applied science. The release of atomic energy is their greatest achievement.

6. The emphasis in literature shifted from "muckraking" before World War I and "debunking" after that struggle to a more constructive note. Newspapers and magazines continue to reach a wide audience.

7. American architecture tends to be functional, and art and drama are becoming less imitative. Musical taste is improving, and Americans are producing their own music, ranging from classical to the latest jazz.

Summary of Important Dates

1903 Wright brothers make first airplane flight.

1907 Japanese laborers excluded from United States by "Gentlemen's Agreement."

1914 Completion of Panama Canal.

1917 Illiterates excluded from this country.

1919 Eighteenth Amendment (prohibition).

1920 Nineteenth Amendment (woman suffrage).

1921 Emergency Quota Act (three per cent of number in country in 1910).

1924 Lodge-Johnson Act (two per cent of number in country in 1890).

1927 First talking motion picture.

1929 Total number of quota immigrants limited to 150,000 (quota based on proportion of total foreign born in 1920).

1933 Twenty-first Amendment (repeal of prohibition).

1945 Atomic energy first released.

Unit Activities

1. See what you can learn about the efforts of the United States Immigration Service to prevent illegal entry into this country. Why is this an important problem? Why is it difficult?

2. List evidences in life in your community of the influence of immigrant groups. If nearby foreign lands influence your community life, list those evidences also. Does your community capitalize on its local color? Many United States communities do — for example, tulip festivals in Holland, Michigan, and fiestas in the southwest.

3. Try to find out the origin of some pastime in which you are interested (chess, playing cards, golf, tennis, a musical instrument, etc.). Report your findings to the class.

4. Use school records and reports and other sources to discover changes in your high school. You might consider enrollment, size of staff, plant and equipment, textbooks and other materials, methods of teaching, extra-

class activities, length of school day, proportion of pupils entering grade 9 that were graduated, graduation requirements and programs of instruction, and legislation governing school attendance. Your findings should make an interesting article for your school or local newspaper.

For Further Reading

Original Sources

Commager, H. S., ed., *Documents of American History*. Appleton-Century-Crofts. Nos. 357, 367, 387, 404, 422, 432, 453.

Handy, W. C., *Father of the Blues: An Autobiography*. Macmillan. The composer of "St. Louis Blues" and other tunes that are almost folksongs tells his own courageous story in an honest, informative way.

Nevins, A., and Commager, H. S., eds., *The Heritage of America*. Little, Brown. No. 229.

Pease, T. C., and Roberts, A. S., eds., *Selected Readings in American History*. Harcourt. Nos. 264–66.

Steffens, L., *Autobiography*. Harcourt. One of the muckrakers describes America — its politics, its crime, and its culture.

General References

Adams, J. T., *The Epic of America*. Little, Brown. Chapter 11.

Hicks, J. D., *The American Nation*. Houghton. Chapter 27.

Morison, S. E., and Commager, H. S., *The Growth of the American Republic*. Oxford. Vol. II, Chapters 12 and 15.

Special Accounts

Adamic, L., *A Nation of Nations*. Harper. Stresses the fact that the culture of this country is a blend of cultures all over the world.

Allen, F. L., *Only Yesterday*, and *Since Yesterday*. Harper. Informal social history of the 1920's and 1930's.

American Nation Series. Harper. Latané, J. H., *America as a World Power*. Pp. 285–303.

Beard, C. A., and M. R., *America in Mid-Passage*. Macmillan. An interpretation of the ten-year period after 1919.

Bowers, D. F., ed., *Foreign Influences in American Life*. Princeton University Press.

Chronicles of America Series. Yale University Press. Orth, S. P., *Our Foreigners*. Perry, B., *The American Spirit in Literature*. Slosson, E. E., *The American Spirit in Education*. Thompson, H., *The Age of Invention* and *The New South*.

Gunther, J., *Inside U.S.A.* Harper.

History of American Life Series. Macmillan. Faulkner, H. U., *The Quest for Social Justice, 1898–1914*. Chapters 7–12. Slosson, P. W., *The Great Crusade and After, 1914–1928*. Chapters 4, 5, 8–15.

Howard, J. T., *Our American Music*. Crowell. The best general account of music in this country.

Kazin, A., *On Native Grounds*. Reynal and Hitchcock. An interpretation of modern prose literature.

Lynd, R. S., and H. M., *Middletown* and *Middletown in Transition*. Harcourt. A sociological story of a Middle Western city in the 1920's and 1930's.

Mellquist, J., *The Emergence of American Art*. Scribner. Deals with the late nineteenth and twentieth centuries. Thirty-five illustrations.

Mumford, L., *The Culture of Cities*. Harcourt. Stresses the need for planning.

Mumford, L., *Sticks and Stones*. Boni and Liveright. American architecture.

Myrdal, G., *American Dilemma*. Harper. Holds that the Negro is interested primarily in securing economic equality.

Stegner, W. E., *One Nation*. Houghton. A discussion of eight minority groups in this country.

Sullivan, L., *Our Times*. Scribner. Volumes I–VI.

Wittke, C., *We Who Built America*. Prentice-Hall. Makes clear the contributions to our culture made by the "new immigration."

Biography

Garwood, D., *Artist in Iowa*. Knopf. The story of Grant Wood.

Graham, S., and Lipscomb, G. D., *Dr. George Washington Carver: Scientist*. Messner.

Malvern, G., *Curtain Going Up! The Story of Katherine Cornell*. Messner.

Miller, M., *Joe Louis: American*. Current Books.

Morrison, H., *Louis Sullivan*. Norton. Praises the architecture of Sullivan and his pupil, Frank Lloyd Wright.

Powell, H., *Walter Camp: The Father of American Football*. Little, Brown.

Imaginative Writing

Barnes, M. A., *Years of Grace*. Houghton. Describes American life in the era preceding "the age of jazz, pep, and personality."

Lewis, S., *Babbitt*. Grosset. Middle class life in the small city.

Steinbeck, J., *The Grapes of Wrath*. Viking. The migration of poor farmers from Oklahoma to California.

Van Druten, J., *I Remember Mama*. Harcourt. A Norwegian-American family in San Francisco.

Poetry

Carmer, C., *America Sings*. Knopf. Songs from all sections of the country.

Pictures

Blanchard, J., *Caravan to the Northwest.* Houghton. Uses pictures to show why people settled in the northwestern part of the United States.

Butterfield, R., *The American Past*. Simon and Schuster.

Pageant of American Series. Yale University Press. Coad, O. S., and Mims, E., *The American Stage*. Gabriel, R. H., *Toilers of Land and Sea*. Hamlin, T. F., *The American Spirit in Architecture*. Keir, M., *The March of Commerce*. Chapters 12, 13, 16, and 17. Krout, J. A., *Annals of American Sport*. Mather, F. J., Morey, C. R., and Henderson, W. J., *The American Spirit in Art*. Weigle, L. A., *American Idealism*. Williams, S. T., *The American Spirit in Letters*.

Rogers, A., and Allen, F. L., *The American Procession*. Harper.

Taylor, D., *A Pictorial History of the Movies*. Simon and Schuster.

 # Sidelights on American History

Drugs to Work Miracles. In a hospital in Washington, two days before Christmas, 1936, a 12-year-old boy lay dying of one of the world's most fatal diseases. His ailment, meningitis, is an infection of the sheath that covers the human spinal cord and brain. Meningitis was so deadly that 99 per cent of all who had it died. In all medical history there had been only 65 known recoveries.

The boy was already unconscious. The doctors expected him to be unconscious until the end. Then something like a miracle occurred. One of the doctors had heard of a new drug developed in Europe. As yet it had been untried in this country, and the doctors administered it to the boy only as a last lone chance. They were utterly amazed when the patient became conscious and began to improve immediately. Two weeks later he was quite well.

The new drug was sulfanilamide, one of several miracle drugs which chemists and medical scientists developed in the next dozen years. Sulfanilamide had been known for a quarter of a century but had never been used in medicine. It was a dye made from coal tar, from which hundreds of other dyes are made. It was first discovered at the University of Vienna, by a young chemist of whose later career nothing whatever is known.

Not until 1930, when two German scientists experimented with the dye to see if it would kill germs, was its value to medicine discovered. Then it amazed the world. It killed the little round germ called streptococcus, which had proved fatal to so many people. A white pellet of sulfanilamide rescued people again and again from the brink of death.

But one germ which sulfanilamide could not kill was the germ of pneumonia. English chemists, therefore, set to work to alter the new drug. Combining it with another element, called pyridine, they tried it on mice which had been given pneumonia. Each mouse had been injected with enough germs to kill 10,000 mice, but those which received the sulfapyridine lived. All the rest died. The new drug cut the human death rate in pneumonia from 25 to 10 in every 100 cases.

Another miracle drug was discovered by Dr. Alexander Fleming of St. Mary's Hospital, London. He noticed one morning that mold had got on to some glass plates on which he was growing bacteria. Wherever there was mold, the bacteria seemed to have disappeared. Curious, Dr. Fleming put the mold into colonies of other germs — germs of blood poisoning, lockjaw, anthrax, and pneumonia. The fuzzy, green-blue mold wiped them out.

Because the Latin name of the rod- or pencil-shaped mold was *penicillium notatum*, Dr. Fleming called his new germ killer penicillin. Today drug companies grow penicillium mold in bottles, as a velvety mat which floats on the surface of a liquid it feeds on. Into this liquid it discharges a mysterious chemical. The chemical is separated from the feeding liquid and dried to a reddish brown powder. Penicillin will not cure malaria, infantile paralysis, cancer, and some other diseases, but against most bacteria — even where sulfanilamide fails — it is the most miraculous drug of all.

Clubs That Serve the Community. Among the many clubs supported by Americans, four were founded expressly for the purpose of serving the community. Rotary International, started by four Chicago business and professional men in 1905, takes its name from the original plan of holding meetings in rotation among its members' places of business. Such a plan is no longer possible, for there are now over 300,000 members in some 6000 clubs, but the aim of Rotary is still community service. The members pledge themselves to maintain high standards in business and professional life. They believe in teaching good citizenship and in promoting friendliness and good will.

Before 1920 three other service clubs had been founded. Kiwanis International, International Association of Lions Clubs, and Optimist International all work for community betterment, particularly through the healthy training of boys and girls. The service clubs sponsor activities for young people, build recreation homes for boys, and train boys and girls to be good citizens. In addition, they engage in projects that range from health education to safety campaigns, from drives for better roads to raising funds for hospitals.

Though the service clubs originated in America, they were so popular that they soon grew into international organizations. There are Lions Clubs, for example, in 17 different countries. The membership of the combined service clubs has grown until it has reached a total of well over three quarters of a million.

The Atomic Age Arrives. In 1942 scientists at the University of Chicago discovered something new about the element uranium. They had known that uranium is radioactive; that is,

it gives off energy all by itself. Now they found that uranium could be used as a basis for creating a chain reaction which could build up a tremendous amount of energy. If such reaction continued unchecked, one pound of uranium could produce the same amount of energy as 2 million pounds of coal. And one of the products of the chain reaction was another radioactive substance — plutonium.

The scientists believed that if "a mass of plutonium of a certain critical size" could be produced, an atomic explosion of unbelievable force could be created. Such an explosion might be used to shorten the world war that was then in progress. To create a sufficient quantity of the various materials needed for atomic bombs, gigantic plants were secretly constructed in the states of Tennessee and Washington. Around the plants were built the "secret cities" of Oak Ridge, Tennessee, and Hanford, Washington, complete with laboratories, dormitories, family houses, and schools. These communities were closely guarded against any leak of scientific information.

At about the same time, a laboratory and another "secret city" were constructed on a lonely desert mesa at Los Alamos, New Mexico. Workers in the laboratory were to find out how to use the new atomic energy in a bomb. What was the "critical size" for the great explosion? How could smaller masses of plutonium be combined to make the critical size? Such questions had to be answered in the new laboratory.

After the plants at Oak Ridge, Hanford, and Los Alamos had performed their appointed tasks, the first atomic bomb in history was exploded on a steel tower in the desert section of southern New Mexico (August, 1945). The tower was completely melted by the heat. Mountains many miles away were illuminated by the flash. The desert sand was fused into a crater of turquoise and jade, half a mile wide.

The secret of the three new cities was so well kept that the world in general knew nothing of them until after two atomic bombs had speeded the end of the war with Japan. Today these cities are still very busy places — and still carefully guarded. Men of science tell us that we know as little about atomic energy as our forefathers knew about electricity in Benjamin Franklin's time. We do know its destructive powers. It is to be hoped that this miraculous force may be developed and directed to constructive purposes for the benefit of all mankind.

Aid to other countries

THE PLAN OF THE BOOK

PART ONE *Early America Develops*	1492 to 1783	**Unit One:** Discovery, Exploration, Development of the English colonies, American Revolution			
	1783 to 1840	**Unit Two:** Framing of Constitution, The new republic, Rise of nationalism, sectionalism, and democracy			
	1789 to 1865	**Unit Three:** Economic developments, Social change and reform, Rise of American culture			
	1840 to 1865	**Unit Four:** Westward expansion, The slavery problem, War Between the States			
PART TWO *Modern America Emerges*	1865 to the 1890's	**Unit Five** Foundations of the American economic system	**Unit Six** Social and cultural developments	**Unit Seven** Government, politics, and foreign affairs	
PART THREE *Modern America Matures*	1890's to the Present	**Unit Eight** American economic system today	**Unit Nine** Social and cultural developments	**Unit Ten** The United States in world affairs	**Unit Eleven** Developments in government and politics

Unit Ten

THE UNITED STATES BECOMES

A WORLD LEADER

The industrial expansion of the United States in the last third of the 1800's caused many Americans to look for markets outside the limits of this continent. In the Far East the United States acquired the Philippines and urged a policy of equal economic opportunity in China. Nearer home, in the early 1900's a broader interpretation of the Monroe Doctrine brought about the establishing of protectorates in many Central American and Caribbean countries. Our goal was not only to extend American trade and investments but also to keep European powers from establishing too much economic and political control in the Western Hemisphere. By the liberation of the Philippines, however, the United States has attempted to carry out more fully the policy of the Open Door in the Far East. Since 1933 the United States has given up the right to interfere in the affairs of other countries in the Western Hemisphere. Instead, we have adopted the policy of the Good Neighbor.

The United States has taken part in two World Wars to prevent one nation or a combination of nations from becoming so powerful as to dominate the world and threaten the American way of life. After World War I the United States failed to become a member in the League of Nations and tried to return to a policy of isolation. Today United States policy is different. This country is a leading member of the United Nations and is wholeheartedly committed to promoting international organization and world peace.

Unfortunately world co-operation is proving difficult to achieve. Various nations mistrust each other's motives and hesitate to rely on a world organization for political and economic security. The road to peace calls for the same full measure of national effort as does war.

Chapter 34

Navy launch

THE UNITED STATES ADOPTS A

POLICY OF IMPERIALISM

In foreign affairs we must make up our minds that, whether we wish it or not, we are a great people and must play a great part in the world. It is not open to us to choose whether we will play that great part or not. We have to play it. All we can decide is whether we shall play it well or ill.

Theodore Roosevelt

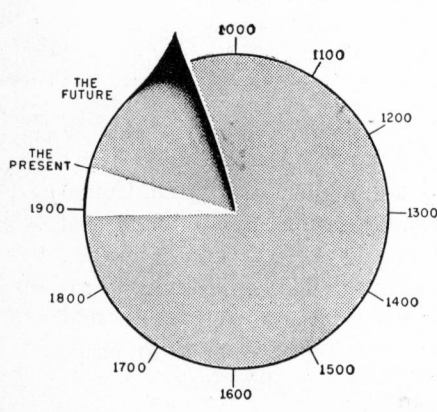

1897 – The Present

For more than a century — through its entire national existence — the United States had followed a policy of isolation. This policy was shattered with startling suddenness by the Spanish-American War. The war grew out of American interest in Cuba, the "Pearl of the Antilles." On several earlier occasions, it may be recalled, American attention had been drawn to this island. During the first half of the 1800's, expansionists had wanted to annex Cuba in order to check the advance of foreign nations in the Western Hemisphere, to benefit American commerce, or to provide a suitable field for the extension of slavery. Interest in Cuba was revived during the rebellion of 1868 (page 476), and again during the closing years of the nineteenth century as a result of the expansion of American in-

616

dustry. By this time Americans had invested about 50 million dollars in Cuban sugar plantations, tobacco fields, and mines. Our annual trade with the island exceeded 100 million dollars.

As a result of the war with Spain over Cuba, the United States extended its authority over lands outside the boundaries of North America. At once it had to face the grave problem of organizing and governing newly-acquired territory. The beginnings of American imperialism overseas will be described in this chapter under the following headings:

1. Our interest in Cuba leads to war with Spain.
2. The United States wins a speedy victory.
3. Cuba and Puerto Rico offer challenging problems.
4. A wise policy helps the Philippines achieve independence.

1 Our Interest in Cuba Leads to War with Spain

Revolt breaks out in Cuba. Near the end of the 1800's, the people of Cuba began to show increasing discontent with Spanish rule. The uprising of 1868, which lasted for ten years, involved great cruelty and destruction of property. It ended in the defeat of the rebels, but Spain was forced to grant some concessions to the Cubans. In 1895 another serious uprising occurred, caused in part by Spanish misrule and in part by an economic crisis. Under the McKinley Act (page 381) Cuban sugar had been entering the United States free of duty. The Wilson-Gorman Tariff (1894), however, placed a duty of 40 per cent on raw sugar imported into the United States. As a result, Cuban trade with America declined, the price of Cuban sugar fell, plantations were closed, and unemployment increased. Unrest flamed into open revolt.

Gomez, the leader of the rebels, directed his campaign toward the destruction of the sugar plantations. By this means he hoped to cut off the sources of government revenue, and also to force the United States to intervene in Cuba to protect American investors. The Spanish commander, General Weyler, found it impossible to crush the scattered bands of revolutionists. He therefore herded those who were not fighting, chiefly women and children, into concentration camps. Here they died of disease and even hunger by the tens of thousands. Fifty thousand perished in the province of Havana alone.

American public opinion is aroused. Public opinion in the United States was at once aroused. American trade with Cuba had been all but destroyed, and American investments were threatened. In addition, certain newspapers were printing sensational and sometimes untrue stories describing the horrors of the Cuban concentration camps. Among these newspapers were the New York *Journal,* owned by William Randolph Hearst, and the New York *World,* owned by Joseph Pulitzer. At the same time Cubans in the United States, many of whom had become American citizens, actively aided the rebels by spreading propaganda and by shipping them arms and ammunition. The United States urged Spain to grant some of the Cuban demands and offered to help the two countries settle their disputes, but this offer aroused only resentment in Spain.

The de Lôme letter makes Americans angry. Two events of February, 1898, fanned American public opinion into frenzy. The first was the publication of a letter written by the Spanish minister to the United States, Señor de Lôme, to a friend in Havana. This letter unfortunately referred to President William McKinley as "weak and a caterer to the rabble, and, moreover, a cheap politician who wishes to leave a door open behind himself and to stand well with the jingoes [those who wanted war] of his party." A spy stole de Lôme's letter from the postoffice in Havana, and it was published in the New York *Journal.* Although de Lôme promptly

Cuban patriot

resigned and his government apologized for his "indiscretion," the damage had been done.

The battleship "Maine" is sunk. Hardly had the American people recovered from the effects of this insult when another incident left them horror-stricken. Because of exaggerated reports of rioting in Cuba, the battleship *Maine* had been sent to the harbor of Havana to protect American lives and property. On the night of February 15, following a terrific explosion, the *Maine* sank in the harbor with the loss of two officers and 258 of the crew. An American naval court of inquiry at once conducted a careful investigation. It reported to the President: "In the opinion of the court the *Maine* was destroyed by the explosion of a submarine mine which caused the partial explosion of two or more of the forward magazines. The court has been unable to obtain evidence fixing the responsibility for the destruction of the *Maine* upon any person or persons."

Americans blame Spain. The American public paid slight attention to the latter part of this report. Nor did it regard as trustworthy the Spanish board of inquiry which declared that the destruction of the ship had been caused by an explosion in the ship's stores of ammunition. Few people even stopped to consider the possibility that Cuban rebels or even private Spanish citizens in Havana might have been responsible for the disaster. The average American, carried away on a wave of emotion, held the Spanish government responsible. "Remember the *Maine*!" became the warlike cry of the press and of people ranging all the way from public leaders to schoolboys.

The United States makes demands. President McKinley, his cabinet, and most of the nation's business interests sincerely hoped to maintain peaceful relations with Spain. But the American people, aroused by the so-called "yellow" or sensational newspapers, demanded war. Even those Republican leaders who wanted peace were afraid of political disaster if they did not yield to public opinion. At the end of March, 1898, the United States Government urged Spain to abandon the policy of putting the Cubans in concentration camps. It also demanded that Spain arrange a truce in the civil war in order to establish immediate peace in Cuba. For a time the Spanish government refused to meet these demands. On April 9, however, at the urgent request of the Pope, it ordered that the fighting be suspended and stated that it was prepared to grant all that the American government had asked.

War is declared. In spite of the apparent surrender of Spain, McKinley delivered a war message to a willing Congress on April 11. Perhaps he doubted the sincerity of the Spanish cabinet. He may have thought that it would be unable to carry out a new, milder policy in the face of hostile public opinion in Spain. At any rate, McKinley asked Congress for authority to use the military and naval forces of the United States to stop hostilities between the government of Spain and the people of Cuba. He considered this authority necessary to protect the commerce and business of the American people, and to end a conflict which was "a constant menace to our peace."

In reply to the President's message Congress eagerly adopted resolutions (1) granting the President's request, (2) proclaiming the independence of Cuba, and (3) calling upon Spain to withdraw its land and naval forces from Cuba. (4) a fourth provision expressly stated that it was not the intention of the United States to "exercise sovereignty, jurisdiction, or control over said island except for the pacification thereof." The United States was determined, when peace had been established, "to leave the government and control of the island to its people." This fourth provision, the so-called Teller Resolution, represented a victory for those in Congress who opposed a policy of imperialism and who believed that we should not annex Cuba. On April 25, 1898, Congress formally declared that war with Spain had existed since the twenty-first of that month.

——— CHECK-UP ———

What events led the United States to go to war with Spain?

1. Why did the Cubans revolt against Spanish rule? How did Spain attempt to suppress the insurrection?
2. How did each of these arouse American public opinion against Spain: the de Lôme letter, the sinking of the "Maine," American newspapers?
3. Why did the United States go to war even though Spain seemed willing to accept our demands concerning Cuba?

2 The United States Wins a Speedy Victory

The Navy acts quickly. From the first it was evident that sea fighting would play an important part in the conflict between Spain and the United States. Two days after the signing of the war resolutions, the United States Atlantic fleet established a blockade of Cuba (April 22). The battleship *Oregon*, which at the time was off the northern Pacific Coast, steamed all the way around South America on a spectacular 14,000-mile voyage to join her sister ships.

Dewey wins a victory in Manila Bay. The first clash, however, occurred far from the island of Cuba. The Pacific fleet had been stationed at Hongkong in China under Commodore George Dewey. The aggressive Assistant Secretary of the Navy, Theodore Roosevelt, had given Dewey instructions to proceed to Manila in the Philippine Islands if war should be declared. On the night of April 30 the fleet arrived at Manila with orders to capture or destroy the Spanish Pacific squadron located there. The next morning Dewey disregarded the mines in the harbor and the batteries on shore and proceeded to bombard the Spanish vessels inside the harbor. Within a short period of time the Spanish ships were destroyed, the shore batteries silenced. and nearly 400 Spanish seamen

killed or wounded. The American ships, on the other hand, were practically untouched, and only seven Americans were wounded. This unexpected victory on the opposite side of the globe was hailed with an outburst of patriotic enthusiasm in the United States. President McKinley extended to Dewey the thanks of the American people for "his splendid achievement and overwhelming victory," and raised him to the rank of rear admiral.

Manila is blockaded and finally taken. After the triumph at Manila Bay, the city of Manila was at the mercy of Dewey. While Dewey was waiting for the arrival of military forces with which to occupy the city, however, an embarrassing incident occurred. Dewey had established a blockade of the city, and four countries — Great Britain, France, Japan, and Germany — sent war vessels to protect their people and their interests. The German squadron was stronger than the American, and the German commander openly neglected to observe the American regulations governing the blockade. As a matter of fact, most European countries were sympathetic toward Spain, and they openly ridiculed the resolution of Congress which stated that we were not interested in acquiring Cuba. Fortunately the British were an exception. The commander of the powerful British squadron in Manila Bay was careful to observe Dewey's blockade. His good will and support helped relieve a tense situation until American troops arrived. Supported by Filipino insurgents who had rebelled against the rule of Spain, the American troops entered the city of Manila on August 13.

Santiago is blockaded. In the meantime our Atlantic fleet under Rear Admiral Sampson cruised off the coast of Cuba and awaited the arrival of the Spanish Atlantic fleet. This squadron, under the command of Admiral Cervera (sair-vay'-rah), had left the Cape Verde Islands on April 29, bound for an unknown destination. When three weeks

Spanish artilleryman

passed without news of Cervera, cities and resorts along the Atlantic coast became panic-stricken, fearing that he would swoop down upon them in a sudden raid. In spite of American watchfulness, Cervera managed to slip into the harbor of Santiago on the southeastern coast of Cuba. The American squadron took up a position outside the harbor and waited for a military force to co-operate in an attack upon Santiago.

The American army is unprepared. Theodore Roosevelt later said that the most striking thing about the Spanish War was the preparedness of the navy and the unpreparedness of the army. The commissary and quartermaster divisions of the War Department seemed to be completely baffled by the job of distributing supplies and food to the troops. Most of the soldiers were equipped with heavy woolen clothing to fight in Cuba under a tropical sun. They complained constantly that the food was unfit to eat. Of the 3000 American deaths in the war, nine tenths were caused by intestinal troubles, typhoid, yellow fever, and other diseases.

Land forces attack Santiago. In the midst of great confusion, some 17,000 officers and men under General Shafter landed in Cuba late in June to begin an attack upon Santiago. Included in this force were the Rough Riders, a volunteer regiment composed largely of cowboys, Indians, and college athletes. The Rough Riders were under the command of Colonel Leonard Wood and Lieutenant Colonel Theodore Roosevelt, who had resigned his office as Assistant Secretary of the Navy to volunteer for service in the army. After some hard fighting the American troops seized San Juan Hill, El Caney, and Kettle Hill, three strategic points commanding the northern and eastern sides of Santiago.

The Spanish fleet at Santiago is destroyed. With the capture of the hills overlooking the city by the Americans, the position of the Spanish fleet in Santiago harbor seemed hopeless. Unless Admiral Cervera attempted to escape, he would have to surrender his fleet when the Americans seized Santiago. Actually, however, the American position was so unsatisfactory and the army so unfit for service that General Shafter was considering a retreat from the outskirts of Santiago. Fortunately for the American cause, Cervera received orders to make a dash for safety. On July 3, 1898, the Spanish fleet steamed out of the harbor at full speed, and turned westward along the shore. The American fleet took up the pursuit, and one after another, the Spanish vessels were crippled and driven ashore. Weakened by the destruction of Cervera's fleet, the Spanish garrison at Santiago surrendered two weeks later.

Puerto Rico is invaded. After the fall of Santiago, General Miles, the commanding general of the United States Army, invaded Puerto Rico. With about 17,000 men he gained control of all the southern and western portions of the island after meeting with practically no opposition. Everywhere the American troops were received with joy by the Puerto Ricans. Except for the fact that Spain had already begun to negotiate for peace, Miles' forces would have completed the conquest of the island.

The war ends. Unable to continue the unequal struggle, Spain asked for peace late in July. On August 12, an armistice was signed. By the terms of this armistice, Spain was to (1) withdraw her forces from Cuba immediately, (2) surrender all authority over Cuba, and (3) cede Puerto Rico and Guam (one of the Mariana Islands in the Pacific) to the United States. In addition, the armistice provided that American troops should occupy Manila "pending the conclusion of a treaty of peace which shall determine the control, disposition, and government of the Philippines."

The Peace of Paris is signed. American and Spanish commissioners met at Paris in October, 1898, to draw up the final treaty of peace. Several points of disagreement arose immediately. The most vexing question involved the Philippine Islands. Arguing that the city of Manila was not occupied until the day after the signing of the armistice, Spain demanded the restoration

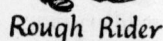

Rough Rider

of the islands. Few people in the United States at the beginning of the war would have favored American expansion in these far distant islands. Now, however, an increasing number of voices urged that we annex the Philippines. Some thought it was the duty of the American people to civilize and Christianize the Filipinos. Others felt that the islands provided an excellent market for American industry as well as a springboard for developing trade with China. President McKinley reached the conclusion that public opinion demanded our taking over the Philippines. He therefore instructed the United States commissioners to pay 20 million dollars for the islands. Spain had no alternative but to accept these terms. The cession of Puerto Rico and of Guam presented no special difficulties, and the treaty of peace was signed by Spain and the United States before 1898 came to a close.

The treaty is ratified. The Treaty of Paris could not go into effect until it had been approved in the Senate by a two-thirds majority. Early in 1899 it was vigorously debated, as opposition developed on several points. Many senators felt that principles set forth in the Declaration of Independence and the Constitution would be violated if this country governed the new territories as though they were colonies. Others feared that colonies would lead the country into entangling alliances with other nations. In the end, however, the forces that favored ratifying the treaty triumphed. When an insurrection broke out in the Philippines, a few wavering senators were convinced that national honor would not permit the United States to withdraw from the islands. On February 6, 1899, the treaty received the necessary two-thirds vote in the Senate. The war was officially over. A new generation of expansionists had dreamed of "manifest destiny," and the dream had become a reality.

The war has important results. For several reasons the Spanish-American War was a landmark in American history:

(1) The protectorate which the United States established over the neighboring

American forces are taking shelter here from Spanish guns on San Juan Hill on July 1, 1898. They soon captured the Spanish guns.

island of Cuba, together with the acquisition of colonies in the Atlantic and in the distant Pacific, ended the American policy of isolation. With almost breath-taking speed the United States had adopted a policy of overseas imperialism. No longer was it a question whether or not we should play a part in the events of the world, but, as Theodore Roosevelt said, "whether we should play that part well or ill."

(2) The victories of the American navy entitled the United States to rank as one of the leading naval powers of the world.

(3) The friendly attitude of Great Britain during the war opened a new chapter in the relations of the two English-speaking peoples. From that time, cordial feeling between the two nations continued to grow.

(4) Northerners and Southerners fought side by side in the war, forgetting in camp life and the heat of battle many of the sectional prejudices that had divided them for more than 30 years.

(5) The war stimulated industrial activity and thus contributed to the new period of prosperity upon which the country entered.

How did the United States gain a speedy victory in the war with Spain?

1. How did the United States Navy strike at Spain in the Philippines? What complications developed after Dewey's victory?
2. How did the United States Navy and Army defeat Spain in Cuba? Which branch of the service was more efficient?
3. What were the terms of the treaty ending the war? Which part of the settlement caused the most debate in Congress?
4. What were the important results of the war?

---

3 **Cuba and Puerto Rico Offer Challenging Problems**

Each new territory offers difficulties. The Spanish-American War left the United States with the knotty problems of organizing and ruling the territories surrendered by Spain. Although Cuba had been promised independence, it was obvious that certain preliminary steps had to be taken before Cuba could stand on her own feet. For Puerto Rico and the Philippines a system of government had to be planned that would be entirely foreign to American tradition. There were nearly a million inhabitants in Puerto Rico, of whom only eleven per cent could read and write. In addition, the island had no experience in self-government. The situation in the Philippines was even more complex.

Conditions in Cuba are improved. To the amazement of the great powers of Europe, the United States proceeded to fulfill its pledge with regard to Cuba. The first step was to correct the frightful conditions which existed at the close of the war. Government was disorganized; cities were unsanitary; and many of the inhabitants were half-clothed, homeless, and starving. Energetic American leaders, of whom General Leonard Wood and Major William Gorgas were outstanding, took

charge of the operations. The sick and hungry were cared for, streets were cleaned and sewers constructed, schools were established, and public finances were put on a sound basis. Havana and Santiago became modern sanitary cities. Mosquitoes, which were found to be responsible for the spread of yellow fever, were exterminated. For the first time, Cuba was free from this dreaded disease.

A Cuban government is organized. The next step was to organize a Cuban government and to reach a decision about Cuba's relation to the United States. Late in 1900 the people of Cuba elected delegates to a constitutional convention in Havana. A constitution modeled upon that of the United States was adopted, but it contained no mention of Cuban relations with the United States. Early in 1901, however, the Congress of the United States added an amendment known as the Platt Amendment to an army appropriation bill. The Platt Amendment provided that the United States would give up its control of the island only when the Cubans agreed to include in their constitution the following essential points:

(1) That the government of Cuba would neither make any treaty by which Cuba would give up its independence nor would it allow any foreign power to obtain control over any of its territory.
(2) That Cuba would contract no debt which could not be paid out of the ordinary revenues of the island.
(3) That Cuba would consent to the right of the United States to intervene "for the preservation of Cuban independence, the maintenance of a government adequate for the protection of life, property, and individual liberty, and for discharging the obligations with respect to Cuba imposed by the Treaty of Paris on the United States. . . ."
(4) That Cuba would sell or lease certain coaling or naval stations to the United States.
(5) That these provisions would be written into a permanent treaty with the United States.

The third section proved to be the heart of the Platt Amendment. At first the Cubans objected strenuously to the establishment of what was clearly a protectorate by the United States over Cuba.

They gave in, however, when they were assured that the United States would intervene in Cuba only when Cuban independence was threatened by internal disorders or foreign invasion. In May, 1902, the first Cuban president was installed and the American troops were withdrawn.

The United States protectorate is used for the benefit of Cuba. The United States formally interfered in Cuban affairs on only one occasion, although troops were sent several times to preserve order or to support the authorities in power. In 1906 the Cuban army was unable to suppress a rebellion, and official intervention was considered necessary. The American military force stayed in control until 1909, when a new president was peacefully inaugurated. After 1909 a "preventive" policy was adopted toward Cuba; that is, a statement that the United States "viewed with alarm" a certain course of action in Cuba was usually enough to cause it to be abandoned. At no time did the United States indicate a desire to use the Platt Amendment as an excuse for annexing Cuba. On the whole, Cuba enjoyed relative peace and prosperity under American protection, and frequently showed that it was grateful to the United States for helping win Cuban independence.

America's economic interest in Cuba increases. Although our military control over Cuba did not last long, American economic influence continued to grow. Near the end of 1903 a trade agreement with Cuba was ratified in spite of strong opposition from sugar growers in the United States. This agreement provided a 20 per cent reduction in tariff rates on Cuban products imported into the United States. American articles brought into Cuba, on the other hand, were favored by a cut of from 20 to 40 per cent in the tariff. Within a few years Cuba was producing two thirds of the sugar imported by the United States. Americans invested heavily in Cuban sugar plantations and refineries, government securities, railroads, public utilities, tobacco fields, and mines. It was estimated that by 1929 American investments in Cuba amounted to more than 1½

Yellow fever was controlled in Cuba after the American doctors, Lazear and Carroll, proved by personal tests that the disease was carried by mosquitoes. Both doctors eventually died from the effects of the disease.

billion dollars, or 40 per cent of the total wealth of the island.

A new Cuban policy is adopted by the United States. Cuba did not escape the severe economic depression which swept the world in the 1930's. There was an oversupply of sugar, and the low price which it brought caused grave political unrest in the island. Because of this country's economic interests in Cuba and our right to intervene "for the protection of life, property, and individual liberty," the United States was vitally concerned in the critical situation. Yet when the Cuban government was overthrown in 1933, the American State Department attempted to follow a hands-off policy. American battleships were sent to Cuban waters, but every effort was made to avoid actual intervention. In 1934, as an illustration of our Good Neighbor policy, Secretary of State Cordell Hull drew up a new treaty with Cuba. By its terms the United States surrendered the right to interfere in the affairs of the island, and the Platt Amendment was abolished. We retained only a naval base at Guantánamo Bay. A new reciprocal trade agreement replaced the agreement of 1903. "The time has come," stated the American am-

Hauling sugar cane

bassador to Cuba, "when Cuba should stand on her own feet, when Cuban people should solve their own destinies, and govern themselves as they see fit."

Puerto Rico becomes an American territory. The task of organizing an administrative system for Puerto Rico was much simpler. The Foraker Act of 1900, which authorized the formation of a civil government, made Puerto Rico an "unorganized territory." Its inhabitants were called citizens of Puerto Rico, and as such were entitled to the protection of the United States although they were not American citizens. A governor, with broad executive power and the right to veto legislation, was appointed for a four-year term by the President of the United States, with the consent of the Senate. He was assisted by an executive council of eleven men chosen in the same way. At least five of the members of the council had to be native inhabitants. This council was also to act as the upper branch of the legislature, while a lower house or assembly was elected by those people in Puerto Rico who were eligible to vote.

As the islanders advanced in civilization, more powers were granted to them. The Jones Act of 1917 made Puerto Ricans citizens of the United States, and created an elective senate to serve as the upper house of the legislature. Acts passed by the legislature, however, could be set aside by either the governor, the President of the United States, or the United States Congress. Moreover, the governor, certain executive heads, and judges of the supreme court of the island were still to be appointed by the President.

In 1928 the Puerto Rican legislature re-quested complete self-government. The United States was thus given an opportunity to point out the benefits which the Puerto Ricans had enjoyed under American supervision. Sanitation had been greatly improved. Education had been made free and compulsory, and illiteracy had been greatly reduced. Roads had been built, and Puerto Rican finances had been placed on a sound basis. Some 20 years later (1947) the Puerto Ricans were granted the right to choose their chief executive by popular vote.

The United States controls Puerto Rican economy. The economic life of Puerto Rico has been under the control of American capital. Most of the land formerly consisted of large estates owned chiefly by Americans, but a Puerto Rican law of 1941 limited land holding by corporations to 500 acres. Most Puerto Ricans own no land; they are employed on the large sugar and tobacco plantations. Complete free trade, which has existed between Puerto Rico and the United States since 1901, has resulted in the expansion of the island's commerce. Since 1901, trade with the United States has increased in value from about 10 million dollars annually to more than 400 million dollars. The economic life of the island was seriously disturbed by the depression of the 1930's. The market for its products — sugar, tobacco, coffee, and fruits — declined, and unemployment increased greatly. Even after recovery from the depression, the standard of living in Puerto Rico was far below that in continental United States. Curiously, one of the chief problems of the island is the rapid increase in population which resulted in part from the improved health conditions introduced under American rule.

The constitutional status of the dependencies is fixed. Soon after the Treaty of Paris in 1899, a difficult question arose regarding our dependencies. Should the Constitution follow the American flag into the insular (island) possessions? Should the inhabitants of the lands which had lately come under our authority have the same privileges that the Constitution gave to

American citizens? The treaty declared that "the civil and political status of the native inhabitants hereby ceded to the United States shall be determined by Congress." Could Congress, then, in spite of the Constitution, limit freedom of speech or religion in the new territories? Must it extend the privileges of jury trials, for example, to the savage Moros in the Philippines?

The provision of the Foraker Act of 1900, reducing the tariff rates on Puerto Rican products, prepared the way for a test of this important question before the highest court in the land. In this case, one of the so-called Insular Cases (Downes vs. Bidwell), the Supreme Court, by a five to four vote, upheld the action of Congress. In other words, it decided that the clause of the Constitution which required that tariff duties must be uniform throughout the United States did not have to be applied to the newly acquired possessions. In other Insular Cases the Court ruled that the Bill of Rights did not have to be applied to the inhabitants of territories which had been placed under the jurisdiction of the United States.

Even after the Puerto Ricans were granted American citizenship, the Supreme Court ruled that the island was not by that act incorporated into the United States; therefore the inhabitants of the island were not entitled to the rights of jury trial guaranteed by the Constitution. Expressed simply, the constitutional rights and liberties enjoyed by American citizens of the mainland did not apply to the insular possessions unless so provided by Congress.

This point of view permitted Congress to grant to each dependency only the powers of self-government that it was politically and economically able to handle. In general these court decisions met with the approval of the American public. In fact, since the cases came up after the endorsement of imperialism in the election of 1900, they led to the observation that "the Supreme Court followed the election returns."

——— CHECK-UP ———

What policies did the United State[s] relations with Cuba and Puerto R[ico]

1. How did the United States im[posi]tions in Cuba? What kind of [government] was established? Why did o[ur economic] interests in Cuba increase?
2. What was the Platt Amendment? How did it affect our relations with Cuba? How did the Good Neighbor policy change these relations?
3. What are the political and economic relations of Puerto Rico with the United States? How have these changed since 1900?
4. How did the Supreme Court decide the question of whether "the Constitution follows the flag"?

4
A Wise Policy Helps the Philippines Achieve Independence

Rebellion complicates the Philippine problem. Although the organization of Puerto Rico carried the United States along unfamiliar paths, even wider departures from American traditions were necessary in the far-flung Philippines. The problem in the Philippines was made more difficult by geography, by racial rivalries, and by religious disagreements, especially between the Mohammedan Moros and the Catholic Malays. The Philippines had a population of more than 7 million people and consisted of over 7000 islands situated some 7000 miles from our Pacific coast. These people represented all stages of civilization from an advanced culture to extreme barbarism. The majority were of Malay origin, though there was a liberal sprinkling of the white and yellow races. It was hard enough to plan a suitable form of government for these distant islands, with their backward tribes and their great variety of races and religions. But the problem was further com-

(Continued on page 628)

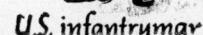

U.S. infantryman

 is placed above. The map contains the following labels:

Siberia

UNION OF SOVIET SOCIALIST REPUBLICS

Arctic Circle

3 ALASKA 1867

CANADA

Hudson Bay

75°

60°

Pribilof Is. 1867

ALEUTIAN IS. 1867

Pacific

CHINA

KOREA

JAPAN

UNITED STATES

Atlantic Ocean

45°

Midway Is.-1867

2 HAWAIIAN IS. 1898

Tropic of Cancer

4 CUBA

5 PUERTO RICO 1898

30°

PHILIPPINES

1

Wake I.-1899

Johnston I.-1898

Kingman Reef-1898

VIRGIN IS. 1917

Yap

MARIANAS IS.

Guam-1898

Palmyra I.-1898

CANAL ZONE 1904

North Latitude

15°

BORNEO

CAROLINE IS.

PALAU IS.

MARSHALL IS.

Howland I.-1857

Baker I.-1857

Jarvis I.-1936

Equator

Ocean

South Latitude

0°

NEW GUINEA

SOLOMON IS.

AMERICAN SAMOA

Manua I.-1899

Swain's-1925

Tutuila I.-1899

SOUTH AMERICA

15°

AUSTRALIA

Tropic of Capricorn

30°

NEW ZEALAND

International Date Line

East Longitude West Longitude

U.N. Trusteeship administered by U.S. after World War II
U.S. possessions are indicated by dates of acquisition or organization

45°

120° 135° 150° 165° 180° 165° 150° 135° 120° 105° 90° 75° 60°

United States and Possessions

Areas outside the United States which this country has held or now holds are shown on these two pages. When the United States secured the Philippine Islands in 1898 (map above and Map 1 on the next page), many statesmen and business leaders felt that this country had acquired a means of obtaining special commercial advantages in China. What came of their expectations? The Philippines are now independent, but the United States still retains military bases there. Certain other islands north and east of Australia (see map above) are now administered by the United States. They were held by Germany before World War I and by Japan in the period between the two World Wars. Why are all these distant islands important to us?

The United States also acquired the Hawaiian Islands in 1898 (Map 2). Our present line of defense in the Pacific runs from the Canal Zone roughly west to Pearl Harbor and north to Alaska (Map 3). The purchase of Alaska in 1867 gave us an area of great strategic value today. Can you see why? Consult a globe in order to answer this question fully. Why is the Canal Zone a vital link in our defense?

In the War with Spain, the United States liberated Cuba (Map 4) and acquired Puerto Rico (Map 5). In 1917 we bought the Virgin Islands from Denmark. We have established military bases in all these places. Why? Explain the political and economic relations today between the United States and each area shown on page 627.

① Philippine Islands

Manila Bay
Dewey
Manila
★
Spanish fleet
LUZON

LUZON

Pacific Ocean

Bataan
Corregidor I.

MINDORO

PANAY
CEBU
SAMAR
LEYTE
NEGROS
BOHOL
PALAWAN

MINDANAO

② Hawaiian Islands

NIIHAU
KAUI
OAHU
MOLOKAI
LANAI
MAUI
KAHOOLAWE
HAWAII

OAHU
Honolulu
★
Pearl Harbor
Diamond Head

Pacific Ocean

③ Alaska

Point Barrow

U.S.S.R.
Bering Strait
Nome
Yukon R.
Fairbanks
CANADA
Klondike
Alaska Highway

Bering Sea

Anchorage

Seward
★ Juneau
Sitka

ATTU
KISKA
PRIBILOF IS.
KODIAK I.
ADAK
UMNAK
UNALASKA
Dutch Harbor
ALEUTIAN IS.

Pacific Ocean

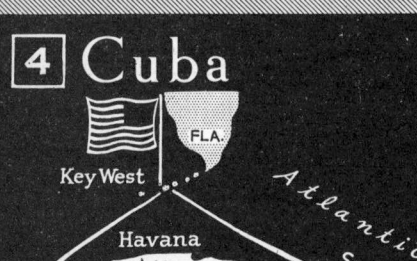

④ Cuba

FLA.
Key West
Havana
★
Atlantic Ocean
Sampson
Schley
Caribbean Sea

Kettle Hill
El Caney
Santiago de Cuba
San Juan Hill
Cervera

Spanish fleet
U.S. fleet

⑤ Puerto Rico

Atlantic Ocean

San Juan
ST. THOMAS
Charlotte Amalie
VIRGIN IS.
ST. JOHN
Ponce
ST. CROIX

Caribbean Sea

★ *Capital cities*
+++ *Modern railroads*

R.M.Chapin

U.S. naval officer

plicated. At home the anti-imperialists were opposing the whole project, and in the islands the natives were in rebellion.

At the outset the natives had welcomed the Americans. After the capture of Manila and the publication of the treaty of peace, however, the Filipino leaders became convinced that for them the war merely meant a change of masters. As a result, open rebellion against the American troops broke out early in 1899. It took three years of stubborn fighting at a cost of about 175 million dollars to show the Filipinos that the United States meant to rule the islands. Americans who opposed imperialism read with shame of the cruel guerrilla warfare adopted first by the rebels and then by the American troops — of fire, looting, and the torture of prisoners. The leader of the rebels, Aguinaldo (ah-geh-nahl'doe), was captured in 1901, but the war dragged on for another year before his followers were finally subdued.

Civil government is organized. Meanwhile President McKinley was developing a Philippine policy. He dispatched a commission to investigate conditions in the Philippines and received an elaborate report on the people, resources, and climate of the islands. The commission concluded that lack of education and political experience, as well as differences in race and language, made the Filipinos unfit at that time to govern themselves. Largely as a result of this report, McKinley sent a second commission under Judge William Howard Taft to establish civil government in the islands. In 1901, Congress co-operated by passing the Spooner Amendment, which gave the President power to govern the islands. Taft then became the first civil governor and later the governor-general of the islands. Four other American commissioners were appointed to head the departments of government, and three Filipinos were added to the commission, thus bringing its membership to seven. The commission organized local and provincial governments throughout the Christian parts of the islands.

The Philippine Islands are governed wisely. Under Governor Taft and his successors an intelligent colonial policy was followed. They encouraged education, stabilized finances, erected public works, and brought about a separation between the Church and state. Church lands were purchased and sold on easy terms to the natives. By 1907, the Philippines had cost the United States some 300 million dollars. Afterwards, taxes collected in the islands were sufficient to meet the expenses of the government.

Self-government is extended. Gradually more control over the government was given to the Filipinos. In 1902, Congress passed the Philippine Government Act, which declared that the inhabitants were citizens of the Philippine Islands and "entitled to the protection of the United States." The act also authorized the Filipinos to elect an assembly which would share the lawmaking powers with the commission. The first Philippine assembly met in 1907. When the Democratic Party, which had been opposed to imperialistic expansion, returned to power in 1913, the Filipinos were given even more power. They were given preference in the civil service and, for the first time, the majority of the commission were natives of the Philippines.

The Jones Act promises independence. Furthermore, the Democrats three years later (1916) passed the Jones Act.[1] This act abolished the commission and authorized the Filipinos to elect their own senate as well as the assembly. It likewise extended suffrage to all adult males who could read and write Spanish, English, or a native dialect. The governor-general and vice-governor, however, were still to be appointed by the President of the United States. The governor-general was to keep his veto power over legislation, and final power was to remain with the President. The Jones Act also promised independence "as soon as a stable government can be established."

[1] The Jones Act of 1916 for the Philippines should not be confused with the Jones Act of 1917, which dealt with Puerto Rico.

Nationalistic sentiments grow in the Philippines. During the 1920's there was increased agitation on the part of certain Filipino leaders for complete independence. They insisted that a stable government had been established, and that therefore the conditions laid down for independence had been fulfilled. During the closing days of Wilson's administration the President recommended that the islands be granted their independence. But the Republican Congress turned down his suggestion. In 1925 the Philippine senate voted unanimously for a direct vote of the people on independence. Commissions sent out under Presidents Coolidge and Hoover reported progress in the Philippines, recommended further concessions, but considered that the times were not suitable for separation from the United States.

American sentiment changes. With the coming of the 1930's there occurred in the United States a notable change in sentiment upon this much-debated question. Those who had favored annexation in 1899 had prophesied that American trade with the Orient would grow as a result of our base in the Philippines. This prediction had failed to come true. Nor had Americans invested capital in the Philippines to any great extent. It was true that the value of commerce between the Philippines and the United States had increased enormously in the first 30 years of the century, but actually our per capita trade with the Philippines was only one eighth as large as that with Puerto Rico. Under a policy of free trade, moreover, the products of the Philippines competed with American-controlled commodities from other sources. Philippine sugar, for example, grown by non-American capital, invaded the market for American-raised sugar from Cuba, Puerto Rico, Hawaii, and the American sugar-raising states. As a result there was a growing opinion that the islands were not economically profitable to the United States. The argument was also advanced that in case of war in the Pacific the defense of the Philippines would be a difficult matter. In fact, if we had to concentrate a fleet in the Philippine waters, we would greatly weaken the defense of our west coast and of the Hawaiian Islands.

Independence is provided for. The new attitude in America was soon reflected in Congress. Early in 1933, a Republican Congress passed the Philippine Independence Act, providing for independence after a ten-year period of probation. To the surprise of many, this project for independence did not meet with approval in the islands, and the Philippine legislature did not accept the offer. In 1934, however, a Democratic administration approved a new independence bill, the McDuffie-Tydings Act. The native legislature accepted the amended bill. Eighteen months later, Manuel Quezon (kay'sahn) was inaugurated as the first President of the new Philippine Commonwealth, and a ten-year prelude to independence began.

Independence is achieved in 1946. In spite of destruction and desolation in the Philippines caused by World War II, the Stars and Stripes were lowered at Manila as promised on July 4, 1946, and a new nation came into existence. Manuel A. Roxas (roe'hoss), inaugurated as the first President of the Philippine Republic, faced grave problems.[2] The 18 million inhabitants of the islands were confronted with severe food shortages. An armed peasant group was in a state of revolt against the government. On the other hand, Congress authorized grants of more than 600 million dollars for reconstruction made necessary by the war. Also, complete independence was made easier by the Bell Act, which provided for eight years of free trade between the United States and the Philippines and then for gradually rising tariffs for the next 20 years. It also gave encouragement to American capital invested in the islands. In spite of much opposition in the new republic, the Bell Act received the approval of the Philippine Congress. In addition, the Philippine government guaranteed the continued existence of American army, navy, and air bases in the islands.

[2] President Roxas died in 1948, and was succeeded by the vice-president, Elpidio Quirino (kee-ree'-noh).

——— CHECK-UP ———

How did the United States help the Philippine Islands in their efforts to become an independent country?

1. Why did the Filipinos revolt against the United States? How did the United States give them increasing opportunities for self-government?

2. Why did the attitude of this country toward Philippine independence change after 1929? How was the problem of independence worked out to the satisfaction of both countries?

3. When did the Philippine Islands finally become independent? What help has the United States given them since independence?

CHAPTER REVIEW

Terms to Understand

imperialism
insurrection
concentration camp
"yellow" newspapers

yellow fever
protectorate
Moros
civil government

People and Things to Know About

de Lôme letter
William McKinley
"remember the *Maine*"
Teller resolution
Admiral George Dewey
Admiral Cervera
Theodore Roosevelt
Rough Riders
San Juan Hill
Peace of Paris (1898)
General Leonard Wood
William Gorgas

Platt Amendment
Good Neighbor policy
Cordell Hull
Foraker Act
Jones Act (1916)
Jones Act (1917)
Insular Cases
Aguinaldo
William H. Taft
McDuffie-Tydings Act
Manuel Quezon
Manuel A. Roxas

Historic Dates to Identify

1898	1902	1934
1900	1916	1946
1901	1917	

Questions to Discuss

1. Contrast the following:
   (a) The attitude of Congress toward Philippine independence before and after 1929.
   (b) United States policy with respect to the independence of Puerto Rico and the Philippine Islands.
   (c) The revolt of the Cubans against Spain and the Filipinos against the United States.
   (d) The attitude of Spain and the United States toward the sinking of the *Maine*.
2. How has the Good Neighbor policy modified the relations of this country with Cuba?
3. Why was Spain unable to offer effective resistance to the United States forces in the West Indies and the Philippines?

Questions to Discuss (Cont.)

4. Why did the Jones Act extend suffrage to adult males in the Philippines who could read and write Spanish or a native dialect as well as to those proficient in English?
5. Why were the relations of the United States to Cuba after the Spanish-American War termed a "benevolent protectorate"?
6. How did the United States help the peoples of the Philippines prepare themselves for independence?

Relating Geography and History

1. On a world map locate:
   (a) The territories acquired by the United States as the result of the Spanish War.
   (b) Manila, Santiago.
2. Why has the United States retained the right to maintain bases in Cuba and the Philippine Islands even though both countries are independent?

Other Things to Do

1. Debate: *Resolved,* That Puerto Rico should be admitted to the union as the forty-ninth state.
2. Find material in the library on Admiral Dewey, Colonel Theodore Roosevelt, or another hero of the War with Spain. Report your findings to the class.
*3. Make a list of territories which the United States has acquired from Spain. Give the name, date of acquisition, and explain how the territory was acquired.
4. Use *Readers' Guide* to find materials on the establishment of the Philippine Republic and the problems confronting the new nation. Report your findings to the class.
5. Debate: *Resolved,* That the Constitution should follow the flag.
6. If there is a veteran of the Spanish War or the Philippine Insurrection in your community, ask him to tell the class about his experiences.

Chapter 35

Canadian "Mountie"

THE UNITED STATES EXTENDS ITS

INFLUENCE IN THE WESTERN HEMISPHERE

In the field of world policy, I would dedicate this nation to the policy of the good neighbor — the neighbor who resolutely respects himself and, because he does so, respects the rights of his obligations and the sanctity of his agreements with a world of neighbors.

Franklin D. Roosevelt

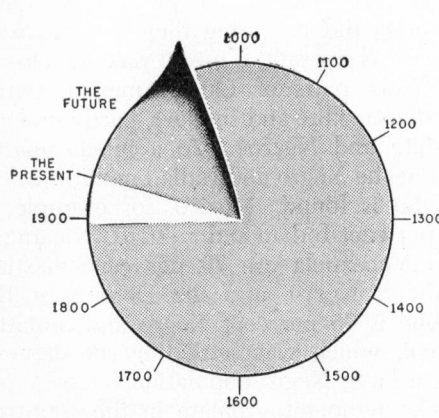

1897–The Present

During most of the 1800's the United States showed little interest in her Latin American neighbors in Central and South America. Communication with South America was none too satisfactory. In fact, a North American visitor, or even products from the United States, often traveled to South America by way of England or some other European port. South America had much closer ties with Europe than with the United States. Actually Europe was closer to many ports of South America than were the largest ports of the United States. Latin America also had much more in common with Europe than with our country. Its languages, its customs, and its culture were to a large extent European.

In the twentieth century there has been a great change in inter-American relations. Under our direction the Caribbean Sea became a world highway of commerce. United States investors put money to work

631

in many Latin American countries. The Monroe Doctrine took on a new meaning; to Latin America our country became the "Colossus of the North," and many of our southern neighbors became suspicious of our intentions. On the other hand, better relations and a better understanding were gradually brought about through Pan-American conferences and the Pan American Union. Then in the 1930's, the United States began a retreat from the imperialistic attitude of the early part of the century. As we gave up protectorates and exchanged more and more products with South American countries, a community of interest developed.

Meantime, relations with our northern neighbor were on a more friendly and intimate basis. We are separated from Canada only by a wide-open border some 3000 miles in length. Since the two countries use the same language (except in Quebec), and have the same basic civilization, they have been closely related commercially and culturally. From time to time some citizens of the United States favored the annexation of Canada, but such opinions found little or no response in Canada. Canada meantime became an independent nation, one of several dominions in the British Commonwealth of Nations.

World War II brought all Americans more closely together than ever before. Fortunately, the spirit of co-operation that resulted from our common interests survived the war. The lack of any other term for referring to the people of the United States has led to the use of the word "American" in a narrow sense. If used properly, however, "American" refers to all the people of North, Central, and South America. The present chapter will deal with the following topics:

1. Latin America is a land of contrasts.
2. The Panama Canal gives the United States a new interest in Latin America.
3. American influence extends throughout the Caribbean.
4. Relations with Mexico grow more friendly.
5. Unity in the Western Hemisphere becomes a reality.

1 Latin America Is a Land of Contrasts

Geography influences Latin American life. The geography of Central and South America has been of unusual importance in the life and history of the peoples who live there. A glance at the map (page 633) shows that most of these countries lie in the tropical zone between the Tropic of Cancer and the Tropic of Capricorn. Here the rainfall is usually heavy, contributing to the growth of jungle. In this vast area only the cool highland plateaus or the cool fringes of coast line have a climate favorable for human habitation. The narrowing area to the south, however, which includes Argentina, Chile, Uruguay, the southern tip of Brazil, and part of Paraguay, lies in the temperate zone. The climate in this area is more nearly like that of the United States.

Latin America has a wide variety of races. Racially there is a wide difference between the people of the United States and their southern neighbors. For the most part, the Spanish conquerors of Latin America did not bring their families with them. As a result, a mixed race developed in many parts of Latin America, partly mestizo (white and Indian), partly mulatto (white and Negro). To a much smaller extent the Negro and Indian mixture called zambo is found. Mexico, for example, is 90 per cent Indian and mestizo. Nicaragua and Venezuela are 70 per cent mestizo. Haiti is Negro, and the Dominican Republic is 75 per cent Negro and mulatto. Brazil, which was settled by Portuguese, has a large Negro population.

The temperate climate in the countries at the southern end of South America, however, encouraged settlement by Europeans. Consequently most of the people in these countries are white. Of the 15 million people living in Argentina and Uruguay, for example, more than 85 per cent belong

Latin America Today

UNITED STATES

BERMUDA IS.

Tropic of Cancer

MEXICO
Tampico
Mexico City ★
Havana
CUBA
HAITI
Port-au-Prince
DOMINICAN REPUBLIC
Ciudad Trujillo

Atlantic Ocean

Pacific Ocean

Caribbean Sea

BR. HONDURAS
HONDURAS
Tegucigalpa
NICARAGUA
GUATEMALA
Guatemala City
San Salvador
EL SALVADOR
Managua
San Jose
COSTA RICA
PANAMA
Panama

Caracas
VENEZUELA
BRITISH GUIANA
SURINAM (DUTCH GUIANA)
FRENCH GUIANA

Bogotá
COLOMBIA

Equator

Quito
ECUADOR

Amazon R.

PERU
Lima ★

BRAZIL

L. Titicaca
La Paz ★
BOLIVIA

PARAGUAY

Rio de Janeiro

Tropic of Capricorn

Asunción

CHILE

Valparaiso
Santiago

ARGENTINA

Buenos Aires ★
URUGUAY
Montevideo

FALKLAND IS.

Scale of Miles
0   250   500   1,000 mi.

★ *Capital Cities*

R. M. Chapin

Cape Horn

Latin America, a land of strong contrasts, has mountainous areas like that shown in the picture above, jungles where fierce and primitive tribes live, and many fine, modern cities like Montevideo, Uruguay, which is shown in the lower picture. The map here shows the countries of modern Latin America and their capitals. What country in Latin America is the same distance from the equator as your state? What factors other than distance from the equator may affect the climate of an area?

to the white race. Outside of Argentina, Uruguay, and Chile, the white population predominates only in Cuba and small Costa Rica. In Latin America as a whole, with a population nearly equal in size to that of the United States, it has been estimated that less than one third is white. Nearly another third is mestizo, a fifth is Negro or mulatto, and nearly another fifth is Indian.

Democracy is the Latin American ideal. The governments of the 20 republics in Latin America differ greatly. Some are pure dictatorships, like Guatemala and the Dominican Republic. Others are ruled by dictators whose power is more or less limited by parliaments. Still others are essentially democratic, such as Mexico, Costa Rica, Colombia, Chile, and Uruguay. Everywhere most of the people are interested in the theory of democracy, and are striving to develop democratic ideals.

Latin America is primarily agricultural. The economy of the Latin American countries is based on agriculture. Because of the great estates in most of the countries, however, 90 per cent of the population is landless and poor. Mexico is the only country where real progress has been made in redistributing the land. After the revolution which took place in Mexico in the twentieth century, 45 million acres, formerly owned by great landowners and corporations, were turned over to the Indian peons who worked the land.

Economic ties with the United States grow stronger. Many of the Latin American states depend mainly upon one or two products. Chief among these are coffee, sugar, wheat, beef, oil, cotton, tin, copper and nitrates. In the 1800's a market for most of these products was found in Europe. In turn, Latin America bought most of its manufactured goods from Europe. Even then, however, the Latin American countries exported a considerable volume of produce to our country, and during recent years trade with the United States both in imports and exports has greatly increased. Today we are largely dependent upon Latin America for sugar, coffee, tropical fruits, and many other products. We have a further interest in the economic development of Latin America because of the investment of some 3 billion dollars of American capital south of the Rio Grande. Besides, the development of the airplane has brought the most distant parts of South America within a day or two of any part of the United States.

Latin America has a distinctive culture. In the development of education and culture the Latin American states vary widely. In Uruguay and Argentina, for example, only about 20 per cent of the population cannot read or write. In Cuba, however, 40 per cent are illiterate; in Colombia and Chile somewhat less than 50 per cent; in Mexico and Panama 60 per cent; in Brazil and Venezuela 70 per cent; and in Haiti 90 per cent. On the other hand, Latin American states have developed a culture peculiarly their own. They have made distinguished contributions in music, art, literature (especially poetry), archeology, and sociology. Buenos Aires is renowned for its musical attractions, and Mexican artists are world famous.

Latin America is Roman Catholic. Our southern neighbors are overwhelmingly Roman Catholic, and the Catholic Church has been a tremendous force in their development. In many countries there is a close connection between Church and state. In others, anti-clerical forces have brought about a separation of Church and state, though Catholicism remains the religion of the great mass of people. Recent immigration, however, has brought in a sprinkling of Protestants as well as a few people who worship in other faiths.

Marimba Drums Guitar Musette Maracas

MUSICAL INSTRUMENTS OF LATIN AMERICA

Why has Latin America been called a land of contrasts?

1. What is the geography of Latin America? The climate? How does the climate of Argentina, Chile, and Uruguay differ from that of most of Latin America?
2. How do the countries of Latin America differ in race?
3. Have all Latin American countries achieved democracy?
4. Is the economic life of Latin America based primarily on agriculture or industry? How have economic ties between Latin America and the United States become stronger?
5. Describe the culture of Latin America. What religion predominates in Latin America?

The Church of Sao Francisco in Bahia, Brazil, is one of thousands built by the Catholic Church throughout Latin America.

---

2 The Panama Canal Gives the United States a New Interest in Latin America

Interest in a canal is revived. As you have read (page 475), during the 1800's Secretary of State Blaine and others tried to bring about closer relations with Latin America, but little came of these attempts. The participation of the United States in the Spanish-American War, however, increased our interest in Latin America. In particular, it gave new life to the idea of building a canal connecting the Caribbean Sea with the Pacific Ocean. The spectacular 14,000-mile trip of the battleship *Oregon* around South America (page 619) and the possession of territory in two hemispheres emphasized the military need for such a link. Obviously the United States must either build powerful fleets for both the Atlantic and Pacific waters, or else build a canal joining the two oceans. It was also evident that in peace times such a waterway would become an important artery of world commerce.

The Hay-Pauncefote Treaty prepares the way. Numerous problems arose before a canal could become a reality. The first problem grew out of the Clayton-Bulwer Treaty (1850), which provided that such a canal was to be under the joint supervision of the United States and Great Britain. Since Great Britain was the mistress of the seas, this treaty practically guaranteed British control in time of war over any canal which should be constructed. Previous efforts to modify the Clayton-Bulwer Treaty had failed, but the new friendliness between Great Britain and the United States at the opening of our century (page 480) suggested that a more favorable arrangement was possible.

Secretary of State John Hay and the British ambassador Pauncefote (pawns'-foot) finally agreed upon a treaty acceptable to both powers (1901). It set aside the Clayton-Bulwer Treaty and permitted the construction of a canal to be controlled and policed by the United States. On the other hand, the canal was to be "free and open to the vessels of commerce and war of all nations" on equal terms.

The Panama route is selected. Now that the United States had a free hand to construct a canal, a question arose as to its location. One suitable route lay across the narrow Isthmus of Panama, which was then owned by the Republic of Colombia. The possibilities of a canal across this neck of land had already attracted attention. As early as 1878, a French company (the Panama Canal Company) had obtained from Colombia the right to build a canal at this point. The French company had failed, however, because of mismanagement and tropical disease, and work on the project had ceased. The French company now offered to sell its rights and equipment to the United States for about 100 million dollars. Meanwhile, United States engineers reported favorably upon a right-of-way through Nicaragua. The possibility that the United States might act on this recommendation caused the French company to reduce its price to 40 million dollars. From a financial point of view the Panama right-of-way was now more attractive, and Congress authorized the President to purchase the rights and property of the Panama Company. He was also authorized to acquire from the Republic of Colombia perpetual control of a narrow strip of land across the isthmus, and there to construct a canal. In case arrangements could not be made for a Panama canal "within a reasonable time and upon reasonable terms," the President was given the power to go ahead with the Nicaraguan route.

Colombia refuses our terms. Secretary Hay arranged the Hay-Herran Treaty with Colombia, and the United States Senate ratified it early in 1903. By the terms of the treaty Colombia was to lease to us a strip of land six miles wide across the isthmus. In return, the United States agreed to pay $10,000,000 in cash and $250,000 annually, beginning nine years after ratification of the treaty. Hoping to obtain better terms from the United States, however, the Colombian Senate adjourned in the fall of 1903 without ratifying the agreement. The failure of the Hay-Herran Treaty provoked ill feeling not only in the United States but also in the province of Panama, which was deprived of an important artery of trade.

Panama revolts from Colombia. In November of 1903 events in Panama took an unexpected turn. Throughout the fall, there were rumors that the inhabitants of Panama would revolt before they would allow the canal project to be given up. A treaty of 1846 with New Granada (part of which later became Colombia), had bound the United States to preserve freedom of transit (passage) across the isthmus. Acting under this treaty, the government at Washington sent the U.S.S. *Nashville* to Panama to make sure that if a revolution occurred, freedom of transit would not be interfered with. On November 3, the day following the arrival of the *Nashville,* the province of Panama revolted from Colombia. Within a week seven United States warships were off the coast of Panama. There was almost no bloodshed in connection with the uprising because the commander of the *Nashville* prevented Colombian military forces from crossing the isthmus to the city of Panama.[1]

A treaty is arranged with Panama. Important events then took place in quick succession. On November 6 the United States recognized the new government in Panama. A week later Bunau-Varilla (boo-no' vah-ree' yah), the former chief engineer of the Panama Company, was received by President Theodore Roosevelt as the minister of the Republic of Panama. On the eighteenth of November a new treaty was ready for ratification. By the terms of this Hay-Bunau-Varilla Treaty, the United States guaranteed the independence of the new republic. We agreed to pay Panama the sum of $10,000,000 outright as well as $250,000 annually, beginning nine years after the ratification of the treaty. In return, Panama granted permanently a zone ten miles wide for the construction of a canal. The properties of the Panama Canal Company and the Panama Railroad Company were also transferred to the United States. The

[1] *The Nashville* arrived at Panama under the following secret orders: "Maintain free and uninterrupted transit. If interruption is threatened by armed force, occupy the line of railroad. Prevent landing of armed force with hostile intent, either government or insurgent, at any point within fifty miles of Panama." These instructions insured, and were meant to insure, the success of the revolution.

United States was granted permission by Panama to fortify the Canal Zone.

President Theodore Roosevelt is criticized. When Congress met the following month, the Panama question apparently was already settled, and the Hay-Bunau-Varilla Treaty was ratified in February, 1904. As might be expected, however, considerable criticism was directed at President Theodore Roosevelt for the attitude of the United States during the revolt in Panama. The presence of American warships in Panama was condemned. The fact that the United States had interfered on the side that opposed Colombia's rights as a nation rather than in support of them appeared questionable to many people. Moreover, the government at Washington had been very hasty in recognizing the new Republic of Panama.

On the other hand, there was no definite evidence that the United States had stirred up the revolution in Panama.[2] Some time after he had retired from the Presidency, Theodore Roosevelt remarked, "If I had followed traditional conservative methods, I should have submitted a dignified state paper of probably two hundred pages to the Congress and the debate would be going on yet, but I took the Canal Zone and then left Congress — not to debate the canal, but to debate me, and while the debate goes on, the canal does also."

The Panama episode disturbs Latin American relations. Our acquisition of the Canal Zone seriously disturbed friendly relations between the United States and Colombia. It also caused indignation and alarm among the other Latin American states. Colombia refused to recognize the independence of Panama and demanded that the question of her rights to the isthmus and her interests in the canal be decided by arbitration. Eventually (1921) an agreement was reached whereby the

[2] On October 10, 1903, Theodore Roosevelt had written a personal letter in which he said, "Privately, I freely say to you that I should be delighted if Panama were an independent state, or if it made itself so at this moment; but for me to say so publicly would amount to an instigation of a revolt, and therefore I cannot say it."

William Howard Taft, later to be President, was sent to Panama as a troubleshooter. This cartoon of the times shows him shoveling out disease and red tape so that construction of the canal can go forward.

United States paid Colombia 25 million dollars.

Construction of the canal is completed. The actual construction of the Panama Canal offered serious engineering difficulties. A lock canal was approved because it would be cheaper and easier to build than a sea-level canal. A further question arose as to whether the work should be carried on by the engineering division of the army or by private contractors. In the end it was decided to make it an army construction project, and in 1908 Colonel G. W. Goethals (go'thalz) assumed complete control.

Another serious obstacle lay in the menace of deadly tropical diseases. Thanks to the tireless energy of the surgeon-general of the army, Dr. W. D. Gorgas, the breeding places of the mosquitoes which carried yellow fever were successfully eliminated. Thus the workmen were able to carry on in comparative safety. After about ten years the great engineering feat was completed, and on August 15, 1914, the canal was formally opened to traffic.

The canal proves its importance. Both from the commercial and military points of view the Panama Canal proved to be of great importance. It made the distance by water from New York to San Francisco shorter by 8000 miles. It shortened the distance from New York to the west coast of South America or to our Pacific possessions by some 4000 miles. The saving in time and in the cost of operating a ship was worth many times the amount which that ship paid in tolls for the privilege of passing through the canal. In addition, the canal was so important for military purposes that the entire expense of construction (about 375 million dollars, plus more than 100 million for fortifications) could be considered part of the cost of national defense. The canal made possible a quick shift of naval strength from one ocean to another. Thus the Atlantic and Pacific fleets could practically be combined into a single unit whenever necessary.

——————— CHECK-UP ———————

How did the United States build the Panama Canal?

1. Why did United States interest in a canal connecting the Pacific Ocean and the Caribbean revive after 1898? What was the reaction in Great Britain to our plan? What treaty prepared the way for building the canal?

2. Why was the Panama route selected? How did the United States acquire the Canal Zone? What was the reaction in Latin America? Why?

3. What difficulties were overcome in the construction of the Panama Canal? Why did the canal prove important?

3 | **American Influence Extends Throughout the Caribbean**

Our interest in the Caribbean grows. As the twentieth century progressed, the United States began to show a keener interest in the affairs of the republics to the south, particularly those in or bordering upon the Caribbean Sea. For one thing, the Spanish War left us a dependency (Puerto Rico) and a protectorate (Cuba) in this region. Another reason for our interest was that the Panama Canal transformed the Caribbean from a closed sea into one of the world's highways of commerce. American statesmen now wanted to make sure that stable governments were maintained in the Caribbean countries, and that European countries did not interfere in the affairs of this hemisphere. They were also interested in obtaining naval and coaling stations for the defense of the Canal Zone.

The United States forces a settlement of the Venezuelan debt. At the time when the location of the new canal was being discussed, an event took place which showed the growing interest of the United States in its southern neighbors and its determination to uphold the principles of the Monroe Doctrine. In 1902 a crisis arose over Venezuela's inability to pay certain debts due European creditors. Germany, Great Britain, and Italy broke off diplomatic relations with Venezuela and established a blockade of its ports to compel payment. The United States Government urged the European powers to submit their claims to arbitration. When Germany ignored this request, President Theodore Roosevelt threatened to order American warships to the Venezuelan coast.[3] Germany finally gave in, and the claims were referred to arbitration committees which recommended that the debts be reduced to about one fifth of the original amount. Since this affair involved no real danger to territory owned by any American country, it seemed clear that we were now taking a new attitude toward developments in the western world.

President Theodore Roosevelt enlarges the Monroe Doctrine. Close on the heels of the Venezuelan crisis came a similar one in the Caribbean island of Hispaniola. On this island there are two states, the Dominican Republic and the Republic of Haiti. European countries, particularly Germany,

[3] Officially the United States took no action, but according to his own account President Roosevelt told the German ambassador that the United States fleet would be sent to Venezuela if Germany did not agree to arbitration.

The Strategic Caribbean

The Panama Canal, an important commercial artery, is also of vital importance to our defense. Why is the canal vulnerable in case of a successful air attack (see inset map)?

less likely. The Monroe Doctrine, therefore, was to do more than simply keep Europe out of the Western Hemisphere. It was now to become a positive doctrine, permitting the United States to assume a position of leadership over the other republics in the Americas. This expanded interpretation of the Monroe Doctrine is known as the Roosevelt corollary.

The Dominican Republic becomes a protectorate. In 1905, President Roosevelt entered into an agreement with the Dominican Republic by which the United States was to guarantee the *territorial integrity* of the republic, that is, we promised that no change would take place in its territory. In return, an American collector was to supervise the customhouses of the re-

stated that they were going to collect — by force if necessary — the debts that the bankrupt Dominican Republic owed them. President Roosevelt took a bold stand. If any nation, said he, had to interfere in the affairs of a Latin American state which was not paying its foreign debts or whose stability was in question, the United States would be the one to interfere — not a European power. Thus there would be less danger of outside interference, and a violation of the Monroe Doctrine would be

public, take charge of its finances, and settle its foreign and domestic debts. When the United States Senate failed to take action upon the agreement, Roosevelt arranged to have the Dominican Republic appoint an American collector who was to receive the protection of American marines. In the end the Senate yielded, and in 1907 approved a slightly revised treaty. Under the American collector, customs receipts doubled and the finances of the republic were placed on a sound basis.[4]

Dollar diplomacy is introduced. For 25 years the Caribbean policy of the United States followed the line of development begun by President Theodore Roosevelt. In order to protect the Panama Canal, the United States Government continued to see that Caribbean countries remained peaceful and met their obligations to foreign powers. It also smoothed the way for the profitable investment of American capital in this region. This policy, commonly called "dollar diplomacy," meant the use of American diplomatic influence to promote our financial and commercial interests abroad. American citizens were encouraged to invest their capital in Latin American countries. In case of financial crisis, the United States protected these investments against loss by administering the customs and supervising the budget of any Latin American republic which was not meeting its obligations.

A protectorate is established over Nicaragua. Hardly a Caribbean country escaped United States supervision at one time or another between 1900 and 1930. Disorder, financial troubles, and the threat of a revolution led President Taft to take a hand in Nicaraguan affairs at the request of its president (1912). United States marines were ordered to Nicaragua to protect American lives and property, and the finances of Nicaragua were placed under American control. These moves were fol-

lowed by a treaty which granted to the United States for the sum of 3 million dollars the right-of-way for an interoceanic canal through Nicaragua. We were also given the lease of a naval base on the Gulf of Fonseca (in the Pacific Ocean), and long-term leases of the Great Corn and Little Corn Islands (in the Caribbean Sea). (See map, page 639.) This agreement failed at the time to receive the approval of the United States Senate, but a treaty with similar provisions (the Bryan-Chamorro Treaty) was ratified in 1916.

The Nicaraguan protectorate is abandoned. American marines remained in Nicaragua almost continuously until the early 1930's. They were withdrawn in 1925, but a fresh revolution, started by dissatisfied groups, brought them back late in the following year. For two years a rebel chieftain named Sandino carried on guerrilla warfare against the Nicaraguan government and a force of more than 5000 United States marines. Fourteen American men-of-war patrolled Nicaraguan waters to prevent the landing of munitions for the rebels. At length Sandino was overcome and order was restored in the republic. In 1933, under the Good Neighbor policy of President Franklin D. Roosevelt, the American troops were withdrawn.

Haiti comes under United States protection. Conditions in the Republic of Haiti also attracted the attention of the United States. After revolutions, demonstrations against foreigners, and trouble between Haiti and the Dominican Republic, the United States intervened in 1911. Three years later the financial situation in Haiti became critical. France and Great Britain made a formal demand for the control of the customhouses, while Germany insisted upon even stronger measures. In 1915 American marines were landed, and the administration of the customs was taken over by the American navy, though the United States announced that it had no intention of seizing the government or the territory of Haiti. A treaty was prepared, placing Haiti under an American protectorate. It provided for our controlling the Haitian customs and for the

---

[4] In 1904 Roosevelt wrote: "I want to do nothing but what a policeman has to do in Santo Domingo. As for annexing the island, I have about the same desire to annex it as a gorged boa constrictor might have to swallow a porcupine wrong end to."

distribution of the revenues between the Haitian government and the countries to whom Haiti was in debt. Expenditures were to be supervised and a native police force was to be officered by the Americans. The treaty, to run for ten years and to be renewable for another ten, was ratified in 1916. A new constitution was also prepared for Haiti, granting foreigners the right to own land. It was ratified by a popular election held under American military supervision after the Haitian assembly had rejected it.

Haitian conditions improve. Conditions in the republic improved greatly under American control. The finances were placed upon a sound basis, and the danger of foreign interference was removed. For the first time in their history, the Haitians had a stable government.[5] Many public improvements were made, including the building of roads, the promotion of education, and the improvement of sanitary conditions. Unfortunately, however, serious charges were directed against the American officials in charge. They were accused of killing many natives without just cause and of inflicting cruel and inhuman punishments upon others.

The protectorate is withdrawn. The 1930's brought about the relaxing of American control in Haiti. A commission was appointed by President Hoover to investigate conditions in the republic. This group suggested that the native Haitians replace American officials as fast as they could be adequately trained for government service. It also recommended that military control, in operation since 1915, be gradually abandoned. President Hoover accepted this liberal recommendation, and in 1931, the Haitian congress assembled — the first to be elected by popular vote in fourteen years. In 1934 a new agreement provided for the relaxing of American military and financial control, and the last of the marines were withdrawn.

The United States continues to intervene in the Dominican Republic. Meanwhile, disorder in the neighboring Dominican Re-

[5] Before American intervention in Haiti, only one of its presidents lived out his term of office and died a natural death in his own country.

public led the United States to take even more drastic steps to strengthen its protectorate over the republic. In 1916 revolutionary disturbances resulted in the landing of American marines on the island. The revolutionists who had gained control of the government were

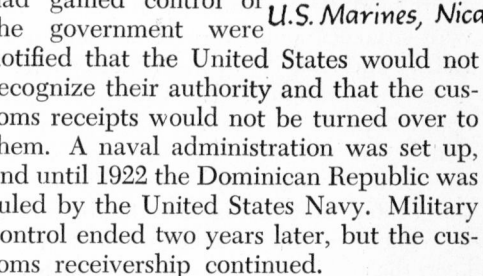

U.S. Marines, Nicaragua

notified that the United States would not recognize their authority and that the customs receipts would not be turned over to them. A naval administration was set up, and until 1922 the Dominican Republic was ruled by the United States Navy. Military control ended two years later, but the customs receivership continued.

American occupation had its good and bad features. Roads, bridges, and wharves were constructed. Education was greatly extended and sanitary conditions were improved. On the other hand, the Dominicans were deprived of their freedom, the Dominican press was placed under censorship, and there were complaints of unreasonable imprisonment and cruel punishments. Under the Good Neighbor policy of Franklin D. Roosevelt's administration, our financial protectorate over the republic was finally withdrawn in 1940.

The Virgin Islands are acquired. American control of the Caribbean was further extended in the year 1917, when the Danish West Indies were purchased at a cost of 25 million dollars. Located at the entrance to the Caribbean, the Virgin Islands were an important link in the defense of the Panama Canal. They were governed by the Navy Department until 1931. At that time they were transferred to the Department of the Interior and a civil government was established. When the United States adopted prohibition in 1919, hard times came to the Virgin Islanders, for the sale of rum was their chief source of revenue. To make matters worse, the use of oil for fuel led to the abandonment of the coaling stations on the islands, resulting in further unemployment. The repeal of prohibition in 1933 (page 592), however, prepared the way for economic recovery in the islands.

The Caribbean becomes an American lake. Thus, as a result of the policy followed by Theodore Roosevelt and his immediate successors, the Caribbean Sea became an American lake. In the 1920's, for example, with possession of Puerto Rico, the Canal Zone, and the Virgin Islands; with protectorates over Cuba, Nicaragua, Haiti, and the Dominican Republic; and with large economic interests in many other Latin American countries, American influence was supreme. No Caribbean state could hope to maintain a political system which did not have the approval of the American government. The influence of the United States was used to discourage the violent overthrow of governments and to keep the peace. As a result, the Caribbean countries at no previous time in their history had enjoyed greater freedom from wars, revolutions, and financial chaos. On the other hand, our use of military force and our control of the civil and economic affairs of these countries aroused the hostility and suspicion of Latin America.

The protectorates are withdrawn. With the development of the Good Neighbor policy in the 1930's, the United States gradually surrendered its control over the Caribbean area. American marines were withdrawn from one state after another. New treaties were drawn up with Cuba (page 623) and Panama (1936) by which our protectorates were withdrawn.

——————— CHECK-UP ———————

How did the United States extend its influence throughout the Caribbean?

1. Why did the United States take a greater interest in the Caribbean area after 1898?
2. What was the real purpose of the Roosevelt corollary to the Monroe Doctrine? How did it cause the United States again and again to intervene in a country's affairs and to establish a protectorate? How did the Latin American countries regard this policy?
3. What is dollar diplomacy?
4. How did this country acquire the Virgin Islands? Why?

4 **Relations with Mexico Grow More Friendly**

Mexico attracts United States investments. American capital was invested in Mexico as it was in the nearby Caribbean republics. Porfirio Diaz was elected president of Mexico in 1877, but he was practically a dictator. Under his iron hand, Mexico had the outward appearances of a well-knit federal state. Underneath the surface, however, lay ignorance and superstition, racial and class hatred, and economic discontent. Although the country was primarily agricultural, almost 90 per cent of the population were landless peons (who lived almost like serfs). Diaz turned the rich natural resources of the country over to foreign capitalists, and they, of course, supported his administration. Americans in particular became interested in the building of railroads, in rubber plantations, in cattle-raising, and in the development of rich silver, lead, copper, and oil resources. By 1910 there were some 50,000 Americans living in Mexico, and American investments had reached a total of a billion dollars.

Huerta becomes provisional president. In the spring of 1911 the aged Diaz was toppled from power by a progressive leader, Francisco Madero. Madero had promised social, economic, and political reforms, but he found his promises difficult to carry out. Rebel forces in the northern states of Mexico opposed him, and Madero waged a losing battle to maintain his position. Early in 1913 he was arrested and shortly afterward shot in cold blood. Victoriano Huerta (wear'tah), who had been Madero's commander in chief, and who was believed to have been responsible for his death, was then proclaimed provisional (temporary) president. Huerta was a strong man of the Diaz type, and was opposed to reform.

Wilson adopts a policy of watchful waiting. Many people wondered what attitude

Mexico's powerful northern neighbor would adopt toward Huerta. President Wilson, who was inaugurated within a month after Madero's death, stated that he would cultivate the friendship and confidence of the republics of Central and South America. But he also added that "We can have no sympathy with those who seek to seize the power of government to advance their own personal interests or ambitions."

True to his word, Wilson failed to follow the example of 26 European nations which recognized the government of Huerta. Unwilling to interfere with the internal affairs of Mexico, Wilson announced a policy of "watchful waiting." His actions did not appear entirely neutral, however, for he allowed arms and munitions to be shipped to Carranza and Pancho Villa (vee'yah) — the men who were leading an opposition movement against Huerta. On the other hand, Wilson turned a deaf ear to requests for direct intervention which were made by American interests in Mexico. Even when American lives were lost below the Rio Grande, and the pressure upon the administration increased, the President remained immovable.[6]

Armed intervention replaces "watchful waiting." In practice the policy of watchful waiting proved difficult to carry out. On one occasion an insult to the American flag led to armed intervention. A squadron of American war vessels under Admiral Mayo had been stationed at Tampico, Mexico, to protect foreign lives and property. In April, 1914, some members of the crew of the U.S.S. *Dolphin,* who had landed in a launch flying the American flag, were arrested by Huerta's officers. The American admiral in charge demanded their immediate release, an apology for their arrest, and a

Primitive farming is still common in Mexico, but modern methods are being introduced.

salute of 21 guns because Mexico had insulted our flag. Huerta gave in to the first two requirements, but refused to salute the flag. The situation was further complicated by the arrival at Veracruz of a German steamer carrying a cargo of machine guns and ammunition for Huerta's forces. Wilson decided that drastic action was necessary. Without awaiting authority from Congress, he ordered American naval forces to occupy Veracruz immediately. At a cost of nineteen American lives the command was carried out, and an army of 6000 men was sent to hold the city.

The ABC powers offer to mediate the Mexican problem. The leading South American nations, Argentina, Brazil, and Chile, were alarmed by the serious turn of affairs. They proposed a conference at which our differences with Mexico could be cleared up and a settlement reached. President Wilson promptly accepted the invitation of the ABC powers, and Huerta had to do the same. A conference was held at Niagara Falls which resulted in Huerta's resignation and his flight to Europe in the summer of 1914. Mexico came under the control of Carranza, and the American forces were withdrawn from Veracruz. When Carranza guaranteed that the lives and property of foreigners in Mexico would be respected, he was recognized by the United States as the head of the Mexican government (1915).

An expedition is launched against Villa. On one other occasion President Wilson had to interfere in Mexico. No sooner had Carranza been elevated to power than his

[6] Great Britain's support of our policy in Mexico was insured when President Wilson gave in on the issue of Panama Canal tolls. In anticipation of the opening of the Canal, Congress had passed a law which exempted American coastwise shipping from paying tolls. Great Britain protested this act on the ground that it was contrary to the terms of the Hay-Pauncefote Treaty. President Wilson secured from Congress the repeal of the Tolls Exemption Act, and in return Great Britain accepted the American policy with respect to Mexico.

Llama pack train, South America

former ally, Villa, turned against him. Partly in revenge for aid given Carranza by the United States, and partly to provoke American interference, Villa seized eighteen Americans in northern Mexico and shot them in cold blood (1916). Shortly afterward he crossed the border with a band of desperados and raided a border town in New Mexico. The town was looted and seventeen Americans lost their lives. A wave of anger swept across the United States and President Wilson announced that an expedition would be sent to Mexico to "get Villa dead or alive." Carranza reluctantly agreed to this, and General John J. Pershing led a force of 6000 men into Mexican territory.

As the American troops advanced farther and farther into Mexico in pursuit of Villa, the hostile attitude of the Mexican people became more and more obvious. Meanwhile, President Wilson had called out the militia of the states. Soon 100,000 national guardsmen were massed along the border ready for action. The United States tried to come to terms with Carranza over the withdrawal of the American troops from Mexico. When the negotiations failed, the situation took on a threatening aspect. Many Americans felt that the United States ought to intervene actively in Mexico, even if such a step meant war. President Wilson, however, was not ready to go so far. The elusive Villa continued to dodge his pursuers, and in 1917, largely because of critical relations with Germany (page 665), American troops were withdrawn from Mexico. In 1920 a new revolt forced Carranza to flee. Once more Wilson was faced with the problem of recognizing a government in Mexico founded upon revolution and violence. Wilson took no action, however, and the vexing question was passed

on to his successor. Eight years of "watchful waiting" seemed to have accomplished little or nothing.

The Mexican constitution raises difficulties for Americans. Diplomatic relations with Mexico were renewed in 1923, but friction between the two countries continued. The Mexican constitution proclaimed in 1917 had struck a severe blow at American interests south of the Rio Grande. It declared that only Mexican citizens and Mexican companies might acquire land or receive the right to develop "mines, waters, or mineral fuels in the Republic of Mexico." The same rights, however, might be granted to foreigners "provided they agreed to be considered Mexicans in respect to such property." Tension between the two countries was increased by the enactment of a law which stated that all petroleum deposits were owned by the Mexican nation. Although the American State Department protested, the Mexican government proceeded to carry out these provisions.

Ambassador Morrow brings about better relations. The appointment of Dwight W. Morrow as ambassador to Mexico, in 1927, brought a marked improvement in relations with our sister republic. Ambassador Morrow was friendly and tactful, and succeeded in gaining the good will of the Mexican people. As a result of a decision of the Mexican Supreme Court, the petroleum law was modified somewhat in favor of United States companies. Mexican regard for Morrow increased when he helped to settle a dispute between the Church and state in Mexico. Thus, during the early 1930's, there was an increase in mutual friendship and understanding between the two countries.

Cárdenas carries out reforms. Other misunderstandings, however, arose between the United States and Mexico. In 1934 Lázaro Cárdenas (car'day-nahs) became President of Mexico. Cárdenas was determined to carry out the reforms of the Mexican Revolution of the early 1900's. He proceeded to nationalize the great estates, including those held by Americans, so that they could be distributed among groups of landless peasants.

In 1938 Cárdenas ordered the seizure of American and British oil properties valued at about 450 million dollars. The United States admitted the right of Mexico to take over the properties, but demanded adequate payment for them. The Mexican government was willing to discuss payment — but only on the basis of the value of the surface property. The subsurface rights (oils and minerals), Mexico claimed, had been given to the national government by the constitution.

Relations with Mexico improve. In the face of these difficulties the United States adopted an attitude of patience toward Mexico. Following the Good Neighbor policy, Secretary of State Cordell Hull tried by every possible means to gain the good will of the Mexican government, and relations became more cordial than ever before. In 1942 Mexico sided with the United States in its war against the Axis powers (page 707). Early in 1943 friendly relations between the two countries were further cemented by an exchange of visits between Presidents Franklin D. Roosevelt and Avila Camacho. In the following year the dispute over the seizure of American oil properties was finally settled when the oil companies accepted an award of some 24 million dollars in full payment. President Harry S. Truman made a good-will tour to Mexico City early in 1947 to visit the new President, Miguel Alemán (ahl-aye-mahn'). He aroused great enthusiasm by placing a wreath at the monument to Mexico's "cadet heroes," who had fought to the death during the Mexican War with the United States rather than surrender to the "Yanquis."

——— CHECK-UP ———

How have relations between the United States and Mexico become more friendly?

1. Why did United States investments increase in the days of President Diaz? What issue grew out of provisions in the Mexican Constitution of 1917?
2. Why did President Wilson adopt a policy of "watchful waiting" in dealing with Mexico? How successful was this policy?
3. Why have relations with Mexico become increasingly friendly since World War I?

5 **Unity in the Western Hemisphere Becomes a Reality**

Conferences improve inter-American relations. An important factor in bringing about a better understanding between the United States and the countries of Latin America was a series of Pan-American Conferences. Started by Secretary of State Blaine in 1889 (page 475), these conferences were revived early in the 1900's when three such meetings were held. When the League of Nations and the World Court came into existence (pages 680, 684), however, nearly all the Latin American countries became members. Under these circumstances Latin America began to look to the League for the protection of its territory and its independence rather than to its powerful North American neighbor and the Monroe Doctrine.

Latin America wants our policy made clear. At a Pan-American Congress held at Santiago, Chile, in 1923, Latin American delegates asked for an interpretation of the Monroe Doctrine and an expression of the attitude of the United States toward the countries of Central and South America. The American delegation, however, was unwilling at this time to define the Monroe Doctrine. The delegation said only that it was a policy of the United States which would be interpreted and enforced by the United States alone. At a later conference held in Havana in 1928, the United States delegation tried to reassure Latin America that it had nothing to fear from American imperialism. The delegation pointed out that we had not used the Monroe Doctrine in an attempt to extend the political influence of the United States or to annex territory. Instead, the delegation insisted, the Doctrine had been used to promote order and security in the New World and to help remove causes which might otherwise have led to more serious international troubles.

Western Canada, like western United States, produces great quantities of grain. Here, powerful farm horses are drawing a reaper through a field of ripe wheat. Canadian farmers also use many tractors and other modern farm equipment.

Secretary of State Hull explains the Good Neighbor policy. Still another Pan-American Conference assembled at Montevideo, Uruguay, in 1933. This assembly proved to be a landmark in the development of this country's Latin American policy, for here Secretary of State Cordell Hull explained the Good Neighbor policy, which President Franklin D. Roosevelt had announced. "My government," said Secretary Hull, "is doing its utmost, with due regard to commitments made in the past, to end with all possible speed engagements which have been set up by previous circumstances." He went on to point out that the administration of Franklin D. Roosevelt was thoroughly opposed to any interference with the freedom or sovereignty of other nations. "No government," he declared, "need fear any intervention on the part of the United States under the Roosevelt administration." At the Montevideo conference the Latin American countries, especially Argentina, expressed a friendliness and freedom from suspicion toward the United States that had not been equaled since the United States adopted a policy of imperialism at the end of the 1800's.

A collective security pact is signed. Three years later (1936) a special conference for the maintenance of peace was held in Buenos Aires and was opened by President Roosevelt in person. It was agreed that a threat of foreign attack against any nation in the Western Hemisphere would be considered a threat to all American republics and should be met by consultation. More important was the action taken at the eighth Pan-American Conference at Lima, Peru, late in 1938. Under the leadership of Secretary of State Hull, this conference adopted the "Declaration of Lima." This was a collective security pact in which all American nations agreed to defend themselves and one another against any threat to their peace, their republican institutions, or their territorial integrity. The conference also favored the lowering of trade barriers, and it condemned racial and religious persecution.

Victoria Square, Montreal, is an attractive area in Canada's largest city.

646

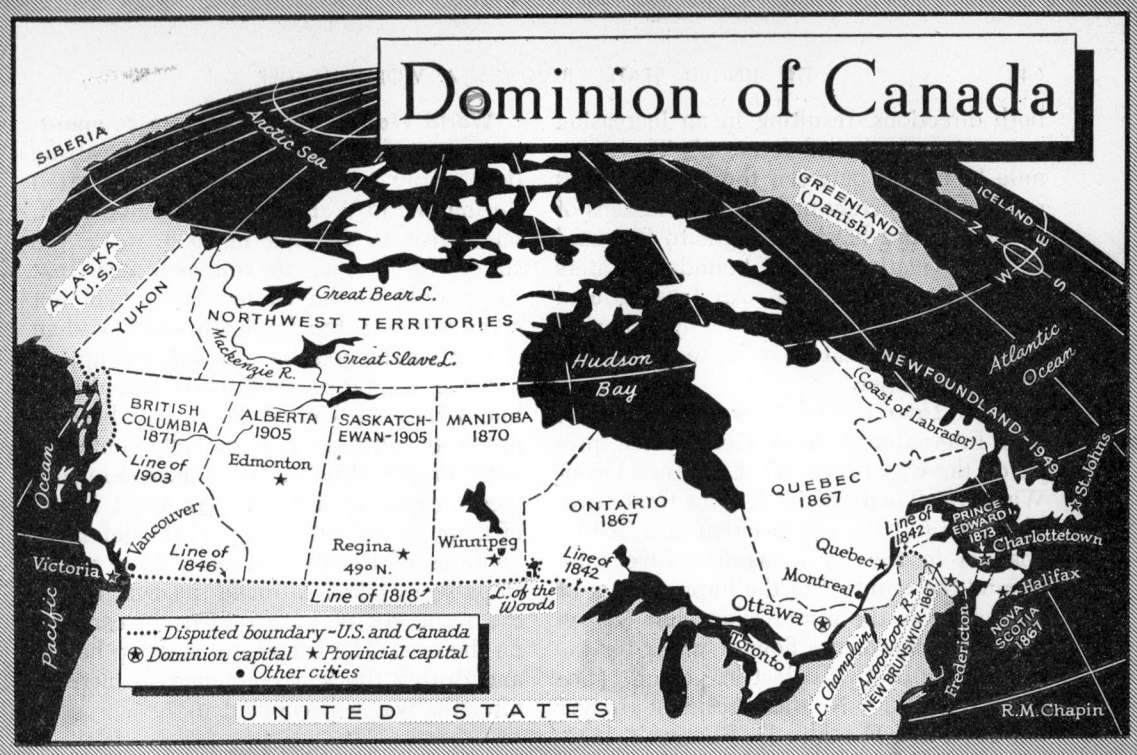

Dominion of Canada

Map labels: SIBERIA, Arctic Sea, ALASKA (U.S.), YUKON, NORTHWEST TERRITORIES, Great Bear L., Mackenzie R., Great Slave L., BRITISH COLUMBIA 1871, Line of 1903, ALBERTA 1905, Edmonton, SASKATCH-EWAN-1905, MANITOBA 1870, Hudson Bay, GREENLAND (Danish), ICELAND, NEWFOUNDLAND-1949, (Coast of Labrador), Atlantic Ocean, Vancouver, Line of 1846, Victoria, Regina, 49° N., Winnipeg, Line of 1842, ONTARIO 1867, QUEBEC 1867, Quebec, Line of 1842, Montreal, Ottawa, Toronto, L. Champlain, PRINCE EDWARD I. 1873, Charlottetown, Halifax, NOVA SCOTIA 1867, NEW BRUNSWICK-1867, Aroostook R., Fredericton, St. Johns, Ocean, Pacific, Line of 1818, L. of the Woods

Legend:
..... Disputed boundary – U.S. and Canada
⊗ Dominion capital ★ Provincial capital
• Other cities

UNITED STATES

R. M. Chapin

Relations between Canada and the United States have been close and friendly since 1814, when their last conflict occurred. The boundary between them has no defenses. Boundary disputes have been settled by arbitration, as follows: 1818 — A treaty between the United States and Great Britain stated that the 49th parallel should be the boundary from the Lake of the Woods to the Rocky Mountains; 1842 — The Webster-Ashburton Treaty determined the boundary between Maine and New Brunswick, as well as the boundary in the area between the Lake of the Woods and Lake Superior; 1846 — A treaty between the United States and Great Britain extended the boundary along the 49th parallel from the Rocky Mountains to the Pacific; 1903 — A tribunal including representatives from the United States, Canada, and Great Britain established the boundary between Alaska and British Columbia.

Inter-American unity during and after World War II will be discussed in Chapter 40. Hope was expressed after the war that Canada, too, might become a member of the Pan American Union, thus filling a place that had been vacant since the Union was started.

The United States and Canada have similar interests. Meanwhile, relations with our northern neighbor had become closer. After World War I, Canada became an independent member of the British Commonwealth of Nations. Though still loyal to the British crown, she was in control of both her domestic and foreign affairs. Since 1927 Canada has carried on diplomatic relations directly with Washington, and rela-

tions between the two countries have been on a very friendly basis. Canadians have migrated to the United States without quota restrictions (page 588), and in turn many Americans have moved into the Canadian agricultural west. For its protection Canada is dependent upon the principles of the Monroe Doctrine as well as upon the British navy and its own resources. About 4 billion dollars of American capital are invested in Canada, and this investment has given the United States a lively interest in that country's economic welfare. In the words of Leighton McCarthy, Canadian Minister to the United States (1943), "Capital, population, and ideas have flowed freely across the border, in both directions, resulting in an increasing unity of outlook and interest." The 3000-mile boundary between the two countries remains completely unfortified. Citizens of both countries have the right to free and equal navigation of the boundary waters and of Lake Michigan. An International Joint Commission has been set up to handle any questions that may arise along the common frontier.

A St. Lawrence waterway is rejected. The International Joint Commission prepared the way for the St. Lawrence Deep-Waterway Treaty of 1932. This treaty provided for (1) the construction of a 27-foot channel in the St. Lawrence River and around the rapids, (2) the improvement of navigation in the upper lakes, and (3) an equal division of the flow of water for the production of hydroelectric power. (See map, page 573.) Neither President Hoover nor President Franklin D. Roosevelt, however, was able to secure the ratification of this treaty by the United States Senate.

Our volume of trade with Canada is great. Trade with Canada is a matter of vital importance, since each country is the other's best customer. Canadian resentment at the Hawley-Smoot Tariff (page 544) was promptly shown by a Canadian tariff directed against the United States (1930). However, a remedy was soon found in the Trade Agreements Act (page 545), and the reciprocal trade agreements drawn up between the United States and Canada were far-reaching in their effects.

World War II brings complete co-operation. The fact that the Monroe Doctrine does apply to Canada was demonstrated during World War II. President Roosevelt, on a visit to Canada in 1938, made the statement, "I give to you assurance that the people of the United States will not stand idly by if the domination of Canadian soil is threatened by any other empire." Two years later, when Canada was at war, but before the United States had become involved, President Roosevelt conferred with Prime Minister Mackenzie King on measures of defense. A Permanent Board of Defense was set up to pool the defensive facilities of the two nations. As a result, steps were taken to make the best use of the resources of both nations in carrying on the war. The friendship built up before and during the war continued to increase after the war was concluded.

——————— CHECK-UP ———————

What changes in policy have led to unity in the Western Hemisphere?

1. Why did Latin America mistrust United States policy under the Monroe Doctrine and the Roosevelt corollary?
2. How did the Good Neighbor policy conciliate Latin America? What is the significance of the Declaration of Lima?
3. How have economic ties between the United States and Canada become stronger? How did conditions during World War II and in the period after the war lead to more complete co-operation between the two countries?

CHAPTER REVIEW

Terms to Understand

protectorate	dollar diplomacy
mestizo	intervention
mulatto	"watchful waiting"
zambo	ABC powers
dictatorship	subsurface rights
peons	collective security pact
anti-clerical	territorial integrity
lock canal	right of intervention
dependency	

People and Things to Know About

temperate zone	Porfirio Diaz
tropical zone	Francisco Madero

People and Things to Know About (Cont.)

Hay-Pauncefote Treaty	Victoriano Huerta
Hay-Bunau-Varilla Treaty	Pancho Villa
	John J. Pershing
Theodore Roosevelt	Dwight W. Morrow
G. W. Goethals	Lázaro Cárdenas
W. D. Gorgas	Avila Camacho
Venezuelan debt settlement	Pan-American Conference
Roosevelt corollary to Monroe Doctrine	Cordell Hull
Woodrow Wilson	Good Neighbor policy
	Declaration of Lima
Franklin D. Roosevelt	St. Lawrence waterway
Virgin Islands	Mackenzie King

Historic Dates to Identify

1903	1917	1938
1914	1933	

Questions to Discuss

1. Why does Latin America tend to look to Spain and France for cultural leadership (literature, music, education)?

2. Compare the following:

   (a) United States relations with Latin America before and after 1930.

   (b) United States and Latin American views on this country's right to intervention.

   (c) United States and Latin American views on our acquisition of the Panama Canal Zone.

3. Why did the United States after 1898 wish to build and fortify an interoceanic canal? Why did Great Britain approve?

4. Compare the reaction to the Roosevelt corollary of businessmen from Spain, Germany, the United States, and Argentina? Of a Republican and a Democrat?

5. How has United States foreign policy changed from 1823, when the Monroe Doctrine was issued, through the period of the Roosevelt corollary, and to the present?

6. Theodore Roosevelt summed up his policy toward other republics in the Western Hemisphere in this phrase: "Speak softly and carry a big stick." What did he mean? Do you think such a policy was justified?

7. How does the idea of land and mineral rights given in the Mexican Constitution of 1917 differ from that held in this country? Do Mexicans have the right to differ from us on this question?

8. Why did President Wilson favor a policy of "watchful waiting" with respect to Mexico?

Relating Geography and History

1. Use a globe or a world map to help you visualize the relation (distance, direction, and nearness to equator) of South America to the United States, Europe, Africa. Compare the distances by water from New York and New Orleans to Rio de Janeiro and Buenos Aires, with the distances of the latter cities from London and Cadiz, Spain.

2. Use the map of the Caribbean area in this text, page 639, to identify United States territories and countries over which this country established a protectorate between 1898 and 1933. By using the map explain why the United States adopted the policy set forth in the Roosevelt corollary? Why was the United States willing to change this policy after 1939?

Other Things to Do

1. Plan a program of Latin American music, or an exhibit of Latin American art and handicraft. By looking in *Readers' Guide* you may find articles discussing efforts to revive old Indian skills in weaving, pottery, hammered silver, and so on.

2. Use *Readers' Guide* to locate articles dealing with United States-Latin American relations since World War II, and report your findings to the class. Consider such problems as (1) ability of this country to absorb Latin American exports, (2) effect on Latin America of post-war inflation in this country, and (3) failure to provide Marshall Plan aid for Latin America.

*3. Make a list of conflicts since 1823 involving the United States and Mexico. Include (1) the issue and date of conflict, (2) United States point of view, and (3) Mexican point of view.

4. Write a letter to the Pan American Union, Washington, D.C., to learn what materials published by that organization are available to your class free or through purchase.

5. Debate: *Resolved*, That the United States should ratify the treaty with Canada to complete the St. Lawrence waterway. Look up additional material on this topic.

Chinese rice farmer

Chapter 36

THE UNITED STATES TAKES AN ACTIVE

PART IN FAR EASTERN AFFAIRS

Asking only the open door for ourselves, we are ready to accord the open door to others.

William McKinley, 1898

The years which followed the Spanish-American War found the interests and the power of the United States expanding in the Far East as well as in the Western Hemisphere. Our annexation of the Philippine Islands had a great effect upon our Far Eastern policy. As you have seen (page 621), one of the convincing arguments in favor of annexing the Philippines had been the nearness of the island to China and their advantage as a springboard for the development of trade with China. The United States soon found, however, that other countries were determined to get this trade for themselves. They were even trying to bring about the partition of China for their own benefit.

Possession of the Philippines also affected our relations with Japan. We found ourselves in Japan's back yard, and the nearest route from our west coast to Manila, capital of the Philippines, was by way of Yokohama, Japan. It was apparent that we would have difficulty in defending the Philippines if we became involved in any Far Eastern conflict. As Theodore Roosevelt expressed it, "The Philippine Islands

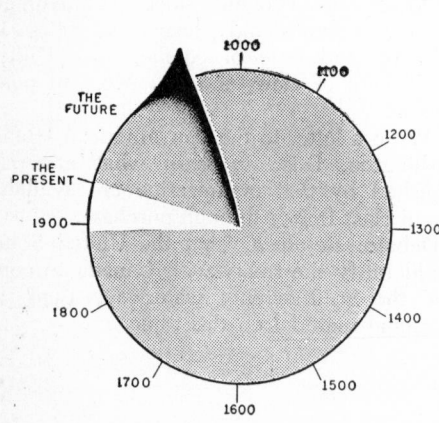

1897 – The Present

form our heel of Achilles." Japan, just beginning to take her place as a world power, considered the western Pacific her own sphere of influence, and resented our presence there.

This chapter will present our relations with the Far East under the following topics:

1. The United States sponsors an Open Door policy in the Far East.
2. Japanese imperialism threatens the Open Door.
3. Japan closes the Open Door.

1 The United States Sponsors an Open Door Policy in the Far East

Secretary of State Hay proclaims the "Open Door." American ships had been carrying on trade with China ever since the early days of the republic, and more recently with Japan.[1] When we obtained a foothold in the Philippines and coaling stations in the Pacific at the close of the 1800's, we had great hopes that this trade would be increased. Unfortunately for our hopes, however, conditions in China were in a state of confusion. After a war between Japan and China revealed how weak China really was, powerful European countries forced China to lease some of her important ports to them (see map, page 655). They also acquired "spheres of interest" over areas in China, where they built railroads and enriched themselves by exploiting the natural resources.

Fearing that leased territories and spheres of interest threatened our commercial rights, Secretary of State John Hay sent communications to the European powers and to Japan in 1899. He asked each nation to state formally (1) that it would not interfere with any port opened by treaty, or with any nation's interests which had been legally established within its sphere of influence, and (2) that there would be no discrimination against citizens of other nations with regard to tariffs, harbor dues, or railway charges. Each nation agreed somewhat reluctantly to the principles set forth in Hay's notes, but only on condition that the other powers would also agree. In 1900 Hay boldly announced that all the nations had given a final and positive acceptance of what he had called the *Open Door policy* in China.

The Chinese rise against foreigners in the Boxer Rebellion. Meanwhile, a tide of resentment against European selfishness was rising in China itself. A patriotic society, known as the "Boxers," began to agitate against the "foreign devils," and their uprising soon developed into organized rebellion. In 1900 bands of Boxers, joined by Chinese government forces, attacked and murdered missionaries and other residents. They gained control of the territory around the capital city, Peking (now Peiping), and cut off communication with the outside world. Foreigners in Peking took refuge in the British legation. The leading nations, including the United States, combined forces and sent an expedition to relieve the city. It arrived just in time to save the besieged diplomats and missionaries.

China now faced a reckoning with the angry foreign powers. Secretary Hay, however, did not want the foreign nations to grab still more of China's territory. He preferred a solution which would "preserve Chinese territorial and administrative entity . . . and safeguard for the world the principle of equal and impartial trade with all parts of the Chinese Empire." In the end, his ideas were followed. Although spared further loss of territory, China was compelled to pay 333 million dollars to the various nations for their losses. The United States was to receive some 24 million dollars, but less than half of this sum was needed to meet the claims of American citizens for losses suffered in the Boxer Rebellion. Later the United States canceled the rest of the debt, and this amount was

[1] Caleb Cushing, a shrewd lawyer and diplomat, negotiated a treaty of commerce with China in 1844. For Perry's journey to Japan, see page 286.

The Russian-Japanese War was brought to an end by a treaty arranged at the peace conference sponsored by Theodore Roosevelt.

used by the Chinese government to provide scholarships for Chinese students who wished to study in China or the United States. For the time, at least, China escaped being divided, and the policy of equal trade privileges and the Open Door for all nations had won a victory.

Russia and Japan fight over Chinese territory. Not long after the Boxer Rebellion, war over Chinese territory broke out between Russia and Japan. Japan had been strengthened by a treaty of alliance made with Great Britain in 1902. Resenting Russian expansion in Manchuria (see map, page 655), Japan declared war on Russia in 1904. Although Japan won some striking victories on land and sea, she was fast nearing the end of her financial resources when President Theodore Roosevelt offered his services as mediator. Russian and Japanese commissioners met with Roosevelt in Portsmouth, New Hampshire, and a peace treaty was signed in September, 1905. Russian interests in Manchuria were transferred to Japan, and Russia recognized Japan's dominant interest in Korea. Russia also ceded to Japan the southern half of the island called Sakhalin (see map, page 655).

Relations between the United States and Japan become less friendly. Our relations with Japan became less friendly after the Russian-Japanese War. For one thing, the Japanese had wanted Russia to pay them a large sum of money as an indemnity, and they felt that President Roosevelt's influence at the peace conference had kept them from getting it. Of equal importance was the problem raised by the American treatment of Japanese immigrants. As has been pointed out (page 587), some of the western states, particularly California, passed laws discriminating against the Japanese who had already arrived. President Theodore Roosevelt tried to smooth over the situation by working out the "Gentlemen's Agreement" with Japan, but resentment against the United States continued.

One of the most important reasons for the growing coolness between Japan and the United States was Japan's attitude toward China. It appeared that Japan was beginning to extend her economic influence in the Far East and was determined to close the Open Door. Moreover, Americans were afraid that Japan had plans for the conquest of the Philippine Islands. By 1907, many people were sure that war between Japan and the United States was not far off.

Our fleet makes a world cruise. To inspire respect for our naval power, and thus make sure that the disagreements with Japan would be settled peaceably, Roosevelt decided to send a fleet of sixteen battleships, six destroyers, and six auxiliary ships on a cruise around the world. Congress at first refused to grant him the necessary funds, but the President had sufficient money to send the fleet to San Francisco, and he declared it would stay there until Congress voted more. In the face of his insistence, Congress gave way. The fleet stopped at South American ports, Hawaii, New Zealand, Australia, the Philippines, China, and Japan. The American sailors were nowhere received with greater enthusiasm than in Yokohama. After a trip through the Suez Canal and across the Atlantic, the fleet steamed back into American waters early in 1909. Greeting the sailors upon their return, President Roosevelt said, "As a war machine the fleet comes back in better shape than it went out. . . . In addition you have shown yourselves the best of all possible ambassadors and heralds of peace. Wherever you have landed you have borne yourselves so as to make us at home proud of being your countrymen."

The Root-Takahira Agreement is signed. While the fleet was on its way, our tense relations with Japan were relieved by the signing at Washington of the Root-Takahira Agreement (1908). Japan recognized American sovereignty in the Philippines, even though the islands were located in an area which Japan regarded as its own sphere of influence. In turn the United States acknowledged Japanese influence in Manchuria and its control of Korea. The agreement also provided that the two powers were determined to support "by all pacific [peaceful] means at their disposal the independence and integrity of China and the principle of equal opportunity for commerce and industry of all nations in that Empire." The special interests of Japan in Manchuria and Korea had already been recognized by other powers, and two years later Korea was made a Japanese possession.

Dollar diplomacy reaches the Far East. President Taft and his Secretary of State, Philander C. Knox, encouraged the investment of American money in China as a means of keeping open the door for American trade. Secretary Knox first proposed that the various great powers join in lending China enough money to acquire the railroads controlled by foreign nations (1909). When Japan and Russia objected to this proposal, Knox tried to obtain for American bankers a share in the foreign loans made to China. Only a small amount of American capital, however, had been invested in China when President Wilson came into office. President Wilson immediately reversed Knox's policy (1913). In Wilson's opinion the conditions under which such loans were made threatened the independence of China, and

"might conceivably go to the length on some unhappy contingency of forcible interference in the financial and even the political affairs of that great Oriental state." Four years later, however, during World War I, the American government approved the participation of American bankers in a Chinese loan.

——— CHECK-UP ———

What became the basic policy of the United States in the Far East?

1. Why did the United States try to persuade other powers to accept an Open Door policy in China? What were the main features of the Open Door policy?
2. How did China react to foreign interference? What were the results?
3 Why did Russia and Japan go to war over Manchuria? What were the results?
4. What problems disturbed friendly relations between the United States and Japan?

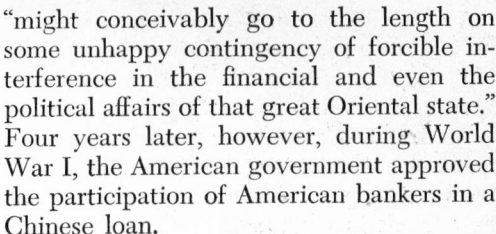

2 **Japanese Imperialism Threatens the Open Door**

World War I strengthens Japan. World War I, which began in August, 1914, played directly into the hands of the Japanese imperialists. Japan immediately took advantage of the fact that Germany was unable to defend her possessions in the Far East. Before the end of 1914 she had taken not only Kiaochow (jyow-jo), which China had leased to Germany, but also the entire province of Shantung (see map, page 655) and the German islands in the Pacific north of the equator. Also taking advantage of the fact that the other European powers had to give their attention to the war, Japan presented China (1915) with the so-called Twenty-one Demands (for special privileges). The Twenty-one Demands were intended to close the Open Door and to make Japan supreme in China.

Korean dress

The United States intervenes. Japan's policy of aggression in China alarmed the United States. Secretary of State Bryan bluntly notified Japan and China that the United States "cannot recognize any agreement or undertaking . . . [which impairs] the treaty rights of the United States and its citizens in China, the political or territorial integrity of the Republic of China, or the international policy relative to China commonly known as the open door policy." As a result of our protests, Japan gave up the extreme demands she had made on China.

Two years later (1917) the United States and Japan attempted to reach an understanding over their aims in China. In the Lansing-Ishii Agreement the two countries declared that they would follow the Open Door policy and guarantee China's independence. On the other hand, the United States gave in to Japan by recognizing that "territorial propinquity [nearness] creates special relations between countries," and by admitting that "Japan has special interests in China."

Japan is allowed to hold her gains. At the peace conference following World War I, Japan was able to consolidate her gains in the Pacific area. The treaty recognized her conquest of the German holdings in Shantung province and also her control of the German islands in the Pacific north of the equator (see map on next page). Japan agreed that eventually she would get out of Shantung, a promise which she later kept. The Pacific islands were granted to Japan in 1919 as a *mandate* under the League of Nations; that is, Japan was to have full authority to establish a government and to develop the islands as she wished, but she would be responsible to the League of Nations for her activities there. Japan was not supposed to fortify the islands, however.[2]

President Wilson did not entirely approve of these terms, but he agreed to them in order to obtain Japan's approval of the peace treaty and the League of Nations. Japan was now a strong power in

---

[2] But Japan violated the mandate and fortified the islands.

the Pacific, and her aggressive attitude toward China was a serious threat to the Open Door and China's independence.

A disarmament conference is held in Washington. Partly because of the situation in the Pacific, President Harding called a disarmament conference to meet in Washington in the autumn of 1921. Naval rivalry had led to an armament race which placed a heavy burden on countries already greatly in debt because of World War I. At first only Great Britain, France, Italy, and Japan were invited to take part in the conference. Later, invitations were extended to all of the powers, except Russia, which were directly interested in the Far Eastern situation.

A four-power treaty is signed. During the conference, much serious thought was given to the situation in the Far East. The object was to remove, if possible, conditions in that area which might lead to international conflict. With this aim in mind the United States, Great Britain, France, and Japan signed a treaty "to respect their rights in relation to their insular possessions and insular dominions in the region of the Pacific Ocean." Any disputes arising among these powers, which could not be settled by their own diplomatic representatives, were to be considered and adjusted in a joint conference of the four powers. Thus the treaty of alliance between Great Britain and Japan, which had been in effect for many years, was replaced by a four-power treaty.[3]

The Open Door policy is preserved. In addition, a nine-power treaty among all the countries represented at the disarmament conference guaranteed the independence of China and the continuation of the Open Door policy. By this treaty equal opportunity in China was again promised for all. The nine powers went further and accepted the principle of China's control over her own tariff. They also called for the creation of a commission which would

---

[3] In case of war, there was no chance that Canada, Australia, or New Zealand would support Japan against the United States. They put pressure on Great Britain to get out of the alliance with Japan, and she was eager to do so.

The Far East About 1939

Railroads
★ Capital cities
Br. British F French P Portuguese
Japanese

U. S. S. R.

Trans-Siberian

SAKHALIN

OUTER MONGOLIA

(MANCHURIA)

MANCHUKUO

KURIL IS.

INNER MONGOLIA

Great Wall

Yellow R.

Mukden

Vladivostok

Peiping (Peking)

CHOSEN (KOREA)

JAPAN

Tientsin

Port Arthur

Br.

Seoul

CHINA

Weihaiwei

Shantung

Tsingtao (Kiaochow)

Kobe

Tokyo

Nagoya

Yokohama

Nanking

Hankow

Nagasaki

Chungking (Wartime capital)

Shanghai

Yangtze R. ★

Kwangchowan

Canton

Br.

F

TAIWAN (FORMOSA)

FRENCH INDO-CHINA

Macau

P

Hong Kong

HAINAN

R. M. Chapin.

Shanghai

RYUKYU IS.

Pacific Ocean

Japanese Mandate 1919

PHILIPPINES

MARIANAS IS.

Guam (U.S.)

PALAU IS.

MARSHALL IS.

CAROLINE IS.

Equator

What world powers had important holdings in the Far East in 1939? Why was Japan at war with China? Why was Japan a rival of both the United States and the U.S.S.R.?

study the question of doing away entirely with extraterritoriality in China (the special privileges enjoyed by foreigners).

As a result of these two treaties, the United States seemed to have acquired wide support for the principle of the Open Door and the independence of China. The United States Senate ratified the various agreements drawn up at the Washington Conference, but it did so with a reservation. The Senate stated that the United States had no intention of departing from its traditional policy of staying aloof from entangling alliances and from participation in the affairs of other nations.

An immigration law brings further trouble. The immigration law of 1924 had serious effects upon our relations with Japan. Since 1907 Japanese immigration to the United States had been restricted under the Gentlemen's Agreement, but there had been no legal restrictions as such. Nevertheless, the Japanese population in the western states continued to grow. Several of them passed anti-Japanese laws, and demanded complete exclusion of the Japanese. In the immigration law of 1924 (page 588), over the objections of President Coolidge and Secretary of State Hughes, Congress declared that "aliens not

Carrying tea, China

eligible for citizenship," which included the Japanese, be barred from admission into the United States and its territories, except for certain classes of individuals.

Japan is angered. Japan was bitter over this discrimination. Her officials called attention to "grave consequences" which would result because the law would endanger the friendly relations between the two countries. In spite of this "veiled threat," Congress passed the bill by large majorities. President Coolidge signed the bill after stating that if the provision calling for Japanese exclusion had stood by itself, he would have vetoed it.

Japan placed on record a "solemn protest" against the clause which put her people in a position less favorable than that of any Europeans. The day that the law went into effect was observed in Japan as a day of national humiliation. It was not exclusion that they resented; exclusion might have been accomplished in various ways. But racial discrimination could never be forgiven by the proud Japanese. The militarists in Japan (those who favored a warlike policy) also held the United States responsible for checking Japan's imperialistic aims in China. Many Japanese felt that their country had sufficient excuse for closing the Open Door in the Far East permanently, by force if necessary.

——————— CHECK-UP ———————

Why did Japanese imperialism threaten the Open Door policy?

1. How did Japan strengthen its position during World War I? What territories were acquired? Why did the United States object to Japan's Twenty-one Demands on China?

2. What agreements concerning the Far East were reached at the Washington Conference?

3. Why did the United States Immigration Act of 1924 anger Japan?

3 Japan Closes the Open Door

Japan takes advantage of civil war in China. The march of events in China during the 1920's again played into the hands of the Japanese militarists. The Manchu dynasty in China had been overthrown in 1911 and a republic established. Beginning in 1923, a new nationalist government in China (called the Kuomintang) tried to build China into a modern state. The Kuomintang (gwo′min-tahng) was first headed by Dr. Sun Yat-sen and later by Chiang Kai-shek (chee-ahng′ kye-shek′). It was not long before the nationalist government clashed with Japanese interests in Manchuria. In 1928 a militarist government in Japan notified both the nationalist government in Nanking and a rival government in Peking that it would not allow the civil war to spread into Manchuria and Mongolia. In Japan the army and navy were responsible, not to the civil government, but directly to the Emperor. The militarists were therefore able to carry out a "positive policy" in China, leaving the civil government to protest its peaceful intentions and its desire to carry out its international obligations. It was the Japanese army and navy that now took over in Manchuria and proceeded to carry out a policy which challenged the League of Nations, the nine-power treaty, the four-power treaty, and the Pact of Paris (page 685).

Japan takes advantage of world conditions. World conditions at the time also favored Japan's policy of aggression. Beginning at the end of 1929, depression gradually enveloped Europe and America. The whole economic structure seemed about to collapse, leaving the leading powers with too many problems at home to permit them to carry out a vigorous policy in the Far East. At the same time, the League of Nations was too weak to deal effectively with a crisis in China. In the

United States public opinion seemed to favor a policy of peace. Certainly, the American people would not have been in favor of using force to preserve the Open Door policy or the independence of China.

Manchuria becomes a puppet state. The Japanese war lords late in 1931 took advantage of this situation to invade Manchuria. Soon all of Manchuria was overrun. China appealed to the League of Nations, but received no effective aid. Meanwhile, in 1932 Secretary of State Henry L. Stimson issued the so-called Stimson Doctrine. This repeated the Bryan warning (page 654) and informed Japan and China that the United States did not intend to "recognize any situation, treaty, or agreement which may be brought about by means contrary to the covenants and obligations of the Pact of Paris of August 27, 1928, to which treaty both China and Japan, as well as the United States, are parties."

In spite of the Stimson Doctrine, Manchuria was promptly proclaimed the sovereign state of Manchukuo — a Japanese puppet state. Secretary Stimson then issued a warning that Japan's violation of the nine-power treaty might release the other powers from the limitation of the naval treaty and fortifications agreement (page 686). Somewhat later (1936), Japan responded by notifying the powers that she no longer considered herself bound by the provisions of the naval treaty.

Japan leaves the League of Nations. In October, 1932, a League committee of investigation (the Lytton Commission) condemned the Japanese attack upon Manchuria and the establishment of the puppet state of Manchukuo. It recommended that Manchuria be established as an independent state within the Chinese republic. It further suggested that the special rights and interests of Japan in Manchuria be recognized and that the nations of the world co-operate to further the internal recovery of China.

When the League Assembly adopted the report of the Lytton Commission, Japan walked out of the Assembly and soon afterward resigned from the League. Japan then insisted that she had the right to act as she saw fit to keep peace and order in eastern Asia. She opposed all attempts on China's part to use the influence of any other nation or nations to resist Japan. When Japan established an oil monopoly in Manchukuo and began to extend her conquests outside of that province, it was evident that the Open Door was closed. Japan claimed that by refusing to recognize Manchukuo the United States had given up any claim to Open Door treatment in that country.

The American Far Eastern policy is relaxed. The administration of President Franklin D. Roosevelt, faced with serious social and economic problems at home, at first adopted a hands-off attitude toward Japanese expansion in China. At the time, the Far Eastern situation did not seem to affect American interests seriously. The Stimson Doctrine was not modified, but the President was not inclined to make the Japanese attitude a matter of international concern. American capital represented only about 6 per cent of all foreign investments in China. Our trade with China amounted to only 2 per cent of our foreign trade, while about 25 per cent of our foreign trade was with Japan. It was to our economic advantage not to provoke Japan, and strong popular feeling against war was at its height in the United States.

Under the circumstances, Secretary of State Cordell Hull agreed with Japanese Foreign Minister Hirota that "no question exists between our two countries that is incapable of amicable solution." Secretary Hull insisted that American treaty rights be recognized but notified the Japanese Foreign Minister in 1934, "The American government has dedicated the United States to

Sampan, China

the policy of the Good Neighbor, and to the practical application of that policy it will continue, on its own part and in association with other governments, to devote its best efforts." The Good Neighbor policy in the Far East was a failure, as we shall see in Chapter 39, and finally was abandoned before we became involved in World War II.

──────── CHECK-UP ────────

How did Japan try to close the open door in China?

1. Why did Japan adopt an unfriendly policy toward the Kuomintang government?

How did conditions throughout the world help to further Japan's policy of aggression in China?

2. How did Japan extend its influence in Manchuria in 1931? What was Manchukuo?
3. What attitude did Secretary of State Stimson take toward Japan's aggression in Manchuria? What was the attitude of the League of Nations?
4. Why did Japan leave the League of Nations? What action did the United States and Japan take with respect to the treaty limiting naval armaments?
5. What attitude did Franklin D. Roosevelt take toward Japan in the early years of his administration? Why?

CHAPTER REVIEW

Terms to Understand

lease
sphere of influence
mandate
puppet state
extraterritoriality
discrimination
militarists

People and Things to Know About

"Boxers"
Gentlemen's Agreement
Open Door policy
John Hay
Boxer Rebellion
Russian-Japanese War
Root-Takahira agreement
Twenty-one Demands
Lansing-Ishii agreement
four-power treaty
nine-power treaty
Immigration Act of 1924
Kuomintang
Sun Yat-sen
Chiang Kai-shek
Manchuria
Henry L. Stimson
Stimson Doctrine
Manchukuo
Washington Conference

Historic Dates to Identify

1899   1900   1905
1921   1924   1932

Questions to Discuss

1. Why was China in the late 1800's unable to defend herself against aggression?
2. Compare the following:
   (a) Japanese and United States policy in China, 1895–1941.
   (b) Monroe Doctrine and the Open Door policy.
3. What goals was the United States seeking at the Washington Conference?
4. Why did Japan initiate a policy of aggres-

Questions to Discuss (Cont.)

sion in the Far East in the early 1930's? What was her goal?

Relating Geography and History

1. On an outline map of eastern Asia and the western Pacific locate the following: China, Japan, Manchuria, Korea, Asiatic Russia, the Philippines, Japanese mandated islands, islands held by the United States before World War II.
2. In 1948 an air force bomber circled the globe in a non-stop flight of a few days, refueling in the air. Compare this flight with the cruise of the fleet around the world early in the century. What conclusions do you reach?

Other Things to Do

1. See if you can learn why Great Britain sought an alliance with Japan before World War I and was willing to renounce this alliance after that war. Report your findings to the class.
*2. Make a list of the steps in our relations with Japan since 1900. Explain each briefly.
3. If you are near a university you may be able to arrange for a student from a Far Eastern country to talk to your class. Perhaps he will be willing to discuss the attitude of Asiatics to the Immigration Act of 1924 or to give his point of view on the present situation in the Far East.
4. Debate: *Resolved,* That the United States has followed a consistent policy in the Far East.

War!

THE UNITED STATES FIGHTS FOR

DEMOCRACY IN WORLD WAR I

The world must be made safe for democracy. Its peace must be planted upon the tested foundations of political liberty. We have no selfish ends to serve. We desire no conquest, no dominion. We seek no indemnities for ourselves, no material compensations for the sacrifices we shall freely make. . . . America is privileged to spend her blood and her might for the principles that gave her birth and happiness and the peace which she has treasured. God helping her, she can do no other.

Woodrow Wilson, 1917

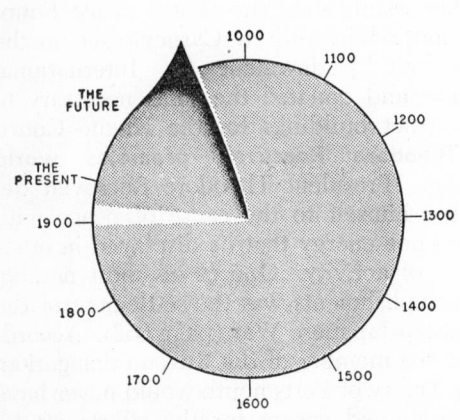

In the early years of the twentieth century opposing forces were at work in the relations among nations. One was pushing in the direction of the preservation of peace; the other was working toward war. Outwardly every important nation protested that it desired peace, and by 1914 the world peace movement had made considerable headway. War had become such a terrible engine of destruction that the nations could be expected to do everything in their power to avoid an appeal to armed force. The desperate efforts put forth after 1900 in one European crisis after another were evidence enough that the world wished to avoid war.

On the other hand, by 1914 Europe was an armed camp, divided into two hostile combinations of nations. The Triple Alliance, consisting of Germany, Austria-Hungary, and Italy, was offset by the Triple Entente, which included Great Britain,

France, and Russia. The ambitions of the European nations aroused jealousies that were a continual threat to peace. The German Empire, recently united by the policy of force known as "blood and iron," was anxious to expand. Germany was convinced that it was being crushed by the ring of Entente Powers, and her people looked forward to "Der Tag" (the day) when she would gain her rightful position of power among the nations of the earth.

For her part Great Britain was thoroughly alarmed by the rapid expansion of German commerce and industry and by the growth of the German navy. She saw her economic supremacy threatened as well as her control of the seas. To make matters worse, France had not forgotten her humiliation at the hands of Germany in the Franco-Prussian War some 40 years before and still looked forward to a day of revenge. Moreover, the leading countries were fully prepared for war. In a crisis some of them were likely to put on armed demonstrations or "rattle the saber." This state of affairs only increased the likelihood that sooner or later the peace of Europe would be shattered.

This chapter will include a discussion of the following topics:

1. The world peace movement makes headway.
2. World War I engulfs Europe and affects the United States.
3. The United States enters the war.
4. The country is mobilized for war.
5. American armed forces play their part in winning the war.

1 The World Peace Movement Makes Headway

The United States takes part in two peace conferences. In the years immediately before the outbreak of World War I, the United States played a prominent part in efforts to promote peace. It took the lead in settling international disputes by arbitration. It also took part in an international peace conference which met in 1899 at The Hague in the Netherlands at the call of the czar of Russia. Here agreements were signed permitting neutral nations to offer their services to prevent war or to bring war to an end. A nation involved in a dispute was given the right to call for a commission of inquiry. The delegates at the conference also agreed that a Permanent Court of Arbitration should be established at The Hague, to which countries might submit their disputes.

In 1907 a second Hague conference representing 44 powers was called by the czar and President Theodore Roosevelt. At this conference new rules were adopted to lessen the horrors of war. The conference also approved a principle known as the Drago Doctrine, which had been suggested by Luis Drago (drah′go), foreign minister for the Argentine. According to the Drago Doctrine, debts should not be collected by force "unless the debtor country refused arbitration, or having accepted arbitration, failed to submit to the award."

Prominent American citizens also contributed handsomely to the cause of peace. For example, Edwin Ginn, a Boston publisher, established the World Peace Foundation, while Andrew Carnegie set up the Carnegie Endowment for International Peace and donated the sums necessary to construct buildings for the Hague Court.

Theodore Roosevelt promotes world peace. President Theodore Roosevelt devoted himself to the cause of peace with the same energy that he displayed in other lines of activity. One of his most notable accomplishments was the settlement of the Russian-Japanese War (page 652). According to a member of the Russian delegation, the Treaty of Portsmouth would never have been signed except for the efforts of the American President. "The man who had been represented to us as impetuous to the point of rudeness," he wrote, "displayed a gentleness, a kindness, and a tactfulness, mixed with self-control, that only a truly great man can command." It was Roosevelt too who urged France to take part in the conference held at Algeciras (al-jeh-see'rass) in Spain (1906) to prevent a break between France and Germany over the control of Morocco, in North Africa. Roosevelt also tried to iron out ill feeling between the United States and Japan (page 587). He further contributed to the peace movement by arranging treaties of arbitration with the leading European countries. For his numerous services in the cause of international peace Roosevelt was awarded the Nobel Peace Prize in 1906.

Other Presidents support the peace movement. President Theodore Roosevelt's successors made further efforts to have disputes between nations submitted to arbitration. President Taft arranged treaties with Great Britain and France which stated that all questions which could be settled by a court of justice should be submitted to arbitration. The Senate, however, refused to approve these treaties.

Undiscouraged by this failure, Secretary of State Bryan, who vigorously supported the peace movement during the Wilson administration, took up the policy of settling international disputes by arbitration. At his suggestion a proposal was made to all nations which had diplomatic representatives at Washington. This proposal suggested that they enter into agreements with the United States to submit to an international commission "all questions of whatever character and nature in dispute between them." In each case a year was to be allowed for the commission to investigate and make a report, and in the meantime the disputing nations were not to resort to war or to increase their military strength. Secretary Bryan negotiated 31 such treaties with the leading powers of the world, not including Germany, Austria, or Turkey, and the Senate promptly ratified them. Despite these efforts, however, the grim gods of war cast everlengthening shadows across the face of Europe. Before the last of the arbitration treaties went into effect, that continent was plunged into the most terrible conflict the world had witnessed up to that time.

—————— CHECK-UP ——————

What support did the United States give to world peace movements?

1. What were the achievements of the Hague Peace Conferences?
2. What private individuals made important contributions to the cause of world peace?
3. What did President Theodore Roosevelt do for the cause of peace? President Taft? Secretary of State Bryan? How successful were their efforts?

2 World War I Engulfs Europe and Affects the United States

World War I begins. A political assassination in the Balkan peninsula [1] furnished the spark which set the world aflame. On June 28, 1914, the Austrian Archduke Francis Ferdinand and his wife were fatally shot by a youthful Serb in Sarajevo (sah'ruh-yeh-vo), a little town in what is now Yugoslavia. Austria held Serbia responsible for the anti-Austrian propaganda in the province of Bosnia which, it was charged, had led to the assassination.[2] For a tense month European diplomats labored to prevent a conflict between the two countries, or, if war was inevitable, to confine it to the Balkans. Austria, however, was not satisfied with Serbia's response to her extreme demands. Having the backing of her powerful ally, Germany, she declared war upon the little Balkan state on July 28.

Europe mobilizes. The war spread across Europe with the speed of a prairie fire. Russia, coming to the aid of Serbia, ordered a general mobilization of its forces two days later. At once Germany sprang to the support of Austria and declared war upon

[1] Countries of the Balkan peninsula included Montenegro, Serbia, Albania, Bulgaria, Rumania, Greece, and Turkey.

[2] Bosnia was a province largely inhabited by Serbs, which had been a part of the old Turkish Empire. It was formally annexed by Austria in 1908. This action caused ill feeling, both in Serbia, which had hoped to annex Bosnia, and in the province itself.

German

Austrian

Russia (August 1). Moreover, w h e n France, the ally of Russia, failed to declare her neutrality within 48 hours, Germany declared war upon France (August 3).

Squeezed between enemy powers to the east and west, Germany put into execution a plan for immediate action and launched a swift thrust at France. To avoid the powerful fortresses along the French border, the German armies invaded neutral Belgium and the tiny state of Luxemburg. The attack on Belgium helped to bring Great Britain into the conflict on the side of her allies, France and Russia (August 4). Because of alliances and promises of gain, other countries became involved in the struggle. At last the Central Powers — Germany, Austria-Hungary, Bulgaria, and Turkey — were pitted against the Allied nations — Great Britain, France, Russia, Serbia, Belgium, Rumania, Japan, Portugal, Montenegro, Greece, and Italy.[3]

The United States declares its neutrality. President Woodrow Wilson at once issued a proclamation of neutrality. He called upon the people of the United States to be "neutral in fact as well as in name" and "impartial in thought as well as in action." To maintain neutrality in fact, however, was not easy. Many naturalized Americans were swayed by love for the lands of their fathers. Thus, while American civilization was closely related to that of England, and the majority of Americans favored the Allies, Americans of German and Austrian origin strongly expressed their sympathy for the Central Powers. Furthermore, Irish-Americans saw a chance to take advantage of Great Britain's involvement in the Euro-

[3] Although Italy had joined the Triple Alliance in the late nineteenth century, her interests more and more became those of the Triple Entente. When the World War broke out, Italy at first hesitated and finally in 1915 entered the conflict on the side of the Allies.

pean war to work for Irish independence.

Widespread propaganda was carried on in the United States by both groups of combatants. Allied propaganda, however, proved to be more effective. This was due partly to widespread sympathy for the Allied cause, and partly to Great Britain's control of the transoceanic cables which carried most of the news published in America about the war.

American economic life is affected. American economic life reacted quickly to the war in Europe. In order to create credit for the purchase of supplies in the United States, English and French holders of American securities proceeded to sell their stocks and bonds on the American exchanges. There followed such a collapse of security values that the New York Stock Exchange was forced to close its doors on July 31, 1914. Unrestricted trading in securities was not resumed for eight months.

As the conflict proceeded, however, such great supplies of war materials were purchased in the United States that our trade with the Allies and neutral European countries increased tremendously. In three years' time the value of American exports to the Allies tripled. American industries were greatly benefited. The increase in industrial activity brought rising wage scales and huge war profits, but it also introduced an era of high prices that worked hardship upon many.

Neutrality proves difficult. Because the United States was the leading source of war materials, neutrality was difficult to maintain. American citizens were free to sell munitions and supplies to both the Central Powers and the Allies. It was the legal right of the nations which were waging war, however, to try to prevent the flow of goods from neutrals to their enemies. Because of superior sea power Great Britain speedily gained control of the sea lanes which led to German ports, thus cutting off direct shipments to that country. In addition, when our trade with neutral European countries swelled suspiciously, British ships began to stop neutral vessels and to seize goods which they believed were going to be reshipped to Germany. The United

States objected to this practice, holding that it "constituted a restriction of the rights of American citizens upon the high seas."

But British interference did not stop at this point. Several months after the outbreak of the war, Great Britain proclaimed a blockade of all German ports. She had earlier given a warning that certain articles would be seized if they were found in the cargoes of ships bound for neutral countries. She now lengthened this list of *contraband* (war supplies or other prohibited articles) until nearly everything that Germany normally imported was prohibited. Furthermore, Great Britain compelled neutral ships to put into British ports for search, and even began the practice of examining American mail. Protests by the United States that the blockade was "ineffective, illegal, and indefensible" fell on deaf ears.

Germany begins submarine warfare. Our grievances against Great Britain, however, soon became unimportant when compared with the troubles caused by Germany's use of submarines. Under the ordinary rules of international law a merchant ship could be stopped by a man-of-war belonging to a nation that was at war. If found carrying contraband, the merchant vessel could be seized and taken to port as a prize. When taking it to port proved to be impracticable, the passengers and crew of the luckless vessel might be removed to a place of safety and the ship sunk. Because of its size and frail construction, the submarine could not follow this practice. Its strength lay in its ability to attack without being seen and to sink a ship without warning. The submarine was, moreover, the only type of vessel which Germany could send to sea in large numbers.

To the dismay of the United States, Germany began to use mines and submarines to strike back at the British. Early in February, 1915, the German government gave two weeks' notice that enemy merchant ships found in a war zone around Great Britain and Ireland would be sunk without warning, and that neutral vessels entering this area did so at their own risk. The American State Department promptly and vigorously protested the German proclamation. It solemnly warned Germany that she would be held to a "strict accountability" for the loss of American lives and property. It further stated that the United States would take action "to secure to American citizens the full enjoyment of their acknowledged rights on the high seas."

The "Lusitania" is sunk. From the American point of view there was an important difference between the German and the British blockades. It was true that Great Britain interfered with American property and trade rights, but claims for property losses could be settled after the war, and damages could be collected for violations of neutral privileges. Germany's policy, on the other hand, involved the destruction of human life, and for this no satisfactory settlement could be made. One incident after another impressed this fact upon the American public. British and American ships were sunk with the loss of American lives. On May 7, 1915, the American public was shocked by the news that the giant Cunard liner *Lusitania* had been struck by a torpedo off the coast of Ireland and had sunk in eighteen minutes. Nearly 1200 men, women, and children, of whom more than 100 were Americans, lost their lives.

Relations with Germany are strained. The sinking of the *Lusitania* nearly brought about a break in relations between the United States and Germany. A strong war group in the United States, centering among the shipping interests of the Northeast, demanded an immediate declaration of war. On the other hand, many Americans were opposed to going to war. Opposition was particularly strong in the Midwest where the people felt farther removed from the European scene than those living along the Atlantic coast, and where many were descended from German immigrants. Germany expressed regret, but explained

German biplane

The "Lusitania," sinking with heavy loss of life from a torpedo hit, is pictured here by a modern artist. Many Americans believed after this catastrophe that war with Germany would be impossible to avoid.

that the *Lusitania* was carrying munitions of war.

Germany agrees to curb the submarines. It was with difficulty that President Wilson, who was trying to carry out a policy of self-control and patience, obtained any satisfaction from the German government. Altogether three notes were written by the United States government in an effort to get Germany to disclaim the sinking of the *Lusitania,* and obtain assurance that such outrages would not occur again. The second note was so strongly worded that Secretary of State Bryan resigned rather than sign it. He believed that it was the first step in a policy that would commit America to war. At the beginning of September, 1915, however, the German ambassador, von Bernstorff, informed the United States Government that "liners will not be sunk by our submarines without warning and without safety of the lives of non-combatants, provided that the liners do not try to escape or offer resistance."

The Central Powers resort to sabotage. In the meantime German efforts in the United States assumed a new form. German agents in America became convinced that the shipment of arms and supplies to the Allies could not be stopped by peaceful means, and they therefore turned to violence. Bombs were placed on ships carrying war goods to Great Britain in order to destroy the vessels in mid-ocean. Strikes were stirred up among the workers in munition plants. A number of such plants were also blown up, while destructive fires broke out mysteriously in shops that were manufacturing other war materials. Such incidents occurred so often that they were obviously part of a well-planned campaign of *sabotage* (malicious destruction of property).

Germany makes the "Sussex" Pledge. The submarine issue was revived in March, 1916, when the unarmed passenger ship *Sussex* was attacked without warning. Several lives were lost, and many persons were injured, including several Americans. President Wilson thereupon notified the Imperial German Government that unless it immediately abandoned its submarine policy, the United States would have to break off diplomatic relations. Early in May, Germany yielded. She renewed the pledge that merchant vessels would not be sunk "without warning and without saving human lives, unless these ships attempt to escape or offer resistance." The German Government offered this *Sussex* pledge, however, with one important reservation. It insisted on the right to change its decision if the United States could not persuade Great Britain to modify her illegal blockade. President Wilson replied that respect for the rights of United States citizens could not depend upon the actions of any other government. Nevertheless, Germany made no more submarine attacks during the remainder of the year. In November, 1916, Wilson was re-elected, largely through the effect of the slogan, "He kept us out of war."

———— CHECK-UP ————

Why did the United States find it difficult to remain neutral in World War I?

1. How did war break out between Austria and Serbia in 1914? Why were many other nations soon involved?

2. How did the war affect economic life in the United States? Which side was best able to obtain supplies from this country? Why?

3. How did each side disregard this country's rights as a neutral? Why? Why did the United States insist that Germany modify its submarine policy?

3 The United States Enters the War

President Wilson urges preparedness. Meanwhile, it became clear that the United States might be drawn into war. In his annual message to Congress in December, 1915, President Wilson stated that he favored "preparedness." While on a speaking tour through the West early in the next year, he uttered this warning: "I assure you that there is not a day to be lost. There may be at any moment a time when I cannot preserve both the honor and peace of the United States." Congress finally passed a National Defense Act (June, 1916). This measure authorized an increase in the regular army, and also provided for a national guard of another 450,000 officers and men, subject to the call of the President. In addition, Congress authorized the expenditure of more than 500 million dollars for battleships, submarines, and destroyers. A Council of National Defense was set up to unify our industries and resources so that in case of war the efforts of our nation would be fully effective. These steps toward preparedness aroused a difference of opinion, for there were many people who believed that a conflict should be avoided at any cost.

Wilson favors "peace without victory." President Wilson wanted to do more than maintain neutrality and national honor. From the beginning he had hoped that the European war might be settled by negotiation, and that he, as the leader of the greatest neutral power, might serve as mediator. In December, 1916, he called upon the warring nations to announce their war aims. When he had received their replies, President Wilson submitted a statement to the Senate in January, 1917, describing the conditions of peace which he felt that America could approve.

The war must be ended, he stated, by a peace worth guaranteeing and preserving, a peace representing security. "It must be a peace without victory," he said. "Victory would mean peace forced upon the loser," he continued. "Only a peace between equals can last." The President believed that such a peace could be achieved only if certain principles were recognized by the nations of the world. Among these were government by the consent of the governed, equal rights for all nations, the freedom of the seas, and the limitation of armaments on land and sea. To the warring powers, however, who were making supreme sacrifices to win the war, Wilson's suggestion of "peace without victory" was altogether unacceptable.

Germany resumes unrestricted submarine warfare. The early months of 1917 saw the failure of Wilson's attempts at peacemaking and an increase in the danger of war for America. On the last day of January, Germany proclaimed a definite war zone around the British Isles, along the French coast, around the Italian coast, and in the eastern Mediterranean. Immediate and unrestricted submarine warfare was announced against all ships which entered this zone, regardless of what nation they represented. Only a single American passenger ship, plainly marked and carrying no contraband, might pass along a certain course in each direction once each week.

Extremists triumph in Germany. This alarming declaration brought an end to the "*Sussex* pledge." To justify the move, Germany stated that since the United States had failed to secure a modification of the British blockade, the German government was released from the pledge. Actually, the new policy meant simply that those extremists in Germany who favored the unrestricted use of submarines were having their way. Submarine warfare, they reasoned, would break the blockade of German ports and isolate Great Britain. The United States, they said, was not prepared to fight, and even if she declared war, Germany would win the war before American soldiers could come to Europe in large numbers. American bankers were already lending large sums of money to the Allies, and great quantities of food, supplies, and munitions were being shipped from the United States to the Allied countries. The German high command believed the war would be over before the United States could do more.

Diplomatic relations are severed. Diplomatic relations with Germany were severed at once, and German Ambassador von Bernstorff was dismissed. The President still refused to believe that the German government really intended to carry out its proclamation. We desired no conflict, he said. We were friendly to the German people. We should not believe that they were hostile to us unless we were forced to acknowledge it because of their hostile acts. Germany, however, lost no time in beginning its program of unrestricted submarine warfare. During the month of February alone, 200 vessels, many of them neutral, were sunk.

Tension grows. There were several reasons why the United States was brought closer and closer to the brink of war:

(1) Something had to be done to protect unarmed American ships which entered the war zone. On March 12 President Wilson issued an order which authorized the arming of American merchantmen.

(2) Meanwhile, a message was intercepted which revealed that the German Foreign Minister, Alfred Zimmermann, had tried to arrange an alliance with Mexico and Japan against the United States, in case the latter entered the war. As bait, Mexico was promised a "restoration" of her "lost territory" of Texas, New Mexico, and Arizona.

(3) American economic stakes in the war could not be entirely ignored. Shipments of munitions rose in value from 40 million dollars in 1914 to well over a billion dollars in 1916. In 1915 the banking house of Morgan floated a British-French loan in the United States for 500 million dollars, and a similar amount was raised in the following year. Because of the blockade, Germany made few purchases and sold comparatively few securities in the United States. If American loans to the Allies were to remain safe investments, the Allies must win the war. There is no evidence, however, that President Wilson's course of action was in any way influenced by this consideration.

War is declared. A quick succession of events, including the overthrow of the Russian czar and the destruction of more American ships, caused President Wilson to call a special session of Congress on April 2, 1917.[4] At this session the President delivered his momentous war message. He urged Congress to take steps not only for the defense of the country but also for the successful conclusion of the war. America was called upon to enter the struggle, not for selfish gain, but to fight for those principles which it had always treasured. "The world must be made safe for democracy. . . . To such a task we can dedicate our lives and our fortunes, everything that we are and everything that we have. . . ."

War resolutions were introduced into both houses of Congress and were passed with overwhelming majorities. When President Wilson placed his signature to the resolutions on April 6, 1917, the United States found itself caught in the whirlpool of European events, fighting against the leading military power of the day.

The American people respond wholeheartedly. The American people were profoundly affected by the declaration of war. The President, fully supported by Congress, bent every effort to win the war. And the American people responded magnificently. Their sacrifices to produce a victorious army, as well as their vigorous support of the government, established a new era in the history of republican government. The efforts of more than 100 million people were directed wholeheartedly to a single purpose: to win the war.

The Allies are encouraged. Equally important were the effects of our declaration of war upon Europe. In April, 1917, the

[4] The overthrow of the Russian czar meant that the United States could now enter the war on the side of the Allies without joining forces with an autocratic government.

French "poilu"

Allies were fighting with their backs to the wall. War-torn France was exhausted. Great Britain's shipping was being destroyed at the rate of about two thirds of a million tons a month. The defeat of the Russian armies had released hundreds of thousands of German soldiers for service on the western front (see map, page 673). In fact, when the United States made its decision to declare war, the Allies were faced with the possibility of defeat — or at best, a deadlock. The news that America had entered the war sent a new surge of hope through the Allied countries. The Central Powers, on the other hand, were indifferent, and Germany considered the American army unimportant. She felt that even if this new enemy across the sea should succeed in putting a really efficient force under arms, submarines could prevent the transports from reaching France.

American air forces were in their infancy when the United States entered World War I. Like other branches of the military service, however, they displayed posters inviting young men to join. Experience gained in the war proved valuable to civilian as well as military aviation.

JOIN THE
AIR SERVICE
and
SERVE
in
FRANCE

DO IT
NOW

But Germany's military leaders soon found that they had greatly underestimated American leadership and the energy of the American people.

——— CHECK-UP ———

How did the United States become involved in World War I?

1. Why did President Wilson urge preparedness and insist that the warring nations respect our rights as a neutral? Why did he favor a "peace without victory"?
2. Why did Germany return to a policy of unrestricted submarine warfare? How did she try to make trouble for this country?
3. Why did the United States go to war in 1917?

4 **The Country is Mobilized for War**

The navy takes part at once. The American navy was able to go into action at once. Less than a month after the declaration of war, American destroyers steamed into Queenstown on the southern coast of Ireland, and they were soon followed by a number of battleships. Under the command of Admiral William S. Sims, the American fleet co-operated with the Allied men-of-war in laying a mine barrage across the northern entrance to the North Sea. With these mines the Allies hoped to combat the movements of the deadly submarines. Naval detachments also swept dangerous waters for mines, attacked submarine bases, and later convoyed transport ships carrying American troops to Europe. In spite of roving German submarines, the American navy convoyed most of America's 2 million "doughboys" across the Atlantic, with practically no loss of life.

A national army is raised. The most pressing problem facing the United States was to raise an army. Within a month after the declaration of war, Congress passed a Selective Service Act. This measure provided for the enlargement of the regular army and national guard by enlistment, and for the raising of a national army by a *selective draft*. All men between the ages of 21 and 30 inclusive (later from 18 to 45) were required to register with local draft boards. About 24 million men were finally enrolled throughout the country. One by one, in the order determined by a great lottery at Washington, these men were called before their local boards. To speed up the draft, the registered men were divided into classes. Those placed in the first class, consisting of unmarried men without dependents, were the ones who were first called for physical examination.

The enlisted and drafted men were quickly whipped into an effective fighting machine. Camps were established for the training of the national guard and the national army. Each camp or cantonment was a small city with complete facilities for housing and training thousands of men in khaki. By the close of 1917 nearly 2 million recruits were being drilled in methods of modern warfare in 32 of these huge camps. At the same time, thousands of selected young men were given instruction as officers either in training camps or in the Students' Army Training Corps organized within the colleges of the country.

Provision is made for financing the war. Congress was also faced with the necessity of providing huge sums of money to carry on the war. The government adopted the general policy of meeting about one third of the war costs by taxation and of borrowing the balance through long-term bond issues. In October, 1917, a revenue bill was passed which (1) increased the income-tax rates, (2) provided that profits should be taxed if they were larger than those of the prewar years 1911–13, and (3) levied taxes on railroad tickets, telegraph and telephone messages, and on certain luxuries.

Eventually the income tax was boosted to a normal level of 12 per cent, while surtaxes ranged as high as 65 per cent on incomes greater than a million dollars. Excess

U.S. "doughboy"

profits taxes ranged from 20 to 60 per cent during the war. Instead of limiting long-term bonds to large denominations for sale to banks, the government issued bonds for amounts as low as $50. There was a vigorous publicity program to interest citizens in the purchase of government bonds. Everybody in the United States — capitalist, laborer, clerk, farmer, and school child — was urged by posters and speeches to buy Liberty bonds "until it hurt." Thrift stamps and war saving certificates reached even the smallest investor. The response of the American people was remarkable. In all, four Liberty Loans and a Victory Loan were floated, which netted the United States government over 21 billion dollars. Of the total amount raised by taxation and borrowing, nearly 10 billion dollars was lent to the Allies.

Industry is mobilized for war. The raising of men and money was accompanied by a mobilization of industry. Every interest in American industrial life was directed to just one purpose — winning the war. The President was granted practically the powers of a dictator. For example: (1) he was authorized by law to obtain supplies for the army at a price which he was to determine; (2) he was given the power to take possession of mines, factories, packing houses, railways, steamships, and all means of communication; and (3) he could license the importation, manufacture, storage, and distribution of all necessities.

Many agencies were established to help the President carry out these emergency powers. The most important were the War Industries Board, the Shipping Board, the Railroad Administration, the War Trade Board, the War Labor Board, the Food Administration, and the Fuel Administration.

The War Industries Board fixed the prices of important war materials including iron and steel products, wool, hides, lumber, cement, ores, and certain metals. It could determine what materials should be given preference in manufacture, and to whom deliveries should be made. The chairman, Bernard M. Baruch (bay-rook'), became the economic dictator of America.

The pressing need for ships to transport

men and supplies was met by the Shipping Board. By September, 1918, the Shipping Board was operating 10 million tons of shipping. This huge amount included German ships which had remained in American ports since the beginning of the war, the ships constructed by the Emergency Fleet Corporation, and still others purchased from allied and neutral countries.

Railroads were co-ordinated under government control (page 519). The War Trade Board undertook to see that the United States obtained an adequate supply of raw materials and to prevent American goods from reaching the enemy.

Labor is mobilized. The attitude of labor was of vital importance in winning the war. In order to reduce labor troubles to a minimum, a National War Labor Board was organized in April, 1918, under former President Taft and Frank P. Walsh. This board was a supreme court for all labor disputes. It kept men at work while their differences with management were being settled. Led by Samuel Gompers, organized labor responded splendidly to the challenge of war.

Food and fuel are regulated. The need for adequate supplies of food was one of the chief problems of World War I. America's entrance into the war meant that the nation must conserve food to help feed the armies in Europe and peoples in the Allied countries. "Food will win the war," was a slogan that swept across the country. A food administration was established under Herbert Hoover, who already was known for his efficient relief work among the suffering Belgians. American families were limited in their consumption of certain foods. People got along with less sugar. Wheatless and meatless days were proclaimed, and practically all breadstuffs were made in part of wheat substitutes. In general, American people gave the food economy program willing support. They not only submitted to food restrictions, but tens of thousands turned their flower gardens and vacant lots into gardens for raising vegetables.

The demand for fuel also made govern-

British "Tommy"   Scottish bagpiper

ment regulation necessary. August, 1917, saw the establishment of a Fuel Administration. Coal was especially needed along the Atlantic seaboard for ships sailing to Europe. So great was the demand for fuel that at one time the administration ordered all manufacturing plants east of the Mississippi River — except those engaged in war industries — to close down for five days. A series of "heatless" Mondays was also proclaimed which lasted through the winter of 1917–18. There was a switch to daylight saving time during the summer months to save fuel. When the people were asked not to use their automobiles on Sundays and holidays so as to conserve gasoline, the response was universal.

Public opinion is mobilized. The winning of the war involved not only the complete control of the nation's industrial life, but the mobilization of public opinion as well. It was essential that the nation wholeheartedly support the war effort. A Committee on Public Information was therefore appointed for the purpose of keeping the morale of the people high. A campaign was carefully planned to mold American opinion and to popularize America's war aims. Pamphlets were prepared that explained the origins and objects of the war. These were printed in many languages and distributed by the millions to the American people.

The Espionage Act is passed. The vast majority of Americans threw themselves enthusiastically into the task of winning the war, but there was a small group which was not in sympathy with the government's war effort. To deal with these people, an

Trench warfare characterized World War I. Men lived and fought for months in trenches until a direct attack on enemy positions was ordered. This was called "going over the top."

——— CHECK-UP ———

How were this country's resources mobilized for war in 1917?

1. What part did the navy play immediately after we declared war? How was a national army raised? What was the Selective Service Act?
2. How was the war financed? How was industry mobilized? How were food and fuel conserved?
3. How was public opinion created to support the war effort? What efforts were made to restrain those who were opposed to United States participation in the war? What criticisms were directed against the Espionage Act?

Espionage Act was adopted in June, 1917. This measure provided severe penalties for anyone who furnished information regarding the national defense or who furthered resistance to the laws of the United States. The following year an amendment to the Espionage Act was even more sweeping in its restrictions. It provided for the punishment of anyone who tried to interfere with the sale of Liberty bonds, who advised reducing production, or who used "abusive language about the form of government of the United States." As a result of this legislation, several hundred people were arrested. Eugene V. Debs, who had been the candidate for President on the Socialist ticket four times, was sentenced to ten years' imprisonment for obstructing the draft in violation of the Espionage Act.

Opinion differed widely on the necessity for such drastic action. Many believed the law was powerless to reach those who were a real danger to the United States, but was an annoyance to thousands of well-intentioned pacifists and conscientious objectors. Others insisted that while freedom of speech and of the press was desirable in time of peace, these rights were dangerous in time of war.

5 American Armed Forces Play Their Part in Winning the War

The American Expeditionary Force reaches France. While the war-weary Allies were cheered by the speed and effectiveness with which America swung into fighting trim, there was a desperate need for increased man power along the western front. President Wilson had named General John J. Pershing supreme commander of the American Expeditionary Force (A.E.F.), and he reached Paris with his staff in June, 1917. The arrival of the first division of American regulars later in the same month and a parade of American troops in Paris on the fourth of July were encouraging. However, a long period of intensive training in the methods of modern trench warfare was required before the newcomers would be prepared to take their places at the Allied front. Although some of our soldiers entered the fighting line in a quiet area in October, 1917, it was another half year before their activity in the war became really significant. By May, 1918, however, Americans were making the perilous passage across the Atlantic at the rate of 10,000 a day. At the close of the struggle there were about 2 million American soldiers on European soil.

The Central Powers meet with success. The early spring of 1918 found the world at the crossroads. On the one side, America was straining every nerve and muscle to make its war efforts effective before the Allies collapsed. On the other, Germany was engaged in a terrific effort to achieve victory before the full weight of the American forces could be felt. In the race against time the fortunes of war seemed to favor the Central Powers. The Italians had suffered a terrible setback in the fall of 1917 at the hands of Germany and Austria. Moreover, as the result of a new revolutionary movement, Russia came under the control of a party of radical communists, or Bolshevists, who were determined to withdraw from the war at any price. In March, 1918, they concluded a humiliating peace with Germany at Brest-Litovsk (brest l-yee-toffsk'). Shortly afterward, Rumania also was forced to accept the harsh terms of the Central Powers. Thus along the whole eastern front German troops were released for service elsewhere.

The Germans launch the offensive of 1918. The German government now planned to concentrate all its forces in the west and to sacrifice possibly another million men in a gigantic drive to end the war. Under Generals von Hindenburg and von Ludendorff, the Germans launched their offensive in March, 1918, along a front extending from the North Sea to Rheims (reems). (See map, page 673.) Under the terrific hammer blows of the German armies the French and British fell steadily backward. Yet, though the Germans advanced 35 miles and took 150,000 prisoners, their great offensive to win a speedy victory was a failure.

The American army reaches the front. There were two principal reasons for the stiff resistance to the German thrusts: a unified Allied command had been established under Marshall Foch (fohsh), and large numbers of American troops were beginning to take an active part in the fighting. General Pershing, who was impressed with the need of stopping the German offensive, offered to place all the American troops temporarily at the disposal of the Allies. Our first division joined the French, on the front near Montdidier, and late in May won the first American victory in storming the fortified position of Cantigny (kahn-tee-nyee'). The second and third divisions also entered the conflict actively; in June they helped sweep the Germans from Belleau (beh-low') Wood and other important areas. When the Germans started the final phase of their drive in mid-July, American troops played a leading role in checking the attack. The American "doughboys" fought with a determination that would have done credit to seasoned veterans, and rolled the Germans back at Château-Thierry (shah-toe-tyeh-ree') in one of the most valiant attacks of the war. The force of the German offensive was spent. Relying principally upon the million American soldiers in France, General Foch now determined to launch an Allied counteroffensive immediately.

An Allied counteroffensive is started. On July 18 a series of counterattacks commenced which continued until France was cleared of the German armies and the war was brought to a close. The first drive along the Marne, conducted by the French and supported by 250,000 Americans, pushed the Germans back to their second-line defenses. A similar American force to the northwest took part in a vigorous campaign against

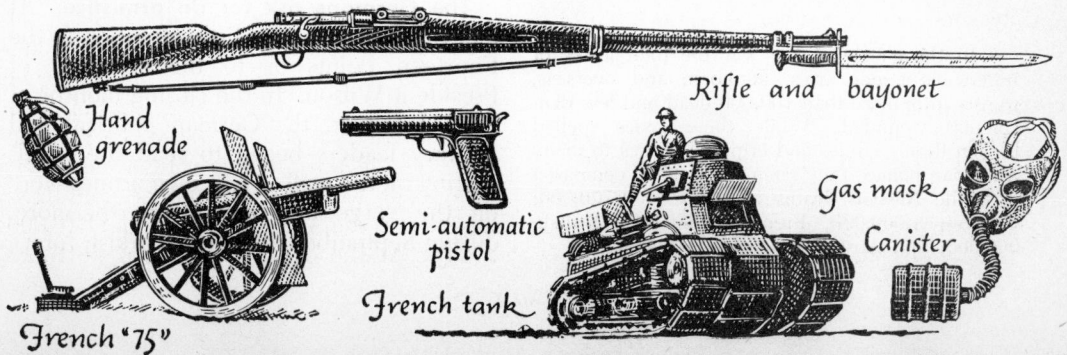

Hand grenade

Rifle and bayonet

Semi-automatic pistol

French tank

Gas mask

Canister

French "75"

the Hindenburg Line. General Pershing now insisted that the American forces be organized as a separate military unit. At the end of August, they were given responsibility for a distinct sector along the Allied front. In September, the Americans launched an attack on St. Mihiel (san mee-yell′), a strongly fortified position held by the Germans since 1914. For three days the battle raged, but the Germans were forced to retreat before the vigorous attacks of the Americans. "The material results of the victory achieved," wrote General Pershing, "were very important. An American army was an accomplished fact, and the enemy had felt its power. No form of propaganda could overcome the depressing effect on the morale of the enemy."

The American army reaches Sedan. In the final Meuse-Argonne (muz arr-gon′) drive beginning ten days later, 1,200,000 Americans smashed the Hindenburg Line. They pushed forward through the Argonne Forest a distance of 30 miles to the important German railroad center of Sedan. Both German and French military experts had regarded the Argonne Forest, heavily fortified with concrete entrenchments, barbed-wire entanglements, and sheltered machine-gun pits, as impenetrable and unconquerable. Every foot of the advance over a front of 23 miles was stubbornly resisted. More ammunition was fired than was used by the Union forces through the entire War Between the States, and over 100,000 Americans were killed or wounded. Yet the American troops continued to push forward. After advancing constantly for 47 days, they reached the outskirts of Sedan and cut the enemy's main line of communications. The progress of the American army was stopped only by the signing of an armistice on November 11.[5]

---

[5] In the course of the war the total losses of Americans under arms, at home and overseas, were a little more than 100,000 dead and less than 250,000 wounded. While these losses spelled broken family circles and crippled bodies to many American homes, they seem small when compared with the Russian deaths in battle of 1,700,000; German, 1,600,000; French, 1,385,000; British, 900,000; and Austro-Hungarian, 800,000.

President Wilson announces the Fourteen Points. Even before the Central Powers had been defeated, an important restatement of the Allies' war aims had been made. As soon as the Russian Bolshevist government had gained control of the Russian state papers, it revealed to an astounded world the secret treaties drawn up by the Allies for the division of the spoils in case of victory over the Central Powers. To offset the bad impression left by Allied greed, Prime Minister Lloyd George of England, in January, 1918, outlined Great Britain's war aims to Parliament in more idealistic terms. Shortly afterward, President Wilson placed before Congress "Fourteen Points" which he considered to be the "only possible program for world peace." They included the following principles:

1. "Open covenants of peace, openly arrived at."

2. Freedom of the seas, in peace and war.

3. The removal of all economic barriers and the establishment of equal opportunities for trade among all nations.

4. The reduction of national armaments "to the lowest points consistent with domestic safety."

5. An impartial adjustment of all colonial claims, in which "the interests of the population concerned must have equal weight with the equitable claims of the government whose title is to be determined."

These were followed by specific points dealing with the future of Russia, Belgium, Alsace-Lorraine, Italy, the Balkan countries, Turkey, and Poland. Last of all came a demand for a "general association of nations . . . for the purpose of affording mutual guarantees of political independence and territorial integrity to great and small states alike."

The Germans ask for an armistice. At first the Germans paid little attention to the Fourteen Points or to the speeches of President Wilson. In the closing months of 1918, however, the German political and military leaders began to read the handwriting on the wall. Their own armies were on the verge of collapse. Furthermore, during September, 1918, the Turkish forces

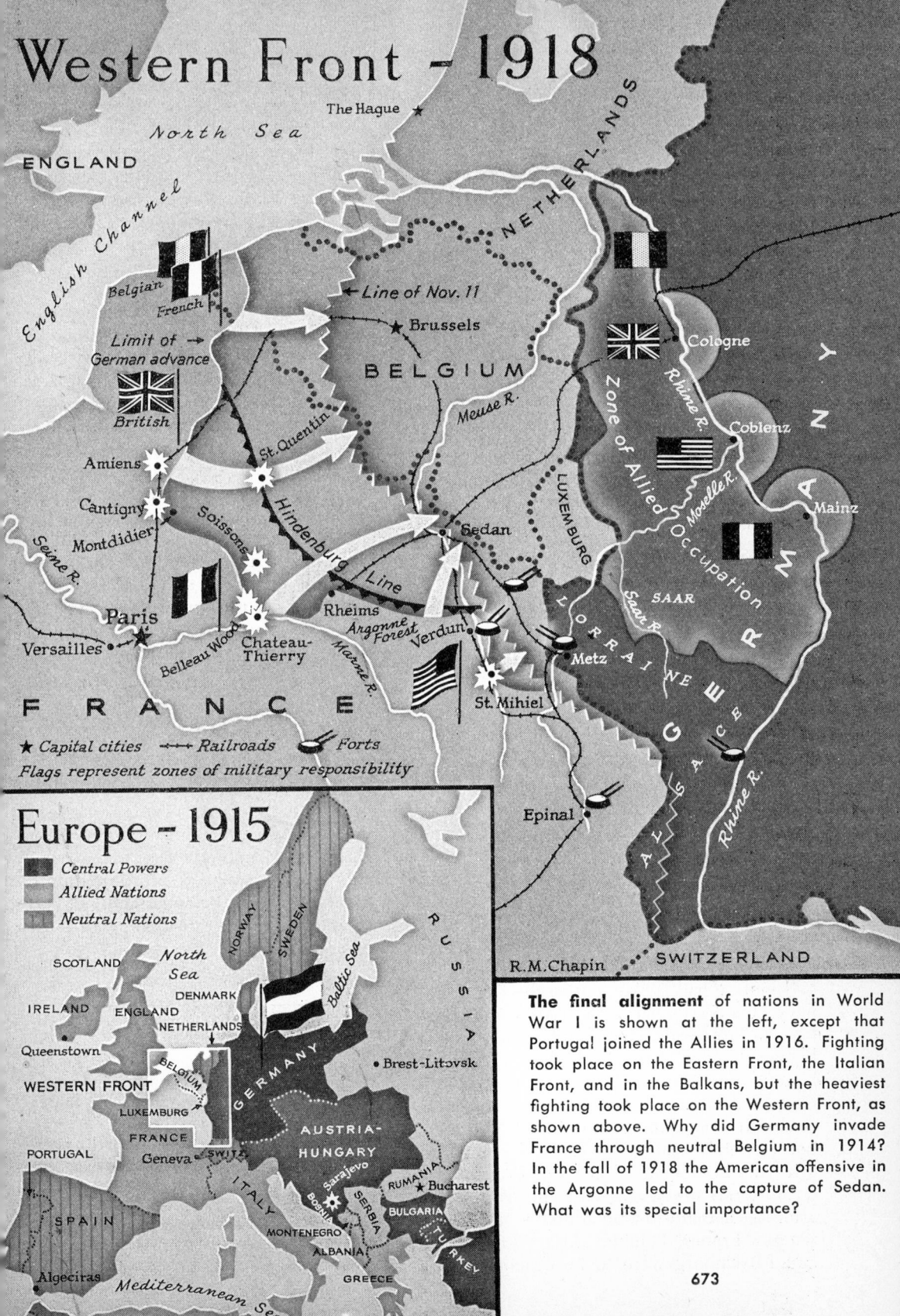

Western Front – 1918

North Sea

The Hague ★

ENGLAND

English Channel

NETHERLANDS

Belgian
French

← Line of Nov. 11

★ Brussels

Limit of →
German advance

BELGIUM

British

Cologne

Zone of Allied Occupation

Rhine R.

Coblenz

Meuse R.

St. Quentin

LUXEMBURG

Moselle R.

Mainz

Amiens

Cantigny

Soissons

Hindenburg

Sedan

Montdidier

Seine R.

Line

SAAR

Saar R.

G E R M A N Y

Paris ★

Rheims

Argonne
Forest

Verdun

L O R R A I N E

Versailles

Belleau Wood

Chateau-
Thierry

Marne R.

St. Mihiel

Metz

A L S A C E

F R A N C E

Rhine R.

★ Capital cities   ↤↦ Railroads   ⚓ Forts
Flags represent zones of military responsibility

Epinal

R.M.Chapin   SWITZERLAND

Europe – 1915

■ Central Powers
▨ Allied Nations
▤ Neutral Nations

NORWAY   SWEDEN

SCOTLAND   *North Sea*

RUSSIA

IRELAND   ENGLAND   DENMARK
NETHERLANDS   *Baltic Sea*

Queenstown

• Brest-Litovsk

BELGIUM

WESTERN FRONT

LUXEMBURG

GERMANY

FRANCE

AUSTRIA-
HUNGARY

PORTUGAL   Geneva   SWITZ.

RUMANIA   • Bucharest

ITALY   Sarajevo

BOSNIA   SERBIA   BULGARIA

SPAIN   MONTENEGRO

ALBANIA   TURKEY

Algeciras   GREECE

Mediterranean Sea

The final alignment of nations in World War I is shown at the left, except that Portugal joined the Allies in 1916. Fighting took place on the Eastern Front, the Italian Front, and in the Balkans, but the heaviest fighting took place on the Western Front, as shown above. Why did Germany invade France through neutral Belgium in 1914? In the fall of 1918 the American offensive in the Argonne led to the capture of Sedan. What was its special importance?

Armistice Day in New York and throughout the country was wildly celebrated by all the people.

in Palestine and Arabia were practically wiped out, while Bulgaria signed an armistice and withdrew from the conflict. Before Germany could recover from the shock of Bulgaria's surrender, Austria-Hungary asked the Allies for terms of peace. Faced with disaster, the German government requested an armistice based on Wilson's Fourteen Points.

An armistice is signed. On November 5, the German government was notified of the willingness of the Allies to make peace. Three days later Marshall Foch read to the German delegates the terms of an armistice, and granted them 72 hours in which to accept it. The demands of the Allies were harsh, but Germany's allies had already laid down their arms, revolution had begun in the leading cities of Germany, and mutiny had broken out in the German navy. On November 9, the Kaiser and the Crown Prince abdicated and on the following day fled to the Netherlands. A few hours before the time limit was up, the German delegates signed the armistice, and at eleven o'clock on the morning of November 11, 1918, peace once more descended upon the battle-scarred fields of France.

The terms are severe. The terms of the armistice actually amounted to German surrender. France, Belgium, Alsace-Lorraine, and Luxemburg were to be evacuated at once. Allied forces were to occupy (1) all German territory west of the Rhine, and (2) the territory on the east bank to a distance of about 18½ miles. (See map, page 673.) A strip of land about six miles wide on both banks of the Rhine was converted into a neutral zone. The Germans were required to surrender a huge amount of war materials, a number of battleships, cruisers, and destroyers, and all of their submarines. They were also forced to renounce the treaties of Brest-Litovsk with Russia and of Bucharest with Rumania. Prisoners were to be sent back to their own countries, and money and valuables taken from invaded countries were to be restored.

Victory is accompanied by wild celebrations. Throughout the war-weary world the ending of hostilities was greeted by joyful celebrations. Happy throngs filled the streets of London and Paris. Even the Germans rejoiced that the suffering and sacrifices of war were over and that Germany had been spared the humiliation of a triumphal march by the victors to Berlin. In the United States a wild carnival of joy greeted the news of the armistice. The greatest war that the world had yet seen was over and America had helped to bring victory to the Allied cause. To Congress President Wilson announced the attainment of "the object upon which all free men had set their hearts." To the American people he joyfully proclaimed: "Everything for which America fought has been accomplished. It will now be our fortunate duty to assist by example, by sober counsel, and by material aid in the establishment of just democracy throughout the world."

--------- CHECK-UP ---------

What part did the American armed forces play in winning the war?

1. What victories were gained by the Central Powers in 1917? How did they hope to end the war in 1918?
2. What contribution did the American Expeditionary Force make to winning the war? The navy?
3. What were the Fourteen Points? Why were they issued? Why did Germany seek an armistice late in 1918?
4. What were the terms of the Armistice?

CHAPTER REVIEW

Terms to Understand

arbitration treaties	propaganda
czar	sabotage
assassination	espionage
neutrality	mine barrage
unrestricted sub-	draft
marine warfare	armistice

People and Things to Know About

Permanent Court of	Woodrow Wilson
Arbitration	*Lusitania*
The Hague	*Sussex* Pledge
Drago Doctrine	"peace without victory"
Theodore Roosevelt	Selective Service Act
Nobel Peace Prize	Liberty bonds
Archduke Francis	Herbert Hoover
Ferdinand	John J. Pershing
Triple Entente	Argonne Forest
Triple Alliance	Fourteen Points
Central Powers	Bolshevists
the Allies	

Historic Dates to Identify

1899   1907   1914   1917
November 11, 1918

Questions to Discuss

1. What important efforts were made by Americans to further the cause of world peace, 1898–1914?
2. Compare the following:
   (*a*) German and British disregard for United States neutral rights.
   (*b*) German and United States views on submarine warfare.
   (*c*) German and British views on the British blockade.
3. Why did the United States proclaim its neutrality in both World Wars, only to be involved in both struggles?
4. Why did President Wilson make an effort to end the war in 1916? Why were the warring nations comparatively uninterested in his efforts?

Questions to Discuss (Cont.)

5. It has been said that "the United States declared war on Germany in 1917 because this country could not afford to have Great Britain lose the war." Do you agree or disagree with this comment? Why?
6. Why did the slogan, "He kept us out of war," help to re-elect Wilson President in 1916?
7. Why did the Allies give great publicity to the Fourteen Points?

Relating Geography and History

On an outline map of western Europe, indicate the line of farthest German advance. Locate the points at which American forces took part in the war.

Other Things to Do

1. Study the causes of World War I in a book which deals at length with that period. List each act that made war more certain in 1914. Explain why each country acted as it did. State your conclusions about the problem of preventing war.
2. Ask veterans of World War I and World War II to describe their experiences in these conflicts. Ask questions to bring out how changed conditions and technological advances affect warfare.
3. Ask a veteran who served on a submarine to speak to the class about the advantages and limitations of this type of craft in modern warfare.
4. Debate: *Resolved,* That the United States should have remained neutral in World War I.
*5. Make a list of contributions by the United States to winning the war. Explain to the class which you think most important, and why.
6. Make a comparison of the armistice terms ending the fighting against Germany in World Wars I and II. In what ways are they similar; in what ways different?

Diplomats

Chapter 38

THE UNITED STATES REJECTS WORLD LEADERSHIP BUT CONTINUES TO WORK FOR PEACE

We had a chance to gain the leadership of the world. We have lost it, and soon we shall be witnessing the tragedy of it all.

Woodrow Wilson

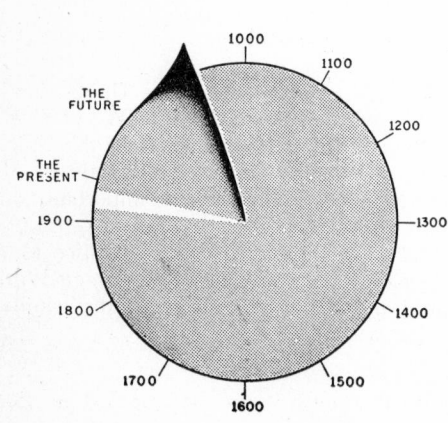

1919-1936

At the end of World War I America was eager for a speedy return to normal conditions. The abrupt change from war to peace, however, created problems almost as difficult as those raised when we entered the conflict. The energies of 4½ million soldiers and 11½ million civilian war workers now had to be redirected to peacetime activities. The industries of the country had to be converted from war to peace. In general, demobilization of the armed forces proceeded smoothly, and so did the change-over in industry, but the process of readjustment continued long after the last gun had been fired in France.

No nation more sincerely desired peace during the postwar years than did the United States. The uselessness of the terrible waste in human lives and property caused by war was clearly impressed upon the minds of the American people. From the standpoint of good business, also, the United States wanted to avoid war. We were developing colonies far from our own borders, and we had large investments, both in older countries laid waste by the war and in less developed regions. Another world conflict would seriously threaten normal commercial, industrial, and financial conditions.

How could we best preserve peace? Was it by joining with the rest of the world in a league of nations, or by returning to the age-old American policy of isolation? Although the United States failed to join the League of Nations, American foreign policy focused on maintaining peace and security. The following topics are a guide to the material in this chapter:

1. President Wilson helps write the Treaty of Versailles.
2. The Senate rejects the Treaty of Versailles and the League of Nations.
3. The United States continues to work for peace.

1 President Wilson Helps Write the Treaty of Versailles

Postwar Europe poses serious problems. America's readjustment after World War I was tied up with the existence of serious problems in Europe. World War I had shaken the world to its very foundations. About 60 million men had been pressed into service, 8 million of whom had lost their lives in battle, and another million had died of disease. Hundreds of billions of dollars in wealth had been wiped out. Large areas had been made unfit for cultivation, and hundreds of towns and villages were in ruins.

These human and economic losses were not the whole story. Europe was in a state of political upheaval. The ruling families in Russia, Germany, and Austria-Hungary had been toppled from power. The new radical government in Russia was declaring its intention of spreading communism throughout the world and of bringing about a world-wide revolution of the oppressed masses. Small national groups everywhere were clamoring for recognition. In the midst of such confusion the peace conference which assembled in Paris in January, 1919, faced a tremendous task. It was called upon to redraw the map of Europe, of Asia, and of Africa. In addition, it had to consider the demands of the various nations, many of which were in direct conflict with each other. It must then try to harmonize all these demands with the peace program laid down by President Wilson in his Fourteen Points.

President Wilson goes to Paris. Although no President had ever left the country during his term of office, President Wilson decided to take part personally in the Paris peace conference. To Congress he justified his course of action with the statement that "the peace settlements which are now to be agreed upon are of transcendent importance both to us and to the rest of the world, and I know of no business or interest which should take precedence of them."

The President believed that his presence at the peace table would do much to bring about peace settlements in keeping with the Fourteen Points. There was a sound basis for this belief. His position was one of world-wide importance. People everywhere found in the things he said an expression of their own ideals. He enjoyed the confidence of those persons in both victor and vanquished countries who sincerely desired peace. On the other hand, it is possible that the final peace treaty might have followed more closely the ideals of the Fourteen Points if the President had remained in Washington. Our peace delegates might then have carried out the President's instructions and he himself would not have been subjected to the "give and take" of direct negotiations with European diplomats.

The President loses the support of Congress. Unfortunately, President Wilson did not go to Europe with the wholehearted support of his own countrymen. Politics had been put aside during the war, and the Republicans as well as the Democrats had given full support to the President's wartime program. But as the end of the con-

The **Big Four** at the Peace Conference were (from left to right) Orlando of Italy, Lloyd George of Great Britain, Clemenceau of France, and President Wilson of the United States.

flict approached, the Republicans were becoming impatient of Wilson's "dictatorial" methods. Instead of trying to retain Republican support for his peace program, Wilson offended the Republicans in Congress still further. In October, 1918, he appealed to the American people to elect a Democratic Congress in the coming congressional elections. To his dismay the Republicans, after a bitter political campaign, carried the Senate, 49–47, and the House, 239 to 194.

President Wilson ignores the Republicans and the Senate. The Republican margin in the Senate, though slim, gave that party the right to name the chairman and the majority of the members on all Senate committees. This power was particularly important in the Foreign Relations Committee, which would deal with any peace treaty concluded with Germany. President Wilson, convinced that his cause was right, refused to accept the 1918 election results as a disapproval of his policies. He angered the Republicans still further by his failure to include any outstanding Republican leaders in the American Peace Commission. Nor did he attempt to win the support of the Senate by appointing any of its members to the Commission.

The "Big Four" dominate the peace conference. The Peace Conference began its meetings early in 1919 at Versailles (vehr-sah'y), just outside Paris. The Treaty of Versailles, which resulted from the conference, was the work of a few men. Although 32 nations, not including the Central Powers, were represented, the treaty was practically written by a group known

as the "Big Four." This group was composed of the prime ministers of Great Britain (Lloyd George), France (Clemenceau), and Italy (Orlando), and President Wilson. Japan was at first a member of the Supreme Council but withdrew as soon as her interests in the Pacific were assured.

The secret treaties are obstacles to a just peace. President Wilson soon ran into difficulty. The Allies called attention to secret agreements they had drawn up during the war for distributing the spoils of war in case the Central Powers were defeated. How could such selfish agreements be made to harmonize with the Fourteen Points? France desired revenge against Germany, Italy claimed land from Austria, and all the Allies were agreed that Germany should pay for the war. How could these desires be made to fit in with Wilson's program for a "peace of justice"? Furthermore, since Germany in its treaties with Russia and Rumania clearly had revealed the type of peace settlement it had in mind for the Allies in case of victory, how could the Allies be expected to write a generous peace?

The covenant of the League of Nations is made a part of the treaty. President Wilson was convinced that the best way to guarantee a lasting peace was through the organization of a league of nations. In such a body injustices of the peace settlement might later be corrected. Consequently, he pressed for the creation of this international body, and his demand received immediate attention. He and his confidential adviser, Colonel Edward M.

House, were appointed as the American representatives on a commission to draw up a covenant (terms of agreement) for such a league. The covenant was reported to the conference in mid-February, 1919, and was promptly adopted.

Opposition to the League of Nations rises in the United States Senate. After he had been assured that the League of Nations would become a part of the peace treaty, President Wilson returned to the United States in February, 1919, to deal with problems here at home. To his disappointment he found a great deal of dissatisfaction in America with his peace plans, especially on the part of certain members of the Senate. The Senators had two reasons for their attitude: (1) they objected to involving the United States in an international association which included the nations of Europe, and (2) they were politically hostile to the President. Before Congress adjourned in March, 37 senators or senators-elect declared that they intended to vote against the treaty if it contained the covenant of the League of Nations. This number was more than enough to defeat the treaty when it came before the Senate for ratification.

Wilson defends the League of Nations. President Wilson refused to be discouraged. In a speech delivered just before he went back to Paris he said, "When the treaty comes back, gentlemen on this side will find the covenant not only in it, but so many threads of the treaty tied to the covenant, that you cannot dissect the covenant from the treaty without destroying the whole vital structure." At the same time, Wilson welcomed suggestions for amending the covenant of the League of Nations. On his return to Paris he succeeded in incorporating into the covenant the proposals of such leading Republicans as Elihu Root, Charles Evans Hughes, and former President Taft, who favored the plan for a league. As a result, it was provided that the Monroe Doctrine and domestic questions of the United States were not to come under the authority of the League. Also any nation was to have the right to withdraw after two years' notice.

The Treaty of Versailles is completed. Back at the peace conference President Wilson found his difficulties greatly increased. The revolt in the United States Senate against his leadership strengthened the demands of Lloyd George and Clemenceau for a "hard" peace. In contrast to Wilson, both of these leaders had the support of their national law-making bodies. Lloyd George had been re-elected in 1918 on a platform in which he promised to hang the German Kaiser. Both he and Clemenceau, the aged "Tiger" of France, were supported by the voters in their demand to make Germany pay the costs of the war. Singlehanded, and for a time ill with influenza, President Wilson fought stubbornly for a peace which he felt would be enduring. At one time he threatened to leave the conference altogether rather than accept the terms of the secret treaties.

Under the circumstances, the Versailles Treaty was probably the best that Wilson could obtain. Though severe in its treatment of Germany, it did establish the League of Nations, and thus provided an instrument by which the terms of the treaty might be modified after the bitterness of the war had died away. By the Versailles and other peace treaties, independent states were created for the benefit of national groups in eastern Europe (Finland, Estonia, Latvia, Lithuania, Poland, and Czechoslovakia. See map, page 711.) Alsace-Lorraine was restored to France, and the boundaries of Serbia (which became Yugoslavia after the war), Belgium, Italy, Greece, and Rumania were enlarged along the lines of nationality. The representatives of Ger-

Yugoslavia   Rumania   Czechoslovakia
NATIONAL COSTUMES

many protested that the provisions of the treaty did not reflect the principles of the Fourteen Points which Germany had accepted in agreeing to the armistice. However, they were powerless to do more than protest, and near the end of June, 1919, they signed the treaty.

The covenant of the League of Nations establishes a world organization. From the American standpoint the most important part of the Treaty of Versailles was the covenant of the League of Nations. To carry on the activities of the League it set up the following machinery: an Assembly, a Council, and a permanent Secretariat (secretarial staff). The Assembly, which possessed final authority, consisted of delegates from the member states, each having one vote. It was to meet at stated intervals at Geneva, Switzerland, "to deal with any matter within the sphere of action of the League or affecting the peace of the world." The Council, to consist of the representatives of nine powers, was to meet as occasion required, and was to have about the same authority as the Assembly. France, Great Britain, Italy, Japan, the United States, and four (later nine) nonpermanent members chosen by the Assembly were to make up the Council. In settling almost all important matters, a unanimous vote of the Council and usually of the Assembly was required. The covenant also provided for a Permanent Court of International Justice, which came to be known as the World Court.[1]

The purpose of the League is to bring about peace and security. The chief purpose of the League was "to achieve international peace and security by the acceptance of obligations not to resort to war." Article X, regarded by many as the heart of the covenant, provided that "The members of the League undertake to respect and preserve as against external aggression the territorial integrity and existing political independence of all members of the League." Article XIII pledged the members (1) to submit to arbitration any disputes that might arise among them, (2) to carry out

[1] The World Court should not be confused with the Hague Court referred to on page 660.

faithfully any awards or decisions made, and (3) to refrain from waging war upon a nation which was carrying out such awards or decisions. Article XVI provided for economic sanctions (penalties) and also military steps against any member which waged war and broke its promises to submit disputes to arbitration. Plans were also laid for an international labor office. To many the dream of a world parliament seemed about to come true.

——— CHECK-UP ———

What were the characteristics of the peace settlement which ended World War I?

1. Why did President Wilson find it difficult to arrange a peace settlement based on the Fourteen Points? Why did he go to Paris in person to help write the treaty? Why did opposition to the treaty arise in the United States Senate?

2. Why did President Wilson put his chief emphasis on having the covenant of the League included in the peace treaty?

3. What was the organization of the League of Nations? What penalties were provided in the covenant to restrain aggressor nations?

---

2 The Senate Rejects the Treaty of Versailles and the League of Nations

The Senate is divided over the League of Nations. When President Wilson submitted the Treaty of Versailles to the Senate (July, 1919), debate on the subject had already started. In their attitude toward the League, senators fell into three main groups: (1) A dozen "irreconcilables," led by William E Borah, Hiram Johnson, and Robert M. La Follette, were determined to defeat the treaty and the League at any cost. (2) Another group of about 40 Democratic senators were in favor of ratifying the treaty without making much change in it. (3) An in-between group, supported
(Continued on page 682)

Woodrow Wilson
(1856-1924)

Teacher

FOR TWENTY-FIVE YEARS before his brief term as Governor of New Jersey and his election to the Presidency, Woodrow Wilson's life was centered in the classroom. In this period he not only proved a stimulating teacher and capable administrator, but he also acquired a thorough knowledge of government and a mastery of the English language. Upsetting the predictions that a mere scholar would prove ineffective in practical politics, Wilson succeeded during his first four years as President in driving a broad program of economic reform through Congress.

The outbreak of World War I necessarily turned Wilson's attention from reform to critical foreign relations. When the United States entered the war against Germany, Wilson's policies transformed America into a fighting nation which contributed magnificently to the final defeat of the Central Powers.

President

World War I brought Wilson his greatest triumphs and his most bitter disappointments. During the grim days of battle he resolved to bring about a settlement which would free the world forever from the scourge of war. For this reason Wilson went in person to the Peace Conference at Paris to fight for a League of Nations which would outlaw future conflicts. He met with a discouraging lack of co-operation at the Conference and bitter opposition at home, but he persisted in his plans. Wilson was essentially a man of intellect and imagi-

World Statesman

nation. He had dreamed a dream that his reason approved and he refused to be turned from it. "I would rather fail in a cause that I know some day will triumph," he declared, "than to win in a cause that I know some day will fail." So he directed all his energies toward winning others to his plan, until his health gave way. He ended his administration broken in health, and he died shortly after; but his ideal of a brotherhood of nations lives on as a challenge to future generations.

by many prominent members of both parties, favored modifying the treaty. They wished to include certain reservations and interpretations which would define more clearly the obligations of the United States under the League covenant. Some of those in the third group favored strong reservations; others were "mild" reservationists. More than 80 senators favored ratification in one form or another.

Senator Lodge opposes the League. From the beginning it seemed unlikely that the treaty would be approved without considerable change. The attitude of the Senate toward any treaty not distinctly favorable to the United States was well known, and in addition the Senate was not controlled by the President's own party. Particularly important was the fact that the chairman of the Senate Foreign Relations Committee, Henry Cabot Lodge, was bitterly hostile to President Wilson. Before he was called upon to consider the Versailles Treaty, Senator Lodge had been a strong supporter of the idea of an association of nations. In the League of Nations, however, Lodge saw — or thought he saw — a threat against American sovereignty. He objected especially to Article X, which, he argued, might involve the United States in a war to protect the territories of some foreign state. Furthermore, he was convinced that the United States alone should decide what questions came within its own jurisdiction. The Republican majority of the Foreign Relations Committee followed Senator Lodge's leadership and opposed the League.

Ratification of the Treaty of Versailles seems doubtful. The American people failed to appreciate the importance of the struggle between President Wilson and the Senate Foreign Relations Committee. When the treaty was submitted to the Senate, there was considerable popular support for ratification. Influential groups, such as the American Federation of Labor, the American Bar Association, the American Bankers' Association, and the Federal Council of Churches, came out in favor of ratifying the treaty and entering the League.

As the struggle over the treaty became more bitter, however, the idealism that had grown up during the war tended to decrease. The people of the United States placed great faith in the advice of Washington, Jefferson, and Monroe against entangling alliances, and were naturally inclined to favor a policy of isolation. The fear that the United States might become entangled in European quarrels increased, and there was an added anxiety that the League plan might result in a superstate which could interfere in America's internal affairs. The treaty was also opposed both by those who felt that it was too severe in its treatment of Germany and by those who agreed with Lloyd George and Clemenceau that it was too lenient.

President Wilson appeals to the people. Meanwhile, the President and the Foreign Relations Committee failed to reach an understanding. The Committee proposed amendments which would require the approval of the Allies and the resubmission of the treaty to Germany. To such amendments President Wilson objected. Modification, he believed, could best be accomplished through the League *after* the treaty had gone into effect. The Foreign Relations Committee, nevertheless, reported the treaty with a number of amendments and reservations. After a lengthy and bitter debate upon the floor of the Senate, fourteen limitations known as the "Lodge Reservations" were approved.

When President Wilson realized that the Senate would not ratify the treaty without serious reservations to the League covenant, he decided to appeal directly to the people. On a tour of important cities in the West he addressed enthusiastic audiences. Senators Johnson and Borah, however, who followed in his footsteps to attack the League, were greeted with equal enthusiasm. These appeals to the people were abruptly cut short late in September, 1919, when the President, worn out by strain and overwork, had a complete physical and nervous breakdown. The public learned later that he had suffered a paralytic stroke. For a long time he lingered at death's door and he was never again able to take any significant part in public life. Thus,

The Treaty of Versailles met with defeat in the Senate. Among those opposed to ratification were (from left to right) Senators Borah of Idaho, Lodge of Massachusetts, and Smoot of Utah.

at the very height of the dispute, the supporters of the League lost their leader.

The treaty is defeated. The Senate vote on the ratification of the treaty took place during the early stage of President Wilson's illness. In November, 1919, his supporters, joined by the "irreconcilables," voted down the treaty with the Lodge reservations. On the other hand, they were unable to secure the ratification of the treaty without the Lodge reservations or with mild reservations acceptable to the President. In 1920, a final vote was taken on the treaty with reservations. The vote of 49 in favor and 35 against was short of the necessary two-thirds approval needed for ratification. A joint resolution of Congress declaring the war at an end was then passed, but it was vetoed by the disabled President as "an ineffaceable stain upon the gallantry and honor of the United States." America remained technically at war until the next presidential administration.

Who was at fault? Opinions differed widely in assigning blame for the rejection of the treaty. President Wilson and his supporters placed the blame squarely upon the shoulders of Senator Lodge and the Foreign Relations Committee. Others believed that the President was at fault for not accepting the treaty with reservations. Our former allies probably would have preferred a treaty with reservations to a treaty for which the United States accepted no responsibility. The League, however, was Wilson's creation, and he could not bring himself to accept an association of nations which lacked the power to act effectively.

President Harding rejects the League. The election of 1920 destroyed President Wilson's last hope that the nation might rebuke the Senate for its rejection of the League of Nations. He had hoped to make the election a "great and solemn referendum" on the treaty and the League, but actually this was not possible under the American system of government. Republicans and others who were opposed to the League voted the Republican ticket. On the other hand, Republicans who favored membership in the League were convinced that the best chance of getting the treaty ratified lay in electing a Republican administration. The country at the time was strongly Republican, and the Republican voter saw no reason for deserting his party over the League issue. The result was an overwhelming Republican victory.

Interpreting the election returns as an expression of the people's disapproval of the League of Nations, the new President, Warren G. Harding, at once made his position clear. In his inaugural address in 1921 he declared that we sought no part "in directing the destinies of the Old World." Somewhat later, in a special message to Congress, he said: "I have no unseemly comment to offer on the League. If it is serving the Old World helpfully, more power to it. But it is not for us. The Senate has so declared, the executive has so declared, the people have so declared. Nothing could be more decisively stamped with finality." In line with this attitude, communications from the secretary-general of the League remained unanswered. In

Elihu Root, Secretary of War and of State in the early 1900's, was later influential in the organization of the World Court.

vitations to join in the work of the League for human welfare were declined, and private citizens were advised to take no share in its programs. In July, 1921, Congress declared the war at an end and reserved to the United States all of the rights it would have acquired by the treaties with Germany, Austria, and Hungary.

America chooses isolation. At the end of 1918 the United States stood at a fork in the road. One guidepost pointed to the old policy of isolation; the other to world leadership. By 1921 the representatives of the American people had chosen the first road. To other nations the United States may well have appeared to be narrow and selfish in its outlook, and unwilling to assume its share of responsibility for establishing a new international order. Many Americans believed that we had won the war only to lose the peace. Others were convinced that the Senate and the country had made a wise decision, in line with the best interests of the nation. Time alone was to tell whether America had taken the right road.

——— CHECK-UP ———

Why did this country reject the Treaty of Versailles and fail to join the League of Nations?

1. What persons and groups in the Senate opposed ratification of the Treaty of Versailles? Why? What was the attitude of the American people?
2. How did President Wilson seek to get the treaty approved? Why did he fail?
3. How did President Harding interpret the election of 1920?

3 The United States Continues to Work for Peace

The United States takes part in League of Nations activities. Although America's attitude was a severe blow to the League of Nations, the League continued to expand until it included more than 50 countries — most of the civilized nations of the world. Its activities became numerous and varied. The League brought about the peaceful settlement of several incidents which might have developed into causes for war. Other activities included efforts to bring about disarmament; control of disease, the slave trade, and the drug trade; and the improvement of labor conditions throughout the world. When it became evident that League commissions and conferences were discussing matters of vital interest to the United States, our State Department began to deal directly with the League staff. Unofficial American observers were sent to Geneva, Switzerland, to sit with League committees dealing with non-political matters. In 1923, formal delegates were sent to represent the United States, and in the following years we were officially represented at many League meetings. By 1931 the United States had five permanent officials at Geneva to look after American interests.

The World Court is established. The covenant of the League of Nations provided for a Permanent Court of International Justice, and this World Court was set up in 1920. The World Court was to have authority over all international disputes submitted to it by states which became members of the court. It might also render "advisory opinions" [2] on questions brought before it by the League Council or Assembly. Membership in the court was not limited to the countries in the League. In the United States there was considerable interest in the World Court because an American statesman, Elihu Root, had helped to outline the court's organization and functions. In addition, the United States definitely favored the settlement of international disputes by arbitration.

The Senate rejects membership in the World Court. Despite this interest, the suggestion that the United States join the World Court led to a long and bitter dispute. As early as 1923, President Harding asked the Senate to approve American membership, but without success. President Coolidge also repeatedly urged acceptance of the World Court plan. In 1926 the Senate finally gave its consent to the proposal, but included a number of reservations which were not acceptable to the other signers of the World Court treaty. Three years later, Elihu Root, who was on a committee appointed to revise the constitution of the court, presented the so-called "Root Formula" to meet the objections of the Senate. This was accepted by the Council and Assembly of the League of Nations and was also satisfactory to the American State Department. But again the old objections to entanglement in European politics were raised, and the Senate failed to take the final step which would make the United States a member of the World Court. In the election of 1932 the platforms of the Republican, the Democratic, and the Socialist Parties all favored our entrance into the Court. President Franklin D. Roosevelt urged action on the matter. Nevertheless, the Senate, early in 1935, again disapproved the proposal.

[2] Opinions given in advance of actual cases tried before the court.

The Paris Peace Pact is adopted. While the controversy over the World Court was in progress, another step was taken which it was hoped would lead to the peaceful settlement of disputes between nations. In 1927, Briand, the French Minister of Foreign Affairs, proposed a treaty with the United States by which both nations would agree never to use war "as an instrument of national policy" in their dealings with one another. Secretary of State Frank B. Kellogg responded that all the principal nations of the world should be invited to join in such a declaration. As a result, the representatives of fifteen powers met at Paris, and in the summer of 1928 signed the Paris Peace Pact, known also as the Kellogg-Briand Pact. Within a few years, more than 60 nations had accepted the pact, which provided:

The High Contracting parties solemnly declare . . . that they condemn recourse to war for the solution of international controversies, and renounce it as an instrument of national policy. . . . The High Contracting parties agree that the solution of all disputes or conflicts . . . shall never be sought except by pacific means.

The United States Senate promptly ratified the treaty. At the same time, fear of European entanglements caused it to add certain interpretations which made the agreement less effective. Since there was no way of enforcing the treaty, the value of the Pact of Paris depended entirely upon whether the nations that signed it were willing to keep to its terms. The fact that it was accepted so widely, however, was regarded at the time as a significant peace gesture.

Disarmament is urged as a means of preventing war. The leading powers also sought to maintain peace by making agreements for the reduction of armaments. Undoubtedly one cause of World War I lay in the fact that the major European powers in 1914 were armed to the teeth. When a dispute did arise, they felt prepared to plunge into war. The race for naval supremacy among the United States, Great Britain, and Japan in the years following

French sailor

the armistice emphasized once more the need for armament agreements.

The Washington Conference provides for naval disarmament. In the autumn of 1921, as you have read (page 654), President Harding called a conference in Washington on the limitation of armaments. Secretary of State Charles Evans Hughes, who was chosen chairman of the conference, startled the world by proposing (1) that limits be set on the battleship strength of the chief navies, (2) that a considerable number of ships already built or in process of construction be scrapped. Since the United States was in a position to outbuild its competitors, and since Secretary Hughes offered to scrap the largest tonnage, the other nations immediately accepted the idea underlying this proposal. A five-power treaty was drawn up which called for a ten-year "holiday" in the construction of capital ships (the class which includes the largest warships). It also fixed the capital ships of these powers at the following tonnages: Great Britain and the United States 525,000 tons each, Japan 315,000 tons, and France and Italy 175,000 tons. Thus the strength of these five nations would be related to one another in a ratio of 5–5–3–1.67–1.67, at least with regard to capital ships. A second agreement outlawed the use of poison gas and provided that submarines were not to be used as commerce destroyers. No action, however, was taken with respect to limiting cruisers, submarines, or land forces.

Later disarmament conferences are failures. The Washington Conference was followed by other disarmament conferences. A conference at Rome in 1924 and another at Geneva three years later failed to achieve definite results. The failure of the Geneva conference led President Coolidge to support a program for American naval construction. At London in 1930 another attempt at

British sailor

naval disarmament was partially successful. A three-power pact was signed by Great Britain, the United States, and Japan, and the "holiday" in the construction of capital ships was extended to the end of 1936. Because France and Italy did not join in this agreement, an "escalator clause" was inserted which permitted the signers to increase their armaments if other nations threatened their security.

Early in 1932 a conference for the reduction of land armaments began its meetings at Geneva. When Germany's request for equality in armament was rejected, Adolf Hitler, the German Nazi leader, announced the withdrawal of his government both from the conference and from the League of Nations (October, 1933).[3] Distrust among the nations of Europe was so great that the conference adjourned near the end of 1934 without any definite accomplishments to its credit.

U.S. sailor (shore duty)

Because the treaty providing for naval limitation was due to expire in 1936, a conference met in London near the close of 1935. Here Japan demanded equality in naval strength with Great Britain and the United States. When this demand was rejected, Japan immediately withdrew. The only accomplishment of the conference was the drawing up of a weak agreement for naval limitation by the United States, Great Britain, and France.

Disarmament proves a failure. Thus, 20 years after World War I the goal of disarmament still was far away. In fact, because of events in the Far East, in Europe, and in Africa, European countries once more were becoming involved in a race to increase and perfect their fighting forces. Greed for empire, as well as fears and hatreds, all helped bring about the failure of attempts to safeguard peace.

[3] Germany had been admitted to the League in 1926.

How did the United States continue to work for world peace?

1. In what ways did the United States co-operate in activities of the League of Nations?
2. What were the functions of the World

Court? What Americans urged that we join the World Court? Why did the Senate reject membership in the court?

3. What was the Kellogg-Briand Pact? Why was its effectiveness limited?
4. What progress was made toward limiting naval armaments? Why did these efforts eventually fail?

CHAPTER REVIEW

Terms to Understand

covenant
secretariat
sanctions
"irreconcilables"
reservations

ratification
superstate
"advisory opinion"
capital ships
"escalator clause"

People and Things to Know About

Woodrow Wilson
"Big Four"
Supreme Council
David Lloyd George
Georges Clemenceau
Treaty of Versailles
League of Nations
Senate Foreign Rela-
  tions Committee
Henry Cabot Lodge
Article X
Article XVI

Warren G. Harding
Geneva, Switzerland
Permanent Court of
  International Justice
Elihu Root
Kellogg-Briand Pact
Washington Confer-
  ence (1921)
Charles Evans Hughes
London Conference
  (1930)

Historic Dates to Identify

1919   1921   1928

Questions to Discuss

1. Contrast the following:
   (a) Difficulties encountered by Presidents Wilson and Washington during their second terms.
   (b) The attitude of Presidents Wilson and Harding toward international co-operation.
2. Why did President Wilson exert less influence at the peace conference after the election of 1918?
3. Why have some people criticized the Treaty of Versailles because it was too harsh; others because it was too mild? What is your opinion?
4. Why did President Wilson feel that the inclusion of the covenant of the League in the peace settlement was more important than the specific terms of the territorial settlements?
5. Why was the Senate more conservative in its reaction to membership by the United States in the League and the World Court than the people of America were?

Questions to Discuss (Cont.)

6. How would you have voted on the League question if you had been a senator in 1919–20? What reasons can you give for your stand?
7. What was the essential weakness in the approach made by the Kellogg-Briand Pact to the problem of maintaining world peace?
8. Why was the United States willing to accept naval equality with Great Britain but not with Japan?

Relating Geography and History

1. After World War I, France wished to annex German territory as far east as the Rhine River or to establish an independent Rhineland Republic? Why?
2. Use an atlas to compare the territory held by Austria-Hungary before 1914 with the territorial arrangements in this area after World War I. What economic problems resulted from breaking up the Austro-Hungarian empire? See Benns, *Europe Since 1914*, or a similar book in your library.

Other Things to Do

1. Report to the class on the secret treaties binding the Allied powers. See Benns, *Europe Since 1914*, or other similar books in your library.
2. Use the encyclopedia to learn the party affiliation, home state, and other facts about the men who were most active in keeping the United States out of the League. Report to the class any reasons you can infer why each of these men took the stand he did.
3. Look in *Readers' Guide* to discover articles discussing the efforts of Presidents Roosevelt and Truman to maintain a bi-partisan foreign policy during and after World War II. Report your findings to the class and compare them with the difficulties encountered by President Wilson.
4. Debate: *Resolved*, That the United States won World War I and lost the peace.

Chapter 39

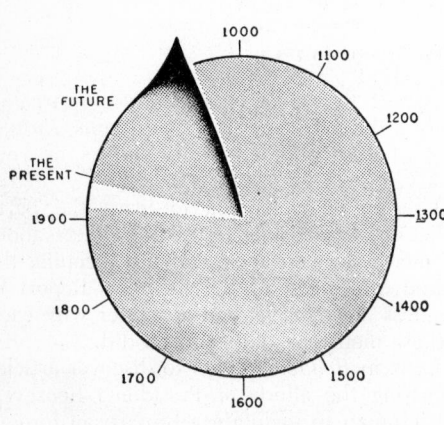

German soldier

AGGRESSOR NATIONS PLUNGE THE

WORLD INTO A SECOND WORLD WAR

There never was a war more easy to stop . . . The strict enforcement of the disarmament clauses of the Peace Treaty would have guarded indefinitely, without violence or bloodshed, the peace and safety of mankind. But this was neglected while the infringements remained petty, and shunned as they assumed serious proportions. Thus the final safeguard of a long peace was cast away.

Winston Churchill

1919-1941

At the end of World War I the Allies reigned victorious. France, Great Britain, Italy, Japan, and the United States, as the most important victorious nations, faced the future with hope and confidence. Yet 20 years after the peace conference, the world was once more plunged into war. Efforts at peacemaking and disarmament had ended in utter failure. The League of Nations — weakened by the decision of the United States not to become a member — had proved powerless to check the mighty new forces unleashed in the world.

What were these forces that divided the victors and lined up Japan and Italy with defeated Germany in a new attempt to conquer the world? In this chapter we shall trace the development of the ambitions, the rivalries, and the greed which threatened world peace and which finally involved the world in a terrible new war. The ominous events which led the United

States into the new conflict will be developed under these topics:

1. The growth of dictator nations leads to war.
2. The United States tries to remain neutral as Germany conquers Europe.
3. The attack on Pearl Harbor brings the United States into the war.

1 The Growth of Dictator Nations Leads to War

World War I leaves a bitter heritage of discontent. Many countries — even those which had been victorious — became discontented soon after the war. The dissatisfaction of some of the nations was increased by the results of the peace conferences. Italy had been promised a share in the spoils by the secret agreements which had brought her into World War I on the side of the Allies. After the war, Italy felt that France, Great Britain, and the United States had kept her from getting the territory she had been promised. Dissatisfied, Italy was more than ready to follow a leader who would help her "obtain a place in the sun."

Although Japan had taken no active part in the war in Europe, she had received a mandate over former German possessions in the Pacific. But Japan, too, believed that she should have received more than she did. The Twenty-one Demands which Japan had made on China during the war had been modified at the insistence of the United States (pages 653-4). Furthermore, many Japanese felt that as a result of the Naval Disarmament Conference in Washington Japan had been placed in an inferior position and had "lost face." Japan like Italy was discontented and bitter over what she considered affronts to her national dignity. Militarists in Japan took over the government from those who were

more friendly to the western nations and who had agreed to disarm.

In many countries the end of World War I brought unemployment, hard times, and great poverty. This was particularly true in Germany. Branded as the nation responsible for war in 1914, disappointed in her dreams of world leadership, and stripped of her colonies, Germany faced the 1920's with deep discontent.

New governments and "have-not" nations disturb the world. In several countries those who were discontented and dissatisfied with their lot overthrew their governments and installed new leaders who promised them better conditions. The new leaders set themselves up as *dictators*; that is, they seized absolute power for themselves and their friends. Most of the dictatorships were established in countries which considered themselves deprived of their fair share of the world's riches or resources. These "have-not" nations and their leaders were not interested in maintaining the *status quo* (leaving matters as they were); they wanted more territory or more colonies and were quick to find excuses for seizing what they wanted.

Germany and Italy were two of the most important "have-not" nations whose dictator governments caused trouble for the world. Japan was a "have-not" nation, too. Although Japan did not change her form of government after World War I, her new leaders were military men who hated democracy and who were not afraid to try to grab what they wanted.

Russia establishes a communist government. Russia was not a "have-not" nation; she was large and rich in resources. During World War I, however, a series of revolutions overthrew the Russian czar and established a new form of government. This new communist government, which was led by Nicholai Lenin (lehn'in), made peace with Germany in 1917. Although the treaty of Brest-Litovsk (page 671) ended the war with Germany, fighting continued for some time between the Communists and the White Russians who opposed the Communists. The Allies favored the White Russians, who were willing to continue the war against Germany, and sent troops and supplies to try to help them. The United States sent expeditionary forces which remained in northern Russia and Siberia until 1919. Finally, foreign troops were withdrawn, and the "Red" armies of the Communists put down all opposition.

Under the czar, Russia had been a backward country, and the people had had few rights or freedoms. The new government, which officially changed the name of the country to the Union of Soviet Socialist Republics (U.S.S.R.), set up a "dictatorship of the proletariat" (working class). Theoretically, under the system of *communism* all property, factories, and businesses are owned by all the people *in common*. Actually, however, Russia was run by the leaders of a single party — the Communist Party — which represented only a very small percentage of all the people. There was strong opposition to communism in Russia, but the Communist leaders ruthlessly killed and imprisoned those who opposed them. They set up a "police state," in which secret police spied on the people and closely regulated their life. As a result, the Russian people enjoyed even less freedom under communism than they had under the czars.

Soviet Russia grows in strength. During the 1920's Soviet Russia continued to stamp out opposition at home and to strengthen the country economically. After the death of Lenin, Josef Stalin became the leader of the Communist Party and the ruler of Soviet Russia. In 1928 Russia began a series of five-year plans aimed at increasing the country's production of both manufactured goods and food. In particular, they tried to increase industrial production and the use of machinery.

One by one the leading countries of the world established diplomatic relations with Russia until by 1930 the United States was the only one of the great powers that had refused to recognize the Soviet gov-

ernment. This policy stemmed in part from the fact that the Soviet government had refused to be responsible for debts incurred by Russia under the rule of the czars. American resentment was also aroused by the encouragement Soviet Russia gave to Communist propaganda in the United States.

In spite of the fact that Soviet Russia and the United States did not maintain normal diplomatic relations, trade between the two countries increased. Long-term credits were granted by American manufacturers to Russia for the purchase of goods in this country. American engineers played a leading part in transforming Russia into an industrial state, and American promoters looked for opportunities to develop Russian natural resources. By 1930 our exports to Russia were nearly six times as great as in the year before the outbreak of World War I.

Soviet Russia is recognized. Official relations between the United States and Russia were resumed at the beginning of Franklin D. Roosevelt's administration (1933). President Roosevelt invited the Russian government to appoint representatives to consider with him "personally all questions outstanding between our countries." Soon afterward he announced that diplomatic recognition had been given the Soviet Union. Commissar Maxim Litvinov, representing Russia, agreed that his country would refrain from communist agitation in the United States. He further promised that if any organization engaged in agitation for communism on American soil, the Russian government would exclude that organization from Russia. Financial questions were to be discussed after recognition. The Soviet government also agreed to respect the civil and religious rights of Americans in Russia.

In general, the immediate results of recognizing Russia proved disappointing. Trade did not increase as expected, while the negotiations to settle the question of debts broke down. In August, 1935, the American Secretary of State was obliged to protest against the "flagrant violation" of the pledges given by the Soviet government to refrain from Communist agitation.

Russian soldier

Mussolini establishes a Fascist government in Italy. After World War I Italy suffered from unemployment and a severe depression. At the same time, many Italians hated communism and were afraid that it would spread from Russia to their own country. Benito Mussolini, a newspaper editor and war veteran, formed an organization of ex-soldiers called Fascists to fight the spread of communism. Mussolini also dreamed of restoring Italy to the power and influence it had during the Roman Empire.

On the excuse of saving Italy from communism, Mussolini and his Fascists marched on Rome in 1922 and seized control of the government. Although he allowed the king to remain, Mussolini immediately set about making himself the absolute dictator of Italy. He glorified war and began to build up Italy's army and navy.

Italy wants more land. Italy considered herself a "have-not" nation. In order to restore Italy to her place as a great power, Mussolini determined to obtain colonies and to develop a great empire. The Japanese aggression in Manchuria in 1931 (page 657) had already proved that the League of Nations was not able to stop a strong nation from carrying out its plans.[1] In 1935, therefore, Mussolini attacked the African kingdom of Ethiopia (map, page 710) and in a few months drove out the native ruler and conquered the country. When the League of Nations tried to apply sanctions (economic penalties), Mussolini took Italy out of the League of Nations. In 1939 Italy also seized Albania and made it a protectorate.

Hitler rises to power in Germany. You have already seen (page 689) that during the 1920's Germany and her people were discontented and unhappy. A republic had been established in Germany after the war, but the Germans associated it with the humiliating terms of the Treaty of Versailles, and it never took firm root. In Germany, as in other countries, the de-

[1] World War II officially began in 1939 with fighting in Europe, but actually there is good reason for dating the beginning of the war with the Japanese aggressions in China.

Galloway

The five-year plans brought women into Russian factories to increase industrial output.

pression which swept the country in the early 1930's caused great hardship. Into this gloomy picture stepped a man who was destined not only to dominate Germany, but to change the course of human history. That man was Adolf Hitler.

Adolf Hitler was an Austrian of humble parentage whose early life had been distinguished chiefly by failures and unhappiness. During World War I, Hitler served in the German army, rising to the rank of corporal. In the years following the war, he plotted with other disappointed Germans to gain political power. He served a term in prison, during which he wrote *Mein Kampf* ("My Struggle"), a curious book which detailed his beliefs and made clear what he planned for Germany when once in power. He and his followers formed the National Socialist German Workers' Party, shortened to Nazis (naht'-zees), which grew from a small minority to the largest single political party in Germany. By holding out glittering promises to all who were discontented, the Nazis attracted many followers. In 1933, Hitler was named to the high office of Chancellor. By illegal means he soon gained control of

691

The Axis dictators, Hitler of Germany (left) and Mussolini of Italy (right), met several times to plan political and military strategy.

all branches of the government, overthrew the constitution of the republic, and declared himself *Der Fuehrer* (the leader) of the German people.

Individuals are unimportant in the Nazi state. Under the dictatorship of Hitler and the Nazis, Germany was transformed into a united, energetic nation. Once more the German people took great pride in their country. Industry boomed and large public works were undertaken. But these gains were won at the cost of human liberties. Every phase of life in Germany was controlled by the Nazi Party. Every individual had to bow to the will of the state, which encouraged the ruthless use of force to establish the supremacy of the "master race." Freedom of speech disappeared, newspapers were muzzled, schools became centers of Nazi propaganda, and freedom of religion was restricted. Labor and industry alike were placed under the close regulation of the state. Claiming that it was their intention to establish a pure Aryan race, the Nazis persecuted the Jews and spoke scornfully of the rights of peoples that did not belong to the "master race."

Hitler attacks the Treaty of Versailles. During the early years of Hitler's rule, other nations paid little attention to the changing scene in Germany. In time it became evident, however, that Hitler's ambitions extended beyond the boundaries of Germany. In his speeches *Der Fuehrer* frequently screamed against the unfair treatment Germany had received under the Treaty of Versailles. At first secretly, and later with no effort at concealment, Hitler set about to destroy the treaty and to make Germany the most powerful military state in the world. In 1935, he proclaimed that Germany would no longer respect the disarmament provision of the Versailles Treaty. Compulsory military service was restored and the German air and naval forces were built up. In 1936 German troops occupied the German Rhineland, which had been demilitarized (stripped of military organization and defense) under the agreement at Versailles.

Germany expands. Hitler was greatly encouraged both by his successes at home and by the fact that other European states seemed unwilling to run the risk of starting a war in order to stop his aggressive moves. He now set about to enlarge the boundaries of Germany. (Follow Germany's expansion on the map, page 711.) In the spring of 1938, Austria was added to Germany without the firing of a shot. In the fall of the same year, Germany forced Czechoslovakia to give up the Sudetenland (soo-day'ten land), a part of Czechoslovakia that had a large German population. For a time it looked as if Great Britain and France would come to the aid of the democratic state of Czechoslovakia. However, they had been following a policy of "appeasement" (pacifying Hitler at any price), and that policy again prevailed. In September, 1938, there was an historic meeting at Munich, attended by Hitler, Prime Minister Neville Chamberlain of England, Premier Daladier of France, and Mussolini, the Fascist dictator of Italy. These men reached an agreement which gave Germany a free rein in the Sudetenland.

After Munich Czechoslovakia was defenseless, and in March, 1939, German troops occupied the country. The Nazis, meanwhile, wrung the Baltic port of Memel (may'mel) from Lithuania.

Hitler meets with more successes. The summer days of 1939 were the lull before a storm. Under the pressure of public opinion, leaders in England and France gradually abandoned the policy of appeasement. The British and French governments pledged themselves to give assistance and even military aid to small countries like Poland, Greece, and Rumania, which stood in danger of attack from Germany. Great Britain and France also began to build up their military, naval, and air forces.

Despite the stiffening attitude of other powers, Hitler, excited over his first successes, was eager for new triumphs. Forgotten already was his solemn promise, given at the Munich Conference: "This is the last territorial claim which I have to make in Europe." This time his attention was fixed upon Poland. He demanded that Poland return the free city of Danzig and give Germany control of a strip of land across the Polish Corridor. Hitler's position had been strengthened by a military alliance with Mussolini. Germany and Italy were now referred to as the Axis powers. As the tension mounted during August, Hitler threw a bombshell into the face of a dismayed Europe with the announcement that he had signed a commercial treaty and a non-aggression pact with Soviet Russia. The announcement caused great astonishment, since the Nazis of Germany and the Communists of Russia had long been bitter enemies. It also dashed all hopes of Britain and France for help from Russia in preventing an attack on Poland.

World War II begins. Events now moved swiftly and certainly toward war. There were

Nazi SS: Elite guard

Swastika

the usual demands, the usual threats. Nazi agents were busily stirring up trouble in Poland. Then came last-minute diplomatic attempts to avoid war. But this time Hitler's opponents refused to back down. On September 1, 1939, *Der Fuehrer* sent his armies across the border into Poland. Two days later, when Germany failed to halt the attack on helpless Poland, Britain and France declared war on Germany. World War II had begun.

——— CHECK-UP ———

How did the ambitions of dictator nations lead to World War II?

1. In what ways did World War I "sow the seeds" of World War II? Why were "have-not" nations a threat to world peace?

2. What events led to the formation of the communist government in Russia? Why was the United States slow to recognize Soviet Russia?

3. Why was Mussolini successful in establishing a Fascist government in Italy? What acts of aggression did Mussolini commit?

4. How did Hitler come to power in Germany? What were some of the basic ideas underlying his dictatorship?

5. Why did Hitler repudiate the provisions of the Treaty of Versailles? Why was this possible?

6. Why did war break out in 1939? Why was Soviet Russia's stand a blow to Great Britain and France?

2 The United States Tries to Remain Neutral as Germany Conquers Europe

American public opinion is divided. During the uncertain days before World War II, Americans had anxiously watched the trend of events. Thanks to radio and excellent news services, the average American was much better informed about European events than in the days just before war broke out in 1914. As one crisis after another threatened to destroy peace, there developed a "tug-of-war" between two groups of people in the United States. One

pucker - up boy!

Mr. **Cordell Hull** of Tennessee was Secretary of State in Roosevelt's cabinet during the difficult period prior to World War II. He held this office until his resignation in 1944.

group expected America to contribute in every possible way to the preservation of peace through some form of international co-operation. The other felt that we would be wise to adopt a complete "hands-off" isolationist policy.

Congress adopts neutrality legislation. Disturbed by the outbreak of war between Italy and Ethiopia and by the failure of peace efforts, the American Congress turned to neutrality legislation as a means of keeping the United States out of war. In the summer of 1935 an emergency measure directed the President to place an embargo upon the shipment of arms to all belligerents (warring countries). He might also advise American citizens that only at their own risk could they travel on ships of nations at war. Actually, the President went further and attempted to discourage transactions of any kind with warring nations. In the following year, Congress outlawed loans and credits to belligerent governments except in case of American republics at war with non-American powers.

In the more permanent Neutrality Act of 1937, Congress continued the provisions of the earlier acts, and adopted the "cash and carry" principle for trading with belligerents. In other words, the President had the right to forbid shipments to belligerents in American vessels, and to limit the trade of belligerents to materials paid for in cash and transported from American ports in foreign vessels. Thus it was hoped that the United States might avoid the pitfalls which led us into the first World War. As relations between rival powers became more tense and the likelihood of war increased, one thing was certain: American public opinion was strongly in favor of keeping out of war.

The administration of Franklin D. Roosevelt states its policy. Although the American people desired to stay free of foreign entanglements, the administration of Franklin D. Roosevelt indicated that it could not remain indifferent to the effects of European diplomatic developments on American interests. A war in Europe was bound to affect the United States, and we might become involved in war against our will.

To make our foreign policy clear in the face of Axis aggression, Secretary of State Hull, in July, 1937, sent a vigorous statement to every foreign office in the world. "We advocate," said Mr. Hull, "abstinence by all nations from use of force in pursuit of policy and from interference in the internal affairs of other nations. We advocate adjustment of problems in international relations by peaceful negotiation and agreement. We advocate faithful observance of international agreements."

President Roosevelt took a more definite stand. In October, 1937, he spoke at Chicago of a "quarantine" of aggressor nations and emphasized our willingness to engage actively in an earnest search for peace. When Europe in September, 1938, seemed on the verge of war over the occupation of the Sudeten portion of Czechoslovakia, the President intervened directly in an effort to preserve peace. He hoped that if he let the aggressor states know where our sympathies lay, their rulers would hesitate before using force. "The conscience and impelling desire of the people of my country," the President cabled to Chancellor Hitler of Germany, "demand that the voice of their government be raised again and yet again to avert and avoid war."

Hitler and Mussolini turn down Roosevelt's plea for peace. Some of President Roosevelt's peace efforts brought violent protests from isolationists and from anti-administration forces. The President insisted, however, that his purpose was only to preserve peaceful relationships among nations. Toward that end he was willing to direct the full strength of the United States by any means short of war. For this reason President Roosevelt again took the initiative in April, 1939, in an attempt to rid the world of its "constant fear of a new war." To his appeal, however, Hitler and Mussolini turned a deaf ear.

The United States faces the outbreak of war. As the fateful days of August, 1939, brought the crisis over Poland, President Roosevelt made further efforts to prevent war. To King Victor Emmanuel III of Italy he sent a personal message urging him and his country to advance the cause of peace. In even stronger appeals to Adolf Hitler and the president of Poland he urged that they settle their difficulties by peaceful means. On September 1, the day when German troops drove into Poland, the President sent last minute pleas to Germany, Poland, Britain, France, and Italy to refrain from bombing civilians and "open" cities (those having no military value). On September 3, when Great Britain and France declared war, Roosevelt expressed an earnest hope for true neutrality, but added: "Even a neutral has a right to take account of facts. Even a neutral cannot be asked to close his mind or his conscience."

Action followed swiftly. With certain exceptions American citizens were not allowed to travel on ships belonging to nations at war. Shipments of arms, munitions, and other war materials to warring nations — either directly or indirectly through neutral countries — was forbidden. The Panama Canal was placed under army rule, and a limited "national emergency" was soon proclaimed. Congress was summoned to meet in special session on September 21.

The neutrality laws are modified. During the special session, politics and party quarrels were largely set aside. The debate in the Senate brought out all the arguments for and against the embargo provisions of the Neutrality Act of 1937, which prohibited the sale of weapons to nations at war.[2] A new act, the Neutrality Act of 1939, was finally passed by substantial majorities in both houses. Its more important provisions were as follows: (1) the embargo on the shipment of arms, munitions, and implements of war was repealed; (2) all commerce with the belligerents was to be on a cash-and-carry basis; (3) the granting of loans to belligerents was prohibited; (4) American vessels were forbidden to enter the war zone; (5) Americans, except in special instances, were not to sail on belligerent ships; and (6) American merchant vessels were not permitted to arm. If the existence of a foreign war was recognized either by the President or by Congress, the law would automatically be brought into effect.

Fascist uniform

By this legislation the United States expressed its determination to keep out of war. But to do so, it had to sacrifice a principle (freedom of the seas) for which it had fought in two earlier wars. The Neutrality Act of 1939 practically drove our merchant marine from the North Atlantic.

Hemispheric solidarity grows. Meanwhile, steps were taken to strengthen cooperation among the republics of the Western Hemisphere. In September, 1939, delegates from the 21 republics met at Panama City in an atmosphere of unparalleled good feeling. The conference adopted a declaration of general neutrality and drew a "safety belt" around the Americas, south of Canada, from 400 to 1200 miles wide. Warring nations were warned that hostile acts must not take place within this zone. No adequate steps

---

[2] The "cash and carry" provision of the Neutrality Act of 1937 had expired May 1, 1939, and had not been renewed.

German "Stuka"
dive bomber

were taken, however, to enforce Pan American neutrality in this extensive area.

"A phony war" follows the conquest of Poland. Although they had promised assistance to Poland, Great Britain and France were able to furnish little actual military aid. German divisions rolled swiftly over that unfortunate country while Nazi bombers hurled death and destruction upon Warsaw and other cities. (See map, page 711.) Poland's fate was sealed when Russian troops invaded from the East. During the seven months following the conquest of Poland, there was so little fighting that the expression "phony war" was used to describe the situation. The armies of Germany and France retired behind strongly fortified lines, and neither side seemed willing to take the offensive. Meanwhile, rumors of peace offers caused "appeasers" in Great Britain and this country to hope that a settlement might be reached.

The blitzkrieg strikes. All this changed, however, with the approach of spring. In April, 1940, Hitler launched an attack on Denmark and Norway. Again British and French attempts at assistance proved feeble. Greatly aided by Nazi sympathizers (called fifth columnists) in these countries, the German armies completed their conquest in three weeks. Then, on May 10, the world was horrified by news that Hitler's forces were invading Netherlands and Belgium. The tactics employed were those of the *blitzkrieg* (lightning war), and were to become all too familiar during succeeding months. The *blitzkrieg* involved the merciless bombing of airports, transportation centers, and cities; the assistance of fifth columnists in the seizure of vital military points; the dropping of parachute troops; the wanton killing of civilians; and startling advances by motorized army divisions.

France collapses. When the Nazi forces swept into northern France, the French army, regarded as the finest in Europe, crumpled before the fierce attack. The confusion was indescribable as troops retreated and roads became choked with crowds of panic-stricken civilians fleeing before the fury of the Nazi thrust. Sensing the fact that France was doomed, Mussolini declared war, an act which President Roosevelt termed a "stab in the back." By the middle of June the collapse of France was complete. According to the terms of the armistice half of France was occupied by Hitler's forces. The remainder was ruled by a government at Vichy under the aged Marshal Petain (pay-tan'). As time went on, the Vichy government gave in more and more to Hitler's demands.

The British fight doggedly on. For a few weeks it seemed that nothing could save England from sharing the fate of France. The British people, however, sturdily rallied under the courageous leadership of Winston Churchill, the statesman who had succeeded Chamberlain as Prime Minister. Through the late summer, fall, and winter of 1940–41, Hitler's air force bombed the little island with terrific attacks designed to "soften" its people for an invasion. But the English refused to become panicky. Their small but efficient air force valiantly fought off the Nazi bombers. To the Royal Air Force, Churchill paid the stirring tribute: "Never in the field of human conflict was so much owed by so many to so few."

The war shifts to the Near East. The spring of 1941 brought a change in Hitler's strategy. He abandoned for the time the plan of invading the British Isles and prepared to strike at Britain through her empire. The scene of battle therefore shifted to the Mediterranean and the Near East. (See map, page 710.) British forces had been successful against the Italians in Ethiopia and Libya, and had reinforced the Greeks in their resistance to Mussolini. When Hitler launched an attack in the Near East, however, the picture changed. British advances in Libya were checked, and they were driven out of Greece, their last foothold on the continent of Europe. The British seemed to suffer from "too little and too late" even though their stubborn resistance upset Hitler's timetable.

The Russian campaign begins. The summer of 1941 was marked by the opening of another great theater of war. On June 22, news reached the world that German armies had launched a surprise attack against Russia. Hitler may have felt the need for supplies which might be obtained in the Ukraine — especially wheat — and the oil of the Caucasus (kaw'kuh-sus). Perhaps he realized the danger of leaving a strong military power at his back in any "all-out" attack upon Britain. The German armies, after forcing their way through the border states of Estonia, Latvia, and Lithuania, launched major drives against the three important cities of Leningrad, Moscow, and Kiev. (See map, page 710.)

The Nazis predicted the collapse of Russia in three weeks. Certainly the great majority of people in England and the United States had very little hope that the Red armies of Josef Stalin could resist Hitler's war machine for any length of time. But to the amazement of the world, the Russians stubbornly resisted. The Red air force escaped the knock-out blow aimed at it, while the Russian armies, apparently much better prepared than the world had thought, kept up the struggle doggedly. Morale remained high and fifth-column activities were insignificant.

Hitler receives a setback in Russia. Fighting a delaying action, the Russian armies fell back to a line of fortification far inside the borders of Russia. As they retreated, they adopted the "scorched earth" policy, stripping the land of all supplies and equipment that might be of value to the Nazi armies. Throughout the summer and fall of 1941, the gigantic struggle continued. Although the Red armies were forced to give ground, they launched counteroffensives to harass the enemy. More important, they blocked Hitler's main objective — the annihilation of the Russian forces. Winter found the German attack not only stalled but forced back in a number of places. The Reds at least had proved that Hitler's forces were not unbeatable, and they had taken a huge toll of Nazi man power. Furthermore, they had given the British a much-needed breathing spell in which to recover from the German air attacks. Now the British were able to step up their own raids on industrial centers and military objectives in Germany and the occupied countries of Europe.

——— CHECK-UP ———

What efforts were made by the United States in the years just before and after the outbreak of World War II to further the cause of peace and to maintain neutrality?

1. How did President Franklin D. Roosevelt try to discourage aggression by the Axis powers and to prevent the outbreak of war?

2. What were the important provisions of the Neutrality Acts of 1935 and 1937? What changes were made by the Neutrality Act of 1939? How did it violate American traditions?

3. Trace the developments in World War II from 1939 to 1941. Why was Germany successful in its attacks on Poland, Denmark and Norway, Holland and Belgium, and France? Why was Germany unsuccessful in its attacks on Great Britain and Russia?

RAF fighter pilots

The Attack on Pearl Harbor Brings the United States into the War

America is aroused by Nazi expansion. The progress of the war had a profound effect upon American thinking and policy. Every Nazi victory brought the war closer to our borders. This was true not only because Germany had conquered much of Europe, but also because such fallen governments as France and Netherlands had territories in the Americas, Africa, and the Far East. If the Nazis seized these colonies, the struggle would be brought to our very borders and we would be deprived of vital raw materials.

Human liberty is threatened. Moreover, Americans became more and more aware that the war represented a fundamental struggle between two opposing ways of life. It was not merely a race for empires, they realized, but an attempt to replace one set of ideas and ideals with another. German activities in the occupied countries of Europe gave proof of the kind of world order the Nazis would establish if the Axis was victorious. The Germans would assume the position of a master race while the defeated peoples would be forced to slave in the fields and factories for the benefit of their conquerors. The spread of such a system would destroy human liberty and the democratic way of life. Even if German conquests fell short of the United States, Hitler would possess such great economic power that he would threaten our safety. Already German and Italian agents were active in Latin American countries. Axis ambitions obviously were not restricted to Europe alone.

The United States takes action for defense. It became increasingly clear, therefore, that the United States had a real stake in the fight that Great Britain in 1940 was carrying on almost alone. The unexpected collapse of France shocked America into action. During the summer and fall of 1940 this country took three important steps: (1) At the request of the President, Congress voted huge sums for increasing our army and air force, and for building a two-ocean navy. (2) In August, Roosevelt exchanged 50 over-age American destroyers for 99-year leases on important air and naval bases in eight British possessions in the Western Hemisphere. Among these were Bermuda, Newfoundland, and Jamaica. (3) Finally, a Selective Service Act established conscription (compulsory enrollment for military service). This was the first time in American history that such a step had been taken in time of peace. Under the provisions of this act men from the ages of 21 to 35 inclusive were made subject to call for training in the American army. As in World War I, the order of call was determined by numbers drawn in Washington, but local boards in each community actually handled the drafting of the young men.

The Havana Conference meets. Steps were taken at the same time to prevent the growth of Nazi influence in Latin America and to determine the position of the American colonies of countries occupied by Germany. The American State Department issued a warning to Berlin and Rome that "The United States would not recognize any transfer and would not acquiesce in any attempt to transfer any geographic region of the Western Hemisphere from one non-American power to another non-American power." At a conference of American republics held in Havana in July, 1940, it was decided that if a European power ceased to govern itself independently, its American possessions should come under a Pan-American

Tanker

trusteeship. Steps were also taken by the conference to prevent fifth-column activities.

American policy is further clarified. President Roosevelt interpreted his re-election in 1940 as an approval by the American people of the policy of all-out aid to Britain, short of war. In his annual message to Congress in January, 1941, the President expressed our national policy as follows: (1) we are committed to all-inclusive national defense; (2) we are committed to full support of all those people who are resisting aggression and are thereby keeping war away from our hemisphere; (3) we feel that principles of morality and considerations for our own security will never permit us to agree to a peace dictated by aggressors and sponsored by appeasers.

The four freedoms are defined. "We look forward," said the President, "to a world founded upon four essential freedoms." These were defined as (1) freedom of speech and expression — everywhere in the world; (2) freedom of every person to worship God in his own way; (3) freedom from want, with economic understandings which will give every nation a healthy peacetime life for its inhabitants; and (4) freedom from fear, calling for such a worldwide reduction of armaments that no nation will be in a position to commit an act of aggression against any neighbor.

Lend-Lease is adopted. In March, 1941, after two months of bitter debate, Congress definitely abandoned isolationism by passing the Lend-Lease Act. This measure authorized the President to sell, lease, lend, or otherwise dispose of war materials to any nation whose defense he considered vital to America's safety. The law also stated that any defense article, including warships, which belonged to a friendly belligerent, could be outfitted or repaired in the United States. Such a defense article could also be manufactured and released to a friendly belligerent. Promptly after the passage of the measure, Congress appropriated seven billion dollars to carry it into effect. From that time, the United States actually became a non-belligerent ally of Great Britain.

British servicewomen operating barrage balloon

Our hostility toward the Axis grows. During the following months the gulf between the United States and the Axis powers grew steadily wider. All ships of the Axis and Axis-dominated countries in our ports were seized. An unlimited national emergency was proclaimed, and all the German and Italian assets in the United States were frozen (could not be used). The offices of German and Italian consuls in the United States were also ordered closed, and in July, 1941, the Axis diplomats left the country. By these last moves our government reduced the danger of Axis plots to slow down aid to Britain.

Production is speeded up. Meanwhile, American production was increased. In December, 1940, the Office of Production Management had been created under the leadership of William Knudsen, of the General Motors Corporation, and Sidney Hillman, noted labor leader. In 1941, other moves were made to speed up production. A priorities act was passed making it possible to allot vital raw materials to the industries producing war products. Secretary of the Interior Ickes (ik'ess) was named National Oil Co-ordinator for the purpose of conserving and distributing petroleum supplies. Appropriations for defense and for aid to Britain were more than doubled for the next year.

The United States patrols the western Atlantic. It was one thing to make goods for England; it was another to get them there. As American production increased, German submarine warfare in the North Atlantic was intensified. The effort to get supplies safely across the ocean placed a strain upon the British navy, which was already having difficulty in keeping open the sea lanes throughout the world. America was unprepared and as yet unwilling to convoy supplies across the Atlantic, but some steps were taken to ease the pressure. In April, 1941, with the permission of the government of Greenland, American air and naval bases were established on that vital stepping-stone of the North Atlantic. A month later, the President announced that navy patrols would help protect vital supplies bound for England. In June American forces relieved the British garrison in Iceland.

The Atlantic Charter is proclaimed. In August, 1941, President Roosevelt and Prime Minister Churchill surprised the world by meeting on shipboard off the coast of Newfoundland. After several days of conferences a program was announced which proposed eight principles as a basis for a new world order. Their program, known popularly as the Atlantic Charter, appears on page 701. Not all of the ideals expressed in the charter have been attained even today. People all over the world, however, took hope from the charter that these high goals might some day be achieved.

Winston Churchill, British Prime Minister, joined President Roosevelt in announcing the aims of the Atlantic Charter.

Merchant ships are armed. Developments in the Battle of the Atlantic soon led to the repeal of the restrictive provisions of the Neutrality Act of 1939. Hitler had announced that every ship, whether with or without convoy, would be torpedoed. The Nazis carried out their threat, sending to the bottom of the ocean American shipping, even within the areas declared vital to American defense. The President, therefore, asked Congress to repeal the section of the Neutrality Act forbidding American ships to arm. Congress, aroused by further attacks on American vessels, went a step beyond the President's request (November, 1941). After bitter and prolonged debate it also repealed the provisions which prevented American ships from entering combat areas. Thus ended the American experiment with legislation designed in advance to keep the United States out of any war.

Japan renews aggression in China. Although the policy of all-out aid to Britain constantly threatened to bring the United States into World War II, an even greater threat to America's uneasy neutrality came from an entirely different direction. While the Axis powers had been engaged in the conquest of Europe, Japan had taken similar steps in eastern Asia. Made bold by its successful seizure of Manchuria and by the gains of the Axis powers in Europe, Japan began an undeclared war on China in 1937. Japanese forces overran all of northern China and seized the important seaports. This was only the first step in Japan's attempt to carry out a long-cherished plan — a plan to gain control of eastern Asia. Such a policy, however, was directly opposed to the Far Eastern policy of the United States and to our commercial and industrial interests. It was also a threat to the Philippines, which had not yet been granted their full independence. The first serious incident occurred at the end of 1937 when Japanese aviators repeatedly bombed and finally sank the United States river gunboat *Panay*. On the same day Japanese airplanes destroyed three American tankers. The Japanese later apologized for the insult to the American flag and paid damages, but it was evident that the attack had

(Continued on page 702)

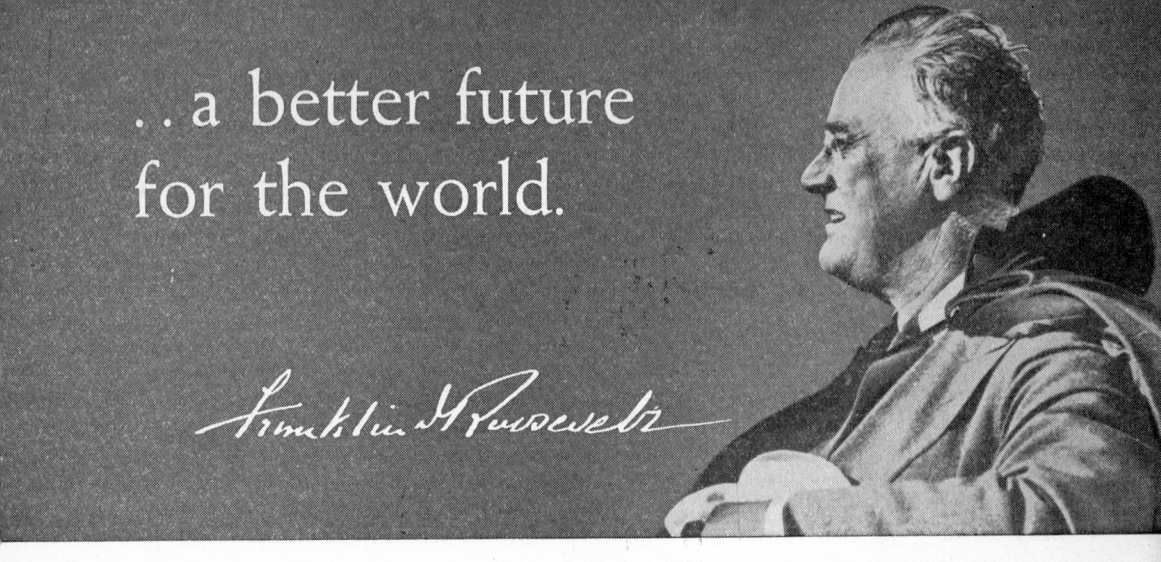

..a better future for the world.

Franklin D. Roosevelt

THE ATLANTIC CHARTER

THE President of the United States and the Prime Minister, Mr. Churchill, representing His Majesty's Government in the United Kingdom, being met together, deem it right to make known certain common principles in the national policies of their respective countries on which they base their hopes for a better future for the world.

First: Their countries seek no aggrandizement, territorial or otherwise;

Second: They desire to see no territorial changes that do not accord with the freely expressed wishes of the peoples concerned;

Third: They respect the right of all peoples to chose the form of government under which they will live; and they wish to see sovereign rights and self-government restored to those who have been forcibly deprived of them;

Fourth: They will endeavor, with due respect for their existing obligations, to further the enjoyment by all states, great or small, victor or vanquished, of access, on equal terms, to the trade and to the raw materials of the world which are needed for their economic prosperity;

Fifth: They desire to bring about the fullest collaboration between all nations in the economic field, with the object of securing for all improved labor standards, economic advancement, and social security;

Sixth: After the final destruction of the Nazi tyranny, they hope to see established a peace which will afford to all nations the means of dwelling in safety within their own boundaries, and which will afford assurance that all the men in all the lands may live out their lives in freedom from fear and want;

Seventh: Such a peace should enable all men to traverse the high seas and oceans without hindrance;

Eighth: They believe that all the nations of the world, for realistic as well as spiritual reasons, must come to the abandonment of the use of force. Since no future peace can be maintained if land, sea, or air armaments continue to be employed by nations which threaten, or may threaten, aggression outside of their frontiers, they believe, pending the establishment of a wider and permanent system of general security, that the disarmament of such nations is essential. They will likewise aid and encourage all other practicable measures which will lighten for peace-loving peoples the crushing burden of armaments.

been a protest against American interests and the presence of Americans in China.

Relations with Japan become less friendly. From the beginning, our State Department protested against any interference with American rights in the areas of China overrun by the Japanese forces. Japanese replies to our complaints announced the desire to meet American wishes, but gave little satisfaction. America thereupon showed its disapproval of the Japanese attitude by lending the Chinese government 25 million dollars. A much more forceful step was taken at the end of July, 1939. The United States formally announced that its trade treaty of 1911 with Japan would be cancelled at the end of six months. This action, which opened the way for an embargo on the shipment of war goods to Japan, was regarded by the latter as "unbelievably abrupt."

In the summer of 1940, a new ministry representing the army came into power in Japan, and American relations with Japan immediately took another turn for the worse. Apparently Japan was now prepared to give up all efforts to satisfy the United States. The United States placed an embargo upon the shipment to Japan of aviation gasoline and later upon scrap iron and steel. A new loan to China was also announced. Japan responded by joining the Axis. The formal alliance with Germany and Italy had for its purpose the establishment of a "new order" in Europe and in Greater East Asia. A mutual assistance pact (an agreement to assist one another) was signed by the three powers. It was apparently aimed at the United States and designed to slow up aid to Britain by threats of war in the Pacific. Within two weeks American citizens were advised by the State Department to leave the Far East. And in the summer of 1941, as Japanese troops poured into Indo-China with the permission of the French Vichy gov-

At Pearl Harbor, on December 7, 1941, Japanese forces settled all questions of American neutrality with an attack that destroyed many ships and airplanes and caused heavy loss of American lives. This picture shows part of the destruction.

ernment, all Japanese assets in the United States were frozen.

Relations with Japan are strained to the breaking point. In the words of Secretary of the Navy Frank Knox, the Far Eastern situation was "extremely strained" in the autumn of 1941. It seemed as if Japan and the United States could not reach an agreement. On the one hand, Japan demanded that the United States (1) abandon all aid to China; (2) reverse its policy of military and economic encirclement of Japan; and (3) cease to interfere with Japan's expansion in Greater East Asia. The United States, in turn, was strongly opposed to (1) Japan's whole policy of aggression in China; (2) the active co-operation of Japan with the other Axis powers; and (3) the further expansion of Japan in East Asia. Nevertheless, negotiations continued. In a "final effort" to reach an understanding with the United States, Japan in November sent a special envoy, Saburo Kurusu, to Washington.

War comes at Pearl Harbor. Negotiations were still going on at Washington when war came to the United States like a fire bell in the night. Suddenly and without warning, waves of Japanese airplanes bombed the great American base of Pearl Harbor, in the Hawaiian Islands, early in the morning of Sunday, December 7. The Americans, caught unaware, fought back heroically. When the attack was ended, a number of naval vessels had been sunk or disabled, squadrons of airplanes had been destroyed, and about 3000 soldiers, sailors, and civilians had been killed.

To startled Americans, who had been stunned by the news of the disaster at Pearl Harbor which blared out from their radios on that Sunday afternoon, events moved with lightning rapidity. A joint session of Congress was summoned on December 8, at which the President in a stirring message asked for a declaration that a state of war existed. Within an hour the declaration was adopted with only one dissenting vote. Three days later, both Germany and Italy declared war upon the United States, thus demonstrating the strength of the ties which bound them to their Asiatic partner.

Congress declared war against Japan on December 8, 1941, in response to a message by President Franklin D. Roosevelt.

Congress at once responded by announcing that a state of war existed between this country and the two Axis powers in Europe. The United States had entered World War II!

——————— CHECK-UP ———————

How did the United States become involved in World War II?

1. Why was the United States aroused by Nazi aggression, especially after the fall of France? What steps were taken to re-arm? To strengthen Western Hemisphere solidarity?

2. What was Lend-Lease? In what other ways short of going to war did the United States help Great Britain?

3. What was the significance of the President's statement about the "four freedoms"? The Atlantic Charter?

4. Why did United States relations with Japan grow less friendly after 1937? On what basic issues did the two countries disagree? How did war come?

CHAPTER REVIEW

Terms to Understand

"have-not" nation
dictator
status quo
communism
proletariat
"police state"
"master race"
demilitarized
non-aggression pact
"new order" in Asia
"cash-and-carry"

"open" cities
"phony war"
appeasement
national emergency
blitzkrieg
"scorched earth"
fifth columnists
"stab in the back"
"a safety belt"
priorities

People and Things to Know About

Nicholai Lenin
Soviet Russia
Josef Stalin
Benito Mussolini
Fascists
Ethiopia
Adolf Hitler
Mein Kampf
Nazis
Axis powers
Czechoslovakia
Sudetenland
Pearl Harbor

Polish Corridor
Munich Conference
Neutrality Acts
Vichy government
Near East
"destroyer for bases"
    trade
"four freedoms"
Lend-Lease
Atlantic Charter
Winston Churchill
Panay

Historic Dates to Identify

1922	1936	1939
1933	1937	1940
December 7, 1941		

Questions to Discuss

1. Contrast the following:

(*a*) United States position on neutral rights in Napoleonic wars, World War I, and World War II.

(*b*) How the United States came to go to war in 1917 and 1941.

(*c*) Advantage to Great Britain and the United States of the "destroyer for bases" deal.

(*d*) Basis on which the United States extended aid to its allies in World War I and in the period 1939–41.

2. Why was Hitler able to rise to power in Germany? Why did he attack the Versailles Treaty?

3. How did Germany and the Soviet Union come to conclude a non-aggression pact in 1939 only to go to war two years later?

Questions to Discuss (Cont.)

4. What was the purpose of President Roosevelt's emphasis on the "four freedoms"?

5. Why did President Roosevelt and Prime Minister Churchill jointly issue the Atlantic Charter?

6. Why did Japan and the United States come into conflict in the Far East?

7. Why did Italy and Japan, allies of Great Britain and France in World War I, "change sides" in World War II?

Relating Geography and History

Refer to available maps and look up related geographical information before attempting to answer these questions:

1. Why did Great Britain find it difficult to extend effective aid to Poland and Norway when these countries were invaded?

2. Why was Germany unable to invade the British Isles?

3. Why did Germany experience far greater difficulties in launching an attack against Russia than one against France?

4. Why did Japan strike at the United States by attacking Pearl Harbor?

Other Things to Do

*1. Make lists, in correct time order, of the events in Europe and the Far East which brought the United States into World War II. In class discussion compare your list with those of other students.

2. Report to the class on the Munich Conference. What stand was taken by each of the powers represented? Why? What powers took no part in the conference? Why? Use Benns, *Europe since 1914,* or some other book in your library for reference.

3. Report to the class on how the RAF won the Battle of Britain. Use Churchill's *Their Finest Hour,* or some other book in your library.

4. Use *Readers' Guide* to find articles on Lend-Lease. Make a graph showing the amount of aid extended to various countries. Show your graph to the class, and make clear whether you consider Lend-Lease a wise policy.

5. Make a chart summing up the provisions of the various Neutrality Acts. Compare this with the provisions of Lend-Lease.

Marine

Chapter 40

AN UNEASY PEACE FOLLOWS THE

WINNING OF WORLD WAR II

Victory in this war is the first and greatest goal before us. Victory in the peace is the next. That means striving toward the enlargement of the security of man here and throughout the world . . . I shudder to think what will happen to humanity, including ourselves, if this war ends in an inconclusive peace, and another war breaks out when the babies of today have grown to fighting age.

Franklin D. Roosevelt, 1943

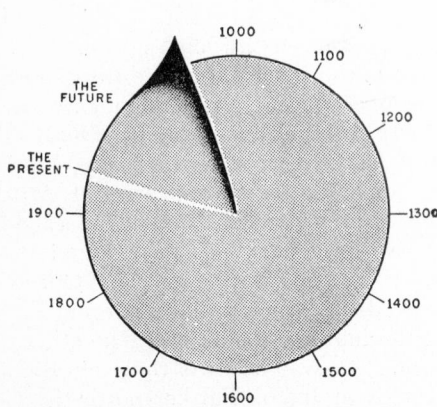

1941 – The Present

The American people met the sudden attack at Pearl Harbor with courage and a strong sense of unity. They knew the declaration of war against the Axis powers meant that days of toil and heartache lay ahead. The air was cleared, however, of the doubts and conflicting opinions that had plagued the country for so many years. No longer was there a place for argument between those who favored taking part in the European war and those who advised a policy of isolation. As a people we had no selfish purpose in entering the war; we had been forced into it by nations whose rulers desired not only our downfall, but the destruction of all those freedoms for which America stood. The whole nation applauded the President's statement in his war message: "I believe I interpret the will of Congress and of the people when I assert that we will not only defend ourselves to the uttermost, but will make very certain that this form of treachery shall never endanger us again."

After the successful conclusion of the war, the United States abandoned the policy it had followed after World War I. It resolutely assumed the burden of becoming a world leader and set itself the task of helping to build a lasting peace. But the path of peace proved to be an uneasy one. High hopes for co-operation between Soviet Russia and her wartime allies vanished in the realities of a new struggle over the ideas and the ideals which would control the world.

The story of the winning of World War II and of the problems which perplexed nations in the postwar world will be told under these topics:

1. World War II is fought and won.
2. The United Nations plan for world peace.
3. Friction grows between Soviet Russia and the West.

1   World War II Is Fought and Won

Japan wins impressive victories. During the months following the declaration of war, the staying power of the American nation was severely tested. Instead of collapsing, as some optimists had freely predicted, Japan continued to win impressive victories. A Japanese invasion force was launched at the Philippine Islands. In addition, another Japanese force of skillful jungle fighters, aided by the indifference of the native population, overran the Malay Peninsula in record time. (See map, page 713.) Attacked from the land side, the great British naval base of Singapore fell in February, 1942. Japanese forces then pressed on through Burma to the very gateway of India and broke the lifeline of supplies to China along the Burma Road. After a bitter struggle, the Netherlands Indies fell to the Japanese, and Australia remained the only

stronghold of the United Nations [1] in the Far East. Japanese invaders, taking advantage of damages to our Pacific fleet at Pearl Harbor, occupied positions as far south as the Solomon Islands. Thus they threatened our line of communications to Australia and New Zealand. In the north, they seized Attu and Kiska in the western Aleutians (June, 1942). (See page 627, map 3.)

The Philippines fall. While the Japanese were thus gaining control of the raw materials and riches of the East Indies, a combined American and Filipino force under General Douglas MacArthur was offering stubborn resistance to the invaders in the Philippines. Early in January, Manila was surrendered, and the American forces retired to the Bataan (buh-tan') peninsula (page 627, map 1). For weeks these forces fought a gallant campaign, and gained precious time in the critical struggle for the Far East. Because of overwhelming odds against them, the American forces on Bataan finally had to surrender. Before the collapse of the American resistance, however, General MacArthur made a dramatic escape to Australia, where he became chief of Allied Nations operations in the southwest Pacific. When Corregidor, an island fortress guarding Manila Bay, surrendered to the Japanese in June, 1942, organized American resistance in the Philippines came to an end. Almost everywhere in the Pacific area, the Rising Sun of Japan seemed in the ascendency.

1942 brings discouraging days. The spring and summer of 1942 also brought dark days in the European and African theaters of war. The Nazis were carrying on a two-pronged *pincers drive* against the Near East. (See map, page 710.) One army under Marshal Rommel was deep in Egypt, threatening the Suez Canal. The other was fighting its way toward the rich Russian oil fields of Baku. Farther north the German Panzer divisions (armored units at-

[1] This term was used at first to describe the 26 nations which united to check Axis aggression. Included were the governments of defeated nations which continued to oppose the Axis. Later the number increased until 50 nations signed the United Nations Charter in 1945.

tacking in co-ordination with airplanes) were driving toward Stalingrad and control of the lower Volga River. Out of Russia came frantic appeals for a "second front" in Europe to relieve the pressure upon Russia.

Latin America supports the United States. Meanwhile, Latin America felt the shock of our entrance into the war. Within two weeks after the attack upon Pearl Harbor, an Inter-American Conference of Foreign Ministers assembled at Rio de Janeiro. The aim of the conference was to bring about diplomatic and economic unity within the Western Hemisphere in the fight against aggression. Because of the influence of the Argentine Republic, however, the conference stopped short with a *recommendation* that the Latin American countries break diplomatic relations with Japan, Germany, and Italy. All except Argentina soon followed the recommendation of the conference. About half of the Latin American nations, including Brazil and all those between the United States and the Panama Canal, declared war upon the Axis. Our neighbors to the south became a tower of strength in the conduct of the war. Brazil not only gave vital assistance in making the South Atlantic safe for shipping, but also sent an expeditionary force to Italy. Mexico prevented the threat of Axis intrigue along our southern border. The Latin American states as a whole co-ordinated their shipping with our own and provided the United States with essential raw materials. With their help, fifth-column activities were suppressed in almost the whole Western Hemisphere.

The home front is mobilized for war. With the coming of war, the United States faced perplexing problems at home. As never before, war became a matter of man power and of production and civilian effort. Men between the ages of 18 and 65 were required to register with local selective service boards. Those between 18 and 45 became liable for military service under the selective service system. Plans were made to use those not drafted into the armed forces in vital war industries for which their training and experience fitted them.

Army nurse   WAVE machinist

Part of the demand for man power was met by women, who engaged in such war jobs as shipbuilding, mining, munitions manufacture, and lumbering. To release men in service for combat duty, women's auxiliary corps were established in the army (WACS), the navy, (WAVES), the coast guard (SPARS), and in the marines.

Changes far greater than those brought about during World War I were cheerfully accepted by the American public. Shortages of vital articles and the threat of inflation resulted in a widespread system of price control and rationing (page 537). With automobile transportation reduced by shortages of gasoline and tires, and with airplane travel severely limited by the needs of the armed services, the average citizen stayed at home or did his traveling in greatly overcrowded trains. The danger of air raids and the activities of submarines led to practice air raids, black-outs, and the dimming of lights in the coastal areas. Farmers strained to produce bumper crops to feed not only the nation and its armed forces but our war-weary allies. Labor worked overtime to make possible our gigantic industrial output (page 508). Men and women everywhere volunteered for all sorts of extra war duties — serving on local boards; acting as air raid wardens, auxiliary policemen and firemen, and plane spotters; assisting in hospitals and Red Cross units; and donating blood for the precious life-saving plasma. Boys and girls took part-time jobs, tended war gardens, helped gather crops, and participated in drives for fats, cans, paper, and other necessary materials. Billions of dollars of war bonds and stamps were purchased. All Americans

General Dwight D. Eisenhower, an American officer, became Allied Commander in Chief in Europe. He is shown here talking with gestures to King George VI of Great Britain while American Generals Omar Bradley (left) and Courtney Hodges stand by.

felt the crushing financial burden of the war through greatly increased taxes.

Industry is placed on a war basis. On the production front miracles were performed. The automobile industry gave up the manufacture of passenger automobiles to produce trucks, tanks, airplanes, engines, artillery, and other things needed by a modern army. Other peacetime industries were likewise converted to war production. The building of ships was greatly speeded up until in the summer of 1943 five ships a day were being launched. Under the efficient direction of William M. Jeffers, a program was developed to take care of America's need for rubber in spite of Japan's conquest of those countries which had formerly supplied us with crude rubber. To mobilize American industry for the war effort, the President appointed Donald Nelson chairman of the War Production Board (WPB). Nelson was given almost complete control over production. In May, 1943, when disputes developed between high-ranking government officials over critical materials and other problems on the home front, President Roosevelt an-

nounced the establishment of a war cabinet to be known as the Office of War Mobilization (OWM). James F. Byrnes, who had resigned from the Supreme Court to become Director of Economic Stabilization, became the head of the new general staff for the home front.

The tide begins to turn. In 1942 the Allies' prospects looked black, but there were a few bright spots in the news which marked the beginning of the turning of the tide. In April, under the leadership of the famous ace, Jimmy Doolittle, a squadron of American planes took off from a carrier and bombed such key Japanese cities as Tokyo, Yokohama, Nagoya, and Kobe. The raid was totally unexpected, and created great panic. In the following month a Japanese invasion fleet was defeated by American naval and air forces in the Battle of the Coral Sea, between New Guinea and the Solomon Islands. In June the Japanese met with a smashing defeat when they attempted to invade Midway Island. (See map, page 713.)

At this very time Prime Minister Churchill was on his way to Washington to discuss with President Roosevelt the conduct of the war. They planned a United Nations strategy which unfolded gradually in the months that followed. Churchill and Roosevelt also met during 1943 in Casablanca, in Washington, and in Quebec.

The United Nations take the initiative. After the summer of 1942, the initiative in the war gradually shifted to the side of the United Nations. In August, American marines seized Henderson Field on Guadalcanal in the Solomon Islands and began to extend American control over the entire island. In October and November, terrific naval and air battles were fought with the Japanese, who seemed willing to pay any price to regain control of Guadalcanal. In a naval battle off Guadalcanal American naval units inflicted crushing losses upon the Japanese fleet.

British desert fighter

These victories practically decided the fate of the Solomons. At the same time, in the African theater, Rommel's attempted breakthrough to the Nile was halted. This prepared the way for a British counter-offensive which did not stop until Rommel had been driven completely out of North Africa. The hard-fighting Russians, too, succeeded in checking Hitler's greatest efforts before Stalingrad, and the Volga remained in Russian hands.

American forces land in Africa. In November, 1942, a new phase of the war began. Carrying out the plans of the Churchill-Roosevelt conference, an American invasion force splashed ashore in North Africa. The French government in North Africa, supposedly loyal to the Vichy government in France, made only a light show of resistance and then sided with the United Nations. All French North Africa except Tunis was soon in American hands. It was not until May, 1943, however, that the American, British, and Free French armies drove into Tunis. There they forced the surrender of the remaining Axis forces in North Africa. (See map, page 710.)

A front is established in Italy. The United Nations were now in control of the western Mediterranean. In July, 1943, General Dwight D. Eisenhower, Allied Commander in Chief, began the invasion of Europe with a large-scale attack upon Sicily. There followed in quick succession the fall of Sicily, the overthrow of Mussolini, the invasion and unconditional surrender of Italy, and the shifting of Italy to the side of the United Nations. The Allied troops, however, had to fight a long and hard campaign to rid Italy of Nazi influence. Nevertheless, the war in Italy pinned down strong elements of Hitler's forces, which were badly needed in both France and Russia.

Naval gun crew

The Russians counterattack (1943). Meanwhile the Russians not only stopped the Nazi summer campaign in 1943, but started an offensive. One German-held stronghold after another fell into Russian hands. By the end of the summer, the Germans had retreated to the line of the Dnieper River.

War in the air is stepped up. While the Axis forces were taking a beating in North Africa and on the Russian front, terrific attacks from the air were directed against the Nazis. The British and American air forces were now in control of the air. Allied planes rained destruction upon the industrial cities in the Ruhr valley, the submarine bases along the coast of occupied France, and even upon Berlin and other industrial centers deep in German territory. The air raids were made for a double purpose: (1) to cripple German factories and transportation facilities, and (2) to weaken Nazi morale. Similar punishment, inflicted upon the industrial cities of Italy from air bases in North Africa, helped to knock Italy out of the war. Radar bombing was first used in the fall of 1943. Radar made possible "precision" bombing under cover of darkness and bad weather.

Submarine warfare is checked. A dark spot in the war picture at this time, however, was the submarine warfare in the Atlantic. Operating in packs, the Nazi undersea craft (U-boats) attacked our supply lines

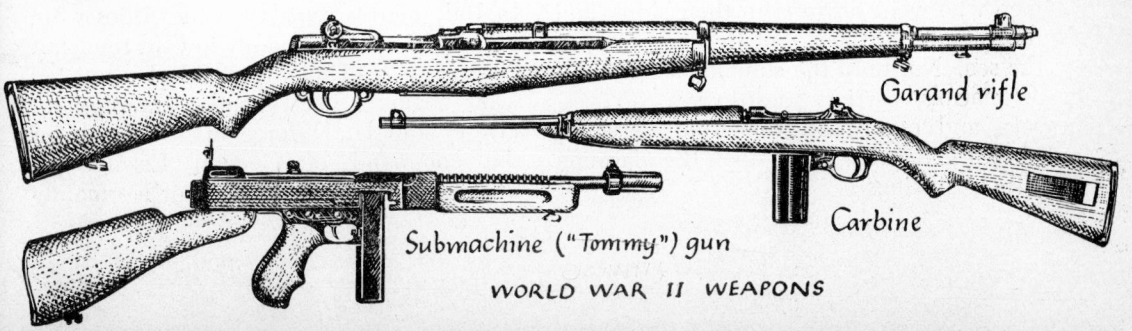

Garand rifle

Carbine

Submachine ("Tommy") gun

WORLD WAR II WEAPONS

Counterattack in the West

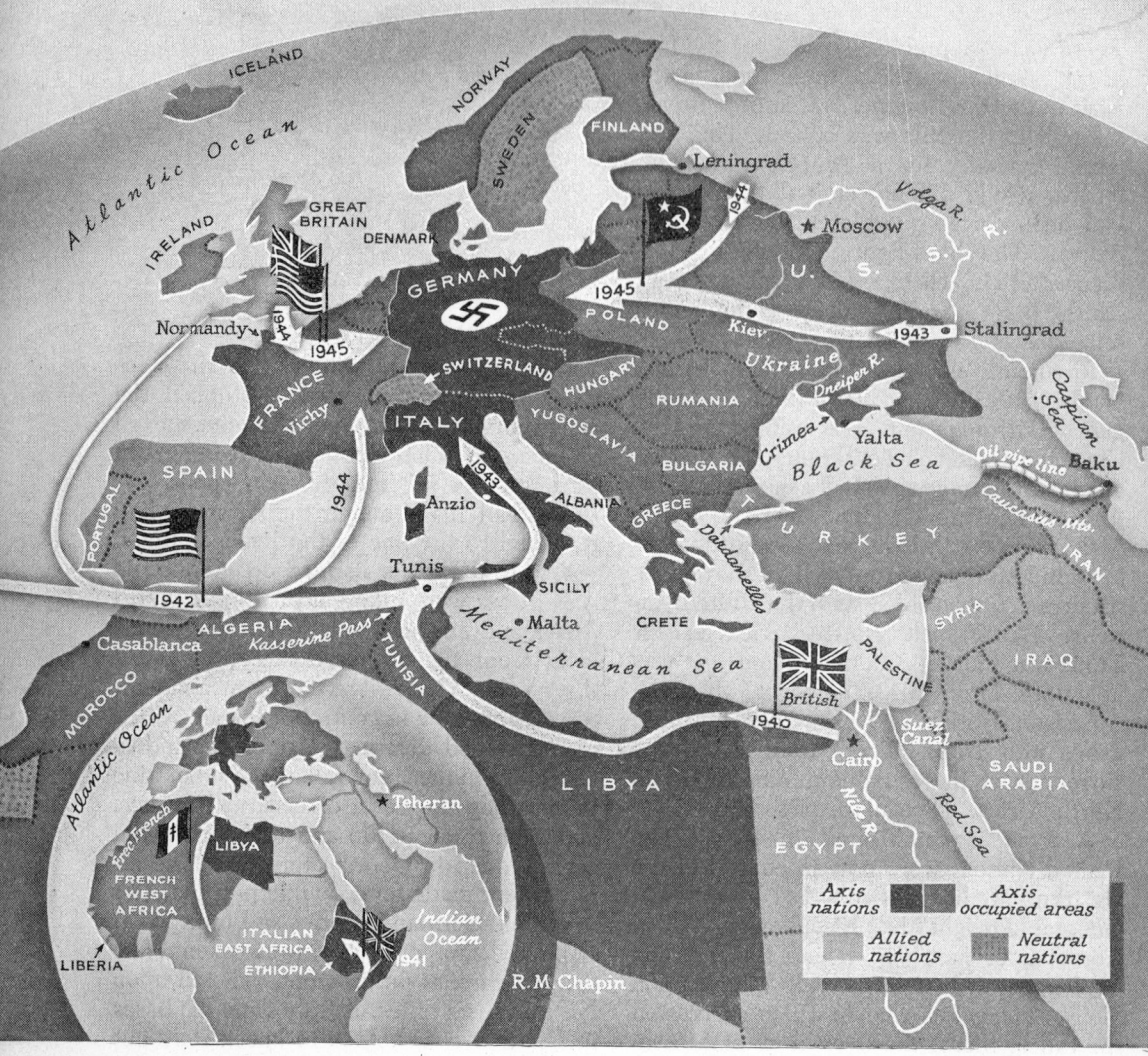

The Axis nations controlled a vast area in 1940. From 1940 through 1944 they were gradually driven back in preparation for final defeat. What nations played major parts in this counterattack and what areas did they liberate? When? Where was the greatest American-British counterattack launched?

and sank hundreds of thousands of tons of shipping each month. The sinking of the ships themselves meant a staggering loss to the United Nations. But much more important were the lives of the gallant seamen who went down with their ships, and the valuable cargoes sent to the bottom of the sea. Not until the summer of 1943 did air patrols, carriers, destroyer-escort vessels, and other anti-submarine measures have a noticeable effect upon the alarming U-boat sinkings.

The war reaches a climax. The war reached its climax in 1944. The Russian drive, starting from deep within the Russian territory, by mid-summer had carried the Soviet armies half-way across Poland. In Italy at this same time the Allies were pushing the Nazis steadily toward the Alps. On June 6 (D-Day), the final phase of the war began. The greatest amphibious (water and land) force in history, under the command of General Eisenhower, stormed ashore on the coast of Normandy in France. (See map, page 710.) Soon American and British armies were pushing toward Germany, spearheaded by the daring tank forces of General Patton's Third Army. The drive was accompanied by continuous pounding from the air, directed particularly against German supply lines.

By August, France had been liberated in the west, while Rumania was knocked out of the war in the east. The Russian armies thereupon started another drive through Hungary toward Budapest. In the north, Finland, which had joined the Nazis in the surprise attack on Russia in 1941, was forced to surrender. With 3 million soldiers on the continent in November, General Eisenhower launched an attack upon the Siegfried Line of Germany. The Allies, however, still had serious obstacles to overcome. Especially severe was the destructive robot and rocket bombing of southern and eastern England. Another setback was the fierce German counterattack in the Battle of the Bulge at the end of the year. But all the time the German armies were being relentlessly destroyed.

The final defeat of Germany is shown on this map. After the liberation of France, the Western Allies broke through the Siegfried Line, captured Remagen, and fanned out in all directions. Meantime, Russian troops were battling westward. The two great forces met on the Elbe River in Germany in the spring of 1945.

Battle of Germany

R. M. Chapin

GI's firing mortar

The United States advances in the Pacific.

Meantime, in the Pacific theater of the war, American forces were taking long steps forward by using leapfrog tactics and leaving behind great pockets of isolated Japanese troops. (See map, next page.) In February, 1944, a great naval force captured the Marshall Islands. In June, Admiral Nimitz invaded Saipan in the Marianas. There he established a base for B-29 superfortress attacks upon Japan's home islands. In October, General MacArthur, having already taken great leaps along the coast of New Guinea, began the invasion of the Philippines. It was at this time that Japan suffered its most crushing naval defeat, losing 69 ships off Leyte. As many more were lost when the Japanese made desperate efforts to reinforce their Leyte garrison in the Philippines. From then on, the force of the Japanese fleet was spent.

The war ends in Europe.

The year 1945 brought the collapse of the Axis powers and the unconditional surrender of both Germany and Japan. In March the Allies made a dramatic seizure of the bridgehead at Remagen, Germany, and thus were able to cross the Rhine River. (See map, page 711.) In the same week the Russians crossed the Oder River in their drive toward Berlin. In April, the Nazi state was cut in two by the joining of the Allied and Russian forces on the Elbe River. In a state of complete collapse, with its armies destroyed and its cities in rubble, Germany accepted unconditional surrender. On May 8 (V–E Day), the war in Europe officially came to an end. Though rejoicing over victory in Europe, the United States now turned its energies wholeheartedly toward finishing the war with Japan.

The Pacific advance continues.

In the Pacific the end came almost as suddenly as the war had begun. Iwo Jima, an island of great importance to our air forces, was seized in February, 1945, at a time when General MacArthur was completing the conquest of the Philippines. Then in July, in the bloodiest campaign in the Pacific area, the conquest of the island of Okinawa was completed. The Japanese fought desperately to defend Okinawa, even to the extent of using great numbers of *suicide planes*. Their pilots made superhuman efforts to crash bomb-laden planes on American warships and succeeded in inflicting heavy damage. In spite of such desperate defensive measures, Japan lost the island, a base of great strategic importance only 400 miles from the home islands.

Japan surrenders.

A meeting of the heads of the United Nations at Potsdam, Germany, in 1945, issued a statement known as the Potsdam Ultimatum. The terms were still unconditional surrender, but the ultimatum stated to Japan the exact meaning of this expression. The only alternative to unconditional surrender was invasion and "the utter devastation of the Japanese homeland." At first, Japan did not seem greatly moved by the Potsdam Ultimatum. Within two weeks, however, a series of historic events brought the Japanese war lords to terms. Early in August, an American plane dropped the first atomic bomb upon Hiroshima, a Japanese city of 375,000. This was a small bomb, but, harnessing the very basic energy of the universe, it was equal in explosive power to 20,000 tons of TNT. At one blow 60 per cent of the city's population was wiped out. Two days later,

Naval aviator

GI's firing "bazooka"

Counterattack in the East

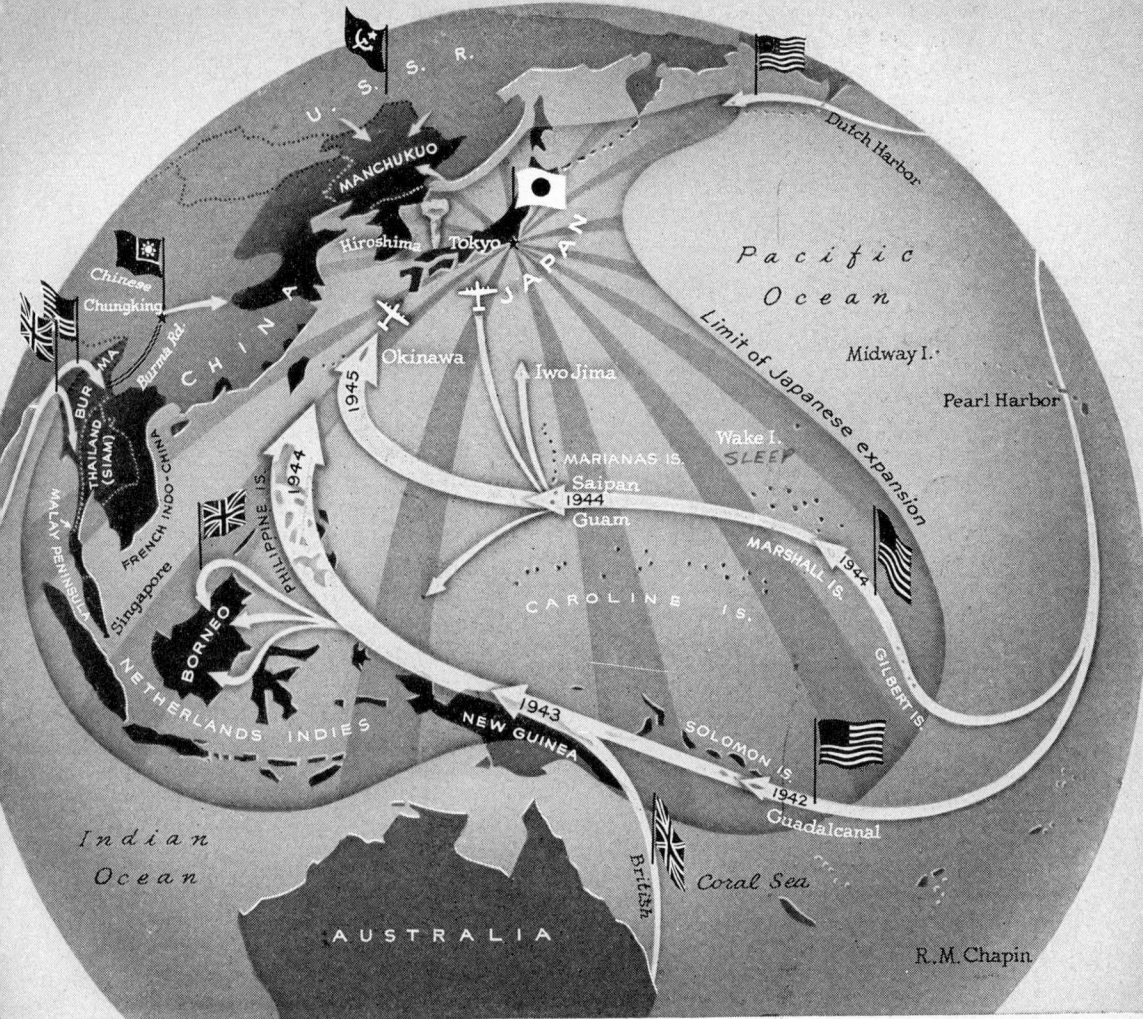

Sea, air, and land operations were used by the Allies to defeat Japan. Occupation of key islands provided air fields which brought still other islands (and eventually the home islands of Japan) under heavy bomber attack. One great achievement of the war was the way our navy solved its supply problem. Thousands of miles west of Pearl Harbor it maintained a fleet superior to that of Japan.

Russia declared war upon Japan, and on the same day another city, Nagasaki, was leveled by a second and more terrifying atomic bomb.

Faced by invasion and utter destruction, Japan stated her willingness to accept the Potsdam Ultimatum. The Japanese asked only that they be allowed to keep their emperor. Arrangements for surrender were completed by August 14 (V–J Day), and the greatest and most terrible war in all history was at last ended. Japan was permitted to keep Emperor Hirohito, but he became merely the spokesman for General MacArthur. The latter was now made the Supreme Allied Commander of the forces which proceeded to occupy the Japanese homeland and to carry out in detail the terms of surrender.

World War II is a global war. American participation in World War II was on a much broader scale than in World War I. Thirteen million Americans were under arms as compared to three million in the earlier war. More than 200,000 were killed in action. The cost, nearly 350 billion dollars, was almost ten times that of World War I. Also, World War II was a global war. American fighting men were to be found in all parts of the earth — South Pacific, West Pacific, China, Burma, Mediterranean Sea, Africa, Europe, and the Atlantic area.

——————— CHECK-UP ———————

How did the United States help to win World War II?

1. What gains were made in 1942 by Japan? By the Germans?
2. How did Latin America take sides against the Axis? How was the United States home front mobilized for war? What contributions did American industry make to winning the war?
3. What attacks were made by United States and United Nations forces in the second half of 1942?
4. How were United Nations offensives launched in North Africa, Sicily and Italy, and France? How did the U.S.S.R. roll back the German armies? What part did air power play in defeating Germany? How were the U-boats checked? How was Germany compelled to surrender unconditionally?
5. Trace the progress of the war against Japan in the Pacific. How was Japan compelled to surrender?

---

2 **The United Nations Plan for World Peace**

Americans favor international co-operation. Long before the end of the war, American leaders were giving thought to the postwar settlement. Public opinion in America definitely began to favor a worldwide organization of nations to prevent future aggression and to avoid another world war. In September, 1943, the House of Representatives, taking account of this swelling tide of public opinion, passed by an overwhelming vote a resolution proposed by Representative James W. Fulbright, of Arkansas. This resolution favored (1) the creation of an international organization with enough power to establish and to maintain just and lasting world peace, and (2) the participation of the United States in such an organization.

Most encouraging of all the declarations of postwar policy, however, was that of the Moscow Conference of Foreign Secretaries in November, 1943. At this meeting the governments of the United States, the United Kingdom, the Soviet Union, and China (1) pledged themselves to continue the war; and (2) recognized the need to set up a general international organization of states, large and small, to maintain international peace and security. Influenced by the Moscow Conference, the United States Senate promptly adopted a resolution calling upon the United States to join with free and sovereign nations in establishing and maintaining such an international organization.

The Cairo and Teheran Conferences aim at lasting peace. Before the end of 1943 two important conferences took place. At Cairo, under the shadow of the pyramids, President Roosevelt, Prime Minister Winston Churchill, and Generalissimo Chiang Kai-shek planned the defeat and the fate of Japan. At Teheran, the capital of Iran, President Roosevelt, Mr. Churchill, and Marshal Stalin laid plans for the destruction of the German armies. At both conferences careful consideration was given to the problem of arranging a lasting peace after the war was over. "We came here with hope and determination," said the three leaders at Teheran. "We leave here friends in fact, in spirit, and in purpose."

The groundwork for a world organization is laid at Dumbarton Oaks. Another step in the program of lasting peace was taken in August, 1944, at a time when the invasion forces were before Paris. At Dumbarton Oaks, an old mansion in Washington, representatives of the United States, Great Britain, Russia, and later China met to draft a charter for a world organization. After seven weeks of debate, their plan for the United Nations was made public. The draft was incomplete, and many important questions were left unsolved, but the general recommendations became the basis of the final plan later adopted at San Francisco.

The Yalta Conference calls the San Francisco Convention. Not until February, 1945, did the "Big Three" — Roosevelt, Churchill, and Stalin — get together again, this time at Yalta in the Russian Crimea (map, page 710). There they planned the combined military operations for the final phase of the war against Germany. They likewise made plans for the occupation and control of Germany after unconditional surrender. Proposals were also discussed for the earliest possible establishment of a permanent international organization to maintain peace. The "Big Three" agreed to call a conference of the United Nations to meet at San Francisco in April, 1945, to prepare a charter for such an organization along the lines suggested at Dumbarton Oaks.

Economic collaboration is planned. Meanwhile, delegates of 44 nations, meeting at Bretton Woods, New Hampshire, planned the machinery for economic cooperation. They proposed an International Bank for Reconstruction and Development, with a capital of nine billion dollars. Of this sum, the United States was to provide something over three billion dollars. The Bretton Woods Conference also proposed an International Monetary Fund to be used to stabilize currencies. It was to have a revolving fund [2] of almost 9 billion dollars, of which the United States would supply 2¾ billion.

The United States avoids the errors of the Versailles conference. In making preparations for the San Francisco Conference, President Roosevelt tried to avoid the mistakes made by President Wilson at the end of World War I. In the first place, the Charter of the United Nations was to be entirely separate from any peace treaty.

[2] A revolving fund is one which is used over and over again as loans are repaid. Members borrow from the fund in time of need (that is, to support currency at a fixed level mutually agreed upon) and then they pay back the sums borrowed as they are able.

World War II was global. While these marines fought for Iwo Jima in the Pacific, other American forces were driving into Germany, halfway around the world.

In the second place, both major political parties were represented in the membership of the American delegation. The delegation included three leading Republicans, Senator Arthur H. Vandenberg, Commander Harold E. Stassen, and Representative Charles A. Eaton; the Dean of Barnard College, Miss Virginia C. Gildersleeve; and four leading Democrats, Secretary of State E. R. Stettinius, Jr., former Secretary Cordell Hull, Senator Tom Connally, and Representative Sol Bloom.

The Charter of the United Nations is prepared. Although President Roosevelt had died a few days earlier, delegates from 46 nations gathered at San Francisco at the end of April, 1945. In a welcoming address from Washington, President Truman warned the conference: "If we do not want to die together in war, we must learn to live together in peace." The first days of the meeting were marked by a sharp struggle over the admission of Argentina and Poland to the conference. Though Argentina had finally declared war upon the Axis, it had been a center of Axis intrigue throughout the period of the war. Backed by the United States, but opposed by Russia, Argentina gained admission to the United Nations. At the same time, a Polish government friendly to Russia was denied admission, though provision was made for Poland to sign the United Nations Charter at a later date.

After two months of debate the delegates completed the preparation of the charter. This was to become effective when ratified by the "Big Five" powers (China, France, Great Britain, Russia, and the United States) and by a majority of the 45 other nations that had signed the charter. Such ratification was completed by October, and the United Nations (UN) became a reality.

The charter is based on Dumbarton Oaks. Following the plans outlined at Dumbarton Oaks, the United Nations Charter included the following provisions:

(1) A General Assembly, in which all member nations were represented, might discuss any question or any matter within the scope of the charter.

(2) A Security Council was to consist of the "Big Five" as permanent members and of six others to be chosen by the Assembly. It was to have authority to investigate international disputes, foster peaceful settlements, and take diplomatic, economic, and military action against aggressors. The Security Council could make decisions on important matters by the affirmative vote of seven members, including all the Big Five. Thus each of the Big Five nations was given a veto power over the actions of the Council. In settling disputes between nations peaceably, however, a party to a dispute was not to have a vote. A Military Staff Committee, under the Security Council, was to be in charge of the military forces of the UN.

(3) An Economic and Social Council, responsible to the General Assembly and including numerous commissions and agencies, was to work to eliminate social and economic problems which might lead to war. None of these agencies was to be hampered by the veto.

(4) An International Court of Justice

was to decide the legal aspects of international disputes submitted to the Court.

(5) A Trusteeship Council was to investigate conditions in territories held in trust by the UN and to advise the Assembly on the supervision of such territories.

(6) Provision was also made for a Permanent Secretariat.

The Senate approves the UN Charter. American enthusiasm for international cooperation was promptly reflected in the Senate. In July, 1945, by an overwhelming vote, the Senate approved the Bretton Woods agreements. After only six days of debate the United Nations Charter was then ratified by a vote of 89 to 2. Thus, by an almost unanimous vote, the United States Senate showed its willingness to cooperate with an international organization in working for the future peace and welfare of the world.

The UN becomes a working organization. During its first years of existence the United Nations grew into a great and going organization. In spite of its failures, it was recognized everywhere as holding the world's best promise of continued peace. It succeeded in settling or contributing to the settlement of numerous disputes — particularly a difficult Palestine problem. It also became a forum for sounding out the opinions of the representatives of the many nations represented. New York City was selected as the permanent headquarters of the UN. Some of the agencies working under the Assembly did notable work, especially the International Trade Organization (ITO) (page 546) and the Human Rights Commission. The latter, under the able direction of its chairman, Mrs. Eleanor Roosevelt, drew up a statement of universal human rights which was adopted by the Assembly at Paris in 1948. Among other things this declaration provided for the "right to life, liberty and security of person," and forbade abridgment of rights because of "race, color, sex, language, religion, political or other opinion."

The United States assumes its place as one of the world's leaders. The attitude of the United States at the end of World War II was in marked contrast to what it had been at the end of World War I. This time there was no attempt to dodge the nation's responsibilities as a leading world power. The people and leaders of both political parties wholeheartedly supported participation in world affairs. The United States looked forward hopefully to the prospect of working with its wartime allies in the building of a permanent peace.

—————— CHECK-UP ——————

What plans were made for an international organization to preserve world peace?

1. What evidence was there that the United States was ready to take part in a world organization after World War II? What other great powers favored such an organization?
2. What preliminary plans were made at Dumbarton Oaks and Bretton Woods? What mistakes of World War I were avoided in drawing up the United Nations Charter?
3. What are the chief provisions of the UN Charter adopted at San Francisco? What are some important achievements of UN?

The General Assembly of the United Nations is shown here at its second meeting, with Dr. Aranha of Brazil presiding.

3 **Friction Grows between Soviet Russia and the West**

Russia and the West fail to see eye to eye. From the beginning it was evident that the success of the United Nations depended upon agreement among the great powers. As time passed, it also became evident that lack of agreement on basic aims was driving the great powers further and further apart. Russia's aims included (1) trying to surround herself with friendly governments, largely as a measure of defense; (2) gaining access to, or bases upon, warm water highways of commerce; (3) carrying out the old Russian policy of expansion; and, above all, (4) extending communism to the rest of the world. Great Britain, on the other hand, was determined to preserve the lifelines of her

empire, and at the same time to give up responsibilities that drained her economic resources. The United States was interested in the preservation of peace and in the protection of the democratic way of life.

On the larger questions which came before the Security Council, the western powers failed completely to reach agreement with Russia. Such questions included the control of atomic and other mass-destruction weapons, general disarmament, and the formation of an international police force. Russia also boycotted the "Little Assembly," established at the suggestion of Secretary of State George C. Marshall to meet when the full Assembly was not in session. During the first few years the UN was in existence, Russia made use of the veto about 30 times, thus bringing nearly to a standstill the work of the Security Council.

The atomic bomb threatens world security. Nothing so disturbed peace of mind, both at home and abroad, as the atomic bomb. Scientists were agreed that whether or not we endeavored to keep the secret of the bomb, other nations were certain to have it within a few years. They also agreed that a surprise attack on this country would inflict terrible damage on industry and cause great loss of life. Our

An atom bomb, exploding under water in a test at Bikini, in the Marshall Islands, has blasted a warship into the air. Such vast power, and the radioactivity that follows it, have become a fearful problem for the world.

political leaders recognized that the United States would probably be the first victim if atomic bombs were used in a surprise attack, because our very system of government prevents us from making such an attack on others. The countries of eastern Europe, however, looked with suspicion upon the United States, which possessed the fearsome weapon and seemed unwilling to share it with its former allies.

The powers disagree on atomic control. The control of atomic power and the atomic bomb became a subject of bitter controversy between the United States and Russia. The General Assembly of the United Nations set up an Atomic Energy Commission to study the best ways of controlling atomic power and weapons. The United States submitted a plan for an International Atomic Energy Authority with complete control over all uses of atomic energy. This plan would give the United Nations agency the right to inspect all atomic energy plants anywhere without being subjected to the veto power of any nation. Soviet Russia, on the other hand, was opposed to any plan which would allow an outside agency to inspect plants in her territory. The Russians suggested that the nations of the world sign an agreement outlawing the use of atomic weapons.

Under the Russian plan each country would enforce the agreement within its own borders. Furthermore, the Russians demanded that the United States destroy all her atomic bombs before any agreement was signed.

Although the United States was ready to destroy or surrender her stockpile of atomic bombs, she was naturally not ready to do so until a workable international agency had been established to enforce atomic control in all countries. World Wars I and II had shown the ineffectiveness of "paper" agreements which lacked means of enforcement. After two years of wrangling over the control of atomic weapons, the UN Atomic Energy Commission reached a "dead end." Russia and the United States could not agree upon terms for atomic disarmament.

The occupation of Germany is planned. Meanwhile, in July, 1945, President Truman, Prime Minister Attlee of Great Britain, and Marshal Stalin of Soviet Russia had held a meeting in Potsdam to lay plans for the future of Germany. At this conference the following results were announced: (1) A program was accepted for the joint control of Germany and of the German capital, Berlin, by Russia, Great Britain, the United States, and France. (2) Germany was to be deprived of the power to make war. (3) Many of the military and political leaders of Germany were to stand trial as war criminals. (4) A five-member Council of Foreign Ministers, representing the five principal powers, was to have the duty of drawing up peace treaties with the enemy countries for submission to the United Nations.

After much effort and debate, the Council of Foreign Ministers succeeded in drawing up treaties with Italy and the so-called satellite states (Finland, Hungary, Bulgaria, and Rumania), but they found the Austrian and German treaties much more difficult. In December, 1947, a meeting of the foreign ministers in London, the fifth since the end of the war, adjourned in complete deadlock over the Austrian and German treaties.

Russian actions create fear and suspicion. The deadlock in the Council of Foreign Ministers over the German and Austrian treaties was just one indication of the growing rift between Soviet Russia and the countries of the West. During the war close co-operation between Soviet and Allied leaders had led to the hope that friendly relations would continue after the war. It soon became evident, however, that Russia had other plans in mind. Although the new governments of the countries in eastern Europe (Poland, Yugoslavia, Rumania, and Hungary) were supposed to be democratic and representative of all political parties, communist-led groups seized control of the governments and made them satellites of Soviet Russia. Wherever Communists came into power, they killed or imprisoned those who were friendly to the West and began destroying freedom of speech and the press. Thus an "iron curtain" of secrecy was lowered over Russia and the Russian-controlled states of eastern Europe. As a result, the cordial feeling that the United States had developed toward Soviet Russia was gradually replaced by fear and suspicion that Russia was once more bent on a program of world revolution.

America's attitude toward Russia stiffens. President Roosevelt had given in to Russian demands many times in order to make sure that Soviet Russia would take part in the work of the United Nations. By the fall of 1946 it was clear that this attitude toward Russia was not working, and the Truman administration turned its back on the Roosevelt policy. In the meetings of the Council of Foreign Ministers in Paris the United States began to take a firm stand against the Russian tactics of delay. Secretary of State Byrnes and the American delegates were strongly supported in this policy of firmness by delegates from France and Great Britain.

The Truman Doctrine tries to check the spread of communism. Early in 1947, when Great Britain announced that she intended to withdraw from Greece, it seemed likely that Russia would move into Greece and Turkey. Thus Russia would gain control of the Dardanelles (map, page 710), and threaten the eastern Mediterranean and the oil-rich Near East. It was under these circumstances that the "Truman Doctrine" was announced (March, 1947). This doctrine stated that the United States would use its resources to prevent the overthrow of any democratic government through interference from outside. The sum of 400 million dollars was appropriated by Congress to support the governments of Greece and Turkey and thus enable them to resist the threat of communism from the north.

Marshall proposes the European Recovery Program. Three months later, Secretary George C. Marshall, who had succeeded James F. Byrnes as Secretary of State, announced a plan to make European recovery a major goal of American policy. Marshall proposed that the United States extend credits amounting to 18 or 20 billion dollars over the next four years to enable Europe to get back on its feet economically. European nations must, however, make definite plans to help themselves. Russia and her Eastern satellites rejected the plan, but sixteen western European nations agreed to increase production, control inflation, and lower trade barriers in order to share in the plan.

Russia's answer to the Marshall Plan was the formation of a bloc (the Cominform),

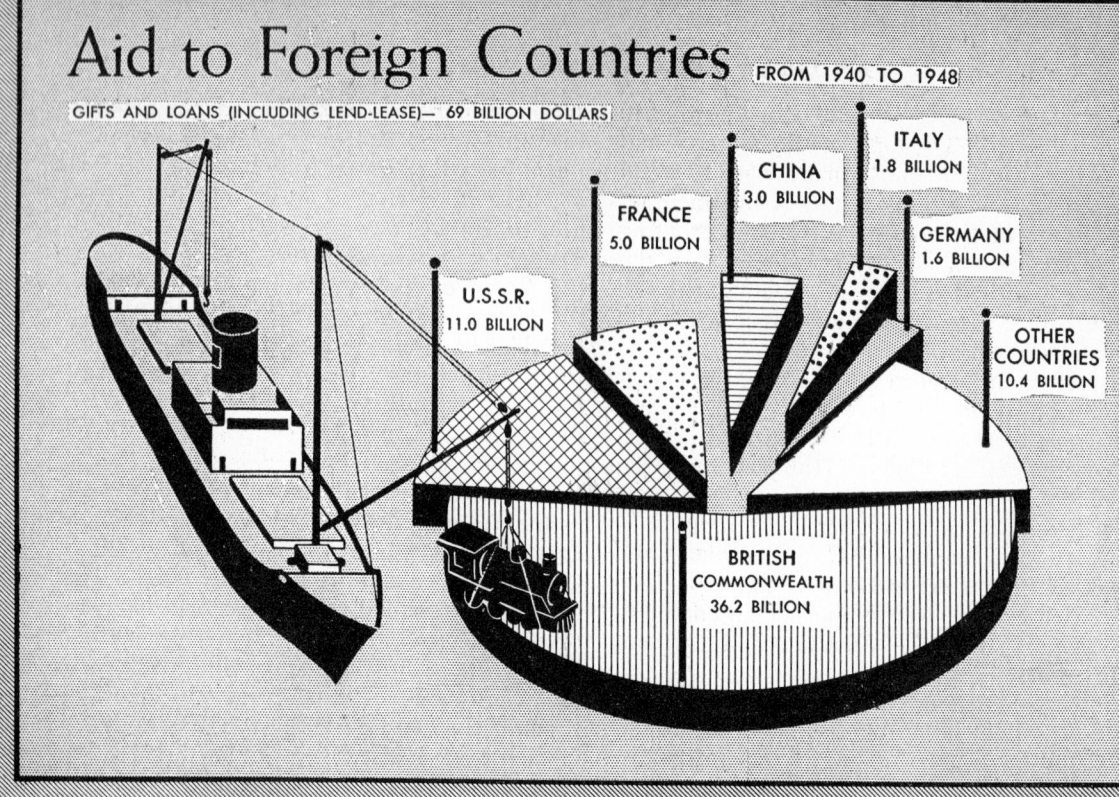

Aid to Foreign Countries FROM 1940 TO 1948

GIFTS AND LOANS (INCLUDING LEND-LEASE)— 69 BILLION DOLLARS

ITALY
1.8 BILLION

CHINA
3.0 BILLION

FRANCE
5.0 BILLION

GERMANY
1.6 BILLION

U.S.S.R.
11.0 BILLION

OTHER
COUNTRIES
10.4 BILLION

BRITISH
COMMONWEALTH
36.2 BILLION

The United States Government either gave or loaned nearly 70 billion dollars to foreign countries between 1940 and 1948. Why? Why did such aid continue after World War II?

consisting chiefly of eastern European nations. The Cominform was "to co-ordinate the activities of Communist parties" in various parts of the world. Spurred on by the success of the Communists in seizing Czechoslovakia in 1948, and by the threats of powerful Communist parties in Italy and France, Congress proceeded to put this European Recovery Program (ERP) into effect. An Economic Co-operation Administration (ECA) under Paul Hoffman, set up to carry out the program, obtained gratifying results.

The Western Hemisphere resists communism. At the same time certain regional understandings and defense pacts were developing within the UN. These agreements served to divide the world even further into East and West. At the end of 1947 the United States Senate ratified the Rio Pact. This was an Inter-American Defense Pact pledging the United States and other American republics to "regard an armed attack on any American state as an attack on all the American states." Meeting in

the Ninth International Conference of American Republics at Bogotá, Colombia, six months later, the American republics made provision for an "Organization of American States." Here a resolution was adopted to take all necessary steps to prevent and uproot communist activities. The republics also made provision for an Inter-American Defense Council to consult on mutual defense arrangements.

East and West engage in a "cold war." Disagreement between East and West developed into what was called a "cold war," a war of ideas and propaganda. There were violent verbal attacks upon the western powers by Soviet representatives, and the Russian government, in turn, was accused of engaging in deception and intrigue. The dispute over the city of Berlin was typical. It had been agreed at Potsdam that this city, like the rest of Germany, would be divided into four zones and governed by the four powers: France, Great Britain, Soviet Russia, and the United States. Unfortunately the city itself was an island in the Russian zone of occupation, not connected with the parts of occupied Germany controlled by the western powers. Because the latter were unable to reach any satisfactory agreement with Russia over the joint government of Germany, they decided to establish a joint government for their three zones, leaving Russia to govern the fourth zone as she pleased. In preparation for this plan the western powers set up a new currency for their area, and extended its use to their sectors in Berlin.

A Berlin blockade is established. The Soviet government feared that a new German government would be set up in western Germany which would keep Russia out of the Ruhr region. They therefore struck back at the western powers by establishing a blockade of Berlin. Rail, water, and road traffic from the West through the Soviet zone to Berlin was cut off. Apparently, the U.S.S.R was leaving the western powers the alternative of getting out of Berlin or of having 2¼ million Berliners starve.

The air-lift is established. Immediately the western powers showed that they were determined to hold their ground. They set up the greatest peace-time "air-lift" in history, and soon several thousand tons of food and other supplies were ferried into Berlin each day by air. By November 1, 1948, about 600 American flying crews were in regular service, transporting supplies for the homes and factories of Berlin. All through the winter of 1948–1949 the air-lift continued, in bad weather as well as good. One important result of this difficult and expensive "Operation Vittles" was to gain the goodwill of the people of Berlin and of Germany in general. Grateful that they had not been deserted by the West, about 80 per cent of the inhabitants of western Berlin rejected communist candidates at an election held in the fall of 1948. The air-lift also raised the prestige of the western powers throughout Europe.

The North Atlantic Pact is approved. Threatened by the extension of communism in Europe and Asia, the western European powers, together with Canada and the United States, began to draw together into a military alliance. In April, 1949, representatives of twelve nations, with a population of a third of a billion people, signed a North Atlantic Pact at Washington. This pact established a security area in the whole North Atlantic. It provided for consultation whenever "the territorial integrity, political independence or security of any of the parties is threatened." It also provided for the use of armed force to resist attack upon any of the parties. Though this pact was proclaimed as a regional agreement under the UN, it was denounced by Russia as "obviously aggressive" and "aimed against the U.S.S.R." At least it served notice upon Russia that the United States would not be neutral in case of an attack upon any North Atlantic country. The North Atlantic Pact was evidence of the worsening relations between the East and the West as well as of the inability of the UN alone to preserve peace.

The foreign ministers meet again to try to solve the question of Germany. In May, 1949, Soviet Russia agreed to lift the blockade of Berlin in return for a four-power conference to consider a settlement of the German question. Foreign ministers Dean Acheson for the United States, Andrei Vishinsky for Soviet Russia, Ernest Bevin for Great Britain, and Robert Schuman for

American and Russian officers argue at the boundary line in Berlin after one of many troublesome episodes in the "cold war."

Chinese soldier

France met at Paris, but little was accomplished. The Russian proposal was to return to the conditions before the Berlin blockade. This the western powers refused to do because a constitution for a German government had been drawn up and adopted by western German leaders early in 1949. Thus the Russian proposal would mean giving up this western German state. Although relations between Soviet Russia and the West had gone from bad to worse, there was consolation in the belief that at least for the time being the advance of communism in Europe had been checked.

American occupation forces govern Japan. Meanwhile, the occupation of Japan had been carried out much more smoothly. One reason was that in Japan the occupation was almost entirely under American control. To be sure, a Far Eastern Commission in Washington and an Allied Council in Tokyo represented the countries which had fought against Japan, but their duties were merely advisory. The real power lay in the hands of General Douglas MacArthur, the American commander, who gave orders to the Japanese emperor and government.

Under General MacArthur's direction, far-reaching changes were undertaken in the political, social, and economic life of Japan. On the surface these reforms seemed to promise much. A democratic constitution and more democratic procedures in government were adopted. Many of the leaders of wartime Japan were tried as war criminals. The emperor's powers were drastically curtailed. Land reforms were undertaken. An attempt was made to break up great industrial combinations which before the war had concentrated economic power in the hands of a few men. It was difficult to tell how successful in the long run these measures would be in building a peace-loving and democratic Japan. In contrast with the four-power occupation of Germany, however, the occupation of Japan seemed a great success.

Korea is divided between Russia and the United States. On the other hand, the situ-

ation in Korea was not unlike that in Germany. Soviet Russia occupied the northern part of Korea, and the United States the southern half. Although both countries had agreed to help form a unified Korean government, the growing suspicion between Russia and the United States made this impossible. Consequently, two separate native governments were established — one communist-controlled in northern Korea and the other a democratic government sponsored by the United States in southern Korea. Each felt that it should be the lawful government for all of Korea. In 1949 the United States and Russia withdrew their occupation forces, but Korea continued to be divided under two separate governments.

Communism triumphs in China. The worst defeat for the foreign policy of the United States and the greatest victory for communism in the postwar world took place in China. Long before Japanese aggression in China, there had been fighting between the Nationalist government of Chiang Kai-shek and Chinese Communists. After Japan invaded China, the Chinese Reds abandoned their attacks on the government and made common cause against the Japanese. The heroic resistance of the Chinese won the admiration of the world. China was made one of the "Big Five" and a permanent member of the Security Council of the United Nations with the same veto power that the other important nations had.

The end of the war did not bring peace to China. The Chinese Communists, who had become stronger during the Japanese invasion, seized Manchuria and parts of northern China after the Japanese surrender. The United States sent General George C. Marshall to China to try to bring about an understanding between the Nationalist government and the Chinese Reds. Marshall did not favor the Communists, but he recognized the inefficiency and corruption in Chiang Kai-shek's government. On his return to this country after the failure of his mission, Marshall recommended that no further aid be given the Chinese and that the United States maintain a "hands-off" attitude toward the Chinese civil war.

Although Russia had recognized and promised to support Chiang Kai-shek's government, the Soviet Union helped the Chinese Communists and gave them captured Japanese military equipment and supplies. Gradually the Communists won more and more territory until finally in 1949 the Nationalist defeats became a disaster. Chiang Kai-shek resigned his office, and the Chinese Reds prepared to take over all of China.

The victory of the Communists in China was a great blow to the prestige of the western allies and a great success for Soviet Russia. Only time would tell how great the Soviet victory had been and whether communist China would become a satellite of the Soviet Union or would stand on its own feet as an independent nation. In any event, the communization of China boded no good for the United States or the other western democracies.

——— CHECK-UP ———

How did increasing friction between Soviet Russia and the western powers lead to a cold war?

1. What were the postwar aims of Soviet Russia? How did these conflict with the postwar goals of Great Britain and the United States? Why were the great powers unable to agree on control of the atomic bomb?

2. What was the Truman Doctrine? The European Recovery Program? How did they help to check the expansion of Soviet influence? What was the purpose of the Atlantic Pact?

3. How did the air-lift defeat the blockade of Berlin? What progress was made toward settling the issues which led to the cold war?

4. How did the occupation of Japan compare with the occupation of Germany? What did it accomplish? How was Korea governed after the war? What events led to the triumph of communism in China?

CHAPTER REVIEW

Terms to Understand

Panzer divisions
selective service
  system
radar bombing
U-boats
D-Day
robot bombing
leapfrog tactics
V-E Day
atomic bomb
TNT
Chinese Reds

V-J Day
stabilize currencies
"Big Three"
"Big Five" powers
Security Council
war criminal
stock pile
cold war
satellites
cominform
air-lift
iron curtain

People and Things to Know About

Burma Road
General Douglas
  MacArthur
Bataan
Corregidor
Coral Sea
Midway
(General) Jimmy
  Doolittle
Winston Churchill
Franklin D. Roosevelt
Chiang Kai-shek

Potsdam Ultimatum
United Nations (UN)
Moscow Conference
Cairo Conference
Teheran Conference
Dumbarton Oaks
Bretton Woods
Yalta Conference
San Francisco
  Convention
Human Rights
Commission

People and Things to Know About (Cont.)

Guadalcanal
Stalingrad
General Rommel
General Eisenhower
Sicily
Normandy
General Patton
Admiral Nimitz
Battle of the Bulge
Iwo Jima
Okinawa
Harry S. Truman
Marshal Stalin

Organization of
  American States
James F. Byrnes
General George C.
  Marshall
Truman Doctrine
European Recovery
  Program
Berlin blockade
Council of Foreign
  Ministers
North Atlantic Pact

Historic Dates to Identify

1942   1945   1949
1944   1947

Questions to Discuss

1. Why was Japan eager to establish control over Southeast Asia and the Dutch East Indies? How did the United States overcome the shortages resulting from these conquests?
2. Why did the Nazis launch offensives directed against Egypt and the Baku region of Russia?

Questions to Discuss (Cont.)

3. Compare the following:

(*a*) Terms ending actual fighting in World Wars I and II.

(*b*) Extent of United States participation in international organizations after World Wars I and II.

(*c*) United States and Soviet views on control of the atom bomb.

(*d*) Control over Germany exercised by the victorious powers after World Wars I and II.

4. Why were the United Nations victorious in the war against Germany? Against Japan?

5. What appear to be the basic goals of Soviet foreign policy? To what extent do these conflict with goals of the United States? What policies of the United States are believed by the Soviet government to threaten its security?

6. What were the underlying purposes of the ECA? Why are these difficult to achieve?

7. How is it possible for the United States to be active in the UN and also active in planning the Organization of American States and the North Atlantic Pact?

8. How important was the communist victory in China?

Relating Geography and History

1. On an outline map, show the maximum Japanese advances in Asia and in the Pacific. Explain to the class why these huge gains were possible. Why was the United States able to force Japan out of the war without conquering each territorial area seized by the Japanese?

2. On an outline map, show the maximum Axis advances in Africa and Europe. Explain to the class how the United Nations launched offensives which destroyed or captured all Axis forces outside Germany and compelled

Relating Geography and History (Cont.)

that country to surrender. Why were the offensives launched where they were?

Other Things to Do

1. Ask a service man who took part in the fighting in the Pacific to describe combined (water-air-land) operations in that area. Ask a service man who took part in the fighting in Africa and Europe to make a similar report. Then discuss how modern warfare is similar to, and differs from, earlier wars.

2. Use *Readers' Guide* to locate articles telling about wartime and postwar developments of submarines, robot and rocket bombs, airplanes, amphibious craft, radar or A-bombs, gas and germ warfare. Report your findings on one of these subjects to the class.

3. For information about the A-bomb and what you and your classmates can do to improve living in the atomic age, read the pamphlet *Operation Atomic Vision*. It is published by the National Association of Secondary-School Principals, N.E.A., 1201 Sixteenth Street, N.W., Washington 6, D.C.

4. By writing to the United Nations Information Center, United Nations, Lake Success, New York, you may obtain information about UN and its many activities.

*5. Make a chart pointing out similarities and differences in the provisions of the Covenant of the League of Nations and the Charter of UN.

6. Use motion pictures, radio broadcasts, and newspaper and magazine reports as sources of information about most recent developments in relations between the Soviet Union and the United States. What progress has been made toward settling the issues underlying this conflict?

TO INCREASE YOUR UNDERSTANDING OF UNIT TEN

Unit Summary

1. In the closing years of the 1800's the United States ventured upon untried paths in its foreign policy. Drawn into a war with Spain because of sympathy for the downtrodden Cubans and because of our interests in Cuba, the United States emerged from the conflict committed to a policy of imperialism.

Steps were taken to set up a protectorate over Cuba and to establish in Puerto Rico and the Philippines forms of government suited to the needs of the people. By the 1930's the United States had given up its protectorate over Cuba, had granted greater self-government to the Puerto Ricans, and had provided for the future independence of the Philippines.

2. During the same period American influence

was greatly extended in the Caribbean region. Under President Theodore Roosevelt the way was cleared for the construction of the Panama Canal. Roosevelt also broadened the Monroe Doctrine. The United States made an attempt to guarantee political and financial stability in the Caribbean countries, a policy that required frequent intervention. By the 1920's the Caribbean had become an American lake. The result was an attitude of fear and hostility toward the United States on the part of these countries to the south. In the early '30's, however, President Franklin D. Roosevelt began a Good Neighbor policy. The United States withdrew from the various republics, while a series of Pan-American conferences cemented more friendly relations. This increased friendliness was extremely important during World War II and the postwar years.

3. The United States also entered the Pacific. By insisting on the Open Door policy, the United States saved China from much foreign exploitation but incurred the hostility of Japan. Japan was angered by our immigration policies but even more by our opposition to her plans to dominate the Far East.

4. Although a general peace movement made headway during the early 1900's, the jealousies and ambitions of European states brought on World War I. After a period of uneasy neutrality (1914–1917), Germany's submarine policy drew the United States into the world conflict. Americans rallied wholeheartedly to the war effort and helped turn the tide of victory against the Central Powers. President Woodrow Wilson then went to the Peace Conference determined to see that his plan for a League of Nations was written into the peace treaty. Though he succeeded in his purpose, Wilson was unable to secure support for the League plan at home. His failure was due to the hostility of Republican leaders in the Senate and to American reluctance to assume world leadership and responsibilities. Though American rejection of the League greatly weakened it, the United States was interested in world peace. During the 1920's and '30's it took part in various conferences and agreements that were intended to bring about disarmament and halt aggression.

5. The rise of aggressor nations upset the uncertain peace of the 1930's and led to the outbreak of World War II in 1939. At first the United States adopted neutrality legislation designed to prevent this nation from becoming involved in the conflict. As the dangers from the Axis Powers grew more threatening, the United States became the "arsenal for democracy." The Japanese attack on Pearl Harbor brought the United States into the war. American industrial production, as well as military might on many fronts, was vital in bringing about the defeat of the Axis. This time the United States accepted the responsibilities of world leadership. It took a leading part in setting up the United Nations and in supporting that organization. When Soviet Russia appeared bent on world domination, the United States backed Western Europe by putting the Truman Doctrine and the Marshall Plan into effect. The serious split between the East and West, however, complicates the possibilities of lasting peace.

Summary of Important Dates

1898 Spanish-American War.
United States acquires Hawaii, Puerto Rico, Guam, the Philippines.

1899 First Hague Conference.

1900 Hay announces acceptance of the Open Door policy.

1903 United States acquires Panama Canal Zone.

1904 Roosevelt's corollary to the Monroe Doctrine stated.

1914 World War I breaks out.
President Wilson announces American neutrality.
Panama Canal completed.

1916 *Sussex* Pledge.

1917 United States enters World War I.
United States acquires Virgin Islands.
Puerto Ricans given American citizenship.

1918 Armistice brings World War I to an end.

1920 League of Nations rejected by the United States.

1921 Washington Arms Conference.

1928 Paris Peace (Kellogg-Briand) Pact.

1932 Stimson Doctrine against Japanese aggression issued.

1933 Beginning of New Deal.
Good Neighbor policy announced.
United States recognizes Soviet Russia.
Hitler comes to power in Germany.

1935 United States begins neutrality legislation.

1939 World War II breaks out in Europe.

1941 United States approves Lend-Lease.
Atlantic Charter drawn up.
Attack on Pearl Harbor brings the United States into World War II.

1944 D-Day marks the invasion of France.

1945 United Nations victories in Europe and Japan mark close of World War II.
First use of atomic bomb.
United Nations Charter drawn up.
1947 Truman Doctrine and Marshall Plan announced.
1948 Cold war intensified; Berlin airlift.
1949 North Atlantic Pact.

Unit Activities

1. Make a list showing all territory acquired by the United States outside its continental limits. For each area, state (1) date acquired, (2) how acquired, (3) why acquired, and (4) present relation of the area to this country. What conclusions can you draw? Can a country exercise influence in an area even though it does not have direct territorial control? Explain.

2. List instances in which the United States has applied the Monroe Doctrine. In each case explain (1) why, and (2) what the outcome was. How was the Monroe Doctrine changed? Why? What is its status under the Good Neighbor Policy?

3. Trace United States foreign policy in the Far East, listing official pronouncements like the Open Door policy and the Stimson Doctrine. What has been the basic goal of this country's policy? Why? What is the goal sought today? What are present obstacles to the realization of this goal?

4. Compare United States participation in the two World Wars, taking into account (1) why this country went to war, (2) extent and type of participation, and (3) to what degree Americans accepted postwar responsibilities. How did the role of this country in world affairs change in one generation?

5. After class discussion, decide on a statement of basic goals of United States foreign policy. To what extent do you approve these goals? Would you wish to change them in any way?

For Further Reading

Original Sources

Commager, H. S., ed., *Documents of American History.* Appleton-Century-Crofts. Nos. 345–51, 355, 358, 360–62, 372, 385, 390, 393, 395, 398, 400, 401, 408–12, 416–18, 420, 423, 435, 436, 442, 447–49, 457, 460, 467, 469, 488–92, 514, 521–27, 534, 535.

Nevins, A., and Commager, H. S., eds., *The Heritage of America.* Little, Brown. Nos. 220–23, 237–45.

Pease, T. C., and Roberts, A. S., eds., *Selected Readings in American History.* Harcourt. Nos. 216–26, 230–35, 237, 242, 245–55, 256, 258, 260, 261, 268, 270.

General References

Adams, J. T., *The Epic of America.* Little, Brown. Chapters 11–13.

Bailey, T. A., *A Diplomatic History of the United States.* Appleton-Century-Crofts. Chapters 30–45.

Faulkner, H. U., *American Economic History.* Harper. Chapters 26 and 27.

Hicks, J. D., *The American Nation.* Houghton. Chapters 14–17, 21–23.

Morison, S. E., and Commager, H. S., *The Growth of the American Republic.* Oxford. Vol. II, Chapters 14, 19–21.

Special Accounts

Agar, H., *A Time for Greatness.* Little, Brown.

American Nation Series. Harper. Latané, J. H., *America as a World Power.* Ogg, F. A., *National Progress.*

Becker, C., *How New Will the Better World Be?* Knopf. This great historian predicted that changes would not be startling.

Benns, F. L., *Europe Since 1914 in Its World Setting.* Appleton-Century-Crofts.

Chronicles of America Series. Yale University Press. Fish, C. R., *The Path of Empire.* Howland, H., *Theodore Roosevelt and His Times.* Seymour, C., *Woodrow Wilson and the World War.* Shelton, O. D., *The Canadian Dominion.* Shepherd, W. R., *The Hispanic Nations of the New World.*

Dolivet, L., *The United Nations.* Farrar. Discusses structure, functions, and powers of UN.

Fay, S. B., *Origins of the World War.* Macmillan. An authoritative account in two volumes of events leading to World War I.

Griswold, A. W., *The Far Eastern Policy of the United States.* Harcourt. A readable survey of developments since 1898.

Hall, W. P., *World Wars and Revolutions; the Course of Europe Since 1900.* Appleton-Century-Crofts. Stresses the role of the United States.

Hersey, J., *Hiroshima.* Knopf. The effect of the atomic bomb on the residents of Hiroshima, and on six of them in particular.

History of American Life Series. Macmillan. Faulkner, H. U., *The Quest for Social Jus-*

tice, 1898–1914. Chapter 13. Slosson, P. W., The Great Crusade and After, 1914–1928. Chapters 1–3.

Horrabin, J. F., An Atlas-History of the Second Great War. Knopf.

Lippmann, W., U. S. Foreign Policy; Shield of the Republic. Little, Brown. States clearly the goals of our foreign policy.

Perkins, D., America and Two Wars. Little, Brown.

Shirer, W. L., Berlin Diary. Knopf. A radio commentator tells what he saw and heard in Nazi Germany.

Simonds, F. H., and Emery, B., The Great Powers in World Politics. American. Shows how the world's system of national states conflicts with internationalism.

Sullivan, L., Our Times. Scribner. Vols. I, IV, and V.

Tomlinson, E., Other Americans; Our Neighbors to the South. Scribner.

Welles, S., The Time for Decision. Harper.

Willkie, W. L., One World. Simon and Schuster.

Imaginative Writing

Anderson, M., and Stallings, L., What Price Glory. Harcourt. A successful play and moving picture of World War I.

Hersey, J. R., A Bell for Adano. Knopf. United States troops in Italy in World War II.

Kantor, M., Happy Land. Coward. An American family that has lost an only son takes comfort in the thought that America must go on.

Nordhoff, C. B., and Hall, J. N., Falcons of France. Little, Brown. Adventures in the Lafayette Flying Corps during World War I.

Remarque, E. M., All Quiet on the Western Front. Little, Brown. A story of World War I by a German author.

Saroyan, W., The Human Comedy. Harcourt. An American family adopts a discharged soldier who had been a friend of their son.

Shiber, E., Paris-Underground. Scribner. An underground group helps British soldiers escape from Nazi-occupied France.

White, W. L., They Were Expendable. Harcourt. PT boats in the Philippines.

Biography

Bowers, C. G., Beveridge and the Progressive Era. Houghton. Beveridge was a prophet of imperialism who dreamed of expanding markets in the Orient.

Butcher, H. C., My Three Years with Eisenhower. Simon and Schuster.

Dodd, W. E., Woodrow Wilson and His Work. Doubleday, Doran. A friendly biography of the President and his times.

Gorgas, M. D., and Hendrick, B. J., William Crawford Gorgas: His Life and Work. Doubleday, Doran. This sanitary expert made possible the construction of the Panama Canal.

Nicolay, H., MacArthur of Bataan. Appleton-Century-Crofts.

Pringle, H. F., Theodore Roosevelt. Harcourt.

Scott, R. L., Runway to the Sun. Scribner. Reminiscences of a famous flyer in World War II.

Poetry

Clarke, G. H., ed., The New Treasury of War Poetry. Houghton.

Pictures

Butterfield, R., The American Past. Simon and Schuster.

Pageant of America Series. Yale University Press. Bassett, J. S., Makers of a New Nation, Chapters 8 and 12. Wood, W., and Gabriel, R. H., In Defense of Liberty, Chapters 9–17.

Rogers, A., and Allen, F. L., The American Procession. Harper.

Stallings, L., The First World War; A Photographic History. Simon and Schuster. Pictures were secured from the pictorial sections and war colleges of the principal powers and from private sources.

 # Sidelights on American History

Jungle Stratagem. For three years after the Treaty of Paris the Filipinos expressed their resentment against American rule in bitter guerrilla warfare. The most sensational event of that difficult period was the capture of the guerrilla leader, Emilio Aguinaldo. He and his troops had resisted the American forces for months from their capital, Malolos, in northern Luzon. When the capital was taken, Aguinaldo disappeared.

The Americans had no idea where Aguinaldo had gone, but his attacks continued. American troops would be surprised in the jungle villages and quickly cut down. American scouts would go out and never return. It was plain to General Funston, the American commander, that the continued resistence was being directed by a capable leader, undoubtedly Aguinaldo. But how, in the trackless jungles of tropical Luzon, could Aguinaldo be found?

The answer came unexpectedly. A Filipino dispatch bearer surrendered himself to American troops. The rebel leader, he said, was hiding far to the northeast in the village of Palanan. He was sending messages to rebel leaders in the southern Philippines. The dispatch bearer offered some of the messages as proof of his statements. Sure enough, the decoded messages also revealed Aguinaldo's hiding place.

And now General Funston devised a trick to surprise and capture the Filipino leader. False answers to the messages advised Aguinaldo that a band of guerrilla troops, with five American prisoners, was proceeding north. The band would arrive at Palanan in a certain number of days. This information was sent to Palanan by a trusted Filipino. Funston and four American officers then proceeded to disguise themselves as prisoners. Taking 80 loyal native scouts, they journeyed by boat to the east coast of Luzon. From there they marched through dense jungle for five days. Received with open arms at Palanan, they fell upon Aguinaldo's bodyguards and overpowered them.

The Filipino leader was taken captive and transported to Manila. There he declared that further rebellion was useless and signed an oath of allegiance to the United States.

The Falling Mountain. Ships passing through the Panama Canal steam through a gap which was carved out of the backbone of a continent. At the time of the building of the canal, this gap was known as Culebra Cut. American army engineers found that Gold Hill, the highest point of Culebra, was part of the Continental Divide — mountains that formed the backbone, as it were, of that part of North America. Here the rivers divided, those on one flank of the mountains running toward the Pacific Ocean, while those on the other flank ran to the Atlantic.

At one point in the construction of the Panama Canal, the Culebra Cut was the cause of real doubt as to whether the sea-to-sea waterway could ever be completed. As the mountain was dug away, huge landslides took place and filled, within a few seconds, excavations that had cost the engineers months of work. Slides were so frequent and so uncontrollable that many engineers predicted utter failure for the canal project. It had been estimated that 95 million cubic yards of earth and rock would have to be removed from Culebra. By the time the project was finished, over 2½ times that amount had been excavated. The cut at the top had to be made three times as wide as had been originally planned.

The job of "breaking the spine" of the continent was given to the American engineer David B. Gaillard, and in recognition of his efforts Culebra Cut was officially renamed Gaillard Cut. Gaillard and his crew of engineers never really conquered the mountain, but its slopes were cut back so far that the landslides occurred less frequently. Although construction of the Panama Canal was formally completed in 1914, a gigantic landslide in 1915 caused the canal to be closed for months. Even today there are occasional slides, and sometimes ships have to wait until the channel is dug out again.

Sergeant York, the One-man Army. Easily the most amazing story of American fighting men in World War I is that of Sergeant Alvin York of Tennessee. York was a corporal on the day in October, 1918, when his platoon of 15 men was ordered to silence a nest of German machine gunners. The Germans had been pouring a withering fire into the infantry companies of York's division (the 82nd), which was trying to hold a ravine. The casualties were heavy and mounting.

York's patrol advanced. The men ran into a German battalion command post, took it by surprise, and captured all the enlisted men and three officers. But the attack brought them into view of enemy machine gunners stationed less than 90 feet away. These yelled to their comrades, "Drop! Drop down!" and opened fire on York's platoon. Six of the fifteen Americans were killed. Three were badly wounded, among them the sergeant in command of the platoon.

As corporal, York was second in rank, and he took over command of the platoon. He ordered the six remaining privates to guard the prisoners. He would take care of the Germans himself! Sharpshooting as he once had done in the mountains of Tennessee, Corporal York picked off twelve of the enemy. Then a German officer and seven men charged him. The American fired once with his rifle and then used his automatic pistol, which held seven shots. All eight Germans dropped in their tracks.

The officer in command of the German machine gun positions immediately surrendered himself and 90 men. York lined them up, placing the officer beside himself at the head of the column, with the unwounded Americans bringing up the rear. On the way back to the American lines they passed other enemy machine gun nests. At York's order, the Germans surrendered.

When he reached the American lines, York found his lieutenant and saluted.

"Corporal York, reporting with prisoners, sir."

"How many prisoners have you got, corporal?" asked the lieutenant, hardly daring to believe his eyes.

"Honest, lieutenant, I don't know," replied York.

When they were counted, there were 132.

Trench Warfare in World War I. It is sometimes said that while World War II was a war of *maneuver*, World War I was a war of *position*. By this is meant that in World War I the real strength of any army depended upon defensive warfare more often than upon offensive. Lightning advances over miles of enemy territory, like those made by mechanized units in World War II, were rare.

World War I was fought from trenches. The armies of both sides dug themselves into the ground whenever their advances were solidly stopped. A network of ditches deeper than the height of a man extended all the way from the French border of Switzerland to the North Sea. And in these trenches the fighting men at the front lived most of the time.

The trenches had underground shelters called "dugouts." There were lookout posts, also, and firing steps where the soldiers stood to shoot if the enemy attacked. Sometimes the soldiers found that the trenches of the enemy were quite near, perhaps only 50 yards away. American soldiers could often hear the Germans talking, quite clearly.

When an attack was to be made, the artillery in the rear would lay down a barrage of shells on the enemy trenches, attempting to destroy them. The men who were to attack would stand in their own trenches, waiting for the "zero hour" when they would go "over the top." Then they would advance through the broken barbed wire and the shell craters of the area between their trenches and those of the enemy — an area referred to as "No Man's Land."

In this kind of warfare, advances were necessarily slow. Sometimes neither side would gain more than a few miles in many months. Battle reports sometimes announced a gain of a few hundred yards as a great victory. Trench warfare conserved man power, but it made decisive victory by either side almost impossible.

A modern political convention

THE PLAN OF THE BOOK

Unit Eleven

POLITICAL LEADERS STRUGGLE

WITH PROBLEMS OF GOVERNMENT

During the 1900's certain distinct trends have been apparent in national politics. Up to our entrance into World War I there was an era of progressive reform, sparked chiefly by Presidents Theodore Roosevelt and Woodrow Wilson. After World War I a conservative reaction set in, which lasted until the great depression. During the 1930's Franklin Roosevelt inaugurated the New Deal program. World War II interrupted this movement of broad social and economic change. In general the two major parties have shared political control more evenly than in the years from 1865 to 1900. Third party movements have been numerous, but none have enjoyed any degree of success.

The people of the United States have made great political gains in the 1900's. Women have received the right to vote, and voters today have much more power than they had in the 1800's. At the local or state level, for example, they can now act directly to obtain legislation they favor. They have obtained increased power to choose members of the state and federal governments. Moreover, voters have increased their influence over those who hold office. In certain states and communities officeholders may be held responsible for their official acts and may be removed from office when they no longer have the confidence of the electorate. All these changes are living proof of the ability of free people to obtain legally the kind of government they want.

In reading this final unit, keep in mind that in America the citizens themselves determine the kind of government and the way of life they want. In the final analysis, the citizens of this country not only determine policies but pay the bill for services received from their government.

Chapter 41

Campaign truck

THE PROGRESSIVE MOVEMENT

INFLUENCES POLITICAL DEVELOPMENT

America stands for opportunity, America stands for a free field and no favor, America stands for a government responsible to the interests of all.

Woodrow Wilson, 1912

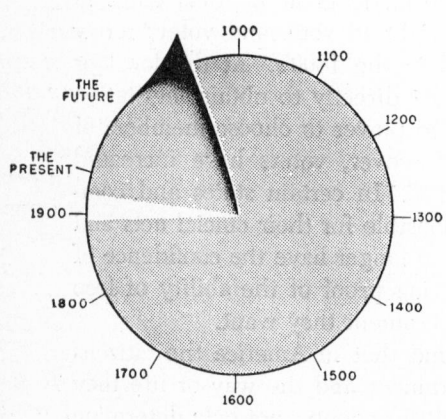

1897-1920

Early in the twentieth century there developed a crusade for reform which is usually referred to as the Progressive Movement. For some time there had been a strong feeling that government had not been serving the best interests of the American people as a whole, and the Progressive Movement grew out of that feeling. Many felt that the United States had been converted into a government of, by, and for the large corporations. They believed that the professional politicians were the willing tools of the moneyed class. As has been pointed out (page 511), one of the main purposes of the Progressive Movement was the protection of the citizen in our modern industrial society through government regulation of big business. Politically this movement aimed to restore greater power to the voters themselves.

The wave of reform started in the West, but in time spread throughout the country. Robert M. La Follette of Wisconsin, Hiram Johnson of California, and A. B. Cummins of Iowa were the best-known leaders of the reform movement, while Theodore Roosevelt did more than anyone else to popularize it. Late in 1901 President McKinley met a tragic death and Roosevelt was suddenly called to the Presidency. With the inauguration of Theodore Roosevelt, a Progressive Era in government started which continued until after World War I. William Howard Taft and Woodrow Wilson completed the trio of Presidents who occupied the White House during this period. The story of the Progressive Movement will be told under the following topics:

1. A Progressive Era begins under Theodore Roosevelt.
2. Reform measures continue under President Taft.
3. Woodrow Wilson calls for a "New Freedom."
4. The Progressive Movement produces political reforms.

Showing intense interest, crowds of people turned out to hear Theodore Roosevelt explain the aims of the reform movement and attack certain practices of business.

1 A Progressive Era Begins under Theodore Roosevelt

Conservative Republicans are strong under President McKinley. The victory of William McKinley over William Jennings Bryan in the election of 1896 (page 468) was a triumph for conservative farmers and businessmen over more extreme groups who favored cheap money, political reforms, and other changes. Even before McKinley was inaugurated the depression of the 1890's began to lift. President McKinley's administration was a time of great prosperity for the whole country. Big business had little to fear from the government in Washington, and business consolidations increased rapidly (page 470). The Dingley Tariff (page 539) raised tariff duties and gave still further protection to industry.

Most of President McKinley's administration, however, was concerned with foreign affairs. The outbreak of war with Spain

in 1898 (page 618) and the problems of governing the newly acquired territories occupied much of the country's attention. The annexation of Hawaii (page 478) and the proclamation of the Open Door policy in China (page 651) were important accomplishments of President McKinley's first term. It was not until 1900 that Congress passed the Gold Standard Act (page 532), which concerned the very question on which the election of 1896 had been fought.

Theodore Roosevelt succeeds to the Presidency. As a result of widespread prosperity, the turn of the century found the Republican Party well established in all branches of the national government. In the election of 1900 President McKinley easily defeated Bryan on the combined issues of free silver and imperialism. Free silver had lost much of its appeal to the American people, and the public seemed to approve America's expansion overseas (Chapter 34).

But the victory of the conservative Republicans was short-lived. Early in September, 1901, while holding a reception at the Pan-American Exposition at Buffalo,

733

President McKinley was shot by a half-crazed anarchist. When he died eight days later, Theodore Roosevelt became the new leader of the American people.[1] Roosevelt's advance to the Presidency alarmed such Republican leaders as "Mark" Hanna and Thomas C. Platt, who feared that he might disturb the well-oiled machinery of business. They were only partly reassured by his statement that he intended "to continue, absolutely unbroken, the policy of President McKinley, for the peace, prosperity, and honor of our beloved country."[2]

Roosevelt's experience had been varied. There was much in Theodore Roosevelt's personality and early record to explain the uneasiness of the conservative leaders. Although Roosevelt was the youngest President the United States had ever had, he had enjoyed a wide political experience. Shortly after his graduation from Harvard he served for three terms in the New York legislature. The next two years he spent on a Dakota ranch. Here he developed a rugged physique, gained sound knowledge and a deep appreciation of the great West, and devoted himself to the writing of historical works. Roosevelt again entered political life in 1889 as a member of the Civil Service Commission under President Harrison. In 1895 he became police commissioner of New York City, and after two strenuous years was appointed Assistant Secretary of the Navy. When the Spanish-American War broke out, Roosevelt resigned to become lieutenant colonel in the Rough Riders (page 620).

Theodore Roosevelt was the typical American. Theodore Roosevelt was the most typically American personality of his

[1] In 1898, Roosevelt, fresh from his triumphs in the Spanish-American War, was elected governor of New York. His energy and independence, however, disturbed the political bosses. They planned to cut short his political career by nominating him to the Vice-Presidency, an office in which there was little opportunity to be influential. Roosevelt objected to their plans, but the Republican Convention in 1900 overwhelmingly nominated him as McKinley's running mate.

[2] It was later jokingly said of Roosevelt that he carried out the policies of McKinley — and buried them!

time. Energetic and resourceful, he was constantly before the public eye. He was responsible for the popularity of such expressions as "the square deal," "the big stick," "malefactors of great wealth," "mollycoddle," and "undesirable citizen." He had little patience with those who held opinions different from his own, and once he had made a decision, he disliked to change his mind. Unlike President McKinley, who had followed public opinion, Roosevelt seemed rather to form it. He was keenly aware of the needs of the people. In fact, he usually managed to assume leadership in the matter of new political and social ideas, without being so far ahead of public opinion that he appeared radical. He read widely and he had a great many interests. He was a naturalist, sportsman, and historian. His writings on various subjects as well as on his own personal experiences cover thirty volumes of published works. He was as much at home with cowboys, prize fighters, or labor leaders as with senators, diplomats, or clergymen. Most of Roosevelt's public experience had been in administrative work, and he loved to exercise authority.

Roosevelt favors the regulation of big business. It has already been pointed out (page 512) that Theodore Roosevelt favored "within reasonable limits" the control and supervision of big business. In his first annual message to Congress he complimented the captains of industry who had built the railroads and developed our industries and commerce. In his opinion there was, however, "a widespread conviction in the mind of the American people that the great corporations were in certain of their features and tendencies harmful to the general welfare." Roosevelt therefore claimed that the nation should have the power to supervise and regulate all corporations that did an interstate business.

For this reason he energetically began a policy of "trust busting." The Northern Securities Company was dissolved, the Expedition and Elkins Acts were passed, and a new cabinet officer, known as the Secretary of Commerce and Labor, was appointed (Chapter 28). On the other hand,

(Continued on page 736)

Theodore Roosevelt
(1858-1919)

Rough Rider

THEODORE ROOSEVELT, though born to ease and luxury, was the foremost advocate of "the strenuous life." From boyhood on through his full and varied life, he was constantly engaged in some sort of fight or crusade. In his youth he waged a long battle to conquer physical weakness. After he completed his education at Harvard, he entered the New York legislature, where, as an unknown legislator, he struggled against political corruption. In a variety of political posts — as a member of the United States Civil Service Commission, head of the New York City police force, Assistant Secretary of the Navy, and Governor of New York — he displayed a vigorous and forceful spirit.

When Theodore Roosevelt became Vice President, it seemed that his crusading days might be ended. But the tragic death of President McKinley opened the doors to the White House and a new field of endeavors. During his two terms Roosevelt fought vigorously for government regulation of big business, a "square deal" for labor, conservation of natural resources, and a better understanding among the nations of the world. Though he retired from the Presidency in 1909, he returned to the political arena three years later and waged a strenuous but unsuccessful campaign as the candidate of the Progressive Party.

President

Besides his ability as a crusader, Roosevelt possessed other outstanding qualities. His interests covered an astounding range and he gained recognition in almost every field to which he turned his attention. Despite his wealthy background he was interested in all types of people and was able to meet them at their level. The cowboys of the West forgot his city background and Harvard accent when they found he could meet the hardships of frontier life and ask no favors. He was equally at ease with the college athletes and the hardy Westerners who were members of the Rough Riders. All sorts of people from all walks of life found a welcome at the White House. Roosevelt deservedly earned the title of "The Most Interesting American."

Big Game Hunter

while Roosevelt was sympathetic toward labor, he supported the workingmen only so long as they obeyed the law. He demanded, in the coal strike of 1902, that the rights of workers be protected, but he also insisted that both capital and labor respect the interests of the public (page 521). "While I am President," said Roosevelt, "I wish the laboring man to feel that he has the same right of access to me that the capitalist has; that the doors swing open as easily to the wage-worker as to the head of a big corporation — and no easier."

Roosevelt wins the election of 1904. Theodore Roosevelt was in a strong position in the election year of 1904. Although his antitrust activities and his interference in the coal strike had antagonized the captains of industry, these actions at the same time had appealed strongly to the general public. Besides, his vigorous foreign policy in the Caribbean and his insistence upon American leadership in the Western Hemisphere won wide praise (Chapter 35). Roosevelt was therefore nominated by the Republican convention without a formal vote. In the Democratic convention, on the other hand, there was a noticeable return to a conservative point of view. The platform denounced the Republican administration as "spasmodic, erratic, sensational, spectacular, and arbitrary." Judge Alton B. Parker, a conservative from New York, was nominated to oppose the progressive Roosevelt.

The contest proved a one-sided affair. Theodore Roosevelt swept the country, receiving 2½ million more votes than Parker. Discontent among the workers, however, was reflected in the size of the Socialist vote. Eugene V. Debs, the Socialist candidate, who first entered a presidential contest in 1900 with less than 100,000 votes, polled over 400,000 votes in this election. Roosevelt won every state outside of the Solid South, and even carried the Democratic state of Missouri. Pleased with the extent of his victory, he made a public announcement on the night of his election which was to plague him in later years. "Under no circumstances," he stated publicly, "will I be a candidate for or accept another nomination."

Fashionable costume of 1909

Theodore Roosevelt's second term increases his popularity. The splendid backing given Roosevelt by the voters encouraged him to continue his progressive policies. Additional lawsuits were undertaken to curb big business. The control over transportation companies was tightened by the passage of the Hepburn Act (page 518). For the protection of the public, the Pure Food and Meat Inspection acts were passed (page 513). Roosevelt also started a vigorous policy of conserving natural resources and reclaiming arid lands (page 565). In the interests of world peace, the President assisted in bringing about a settlement of the Russian-Japanese War, sent delegates to the Second Hague Conference, and sponsored a series of arbitration treaties (pages 652, 660). A panic and depression in 1907 gave Roosevelt's opponents an opportunity to criticize him, but with the people as a whole he stood at the height of his popularity.

Theodore Roosevelt chooses his successor. As the election of 1908 approached, there was no indication that Theodore Roosevelt regretted his announcement that he would not again be a candidate for President. It seems certain that he could have been nominated and elected; in fact, there was a widespread movement to force the nomination upon him, but he firmly opposed it. His Secretary of War, William Howard Taft, seemed to be the most available candidate. Roosevelt made sure of sufficient delegates at the Republican convention to nominate Taft on the first ballot. He also dictated a platform, adopted by the convention, which said on the important question of the tariff (page 541): "The Republican Party declares unequivocally for a revision of the tariff by a special session of Congress immediately following the inauguration of the next President." The platform also promised that the Sherman Antitrust Law and the Interstate Commerce Act would be strengthened, and that there would be currency reform.

Taft defeats Bryan. After an eight-year interval, William Jennings Bryan again controlled the Democratic convention. The Democratic platform condemned private monopolies. It called for a reduction of tariff duties and the enactment of an income-tax law. It also opposed the use of injunctions in labor disputes. On the first ballot Bryan was nominated for the Presidency by an overwhelming majority.

Until this election it had been customary for the American Federation of Labor to take no stand on the presidential election, but Samuel Gompers, president of the A. F. of L., departed from the policy of neutrality. He gave his support and promised the labor vote to the Democratic Party. Nevertheless, in the election which followed, Taft received 1¼ million more votes than his opponent. The Republicans also won both houses of Congress by a large majority. Having expressed complete confidence in Taft, Theodore Roosevelt departed to hunt big game in Africa and to make a triumphal tour of European capitals.

——————— CHECK-UP ———————

What progressive measures characterized the administration of Theodore Roosevelt?

1. What were the chief features of President McKinley's administration? Why was Theodore Roosevelt selected as his running mate in 1900?
2. What experience had Theodore Roosevelt had before becoming Vice-President? Why was he popular as President? What was his conception of a "square deal" for labor and capital?
3. What were the major accomplishments of Theodore Roosevelt's second administration? Why was Taft nominated by the Republican Party in 1908?

2 Reform Measures Continue Under President Taft

President Taft's position is difficult. In spite of Theodore Roosevelt's hearty support of Taft, a feeling of dissatisfaction with the new President was soon evident. To be successor to the energetic Roosevelt was no easy task for any man, and Taft, by contrast, seemed slow-moving and conservative. His mind was of the judicial type. He made decisions only after careful study, and he showed no interest in exercising any powers as executive that were not specifically granted by the Constitution or by law. Few Presidents possessed better qualifications for the office than Taft. At any other time he no doubt would have made an unusually satisfactory President. He was good-natured, unaffected, democratic, and courageous. But after the Roosevelt era Taft's administration was disappointing, and it ended in disaster. Before the end of his term the disagreement between the progressives and conservatives split the Republican Party.

Taft seems to support the conservatives. The Payne-Aldrich Tariff was the first step in Taft's downfall (page 541). In his campaign Taft had made it clear that the statement on the tariff in the party platform meant revision downward, and the American people accepted this interpretation without question. Although the tariff bill in its final form provided for a slight revision upward, Taft defended it as "the best tariff law the Republicans ever made, and therefore the best the country ever had." Moreover, in an unfortunate dispute over the conservation of natural resources, Taft again seemed to be on the side of the

Fashions in men's hats, 1900's

President Taft was well liked for his friendly nature. With him in this front porch picture are his two sons. Charles (left) became a lawyer and church leader, Robert (right) a prominent Republican senator.

conservatives (page 566). The dismissal of Chief Forester Gifford Pinchot widened the split between the progressive and the conservative Republicans. This incident also influenced Theodore Roosevelt to lend a sympathetic ear to his friend Pinchot and the grievances of the progressive wing of the Republican Party.

President Taft secures the passage of progressive measures. Although Taft seemed to be allied with the conservatives, a number of progressive measures were adopted during his administration. A postal savings bank was established which made every post office a bank. Over the protests of the express companies, the parcel post was established, and its business grew rapidly. Another act of Congress required that funds spent on federal political campaigns should be made public. A beginning was made in the struggle to ban child labor. To improve the welfare of miners, a Bureau of Mines was established in the Department of the Interior. A separate Department of Labor, whose head was a member of the President's cabinet, was also created. The civil service was greatly enlarged, and a law was passed which limited the working day to eight hours for all workers under contract with the government. In 1912 Arizona and New Mexico were admitted to the Union, bringing the total to 48 states. The next year the Sixteenth Amendment, authorizing a tax on in-

comes, became a part of the Constitution. Numerous arbitration treaties were also drawn up with foreign powers (page 661).

The Speaker of the House is deprived of power. During the Taft administration, the differences between the progressive and conservative wings of the Republican Party deepened. The progressives, who favored giving the voters more control over the nation's political and economic life, were called insurgents. The conservatives were referred to as reactionaries, "standpatters," or the "old guard." Within the House of Representatives the progressives won an important test of strength. Until 1910 the Speaker of the House was one of the most powerful officers of the government. He appointed all House committees. He was also chairman of the Rules Committee, which decided on the procedure of the House and determined its order of business. As the presiding officer of the House during debate, he determined who should speak by recognizing or refusing to recognize whom he pleased.

Speaker "Joe" Cannon, a conservative, was believed to have used this power to stifle progressive legislation. Therefore Representative George W. Norris of Nebraska proposed an amendment to the House rules (1910). The purpose of this amendment was to enlarge the Rules Committee and to bar the Speaker of the House from membership on it. Speaker Cannon ruled the motion out of order. But after an all-night debate the insurgent Republicans, supported by the Democrats, overruled his decision and passed the amendment. In the following year the Speaker was also deprived of the power of appointing the remaining committees. From that time on, the Speaker was the presiding officer of the House, not its dictator.

The Progressives organize. In 1911 the Republican progressives organized the National Progressive Republican League. Its purpose was to secure the passage of progressive political, social, and economic legislation. The league also promoted the nomination of Senator Robert M. La Follette for President because "his experience, his character, his courage, his record in constructive legislation, his administrative ability meet the requirement of leadership such as a presidential candidacy demands." Theodore Roosevelt, who had delivered a number of progressive speeches since his return to the United States, willingly supported the principles of this league, but declined an invitation to join. As a matter of fact, many progressives looked longingly toward Roosevelt as the only man who could lead them to victory. To enter the presidential contest, however, would seem to be not only a violation of his pledge of 1904, but a betrayal of Taft, to whom he had given unqualified support. It could also be considered a slap at Senator La Follette.

Theodore Roosevelt becomes a candidate. Early in 1912 a series of events caused Theodore Roosevelt to change his mind. Senator La Follette made a lengthy and rambling speech which caused Gifford Pinchot to telegraph Roosevelt that in his judgment La Follette could no longer be regarded as a serious candidate. At the same time seven Republican governors and a group of influential citizens joined to ask Roosevelt to heed public demand and become a candidate. Before Roosevelt answered, Taft slightingly referred to the progressive leaders as "political emotionalists." This attack aroused Roosevelt's fighting spirit and on February 24 he announced, "My hat is in the ring." La Fol-

lette's chances for the nomination disappeared with the announcement of Roosevelt's candidacy.

The Republican convention renominates President Taft. A struggle for delegates to the Republican convention started immediately. President Taft had an advantage in that he controlled the Republican National Committee. When the convention met at Chicago in June, 1912, the seats of more than 200 delegates were contested. The Republican National Committee, which was determined to nominate Taft, was in control of the situation, and it awarded only nineteen of the contested seats to Roosevelt delegates. When the Roosevelt delegates found themselves clearly in the minority, they refused to take any further part in the convention. The remaining delegates nominated President Taft and drew up a party platform praising his administration for its large amount of constructive legislation. In the opinion of Roosevelt, however, the nominee of the convention was merely "the beneficiary of [a] successful fraud."

The Democratic convention names Woodrow Wilson. Democratic leaders imme-

"Bob" La Follette was a leader of progressive forces for years. He is shown here as he looked at a political convention in 1924.

diately saw the opportunity given them by the division in the ranks of the Republican Party. When the convention met at Baltimore in June, a split developed between the progressive and the conservative delegates similar to that in the Republican Party. The progressively-minded Bryan was not a candidate, but as leader of the party he was able to control the convention. The balloting for a candidate became a struggle between J. Beauchamp (Champ) Clark of Missouri, Speaker of the House of Representatives, and Woodrow Wilson. Clark occupied a middle-of-the road position between progressives and reactionaries, while Wilson had already won a reputation as a progressive governor of New Jersey. On the forty-sixth ballot, largely because of Bryan's influence, Wilson was chosen as the Democratic standard-bearer.[3] The platform adopted by the Democratic convention was progressive in tone. It called for a reduction in tariff rates, stricter antitrust legislation, banking and currency reform, publicity for campaign contributions, and conservation.

The Progressive Party is organized. Meanwhile, the Roosevelt delegates who had refused to take part in the Republican convention returned home to plan a Progressive Party which would nominate a progressive candidate. Delegates were chosen to a party convention, and plans were made to place the names of Progressive electors on the ballots for the November election. To organize a party for a presidential election in the brief time before the election was a problem which few men other than Theodore Roosevelt would have attempted.

The Progressive convention, which met at Chicago in August, was marked by great enthusiasm. Theodore Roosevelt was nominated for the Presidency, with Hiram Johnson of California as his running mate. In its platform the Progressive Party gave its support to all the new experiments in democracy, including woman suffrage and

a swifter method of amending the federal Constitution. It also favored rigid government control of corporations, downward revision of the tariff, conservation of natural resources, development of the agricultural interests, and a broad program of social legislation. Such social reforms were to include minimum-wage laws, the prohibition of child labor, social insurance, and the eight-hour day.

The campaign is dramatic. President Taft exerted little energy in the campaign, but Wilson turned out to be an excellent campaigner. He was well-informed and was able to express himself in a clear, convincing style that inspired confidence. Theodore Roosevelt fought with his usual vigor. He called one of his opponents reactionary and the other visionary. During the campaign, while in Milwaukee to deliver a speech, he was shot by a fanatic. Against the advice of his friends, with a bullet in his chest, he delivered an address which marked the dramatic climax of the campaign.

Woodrow Wilson wins the election. Because of the split in the Republican Party, Woodrow Wilson won an overwhelming victory. President Taft carried only the two states of Vermont and Utah, while Theodore Roosevelt won the states of Pennsylvania, Michigan, Minnesota, South Dakota, and Washington. He also won eleven of the thirteen electoral votes of California. Wilson carried the remaining states, with a total electoral vote of 435. In addition, the Democrats won a majority in both houses of Congress. In spite of defeat, however, the election was a personal triumph for Theodore Roosevelt. His organization had been hastily developed, he lacked the support of La Follette, and he failed to win over the progressive wing of the Democratic Party from Wilson. Nevertheless, Theodore Roosevelt polled four times as many votes as any independent candidate had received during the preceding half century. The Socialist candidate, Debs, received nearly 900,000 votes on a program that called for government ownership of the means of production and distribution.

---

[3] At a critical moment in the balloting, Bryan shifted the Nebraska vote from Clark to Wilson because he would not support a candidate who was backed by Tammany Hall.

Why did rivalry between progressives and conservatives come to a head during President Taft's administration?

1. Why were the progressives dissatisfied with President Taft's position on the Payne-Aldrich tariff? What progressive measures did Taft support?

2. Why did the progressives revolt against the concentration of power in the hands of the Speaker of the House? What changes were made?

3. How did Theodore Roosevelt in 1912 come to be a candidate for President on the Progressive ticket? What candidates opposed him? Who won the election? Why?

President Woodrow Wilson and his fiancée, Mrs. Galt, attended the second game of the 1915 World Series. President Wilson was highly popular at this time and was re-elected to the Presidency the following year.

3 Woodrow Wilson Calls for a "New Freedom"

Wilson's reputation as a progressive was well deserved. The new President was a Virginian of Scotch-Irish Presbyterian ancestry. After graduating from Princeton Woodrow Wilson had studied law at the University of Virginia. He did not find the practice of law to his liking, and entered Johns Hopkins at the age of 27 for graduate study in history. There his work was so brilliant that he won an appointment to teach at Bryn Mawr. Later he became president of Princeton University. Probably no American in public life was better informed than Woodrow Wilson on American history and on the workings of government. Furthermore, his capacity for leadership was recognized before he was elected to the Presidency. As governor of New Jersey he had acted on the theory that he was responsible not to the political leaders, but only to the people who had elected him. He succeeded in bringing the state legislature completely under his control. By carrying out a thoroughgoing program of reform, he came to be known as the most progressive and independent governor in the East.

President Wilson exercises leadership. As President, Woodrow Wilson regarded himself not only as the leader of his party but also as the representative of the whole people. In the campaign President Wilson had proposed a program of political and economic reform which he called the "New Freedom." In his inaugural address he made a stirring appeal to the American people to support him in this program of reform. He believed that he was personally responsible for carrying this program into effect. When Wilson rewarded Bryan by making him Secretary of State, many expected that Bryan would dominate the administration. Political prophets also predicted freely that Wilson would find Congress more difficult to deal with than the New Jersey legislature. The prophets were amazed, however, when he established complete control over the cabinet and succeeded in leading Congress "like a school-master." President Wilson believed firmly in democracy — that the people could be trusted in the long run to reach a sound decision. His state papers, which showed his lofty idealism and were expressed in a splendid literary style, gained a wide hearing. His ability to touch the heart-strings of the average man soon made him a leader of public opinion.

Opinions differ as to President Wilson's personal characteristics. People differ widely in their interpretations of Wilson's personal characteristics. In the opinion of his friends he was courageous, conscientious, patient, and open-minded. His enemies, on the other hand, hated and distrusted him. They said that he was aloof and insincere. They accused him of surrounding himself with small men so that he might appear big, and of being impatient with advice that did not agree with his own beliefs. Basing his opinions on sound scholarship and knowledge, he was not easily turned from his purpose. As a result, his enemies called him stubborn.

Important legislation is passed. Scarcely had the new administration been inaugurated when President Wilson spurred Congress to adopt a vigorous program of legislation. One after another, such laws as the Underwood Tariff (page 542), the Federal Reserve Act (page 533), and the Clayton Act (page 514) were passed. In addition to these major laws, legislation was passed for the benefit of the farmers (page 556), and the Smith-Lever Act extended government aid for agricultural education in land-grant colleges (page 552). A civil government was inaugurated in the Canal Zone, and the Jones Act (page 628) provided a new form of government for the Philippines. There were benefits for labor, too, in the Clayton Act and the Adamson Act (pages 522, 523), and in a law which set up a board of arbitration to aid in labor disputes. By the close of President Wilson's first term an impressive list of measures had been driven through Congress by this determined President.

President Wilson is renominated in 1916. As the election of 1916 approached, Wilson's fortunes ran high. On the whole his Mexican policy (page 642) met with the approval of the country, though many criticized his failure to protect American interests more fully. He had also displayed skill in handling the complicated situation growing out of the European war. By the *Sussex* Pledge (page 664) he appeared to have won a diplomatic victory in the submarine dispute with Germany. For a time, at least, American lives on the high seas seemed safe. In addition, the President had taken the leadership of the movement for preparedness, and the federalized militia was getting valuable training along the Mexican frontier. Wilson's friends could likewise point with pride to his success in carrying out his program of domestic reform. It was not surprising, therefore, that the Democratic convention renominated him with enthusiasm.

Hughes is nominated by the Republicans. The Republican convention, which met in Chicago, chose Supreme Court Justice Charles Evans Hughes, former governor of New York, as its candidate. The Republican platform called for a policy of aggressive neutrality in the European war. It emphasized the need for preparedness and criticized the Underwood Tariff. President Wilson was charged with having been criminally neglectful of American interests in Mexico. Instead of placing a separate candidate in the field, the Progressives followed the suggestion of Theodore Roosevelt and gave their support to the Republican nominee. Hughes toured the country, finding fault with the foreign policy of the administration, but he failed to outline a policy that would be a good substitute. In his visit to California, furthermore, Hughes made a serious blunder in failing to make friends with the Progressives led by Hiram Johnson.

President Wilson wins over Hughes. President Wilson, on the other hand, contented himself with delivering a number of speeches from the front porch of his summer home at "Shadow Lawn" in New Jersey. The Democratic Party adopted the slogan, "He kept us out of war," which was particularly convincing in the Middle West. The election was one of the closest in American history. Early in the morning after the election, victory was conceded to Hughes. As more returns came in from the West, however, it became evident that the final count would be close. Not until official returns were received from California several days later was it known definitely that President Wilson had carried that state and the election by a very narrow margin. The victory was a great personal triumph for President Wilson. His success in 1912 was made possible by a split in the Republican Party, but he won in 1916 against a reunited party. Moreover, he had won in spite of the fact that at that time the great majority of the voters in the country were considered Republicans.

The Democrats lose the congressional elections of 1918. Between the election of 1916 and the congressional elections of 1918, the United States devoted all its energies to winning World War I. For this purpose Congress granted President Wilson extraordinary powers. By November, 1918, negotiations for an armistice were under way, and victory for the Allied cause was certain. As has previously been explained (page 677), President Wilson made serious mistakes in planning for the peace. He ignored the Republican support which he had received for his war measures, and he called upon the country to elect a Democratic Congress to aid him in the difficult peace decisions which lay ahead.

By 1918 the Republican Party was fully reunited. Its leaders, including Taft, Theodore Roosevelt, and Lodge, immediately accepted the President's challenge and carried on a vigorous campaign for the election of a Republican Congress. In the election the country, knowing that victory was sure, reverted to its normal political tone, and the Republicans won the day. When President Wilson went to Europe for the peace negotiations, he went without the support of either the voters or the Senate.

The Treaty of Versailles figures in the election of 1920. The Treaty of Versailles and the question of whether the United States should ratify it occupied the attention of the country in the period just before the election of 1920 (page 680). For a year before the election, Wilson was a sick and broken man, and the Democratic Party was without his leadership. When

Charles Evans Hughes, defeated for the Presidency in 1916, later served for eleven years as Chief Justice of the Supreme Court.

the Senate rejected the League of Nations, the President hoped that the election of 1920 would become a solemn referendum on the treaty. To be sure, the treaty became the leading issue, but it was lost sight of by the ordinary voter, who in 1920 found little or no reason for voting against the candidate of his own party. "Any good Republican can be nominated for President and can defeat any Democrat," boasted Boies Penrose, the Republican leader in Pennsylvania.

The Republicans nominate Harding. In the Republican convention many leaders were passed over in favor of Warren G. Harding, Senator from Ohio, for President. Governor Calvin Coolidge of Massachusetts was nominated for the Vice-Presidency. While the platform promised international co-operation without injury to American sovereignty, it backed up the Senate in rejecting the Treaty of Versailles. The Democratic convention favored immediate acceptance of the League of Nations without any changes which would make its provisions less effective. Governor James M. Cox of Ohio was nominated for the Presidency on the forty-fourth ballot, with Franklin D. Roosevelt of New York occupying second place on the ballot.

Harding is elected. The election, the first in which women voters all over the country participated, resulted in an overwhelming defeat for the Democrats. The vote was about 16 million to 9 million. The Republicans carried all the northern and western states, the border states (with the exception of Kentucky) and even the state of Tennessee, for a total of 404 electoral votes. Debs, though still behind prison bars for violating the Espionage Act during the war, received nearly a million Socialist votes. A Farmer-Labor party entered the field to win benefits for the farmers, but polled only a quarter of a million votes. The election of 1920 marked an important milestone in national development. The American people had spoken; the League of Nations was rejected; war idealism was a thing of the past; and the Progressive Era was over.

——— CHECK-UP ———

What liberal gains were made during Woodrow Wilson's administrations?

1. What experience did Woodrow Wilson have before becoming President? What important legislation was passed during his first administration?

2. Why was the election of 1916 much closer than that of 1912? Why was there less progressive legislation during Wilson's second administration than during the first?

3. Why did the Republicans sweep the elections of 1920?

Voting booth

BALLOT BOX

Register of names

4 The Progressive Movement Produces Political Reforms

Lawmaking power is extended to the voter. The Progressive Movement of the early century was accompanied by a number of political reforms. These started in the state and local governments, but extended also to the federal system. The purpose of one important reform was to give the voter a larger voice in lawmaking; it thus furnished a check upon a legislature that was controlled by political bosses or dominated by big business interests. This reform involved the use of two devices known as the *initiative* and the *referendum*. By the initiative a stated percentage (usually five to eight per cent) of the voters in a state might initiate, or start, a law. If the state legislature then failed to pass the measure, it could be brought before (referred to) the voters in a referendum for their approval. Also, if a certain percentage of the voters should petition for a referendum, a law already before the lawmaking body must be submitted to popular vote before it could go into effect. Starting in South Dakota in 1898, the initiative and referendum spread until half the states, mostly in the Midwest and the West, had adopted this method of legislation in one form or another.

The recall checks the politician. Another device, the *recall*, made it possible for voters to remove an official before his term expired. On petition of a substantial percentage of the voters (usually 25 per cent), a special election must be held to determine whether the officer should complete his term or be replaced by another. Beginning in the early 1900's, the recall was presently adopted in twelve states. In seven of these it applied to judicial as well as executive officers. Oregon was the first state to provide that all state officers be subject to the recall. The device has been used chiefly to remove municipal officers, though in 1921 the governor and the higher state officials in North

Dakota were removed by recall. It was predicted that if the recall were extended to the judicial branch of the government there would be serious consequences, but that prediction failed to come true.

Direct primaries give the voter a voice in nominations. The *direct primary* was another practice widely adopted in the drive to make government more responsive to the people. Introduced by Governor La Follette of Wisconsin in 1903, it was designed to give the voters a chance to nominate candidates. Previously the important privilege of naming candidates for public office had fallen upon party caucuses or conventions which were easily controlled by professional politicians. Under the direct primary plan, candidates were nominated by petition. Then all the enrolled voters of a party had a chance to choose the party's standard-bearers in a preliminary or primary election.

Direct primaries are not without disadvantages. The new system spread rapidly through the western states and was finally adopted by all but five states in the Union. It turned out to be a disappointment to its supporters, however, because the party organizations still found it possible to nominate their favorites. Moreover, the men who were successful in the primary race found that they had to pay the costs of two campaigns. Thus the use of the primary system tended to limit the candidates to those who possessed strong financial backing. After experimenting with the direct primary, New York State partially abandoned the system in 1921.

Nevertheless, the direct primary gave the voters a weapon, if they chose to use it, with which to force the choice of candidates who met their approval. In a number of states a form of the direct primary was to be found in the presidential preferential system. By this device the voters indicated their preference for a candidate to be supported by the delegates attending the national nominating conventions.

The Seventeenth Amendment provides for direct election of senators. The attention of the reformers was also directed toward the method of electing senators. It was widely believed that the state legis-

Voting machines were invented to reduce corrupt balloting practices during elections.

latures, which under the Constitution had the duty of choosing senators, sometimes were influenced by money or big business. The Senate was criticized as a millionaires' club, and it was customary to speak of sugar senators, lumber senators, oil senators, or railroad senators. On numerous occasions the House passed resolutions calling for a constitutional amendment which would permit the election of senators by the people, but the proposal was always defeated in the Senate. Nevertheless, the idea continued to gain supporters. As early as 1899 the people of Nevada chose a candidate for senator whom the state legislature was pledged to elect. By 1912, some three fourths of the states had followed Nevada's example. In the same year the Senate yielded and passed the resolution favoring an amendment which would permit the direct election of senators. The resolution was promptly ratified by the states (1913) and became the Seventeenth Amendment. As in the case of the direct primary, popular election of senators has not accomplished all that its supporters expected.

Alfred E. Smith (right), governor of New York for four terms, became a candidate for the Presidency in 1928 (see page 753).

Financial interests and party bosses continued to have much influence in the process of choosing senators.

The short-ballot movement spreads. Reformers knew that the long ballots used in most elections made boss rule easier. Ballots frequently contained hundreds of names. The average voter could not hope to become acquainted with the qualifications of all the candidates. Therefore the temptation to vote the straight party ticket was very strong. The National Short Ballot Association was formed in 1910 to reduce the number of elective officers. The duties of many state and local officials, the association reported, were outlined by law and did not involve decisions dealing with general policies. Such officials, it concluded, should be appointed rather than elected. The election of fewer candidates, on the other hand, would not only place the responsibility for good government where it belonged, but would also encourage intelligent voting. Although professional politicians opposed the short ballot, a number of states made considerable progress by consolidating departments and reducing the number of elective officers. In New York State, for example, under the leadership of Governor Alfred E. Smith, the number of state elective officers was

cut down to four — governor, lieutenant-governor, attorney general, and comptroller. The governor was given authority to appoint the remaining heads of departments, who were then responsible to him.

Municipal reform is demanded. The most glaring abuses of democratic government in the United States have developed in its cities. As we have seen, the growth of industry and the increase of immigration swelled the size of cities and added to the list of services which their inhabitants required. The expense of city government, therefore, increased enormously. Great ability and a high degree of honesty and efficiency were required for the management of municipal affairs. Yet city officials generally were chosen by the parties organized along national lines. The governments of many cities were controlled by party bosses who were chiefly interested in the advancement of their own political organizations. In all too many cases the taxpayers were robbed by corrupt officials.

Commission government is introduced. One important reform in city government came as a result of a great disaster. In 1900, the city of Galveston, Texas, was almost wiped out by a tidal wave. As the mayor and council were unable to cope with the crisis, the government of the city was turned over to five commissioners, who were given full authority for a year. This commission form of government was so satisfactory that Galveston continued under the plan. In the course of time more than 400 cities adopted the same form of government. The commissioners, usually five in number, were elected by the voters without regard to party connections. Each commissioner was made responsible for the direction of one department of the city government, while the commission as a whole carried out the duties formerly given to the city council.

The city-manager plan grows. Other American cities have experimented with a modification of the commission form of government known as the city-manager plan. The first large city to try it was Dayton, Ohio, in 1914, and it has since been tried in some 500 cities. The commissioners or the city council employ a city manager, usually an outsider, who has no political connections, but is an expert in municipal operation. He has authority to administer the affairs of the city, but is responsible to the council or commission. Although these plans contributed to better city government, the activities of political machines still menace the American city.

——————— CHECK-UP ———————

What political reforms characterized the first 20 years of the twentieth century?

1. What were the initiative, referendum, and recall? How did they extend the power of the voter?

2. What was the direct primary? The direct election of senators? What advantages were claimed for each? Was each of these reforms as successful as had been expected? Why?

3. What is the short ballot? Why do political reformers claim that only policy-determining officials should be elected?

4. How have the commission and city-manager type of government served to increase the efficiency of municipal government?

CHAPTER REVIEW

Terms to Understand

anarchist
"square deal"
progressives
conservatives

parcel post
postal savings bank
"hat in the ring"

People and Things to Know About

William McKinley
Theodore Roosevelt
William Howard Taft
Woodrow Wilson
Robert M. La Follette
Charles Evans Hughes
Progressive Movement
Progressive Party
Seventeenth Amendment

"New Freedom"
commission government
city manager
initiative
referendum
recall
direct primary
preferential primary
short ballot

Historic Dates to Identify

1912   1913   1920

Questions to Discuss

1. Contrast the following:

(a) The Republican victory of 1860 and the Democratic victory of 1912.

(b) Liberal gains under the administrations of Theodore Roosevelt and William Howard Taft.

(c) First and second administrations of Woodrow Wilson.

(d) Popular sentiment in 1912 and 1920.

2. Why was Theodore Roosevelt popular as President? Why was Taft unpopular? Can you think of other Presidents who have been popular (or unpopular) for similar reasons?

3. In which campaign, 1912 or 1916, did the Democratic Party, through its own efforts,

Questions to Discuss (Cont.)

make the best showing? Can you prove your point? (See *World Almanac*)

4. Of the four methods for extending the power of the voters (initiative, referendum, recall, direct primary) which are found in your state?

5. Why were the commission and city-manager forms of government adopted by many cities which had suffered from inefficient municipal government?

Other Things to Do

*1. Make a list of Vice-Presidents who became President because of the death of the President in office. In each case, indicate the reasons why the Vice-President was placed on the ticket, whether the party was pleased to have him become President, and his achievements.

2. Write an editorial explaining why you feel that Theodore Roosevelt was "robbed" of the Republican nomination in 1912, and why he should have run on a third party ticket.

3. Read a biography of Theodore Roosevelt, and report on interesting episodes in his life.

4. Read a biography of William Howard Taft, and report on his career before or after being President.

5. Debate: *Resolved,* That more constructive legislation was enacted during Woodrow Wilson's administration than during any other presidential administration.

6. Obtain a sample ballot used in a recent election. Is it a long or a short ballot? Are officials elected who might better be appointed? Seek the advice of leading citizens in your community on this question.

Chapter 42

Political symbols

A CONSERVATIVE REACTION FOLLOWS

THE ERA OF PROGRESSIVE REFORM

America's present need is not heroics but healing; not nostrums but normalcy, not revolution but restoration . . . not surgery but serenity.

Warren G. Harding, 1920

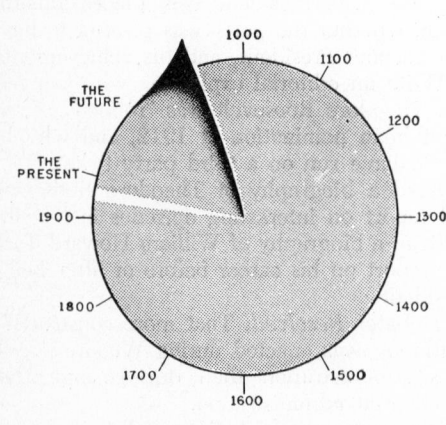

1921-1933

From 1921 to 1933 the Republicans were again in control of the national administration. This period proved to be an era of conservatism. During the first 20 years of the century, as we have seen, Theodore Roosevelt and then Woodrow Wilson had led the country toward political and social reform. World War I followed, and the American people were lifted to great heights of patriotism and idealism. The reaction which followed the war was entirely natural. For a while the American people seemed to have no further desire for reform measures, no interest in making further sacrifices for the welfare of mankind. This change in public sentiment was largely responsible for the triumph of the Republicans under Harding in the election of 1920. During President Harding's administration there was a post-war lowering of the tone of public morality. This was followed by prosperity under President Coolidge and then by panic and depression under President Hoover.

This period of Republican control of the government will be treated under the following topics:

1. President Harding tries to solve postwar problems.
2. The country is prosperous under President Coolidge.
3. President Hoover is faced with a great depression.

---

1 President Harding Tries to Solve Postwar Problems

President Harding supports the party organization. President Harding prided himself upon being an average American citizen. Before entering politics he had been owner and editor of the Marion (Ohio) *Star,* and in the words of Mrs. Harding, they were "just folks." In public life Harding had shown no signs of leadership, but he had been a faithful supporter of the Republican party organization.

The return to "normalcy" meets many problems. Although President Harding had declared that it was his intention to restore the United States to "normalcy," he found many difficulties in his way. He was faced with problems of demobilization — the disposal of ships and the care of war veterans, for example — which demanded immediate attention. Industry was changing over from wartime to peacetime production. Disputes arose between labor and capital, and strikes increased. Farmers suffered from the loss of their wartime market. Taxes were at a high level. The enforcement of prohibition proved difficult. America's relations with the League of Nations were far from clear, and the settlement of war debts presented a knotty problem (pages 542, 534). Through this maze of difficult situations, President Harding was obliged to thread his way, surrounded by advisers whom he trusted at first, but who later proved unworthy of his confidence.

The merchant marine presents a difficult problem. One demobilization problem which the Harding administration had to face was what to do with the American merchant marine. During the war there had been a demand for ships and yet more ships. The end of the conflict found the United States Shipping Board with thousands of vessels for which there was little or no use. The wooden ships were written off as a total loss in 1920. A Merchant Marine Act of the same year permitted the sale of the merchant marine to American shippers on easy terms, but there was little or no demand for the ships at any price. Though this law was passed near the end of President Wilson's second term, the problems of administration were left for Harding. Some of the steel ships continued to be operated at a loss by the government. Hundreds of others were laid up in rivers and bays to deteriorate.[1]

The Veterans' Bureau is created. There was still another problem of World War I with which President Harding and his successors had to deal. This was the demand of the war veterans for "adjusted compensation." They felt that the low pay soldiers received during the war should be equalized with the pay of those who had remained at home and worked at less dangerous occupations. In 1921 veterans' affairs were placed under the United States Veterans' Bureau. This bureau was granted liberal support by Congress. It handled the claims of veterans for compensation and hospitalization, took care of the sick and wounded,

---

[1] The shipping problem did not end with Harding's administration. In 1928 the Jones-White Merchant Marine Act provided what amounted to a subsidy for American shippers, who were to be given long-term mail-carrying contracts at high rates. In 1936 Congress went a step further and passed a Ship Subsidy Act. Its object was to establish a well-balanced merchant marine, promote the commerce of the United States, and aid in national defense. The act provided for a United States Maritime Authority of five members. To American companies which met the requirements of the law, this board was to pay as a subsidy (1) the difference in cost of construction between American and foreign built ships and (2) the difference in operating costs between the American company and its principal foreign competitor.

and administered the government insurance program for veterans. In addition to the aid given veterans by the federal government, many states voted cash "bonuses."

Soldiers' bonus legislation is passed. In spite of the fact that the American government had been more generous in its treatment of war veterans than any of the European powers, the demand for adjusted compensation grew steadily. Members of Congress lent a willing ear to the demands of veterans' organizations, such as the American Legion. In 1922 a bonus bill was defeated only by the veto of President Harding. His objection was based upon the fact that Congress had made no provision for raising the money with which to meet the expense of the bonus. In 1924, however, a bonus bill was passed over President Coolidge's veto. This act provided that 20-year adjusted service certificates, similar to endowment insurance policies, be issued to the veterans. The amount of each certificate depended upon the veteran's length of service and the proportion of his service spent overseas. The

President Warren G. Harding (right) died in 1923 after an unhappy term of office. He was succeeded by President Calvin Coolidge (left), who completed Harding's administration, was re-elected in 1924, and led the country in a quiet way through the period often called "the golden 20's."

average face value of the certificates was more than $1000, and in the meantime veterans could use the certificates as security in borrowing money.

The bonus question plagues later administrations. In the summer of 1932, as the depression became more acute, the veterans demanded the immediate payment in full of their adjusted service certificates. This payment of about 2 billion dollars, they argued, would place a large amount of money in circulation. The Patman Bill providing for the issuance of the necessary currency passed the House, but was defeated in the Senate. In the meantime, 10,000 or more veterans from all parts of the country, encouraged by the attitude of their congressmen, assembled at Washington to demand the passage of the bonus legislation. Many of these veterans believed that they were trying to collect an honest debt, and stayed on at Washington after the defeat of the Patman Bill. At the end of July the federal government resorted to the use of troops, tanks, and gas bombs to drive the "bonus expeditionary force" from Washington. The episode was evidence of the mounting discontent among the unemployed ex-servicemen. Bonus agitation continued. In January, 1936, Congress passed, over President Roosevelt's veto, an act providing that the balance due to the veterans on their adjusted service certificates should be paid in "baby bonds" and cash.

Gains are made during the Harding administration. Among the accomplishments of the Harding administration was the passage of the National Budget Act, creating a Bureau of the Budget (page 538). Secretary of the Treasury Mellon also carried out a broad program of tax reduction. Congress passed an act (1922) setting up a war debt commission to agree with the European countries upon the amounts of the war debts owed us and the rate of interest that each should pay (page 542). To protect the farmer from falling prices, an emergency tariff act was passed in 1921. This was followed in the next year by the Fordney-McCumber Tariff, which restored the system of high protection in operation before the Underwood Tariff (page 544). The flood of postwar immigration led to the restriction of immigration, first by the act of 1921, and three years later by the Lodge-Johnson Act (page 588). In the field of foreign affairs President Harding invited the leading powers to attend the Washington Conference, which limited naval construction and drew up treaties governing affairs in the Pacific (page 654, 686). Though the President recommended further international co-operation, Congress refused to go along. It rejected the proposal that the United States become a member of the World Court (page 685).

Public scandals hurt the Harding administration. Like President Grant (page 451), President Harding was also badly served by his associates. Harding was genial and kindly, but lacked the high mental and moral qualifications necessary to exercise real leadership. Selfish politicians were largely responsible for his nomination, and since loyalty to his friends was one of Harding's strong characteristics, the way was paved for graft and corruption on a large scale. The director of the Veterans' Bureau, Charles R. Forbes, was found guilty of "almost unparalleled waste, recklessness, and misconduct" in handling construction contracts and in purchasing supplies. While Forbes headed the bureau, a quarter of a billion dollars of government funds were stolen or squandered. The Alien Property Custodian, Thomas W. Miller, was dismissed from office and later found guilty of conspiring to cheat the government. "Jess" Smith, a politician from Ohio, formerly associated with Harding, committed suicide when his own activities seemed about to be uncovered. Attorney General Daugherty also became a center of attack, particularly in regard to the illegal withdrawal of alcohol. A member of the Senate investigating committee charged that the morale of the Department of Justice under Daugherty had been undermined by the promotion of unfaithful employees, and the dismissal or demotion of those who were conscientious in their duties. Daugherty was eventually asked

"Bonus marchers" gathered on the steps of the Capitol and elsewhere in Washington as Congress debated a bonus bill in 1932.

to resign by Harding's successor, President Coolidge.

The Teapot Dome scandal involves Secretary Fall. The most serious scandal under Harding involved the Department of the Interior. Shortly after his inauguration (March 4, 1921), President Harding transferred the control of certain naval oil reserves in Wyoming and California from the Navy to the Interior Department. In this transfer he had the approval of Secretary of the Navy Denby. Secretary of the Interior Fall then leased the Teapot Dome lands in Wyoming to Harry F. Sinclair and leased the Elk Hills Reserve in California to a corporation controlled by E. M. Doheny. After Fall had resigned from the cabinet, however, these transactions aroused suspicion. Later it was found that Fall, without posting security or paying interest, had received "loans" of $100,000 from Doheny and of about $300,000 from Sinclair. The Supreme Court in 1927 canceled the leases because they were tainted with "conspiracy, corruption, and fraud." Fall was finally tried and convicted of accepting a bribe, fined $100,000, and sentenced to a year in jail.

President Harding is succeeded by Calvin Coolidge. The details of widespread corruption in the administration were beginning to leak out and to shock the public when President Harding made a trip to Alaska in 1923. On August 2, while in California on his way home, the heavy-hearted President died and was succeeded by Vice-President Coolidge. "We saw him gradually weaken not only from physical exhaustion but from mental anxiety," said Herbert Hoover in 1931. "Warren Harding had a dim realization that he had been betrayed by a few of the men whom he had trusted."

──────── CHECK-UP ────────

What were the nation's important postwar (World War I) problems?

1. What did President Harding claim as the goal of his administration? What problems made the attainment of this goal difficult?

2. Why did the merchant marine create a problem after the war? What efforts were made to solve this problem?

3. What services did the government provide for veterans? Why did they demand adjusted compensation? How was their demand met?

4. What were the accomplishments of the Harding administration? What scandals shocked the nation?

┌───┬─────────────────────────────┐
│   │ **The Country Is Prosperous** │
│ 2 │   │
│   │ **Under President Coolidge** │
└───┴─────────────────────────────┘

President Coolidge is associated with the "golden twenties." Calvin Coolidge stood for New England honesty, thrift, and simplicity. A graduate of Amherst College, he had settled down to practice law in western Massachusetts. He served in both branches of the state legislature. In 1915 he was elected lieutenant governor, and in 1918 he became governor of Massachusetts. Largely because of the nation-wide reputa-

tion he acquired during a Boston police strike,[2] Coolidge received the vice-presidential nomination on the Republican ticket in 1920.

Upon entering the White House, President Coolidge adopted a policy of non-interference in business, and in general continued Harding's policies. The golden prosperity of the twenties has come to be associated with his administration. All sections of the country and all classes of the population, except the farmers, shared in this Coolidge prosperity.

President Coolidge faces Davis in the election of 1924. In 1924 the Republican convention chose Coolidge almost unanimously for the Presidency. Charles G. Dawes was nominated for the Vice-Presidency. At the Democratic convention, on the other hand, there was a bitter contest. William G. McAdoo of California and Alfred E. Smith of New York were the leading candidates for the nomination. Each of them controlled enough votes to prevent the nomination of the other, and more than 100 ballots were cast before the two leading candidates withdrew in order to break the deadlock. John W. Davis of West Virginia was finally nominated on the 103rd ballot, and Governor Charles W. Bryan of Nebraska was promptly chosen for the Vice-Presidency.

The campaign of 1924 was made more lively by the fact that Senator Robert M. La Follette was running for the Presidency on a progressive platform. La Follette was endorsed by the Party of Progressive Action (which represented the conservative wing of the Farmer-Labor Party), by the American Federation of Labor, and by the Socialists. As the leader of the insurgents

[2] The mayor of Boston restored order by calling out on police duty those companies of the Massachusetts militia stationed in the city. On September 11, 1919, after disorder had been put down, Coolidge took control and sent militia units from other parts of the state into Boston. To President Gompers of the American Federation of Labor, Coolidge telegraphed, "There is no right to strike against the public safety by anybody, anywhere, any time." The governor's action won widespread approval, though he never claimed credit for settling the strike.

The cabinet of President Coolidge (front, center) included several famous men. Can you recognize a later President? A later Chief Justice of the Supreme Court?

in Congress, he appealed to the discontented farmers, to labor, and to those who favored political and social reform.

It was in the campaign of 1924 that the radio was first used extensively in a presidential campaign. By this means the candidates were able to reach Americans in their homes throughout the country.

President Coolidge wins. The hope of the Democrats that La Follette would split the Republican Party proved futile. President Coolidge won the election with a majority of the popular votes cast. Outside of the Solid South the Democrats carried only the state of Oklahoma, and La Follette carried only his own state of Wisconsin. In eleven western states, however, La Follette polled more votes than Davis. In the congressional elections the Republicans returned a majority to both houses.

President Coolidge stands for "laissez faire." The second Coolidge administration was noted chiefly for the fact that prosperity continued. Coolidge's fundamental theories were economy in government and noninterference in industry and agriculture. Tax reduction continued, and substantial amounts were paid on the national debt. The President was sympathetic toward the farmer's cause, but by his veto of the McNary-Haugen Bill (page 556) he showed that he did not favor carrying the government into the market to raise the price of farm products. President Coolidge's policies aroused the opposition of western congressmen, and they undertook to embarrass the Chief Executive on numerous occasions. For the first time since the administration of Grant, the Senate refused to approve a cabinet appointment.

Though relations with Mexico and Nicaragua continued to be troubled, a successful Pan-American Congress was held during this administration (page 645). A number of arbitration treaties were drawn up, and the Kellogg-Briand Peace Pact was drafted (page 685). When the Geneva Disarmament Conference (page 686) broke down, President Coolidge was won over to a program of increased naval construction.

Hoover opposes Smith in the election of 1928. In August, 1927, President Coolidge announced that he would not be a candidate for re-election in 1928. "I do not choose to run for President in 1928," was his brief statement. For a time there was a move to draft him, but it soon became evident that he would not be a candidate. Herbert Hoover, his Secretary of Commerce, was nominated for the Presidency by the Republican convention on the first ballot, and Senator Charles Curtis of Kansas for the Vice-Presidency. The Democrats nominated Alfred E. Smith of New York on the first ballot, with Senator Joseph T. Robinson of Arkansas as his running mate. Both presidential candidates had risen from the people, Hoover from an Iowa farm, and Smith from the sidewalks of New York. Hoover was known as an efficient administrator, and was called the engineer in politics. Smith was loved for his human qualities, and as governor of New York he had acquired a wide knowledge of the workings of government.

President Herbert Hoover (left) held a conference in 1929 on transcontinental aviation routes. It was attended by Colonel Charles A. Lindbergh (right), then a great hero to the American people (page 498).

Hoover wins decisively. There was very little difference between the platforms of the two parties. The election, therefore, centered largely on the candidates themselves. In spite of Governor Smith's popularity in New York, strong opposition to him developed on three counts. He had connections with Tammany Hall, he was opposed to prohibition, and he was a Roman Catholic. These factors help to explain the decisive victory won by Hoover. Prosperity, for which the Republicans claimed full credit, also contributed to the Republican landslide. Hoover not only polled over 21 million votes to 15 million for Smith, but he even carried Smith's own state of New York, which four times had elected Smith to the governorship. The Republicans invaded the Solid South and carried Virginia, North Carolina, Tennessee, Florida, and Texas. The electoral vote was 444 to 87. In spite of his overwhelming defeat, however, Smith received a larger percentage of the total vote than either

Cox in 1920 or Davis in 1924. He also carried New York City, Boston, Cleveland, and other industrial centers. The new Congress was overwhelmingly Republican.

——————— CHECK-UP ———————

What were the distinguishing features of President Coolidge's administration?

1. What kind of person was President Coolidge? How did he happen to become President?
2. What were the chief goals sought by the Coolidge administration? What were its chief accomplishments?
3. Why did the Republicans win the election of 1928?

---

3 President Hoover Is Faced with a Great Depression

Important developments mark President Hoover's administration. Like Coolidge, President Hoover was a firm believer in the policy of *laissez faire*. He appreciated the great resources of the United States, fully approved the capitalistic system of industry, and looked forward to a period of continued prosperity. Believing that production would continue to increase, he foresaw a new day for the working classes when they would enjoy more leisure, more automobiles, more radios, and more of the luxuries of life. Some important developments during his administration were the further restriction of immigration (page 588), the enactment of the Agricultural Marketing Act (page 556) and the Hawley-Smoot Tariff (page 544). In the field of foreign affairs, the administration provided for a moratorium on war debts (page 534), renewed efforts to bring the United States into the World Court, participated in the London Conference, 1930 (page 686), and adopted a vigorous policy in relation to Japanese imperialism (page 657).

Hoover's administration was also associated with social reform. The President's Research Committee on Social Trends carried on three years of intensive research surveying American civilization. The committee report, which covered several volumes, was a monument to the Hoover administration. Again, the National Commission of Law Observance and Law Enforcement was appointed to study the problem of better law enforcement.

The "lame duck" session is abolished. During the Hoover administration the Twentieth Amendment was proposed to Congress. The short session of Congress (from December following a presidential election to March 4 when the new President was inaugurated) had long been criticized as one of the weaknesses of our political system. In 1932, for example, more than 150 representatives, who had not been re-elected in November, continued to serve during the short session from December, 1932, to March 4, 1933. These so-called "lame ducks" stood for principles which the voters had rejected at the polls. Naturally such congressmen accomplished little, and the federal government did practically nothing except mark time until the new administration began. A century and more ago, when transportation was difficult, it was necessary to have a long interval between the election of congressmen and the beginning of their new terms. This situation had long since ceased to exist.

In March, 1932, therefore, after ten years of effort on the part of Senator George W. Norris, both houses of Congress approved an amendment to do away with the "lame duck" or short session of Congress. Congress also provided for the selection of a President or Vice-President in case the President-elect or Vice-President-elect should die or fail to qualify for office. The measure was ratified by the states with unusual swiftness. In February, 1933, the Twentieth Amendment was proclaimed a part of the Constitution to become effective on the fifteenth of the following October. The Twentieth Amendment provided that congressmen who were elected in November were to take office on January 3 instead of March 4. It also provided that the President and Vice-President were to be inaugurated on January 20.

Disaster overtakes the Hoover administration. In spite of the sound accomplishments of the Hoover administration, the effects of the stock market crash of 1929 and the depression which followed it were so tremendous that everything else was almost forgotten. Hurried emergency steps were taken to strengthen the financial structure of the country, to prop up its tottering banks, railroads, and industries, and to relieve unemployment (page 516). These steps involved large appropriations of money. Since government revenue was dwindling, Congress found that new taxation was necessary if the budget were to be balanced. Thus the administration, which began under such favorable circumstances and with glowing prophecies for everlasting prosperity, drew to its close under conditions as critical as any the nation had ever experienced.

President Hoover is renominated in 1932. As the election of 1932 approached, discontent, unemployment, and financial ruin were widespread. By the irony of fate the voters now placed responsibility for the

Steel production and other industrial activity continued at high levels during the early Hoover administration. After the crash of 1929, production collapsed.

As depression deepened, the unemployed sought shelter where they could, and tried to find work. In New York City, a "box car village" housed homeless men.

depression upon the Republican Party, which had claimed credit for the prosperity of the "golden twenties." The chief issue of the election was the depression, although the question of prohibition frequently took the center of the stage. At the Republican convention President Hoover was renominated on the first ballot. The Republican platform proposed that the liquor question again be submitted to the voters. This was to be done through a constitutional amendment drawn up in such a way that "the gains already made in dealing with the evils inherent in the liquor traffic" would be preserved. The platform also contained a glowing tribute to President Hoover for his efforts to overcome the effects of the depression.

The Democrats draft a platform. Those who expected the Democratic convention to be split by disagreement, as in 1924, proved to be poor prophets. The Democratic platform was the briefest in the history of the party. It declared that the chief causes of America's economic and social distress were "the disastrous policies pursued by our government since the World War." It came out in favor of economy and a sound currency. It called for a competitive tariff for revenue, with reciprocal tariff agreements with other nations. It also favored unemployment and

old age insurance under state laws, steps to aid agriculture, and strict enforcement of the antitrust laws. Participation in the World Court, independence for the Philippines, and outright repeal of the Eighteenth Amendment prohibiting the sale of liquor likewise were proposed.

The Democrats nominate Franklin D. Roosevelt. On the first ballot for the presidential nomination, Governor Franklin D. Roosevelt of New York was far in the lead, although short of the two-thirds majority required for the Democratic nomination. On the fourth ballot William G. McAdoo of California shifted the votes of California from John N. Garner of Texas to Roosevelt, and started a stampede which gave the nomination to Roosevelt. Garner in turn was nominated for the Vice-Presidency on the first ballot. Governor Roosevelt set a precedent by flying from Albany to Chicago to address the convention before it adjourned.

Franklin D. Roosevelt calls for a "new deal." At first the Republican campaign was slow, while the Democrats were aggressive. Governor Roosevelt proposed a "new deal" which included: (1) a program for farm relief, (2) bringing the railroads back to life, (3) tariff revision with the hope of restoring foreign markets, and (4) the control of public utilities. Without alarming the conservatives by radical proposals, he managed to reach the ear of "the forgotten man." It was only during the latter part of the campaign that President Hoover began a series of vigorous speeches in defense of his administration. Progressive Republicans, such as Johnson, Norris, and the La Follettes, however, gave their support to Roosevelt.

Roosevelt wins. In the election the Democrats won an overwhelming victory. They received over 7 million votes more than the Republicans, and carried all the states except Pennsylvania, Connecticut, Delaware, Maine, New Hampshire, and Vermont. The electoral vote was 472 for Roosevelt and 59 for Hoover. Republican senators and congressmen with long records of service were defeated. State after state, normally Republican, elected Democratic legislatures and governors. The Socialists were expecting an unusually large vote as an expression of widespread discontent, but their candidate, Norman Thomas, polled fewer than 900,000 votes. The problem of lifting the country out of the depths of the depression now rested squarely on the shoulders of the Democrats and their leader, Franklin D. Roosevelt.

——— CHECK-UP ———

How did depression defeat President Hoover's plans?

1. What future did President Hoover foresee for the United States at the beginning of his administration? What were some of the important accomplishments of his Presidency?

2. What was the "lame duck" amendment? Why was it added to the Constitution?

3. What were the issues of the election of 1932? How did the Democrats propose to meet the problems rising out of the depression? Why did they win the election?

CHAPTER REVIEW

Terms to Understand

normalcy
bonus
adjusted compensation

"golden twenties"
"lame duck"

People and Things to Know About

Teapot Dome
Twentieth Amendment
Warren G. Harding
Franklin D. Roosevelt
New Deal

Calvin Coolidge
Herbert Hoover
Alfred E. Smith
George W. Norris

Historic Dates to Identify

1920   1932

Questions to Discuss

1. Why does a nation prefer "normalcy" to other goals after a war? Was this goal achieved more nearly after World War I than after World War II?

2. Compare the following:

   (a) The Grant and Harding administrations.

   (b) Policies with respect to taxation and debt reduction after World Wars I and II.

3. Why does the government subsidize an American merchant marine even though

Questions to Discuss (Cont.)

foreign shippers would be glad to handle our overseas trade?

4. How did these Presidents differ in their ideas of the proper relation of government to business: Theodore Roosevelt, Wilson, Harding, Coolidge, Hoover, Franklin D. Roosevelt?

5. To what extent was it fair for the American people to hold the Hoover administration responsible for the depression?

Other Things to Do

1. Refer to the *World Almanac* for a statement of current expenditures by the federal government. What proportion of these expenditures are directly or indirectly related to war? Show your findings in a graph.

2. Read about the "golden twenties" in *Only Yesterday* by Frederick Allen. Read to the class excerpts which you find interesting.

3. Draw a cartoon dealing with one of the Presidents or one of the elections discussed in this chapter.

*4. Make a list (1) of Presidents defeated for re-election because of hard times during their administration, and (2) of Presidents re-elected because they claimed credit for prosperity. What are your conclusions?

CCC worker

FRANKLIN D. ROOSEVELT INTRODUCES

A NEW DEAL

This great nation will endure as it has endured, will revive and will prosper.
Franklin D. Roosevelt, 1933

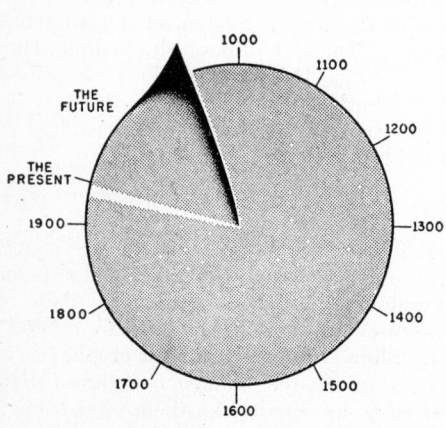

1933 - 1945

Few Presidents, even in time of war, have faced problems as serious and complex as those which confronted President Franklin D. Roosevelt on March 4, 1933. The country — in fact, the whole world — was suffering from a very severe depression. Business activity in the United States was at little more than half its normal level. The purchasing power of the farmers, a fourth of the population, had been almost destroyed. In the cities the families of about 13 million unemployed men were living in distressing poverty. The railroads in the United States showed a deficit for 1932 of 150 million dollars; yet these railways must be kept out of bankruptcy to insure the safety of savings bank deposits, trust funds, and insurance company reserves. For the third successive year the national budget was out of balance, and for the next twelve months the Treasury was faced with a probable deficit of one billion dollars. The climax of the nation's woes was reached on inauguration day. Because of a breakdown of confidence in the financial stability of the country, a bank holiday had been proclaimed in nearly every state of the Union. Out of such economic and social chaos the new administration was pledged to bring order.

The incoming President had to deal with foreign questions, too, and these were equally perplexing. The value of our export trade for 1932 was the smallest since 1905. It was necessary to clear up the war debt situation so that Europe might become an outlet for our surplus agricultural and manufactured products. The administration had to decide what part the United States would play in an approaching world economic conference at London. The foreign outlook was further complicated by questions about our obligations in the Far East under the Nine-Power Treaty and the Pact of Paris (page 657), about our relations with Soviet Russia and the Latin American countries, and about our relation to the World Court (pages 646, 685, 690).

In the near future, the rise of totalitarian governments in the Old World was to present problems yet undreamed of in 1933. Within a decade the policies pursued by the dictators would lead to a second world war. The action taken by the administration of Franklin D. Roosevelt in dealing with the many troublesome problems just listed will be considered under the following headings:

1. Action characterizes the early days of the New Deal.
2. New Deal gains are consolidated during Roosevelt's second term.
3. President Franklin D. Roosevelt breaks the two-term tradition.

1 Action Characterizes the Early Days of the New Deal

The new President is well qualified. To the solution of the problems with which he was faced in 1933, President Franklin D. Roosevelt, a distant cousin of "Teddy" Roosevelt, brought a buoyancy of spirit and freshness of viewpoint which gave new courage to the nation. Roosevelt was born in New York State of a well-to-do family. He was graduated from Harvard in 1904 and then studied law. His political career included a term in the New York legislature, an appointment to the post of Assistant Secretary of the Navy under President Wilson, and two terms as governor of New York. Though badly crippled by infantile paralysis when he was 39 years old, Roosevelt refused to be beaten by his misfortune. The very determination and courage with which he met his own problems was to stand him in good stead as the nation's leader.

President Roosevelt organizes a "brain trust." For Secretary of State Roosevelt selected Cordell Hull of Tennessee, a former member of Congress and an opponent of the trade barriers which had been created throughout the world. The Postmaster General was James A. Farley, who had managed President Roosevelt's election campaign and was chairman of the Democratic National Committee. Harold L. Ickes, formerly associated with the Progressive Movement in the days of Theodore Roosevelt, became Secretary of the Interior. The post of Secretary of Agriculture was filled by Henry A. Wallace, a member of an Iowa family long interested in the farmer and his problems. Frances Perkins, former New York Commissioner of Labor and the first woman to hold a cabinet post, became Secretary of Labor. Henry Morgenthau, Jr., soon became Secretary of the Treasury.

Besides the cabinet, President Roosevelt gathered around him a number of advisers, many of them college professors. This group soon earned the popular title of "brain trust." Although its membership shifted from time to time, the most prominent advisers during Roosevelt's first administration were Professors Raymond Moley, Rexford Tugwell, A. A. Berle, George F. Warren, and Felix Frankfurter. Upon their advice the President counted heavily when forming his policies.

Frances Perkins, Secretary of Labor from 1933 to 1945, was the first woman cabinet member. (See page 780.)

The inaugural address calls for action. President Roosevelt's inaugural address, clear, brief, and frank, sounded the keynote of his policies. "This is pre-eminently the time to speak the truth, the whole truth, frankly and boldly . . . " he stated. "Values have shrunk to fantastic levels; taxes have risen; our ability to pay has fallen; government of all kinds is faced by serious curtailment of income; the means of exchange are frozen in the currents of trade; the withered leaves of industrial enterprise lie on every side; farmers find no markets for their products; and the savings of many years in thousands of families are gone. More important, a host of unemployed citizens face the grim problem of existence, and an equally great number toil with little return. Only a foolish optimist can deny the dark realities of the moment . . . This nation calls for action, and action now."

The President meets the financial crisis. President Roosevelt gave the country a rare example of action in meeting the financial crisis (page 534). Panicky fear was quickly driven away. Confidence was restored in the banks which opened, and bank failures practically ceased. Bank deposits were now generally insured, and the banking business was placed upon a solid foundation (page 535). The country was taken off the gold standard, and the value of the currency, backed by a reserve of gold and silver bullion, was fixed at 59.06 cents in terms of its former gold value (page 536). The President handled this critical situation very effectively. As a result, his prestige among the American people rose.

The economy plank is abandoned. As part of the program of restoring public confidence, President Roosevelt attempted to lower the expenditures of the government so that they would be brought into closer relationship with its income. At once Congress granted the President the power to reduce payments of pensions and other veterans' benefits, and to reduce government salaries. President Roosevelt promptly put his program of economy into effect. A year later, however, Congress passed the Independent Offices Appropriation Act over the President's veto, thus practically wiping out the effect of Roosevelt's economy drive. This measure restored federal salaries and most of the veterans' benefits. Later in the Roosevelt administration, economy was abandoned as an official policy, and huge appropriations were made for relief and recovery.

Action is taken on the liquor and farm problems. A campaign pledge was carried out and revenue provided for the government by modifying the Volstead Act to permit the manufacture and sale of beer and light wines (page 592). Before the end of 1933, the Eighteenth Amendment was repealed, and national prohibition became a matter of history. Meanwhile President Roosevelt also tackled the question of farm relief, and in May Congress passed the Agricultural Adjustment Act (page 557). Aided by the AAA and the natural trend toward economic recovery, farm income started upward.

Relief is sought for unemployment. Early in his administration President Roosevelt turned to the baffling question of unemployment relief. Private agencies and local units of government had been unable to handle the crushing load placed upon them, and, therefore, unemployment relief had grown to a problem of national importance. On March 21, 1933, the President recommended three types of legislation to relieve the unemployment situation: (1) the enrollment of workers for public employment, (2) direct grants to states for relief work, and (3) a broad public works program that would create employment for labor. To carry out the first proposal a Civilian Conservation Corps (CCC) of some 300,000 unemployed men, mostly young men who had never held jobs, was organized for a period of two years. These men were employed on reforestation projects, the prevention of floods and soil erosion, and work in the national parks. The members of the CCC were to be paid $30 per month, and to be clothed, fed, and sheltered. At first the CCC movement was scoffed at as a useless gesture; later it was praised on all sides and its life extended until the outbreak of World War II.

Relief aid is extended to the states. The second part of the President's program involved grants of nearly a billion and a half dollars to the states to aid in direct local relief. A Federal Emergency Relief Administration (FERA) was set up to take charge of alloting this money. Senator Wagner, sponsor of the original bill, explained that "the plan embodied in the bill is designed to stimulate the maximum of local effort in the provision of relief and to supplement that effort with federal assistance."

Relief is provided through work projects. By the provisions of the National Industrial Recovery Act of June, 1933, more than 3 billion dollars was to be spent for public works. This outpouring of public funds was of course intended to increase employment directly, but its purpose was also to aid industrial recovery by promoting activity in the heavy industries that turned out such products as steel, cement, brick, lumber, and machinery. To put this program into operation, a Public Works Administration (PWA) was established, with Secretary of the Interior Ickes at its head. An offshoot of the PWA was the Civil Works Administration (CWA), which was to create employment and supplement other relief measures provided for by Congress. During the unusually severe winter of 1933–34 the CWA found employment for some 4 million men and women.

The PWA, however, was unable to reduce unemployment rapidly. In order to relieve the pressure of the huge relief rolls upon state and municipal governments, an Emergency Relief Appropriation Act was passed in April, 1935. It set aside $4,800,000,000, the largest peacetime appropriation ever made, to "provide relief, relief work, and to increase employment by providing for useful projects." People fit for employment were to be taken off local relief and put on federal work relief. The money was to be spent at the discretion of the President, though actually Secretary Ickes and Harry L. Hopkins, federal relief director, were the ones who decided how it should be spent. In addition to the federal agencies already in existence, the Works Progress Administration (WPA) was now set up to aid in carrying out the work projects. One of the most discouraging features of the New Deal was the fact that unemployment continued in spite of the efforts of government relief agencies, in spite of the recovery of business, and in spite of the increase in industrial pay rolls. As late as 1939 there were more than 8 million unemployed.

The National Recovery Administration is established. The National Industrial Recovery Act was the climax of the President's program to meet the immediate crisis (page 516). General Hugh S. Johnson became the first administrator of the National Recovery Administration (NRA). He conducted a vigorous drive in the summer of 1933, which resulted in the adoption of nearly 300 NRA codes covering all major industries. The "blue eagle" was the mark of identification of those who co-operated through the signing of the NRA codes.

WE DO OUR PART
NRA "blue eagle"

Posters carrying the blue eagle were displayed in their shops and factories, while their goods bore the slogan "We do our part." Some of the provisions of the National Industrial Recovery Act were especially favorable to labor. After the act had been declared unconstitutional by the Supreme Court (page 516), Congress passed other acts designed to carry out its labor provisions (page 525).

Permanent reforms are pushed. Most of the policies of the New Deal so far discussed were emergency measures which were intended to bring the country out of the gloom and inactivity into which it had sunk by 1933. But there were other cards in the New Deal, some of which involved permanent reforms and planning. Among these were the banking acts of 1933 and 1935 (page 535) and the measures which regulated the sale of securities (page 536). Other experiments of the New Deal were launched to conserve our natural resources and to provide "a more abundant life" for American citizens. Outstanding among them was the Tennessee Valley Authority (TVA) (see page 570). Construction was pushed forward also on great dams and reclamation projects like Hoover (Boulder) Dam in Arizona and the Grand Coulee Dam on the Columbia River in Washington (page 571). In large cities slums were torn down in order to build more livable quarters. In the coal fields neat homes were planned to replace the miserable hovels of the miners. In order to free people from the insecurity of old age and the fear of unemployment, the Social Security Act was passed in 1935 (page 593).

International good feeling is promoted. The Roosevelt Administration had to deal with so many problems of recovery and relief at home that at first there was little chance to think about the international aspects of recovery. Elaborate plans were made for a world economic conference to be held at London in the summer of 1933, but the meeting was not a success. President Roosevelt apparently felt that if the United States co-operated in the international movement to restore monetary standards, her domestic recovery would suffer. At any rate, he withdrew his support, and the conference broke up without reaching any important agreements.

Of greater importance in promoting international good feeling were the recognition of Russia (page 690), the negotiation of a new treaty with Cuba (page 623), the development of the Good Neighbor policy toward the Caribbean nations (page 646), and the negotiation of a number of reciprocal trade agreements (page 545).

Opposition to the New Deal rises. Thus, in the course of four years, President Roosevelt, with the aid of Democratic Congresses, had pushed through a program of legislation that made drastic changes in the traditional American social and economic system. At first the New Deal was enthusiastically received by the great majority of Americans. In the mid-term elections of 1934 the country showed its approval of the President's policies by returning an overwhelming majority of Democrats to Congress. As conditions improved, however, criticism from certain groups, particularly businessmen and some newspapers, became increasingly common. The President was charged with breaking his campaign pledges, with seeking to set up a socialistic form of government, and even with attempting to be dictatorial. Some business leaders protested that the government had too much power over business, and pointed out the dangers of the loss of "rugged individualism." On the political side, the administration was accused of creating many new political jobs and giving them to those who supported New Deal policies. It was also accused of using relief funds to make itself more powerful. The most frequent argument against the New Deal, however, was its high cost. Because of relief expenditures, emergency loans, and the multiplication of government bureaus, the cost of government increased more rapidly than the national income. By 1936 the national debt approached 34 billion dollars (page 539).

─────── CHECK-UP ───────

How did the New Deal act to combat the great depression?

1. Who were the President's chief advisers? What steps were taken to meet the financial crisis? To raise farm income?
2. What measures were enacted to relieve unemployment? Why was the "economy plank" in the 1933 Democratic platform disregarded?
3. What permanent reforms were begun during the first four years of the New Deal? What measures increased international good will?
4. What groups came to oppose the New Deal? Why?

---

2 New Deal Gains Are Consolidated During Roosevelt's Second Term

Supreme Court decisions check the New Deal. At the same time that the tide of public criticism was rising, the Supreme Court dealt the New Deal a series of crushing blows. Much of the New Deal legislation had been hastily written to meet emergency conditions which seemed to justify some departures from well-beaten paths. By the time these laws came before the Supreme Court, however, the atmosphere of panic had disappeared. The New Deal acts had to bear the close examination of experienced justices, four of whom were definitely conservative Early in 1935, by the close vote of five to four, the Court upheld the government in its cancellation of the gold clause (page 537). In May, however, the Court found the Railroad Pension Act unconstitutional. In the same month, by unanimous decision, the Court ruled the NRA unconstitutional.

This smashing blow at the New Deal structure was followed in January, 1936, by a decision which by a six to three vote outlawed the AAA (page 558). In the next month the Court upheld the government's right to sell power through the TVA, but the experiment in the Tennessee valley had important social and economic aspects, not dealt with in this decision.

It was evident from these decisions that the Supreme Court believed in a strict (rather than a liberal) interpretation of the interstate commerce and the due process clauses of the Constitution. Equally apparent was the Court's opposition to the federal government's interference with either state rights or property rights, and to its use of the national emergency as an excuse for interpreting the Constitution more liberally.

New Dealers defend their policies. President Roosevelt and New Deal spokesmen defended their policies vigorously. They insisted that human rights were more sacred than property rights. They branded their critics as tories, who would not allow the masses to have economic freedom. They pointed with pride to the signs of recovery — higher prices, increased business

New Deal laws were cautiously reviewed by the Supreme Court. Here (right to left) Justice Brandeis, Chief Justice Hughes, and Justice Van Devanter testify in 1935 before the Senate Judiciary Committee.

activity and higher dividends, swelling farm incomes, and growing savings accounts. The decisions of the Supreme Court were met with threats to amend the Constitution so that Congress would have the power to legislate for the general welfare. Some people suggested the possibility of a change in the membership of the Supreme Court so that the country could go "Forward with the Constitution."

Landon opposes Roosevelt in the election of 1936. As the election of 1936 approached, it was evident that the campaign would be bitter. Big business was hostile to the New Deal, and there was every indication that the Republicans would make the Supreme Court a lively issue. When the Republican convention met at Cleveland early in June, Governor Alfred M. Landon of Kansas was nominated for the Presidency on the first ballot. He had been one of the few Republican governors elected in the Democratic years 1932 and 1934, and he had managed to balance the budget of his own state. Colonel Frank Knox, a newspaper publisher from Illinois, was promptly nominated for the Vice-Presidency.

The Democratic convention, held some two weeks later, was a Roosevelt jubilee. His nomination was seconded by representatives of every state and territory. Vice-President Garner was again named as his running mate. This Democratic Convention was memorable for adopting the policy of a majority vote for nomination. This replaced the two-thirds rule in force since the days of Andrew Jackson.

In the election of 1936, there was a new left-wing Union Party, which favored the election of William Lemke of North Dakota. The Union Party seemed a threat in the Central Northwest to the otherwise confident Democrats. The Socialist Party, under Norman Thomas, and the Communist Party, led by Earl Browder, also entered the contest.

The Democrats sweep the country. In general the platforms of the two major parties differed in that the Republican platform was anti-New Deal while the Democratic supported the Roosevelt pro-

gram and urged that it be continued. Both parties sought the votes of labor, the farmers, and the veterans of World War I. As the campaign progressed, the Republicans focused attention on (1) the need for government economy, (2) the danger which might result from any reduction of the authority of the Supreme Court, and (3) the importance of preserving the Constitution and the "American way of life." When the election was over, however, it was evident that the great majority of American citizens endorsed the President and his policies. President Roosevelt carried every state in the Union except Vermont and Maine and obtained 523 electoral votes to 8 for Landon. The Democrats also succeeded in keeping their control of both houses of Congress by wide majorities.

The President attacks the Supreme Court. Relations between President Roosevelt and Congress were less cordial during the second administration than in the early days of the New Deal. Conservative Democrats, especially those from the South, became more and more unwilling to follow the leadership of the liberals in the administration. The President's attempt to reform the Supreme Court contributed to this situation. Early in his second term President Roosevelt startled the country by asking for the power to appoint (up to a total of 15) a new Supreme Court justice for each one who did not retire upon reaching the age of 70. Since six of the Supreme Court judges were 70 or older, this plan would permit the President to appoint enough liberal judges to obtain decisions favorable to the New Deal. For several months there was heated discussion, in which President Roosevelt was accused of trying to "pack" the Supreme Court. The Court itself proceeded to make several liberal decisions. It reversed an earlier opinion in which it declared a New York minimum wage law illegal, and it upheld the Wagner Labor Disputes Act (page 525) and the Social Security Act (page 593). After weeks of bitter debate, during which Senator Joseph Robinson from Arkansas, the leader of the administration forces, died suddenly, the Senate refused to pass the bill providing for an enlarged Supreme Court.

The Supreme Court becomes liberal.
While President Roosevelt lost his battle to enlarge the Supreme Court, death and resignations during the next few years gave him an opportunity to change its membership almost completely. During the second Roosevelt administration the Court handed down a series of decisions which approved New Deal aims and measures. The interstate commerce clause of the Constitution was so extended that it granted Congress sweeping power over the nation's economic life. Other decisions showed a more liberal attitude toward civil liberties and social reform.

Congress enacts important legislation.
Also during Roosevelt's second administration Congress passed a number of significant laws. Of special importance was the Fair Labor Standards Act of 1938 (page 526), and the second Agricultural Adjustment Act (page 559). In 1938 Congress also enacted a Food, Drug, and Cosmetics Act, providing for stricter regulation and higher standards of manufacture and sale than those of 1906 (page 513). This act provided heavy penalties for misbranding products and for false and misleading advertising claims. In 1939 the Social Security Act was amended to increase benefits. Not only were pensions increased for workers at the age of 65, but dependents also were provided for.

Another important new law was the Hatch Act which was passed "to prevent pernicious political activities." By this measure federal administrative officers were barred from taking part in the nomination or election of any candidate for President, Vice-President, or Congress. The Hatch Act provided punishment for anyone who used political pressure upon job-holders, notably upon WPA workers. Congress also passed a government reorganization act, which gave the President power to regroup or abolish entirely all but eighteen federal bureaus and agencies, if he felt that such action were necessary to increase economy or efficiency. The act was part of an effort, sponsored by Presi-

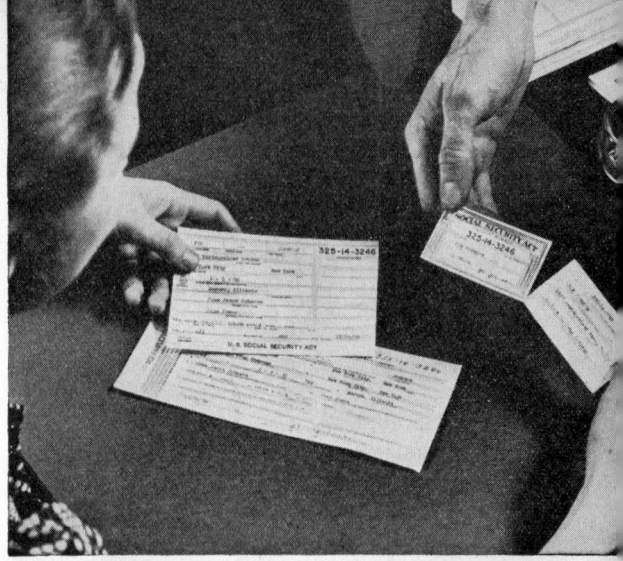

The Social Security Act of 1935 helped to provide pensions for aged people and unemployment insurance for many workers. Each applicant is given a card showing his identification number.

dents since the days of Theodore Roosevelt, to correct unnecessary and expensive duplication and overlapping in the federal administrative service.

——————— CHECK-UP ———————

How did the New Deal consolidate its reform program?

1. What New Deal measures were declared unconstitutional by the Supreme Court, and for what reasons? How did New Dealers justify their program?
2. What were the issues in the election of 1936? What was the outcome?
3. How did the President propose to meet the opposition of the Supreme Court? How was his proposal received by Congress? How did the Supreme Court become more liberal?
4. What important legislation was enacted during President Franklin D. Roosevelt's second term?

3 **President Franklin D. Roosevelt Breaks the Two-Term Tradition**

The Republicans choose Willkie in 1940.
The election of 1940 took place at a time

765

Wendell Willkie, Republican candidate, helped make the campaign of 1940 one of the most colorful in our history. His home town, Elwood, Indiana, greeted him uproariously.

when issues within this country were largely overshadowed in importance by the spread of war throughout Europe (Chapter 39). At the Republican convention held at Philadelphia, the delegates chose as their presidential candidate Wendell L. Willkie, president of the Commonwealth and Southern Corporation. They selected Senator Charles L. McNary of Oregon as his running mate. Willkie was a lawyer who had been associated with business rather than politics. It was expected that he would attract the support of businessmen while McNary would draw the vote of the West and of liberal groups.

Franklin D. Roosevelt is nominated for a third term. Long before the Democratic convention assembled at Chicago in July, there was much talk of a third term for President Roosevelt. The two-term precedent established by Washington and Jefferson nearly a century and a half before had never been broken. Roosevelt's opponents insisted that the discarding of this custom would be a dangerous and unnecessary break with cherished American traditions. Others, however, felt that the threatening world situation called for a continuation of the administration's foreign policy. Adopting the slogan, "Don't swap horses

in mid-stream," they agreed that the breaking of this unwritten law was justified. To the convention the President sent a message that he had never had any desire or purpose to continue in the office of the President, to be a candidate for that office, or to be nominated by the convention for that office. Nevertheless, the delegates chose President Roosevelt on the first ballot, and, at his suggestion, nominated Henry A. Wallace for the Vice-Presidency.

Roosevelt triumphs. Among the topics that were debated during the months that followed were the third-term issue, the government's attitude toward business, the trend of foreign affairs (made critical by the aggressive attacks of Germany and Italy in Europe), and America's defense problem. As an issue foreign policy was not too important, since both candidates strongly urged a program of defense and aid to Britain. Mr. Willkie undertook a whirlwind campaign tour during which he covered some 30,000 miles in 34 states. The President, on the other hand, limited his campaign to a few addresses near the close of the contest. The balloting in the 1940 election represented the greatest outpouring of votes in American political history. More than 27 million votes were cast for President Roosevelt, while well over 22
(Continued on page 768)

Breaking a long tradition, the Democrats in 1940 nominated Franklin D. Roosevelt for a third term as President. Delegates roared approval of the nomination.

Franklin D. Roosevelt
(1882-1945)

President

"THE ONLY THING we have to fear is fear itself." The indomitable courage behind these words typifies the private life and public career of Franklin D. Roosevelt.

Born in Hyde Park, New York, Franklin Roosevelt prepared at Groton, graduated from Harvard, and studied law at Columbia. His political career began in 1910, when he was elected to the New York legislature. Two years later he actively supported Woodrow Wilson for President. Always fond of ships and the sea, he accepted the post of Assistant Secretary of the Navy and held this position for eight years (1913-21). During World War I his efforts contributed greatly to overcoming the German submarine menace. In 1920 he was the unsuccessful Democratic candidate for Vice President.

Shortly afterward, Roosevelt was stricken with infantile paralysis. Instead of being hopelessly crushed by this cruel blow, he emerged from it with a stronger will power and deeper sympathies. Through conversations with streams of visitors he kept his interests alive and his thinking stimulated. He was prevailed upon to run for Governor of New York in 1928 and served for two terms in this office. His administration was "quietly successful."

Conservationist

When Roosevelt was elected to the Presidency in 1932, his courage was a tonic to a disheartened people. On the home front he launched a broad program of "relief, recovery, and reform." In the western hemisphere he inaugurated the Good Neighbor policy. When World War II broke out, he led the nation from isolation to an understanding of the issues involved. And when the United States was drawn into the conflict, he became the architect of victory and of plans for future peace.

World Statesman

It is still too early to evaluate his accomplishments fully. Franklin D. Roosevelt and his policies won enthusiastic praise but they also called forth bitter criticism. It is certain, however, that in leading the United States along new paths, he left his imprint upon national development as indelibly as President Andrew Jackson did a century before.

million were given to Willkie. Roosevelt carried 38 states with a total of 449 electoral votes. In Europe, Roosevelt's re-election was regarded as a blow to the Axis countries.

Friction between President and Congress increases. During the greater part of his third term President Roosevelt had to give his whole attention to the task of fighting a global war (Chapter 40). As the war progressed, relations between the President and Congress grew even more strained. After the Congressional elections had taken place in 1942, the Democratic majorities in Congress were sharply reduced. The Republicans, as well as Democratic opponents of the New Deal, became bolder in their opposition to the President. In general, Congress supported the President's war measures (though it refused to grant him additional war powers) but challenged his domestic program. The farm bloc, in particular, was hostile to the President's anti-inflation program (page 537). Congress opposed him when he tried to place a limit of $25,000 on salaries, and rebuked him by passing the Connally-Smith Anti-Strike Act over his veto (page 527). Congress also showed its hostility to the whole New Deal program by abolishing the National Resources Planning Board (NRPB), which had been working on a broad plan of social security for the postwar period. The widest rift between Congress and the President developed early in 1944. President Roosevelt vetoed a tax bill which he said provided "relief not for the needy but for the greedy." Strongly resenting the language of the President, Congress immediately passed the bill over his veto by overwhelming majorities. At this time the administration had lost control of Congress to a combination of Republicans and conservative Democrats.

Franklin D. Roosevelt is nominated for a fourth term. The election of 1944 occurred at the height of World War II. The chief issue was whether or not the American people wanted a change. Governor Thomas E. Dewey of New York and his running mate on the Republican ticket, Governor John W. Bricker of Ohio, maintained

that the people did. The Democratic Party, which placed President Roosevelt in nomination for a fourth term, believed otherwise. The administration's conduct of the war since Pearl Harbor left little room for criticism and the President's foreign policy met with general approval. As a result, the issues of the campaign were narrowed down to domestic policies. Yet many voters who desired a change on the home front thought it more important that at this critical time our foreign policy be continued without change. They therefore voted for Franklin D. Roosevelt and the vice-presidential candidate, Senator Harry S. Truman, of Missouri. Also, the Political Action Committee (PAC) of the CIO gave strong support to the Democratic ticket.

Roosevelt wins the election. President Roosevelt won the election by a closer margin than in any of his previous victories. The President and Senator Truman received over 25,500,000 votes to 22,000,000 for Governors Dewey and Bricker. The electoral vote was 432 to 99. The Democrats retained their majority in the Senate and increased their strength in the House. Notable among the congressmen who were defeated were certain "isolationists" who had opposed the President's world policies. Thus the nation endorsed the President's objectives, which he had stated as (1) to win the war, (2) to win it "in such a way that there could be no further wars in the foreseeable future," and (3) to provide occupations and a decent standard of living for all Americans.

The President's death shocks the world. President Franklin D. Roosevelt was inaugurated for a fourth term in January, 1945. Less than three months later, on April 12, he died suddenly of cerebral hemorrhage at Warm Springs, Georgia. His death was a shock, not only to Americans but to freedom-loving people everywhere. He died on the very eve of military victory to which he had made notable contributions. He had led the American people step by step from isolation to world co-operation. He had built up the greatest coalition in history for the defense of man's freedom; he had helped direct our armies to victory;

and he had prepared the way for our entering a world organization. It was too early to evaluate the successes and failures of Franklin D. Roosevelt as President, but the nation mourned a leader who had left a lasting imprint on America and the world.

——————— CHECK-UP ———————

What were the great problems of President Franklin D. Roosevelt's last two administrations?

1. Why was President Roosevelt nominated for a third term in 1940? Who was his Republican opponent? What were the issues of the campaign?

2. Why was there increasing friction between Congress and the President? On what issues did Congress reject his leadership?

3. Why was President Roosevelt nominated for a fourth term? Who was his Republican opponent? What was the issue of the campaign?

4. Why did President Roosevelt's death shock the world?

CHAPTER REVIEW

Terms to Understand

"brain trust"   "rugged individualism"
"blue eagle"   "packing" the Supreme
farm bloc   Court
anti-inflation program

People and Things to Know About

Cordell Hull   Harry L. Hopkins
Raymond Moley   Hugh S. Johnson
Senator Wagner   Volstead Act
New Deal   FERA
CCC   Alfred M. Landon
PWA   Wendell L. Willkie
CWA   Thomas E. Dewey
James A. Farley   Political Action Com-
Harold L. Ickes   mittee
Hatch Act

Historic Dates to Identify

1933   1940   1945

Questions to Discuss

1. Compare the following:

(a) Measures taken by Congress to combat the depression of 1929 and congressional action in earlier depressions.

(b) Franklin D. Roosevelt's "brain trust" and Andrew Jackson's "kitchen cabinet."

(c) Party attitude toward a third term for Franklin D. Roosevelt and Ulysses S. Grant.

(d) Relations between Franklin D. Roosevelt and his Democratic Congress during the first term and later.

2. Why were President Roosevelt's domestic policies more widely popular during his first term than later?

3. Why were federal rather than state funds used for the emergency relief measures of the New Deal?

Questions to Discuss (Cont.)

4. What other Presidents than Franklin D. Roosevelt found their policies blocked by the Supreme Court? What did each of them do?

5. How is it possible for a President who has been re-elected to experience difficulty in persuading a Congress controlled by his own party to enact legislation promised in the party platform?

6. Why are unemployment and falling prices a far more serious problem today than they were 100 years ago?

Other Things to Do

1. Debate: *Resolved,* That the President of the United States should be elected for a single term of six years.

2. Many members of the New Deal have written books dealing with this period. Read in some of these books and report interesting findings to the class. Can you find instances where the authors fail to agree on "what happened and why"?

3. Make a survey of your community to find work done by CCC, WPA, and PWA. Then make a table locating and describing each project. Do the projects seem to have had permanent worth to the community as well as immediate value in relieving unemployment?

4. Read in *One World* by Wendell Willkie, and report on interesting passages.

5. Look in newspaper and magazine files for 1940 to discover contemporary reactions to the third term issue. Include cartoons in your study. Report your findings to the class.

*6. Sum up in a paragraph or two the underlying ideas of President Roosevelt's New Deal. Give illustrations of how these ideas were put into practice, and state your reactions to Roosevelt's program.

Chapter **44**

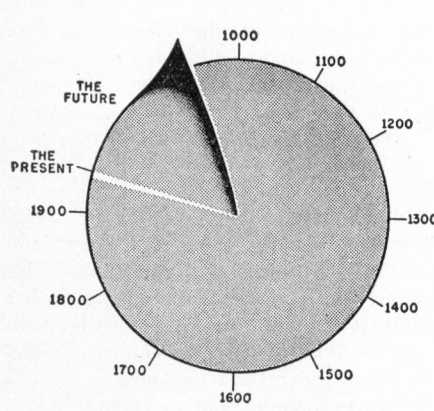

Polling public opinion

THE UNITED STATES

FACES POSTWAR PROBLEMS

The goal of our people and their Government is a permanent world peace. The method by which that goal may be obtained has been, and will continue to be, the subject of disagreement in our democratic society. But if need be, we stand united in readiness to defend ourselves and to co-operate with like-minded peoples against whatever forces may threaten world peace or our freedoms.

Senate Committees on Armed Services and Foreign Relations, 1951

1945 - The Present

Vice-President Harry S. Truman, who succeeded Franklin D. Roosevelt as President, was in many respects a decided contrast to the distinguished Roosevelt. President Truman came from a middle class family and had experience both as a farmer and as a retail merchant before going into politics. In his behavior and even in his reactions to the great honor that had been thrust upon him, Truman seemed much more an "average American" than the late President. To many people this was one of his greatest assets.

Any man might well have looked at the future with doubt and misgiving. As executive head of the nation which even then was emerging as the most powerful in the world, President Truman was faced with serious responsibilities and problems. He would have to lead the United States through the successful conclusion of World War II and through all the perplexing problems of the return to peacetime conditions. But most important of all, President Truman would have a large responsibility in making sure that the United States played its proper part in world co-operation if a third world war was to be avoided.

This chapter will be concerned with the United States after World War II and will describe the problems faced by the nation. The material will be divided into the following topics:

1. Serious decisions challenge the nation after World War II.
2. The Democrats continue in control.

1 Serious Decisions Challenge the Nation after World War II

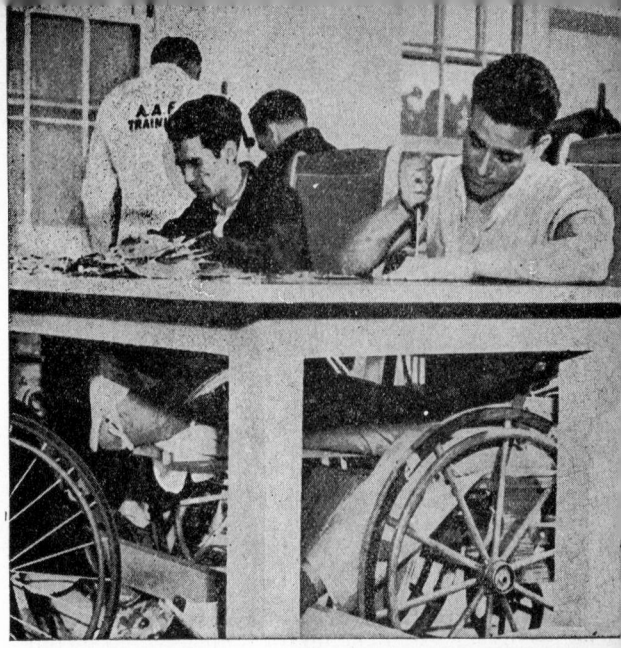

Aid for veterans is a vast undertaking. Many private as well as public agencies share this responsibility.

Harry S. Truman succeeds President Roosevelt. Born in the small Missouri town of Lamar, Harry S. Truman received his early education in Independence, Missouri. A veteran of World War I, he served in the elective offices of county judge and presiding judge of Jackson County, Missouri. In 1934 he was elected to the United States Senate and six years later was re-elected to that body.

As a member of the Senate, Truman served on several investigating committees and won praise for his efficiency and hard work as chairman of a senate committee inquiring into the spending of funds for national defense. He was not an eloquent orator but he was admired for his plain-speaking and fearlessness. When Franklin D. Roosevelt was nominated for a fourth term (1944) it seemed advisable to choose a Vice-Presidential candidate from the Middle West, and Truman received the Democratic nomination. Roosevelt's sudden death four months after his election placed Harry S. Truman in the White House. He was the seventh Vice President to be elevated to the highest office in the land through the death of a President.

Perplexing problems confront President Truman. With final victory yet to be won and the plans for world peace still in their infancy, the new President faced a difficult and uncertain future. Truman assumed the heavy responsibilities of his office in a spirit of courage and humility. His enthusiasm and sincerity helped to make up for his lack of experience. The country accepted his leadership and he soon had a cabinet of his own choosing to help him meet the difficult problems that lay ahead. At first, because of his service in the Senate, Truman and Congress were on unusually friendly terms. Later, when Congress failed to carry out the program which the President requested, relations between Truman and the legislative branch became strained.

Victory brings problems of demobilization and reconversion. As the defeat of the Axis powers became assured, the Truman administration faced a whole set of new problems. Although it was evident that sizeable military forces would be required to occupy Japan, Germany, and Italy even after hostilities ended, there was strong public pressure to demobilize our military forces. As a result, a speeded-up system of discharge was put into effect even before the war with Japan ended. A G.I. Bill of Rights, enacted by Congress in 1944, provided many benefits for the discharged soldier. These included mustering-out pay, hospitalization, loans for the purchase of homes, farms, or a business, and extensive educational benefits. By 1951, when the enrollment privilege expired, more than 8 million veterans of World War II had attended schools or colleges under the G. I. Bill, at a cost to the government of 14 billion dollars for tuition and subsistence.

Under the guidance of the Office of Mobilization and Reconversion, industry shifted from wartime to peacetime conditions as effectively and painlessly as could be expected. Nevertheless, certain difficulties were encountered. Workers who had received additional pay for overtime labor during the war demanded higher wages to make up for their lowered income. Strikes became widespread throughout the nation. This pressure on the part of labor resulted in several wage increases (page 528). Higher wages, plus the fact that people had been unable to purchase many articles during the war, resulted in increased demand for goods and higher

Buyers' strikes were organized in a few places to resist soaring costs of living. Little came of these and other efforts.

prices. The easing of price control (page 538) made the problem of inflation and higher prices more acute. Wages, however, especially for organized labor, rose more rapidly than prices, and purchasing power increased. Business activity and employment remained at a high level, and the national income continued to rise.

The wage level continues upward. Higher living costs brought about a fourth round of collective bargaining in 1949. This was reflected not so much by wage increases as by recognition on the part of management of responsibility for the health and security of the workers. New wage contracts carried so-called fringe benefits — that is, payment of pensions and social insurance entirely by management as part of normal business costs. A long-drawn-out and crippling dispute in the bituminous coal mines ended in March, 1950, with some gains for the miners. Two months later a 100-day strike at the Chrysler plants concluded with a pension grant and other fringe benefits for employees. In 1950, a fifth round of wage increases raised the hourly wage level for organized workers another 10 to 15 cents. General Motors introduced a new idea in its wage contract by tying wage increases to the cost of living index.

Price increases lead to controls. Wage increases, in turn, were accompanied by new price increases (page 537). Prices held fairly stable in 1949, but after the invasion of South Korea in June, 1950 (page 773), the price trend was markedly upward. Measures suggested for controlling inflation included: (1) increased production; (2) increased taxation, designed to drain off buying power at a time when the production of war goods was cutting down the production of consumer goods; (3) curbing of private credit, thus cutting down the demand for consumer goods; and (4) direct wage and price controls. In September, 1950, Congress passed the Defense Production Act, giving the President extraordinary economic powers, including the power to fix wage and price ceilings. An Economic Stabilization Agency (ESA) was set up. In January, 1951, general wage and price ceilings were announced. Prices, except for agricultural products (which were protected by parity provisions) were fixed at the highest levels reached between December 19 and January 25. Wages were frozen at the January 25 levels, though cost-of-living increases of 10 per cent were permitted. Experiments with price roll-backs, affecting particularly automobiles and beef, ran into stiff resistance. The Defense Production Act expired at the end of June, 1951, at which time the President asked for strengthened controls. Congress, however, finally enacted a watered-down measure, which weakened rather than strengthened all controls.

Relations with Russia grow worse. Meantime, the hopes which had attended the framing and ratification of the United Nations Charter were giving way to fear and anxiety (pages 715–717). Relations with the U.S.S.R. went from bad to worse, (1) as Russia extended her authority over neighboring countries (page 719), (2) when she seemed determined to drive the western democracies out of Berlin (page 721), and (3) when the democracies responded by drawing together in the North Atlantic Pact (page 721). It soon became evident that Russia had chosen the Far East as the most likely place for the next move for the extension of communism.

North Korea becomes an aggressor. Near the end of June, 1950, the "cold war" was suddenly converted into a shooting war. Without warning the troops of Communist North Korea invaded South Korea (page 722). The South Korean government had been sponsored by the United Nations and had received American aid and support. If it were now permitted to fall before Communist aggression, it would be not only a blow to UN prestige, but also an encouragement to further Communist expansion by force.

The UN and the U.S. take action. At once the UN Security Council took action. Early in the year the Russian delegate had walked out of the Council because of its refusal to recognize the Communist government as the legal government of China (page 722). Taking advantage of the absence of Russia, with her ever-present veto threat, the Council called upon the North Koreans to end hostilities and to withdraw its invasion forces. It also called upon UN members for assistance. Promptly American air and ground forces, under the command of General Douglas MacArthur, were ordered into Korea to support the South Korean government. At the same time the Seventh Fleet was ordered to Formosa, still under the control of Nationalist China, to prevent a Communist attack upon that important outpost. Great Britain, Canada, the Netherlands, Australia, New Zealand, and Nationalist China promptly offered their support to what President Truman called a UN police action. Soon sixteen nations were fighting side by side under the new UN flag. Congress gave evidence of its support by extending the life of the draft by almost unanimous vote.

The war in Korea drags on. For the next year the fighting in Korea was indecisive. In the first stage the North Koreans held the advantage in manpower and equipment. The UN forces gathered slowly, and though they possessed superior air and naval power, they were driven back to a narrow beachhead around Pusan in the southeast of the peninsula. In September, 1950, General MacArthur launched a brilliant counterattack which carried the UN forces all the way to the Manchurian border. Then, when victory and the end of the war seemed near, Communist China (page 722) joined forces with the North Koreans, and General MacArthur was faced with what he termed "an entirely new war."

Again the UN forces were driven back below the 38th parallel and again the South Korean capital, Seoul, fell into the hands of the Communists. The Communists prepared a spring offensive in 1951 designed to drive the UN forces out of Korea, but it ground to a halt below Seoul. Meantime the United Nations, upon American urging, condemned Communist China as an aggressor and called upon the Peiping Government to stop its attacks and withdraw. General Matthew B. Ridgeway, who now replaced General MacArthur in command, carried out a counteroffensive planned to inflict heavy losses upon the trained

Chinese soldiers at the lowest possible cost to the UN forces. Above the 38th parallel a deadlock developed which neither side seemed able to break. The United Nations had now attained its limited objective of halting aggression and the Communists were at last prepared to talk peace. Negotiations for a cease-fire dragged on during the summer and fall of 1951, but progress was discouragingly slow.

General MacArthur is removed from command. At the height of the Chinese build-up for the spring offensive, General MacArthur was suddenly removed from his Far East command. For a long time friction had been growing between the General and President Truman over the former's tendency to make announcements of policy without first consulting the State or Defense Departments. General MacArthur's rather brusque dismissal added fuel to a "great debate" over our foreign policy. General MacArthur advocated a more aggressive policy in the Far East, including the bombing of Chinese bases in Manchuria, a blockade of the Chinese coast, support of the Chinese Nationalist forces, and defense of Formosa. The Truman administration, on the other hand, supported a policy of halting aggression in Korea, preventing the Korean incident from developing into World War III, and leaving the door open for a negotiated peace. The American

people, moved in part by enthusiasm for General MacArthur's record as a soldier, and in part by approval of a more aggressive policy in Korea, welcomed him with great acclaim upon his return to America. A long Senate inquiry into the dismissal followed which brought out sharply the differences in points of view on Far Eastern policy. At the end of the hearings, however, the Senate Committees on Armed Services and Foreign Relations unanimously approved the following warning to the Communist world: "The issues which might divide our people are far transcended by the things which unite them. If threatened danger becomes war, the aggressor would find at one stroke arrayed against him the united energies, the united resources, and the united devotion of all the American people."

The North Atlantic Pact is strengthened. While the "great debate" on foreign policy was going on, steps were being taken to strengthen the defenses of Western Europe. The Truman administration believed that our main defensive effort should be in Europe. The extension of Soviet power in Europe and the Middle East, it was argued, would be a disastrous blow to our security. Early in 1951, General Dwight D. Eisenhower, as Supreme Commander of the North Atlantic Defense Force, toured Europe to rally the democracies in the de-

Surrounded by the flags of the participating nations, President Harry S. Truman opens the Japanese Peace Treaty Conference at San Francisco. Governor Earl Warren of California stands at the right in the background.

fense effort. Congress approved the President's proposal to station six American divisions in Europe, and for the fiscal year beginning in 1951 the President asked Congress to vote nearly 7 billion dollars for military and economic aid for Western Europe and 1½ billions for our other allies. In September, 1951, the admission of Greece and Turkey into the North Atlantic community of nations was approved, subject to ratification by the member nations. The rearming of Western Germany, however, remained a thorny question in the program of strengthening European defenses.

The United States begins to mobilize. As tension mounted between East and West, steps were taken to mobilize this country's manpower and resources. Three months after South Korea was invaded the President proclaimed a state of national emergency. He now looked forward to an army of 3,500,000 men, a rapid speed-up in the production of military equipment, and an increase in the annual defense budget from 13 to 42 billion dollars. A new Office of Defense Mobilization (ODM) was set up under Charles Edward Wilson. It was to have charge of production, procurement of materials, manpower, transportation, and economic stabilization. In June, 1951, the draft law was extended to 1955. The draft age was lowered to 18½, the term of service was increased to two years, and provision was made for a system of universal military training.

Peace with Japan is achieved. At the close of the summer (1951) the defensive position of the democratic powers was also strengthened in the Pacific area. At the end of August, a mutual defense pact was signed at Washington by Secretary of State Dean Acheson and Foreign Minister Carlos Romulo of the Philippines. Two days later the United States signed a similar defensive pact with Australia and New Zealand. Of even greater importance, however, was the signing of a peace treaty with Japan at San Francisco in September by 48 of the powers (not including the Russian bloc, India, or China) which had been at war with that nation. Largely the work of Ambassador John

Foster Dulles, the treaty extended generous terms to Japan. In turn, it prepared the way for a Japanese-American security pact providing for the retaining of U.S. troops and bases in Japan. Thus Japan became the cornerstone of a new defensive structure designed to prevent further Communist aggression in the Pacific. Only time would tell whether these strengthened defenses would deter the aggressor and prevent the outbreak of World War III.

─────── CHECK-UP ───────

What problems confronted the United States in the years following World War II?

1. What background and experience did President Truman have before he became President? What problems of demobilization and reconversion did victory bring? What have been the chief developments in connection with wages and prices since the end of World War II?

2. Why did relations with Russia become more strained? What led the UN and the United States to take action in Korea? What developments have taken place in Korea?

3. How has the United States strengthened its defenses through (a) the North Atlantic Pact, (b) its own mobilization, (c) treaties with countries in the Far East, against the threat of aggression?

2 The Democrats Continue in Control

The Republicans regain control of Congress. In the postwar period, when serious economic problems and foreign policy were challenging the Administration and the American people, control by the Democrats continued, though not unchallenged. Even President Franklin D. Roosevelt had had trouble in holding together under the Democratic standard such groups as New Dealers, southern Democrats, labor groups and independent voters. Now, as the mid-term elections of 1946 approached, divisions within the Democratic Party became more pronounced. Moreover, President Truman's popularity had declined. As a result the Republicans won a sweeping victory. They obtained a majority of six in the Senate, and, by regaining more than 100 seats in the House, won control of that body. The President was therefore forced to deal with a hostile Congress, while Republican chances for victory in the presidential election of 1948 seemed greatly improved.

The new Congress makes important decisions in foreign affairs. The work of the newly elected Republican Congress was of special importance, since it became the chief issue in the election of 1948. President Truman later condemned this Eightieth Congress as the worst since the radical Republican Congress under President Johnson (page 324). Actually, its record was most creditable in the field of foreign affairs. It approved the Truman Doctrine for aid to Greece and Turkey (page 719). It also approved the European Recovery Program, although the House was not eager to grant the funds that ERP would need. The Eightieth Congress made provision for

President Truman's appeal to the average voter was stronger in 1948 than most political analysts realized. Here he is being cheered by a New Jersey audience.

uniting the armed forces of the United States under a single Secretary of Defense, and it passed a compromise draft measure to build up the strength of the military forces in peacetime. It passed legislation permitting a limited number of displaced persons to enter this country, although the provisions of the act were criticized as unfair to certain peoples. It also renewed the Reciprocal Trade Agreements Act (page 546), but with restrictions and for only a single year. In addition, the Senate ratified peace treaties with Italy, Hungary, Rumania, and Bulgaria.

Important domestic legislation is passed. The Eightieth Congress also dealt with a number of important domestic problems. One piece of legislation was the bitterly debated Taft-Hartley Labor Relations Act (page 529). Another measure provided for a tax reduction of 4.8 billion dollars, passed — like the Taft-Hartley Act — over a strong presidential veto. The bill for tax reduction was attacked because of the greater relief it gave to the larger taxpayers.

Another act of Congress provided a new order of presidential succession in the absence of a Vice-President (page 463). A constitutional amendment limiting future Presidents to two terms was also sent to the states for ratification.[1] A special session called in the summer of 1948 approved a loan of 64 million dollars to the United Nations for a headquarters building in New York, as well as mild anti-inflation and housing measures. According to its critics in the Democratic Party, however, the Eightieth Congress had failed to attack outstanding problems — wage and price controls, the high cost of living, housing, civil rights, minimum wages, and social security.

President Truman's chances for re-election look slim. President Truman was renominated — without great confidence or enthusiasm — by the Democratic convention in July, 1948. The outlook for his re-election appeared far from encouraging. He had lost the support of the left wing Democrats, who now formed a third party. This new

[1] This amendment was ratified by 36 states and became Amendment 22 in 1951.

Progressive Party nominated Henry Wallace for President and Glen Taylor of Idaho as his running mate. Moreover, President Truman's program for promoting civil rights ran counter to the traditions of the southern Democrats. Many of these declined to support Truman. They organized the States Rights Democrats (Dixiecrats) and nominated Governor J. Strom Thurmond of South Carolina and Governor Fielding L. Wright of Mississippi. In June the Republicans had again nominated Governor Thomas E. Dewey of New York, with Governor Earl Warren of California as running mate. Never had the Republicans entered a presidential contest with greater confidence. Governor Dewey conducted a campaign which was intended only to hold his advantage. President Truman, almost single-handed, conducted a vigorous uphill, 30,000-mile campaign. Apparently he had little chance of success; indeed, few persons aside from President Truman himself were willing to predict a Democratic victory.

The election is a complete upset. When the election returns came in, the predictions of the political prophets, pollsters, and radio and newspaper commentators proved to be completely wrong. Apparently the forces of labor had voted against the Republicans to indicate their dislike of the Taft-Hartley Act. It appeared that middle-western farmers had cast their votes for the party which had supported farm prices and under which they had enjoyed the greatest prosperity in history, while housewives voted against a Congress which they held responsible for high prices. Instead of being defeated, President Truman and Senator Alben Barkley of Kentucky emerged with 24 million popular votes to somewhat less than 22 million for Dewey and Warren. The Democratic candidate received 304 out of the 531 electoral votes. Actually, the election was closer than these figures indicate, for the shift of a few thousand votes in California, Illinois, and Ohio would have changed the result. Thirty-eight electoral votes from four southern states went to Governor Thurmond of the Dixiecrats. The Democrats won both houses of the Eighty-

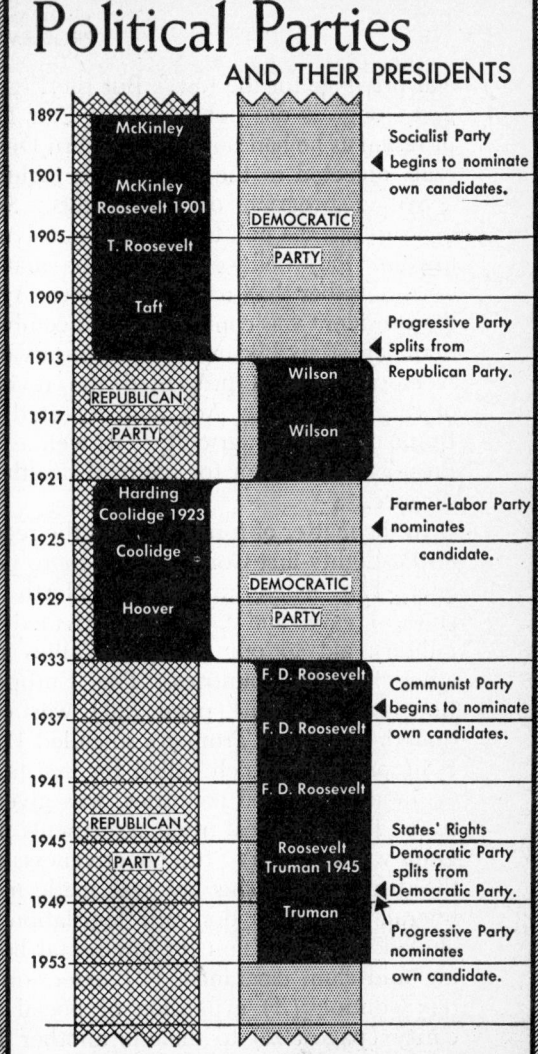

The Democratic Party has been unusually successful since 1932. Why? Why were many Republican Presidents elected between 1868 and 1912? (See chart, page 466.)

first Congress by large majorities. The election of 1948 was indeed a personal triumph for President Truman.

The Eighty-first Congress opposes Truman's Fair Deal but passes important legislation. The President interpreted the election results to mean that the American people would support him in putting through a program of legislation which he termed a "Fair Deal." He defined it as "the welfare of all the people against special privilege for the few." But the Eighty-first Congress did not adopt his Fair Deal program as he had hoped. Southern Democrats objected to the fact that it included a strong program of civil rights. Such measures as the poll tax and the anti-lynching bill, they believed, should be matters of state rather than national concern. Again the President was confronted by a combination of Republicans and conservative Democrats which prevented the revision of the Taft-Hartley Act, and defeated the Brannan Plan for agriculture as well as the President's program for national health insurance.

In the matter of foreign affairs the record of the Eighty-first Congress was more positive. The Senate ratified the North Atlantic Treaty, and Congress provided for military aid to our European allies and other friendly countries. The European Recovery Program (page 720) was continued. President Truman's so-called Point Four program, which called for assistance to under-developed countries, was given a start. The reciprocal trade agreements program was restored to full effectiveness, and the displaced persons law was made more liberal. Important domestic legislation included: (1) provision for low-rental housing and slum clearance; (2) extension of rent control; (3) expansion of Social Security (page 592) to include another 10,000,000 persons, and benefit increases of about 75%; (4) an increase in minimum wages to 75 cents per hour (page 526); (5) further aid to farmers; (6) a tax increase to meet the Korean emergency; (7) an increase of FDIC coverage to $10,000 (page 535); (8) a system of war economy controls; and (9) an Internal Security Act designed to bring communist activities under control. The President vetoed this last measure as unworkable, but it was promptly passed over his veto. Meantime, under the Smith Act of 1940 eleven of the leading communists in the United States were placed on trial for advocating the overthrow of government in the United States by force or violence. After a long-drawn-out trial they were convicted, and in due course of time their conviction was upheld by the United States Supreme Court.

The Republicans gain in the election of 1950. In the mid-term Congressional elections the administration again suffered a severe setback. Criticism of the foreign policy of the President and of Secretary of State Dean Acheson contributed to the Democratic losses. Specifically, dissatisfaction was expressed with the Far Eastern policy, with the loss of China to the Communists, and with developments in Korea. Attacks leveled at the President's Fair Deal program and his "welfare state" also gained votes for the Republicans. Support of labor for its candidates proved disappointing, and the farmers seemed to be drifting back to Republican ranks. As a result of the election the Democratic majority in the Senate was reduced to the narrow margin of two, and in the House it was down to 36. Some of the President's ardent supporters had met with defeat, and, on the other hand, some of his chief opponents had been re-elected. Only the Solid South saved the Democrats from complete rout. The Southern Democrats, however, were by no means pro-administration, and in the new Congress the Republican-Southern Democrat coalition grew in strength. In 1951, the 82nd Congress became better known for its investigations than for legislation. Reference has already been made to the lengthy hearings in the Senate on the dismissal of General MacArthur. In addition, a Senate Crime Investigation Committee held some sensational hearings on organized crime in interstate commerce.

As the year 1951 drew to a close, the world faced a crucial situation. Never had it been so difficult for even the most careful observer to tell what the following years would bring forth. It might be an attack with atomic bombs or with even more terrifying weapons. Or the cold war might drag on, each participant awaiting the event that would change the whole picture. One thing was certain — our primary aims were support of the free world and the preservation of peace.

——————— CHECK-UP ———————

What have been the highlights of Democratic control since World War I?

1. What was the result of the congressional election of 1946? What did the Republican Congress accomplish in the area of foreign affairs? In the field of domestic affairs? Why did the Democrats criticize the Eightieth Congress?

2. What new parties took part in the 1948 presidential campaign? Why did most "experts" doubt that President Truman could be re-elected? How was his victory possible?

3. What was the Fair Deal? Why did it meet opposition in Congress? What legislation did the Eighty-first Congress adopt? What were the results of the congressional election of 1950?

CHAPTER REVIEW

Terms to Understand

reconversion   left-wing Democrats
civil rights   filibuster

People and Things to Know About

Harry S. Truman
G. I. Bill of Rights
Seoul
Great Debate
Eightieth Congress
Henry A. Wallace
J. Strom Thurmond
Thomas E. Dewey
Dixiecrats
Fair Deal
Charles E. Wilson
Point Four

Historic Dates to Identify

1945   1948   1950

Questions to Discuss

1. Compare the following:

(a) President Truman and President Franklin D. Roosevelt.

(b) Postwar problems after the War Between the States, World War I, and World War II.

(c) United States foreign policy after World Wars I and II.

(d) The presidential elections of 1860, 1912, and 1948.

2. Why were the five great powers given the right of veto in the UN?

3. Some people believe that the rapid demobilization of the United States armed forces after World War II was a mistake. Why do they make this statement?

4. Since the labor force and production for civilian use increased, why were prices higher after World War II than they were during the war?

5. Why was co-operation with Soviet Russia more difficult after World War II than during that conflict?

6. Do you agree with the UN's policy of taking action against the North Koreans? Why?

Other Things to Do

1. History is made each day, and the only way to keep abreast of affairs is to be currently informed. What are most recent developments in these problem areas? (1) Relations between Soviet Russia and the United States, (2) Control of atomic energy, (3) Unification of the armed forces, and (4) Labor-management relations and legislation. How can you find recent information about these problems? Share your findings with the class.

2. Make a collection of cartoons dealing with relations between the United States and Soviet Russia. Arrange a bulletin board display, and have the class evaluate the cartoons.

3. Use *Readers' Guide* to discover articles dealing with pre-election predictions (1948), which attempt to explain why the "experts" were wrong. Report your findings to the class.

4. Debate: *Resolved,* That the filibuster should be abolished in the United States Senate.

°5. Make a chart comparing the Square Deal, the New Freedom, the New Deal, and the Fair Deal. In each case, state the President responsible for it, the basic purpose, and the chief accomplishments.

6. Take part in a panel discussion on the outlook for the United Nations. In preparation for this discussion consider the achievements of the UN to date, the problems it has encountered, the split between East and West, and the development of security pacts between groups of nations. Make use of newspapers and magazines, as well as materials from the UN.

Unit Summary

1. McKinley's election in 1896 defeated the free silver movement and seemed to herald a period of conservative politics, favorable to big business. His death, which brought Theodore Roosevelt to the White House, changed the picture completely. Roosevelt's administration, with its attack on monopolies, its "square deal" for labor, and its emphasis on conservation, introduced an era of reform into national politics.

2. William Howard Taft, chosen by Roosevelt as his successor, carried on many progressive policies. However, his stand on the tariff and other events in his administration seemed to ally him with the conservative wing of the Republicans. As a result, a Progressive Party was formed. With Roosevelt as its standard bearer, it entered the campaign of 1912. Profiting from the split in the Republican Party, Wilson won the election. He succeeded in pushing through a broad program of reform, but the outbreak of World War I and our entrance into it thrust progressive politics into the background. Wilson's attempt to win American approval of the League of Nations failed, and he ended his administration broken in health.

3. During the first two decades of the 1900's considerable progress was made in bringing government more directly under the control of the public. Certain reform measures were put into practice — the direct primary; the initiative, referendum, and recall; the direct election of senators; and women's suffrage.

4. Harding's election in 1920 marked the beginning of an era of conservative politics which continued through the administrations of Coolidge and Hoover. This was a period of prosperity and of *laissez faire* toward business. Hoover's administration was clouded by the depression which began in 1929. Hoover became the scapegoat for this national misfortune and was defeated in the election of 1932.

5. To a country plagued by financial paralysis, business failures, and widespread unemployment, Franklin D. Roosevelt announced a New Deal. His program of relief, recovery, and reform brought some measure of help to

the nation. The program was highly praised and bitterly criticized As the 1930's came to an end, international problems became of first importance. With America's entrance into World War II, Roosevelt's efforts were bent toward winning the war and establishing a permanent peace. His death, shortly after the beginning of his fourth term, placed Harry Truman in the White House. Truman's administration was made difficult by the problems of postwar readjustment and by a disturbing split in aims and policies between the western powers and Soviet Russia. Truman won a surprising victory in 1948, but met opposition to his Fair Deal and increasing international tension during his second term.

Summary of Important Dates

1898 Initiative and referendum introduced in South Dakota.
1903 Direct primary introduced in Wisconsin.
1910 Powers of Speaker of House reduced.
1912 Progressive Party tries to elect Theodore Roosevelt.
1913 Seventeenth Amendment (direct election of Senators).
1920 Nineteenth Amendment (woman suffrage).
1921 Harding's inauguration marks beginning of era of conservatism.
National Budget Act passed.
1932 Twentieth Amendment proposed by Congress ("lame duck" sessions abolished).
1933 Franklin D. Roosevelt inaugurates the New Deal.
1939 Hatch Act limits political activities of federal employees.
Reorganization Act passed.
1940 Roosevelt breaks the third term tradition.
1947 Presidential succession is changed.
1951 Twenty-second Amendment (limitation on Presidential term).

Unit Activities

1. List reforms since 1900 which have furthered political democracy in this country. In each case (1) explain the purpose sought and (2) make clear whether the reform has worked in practice as well as was expected.

2. Use *Readers' Guide* to find the platforms of major and minor parties in the last presidential election. List the reforms proposed. Have a class discussion to discover which are favored by the group. Which are likely to be enacted into law in the near future?

3. Get in touch with the leaders of the political parties represented in your community. Invite these men to explain to the class how the party is organized, how it reaches decisions and how it "gets out the vote." Before listening to these men, some members of the class should read Kent, *The Great Game of Politics,* or a similar book in your library, and report to the group. After listening to the speakers, the class should discuss the comparative advantages of being a party man and an independent voter.

4. List examples of how Congress failed to follow the President's leadership (1) when the President belonged to the majority party in both houses of Congress, and (2) when the President belonged to the minority party. Try to explain why, in each case, the Chief Executive and legislative bodies failed to co-operate. What can the President do to insure greater co-operation?

For Further Reading

Original Sources

Commager, H. S., ed., *Documents of American History.* Appleton-Century-Crofts. Nos. 376, 379–84, 389, 391, 406, 429, 452, 454, 475, 476, 479, 484, 508, 509, 531, 532.

Nevins, A., and Commager, H. S., eds., *The Heritage of America.* Little, Brown. Nos. 233–36, 246, 247, 249–51.

Pease, T. C., and Roberts, A. S., eds., *Selected Readings in American History.* Harcourt. Nos. 229, 236, 238, 239.

Roosevelt, T., *Theodore Roosevelt.* Scribner. This autobiography stresses politics.

Smith, Alfred E., *Up to Now.* Viking. The autobiography of a great Democrat and an able governor of New York.

General References

Adams, J. T., *The Epic of America.* Little, Brown. Chapter 12.

Hicks, J. D., *The American Nation.* Houghton. Chapters 18–20, 24, 30.

Morison, S. E., and Commager, H. S., *The Growth of the American Republic.* Oxford, Vol. II, Chapters 16–18, 22–23.

Special Accounts

American Nation Series. Harper. Latané, J. H., *America as a World Power.* Ogg, F. A., *National Progress.*

Beals, C., *Pan America: A Program for the Western Hemisphere.* Stresses the need for building up the standard of living in South America.

Chase, S., *Where's the Money Coming From?* Twentieth Century Fund.

Chronicles of America Series. Yale University Press. Howland, H., *Theodore Roosevelt and His Times.* Orth, S. P., *The Boss and the Machine.* Seymour, C., *Woodrow Wilson and the World War.*

Dietz, D., *Atomic Energy in the Coming Era.* Dodd, Mead.

History of American Life Series. MacMillan. Faulkner, H. U., *The Quest for Social Justice 1898–1914.* Chapters 4 and 5. Slosson, P. W., *The Great Crusade and After, 1914–1928.* Chapters 3 and 6.

Hoover, I. H., *Forty-two Years in the White House.* Houghton.

Kohlsaat, H. H., *From McKinley to Harding.* Scribner.

Lilienthal, D. E., TVA: *Democracy on the March.* Harper.

Sullivan, L., *Our Times.* Scribner. Volumes I–VI.

United Nations Bulletin. International Documents Service, Columbia University Press, 2960 Broadway, New York City 27. This Service is the general agent for UN publications. The *UN Bulletin* is a semi-monthly illustrated periodical which discusses current developments.

United Nations Department of Public Information, Lake Success, New York. Inquiries regarding recently issued publications, posters, filmstrips, etc., should be addressed to the Educational Liaison Section at the above address.

The following organizations issue useful bibliographies, pamphlets, etc., about UN:

American Association for the United Nations, 45 East 65th Street, New York City 21.

Carnegie Endowment for International Peace, 405 West 117th Street, New York City 27.

Foreign Policy Association, 22 East 38th Street, New York City, 16.

National Education Association, 1201 Sixteenth Street, N.W., Washington 6, D.C.

Woodrow Wilson Foundation, 45 East 65th Street, New York City 21.

World Peace Foundation, 40 Mt. Vernon Street, Boston 8, Massachusetts.

Biography

Andrews, M. R. S., *His Soul Goes Marching On.* Scribner. Theodore Roosevelt.

Bowers, C. G., *Beveridge and the Progressive Era.* Houghton. Beveridge was a leader in the Progressive Party.

Dodd, W. E., *Woodrow Wilson and His Work.* Doubleday.

Harlow, A. F., *Theodore Roosevelt, Strenuous American.* Messner.

Perkins, Frances, *The Roosevelt I Knew.* Viking. A cabinet member writes about F. D. R.

Pringle, H. F., *The Life and Times of William Howard Taft.* Farrar. An interesting account of the life of the friendly President.

Pictures

Butterfield, R., *The American Past.* Simon and Schuster.

Pageant of America Series. Yale University Press. Bassett, J. S., *Makers of a New Nation.* Chapters 8–12.

Rogers, A., and Allen, F. L., *The American Procession.* Harper.

Sidelights on American History

First Woman Cabinet Member. It was in 1869 in the territory of Wyoming that American women were first given the right to vote, and the first woman Congressman took her seat in the House of Representatives in 1917. But it was not until 1933 that, for the first time in American history, a woman became a member of the President's cabinet. In that year President Franklin D. Roosevelt, at the beginning of his first term, appointed Frances Perkins to be his Secretary of Labor.

Miss Perkins was a New Englander, and her past training had been mostly in the field of social work. That is, she had worked for organizations that concerned themselves with the welfare of the poor or the underprivileged and tried, by legislation or other means, to give such people more advantages. As part of her activity as a social worker, Miss Perkins had investigated working conditions in sweatshops and cellar bakeries, inspected living conditions in tenements, and organized drives to secure the passage of legislation which would make working conditions safer everywhere.

This sort of career put her into frequent touch with men in politics, and she came to know and work with many prominent Americans. Al Smith, when he was the governor of New York, put her on the Industrial Commission of that state, and here she gained much experience in industrial and labor legislation. Other political figures whom she came to know were Senator Robert F. Wagner, whose name is linked with the Wagner Labor Act, Big Tim Sullivan, a leader of Tammany Hall, and Franklin D. Roosevelt, who, as governor of New York State, appointed Miss Perkins as Industrial Commissioner of that state.

As the country's first woman Secretary of Labor, Miss Perkins had to face much unjust criticism merely because she was a woman. Many Americans believed that the post of Secretary of Labor was a job for a man only. William Green, the head of the American Federation of Labor, declared: "Labor will never be reconciled to a woman."

It cannot be said, however, that Labor never became reconciled to Miss Perkins, for she served as President Roosevelt's Secretary of Labor for over twelve years. During that period she won the respect of many labor leaders.

Perhaps Miss Perkins' road as Secretary of Labor would have been easier if she had had a stronger sense of personal publicity. She never attempted to be dramatic or to glamorize herself in the public eye, as so many political figures do. Probably there was no harder working member of the President's cabinet. She took her job seriously and gave to it everything she had. She worked so much that the chauffeur who was assigned to her official car quit his job. "I was too tired," he explained. "Miss Perkins just worked herself and me night and day."

Conservation Pioneer. Today almost everybody knows the meaning of "conservation of natural resources." Americans have not always been aware of the need for conservation, however. The early settlers never dreamed that some day our vast prairies might lack good farm lands, or that our forests would sometime be too small for our needs. It was late in the 1800's when Americans woke up to the fact that we were heedlessly wasting our soil, our forests, and our minerals, and that for the good of all something ought to be done.

One of the first Americans to do something personally and directly about conservation was Gifford Pinchot. Pinchot graduated from Harvard College in 1889. Young as he was, he knew then that conservation was to be his work, the career of his entire lifetime. He journeyed to Europe and studied forestry conservation under the leading experts, who were then far ahead of Americans in this field. Then he returned to his native country to begin the first systematic forestry work in the United States. This he did in a tract of woodland in Biltmore, North Carolina. The project established Pinchot as the pioneer in forestry conservation in North America.

Except for a few years in politics (he became the governor of Pennsylvania in 1922) Pinchot devoted his life to the cause of conservation. When the first bureau of forestry was created by the Department of Agriculture, Pinchot was made its head. To run the newly established National Forestry Service President Roosevelt chose Gifford Pinchot, because he knew that to Pinchot conservation was practically a religion.

Pinchot believed that vast areas of the public lands owned by the federal government should be permanently set aside for economic reasons — because they contained valuable water power, for example, or minerals, or timber, or oil. Until his day, public lands had usually been set aside for recreational reasons only, areas like the great western national parks and national forests — Yellowstone, Glacier, and Yosemite. Altogether these totaled about 45 million acres, but Pinchot urged that much more land be set aside. Through his efforts 148 million additional acres (totaling an area larger than all of California) were permanently removed from public sale during the Presidency of Theodore Roosevelt. These areas were dedicated to the preservation of natural resources under the best conservation practices.

Largely because of Pinchot's work, many forestry schools were established in our colleges, and the preservation of natural resources became a popular career.

Pinchot served 12 years as head of the Forestry Service. All the rest of his life he crusaded for conservation. On his 80th birthday he published a new book on the subject. He declared before his death in 1946 that world peace depended on world conservation. Continued wasting of natural resources, he believed, brought hunger and want to the peoples of the world and was therefore the basic cause of war.

America has had other great conservationists, but it was Gifford Pinchot more than anyone else who made Americans aware of the necessity for preserving our natural resources for the use of future generations.

CCG52

YOUR GOVERNMENT

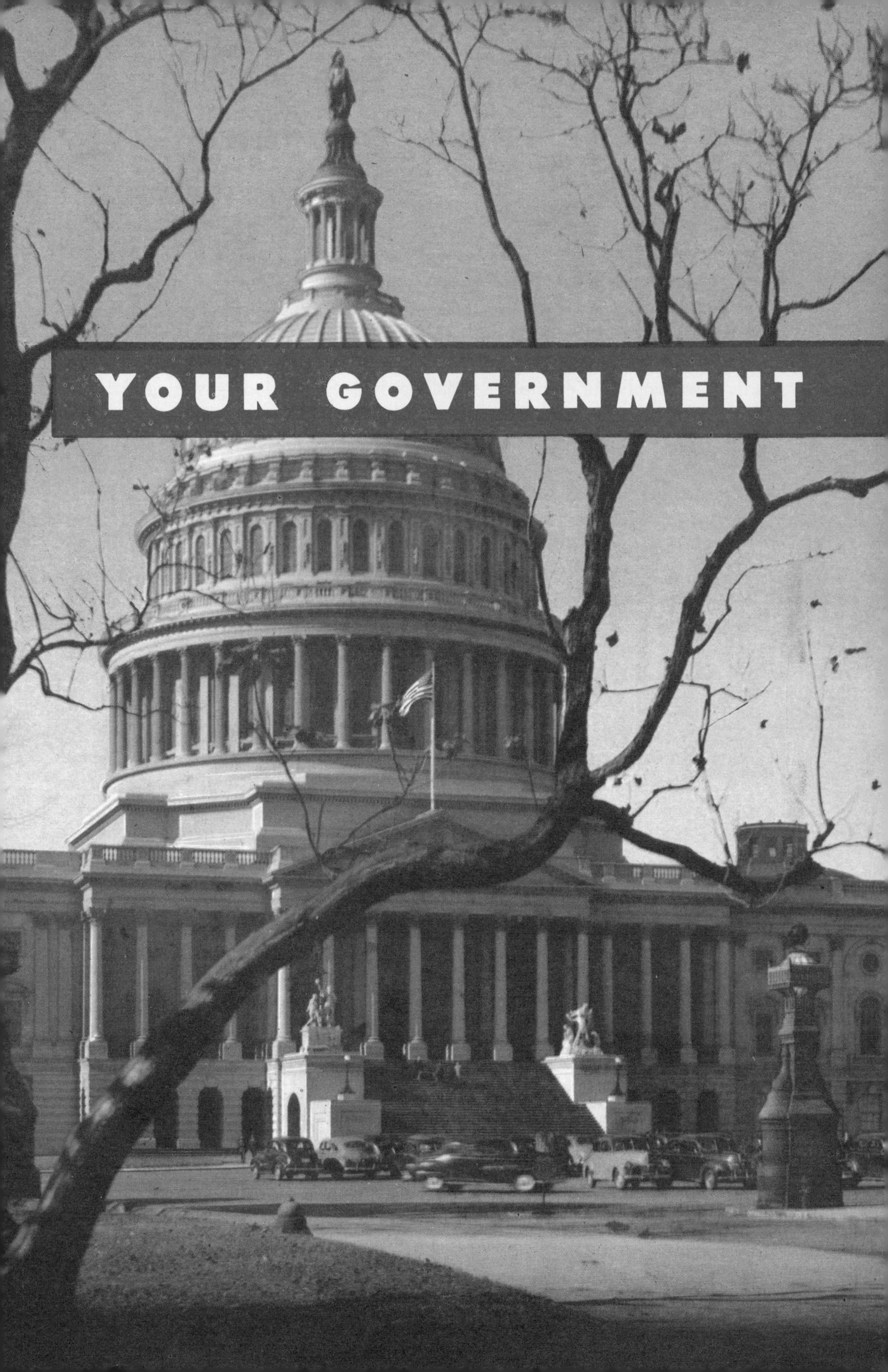

YOU HAVE THREE GOVERNMENTS

Government in the United States is carried on for the benefit and well-being of American citizens. It operates at three distinct levels: local, state, and federal. The authority and duties of these three levels overlap somewhat, but they are distinct enough to give each citizen the services of three separate governments. His water supply, for example, is usually provided by his local government — that is, by the city, town, or village in which he lives. His state government, on the other hand, decides how he will get a license for his automobile. The delivery of his mail is a service performed by government at the federal level. These and other functions of the three levels of American government are shown in the charts on this page and the next.

A striking change has taken place since 1789 in the relative size and importance of the three levels of our government. Quite clearly, each has a vital place in the whole system. But over the years the federal government has become by far the largest. Nowadays the federal government collects in taxes and spends three times as much money as the other two levels together.

The growth of the federal government occurred as the country expanded from a mere handful of people on the eastern seaboard to a shifting, growing population of over 150 million people scattered through 48 states. As transportation and communication speeded up, and as our whole economic life became more complex, more authority and more functions were assigned to the federal government. Foreign relations have also caused the federal government to grow in importance. The federal government has always had charge of our affairs with other countries. As the United States became more influential in world affairs, the President, the Congress, and the Department of State had more responsible roles to play.

xviii

LOCAL GOVERNMENT PROVIDES,
among other services:

Police Protection
Fire Protection
Water Supply
Sanitation
Street Maintenance
Public Schools

and spends, out of the tax dollar, about 11¢

Local Water Supply

STATE GOVERNMENT PROVIDES,
among other services:

Schools and Colleges
Welfare Services
Highway Maintenance
State Police
Hospitals
Prisons

and spends, out of the tax dollar, about 15¢

State Police

Despite the present large size of the federal government, it is well to keep in mind that the states have at all times been an important part of our governmental system. Local governments could not exist and function without the powers granted to them by the states. And the federal government could not have come into existence had not the states consented to give up some of their powers for the larger good of all citizens.

In the charts on the next few pages you will see what some of the machinery of the federal government is like. As you look at the charts, you need to bear in mind two fundamental ideas that were written into the Constitution many years ago and that still have vital importance. First, the legislative branch makes the laws, the executive branch enforces the laws, and the judicial branch interprets the laws. Second, under the principle known as separation of powers, each branch has its own separate functions and may not interfere with the functions of the other two except in certain ways that are specified in the Constitution.

Turn now to the next two pages and study the chart showing the organization of the executive branch of the federal government — that part of the government directly supervised by the President. Then turn to the Constitution and read Article II, the Executive Department (page xxxix), to learn about the duties and the authority of the President and about the method by which he is elected.

xix

FEDERAL GOVERNMENT PROVIDES,
among other services:

Military Security
Social Security
Postal Service
Flood Control, Conservation
Financial Support to Agriculture,
   Industry, Trade, and Education

and spends, out of the tax dollar, about 74¢

Rural Mail Carrier

THE PRESIDENT

EXECUTIVE OFFICES OF THE PRESIDENT

Council of Economic Advisers   •   National Security Council

Bureau of the Budget • National Security Resources Board

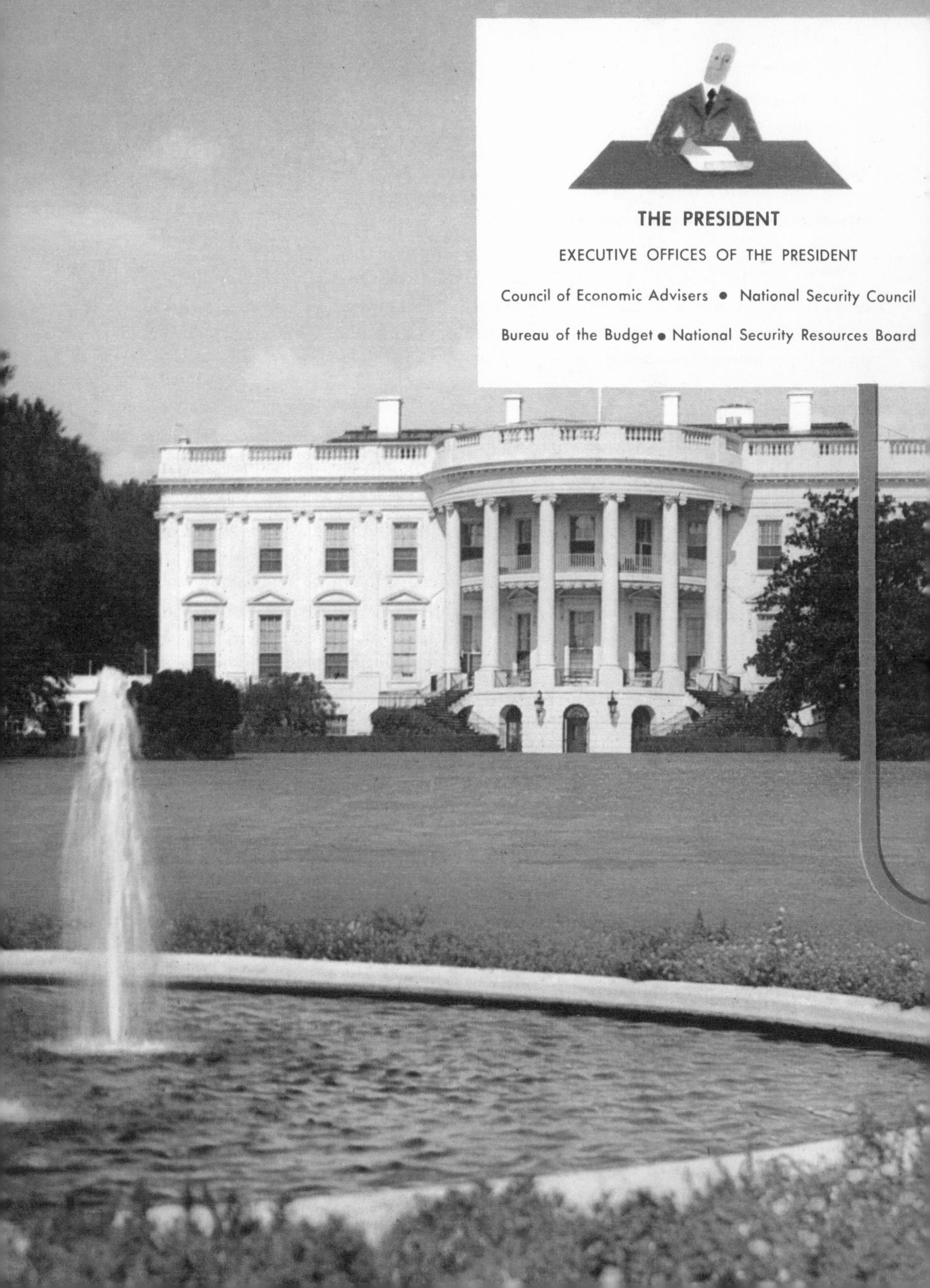

the Federal Government

THE CABINET

DEPARTMENT OF AGRICULTURE
POST OFFICE DEPARTMENT
DEPARTMENT OF NATIONAL DEFENSE
DEPARTMENT OF THE TREASURY
DEPARTMENT OF LABOR
THE PRESIDENT
VICE-PRESIDENT
DEPARTMENT OF STATE
DEPARTMENT OF COMMERCE
DEPARTMENT OF JUSTICE
DEPARTMENT OF THE INTERIOR

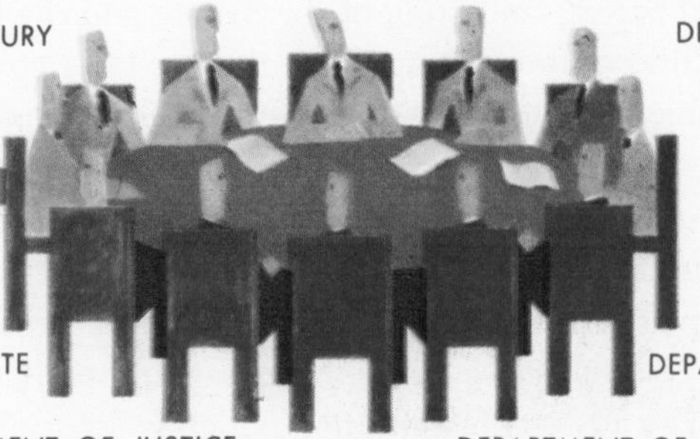

INDEPENDENT OFFICES AND ESTABLISHMENTS

Federal Reserve System
Federal Security Agency
Federal Mediation and Conciliation Service
Federal Communications Commission
Interstate Commerce Commission
Atomic Energy Commission
Federal Works Agency
Federal Deposit Insurance Corporation
Reconstruction Finance Corporation
Securities and Exchange Commission
Housing and Home Finance Agency
Civil Aeronautics Board
Selective Service System
Veterans Administration
National Capital Park and Planning Commission
Civil Service Commission

THE CONGRESS

Americans have always been firmly attached to the idea of representative government. Our forefathers were so greatly interested in its operation that they dealt with it in the first Article of the Constitution. That Article sets forth the powers and duties of the country's highest legislative body — the Congress of the United States, consisting of the Senate and the House of Representatives.

The first duty of Congress is to pass laws governing any activity like interstate commerce which falls within the authority of the federal government. The procedures which a bill may follow in order to become a law are shown in the chart opposite this page. To speed up and smooth out the process of lawmaking, both the Senate and the House of Representatives maintain Standing Committees to study bills before they are introduced for debate. When Senate and House fail to agree on a bill, a Conference Committee is appointed to work out a compromise. For advice on legislation which is especially important and complicated, Congress establishes Joint Committees of the House and Senate.

Political parties exercise great influence and perform useful functions in Congress. Members from the party holding a majority of seats in the House elect the Speaker of the House. The Vice-President of the United States serves as President of the Senate, but the majority party in the Senate elects a President Pro-Tempore to fill that post when the Vice-President is absent. The majority party also selects the chairmen and most of the other members for all congressional committees, a very important privilege.

In order to secure as many votes as possible for legislation favored by the party, members of both the minority and majority parties are selected to talk and work persuasively among the other congressmen. These members, in both the Senate and House, are called "floor leaders" and "whips." An individual member of Congress often votes for or against a certain bill according to the viewpoint of his party, but he is free to ignore his party if he chooses.

Turn now to the chart on the next two-page spread to see how Congress is organized. Then read Article I of the Constitution (page xxxiii), which outlines the powers and duties assigned to the Legislative Department.

A senator (RIGHT) chats with a voter. This is one of several means used by congressmen to sound out public opinion.

How A Bill in Congress Becomes a Law

Bill is introduced in House and referred to appropriate committee.

It may be reported out with or without change —or it may be shelved.

Rules ("traffic") Committee may delay bill, but this power is now limited.

Senate committee considers bill, may shelve it or report it out to the floor.

House then debates the bill. If it is passed (with or without revision), bill is sent to the Senate.

Chairman of original committee may bring bill to floor of House.

If Senate passes bill differing from House bill, both versions go to Conference Committee.

Conference Committee may adopt a compromise. This is submitted to House and Senate.

If House and Senate accept the compromise, the bill goes to the President for signature.

This chart shows typical procedure for bills originating in the House of Representatives. Bills which originate in the Senate follow similar procedure.

If President signs, bill becomes law. If he vetoes, Congress can override his veto by two-thirds majority.

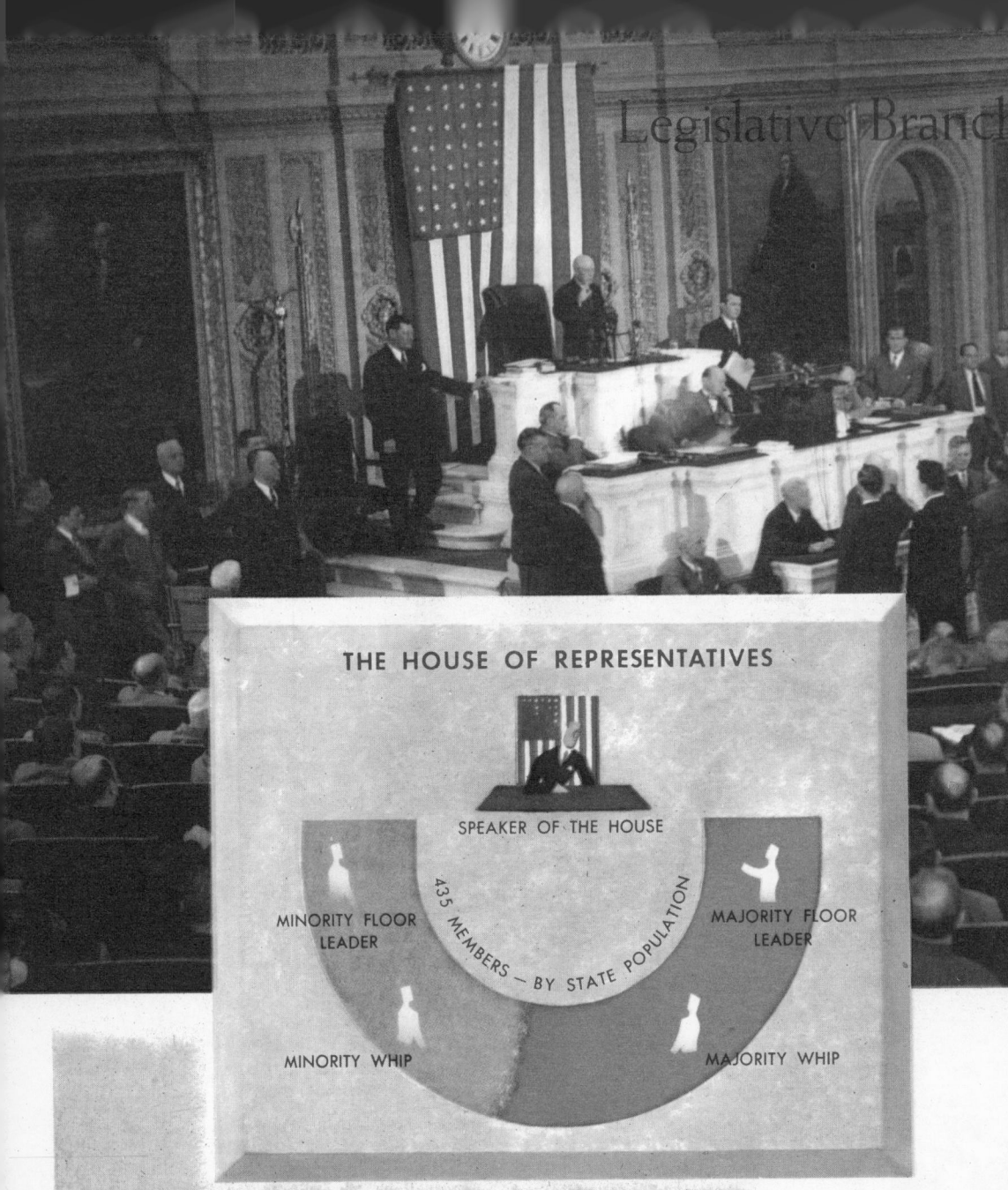

THE HOUSE OF REPRESENTATIVES

SPEAKER OF THE HOUSE

435 MEMBERS — BY STATE POPULATION

MINORITY FLOOR
LEADER

MAJORITY FLOOR
LEADER

MINORITY WHIP

MAJORITY WHIP

STANDING COMMITTEES

Agriculture
Appropriations
Armed Services
Banking and Currency
District of Columbia
Education and Labor
Expenditures in the Executive
    Departments
Foreign Affairs
House Administration

Interstate and Foreign Commerce
Judiciary
Merchant Marine and Fisheries
Post Office and Civil Service
Public Lands
Public Works
Rules
Un-American Activities
Veterans' Affairs
Ways and Means

JOINT COMMITTEES

Atomic Energy
Foreign Economic Cooperc
Internal Revenue Taxation

THE SENATE

PRESIDENT OF THE SENATE

MINORITY FLOOR
LEADER

96 MEMBERS — 2 FROM EACH STATE

MAJORITY FLOOR
LEADER

MINORITY WHIP

MAJORITY WHIP

E HOUSE AND SENATE

bor-Management Relations
e Economic Report
and Others

STANDING COMMITTEES

Agriculture and Forestry

Appropriations

Armed Services

Banking and Currency

District of Columbia

Expenditures in the Executive
    Departments

Finance

Foreign Relations

Interior and Insular Affairs

Interstate and Foreign Commerce

Judiciary

Labor and Public Welfare

Post Office and Civil Service

Public Works

Rules and Administration

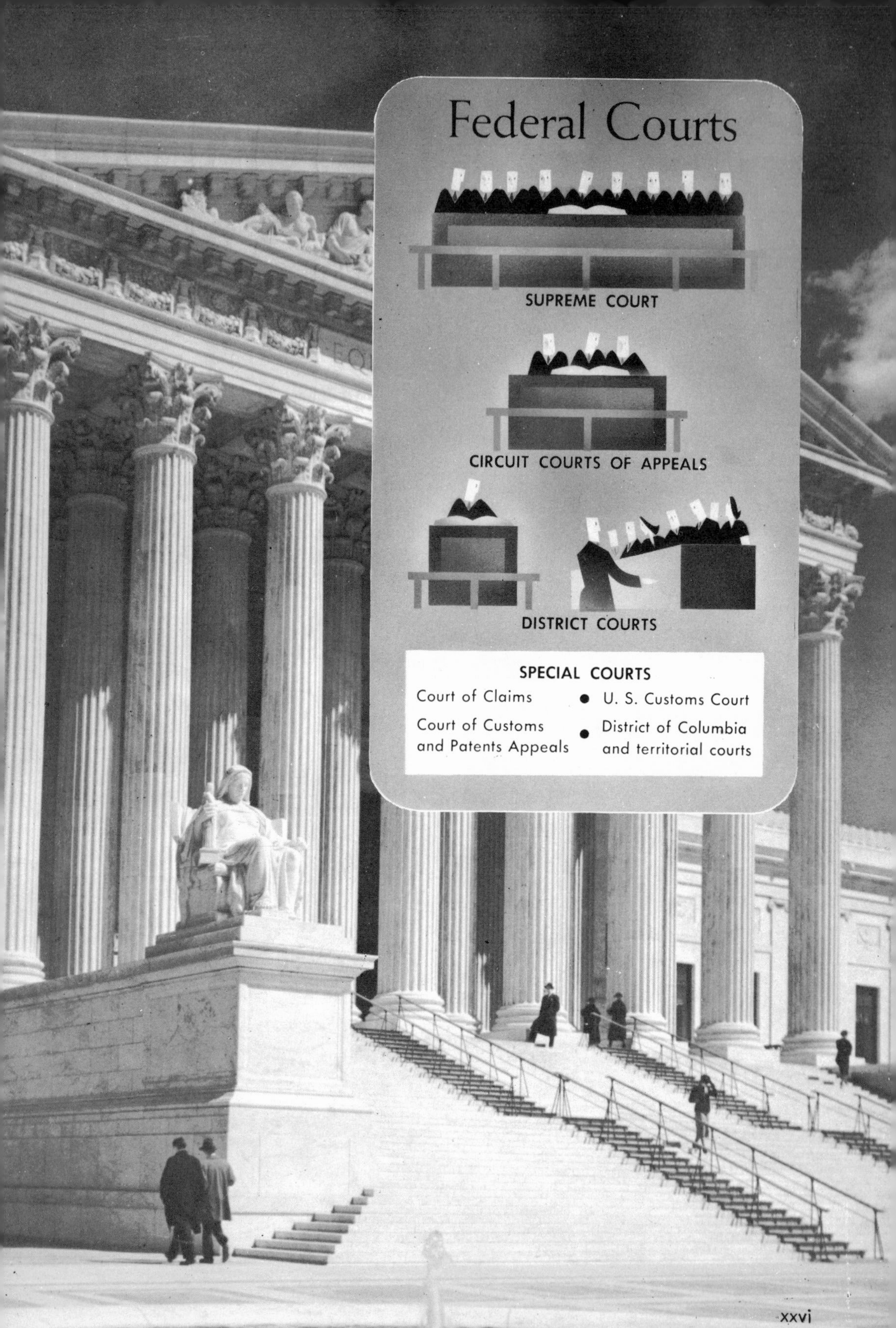

Federal Courts

SUPREME COURT

CIRCUIT COURTS OF APPEALS

DISTRICT COURTS

SPECIAL COURTS

Court of Claims

Court of Customs
and Patents Appeals

• U. S. Customs Court

• District of Columbia
and territorial courts

THE JUDICIAL BRANCH

The Constitution established a Supreme Court of the United States, and directed Congress to create lesser courts as they became necessary. The chart on the facing page shows the kinds of federal courts now in existence. They differ from one another mainly according to the nature of the cases with which they deal. They are alike in that they hand down justice to those who are charged with breaking laws which fall within the authority of the federal government. Turn now to Article III of the Constitution (page xli) and read what it says about the Judicial Department. Notice especially in Section 2 the kinds of cases that fall under the authority of the federal court system.

The most famous and most influential of American Courts is the Supreme Court of the United States. Its decisions in any case it tries are final unless it chooses to reverse its own ruling. Cases originating in the lesser federal courts, or in state courts when the cases involve the Constitution, may under certain conditions be carried up to the Supreme Court for final judgment. Also, the Supreme Court established early in our history its right to decide whether the acts of Congress and of state legislatures were in accord with the Constitution.

THE HANDLING OF FOREIGN AFFAIRS

The relations of the United States with other countries are a particular responsibility of the federal government, which must shape foreign policy and conduct foreign affairs in a way which will ultimately satisfy a majority of American citizens. Committees on foreign relations in the House and the Senate take a hand in that task, but the largest measure of responsibility rests with the President. He is assisted by many of the offices and departments in the Executive Branch (see chart on pages xx-xxi), but most of his advice and help in foreign relations comes from the Department of State.

The chart on the next two pages shows how the Department of State is organized and illustrates the worldwide character of its work. Night and day, year in and year out, messages come to the State Department from the embassies, legations, and other foreign offices of the United States. The messages come by cable, radio, telephone, telegram, courier, or diplomatic pouch, and tell department officials what is going on all over the world. The State Department in turn dispatches daily an endless stream of inquiries, instructions, and advice to its foreign offices, which make known wherever they are located the official views and policies of the United States Government.

The Department of State

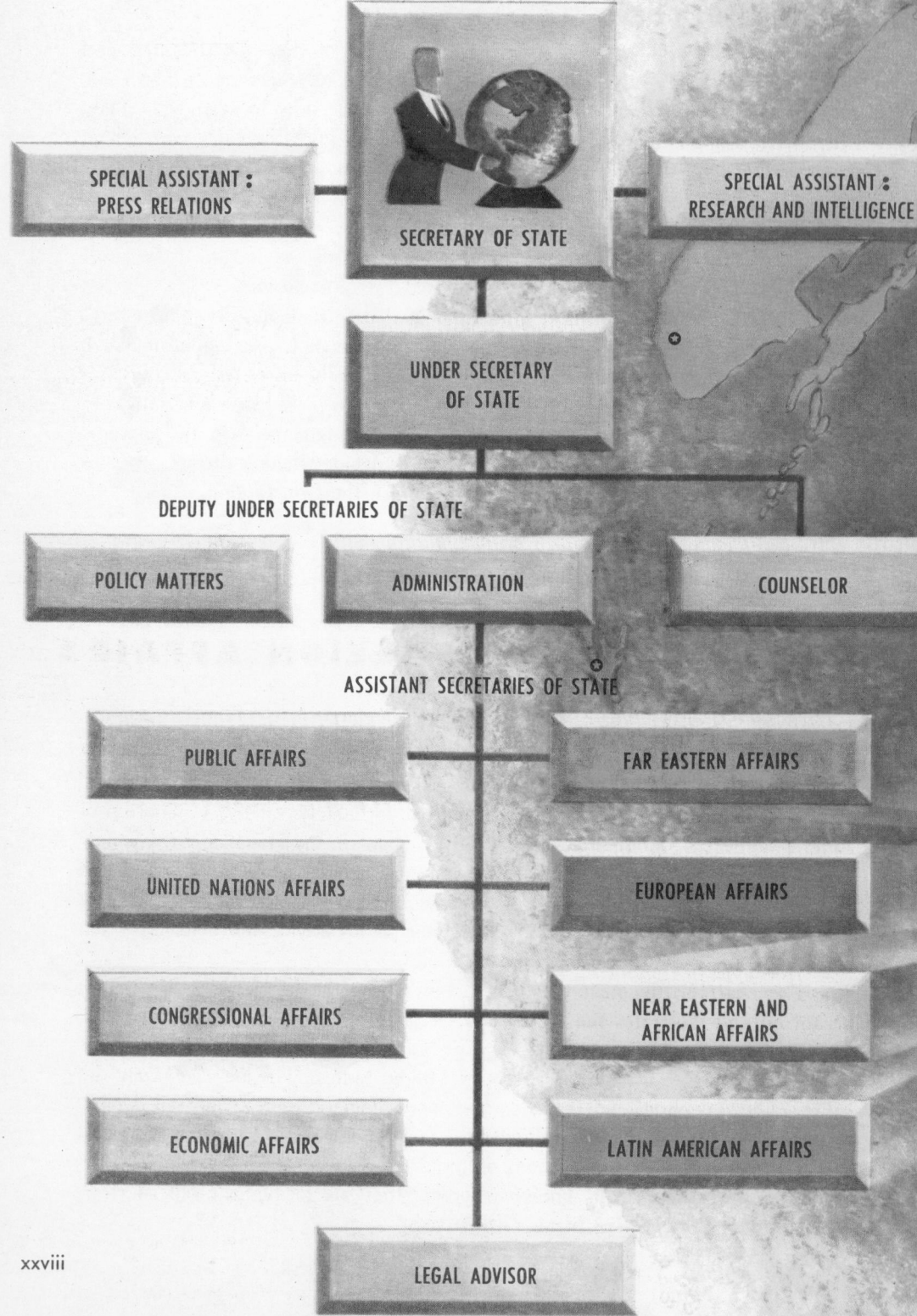

SECRETARY OF STATE

SPECIAL ASSISTANT:
PRESS RELATIONS

SPECIAL ASSISTANT:
RESEARCH AND INTELLIGENCE

UNDER SECRETARY
OF STATE

DEPUTY UNDER SECRETARIES OF STATE

POLICY MATTERS

ADMINISTRATION

COUNSELOR

ASSISTANT SECRETARIES OF STATE

PUBLIC AFFAIRS

FAR EASTERN AFFAIRS

UNITED NATIONS AFFAIRS

EUROPEAN AFFAIRS

CONGRESSIONAL AFFAIRS

NEAR EASTERN AND
AFRICAN AFFAIRS

ECONOMIC AFFAIRS

LATIN AMERICAN AFFAIRS

LEGAL ADVISOR

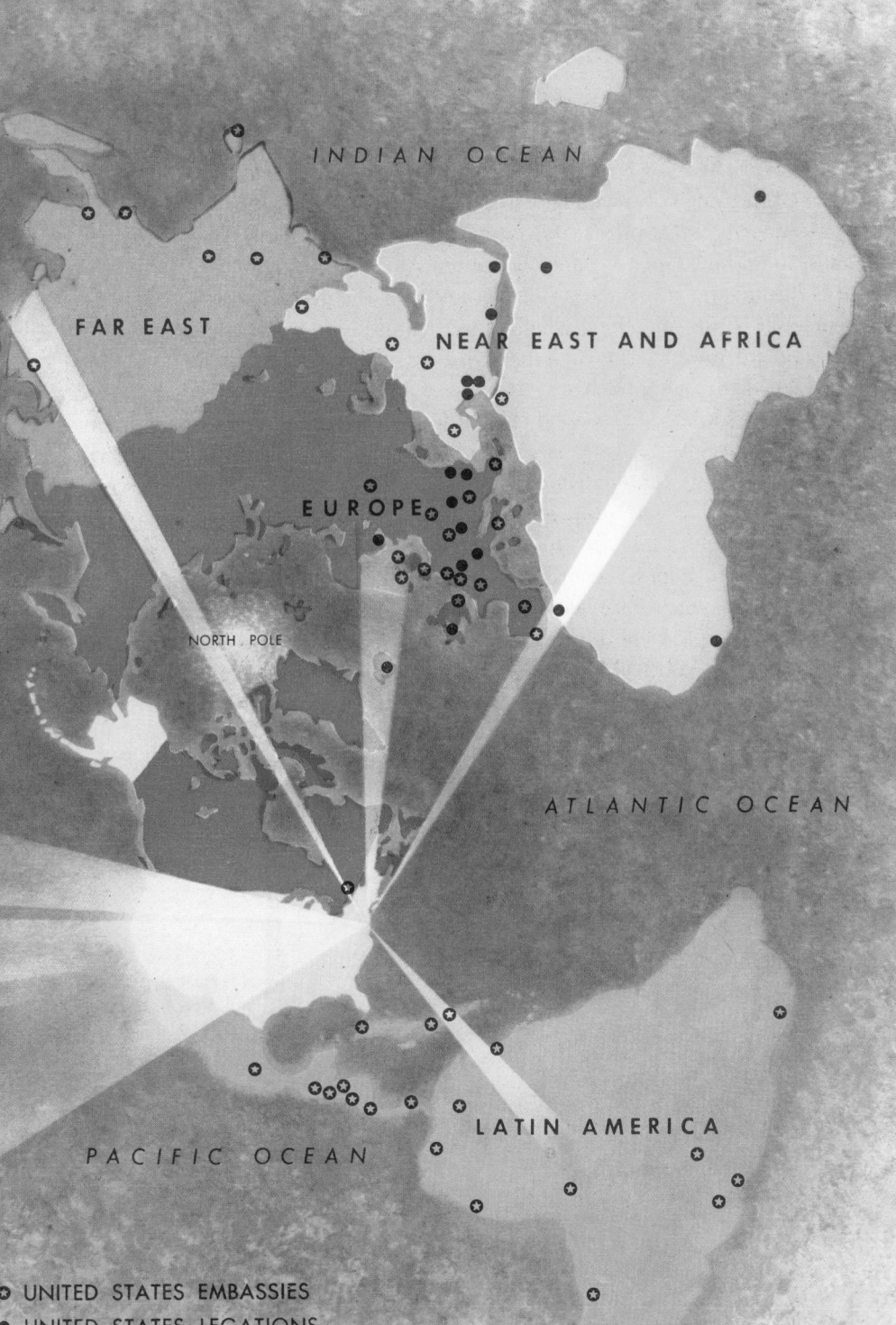

INDIAN OCEAN

FAR EAST

NEAR EAST AND AFRICA

EUROPE

NORTH POLE

ATLANTIC OCEAN

PACIFIC OCEAN

LATIN AMERICA

✪ UNITED STATES EMBASSIES
● UNITED STATES LEGATIONS

YOU AND YOUR GOVERNMENT

In the foregoing pages you have seen how many of the agencies and officials of American government use the powers and carry out the duties assigned to them. The most important thing to remember about American government, however, is that it is democratic government — government of the people, by the people, for the people. It is not something wholly apart from the body of citizens. In other words, *you* are the government when you use the powers and carry out the duties assigned to each citizen.

Some of the things that a good citizen does are pictured on page xxxii. One of the most important is to vote, as soon as you are old enough, for public officials who will try to do the things which you believe should be done. Another is to keep well informed about public issues and the record of public officials so that you will be able, when you vote, to vote intelligently. Still another is to use every available means to express your opinion about public issues so that a public official may hear your voice along with many others, and thus learn what a majority of the people want done. When you carry out these and other functions of good citizenship you will be joining with the millions of individual Americans who have made your country what it is today and who will decide what it is to become in the future.

A new voter studies the ballot before voting. The polling place is a rural schoolhouse.

THE YOUNG MAN above and the young woman at the left are about to vote, one of the most important functions of citizenship in a democracy. If they have studied the issues carefully, and know the records of the officials up for election, their votes will be important. Among other uses, their votes will help to lay down a course of action for American government which will meet the approval of a majority of intelligent American citizens.

What the Good Citizen Does

VOTES INTELLIGENTLY

KEEPS WELL INFORMED

HELPS CREATE PUBLIC OPINION

PAYS TAXES

SERVES ON JURIES

SERVES IN PUBLIC OFFICES

PERFORMS MILITARY SERVICE

HELPS IN WORK OF POLITICAL PARTIES

THE CONSTITUTION OF THE UNITED STATES OF AMERICA

Adopted in 1787-1788

A VAST NUMBER of books, articles, and legal opinions have been written about our Constitution. Some men have spent most of their lives trying to understand all of its possible meanings, or even a small part of them. The average citizen, of course, has neither the time nor the legal training to study the subject so deeply. But there are certain minimum essentials about the Constitution which every citizen should try to understand. They are the bedrock on which American democracy is built.

The following pages will start you in the direction of understanding these minimum essentials of this greatest public document of the American people.

The Constitution is printed below in the wider column at the left. The actual words of the document are printed in regular type (like this: We the People). For easier reading, various headings and subheadings have been added in bolder type (like this: **Legislative Department, Congress in General,** and **Election and Term of Members**). Certain portions of the Constitution which are no longer in effect are printed in italic type (like this: *which shall be determined*).

Throughout the text you will find superior numbers (like this: [2]). These refer to the numbers in the narrower column at the right, where there are notes to help you understand what the Constitution means.

THE TEXT OF THE CONSTITUTION

PREAMBLE

We the People of the United States,[1] in order to form a more perfect union, establish justice, insure domestic tranquillity, provide for the common defence, promote the general welfare, and secure the blessings of liberty to ourselves and our posterity, do ordain and establish this Constitution for the United States of America.[2]

ARTICLE I
Legislative Department

SECTION 1. Congress in General

All legislative powers herein granted shall be vested in a Congress of the United States, which shall consist of a Senate and House of Representatives.[3]

SECTION 2. The House of Representatives

a. Election and term of members. The House of Representatives shall be composed of members chosen every second year by the people of the several States,[4] and the electors [5] in each state shall have the qualifications requisite for electors of the most numerous branch of the State Legislature.[6]

NOTES

1. These opening words of the Constitution clearly indicate that the sovereign power (the power to establish a government or change it) belongs to the people.
2. The preamble states objectives. It does not confer power.
3. Under the Great Compromise (page 134) the Senate was to represent the states equally; in the House, membership was to be divided among the states according to population.
4. There is a new House every two years. When the government started, only the House was popularly elected. The Constitution does not state the qualifications for voters. That power was left to the states, subject later to the 15th and 19th Amendments.
5. "Electors" here means voters. For another meaning, see page 140.
6. In most states, the larger branch of the state legislature was popularly elected.

b. Qualification of members. No person shall be a Representative who shall not have attained to the age of twenty-five years, and been seven years a citizen of the United States, and who shall not, when elected, be an inhabitant of that State in which he shall be chosen.

c. Apportionment of representatives and of direct taxes. Representatives and direct taxes [1] shall be apportioned among the several States which may be included within this Union, according to their respective numbers, *which shall be determined by adding to the whole number of free persons, including those bound to service for a term of years,*[2] *and excluding Indians not taxed,*[3] *three fifths of all other persons.*[4] The actual enumeration shall be made within three years after the first meeting of the Congress of the United States, and within every subsequent term of ten years, in such manner as they shall by law direct.[5] The number of Representatives shall not exceed one for every thirty thousand, but each State shall have at least one representative; *and until such enumeration shall be made, the State of New Hampshire shall be entitled to choose three; Massachusetts, eight; Rhode Island and Providence Plantations, one; Connecticut, five; New York, six; New Jersey, four; Pennsylvania, eight; Delaware, one; Maryland, six; Virginia, ten; North Carolina, five; South Carolina, five; and Georgia, three.*

d. Filling vacancies. When vacancies happen in the representation from any State, the Executive authority thereof shall issue writs of election to fill such vacancies.[6]

e. Officers; impeachment. The House of Representatives shall choose their Speaker and other officers; and shall have the sole power of impeachment.[7]

Section 3. The Senate

a. Number and election of members. The Senate of the United States shall be composed of two Senators from each state, *chosen by the legislature thereof,*[8] for six years; and each Senator shall have one vote.

b. Classification. Immediately after they shall be assembled in consequence of the first election, they shall be divided as equally as may be into three classes. *The seats of the Senators of the first class shall be vacated at the expiration of the second year, of the second class at the expiration of the fourth year, and of the third class at the expiration of the sixth year,* so that one third may be chosen every second year;[9] and if vacancies happen by resignation, or otherwise, during the recess of the legislature of any State, the Executive thereof may make temporary appointments until the next meeting of the legislature, which shall then fill such vacancies.[10]

c. Qualifications of members. No person shall be a Senator who shall not have attained to the age of thirty years, and been nine years a citizen of the United States,[11] and who

1. A direct tax is usually paid by the person on whom it is imposed; an indirect tax is usually shifted to the consumer by the person againt whom it is levied. Amendment 16 now permits Congress to levy an income tax without such apportionment.

2. This phrase refers to indentured servants.

3. Indians are now citizens (page 354).

4. "Persons" here means slaves.

5. A national census is taken every ten years. A law now provides that Congress shall reapportion membership among the states after each census.

6. A special election is held in the state to fill a vacancy in the House.

7. Only the House has power to impeach (accuse) a civil officer of the United States for "treason, bribery, or other high crimes and misdemeanors." See Article II, Section 4. The Senate tries cases of impeachment. See Article I, Section 3, clause "f."

8. Under Amendment 17 senators are now elected by voters who have the same qualifications as voters for members of the House. Thus, both houses are now popularly elected.

9. There is never a new Senate. The terms of only one-third of its members expire in any election year.

10. Amendment 17 provides for special elections to fill Senate vacancies, as in the case of the House. The state legislature, however, may give the governor power to make a temporary appointment until an election is held.

11. Age qualifications for a senator are higher than for a representative. Thus, the Senate includes older and more experienced men. This fact, as well as the longer term of senators and the continuous nature of the Senate, makes for a more stable and experienced legislative body.

shall not, when elected, be an inhabitant of that State for which he shall be chosen.

d. President of Senate. The Vice President of the United States shall be President of the Senate, but shall have no vote, unless they be equally divided.[1]

e. Other Officers. The Senate shall choose their own officers, and also a President *pro tempore*,[2] in the absence of the Vice President, or when he shall exercise the office of President of the United States.

f. Trial of impeachment. The Senate shall have the sole power to try all impeachments. When sitting for that purpose, they shall be on oath or affirmation. When the President of the United States is tried, the Chief Justice shall preside; and no person shall be convicted without the concurrence of two thirds of the members present.[3]

g. Judgment in case of conviction. Judgment in cases of impeachment shall not extend further than to removal from office, and disqualification to hold and enjoy any office of honor, trust or profit under the United States; but the party convicted shall nevertheless be liable and subject to indictment, trial, judgment and punishment, according to law.[4]

Section 4. Election and Meetings of Congressmen

a. Method of holding elections. The times, places and manner of holding elections for Senators and Representatives shall be prescribed in each State by the legislature thereof; but the Congress may at any time by law make or alter such regulations, except as to the places of choosing Senators.[5]

b. Meeting of Congress. The Congress shall assemble at least once in every year, *and such meeting shall be on the first Monday in December,* unless they shall by law appoint a different day.[6]

Section 5. Rules of Procedure

a. Organization. Each house shall be the judge of the elections, returns and qualifications of its own members,[7] and a majority of each shall constitute a quorum to do business; but a smaller number may adjourn from day to day, and may be authorized to compel the attendance of absent members, in such manner, and under such penalties as each house may provide.

b. Rules of proceedings. Each house may determine the rules of its proceedings,[8] punish its members for disorderly behavior, and, with the concurrence of two thirds, expel a member.[9]

c. Journal. Each house shall keep a journal of its proceedings, and from time to time publish the same, excepting such parts as may in their judgment require secrecy;[10] and the yeas and nays of the members of either house on

1. This is the only duty assigned in the Constitution to the Vice-President. In recent years dignity has been added by the President's invitation to take part in cabinet meetings.

2. *Pro tempore* means "for the time being."

3. Impeachment is one of the cases in which a two-thirds vote of those present is required.

4. If the Senate finds the officer guilty as charged, it may remove him from office and disqualify him from holding another office under the United States. The person convicted may also be tried for the same offense before the regular courts.

5. Except in Maine, which holds its election in September, congressional elections are held on the Tuesday after the first Monday in November of the even numbered years. Congress has also provided for a secret ballot, and permits the use of voting machines.

6. Before 1933 the first regular session of a Congress began in December of the odd-numbered year and its last regular session began in December of the even-numbered year. For a change in this procedure, turn to Amendment 20, page xlix.

7. Either house may refuse to seat a newly-elected member. Also, disputed elections may finally be settled in the House or Senate as the case may be.

8. Extensive rules of procedure have grown up in Congress. They cover the duties of officers and committees and the order and means of conducting business. In general, Senate rules are less strict than House rules.

9. Expulsion from either house requires a two-thirds vote.

10. Of greater importance than the journal is the *Congressional Record,* issued daily during sessions of Congress.

any question shall, at the desire of one fifth of those present, be entered on the journal.[1]

d. **Adjournment.** Neither house, during the session of Congress, shall, without the consent of the other, adjourn for more than three days, nor to any other place than that in which the two houses shall be sitting.

SECTION 6. Compensation, Privileges, and Restrictions

a. **Pay and privileges of members.** The Senators and Representatives shall receive a compensation for their services, to be ascertained by law, and paid out of the Treasury of the United States.[2] They shall in all cases, except treason, felony and breach of the peace, be privileged from arrest during their attendance at the session of their respective houses, and in going to and returning from the same;[3] and for any speech or debate in either house, they shall not be questioned in any other place.

b. **Holding other offices prohibited.**[4] No Senator or Representative shall, during the time for which he was elected, be appointed to any civil office under the authority of the United States which shall have been created, or the emoluments[5] whereof shall have been increased during such time; and no person holding any office under the United States shall be a member of either house during his continuance in office.

SECTION 7. Mode of Passing Laws

a. **Revenue bills.** All bills for raising revenue shall originate in the House of Representatives;[6] but the Senate may propose or concur with amendments as on other bills.

b. **How bills become laws.** Every bill which shall have passed the House of Representatives and the Senate shall, before it become a law, be presented to the President of the United States;[7] if he approve he shall sign it, but if not he shall return it, with his objections to that house in which it shall have originated, who shall enter the objections at large on their journal, and proceed to reconsider it. If after such reconsideration two thirds of that house shall agree to pass the bill, it shall be sent, together with the objections, to the other house, by which it shall likewise be reconsidered, and if approved by two thirds of that house, it shall become a law. But in all such cases the votes of both houses shall be determined by yeas and nays, and the names of the persons voting for and against the bill shall be entered on the journal of each house respectively. If any bill shall not be returned by the President within ten days (Sundays excepted) after it shall have been presented to him, the same shall be a law, in like manner as if he had signed it, unless the Congress by their adjournment prevent its return, in which case it shall not be a law.[8]

c. **Approval or disapproval by the President.** Every order, resolution, or vote to which the concurrence of the Senate

1. One fifth of those present can make the members of either house stand up and be counted.

2. This provision served to strengthen the federal government in its early days. Unless the new government succeeded, the members of the early Congress would receive no pay. In 1951 the compensation of congressmen was $12,500 per year ($30,000 for the Speaker of the House), plus liberal allowances for travel, clerk hire, stationery, and other uses. Congressmen also enjoy the franking privilege, or the right to send free any mail stamped with their name.

3. Members of Congress are free from arrest in any civil process. For almost any criminal offense they may be arrested.

4. This section places certain limitations upon members of Congress.

5. This means salary or other compensation.

6. Tariff or income-tax measures are examples of revenue bills. By custom, bills appropriating money also originate in the House. Actually the Senate exerts much influence over revenue bills through its power of amendment.

7. Before a bill is sent to the President, it must be passed in identical form by both houses. Frequently, when the two houses cannot agree on the same form of a bill, the differences are ironed out in a Conference Committee composed of members of both houses.

8. If a President takes no action on a bill for ten days (Sundays excepted), it becomes a law without his signature provided Congress is still in session. If Congress has adjourned, the bill is dead. This is known as a "pocket veto."

and House of Representatives may be necessary (except on a question of adjournment) shall be presented to the President of the United States; and before the same shall take effect, shall be approved by him, or being disapproved by him, shall be repassed by two thirds of the Senate and House of Representatives, according to the rules and limitations prescribed in the case of a bill.[1]

Section 8. Powers Granted to Congress[2]

The Congress shall have power

a. To lay and collect taxes, duties, imposts, and excises, to pay the debts and provide for the common defence and general welfare of the United States; but all duties, imposts and excises shall be uniform throughout the United States;[3]

b. To borrow money on the credit of the United States;[4]

c. To regulate commerce with foreign nations, and among the several States, and with the Indian tribes;[5]

d. To establish an uniform rule of naturalization, and uniform laws on the subject of bankruptcies throughout the United States;[6]

e. To coin money, regulate the value thereof, and of foreign coin, and fix the standard of weights and measures;

f. To provide for the punishment of counterfeiting the securities and current coin of the United States;

g. To establish post offices and post roads;

h. To promote the progress of science and useful arts, by securing for limited times to authors and inventors the exclusive right to their respective writings and discoveries;[7]

i. To constitute tribunals inferior to the Supreme Court;

j. To define and punish piracies and felonies committed on the high seas and offences against the law of nations;

k. To declare war,[8] grant letters of marque and reprisal,[9] and make rules concerning captures on land and water;

l. To raise and support armies,[10] but no appropriation of money to that use shall be for a longer term than two years;

m. To provide and maintain a navy;

n. To make rules for the government and regulation of the land and naval forces;

o. To provide for calling forth the militia to execute the laws of the Union, suppress insurrections and repel invasions;

p. To provide for organizing, arming, and disciplining the militia, and for governing such part of them as may be employed in the service of the United States, reserving to the States respectively the appointment of the officers,

1. A joint resolution, for example, must be passed and approved in the same manner as a bill.

2. Section 8 is one of the most important in the Constitution. A few other powers are granted to Congress, but here are gathered together its most important powers.

3. The taxing power had not been exercised by Congress under the Articles of Confederation. It was of great importance in the growth of the national government. Included are duties on imported goods, excises on goods produced in this country, as well as other taxes.

4. Borrowing is generally by the issuance of government bonds or certificates of indebtedness.

5. This is another very important power not exercised by Congress under the Confederation.

6. Bankruptcy legislation was largely left to the states until 1898. This is an example of a concurrent power (page 140).

7. This clause is the basis of our patent and copyright laws.

8. Congress alone has the power to declare war. Still, a situation may develop in which Congress has little or no choice.

9. This power to commission privateers to prey upon enemy commerce, which was important in the War of 1812, is no longer exercised by Congress.

10. The military powers of Congress are extensive.

and the authority of training the militia according to the discipline prescribed by Congress;[1]

q. To exercise exclusive legislation in all cases whatsoever, over such district (not exceeding ten miles square) as may, by cession of particular States, and the acceptance of Congress, become the seat of the government of the United States,[2] and to exercise like authority over all places purchased by the consent of the legislature of the State in which the same shall be for the erection of forts, magazines, arsenals, dock-yards, and other needful buildings; — and

r. To make all laws which shall be necessary and proper for carrying into execution the foregoing powers, and all other powers vested by this Constitution in the government of the United States, or in any department or officer thereof.[3]

SECTION 9. Powers Denied to the Federal Government

a. *The migration or importation of such persons as any of the States now existing shall think proper to admit, shall not be prohibited by the Congress prior to the year one thousand eight hundred and eight,[4] but a tax or duty may be imposed on such importation, not exceeding ten dollars for each person.*

b. The privilege of the writ of habeas corpus [5] shall not be suspended, unless when in cases of rebellion or invasion the public safety may require it.

c. No bill of attainder [6] or ex post facto law [7] shall be passed.

d. No capitation, or other direct, tax shall be laid, unless in proportion to the census or enumeration herein before directed to be taken.[8]

e. No tax or duty shall be laid on articles exported from any State.

f. No preference shall be given by any regulation of commerce or revenue to the ports of one State over those of another: nor shall vessels bound to, or from, one State be obliged to enter, clear, or pay duties in another.[9]

g. No money shall be drawn from the Treasury, but in consequence of appropriations made by law; [10] and a regular statement and account of the receipts and expenditures of all public money shall be published from time to time.

h. No title of nobility shall be granted by the United States: [11] and no person holding any office of profit or trust under them shall, without the consent of the Congress, accept of any present, emolument, office, or title, of any kind whatever, from any king, prince, or foreign state.

SECTION 10. Powers Denied to the States[12]

a. No State shall enter into any treaty, alliance, or confederation; grant letters of marque and reprisal; coin money; emit bills of credit; make any thing but gold and silver coin

1. In recent times the federal government has broadened its power over the militia.

2. This provision enables Congress to legislate for the District of Columbia.

3. This is the so-called "elastic clause." Whether it was to be interpreted strictly or broadly soon became a matter of bitter dispute between political parties (page 142). It is the basis for much legislation not authorized in any other provision. The taxing power and the commerce clause, in particular, have brought forth legislation not foreseen by the framers of the Constitution.

4. Congress, in its regulation of commerce, was not to prevent the importation of slaves for a period of 20 years (page 136).

5. The purpose of this writ is to prevent unreasonable imprisonment by having a person brought before a court to determine whether he is legally held. The Constitution does not say who may suspend it. Lincoln exercised this power, but the Supreme Court held that he could do so only when authorized by Congress.

6. This is a legislative measure which condemns a person without a trial in court.

7. This provision applies to a law making an act a crime which was not criminal when committed, or increasing the penalty for a crime already committed.

8. Except for an income tax, which the courts at first held not to be a direct tax, Congress has not exercised this power since 1861. Amendment 16 specifically authorized an income tax.

9. The purpose of this clause is to establish uniformity for all ports.

10. See note 6 on page xxxvi.

11. Even without this limitation Congress probably would never have been tempted to set up an order of nobility.

12. For the powers reserved to the states, turn to Amendment 10.

a tender in payment of debts; pass any bill of attainder; ex post facto law, or law impairing the obligation of contracts, or grant any title of nobility.[1]

b. No State shall, without the consent of the Congress, lay any imposts or duties on imports or exports, except what may be absolutely necessary for executing its inspection laws; and the net produce of all duties and imposts, laid by any State on imports or exports, shall be for the use of the treasury of the United States; and all such laws shall be subject to the revision and control of the Congress.

c. No State shall, without the consent of Congress, lay any duty of tonnage, keep troops,[2] or ships of war in time of peace, enter into any agreement or compact with another State, or with a foreign power, or engage in war, unless actually invaded, or in such imminent danger as will not admit of delay.[3]

ARTICLE II
Executive Department

SECTION 1. President and Vice President

a. Term of office. The executive power shall be vested in a President of the United States of America. He shall hold his office during the term of four years,[4] and, together with the Vice President, chosen for the same term, be elected as follows:

b. Electors. Each State shall appoint, in such manner as the legislature thereof may direct, a number of electors, equal to the whole number of Senators and Representatives to which the State may be entitled in the Congress; but no Senator or Representative, or person holding an office of trust or profit under the United States, shall be appointed an elector.[5]

Former method of electing President and Vice President.[6] *The electors shall meet in their respective States, and vote by ballot for two persons, of whom one at least shall not be an inhabitant of the same State with themselves. And they shall make a list of all the persons voted for, and of the number of votes for each; which list they shall sign and certify, and transmit sealed to the seat of the government of the United States, directed to the President of the Senate. The President of the Senate shall, in the presence of the Senate and House of Representatives, open all the certificates, and the votes shall then be counted. The person having the greatest number of votes shall be the President, if such number be a majority of the whole number of electors appointed; and if there be more than one who have such majority, and have an equal number of votes, then the House of Representatives shall immediately choose by ballot one of them for President; and if no person have a majority, then from the five highest on the list the said house shall in like manner choose the President. But in choosing the President the votes shall be taken by States,*

1. Some of these powers are also denied to the national government; others may be exercised by the federal government, but not by the states.

2. This does not prevent the state from having its own militia. See Amendment 2.

3. Clauses "b" and "c" enumerate powers which may only be exercised by the state with the consent of Congress or in an emergency.

4. The framers of the Constitution could not foresee the growth of power and prestige of the office of President. The four-year term without limitation as to reelection was a compromise between various plans.

5. Instead of placing the election of the Chief Executive directly in the hands of the voters, the Constitution provided for the selection of electors. The electors, in turn, would choose a President. Actually, the selection of electors today is not too important, since their vote is a formality (see the following note). Usually electors are prominent party members.

6. This section has been changed by Amendment 12, adopted in 1804. The Constitution makes no provision for the nominating conventions, but they have become as well established through custom as though they had been directly provided for. (See note 2, page xlvi.)

At the presidential elections in November, voters cast their ballots for electors who are pledged to vote for the candidates nominated by the conventions. The party which polls the greatest number of popular votes in a state gets *all* of the electoral votes of that state, and the other parties get none. The candidate who gets the greatest number of popular votes in the nation as a whole, therefore, does not necessarily win the election. For the present procedure in the electoral college, turn to Amendment 12, and the accompanying notes.

the representation from each State having one vote; a quorum for this purpose shall consist of a member or members from two thirds of the States, and a majority of all the States shall be necessary to a choice. In every case, after the choice of the President, the person having the greatest number of votes of the electors shall be the Vice President. But if there should remain two or more who have equal votes, the Senate shall choose from them by ballot the Vice President.

c. Time of elections. The Congress may determine the time of choosing the electors, and the day on which they shall give their votes; which day shall be the same throughout the United States.[1]

d. Qualifications of the President. No person except a natural born citizen, *or a citizen of the United States, at the time of the adoption of this Constitution,* shall be eligible to the office of President;[2] neither shall any person be eligible to that office who shall not have attained the age of thirty-five years, and been fourteen years a resident within the United States.

e. Vacancy. In case of the removal of the President from office or of his death, resignation, or inability to discharge the powers and duties of the said office,[3] the same shall devolve on the Vice President,[4] and the Congress may by law provide for the case of removal, death, resignation, or inability, both of the President and Vice President, declaring what officer shall then act as President, and such officer shall act accordingly, until the disability be removed, **or a President shall be elected.**[5]

f. The President's salary. The President shall, at stated times, receive for his services, a compensation, which shall neither be increased nor diminished during the period for which he shall have been elected, and he shall not receive within that period any other emolument from the United States, or any of them.[6]

g. Oath of office. Before he enter on the execution of his office, he shall take the following oath or affirmation: — "I do solemnly swear (or affirm) that I will faithfully execute the office of President of the United States, and will to the best of my ability, preserve, protect, and defend the Constitution of the United States."

SECTION 2. Powers of the President[7]

a. Military powers; reprieves and pardons. The President shall be commander in chief of the army and navy of the United States, and of the militia of the several States, when called into the actual service of the United States;[8] he may require the opinion, in writing, of the principal officer in each of the executive departments,[9] upon any subject relating to the duties of their respective offices, and he shall have power to grant reprieves and pardons for offences against the United States, except in cases of impeachment.

1. The popular vote for electors takes place on the Tuesday after the first Monday of November in each "leap year." In mid-December the electors meet in their state capitals and cast their electoral votes.

2. Today, of course, the President must be a natural born citizen, though the courts may interpret the clause to include some not actually born within the United States.

3. The Constitution does not state who shall determine this disability, and Congress has not attempted to legislate on the subject.

4. Tyler, the first Vice-President to succeed to the Presidency, took the title as well as the powers and duties of that office. This precedent has since been followed.

5. By act of 1947 Congress fixed the Speaker of the House and the President *pro tempore* of the Senate as next in line of succession. (See page 463 for the previous arrangement.)

6. In 1949 Congress fixed this salary at $100,000 per year plus a tax-free expense account of $50,000.

7. Section 2 and Section 3 make up another of the all-important parts of the Constitution.

8. As commander in chief, the President becomes very powerful in time of war.

9. No provision is made in the Constitution for a cabinet or for cabinet meetings. The existence of executive departments is implied here, however, and the cabinet developed during Washington's time (page 146).

b. Treaties; appointments. He shall have power, by and with the advice and consent of the Senate, to make treaties, provided two thirds of the Senators present concur; [1] and he shall nominate, and by and with the advice and consent of the Senate, shall appoint ambassadors, other public ministers and consuls, judges of the Supreme Court, and all other officers of the United States, whose appointments are not herein otherwise provided for, and which shall be established by law; [2] but the Congress may by law vest the appointment of such inferior officers as they think proper in the President alone, in the courts of law, or in the heads of departments. [3]

c. Filling vacancies. The President shall have power to fill up all vacancies that may happen during the recess of the Senate, by granting commissions which shall expire at the end of their next session.

Section 3. Duties of the President

He shall from time to time give to the Congress information of the state of the Union, and recommend to their consideration such measures as he shall judge necessary and expedient; [4] he may, on extraordinary occasions, convene both houses, or either of them, [5] and in case of disagreement between them with respect to the time of adjournment he may adjourn them to such time as he shall think proper; he shall receive ambassadors and other public ministers; [6] he shall take care that the laws be faithfully executed, [7] and shall commission all the officers of the United States.

Section 4. Impeachment

The President, Vice President and all civil officers of the United States shall be removed from office on impeachment for, and conviction of, treason, bribery, or other high crimes and misdemeanors.

ARTICLE III
Judicial Department

Section 1. The Federal Courts

The judicial power of the United States shall be vested in one Supreme Court, and in such inferior courts as the Congress may from time to time ordain and establish. [8] The judges, both of the Supreme and inferior courts, shall hold their offices during good behavior, [9] and shall, at stated times, receive for their services, a compensation, which shall not be diminished during their continuance in office.

Section 2. Jurisdiction of the Federal Courts

a. Federal courts in general. The judicial power shall extend to all cases, in law and equity, arising under this Constitution, the laws of the United States, and treaties made, or which shall be made, under their authority; — to all cases affecting ambassadors, other public ministers and consuls;

1. The President or his appointees draw up the treaty, which is then submitted to the Senate for ratification.

2. Ratification of treaties requires a two-thirds vote; ratification of appointments a simple majority.

3. Congress has, with the approval of the President, placed the appointment of the great majority of federal officeholders in the hands of the Civil Service Commission (page 459).

4. Annual and special messages are based upon this provision. Washington and Adams delivered their messages to Congress in person. Beginning with Jefferson, and continuing up to Wilson, the Presidents sent written messages to be read by the clerks.

5. Special sessions are here provided for.

6. This clause really gives the President the power to recognize or refuse to recognize a foreign government.

7. This clause is the basis of the President's executive power. Actually, the laws are carried out by the various departments, the heads of which make up the cabinet, and by special commissions and agencies.

The President exercises other powers. For the veto power see note 8, page xxxvi. The power of appointment carries with it the power of removal, which is not subject to approval by the Senate. From time to time, especially in national emergencies, special powers have been conferred upon the President. As leader of his party, and as spokesman for the people, a strong President may accomplish many things not provided for in the Constitution.

8. Under the Articles of Confederation there were no national courts. The organization of the Supreme Court, and the establishment of lower courts, is left to Congress. There are two main levels of inferior courts — Circuit Courts of Appeal and District Courts.

9. Judges are appointed virtually for life.

— to all cases of admiralty and maritime jurisdiction; — to controversies to which the United States shall be a party; — to controversies between two or more States; — *between a State and citizens of another State;* — between citizens of different States; — between citizens of the same State claiming lands under grants of different States, and between a State, or the citizens thereof, and foreign states, citizens or subjects.[1]

b. **Supreme Court.** In all cases affecting ambassadors, other public ministers and consuls, and those in which a State shall be a party, the Supreme Court shall have original jurisdiction.[2] In all the other cases before mentioned, the Supreme Court shall have appellate jurisdiction, both as to law and fact, with such exceptions, and under such regulations as the Congress shall make.

c. **Rules respecting trials.** The trial of all crimes, except in cases of impeachment, shall be by jury;[3] and such trial shall be held in the State where the said crimes shall have been committed; but when not committed within any State, the trial shall be at such place or places as the Congress may by law have directed.

SECTION 3. Treason

a. **Definition of treason.** Treason against the United States shall consist only in levying war against them, or in adhering to their enemies, giving them aid and comfort.[4] No person shall be convicted of treason unless on the testimony of two witnesses to the same overt act, or on confession in open court.[5]

b. **Punishment of treason.** The Congress shall have power to declare the punishment of treason, but no attainder of treason shall work corruption of blood, or forfeiture except during the life of the person attainted.[6]

ARTICLE IV
The States and the Federal Government
SECTION 1. State Records

Full faith and credit shall be given in each State to the public acts, records, and judicial proceedings of every other State.[7] And the Congress may by general laws prescribe the manner in which such acts, records, and proceedings shall be proved, and the effect thereof.

SECTION 2. Privileges and Immunities of Citizens

a. **Privileges.** The citizens of each State shall be entitled to all privileges and immunities of citizens in the several States.[8]

b. **Extradition.** A person charged in any State with treason, felony, or other crime, who shall flee from justice and be found in another State shall, on demand of the executive authority of the State from which he fled, be delivered up, to be removed to the State having jurisdiction of the crime.[9]

1. In general two classes of cases come before the federal courts: (1) because of the nature of the case, for example, a case arising under the Constitution, federal laws, treaties, or affecting ships on the high seas or in United States waters; (2) because of the nature of the parties involved, — the United States, a state, an ambassador, citizens of different states, etc. (See note 1, page xlvi.)

2. Most federal cases start in the lower courts, such as the United States District Court. Only the special cases listed here may be started in the Supreme Court. Much of the Supreme Court's work has to do with cases appealed from lower federal courts or from state courts (appellate jurisdiction).

3. Here a jury trial is provided only for criminal cases, but Amendments 5, 6, and 7 have added to this clause.

4. Instead of leaving the definition of treason to Congress, the Constitution limits treason to specific offenses.

5. For conviction, there must be two witnesses to the same actual act of treason, or confession in open court.

6. Congress may provide the punishment of treason, but punishment cannot extend to the descendants of the traitor.

7. For example, a will drawn up legally in New Jersey would be examined and approved in Connecticut courts even though it did not meet the requirements of Connecticut law. On the other hand, some of the states are reluctant to accept divorce decrees of Nevada courts, where the laws are very lenient.

8. A citizen of Oregon, for example, going into California, would be entitled to all the privileges of a citizen of California but no more. See Amendment 14.

9. Usually the governor gives up such a person without question. He may, however, exercise his judgment, and there is no way to force him to surrender the accused.

c. Fugitive workers. *No person held to service or labor in one State, under the laws thereof, escaping into another shall, in consequence of any law or regulation therein, be discharged from such service or labor, but shall be delivered upon claim of the party to whom such service or labor may be due.*[1]

SECTION 3. New States and Territories

a. Admission of new States. New States may be admitted by the Congress into this Union; but no new State shall be formed or erected within the jurisdiction of any other State; nor any State be formed by the junction of two or more States, or parts of States, without the consent of the legislatures of the States concerned, as well as of the Congress.[2]

b. Power of Congress over territory and property. The Congress shall have power to dispose of and make all needful rules and regulations respecting the territory or other property belonging to the United States; and nothing in this Constitution shall be so construed as to prejudice any claims of the United States, or of any particular State.

SECTION 4. Guarantees to the States

The United States shall guarantee to every State in this Union a republican form of government,[3] and shall protect each of them against invasion;[4] and on application of the legislature, or of the executive (when the legislature cannot be convened) against domestic violence.[5]

ARTICLE V

Method of Amendment

The Congress, whenever two thirds of both houses shall deem it necessary, shall propose amendments to this Constitution, or, on the application of the legislatures of two thirds of the several States, shall call a convention for proposing amendments, which, in either case, shall be valid to all intents and purposes, as part of this Constitution, when ratified by the legislatures of three fourths of the several States, or by conventions in three fourths thereof,[6] as the one or the other mode of ratification may be proposed by the Congress; provided that *no amendments which may be made prior to the year one thousand eight hundred and eight shall in any manner affect the first and fourth clauses in the ninth section of the first article; and that* no State, without its consent, shall be deprived of its equal suffrage in the Senate.[7]

ARTICLE VI

General Provisions

a. Public debt. All debts contracted and engagements entered into, before the adoption of this Constitution, shall be as valid against the United States under this Constitution, as under the Confederation.

1. So far as this refers to slaves (and the return of fugitive slaves was its original purpose) this section has been replaced by Amendment 13.

2. The additional power of admitting new states is conferred here upon Congress. However, a state may not be deprived of any of its territory without its consent.

3. Congress may exercise this power by refusing to admit senators and representatives from a state. In an emergency the President could send in federal troops to preserve a republican form of government.

4. Invasion of a state, except from a neighboring state, would also mean invasion of the nation, and would call for action on the part of the national government.

5. Domestic violence is different. Here the federal government would intervene only upon request, unless national interests were threatened. In the latter case, the President might intervene even over the protests of the state. (See page 394.)

6. The Constitution may be amended in any one of four ways:

(1) An amendment may be proposed by two thirds of both houses of Congress and ratified by the legislatures of three fourths of the states.

(2) An amendment may be proposed as above and ratified by special conventions in three fourths of the states.

(3) An amendment may be proposed by a special convention, called upon application of two thirds of the state legislatures, and ratified by three fourths of the state legislatures.

(4) An amendment may be proposed as in (3) above and ratified in three fourths of the states by special conventions. All 22 amendments were added by the first method except Amendment 21, which was added by the second.

7. Note this further protection for the small states.

b. Supremacy of the Constitution. This Constitution, and the laws of the United States which shall be made in pursuance thereof; and all treaties made, or which shall be made, under the authority of the United States, shall be the supreme law of the land;[1] and the judges in every State shall be bound thereby, anything in the Constitution or laws of any State to the contrary notwithstanding.

c. Oath of office; no religious test. The Senators and Representatives before mentioned, and the members of the several State legislatures, and all executive and judicial officers, both of the United States and of the several States, shall be bound by oath or affirmation, to support this Constitution; but no religious test shall ever be required as a qualification to any office or public trust under the United States.[2]

ARTICLE VII
Ratification of the Constitution
The ratification of the conventions of nine States shall be sufficient for the establishment of this Constitution between the States so ratifying the same.[3]

AMENDMENTS TO THE CONSTITUTION

Amendment 1 (1791)[4]
Freedom of Religion, Speech, and the Press; Right of Assembly

Congress shall make no law respecting an establishment of religion, or prohibiting the free exercise thereof; or abridging the freedom of speech, or of the press; or the right of the people peaceably to assemble, and to petition the government for a redress of grievances.[5]

Amendment 2 (1791)
Right to Keep and Bear Arms

A well-regulated militia, being necessary to the security of a free State, the right of the people to keep and bear arms, shall not be infringed.[6]

Amendment 3 (1791)
Quartering of Troops

No soldier shall, in time of peace be quartered in any house, without the consent of the owner, nor in time of war, but in a manner to be prescribed by law.[7]

Amendment 4 (1791)
Limiting the Right of Search

The right of the people to be secure in their persons, houses, papers, and effects, against unreasonable searches and seizures, shall not be violated, and no warrants shall issue but upon probable cause, supported by oath or affir-

1. The *supreme law* of the land consists of: (a) the Constitution, (b) laws of Congress passed in accordance with the Constitution, and (c) treaties. The supreme law has superiority over any state and local laws that may happen to conflict with it. The Constitution does not say who shall determine whether a law of Congress is passed in accordance with the Constitution. Chief Justice John Marshall (page 166) concluded that this power resided in the Supreme Court. Since his time the Supreme Court has assumed the power to declare a law of Congress unconstitutional.

2. Any religious qualification for federal office is ruled out.

3. This was a revolutionary provision, for delegates to the Constitutional Convention had been instructed to revise the Articles of Confederation, and unanimous consent of the states was required for such amendments.

4. The first ten amendments are known as the Bill of Rights. In general they protect the individual, both citizen and alien, against the exercise of undue power by the federal government. State constitutions protect the individual against excessive state authority.

5. Each individual is free to worship as he sees fit. He may also speak, write, or print anything he wants to, except that he may not slander or libel other people nor advocate violent overthrow of the government. Citizens may also meet together for any lawful purpose provided they do not interfere with the rights of others. Finally, the people are free to petition the government to correct any grievances or abuses.

6. This prevents anyone from taking away our liberties by force. States, of course, have laws about the sale and use of firearms.

7. This amendment forbids the government to assign troops to private homes for food and shelter, except by special law passed in time of war.

mation, and particularly describing the place to be searched, and the persons or things to be seized.[1]

Amendment 5 (1791)
Guaranty of Trial by Jury;
Private Property to be Respected

No person shall be held to answer for a capital, or otherwise infamous crime, unless on a presentment or indictment of a grand jury, except in cases arising in the land or naval forces, or in the militia, when in actual service in time of war or public danger; nor shall any person be subject for the same offense to be twice put in jeopardy of life or limb; nor shall be compelled in any criminal case to be a witness against himself, nor be deprived of life, liberty, or property, without due process of law; nor shall private property be taken for public use without just compensation.[2]

Amendment 6 (1791)
Rights of Accused Persons

In all criminal prosecutions, the accused shall enjoy the right to a speedy and public trial, by an impartial jury of the State and district wherein the crime shall have been committed, which districts shall have been previously ascertained by law, and to be informed of the nature and cause of the accusation; to be confronted with the witnesses against him; to have compulsory process for obtaining witnesses in his favor, and to have the assistance of counsel for his defense.[3]

Amendment 7 (1791)
Rules of the Common Law

In suits at common law, where the value in controversy shall exceed twenty dollars, the right of trial by jury shall be preserved, and no fact tried by a jury, shall be otherwise re-examined in any court of the United States than according to the rules of common law.[4]

Amendment 8 (1791)
Excessive Bail, Fines, and Punishment Prohibited

Excessive bail shall not be required, nor excessive fines imposed, nor cruel and unusual punishments inflicted.[5]

Amendment 9 (1791)
Rights Retained by the People

The enumeration in the Constitution of certain rights, shall not be construed to deny or disparage others retained by the people.[6]

Amendment 10 (1791)
Powers reserved to States and People

The powers not delegated to the United States by the

1. The government may not search a home or a person, or arrest a person, without reasonably good cause, and then only when the official who makes the search or arrest has a legal warrant to do so.

2. (a) An individual may not be brought to trial for ordinary crimes except after indictment (accusation) by a grand jury. (b) He may not be brought to trial a second time for the same offense. (c) He is not obliged to testify against himself. (d) He may not have his "life, liberty, or property" taken from him except by regular legal proceedings. (e) His private property may not be taken for use by the government without fair payment for it.

3. If anyone is accused of a crime, (a) he is entitled to a speedy public trial before an impartial jury; (b) he must be clearly told what the charge against him is; (c) the witnesses against him must give their testimony in his presence; (d) the government must co-operate with him in securing witnesses in his favor; and (e) he must be allowed to have the help of a lawyer.

4. Except in cases involving less than $20, civil suits (as contrasted with criminal cases) may be tried before a jury.

5. When accused of a crime, a person may in most instances have someone put up money for him so that he will not have to remain in jail. This money is called bail. Bail, fines, and punishments must be kept at a reasonable level.

6. It was impossible to list in the Constitution all the rights to be retained by the people. This amendment states that rights not specifically listed above are not to be surrendered simply because they are not mentioned. Similarly, Amendment 10 makes clear that any powers not granted to the federal government and not denied to the states are reserved to the states or to the people.

Constitution, nor prohibited by it to the States, are reserved to the States respectively, or to the people.

Amendment 11 (1798)
Limiting the Powers of Federal Courts

The judicial power of the United States shall not be construed to extend to any suit in law or equity, commenced or prosecuted against one of the United States by citizens of another State, or by citizens or subjects of any foreign state.[1]

Amendment 12 (1804)
Election of President and Vice President [2]

The electors shall meet in their respective States and vote by ballot for President and Vice President, one of whom, at least, shall not be an inhabitant of the same State with themselves; they shall name in their ballots the person voted for as President, and in distinct ballots the person voted for as Vice President, and they shall make distinct lists of all persons voted for as President, and of all persons voted for as Vice President, and of the number of votes for each, which lists they shall sign and certify, and transmit sealed to the seat of the government of the United States, directed to the President of the Senate; — the President of the Senate shall, in the presence of the Senate and House of Representatives, open all the certificates and the votes shall then be counted; — the person having the greatest number of votes for President shall be the President, if such number be a majority of the whole number of electors appointed; and if no person have such majority, then from the persons having the highest numbers not exceeding three on the list of those voted for as President, the House of Representatives shall choose immediately, by ballot, the President. But in choosing the President, the votes shall be taken by States, the representation from each State having one vote; a quorum for this purpose shall consist of a member or members from two thirds of the States, and a majority of all the States shall be necessary to a choice. And if the House of Representatives shall not choose a President whenever the right of choice shall devolve upon them, *before the fourth day of March next following*, then the Vice President shall act as President, as in the case of the death or other constitutional disability of the President. — The person having the greatest number of votes as Vice President, shall be the Vice President, if such number be a majority of the whole number of electors appointed, and if no person have a majority, then from the two highest numbers on the list, the Senate shall choose the Vice President;[3] a quorum for the purpose shall consist of two thirds of the whole number of Senators, and a majority of the whole number shall be necessary to a choice. But no person constitutionally ineligible to the office of President shall be eligible to that of Vice President of the United States.

1. Amendment 11 modifies Article III, Section 2, clause "a" (page xlii) so as to prevent a state from being brought into court by a citizen of another state or of a foreign country.

2. Amendment 12, the result of confusion at the time of Jefferson's election (page 159), establishes the present procedure in the electoral college (See note 6, page xxxix.) Today the national committees arrange for party conventions. The conventions of the major parties have more than a thousand delegates, with as many more alternates. They nominate candidates for the Presidency and Vice-Presidency, draw up a party platform, and appoint a new national committee for the next four years.

The President and the Vice-President are voted for separately by the electors in the state capitals. The lists of candidates, with the votes for each, are sent to the President of the Senate, who opens them in the presence of both houses. The votes are then counted, but the amendment fails to say by whom. See page 455 for the dispute over the election of 1876. An answer to this question was attempted by the Electoral Count Act of 1887 (see page 464).

If no candidate for President receives a majority, the election goes to the House, where the members vote by states for the three highest candidates. (See page 195 for the way this worked out in the election of 1824.) Each state casts one vote. Thus Nevada has the same vote as New York. A quorum consists of at least one member from two thirds of the states, and a majority of all the states is necessary for a choice.

3. If no candidate for Vice-President receives a majority, the Senate chooses a Vice-President from the two highest candidates. Again, a quorum consists of two thirds, and a majority of the whole number of senators is necessary for a choice.

Amendment 13 (1865)

Slavery Abolished [1]

Section I. Abolition of Slavery

Neither slavery nor involuntary servitude, except as a punishment for crime whereof the party shall have been duly convicted, shall exist within the United States, or any place subject to their jurisdiction.

Section 2. Enforcement

Congress shall have power to enforce this article by appropriate legislation.

Amendment 14 (1868)

Citizenship Defined

Section I. Definition of Citizenship

All persons born or naturalized in the United States, and subject to the jurisdiction thereof, are citizens of the United States and of the State wherein they reside.[2] No State shall make or enforce any law which shall abridge the privileges or immunities of citizens of the United States; nor shall any State deprive any person of life, liberty, or property, without due process of law; nor deny to any person within its jurisdiction the equal protection of the laws.[3]

Section 2. Apportionment of Representatives

Representatives shall be apportioned among the several States according to their respective numbers, counting the whole number of persons in each State, excluding Indians not taxed. But when the right to vote at any election for the choice of electors for President and Vice President of the United States, Representatives in Congress, the executive and judicial officers of a State, or the members of the legislature thereof, is denied to any of the male inhabitants of such State, being twenty-one years of age, and citizens of the United States, or in any way abridged, except for participation in rebellion, or other crime, the basis of representation therein shall be reduced in the proportion which the number of such male citizens shall bear to the whole number of male citizens twenty-one years of age in such State.[4]

Section 3. Disability Resulting from Insurrection

No person shall be a Senator or Representative in Congress, or Elector of President and Vice-President, or hold any office, civil or military, under the United States, or under any State, who, having previously taken an oath, as a member of Congress, or as an officer of the United States, or as a member of any State legislature, or as an executive or judicial officer of any State, to support the Constitution of the United States, shall have engaged in insurrection or rebellion against the same, or given aid or comfort to the

1. Amendments 13, 14, and 15 resulted from the War Between the States. In general, Amendment 13 freed the slaves, Amendment 14 was intended to guarantee civil rights to the freedmen, and Amendment 15 extended to them the right to vote.

2. This is the only definition of citizenship to be found in the Constitution.

3. These clauses have become very important. Intended primarily as a protection for the freedmen, they have also become a protection to corporations, since the Supreme Court has held a corporation to be a *person* within the meaning of this amendment (page 387). The Supreme Court has declared unconstitutional many state laws which it held deprived a corporation of property without *due process of law*, or denied to a corporation the *equal protection of the laws.*

4. This section was intended as a practical solution of the political problem created by the freeing of the slaves. Each freedman would now count as one in apportioning representatives. The effect would be to increase the representation of the southern (Democratic) states. Something had to be done, thought the radical Republicans, to make sure that the Negroes, who were favorable to the Republican Party, were protected in the right to vote. (page 325). Under this section, if a state had a male population 30 per cent Negro, and if the Negroes were not given the right to vote, then the state would lose 30 per cent of its representatives in Congress. This provision of the 14th Amendment has never been put into effect.

enemies thereof. But Congress may by vote of two thirds of each house, remove such disability.[1]

Section 4. Public Debt of the United States Valid; Confederate Debt Void

The validity of the public debt of the United States, authorized by law, including debts incurred for payment of pensions and bounties for services in suppressing insurrection or rebellion, shall not be questioned. But neither the United States nor any State shall assume or pay any debt or obligation incurred in aid of insurrection or rebellion against the United States, or any claim for the loss or emancipation of any slave; but all such debts, obligations, and claims shall be held illegal and void.[2]

Section 5. Enforcement

The Congress shall have power to enforce by appropriate legislation the provisions of this article.[3]

Amendment 15 (1870)
Right of Suffrage

Section 1. The Suffrage

The right of citizens of the United States to vote shall not be denied or abridged by the United States or any State on account of race, color, or previous condition of servitude.[4]

Section 2. Enforcement

The Congress shall have power to enforce this article by appropriate legislation.

Amendment 16 (1913)
Income Tax

The Congress shall have power to lay and collect taxes on incomes, from whatever source derived, without apportionment among the several States, and without regard to any census or enumeration.[5]

Amendment 17 (1913)
Direct Election of Senators

a. Election by the people. The Senate of the United States shall be composed of two Senators from each State, elected by the people thereof, for six years; and each Senator shall have one vote. The electors in each State shall have the qualifications requisite for electors of the most numerous branch of the State legislatures.[6]

b. Vacancies. When vacancies happen in the representation of any State in the Senate, the executive authority of such State shall issue writs of election to fill such vacancies: PROVIDED that the legislature of any State may empower the executive thereof to make temporary appointments until the people fill the vacancies by election as the legislature may direct.

1. In other words, if any person who had held an office which required an oath to support the Constitution of the United States had violated that oath by taking up arms against the United States or by giving aid and comfort to the enemy, then he could not hold any office which would again require such an oath. This limitation deprived the southern states of many possible leaders during Reconstruction.

2. Section 4 silenced any doubt about the validity of the national debt, but outlawed the whole Confederate debt. Confederate bonds were now worthless, and those who had loaned money in support of the Confederacy were thereby punished. Nor would there be any repayment for the loss of the slaves, now become freedmen.

3. Section 5 gave to Congress power to enforce the provisions of Amendment 14.

4. Amendment 15 places another limitation upon the power of the states. They may not deny the right to vote to anyone because of race, color, or previous condition of servitude.

5. The income-tax law of 1894 had been declared unconstitutional by the Supreme Court on the ground that it was a direct tax, not apportioned among the states according to population (see page 383). Amendment 16 specifically grants to Congress the power to levy a tax on incomes derived from any source, and without apportionment among the states according to population.

6. Amendment 17 provides for direct election of United States Senators. The qualifications needed to vote for senators shall be the same as for the lower branch of the state legislature. See note 10, page xxxiv.

c. Not retroactive. This amendment shall not be so construed as to affect the election or term of any Senator chosen before it becomes valid as part of the Constitution.

Amendment 18 (1919)
National Prohibition [1]

Section 1. Prohibition of Intoxicating Liquors

After one year from the ratification of this article the manufacture, sale, or transportation of intoxicating liquors within, the importation thereof into, or the exportation thereof from the United States and all territory subject to the jurisdiction thereof for beverage purposes is hereby prohibited.

Section 2. Enforcement

The Congress and the several States shall have concurrent power to enforce this article by appropriate legislation.

Section 3. Limited Time for Ratification

This article shall be inoperative unless it shall have been ratified as an amendment to the Constitution by the legislatures of the several States, as provided in the Constitution, within seven years from the date of the submission hereof to the States by the Congress.

Amendment 19 (1920)
Extending the Vote to Women

Section 1. Woman Suffrage

The right of citizens of the United States to vote shall not be denied or abridged by the United States or by any State on account of sex.[2]

Section 2. Enforcement

The Congress shall have power to enforce this article by appropriate legislation.

Amendment 20 (1933)
The "Lame Duck" Amendment

Section 1. Terms of President, Vice President, and Congress

The terms of the President and Vice President shall end at noon on the 20th day of January, and the terms of Senators and Representatives at noon on the 3d day of January, of the years in which such terms would have ended if this article had not been ratified; and the terms of their successors shall then begin.[3]

Section 2. Sessions of Congress

The Congress shall assemble at least once in every year, and such meeting shall begin at noon on the 3d day of January, unless they shall by law appoint a different day.[4]

1. Amendment 18 has been repealed by Amendment 21, but it has several points of interest. It did not go into effect until one year after ratification. Wartime prohibition restrictions, however, deprived those interested of the expected advantages of this provision. Section 2 provided for concurrent power of enforcement. Yet, the Volstead Act, passed by Congress (page 592), was so strong that little power was left to the states. In Section 3 the idea was introduced of limiting the time for ratification by the state legislatures.

2. By Amendment 19 the power of the states to determine who may vote has been further limited. In this case the right to vote may not be denied because of sex. Both in this amendment and in Amendment 15 Congress is given power to enforce the provisions by appropriate legislation.

3. The Twentieth or "Lame Duck" Amendment represents the successful ending of a long struggle on the part of Senator George W. Norris to do away with the so-called "lame-duck" session of Congress. (See page 755.) Before 1933 many members of the "short session" of Congress meeting in December of even-numbered years had been defeated in the November elections. Congress as a whole, therefore, often stood for principles already rejected by the voters. Amendment 20 did away with this "lame duck" Congress. The terms of senators and representatives ended on January 3 instead of on March 4. Also, the last year of President Franklin D. Roosevelt's first term was shortened from March 4th to January 20.

4. Thereafter, too, the sessions of the newly-elected Congress began on January 3 following the election, instead of thirteen months after election, with the whole short session of the old Congress intervening.

Section 3. Presidential Succession

If, at the time fixed for the beginning of the term of the President, the President elect shall have died, the Vice President elect shall become President. If a President shall not have been chosen before the time fixed for the beginning of his term, or if the President elect shall have failed to qualify, then the Vice President elect shall act as President until a President shall have qualified; and the Congress may by law provide for the case wherein neither a President elect nor a Vice President elect shall have qualified, declaring who shall then act as President, or the manner in which one who is to act shall be selected, and such person shall act accordingly until a President or a Vice President shall have qualified.[1]

Section 4. Choice of President by the House

The Congress may by law provide for the case of the death of any of the persons from whom the House of Representatives may choose a President whenever the right of choice shall have devolved upon them, and for the case of the death of any of the persons from whom the Senate may choose a Vice President whenever the right of choice shall have devolved upon them.[2]

Section 5. Date Effective

Sections 1 and 2 shall take effect on the fifteenth day of October following the ratification of this article.

Section 6. Limited Time for Ratification

This article shall be inoperative unless it shall have been ratified as an amendment to the Constitution by the legislatures of three fourths of the several States within seven years from the date of its submission.[3]

Amendment 21 (1933)

Repeal of Prohibition

Section 1. Repeal of Amendment 18

The eighteenth article of amendment to the Constitution of the United States is hereby repealed.[4]

Section 2. States Protected

The transportation or importation into any State, territory, or possession of the United States for delivery or use therein of intoxicating liquors, in violation of the laws thereof, is hereby prohibited.[5]

Section 3. Limited Time for Ratification

This article shall be inoperative unless it shall have been ratified as an amendment to the Constitution by conventions in the several States, as provided in the Constitution, within seven years from the date of the submission hereof to the States by the Congress.[6]

1. Section 3 makes provision for filling the office of President in case of death or failure to qualify before the time fixed for the beginning of his term.

2. In case the election is thrown into Congress because no candidate for either President or Vice-President receives a majority of the electoral vote, Congress may make provision for any situation arising from the death of any of the candidates.

3. As in the case of Amendment 18, a time limit was placed upon the state legislatures for the ratification of this amendment.

4. In spite of widespread dissatisfaction with the workings of Amendment 18, it was generally believed that the very difficulty of amending the Constitution would prevent its repeal. The situation in 1933, however, was very unusual because of the depression. The administration felt that some of the arguments in favor of the 18th Amendment were no longer as strong as they had been. It was now desirable to put man-power to work, to find uses for grain, and to gain sources of revenue.

5. Section 2 was designed to protect states which had laws prohibiting the use of liquor.

6. Section 3 was unique in that Congress made provision for the submission of this amendment to conventions in the states. Ratification proceeded with unusual speed, and Amendment 21 was proclaimed a part of the Constitution before the end of 1933. This in effect gave the people, in electing their conventions, the opportunity to express their opinions on the question.

Amendment 22 (1951)
Presidential Term Limited

Section 1. Definition of Limitation

No person shall be elected to the office of the President more than twice, and no person who has held the office of President, or acted as President, for more than two years of a term to which some other person was elected President shall be elected to the office of the President more than once. But this article shall not apply to any person holding the office of President when this article was proposed by the Congress, and shall not prevent any person who may be holding the office of President, or acting as President, during the term within which this article becomes operative from holding the office of President, or acting as President during the remainder of such term.[1]

Section 2. Limited Time for Ratification

This article shall be inoperative unless it shall have been ratified as an amendment to the Constitution by the legislatures of three-fourths of the several States within seven years from the date of its submission to the States by the Congress.

1. The framers of the Constitution included no limitation on the number of terms a President might serve. Presidents Washington and Jefferson, however, decided against a third term. This practice became an unwritten custom which was observed by succeeding Presidents until 1940, when Franklin D. Roosevelt was elected for a third term. The Twenty-second Amendment does not apply to President Truman.

IMPORTANT DATES IN
THE MAKING OF MODERN AMERICA

1096 The first Crusade.
1271–95 Marco Polo visits the Far East.
1492 Columbus discovers New World.
1493 Pope draws demarcation line.
1497 John Cabot explores the North American coast.
1498 Vasco da Gama reaches India.
1500 Cabral discovers Brazil.
1513 Balboa reaches the Pacific.
1519 Cortez starts conquest of Mexico.
    Magellan starts around World.
1532 Pizarro begins conquest of Peru.
1534–35 Cartier explores the St. Lawrence River.

1539 De Soto begins exploration of North America.
1588 English defeat Spanish Armada.
1607 Jamestown is founded.
1608 Champlain founds Quebec.
1609 Hudson explores Hudson River.
1619 House of Burgesses in Virginia meets for first time. Negroes introduced into Virginia.
1620 Pilgrims land at Plymouth.
1624 Virginia becomes royal colony.
1630 Massachusetts Bay colony established.
1634 Maryland founded.
1636 Rhode Island and Connecticut founded.

    Harvard College established.
1639 Fundamental Orders of Connecticut.
1643 New England Confederation established.
1647 School law adopted by Massachusetts.
1649 Maryland Toleration Act.
1660–63 Navigation Acts passed.
1664 English take New Netherland.
1665 Beginning of New Jersey.
1670 Charles Town (Charleston) South Carolina, founded.
1673 Marquette and Joliet explore the Mississippi.
1681 Beginning of Pennsylvania.

1682 La Salle reaches mouth of the Mississippi.
Philadelphia is founded.
1684 Dominion of New England established.
1688 "Glorious Revolution" in England ends Dominion of New England.
1689 War begins between England and France.
1693 College of William and Mary founded.
1699 Colonial industry restricted by Woolens Act.
1704 Delaware founded.
Boston news-letter published.
1732 The Hat Act passed.
1733 Georgia founded.
Molasses Act passed.
1735 Zenger Case establishes freedom of the press.
1750 Iron Act passed.
1754 French and Indian War begins.
Albany Plan of Union proposed.
1755 Braddock defeated.
1757 William Pitt plans victory.
1759 The English capture Quebec.
1763 Treaty of Paris; French driven out of America.
Proclamation line established.
Parson's cause argued.
1764 Sugar and Currency Acts passed.
1765 Stamp Act passed.
Stamp Act Congress meets.
1766 Stamp Act repealed.
1767 Townshend Acts passed.
1770 Boston Massacre occurs.
1772 Committees of Correspondence formed.
1773 Boston Tea Party.
1774 Intolerable Acts passed.
First Continental Congress meets.
First settlement in Kentucky.
1775 Battles of Lexington and Concord take place.
Second Continental Congress meets.
Battle of Bunker Hill occurs.
1776 Declaration of Independence is issued.
Common Sense is published.
Battle of Trenton takes place.

1777 Burgoyne surrenders at Saratoga.
Howe takes Philadelphia.
1778 Treaty of alliance made with France.
1778–79 George Rogers Clark wins the West.
1781 Cornwallis surrenders at Yorktown.
Articles of Confederation go into effect.
1783 Treaty of Paris; United States wins its independence.
1785 Land ordinance is passed.
1787 Northwest Ordinance adopted.
Constitution drafted.
1789 **George Washington becomes President.**
First Congress meets.
French Revolution begins.
Slater starts United States factory system.
System of United States courts organized.
1791 Bill of Rights added to Constitution.
First United States Bank created.
Vermont becomes a state.
1792 Kentucky becomes a state.
1793 Washington issues proclamation of neutrality.
Cotton gin invented.
Genêt Affair.
1794 Whisky Rebellion occurs.
1795 Completion of Jay and Pinckney treaties.
1796 Tennessee admitted.
1797 **John Adams becomes President.**
1798 Alien and Sedition Acts passed.
Virginia and Kentucky Resolutions adopted.
1801 John Marshall appointed Chief Justice.
Thomas Jefferson becomes President.
Expedition sent against Barbary pirates.
1803 Marshall renders decision in Marbury *vs.* Madison.
Louisiana is purchased.
Ohio becomes a state.
1804 Lewis and Clark start expedition.
1805–06 Zebulon Pike continues exploration.
1807 The Embargo Act passed.
Fulton's steamboat is successful.

1809 Non-intercourse replaces embargo.
James Madison becomes President.
1811 Cumberland road started.
Indians defeated at Tippecanoe.
1812 Louisiana admitted.
1812–14 War with Great Britain.
1814 Hartford Convention.
Treaty of Ghent ends war.
1815 Jackson victorious at New Orleans.
1816 Protective tariff adopted.
Steamboat goes up Mississippi.
Second United States Bank chartered.
Indiana becomes a state.
1817 **James Monroe becomes President.**
Era of Good Feelings begins.
Mississippi admitted.
Rush-Bagot Agreement.
1818 Illinois admitted as state.
Canadian boundary settled.
1819 Florida acquired from Spain.
Alabama becomes a state.
Panic sweeps the country.
1820 Missouri Compromise.
Maine admitted.
1821 First public high school.
Missouri becomes a state.
1822 United States recognized independence of Latin American states.
1823 Monroe Doctrine proclaimed.
1825 **John Quincy Adams becomes President.**
Erie Canal opened.
1828 Tariff of Abominations.
Exposition and Protest issued.
1829 **Andrew Jackson becomes President.**
1830 Successful run made on B&O railroad.
Webster-Hayne debate.
1831 First nominating convention held.
First issue of *The Liberator* appears.
McCormick reaper invented.
1832 South Carolina nullifies the tariff.
Jackson vetoes the Bank Bill.
1833 Compromise tariff passed.

New York *Sun* starts *penny* daily.

1836 Texas declares its independence.
Arkansas becomes a state.
Specie Circular issued.

1837 **Martin van Buren becomes President.**
Panic grips the nation.
Michigan admitted.
First free state university in Michigan.
Horace Mann starts educational reforms.

1840 Triumph of Whigs; end of Jacksonian Era.
Independent Treasury established.

1841 **William Henry Harrison becomes President and is succeeded by John Tyler.**

1842 Webster-Ashburton Treaty signed.

1844 Telegraph successfully used.

1845 Texas annexed; admitted.
James K. Polk becomes President.
Florida admitted as state.
Famine results in wave of Irish immigration.

1846 Oregon boundary fixed at 49th parallel.
Mexican War begins.
Howe perfects sewing machine.
Hoe cylinder press invented.
Smithsonian Institution founded.
Ether used successfully.
Iowa becomes a state.

1847 Mormons move to Great Salt Lake.

1848 End of Mexican War; United States gains Mexican Cession.
Women's Rights Convention at Seneca Falls.
Wisconsin admitted.

1849 **Zachary Taylor becomes President.**
California gold rush.

1850 **Millard Fillmore succeeds to the Presidency.**
Compromise of 1850.
California admitted.

1852 *Uncle Tom's Cabin.*

1853 **Franklin Pierce becomes President.**
Gadsden Purchase made.
"Great Republic" built at height of clipper era.

1854 Perry opens Japan to West.
Immigration passed 400,-000 mark.
Kansas-Nebraska Act.
Beginning of Republican Party.

1856 Civil war rages in Kansas.
Bessemer process introduced.

1857 **James Buchanan becomes President.**
Dred Scott decision rendered.
Missouri Compromise declared unconstitutional.
Impending Crisis published.

1858 Lincoln-Douglas debates.
Minnesota admitted.

1859 John Brown raids Harper's Ferry.
First oil well drilled.
Fifty-niners move into Nevada and Colorado.
Oregon becomes a state.

1860 Lincoln elected President.
South Carolina secedes.
Pony Express established.

1861 Southern Confederacy formed.
Abraham Lincoln becomes President.
Fort Sumter fired upon.
Trent affair threatens relations with Great Britain.
Kansas admitted as state.

1861–65 **War Between the States.**

1862 Duel between ironclads *Monitor* and *Merrimac*.
Homestead Act passed.
Morrill Act provides for land grant colleges.
Department of Agriculture created.
Peninsular Campaign fails.
Mississippi opened to Vicksburg.

1863 Emancipation Proclamation issued.
Battle of Gettysburg.
Surrender of Vicksburg.
National banking system adopted.
West Virginia admitted.

1864 Grant opens drive toward Richmond.
Sherman takes Atlanta and Savannah.
Pullman sleeping car introduced.
Nevada admitted as state.

1865 Sherman marches north into the Carolinas.
Lee surrenders at Appomattox.
Lincoln assassinated.
Andrew Johnson becomes President.
Maximilian affair in Mexico.
Johnson attempts liberal plan of reconstruction.
13th Amendment adopted.

1866 Atlantic cable successfully laid.
National Labor Union organized.

1867 Reconstruction Act passed.
Granger movement started.
Alaska purchased.
Johnson impeached.
Nebraska admitted.

1868 14th Amendment adopted.
Johnson acquitted.

1869 **Ulysses S. Grant becomes President.**
First transcontinental railroad completed.
Territory of Wyoming gave suffrage to women.
New York Central lines merged.
Knights of Labor founded.
Gold conspiracy ends in Black Friday.

1870 15th Amendment adopted.

1871 Treaty of Washington signed.

1872 Westinghouse airbrake developed.
Duplex telegraph introduced.
Congress passes Amnesty Act.

1873 Panic checks business activity.
"Crime of '73" demonetizes silver.

1874 Chautauqua movement started.
Woman's Christian Temperance Union organized.

1875 B&O Railroad reaches Chicago.

1876 Custer's force wiped out by Indians.
Telephone invented.
Centennial Exposition.
National baseball league organized.
Colorado admitted.
Disputed election.

1877 **Rutherford B. Hayes becomes President.**
Federal troops removed from South.
Railroad strike occurs.
Successful phonograph produced.

1878 Bland-Allison Act passed.
New York Symphony Orchestra organized.

1879 Specie payment resumed.
Edison introduces electric lamp.

1881 **James A. Garfield becomes President and is succeeded by Chester A. Arthur.**
American Red Cross founded.
Boston Symphony Orchestra founded.

1882 Chinese immigrants excluded.
Standard Oil Trust organized.
Carnegie joins with Frick.

1883 Pendleton Act sets up Civil Service Commission.
Metropolitan opera opened.

1885 **Grover Cleveland becomes President.**

1886 American Federation of Labor organized.
Haymarket affair.
Presidential Succession Act passed.
Granger laws ruled unconstitutional.

1887 Interstate Commerce Act.
Indians given land by Dawes Act.
Electoral Count Act passed.
Experimental stations set up by Hatch Act.

1889 **Benjamin Harrison becomes President.**
Pan-American Conference held at Washington.
Jane Addams founds Hull House.
Montana, North and South Dakota, and Washington admitted.

1890 McKinley tariff enacted.
Sherman Silver Act.
Sherman Antitrust Act.
Wyoming admitted; grants full political rights to women.
Source of immigration shifting to southern and eastern Europe.
Frontier ceases to exist.

Idaho becomes state.

1891 Populist Party organized.
Withdrawal of timber lands authorized.

1892 Homestead strike.

1893 **Grover Cleveland becomes President.**
Great Northern Railroad completed.
First Ford car built.
Columbia Exposition at Chicago.
Panic paralyzes business.
Sherman Silver Act repealed.

1894 Wilson-Gorman tariff passed.
First motion-picture projector.
Pullman strike in Chicago.

1895 Venezuelan boundary dispute.
Insurrection breaks out in Cuba.

1896 Rural free delivery introduced.
Utah admitted as state.
Bryan defeated in free silver campaign.

1897 **William McKinley becomes President.**
Dingley Act passed.
Gold rush to Klondike.

1898 Spanish-American War.
Philippines, Puerto Rico, and Guam acquired.
Hawaii annexed.

1899 Tutuila acquired.
First Hague Peace Conference held.
Treaty of Paris ratified.

1900 Open Door policy announced.
Boxer Rebellion.
Gold Standard Act.
Commission government introduced.

1901 McKinley assassinated.
Theodore Roosevelt succeeds to the Presidency.
United States Steel organized.
Hay-Pauncefote Treaty adopted.

1902 Troops withdrawn from Cuba.
Coal strike settled.
Suit against Northern Securities Company.
Newlands Reclamation Act passed.
Tarbell's History of *The Standard Oil Company.*

1903 Alaskan boundary settled.
Successful airplane flight.

United States acquires Canal Zone.
Elkins Act passed.
Recall adopted in Los Angeles.
Direct primary introduced.

1904 Roosevelt corollary stated.
World's Fair held at St. Louis.

1905 IWW organized.
Treaty of Portsmouth ends Russo-Japanese War.

1906 Meat Inspection Act.
Pure Food and Drugs Act.
Hepburn Act regulates railroads.

1907 Financial panic occurs.
Roosevelt Dam opened.
Oklahoma becomes a state.
Second Hague Conference.
Gentlemen's Agreement.

1908 Conservation conference held.
Fleet cruises around world.
Root-Takahira Agreement adopted.

1909 **William H. Taft becomes President.**
Payne-Aldrich Tariff.

1910 Mann-Elkins Act passed.
Speaker of House stripped of power.

1911 Rule of reason laid down.

1912 Progressive Party organized.
South takes lead in cotton manufacture.
Arizona and New Mexico admitted.

1913 Parcel post started.
Woodrow Wilson becomes President.
Federal Reserve Act.
Underwood Tariff.
16th & 17th Amendments proclaimed.
Policy of "Watchful waiting" begins.

1914 Federal Trade Commission and Clayton Acts passed.
Smith-Lever Act passed.
Panama Canal opened.
World War I begins.

1915 *Lusitania* sunk.
Telephone from N.Y. to San Francisco.

1916 Jones Act for Philippines.
Germany gives *Sussex* pledge.

1917 U.S. enters World War I.
Railways taken over.
Virgin Islands acquired.

Smith-Hughes Act passed.
Literacy test for immigrants.
Jones Act for Puerto Rico.
Revolution in Russia.
1918 Fourteen Points announced.
Battles of Chateau-Thierry, St. Mihiel, Argonne.
Armistice signed.
1919 Treaty of Versailles drawn up.
18th Amendment adopted.
1920 World Court set up.
League of Nations finally rejected.
19th Amendment adopted.
Transportation Act passed.
Station KDKA on the air.
1921 **Warren G. Harding becomes President.**
National Budget Bureau established.
Veterans' Bureau set up.
Emergency Quota Act passed.
Washington Conference.
1922 War debts funded.
Fordney-McCumber Act.
Teapot Dome leased.
1923 **Calvin Coolidge succeeds to the Presidency.**
Pan-American Congress at Santiago.
1924 Immigration further restricted.
Indians made citizens.
Soldiers' bonus bill passed.
1927 McNary-Haugen Bill vetoed.
Sound films introduced.
Lindbergh flies to Paris.
1928 Pan-American Congress held at Havana.
Paris Peace Pact signed.
1929 **Herbert Hoover becomes President.**
National origins quotas adopted.
Agricultural Marketing Act passed.
Stock market crash.
1930 Hawley-Smoot Tariff passed.
London Naval Conference held.
1931 Hoover moratorium.
Japan invades Manchuria.
1932 Reconstruction Finance Corporation set up.
Stimson Doctrine announced.
Glass-Steagall Act passed.
1933 **Franklin D. Roosevelt be-**

comes President.
Bank Holiday proclaimed.
FDIC set up.
Gold standard abandoned.
Agricultural Adjustment Act passed.
National Recovery Administration set up.
Tennessee Valley Authority created.
Civilian Conservation Corps set up.
20th and 21st Amendments proclaimed.
Good Neighbor policy announced.
Russia recognized.
Hitler named chancellor.
Farm Credit Administration established.
1934 Securities and Exchange Commission set up.
Trade Agreements Act passed.
National Resources Planning Board appointed.
Federal Communications Commission set up.
Silver purchase act passed.
Cuban treaty adopted.
1935 Social Security Act passed.
Wagner Act passed.
ICC given control over motor carriers.
Dollar devaluation upheld.
Banking Act passed.
Control extended over power companies.
Beginning of CIO.
London Naval Conference held.
1936 AAA unconstitutional.
TVA upheld.
Hoover Dam opened.
Panama Treaty adopted.
1937 Recession takes place.
Controversy over Supreme Court.
Neutrality Act passed.
Panay incident occurred.
1938 Congress of Industrial Organizations (CIO) organized.
Second AAA provided for.
Fair Labor Standards Act passed.
Food, Drug, and Cosmetics Act.
Civil Aeronautics Act.
Pan-American Congress at Lima.
Munich crisis in Europe.
1939 World War II starts.
Neutrality Act modified.

Hemisphere solidarity established.
1940 Fall of France.
Wheeler-Lea Act passed.
Havana Conference held.
1941 Lend-Lease adopted.
Four freedoms proclaimed.
Rio Conference held.
Atlantic Charter proclaimed.
Germany invades Russia.
Pearl Harbor attacked by Japan.
1942 Corregidor falls.
Anti-inflation program adopted.
Guadalcanal invaded.
Invasion of Africa.
1943 Invasion of Sicily and Italy.
Cairo and Teheran Conferences held.
1944 D-Day in Europe.
France liberated.
Marshalls and Marianas invaded.
Dumbarton Oaks conference held.
Taxes reduced over veto.
1945 Yalta Conference held.
Germany and Japan collapse.
Atom bombs dropped.
Harry S. Truman succeeds to the Presidency.
San Francisco Conference.
UN Charter approved.
1946 Postwar strikes followed by wage increases.
Price controls end.
Philippines independent.
1947 Taft-Hartley Act passed.
Presidential Succession changed.
Truman Doctrine adopted.
Marshall Plan announced.
Rio Pact ratified.
1948 ITO Charter drawn up.
Communists seize Czechoslovakia.
Berlin blockade established.
1949 North Atlantic Pact approved.
Communists triumph in China.
Government reorganization approved.
Housing measure adopted.
1950 UN intervention in Korea.
Economic Stabilization Agency set up.
1951 22nd Amendment adopted.
Japanese Treaty signed.

THE STATES OF THE UNITED STATES OF AMERICA

NO.	STATE NAME	DATE OF ADMISSION	POPULATION (1950 CENSUS)	NUMBER OF REPRESENTATIVES (1950 APPORTIONMENT)	AREA IN SQUARE MILES	CAPITAL	LARGEST CITY
1	Delaware	1787	318,085	1	2,057	Dover	Wilmington
2	Pennsylvania	1787	10,498,012	30	45,333	Harrisburg	Philadelphia
3	New Jersey	1787	4,835,329	14	7,836	Trenton	Newark
4	Georgia	1788	3,444,578	10	58,876	Atlanta	Atlanta
5	Connecticut	1788	2,007,280	6	5,009	Hartford	Hartford
6	Massachusetts	1788	4,690,514	14	8,257	Boston	Boston
7	Maryland	1788	2,343,001	7	10,577	Annapolis	Baltimore
8	South Carolina	1788	2,117,027	6	31,055	Columbia	Columbia
9	New Hampshire	1788	533,242	2	9,304	Concord	Manchester
10	Virginia	1788	3,318,680	10	40,815	Richmond	Richmond
11	New York	1788	14,830,192	43	49,576	Albany	New York
12	North Carolina	1789	4,061,929	12	52,712	Raleigh	Charlotte
13	Rhode Island	1790	791,896	2	1,214	Providence	Providence
14	Vermont	1791	377,747	1	9,609	Montpelier	Burlington
15	Kentucky	1792	2,944,806	8	40,395	Frankfort	Louisville
16	Tennessee	1796	3,291,718	9	42,246	Nashville	Memphis
17	Ohio	1803	7,946,627	23	41,222	Columbus	Cleveland
18	Louisiana	1812	2,683,516	8	48,523	Baton Rouge	New Orleans
19	Indiana	1816	3,934,224	11	36,291	Indianapolis	Indianapolis
20	Mississippi	1817	2,178,914	6	47,716	Jackson	Jackson
21	Illinois	1818	8,712,176	25	56,400	Springfield	Chicago
22	Alabama	1819	3,061,743	9	51,609	Montgomery	Birmingham
23	Maine	1820	913,774	3	33,215	Augusta	Portland
24	Missouri	1821	3,954,653	11	69,674	Jefferson City	St. Louis
25	Arkansas	1836	1,909,511	6	53,102	Little Rock	Little Rock
26	Michigan	1837	6,371,766	18	58,216	Lansing	Detroit
27	Florida	1845	2,771,305	8	58,560	Tallahassee	Miami
28	Texas	1845	7,711,194	22	267,339	Austin	Houston
29	Iowa	1846	2,621,073	8	56,280	Des Moines	Des Moines
30	Wisconsin	1848	3,434,575	10	56,154	Madison	Milwaukee
31	California	1850	10,586,223	30	158,693	Sacramento	Los Angeles

		DATE OF ACQUISITION	POPULATION		AREA IN SQUARE MILES	CAPITAL	PRINCIPAL CITY
32	Minnesota	1858	2,982,483	9	84,068	St. Paul	Minneapolis
33	Oregon	1859	1,521,341	4	96,981	Salem	Portland
34	Kansas	1861	1,905,299	6	82,276	Topeka	Wichita
35	West Virginia	1863	2,005,552	6	24,181	Charleston	Huntington
36	Nevada	1864	160,083	1	110,540	Carson City	Reno
37	Nebraska	1867	1,325,510	4	77,237	Lincoln	Omaha
38	Colorado	1876	1,325,089	4	104,247	Denver	Denver
39	North Dakota	1889	619,636	2	70,665	Bismarck	Fargo
40	South Dakota	1889	652,740	2	77,047	Pierre	Sioux Falls
41	Montana	1889	591,024	2	147,138	Helena	Great Falls
42	Washington	1889	2,378,963	7	68,192	Olympia	Seattle
43	Idaho	1890	588,637	2	83,557	Boise	Boise
44	Wyoming	1890	290,529	1	97,914	Cheyenne	Cheyenne
45	Utah	1896	688,862	2	84,916	Salt Lake City	Salt Lake City
46	Oklahoma	1907	2,233,351	6	69,919	Oklahoma City	Oklahoma City
47	New Mexico	1912	681,187	2	121,666	Santa Fe	Albuquerque
48	Arizona	1912	749,587	2	113,909	Phoenix	Phoenix
	District of Columbia		802,178		69		
Total			150,697,361	435	3,022,387		

PRINCIPAL TERRITORIES AND DEPENDENCIES OF THE UNITED STATES

TERRITORY OR DEPENDENCY	DATE OF ACQUISITION	POPULATION (LATEST AVAILABLE FIGURES)	AREA IN SQUARE MILES	CAPITAL, OR PRINCIPAL CITY
Alaska	1867	128,648	586,400	Juneau
Hawaiian Islands	1898	499,794	6,454[1]	Honolulu
Puerto Rico	1899	2,210,708	3,435	San Juan
Guam	1899	59,498	206	Agana
American Samoa	1900	18,937	76	Pago Pago
Panama Canal Zone	1904	52,822	553	Balboa
Virgin Islands	1917	26,665	133	Charlotte Amalie
Total		2,997,072	597,257	

[1] Includes Baker, Canton, Enderbury, Howland, Jarvis, Johnston, Midway, and other islands.

PRESIDENTS AND VICE-PRESIDENTS OF THE UNITED STATES

PRESIDENT	BORN	DIED	DATE OF INAUGURATION	PARTY ELECTING PRESIDENT	STATE	VICE-PRESIDENT	STATE
George Washington	1732	1799	1789	None	Virginia	John Adams	Massachusetts
George Washington	1732	1799	1793	None	Virginia	John Adams	Massachusetts
John Adams	1735	1826	1797	Federalist	Massachusetts	Thomas Jefferson	Virginia
Thomas Jefferson	1743	1826	1801	Dem.–Republican	Virginia	Aaron Burr	New York
Thomas Jefferson	1743	1826	1805	Dem.–Republican	Virginia	George Clinton	New York
James Madison	1751	1836	1809	Dem.–Republican	Virginia	George Clinton	New York
James Madison	1751	1836	1813	Dem.–Republican	Virginia	Elbridge Gerry	Massachusetts
James Monroe	1758	1831	1817	Dem.–Republican	Virginia	Daniel D. Tompkins	New York
James Monroe	1758	1831	1821	Dem.–Republican	Virginia	Daniel D. Tompkins	New York
John Quincy Adams	1767	1848	1825	Nat.–Republican	Massachusetts	John C. Calhoun	South Carolina
Andrew Jackson	1767	1845	1829	Democratic	Tennessee	John C. Calhoun	South Carolina
Andrew Jackson	1767	1845	1833	Democratic	Tennessee	Martin Van Buren	New York
Martin Van Buren	1782	1862	1837	Democratic	New York	Richard M. Johnson	Kentucky
William H. Harrison	1773	1841	1841	Whig	Ohio	John Tyler	Virginia
John Tyler	1790	1862	(1841, April)	Whig	Virginia		
James K. Polk	1795	1849	1845	Democratic	Tennessee	George M. Dallas	Pennsylvania
Zachary Taylor	1784	1850	1849	Whig	Louisiana	Millard Fillmore	New York
Millard Fillmore	1800	1874	(1850, July)	Whig	New York		
Franklin Pierce	1804	1869	1853	Democratic	New Hampshire	William R. King	Alabama
James Buchanan	1791	1868	1857	Democratic	Pennsylvania	John C. Breckinridge	Kentucky
Abraham Lincoln	1809	1865	1861	Republican	Illinois	Hannibal Hamlin	Maine
Abraham Lincoln	1809	1865	1865	Republican	Illinois	Andrew Johnson	Tennessee
Andrew Johnson	1808	1875	(1865, April)	Republican	Tennessee		
Ulysses S. Grant	1822	1885	1869	Republican	Illinois	Schuyler Colfax	Indiana
Ulysses S. Grant	1822	1885	1873	Republican	Illinois	Henry Wilson	Massachusetts

PRESIDENT	BORN	DIED	DATE OF INAUGURATION	PARTY ELECTING PRESIDENT	STATE	VICE-PRESIDENT	STATE
Rutherford B. Hayes	1822	1893	1877	Republican	Ohio	William A. Wheeler	New York
James A. Garfield	1831	1881	1881	Republican	Ohio	Chester A. Arthur	New York
Chester A. Arthur	1830	1886	(1881, Sept.)	Republican	New York		
Grover Cleveland	1837	1908	1885	Democratic	New York	Thomas A. Hendricks	Indiana
Benjamin Harrison	1833	1901	1889	Republican	Indiana	Levi P. Morton	New York
Grover Cleveland	1837	1908	1893	Democratic	New York	Adlai E. Stevenson.	Illinois
William McKinley	1843	1901	1897	Republican	Ohio	Garrett A. Hobart	New Jersey
William McKinley	1843	1901	1901	Republican	Ohio	Theodore Roosevelt	New York
Theodore Roosevelt	1858	1919	(1901, Sept.)	Republican	New York		
Theodore Roosevelt	1858	1919	1905	Republican	New York	Charles W. Fairbanks	Indiana
William H. Taft	1857	1930	1909	Republican	Ohio	James S. Sherman	New York
Woodrow Wilson	1856	1924	1913	Democratic	New Jersey	Thomas R. Marshall	Indiana
Woodrow Wilson	1856	1924	1917	Democratic	New Jersey	Thomas R. Marshall	Indiana
Warren G. Harding	1865	1923	1921	Republican	Ohio	Calvin Coolidge	Massachusetts
Calvin Coolidge	1872	1933	(1923, August)	Republican	Massachusetts		
Calvin Coolidge	1872	1933	1925	Republican	Massachusetts	Charles G. Dawes	Illinois
Herbert Hoover	1874		1929	Republican	California	Charles Curtis	Kansas
Franklin D. Roosevelt	1882	1945	1933	Democratic	New York	John N. Garner	Texas
Franklin D. Roosevelt	1882	1945	1937	Democratic	New York	John N. Garner	Texas
Franklin D. Roosevelt	1882	1945	1941	Democratic	New York	Henry A. Wallace	Iowa
Franklin D. Roosevelt	1882	1945	1945	Democratic	New York	Harry S. Truman	Missouri
Harry S. Truman	1884		(1945, April)	Democratic	Missouri		
Harry S. Truman	1884		1949	Democratic	Missouri	Alben W. Barkley	Kentucky

INDEX

In addition to the usual entries, this Index contains many references to maps, charts, and pictures. These may be identified as follows:

m refers to a map
c refers to a chart
p refers to a picture

About the Making of This Book

THE TYPE FACE in which the greater part of this book is set, and which you are reading now, is called "Caledonia." This attractive modern face, regarded as one of the most legible ever designed, is based on an older type style called "Scotch," which also has a reputation for good legibility. Caledonia was designed by an American, W. A. Dwiggins, probably the leading modern originator of book designs and type faces.

MOST OF THE HEADINGS (like this: **Modern America**) have been set in a "sans serif" type face. Sans serif letters do not have small tops and bottoms ("serifs," that is) as do the "Roman" letters you are now reading. Also, every part of a sans serif letter is of equal thickness, whereas Roman letters are a little heavier here and a little lighter there. These distinctive sans serif headings provide points of contrast where contrast is needed. Further, they vary in weight from quite light to very black, permitting a useful range of emphasis among the headings. The sans serif type face most commonly used in this book is "Linotype Spartan."

OTHER TYPE FACES which harmonize agreeably with Caledonia and Spartan have been used at various places in the book because they have special usefulness for special purposes. An example may be found in the text of the Declaration of Independence (pages 103–105), which is set in a type face called Weiss.

THE MANUFACTURE of a book depends on the work of people in many parts of the world, and on discoveries of long ago. The lines of type letters that are set on the linotype machine and put together to make a book like this are made from "type metal" containing lead, tin, and antimony. Lead is mined in the United States but much of it comes also from Mexico, Argentina, Australia, Burma, and France. Most of our tin comes from Bolivia, but some comes from the former Netherland East Indies, the Belgian Congo, and the Malay Peninsula. Antimony comes from China and Mexico.

PAPER-MAKING was started by the Chinese many centuries ago. Throughout the years, and in many parts of the world, countless improvements were made in paper. By this time, there are many products that go into the making of paper like that on which this book is printed: wood pulp from Canada, Norway, Sweden, and Finland, as well as from our own forests; clay from Georgia or from the "White Cliffs of Dover" in England; alum from the Andes Mountains or from Italy; dyes from around the Mediterranean Sea, the Canary Islands, Asia Minor, and elsewhere; borax from the Death Valley region in California; titanium from India.

MANY PAGES OF A BOOK are printed at one time on huge sheets of paper. Then the sheets are folded, trimmed, sewn together, and bound into hard covers. The cotton for the cloth covers of this book was grown in our southern states, then woven and prepared in New England. But even for the bindings we rely on far-distant workers. The thread that sews the pages together (it is hidden by the cover) is made from a special grade of cotton grown in Egypt, where the same kind of cotton was being grown many centuries before Columbus discovered America.